Handbook of Research on Advanced Hybrid Intelligent Techniques and Applications

Siddhartha Bhattacharyya
RCC Institute of Information Technology, India

Pinaki Banerjee
Goldstone Infratech Limited, India

Dipankar Majumdar
RCC Institute of Information Technology, India

Paramartha Dutta
Visva-Bharati University, India

A volume in the Advances in Computational
Intelligence and Robotics (ACIR) Book Series

Information Science
REFERENCE
An Imprint of IGI Global

Published in the United States of America by
　　　Information Science Reference (an imprint of IGI Global)
　　　701 E. Chocolate Avenue
　　　Hershey PA, USA 17033
　　　Tel: 717-533-8845
　　　Fax: 717-533-8661
　　　E-mail: cust@igi-global.com
　　　Web site: http://www.igi-global.com

Library of Congress Cataloging-in-Publication Data

Handbook of research on advanced hybrid intelligent techniques and applications / Siddhartha Bhattacharyya, Pinaki Banerjee, Dipankar Majumdar, and Paramartha Dutta, editors.
　　pages cm
 Includes bibliographical references and index.
 ISBN 978-1-4666-9474-3 (hardcover) -- ISBN 978-1-4666-9475-0 (ebook) 1. Expert systems--Handbooks, manuals, etc.
2. Hybrid computer simulation--Handbooks, manuals, etc. 3. Artificial intelligence--Handbooks, manuals, etc. 4. Fuzzy systems--Handbooks, manuals, etc. I. Bhattacharyya, Siddhartha, 1975- editor. II. Banerjee, Pinaki, 1964- editor. III. Majumdar, Dipankar, 1976- editor.
 QA76.76.E95H35535 2016
 006.3'3--dc23
　　　　　　　　　　　2015028207

This book is published in the IGI Global book series Advances in Computational Intelligence and Robotics (ACIR) (ISSN: 2327-0411; eISSN: 2327-042X)

British Cataloguing in Publication Data
A Cataloguing in Publication record for this book is available from the British Library.

For electronic access to this publication, please contact: eresources@igi-global.com.

Advances in Computational Intelligence and Robotics (ACIR) Book Series

ISSN: 2327-0411
EISSN: 2327-042X

MISSION

While intelligence is traditionally a term applied to humans and human cognition, technology has progressed in such a way to allow for the development of intelligent systems able to simulate many human traits. With this new era of simulated and artificial intelligence, much research is needed in order to continue to advance the field and also to evaluate the ethical and societal concerns of the existence of artificial life and machine learning.

The **Advances in Computational Intelligence and Robotics (ACIR) Book Series** encourages scholarly discourse on all topics pertaining to evolutionary computing, artificial life, computational intelligence, machine learning, and robotics. ACIR presents the latest research being conducted on diverse topics in intelligence technologies with the goal of advancing knowledge and applications in this rapidly evolving field.

COVERAGE

- Pattern Recognition
- Fuzzy Systems
- Artificial life
- Cognitive Informatics
- Computational Logic
- Intelligent control
- Robotics
- Synthetic Emotions
- Heuristics
- Adaptive and Complex Systems

IGI Global is currently accepting manuscripts for publication within this series. To submit a proposal for a volume in this series, please contact our Acquisition Editors at Acquisitions@igi-global.com or visit: http://www.igi-global.com/publish/.

Titles in this Series

For a list of additional titles in this series, please visit: www.igi-global.com

Innovative Research in Attention Modeling and Computer Vision Applications
Rajarshi Pal (Institute for Development and Research in Banking Technology, India)
Information Science Reference • copyright 2016 • 457pp • H/C (ISBN: 9781466687233) • US $200.00 (our price)

Handbook of Research on Emerging Perspectives in Intelligent Pattern Recognition, Analysis, and Image Processing
Narendra Kumar Kamila (C.V. Raman College of Engineering, India)
Information Science Reference • copyright 2016 • 484pp • H/C (ISBN: 9781466686540) • US $255.00 (our price)

Research Advances in the Integration of Big Data and Smart Computing
Pradeep Kumar Mallick (Institute for Research and Development, India)
Information Science Reference • copyright 2016 • 380pp • H/C (ISBN: 9781466687370) • US $210.00 (our price)

Handbook of Research on Swarm Intelligence in Engineering
Siddhartha Bhattacharyya (RCC Institute of Information Technology, India) and Paramartha Dutta (Visva-Bharati University, India)
Engineering Science Reference • copyright 2015 • 744pp • H/C (ISBN: 9781466682917) • US $335.00 (our price)

Handbook of Research on Advancements in Robotics and Mechatronics
Maki K. Habib (The American University in Cairo, Egypt)
Engineering Science Reference • copyright 2015 • 993pp • H/C (ISBN: 9781466673878) • US $515.00 (our price)

Handbook of Research on Advanced Intelligent Control Engineering and Automation
Ahmad Taher Azar (Benha University, Egypt) and Sundarapandian Vaidyanathan (Vel Tech University, India)
Engineering Science Reference • copyright 2015 • 795pp • H/C (ISBN: 9781466672482) • US $335.00 (our price)

Handbook of Research on Artificial Intelligence Techniques and Algorithms
Pandian Vasant (Universiti Teknologi Petronas, Malaysia)
Information Science Reference • copyright 2015 • 796pp • H/C (ISBN: 9781466672581) • US $495.00 (our price)

Handbook of Research on Synthesizing Human Emotion in Intelligent Systems and Robotics
Jordi Vallverdú (Universitat Autònoma de Barcelona, Spain)
Information Science Reference • copyright 2015 • 469pp • H/C (ISBN: 9781466672789) • US $245.00 (our price)

Recent Advances in Ambient Intelligence and Context-Aware Computing
Kevin Curran (University of Ulster, UK)
Information Science Reference • copyright 2015 • 376pp • H/C (ISBN: 9781466672840) • US $225.00 (our price)

www.igi-global.com

701 E. Chocolate Ave., Hershey, PA 17033
Order online at www.igi-global.com or call 717-533-8845 x100
To place a standing order for titles released in this series, contact: cust@igi-global.com
Mon-Fri 8:00 am - 5:00 pm (est) or fax 24 hours a day 717-533-8661

Dr. Siddhartha Bhattacharyya would like to dedicate this book to:
My respected father Late Ajit Kumar Bhattacharyya, my respected mother Late Hashi Bhattacharyya, Rajrupa, Rishika and Abhinandan.
Mr. Pinaki Banerjee would like to dedicate this book to:
My respected father Late Anil Chandra Banerjee and my respected mother Mrs. Sandhya Banerjee.
Dr. Dipankar Majumdar would like to dedicate this book to:
The authors who have made their sincere contributions in making it a success.
Dr. Paramartha Dutta would like to dedicate this book to:
My respected father Late Arun Kanti Dutta and my respected mother Mrs. Bandana Dutta.

Editorial Advisory Board

List of Contributors

Table of Contents

Detailed Table of Contents

Section 1
Hybrid Intelligent Techniques: Concepts and Fundamentals

Chapter 1

    Siddesha S, Sri Jayachamarajendra College of Engineering, India
    S K Niranjan, Sri Jayachamarajendra College of Engineering, India
    V N Manjunath Aradhya, Sri Jayachamarajendra College of Engineering, India

Arecanut is an important cash crop of India and ranks first in the production. Arecanut crop bunch segmentation plays very vital role in the process of harvesting. Work on arecanut crop bunch segmentation is of first kind in the literature and this chapter mainly focuses on exploring different color segmentation techniques such as Thresholding, K-means clustering, Fuzzy C Means (FCM), Fast Fuzzy C Means clustering (FFCM), Watershed and Maximum Similarity based Region Merging (MSRM). The effectiveness of the segmentation methods are evaluated on our own collection of Arecanut image dataset of size 200.

Chapter 2

    K. Mahantesh, SJB Institute of Technology, India
    Manjunath Aradhya V N, Sri Jayachamarajendra College of Engineering, India

The difficulty of searching for patterns in data is still exploratory and, ever increasing image datasets with high intra-class variations has created a large scope for generalizing image classification problems. This chapter initiates the inclusivity of discrete latent variables leading to mixture of Gaussians capturing multimodal distributions from segmented regions. Further, these mixtures are analyzed in maximum likelihood framework to extract discriminatory features in compact and de-correlated feature space. Conversely, it is less evident in literature that combining these features with diverse distance measure techniques and neural network classifiers improves the classification performance. In this chapter, we study, explore and demonstrate the idea of subspace mixture models as hybrid intelligent technique for image retrieval systems.

Chapter 3

Petre Anghelescu, University of Pitesti, Romania

In this chapter, bio-inspired techniques based on the cellular automata (CAs) and programmable cellular automata (PCAs) theory are used to develop information security systems. The proposed cryptosystem is composed from a combination of a CA as a pseudorandom number generator (PRNG) and a PCA that construct the ciphering functions of the designed enciphering scheme. It is presented how simple elements named „cells" interact between each other using certain rules and topologies to form a larger system that can be used to encrypt/decrypt data sent over network communication systems. The proposed security system was implemented in hardware in FPGA devices of type Spartan 3E – XC3S500E and was analyzed and verified, including NIST statistical tests, to assure that the system has good security and high speed. The experimental results proves that the cryptographic techniques based on bio-inspired algorithms provides an alternative to the conventional techniques (computational methods).

Chapter 4

Priya Gupta, BITS, India
Anu Gupta, BITS, India
Abhijit Asati, BITS, India

In this chapter, the design and comparative analysis is done in between the most well-known column compression multipliers by Wallace and Dadda in sub-threshold regime. In order to reduce the hardware which ultimately reduces area, power and overall power delay product, an energy efficient basic modules of the multipliers like AND gates, half adders, full adders and partial product generate units have been analyzed for sub-threshold operation. At the last stage ripple carry adder is used in both multipliers. The performance metrics considered for the analysis of the multipliers are: power, delay and PDP. Simulation studies are carried out for 8x8-bit and 16x16-bit input data width. The proposed circuits show energy efficient results with Spectre simulations for the TSMC 180nm CMOS technology at 0.4V supply voltage. The proposed multipliers so implemented outperform its counterparts exhibiting low power consumption and lesser propagation delay as compared to conventional multipliers.

Chapter 5

J. Jagan, VIT University, India
Prabhakar Gundlapalli, Nuclear Power Corporation of India Limited, India
Pijush Samui, VIT University, India

The determination of liquefaction susceptibility of soil is a paramount project in geotechnical earthquake engineering. This chapter adopts Support Vector Machine (SVM), Relevance Vector Machine (RVM) and Least Square Support Vector Machine (LSSVM) for determination of liquefaction susceptibility based on Cone Penetration Test (CPT) from Chi-Chi earthquake. Input variables of SVM, RVM and LSSVM are Cone Resistance (qc) and Peak Ground Acceleration (amax/g). SVM, RVM and LSSVM have been used as classification tools. The developed SVM, RVM and LSSVM give equations for determination of liquefaction susceptibility of soil. The comparison between the developed models has been carried out. The results show that SVM, RVM and LSSVM are the robust models for determination of liquefaction susceptibility of soil.

Speech is the natural communication means, however, it is not the typical input means afforded by computers. The interaction between humans and machines would have become easier, if speech were an alternative effective input means to the keyboard and mouse. With advancement in techniques for signal processing and model building and the empowerment of computing devices, significant progress has been made in speech recognition research, and various speech based applications have been developed. With rapid advancement of the speech recognition technology, telephone speech technology are getting more involved in many new applications of spoken language processing. From the literature it has been found that the spectro-temporal features gives a significant performance improvement for telephone speech recognition system in comparison to the robust feature techniques used for the recognition purpose. In this chapter, the authors have reported the use of various spectral and temporal features and the soft computing techniques that have been used for the telephonic speech recognition.

#### Chapter 7

Inspired from nature, evolutionary algorithms have been proven effective and unique in different real world applications. Comparing to traditional algorithms, its parallel search capability and stochastic nature enable it to excel in search performance in a unique way. In this chapter, evolutionary algorithms are reviewed and discussed from concepts and designs to applications in bioinformatics. The history of evolutionary algorithms is first discussed at the beginning. An overview on the state-of-the-art evolutionary algorithm concepts is then provided. Following that, the related design and implementation details are discussed on different aspects: representation, parent selection, reproductive operators, survival selection, and fitness function. At the end of this chapter, real world evolutionary algorithm applications in bioinformatics are reviewed and discussed.

Chapter represents discovering behavioural patterns within non-temporal and temporal data subsets related to customer churn. Traditional approach, based on using conventional data mining techniques, is not a guarantee for discovering valuable patterns, which could be useful for decision support. Business case, as a part of the text, illustrates such type of situation, where an additional data set has been chosen for finding useful patterns. Chosen data set with temporal characteristics was the key factor after applying REFII model on it, for finding behavioural customer patterns and for understanding causes of the increasing churn trends within observed portfolio. Text gives a methodological framework for churn problem solution, from customer value calculation, to developing predictive churn model, as well as using additional data sources in a situation where conventional approaches in churn analytics do not provide enough information for qualitative decision support. Revealed knowledge was a base for better understanding of customer needs and expectations.

Chapter 9

Bassem Mahmoud Mokhtar, Alexandria University, Egypt
Mohamed Eltoweissy, Virginia Military Institute, USA

The ever-growing and ever-evolved Internet targets supporting billions of networked entities to provide a wide variety of services and resources. Such complexity results in network-data from different sources with special characteristics, such as widely diverse users, multiple media, high-dimensionality and various dynamic concerns. With huge amounts of network-data with such characteristics, there are significant challenges to a) recognize emergent and anomalous behavior in network-traffic and b) make intelligent decisions for efficient network operations. Endowing the semantically-oblivious Internet with Intelligence would advance the Internet capability to learn traffic behavior and to predict future events. In this chapter, the authors discuss and evaluate the hybridization of monolithic intelligence techniques in order to achieve smarter and enhanced networking operations. Additionally, the authors provide systematic application-agnostic semantics management methodology with efficient processes for extracting and classifying high-level features and reasoning about rich semantics.

Chapter 10

João Sousa Andrade, Instituto Superior Tecnico, Portugal
Artur M. Arsénio, Universidade da Beira Interior, Portugal

Infectious diseases, such as the recent Ebola outbreak, can be especially dangerous for large communities on today's highly connected world. Countermeasures can be put in place if one is able to predict determine which people are more vulnerable to infections or have been in contact with the disease, and where. Contact location, time and relationship with the subject are relevant metrics that affect the probability of disease propagation. Sensors on personal devices that gather information from people, and social networks analysis, allow the integration of community data, while data analysis and modelling may potentially indicate community-level susceptibility to an epidemic. Indeed, there has been interest on social networks for epidemic prediction. But the integration between large-scale sensor networks and these initiatives, required to achieve epidemic prediction, is yet to be achieved. In this context, an opportunistic system is proposed and evaluated for predicting an epidemic outbreak in a community, while guaranteeing user privacy.

Section 2
Hybrid Intelligent Techniques: Applications

Chapter 11

Sourav De, The University of Burdwan, India
Siddhartha Bhattacharyya, RCC Institute of Information Technology, India
Susanta Chakraborty, Indian Institute of Engineering Science and Technology, India

A self-supervised image segmentation method by a non-dominated sorting genetic algorithm-II (NSGA-II) based optimized MUSIG (OptiMUSIG) activation function with a multilayer self-organizing neural network (MLSONN) architecture is proposed to segment multilevel gray scale images. In the same way, another NSGA-II based parallel version of the OptiMUSIG (ParaOptiMUSIG) activation function with a parallel self-organizing neural network (PSONN) architecture is purported to segment the color images in this article. These methods are intended to overcome the drawback of their single objective based counterparts. Three standard objective functions are employed as the multiple objective criteria of the NSGA-II algorithm to measure the quality of the segmented images.

Chapter 12

Sandip Dey, Camellia Institute of Technology, India
Siddhartha Bhattacharyya, RCC Institute of Information Technology, India
Ujjwal Maulik, Jadavpur University, India

In this article, a genetic algorithm inspired by quantum computing is presented. The novel algorithm referred to as quantum inspired genetic algorithm (QIGA) is applied to determine optimal threshold of two gray level images. Different random chaotic map models exhibit the inherent interference operation in collaboration with qubit and superposition of states. The random interference is followed by three different quantum operators viz., quantum crossover, quantum mutation and quantum shifting produce population diversity. Finally, the intermediate states pass through the quantum measurement for optimization of image thresholding. In the proposed algorithm three evaluation metrics such as Brinks's, Kapur's and Pun's algorithms have been applied to two gray level images viz., Lena and Barbara. These algorithms have been applied in conventional GA and Han et al.'s QEA. A comparative study has been made between the proposed QIGA, Han et al.'s algorithm and conventional GA that indicates encouraging avenues of the proposed QIGA.

Chapter 13

K R Singh, Yeshwantrao Chavan College of Engineering, India
M M Raghuwanshi, Yeshwantrao Chavan College of Engineering, India
M A Zaveri, Sardar Vallabhbhai National Institute of Technology, India
James Peters, University of Manitoba, Canada

Computer vision is a process of electronically perceiving and understanding of an image like human vision system (HVS) do. Face recognition techniques (FRT) determines the identity of the individual by matching the facial images with the one stored in the facial database. The performance of FRT is greatly affected by variations in face due to different factors. It is interesting to study how well these issues are being handled by RST and near set theory to improve the performance. The variation in illumination and plastic surgery changes the appearance of face that introduces imprecision and vagueness. One part of chapter introduces the adaptive illumination normalization technique using RST that classifies the image illumination into three classes based on which illumination normalization is performed using an appropriate filter. Later part of this chapter introduces use of near set theory for FRT on facial images that have previously undergone some feature modifications through plastic surgery.

Pramit Ghosh, RCC Institute of Information Technology, India
Debotosh Bhattacharjee, Jadavpur University, India
Mita Nasipuri, Jadavpur University, India

This chapter describes an automatic intelligent diagnostic system for Tuberculosis. Sputum microscopy is the most common diagnostic technique to diagnose Tuberculosis. In Sputum microscopy, Sputum are examined using a microscope for Mycobacterium tuberculosis. This manual process is being automated by image processing, where classification is performed by using a hybrid approach (color based and shape based). This hybrid approach reduces the false positive and false negative rate. Final classification decision is taken by a fuzzy system. Image processing, soft-computing, mechanics, and control system plays a significant role in this system. Slides are given as input to the system. System finds for Mycobacterium tuberculosis bacteria and generates reports. From designing point of view ARM11 based, 32 bit RISC processor is used to control the mechanical units. The main mathematical calculation (including image processing and soft computing) is distributed between ARM11 based group and Personal Computer (Intel i3). This system has better sensitivity than manual sputum microscopy.

Vishal Shreyans Shah, VIT University, India
Henyl Rakesh Shah, VIT University, India
Pijush Samui, VIT University, India

This chapter examines the capability of Minimax Probability Machine Regression (MPMR) and Extreme Learning Machine (ELM) for prediction of Optimum Moisture Content (OMC), Maximum Dry Density (MDD) and Soaked California Bearing Ratio (CBR) of soil. These algorithms can analyse data and recognize patterns and are proved to be very useful for problems pertaining to classification and regression analysis. These regression models are used for prediction of OMC and MDD using Liquid limit (LL) and Plastic limit (PL) as input parameters. Whereas Soaked CBR is predicted using Liquid limit, Plastic limit, OMC and MDD as input parameters. The predicted values obtained from the MPMR and ELM models have been compared with that obtained from Artificial Neural Networks (ANN). The accuracy of MPMR and ELM models, their performance and their reliability with respect to ANN models has also been evaluated.

Shikha Mehta, Jaypee Institute of Information Technology, India
Monika Bajaj, University of Delhi, India
Hema Banati, Dyal Singh College, India

Formal learning has shifted from the confines of institutional walls to our home computers and even to our mobiles. It is often felt that the concept of e-learning can be successfully applied to theoretical subjects but when it comes to teaching of science subjects like chemistry where hands on practical training is must, it is inadequate. This chapter presents a hybrid approach (amalgamation of concepts of machine learning technique with soft computing paradigm) to develop an intelligent virtual chemistry laboratory (IVCL) tool for simulating chemical experiments online. Tool presents an easy to use web based interface, which takes as input the reactants and presents results in the form of - type of reaction occurred and the list of possible products. Technically, the IVCL tool utilizes naïve bayes algorithm to classify the type of reactions and then applies genetic algorithm inspired approach to generate the products. Subsequently it employs system of equations method to balance the reactions. Experimental evaluations reveal that proposed IVCL tool runs with 95% accuracy.

Chapter 17

In Content-Centric Networks (CCNs) as a promising network architecture, new kinds of anomalies will arise. Usually, clustering algorithms would fit the requirements for building a good anomaly detection system. K-means is a popular anomaly detection method; however, it suffers from the local convergence and sensitivity to selection of the cluster centroids. This chapter presents a novel fuzzy anomaly detection method that works in two phases. In the first phase, authors propose an hybridization of Particle Swarm Optimization (PSO) and K-means algorithm with two simultaneous cost functions as well-separated clusters and local optimization to determine the optimal number of clusters. When the optimal placement of clusters centroids and objects are defined, it starts the second phase. In this phase, the authors employ a fuzzy approach by the combination of two distance-based methods as classification and outlier to detect anomalies in new monitoring data. Experimental results demonstrate that the proposed method can yield high accuracy as compared to preexisting algorithms.

Chapter 18

Registration of medical images like CT-MR, MR-MR etc. are challenging area for researchers. This chapter introduces a new cluster based registration technique with help of the supervised optimized neural network. Features are extracted from different cluster of an image obtained from clustering algorithms. To overcome the drawback regarding convergence rate of neural network, an optimized neural network is proposed in this chapter. The weights are optimized to increase the convergence rate as well as to avoid stuck in local minima. Different clustering algorithms are explored to minimize the clustering error of an image and extract features from suitable one. The supervised learning method applied to train the neural network. During this training process an optimization algorithm named Genetic Algorithm (GA) is used to update the weights of a neural network. To demonstrate the effectiveness of the proposed method, investigation is carried out on MR T1, T2 data sets. The proposed method shows convincing results in comparison with other existing techniques.

Preface

Many real life problems suffer from uncertainty, imprecision, vagueness to name a few. Conventional computing paradigms often fall short of offering comprehensive solutions to them. Even latest soft computing paradigms appear not too robust to handle the situations. This is primarily because each individual constituent of Soft Computing suffers from shortcomings, someway or other. In this backdrop, limitations of one such Soft Computing constituent may often be found to be supplemented by another constituent giving rise to hybridization. Hybrid computing is a paradigm which addresses fused impact of a member of Soft Computing constituents these issues to a considerable extent. This book is intended to encompass such hybrid computing techniques reported in the literature.

Soft Computing, as the name suggests, deals with the soft meaning of concepts. This is a relatively new computing paradigm which entails a synergistic integration of essentially four other computing paradigms, viz., neural networks, fuzzy logic, rough sets and evolutionary computation, incorporating probabilistic reasoning (belief networks, genetic algorithms and chaotic systems). These computing paradigms are conjoined to provide a framework for flexible information processing applications designed to operate in the real-world. Bezdek referred to this synergism as computational intelligence. According to Prof. Zadeh, soft computing is "an emerging approach to computing, which parallels the remarkable ability of the human mind to reason and learn in an environment of uncertainty and imprecision." Soft computing technologies are robust by design, and operate by trading off precision for tractability. Since they can handle uncertainty with ease, they conform better to real-world situations and provide lower cost solutions. The four components of soft computing differ from one another in more than one way. They operate either independently or in unison depending on the domain of applications. Hybrid computing stems from the synergistic integration of the different soft computing tools and techniques as has already been indicated. The fusion of these techniques towards achieving enhanced performance and more robust solutions can be achieved through appropriate hybridization.

An intelligent machine inherits the boon of intelligence by virtue of the various methodologies offered by Soft Computing paradigm encompassing fuzzy and rough set theory, artificial neurocomputing, evolutionary computing, as well as approximate reasoning. At times, situation demands in reality, where any of the techniques listed above does not provide any comprehensible solution but an effective symbiosis of more than one of the above techniques offers a formidable solution. This gives rise to the advent to several hybrid methodologies. Of late, there is enormous growth of research exploration of injecting elements of intelligence using efficient hybrid techniques. All these initiatives indicate that the individual soft computing techniques do not behave in conflicting manner rather behave complimentary to one another. In fact, recent reports reveal the inherent strength of such hybridization of computation methods.

The objective of the present endeavor is to bring a broad spectrum of application domains under the purview of hybrid intelligence so that it is able to trigger further inspiration among various research communities to contribute in their respective fields of applications, thereby orienting these application fields towards intelligence.

Once the purpose, as stated above, is achieved a larger number of research communities may be brought under one canopy to ventilate their views and ideas in a more structured manner. In that case, the present endeavor may be seen as the beginning of such an effort in bringing various research applications close to one another.

The target audience of the intended book is the relevant research community. To be precise, the book is aimed to establish the missing link between the research standing in the relevant field and that is upcoming. Hybridization would surely and certainly help the readers grasp the essence and utility of the different soft computing techniques in vogue.

The proposed book would come to the benefits of several categories of students and researchers. At the students' level, this book can serve as a treatise/reference book for the special papers at the masters level aimed at inspiring possibly future researchers. Newly inducted PhD aspirants would also find the contents of this book useful as far as their compulsory coursework is concerned.

At the researchers' level, those interested in interdisciplinary research would also benefit from the book. After all, the enriched interdisciplinary contents of the book would always be a subject of interest to the faculties, existing research communities and new research aspirants from diverse disciplines of the concerned departments of premier institutes across the globe. This is expected to bring different research backgrounds (due to its cross platform characteristics) close to one another to form effective research groups all over the world. Above all, availability of the book should be ensured to as much universities and research institutes as possible to promote effective research of interdisciplinary nature.

The book is organized into two broader sections depending on the type of contributions. These are 1) Hybrid Intelligent Techniques: Concepts and Fundamentals and 2) Hybrid Intelligent Techniques: Applications. Section 1 comprises first ten chapters while Section 2 comprises rest eight following.

Chapter 1 illustrates a study of different cash crop bunch segmentation techniques that play very vital role in the process of harvesting. The cash crop under consideration happens to be the arecanut crop available in India. Different color segmentation techniques such as thresholding, K-means clustering, Fuzzy C Means (FCM), Fast Fuzzy C Means clustering (FFCM), Watershed and Maximum Similarity based Region Merging (MSRM) techniques are discussed in this chapter.

The inclusivity of discrete latent variables leading to mixture of Gaussians capturing multimodal distributions from segmented regions is initiated in Chapter 2. Further, these mixtures are analyzed in maximum likelihood framework to extract discriminatory features in compact and de-correlated feature space. In addition, this chapter demonstrates the idea of subspace mixture models in image retrieval systems.

In Chapter 3 bio-inspired techniques based on the cellular automata (CAs) and programmable cellular automata (PCAs) theory are used to develop information security systems composed of a combination of a CA as a pseudorandom number generator (PRNG) and a PCA that construct the ciphering functions of the designed enciphering scheme. The experimental results prove that the cryptographic techniques based on bio-inspired algorithms provide a formidable alternative to the conventional techniques.

Chapter 4 presents the design and comparative analysis between the most well-known column compression multipliers by WALLACE and DADDA in sub-threshold regime. The proposed multipliers outperform their counterparts exhibiting low power consumption and lesser propagation delay as compared to conventional multipliers.

Chapter 5 adopts Support Vector Machine (SVM), Relevance Vector Machine (RVM) and Least Square Support Vector Machine (LSSVM) for determination of liquefaction susceptibility based on Cone Penetration Test (CPT) from Chi-Chi earthquake. The results show that SVM, RVM and LSSVM are the robust models for determination of liquefaction susceptibility of soil.

An overview and the use of various spectral and temporal features and the soft computing techniques that have been used for the telephonic speech recognition are elucidated in Chapter 6.

In Chapter 7, evolutionary algorithms are reviewed and discussed from concepts and designs to applications in bioinformatics. In addition, it also focuses on real world evolutionary algorithm applications in bioinformatics.

Chapter 8 presents discovering behavioral patterns within non-temporal and temporal data subsets related to customer churn. Traditional approach, based on using conventional data mining techniques, is not a guarantee for discovering valuable patterns, which could be useful for decision support. Chosen data set with temporal characteristics is the key factor after applying REFII model on it, for finding behavioral customer patterns and for understanding causes of the increasing churn trends within observed portfolio. It concludes that revealed knowledge is a base for better understanding of customer needs and expectations.

In Chapter 9, the authors discuss and evaluate the hybridization of monolithic intelligence techniques in order to achieve smarter and enhanced networking operations. Additionally, the authors provide systematic application-agnostic semantics management methodology with efficient processes for extracting and classifying high-level features and reasoning about rich semantics.

Infectious diseases, such as the recent Ebola outbreak, can be especially dangerous for large communities on today's highly connected world. Sensors on personal devices that gather information from people, and social networks analysis, allow the integration of community data, while data analysis and modeling may potentially indicate community-level susceptibility to an epidemic. In this context, an opportunistic system is proposed in Chapter 10 and evaluated for predicting an epidemic outbreak in a community, while guaranteeing user privacy.

A self supervised image segmentation method by a non-dominated sorting genetic algorithm-II (NSGA-II) based optimized MUSIG (OptiMUSIG) activation function with a multilayer self organizing neural network (MLSONN) architecture is proposed in Chapter 11 to segment multilevel gray scale images. In the same way, another NSGA-II based parallel version of the OptiMUSIG (ParaOptiMUSIG) activation function with a parallel self organizing neural network (PSONN) architecture is purported to segment the color images in this article. These methods are intended to overcome the drawback of their single objective based counterparts.

In Chapter 12, a genetic algorithm inspired by quantum computing (QIGA) is presented which is applied to determine optimal threshold of two gray level images. Different random chaotic map models exhibit the inherent interference operation in collaboration with qubit and superposition of states.

Chapter 13 bears two parts. One part of chapter introduces the adaptive illumination normalization technique using RST that classifies the image illumination into three classes based on which illumination normalization is performed using an appropriate filter. Later part of this chapter introduces use of near set theory for FRT on facial images that have previously undergone some feature modifications through plastic surgery.

Chapter 14 describes an automatic intelligent diagnostic system for Tuberculosis in the form of Sputum microscopy. In Sputum microscopy, Sputum are examined using a microscope for Mycobacterium tuberculosis. This manual process is being automated by image processing, where classification is performed by using a hybrid approach (color based and shape based).

Chapter 15 examines the capability of Minimax Probability Regression Machine (MPMR) and Extreme Learning Machine (ELM) for prediction of Optimum Moisture Content (OMC), Maximum Dry Density (MDD) and Soaked California Bearing Ratio (CBR) of soil. These algorithms can analyze data and recognize patterns and are proved to be very useful for problems pertaining to classification and regression analysis.

A hybrid approach (amalgamation of concepts of machine learning technique with soft computing paradigm) to develop an intelligent virtual chemistry laboratory (IVCL) tool for simulating chemical experiments online is presented in Chapter 16. The developed tool presents an easy to use web based interface, which takes as input the reactants and presents results in the form of type of reaction occurred and the list of possible products.

Chapter 17 presents a novel fuzzy anomaly detection method that works in two phases. In the first phase, authors propose a hybridization of Particle Swarm Optimization (PSO) and K-means algorithm with two simultaneous cost functions as well-separated clusters and local optimization to determine the optimal number of clusters. When the optimal placement of clusters centroids and objects are defined, it starts the second phase. In this phase, the authors employ a fuzzy approach by the combination of two distance-based methods as classification and outlier to detect anomalies in new monitoring data.

Registration of medical images like CT-MR, MR-MR etc. are challenging area for researchers. Chapter 18 introduces a new cluster based registration technique with help of the supervised optimized neural network. Features are extracted from different cluster of an image obtained from clustering algorithms. To overcome the drawback regarding convergence rate of neural network, an optimized neural network is proposed in this chapter.

It may be noted that there are good amount of contributions of the applications of hybrid intelligent techniques in various fields. However, any such previous effort has remained application specific i. e. aimed at identifying a specific application domain where the ingredients of hybrid intelligent techniques have been applied quite effectively. But, to the best of our knowledge, efforts to bring in multiple domains engineering and science within one framework as is evident from the diversified nature of the chapters in this book are not very frequent. In that sense, this appears to be the first such effort to accommodate cross platform applications of hybrid intelligent techniques. Speaking from the scholastic point of view, this is a noteworthy achievement in which the present endeavor may be thought of as the maiden facilitator.

Siddhartha Bhattacharyya
RCC Institute of Information Technology, India

Pinaki Banerjee
Goldstone Infratech Limited, India

Dipankar Majumdar
RCC Institute of Information Technology, India

Paramartha Dutta
Visva-Bharati University, India

Section 1
Hybrid Intelligent Techniques:
Concepts and Fundamentals

Chapter 1
A Study of Different Color Segmentation Techniques for Crop Bunch in Arecanut

Siddesha S
Sri Jayachamarajendra College of Engineering, India

S K Niranjan
Sri Jayachamarajendra College of Engineering, India

V N Manjunath Aradhya
Sri Jayachamarajendra College of Engineering, India

ABSTRACT

Arecanut is an important cash crop of India and ranks first in the production. Arecanut crop bunch segmentation plays very vital role in the process of harvesting. Work on arecanut crop bunch segmentation is of first kind in the literature and this chapter mainly focuses on exploring different color segmentation techniques such as Thresholding, K-means clustering, Fuzzy C Means (FCM), Fast Fuzzy C Means clustering (FFCM), Watershed and Maximum Similarity based Region Merging (MSRM). The effectiveness of the segmentation methods are evaluated on our own collection of Arecanut image dataset of size 200.

INTRODUCTION

Agriculture plays a major role in any nation's economy and it is the primary livelihood of the mankind. Indian economy is based on agriculture as it is a traditional occupation. A stable agricultural industry ensures a country with food security, source of income and source of employment. This could be achieved by improving agriculture production and its quality by practicing precision agriculture. Precision agriculture, as a crop management concept, could meet much of the increasing environmental, economic, market and public pressures (Stafford 2000). The impact of precision agriculture technologies on agricultural production is expected in two areas: profitability for the producers and ecological

DOI: 10.4018/978-1-4666-9474-3.ch001

and environmental benefits to the public (Zhang et al. 2002). The objectives of precision agriculture are profit maximization, its input rationalization and environmental damage reduction, by adjusting the agriculture practices to the site demands.

In the field of precision agriculture considerably quite a large effort on research has been focused. This leads the agricultural and engineering companies for manufacturing advanced machine vision devices to facilitate the practice of precision agriculture (Scarlet 2001). The spatial and temporal soil variability and crop management within a farm has been admired for centuries. In the past, the fields are small in size and their demarcations are defined by natural boundaries, like soil type and water courses. This made farmers to change their soil and crop treatments manually. With the enhancement in the area of field, the crop production was substantially increased and to cope up with the large scale of crop production automation coined more importance in the later part of the previous century (Godwin and Miller 2003). Without incorporating and developing the new technology for filed spatial variability and crop management (Goense et al. 1996), it was impossible automate the precision agriculture. With the advancement in technology which vitally made the impact for the development of the precision agriculture concept, in the late 1970s, the Global Positioning System (GPS) using satellites placed in orbit by the Department of Defense in the US. This system helped in locating any position on earth using latitude, longitude and altitude, 24 hours a day, up to the perfect accuracy of a few centimeters. With this information available to machines in the field, the treatment for the crops can be applied locally at the time of field operations within the field for the required amount of area (Stafford 1994). Precision agriculture is the future way ahead for formers to produce quality crop for the millennium. This is because the production of crop become more and more precise, the technologies are highly optimized which results in cost reduction and impact over the environment (Stafford et al. 1996).

Three main obstructions which needed to overcome during the implementation of precision agriculture (Matthews 1983; Stafford 2000)

1. Precision agriculture deals with intensive information related to mapping of different types of soil, crop and factors related to environment of the field. This produces huge data quantities which would be processed by the user. Along with the field data some more data is added based on the experience like weather and market information data. This overload of data has to be maintained and managed properly by suitable data integration, expert and decision support systems (Stafford 1994). To achieve this development some standardization of data formats and transfer protocols need to be followed.
2. There is an absence of balanced systems and methods for deciding application necessities on a restricted premise and a parallel absence of experimentally approved evidences for the benefits guaranteed for the concept. Both of these must be addressed by researching in the area of soil, crop science and agronomic exploration and experimentation.
3. Although information needed on soil, yield and ecological elements can be obtained, most strategies are expensive and intense labor-oriented, (like laboratory set up and subject expert for the analysis of soil). The information can be created through programmed sensor frameworks sensing particular components or suitable substitutes.

Accordingly, improvement of quick sensing frameworks must be needed before practicing precision agriculture. With the improvement of frameworks that can give information at fine spatial determination, the advancement of more exact application innovations and exact and dependable position reckoning has ended up important. Agricultural engineers must take a lead in overcoming the first and third hindrances however, in the most recent decade of research in precision agriculture has demonstrated, that the topic is multidisciplinary thus the inter disciplinary groups are expected to develop solutions for these issues (Stafford 2000).

Precision agriculture is an integrated crop management system that endeavors to match the sort and amount of inputs with the genuine product requirements for small regions within the farm field area. The benefits of precision agriculture in relation with economy and environmental could be envisioned through decreased utilization of water, fertilizers, herbicides and pesticides along with farm equipments. This avoids in managing the entire field based on some theoretical condition, which may not exist any-place in the field (Godwin and Miller 2003). A precision agriculture approach perceives site-particular differences inside fields and adjusts the management procedures as needed (Goovaerts 2000).

Precision agriculture plays a vital role in cropping systems like yield monitoring, its variability, crop variety comparisons, yield damage reports, and field efficiency (Koch and Khosla 2003). In recent years, with the advancement in machine vision, applications of digital image processing and pattern recognition approaches have become powerful and essential in the field of precision agriculture, which involves com-putation and processing of intense data in order to provide timely and accurate information (Cox 2002).

With advancement in machine vision in the field of precision agriculture minimizes the human in-tervention and provides proper information for decision making process. The main problem in machine vision is in determining the presence of particular object, feature or activity in the image data. Even this can normally solved without human intervention, but the outcome results are not as per the expectation (Cox 2002). The available approaches for this problem can be solved for only specific objects, like simple geometric objects, human faces, printed or hand-written characters, or vehicles, and in particular for specific situations, where the images are captured in a well-defined illumination, background, and the direction of the object relative to the camera.

Agricultural automation may take advantage of machine vision resources, which can be applied to a number of different tasks, such as inspection, classification of plants, estimated production, automated collection and guidance of autonomous machines. Crop image segmentation issue on colour difference between mature crops and backgrounds under natural illumination condition is an important and difficult content of crop-harvesting machine vision.

Dealing with voluminous data and detection of proper crop bunch is very much desired in the process of harvesting. Machine vision approaches have been implemented in precision agriculture for various applications. The research works have been also done for harvesting, disease detection in case of crops like Tobacco (Guru et al. 2012), Tomato (Schillaci et al. 2012; Yin et al.2009), Potato (Hassankhani and Navid 2012), Coffee (Johnson et al. 2004), Tea (Singh and Kamal 2013), Mango (Chhabra et al. 2012) etc. Only a few attempts have been made for crops like Arecanut for classification, harvesting, grading and disease detection. Arecanut or Betelnut (Areca catechu L.,) is an important cash crop in the Western Ghats, Eastern Ghats, East and North Eastern regions of India. India ranks first in terms of both area (47%) and production (47%) of Arecanut. Indian productivity is also on par with the world productivity at 1.27 tonnes/ha (Gracy et al. 2010). Mainly, Arecanut is an important component of the religious, social and cultural celebrations and economic life of people in India. Also Arecanut is also used in Ayurvedic and Veterinary medicines.

Crop harvesting is the process of extraction of matured crops from the plant. The selection of right time and right maturity of crop adds quality to the crop. The assessment of proper crop for harvesting is a crucial decision making process. Automating the process mainly needs a solid machine vision model which helps in selecting the crop from the plant. This selection and extraction of crops from the plant can be carried out using image segmentation techniques.

From the literature survey it is evident that very few works have been done on crop segmentation part and in case of arecanut only few works have been done and those involves segmentation of a single nut from the background. So automatic segmentation (Gao et al. 2001) of crop bunches from the arecanut crops are very much needed as the plants are tall and needs skilled labor for harvesting. This increased labor cost in harvesting made small and middle level farmers life very tough. Also it is very dangerous for the labors who involved in harvesting; several cases have been reported by farmers that so many labors got injured by falling from the tree. This is due to the reason that, areca trees trunks are very thin and it grows to the height of 20-30 feet. This triggers us for proposing an automated harvesting process and this basically works based on the machine vision technique. This creates a huge scope for detecting and extraction of crop bunch from the plant using some solid color image segmentation techniques.

Color image segmentation is a prime and very important task in most of the machine vision problems. Color image segmentation is very much needed in the field of precision agriculture especially for harvesting process. One of the main problem with color segmentation in arecanut crop bunch is the complex background i.e., the background consists of other trees or leaves, flowers etc. of these some may have the same color as the crop bunch. Separation of areca crop bunches from the background is very challenging task.

This chapter initiates the exploration of various color segmentation methods (Sridevi and Mala 2012; Elbalaoui et al. 2013) and studies the effectiveness for areca crop bunch segmentation which are based on feature, image domain and edge (Lucchese and Mitra 2001; Pratt 2008). Under these different color segmentation techniques like Threshold (Pratt 2008; Sridevi and Mala 2012), K-Means clustering (Vijay et al 2014), Fuzzy C Means clustering (Cheng 1995; Pantofaru and Herbert 2005; Gonzalez and Woods 2009; Muthukannan and Latha 2012), Fast Fuzzy C Means clustering (Bhoyar and Kakde 2010; Singh and Singh 2010), Watershed segmentation (Belaid and Mourou 2009; Sridevi and Mala 2012), and Maximum Similarity based Region Merging (Ning et al 2009).

BACKGROUND

A novel and robust color space conversion and color index distribution analysis technique for automated date maturity evaluation for harvesting the date fruits was proposed (Lee et al. 2008b). Also Computer vision technology for detecting fruit size, color, bruise, and surface defects evaluation of fruit for the overall quality were discussed. Image analysis and color quantization techniques are used in evaluating fruit maturity for the harvesting process is demonstrated using Medjool date samples collected from field testing (Lee et al. 2008a).

Another system was developed using a genetic algorithm based neural network detecting technique for evaluating maturity of strawberry fruits during harvesting procedure (Xu 2009). A robust and an intelligent algorithm operated on the multispectral images for the estimatation of accurate percentages of green (under-ripe), yellow (proper ripe), and brown (over-ripe) colored coffee cherries displayed on the canopy surface (Furfaro et al. 2007). From the airborne multispectral imagery a feasibility of monitoring the coffee field ripeness was proposed and different approaches are discussed (Johnson et al. 2004).A multivariate based three class problem was incorporated considering a Bayesian classifier for data fusion to classify fresh non damaged tomatoes based on their ripening stages (Baltazar et al. 2008).

Attempts have been made using machine vision in several crop management activities like crop to soil mapping, weed and disease detection, crop grading, and classification for harvesting. A machine vision–based guidance system was developed for grain harvesting (Benson et al. 2003; Mondal and Tiwari 2007). This system involve some stages like image acquisition from the sensor, digitization of the image, segmentation using adaptive using gray level histogram based techniques. Post segmentation process involves filtering using low-pass filters to remove noise. Blob analysis is done for classifying the connected pixels of the same image as a single object.

An automatic classification method for Betelnut/Arecanut is proposed in (Liu et al. 2009). The classification is done by extracting color, shape and texture features of Arecanut. The segmentation of the individual arecanut is done as preprocessing step using bilinear interpolation and wavelet decomposition. Arecanut image has been captured using CCD camera with YCbCr color mode. The image captured by keeping the arecanuts in white background to increase the contrast between object and the background region. As preprocessing mainly works on Y component, the arecanut is segmented based on Y component. Segmentation is achieved by considering only the low frequency image as the expected image and removing the high frequency components.

A method proposed for classification of Arecanut into two classes based on color (Danti and Suresha 2012b). The proposed method has three steps, segmentation, masking and classification. Three sigma control limits are used on the YCBCR image for the effective segmentation of Arecanuts. Classification is made based on the red and green color components of the segmented region of the Arecanuts. The segmentation is on individual arecanut images. The RGB image is first converted to YCBCR mode, the red and blue components from the arecanut image cropped manually for determining the lower and upper control limits of the red and blue colors. Shadow was removed using 3 sigma controls by setting the background color as black. Morphological operations are used for removing the noise on the binary image which was converted by segmented image.

Use of texture features have also been studied for classification of Arecanut (Danti and Suresha 2012c). The segmentation of arecanut from its background is the first step. This is done by converting the RGB image to HIS and YCbCr color model and then the saturation channel from HSI color model is extracted. Threshold based segmentation is carried out based on global image threshold using Otsu method is used. Classification is done using mean around features, gray level co-occurrence matrix (GLCM) features and combined (Mean around & GLCM) features.

Decision trees classifier is used for classification purpose. An approach has been proposed for grading of Arecanuts (Danti and Suresha 2012a). Three sigma control limits on color features are determined for effective segmentation of Arecanuts. Color features are used for the grading of Arecanuts with the help of support vector machines (SVMs) into two grades i.e. boiling and Non-boiling nuts. In the above mentioned work, the segmentation is again done for individual Arecanuts.

An application was developed by neural networks and image processing techniques for detecting and classifying the quality of Arecanuts. Defects with diseases or insects of Arecanuts were segmented by a detection line (DL) method. Six geometric features, three color features, and defect areas were used in the classification procedure. A back-propagation neural network classifier was employed to sort the quality of Arecanuts. Here the segmentation work is done for detecting the diseases spots on the Arecanuts (Huang 2012).

From the above literature survey, it is quite evident that few work has been carried out on segmentation of Arecanut is inadequate and fragmentary. It also reveals that no attempts have been made for segmentation of crop bunches of Arecanut.

Among these the segmentation of Arecanut bunch crops it's of first kind in the literature.

NEED FOR MACHINE VISION IN HARVESTING

Harvesting is a vital and very important stage in production of any crop. If the crop production is qualitative then it should follow a selective harvesting process. Selective harvesting deals with the collection of only proper ripe crops from the plant. Hence, before the process of harvesting a crop, farmers should consider proper and accurate factors like unripe, ripe and over-ripe of crops. Due the human sensory limitations, the manual judgment of crop ripeness by human will not guarantee the accurate and precise result. Also the variability of lighting condition will minimize the efficiency in evaluating crop ripeness over the time. Therefore with these issues, there is a need to develop a robust model against ecological conditions (sunny, cloudy and rainy) to evaluate ripeness of crop during the harvesting process. The visual properties of crop like color, shape and textures need to be exploited for the evaluation of the ripeness of crop for harvesting process.

With this backdrop, there is need for exploring machine vision based algorithmic models for crop bunch segmentation of arecanut crop. The prime applications of arecanut crop bunch segmentation include monitoring and mapping crop yields. Crop-yield monitors to watch both quantitative and qualitative parameters, a great need of timely harvesting based on crop ripeness. Due to the excessive labor cost and chances of making wrong decision at the time crop selection, harvesting and grading, there is an increasing demand for machine vision based technology. Implementation of suitable machine vision techniques in precision agriculture for proper crop management helps farmers to serve the society by providing quality crops (Lee et al. 2011).

Arecanut harvesting is done manually in present scenario and is very cumbersome and dangerous process in case for non-expertise labors. Automation of harvesting process mainly concentrates on extraction or segmentation the crop bunch from the arecanut tree image. Image segmentation is a process of partitioning an image into its constituent regions to extract data from the attributes of the image. A good segmentation should result in regions in which the image elements should have uniform properties in terms of brightness, color or texture etc. Though the image is to be portioned into regions, the considerable changes within the regions should be observable visually. The quality of the segmentation can be measured by the elements of the same region should be similar and should have clear difference between elements of the other regions.

Now there are a number of wide varieties of image segmentation techniques are available, among these some are for general purpose and some are designed for specific types of images for the specific filed. Mainly the techniques were classified as: spatial clustering with measurement space guide, region growing schemes based on single linkage, region growing schemes based on hybrid linkage, region growing schemes with centroid linkage, spatial clustering techniques, and split-and-merge methods (Haralick and Shapiro 1985).

The proposed work concentrates at extracting the crop bunch of arecanut from the given image using different color segmentation approaches which are classified mainly into three classes based on

1. Feature space,
2. Image domain, and
3. Edge-based (Fu and Mui 1981; Lucchese and Mitra 2001 ; (Pantofaru and Herbert 2005).

The feature-space based method is composed of two steps, feature extraction and clustering. Feature extraction is the process to find some characteristics of each pixel or of the region around each pixel, pixel value, pixel color component, windowed average pixel value, windowed variance etc. After we get some typical properties around every pixel, clustering procedure is executed to divide the image into compelling parts focused around these properties. Image space based technique experiences the image and finds the border between segments by few rules. The primary attention to separate two pixels into specific segment is the pixel value differences, so this sort of routines couldn't manage textures well. The main methods in this class are split and merge, region growing, and watershed. The third class is edge-based image segmentation method, which has edge detection and edge linking techniques (Haralick and Shapiro 1985; Lucchese and Mitra 2001).

In spite of the fact that there have been numerous sorts of existed strategies, some basic issue still can't be solved. For class (1), the exact boundaries between segments are still difficult to focus on the grounds that features take properties around however not precisely on every pixel. Class (2) just uses the pixel value, which may bring about over-segmentation on texture regions. The edge detection makes class (3) ends up with over-segmentation issue. The segmentation process can be divided into different category based on the attributes selected like pixel intensity, homogeneity, discontinuity, cluster data, topology etc. Each approach has its own advantages and disadvantages. The result of one approach may not be the same as compared with other. Methods that are specialized to particular applications can often achieve better performance. Selection of an appropriate method to a segmentation problem is very challenging dilemma.

The segmentation procedures can be semi-interactive or automatic. With the major difficulty of ill-posed nature of segmentation it is hard to obtain single answer for segmentation of given image as the interpretation varies from individual approaches. In some cases manual interaction to segment the image may be error-prone (for example, in case of seed selection) while the fully automated approach can give error output (for example in case of watershed segmentation)and in some cases interactive methods can be laborious and time consuming. So a single approach to segment all variety of images may be practical unachievable. The prior knowledge on the image can give better results and gives user the choice to decide proper method to segment the image.

DATASET CREATION

Creation of a suitable dataset is crucial for any research as the dataset is the primary thing for designing and testing the system. A newly designed system has to be empirically tested for various characteristics to assess its effectiveness in meeting requirements. Automation of any stage of precision agriculture for any crop has to be empirically tested for its various characteristics to assess its effectiveness in meeting the requirements for which it has been designed. The arecanut image data set is not readily available. This scarcity is mainly due to the huge manual effort required to collect a sufficiently large number of arecanut images. Due to the non-availability of a sufficiently large benchmarking dataset of arecanut images, it is difficult to compare the performances of different systems. In view of this, we have made an attempt to create a dataset of 200 arecanut images. These images are collected across the Karnataka state by visiting few districts and the images are captured from the ground by focusing the areca nut crop bunch at the top of the tree. This is very laborious process. The images were captured from the ground using NIKON COOLPIX L810 Digital camera with 26X Zoom. The input arecanut image, which has crop bunch along with different parts of arecanut plant like leaves, branches, stem and other tress in the background. Extracting the region of interest i.e., the crop bunch is a really very challenging task. To evaluate the performance of the segmentation techniques, one need to compare the segmented output samples with the ground truth samples. Performance evaluation of the segmentation algorithm is very important step in deciding which method is better by comparing with other methods. In the present case, due to the non availability of arecanut ground truth image dataset, we have created the ground truth dataset and did the performance comparison with other methods.

EXPLORATION OF DIFFERENT SEGMENTATION METHODS

Threshold Method

Intensity is the property shared by the pixels of a region. These regions can be naturally segmented through thresholding, which separates the regions with light and dark pixels.

Threshold based segmentation is the simplest segmentation technique which partitions different regions with different intensity levels based on the threshold value given. Thresholding algorithms are selected manually based on the priori knowledge or automatically by image information. These algorithms further classified based on edge, region and hybrid methods. Segmentation of image using thresholding is simple and promising for segmentation in case of images having light objects with dark background. Thresholding operation converts a multilevel image into a gray scale image and for the selection of a proper threshold *T*, further it divide the pixels of image into different regions and separate the light and useful objects from background. Any pixel (*x, y*) considered as a part of object only when its intensity exceed or in the range of the threshold value, given by, $f(x,y) \geq T$ otherwise the pixel belongs to background. Thresholding technique can be mathematically represented by (Gonzalez and Woods 2009),

$$T = \left\{ x, y, L(x,y), f(x,y) \right\} \tag{1}$$

where (x,y) is the pixel location, $L(x,y)$ is the local property of the input image and $f(x,y)$ is the intensity value of the pixel (x,y).

Based on the selected threshold value, two classes are there, global and local thresholding. Global thresholding method has a fixed threshold value *T*. The threshold value should be proper to get an appropriate Region of Interest (ROI) of the image (Sridevi and Mala 2012). The output image *g* for the given input image *f* is obtained using the following (Gonzalez and Woods 2009),

$$g(x,y) = \begin{cases} 1, & \nabla f(x,y) \geq T \\ 0, & otherwise \end{cases} \tag{2}$$

Global threshold method will work only with images having even background illumination.

To overcome the issue with global thresholding method for non uniform background illumination, local thresholding was adopted using mean and standard deviation (SD) of the neighborhood pixels. It selects the threshold value based on the calculating the mean $\left(m_{xy} \right)$ and standard deviation σ_{xy}. The output image *g* for the given input image *f* is obtained using the following (Gonzalez and Woods 2009),

$$g(x,y) = \begin{cases} 1, & f(x,y) \geq a\sigma_{xy} + f(x,y) > bm_{xy} \\ 0, & otherwise \end{cases} \qquad (3)$$

Local thresholding method uses multiple threshold values to manage the uneven illumination (Agarwal and Xaxa 2014).

In the case of crop bunch segmentation, the image is a color image. In this image each pixel is characterized by three RGB values. Hence 3D histogram has been constructed and is analogous to the method used for one variable. Histograms are plotted for each of color values the red, green and blue and the threshold point are found. The object in the segmented image is distinguished by assigning the average pixel value to the regions separated by thresholds.

Major issue with this method is, it considers only the intensity and does not draw any relation between the pixels. So there is no confirmation that the pixels selected by this are neighbor to one another. Also this nature of this method can introduces unrelated pixels within the same region i.e. nearby the boundaries. Due to this the noise will be maximized due to the variation of intensities of pixels within the region. This sometimes results in either under segmentation or over segmentation issues. This issue is very obvious when dealing with natural images.

From the experimentation and the result it is observed that the results are not as per the expectation. Here the complexity arises in selection of proper threshold values which separates the background from foreground. In the proposed case, it is very difficult to get the proper threshold value as the background is complex, as it consists of leaves, flowers which are having similar color compared to the arecanut crop bunch.

The Segmentation results of arecanut crop bunch using Thresholding are shown in Figure 1 and the performance of this technique is shown in Table-1.

K-Means Clustering

Clustering is a normally a techniques used for classification of samples. Given a vector of N measurements depicting every pixel or collection of pixels (i.e., district) in an image, a similarity of the measurement vectors and in this manner their grouping in the N-dimensional estimation space infers comparability of the similar pixels or pixel groups. Thus, clustering in measurement space indicates the similar regions of an image, and may be used for segmentation purposes.

The measurement vectors describe some useful features of the image and are also known as a feature vectors. Similarity between regions of the image or pixels implies in the feature space. Clustering methods are some of the earliest data segmentation techniques to be developed (Vijay et al 2014).

Normally the clustering algorithms suffer from two major issues

1. Predefinition of number of clusters, which makes inadequate using a huge image data base during batch processing.
2. Representation of clusters by their centroid and built based on Euclidean distance inducing a hyper sphere cluster shape, which is incapable of capturing the actual structure of the data. This is especially arises during the case of color clustering with arbitrarily shaped clusters (Celenk 1990; Xi et al.2007).

Figure 1. Results of Arecanut crop bunch segmentation using Threshold method

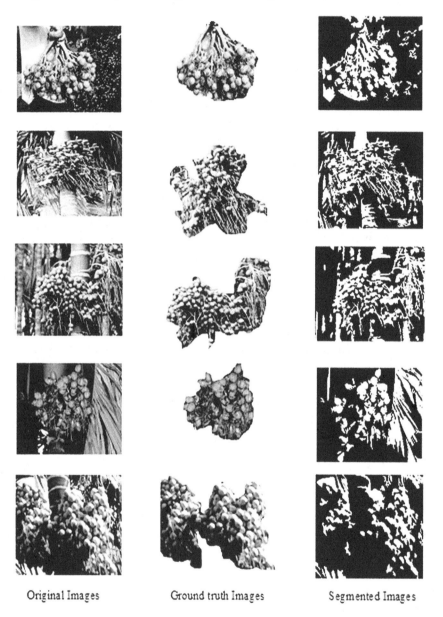

Original Images	Ground truth Images	Segmented Images

The K-Means clustering method is one of the well-known methodologies connected to comprehend low-level image segmentation. In K-Means clustering a specific number of disjoint, flat (non-hierarchical) clusters were generated. It is well suits to the situation related to globular cluster generation. It is an unsupervised, numerical, iterative and non-deterministic method.

This algorithm is joined and its point is to optimize the partitioning choices focused around a user defined initial set of clusters. The applications of the clustering algorithms to division of complex color textured images are confined by two issues. The main issue is created by the beginning condition (the initialization of the initial cluster), while the second is produced by the way that no spatial (regional) attachment is connected amid the space partitioning procedure.

There are two preprocessing steps that are required for the implementation of K-means clustering algorithm: The stage begins first by making device independent color space transformation structure. Device independent color space, the coordinates used to point out the color will deliver the same shade regardless of the device used to draw it. Hence, making the color change structure that characterizes the shade space transformation is needed. At that point, the connection of device independent color space change, which changes over the color values in the image to the color space defined in the color change structure. The color change structure determines different parameters of the change. A device color space is the one where the resultant color relies on upon the supplies used to create it. Case in point the color created utilizing pixel with a given RGB qualities will be adjusted as the splendor and differentiation on the presentation device utilized. Hence the RGB framework is a shade space that is reliant (Agarwal and Xaxa 2014).

Generally, iterative frameworks are used for implementing spatial partitioning methods for either minimizing the variation within the clusters or try to identify the optimal partitions on a set of Gaussian Mixture Models (Farnoosh and Zarpak 2008). It is a nonhierarchical clustering technique and has a simple process to classify the given data set through a number of K clusters known apriori. K-Means algorithm iteratively updates space partition of the input data, where the elements exchanged between clusters based on a predefined metric (Euclidian distance and the vector under analysis) for satisfying the criteria of minimization of variation inside each cluster and maximization of variation among the resulting K clusters. The *K*-means clustering is a partitioning method for combining objects to minimize the within-group variance. By minimizing dissimilarity of a local subset, the algorithm will yield an optimal dissimilarity of all subsets globally (Gonzalez and Woods 2009).

The algorithm has following steps to image threshold:

1. Initialize the (K) class centers. Use an unequal-distance method to define the initial class centers:

$$Cen_i^0 = GV_{min} + \left[\left(\frac{(j - j/2)(GV_{max} - GV_{min})}{K} \right) \right] \qquad (1)$$

where $j = 1, 2, ... K$ and where Cen_i^0 is the initial class center for the *jth* class, GV_{max} and GV_{min} are the maximum and minimum of the gray value GV in the sample space.

2. Assign each point to its closest class center. The criterion to assign a point to a class is based on the Euclidean distance in the feature (*GV*) space using:

$$Dist_{i,j} = abs\left(GV_j - Cen_i \right) \qquad (2)$$

where $i = 1, 2, ... M$ and $j = 1, 2, ... N$ and where $Dist_{i,j}$ is the distance from the *jth* point to the *ith* class, and *N* is the total number of points in the sample space.

3. Calculate the (K) new class centers from the mean of the points that are assigned to it. The new class centers are calculated by N_i

$$Cent_i^m = \frac{1}{N_j} \sum_{i=1}^{N_i} GV_j \tag{3}$$

where $j = 1, 2, ... K$ and where N_i, is the total number of points that are assigned to the ith class in step 2.

4. Repeat step 2 if any class centers change, otherwise end the circulation.
5. The threshold value is defined as the average of the Kth class center and the $(K-1)th$ class center:

$$Thresh = \frac{1}{2} \left[Cent_K + Cent(K-1) \right] \tag{4}$$

This method is having some limitations; it is difficult to assume the value of K, it will not work well with global clusters, result may have different final clusters due to different initial partitions and this will not well suits to clusters of different size and density.

The result obtained by this technique is not better for segmentation purpose. This is due to the partitions created having similarities in color and to the complex background. This also fails in minimizing the within-group variance.

The Results of arecanut crop bunch segmentation using K-Means Clustering method with K=2 is shown in Figure 2 and the performance of this technique is shown in Table 1.

Fuzzy C-Means (FCM) Method

In case of hard clustering, the sample data is partioned into distinct clusters, among those each data element belongs to specifically to only one cluster. Fuzzy clustering sometimes also known as soft clustering where, data elements can be grouped in to more than one cluster, and those associated with each element is the belongs to the set of membership levels. This highlights the strength of association between the particular data element with a specific cluster. During the process Fuzzy clustering assigns the different membership levels and later using these membership levels assigns the data elements to one or more clusters. Fuzzy c-means (FCM) algorithm incorporates the spatial information of the data into the membership function for clustering. The spatial function is arrived from the summation of the each pixel under consideration with its neighborhood as membership function (Chuang et al. 2006).

Fuzzy Segmentation is considered as one of the interest area of research. Most analytic fuzzy clustering approach is derived from the fuzzy C-means (FCM) algorithm (Chaabane et al. 2008; Muthukannan and Latha 2012). The segmentation carried out using the thresholding technique, while the fine segmentation assigns the unclassified pixels to the closet class using Fuzzy C means (Chaabane et al. 2008; Yang et al. 2005).

Figure 2. Results of Arecanut crop bunch segmentation using K-means with K=2

Original Image	Ground Truth	Segmented image

The algorithm can be given mathematically as follows,

$$J_m\left(X,Y\right) = \sum_{i=1}^{n}\sum_{j=1}^{c} u_{ji}^m d^2\left(p_i, q_j\right) \tag{5}$$

with

$$\sum_{i=1}^{c} u_{ij} = 1, 1 \leq i \leq n,$$

Table 1. Comparison and evaluation of different segmentation methods

Evaluation Parameters	Threshold					K-Means				
	1	**2**	**3**	**4**	**5**	**1**	**2**	**3**	**4**	**5**
Correlation	-0.29	-0.09	-0.15	-0.12	0.112	0.03	-0.16	-0.09	0.04	-0.20
RSME	13.61	13.15	12.88	12.99	13.94	11.89	11.76	11.55	13.18	11.02
Jaccard Coefficient	0.545	0.651	0.691	0.623	0.538	0.09	0.610	0.677	0.565	0.632
Dice Coefficient	0.004	0.005	0.005	0.005	0.004	0.005	0.004	0.004	0.004	0.004
Evaluation Parameters	**FCM**					**FFCM**				
	1	**2**	**3**	**4**	**5**	**1**	**2**	**3**	**4**	**5**
Correlation	-0.18	-0.06	0.07	-0.11	0.05	0.039	0.002	0.05	0.02	0.003
RSME	13.38	13.04	12.14	13.08	13.19	13.72	13.75	13.43	13.49	12.46
Jaccard Coefficient	0.601	0.659	0.730	0.605	0.603	0.999	1.000	0.999	0.999	1.000
Dice Coefficient	0.005	0.005	0.005	0.005	0.005	0.007	0.007	0.007	0.008	0.008
Evaluation Parameters	**MSRM**									
	1		**2**		**3**		**4**		**5**	
Correlation	0.430		0.330		0.400		0.300		0.600	
RSME	5.690		5.180		8.530		5.800		7.820	
Jaccard Coefficient	0.990		1.000		0.990		0.990		1.000	
Dice Coefficient	0.005		0.005		0.006		0.005		0.006	

$$u_{ij} \geq 0, 1 \leq i \leq n, 1 \leq j \leq c ,$$

$$\sum_{i=1}^{n} u_{ij} > 0, 1 \leq j \leq c$$

where $P = \left\{ p_1, p_2, ... p_n \right\} \subset R^s$, s is the dimension of space, n is the number of unclassified pixels, c is the number of clusters $(1 < c < n)$, m is the fuzzy factor .., $d_{ij} = \left\| p_i - q_j \right\|$ is the distance between sample p_i and clustering center q_j with $(1 < j < c)$. p_{ij} is the membership of the jth sample of the ith cluster center. The segmentation results are as shown in Figure 3 and the performance of this technique is shown in Table 1.

The FCM algorithm utilizes shared distances to compute the fuzzy weights. At the point when a feature vector is of equal distance from two cluster centers, it weights the same on the two clusters regardless of what is the distribution of the clusters. It can't separate the two clusters with distinctive distributions of feature vectors. Hence, the FCM algorithm is well suited to data that is pretty much uniformly distributed around the cluster centers. The FCM algorithm divides the two clusters with characteristic shapes but close boundaries into a large cluster.

In this case, the result obtained is quite better compare to the previous two methods. The unclassified pixels are grouped together based on the fuzzy c means. While grouping the foreground pixels there is an overlapping with background pixels.

Figure 3. Results of Arecanut crop bunch segmentation using Fuzzy C Means (FCM) clustering method

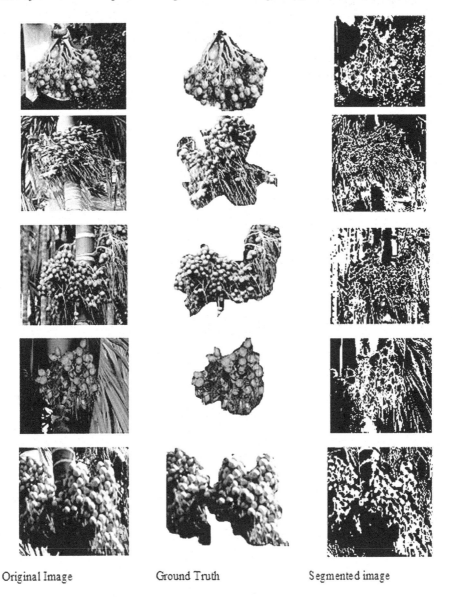

Original Image   Ground Truth   Segmented image

Fast Fuzzy C-Means (FFCM) Method

Fuzzy C Means clustering algorithm is widely used for image segmentation purpose. This concentrates those points which belong to two or more classes with respective membership. This algorithm gives good segmentation results, only when the input image should be noiseless. This fails to properly segment the images which are corrupted by noise.

To avoid these issues, a modified Fuzzy C Means segmentation method based on spatial constraints can be used (Capitaine and Frelicot 2011). The modified FCM segmentation algorithm will be compensating the intensity non homogeneities by modifying the objective function (Chen and Lu 2002; Pratt 2008).

The FFCM algorithm has following steps:

1. Computing the agglomerated histogram of the color image: Let n be the number of colors in the agglomerated histogram and c is the number of major segments with $(c < n)$, H_k is the number of pixels having color X_k represents the cluster k. The modified FCM with histogram data is given by,

$$Y_i = \frac{\sum_{j=1}^{n} u_{ji}^m \cdot p_j \cdot H_k}{\sum_{j=1}^{n} u_{ji}^m \cdot H_k} \tag{6}$$

where $j = 1, 2, \ldots c$.

2. Generation of Fuzzy functions using the following equation by replacing N by n

$$m_{ij} = \left[\sum_{j=1}^{c} \left(\frac{d_{ik}}{d_{jk}} \right)^{\frac{2}{m-1}} \right]^{-1}, \quad i = 1, 2, \ldots c \text{ and } k = 1, 2, \ldots N \tag{7}$$

3. Construct the partition matrix for FCM of size $cx(n+1)$ using the following equation

$$m = \frac{1}{1 + \alpha d^2} \tag{8}$$

where m is the membership value for every pixel of the image, d is the Euclidean distance between the color coefficients and the cluster seed, the color coefficients and the cluster seeds are scaled to the interval [0,1] and α is an arbitrary constant to control the memberships on the distances i.e., the fuzziness, such that $0 \leq \alpha \leq 1$.

4. Determine the cluster centers using equation (6), store the cluster centers.
5. New partition or the membership values can be computed using the cluster centers from Step 4 and equation (7).
6. Steps 4 and 5 are repeated till the error of the respective cluster centers should become below the threshold.
7. Hardening the converged partition will yield the segmented image.

In this technique the results are better compared to Fuzzy C Means but not sufficient. This is once again based on generation of histogram for color image, which again sets a complexity in selection of proper threshold values between back ground and fore ground.

The corresponding arecanut crop bunch segmentation results are shown in Figure 4 and the performance of this technique is shown in Table 1.

Figure 4. Results of Arecanut crop bunch segmentation using Fast Fuzzy C Means (FFCM) method

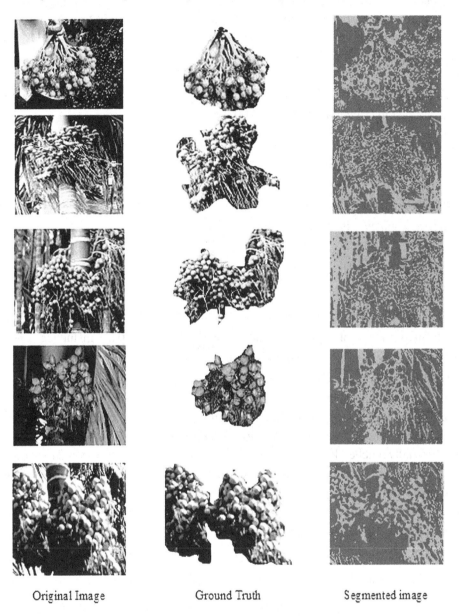

| Original Image | Ground Truth | Segmented image |

Watershed Algorithm

Due to the problem of selecting a proper threshold values in case of histogram generation, the region based algorithms are used. Region based segmentation algorithms operates based on grouping the pixels iteratively with its neighbors which are having similar values and splitting the group whose pixels are having dissimilar values (Kim and Kim 2003; Schettini 1993).

Watershed transformation is one of the region based segmentation approaches. The idea is coined from the field of geography which includes landscape or topographic relief flooded by water. Watersheds divide the lines of regions of attraction where rain is falling. This can be imagined when the landscape immersed in a lake, with holes in local minima. The catchment basins starts filling up with water from local minima and at some parts water emerges from different basins would meet and builds the dam. This process will be stopped when the water level reaches the highest peak of the landscape. Based on this, the landscape splits into different regions separated by dams known as watershed (Gonzalez and Woods 2009).

Let $f(x, y)$ with $(x, y) \in R^2$, be a real scalar function describing an image *I*. The morphological gradient of I is defined in (Belaid and Mourou 2009) by,

$$\delta_D f = \left(f \oplus D \right) - \left(f \ominus D \right) \tag{9}$$

where $\left(f \oplus D \right)$ and $(f \ominus D)$ are the elementary dilation and erosion of *f* by the structuring element *D*. The morphological Laplacian is given by

$$\Delta_D f = \left(f \oplus D \right) - 2f + \left(f \ominus D \right) \tag{10}$$

This morphological Laplacian influence zones of minima and suprema: regions with $\Delta_D u < 0$ are considered as influence zones of suprema, while regions with $\Delta_D u > 0$ are influence zones of minima. $\Delta_D u = 0$ interprets edge locations, and represent an essential property for the construction of morphological filters. The idea here is to apply either dilation or erosion to the image *I*, depending on whether the pixel is located within the influence zone of a minimum or a maximum.

The Catchment basin *C(M)* associated to a minimum *M* is the set of pixels *p* of Ω an open bounded domain of *R*, such that a water drop falling at *p* flows down along the relief, following a certain descending path, and eventually reaches *M*. The catchment basins of an image *I* correspond then to the influence zones of its minima, and the watershed will be defined by the lines that separate adjacent catchment basins (Belaid and Mourou 2009; Gonzalez and Woods 2009).

Computation of watersheds and the most commonly used is based on an immersion process analogy. This immersion process can be formulated as follows, Let h_{min} and h_{max} are the smallest and the largest values taken by *f*. Let $T_h = \left\{ p \in \Omega, f(p) \leq h \right\}$ be the threshold set of *f* at level *h*. A recursion with the gray level h increasing from h_{min} and h_{max}, in which the basins associated with the minimum of *f* are successively expanded. Let X_h is the union of the set of basins computed at level *h*. A connected component of threshold set $T_h + 1$ at level $h + 1$ can be a new minimum, or an extension of a basin in X_h. By denoting min_h, the union of all regional minima at level *h*, the following recursion defines the watershed by immersion.

$$\begin{cases} x_{h_{min}} = T_{h_{min}} \\ \forall h \in \left[h_{min}, h_{max} - 1 \right], X_{n+1} = min_{h+1} UIZ_{Th+1}(X_n) \end{cases}$$

with $IZ_{Th+1} = \bigcup_{i=1}^{k} iZ_{Th+1}\left(X_{n_i} \right), k -$ is the number of minima of *I* and $iZT_{h+1}\left(X_{hi} \right)$

$$iZ_\Omega\left(Y_i\right) = \left\{Z \in \Omega, \forall k \neq i, d_\Omega\left(Z, Y_i\right) \leq d_\Omega\left(Z, Y_k\right)\right\} \tag{11}$$

The set of the catchment basins of a gray level image I is equal to the set $X_{h\max}$. At the end of this process, the watershed of the image I is the complement of $X_{h\max}$ in Ω (Belaid and Mourou 2009).

The main issue with watershed technique is that it is highly sensitive to local minima. And at each minima a watershed is created. If there is a noise in the image, it creates a watershed which is not desired. So the image with noise will have an impact on the segmentation. In order to rectify this issue the sigma setting of the Gaussian filter is adjusted to smoothen the image, which minimizes the noise and the local minima in turn. This enhances the usefulness of the watershed segmentation. The level of this sigma can be balanced by the user. While setting up the sigma value if the Gaussian filter care has to be taken with the value of sigma, if the value of sigma is too high, the watershed location will be shifted to some other location due to the impact of Gaussian blurring.

This algorithm is based on region, and tried to create different regions present in the given input image. Later based on the similarities, the region can be split or merged. Once again the complexity of background in the input image creates regions which are the combination of foreground and background in certain points due to similarities.

The watershed segmentation results are shown in Figure 5 and the performance watershed technique is shown in Table 1.

Maximal Similarity Based Region Merging (MSRM)

From the analysis and experimentation of the above methods, it is evident that single segmentation techniques will not suited to the requirement. This makes the automatic segmentation very complex and leads to the need of suitable hybrid segmentation techniques. Automatic segmentation of object from background is very hard in case of natural images with color and texture features. Because of this difficulty, semi-automatic segmentation methods with user interactions have been become very popular. The low level image segmentation methods like mean shift (Cheng 1995; Bailer et al. 2005; Zheng et al. 2009), watershed (Belaid and Mourou 2009) etc. will divide the image into small regions. Even these may suffer with over segmentation issues, these methods provide a good reason for the low level operation such as region merging. This is a Hybrid technique which works using the combination of mean shift and region merging technique. The MSRM method is based on the initial segmentation of mean shift. The interaction information is through markers, which is the input provided by the user by indicating roughly the object and background. The markers are simple strokes. Once the strokes are marked on the mean shifted input image, this method calculates the similarity of various regions and merges them based on maximal similarity rule. At the end of merging process, the object is extracted from the background (Singh and Singh 2010).

The mean shift algorithm is defined as in (Bailer et al. 2005; Zheng et al. 2009),

Let $S \subset X$ be a finite set or data or sample. Let K *be* a kernel and $w = S \rightarrow (0, \infty)$ a weight function. The sample mean with kernel K at $x \in X$ is defined as,

Figure 5. Results of Arecanut crop bunch segmentation using Watershed method

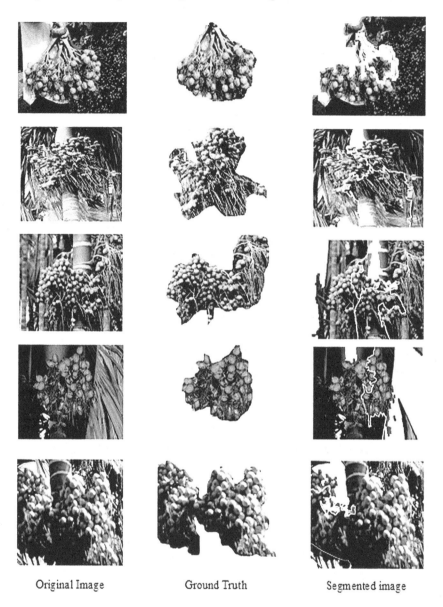

Original Image   Ground Truth   Segmented image

$$m(x) = \frac{\sum\limits_{s \in S} K(s-x)w(s)s}{\sum\limits_{s \in S} K(s-x)w(s)} \tag{12}$$

Let $T \subset X$ be a finite set or (cluster centers). The evolution of T is the form of iterations $T \leftarrow m(t)$ with $m(T) = \{m(t); t \in T\}$ known as a mean shift algorithm (Bailer et al. 2005). For each $t \in T$, there is a sequence $t, m(t), m(m(t)), ...$ is called as the trajectory of t. The weight $w(s)$ can be either fixed all through the process or re-evaluated after each iteration. It may also be a function of the current 'T'. The algorithm works till it reaches a fixed point $(m(T) = T)$.

In this work, the EDISON system was used to carry out mean shift segmentation (EDISON v1.1 2002). Once the mean shift segmentation is done, there are small regions available. To guide the region merging process, the regions should be represented by certain descriptors with a rule for merging. A region can be described by some features like color, texture, edge, shape and size. Color histogram is used as an effective feature for representing the object color statistics. The RGB color space is used for color histogram and each color channel i.e., R,G,B are quantize into 16 levels and histogram of each color is computed in the feature space of 16x16x16= 4096 bins.

In the interactive program part, users will mark the some regions as object and some as background. The similarity measure (R, Q) between two regions R and Q to accommodate the comparison between various regions is defined as,

$$\rho(R,Q) = \sum_{u=1}^{4096} \sqrt{Hist_R^u \cdot Hist_Q^u} \tag{13}$$

where $Hist_R^u$ and $Hist_Q^u$ are normalized histograms of R and Q, and u represents the uth element of them. ρ is a divergence measure known as Bhattacharyya coefficient (Fukunaga 1990) having a straight forward geometric interpretation. It is the cosine of the angle between the unit vectors.

$$\left(\sqrt{Hist_R^1}, \ldots, \sqrt{Hist_R^{4096}}\right)^T and \left(\sqrt{Hist_Q^1}, \ldots, \sqrt{Hist_Q^{4096}}\right)^T .$$

The higher the value of Bhattacharyya coefficient between R and Q, the higher the similarity between them.

In the integrative image segmentation, user has to specify the object and the background. This can be marked by drawing some markers, such as a line, curve or a stroke to highlight the object and the background. One the marking is done, each region is labeled with three regions such as, marked object, marked background and non-marked region. For the total extraction of the object, user needs to assign each non-marker region with a correct label of object region or background region automatically.

After marking process is done, the challenge lies in extraction of object contour from background. To identify all non-marker regions with the guidance of object and background markers, an adaptive maximal similarity based merging is used. Let Q be an adjacent of R and denote by $S_Q = \left\{S_i^Q\right\}, i = 1, 2, \ldots, q$ the set of $Q's$ adjacent regions. The similarity between Q and all its adjacent regions, i.e., $\rho\left(Q, S_i^Q\right), i = 1, 2, \ldots q$ are calculated. Obviously R is a member of S_Q. If the similarity between R and Q is the maximal one among all the similarities $\rho\left(Q, S_i^Q\right)$, we will merge R and Q. and the merging rule is given by,

$$Merge\ R\ and\ Q\ if\ \rho(R,Q) = \max_{i=1,2,\ldots q}\rho\left(Q, S_i^Q\right) \tag{14}$$

The MSRM process has two stages; first stage is about merging marker background regions with their adjacent regions. After this merging some non-marker background regions will be merged with the respective background markers. The second stage is focused on non-marker regions which are still remaining after first stage. This procedure is iteratively implemented and the iteration stops when the entire non marker region set will not find new regions for merging (Ning et al 2009).

The corresponding results are shown on Figure 6 and the comparison of performance of this hybrid technique with other techniques is shown in Table 1.

This hybrid segmentation technique gives somewhat promising result compared to the previous methods. This drives the need of hybrid segmentation techniques further for the problems related to natural image segmentation.

Figure 6. Results of Arecanut crop bunch segmentation using Maximal Similarity based Region Merging (MSRM) method

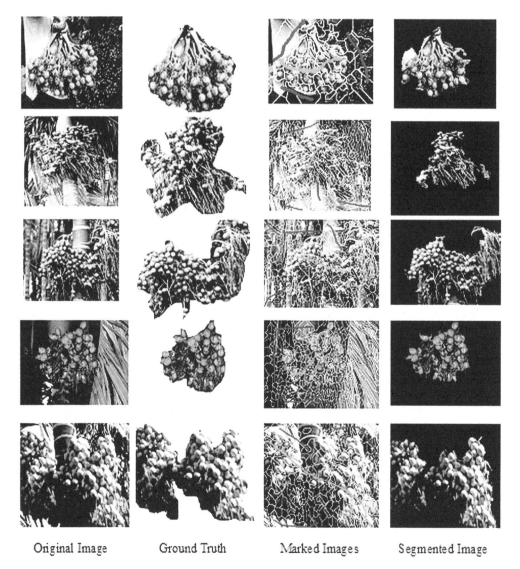

Original Image Ground Truth Marked Images Segmented Image

DISCUSSION AND CONCLUSION

The different segmentation techniques explored in this chapter are having certain limitations (Khan and Ravi 2013). The threshold segmentation method neglects the spatial information of the image, it highly noise sensitive and selection of the threshold value is crucial and based on this it suffers either over segmentation or under segmentation issues. Sometimes this leads to pseudo edges or missing edges. In K-means clustering approach the selection of desired number of clusters based on needs to be set earlier. This creates ambiguity while setting of the number of clusters. Fuzzy C-means method raises the ambiguity among the choice of features for better results for the given image. This is somewhat slow; this can be overcome by using certain histograms as in Fast Fuzzy C Means clustering method (Chaabane et al. 2008). Watershed methods even though give good results, it suffers from over segmentation and it unnecessarily segments into a number of regions (Belaid and Mourou 2009). It provides the connected component at the cost of computation time. This faces difficulty when segmenting the image with noise. Maximal Similarity based Region Merging method is semi automatic and needs human intervention for marking the background and the object; this makes this method computationally slow. It is intolerant to noise and moderately detects multiple objects. After exploring the above mentioned color segmentation techniques since we got better results using MSRM in comparison with other techniques, we have evaluated the MSRM technique using the evaluation parameters such as, Correlation, Jaccard coefficient, mean square error (RMSE) and Dice coefficient.

The correlation used as a measure of the similarity between ground truth image and a segmented image. The value of the correlation coefficient is between -1 and 1, where -1 indicates the similarity measure is away from the desired result. The Jaccard similarity coefficient, also known as the Tanimoto coefficient, measures the cover of two sets. It is characterized as the measure of the intersection of the sets partitioned by the span of their union. The Jaccard coefficient is zero if the two sets are disjoint, and is one if they are identical. So when applied this to evaluate the agreement of segmentation results, the goal is to get as close to 1 as possible. The simplest of image quality measurement is Mean square Error (MSE). The large value of MSE means that image is poor quality and The Root MSE (RMSE) is calculated using the formula, $RMSE = \sqrt{MSE}$. The Dice coefficient is similar to Jaccrd coefficient and represents the size of the union of 2 sets divided by the average size of the two sets. Dice coefficient with value of 0 indicates no overlap; and a value of 1 indicates perfect agreement. Higher numbers indicate better agreement.

The maximal similarity based region merging segmentation (MSRM) method is better compared to other methods and the corresponding evaluation is shown in Table 1 for images shown in Figure 6. From Table 1 it is evident that MSRM provides fair segmentation result and needs some improvement. This further drives for the need for some robust color segmentation algorithm for the purpose of Arecanut crop bunch segmentation.

FUTURE RESEARCH

Based on the experimentation on different color segmentation techniques it is clear that there will be a need of efficient and robust color segmentation techniques is essential for natural images. Also with single algorithm the results are not promising, this makes the essentiality of some hybrid color segmentation techniques which is either the fusion of existing algorithms. In the last technique the approach is semi-automatic which require human intervention in choosing the back ground and the object of interest. So based on these issue the future direction of this work focused at the following:

1. Automation of object and background selection part of MSRM algorithm.
2. Exploring graph based segmentation methods for the better results (Baldevbhai and Anand 2012; Shi and Malik 2000).
3. Exploring more hybrid segmentation methods i.e., fusion of segmentation methods.
4. Formulation of robust color segmentation techniques for images with complex background.
5. Exploration and experimentation of new segmentation techniques on different color spaces and hybridization of the color spaces.

REFERENCES

Agarwal, S., & Xaxa, D. K. (2014). Survey on Image Segmentation Techniques and Color Models. [IJCSIT]. *International Journal of Computer Science and Information Technologies*, 5(3), 3025–3030.

Bailer, W., Schallauer, P., Haraldsson, H. B., & Rehatschek, H. (2005). Optimized Mean Shift Algorithm for Color Segmentation in Image Sequences. In IS&T/SPIE Electronic Imaging (Vol. 5685, pp. 593–600).

Baldevbhai, P. J., & Anand, R. S. (2012). Review of Graph, Medical and Color Image base Segmentation Techniques. *IOSR Journal of Electrical and Electronics Engineering (IOSRJEEE)*, 1(1), 1-19.

Baltazar, A., Aranda, J. I., & Gonzalez-Aguilar, G. (2008). Bayesian classification of ripening stages of tomato fruit using acoustic impact and colorimeter sensor data. *Computers and Electronics in Agriculture*, 60(2), 113–121. doi:10.1016/j.compag.2007.07.005

Belaid, L. J., & Mourou, W. (2009). Image Segmentation: A Watershed Transformation Algorithm. *Journal of Image Analysis and Stereology by International Society for Stereology*, 28(2), 93–102. doi:10.5566/ias.v28.p93-102

Benson, E. R., Reid, J. F., & Zhang, Q. (2003). Machine vision–based guidance system for an Agricultural small–grain harvester. *Transactions of the American Society of Agricultural Engineers*, 46(4), 1255–1264. doi:10.13031/2013.13945

Bhoyar, K., & Kakde, O. (2010). Colour Image Segmentation using Fast Fuzzy C-Means Algorithm. *Electronic Letters on Computer Vision and Image Analysis*, 9(1), 18–31.

Capitaine, H. L., & Frelicot, C. (2011). A fast fuzzy c-means algorithm for color image segmentation. *Proceedings of International Conference of the European Society for Fuzzy Logic and Technology (EU-SFLAT'2011)*, France (pp. 1074-1081). doi:10.2991/eusflat.2011.9

Celenk, M. (1990). A color clustering technique for image segmentation. *Computer Vision Graphics and Image Processing*, 52(2), 145–170. doi:10.1016/0734-189X(90)90052-W

Chaabane, B. S., Sayadi, M., Fnaiech, F., & Brassart, E. (2008). *Color Image Segmentation using Automatic Thresholding and the Fuzzy C-Means Techniques. Electro technical conference, 14th IEEE Mediterranean* (pp. 857–861). Ajaccio: ISBN.

Chen, T. Q., & Lu, Y. (2002). Color image segmentation - an innovative approach. *Pattern Recognition, 35*(2), 395–405. doi:10.1016/S0031-3203(01)00050-4

Cheng, Y. Z. (1995). Mean shift, Mode seeking and clustering. *IEEE Transactions on Pattern Analysis and Machine Intelligence, 17*(8), 790–799. doi:10.1109/34.400568

Chhabra, M., Gour, R., & Reel, P. S. (2012). Detection of Fully and Partially Riped Mango by Machine vision. *Proceeding of the International Conference on Recent Trends in Information Technology and Computer Science ICRTITCS* (pp. 26-31). doi:10.1007/978-81-322-0491-6_15

Chuang, K. S., Tzeng, H. L., Chen, S., Wu, J., & Chen, T. J. (2006). Fuzzy c-means clustering with spatial information for image segmentation. *Journal of Computerized Medical Imaging and Graphics, 30*(1), 9–15. doi:10.1016/j.compmedimag.2005.10.001 PMID:16361080

Cox, S. (2002). Information technology: The global key to precision agriculture and sustainability. *Computers and Electronics in Agriculture Journal, 36*(2-3), 93–111. doi:10.1016/S0168-1699(02)00095-9

Danti, A., & Suresha, M. (2012a). Arecanut Grading Based on Three Sigma Controls and SVM, Proceedings of the IEEE-International Conference On Advances In Engineering, Science And Management (ICAESM), Nagapattinam, Tamilnadu, India (pp. 372-376).

Danti, A., & Suresha, M. (2012b). Segmentation and classification of raw arecanuts based on three sigma control limits. Journal Procedia Technology. *Sciverse Science Direct, 4*, 215–219.

Danti, A., & Suresha, M. (2012c).Texture Based Decision Tree Classification for Arecanut, *Proceedings of the CUBE International Information Technology Conference* (pp. 113-117). ACM Publications.

Elbalaoui, A., Fakir, M., Idrissi, N., & Marboha, A. (2013). Review of Color Image Segmentation. *International Journal of Advanced Computer Science and Applications* (Special Issue on Selected Papers from Third international symposium on Automatic Amazigh processing), 15-21. doi:10.14569/SpecialIssue.2013.030204

Farnoosh, R., & Zarpak, B. (2008). Image Segmentation using Gaussian mixture model. *International Journal of Engineering Science, 19*(1-2), 29–32.

Fu, K. S., & Mui, J. K. (1981). A Survey on image segmentation. *Pattern Recognition Journal, 13*(1), 3–16. doi:10.1016/0031-3203(81)90028-5

Fukunaga, K. (1990). *Introduction to statistical Pattern recognition* (2nd ed.). Academic press.

Furfaro, R., Ganapol, B. D., Johnson, L. F., & Herwitz, S. R. (2007). Neural Network Algorithm for Coffee Ripeness Evaluation Using Airborne Images. *Applied Engineering in Agriculture, 23*(3), 379–387. doi:10.13031/2013.22676

Gao, H., Siu, W. C., & Hou, C. H. (2001). Improved Techniques for Automatic Image Segmentation. *IEEE Transactions on Circuits and Systems for Video Technology, 11*(12), 1273–1280. doi:10.1109/76.974681

Godwin, R. J., & Miller, P. C. H. (2003). A Review of the Technologies for Mapping Within-field Variability. *Biosystems Engineering Journal, 84*(4), 393–407. doi:10.1016/S1537-5110(02)00283-0

Goense, D., Hofstee, J. W., & Bergeijk, J. V. (1996). An information model to describe systems for spatially variable field operations. *Computers and Electronics in Agriculture Journal, 14*(2-3), 197–214. doi:10.1016/0168-1699(95)00048-8

Gonzalez, R. C., & Woods, R. E. (2009). *Digital Image Processing* (3rd ed.). Pearson Prentice Hall.

Goovaerts, P. (2000). Estimation or simulation of soil properties- An optimization problem with conflicting criteria. *Geoderma, 3*(3-4), 165–186. doi:10.1016/S0016-7061(00)00037-9

Gracy, C. P., Nagashree, N., Nayak, A., & Girisha, K. (2010). Recent Posts on Indian Scenario of arecanut. Retrieved from http://krishisewa.com/cms/articles/production-technology/61-arecanut.html

Guru, D. S., Mallikarjuna, P. B., Manjunath, S., & Shenoi, M. M. (2012). Machine vision based classification of tobacco leaves for automatic harvesting. *Intelligent Automation and Soft Computing Journal, 18*(5), 581–590. doi:10.1080/10798587.2012.10643267

Haralick, R. M., & Shapiro, L. G. (1985). Image segmentation techniques. *Computer Vision Graphics and Image Processing, 29*(1), 100–132. doi:10.1016/S0734-189X(85)90153-7

Hassankhani, R., & Navid, H. (2012). Potato Sorting Based on Size and Color in Machine Vision System. *The Journal of Agricultural Science, 4*(5), 235–244.

Huang, K. Y. (2012). Detection and classification of areca nuts with machine vision. *Journal Computers and Mathematics with Applications, 64*(5), 739–746. doi:10.1016/j.camwa.2011.11.041

Johnson, L. F., Herwitz, S. R., Lobitz, B. M., & Dunagan, S. E.L. F. Johnson; S. R. Herwitz; B. M. Lobitz; S. E. Dunagan. (2004). Feasibility of Monitoring Coffee Field Ripeness with Airborne Multispectral imagery. *Applied Engineering in Agriculture, 20*(6), 845–849. doi:10.13031/2013.17718

Khan, A. M., & Ravi, S. (2013). Image Segmentation Methods: A Comparative Study. *International Journal of Soft Computing and Engineering, 3*(4), 84-92.

Kim, J. B., & Kim, H. J. (2003). Multiresolution-based watersheds for efficient image segmentation. *Pattern Recognition Letters, 24*(1–3), 473–488. doi:10.1016/S0167-8655(02)00270-2

Koch, B., and Khosla, R.(2003). The Role of Precision Agriculture in Cropping Systems. *Journal of Crop Production*, 9(1/2), 361-381.

Lee, D., Archibald, J. K., Chang, Y., & Greco, C. R. (2008b). Robust color space conversion and color distribution analysis techniques for date maturity evaluation. *Journal of Food Engineering, 88*(3), 364–372. doi:10.1016/j.jfoodeng.2008.02.023

Lee, D., Archibald, J. K., & Xiong, G. (2011). Rapid Color Grading for Fruit Quality Evaluation Using Direct Color Mapping. *IEEE Transactions on Automation Science and Engineering, 8*(2), 292–302. doi:10.1109/TASE.2010.2087325

Lee, D. J., Chang, Y., Archibald, J. K., & Greco, C. G. (2008a). Color quantization and image analysis for automated fruit quality evaluation. Proceedings of the IEEE International Conference on Automation Science and Engineering (pp. 194-199). doi:10.1109/COASE.2008.4626418

Liu, T., Xie, J., He, Y., Xu, M., & Qin, C. (2009). An Automatic Classification Method for Betel Nut Based on Computer Vision, *Proceedings of the IEEE International Conference on Robotics and Biomimetics*, Guilin, China (pp. 19-23). doi:10.1109/ROBIO.2009.5420823

Lucchese, L., & Mitra, S. K. (2001). Color image segmentation: a state-of-the-art survey. In Proceedings of the Indian National Science Academy (INSA-A), New Delhi, India (Vol. 67, pp. 207–221).

Matthews, J. (1983). Some challenges for engineers in agriculture. *Journal of the Royal Agricultural Society of England*, *144*, 146–158.

Mondal, P., & Tiwari, V. K. (2007). Present status of Precision Farming: A Review. *International Journal of Agricultural Research*, *2*(1), 1–10. doi:10.3923/ijar.2007.1.10

Muthukannan, K., & Latha, P. (2012). Clustering Techniques based Crops Image Segmentation. *International Journal of Computer Applications (IJCA)*, *2*, 33-37.

Ning, J., Zhang, L., Zhang, D., & Wu, C. (2009). Interactive image segmentation by maximal similarity based region merging. *Pattern Recognition*, *43*(2), 445–456. doi:10.1016/j.patcog.2009.03.004

Pantofaru, C., & Herbert, M. (2005). A Comparison of image segmentation algorithms [Tech. Report] (CMU-RI-TR-05-40).

Pratt, W. K. (2008). *Image segmentation - Text book of Digital image Processing* (4th ed., pp. 579–622). Wiley.

Scarlet, A. J. (2001). Integrated control of agricultural tractors and implements: A review of potential opportunities relating to cultivation and crop establishment machinery. *Computers and Electronics in Agriculture Journal*, *30*(1-3), 167–191. doi:10.1016/S0168-1699(00)00163-0

Schettini, R. (1993). A segmentation algorithm for color images. *Pattern Recognition Letters*, *14*(6), 499–506. doi:10.1016/0167-8655(93)90030-H

Schillaci, G., Pennisi, A., Franco, F., & Longo, D. (2012). Detecting tomato crops in greenhouses using a vision based method. *Proc. International Conference on Safety Health and Welfare in Agriculture and in Agro-food Systems*, Ragusa – Italy (pp. 252-258).

Shi, J., & Malik, J. (2000). Normalized Cuts and Image Segmentation. *IEEE Transactions on Pattern Analysis and Machine Intelligence*, *22*(8), 888–905. doi:10.1109/34.868688

Singh, G., & Kamal, N. (2013). Machine Vision System for Tea Quality Determination – Tea Quality Index (TQI). IOSR Journal of Engineering, 3(7), 46-50.

Singh, K. K., & Singh, A. (2010). A Study of Image Segmentation Algorithms for Different Types of Images. *International Journal of Computer Science Issues*, *7*(5), 414–417.

Sridevi, M., & Mala, C. (2012). A Survey on Monochrome Image Segmentation Techniques. *Procedia Technology* (Vol. 6, pp. 548-555).

Stafford, J. V. (2000). Implementing Precision Agriculture in the 21st Century [Keynote address]. Proceedings of AgEng (Vol. 76, 267-275).

Stafford, J. V., & Ambler, B. (1994). In-Field location using GPS for spatially variable field operations. *Computers and Electronics in Agriculture Journal, 11*(1), 23–36. doi:10.1016/0168-1699(94)90050-7

Stafford, J. V., Ambler, B., Lark, R. M., & Catt, J. (1996). Mapping and interpreting the yield variation in Cereal Crops. *Computers and Electronics in Agriculture Journal, 14*(2-3), 101–119. doi:10.1016/0168-1699(95)00042-9

Vijay, J., Sohani, M., Shrivas A. (2014). Color Image Segmentation Using K-Means Clustering and Otsu's Adaptive Thresholding. *International Journal of Innovative Technology and Exploring Engineering*, 3(9), 72-76.

Xi, Y., Feng, D. D., Wang, T., Zhao, R., & Zhang, Y. (2007). Image segmentation by clustering of spatial patterns. *Pattern Recognition Letters, 28*(12), 1548–1555. doi:10.1016/j.patrec.2007.03.012

Xu, L. (2009). Strawberry Maturity Neural Network Detecting System Based on Genetic Algorithm. *Computer and Computing Technologies in Agriculture II, 2*, 1201–1208.

Yang, Y., Zheng, Ch., & Lin, P. (2005). Fuzzy C-means clustering algorithm with novel penalty term for image segmentation. *Opto-Electronics Review, 13*(4), 309–315.

Yin H., Chai, Y., Yang, S. X., and Mitta, G. S. (2009). Ripe tomato extraction for a harvesting robotic system. In *Systems, Man and Cybernetics* (pp. 2984-2989). IEEE.

Zhang, N., Wang, M., & Wang, N. (2002). Precision agriculture worldwide - an overview. *Journal of Computers and Electronics in Agriculture, 36*(2-3), 113–132. doi:10.1016/S0168-1699(02)00096-0

Zheng, L., Zhang, J., Wang, Q. (2009). Mean-shift-based color segmentation of images containing green vegetation. *Journal of computers and electronics in agriculture*, 65(1), 93-98.

Chapter 2
An Impact of Gaussian Mixtures in Image Retrieval System

K. Mahantesh
SJB Institute of Technology, India

Manjunath Aradhya V N
Sri Jayachamarajendra College of Engineering, India

ABSTRACT

The difficulty of searching for patterns in data is still exploratory and, ever increasing image datasets with high intra-class variations has created a large scope for generalizing image classification problems. This chapter initiates the inclusivity of discrete latent variables leading to mixture of Gaussians capturing multimodal distributions from segmented regions. Further, these mixtures are analyzed in maximum likelihood framework to extract discriminatory features in compact and de-correlated feature space. Conversely, it is less evident in literature that combining these features with diverse distance measure techniques and neural network classifiers improves the classification performance. In this chapter, we study, explore and demonstrate the idea of subspace mixture models as hybrid intelligent technique for image retrieval systems.

INTRODUCTION

The advances in internet and image acquisition techniques has given away tremendous increase in digital image collections usually generated by scientific, educational, medical, industrial and other applications. The application potential of managing these large image databases has drawn substantial attention of researchers to develop various techniques to browse, store and retrieve images from large image archives. Earlier, text based techniques are generally used to organize images with semantic hierarchies to facilitate easy navigation and browsing (Blaser 1979). However, manually annotating images for wide spectrum of images is obviously a cumbersome and expensive task for large image datasets which is often subjective to human perception, context sensitive and incomplete (Chang and Hsu 1992). Since text-based methods failed to support a variety of task-dependent queries, content-based image retrieval (CBIR) was introduced as an effective alternate in the early 1980's (Ritendra et al. 2008).

DOI: 10.4018/978-1-4666-9474-3.ch002

In CBIR, images are indexed by their visual content, such as color, texture & shapes. The problem of extracting/matching images has remained primarily statistical in nature, image retrieval systems employ pattern recognition methods to define the visual content with partial semantics (Gupta and Santini 1997). Many sophisticated algorithms designed to describe color, shape, and texture features, cannot adequately model image semantics and portray limitations while dealing broad content image databases (Mojsilovic and Rogowitz 2001). Extensive research on CBIR systems reveals low level contents with single and/or combination of multiple features often fail to describe the high level semantic concepts in user's mind (Zhou and Huang 2000). While this intrinsic difficulty in solving the core problem cannot be denied, we believe that the current state-of-the-art in CBIR holds enough promise and maturity to be useful for real-world applications, if aggressive attempts are made.

Few Existing Systems

Due to the advancements made in digital communication and the availability of image capturing devices (e.g. digital cameras and image scanners), the size of digital image collection is increasing rapidly. Usually, the keyword indexing-based retrieval systems are used to browse such images and a number of keyword-based general WWW search engines allow indicating that the media type must be images. Hot-Bot (http://hotbot.lycos.com/) and NBCi (http://www.nbci.com/) are examples of these. A number of other general search engines are more specifically for images, such as Yahoo!'s Picture Gallery (http://gallery.yahoo.com/) or the multimedia searcher of Lycos, but they are still only keyword-based. There are many special image collections on the web that can be searched with a number of alphanumerical keys e.g. ImageFinder (Guojun et al. 2007). ADL (Alexandria Digital Library) searches images with texture features which mainly focus on earth and social science applications (Manjunath et al. 1995). DEC Research Lab developed AltaVista Photofinder based on visual characteristics such as dominant colors, shapes and textures (Altavista). Berkeley Digital Library Project (BDLP) uses alphanumeric keys with content based search depending upon 13 color bins, six values with each bin and percentage of colors in each bin; all features are put into relational database (Chad et al. 1996). The features used for querying in Blobworld are the color, texture, location, and shape of regions (blobs) and of the background, Singular value decomposition (SVD) is used to project the histogram vectors onto a lower-dimensional subspace. The retrieved images are presented together with the segmented versions and the demo provides retrieval from a collection of 10000 corel stock photos (Serge et al. 1999). The ImageMiner system classifies landscapes, and body plans have been used to recognize animals and people (David et al. 1997). NETRA segments images in the database into homogeneous color regions later color, texture, shape, and spatial location features are extracted and finally SS-tree indexing is used to order the retrieval results (Wei et al. 1999).

BACKGROUND

The pattern recognition task of assigning an object to a class is referred to be a classification task. Over the past decade, significant attempts had been made to extract adequate features (patterns) and designing efficient classifiers to categorize object classes in an ever increasing datasets. The visual features such as Color (Wang et al. 2012), Shape (Safar et al. 2000), and Texture features (Ojala et al. 1994) are widely explored as image contents for image representation and retrieval. Global features failed to represent spatial distributions and hence consequently Color Coherence Vector (CCV), color correlograms, spatial color histogram, and spatial chromatic histogram proposed in (Cinque and Ciocca 2001) has incorporated the spatial color information in the descriptors. Texture provides high level semantic information obtained through local statistical measures for image classification (Sethi and Coman 2001). Wavelet sub-bands features are re-modeled as Hidden Markov Model (HMM) with different orientations and obtained rotation invariant texture features (Chen and Kundu 1994). Shape features are impressive in many domain specific images such as man-made objects. However, it is difficult to apply shape features compared to color and texture due to the inaccuracy of segmentation (Mehrotra and Gary 1995). Zhang (Zhang et al. 2006) uses segmentation for better representation of local image features and identifying salient points for improving classification rate.

A normalized cut criterion calculates the dissimilarity between the different groups As well as within the groups for perceptual grouping of images (Shi & Malik 2000). Boykov and Jolly (Boykov et al. 2001) segmented an image by computing a min-cut/max-flow on a graph which encodes both the user constraints and pair-wise pixel similarity. Logistic classifier was designed to predict edge strength using gradient operators for brightness, color and texture bands (Fowlkes et al. 2004). Boosted Edge Learning makes an effort to learn edge classifier in the form of a probabilistic boosting tree with many features computed on image patches (Tu et al. 2006). The Oriented Watershed Transform (OWT) is used to produce a set of initial regions; Ultrametric Contour Map (UCM) extracts boundaries from these regions. The sequence of OWT-UCM operations converts these contours to hierarchical region tree, and for a given threshold segmented output is a set of closed contours (Fowlkes et al. 2009). A globalized framework is developed using spectral clustering on multiscale color and texture cues. Local cues are computed by applying oriented gradient operators at every location in the image, which creates an affinity matrix with its coefficients as similarity distances between pixels. Contour information is encoded along with the fixe number eigen vectors from the affinity matrix (Fowlkes et al. 2011). In (Ren & Bo 2012), contours are extracted by computing sparse code gradients using orthogonal matching pursuit and K-SVD for dictionary learning. Sparse codes effectively measure local contrasts in locating contours in depth and outperform the state-of-the-art global Pb (gPb) operator. Wang and Sun (Wang et al. 2010) segmented color images based on low-level features such as color and texture. Since, color and texture of each segment possess non-uniform statistical characteristics and thus aimed at segmenting natural scenes.

SIFT (Shift Invariant Feature Transform) and color histogram in HSV color space are extracted as features and comparison of six different classifiers such as Principal Component Analysis (PCA), Fisher Linear Discriminant Analysis (FLDA), Local Fisher Discriminant Analysis (LFDA), Isometric Mapping (ISOMAP), Locally Linear Embedding (LLE), and Locality Preserving Projections (LPP) is carried out in (Zhuo et al. 2014). Color and texture features extracted using Color co-occurrence matrix (CCM) and difference between pixels of scan pattern (DBPSP) are given to neural network classifier to classify images in multimedia dataset (ElAlami 2014).

If the goal of feature extraction is to map input patterns onto points in a feature space, the purpose of classification is to assign each point in the space with a class label or membership scores to the defined classes. Hence, once a pattern is mapped (represented), the problem becomes one of the classical classification to which a variety of classification methods can be applied. Work on artificial neural networks (ANN's), commonly referred to as "neural networks", has been motivated right from its inception by the recognition that the human brain computes in an entirely different way from the conventional digital computer (Patterson 1995). From the late 1980s, artificial neural networks (ANNs) have been widely applied to pattern recognition due to the rediscovery and successful applications, which are able to separate class regions of arbitrarily complicated distributions. The Support Vector Machines (SVM) (Burges 1988) is a new type of hyperplane classifier, developed based on the statistical learning theory of Vapnik (Vapnik 1995). Multi-kernels SVM is used as classifier with bag of visual words and low level features and initiated multi-instance learning (Xiaoqiang et al. 2014). Nearest Neighbor (NN), SVM & Logistic Regression (LOG-REG) are used as classifiers across features obtained during learning filters by performing direct convolution of Leung Malik (LM) filter bank with an image and sparse features with iterative thresholding (Gonzalez et al. 2014).

In recent years, the trend on "similarity learning" is observed. The use of prior knowledge within a constellation model framework was suggested by Fei Fei (Fei-Fei et al. 2004), who extended the work of Fergus (Fergus et al. 2003) into a full Bayesian setting, thereby introducing prior distributions. Bag of Features (BoF) representing image as unorderly collection of local features, have demonstrated impressive levels of performance (Csurka et al. 2004). Though BoF improved classification rate but failed to give local information, this was overcome by partitioning image into pyramid like smaller sub-regions and computed histograms of these fragments as features reporting most successful results (Lazebnik et al. 2006). Kernel codebook approach describes an image as a bag of discrete visual code-words, where the frequency distributions of these words can be used for image categorization (Van et al. 2008). Difficulty of training restricted Boltzmann machines (RBMs) to develop effective image representation is connected with mixture models to improve classification performance (Kihyuk et al. 2011).

PCA provides its projected components as effective features for face recognition. Due to its unsupervised nature, class label information of the data is missing in PCA (Turk and Pentland 1991). Marian (Marian et al. 2002) proposed face recognition by ICA, in which faces are represented as a linear combination of basis images found using PCA depending on pixels pair wise relationships. Langlois (Langlois et al. 2010) presents an introduction to independent component analysis (ICA): InfoMax and FastICA algorithms and implementation using Mathematica software. Class label information of the data can be better utilized by applying Fisher's Linear Discriminant Analysis (FLD) (Belhumeur et al. 1997). The main objective of using subspace based approach is to reduce the dimension of feature space, maximize between-class variations and minimizes within-class scatter and most importantly making algorithms insensitive to higher order statistics.

MAIN FOCUS OF THE CHAPTER

The problem of facilitating a machine to learn and recognize object and its category is one of the most challenging tasks in computer vision and pattern recognition. The prime issues can be listed as follows:

1. Understanding image user's needs and information-seeking behavior.
2. To identify suitable ways of describing image content in varying conditions and ever expanding datasets.
3. To deal with the higher dimensional feature spaces for practical application of recognition systems.

Several approaches addressing the above mentioned issues have limited its ability to capture interesting correlations in the data. Yet, Gaussian distributions in the sense of having too many parameters failed to provide good approximations to multimodal distributions. A problem of identifying dominant correlations in the higher dimensional data still needs to be explored.

The main focus of this chapter is threefold:

1. To study the complex distributions with many input variables of the image features.
2. To introduce semantic learning by combining discriminative and generative models as a hybrid approach.
3. To study, analyse and explore Gaussian mixtures in image retrieval system.

SOLUTIONS AND RECOMMENDATIONS

In this chapter, we present a hybrid approach in automatic discovery of regularities in data and with the use of these regularities actions are taken to classify the image data into different categories. We emphasize to study the complex class distribution structures, which tend to increase in sparsity for deriving the useful visual features describing image content. Gaussian distribution being intrinsically unimodal fails to give good approximation with multiple parameters governing complexity of the data. In this regard, multimodal distributions are obtained by introducing latent variables leading to mixture of Gaussians. Expectation Maximization (EM) algorithm can be applied to these Gaussian mixtures to get best maximum likelihood estimators. Being motivated by these factors, we first segment all image categories in hybrid color space (HCbCr - LUV) to identify the color homogeneity between the neighboring pixels and then FCM technique is applied for partitioning image pixels into its coordinated clusters. Further, transformation matrix is obtained for each cluster by applying subspace methods such as Principal Component Analysis (PCA) & Fisher's Linear Discriminant (FLD) to all segmented classes. These clusters can be viewed as mixture of several Gaussian classes (latent variables) and Expectation Maximization (EM) algorithm is applied to these Gaussian mixtures giving best maximum likelihood estimators and thereby incorporating prior information with discriminative features in reduced feature space during learning process. For subsequent classification, the effectiveness of two different classifiers are explored, firstly by considering similarity/distance measure techniques and secondly neural network architectures such as Generalized Regression Neural Network (GRNN) & Probabilistic Neural Network (PNN) to obtain an average classification rate.

We also present a brief overview on impact of segmentation towards identifying these latent variables and its continued effect on recognition rates. More prominently, subspace mixture models can be used as a powerful framework to capture the dominant correlations in the dataset by expressing the forms and properties of complex distributions. The following sections briefly presents the above mentioned mixture models along with segmentation as preprocessing technique and performing classification in reduced feature space.

Pre-Processing

Image segmentation is considered as one of the important pre-processing tasks in the process of recognition and retrieval. Color uniformity is considered as a significant criterion for partioning the image into considerable multiple disjoint regions and the distribution of the pixel intensities are investigated in different color spaces. Hence in our earlier work, we examined color homogeneity of pixels in different

Table 1. Algorithm of proposed image segmentation model

Algorithm: Proposed complex hybrid color space model.
Input: RGB Color Image.
Output: Segmented Image.
Method:
Step 1: Transform RGB image into Y CbCr and HSI Color spaces.
Step 2: Consider CbCr of Y CbCr & H of HSI.
Step 3: Compute high dimensional hybrid HCbCr three 2-D matrices.
Step 4: Transform hybrid HCbCr to LUV color space.
Step 5: Apply direct clustering method k-means/FCM (k=3) for U & V components.
Step 6: Stop.
Method ends.

color spaces and derived hybrid color space model (Mahantesh et al. 2013). In this method, chrominance and human color vision perception components are extracted, which is crucial and found to be very effective for image segmentation. Algorithm of the derived complex hybrid color space model is as shown in Table 1.

The derived color space built by means of a sequential supervised feature selection scheme exhibits both psycho-visual and physical color significance, named complex hybrid color spaces. Pixels are discriminated between the pixel classes in the hybrid color space using k-means & FCM for better classification. After deriving multidimensional color space, identifying groups or clusters of data points can be carried out with a set of observed data and random D-dimensional euclidean values. Intuitively, we can think of a cluster as a set of data points with smaller inter-point distances in comparison distances outside the clusters. Here, in our work we have considered two such clustering methods known as k-means and FCM techniques which vary slightly from each other in assigning the data points to the respective clusters. In the following paragraphs, we shall see how FCM is different and dominated above k-means with its brief working principle.

K-Means Clustering

K-means is basically a two stage objective oriented clustering technique to obtain clusters by satisfying objective function. Some of the important steps can be mentioned as:

Step 1: Choose some initial cluster centers μ_k and initiate binary indicator variable r_{nk} w.r.t a data points.
Step 2: Define objective function J sometimes known as distortion measure.
Step 3: In the first phase, we minimize J w.r.t r_{nk} keeping μ_k constant.
Step 4: In the second phase, we minimize J w.r.t μ_k keeping r_{nk} constant.
Step 5: Steps 3 to 4 repeated until better convergence.

Fuzzy C-Means

Fuzzy C-Means (FCM) is an optimization clustering technique to obtain membership values along with the centroids of the individual clusters. The key steps entailed in FCM process to extract pixel-level color feature is as given below:

Step 1: Initialize the membership values randomly.
Step 2: Compute the centroids of each clusters.
Step 3: Update the membership values using the current values of the centroids.
Step 4: Compute the difference between previous and current membership values.
Step 5: If computed value is less than threshold value go to Step 2, else end the process.

Fuzzy clustering uses weighted centroids which are based on the analysis of its probabilities for assigning the data point to its group. Whereas, in k-means there lays an ambiguity of assigning the same data point to its group due to distance function calculations. FCM almost produces close result to k-means and recent survey has revealed that FCM is best suitable in understanding patterns and feasible for segmentation in image retrieval applications (Sanjay et al. 2013). The detailed study and experimental simulations revealed that, direct clustering method such as FCM applied to images in derived hybrid color space generates perceptually meaningful regions (Mahantesh et al. 2013), and further carried forwarded as preprocessing step for feature extraction and classification stages in upcoming sections.

Gaussian Mixture Models

The proposed method is based on mixture models in which Expectation Maximization (EM) algorithm is used to learn the mixture of Gaussians. Intent to provide good approximation to multimodal distributions fails due to its intrinsic unimodal property of Gaussian distributions and also very limited in representing adequate number of distributions. Latent variables also called as hidden or unobserved variables can be used in mixture distribution which allows us to solve both of the aforesaid issues. Discrete latent variables can also be interpreted as assigning data points towards specific components of mixtures. EM algorithm is one of the techniques for finding maximum likelihood estimation in latent variable (Bishop 2006).

A simple Gaussian distribution being unsuccessful in capturing the dominant clumps of the given dataset (e.g. four clumps as shown in Figure 1(a)), whereas a linear superposition of Gaussians succeeds in better characterization. Hence, mixture distributions are formulated considering superpositions of

Figure 1. Illustrations of: (a) Gaussian mixture distribution in one dimension showing '4' Gaussians; (b) Gaussian mixtures estimated by EM (for '4' clusters)

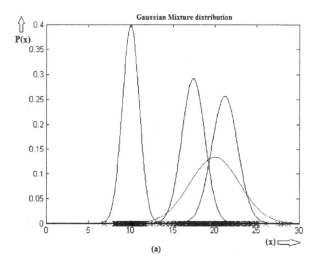
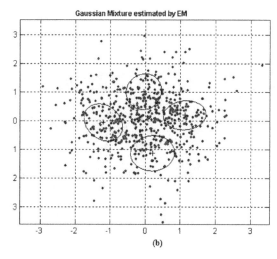

several such combinations of basic Gaussian distributions. Figure 1(a), illustrates the mixture of four Gaussians for a data of 600 random points. We observe that a linear combination of four Gaussians give rise to complex densities and further approximated using adequate number of mixtures involving fine-tuning of their means and covariance. Gaussian Mixtures estimated by EM algorithm for four clusters is as shown in Figure 1 (b).

During learning process of classification, we discovered centers and variances of the Gaussian components associated with mixing coefficients are employed as regulating parameters. Gaussian mixtures used to analyse complex probability distribution are formulated in terms of discrete latent variables and further defined as the weighted sum of 'M' Gaussian components as follows:

$$P\left(\frac{X}{\lambda}\right) = \sum_{i=1}^{M} w_i * g\left(\frac{X}{\mu_i}, \Sigma_i\right) \tag{1}$$

where 'w_i' is mixture weights and function 'g' is Gaussian density components of D-variate Gaussians.

Illustration of Density Modelling with a Gaussian Mixture Model

We considered the problem of modelling randomly generated data by a mixture of three Gaussians in 2 dimensions with known priors (0.3, 0.5 and 0.2), centres (2, 3.5), (0, 0) & (0,2) and the variances (0.2, 0.5 and 1.0). Figure 2 (a and b) contain a scatter and surface plot (3-D view of density function) of the data respectively. A Gaussian mixture model with three components is trained using EM, 1-standard deviation circles for the three components of the mixture model is shown in Figure 3.

In a task such as object recognition, in which important information may be contained in the high-order relationships among pixels, it seems reasonable to expect that better basis images may be found by methods sensitive to these high-order statistics. The goal of proposed model is to partition set of all classes into several clusters using Gaussian mixture model and to obtain transformation matrix for each

Figure 2. Illustrations of: (a) scatter plot of the data; (b) surface plot

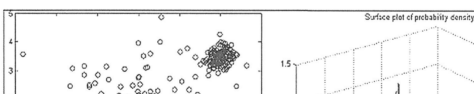

Figure 3. Plot of data and mixture centres

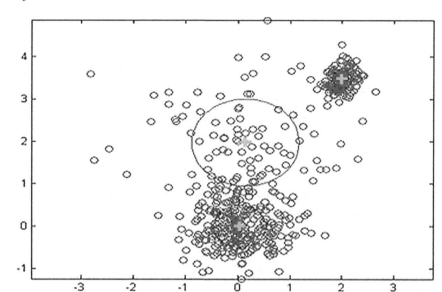

cluster in reduced feature space to minimize the effect of higher dimension. In this regard, we investigate subspace based algorithm on GMM such as PCA & FLD Mixture Models for efficient recognition and retrieval. Detailed description necessary to understand the above mentioned models are provided in the following paragraphs.

PCA Mixtures

The main objective of this model is to partition set of all classes into several clusters and to obtain PCA transformation matrix for each cluster. Let $x=x_1, x_2, \ldots, x_N$ be N-dimensional observed data belonging to different object category (e.g. n=101/256 classes belonging to Caltech dataset). Here, a class and its density function of the N-dimensional data x is represented as

$$P(x) = \sum_{k=1}^{K} P\left(\frac{x}{k}, \theta_k\right) P(k) \tag{2}$$

where $P(x/k, \theta_k)$ and $P(k)$ represent the conditional density and apriory probability of the kth cluster respectively, and θ_k is the unknown model parameters which is to be calculated through EM learning. The multivariate Gaussian distribution function to model $P(x/k, \theta_k)$ can be calculated using:

$$\eta\left(\frac{x}{\mu_k}, \Sigma_k\right) = \frac{1}{(2\pi)^{\frac{D}{2}} |\Sigma|^{\frac{1}{2}}} e^{-\frac{1}{2}(x-\mu_k)^T \Sigma^{-1}_k (x-\mu_k)} \tag{3}$$

where μ_k and Σ_k are mean and covariance matrix of kth cluster respectively. A distribution can be written as a linear superposition of Gaussian in the form:

$$P(x) = \sum_{k=1}^{K} \pi_k \eta \left(\frac{x}{\mu_k}, \Sigma_k \right) \tag{4}$$

where π_k is called the mixing coefficient that is set to the fractions of data points assigned to k^{th} cluster. Now log of the likelihood function is given by:

$$\ln P \left(\frac{X}{\pi}, \mu, \Sigma \right) = \sum_{n=1}^{N} \ln \sum_{k=1}^{K} \pi_k \eta \left(\frac{x_n}{\mu_k}, \Sigma_k \right) \tag{5}$$

A powerful method for finding the maximum likelihood solution for GMM is EM algorithm (Bishop 2006). To find a suitable initialization for a GMM, the means μ_k, covariances Σ_k and mixing coefficients π_k are initialized by running K-means clustering algorithm, which are then subsequently estimated using EM. We now vary between the following two steps which are called Expectation (E) step and the Maximization (M) step. In the E-step, current values of the parameters are used to evaluate the posteriori probabilities given by:

$$\xi(z_{nk}) = \frac{\pi_k \eta \left(\frac{x}{\mu_k}, \Sigma_k \right)}{\sum_{j=1}^{K} \pi_j \eta \left(\frac{u}{\mu_j}, \Sigma_j \right)} \tag{6}$$

In the M-step, we use these probabilities to re-estimate the means μ_k^{new}, covariance matrix Σ_k^{new}, and mixing coefficient π_k^{new} respectively as follows:

$$\mu_k^{new} = \frac{1}{N_k} \sum_{n=1}^{N} \xi(z_{nk}) x_n \tag{7}$$

$$\Sigma_k^{new} = \frac{1}{N_k} \sum_{n=1}^{N} \xi(z_{nk}) \left(x_n - \mu_k^{new} \right) \left(x_n - \mu_k^{new} \right)^T \tag{8}$$

$$\pi_k^{new} = \frac{N_k}{N} \tag{9}$$

Each revised parameters resulting after the execution of E-step followed by an M-step certainly increases the log likelihood function and confirmed convergence till the change in the log likelihood falls below some threshold. Now, k^{th} eigen value and eigen vector parameters are obtained using eigen value analysis $\Sigma_k W_{kj} = \lambda_{kj} W_{kj}$, for every values of $k = 1 \ldots K$. The PCA transformation matrix W_k can be obtained by carefully selecting 'p' dominant eigen vectors of kth cluster.

Figure 4. (a) and (b): Sample and its segmented images of Caltech-101 dataset belonging to the same class; (c) and (d): discrete representations of PCA mixture features

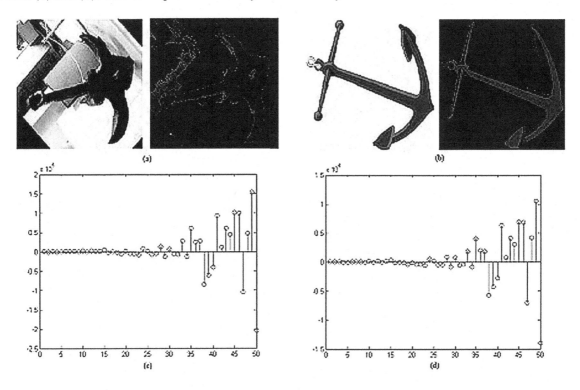

Figures 4 and 5 illustrate original and segmented images along with discrete representation of PCA mixtures for within the class and between class, respectively. To illustrate with an example, we had also made use of the scatter plotmatrix technique to analyze the PCA mixtures. If feature matrix X is P-by-M and Y is P-by-N, plotmatrix will produce a N-by-M matrix of axes. In our case, feature matrix FM of size 50X4 representing individual mixtures column-wise produces plots with 4X4scatter matrix by comparing the mixtures of individual columns with all the mixtures.

Figures 6 and 7 show the scatter plots with histograms of mixtures as principal diagonal plots and the remaining plots are the scatter plots (coefficients identified as upper triangle plots seem to be rotated by 90-degrees compared to the lower triangle plots). From the histogram analysis and comparison of within-class images, we conclude that all mixture histograms for within-class are almost identical (please refer diagonal histogram plots in Figure 6). Objects belonging to the same class generate class mixture histograms which appear to be identical and exhibit unique features. Whereas, between-class mixture histograms acquire distinct features (please refer diagonal histogram plots in Figure 7). It is also noticed that, most discriminative mixture histograms are obtained at higher order mixtures.

FLD Mixtures

Fisher Linear Discriminant Analysis proposed by R. A. Fisher is one of the most popular feature extraction methods in pattern recognition (Belhumeur et al. 1997). Principal component analysis, which is based on the assumptions of uncorrelatedness and normality, FLD is rooted in the hypothesis of extracting a

Figure 5. (a) and (b): Sample and its segmented images of Caltech-101 dataset belonging to the different classes; (c) and (d): discrete representations of PCA mixture features

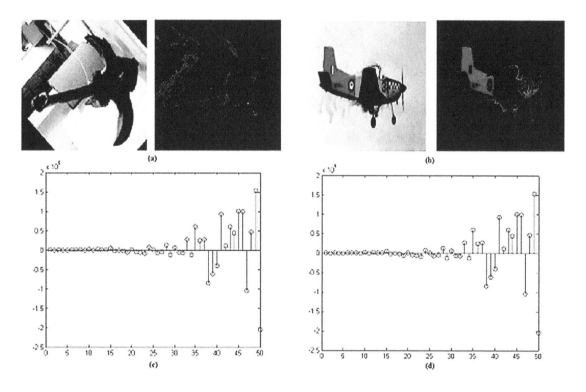

set of class specific projections. However in reality, it becomes tedious to compute Fisher projections as the dimension of patterns increases with increase in class labels. For better understanding of the concept, a brief theory on Linear Discriminant Analysis (LDA) is given in the following paragraphs followed by the discussions to integrate FLD & Gaussian mixtures.

Figure 6. Within class scatter plot matrix for segmented images shown in Figures 4 (a) and (b)

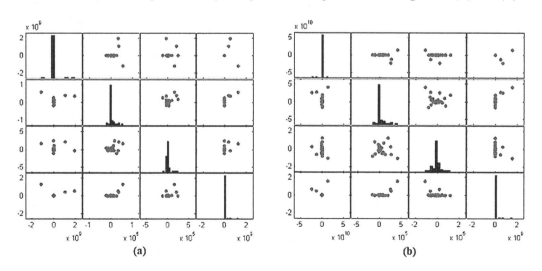

Figure 7. Between class scatter plot matrix for segmented images shown in Figures 5 (a) and (b)

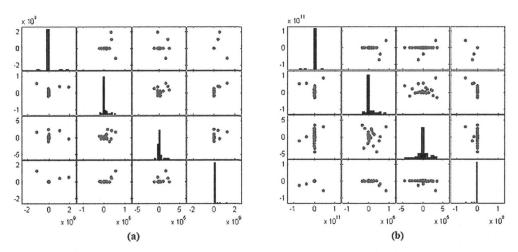

(a)   (b)

The main objective of LDA is to reduce dimensionality while preserving the class discriminatory information to a large extent. In order to achieve this, Fisher suggested maximizing the mean difference by normalizing the measure of within class data scatter for better classification. Since PCA is an unsupervised technique, the main disadvantage is missing class label information of the data. With the utmost concern of utilizing class label information and finding informative projections, Fisher Linear Discriminant Analysis (FLDA) considers the objective function *'W'* (as given in equation 10) and perpetually tries to maximize it.

$$W = \arg\max_{w} \frac{\left| w^T S_B w \right|}{\left| w^T S_w w \right|} \tag{10}$$

where S_B & S_w are "Between-class" and "Within-class" scatter matrices respectively. Since these matrices are proportional to the covariance matrices, constant 'w' which is a generalized eigen vector set will not have any effect on solution w.r.t defined objective function *'W'*. Letting x_1, x_2... x_k be samples of *'k'* set of images belonging to *'c'* classes, scatter matrices can be defined as:

$$s_B = \sum_{i=1}^{c} N_i \left(\mu_i - \overline{x} \right) \left(\mu_i - \overline{x} \right)^T \tag{11}$$

$$s_w = \sum_{i=1}^{c} \sum_{x_k \in X_i} \left(\mu_i - \overline{x} \right) \left(\mu_i - \overline{x} \right)^T \tag{12}$$

where μ_i is the mean image of class X_i, $\overline{x}$ is overall mean of data-cases and N_i is number of samples in each class. Firstly, PCA is applied to the resultant within class singular covariance for dimensionality reduction and later FLDA is applied to obtain nonsingular scatter matrix S_W.

Figure 8. Plots of FLD mixture feature coefficients (a) 1ˢᵗ mixture (b) 2ⁿᵈ mixture (c) 3ʳᵈ mixture (d) 4ᵗʰ mixture

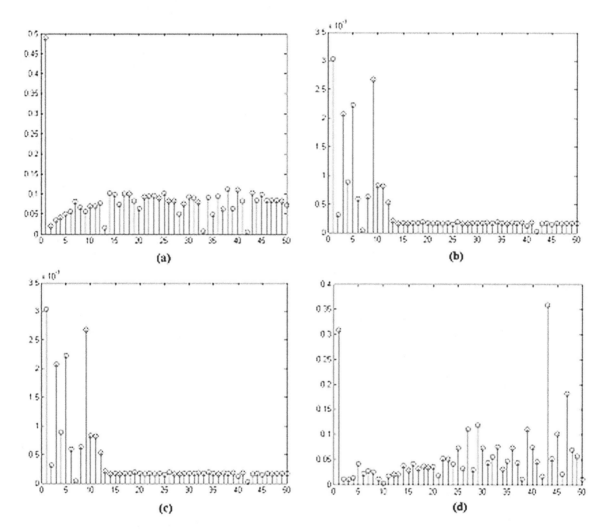

(a)

(b)

(c)

(d)

FLD mixture model makes use of several transformation matrices among overall classes. This can be achieved by applying PCA mixture model to the set of means μ_i of each category with different k-mixtures. Cluster mean C_k, transformed matrix T_k & diagonal matrix U_k are obtained along with λ_{kd} as diagonal elements w.r.t the dth largest eigen value of covariance matrix. With these set of outcomes we can formulate the scatter matrices for k^{th} mixture components as follows:

$$S_{B_k} = T_k U_k T_k^T \tag{13}$$

$$s_{w_k} = \sum_{l \in l_k} \frac{1}{n_l} \sum_{x \in c_i} \left(x - \mu_l \right) \left(x - \mu_l \right)^T \tag{14}$$

Using equations 13 & 14, we compute transformation matrix W_k for k^{th} mixture component with a continued argument of maximizing the following objective function.

$$SJ_k(U) = \frac{\left|U^T S_B U\right|}{\left|U^T S_{w_k} U\right|} \tag{15}$$

To illustrate with an example, we demonstrated the proposed FLD mixture model on an image of size 256X256 for '40 Gaussians and obtained transformation matrix capturing 50 dominant eigen vectors as feature coefficients for each mixtures. Figure 8 shows the plots of features obtained from FLD mixture model for different mixtures.

Figure 9 shows sample images of Caltech-256 dataset and its corresponding scatter plot matrix signifying distinctiveness in mixture histograms between the class object categories. Figures 10 and 11 demonstrate, original and segmented images as (a) and (b) along with the discrete representation as (c) and (d) for FLD mixtures for k = 4 mixtures. It exhibits almost similar discrete data points for within-class image features and distinct features for between-class feature data points.

Figure 9. 1ˢᵗ row: sample images of Caltech-256 dataset (between class); 2ⁿᵈ row: scatter plot matrix using FLD mixture models

Figure 10. (a) and (b): Original and segmented images within the class; (c) and (d): discrete representation of FLD features

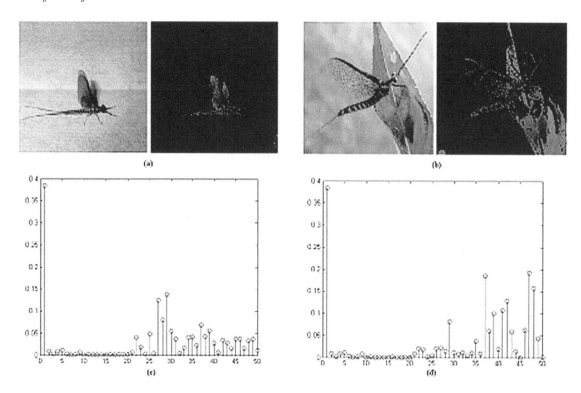

Figure 11. (a) and (b): Original and segmented images between the class; (c) and (d): discrete representation of FLD features

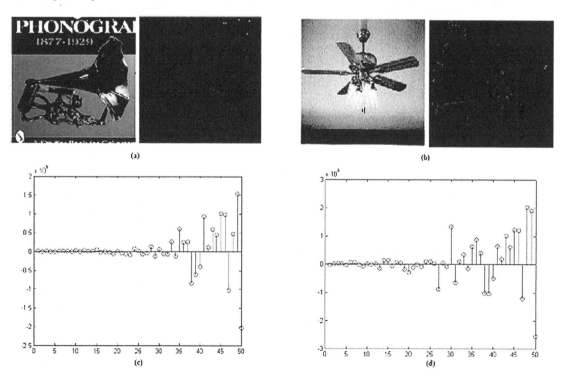

To conclude this section, the clusters viewed as mixture of several Gaussian classes (latent variables) and Expectation Maximization (EM) algorithms applied to these Gaussian mixtures give best maximum likelihood estimators and thereby attain highly discriminative features in reduced feature space. Further, during classification stage, these features can be used to assign the class label information to an image in large image datasets.

Classification Methods

Classification is a major task in order to calculate visual similarities between a query and database image, many classification techniques have been developed for image retrieval based on empirical estimates of the distribution of features in recent years (Ritendra et al. 2008). Many of the recognition systems with effective feature descriptor fail due to inefficient classification techniques. In this regard, we proposed the effectiveness of two different classifiers, firstly by considering similarity/distance measure techniques and secondly neural network architectures such as GRNN & PNN to obtain an average classification rates. Detailed explanation can be found in the following sections.

Distance Measures

Similarity/distance is defined as a quantitative degree that enumerates the logical separation of two objects represented by a set of measurable attributes/characteristics. To enumerate few of the important properties that is commonly found in most useful distance computation tasks are as follows:

1. Symmetry, $d(x, y) = d(y, x)$.
2. Positive definite, $d(x, y) > 0$, for $x \neq y$, and $d(x, x) = 0$.
3. Triangle inequality, sometimes useful in making a metric $d(x, y) \leq d(x, z) + d(z, y)$.
4. In addition to that:
    a. $d(x, y)$ should have a physically meaningful interpretation.
    b. $d(x, y)$ should be efficiently computable.

In this work, we studied & explored various different similarity/distance measure techniques namely, Minkowski, Mahalonobis, Manhattan, Euclidean, Squared Euclidean, Mean Square Error (Mean SSE), Angle, Correlation co-efficient, Mahalonobis between normed vector, Weighted Manhattan, Weighted SSE, Weighted angle, Canberra, Modified Manhattan, Modified Squared Euclidean (Mod-SSE), Weighted Modified SSE and Weighted Modified Manhattan.

Since, different similarity distance measures will affect the recognition rate. It was observed that Minkowski, Eucledian, Modified Squared Eucledian, Correlation coefficient and Angle Based distances seems to be significant in improving an average recognition rates.

Neural Network Classifiers

Artificial Neural Networks (ANN), an information processing paradigm inspired by the biological nervous systems towards learning process is configured for a specific application, such as pattern recognition or data classification. A novel structure of large number of highly interconnected processing elements (neurons) and its synaptic connections are the key elements of this paradigm (Patterson 1995). As neural networks are extremely fast and efficient, we have considered GRNN and PNN to classify and label the query image.

Generalized Regression Neural Network (GRNN)

Neural networks have been motivated right from its inception by the recognition that the human brain computes in an entirely different way from the conventional digital computer. GRNN are paradigms of the Radial Basis Function (RBF) used to functional approximation and was rediscovered to perform general regressions. In our experiments, GRNN are used to calculate weighted average of the trained feature vectors which appears to be close to the given input case for better classification (Wasserman 1993).

GRNN consists of four layers, which are named as input layer, pattern layer, summation layer and output layer as shown in Figure 12. The number of input units depends on the total number of observation parameters i.e. an input vector 'X' (feature matrix F_i). The input layer connected to the pattern layer consists of neurons provides training patterns and its output to the summation layer to perform normalization of the resultant output set.

Each of the pattern layers is connected to the summation neurons and calculates the weight vector using the following equations.

$$W_i = e^{\left[\dfrac{-\left\| x - x_t \right\|^2}{2h^2} \right]} \tag{16}$$

$$y(x) = \frac{\sum_{i=1}^{n} T_i W_i}{\sum_{i=1}^{n} W_i} \tag{17}$$

where the output $y(x)$ is weighted average of the target values T_i of training cases x_i close to a given input case x.

Figure 12. Generalized Regression Neural Network (GRNN) architecture

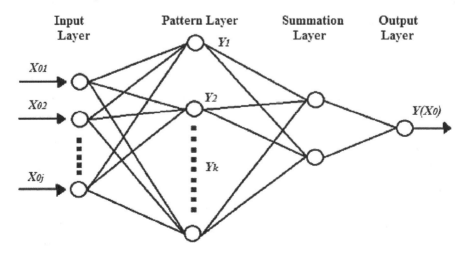

Figure 13. Probabilistic Neural Network (PNN) architecture

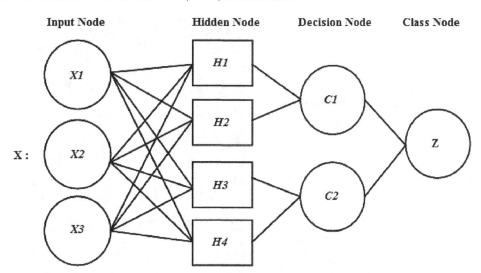

Probabilistic Neural Network (PNN)

Due to its excellent generalization performance, SVM is most promising classifiers in machine learning. However, SVM's are slow and still remains to be a bottleneck for large datasets and multiclass classification. We have made use of PNN, since it is based on concepts used for conventional pattern recognition problems. It models the Bayesian classifier & minimizes the risk of misclassification. Bayes' classifier is usually criticized due to lack of information about the class probability distributions and makes use of nonparametric techniques, whereas the inherent advantage of PNN is the better generalization and convergence properties when compared to that of Bayesian classifier in classification problems (Donald 1990).

PNN Architecture (shown in Figure 13) is similar to that of supervised learning architecture, but PNN does not carry weights in its hidden layer. Each node of hidden layer acts as weights of an example vector. The hidden node activation is defined as the product of example vector 'E' &input feature vector 'F' given as $h_i=E_i \times F$. The class output activations are carried out using the following equation:

$$C_j = \frac{\sum_{i=1}^{n} e^{\frac{(h_i-1)}{\gamma^2}}}{N} \tag{18}$$

where 'N' is example vectors belonging to class 'C', 'h_i' is hidden node activation and 'γ' is smoothing actor.

Experimental Setup

We considered identical conditions in order to conduct experiments on each image category. Each category dataset are divided into train and test datasets, first 'N' number of training images are drawn orderly as labeled set and remaining images in dataset are considered as test images. We then learn models based on the proposed approaches for different set of mixtures and evaluated their performances on the test images.

Figure 14. Column 1: original image; column 2: resultant segmented image

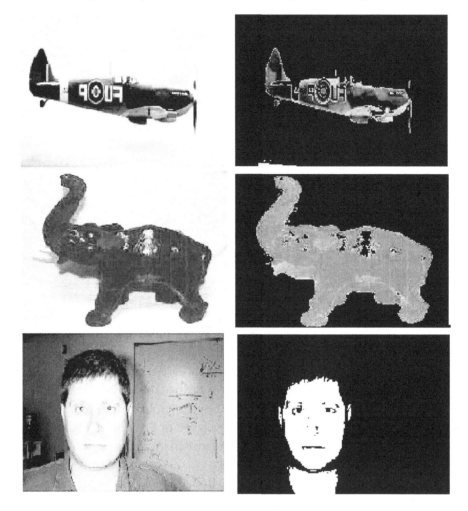

EXPERIMENTAL RESULTS AND PERFORMANCE ANALYSIS

All our experiments are carried out on a PC machine with an intel core2duo 2.20 GHz processor and 3GB RAM under Matlab 10.0 programming platform. We demonstrated our proposed methods on three most popular and extensively used datasets namely Corel-1K, Caltech-101 & Caltech-256. Corel-1K comprises of 1000 natural scene images classified into 10 object classes and 100 images per class (Jia et al. 2001). Caltech-101 contains a total of 9144 images, divided between 101 distinct objects (including faces, watches, ants, pianos, etc.) with varying pose, color and lighting intensity and a background category (for a total of 102 categories) ranging from 31 to 800 images per category (Fei-Fei et al. 2004). Griffin (Griffin et al. 2007), introduced a challenging set of 256 object categories containing a total of 30607 images with high variations in intensity, clutter, object size, location, pose, and also increased number of categories with at least 80 images per category.

The system is initialized by transforming RGB image to complex hybrid color space and then FCM technique is applied to generate collection of fuzzy clusters based on color homogeneity of the pixels (as per the discussions made in preprocessing section). Figure 14, illustrates few samples of original and resultant segmented images of a Caltech-101 dataset. Later, segmented image is given to EM algorithm to obtain mixture of eigen values which takes several iterations in finding better convergence.

Some of the trial runs conducted as preliminary experiments revealed that, mixing different normal distributions at $k=4$ mixtures influences better convergence for fitting a mixture model in unsupervised context and found effective in identifying hidden structures by providing better estimates for unlabeled data. Incidentally, mixture of four Gaussians is considered to be as an optimal choice of for improving classification performance.

Caltech-101 and Caltech-256 Datasets

As per the standard procedural settings mentioned in (Griffin et al. 2007; Holub et al. 2005; Jianchao et al. 2009), we divided the entire caltech-101/256 datasets into 15 and 30 images/category as labeled dataset and the remaining images are tested to obtain an average of per class recognition in each stage for each of the classifiers (Distance Measures (DM) & Neural Networks (NN)). Surprisingly, 18 classes out of 101 object category reached 100% recognition rate which was found better in comparison with 11 classes due to Locality-constrained Linear Coding technique (Jinjun et al. 2010). Figure 15 shows few sample images of Caltech-101 dataset with high and low recognition rates.

Table 2 summarizes the proposed model's performance on the Caltech-101 dataset. The performance of feature vectors obtained due Gaussian mixture model is well above the Fisher score features extracted using 3 different detectors and classifying them using SVM (Holub et al. 2005). Whereas, Serre constructed C2 features combining simple features S1 and complex features C1. S1 responses generated due to Gabor filters and C1 generated due to shift and size of the object very similar to the primary visual cortex showed deprived results (Serre et al. 2005). In order to get the benefit of posterior log-odds for each class, earlier NBNN found a drift to local NBNN capturing selective features from different set of descriptors (Sancho and David 2012). Proposed set of mixtures proved competent enough to outperform local NBNN and found highly competitive in comparison with SVM-KNN classifier mentioned in (Hao et al. 2006). Relevance sparsity model found its best recognition rate of 43.8% due to the investigations

Figure 15. Few sample images of Caltech-101 dataset with (a) high and (b) low recognition rates

Table 2. Performance analysis of the proposed and existing methods for Caltech-101 dataset

Methods	Classification Rates (%)			
	15 Train		**30 Train**	
Visual Cortex model [Serre et al. 2005]	35		42	
Disciminative model [Holub et al. 2005]	37		43	
Relevance Sparsity model [German et al. 2014]	-		43.8	
SVM-KNN [Hao et al. 2006]	45		-	
Local NBNN [Sancho et al. 2012]	47.8		55.2	
Coslets [Mahantesh et al. 2015]	46		54	
Weighted Descriptor model [Mahantesh et al. 2014]	47		53	
Proposed Methods	**Without Segmentation**	**With Segmentation**	**Without Segmentation**	**With Segmentation**
PCA+GMM+GRNN	30	38	37	48
FLD+GMM+GRNN	18	26	28	37
PCA+GMM+PNN	29	37	31	44
FLD+GMM+PNN	19	27	29	35
PCA+GMM+NN(average)	36	45	46	53
FLD+GMM+NN(average)	29	42	44	51
PCA+GMM+ Distance Measures	43	49	49	57
FLD+GMM+ Distance Measures	42	46	47	53

carried out on sparsity constraints by convolving linear filters within an image (German et al. 2014). Whereas, combining Gaussians with complex densities has achieved 57% recognition rate at its best and has outperformed our own earlier transform based methods found in (Mahantesh et al. 2014 & 2015).

Figure 16 showing sample images of Caltech-256 dataset along with its recognition rates are quite evident that objects with fairly discriminating background (Figure 16a) has achieved good results in comparison with objects with more complex background (Figure 16b). We would rather like to consider this problem as a scope for segmentation, but still proposed models are capable of extracting discriminatory features even with an increasing number of categories and more cluttered objects has raised the level of difficulty and making it even more challenging for retrieval.

Table 3 summarizes the classification rates obtained on Caltech-256 dataset and gives performance evaluation of proposed model against some of the most popular and leading techniques. Mixture of Gaussians found to be very adequate in storing stable parameters compared to the kernel codebook approach where Gaussian distributions extracted as features using SIFT descriptors and are further smoothened using kernels to generate codebook (Van et al. 2008). Griffiin (Griffin et al. 2007), highlighted the importance of segmentation and demonstrated spatial pyramid matching (SPM) with correlation clas-

Figure 16. Few sample images of Caltech-256 dataset with (a) high and (b) low recognition rates

Table 3. Performance analysis of the proposed and existing methods for Caltech-256 dataset

Methods	Classification Rates (%)			
	15 Train		30 Train	
Kernel Codebook [Van et al. 2008]	-		27.17	
SPM + Correlation Classifier [Griffin et al. 2007]	28.3		34.1	
Local NBNN [Sancho et al. 2012]	33.5		40.1	
LSPM + Sparse coding [Jianchao et al. 2009]	28.3		34.1	
Coslets [Mahantesh et al. 2015]	26		31	
Weighted Descriptor model [Mahantesh et al. 2014]	25		32.7	
Proposed Methods	**Without Segmentation**	**With Segmentation**	**Without Segmentation**	**With Segmentation**
PCA+GMM+GRNN	20	25	24	30
FLD+GMM+GRNN	17	23	22	28
PCA+GMM+PNN	21	26	25	31
FLD+GMM+PNN	18	24	23	29
PCA+GMM+NN(average)	23	27	28	32
FLD+GMM+NN(average)	22	25	31	36
PCA+GMM+ Distance Measures	23	29	29	35
FLD+GMM+ Distance Measures	24	28	29	34

sifier to obtain highly competitive results compared to our method and also noticed that performance on Caltech-256 is roughly half of the Caltech-101 dataset performances. Proposed mixture model leads Linear SPM technique which is an extension of SVM using SPM kernel approach in combination with sparse codes which has been identified as one of the most successful techniques in image classification (Jianchao et al. 2009).

In order to draw comparison with few of the very recent techniques and some unusual parametric settings, we considered 15 and 30 images/category for training and not more than 20 & 50 images/category for testing as mentioned in (Bao-Di et al. 2013; Liu et al. 2012). For Caltech 101 dataset, we obtained highest classification rate of 67% & 73% respectively in accordance with 67% & 74% of DLMM (Bao-Di et al. 2013), 66% & 72% of ScSPM (Liu et al. 2012) techniques. Similarly for Caltech-256 dataset, we obtained highest recognition rates of 29.6% & 36% outperforming 29% & 35% of (Bao-Di et al. 2013) and 28% & 34% of (Liu et al. 2012) considering 15 & 30 images/category as labeled images respectively.

Corel-1K Dataset

Figure 17 shows few sample images of Corel-1K dataset with 100% recognition rate. Table 4 shows the results obtained subspace methods on Corel-1K dataset highlighting improved discriminativity in terms of high classification rate and faster learning rate with 30 train samples per category in comparison with 50 training samples as mentioned in (Jianchao et al. 2009; Lu and Ip 2009; Shenghua et al. 2010). With respect to the tabulated results, proposed method found to be very aggressive in comparison with several state of the art techniques for datasets comprising lesser number of classes.

Figure 17. Few sample images of Corel-1K dataset with 100% recognition rate

Table 4. Performance analysis of the proposed and existing methods for Corel-1K dataset

Methods	Classification Rates (%)	
Learning Context model [Lu and Ip 2009]	77.9	
LSPM & Sparse Coding [Jianchao et al. 2009]	86.2	
Laplacian Sparse Coding [Gao et al. 2010]	88.4	
Coslets [Mahantesh et al. 2015]	94	
Weighted Descriptor model [Mahantesh et al. 2014]	93.55	
Proposed Methods	**Without Segmentation**	**With Segmentation**
PCA+GMM+GRNN	78	89
FLD+GMM+GRNN	69	78
PCA+GMM+PNN	84	92
FLD+GMM+PNN	79	87
PCA+GMM+NN(average)	83	94
FLD+GMM+NN(average)	77	89
PCA+GMM+Distance Measures	84	96
FLD+GMM+Distance Measures	83	95

In all the experiments it is worth noting that segmentation as preprocessing has significantly augmented the recognition performance. An effort to integrate over all possible positions and orientations of an object in reduced feature space and the choice of $k = 4$ mixtures is highly noteworthy to achieve better classification rate. Due to the lesser number of components present in learning data, it results in faster evaluation of testing phase with increase in numerical stability.

CONCLUSION AND FUTURE RESEARCH DIRECTIONS

An idea of combining Gaussians with complex densities provides a hybrid framework to handle multi-modality features and a motive of applying EM to Gaussian mixtures has proved successful in exploiting preeminent likelihood parameters from the derived latent variable models. Representation of complicated distribution to its simplest form has paved the way for mixture models to be used extensively for cluster analysis.

As presented above, efforts are made to develop an efficient image segmentation technique as a part of preprocessing step along with the combination of mixture models & subspace methods are explored for feature extraction. The recognition accuracies are shown in various similarity/distance measures along with neural network classifiers. Algorithms are tested on very large benchmark datasets widely used by research communities. This was coupled with performance evaluation process that studied the efficacy of these algorithms (including some existing algorithms) under several important real time test conditions. We would like to conclude that, it is not only necessary to develop better pattern recognition methods to capture the visually important features from the image, but also to develop them such that they are simple, efficient and easily mapped to human queries.

While the proposed framework determines the significant features by studying complex distributions present in the image data which is usually linear in nature, this section overlay the platform to develop and explore ideas to extract non-linear discriminatory features by initiating kernel based approaches. In future, one can investigate the classification performance of our model for different distances measures, SVM and various Neural Network architectures. Finally, we would like to conclude this chapter with an overview of developing an automatic image retrieval system suitable for real time situations and an indication for some possible future avenues.

REFERENCES

Alami, M. E. (2014). A new matching strategy for content based image retrieval system. *Applied Soft Computing*, *14*, 407–418. doi:10.1016/j.asoc.2013.10.003

Altavista. (n. d.). Retrieved from http://www.altavista.com/sites/search/simage

Bartlett, M.S., Movellan, J.R., & Sejnowski, T.J. (2002). Face recognition by independent component analysis. *Neural Networks, IEEE Transactions,* 13(6), 1450-1464).

Belhumeur, P. N., Hespanha, J. P., & Kriegman, D. J. (1997). Eigenfaces vs fisherfaces: Recognition using class specific linear projection. *IEEE Transactions on Pattern Analysis and Machine Intelligence*, *19*(7), 711–720. doi:10.1109/34.598228

Belongie, S., Hellerstein, J.M., Carson, C., Thomas, M., & Malik, J. (1999). Blobworld: A system for region-based image indexing and retrieval. *Proceedings of the Third International Conference VISUAL* (pp. 509– 517).

Bishop, C. (2006). *Pattern Recognition and Machine Learning*. Springer.

Blaser, A. (Ed.), (1979). Database Techniques for Pictorial Applications, Lecture Notes in Computer Science (Vol. 81). Springer Verlag.

Boykov, Y. V., & Jolly, M. P. (2001). Interactive graph cuts for optimal boundary & region segmentation of objects in n-d images. *Proceedings of IEEE International Conference on Computer Vision* (Vol. 1, pp. 105–112). doi:10.1109/ICCV.2001.937505

Burges, C. (1988). A tutorial on support vector machines for pattern recognition. *Knowledge Discovery and Data Mining*, *2*, 1–47.

Carson, C., & Ogle, V. E. (1996). Storage and retrieval of feature data for a very large online mage collection. *IEEE Computer Society Bulletin of the Technical Committee on Data Engineering*, *19*(4), 19–27.

Chang, S. K., & Hsu, A. (1992). Image information systems: Where do we go from here. *IEEE Transactions on Knowledge and Data Engineering*, *5*(5), 431–442. doi:10.1109/69.166986

Chen, J. L., & Kundu, A. (1994). Rotational and gray-scale transform invariant texture identification using wavelet decomposition and hidden Markov model. *IEEE Transaction in Machine Intelligence, 16*(2), 208–214. doi:10.1109/34.273730

Cinque, L., Ciocca, G., Levialdi, S., Pellicanò, A., & Schettini, R. (2001). Color-based image retrieval using spatial-chromatic histogram. *Image and Vision Computing, 19*(13), 979–986. doi:10.1016/S0262-8856(01)00060-9

Csurka, G., Dance, C., Fan, L., Willamowski, J., & Bray, C. (2004). Visual categorization with bags of keypoints. Proceedings of *Workshop on Statistical Learning in Computer Vision, ECCV* (pp 1-22).

Datta, R., Joshi, D., Li, J., & Wang, J. Z. (2008). Image retrieval: Ideas, influences, and trends of the new age. *ACM Computing Surveys, 40*(2), 1–60. doi:10.1145/1348246.1348248

Donald, F. (1990). Probabilistic Neural Networks. *Neural Networks, 3*(1), 109–118. doi:10.1016/0893-6080(90)90049-Q

Dubey, S. K., & Ghosh, S. (2013). Comparative analysis of k-means and fuzzy cmeans algorithms. *International Journal of Advanced Computer Science and Applications, 4*, 35–39.

Fei-Fei, L., Fergus, R., & Perona, P. (2004). Learning generative visual models from few training examples. Proceedings of *Workshop on Computer Vision and Pattern Recognition.*

Fergus, R., Perona, P., & Zisserman, A. (2003). Object class recognition by unsupervised scale invariant learning. *Proceedings of the IEEE Computer Society Conference on Computer Vision and Pattern Recognition* (Vol.2, p. 264). doi:10.1109/CVPR.2003.1211479

Forsyth, D. A., & Fleck, M. M. (1997). Body plans. *Proceedings of the IEEE Conference on Computer Vision and Pattern Recognition* (pp. 678–683). doi:10.1109/CVPR.1997.609399

Fowlkes, C., Malik, J., Arbelaez, P., & Maire, M. (2009). *From contours to regions: An empirical evaluation* (pp. 2294–2301). IEEE CVPR.

Fowlkes, C., Malik, J., Arbelaez, P., & Maire, M. (2011). Contour detection and hierarchical image segmentation. *IEEE PAMI, 33*(5), 898–916. doi:10.1109/TPAMI.2010.161 PMID:20733228

Fowlkes, C., Martin, D., & Malik, J. (2004). Learning to detect natural image boundaries using local brightness, color and texture cues. *IEEE-PAMI, 26*(5), 530–549. doi:10.1109/TPAMI.2004.1273918 PMID:15460277

Gao, S. Wai Hung Tsang, I., Tien Chia, L., & Zhao, P. (2010). Local features are not lonely. Laplacian sparse coding for image classification. In IEEE CVPR (pp 3555-3561).

Griffin, G., Holub, A., & Perona, P. (2007). *Caltech 256 object category dataset* [Technical Report UCB/CSD-04-1366]. California Institute of Technology.

Gupta, A., Santini, S., & Jain, R. (1997). In search of information in visual media. *Communications of the ACM, 40*(12), 34–42. doi:10.1145/265563.265570

Holub, A., Welling, M., & Perona, P. (2005). Exploiting unlabelled data for hybrid object classification. Proceedings of the *NIPS Workshop* (Vol.7).

Jianchao, K. Y., Gongz, Y., & Huang, T. (2009). Linear Spatial Pyramid Matching Using Sparse Coding for Image Classification. In IEEE CVPR (pp 1794-1801).

Langlois, D., Chartier, S., & Gosselin, D. (2010). An introduction to independent component analysis: Infomax and fastica algorithms. *Tutorials in Quantitative Methods for Psychology, 6*(1), 31–38.

Lazebnik, S., Schmid, C., & Ponce, J. (2006). *Beyond bags of features: Spatial pyramid matching for recognizing natural scene categories.* CVPR.

Li, J. (2001). SIMPLIcity: Semantics-sensitive Integrated Matching for Picture Libraries. *IEEE Transactions on Pattern Analysis and Machine Intelligence, 23*(9), 947–963. doi:10.1109/34.955109

Liu, B., Wang, Y., Zhang, Y., & Zheng, Y. (2012). Discriminant sparse coding for image classification: *Proceedings of the 37th International Conference on Acoustics, Speech and Signal Processing* (pp. 2193–2196).

Liu, B.-D., Wang, Y.-X., Zhang, Y.-J., & Shen, B. (2013). Learning dictionary on manifolds for image classification. *Pattern Recognition, 46*(7), 1879–1890. doi:10.1016/j.patcog.2012.11.018

Lu, G., Liu, Y., Zhang, D., & Ma, W.-Y. (2007). A survey of content based image retrieval with high-level semantics. *Pattern Recognition, 40*(1), 262–282. doi:10.1016/j.patcog.2006.04.045

Lu, Z., & Ip, H. H. (2009). Image categorization by learning with context and consistency. In IEEE CVPR, (pp 2719-2726).

Mahantesh, K., Manjunath Aradhya, V. N., & Niranjan, S. K. (2013). An impact of complex hybrid color space in image segmentation. *Proceedings of 2nd International Symposium on Intelligent Informatics* (Vol.235, pp.73-82).

Mahantesh, K., Manjunath Aradhya, V. N., & Niranjan, S. K. (2015). Coslets: A Novel Approach to Explore Object Taxonomy in Compressed DCT Domain for Large Image Datasets. *Proceedings of 3rd International Symposium on Intelligent Informatics* (Vol. 320, pp. 39-48).

Mahantesh, K., Yashaswini, T. S., & Manjunath Aradhya, V. N. (in press). A Weighted Dominant Visual Descriptor for Object Categorization in Large Image Datasets. Proceedings of the *2nd International Conference on Applied Information and Communications Technology (ICAICT 2014)*, Muscat, Oman.

Manjunath, B. S. (1995). Image browsing in the Alexandria digital library project. *D-Lib Magazine.* Retrieved from http://www.dlib.org/dlib/august95/alexandria/08manjunath.html

Mc Cann, S., & *Lowe, D. G.* (2012). Local Naive Bayes Nearest Neighbor for Image Classification.

Mehrotra, R., & Gary, J. E. (1995). Similar-shape retrieval in shape data management, *IEEE. Computation, 28*(9), 57–62.

Mojsilovic, A., & Rogowitz, B. (2001). Capturing image semantics with low-level descriptors. *Proceedings of the ICIP* (pp. 18-21).

Ojala, T., Pietikainen, M., & Harwood, D. (1994). Performance evaluation of texture measures with classification based on Kullback discrimination of distributions. *Proceedings of International Conference on Pattern Recognition* (pp 582-585). doi:10.1109/ICPR.1994.576366

Patterson, D. W. (1995). *Artificial neural networks*. Prentice Hall.

Rahmani, Z. H., & Cholleti, S. R., & goldman, S. A. (2006). Local image representations using pruned salient points with applications to CBIR. *Proceedings of the ACM International Conference on Multimedia* (pp 287-296).

Ren, X., & Bo, L. (2012). Discriminatively trained sparse code gradients for contour detection. *Advances in Neural Information Processing Systems*, *25*, 593–601.

Rigamonti, R., Lepetit, V., González, G., Türetken, E., Benmansour, F., Brown, M., & Fua, P. (2014). On the relevance of sparsity for image classification. *Computer Vision and Image Understanding* (Vol. *125*, pp. 115–127). doi:10.1016/j.cviu.2014.03.009

Safar, M., Shahabi, C., & Sun, X. (2000). Image Retrieval by Shape: A Comparative Study. *Proceedings of IEEE International Conference on Multimedia and Expo* (pp 141-144). doi:10.1109/ICME.2000.869564

Serre, T., Wolf, L., & Poggio, T. (2005). Object recognition with features inspired by visual cortex. Proceedings of *IEEE Computer Society Conference on Computer Vision and Pattern Recognition* (Vol. 2, pp. 994-1000). doi:10.1109/CVPR.2005.254

Sethi, I. K., & Coman, I. L. (2001). Mining association rules between low-level image features and high-level concepts. *Proceedings of the SPIE Data Mining and Knowledge Discovery*, *3*, 279–290.

Shi, J., & Malik, J. (2000). Normalized cuts and image segmentation. *IEEE Transactions on Pattern Analysis and Machine Intelligence*, *22*(8), 889–905.

Sohn, K., Jung, D. Y., Lee, H., & Hero, A. O. (2011). Efficient Learning of Sparse, Distributed, Convolutional Feature Representations for Object Recognition. Proceedings of the *IEEE International Conference on Computer Vision* (pp 2643 – 2650).

Tu, Z., Dollar, P., & Belongie, S. (2006). Supervised learning of edges and object boundaries. *IEEE-CVPR*, *2*, 1964–1971.

Turk, M., & Pentland, A. (1991). Eigenfaces for recognition. *Journal of Cognitive Neuroscience*, *3*(1), 7186. doi:10.1162/jocn.1991.3.1.71 PMID:23964806

Van Gemert, J. C., Geusebroek, J. M., Veenman, C. J., & Smeulders, A. W. M. (2008). Kernel codebooks for scene categorization. *Proceedings of the ACM - European Conference on Computer Vision: Part III* (pp. 696 – 709).

Vapnik, V. (1995). *The nature of statistical learning theory*. New York. doi:10.1007/978-1-4757-2440-0

Wang, J., Yang, J., Yu, K., Lv, F., Huang, T., & Gong, Y. (2010). Locality-constrained Linear Coding for Image Classification. In IEEE CVPR (pp 3360 – 3367).

Wang, X. Y., & Sun, Y. F. (2010). A color- and texture-based image segmentation algorithm. *Machine Graphics and Vision*, *19*(1), 3–18.

Wasserman, P. D. (1993). *Advanced methods in Neural Computing* (pp. 155–161).

Wei-Ying, M., & Manjunath, B. S. (1999). Netra: A toolbox for navigating large image databases. *Multimedia Systems*, *7*(3), 184–198. doi:10.1007/s005300050121

Xing-yuan, W., Zhi-feng, C., & Jiao-jiao, Y. (2012). An effective method for color image retrieval based on texture. *Computer Standards & Interfaces*, *34*(1), 31–35. doi:10.1016/j.csi.2011.05.001

Zhang, H., Berg, A.C., Maire, M., Malik, J. (2006). Discriminative Nearest Neighbor Classification for Visual Category Recognition. *IEEE-CVPR* (Vol.2, pp. 2126-2136).

Zhao, X., Liu, Y., Wang, D., Li, D., & Wang, J. (2014). Multiple kernel-based multi-instance learning algorithm for image classification. *Visual Communication & Image Retrieval*, *25*(5), 1112–1117. doi:10.1016/j.jvcir.2014.03.011

Zhou, X. S., & Huang, T. S. (2000). CBIR: from low-level features to high level semantics, *Proceedings of the SPIE, Image and Video Communication and Processing* (Vol. 3974, pp. 426-431).

Zhuo, L., Cheng, B., & Zhang, J. (2014). A comparative study of dimensionality reduction methods for large-scale image retrieval. *Neurocomputing*, *141*, 202–210. doi:10.1016/j.neucom.2014.03.014

Chapter 3
Cryptographic Techniques Based on Bio-Inspired Systems

Petre Anghelescu
University of Pitesti, Romania

ABSTRACT

In this chapter, bio-inspired techniques based on the cellular automata (CAs) and programmable cellular automata (PCAs) theory are used to develop information security systems. The proposed cryptosystem is composed from a combination of a CA as a pseudorandom number generator (PRNG) and a PCA that construct the ciphering functions of the designed enciphering scheme. It is presented how simple elements named „cells" interact between each other using certain rules and topologies to form a larger system that can be used to encrypt/decrypt data sent over network communication systems. The proposed security system was implemented in hardware in FPGA devices of type Spartan 3E – XC3S500E and was analyzed and verified, including NIST statistical tests, to assure that the system has good security and high speed. The experimental results proves that the cryptographic techniques based on bio-inspired algorithms provides an alternative to the conventional techniques (computational methods).

INTRODUCTION

Because the communications and computer systems become each time more pervasive, cryptographic techniques plays an essential role, requiring new solutions, in order to provide *data authentication*, *integrity* and *confidentiality* in insecure environments. The interconnection of these pervasive devices leads to Mark Weiser's famous vision of ubiquitous computing (Weiser, 1999) and in this way within any minute, a huge amount of information is exchanged through the Internet or over other insecure communication channels. Many kinds of information exchanges, for example text, audio/video content, in multimedia communications, should be protected from *unauthorized copying*, *intercepting* and *tampering* as they are traversing on public digital networks. Accordingly, cryptography has become more important in data security. Also, in the recent years, researchers have remarked the similarities between

DOI: 10.4018/978-1-4666-9474-3.ch003

bio-inspired systems (particularly cellular automata), chaos and cryptography (Dachselt, & Schwarz, 2001; Fuster-Sabater, & Cabalerro-Gil, 2010; Kocarev, & Lian, 2011). Some of the cellular automata features as *ergodicity* and *sensibility to the initial conditions* and *control parameters* can be correlated with the cryptographic properties as *confusion* and *diffusion*.

The essence of the theoretical and practical efforts which are done in this new field is represented by the idea that bio-inspired based encryption techniques are capable to have similar performances regarding the classic methods based on computational techniques. In this paper is presented an encryption system that uses a combination of two cellular automata*: a first class of cellular automaton* that generates the evolution rules for the second class of *five programmable cellular automata* arranged in pipeline. The entire security system was implemented both in software using C# programming language and in hardware on a FPGA of type Spartan 3E – XC3S500E in which the plaintext/ciphertext is received/transmitted using User Datagram Protocol (UDP).

This chapter is organized in eight sections. In the *background section*, are described some basic theoretical foundations of the proposed work that includes CAs and PCAs. The *third section*, provides a brief overview of the classical cryptography and bio-inspired systems in cryptography. The *next section*, on *reconfigurable hardware devices*, introduces the existing reconfigurable hardware devices approaches for supporting bio-inspired algorithms and presented also the reasons for using them in the application presented in this chapter. Then, the section *bio-inspired based algorithm for cryptography*, describes the proposed bio-inspired encryption algorithm used to encrypt and decrypt data sent over the communication networks. Additionally, in section *testing and experimental results*, are made the investigations of statistical properties of the encrypted sequences (performed using NIST statistical tests), distribution of text (plaintext and ciphertext) and encryption/decryption speed. In the next section, are presented the future research direction of the research presented in this chapter. Finally, section eight, conclude the chapter.

BACKGROUND

The intersection of biology and computer science has been a productive field for some time. On one hand, CAs is a bio-inspired paradigm highly addressing the soft computing and hardware for a large class of applications including information security. On the other hand, PCAs is a modified CAs structure including switches in order to allow the self-organizing of the cellular structure.

Cellular Automata (CA)

CAs, first introduced by von Neumann and Stanislav Ulam (Neumann, 1966) in the '50s, exhibit useful and interesting characteristics and has attracted researchers from different field of interests, who applied it in different ways. The most notable characteristics of CAs are: *massive parallelism, locality of cellular interactions* and *simplicity of basics components*. CAs perform computations in a distributed way on a spatial grid and differ from a standard approach to parallel computations whereby a problem is split into independent sub-problems later to be combined in order to yield a final solution. CAs suggest a new approach in which a complex global behavior can be modelled by non-linear spatially extended local interactions.

Thus far, CAs have been used primarily to model the systems consisting of a number of elements obeying identical laws of local interactions (e.g. problems of fluid dynamics, plasma physics, chemical systems, crystals growth, economics, two-directional traffic flow, image processing and pattern recognition, parallel processing, random number, evolution of spiral galaxies, modeling of very complicated physical or chemical processes, molecular computing) (Adamatzky, 1994; Ilachinski, 2001; Wolfram, 2002).

The wide applicability of CA is somehow limited because the methodologies for designing CA, intended to solve specific predefined tasks, are still underdeveloped. Such designing techniques would be extremely useful since there exist many problems for which local interactions, that would drive CA to solve these problems, are not known in advance. To the best of my knowledge, some works has already been done in this area, mainly using genetic algorithms to find evolution rules for the specific CAs.

CAs are mathematical idealizations of physical systems in terms of discrete time and space, where interactions are only local and where each cell can assume the value either 0 or 1 (Sung-Jin, 2004). In fact, CA represents a particular class of dynamical systems that enable to describe the evolution of complex systems with simple rules, without using partial differential equations. Each cell of the CA is restricted to local neighborhood interactions only, and as a result it is incapable of immediate global communication. The neighborhood of the cell is taken to be the cell itself and some or all of the immediately adjacent cells. The CA evolves in discrete steps, with the next value of one site determined by its previous value and that of a set of sites called the neighbor sites. The extent of the neighborhood can vary, depending among other factors upon the dimensionality of the CA under consideration. Classical examples for cell neighborhoods are presented in *Figure 1* (left side, von Neumann Neighborhood - with 3 cells for one-dimensional CA respective 5 cells for bi-dimensional CA and right side, Moore neighborhood with 3 cells for one-dimensional cellular automata respective 9 cells for bi-dimensional cellular automata considers both kinds the direct and the diagonal neighbors).

The state of each cell is updated simultaneously at discrete time steps, based on the states in its neighborhood at the preceding time step. The algorithm used to compute the next cell state is referred to as the CA local rule.

Figure 1. CA classical neighborhoods (a) von Neumann neighborhood, (b) Moore neighborhood

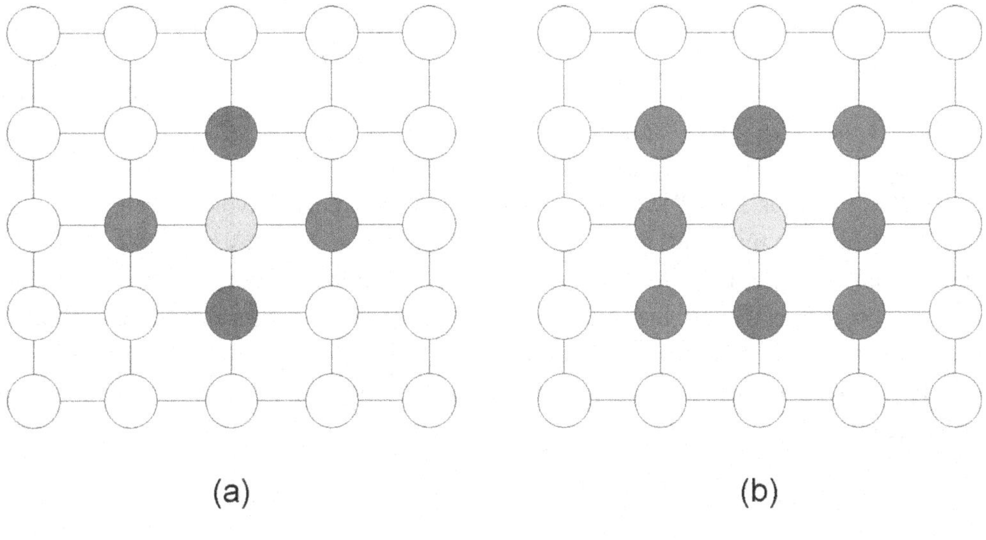

(a)　　　　　　　　(b)

Figure 2. CAs state transitions depending on the neighborhood states

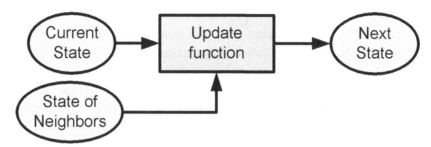

Typically, a CA consists of a graph where each node is a finite state cell. This graph is usually in the form of a two-dimensional lattice whose cells evolve according to a global update function applied uniformly over all the cells. As arguments, this update function takes the cell's present state and the states of the cells in its interaction neighborhood as shown in Figure 2.

The next-state function describing a rule for a three neighborhood CA cell where assuming that

i is *position of an individual cell in an one dimensional array*,
t is *time step*, and
$a_i(t)$: *output state* of the *i-th cell* at *the t-th time step*

can be expressed as follows:

$$a_i\big(t+1\big) = f\Big[a_i(t), a_{i+1}(t), a_{i-1}(t)\Big] \tag{1}$$

where f denotes the *local transition function* realized with a combination logic and is known as a rule of the CA.

If the *rule of a CA* involves *only XOR logic*, then it is called a *linear rule*.

Rules involving *XNOR logic* are referred to as *complement rules*.

A CA with all its cells having *linear rules* is called a *linear CA*, whereas a CA having a *combination of XOR and XNOR rules* is called additive CA.

If *all the cells obey the same rule*, then the CA is said to be a *uniform CA, otherwise*, it is a *hybrid CA*.

A CA is said to be a *null boundary CA* if both the *left* and *right neighbor* of the *leftmost* and *rightmost terminal cell* is *connected to logic 0-state*.

For example, in case of one-dimensional, three neighborhood and two-state cell, the number of all possible *uniform CA* rules is 256 (2^8). These rules are enumerated using Wolfram's naming convention (Wolfram, 1986) from rule number 0 to rule number 255 and can be represented by a 3-variable Boolean function. As an example, in Table 1, are presented five fundamental rules that are obtained using 3-neighborhood (the cell on the left, the cell itself and the cell from the right side of the cell in question). This means that the rule for this three cell neighborhood must contain 8 bits. These rules, arranged in a certain mode, are used in the proposed encryption system presented in later sections to construct the cryptographic algorithm.

Table 1. An example of CA evolution rules construction

Rules (Decimal Number)	7 111	6 110	5 101	4 100	3 011	2 010	1 001	0 000
90	0	1	0	1	1	0	1	0
150	1	0	0	1	0	1	1	0
51	0	0	1	1	0	0	1	1
60	0	0	1	1	1	1	0	0
102	0	1	1	0	0	1	1	0
	2^7	2^6	2^5	2^4	2^3	2^2	2^1	2^0

The space of evolution rules depends on the number of possible states of the current cell and the number of its neighbors. This leads to an exponential growing of the rules space (see Table 2).

The systematic study of CA was initialized by S. Wolfram in (Wolfram, 2002) in which he studied the relationships between CA and different dynamical systems. According to (Wolfram, 2002) there are four classes of CA whose comportment can be compared with the similar behavior of the dynamic systems (given in parenthesis):

Class I: The CA evolution from all initial configurations reaches the same final state and stays there (limit points).

Class II: The CA encounters simple or cyclic structures, but which one depends on the initial configuration (limit cycles).

Class III: The CA from majority of initial states lead to arbitrary patterns (chaotic behavior of the kind associated with strange attractors).

Class IV: The CA from some of initial configurations generates global complex structures (very long transients with no apparent analog in continuous dynamic systems). This behavior basically means that CA can be shown to be capable of universal computation.

Table 2. The size of the rules in function of neighborhood dimension

Size of the Cell Neighborhood	Decimal Rule Size (Maximum Value)	Rule Bit Size
2	16	4
3	256	8
4	65536	16
5	4294967296	32
6	18446744073709551616	64
7	3.40E+38	128
8	1.16E+77	256
9	1.34E+154	512

Figure 3. PCA with 3-neighbors and all non-completed additive evolution rules

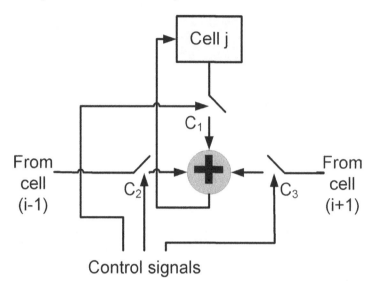

This classification mainly refers to 1-D CAs, but similar ones can be made for 2-D or 3-D cases. Classifications of CA are done by means of empirical observations of CA evolutions (space-time patterns). The very large phenomenology of the CA model, its apparently big complexity and massive parallelism (however, this parallelism, when emulated in software or in sequential hardware, disappears) offer a good basis for applications in cryptography and not only.

Programmable Cellular Automata (PCA)

The programmable cellular automata (PCA) was firstly introduced in (Nandi et al., 1994) as a modified CA structure. These PCA allows spatial and temporal variations in the state transition rules within a CA according to some external control scheme and signals. Practically, PCA dynamically change the CA rules. As an example, using such a cell structure as in Figure 3, all possible non-complemented additive rules can be achieved through the combinations of the control signals of C_1, C_2 and C_3 switches.

Thus the PCA architecture is very much flexible and enable to emulate via control signals different hybrid CA configurations (Anghelescu et al., 2010). In practice, a control program, stored in memory, can be employed to activate the switches. For example, the state 1 or 0 of the bit i-th of a memory word either opens or closes the switch that controls that cell. Basically, such a structure is referred as a PCA. In this paper, PCA is used to implement the proposed encryption algorithm.

All in all, the CAs and PCAs offer a good basis for applications in cryptography and represent a "converse pole" as computing architecture in comparison with sequential model: are parallel systems without central processing unit in which the computation powerful of his elements are much reduced.

LITERATURE REVIEW

In present, promising applications for cryptographic algorithms may be classified into two categories:

Category I: Processing of large amount of data at real time potentially in a high speed network. Examples include telephone conversations, telemetry data, video conferencing, streaming audio or encoded video transmissions and so forth.

Category II: Processing of very small amount of data at real time in a moderately high-speed network transmitted unpredictably. Examples include e-commerce or m-commerce transactions, bank account information extraction, e-payments and micro-browser-based (WAP-style), HTML page browsing and so forth.

Cryptographic realizations could be done in software or in hardware (Henriquez et al., 2006). In *software platforms* can be used for those security applications where the data traffic is not too large and thus low encryption rate is acceptable. On the other hand, *hardware methods* offer high speed and bandwidth, providing real time encryption if needed.

A good overview on the all major cryptographic techniques can be found in reference (Menezes et al., 1996; Stallings, 2003; Cusick & Stanica, 2009; Koc, 2009). Accordingly, the cryptographic methods are divided into two categories: symmetric-key (or secret-key) and asymmetric-key (or public-key). In symmetric cryptography the same key is used for both encryption and decryption, whereas in asymmetric cryptography there are two keys: one for encryption (which is public known), and other for decryption (which must remain secret). Based on these algorithms there are mainly two classes of symmetric-key encryption schemes: block ciphers and stream ciphers. Block ciphers breaks up the message into blocks of the fixed length and encrypt one block at a time. On the contrary, the stream ciphers encrypt a single bit of plain text at a time. Encryption is accomplished by combining the cipher sequence with the plaintext, usually with the bitwise XOR logic operation. There are several methods in order to generate the cipher sequence beginning from the secret key: LFSR (Linear Feedback Shift Register) generator, BBS (Blum Blum Shub) generator, and so forth (Menezes et al., 1996).

As we said above, there are several mathematical techniques that can be used for cryptographic purpose, and one of them is the use of bio-inspired systems or discrete dynamical systems (Schmitz, 2001). In the domain of researches having as subject the association between the cellular automata and cryptography was reported more encryption systems based on the cellular automata theory. CA were proposed for both secret-key and public-key cryptography. Remarkable is the fact that the relationship between the CA and cryptography was revealed by Shannon in his fundamental early work (Shannon, 1949):

Good mixing transformations are often formed by repeated products of two simple non-commuting operations. Hopf has shown, for example, that pastry dough can be mixed by such a sequence of operations. The dough is first rolled out into a thin slab, then folded over, then rolled, and the folded again, etc.

It seems that Shannon discusses about a system composed from simple components that interaction between them – with a transparent local comportment – but the global comportment of the entire system unsuspected, things that are well known in the CA theory.

So that, a very simple variant used for encryption using cellular automata is reported by Stephen Wolfram in (Wolfram, 1986) and (Wolfram, 2002) and is based on the fact that the CA from class III (conform the Wolfram classification) are dynamical chaotic systems. In this case, the evolution of the cellular automaton depends considerable of the initial state, but we can say that after some time the state is forgotten in sense in which cannot be found from current configuration analyses. Anyway, if we repeat the initial state, the evolution will be the same. Wolfram use a uniform 1D CA with three neighborhoods, and rule 30 to generate pseudorandom number sequences (CA-PRNG). The encryption system proposed by Wolfram can be included in category "Chaotic stream ciphers based on the pseudorandom number generator" (PRNG). The based principle of these ciphers is to obtain the encryption text by mixing the output of these pseudorandom number generators with the message (Lee et al., 2003; Koc, 2009).

Another solution used for encryption with cellular automata is presented in (Hortensius et al., 1989) and (Nandi et al., 1994). These used non-uniform CA with two rules 90 and 150, and it was found that the quality of pseudorandom number generated was better that the quality of the Wolfram system. (Tomassini & Perrenoud, 2000) proposed to use non-uniform, 1D CAs with four rules 90, 105, 150 and 165, which provide high quality pseudorandom number sequences and a huge space of possible secret keys which is difficult for cryptanalysis.

Another variant of encryption system based on the cellular automata, which consider also the inverse iteration, is presented in (Adamatzky, 1994) and (Martin, 2004). Here is used a bi-dimensional cellular automaton and the dates are the initial state of the cellular automaton. Using a reversible evolution rule the initial message is modified progressive. The message is decrypted rolling the inverse rule the same number of iterations as to encryption. This encryption system can be included in category of "Stream ciphers based on inverse iteration-with reaction". These systems can be also based on a series of evolution rules that served as chaotic system, rules used for encryption and decryption (Lu et al., 2004).

Other cryptosystem realized with the help of cellular automata combine the direct and inverse iteration (Gutowitz, 1994), "Block ciphers based on the direct and inverse iteration" (Masuda & Aihara, 2002) – these ciphers was as a general rule proposed for image encryption. Here is used a bi-dimensional cellular automaton, the message being the initial state of this. The codification implied the inverse iteration of a rule, the key is a rule. This rule is not necessary to be reversible: for inverse iteration is chosen randomly one of the possible states of the cellular automaton. For decryption we must know the rule that is direct iterated and use the same number of steps (Anghelescu et al., 2010; Anghelescu et al., 2013).

(Tripathy & Nandi, 2009) have designed a lightweight CA-based symmetric-key encryption that supports 128-bit block size with 128-, 192- and 256-bit keys. The motivation for embarking on CA for their cipher design is due to the fact that CA provides a high level of parallelism and therefore, able to achieve high speeds. The cipher has also been proved to be resistant against timing analysis attacks.

A hybrid CA with 2 rules 30 and 134 is proposed as cryptographic hash functions in (Jamil et al., 2012), in which elementary CA rules are used for mixing bits of the message. The cipher has also been analyzed using NIST tests and passes all the statistical tests.

The deterministic chaotically dynamic of CA is similar with pseudorandom systems used in classical methods and the complexity of a dynamical system that determine the efficiency of the entire information protection process is equivalent with the algorithm complexity from classical encryption methods.

Wolfram (Wolfram, 2002) pointed out that the future researches in this domain must be oriented to find solutions to complete the classical encryption systems with the other based on the bio-inspired systems (for example cellular automata theory), and less to design work of new methods developed "ad-hoc".

From the above discussion, seeing the promised potential of using of the CA in the field of cryptography, we believe that research on bio-inspired cryptography will be helpful to benefit the conventional cryptology and open a broader road to the design of ciphers with very good properties.

RECONFIGURABLE HARDWARE AND CA

The reconfigurable devices as piece of hardware able to dynamically adapt to algorithms and become through electrically program, almost any kind of digital circuit or system, was firstly introduced by G. Estrin in 1960. His invention consists on a hybrid machine composed by a general purpose microprocessor interconnected with programmable logic devices (Bobda, 2007). In general, reconfigurable devices tend to be a good choice when dealing with algorithms that implies high parallelism as CA based algorithms are. VLSI (also known as ASIC - Application Specific Integrated Circuit) and FPGAs (Field Programmable Gate Arrays) are two distinct alternatives for implementing cryptographic algorithms in hardware. An electronic device is said to be configurable (or programmable) when its functionality is not pre-defined at fabrication-time, but can be further specified by a configuration bit-stream (or a program). Reconfigurable devices permit configuration several times, supporting system upgrades and refinements in a relatively small time scale. Given this architectural flexibility and upgradeability, they constitute the best candidate for supporting bio-inspired architectures: they offer a set of features that permit the implementation of flexible architectures, while still guaranteeing high performance execution (Upegui, 2010).

A FPGA consists of an array of logic elements together with an interconnect network which can be configured by the user at the point of application. The basic structure of a FPGA circuit that contain an array/matrix of configurable logic blocks of potentially different types, including general logic, memory and multiplier blocks, surrounded and connected via programmable interconnects is presented in Figure 4.

User programming specifies both the logic functions of each block and the connections between the blocks. In one sense, FPGAs represent an evolutionary improvement in gate array technology which offers potential reductions in prototype system costs and product time-to-market. However, recent applications of FPGA technology suggest their impact on electronic systems may be much more profound. Consider the fact that reprogrammable FPGAs are capable of dynamically changing their logic and interconnect structure to adapt to changing system requirements. This offers a new computing paradigm which blurs the traditional lines between hardware and software. The main advantage of FPGAs is their re-configurability, i.e., they can be used for different purposes at different stages of a computation and they can be, at least partially, reprogrammed on run-time. The two most popular FPGA manufacturers are Xilinx and Altera. Today, due to cost decreases and the flexibility of a programmable solution, high-density FPGAs are often employed for system-level prototyping.

All in all, the using of FPGA devices for bio-inspired based cryptosystems is motivated by *four reasons*: *encryption speed* (encryption algorithms based on multiple cells interconnected contain many operations on that uses communications between adjacent cells and these can be executed in parallel or pipelined mode in hardware, while not suitable in software); *security assured* (there is no physical protection for an encryption algorithm written by software and an intruder can go in with various debugging tools to modify the algorithm without anyone ever realizing it; hardware encryption devices can be securely encapsulated to prevent this.); *flexibility* (all the implemented functions could be upgraded at any time); *analogy between the re-configurability and CA (*all the CA cells could be updated in parallel, in a single time clock*).

Figure 4. Basic FPGA structure

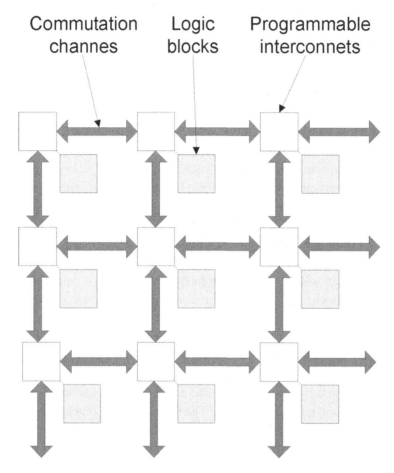

BIO-INSPIRED BASED ALGORITHM FOR CRYPTOGRAPHY

In this section is presented the proposed cryptosystem used to encrypt/decrypt data sent over the communication networks. This cryptosystem uses a *one-dimensional CA* and a *combination of five one-dimensional PCAs* arranged in pipeline and a *control logic* that manage all the operations of the CA and PCAs. The basic structure of the cryptosystem is presented in Figure 5.

Figure 5. Basic structure of the cryptosystem

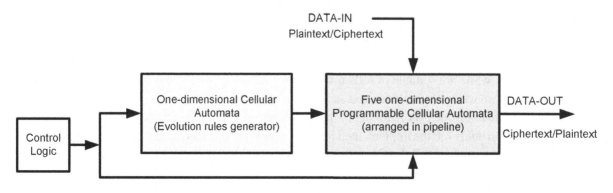

Because a lot of simulations and research has been carried out using 8-bit PCAs, an 8-bit PCAs was chosen for this project. In the block cipher scheme, one 8-bit message block is enciphered by one enciphering function. The enciphering function has five fundamental transformations (FTs) in order to operate on 8-bit data. This FTs are constructed using five PCAs arranged in pipeline. The block cipher scheme can be mathematically expressed as follows:

If

M is a *block of text* (*8 bits plaintext*),
C is a *block of text* (*8 bits ciphertext*),
E is an *enciphering function*

Then encryption:

$$C = E \bullet M \tag{2}$$

Decryption:

$$M = E^{-1} \bullet C \tag{3}$$

where: ● denotes a function symbol.

The algorithm discussed here to encrypt/decrypt data sent over communication networks can be divided into two-phases: an *encryption phase* and a *decryption phase*.

In the *encryption phase* the initial PCA configurations that practically contain inside the plaintext are evolved a number of predefined steps (between 1 and 7). The PCAs control signals are generated using the interconnections with the first CA that acts like a pseudo-random number generator (PRNG). The encryption phase for the pipelined PCAs block cipher is presented in Figure 6.

In the *decryption phase* the initial PCA configurations that contain inside the ciphertext are evolved a number of steps that must be accordingly with the differences between 8 and number of steps used for encryption phase. The diagram of the decryption phase for the pipelined PCAs block cipher is presented in Figure 7.

In the decryption phase *decrEvolSteps is 8 - encrEvolSteps* because the PCAs discovered and used in this cryptosystem generates for any initial state (that could be plaintext or ciphertext) cycles of even length that will repeat themselves after 8 steps. The PCAs used in this cryptographic algorithm is a *hybrid PCA* and is configured with the combination of the rules 51, 60 and 102 presented in the Table 1. In Figure 8 is presented an example of cycles generated by the PCA configured with rules cell 1 – rule 60, cell 2 – rule 51, cell 3 – rule 60, cell 4 – rule 60, cell 5 – rule 60, cell 6 – rule 51, cell 7 – rule 51, cell 8 – rule 51 and initial states 128 in the left side and 242 in the right side.

As it is shown in Figure 8, the PCA has two equal cycles of length 8. This property is a basic requirement of the cryptographic scheme. For example, in the enciphering phase, if it is used this PCA as enciphering function and define a plaintext as its initial state, it goes to its intermediate state after four

Figure 6. The diagram of the encryption phase   *Figure 7. The diagram of the decryption phase*

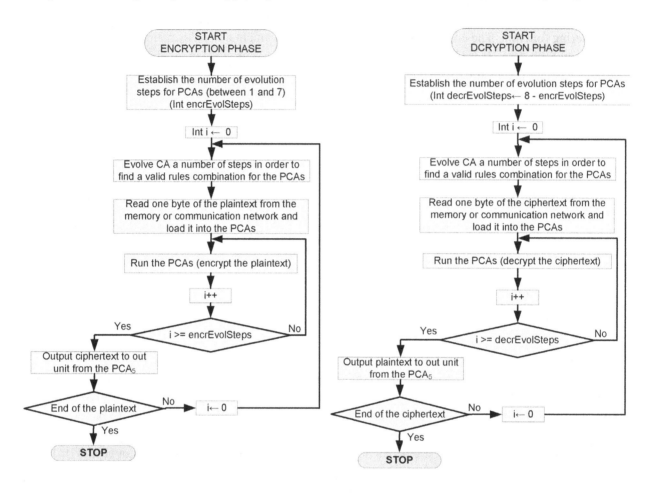

cycles. In the deciphering phase, after running another four cycles, the intermediate state returns back to its initial state, so the cipher text is deciphered into plaintext. Because the PCA does not generate sequences of maximum-length for all the possible combinations (512) of the rules it is necessary to apply from the first CA used as PRNG only the combinations of the three rules 51, 60 and 102 that generate cycles of length 8. The rules with 8-cycle length are only 156 and are presented in detail in my previous paper (Anghelescu et al., 2010).

Figure 8. The transitions diagram of the PCA with initial states 128 (left side) and 242 (right side)

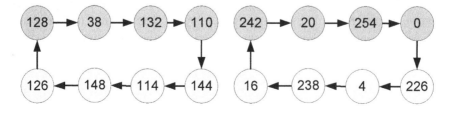

Figure 9. Bio-inspired cryptosystem: general architecture

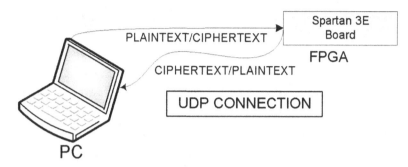

Figure 10. FPGA board used for test the bio-inspired based cryptosystem

In concordance with the CA theory, a single PCA cell was designed and then was multiplied in the FPGA circuits. The cell consists of a D flip-flop and a logic combinational circuit (LCC). The LCC includes multiplexers and XNOR logic gates to implement the rules of CA and to control the loading of data and operation of the CA. The entire scheme of that cell is presented in detail in paper (Anghelescu et al., 2013). The CA that select which rules are applied to the cells of the PCAs is realized by using a combination of rules 90 and 150 presented in Table 1. It has established in paper (Hortensius & Podaima, 1990) that the maximum-length CAs with rules 90 and 150 generates patterns having a high quality of pseudo-randomness. The control logic is the heart of the design and includes the communication interface between the FPGA and PC using UDP protocol and controls all operations of the cryptosystem. UDP is a simple to implement protocol because it does not require keeping track of every packet sent or received and it does not need to initiate or end a transmission.

TESTING AND EXPERIMENTAL RESULTS

A lot of experiments were carried out throughout the development of the cryptosystem, motivated by three reasons:

First: For investigation of the CA and PCA comportment,
Second: For assuring that the generated sequences respect the CA and PCA theory and
Third: To assure that the pipeline PCA based cryptosystem has a good security and high speed.

Figure 11. Results for encryption and decryption phases

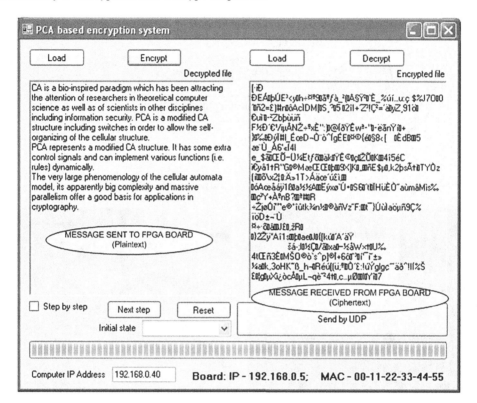

The general structure of the cryptosystem is presented in Figure 9.

In order to put in practice the principle of working of the cryptosystem was proposed an architecture which is able to satisfy both of the requirements for communication and for specifications related on PCA. FPGA circuits are used to implement the pipeline PCA block cryptosystem. The cryptosystem is implemented using VHDL code and is written in Xilinx ISE and Active HDL using structural and behavioral specifications. The hardware implementation of the PCA cryptosystem was realized using a Spartan 3E XC3S500E FPGA board from Xilinx (Xilinx, 2011) (see Figure 10).

The FPGA board is interfaced with a host computer using RJ-45 connector and UDP protocol. The UDP allows high speed data transfer from the PC to the cryptosystem and inverse. In Figure 11 is presented an illustrative example for the cryptographic phases (encryption and decryption process) applied to a text file.

The message (plaintext or ciphertext) is divided into 1Kb packages and is sent to the FPGA board using the UDP client – server connection. As the bytes reaches destination they are immediately encrypted using the correspondent bytes of the PCA's state and then saved into the 1Kb RAM memory of the board. In the FPGA, the message received is treated character by character as we explained above and the encryption/decryption results are sent back by the FPGA to the PC to be displayed, stored and analyzed. In hardware, the encryption rules are applied using the CA as PRNG or are downloaded to the RAM memory before encryption. When the encryption process begins, rules are generated or read out in sequence and sent to the PCAs. The process of generated or read rules does not introduce delays in the cryptographic algorithm because are generated/read in parallel with the encryption/decryption of a block of message.

Figure 12. Distribution of the plaintext in ASCII interval

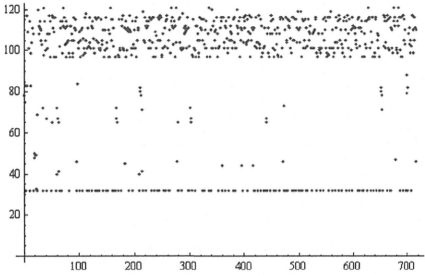

To show that the bio-inspired based cryptosystem has the property of *confusion* specific for classical cryptography it is possible to identify the distribution of the plaintext and ciphertext in ASCII intervals. This cryptosystem will map the given plaintext into a random ciphertext, which means that no pattern appears in the ciphertext. In the Figure 12 and Figure 13, the distribution of the ASCII values for a plaintext and ciphertext is presented. In Figure 12, plaintext distribution, most of the characters are lowercase, so the distribution is dense in the interval 97 and 122. In Figure 13, ciphertext distribution, the ciphertext is distributed almost uniform in the complete interval of ASCII values, and not only in the *zone of alphanumeric intervals,* and hence the developed cryptosystem also maps plaintext to a random ciphertext.

Figure 13. Distribution of the ciphertext in ASCII interval

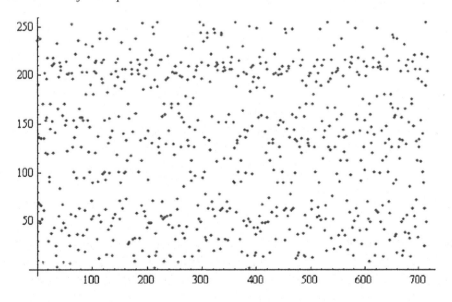

Table 3. Results for NIST statistical tests

Crt. No.	Test Applied	Interpretation	Crt. No.	Test Applied	Interpretation
1.	Frequency Test	PASS	9.	Maurer's Universal Statistical	PASS
2.	Frequency Test within a Block	PASS	10.	Linear Complexity Test	PASS
3.	Runs Test	PASS	11.	Serial Test	PASS
4.	Test for the Longest Run of Ones in a Block	PASS	12.	Approximate Entropy Test	PASS
5.	Binary matrix Rank Test	PASS	13.	Cumulative Sums Forward	PASS
6.	Discrete Fourier Transform	PASS	14.	Cumulative Sums Reverse	PASS
7.	Non-Overlapping Template Matching Test	PASS	15.	Random Excursions Test	PASS
8.	Overlapping Template Matching Test	PASS	16.	Random Excursions Variant	PASS

In the PCA encryption algorithm, the same ciphertext may be generated from different plaintext, and any ciphertext may give rise as well to different plaintext depending on the different PCA's rule configuration.

The PCA based encrypted sequences was tested using a set of 16 statistical tests conceived by the National Institute of Standards and technology (NIST) (Rukhin et al., 2010). The NIST test generates probabilistic results with respect to some characteristics that describe the pseudo-random number generators. The encrypted sequences pass the NIST tests and the system is accepted as possible random (Table 3).

The encrypted sequences pass the NIST tests and the cryptosystem is accepted as possible random. The timing analyzer was used to determine the critical path and the maximum operating frequency (33Mbps at 50MHz CLK Xilinx FPGA – XC3S500E). The encryption system discussed above can be applied in data communication networks, both in private network (Local Area Network – LAN) and public network (Wide Area Network – WAN).

FUTURE RESEARCH DIRECTIONS

In the immediate future, in order to assure flow control and guarantees that all sent packets will reach the destination in the correct order, the bio-inspired based cryptosystem will be implemented using the TCP protocol instead of UDP protocol. Also, the FPGA board will be connected to a router in order to assure encryption and decryption of messages from any computer connected to the Internet. The value for encryption/decryption speed will be improved by using increased FPGA clock speed and increased space RAM memories in order to store more encrypted/decrypted TCP/UDP packages into the FPGA before starting sending back the messages to the PC in the transmission phase.

CONCLUSION

In the present work, is demonstrated the ability of bio-inspired based algorithms to combine the two necessary properties *diffusion* (sensitivity to the initial conditions and/or control parameters) and *confusion* (the output has the same distribution for any plaintext used like input) in order to obtain cryptographic solutions. The major aspect treated in this paper is the cryptosystem description based on the CA and PCA paradigms, where an original model is proposed to cooperate and create a cryptographic system. The basic algorithms for each encryption and decryption involved in the cryptosystem architecture are described, too. According to the results obtained with respect to security analysis, the proposed method is expected to be useful for real-time encryption/decryption and transmission applications. The general conclusion of this work is that it is possible to build evolutionary cryptosystems based on a simple mathematical models specific of CA and PCA by introducing the local interaction between cells, local evolution rules, and massive parallelism.

REFERENCES

Adamatzky, A. (1994). *Identification of Cellular Automata*. London: Taylor & Francis Ltd.

Anghelescu, P., Ionita, S., & Iana, V. (2013). High-speed PCA Encryption Algorithm using Reconfigurable Computing. *Journal of Cybernetics and Systems*, 44(4), 285–304.

Anghelescu, P., Ionita, S., & Sofron, E. (2010). Encryption Technique with Programmable Cellular Automata. *Journal of Cellular Automata*, 5(1-2), 79–106.

Bobda, C. (2007). *Introduction to Reconfigurable Computing – Architectures, algorithms and applications*. Springer.

Cho, S.-J., Choi, U.-S., Hwang, Y.-H., Kim, H.-D., Pyo, Y.-S., Kim, K.-S., & Heo, S.-H. (2004). Computing Phase Shifts of Maximum-Length 90/150 Cellular Automata Sequences. Proceeding of the 6th *International Conference on Cellular Automata for Research and Industry, ACRI 2004*, Amsterdam (pp. 31-39). doi:10.1007/978-3-540-30479-1_4

Cusick, T., & Stanica, P. (2009). *Cryptographic Boolean functions and applications*. Elsevier.

Dachselt, F., & Schwarz, W. (2001). Chaos and Cryptography. *IEEE Transactions on Circuits and Systems*, 48(12), 1498–1509. doi:10.1109/TCSI.2001.972857

del Rey, Á.M. (2004). A Novel Cryptosystem for Binary Images. *Grant SA052/03, Studies in Informatics and Control*, 13(1).

Fuster-Sabater, A., & Cabalerro-Gil, P. (2010). Chaotic Cellular Automata with Cryptographic Application. Proceedings of the 9th *International Conference on Cellular Automata for Research and Industry* (pp. 251–260). Springer-Verlag Berlin Heidelberg

Gutowitz, H. (1994). *Methods and Apparatus for Encryption, Decryption and Authentication using Dynamical Systems*.

Rodriguez-Henriquez, F., Saqib, N.A., Días Pérez, A.D., & Koc, C.K. (Eds.), (2006). Cryptographic algorithms on reconfigurable hardware. Springer Science + Business Media, LLC.

Hortensius, P. D., McLeod, R. D., & Card, H. (1989). Parallel Random Number Generation for VLSI Systems using Cellular Automata. *IEEE Transactions on Computers*, 38(10), 1466–1473. doi:10.1109/12.35843

Hortensius, P. D., & Podaima, R. D. (1990). Cellular Automata Circuits for Built-in Self-test. *IBM Journal of Research and Development, 34*(2/3), 389–405. doi:10.1147/rd.342.0389

Ilachinski, A. (2001). Cellular Automata – A Discrete Universe. Singapore: World Scientific Publishing Co. Pte. Ltd.

Jamil, N., Mahmood, R., & Muhammad, R. (2012). A New Cryptographic Hash Function Based on Cellular Automata Rules 30, 134 and Omega-Flip Network. Proceedings of the *2012 International Conference on Information and Computer networks (ICICN 2012)*, Singapore (Vol. 27, pp. 163-169). IACSIT Press.

Koc, C.K. (Ed.), (2009). Cryptographic engineering. Springer Science + Business Media, LLC. doi:10.1007/978-0-387-71817-0

Kocarev, L., & Lian, S. (2011). *Chaos-Based Cryptography – Theory, Algorithms and Applications.* Springer-Verlag Berlin Heidelberg. doi:10.1007/978-3-642-20542-2

Lee, P. H., Pei, S. C., & Chen, Y. Y. (2003). Generating chaotic stream ciphers using chaotic systems. *The Chinese Journal of Physiology, 41*, 559–581.

Lu, H., Wang, S., Li, X., Tang, G., Kuang, J., Ye, W., & Hu, G. (2004). A new spatiotemporally chaotic cryptosystem and its security and performance analyses. *Chaos (Woodbury, N.Y.), 14*(3), 617–629. doi:10.1063/1.1772731 PMID:15446972

Masuda, N., & Aihara, K. (2002). Cryptosystems with discretized chaotic maps. *IEEE Trans. Circuits Syst. I, 49*(1), 28–40. doi:10.1109/81.974872

Menezes, A., Oorschot, P., & Vanstone, S. (1996). *Handbook of applied cryptography.* CRC Press. doi:10.1201/9781439821916

Nandi, S., Kar, B. K., & Chaudhuri, P. P. (1994). Theory and applications of cellular automata in cryptography. *IEEE Transactions on Computers, 43*(12), 1346–1356. doi:10.1109/12.338094

Rukhin, A., Soto, J., Nechvatal1, J., Smid, M., Barker, E., Leigh, S., Levenson, M., Vangel, M., Banks, D., Heckert, A., Dray, J., Vo, S. (2010). *A Statistical Test Suite for Random and Pseudorandom Number Generators for Cryptographic Applications* (NIST Special Publication 800-22).

Schmitz, R. (2001). Use of Chaotic Dynamical Systems in Cryptography. *Journal of the Franklin Institute, 338*(4), 429-441.

Shannon, C. (1949). Communication Theory of Secrecy Systems. *Bell Sys. Tech. J., 28*, 656–715. Retrieved from netlab.cs.ucla.edu/wiki/files/shannon1949.pdf

Stallings, W. (2003). *Cryptography and Network Security* (3rd ed.). Prentice Hall.

Tomassini, M., & Perrenoud, M. (2000). Stream Ciphers with One- and Two-Dimensional Cellular Automata. In M. Schoenauer at al. (Eds.), Parallel Problem Solving from Nature - PPSN VI, LNCS (Vol. 1917, pp. 722-731).

Tripathy, S., & Nandi, S. (2009). LCASE: Lightweight cellular automata-based symmetric key encryption. *International Journal of Network Security, 8*(2), 243–252.

Upegui, A. (2010). Dynamically Reconfigurable Hardware for Evolving Bio-Inspired Architectures. In R. Chiong (Ed.), *Intelligent Systems for Automated Learning and Adaptation: Emerging Trends and Applications* (pp. 1–22). doi:10.4018/978-1-60566-798-0.ch001

von Neumann, J. (1966). *Theory of Self-Reproducing Automata* (Ed., Burks, A.W.). London: Univ. of Illinois Press.

Weiser, M. (1999). The computer for the 21st century. *Mobile Computing and Communications Review*, *3*(3), 3–11. doi:10.1145/329124.329126

Wolfram, S. (1986). Cryptography with Cellular Automata. *Springer, Advances in Cryptology: Crypto '85 Proceedings. LNCS, 218*, 429–432.

Wolfram, S. (2002). *A new kind of science*. Champaign, IL: Wolfram Media Inc.

Xilinx. (2011). Spartan 3E Starter kit board data sheet. Retrieved from http://www.xilinx.com/support/documentation/boards_and_kits/ug230.pdf

Chapter 4
Detailed Analysis of Ultra Low Power Column Compression WALLACE and DADDA Multiplier in Sub–Threshold Regime

Priya Gupta
BITS, India

Anu Gupta
BITS, India

Abhijit Asati
BITS, India

ABSTRACT

In this chapter, the design and comparative analysis is done in between the most well-known column compression multipliers by Wallace and Dadda in sub-threshold regime. In order to reduce the hardware which ultimately reduces area, power and overall power delay product, an energy efficient basic modules of the multipliers like AND gates, half adders, full adders and partial product generate units have been analyzed for sub-threshold operation. At the last stage ripple carry adder is used in both multipliers. The performance metrics considered for the analysis of the multipliers are: power, delay and PDP. Simulation studies are carried out for 8x8-bit and 16x16-bit input data width. The proposed circuits show energy efficient results with Spectre simulations for the TSMC 180nm CMOS technology at 0.4V supply voltage. The proposed multipliers so implemented outperform its counterparts exhibiting low power consumption and lesser propagation delay as compared to conventional multipliers.

DOI: 10.4018/978-1-4666-9474-3.ch004

INTRODUCTION

During the last decade, extensive consideration has been given to the use of hybrid intelligence design technique which is suitable to design energy efficient digital modules for very large scale integration (VLSI) implementation. The computing efficiency of this modern technique offers a highly efficient solution to the hybrid intelligence based applications, digital signal processing (DSP) processors and biomedical applications like hearing aids, pacemakers etc.

In order to maintain the rapid increase of energy efficient fidelity applications, emphasis will be on incorporation of low power energy efficient modules in future system design. The design of such modules will have to partially rely on reduced power dissipation in fundamental hybrid intelligence units. Most of the hybrid intelligent applications need to design low power arithmetic circuit towards the development of power-efficient systems such as adders and multipliers. These underscores urges us to design a low power multipliers.

Multiplication is often an essential function in digital systems. Low power multiplication has always been a fundamental requirement of energy efficient processors and systems. In DSP application, multiplications are one of the most utilized arithmetic operations, as part of filters, convolvers, and transform processors. Improving multiplier design directly benefits the low power embedded processors used in consumer and industrial electronic products. In the past five decades, engineering ingenuity has moved multiplication away from the slow add-and-shift techniques to faster, parallel multiplication schemes. In the first large-scale digital systems, multiplication was performed as a series of additions and shifts. The requisite hardware consisted only of a parallel adder and a few registers.

The performance of multiplier was significantly improved with the introduction of Booth's method proposed by (Andrew D. Booth, 1951). Booth's method and the modified Booth method do not require a correction of the product when either (or both) of the operands is negative for two's complement numbers. During the 1950's, multiplier designs moved away from the slow sequential multiplication to faster simultaneous or parallel multipliers.

The two classes of parallel multipliers were defined by (R. De Mori, 1965). The first class of parallel multiplier uses a rectangular array of identical combinational cells to generate and sum the partial product bits. Multipliers of this class are called iterative array multipliers or, more simply, array multipliers. The delay is generally proportional to the word length of the multiplier input. Due to the regularity of their structures, array multipliers are easy to layout and have been implemented frequently. The second class of parallel multiplier reduces a matrix of partial product bits to two words through the strategic application of counters or compressors. These two words are then summed using a fast carry-propagate adder to generate the final binary product. This class of parallel multiplier is sometimes termed a column compression multiplier. Since the delay is proportional to the logarithm of the multiplier word length, these are also the fastest multipliers. Consequently, there exits considerable interest has centred on two's complement multipliers, since two's complement representation of numbers is almost used universally. Two's complement representation adds complexity to the multiplication algorithm because the sign of the number is embedded in the number itself.

In order to design an array multiplier for two's complement operands, Booth's algorithm can be employed. The implementation of a Booth's algorithm array multiplier computes the partial products by examining two multiplicand bits at a time. Except for enabling usage of two's complement operands, this Booth's algorithm array multiplier offers no performance or area advantage in comparison to the basic array multiplier. Better delays can be achieved by implementing a higher radix modified Booth algorithm.

Figure 1. Generation of partial products of 4x4 two's complement multiplier by Baugh Wooley's method

$$a[3] \ a[2] \ a[1] \ a[0]$$

$$X \quad b[3] \ b[2] \ b[1] \ b[0]$$

					$\overline{a[3]b[0]}$	a[2]b[0]	a[1]b[0]	a[0]b[0]	pp0
			$\overline{a[3]b[1]}$	a[2]b[1]	a[1]b[1]	a[0]b[1]			pp1
		$\overline{a[3]b[2]}$	a[2]b[2]	a[1]b[2]	a[0]b[2]				pp2
	$a[3]b[3]$	$\overline{a[2]b[3]}$	$\overline{a[1]b[3]}$	$\overline{a[0]b[3]}$					pp3
1	0	0	1						

prod[7]   prod[6]   prod[5]   prod[4]   prod[3]   prod[2]   prod[1]   prod[0]

The partial products of two's complement multiplication are generated by an algorithm described by Baugh-Wooley. In Baugh-Wooley's algorithm, two's complement multiplication is converted to an equivalent parallel array addition problem in which each partial product bit is the AND operation of a multiplier bit and a multiplicand bit, and the signs of all partial product bits are positive, allowing the products to be formed using array addition techniques. In conventional multiplication, there are partial product bits with negative as well as positive signs. (Baugh et al., 1973) revealed that instead of subtracting the partial products that have negative signs, the negation of partial products can be added. The modified Baugh-Wooley method is shown in Figure below. This organization of partial product bits produces an easy to remember strategy for two's complement multiplication, which is first to invert the bits along the left edge and the bottom row, with the exception of the bottom left partial product bit and second to add a single one to the n+1 and 2n columns. Note that the one in the 2n column is not actually part of the final product and can be ignored. The negated partial product bits can be produced using a NAND gate instead of an AND gate, which may reduce the area slightly in CMOS. Generation of partial products of 4x4-bit two's complement multiplier by Baugh Wooley's method is shown in Figure 1.

In this chapter, the complicated reduction of partial products analysis is done in between the most well-known column compression multipliers by (Wallace et al., 1964; Dadda, 1965) algorithms. The main objective is to implement energy efficient Wallace and Dadda multiplier based on universally used Two's complement numbers representation operated in sub-threshold regime. The sub-threshold operation involves, scaling voltage below the device threshold which yields significantly lower power consumption compared to super-threshold counterparts. It can be used for wide range of low power based energy applications.

This Wallace and Dadda multiplier operated in sub-threshold region minimizes the switching and leakage energy but it would be slow. Hence there is an interesting trade between speed and switching energy. For leakage-aware CMOS circuits, it is a major challenge to find the optimal tradeoff between high switching speeds and low leakage currents. To increase the speed of the multipliers, more complex, more power-hungry architecture could be used for their implementations.

The multiplication process begins with the generation of all partial products in parallel using an array of AND gates. The basic building blocks of multiplier structure employs multiplicand block design (an N*N bit product) which comprise of AND gate array for computing the partial products, multiplier result block design for partial products addition along with adder in the final stage of addition. These parts of the circuit decide the overall circuit performance, power consumption and area. Extensive research has been done to improve the performance of these building blocks.

Initially in this chapter, different varieties of logic families and body biasing scheme have been explored to develop Wallace and Dadda multipliers by (D. Markovic et al., 2000; U. Ko. et al., 1995; R. Zimmermann & W. Fichtner., 1997). Both multipliers uses full adders and half adders to reduce the partial product tree to two rows, and then a final adder is used to add these two rows of partial products. So basically AND gates, half adder (HA), full adder (FA), partial product generate (PPG) are the common cells for both multipliers. As discussed earlier that these adder levels have significant impact on power and delay of the entire multipliers design. So early analyses of these adders are done in identifying the block occupying a large portion of the total power and delay. Therefore, selecting an appropriate adder cell can significantly improve the overall performance of the designed Wallace and Dadda multipliers. Finally, the resultant most energy efficient logic family and biasing scheme for basic blocks are being used to the final implementation of multipliers in sub-threshold regime.

In Section 2, basics of multipliers and their reduction schemes have been discussed. In Section 3, the impact and the usage of logic families with/without reverse body biasing (RBB) scheme in sub-threshold regime have been discussed. The basic gates are described in detail with major emphasis on accommodations for energy efficiency. Measurement shows the basic gates are functional at 400 mV power supply voltage. For further improvement in overall performance of the logic gates, RBB scheme has been applied. This RBB scheme takes advantage of the unique sensitivity in sub-threshold regime, such that the robustness at low voltages is seen to be improved dramatically with its application. Also, the fluctuations induced by process and temperature variability due to RBB can be eliminated with minimal energy penalties. Section 4 describes the literature survey of the column compression Wallace and Dadda multipliers. Section 5 presents the detailed analysis of the standard cell library for the implementation of Wallace and Dadda multipliers in sub-threshold regime. In Section 6, the implementation of proposed 8x8-bit, 16x16-bit Wallace and Dadda multipliers have been done using hybrid logic styles at 0.4V supply voltage. These techniques are characterized in terms of power, performance and PDP for each circuit logic families. Section 7 gives the detailed analysis of the power efficient multipliers, describes the simulation methodology used and overall experimental results and Section 8 presents a summary of the chapter, the concluding remarks followed by future scope.

BASICS OF MULTIPLIERS

The column compression multipliers, also known as tree multipliers, are highly useful in high speed computations due to their propagation delay. The propagation delay is proportional to the logarithm of the operand word length in comparison to array multipliers whose delay is directly proportional to operand word length discussed by (P. R. Cappello, 1983). Column compression multipliers are faster than array multipliers but have an irregular structure and so their design is difficult. With the improvement in VLSI design techniques and process technology, designs which were previously infeasible or too difficult to be implemented by manual layout can now be implemented through automated synthesis.

The internal basic modules are similar for both architectures (Wallace and Dadda) with the difference occurring in the procedure of reduction of the partial products and the size of the final adder. In Wallace's scheme, the partial products are reduced as soon as possible. On the other hand (Townsend et al., 2003) discuss that the Dadda's method does minimum reduction necessary at each level and requires the same number of levels as Wallace multiplier. As a result, final adder in Wallace multiplier is slightly smaller in size as compared to the final adder in Dadda multiplier.

1. Dadda Multiplier Architecture

The Dadda multiplier is a hardware multiplier design invented by computer scientist Luigi Dadda in 1965. It is similar to the Wallace multiplier, but it is slightly faster (for all operand sizes) and requires fewer gates (for all but the smallest operand sizes. In fact, Dadda and Wallace multipliers have the same three steps:

1. Multiply (logical AND) each bit of one of the arguments, by each bit of the other, yielding results. Depending on position of the multiplied bits, the wires carry different weights, for example wire of bit carrying result of is 32.
2. Reduce the number of partial products to two layers of full and half adders.
3. Group the wires in two numbers, and add them with a conventional adder.

The Dadda multiplier architecture can be divided into three stages. The first stage involves generation of partial products by two's complement parallel array multiplication algorithm presented by Baugh-Wooley et al. (1973). In their algorithm, signs of all partial product bits are positive. It's different from conventional two's complement multiplication which generates partial product bits with negative and positive signs. The final product obtained after the reduction is also in two's complement form. Figure 1 shows generation of partial products for 4x4-bit multiplier by Baugh-Wooley method. Figure 2 shows the arrangement of the partial products for an 8x8-bit multiplier. The dots represent the partial products.

In the second stage, the partial product matrix is reduced to a height of two using the column compression procedure developed by Dadda. The iterative procedure for doing this is as follows:

1. Assuming the minimum column height i.e. $h_1 = 2$ and calculating remaining column height using formula $h_{j+1} =$ floor $(1.5*h_j)$ for increasing values of j. Continue this until the largest j is reached such that maximum column height for the multiplier to be designed is attained. Using this equation we get $h_1=2$, $h_2=3$, $h_3=4$, $h_4=6$, $h_5=9$ and so on. For example, in the first stage of the 8x8-bit Dadda multiplication shown in Figure 2(a), the maximum height of columns is 8 therefore; the value of h_j is 6 means heights of the columns are reduced to a maximum of 6. Similarly in the second stage, shown in Figure 2(b) the maximum height of column is 6 and value of h_j is 4 heights of the columns are reduced to a maximum of 4.

Figure 2. Column compression scheme for 8x8-bit Dadda multiplier

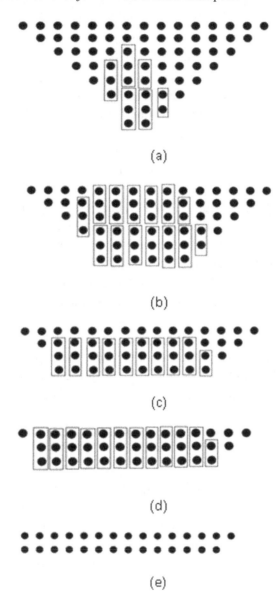

(a)

(b)

(c)

(d)

(e)

2.   All the columns, with heights greater than h_j, are reduced to a height of h_j using either half adder or full adder. If the column height has to be reduced by one, use a half adder else use a full adder and continue this step till the column height is reduced to h_j.

3.   Stop the reduction if the height of the matrix becomes two, after which it can be fed to final adder.

Figure 2 (b), (c), (d) and (e) show the reduction stages for an 8x8-bit Dadda multiplier. Once the height of matrix is reduced to two, a 2N-2 bit adder is used to generate the final product. RCA is used for final adder stage.

Array Reduction

Array reduction is based on the Dadda's algorithm. The column height or size of the queues is reduced by using full adders and half adders till the length of all queues (height of all columns) is two or less.

For N*N Dadda multipliers, if i is the number of iteration, 2N-1 is the sizes of all queues and their maximum is stored in L[i]. The value of column height (h_j) is find out using formula $h_{j+1} =$ floor $(1.5*h_j)$ as discussed in the above part of the iterative procedure. The maximum calculated value of column height is stored in H[i]. After the calculation of H[i], the reduction of the array is started sequentially checking the sizes of all the queues in the array. If the size of the queue is lesser than or equal to H[i], no changes are made to the queue. If the size of the queue is greater than H[i], the queue needs to be reduced to H[i] using half adders and full adders.

The difference in the length between queue and H[i] decides the use of either of these adders for e.g. half adder is used if difference is one. The first two elements of the queue used as the input of the half adder. The output sum is en-queued to the same queue while carry out is en-queued to the adjacent queue in sequence, thus use of single half adder reduces the size of the queue by one. In the similar way, full adder is used to reduce the queue if difference in the length between queue and H[i] is greater than or equal to two. The first three elements of the queue used as the input of the full adder. The output sum is en-queued to the same queue and carry out is en-queued to the adjacent queue in sequence, thus use of single full adder reduces the size of the queue by two.

The iterations continue recursively till the size of the queue becomes equal to H[i]. The next queue iterations in sequence are taken up for reduction after one queue is reduced till at most two elements remain in each queue. When the length of all queues (height of all columns) is two or less then the reduction phase is completed.

Figure 3 shows the queues reduction scheme for 4x4-bit Dadda multiplier and their step by step explanations given below

Iteration One: Figure 3 (a) shows the state of the queues before the start of the reduction in which the maximum length (L [1]) for this iteration is 4 and H[1] can be calculated to be 3. All the queues with sizes greater than 3 need to be reduced. Starts form the Queue 4; the first two elements (enclosed by the square) of the queues are de-queued and summed by half adder ('ha0'). The output sum bit of the half adder is assigned as 'ha0s' and the carry out bit of the same half adder is assigned as wire 'ha0c'. The output sum 'ha0s' is compressed to Queue 4 and carry 'ha0c' is compressed to Queue 5 as shown in Figure 3(b) according to the algorithm. The compressed elements are above the arrow in the queue. One more element is added in the Queue 5 due to which the length of the queue increases to 5. Full adder ('fa0') is used to reduce its length to 3. The first three elements (enclosed by the square) of queue are de-queued and summed by 'fa0'. The output sum bit of the full adder is assigned as 'fa0s' en-queuing to Queue 5 and the carry out bit of the same full adder is assigned as 'fa0c' Queue 6. Now the length of all queues is less than or equal to three, so the iteration phase for this stage is done as shown in Figure 3(c).

Iteration Two: For the second iteration the maximum length (L[2]) is 3 and height H[2] can be calculated to be 2. All the queues with sizes greater than 2 need to be reduced. From the starting of the Queue, the first queue with length greater than 2 is Queue 3 (length is only exceeded by one). In the Queue 3, the first two elements (enclosed by the square) of the queues are de-queued and summed by half adder ('ha1') to reduce the length to 2. The output sum bit of the half adder is as-

Figure 3. 4x4-bit Dadda multiplier queues reduction scheme

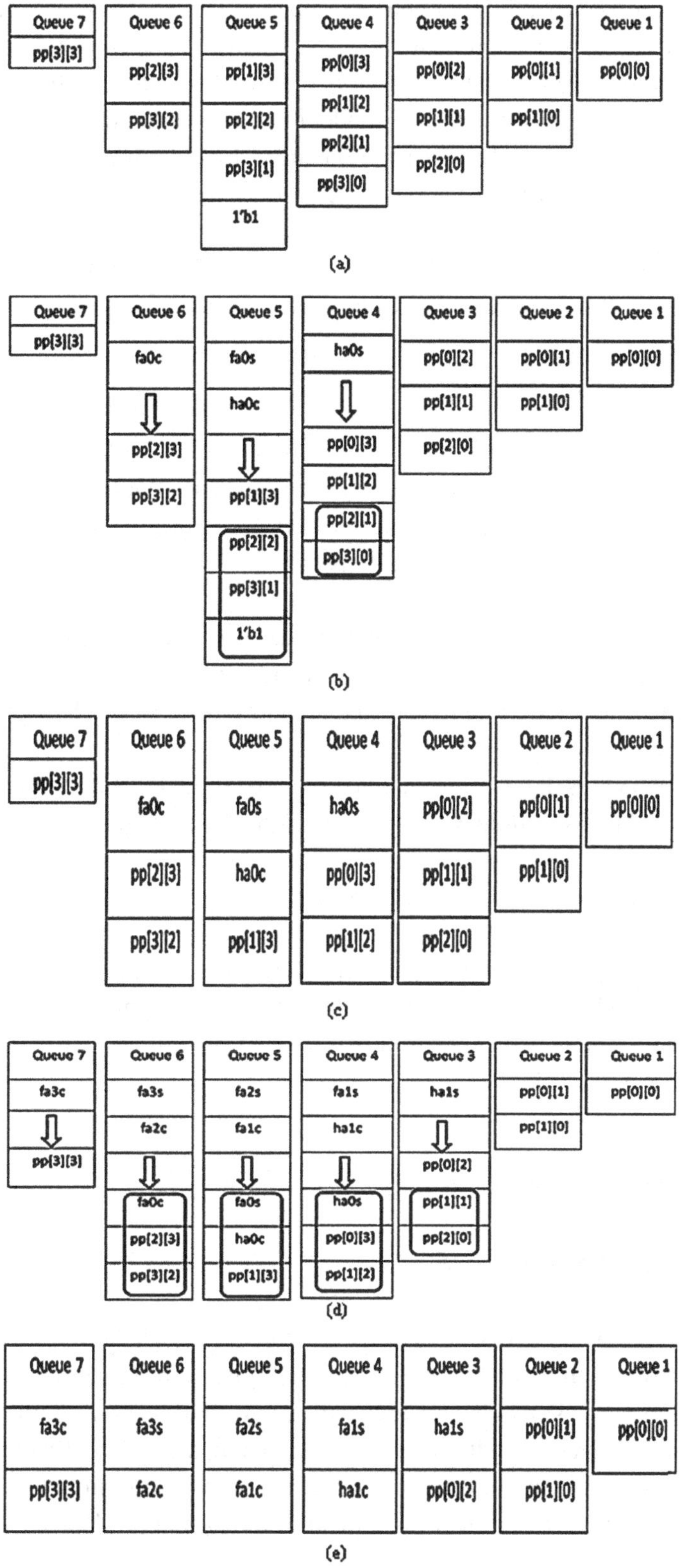

Queue 7	Queue 6	Queue 5	Queue 4	Queue 3	Queue 2	Queue 1
pp[3][3]			pp[0][3]	pp[0][2]	pp[0][1]	pp[0][0]
	pp[2][3]	pp[1][3]	pp[1][2]	pp[1][1]	pp[1][0]	
	pp[3][2]	pp[2][2]	pp[2][1]	pp[2][0]		
		pp[3][1]	pp[3][0]			
		1'b1				

(a)

Queue 7	Queue 6	Queue 5	Queue 4	Queue 3	Queue 2	Queue 1
pp[3][3]	fa0c	fa0s	ha0s	pp[0][2]	pp[0][1]	pp[0][0]
	⇩	ha0c	⇩	pp[1][1]	pp[1][0]	
	pp[2][3]	⇩	pp[0][3]	pp[2][0]		
	pp[3][2]	pp[1][3]	pp[1][2]			
		pp[2][2]	pp[2][1]			
		pp[3][1]	pp[3][0]			
		1'b1				

(b)

Queue 7	Queue 6	Queue 5	Queue 4	Queue 3	Queue 2	Queue 1
pp[3][3]	fa0c	fa0s	ha0s	pp[0][2]	pp[0][1]	pp[0][0]
	pp[2][3]	ha0c	pp[0][3]	pp[1][1]	pp[1][0]	
	pp[3][2]	pp[1][3]	pp[1][2]	pp[2][0]		

(c)

Queue 7	Queue 6	Queue 5	Queue 4	Queue 3	Queue 2	Queue 1
fa3c	fa3s	fa2s	fa1s	ha1s	pp[0][1]	pp[0][0]
⇩	fa2c	fa1c	ha1c	⇩	pp[1][0]	
pp[3][3]	⇩	⇩	⇩	pp[0][2]		
	fa0c	fa0s	ha0s	pp[1][1]		
	pp[2][3]	ha0c	pp[0][3]	pp[2][0]		
	pp[3][2]	pp[1][3]	pp[1][2]			

(d)

Queue 7	Queue 6	Queue 5	Queue 4	Queue 3	Queue 2	Queue 1
fa3c	fa3s	fa2s	fa1s	ha1s	pp[0][1]	pp[0][0]
pp[3][3]	fa2c	fa1c	ha1c	pp[0][2]	pp[1][0]	

(e)

signed as 'ha1s' en-queued to Queue 3 and the carry out bit of the same half adder is assigned as 'ha1c' being compressed to adjacent queue to Queue 4. Due to this carry bit the length of Queue 4 is increased to four which is more than the allowed size. In the Queue 4, the first three elements (enclosed by the square) of the queues are de-queued and summed by full adder ('fa1') to reduce its length to 2. The output sum bit of the full adder is assigned as 'fa1s' en-queued to Queue 4 and the carry out bit of the same full adder is assigned as 'fa1c' being compressed to adjacent queue to Queue 5. Due to this carry bit the length of Queue 5 is increased to four which is more than the allowed size. The same above procedure is followed recursively as Queue 4. Queue 6 also faces the same conditions and undergoes the same procedure outlined above. Figure 3(d) shows the elements decompressed and compressed to Queues 3, 4, 5 and 6. Figure 3(e) shows the final state of the queues at the end of stage.

Final Stage Adder

Ripple carry adder is used for the final summation of the elements in the queues when the size of all queues has been reduced to two or less. The first elements of all queues form the first input to the adder and the second elements form the second input to the adder.

Concluding Remarks: The reduction rules for the Dadda tree, however, are as follows:
1. Take any three wires with the same weights and input them into a full adder. The result will be an output wire of the same weight and an output wire with a higher weight for each three input wires.
2. If there are two wires of the same weight left, and the current number of output wires with that weight is equal to 2 (modulo 3), input them into a half adder. Otherwise, pass them through to the next layer.
3. If there is just one wire left, connect it to the next layer.

Dadda multipliers are the refinement of parallel, in contrast to the Wallace reduction. Dadda multiplier performs the least reduction at each stage. The maximum height of each stage is determined by working back from final stage which consists of two rows of partial products. The height of each stage should be in the order 2, 3, 4,6,9,13,19,28,42,63 etc.

For Dadda multipliers the number of full adders and half adders required depends on the value of N.

No of Full Adders = N2 -4N+3 and No of Half Adders = N-1

2. Wallace Multiplier Architecture

The Wallace multiplier architecture can be divided into three stages. The first stage involves generation of partial products by two's complement parallel array multiplication algorithm. In their algorithm, signs of all partial product bits are positive. It's different from conventional two's complement multiplication which generates partial product bits with negative and positive signs. The final product obtained after the reduction is also in two's complement form. Figure 4 shows column compression scheme for an 8x8-bit multiplier. The dots represent the arrangement of the partial products.

Figure 4. Column compression scheme for 8x8-bit Wallace multiplier

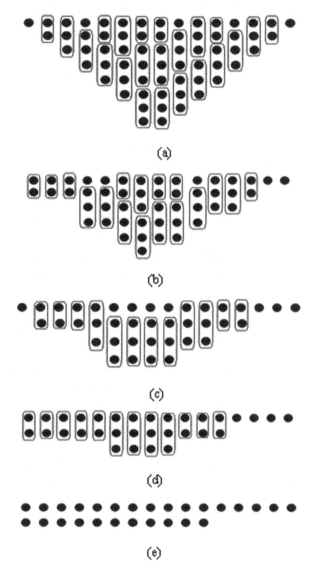

In the second stage, the partial product matrix is reduced to a height of two using the column compression procedure developed by Wallace. The iterative procedure for doing this is as follows:

Find out the maximum height of columns in the dot matrix array. If it is greater than 2, reduce the height by following the recursive procedure described below.

1. Check the height of each column. If it is 1, no reduction is done. If it is 2, use a half adder else use a full adder and check the height of column again. Continue the reduction till the height of column becomes ≤ 1.

2. Repeat the above step for all other columns and at the end, en-queue the 'sum' strings of all half adders and full adders into the same columns and carry strings into the adjacent columns.

3. Again find out the maximum height of columns and continue the reduction using the above recursive procedure till maximum height reaches 2.

Figure 4 (b), (c), (d) and (e) show the reduction stages for an 8x8-bit Wallace multiplier. Once the height of matrix is reduced to two, an RCA is used to generate the final product.

Array Reduction

It needs to be reduced according to Wallace's algorithm. The size of the queues (height of columns) is reduced by using full adders and half adders. The loop stops executing when the length of all queues (height of all columns) is two or less.

Let 'a [2N]' represents an array of '2N' queues to store the names of partial products during reduction. Let a[i]→size represents the size of ith queue. At the start of every iteration, the sizes of all the 2N queues are checked and their maximum is stored in 'max'. Let temp_size [i] holds the size of ith queue a[i] → size and it is reassigned with new size after every iteration. Every de-queue operation will decrement the size of queue, a[i] → size by 1 and every en-queue will increment its size by 1 and temp_size[i] will be decremented by 1 for every de-queue.

If temp_size[i] = 2, queue a[i] is reduced using a half adder. The first two elements are decompressed and used as input to the half adder, temp_size[i] is decremented by 2 and becomes 0. The sum from the half adder is compressed to the same queue and the carry out is compressed to the next queue in sequence.

If temp_size[i] > 2, full adder is used to reduce the queue. When a full adder is used, the first three elements of the queue are decompressed and are supplied as inputs to the full adder. The sum from the full adder is compressed to the same queue while the carry out is compressed to the next queue in sequence and temp_size[i] is decremented by 3. If temp_size[i] becomes ≤ 1, the reduction of queue a[i] is stopped else the above procedure is followed recursively. After a queue is reduced, the next queue in sequence is taken up for reduction. At the end of iteration, maximum height of dot matrix array is found out and is stored in 'max'. The iterations continue till 'max' becomes ≤ 2 i.e. at most two elements remain in each queue. Once such a state has been reached, the reduction phase is completed.

The array reduction using queues is explained with the help of an example. A 4x4-bit Wallace multiplication is taken as the example. Figure 5 shows the step by step 4x4-bit Wallace multiplier queues reduction scheme.

The Figure 5 (a) shows the state of the queues before the start of the reduction. The reduction of the queues for a 4x4-bit multiplier is explained below:

Iteration One: On checking the sizes of all the queues, it is observed that the maximum size 'max' for this iteration is 4. Since the size of Queue1 = 1, no reduction is done. The size of Queue2 is 2; hence a half adder is used for reduction. The first two elements of the queue are decompressed and summed in a half adder ('ha0') by printing a half adder. Now temp_size [1] of this queue becomes 0. The sum bit of the half adder is assigned to a wire 'ha0s' and the carry out bit is assigned to the wire 'ha0c'. In accordance with the algorithm, 'ha0s' is compressed to Queue2 and 'ha0c' is compressed to Queue3. Since temp_size [2] for Queue3 is 3, a full adder ('fa0') is used for reduction. The addition of the full adder leads to de-queuing of the first three elements of Queue3 and en-queuing of the sum of the full adder'fa0s' to Queue3 and the carry out of the full adder 'fa0c' to Queue4. Now for reduction of Queue4, consider temp_size [3] of this Queue which is 4. So,

Figure 5. 4x4-bit Wallace multiplier queues reduction scheme

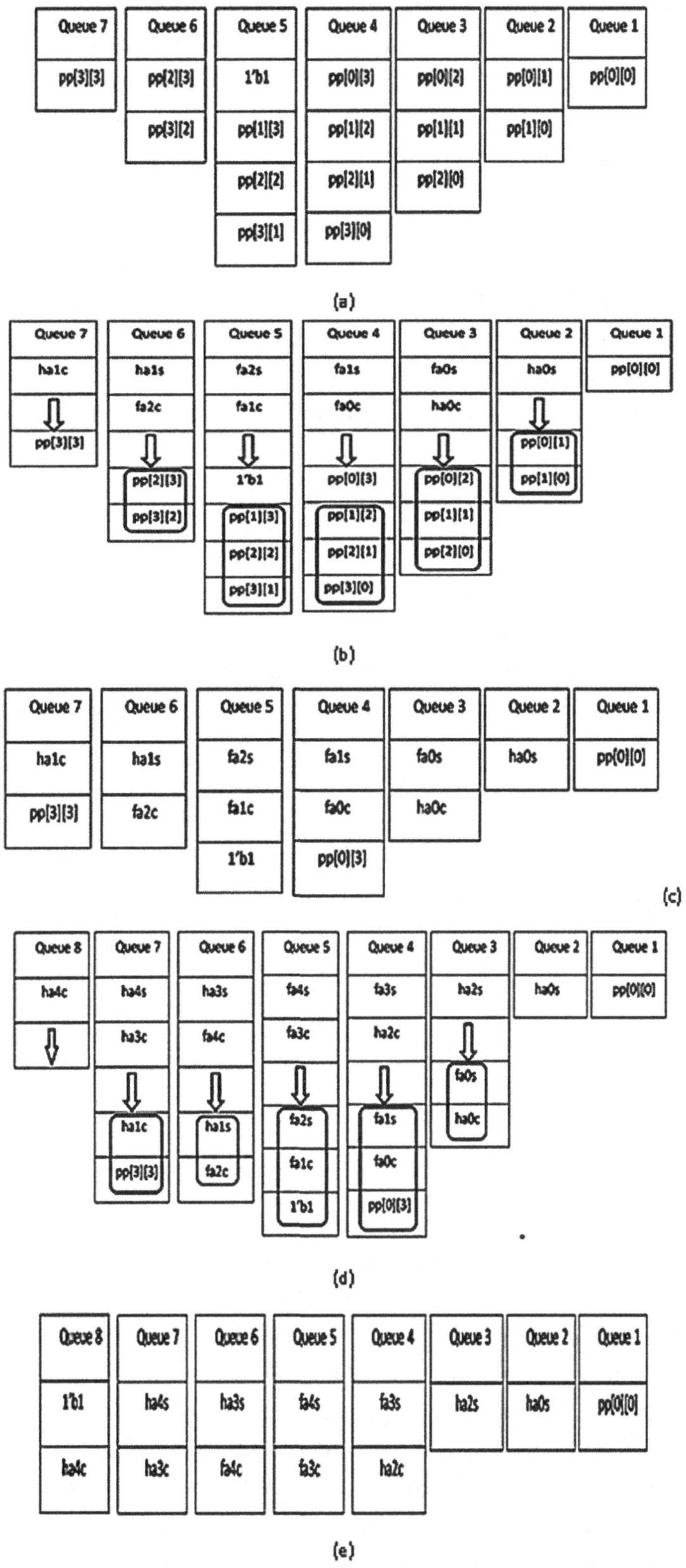

(a)

(b)

(c)

(d)

(e)

a full adder ('fa1') is used for reduction and its sum 'fa1s' is compressed into Queue4 and carry 'fa1c' is compressed into Queue5. Now temp_size [2] is decremented by 3 and becomes 1 and so the reduction stops. The reduction of Queues 5 and 6 follow similar procedure described above and the reduction of all Queues in this iteration is shown in Figure 5(b). The elements above the arrow in the queue are the ones which are compressed in this iteration. The state of the queues at the end of this iteration is shown in Figure 5(c)

Iteration Two: On checking the sizes of all the queues, it is observed that the maximum size 'max' for the second iteration is 3. The variable temp_size[i] is assigned the new size of ith array a[i]→size. All queues with sizes greater than 1 need to be reduced. The program starts checking the sizes of the queues sequentially. Queue 3 has a size of 2 and hence a half adder ('ha2') is used for reduction. Full adders are used for the reduction of Queues 4 and 5 since their size is 3. Queues 6 and 7 are reduced using half adders. Figure 5(d) shows the elements decompressed and compressed to all the Queues in this iteration. The final state of the queues at the end of this iteration is shown in Figure 5(e).

Final Stage Adder

Once the size of all queues has been reduced to two or less, the elements in the queues are ready to be summed using adder. If a[i]→size is 1, the only element in the Queue a[i] is de-queued and assigned to prod[i], where 'prod' is an array holding the '2N' bit product of an N*N multiplier. The first elements of all queues form the first input to the adder and the second elements form the second input to the adder.

3. Ripple Carry Adder (RCA)

An energy efficient RCA is used in the final stage of reduction of partial products by Dadda and Wallace algorithms in sub-threshold regime.

An N-bit RCA is built using N number of full adders where carry input (C_{in}) of each of the full adders is the carry output (C_{out}) of the previous full adders. An example of 8-bit RCA is shown in Figure 6. C_{in} of the 1st full adder is assumed to be 0 and the C_{out} of each of the full adders ripple to the next adder.

REVERSE BODY BIASING (RBB) EFFECTS ON LOGIC GATES: AN OBSERVATION

The sub-threshold leakage current is the drain-source current of a transistor operating in the weak inversion region in which the current flows due to the diffusion current of the minority carriers in the channel. The four main sources of leakage current in a MOS transistor are: On-state gate leakage, Off-state gate leakage, gate induced drain leakage (GIDL), sub-threshold leakage current (weak inversion) (I_{SUB}). Figure 7 shows the leakage currents in CMOS logic gates. In current CMOS technologies, the sub-threshold leakage current, I_{SUB}, is much larger than the other leakage current components. Due to this leakage current overall performance of the digital circuits affects a lot.

Body biasing scheme is one of the most energy efficient technique which manage threshold voltage (V_{th}) and power supply voltage (V_{dd}) at the same time, in order to minimize the power dissipation and improve the performance of digital VLSI circuits in sub-threshold region of operation. For instance, ef-

Figure 6. An example of 8-bit Ripple Carry Adder

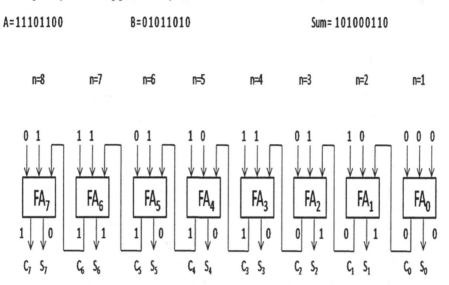

Figure 7. Leakage currents in CMOS logic gates

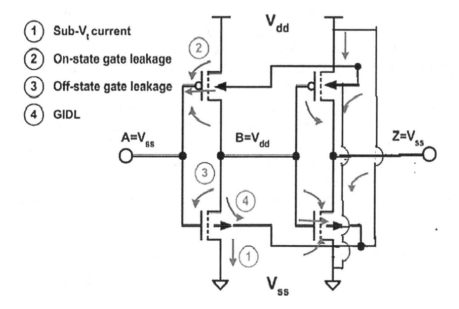

fective body biasing techniques can adjust the transistor V_{th} to compensate for changes in the transistor as the product ages. It can also adjust the transistor V_{th} for temperature fluctuation, maintaining a uniform performance and thus adjusting leakage current. The body biasing scheme and proved that swapped or RBB scheme is well suited for devices with low threshold voltages and power supply voltages below threshold discussed by (S. Narendra et al., 2004). Therefore it works efficiently in sub-threshold regime. To verify their insight effects into the device response at the gate and drain or source terminals, the detailed analysis of basic gates with/without RBB scheme have been observed.

In this scheme the bulk terminal of both the devices would get interchanged i.e. PMOS tied to ground and NMOS tied to V_{dd} in weak inversion region, there is a noticeable increase of the drain current which leads to increased switching speeds and potentially dissipating less power while above threshold swapping the bulk terminal connections degrades the delays significantly. Whereas in the conventional configuration the bulk terminal of both NMOS and PMOS devices are tied to ground and V_{dd} respectively. This type of bulk connection prevents forward body biasing (FBB) at the source or drain-to-bulk p/n+ junctions in normal region of operation (V_{dd} above than threshold voltage). In this manner, the ability to increase sub-threshold currents is called examination of the OFF current (I_{OFF}) with modified bulk potential. Thus this extra current improves the overall performance of the circuits as discussed by (P.Ramanathan & P.T.Vanathi, 2009). It is clearly mentioned that the frequencies of CMOS logic gates with RBB scheme are higher than conventional body biasing scheme at low voltages. Hence RBB scheme also affects the overall PDP.

The principle objective of designing the digital circuit operated in sub-threshold regime is to minimize the overall PDP. The PDP based metric is generally used in arithmetic circuits because they operates at optimum energy under a given frequency. It is a good measure for comparing the logic styles that are used in low power digital system. In paper (Priya G. et al., 2014), the basic logic gates with/without RBB scheme have been implemented. The designed logic gates using static CMOS logic style, transmission gate (TG), pass transistor (PT), swing restored pass-transistor logic (SRPL), complementary pass-transistor logic (CPL) and double pass-transistor logic (DPL) were simulated using the BSIM3 (V3.24) model at minimum 0.4V power supply using 180nm technology. Measured PDP summary with/without RBB scheme for optimized logic gates and overall comparison of different logic families shown in Table 1.

The cumulative result concludes as hybrid PT (PT with RBB scheme), TG, Static CMOS, SRPL and DPL are most the energy efficient logic families that can be used to implement arithmetic circuits in sub-threshold regime whereas CPL shows the least efficient result amongst all. The comparison among logic gates illustrate that XOR logic gate gives the efficient results in all logic families with RBB scheme as compared to conventional logic XOR gate whereas AND logic gate with RBB scheme showed energy efficient results in all PT/TG logic families except static CMOS logic family. OR gate does not show any effect with RBB scheme as all values are similar in both cases. After the analysis, it is found that to implement energy efficient arithmetic circuits, conventional PT/ TG logic family does not evaluate

Table 1. PDP (watt*Sec) summary for optimized logic gates of different logic families

Logic Families	Without RBB Scheme			With RBB Scheme		
	AND	OR	XOR	AND	OR	XOR
Static CMOS+RBB	1.92E-17	2.63E-17	6.23E-16	8.232E-18	1.802E-17	7.25E-16
TG+RBB	4.95E-18	9.46E-18	4.51E-16	5.846E-18	5.406E-18	9.43E-16
PT+RBB	3.66E-18	5.86E-18	2.29E-16	1.132E-17	2.04E-18	3.97E-16
SRPPL+RBB	3.43E-17	2.45E-17	1.16E-15	2.79E-17	2.47E-17	1.45E-15
CPL+RBB	6.84E-17	6.16E-17	1.83E-15	6.89E-17	6.17E-17	2.45E-15
DPL+RBB	1.65E-16	1.85E-17	7.87E-15	1.80E-17	2.34E-17	1.01E-15

Priya G. et al. (2014).
Note: 180nm Technology at 0.4 V.

any results due to their voltage degradation and poor noise margin. However, PT /TG logic family with RBB schemes works efficiently in sub-threshold regime and meets the requirement of energy efficient arithmetic circuits.

In our investigations, Hybrid DPL was found to be the most efficient pass-transistor logic style. Complementary CMOS, however, proves to be superior to hybrid TG (TG with RBB scheme) in all respects with only few exceptions. The investigation results presented show that for lower bit operands, complex logic gates and under realistic circuit conditions complementary static CMOS performs much better than DPL and other pass-transistor logic styles if low power is of concern. Whereas hybrid TG logic have best results for higher bit operands. The most energy efficient logic gates are being used for the final implementation of column compressors Wallace and Dadda multipliers.

LITERATURE SURVEY

Portable devices which are battery-operated require two kinds of power: dynamic power and leakage power. When the circuit in active mode it consumes dynamic power and it consumes leakage power when the circuit is in inactive or standby mode.

Many papers have been published based on the optimization of low-power arithmetic units in sub-threshold region based on different methodology and design techniques to improve the power dissipation, performance, and area which shows the importance of the area. Their main aim was at offering low power consumption, high speed and reduced PDP.

(J. Rabaey et al., 1995; A. P. Chandrakasan et al., 1992; A. P. Chandrakasan & R.W. Brodersen., 1995; S. Narendra, 2001; Fisher et al., 2008; & Priya G., 2013) have been discussed on ultra low power based VLSI circuit design which is a primary design metric for manufactures. Due to technological advancement, power reduction is highest in jurisdiction when compared to speed and area. Higher power consumption increases the on-chip temperature which results in reduced operating life of the chip and battery life. To satisfy the low power requirement of the CMOS based circuits, (Allan L. silburt et al., 1988) introduced sub-threshold logic scheme, which involves scaling voltage below the device threshold. Extensive research is going on the subjects of sub/near-threshold digital design and their challenges, the goal of this chapter however is to cover a border range of sub-threshold based Wallace and Dadda multiplier designs, to show the interrelation of different solutions and their effective methods for low power digital design and review the recent updates and new advances in ultra low power era.

As the whole logic core of chip operates at a power supply falling from nominal level to the value less than threshold of MOS transistor i.e. $V_{dd} < V_{th}$, the power dissipation can greatly be reduced according to the square law dependence on the supply voltage, however the penalty of speed degradation is also obvious. Despite fabricated in deep submicron CMOS technologies, when MOS transistor in the circuits are forced to operate in sub-threshold region (weak inversion region), the drain to source ON current can drop much lower than 100 nA, resulting in ultra low frequency.

All the MOS transistors which operate in the weak inversion region will have a very small amount of sub-threshold leakage current, which is utilized as conduction current to obtain the ultra-low power consumption. Equation (1) shows that sub-threshold leakage current is exponentially dependent on V_{th} hence it increases with decrease in V_{th}.

$$I_{leak} = I_0 e^{\frac{V_{GS}-V_{th}}{nV_T}} \left(1 - e^{-\frac{V_{DS}}{V_T}} \right) \tag{1}$$

where $I_0 = \mu_0 C_{ox} \dfrac{W}{L} V_{th}^2 e^{1.8}$.

The sub-threshold leakage current is exponentially related to the gate voltage as shown in equation (1). This exponential relationship is expected to give an exponential reduction in power consumption, but also an exponential increase in delay. Due to this more leakage currents and dissipation of heat increases the on-chip temperatures which cause more power dissipation stated by (W. Daasch., 2002; Vivek De., 1999) stated that decreased V_{th} leads to the exponential increase in the sub-threshold leakage current and hence increases leakage power. These types of scaling in threshold and terminal voltages trade-offs ultimately mean that the problem facing process and circuit engineering become more complicated with each generation. Hence Sub-threshold design approaches are appealing for a wide range of low power or energy applications discussed by (Priya G., 2013).

Sub-threshold circuits are ideal for applications where performance is of secondary importance but minimizing energy consumption is a key in the digital domain as well as analog and mixed signal domain. The very first application that needed to limit the power consumption of integrated circuits at the microwatt level was the electronic watch developed by (Vittoz E., 1972); the frequency divider is the main part of the electronics in a quartz crystal wristwatch which consume power in a range of few microwatts to ensure a sufficient life time of the available energy source. The wristwatch does not need high speed circuits. It may be desirable to increase the maximum frequency at low voltage. In the late 80s, a new wave of interest for weak inversion (or sub-threshold) circuits was triggered by (Mead C., 1989). He promoted them as the best way to implement analog VLSI systems that mimic the operation of the brain. With the increasing demand for energy-efficient designs, research related to sub-threshold has attained considerable importance. Sub-threshold digital circuits remained totally ignored until the mid90's, with the newly recognized need of limiting the power consumption, in particular for portable systems.

While both digital and analog circuits have been designed in the sub-threshold region, the focus of this chapter will be digital sub-threshold circuits. In current scenario (Udaiyakumar R. et al., 2012) have been discussed in their research work that more than 50% power dissipation occurs due to leakage current of the entire chip, hence an additional analysis is required to design a low power multipliers in sub-threshold region. The energy efficient arithmetic circuits are designed to handle the data in units; each unit has a fixed number of binary digits which compromises with available memory capacity, operating speed, required accuracy of numerical data, and other considerations discussed by (Shaw Robert F., 1950). These circuits are the combination of arithmetic elements like registers, multiplier, adder, divider, memory bus switching etc. Arithmetic addition is one of the widely used fundamental arithmetic operations within contemporary electronic systems and it is the nucleus of the four basic arithmetic operations, addition, multiplication, subtraction and division. Addition is performed to increment program counters, multiplication is performed with multiple addition, subtraction is performed as an addition when negative numbers are represent in their 2'complement form, division is done by successive subtraction, and it requires no extra correction operations, if either dividend or divisor is negative that can also be performed by using adder circuits (Ross HD, 1953; Eshtawie M. et al., 2010).

Adders are one of the essential components for designing all types of processors, namely, digital signal processors (DSP), microprocessors, arithmetic logical units (ALU), floating point arithmetic units, memory addressing and program counting and so forth. In DSP based applications a high throughput (multiplier and accumulation) MAC element is used to perform the critical operations which involve many multiplication and accumulations. For designing the MAC, various architectures of multipliers, accumulator and CSA's are considered. Many MAC unit design has been invented with low standby power consumption and high speed so as to gain better system performance discussed by (Dakua P. et al., 2012). Multipliers (in the MAC unit) are the major power consuming units. Using the modified MAC module together with clock gating has made more than 50% power saving. This saving produces 48% reduction in the overall power consumption of the pseudo inverse module as discussed by (Khan Z. et al., 2006). In most of the digital systems, adder and multiplier lies in the critical path that affects the overall speed of the system and the performance of adder may determine the whole system performance. The choice of arithmetic module architecture is of utmost importance, since its performance determines the whole system response. In recent years some techniques that trade power for accuracy by removing or reconfiguring blocks of the arithmetic circuits have been made available. This is especially important on low power battery-operated devices, where a longer life could be preferred to a higher output precision.

A number of modifications are proposed in the literature to optimize the power delay product of the Wallace and Dadda multipliers. The delay for an N×N-bit Wallace multipliers can be reduced to log N, making it faster than the array multiplier as discussed in (J. Rabaey et al., 2002). In Wallace's method, a pseudo-adder (a row of N full adders with no carry chain) is used to sum three operands into a two operand result with only one single full adder delay. The procedure is repeated continuously to generate two rows of partial products from N row partial products for an N×N multiplier. These two rows are then combined using a fast carry propagating adder (CPA). Dadda generalized and extended Wallace's results by noting that a full adder can be thought of as a circuit which counts the number of ones in the input, and then outputs that number in 2-bit binary form. In the Wallace method, the partial products are reduced as soon as possible. In contrast, Dadda's method does the minimum reduction necessary at each level to perform the reduction in the same number of levels as required by the Wallace method resulting in a design with fewer full adders and half adders.

The disadvantage of Dadda's method is that it requires a slightly wider, fast CPA and has a less regular structure than Wallace's. A closer examination of the delays within these two multipliers and the detailed analysis for several sizes of Wallace and Dadda has been discussed by (W. J. Townsend et al., 2003). The result indicates that despite the presence of larger CPA, Dadda's design yields a slightly faster multiplier. (P. Ramanathan et al., 2009) has been discussed a new technique of implementing digital multipliers using decomposition logic. When compared to the Dadda multiplier, the proposed multiplier was faster and energy efficient with a negligible power penalty in spite of extra logic circuitry. A guideline to choose the appropriate decomposition structure for larger multipliers has also been provided. A pipelined implementation of the decomposition multiplier structure has been presented, using a new concept of adders having latched outputs which reduces the overhead costs in pipelined implementations. The decomposition logic presented here can be extended to other multiplier designs such as the Booth multiplier.

In order to minimize the area of multipliers, (Waters and Swartzlander, 2010) presented a reduced complexity Wallace multiplier by reducing the number of half adders in the reduction process. We call this design "RCW (reduced complexity Wallace) multiplier" from now on. The speed of the RCW multiplier is expected to be the same as of traditional Wallace (TW) multiplier due to the equal number of reduction stages in both multipliers. The RCW uses a larger final adder as compared to the TW multiplier. However, the focus of their research is to reduce the delay by using a faster final adder while still using the same reduction tree as RCW. Whereas (Shahzad Asif et al., 2014) discussed a novel a strategy to reduce the area of RCW multiplier. This innovative method allows for an effective utilization of half adders in such a way that the size of the final adder is reduced. The synthesized result shows that the Wallace multiplier has the smallest area as compared to the other Wallace based multipliers.

In the proposed system, the two multipliers, Wallace and Dadda tree multiplier are hybridized respectively with RCA to operate in sub threshold regime. The main focus remains to optimize overall PDP using hybrid logic families (combination of more than two different familielies in one design) with modification of design in subthreshold regime. Modified booth multiplier is proposed to reduce the partial products whereas Wallace tree multiplier is accompanied for fast addition and RCA is used for final accumulation. AND gate, half adder, full adder, partial product generate are the standard cells for Wallace and Dadda multipliers as already discussed in the introduction section. Selecting an appropriate adder cell can significantly improve the overall performance of the Wallace and Dadda multipliers. The proposed circuits show an energy efficient agreement with Spectre simulations using BSIM3v3 and BSIM4 models for the TSMC 180nm CMOS technology at 0.4V supply voltage.

Apart from this the comparative analysis of the proposed design using semi-custom and full custom design technique is also done which follows the cadence design flow. Their post synthesis results which include propagation delay, power consumption and PDP were compared with that of proposed Wallace and Dadda multiplier in sub-threshold regime. The Verilog codes have been synthesized using 180 nm technology library. It is observed that the multipliers in sub-threshold regime gives lower PDP when compared in super-threshold regime. Dadda multiplier with ripple carry adder in the final stage gives better performance than Wallace multiplier in both region of operation.

PROPOSED STANDARD CELL LIBRARY: SUB-THRESHOLD REGIME

In this section, the impact and the usage of multiplier's standard cells in sub-threshold regime are proposed and analyzed. The AND Gate, Half Adder, Full Adder, Partial Product Generate are the common standard cells to implement energy efficient column compression Wallace/Dadda multipliers.

In order to verify the functionality and to see their insight effects on the circuit performance in sub-threshold regime, all these standard cells with/without RBB scheme have been implemented and compared with conventional body biasing scheme in 180nm Technology. Measurement shows all these basic modules are functional at 400 mV.

1. AND Gate

The AND gate is used in the first part of Wallace and Dadda multipliers to generate all partial products. Multiple AND gates are proposed by modifying logical efforts of conventional logic families to reduce the overheads (transistor count and power dissipation) of implementing column compression multiplier design. For further improvement in overall performance, RBB scheme has been applied in all the logical families and observed their insights effects.

Figure 8 shows the schematic diagram of AND gate and their implementation using different logic families.

Figure 8. Schematic diagram of AND Gate

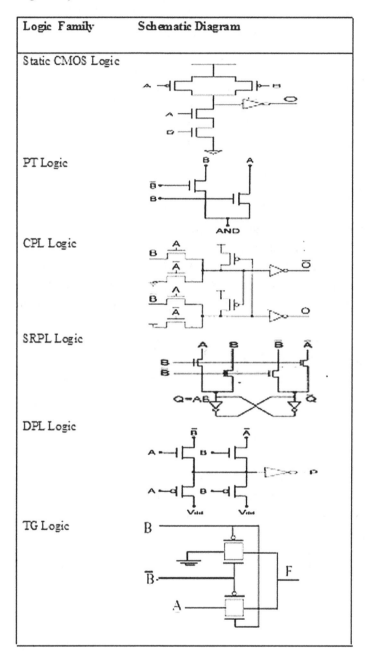

The designed AND logic gate using static CMOS, TG, PT, SRPL, CPL and DPL logic families with/without RBB scheme were simulated using the BSIM3 (V3.24) model at minimum 0.4V power supplyand their simulated results have already been mentioned above in Table 1. From the analysed results it is clear that the AND gate using static CMOS logic without RBB scheme and TG logic family with/without RBB scheme achieve significant improvement in terms of overall PDP and on average at different feature sizes.

Figure 9. Half adder circuit

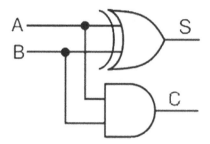

2. Half Adder (HA)

In electronics, an adder is a digital circuit that performs addition of numbers. For single bit adders, there are two general types: half adder and full adder.

A half adder has two inputs, generally labeled A and B, and two outputs, the sum (S) and carry (C). S is the two-bit XOR of A and B, and C is the AND of A and B. Essentially the output of a half adder is the sum of two one-bit numbers, with C being the most significant of these two outputs. Figure 9 shows gate level HA circuit.

A HA is a logical circuit that performs an addition operation on two binary digits. It produces a sum and a carry value which are both binary digits.

$$S = A \oplus B$$

$$C = A \cdot B$$

The HA is used in the second phase reduction of Wallace/Dadda multipliers in sub-threshold regime. These are basically used to reduce the number of partial product elements in the particular column of the group. The PDP of HA affects the overall performance of multiplier. Therefore, it is necessary to reduce for overall performance improvement.

After the extensive analysis, it is found that HA using conventional static CMOS logic family gives the best results in sub-threshold regime. The internal transistor level schematic diagram of Static CMOS HA with modifying logical efforts is shown in Figure 10 and their insight effects with/without RBB scheme is given in Table 2.

3. Full Adder (FA)

The second type of single bit adder is the full adder. The full adder takes into account a carry input such that multiple adders can be used to add larger numbers. To remove ambiguity between the input and output carry lines, the carry in is labeled Ci or Cin while the carry out is labeled Co or Cout as shown in Figure 11.

A full adder is a logical circuit that performs an addition operation on three binary digits. The full adder produces a sum and carries value, which are both binary digits. It can be combined with other full adders (see below) or work on its own.

Figure 10. Schematic diagram of static CMOS half adder

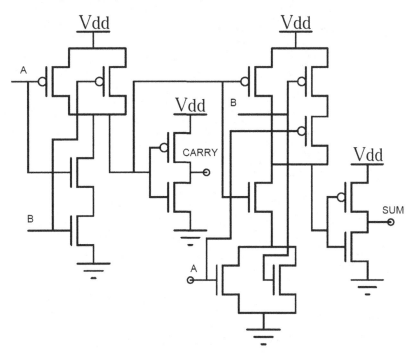

$$S = \left(A \otimes B \right) \otimes C$$

$$Co = \left(A \cdot B \right) + \left(C_i \cdot \left(A \otimes B \right) \right) = \left(A \cdot B \right) + \left(B \cdot C_i \right) + \left(C_i \cdot A \right)$$

Note that the final OR gate before the carry-out output may be replaced by an XOR gate without altering the resulting logic. This is because the only discrepancy between OR and XOR gates occur when both inputs are 1; for the adder shown here, one can check this is never possible. Using only two types of gates is convenient if one desires to implement the adder directly using common IC chips. A full adder can be constructed from two half adders by connecting A and B to the input of one half adder, connecting the sum from that to an input to the second adder, connecting Ci to the other input and or the two carry outputs. Equivalently, S could be made the three-bit XOR of A, B, and Ci and Co could be made the three-bit majority function of A, B, and Ci. The output of the full adder is the two-bit arithmetic sum of three one-bit numbers.

Table 2. Analyzed results for Half Adder at 0.4V using 180nm technology

Logic Family	Power (nW)	Delay (ns)	Power*Delay (watt*Sec 10^{-15})
Static CMOS (With RBB)	8.1003	16.41	0.132
Static CMOS (Without RBB)	0.5312	52.69	0.0279

Figure 11. Full adder circuit

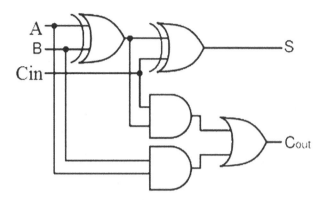

Figure 12. Schematic of MCMOS full adder

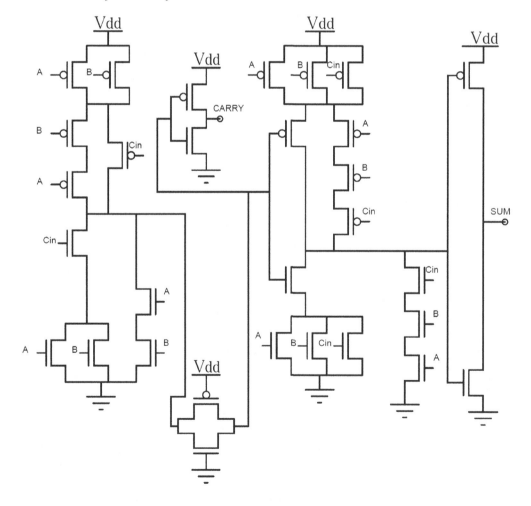

In order to demonstrate the efficiency of the new design, the power consumption and other general characteristics of the FA design have been analyzed against variety of low power full adder cells proposed in past literature. Energy efficient FA has been implemented which is capable of doing fast multiplication proposed by (Priya et al., 2013). The designed FA exclusively operated on sub-threshold conduction currents to perform circuit operations, yielding a dramatic improvement in power consumption compared to traditional circuit design approaches.

Figure 12 to Figure 15 show the schematic diagrams of energy efficient FA using modified static CMOS (MCMOS) logic static CMOS mirror logic, static energy recovery full adder (SERF) logic and TG logic families respectively.

These gates are successfully operated in sub-threshold regime using 180nm technology and their comparative results with/without RBB scheme in terms of power, delay and PDP are shown in Table 3.

From the simulated results given in Table 3, it is clear that the two proposed approximate designs using static CMOS mirror logic without RBB scheme and TG logic family with/without RBB scheme achieve significant improvement in terms of overall PDP.

4. Partial Product Generate Circuit (PPG)

Partial product generation is the very first step in multiplier. These are the intermediate terms which are generated based on the value of multiplier. If the multiplier bit is '0', then partial product row is also zero, and if it is '1', then the multiplicand is copied as it is. From the 2nd bit multiplication onwards, each

Figure 13. Schematic of static CMOS mirror full adder

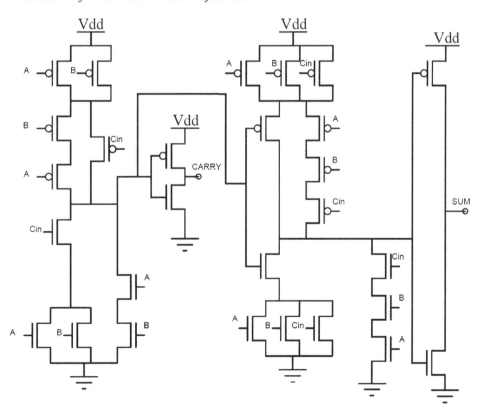

Figure 14. Schematic of SERF adder

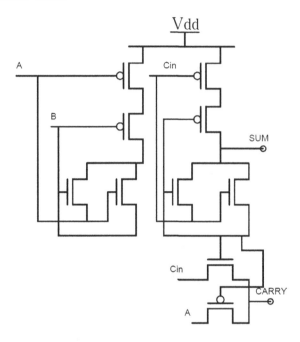

partial product row is shifted one unit to the left as shown in the above mentioned example. In signed multiplication, the sign bit is also extended to the left. Partial product generators for a conventional multiplier consist of a series of logic AND gates as shown in Figure 16.

Figure 15. Schematic of TG full adder

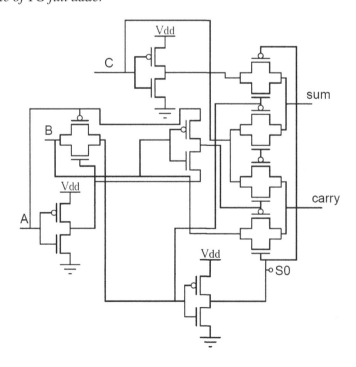

Figure 16. Partial product generation logic

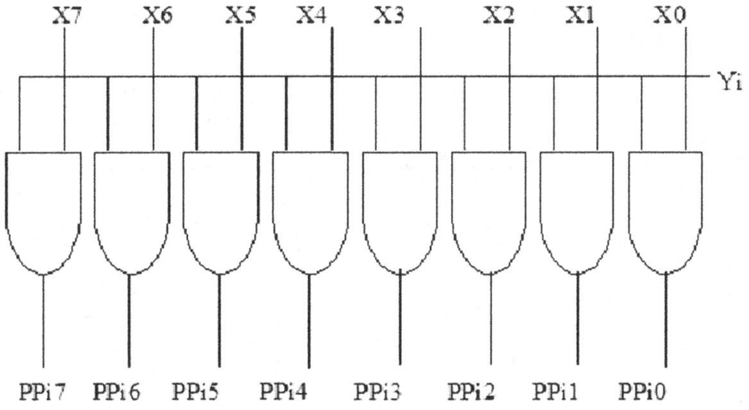

Table 3. Analyzed results for full adder at 0.4 V

Logic Family	With RBB Scheme			Without RBB Scheme		
	Power (nW)	Delay (ns)	Power*Delay (Watt*Sec 10⁻¹⁵)	Power (nW)	Delay (ns)	Power*Delay (Watt*Sec 10⁻¹⁵)
Static CMOS Mirror Logic	14.06	22.58	0.1856	0.574	80.51	0.0462
Conventional Static CMOS	42.04	10.365	0.4357	12.5	71.655	0.896
New SERF	53.91	2044.0	110.19	8.551	2187.5	18.705
TG Logic	0.588	22.55	0.0132	0.314	59.846	0.0187
MCMOS Static with TG	47.20	15.465	0.7299	18.81	55.88	1.051

Conventionally, in the Wallace and Dadda multipliers the partial products are re-adjusted in a reverse pyramid style, which makes it easy to analyze the tree for efficient reduction. This module is used to reduce the partial products matrix to an addition of only two operands. Careful optimization of the partial-product generation can lead to some substantial delay and area reduction. The final multiplication product is the result of the addition of all partial products. The internal architecture of the partial product generate module for 8x8-bit, 16x16-bit Wallace and Dadda multipliers consist of bunch of energy efficient AND gates as shown in Figure 17 (a) and Figure 17 (b) .

It is found that static CMOS AND gate without RBB scheme design is most energy efficient to implement power aware column compression 8x8-bit and 16x16-bit multipliers. The overall analyzed result for partial products generate module using 180nm technology is shown in Table 4.

Table 4. Analyzed results for partial product generate module at 0.4V

Module Name	Power (nW)	Delay (ns)	Power*Delay (Watt*Sec 10⁻¹⁸)
PPG_for_8x8-bit Multiplier	1.323	22.57	29.86
PPG_for_16x16-bit Multiplier	3.854	24.07	92.77

Figure 17a. Partial product generate module for Wallace and Dadda multipliers: 8x8-bit

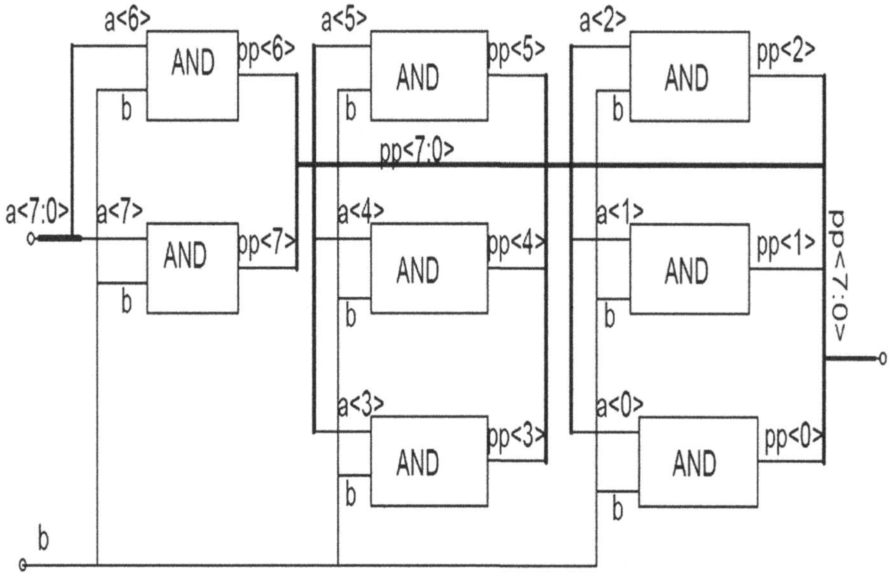

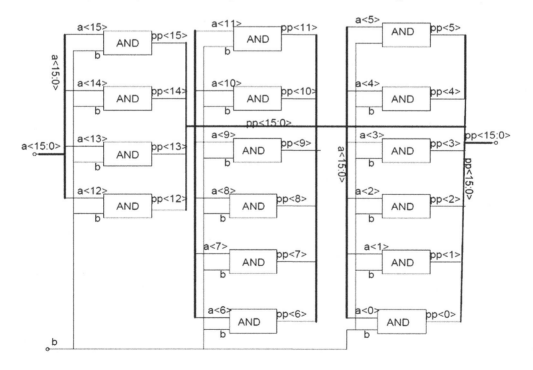

Figure 17b. Partial product generate module for Wallace and Dadda multiplier: 16x16-bit

PROPOSED DADDA AND WALLACE MULTIPLIERS

In this section, modification in the Wallace/Dadda multiplier is presented to further reduce its overall PDP in sub-threshold regime by reducing the complexity of the conventional architecture. Proposed Wallace and Dadda multiplier has the same number of stages and the same rule for maximum number of rows in a stage as in the other multipliers discussed in this chapter. Both architectures are similar with the difference occurring in the procedure of reduction of the partial products and the size of the final adder. In Wallace's scheme, the partial products are reduced as soon as possible. On the other hand, Dadda's method does minimum reduction necessary at each level and requires the same number of levels as Wallace multiplier. As a result, final adder in Wallace multiplier is slightly smaller in size as compared to the final adder in Dadda multiplier. The Block diagram of proposed energy efficient column compression multipliers (Wallace/Dadda) is shown in Figure 18. A Wallace/Dadda multiplier is usually composed of three parts

- Partial product generate module
- A Half Adder (HA) and Full Adder (FA) tree to reduce the partial products matrix to an addition of only two operands
- A Ripple Carry Adder (RCA) for the final computation of the binary result.

Figure 18. Block diagram of energy efficient n-bit column compression multiplier

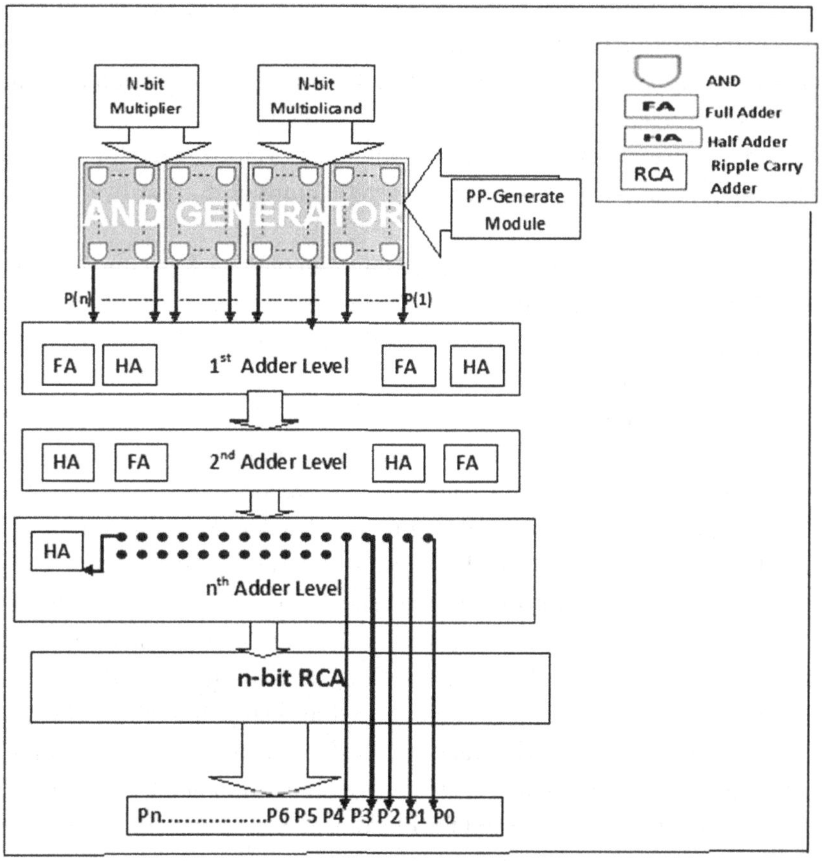

In the Wallace and Dadda multipliers, the reduction part uses half-adders, full-adders and ripple carry adders; each partial product bit is represented by a dot as shown in Figure 18. Reduction is performed depending on the number of elements in that particular column of the group. Three dot products is used to represent a FA, whereas only two dot products is used to represent a HA. If a column has only one element then that is passed on to the next stage without any reduction. If the last group of a stage contains less than three rows then no reduction is performed on that group. The last part performs the function to add the remaining two rows using an exact RCA to compute the final binary result. Since all the basic cells are same in both 8x8-bit/16x16-bit Wallace and Dadda multipliers. So in the energy efficient multiplier designs static CMOS logic without RBB scheme is used for AND gate, HA, whereas static CMOS mirror logic family without RBB scheme is used for Full adder. The least significant bit (LSB) of the product, $P0$, is produced by the partial product generation block by computing $A0 \times B0$. In the first stage of the reduction process, product bit $P1$ is computed by using the additional half adder. In the second stage, $P2$ is computed. Similarly, stage 3 and stage 4 compute the product bits $P3$ and $P4$, respectively. Thus, when the partial product tree is reduced to two rows, five LSBs ($P4 - P0$) of the product are already computed as shown in Figure 18.

ASIC IMPLEMENTATION AND SIMULATION RESULTS

Many sub-threshold based ultra-low power systems also are very specialized. For example, sub-threshold wireless micro-sensors sense data, process it using signal processing algorithms, and then communicate the data wirelessly across a network. It is easy to conceive that the signal processing algorithms on the chip would vary based on the type of data coming from the sensor, the sensor's environment, or the sensor's specific application. The energy efficient, solution for this application would be the most efficient hardware essentially is hardwired to do its specific task known as an application- specific integrated circuit (ASIC) implementation which is an integrated circuit (IC) customized for a targeted specific use, rather than intended for general-purpose use. The targeted nature of this hardware makes it impossible to reuse in a different ULP application.

ASICs achieve very power efficient operation, but they can only perform the function for which they were originally defined. On the other hand, targeting an ASIC or application-specific instruction set processor (ASIP) to low volume applications requires the non-recoverable engineering costs to design and fabricate a new chip for each new application, making the cost prohibitive. The proposed circuit was also designed a gate level and simulated in Verilog-HDL. The Verilog-HDL language supports modeling needs at the algorithm or behavioral level, and at the implementation or structural level. It provides a versatile set of description facilities to model arithmetic circuits from the system level to the gate level.

In many respects Verilog is a very powerful, high-level, concurrent programming language. At the implementation level structural models can be build using component instantiation statements that connect and invoke subcomponents. The Verilog generate statement provides ease of block replication and control. Verilog, as a consensus description language and design environment, offers design tool portability, easy technical exchange, and technology insertion. The complete ASIC implementation of the 8x8-bit and16x16-bit of Wallace and Dadda design is also done using the Cadence design flow. Both the design has been developed using Verilog-HDL and synthesized in encounter RTL compiler using typical library of 180 nm technology. The test bench is created for simulation and logic verification by NCSIM simulator. The Cadence SoC Encounter is used for Placement & Routing (P&R). Parasitic extraction is

Table 5. SOC (post route) results at 180nm technology

Module Name	SOC Results (Post Layout)		
	Power (mW)	Delay (ns)	Power*Delay (Watt*Sec 10^{-15})
8x8-bit Wallace Multiplier	0.05797	6.319	366.312
8x8-bit Dadda Multiplier	0.05462	4.424	241.638
16x16-bitWallace Multiplier	0.1522	12.912	1965.20
16x16-bit Dadda Multiplier	0.1448	12.084	1749.76

performed using Encounter Native RC extraction tool. The extracted parasitic RC (SPEF format) is back annotated to common timing engine in encounter platform for static timing analysis. ASIC implementation results after post-layout simulation using semi-custom design techniques are shown in Table 5.

The ASIC Implementation is to be done to differentiate the performance evaluation of the proposed design in sub-threshold and super-threshold regime at the same technology. The stimulation results were carried out of two 8x8-bit and 16x16-bit Wallace and Dadda multiplier designs in sub-threshold regime. The proposed energy efficient multiplies operates at 0.4V. In fact, in addition to normal transistors, circuits are tested in corner cases with fast and slow transistors and their combinations too. In each stage one of the components FF, SS, FS, and SF is replaced instead of normal transistors in circuit and is perused in each circuit function. Since the delay of proposed multiplier circuit is proportional to the logarithm of the number of bits in the multiplier and also delay of used standard cells. To measure the critical path delay and to verify the functionality of proposed Wallace and Dadda multipliers, n-number of test patterns has been applied to the multiplier. The worst delay has been observed for the inputs from 11111111x00001000 for 8x8-bit Wallace and Dadda and 1111111111111111x0000000000001000 for 16x16-bit Wallace and Dadda multipliers. Table 6 summarized the power, delay and PDP of 8x8-bit and 16x16-bit Wallace Dadda multipliers using hybrid logic families in subthreshold regime. The analyzed results compared with different existing low power technique based multiplier results.

Table 6. Comparison with other published results in terms power, delay and PDP in sub-threshold regime

Module (References)	Size	Power (nW)	Delay (ns)	PDP(10^{-15})
Wallace Multiplier (Shahzad Asif et al., 2014)	8x8-bit	1960000.0	2.66	5213.6
Wallace Multiplier (Shahzad Asif et al., 2014)	16x16-bit	11200000.0	3.75	42000.00
Dadda Multiplier (Shahzad Asif et al., 2014)	8x8-bit	1940000.0	2.64	5121.6
Dadda Multiplier (Shahzad Asif et al., 2014)	16x16-bit	11220000.0	3.80	42636.00
Dadda Multiplier (P. Ramanathan et al., 2009)	8x8-bit	76700.00	4.00	306.8
Dadda Multiplier (P. Ramanathan et al., 2009)	16x16-bit	196000.00	5.05	989.81
Proposed Wallace Multiplier	8x8-bit	15.29	414.1	6.331
Proposed Wallace Multiplier	16x16-bit	43.941	518.5	22.78
Proposed Dadda Multiplier	8x8-bit	13.11	347.4	4.908
Proposed Dadda Multiplier	16x16-bit	34.571	452.4	15.63

Figure 19. Comparison graph of 8x8-bit, 16x16-bit Wallace and Dadda multipliers

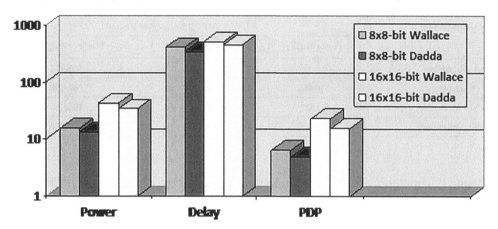

Table 6 shows the comparative simulation results of the proposed design with the existing published results in sub-threshold regime. The proposed multiplier architectures exhibit an overall reduction in PDP as compared to conventional multiplier architecture. In addition, it has been observed that the PDP improvement for Dadda multiplier is better than Wallace multiplier in sub-threshold regime. The PDP comparison graphs of proposed Wallaec and Dadda are shown in Figure 19.

CONCLUSION AND FUTURE WORK

This chapter presents an overview on ultra-low sub-threshold leakage technique and their effects on RBB schemes by reviewing the other recent work on low leakage techniques. There is a tight tradeoff among the power consumption, speed and supply voltage in the design of CMOS circuits. Scaling of CMOS technology in nanometer scale faces great challenges due to sub threshold leakage power. Scaling down threshold voltage, device dimensions and supply voltage for achieving high performance, power dissipation has largely contributed to increase in leakage power.

For more analysis, the 8x8-bit, 16x16-bit Wallace and Dadda multipliers have been implemented in 180nm technology at 0.4 volt power supply. The main focus of this chapter was to optimize overall PDP using hybrid logic families (combination of more than two different famililies in one design) in subthreshold regime. The designed mulipliers have also been optimized the number of transitor. The simulated results show that the proposed Wallace and Dadda multiplier have improved results as compared to existing published results. It has also been observed that the proposed Dadda multipliers show an improve results as compare to proposed Wallace multipliers in sub-threshold regime. The overall PDP improvement for designed 8x8-bit Dadda is 22.47%, while for 16x16-bit Dadda PDP improvement is 31.38% as compared to 8x8-bit, 16x16-bit Wallace multipliers respectively. Thus the Dadda multiplier has improved PDP, power, performance as compared to the Wallace multiplier. Since the designed power efficient multipliers in sub-threshold regime use the RCA in the final stage, in the same way, the proposed multipliers can also implemented using parallel prefix adders which supplements the logarithmic delay of the compression tree for future work and analysis. Dadda multiplier with parallel prefix adders in the final stage will gives better performance in terms of delay, area and power than Wallace multiplier.

REFERENCES

Asif, S., & Kong, Y. (2014). Low-area Wallace multiplier. *VLSI Design, 2014,* 1–6. doi:10.1155/2014/343960

Baugh, C. R., & Wooley, B. A. (1973). A Two's complement parallel array multiplication algorithm. *IEEE Transactions on Computers, C-22*(12), 1045–1047. doi:10.1109/T-C.1973.223648

Booth, A. D. (1951). A signed binary multiplication technique. *The Quarterly Journal of Mechanics and Applied Mathematics, 4*(2), 237–240. doi:10.1093/qjmam/4.2.236

Cappello, P. R., & Steiglitz, K. (1983). A VLSI layout for a pipe-lined Dadda multiplier. *ACM Transactions on Computer Systems, 1*(2), 157–17. doi:10.1145/357360.357366

Chandrakasan, A. P., & Brodersen, R. W. (1995). Minimizing power consumption in digital CMOS circuits. *Proceedings of the IEEE, 83*(4), 498–523. doi:10.1109/5.371964

Chandrakasan, A. P., Sheng, S., & Brodersen, R. W. (1992). Low- power CMOS digital design. *IEEE Journal of Solid-State Circuits, 27*(4), 473–484. doi:10.1109/4.126534

Daasch, W., Lim, C., & Cai, G. (2002). Design of VLSI CMOS Circuits under Thermal Constraint. *IEEE Transactions on Circuits and Systems II: Analog and Digital Signal Processing, 49*(8), 589–593. doi:10.1109/TCSII.2002.806247

Dadda, L. (1965). Some schemes for parallel multipliers. *Alta Frequenza, 34,* 349–356.

Dakua, P., & Sinha, A., & Gourab. (2012). Hardware implementation of MAC unit. *International Journal of Electronics Communication and Computer Engineering, 3,* 79–82.

De, V. & Borkar S. (1999, August). *Technology and Design Challenges for Low Power and High Performance.* Paper presented at Proceedings of International Symposium on Low Power Electronics. San Diego, CA, USA. doi:10.1145/313817.313908

De Mori, R. (1965). Suggestions for an IC fast parallel multiplier. *Electronics Letters, 5*(3), 50–51. doi:10.1049/el:19690034

Eshtawie, M., Hussin, S., & Othman, M. (2010, June). *Analysis of results obtained with a new proposed low area low power high speed fixed point adder.* Paper presented at IEEE International Conference on Semiconductor Electronics (ICSE), Melaka, Malaysia. doi:10.1109/SMELEC.2010.5549387

Fisher, S. Teman, A. Vaysman, D. , Gertsman, A. , Yadid-Pecht O., & Fish A. (2008, December). *Digital sub-threshold logic design - motivation and challenges.* Paper presented at 25th IEEE Convention of Electrical and Electronics Engineers in Israel, Eilat.

Khan, Z., Arslan, T., Thompson, J., & Erdogan, A. (2006). Analysis and implementation of multiple–input, multiple–output VBLAST receiver from area and power efficiency perspective. *IEEE Transactions on Very Large Scale Integration (VLSI). Systems, 14,* 1281–1286.

Ko, U., Balsara, P. T., & Lee, W. (1995). Low-power design techniques for high-performance CMOS adders. *IEEE Transactions on Very Large Scale Integration (VLSI). Systems, 3,* 327–333.

Markovic, D., Nikolic, B., & Oklobdzija, V. G. (2000). A general method in synthesis of pass-transistor circuits. *Microelectronics Journal, 31*(11-12), 991–998. doi:10.1016/S0026-2692(00)00088-4

Mead C. (1989). Analog VLSI and neural systems. *Addison-Wesley VLSI Systems Series,* 1- 371.

Narendra, S., Shekhar, B., & Vivek, D., Dimitri A., & Anantha C., (2001, August). Scaling *of stack effect and its application for leakage reduction.* Proceedings of the International Symposium on Low Power Electronics and Design, Huntington Beach, CA.

Narendra, S., Tschanz, J., Hofsheier, J., Bloechel, B., Vangal, S., Hoskote, Y., . . . De, V. (2004). *Ultra-Low voltage circuits and processor in 180 nm to 90 nm technologies with swapped- body biasing technique.* Paper presented at IEEE International Conference on Solid-State Circuits, San Francisco, CA.

Priya, G., Akshay, K., Pratishtha, D., & Anu, G. (2013, August). *Design and Implementation of low power TG full adder design in sub-threshold regime.* Paper presented at IEEE International Conference on Intelligent Interactive Systems and Assistive Technologies, Coimbatore, India.

Priya, G., Anu, G., & Abhijit, A. (2013). A review on ultra low power design technique: Sub-threshold logic. *International Journal of Computer Science and Technology-IJCST., 4*(2), 64–71.

Priya, G., Anu, G., & Abhijit, A. (2014). Design and implementation of n-bit sub-threshold kogge stone adder with improved power delay product. *European Journal of Scientific Research, 123*(1), 106–116.

Rabaey, J., Pedram, M., & Landman, P. (2002). *Low power design methodologies. The Springer International Series in Engineering and Computer Science. 336.* Boston, MA: Kluwer Academic Publishers/ Springer.

Ramanathan, P., Vanathi, P. T., & Agarwal, S. (2009). High speed multiplier design using decomposition logic. *Serbian Journal of Electrical Engineering, 6*(1), 33–42. doi:10.2298/SJEE0901033R

Ross, H. D. (1953). The arithmetic element of the IBM type 701 computer. *Proceedings of the IRE,* 1287-1294. doi:10.1109/JRPROC.1953.274302

Shaw Robert, F. (1950). Arithmetic operations in a binary computer. *Proceedings of the review of Scientific Instruments, 21:* 687-693.

Silburt, A.L., Boothroyd, A.R., & Digiovanni, M. (1988). Automated parameter extraction and modeling of the MOSFET below threshold. *IEEE Transactions on Computer-Aided Design,* 1, 484-488.

Townsend, W. J., & Earl, E. Swartzlander & J.A. Abraham. (2003). A comparison of Dadda and Wallace multiplier delays. *Proceedings of the SPIE in Advanced Signal Processing Algorithms, Architectures and Implementations (Vol. 5205,* pp. 552-560). Univ. of Texas, Austin, USA.

Udaiyakumar, R., & Sankaranarayanan, K. (2012). Certain investigations on static power dissipation in various nano-scale CMOS D Flip-Flop structures. *IACSIT International Journal of Engineering and Technology,* 2, 644–651.

Vittoz, E., Gerber, B., & Leuenberger, F. (1972). Silicon-Gate CMOS frequency divider for the electronic wrist watch. *IEEE Journal of Solid-State Circuits, SC-7*(2), 100–104. doi:10.1109/JSSC.1972.1050254

Wallace. C. S. (1964). A suggestion for a fast multiplier. *IEEE Transactions on Electronic Computers.* EC-13(1).14-17.

Waters, R. S., & Swartzlander, E. E. (2010). A reduced complexity Wallace multiplier reduction. *IEEE Transactions on Computers*, *59*(8), 1134–1137. doi:10.1109/TC.2010.103

Zimmermann, R., & Fichtner, W. (1997). Low-power logic styles: CMOS versus pass-transistor logic. *IEEE Journal of Solid-State Circuits*, *32*(7), 1079–1090. doi:10.1109/4.597298

APPENDIX: CADENCE RTL COMPILER

INTRODUCTION

Cadence RTL compiler is a synthesis tool used to synthesize the Verilog code to physical cells as per the required technology, in this case UMC 90nm.It also allows us to apply constraints on the circuit like timing constraints, power constraints etc. The following steps will allow you to synthesize your Verilog code which was simulated in Cadence NCLaunch.

Note: It should be kept in mind that RTL compiler does not check the functionality

The Cadence RTL Compiler does the following things:

- Generate fast, area-efficient ASIC designs by employing user-specified standard cell
- Explore design tradeoffs involving design constraints such as timing, area, and power under various loading, temperature, and voltage conditions.
- Synthesize and optimize finite state machines, synchronous and asynchronous designs.
- Manage complexity by creating and partitioning hierarchical designs automatically, optimizes designs faster and utilize higher capacity with Automated Chip Synthesis.
- Benefit from the easy-to-use, customizable UNIX style user interface, TCL, and intuitive visual interface.
- Enjoy support for industry standard languages.
- Design using hundreds of libraries offered by over 60 semiconductor and library vendors

The flow chart for synthesis process is shown in Figure 20.
The Figure 21 depicts the flowchart for entire synthesis process.

Figure 20. Flow chart for synthesis process

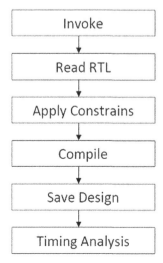

Figure 21. Synthesis procedure from reading the HDL source to translation

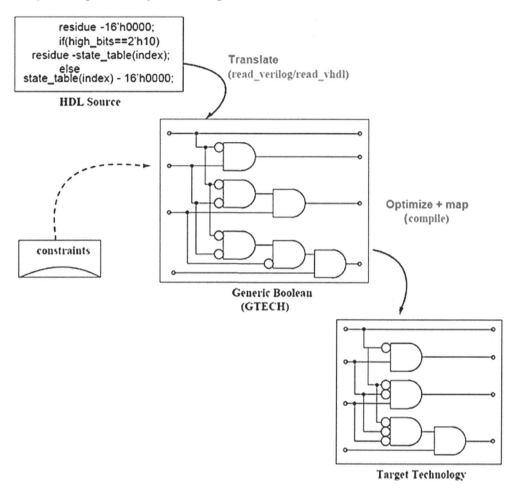

The Figure depicts the synthesis procedure from reading the HDL source to translation to mapping to the particular technology.

The broad steps of synthesis are:

- **Hierarchical Compile**
  - Compile strategy
  - Top level only compilation
  - Incremental compile
- **Design Optimization**
  - High-level optimization
    - Arithmetic expressions optimization
  - Full compile
    - Flattening and structuring
    - Mapping:
    - Delay optimization

- ▪ Design rule fixing
    - ▪ Area specific optimization
  - ◦ Sequential optimization for complex flip-flops and latches
  - ◦ Finite State Machine (FSM) optimization
  - ◦ Time borrowing for latch-based designs
- **Timing Analysis Features**
  - ◦ Timing exceptions
  - ◦ Case analysis to set constant paths
  - ◦ Incremental timing update
  - ◦ Support for synchronous and asynchronous designs
- **Intuitive User Interface/Ease-of-Use**
  - ◦ Report generation
  - ◦ Command log files
  - ◦ Scripting

BUDGETING AUTOMATED CHIP SYNTHESIS

Steps to run the tool:

Path to Manual

```
/edatools/cadence_new/rc72/doc/rc_user/rc_user.pdf
/edatools/cadence_new/rc72/doc/rc_ta/rc_ta.pdf
```

Prerequisites

Before invoking the tool user has to make sure that following folders are created:

```
Create the following folders in your home folder:
>mkdir rc_compiler
>cd rc_compiler
Inside rc_compiler folder:
>mkdir rtl scripts com_files results (four different folders)
rtl: Stores the verilog code. e.g fareg.v
com_files: Stores the technology library files (.lib files)
scripts: Store the script file with the set of commands e.g fareg.tcl
results: Stores the synthesised netlists, reports and log files.
copy the following files in com_files folder
```

CORE

Typical Case

```
/linuxeda/dk/umc90nm/faraday90nm/LLLowK1p9m/core/FSD0K_A_GENERIC_CORE_1D0V_
DP_2007Q2v1.3/FSD0K_A_GENERIC_CORE_1D0V_DP_2007Q2v1.3/fsd0k_a/2007Q2v1.3/GE-
NERIC_CORE_1D0V/FrontEnd/synopsys/fsd0k_a_generic_core_1d0vtc.lib
```

Worst Case: Setup Time Analysis

```
/linuxeda/dk/umc90nm/faraday90nm/LLLowK1p9m/core/FSD0K_A_GENERIC_CORE_1D0V_
DP_2007Q2v1.3/FSD0K_A_GENERIC_CORE_1D0V_DP_2007Q2v1.3/fsd0k_a/2007Q2v1.3/GE-
NERIC_CORE_1D0V/FrontEnd/synopsys/fsd0k_a_generic_core_0d9vwc.lib
```

Best Case: Hold Time Analysis

```
/linuxeda/dk/umc90nm/faraday90nm/LLLowK1p9m/core/FSD0K_A_GENERIC_CORE_1D0V_
DP_2007Q2v1.3/FSD0K_A_GENERIC_CORE_1D0V_DP_2007Q2v1.3/fsd0k_a/2007Q2v1.3/GE-
NERIC_CORE_1D0V/FrontEnd/synopsys/fsd0k_a_generic_core_1d1vbc.lib
```

These library files contain the standard cell definitions i.e. the definition of the various combinational and sequential elements to be used during mapping.

I/O

Typical Case

```
/edatools/dk/umc90nm/faraday90nm/LLLowK1p9m/IO/FOD0K_B25_T25_GENERIC_IO_
DP_2008Q3v2.0/fod0k_b25/2008Q3v2.0/T25_GENERIC_IO/FrontEnd/synopsys/fod0k_b25_
t25_generic_ tt1p2v25c.lib
```

Worst Case: Setup Time Analysis

```
./edatools/dk/umc90nm/faraday90nm/LLLowK1p9m/IO/FOD0K_B25_T25_GENERIC_IO_
DP_2008Q3v2.0/fod0k_b25/2008Q3v2.0/T25_GENERIC_IO/FrontEnd/synopsys/fod0k_b25_
t25_generic_io_ss1p08v125c.lib
```

Best Case: Hold Time Analysis

```
/edatools/dk/umc90nm/faraday90nm/LLLowK1p9m/IO/FOD0K_B25_T25_GENERIC_IO_
DP_2008Q3v2.0/fod0k_b25/2008Q3v2.0/T25_GENERIC_IO/FrontEnd/synopsys/fod0k_b25_
t25_generic_io_ff1p32vm40c.lib
```

This library contains information regarding the input output pads to be used in the design.

To invoke the tool use the following commands in csh window:

```
>cd rc_compiler
>source /edatools/scripts/cadencerc62.csh ---for Solaris systems
>source /linuxeda/scripta/caence/rc.csh ----for linux systems
```

SCRIPT FILE FOR SYNOPSYS DESIGN CONSTRAINTS (.SDC) GENERATION

```
set_attribute information_level 7
set root_dir /pgassignments/aditya/rc_compiler
set synth_dir /pgassignments/aditya/rc_compiler/results
set rtl_path /pgassignments/aditya/rc_compiler/rtl
set lib_path /pgassignments/aditya/rc_compiler/com_files
set com_fl_path /pgassignments/aditya/rc_compiler/com_files
set file_list {fareg.v}
set top_module {fareg}
set_attribute gen_module_prefix G2C_DP_COMP
set_attr hdl_search_path $rtl_path
set_attr lib_search_path $lib_path
set library {fsd0k_a_generic_core_1d0vtc.lib
fod0k_b25_t25_generic_io_tt1p2v25c.lib}
set_attribute library $library
load -v2001 $file_list
elaborate $top_module
current_design  $top_module
dc::set_time_unit -picoseconds
dc::set_load_unit -femtofarads
dc::create_clock -name CLK -period 4000 -waveform {0 2000}
dc::set_clock_latency 200.0 [dc::get_clocks CLK]
dc::set_clock_transition 20.0 [dc::get_clocks CLK]
dc::set_input_delay 200.0 -clock CLK [dc::all_inputs]
dc::set_output_delay 200.0 -clock CLK [dc::all_outputs]
set_attribute max_dynamic_power 0.0 $top_module
set_attribute max_leakage_power 0.0 $top_module
set_attribute delete_unloaded_seqs false $top_module
```

```
set_attribute max_fanout 17 $top_module
set_attribute max_capacitance 10 $top_module
set_attribute max_transition 37 $top_module
set MAP_EFF low
synthesize -to_mapped -effort $MAP_EFF -no_incr
cd designs/fareg
report area > $synth_dir/fareg_area.rep
report summary > $synth_dir/fareg_sum.rep
report timing -num_paths 4 > $synth_dir/fareg_slack.rep
report gates > $synth_dir/fareg_gates.rep
cd ..
cd ..
write -mapped fareg > $synth_dir/fareg_NL.v
write_sdc fareg > $synth_dir/fareg.sdc
```

SCRIPT FILE FOR SETUP TIME ANALYSIS

```
set_attribute information_level 7
set root_dir /pgassignments/aditya/rc_compiler
set synth_dir /pgassignments/aditya/rc_compiler/results
set rtl_path /pgassignments/aditya/rc_compiler/rtl
set lib_path /pgassignments/aditya/rc_compiler/com_files
set com_fl_path /pgassignments/aditya/rc_compiler/com_files
set file_list {fareg.v}
set top_module {fareg}
set_attribute gen_module_prefix G2C_DP_COMP
set_attr hdl_search_path $rtl_path
set_attr lib_search_path $lib_path
set library {fsd0k_a_generic_core_0d9vwc.lib
fod0k_b25_t25_generic_io_ss1p08v125c.lib}
set_attribute library $library
load -v2001 $file_list
elaborate $top_module
dc::current_design $top_module
dc::set_time_unit -picoseconds
dc::set_load_unit -femtofarads
dc::create_clock [dc::get_ports CLK] -name CLK -period 4000 -waveform {0 2000}
dc::set_clock_latency 200.0 [dc::get_clocks CLK]
dc::set_clock_transition 50.0 [dc::get_clocks CLK]
dc::set_clock_uncertainty 300.0 -setup [dc::get_clocks CLK]
dc::set_input_delay 200.0 -clock CLK -max [dc::all_inputs]
dc::set_output_delay 100.0 -clock CLK -max [dc::all_outputs]
```

```
set_attribute max_dynamic_power 0.0 $top_module
set_attribute max_leakage_power 0.0 $top_module
set_attribute delete_unloaded_seqs false $top_module
set_attribute max_fanout 17 $top_module
set_attribute max_capacitance 10 $top_module
set_attribute max_transition 37 $top_module
set MAP_EFF low
synthesize -to_mapped -effort $MAP_EFF -no_incr
cd designs/fareg
report area > $synth_dir/fareg_area.rep
report summary > $synth_dir/fareg_sum.rep
report timing -num_paths 4 > $synth_dir/fareg_slack.rep
report gates > $synth_dir/fareg_gates.rep
cd ..
cd ..
write -mapped fareg > $synth_dir/fareg_NL.v
write_sdc fareg > $synth_dir/fareg.sdc
```

SCRIPT FILE FOR HOLD TIME ANALYSIS

```
set_attribute information_level 7
set root_dir /pgassignments/aditya/rc_compiler
set synth_dir /pgassignments/aditya/rc_compiler/results
set rtl_path /pgassignments/aditya/rc_compiler/rtl
set lib_path /pgassignments/aditya/rc_compiler/com_files
set com_fl_path /pgassignments/aditya/rc_compiler/com_files
set file_list {fareg.v}
set top_module {fareg}
set_attribute gen_module_prefix G2C_DP_COMP
set_attr hdl_search_path $rtl_path
set_attr lib_search_path $lib_path
set library {fsd0k_a_generic_core_1d1vbc.lib
fod0k_b25_t25_generic_io_ff1p32vm40c.lib}
set_attribute library $library
load -v2001 $file_list
elaborate $top_module
dc::current_design $top_module
dc::set_time_unit -picoseconds
dc::set_load_unit -femtofarads
dc::create_clock [dc::get_ports CLK] -name CLK -period 4000 -waveform {0 2000}
dc::set_clock_latency 200.0 [dc::get_clocks CLK]
dc::set_clock_transition 50.0 [dc::get_clocks CLK]
```

```
dc::set_clock_uncertainty 20.0 -hold [dc::get_clocks CLK]
dc::set_input_delay 200.0 -clock CLK -max [dc::all_inputs]
dc::set_output_delay 100.0 -clock CLK -max [dc::all_outputs]
set_attribute max_dynamic_power 0.0 $top_module
set_attribute max_leakage_power 0.0 $top_module
set_attribute delete_unloaded_seqs false $top_module
set_attribute max_fanout 17 $top_module
set_attribute max_capacitance 10 $top_module
set_attribute max_transition 37 $top_module
set MAP_EFF low
synthesize -to_mapped -effort $MAP_EFF -no_incr
cd designs/fareg
report area > $synth_dir/fareg_area.rep
report summary > $synth_dir/fareg_sum.rep
report timing -num_paths 4 > $synth_dir/fareg_slack.rep
report gates > $synth_dir/fareg_gates.rep
cd ..
cd ..
write -mapped fareg > $synth_dir/fareg_NL.v
write_sdc fareg > $synth_dir/fareg.sdc
```

EXPLANATION OF THE SCRIPT FILE

```
set_attribute information_level 7
# The information level 7 specifies that you are going to supply the maximum
amount of information to the compiler through the script file.
set root_dir /pgassignments/aditya/rc_compiler
#The "set root_dir" command specifies the root directory or the absolute path
from where you
#are going to source the RC compiler. The path is set as /home/ aditya/rc_compiler
set synth_dir /pgassignments/aditya/rc_compiler/results
#The "set  synth_dir" command specifies the synthesis directory. This is the
directory
where the reports generated by the RC compiler will be stored. The path has
been set as
/home/ aditya/rc_compiler/results
set rtl_path /pgassignments/aditya/rc_compiler/rtl
#The set rtl_path" command tells the RC compiler to look for the RTL (verilog
file) in the "rtl" folder inside "rc_compiler". The "rtl" folder is supposed
to contain the RTL code file.
set lib_path /pgassignments/aditya/rc_compiler/com_files
```

```
#The RC compiler needs library files for synthesizing the RTL code and gener-
ating the
#synthesized netlist. The "set lib_path" command tells the RC compiler to look
for the
#library files in the folder named "com_files" inside "rc_compiler"
set com_fl_path /pgassignments/aditya/rc_compiler/com_files
#The set com_fl_path command sets the library files path to the above direc-
tory.
set file_list {fareg.v}
# Mention the name of the HDL file or files. In this case the only file is
fareg.v
set top_module {fareg}
#The top module  is  supposed  to  be  the  module which  calls  or
instantiates  all  other modules. In this design the top level module is
fareg.
set_attribute gen_module_prefix G2C_DP_COMP
set_attr hdl_search_path $rtl_path
#The command "set_attr  hdl_search_path $rtl_path" sets the rtl search path to
the value of the variable rtl_path which has been previously set.
set_attr lib_search_path $lib_path
set library {fsd0k_a_generic_core_1d0vtc.lib
fod0k_b25_t25_generic_io_tt1p2v25c.lib}
set_attribute library $library
#The "set_attribute library $library" sets the library path to the value of
the variable library which has been set previously.
load -v2001 $file_list
#The above command lines loads or reads the source files for the design. Note
that by default RTL compiler uses Verilog 1995 standard. The -v2001 command
tells the compiler to use Verilog 2001 standard. In the present problem, we
have used the generate statement and since the generate statement is defined
only in Verilog 2001 standard, hence it is mandatory to specify - v2001 in the
above command.
elaborate $top_module
# This step elaborates the top level module. The elaboration step flattens the
netlist that is it breaks the top modules into various sub modules until it
reaches the leaf cells in the bottom of the hierarchy.
dc::current_design $top_module
Since we are using Synopsys Design Constraint Commands which are written using
"dc::" prefix, we've to set the current design to $top_module
dc::set_time_unit -picoseconds
#This command forces the sdc time units to picoseconds. The time units of Ca-
dence RTL Compiler are ps where as default sdc time units are ns.
dc::set_load_unit -femtofarads
```

```
#This command forces the sdc load units to femtofarads. The load units of RTL
Compiler are femtofarads where as default sdc load units are picofarads.
dc::create_clock [dc::get_ports CLK] -name CLK -period 4000 -waveform {0 2000}
#It creates a clock name CLK with period 4000ps and duty cycle 50%
dc::set_clock_latency 200.0 [dc::get_clocks CLK]
# set_clock_latency command is used to define the estimated clock insertion
```
delay during synthesis. This is primarily used during the pre-layout syn-
thesis and timing analysis. The estimated delay number is an approximation of
the delay produced by the clock tree network insertion
```
dc::set_clock_transition 50.0 [dc::get_clocks CLK]
```
It is used during the pre-layout synthesis, and for timing analysis. Using
this command forces DC to use the specified transition value (that is fixed)
for the clock port or pin. Setting a fixed value for transition time of the
clock signal in pre-layout is essential because of a large fanout associated
with the clock network. Using this command enables DC to calculate realistic
delays for the logic being fed by the clock net based on the specified clock
signal transition value.
```
   dc::set_clock_uncertainty 20.0 -hold [dc::get_clocks CLK]
```
set_clock_uncertainty command lets the user define the clock skew information.
Basically this is used to add a certain amount of margin to the clock, both
for setup and hold times. During the pre-layout phase one can add more margin as compared to the post-layout phase. It is strongly recommended that users specify a certain amount of margin both for pre-layout and the post layout
phased. The main reason for doing this is to make the chip less susceptible
to the process variations that may occur during manufacturing.
```
dc::set_input_delay 200.0 -clock CLK -max [dc::all_inputs]
```
set_input_delay specifies the input arrival time of a signal in relation to
the clock. It is used at the input ports, to specify the time it takes for the
data to be stable after the clock edge.
```
dc::set_output_delay 100.0 -clock CLK -max [dc::all_outputs]
```
set_output_delay command is used at the output port, to define the time it
takes for the data to be available before the clock edge. The timing specification of the design usually contains this information.
```
set_attribute max_dynamic_power 0.0 $top_module
set_attribute max_leakage_power 0.0 $top_module
```
 #There are mainly two kinds of power dissipations in a design which the RC
compiler reports i.e. dynamic power (switching power) and leakage power (due
to leakage currents). Both the powers can be optimized for by setting the
above two attributes. Setting the two powers to 0.0 doesn't mean it minimizes
the dissipation to zero. It just optimizes the design for minimum power.
```
set_attribute delete_unloaded_seqs false $top_module
```
#By default, RC compiler removes flip flops and logic if they do not transi-
tively fan in out to output ports. To prevent this, use the delete_unloaded_

```
seqs attribute.
set_attribute drc_first true
##Note: By default, timing has the highest priority and the compiler will not
fix DRC violations if doing so causes timing violations. However the priority
can be overridden by setting the drc_first attribute to true. In this case all
violations will be fixed.
set MAP_EFF low
synthesize -to_mapped -effort $MAP_EFF -no_incr
# During synthesis the compiler maps the combinational and sequential instanc-
es used in the design to the technology mapped instances. The mapping or opti-
mization effort defines the level of effort the compiler puts in during syn-
thesis. That is the higher the effort the higher the optimization done by the
compiler. The "synthesize -to_mapped" command is used to specify the extent of
optimization effort. Set MAP_EFF low sets the level of optimization to low.
report area fareg > $synth_dir/fareg_area.rep
cd designs/fareg
report summary > $synth_dir/fareg_sum.rep
report timing -num_paths 4 > $synth_dir/fareg_slack.rep
report gates > $synth_dir/fareg_gates.rep
report power > $synth_dir/fareg_power.rep
cd ..
cd ..
# The above lines generate area, summary, slack, gate and power reports. These
report files will be generated in the results folder.
write -mapped multiplier > $synth_dir/fareg.v
write_sdc multiplier > $synth_dir/fareg.sdc
# The above lines generate the netlist (NL) and SDC files which will be used
by SOC
Encounter for placement and routing.
```

BACK ANNOTATION

```
#Note: An external clock does not directly drive any points within the design,
but is only
#used as a reference for external delays. Combinational designs don't have any
clocks
but still the above constraint must be defined for such designs because it is
used as
reference for Slack calculation .
After the synthesis, it is required to check the functionality of the design
so the fa8_NL.v needs to be simulated in NCLaunch
Following Modifications are required:
```

```
1.Include the Verilog simulation files at the top of the fa8_NL.v
`include "fsd0k_a_generic_core_21.lib"
This file is available at
```

CORE

```
/edatools/dk/umc90nm/faraday90nm/LLLowK1p9m/core/FSD0K_A_GENERIC_CORE_1D0V_
DP_2007Q2v1.3/FSD0K_A_GENERIC_CORE_1D0V_DP_2007Q2v1.3/fsd0k_a/2007Q2v1.3/GE-
NERIC_CORE_1D0V/FrontEnd/verilog/fsd0k_a_generic_core_21.lib
Copy this file in the folder where you are invoking NCLaunch Tool
```

Renote: It is to be kept in mind the now the time scale has been changed to 10ps so the Verilog test bench needs to be edited accordingly.

The rest of the procedure can be referred from Chapter-1 NCLaunch

This is the end of synthesis process. Now feed the NETLIST file (fa8_NL.v) along the SDC file (fa8_chip.sdc) generated by the compiler to SOC encounter for Placement and Routing process.

Chapter 5
Utilization of Classification Techniques for the Determination of Liquefaction Susceptibility of Soils

J. Jagan
VIT University, India

Prabhakar Gundlapalli
Nuclear Power Corporation of India Limited, India

Pijush Samui
VIT University, India

ABSTRACT

The determination of liquefaction susceptibility of soil is a paramount project in geotechnical earthquake engineering. This chapter adopts Support Vector Machine (SVM), Relevance Vector Machine (RVM) and Least Square Support Vector Machine (LSSVM) for determination of liquefaction susceptibility based on Cone Penetration Test (CPT) from Chi-Chi earthquake. Input variables of SVM, RVM and LSSVM are Cone Resistance (qc) and Peak Ground Acceleration (amax/g). SVM, RVM and LSSVM have been used as classification tools. The developed SVM, RVM and LSSVM give equations for determination of liquefaction susceptibility of soil. The comparison between the developed models has been carried out. The results show that SVM, RVM and LSSVM are the robust models for determination of liquefaction susceptibility of soil.

INTRODUCTION

Liquefaction and its upshots are the major crisis dealing by the geotechnical engineers. Liquefaction is the observable fact in which the stiffness and the strength of the soil gets reduced rapidly most commonly on ground shaking during earthquake. The shear wave produced by earthquake makes the loose sand

DOI: 10.4018/978-1-4666-9474-3.ch005

to contract which tends in increasing the pore pressure, which in turn triggers the soil liquefaction. In the liquefied soil the effective confining stress becomes zero, automatically the strength of the soil will be zero. This clears that the liquefied soil cannot support the weight of the structure above it. Precisely, we can say the prime factors which influences the liquefaction initiation is excess pore pressure, shear strength and strain of the soil. Flow liquefaction and cyclic mobility are its varieties. Moreover, flow liquefaction occurs when the static shear stress becomes greater than shear strength of the liquefied soil, whereas for cyclic mobility static shear stress becomes lesser than shear strength. Hence, in the event of providing a quick fix for the issue on determining the liquefaction susceptibility of soil, this study has been engaged.

The Static Cone Penetration Test (SCPT) is one of the most fair and familiar in-situ tests for exploring the geotechnical properties of the soil. Furthermore, the efficiency of the SCPT is very impressive in site characterization too. The (SCPT) had been performed as per IS: 4968 Part III. The test comprises of driving a cone assembly basically consisting of a steel cone with 60 degrees apex angle and a base diameter of 35.7mm giving a cross sectional area of about $10cm^2$ and an independent cylindrical friction jacket of a slightly larger diameter than that of the cone and length 10cm giving a surface area of about $115cm^2$. The test is conducted at depth intervals of 10cm. At each depth first the cone alone and subsequently the cone and friction jacket combined are pushed into the ground via sounding rods and the corresponding loads required for penetration are recorded. In this process the cone assembly gets extended out fully. Thereafter, for conducting the test at the next depth, the cone assembly has to close up to the initial state which is achieved by pushing the mantle tube till the cone reaches the next intended depth of test. The above procedure is then repeated at the next depth and so on. In this manner, a continuous penetration of the cone assembly into the ground is achieved. The obtained cone resistance from the performed SCPT will be entertained as input for developing the models. The SCPT test has been carried out and the soil properties are driven out. Those properties of the soil will be segregated according to the requirement and it will sail as the input along with the techniques which will be described in the further section.

SVM is one of the pioneer method developed by Vapnik (1995) based on statistical learning theory. The function can be either classification or regression function. SVM uses the nonlinear mapping to transform the original training data into a higher dimension. It seeks out for the best separating hyperplane which is called as the optimal hyperplane that separates the tuples from one class to the other optimally. The support vectors are those which lie on the hyperplane. SVM has its own ability to model complex nonlinear decision boundaries with high accuracy, however it can be slow. It is much less prone to overfitting than other methods. The target values of SVM are -1 and +1.The distance from the hyperplane to the closest data points is margin. In order to maximize the margin for good generalization, kernel function and Lagrange mulitpliers were used. The radial basis function acts as the kernel function. In SVM, the target function tries to acquire minimal error on the training set and also attempt to maximize the margin simultaneously, which leads to avoid overfitting. This mechanism tends to the good generalization of support vectors.

The RVM was developed by Tipping (2000) based on the Bayesian theorem in a simple manner. RVM has its unique advantages; however it is the functional form of SVM. The Bayesian framework along with some basis functions of SVM offers the additional merits. It has the package of profits like probabilistic predictions, noise estimation, and utilization of arbitrary functions and so on. The RVM adopts the Gauissian prior with a distinct parameter. For generalization the logistic sigmoid function adopts the Bernoulli distribution. The optimal parameters are then derived. In RVM the target values assigned are 0 and +1. The important note is that there is no noise variance in RVM.

Least Square Support Vector Machine (LSSVM) was developed by Suykens (1999). LSSVM is the Least squares version of Support Vector Machine (SVM). For the classification problems LSSVM makes the equality constraints which make the solutions to follow directly from the set of linear equations instead of solving quadratic programming problems like SVM. The LSSVM makes data in high dimensional input spaces. The LSSVM simplifies the problem via equality constraints and least squares. LSSVM take on optimization problem for resolving the weight and bias, the factors used for obtaining the target. Lagrangian multipliers solve the optimization problems. The dual problem formulation, Kernel basis function, etc., for solving the problems are also been explored here. The radial basis function acts as the kernel function. In RVM the target values assigned are -1 and +1.

This chapter takes up the modeling of liquefaction susceptibility of soil with the involvement of the machine learning techniques like SVM, RVM and LSSVM, since the laboratory test of which application are very pricey, strenuous and depletes the time. Furthermore, it reveals the capability of the engaged SVM, RVM and LSSVM techniques with their own benefits. These techniques convey the equations which will be helpful for future purpose. In addition, the statistical analysis for the input parameters of the dataset was also performed.

BACKGROUND

Robertson and Campanella (1985) developed first CPT based method for determination of liquefaction susceptibility of soil. The value of CRR was determined from the plot of earthquake magnitude versus the magnitude scaling factor. Later it was reproduced by Yould and Noble (1997a). For the calculation of CRR from CPT data along with empirical liquefaction data from compiled case histories had been reproduced by Robertson and Wride (1998). In this method, normalization of tip resistance (q_{c1N}) was done by using the following relations:

$$q_{c1N} = C_q \left(\frac{q_c}{P_a} \right) \tag{1}$$

where

$$C_q = \left(\frac{P_a}{\sigma'_v} \right) \tag{2}$$

where C_q = normalizing factor for cone penetration resistance, P_a = 1 atm of pressure in the same units used for σ'_v, n = exponent that varies from 0.5 to 1, depending on the grain characteristics of the soil (Olsen, 1997) and q_c = field cone penetration resistance measured at the tip. The above CPT method has been revised and updated by many researchers (Seed and Alba, 1986; Stark and Olson, 1995; Olsen, 1997; Robertson and Wride, 1998; Moss et al., 2006).

Occurrence of liquefaction affects the foundation of structure can cause a wide range of structural damages starting from minor settlement, and ending to general failure due to loss of bearing capacity. Shanin et al., (2000) predicted the settlement of shallow foundations on cohesionless soil. Baziar and

Jafarian (2007) developed an ANN model to correlate some of the soil parameters with the strain energy required liquefaction triggering. The main advantage of the energy-based approach is that the shear energy required to liquefy a soil deposit is not dependent on the stress history. Another approach is based on extracting accurate classification rules from ANN via Ant Colony Optimization for generating the prediction rules for soil liquefaction (Adil et al., 2009). Moreover, ANN has its own deficiency such as black box approach, low generalization capability, overfitting, etc. (Park & Rilett 1999; Kecman, 2001). Kayadelen (2011) utilized Genetic Expression Programming (GEP) and Adaptive Neuro-Fuzzy (ANFIS) techniques with the standard penetration test value and other properties of soil. He successfully determined the complex relationship between seismic properties of soils and their liquefaction potential. Usama and Yased (2014) followed the Lattice Boltzmann method (LBM) and Discrete Element Method (DEM) for modeling the response of a saturated soil deposit subjected to seismic excitation. The three-dimensional pore-scale which was presented for the dynamic response and liquefaction of saturated granular soils. The Finite Element Method (FEM) and Finite Difference Method (FDM) were coupled for estimating the effectiveness of combined displacement error and pore water pressure (Tang et al., 2015). This method was established for soil seismic liquefaction analysis.

There are more uncertainties in the available methods. In the event of overwhelming those uncertainties, the recipe of SVM, RVM and LSSVM were procured. The following sections will give the procedures of the mentioned techniques and their proficiency in determining the liquefaction susceptibility of soil.

Details of SVM

Recently, SVM has emerged as an elegant pattern recognition tool and a better alternative to ANN methods. The method has been developed by Vapnik (1995) and is gaining popularity due to many attractive features. The formulation is based on Structural Risk Minimization (SRM), which has been shown to be superior to the empirical risk minimization (ERM) used in conventional neural networks. The method classifies patterns through the construction of optimal hyperplanes which separates the data belonging to different classes. This section describes an introduction to this relatively new technique. Details of this method can be found in Boser et al. (1992), Cortes and Vapnik (1995), Gualtieri et al. (1999), Vapnik (1998). A binary classification problem is considered having a set of training vectors (D) belonging to two separate classes.

$$D = \left\{ \left(x^1, y^1 \right), ..., \left(x^n, y^n \right) \right\} x \in R^n, y \in \left\{ -1, +1 \right\} \tag{3}$$

where $x \in R^n$ is an n-dimensional data vector with each sample belonging to either of two classes labelled as $y \in \{-1, +1\}$ and l is the number of training data. The main aim is to find a generalized classifier that can distinguish the two classes (-1, +1) from the set of the training vectors mentioned above (D) and also can classify equally well the unseen data. For determination of liquefaction susceptibility, x = [a_{max}/g and q_c] where a_{max}=Peak Ground Acceleration (PGA), g= acceleration due to gravity, q_c=cone resistance and y= [-1, +1] -1=liquefaction, +1=No liquefaction. For a set of data, this would mean a linear hyper plane defined by equation (2) which can distinguish the two classes.

$$f(x) = w \cdot x + b = 0 \tag{4}$$

where $w \in R^n$ determines the orientation of a discriminating hyperplane, $b \in r$ is a bias. Where, $R^n =$ n dimensional vector space; and r = one dimensional vector space. An example of hyperplane is shown in Figure 1. Soil parameter, $x_1 = q_c$ and Earthquake parameter, $x_2 = a_{max}/g$.

For the linearly separable case, a separating hyperplane can be defined for the two classes as

$$w \cdot x_i + b \geq 1 \left(for\ y_i = +1 \right) No\ liquefaction$$
$$w \cdot x_i + b \leq -1 \left(for\ y_i = -1 \right) Liquefaction$$

(5)

The above two equation can be combined as

$$y_i \left(w \cdot x_i + b \right) \geq 1$$

(6)

Sometimes, due to the noise or mixture of classes introduced during the selection of training data, variables $\xi_i > 0$, called slack variables, are used due to the effects of misclassification (Yoonkyung & Koo, 2002; Aixin et al., 2002; Dell & Sun, 2003). So the above equation can be written as

$$y_i \left(w \cdot x_i + b \right) \geq 1 - \xi_i$$

(7)

The perpendicular distance from the origin to the plane $w \cdot x_i + b = -1$ is $\dfrac{|1+b|}{\|w\|}$. Similarly, the perpendicular distance from the origin to the plane $w \cdot x_i + b = 1$ is $\dfrac{|b-1|}{\|w\|}$.

Figure 1. An example of hyperplane

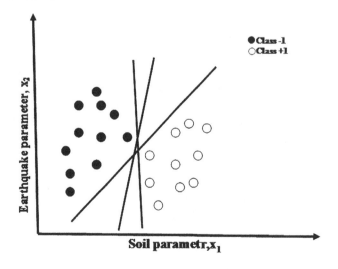

The margin (ρ(w, b)) between the planes is simply

$$\rho\left(w,b\right) = \frac{2}{\|w\|} \tag{8}$$

The optimal hyperplane is located where the margin between two classes of interest is maximized and the error is minimized. This is shown in Figure 2.

The maximization of this margin leads to the following constrained optimization problem
Minimize:

$$\frac{1}{2}\|w\|^2 + C\sum_{i=1}^{l}\xi_i$$

Subjected to:

$$y_i\left(w \cdot x_i + b\right) \geq 1 - \xi_i \tag{9}$$

The constant $0 < C < \infty$, a parameter defines the trade-off between the number of misclassification in the training data and the maximization of margin. A large C assigns higher penalties to errors so that the SVM is trained to minimize error with lower generalization while a small C assigns fewer penalties to errors; this allows the minimization of margin with errors, thus higher generalization ability (Olivier et al., 1999; Furey et al., 2000; Foody & Ajay, 2004; Anderson et al., 2003; Carl &Peter, 2003). If C goes to infinitely large, SVM would not allow the occurrence of any error and result in a complex model, whereas when C goes to zero, the result would tolerate a large amount of errors and the model would be

Figure 2. Margin widths of different hyperplanes

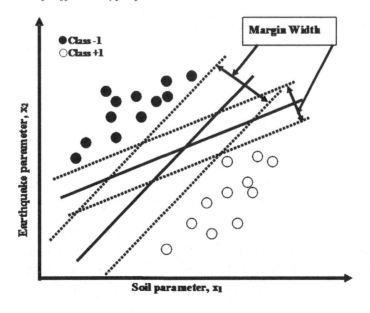

less complex (Simon &Daphne, 2001; Chih & Chih, 2002; Zhang et al., 2003; Farid & Lorenzo, 2004; Asghari & Huosheng, 2008) . In order to solve the above optimization problem (7), the Lagrangian is constructed as follows:

$$L\left(w,b,\alpha,\beta,\xi\right) = \frac{\|w\|^2}{2} + C\left(\sum_{i=1}^{l}\xi_i\right) - \sum_{i=1}^{l}\alpha_i\left\{\left[\left(w\cdot x_i + b\right)\right]y_i - 1 + \xi_i\right\} - \sum_{i=1}^{l}\beta_i\xi_i \qquad (10)$$

where α, β are the Lagrange multipliers. The solution to the constrained optimization problem is determined by the saddle point of the Lagrangian function $L(w,b,\alpha,\beta,\xi)$, which has to be minimized with respect to w, b and ξ. Thus, differentiating $L(w,b,\alpha,\beta,\xi)$ with respect to w, b and ξ and setting the results equal to zero, the following three conditions have been obtained:

Condition 1:

$$\frac{\partial L\left(w,b,\alpha,\beta,\xi\right)}{\partial w} = 0 \Rightarrow w = \sum_{i=1}^{l}\alpha_i y_i x_i$$

Condition 2:

$$\frac{\partial L\left(w,b,\alpha,\beta,\xi\right)}{\partial b} = 0 \Rightarrow \sum_{i=1}^{l}\alpha_i y_i = 0$$

Condition 3:

$$\frac{\partial L\left(w,b,\alpha,\beta,\xi\right)}{\partial \xi} = 0 \Rightarrow \alpha_i + \beta_i = C \qquad (11)$$

Hence from equations 8, 9 the equivalent optimization problem becomes (Osuna et al. 1997), Maximize:

$$\sum_{i=1}^{l}\alpha_i - \frac{1}{2}\sum_{i=1}^{l}\sum_{j=1}^{l}\alpha_i\alpha_j y_i y_j\left(x_i\cdot x_j\right)$$

Subjected to:

$$\sum_{i=1}^{l}\alpha_i y_i = 0 \text{ and } 0{\leq}\alpha_i{\leq}C, \text{ for } i=1, 2,\ldots, 1 \qquad (12)$$

Solving equation (12) with constraints determines the Lagrange multipliers. According to the Karush-Kuhn-Tucker (KKT) optimality condition (Fletcher, 1987); some of the multipliers will be zero. The nonzero multipliers are called support vectors. This is explained in figure 3.

Figure 3. Support vectors with maximum margin

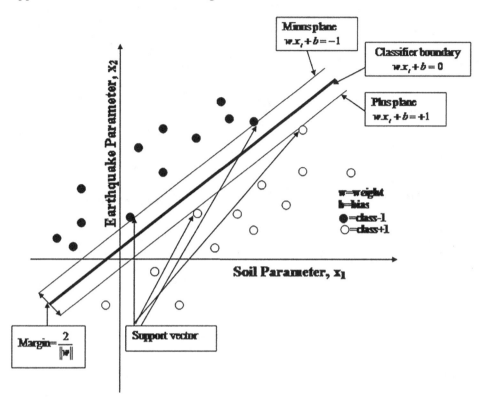

In conceptual terms, the support vectors are those data points that lie closest to the optimal hyperplane and are therefore the most difficult to classify. The value of w and b are calculated from $w = \sum_{i=1}^{l} y_i \alpha_i x_i$ and $b = -\frac{1}{2} w \left[x_{+1} + x_{-1} \right]$, where x_{+1} and x_{-1} are the support vectors of class labels +1(No liquefaction) and -1(liquefaction) respectively. The classifier can then be constructed as:

$$f(x) = sign(w \cdot x + b) \tag{13}$$

where sign (●) is the signum function. It gives +1(No liquefaction) if the element is greater than or equal to zero and -1(liquefaction) if it is less than zero.

In case where linear supporting hyper plane is inappropriate, SVM maps input data into a high dimensional feature space through some nonlinear mapping (Boser et al., 1992).This method easily converts a linear classification learning algorithm into a nonlinear one, by mapping the original observations into a higher-dimensional nonlinear space so that linear classification in the new space is equivalent to nonlinear classification in the original space.

Figure 4. Concept of nonlinear SVM for classification problem

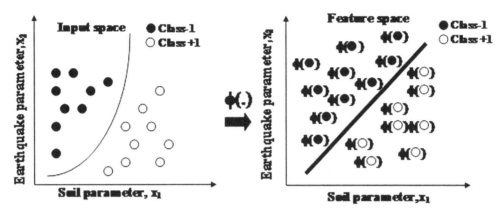

After replacing x by its mapping in the feature space, the optimization problem of equation (12) becomes Maximize:

$$\sum_{i=1}^{l} \alpha_i - \frac{1}{2} \sum_{i=1}^{l} \sum_{j=1}^{l} \alpha_i \alpha_j y_i y_j \left(\Phi \left(x_i \right) \cdot \Phi \left(x_j \right) \right)$$

Subjected to:

$$\sum_{i=1}^{l} \alpha_i y_i = 0 \text{ and } 0 \leq \alpha_i \leq C, \text{ for } i=1, 2,..., l \tag{14}$$

Kernel function $K \left(x_i \cdot x_j \right) = \Phi \left(x_i \right) \cdot \Phi \left(x_j \right)$ has been introduced instead of feature space to reduce computational demand (Cortes & Vapnik, 1995; Cristianini & Taylor, 2000; Yuh & Mangasarian, 2001). The Kernel representation offers a powerful alternative by using linear machines in hypothesizing complex real world problems as opposed to ANN based learning paradigms, which use multiple layers of threshold linear functions (Cristianini & Taylor, 2000). Polynomial, radial basis functions and certain sigmoid functions has been used as a kernel functions (Bryan et al., 2008; Fraser et al., 2014; Czarnecki & Tabor, 2014; Cheng et al., 2014). To get the equation (11), same procedures have been applied as in linear case. An important characteristic of this optimization problem is that the solution is global and deterministic (i.e. given the same training set and values of C, the same solution is always found; that is, no stochastic events are present during the building of the model), which is in contrast to ANN.

The above SVM has been used to predict liquefaction susceptibility of soil based on CPT. The database has been collected from the work of Goh (1994) and Ku et al., (2004). The database contains information about cone resistance (q_c), PGA and status of soil. The total dataset which was taken into consideration are categorized in Table 1.

The statistical analysis of the input parameter was reckoned and it is figured out in Table 2.

In carrying out the formulation, the data has been branched into two sub-sets: such as

Table 1. Total dataset used for developing and evaluating the model

q_c	a_{max}/g	Liquefaction Observed	q_c	a_{max}/g	Liquefaction Observed
1.27	0.79	yes	8.3	0.19	no
1.97	0.79	yes	12.77	0.19	no
1.79	0.79	yes	2.96	0.19	yes
1.35	0.79	yes	1.73	0.21	yes
13.89	0.79	no	8	0.19	no
20.05	0.79	no	8.74	0.19	no
0.94	0.43	yes	10.05	0.19	no
1.47	0.43	yes	11.26	0.19	no
11.56	0.43	no	7.52	0.21	no
12.89	0.43	no	6.61	0.19	no
3.86	0.43	yes	8.32	0.19	no
16.3	0.43	no	11.58	0.19	no
1.41	0.43	yes	2.09	0.19	yes
0.9	0.43	yes	2.69	0.19	yes
1.87	0.43	yes	3.05	0.19	yes
5.77	0.43	yes	10.61	0.19	no
2.54	0.19	yes	14.74	0.19	no
7.46	0.19	no	13.65	0.19	no
7.62	0.19	no	1.28	0.12	yes
8.03	0.19	no	5.46	0.12	no
6.8	0.19	no	5.16	0.12	no
7.02	0.19	no	2.65	0.12	yes
7.72	0.19	no	7.4	0.12	no
7.68	0.19	no	7.47	0.12	no
6.23	0.19	no	7.68	0.12	no
12.15	0.19	no	6.54	0.12	no
2.54	0.19	yes	5.59	0.12	no
8.15	0.19	no	6.85	0.12	no
10.08	0.19	no	6.68	0.12	no
16.89	0.19	no	6.12	0.12	no
1.62	0.19	yes	7.18	0.12	no
2.45	0.19	yes	5.91	0.12	no
9.19	0.19	no	6.62	0.12	no
13.65	0.19	no	7.99	0.12	no
17.08	0.19	no	7.38	0.12	no
1.82	0.19	yes	7.03	0.12	no
8.25	0.19	no	6.73	0.12	no
2.54	0.19	yes	5.47	0.12	no

continued on following page

Table 1. Continued

q_c	a_{max}/g	Liquefaction Observed		q_c	a_{max}/g	Liquefaction Observed
6.32	0.12	no		2.78	0.19	yes
0.92	0.12	yes		14.67	0.19	no
0.64	0.12	yes		0.64	0.12	yes
6.05	0.12	no		3.26	0.12	yes
6.76	0.12	no		7.04	0.12	no
2.01	0.12	yes		6.64	0.12	no
1.89	0.12	yes		7.58	0.12	no
7.43	0.12	no		5.21	0.12	no
7.72	0.12	no		5.38	0.12	no
7.12	0.12	no		7.41	0.12	no
6.08	0.12	no		6.49	0.12	no
7.76	0.12	no		1.5	0.12	yes
0.2	0.12	yes		2.49	0.12	yes
5.93	0.12	no		1.54	0.12	yes
7.57	0.12	no		6.61	0.12	no
0.23	0.12	yes		9.48	0.12	no
7.24	0.12	no		7.94	0.12	no
8.83	0.12	no		0.18	0.12	yes
0.72	0.79	yes		6.21	0.12	no
11.66	0.79	no		3.2	0.16	yes
14.45	0.79	no		1.6	0.16	yes
11.32	0.43	no		7.2	0.16	yes
6.01	0.43	yes		5.6	0.16	yes
11.96	0.43	no		5.45	0.16	yes
8.27	0.19	no		8.84	0.16	yes
2.7	0.19	yes		9.7	0.16	yes
6.67	0.19	no		8	0.16	no
2.22	0.19	yes		14.55	0.16	no
2.62	0.19	yes		10	0.23	no
12.43	0.19	no		16	0.23	no
6.7	0.19	no		15.38	0.23	no
2.66	0.19	yes		1.79	0.23	yes
7.41	0.19	no		4.1	0.23	yes
1.18	0.19	yes		7.95	0.23	yes
8.01	0.19	no		8.97	0.23	yes
6.83	0.21	no		1.7	0.4	yes
2.61	0.19	yes		9.4	0.4	yes
8.3	0.19	no		5.7	0.4	yes
3	0.19	yes		7.6	0.4	yes

continued on following page

Table 1. Continued

q_c	a_{max}/g	Liquefaction Observed	q_c	a_{max}/g	Liquefaction Observed
1.5	0.4	yes	1.45	0.2	yes
1	0.4	yes	2.15	0.2	yes
5	0.4	yes	2.6	0.2	yes
2.5	0.4	yes	2.73	0.2	yes
2.6	0.4	yes	1.78	0.2	yes
3.2	0.4	yes	7.64	0.2	no
5.8	0.4	yes	25.6	0.8	no
3.5	0.4	yes	24.7	0.8	no
8.4	0.4	yes	31.4	0.8	no
1.7	0.4	yes	1.43	0.8	yes
3.5	0.4	yes	2.48	0.8	yes
4.1	0.4	yes	4.03	0.8	yes
5.5	0.4	yes	3.3	0.8	no
9	0.4	yes	8.8	0.8	no
7	0.4	yes	6.7	0.8	no
1.18	0.4	yes	1.65	0.2	yes
4.24	0.4	yes	3.65	0.2	yes
11.47	0.4	no	1.03	0.2	yes
15.76	0.4	no	5	0.2	yes
11.39	0.2	no	2.91	0.2	yes
12.12	0.2	no	6.06	0.2	yes
17.76	0.2	no	13.24	0.2	no
2.65	0.2	yes	13.06	0.2	no
4.4	0.2	yes	16.59	0.2	no
3	0.2	yes	10.59	0.2	no
9	0.2	yes	9.12	0.2	no
2	0.1	yes	11.29	0.2	no
1.1	0.2	yes	1.94	0.2	yes
15.5	0.1	no	5	0.2	yes
6.5	0.1	no	2.24	0.2	yes
9	0.1	no	14.12	0.1	no
2.5	0.1	no	18.94	0.1	no
16.5	0.1	no	3.52	0.2	yes
13.65	0.1	no	2.73	0.2	yes
8.47	0.2	no	3.29	0.2	yes
4.55	0.2	no	4.12	0.2	yes
5.79	0.2	no	2.94	0.2	yes
2.48	0.2	yes	3	0.2	yes
1.57	0.2	yes	5.85	0.2	yes

continued on following page

Table 1. Continued

q_c	a_{max}/g	Liquefaction Observed
9	0.2	yes
1.8	0.2	yes
2.55	0.2	yes
4.5	0.2	yes
4.24	0.2	yes
8	0.2	no

q_c	a_{max}/g	Liquefaction Observed
5.22	0.22	yes
3.73	0.22	yes
3.11	0.22	yes
1.32	0.22	yes
5.22	0.22	yes

Table 2. Statistical analysis of the input parameter

Variable	Mean	Standard Deviation	Skewness	Kurtosis
q_c	6.58	4.85	1.44	6.38
a_{max}/g	0.25	0.17	2.04	6.45

1. **A Training Dataset:** This is required to construct the model. In this study, 170 data out of the 243 are considered for training dataset.
2. **A Testing Dataset:** This is required to evaluate the performance of the model. In this study, the remaining 73 data are considered as testing dataset.

The data are normalized between 0 and 1. Radial basis function has been used kernel function. The expression of radial basis function is given below:

$$K\left(x_k, x\right) = \exp\left\{-\frac{\left(x_k - x\right)\left(x_k - x\right)^T}{2\sigma^2}\right\} \tag{15}$$

where σ width of radial basis function.

DETAILS OF RVM

This section presents the methodology of RVM for prediction of liquefaction susceptibility of soil based on CPT. RVM was developed by Tipping (2000). Let us consider a set of example of input vectors $\{x_i\}_{i=1}^N$ is given along with a corresponding set of targets $\{y_i\}_{i=1}^N$. For classification problem, y_i should be 0 for "Liquefaction" and +1 for "No Liquefaction". To use these data for classification purpose, a value of 0 is assigned to the liquefied sites while a value of +1 is assigned to the non-liquefied sites so as to make this a two-class classification problem. PGA and q_c have been used as input variables. So, $x = \left[PGA, q_c\right]$.

The RVM constructs a logistic regression model based on a set of sequence features derived from the input patterns, i.e.

$$p\left(C_1/x\right) \approx \sigma\left\{y\left(x;w\right)\right\}, \text{ with } y\left(x;w\right) = \sum_{i=1}^{N} w_i \Phi_i\left(x\right) + w_0 \tag{16}$$

where φ_i is an ith component of the basis vector function

$$\Phi\left(x\right) = \left(\Phi_1\left(x\right), \Phi_2\left(x\right), \ldots, \Phi_N\left(X\right)\right)^T = \left[1, K\left(x_i, x_1\right), K\left(x_i, x_2\right), \ldots, K\left(x_i, x_N\right)\right]^T,$$

$w = \left(w_0, \ldots, w_N\right)^T$ are a vector of weights, $\sigma\left\{y\right\} = \left(1 + \exp\left\{-y\right\}\right)^{-1}$ is the logistic sigmoid link function and $K\left(x_i, x_j\right)_{j=1}^{N}$ are kernel terms. Assuming a Bernoulii distribution for $P\left(t/x\right)$, the likelihood is written as (Tipping 2000; Bishop & Tipping, 2000):

$$P\left(t/w\right) = \prod_{i=1}^{N} \sigma\left\{y\left(x_i; w\right)\right\}^{t_i} \left[1 - \sigma\left\{y\left(x_i; w\right)\right\}\right]^{1-t_i} \tag{17}$$

We cannot integrate the weights analytically. The RVM adopts the following separable Gaussian prior, with a distinct hyper-parameter, α_i, for each weight (Chen et al., 2001; Christopher et al., 2005; Ron & Daniel, 2006; Xiaodong et al., 2009; Mianji & Zhang, 2011),

$$p\left(w/\alpha\right) = \prod_{i=1}^{N} N\left(w_i/0, \alpha_i^{-1}\right)$$

The optimal parameters of the model are then derived by minimizing the penalized negative log-likelihood,

$$\log\left\{P\left(t/w\right)p\left(w/\alpha\right)\right\} = \sum_{i=1}^{N}\left[t_i \log y_i + \left(1 - t_i\right)\log\left(1 - y_i\right)\right] - \frac{1}{2}w^T A w \tag{18}$$

where $A = diag\left(\alpha\right)$.

If we differentiate twice equation (17), the expression is given below:

$$\nabla w \nabla w \log p\left(w/t, \alpha\right) = -\left(\Phi^T B \Phi + A\right) \tag{19}$$

where $B = diag\left(\beta_1, \ldots, \beta_N\right)$ is a diagonal matrix with $\beta_n = \sigma\left\{y\left(x_n\right)\right\}\left[1 - \sigma\left\{y\left(x_n\right)\right\}\right]$

The following equation has been used for updating hyper-parameter

$$\alpha_i^{new} = \frac{1 - \alpha_i \sum_{ii}}{\mu_i^2} \tag{20}$$

where μ_i is the ith posterior mean weight, $\sum_{ii}$ is the ith diagonal element of the posterior weight covariance (Shovan et al., 2005; Silva & Ribeiro, 2006; Demir & Erturk, 2007; Achmad et al., 2009; Phillipsa et al., 2011). The process is repeated until the ultimate goal is met. The property of this optimization problem is that the value of many w will be zero. The nonzero weights are called relevance vectors. Probability (P) has been determined by using the following equation.

$$P = \frac{1}{1 + \left(\dfrac{1}{e^y}\right)} \tag{21}$$

The database has been collected from the work of Goh (1994) and Ku et al., (2004). The database contains information about cone resistance (q_c), PGA and status of soil. In carrying out the formulation, the data has been divided into two sub-sets: such as

1. **A Training Dataset:** This is required to build up the model. In this study, 170 data out of the 243 are considered for training dataset.
2. **A Testing Dataset:** This is required to estimate the model performance. In this study, the remaining 73 data are considered as testing dataset.

The data are normalized between 0 and 1. Radial basis function has been used kernel function. The expression of radial basis function is given below:

$$K\left(x_k, x\right) = \exp\left\{-\frac{\left(x_k - x\right)\left(x_k - x\right)^T}{2\sigma^2}\right\} \tag{22}$$

where σ width of radial basis function.

DETAILS OF LSSVM

The LSSVM is a statistical learning method which has a self-contained basis of statistical-learning theory and excellent learning performance (Suykens & Vandewalle, 1999; Suykens et al., 2002; Gestel et al., 2002; Tony et al., 2004). A binary classification problem is considered having a set of training vectors (D) belonging to two separate classes.

$$D = \left\{ \left(x^1, y^1 \right), \ldots\ldots, \left(x^n, y^n \right) \right\} x \in R^n, y \in \left\{ -1, +1 \right\} \tag{23}$$

where $x \in R^n$ is an n-dimensional data vector with each sample belonging to either of two classes labelled as $y \in \left\{ -1, +1 \right\}$, and n is the number of training data. Maximum peak ground acceleration (a_{max}/g) and q_c as input parameters. Therefore, For MODEL II $x = \left[\dfrac{a_{max}}{g}, q_c \right]$. In the current context of classifying soil condition during earthquake, the two classes labeled as (+1, -1) may mean non liquefaction and liquefaction. The SVM approach aims at constructing a classifier of the form:

$$y(x) = sign \left[\sum_{k=1}^{N} \alpha_k y_k \psi \left(x, x_k \right) + b \right] \tag{24}$$

where, α_k are positive real constants, b is a real constant and $\psi \left(x, x_k \right)$ is kernel function and sign is the signum function. It gives +1 if the element is greater than or equal to zero and -1 if it is less than zero. For the case of two classes, one assumes

$$w^T \phi \left(x_k \right) + b \geq 1, \; if \; y_k = +1 \left(No \; Liquefaction \right)$$

$$w^T \phi \left(x_k \right) + b \leq 1, \; if \; y_k = -1 \left(Liquefaction \right) \tag{25}$$

which is equivalent to

$$y_k \left[w^T \phi \left(x_k \right) + b \right] \geq 1, \; k = 1, \ldots, N \tag{26}$$

where $\phi(.)$ is a nonlinear function which maps the input space into a higher dimensional space. According to the structural risk minimization principle, the risk bound is minimized by formulating the following optimization problem:

Minimize:

$$\frac{1}{2} w^T w + \frac{\gamma}{2} \sum_{k=1}^{l} e_k^2$$

Subjected to:

$$y_k \left[w^T \phi \left(x_k \right) + b \right] = 1 - e_k, \; k = 1, \ldots, N \tag{27}$$

where, γ is the regularization parameter, determining the trade-off between the fitting error minimization and smoothness and e_k is error variable.

In order to solve the above optimization problem (Equation 27), the Lagrangian is constructed as follows:

$$L\left(w,b,e,\alpha\right) = \frac{1}{2}w^T w + \frac{\gamma}{2}\sum_{k=1}^{l}e_k^2 - \sum_{k=1}^{N}\alpha_k\left\{y_k\left[w^T\phi\left(x_k\right)+b\right]-1+e_k\right\} \qquad (28)$$

where α_k are Lagrange multipliers, which can be either positive or negative due to the equality constraints as follows from the Kuhn-Tucker conditions (Fletcher, 1987; Kruif & Vries, 2003; Daisuke & Shigeo, 2003; Arun & Gopal, 2009; Valyon & Horvath, 2004; Nurettin, 2005). The solution to the constrained optimization problem is determined by the saddle point of the Lagrangian function L (w,b,e,α), which has to be minimized with respect to w, b, e_k and α_k (Suykens et al., 2001; Vikramjit et al., 2007, Lijuan, 2009; Yuangui et al., 2006). Thus, differentiating L (w,b,e,α) with respect to w, b, e_k and α_k and setting the results equal to zero, the following three conditions have been obtained:

$$\frac{\partial L}{\partial w} = 0 \Rightarrow w = \sum_{k=1}^{N}\alpha_k y_k \phi\left(x_k\right)$$

$$\frac{\partial L}{\partial b} = 0 \Rightarrow \sum_{k=1}^{N}\alpha_k y_k = 0$$

$$\frac{\partial L}{\partial e_k} = 0 \Rightarrow \alpha_k = \gamma e_k$$

$$\frac{\partial L}{\partial \alpha_k} = 0 \Rightarrow y_k\left[w^T\phi\left(x_k\right)+b\right]-1+e_k = 0, k = 1,...,N \qquad (29)$$

The above equation (29) can be written immediately as the solution to the following set of linear equations (Fletcher, 1987).

$$\begin{bmatrix} I & 0 & 0 & -Z^T \\ 0 & 0 & 0 & -Y^T \\ 0 & 0 & \gamma I & -I \\ Z & Y & I & 0 \end{bmatrix}\begin{bmatrix} w \\ b \\ e \\ \alpha \end{bmatrix} = \begin{bmatrix} 0 \\ 0 \\ 0 \\ 1 \end{bmatrix} \qquad (30)$$

where

$$Z = \left[\phi\left(x_1\right)^T y_1;...;\phi\left(x_N\right)^T y_N\right],$$

$$Y = \left[y_1; ...; y_N \right] I = \left[1; ...; 1 \right],$$

$$e = \left[e_1; ...; e_N \right],$$

$$\alpha = \left[\alpha_1; ...; \alpha_N \right].$$

The solution is given by

$$\begin{bmatrix} 0 & -Y^T \\ Y & \Omega + \gamma^{-1}I \end{bmatrix} \begin{bmatrix} b \\ \alpha \end{bmatrix} = \begin{bmatrix} 0 \\ 1 \end{bmatrix} \tag{31}$$

where $\Omega = Z^T Z$ and the kernel trick can be applied within the Ω matrix.

$$\Omega_{kl} = y_k y_l \phi \left(x_k \right)^T \phi \left(x_l \right)$$

$$= y_k y_l K \left(x_k, x_l \right), k,l = 1, ..., N \tag{32}$$

where $K \left(x_k, x_l \right)$ is kernel function.

The classifier in the dual space takes the form

$$y \left(x \right) = sign \left[\sum_{k=1}^{N} \alpha_k y_k K \left(x, x_k \right) + b \right] \tag{33}$$

In carrying out the formulation, the data has been divided into two sub-sets: such as

1. **A Training Dataset:** This is required to develop the model. In this study, 170 data out of the 243 are considered for training dataset.
2. **A Testing Dataset:** This is required to estimate the performance of the developed model. In this study, the remaining 73 data are considered as testing dataset.

The data are normalized between 0 and 1. Radial basis function has been used kernel function. The expression of radial basis function is given below:

$$K \left(x_k, x \right) = \exp \left\{ -\frac{\left(x_k - x \right) \left(x_k - x \right)^T}{2\sigma^2} \right\} \tag{34}$$

where σ width of radial basis function.

SOLUTIONS AND RECOMMENDATIONS

In order to develop the SVM, the design values of C and σ have been determined by trial and error approach. The developed SVM gives best performance at C=100 and σ=0.01. The developed SVM gives training performance=100% and testing performance = 91.78%. The developed SVM gives the following equation for prediction of liquefaction susceptibility of soil.

$$y = sign\left(\sum_{k=1}^{173} \alpha_k \exp\left\{-\frac{\left(x_k - x\right)\left(x_k - x\right)^T}{0.0002}\right\}\right) \tag{35}$$

The value of α_k is given by Figure 5.

The developed SVM gives a chart for prediction of liquefaction susceptibility of soil.

The developed RVM gives training performance=91.76% and testing performance = 97.26%. The developed RVM gives the following equation for prediction of liquefaction susceptibility of soil.

$$y = \left(\sum_{k=1}^{173} w_i \exp\left\{-\frac{\left(x_k - x\right)\left(x_k - x\right)^T}{0.32}\right\}\right) \tag{36}$$

Figure 7 shows the value of w.

The developed RVM gives a chart for classifying liquefiable and non-liquefiable soils. This is represented in Figure 8.

Figure 5. Values of α_k

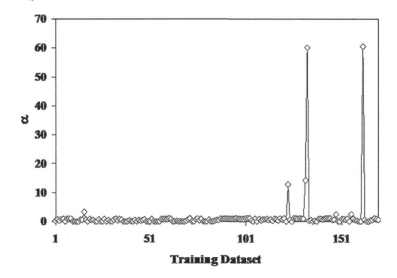

Figure 6. Chart for classifying liquefiable and non-liquefiable soil

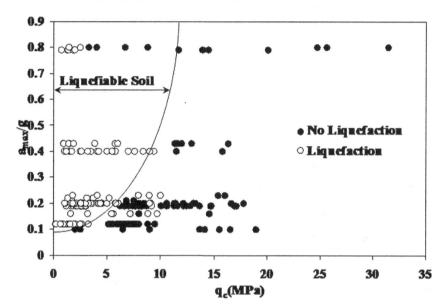

Figure 7. Values of w

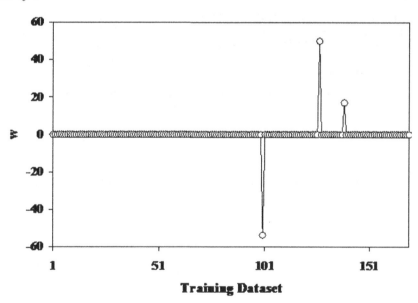

For developing the LSSVM, the design values of γ and σ is 100 and 0.1 respectively. The performance of training and testing dataset has been determined by using the design values of γ and σ. The developed LSSVM gives training performance=95.88% and testing performance = 95.89%. The developed LSSVM gives the following equation.

$$y = \sum_{i=1}^{170} \alpha_i \exp\left\{ -\frac{(x_i - x)(x_i - x)^T}{0.02} \right\} + 0.6646 \tag{37}$$

The value of α_i has been is given Figure 9.
The result of LSSVM has been plotted in Figure 10.

Figure 8. Chart for classifying liquefiable and non-liquefiable soil

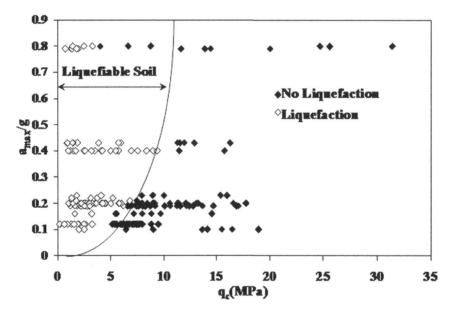

Figure 9. Values of α_i

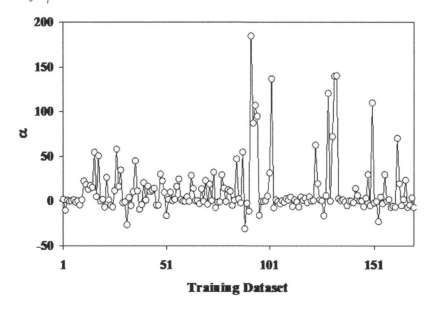

Figure 10. Chart for classifying liquefiable and non-liquefiable soil

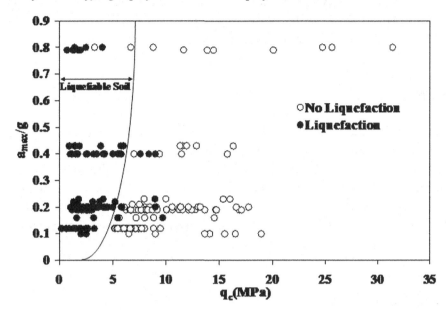

The comparison between the developed SVM, RVM and LSSVM has been done and it is classified in Table 3.

Table 2 shows the comparison between the developed SVM, LSSVM and RVM models. It is clear from Table 1 that the performance of LSSVM is best. The performance of SVM and RVM is comparable. The developed SVM and LSSVM use two tuning parameters. However, the developed RVM uses only one tuning parameter. The developed SVM and RVM use 121 and 3 training datasets for final prediction. So, the SVM and RVM models produce sparse solution. Sparseness means that a significant number of the weights are zero (or effectively zero), which has the consequence of producing compact,

Table 3. Comparison between the developed SVM, LSSVM, and RVM models

Model	Design Values	Training Performance (%)	Testing Performance (%)	No of Training Dataset Used for Final Prediction	Equation
SVM	C=100 and σ=0.01	100%	91.78%	121	$y = sign\left(\sum\limits_{k=1}^{173} \alpha_k \exp\left\{-\dfrac{\left(x_k - x\right)\left(x_k - x\right)^T}{0.0002}\right\}\right)$
LSSVM	γ=100 and σ=0.1	95.88%	95.89	170	$y = \sum\limits_{i=1}^{170} \alpha_i \exp\left\{-\dfrac{\left(x_i - x\right)\left(x_i - x\right)^T}{0.02}\right\} + 0.6646$
RVM	σ=0.4	97.26%	91.76%	3	$y = \left(\sum\limits_{k=1}^{173} w_i \exp\left\{-\dfrac{\left(x_k - x\right)\left(x_k - x\right)^T}{0.32}\right\}\right)$

computationally efficient models, which in addition are simple and therefore produce smooth functions. The developed LSSVM and SVM use the classes of training dataset in the final equation. However, the developed RVM does not use the classes of training dataset in the final equation.

CONCLUSION

This chapter has described the efficiency of SVM, RVM and LSSVM on the classification of liquefaction susceptibility of soil. The described procedures were executed and the performance of SVM, RVM and LSSVM obtained were remarkable and promising. The evolved models can be a benefit for the geotechnical engineers. These impressive models can act as the quick tool for determining the liquefaction susceptibility of soils. These extracted equations can be utilized for finding the soil will liquefy or not. Moreover, SVM, RVM and LSSVM methods can be used as a solvent for distinguished geotechnical problems.

ACKNOWLEGMENT

We thank BRNS for funding this project under the grant no 2011/36/46-BRNS/1966 dated 19.11.2011.

REFERENCES

Chih-Wei Hsu., & Chih-Jen Lin (2002). A Comparison of Methods for Multiclass Support Vector Machines. *IEEE Transactions on Neural Networks*, *13*(2), 415–425. doi:10.1109/72.991427 PMID:18244442

Anderson, D. C., Li, W., Payan, D. G., & Noble, W. S. (2003). A New Algorithm for the Evaluation of Shotgun Peptide Sequencing in Proteomics: Support Vector Machine Classification of Peptide MS/MS Spectra and SEQUEST Scores. *Journal of Proteome Research*, *2*(2), 137–146. doi:10.1021/pr0255654 PMID:12716127

Foody, G. M., & Mathur, A. (2004). A Relative Evaluation of Multiclass Image Classification by Support Vector Machines. *IEEE Transactions on Geoscience and Remote Sensing*, *42*(6), 1335–1343. doi:10.1109/TGRS.2004.827257

Baziar, M. H., & Jafarian, Y. (2007). Assessment of liquefaction triggering using strain energy concept and ANN model: Capacity energy. *Soil Dynamics and Earthquake Engineering*, *27*(12), 1056–1072. doi:10.1016/j.soildyn.2007.03.007

van Gestel, T., Suykens, J. A. K., Baesens, B., Viaene, S., Vanthienen, J., Dedene, G., . . . Vandewalle, J. (2004). Benchmarking Least Squares Support Vector Machine Classifiers. *Machine Learning*, *54*(1), 5–32. doi:10.1023/B:MACH.0000008082.80494.e0

Boser, B. E., Guyon, I. M., & Vapnik, V. N. (1992). A training algorithm for optimal margin classifier. *Proceedings of the fifth annual workshop on Computational learning theory,* Pittusburgh, PA, USA (pp. 27-29). doi:10.1145/130385.130401

Catanzaro, B., Sundaram, N., & Keutzer, K., (2008). Fast support vector machine training and classification on graphics processors. *Proceedings of the 25th international conference on Machine learning*, New York, USA (pp. 104-111).

Chen, S., Gunn, S. R., & Harris, C. J. (2001). The relevance vector machine technique for channel equalization application. *IEEE Transactions on Neural Networks*, *12*(6), 1529–1532. doi:10.1109/72.963792 PMID:18249985

Cheng, G., Han, J., Zhou, P., & Guo, L. (2014). Multi-class geospatial object detection and geographic image classification based on collection of part detectors. *ISPRS Journal of Photogrammetry and Remote Sensing*, *98*, 119–132. doi:10.1016/j.isprsjprs.2014.10.002

Christopher Bishop, M., & Michael Tipping, E. (2000). Variational relevance vector machines. *Proceedings of the Sixteenth conference on Uncertainty in artificial intelligence*, San Francisco, CA, USA (pp. 46-53). Morgan Kaufmann Publishers Inc.

Wang, X., Ye, M., & Duanmu, C. J. (2009). Classification of data from electronic nose using relevance vector machines. *Sensors and Actuators. B, Chemical*, *140*(1), 143–148. doi:10.1016/j.snb.2009.04.030

Acur, N. (2005). Classification of ECG beats by using a fast least square support vector machines with a dynamic programming feature selection algorithm. *Neural Computing & Applications*, *14*(4), 299–309. doi:10.1007/s00521-005-0466-z

Melgani, F., & Bruzzone, L. (2004). Classification of Hyperspectral Remote Sensing Images with Support Vector Machines. *IEEE Transactions on Geoscience and Remote Sensing*, *42*(8), 1778–1790. doi:10.1109/TGRS.2004.831865

Lee, Y., & Lee, C.-K. (2003). Classification of multiple cancer types by multicategory support vector machines using gene expression data. *Bioinformatics (Oxford, England)*, *19*(9), 1132–1139. doi:10.1093/bioinformatics/btg102 PMID:12801874

Xie, L., Ying, Y., & Ying, T. (2009). Classification of tomatoes with different genotypes by visible and short-wave near-infrared spectroscopy with least-squares support vector machines and other chemometrics. *Journal of Food Engineering*, *94*(1), 34–39. doi:10.1016/j.jfoodeng.2009.02.023

Cortes, C., & Vapnik, V. N. (1995). Support-vector networks. *Machine Learning*, *20*(3), 273–297. doi:10.1007/BF00994018

Moss, R. E., Seed, R. B., Kayen, R. E., Stewart, J. P., Der Kiureghian, A., & Cetin, K. O. (2006). CPT-based Probablistic and Deterministic Assesment of in situ Seismic soil liquefaction potential. *Journal of Geotechnical and Geoenviromental Engineering, 132*(8), 1032–1051. doi:10.1061/(ASCE)1090-0241(2006)132:8(1032)

Cristianini, N., & Shawe Taylor, J. (2000). *An introduction to Support vector machine*. London: Cambridge University press.

Czarnecki, W. M., & Tabor, J. (2014). Two ellipsoid Support Vector Machines. *Expert Systems with Applications*, *41*(18), 8211–8224.

ZhangD, . (2003). Question classification using support vector machines. *Proceedings of the 26th Annual International ACM SIGIR conference on Research and development in informaion retrieval*, New York, USA (pp. 26-32).

Demir, B., & Erturk, S. (2007). Hyperspectral Image Classification Using Relevance Vector Machines. *Geoscience and Remote Sensing Letters, 4*(4), 586–590. doi:10.1109/LGRS.2007.903069

Widodo, A., Kim, E.Y., Son, J.-D., Yang, B.-S., Tan, A.C.C., Gu, D.-S., . . . Mathew, J. (2009). Fault diagnosis of low speed bearing based on relevance vector machine and support vector machine. *Expert Systems with Applications, 36*(3), 7252–7261. doi:10.1016/j.eswa.2008.09.033

Fletcher, R. (1987). *Practical methods of optimization*. Chichester, New York: Wiley.

Fraser, G. D., Chan, A. D. C., Green, J. R., & Macisaac, D. T. (2014). Automated biosignal quality analysis for electromyography using a one-class support vector machine. *IEEE Transactions on Instrumentation and Measurement, 63*(12), 2919–2930. doi:10.1109/TIM.2014.2317296

Tsujinishi, D., & Abe, S. (2003). Fuzzy least squares support vector machines for multiclass problems. *Neural Networks, 16*(5–6), 785–792. PMID:12850035

Baykasoğlu, A., Çevik, A., Özbakır, L., & Kulluk, S. (2009). Generating prediction rules for liquefaction through data mining. *Expert Systems with Applications, 36*(10), 12491–12499. doi:10.1016/j.eswa.2009.04.033

vanGestel, T., Suykens, J., Lanckriet, G., Lambrechts, A., Moor, B., & Vandewalle, J. (2002). Bayesian Framework for Least-Squares Support Vector Machine Classifiers, Gaussian Processes, and Kernel Fisher Discriminant Analysis. *Neural Computation, 14*(5), 1115–1147. doi:10.1162/089976602753633411 PMID:11972910

Goh, A. T. C. (1994). Seismic liquefaction potential assessed by neural networks. *Journal of Geotechnical Engineering, 120*(9), 1467–1480. doi:10.1061/(ASCE)0733-9410(1994)120:9(1467)

Gold, C., & Sollich, P., (2003). Model selection for support vector machine classification. *Neurocomputing, 55*(1–2), 221–249.

Gualtieri, J. A., Chettri, S. R., Cromp, R. F., & Johnson, L. F. (1999). Support vector machine classifiers as applied to AVIRIS data. *Proceedings of the 8th JPL Airborne Earth Science Workshop*.

Kayadelen, C. (2011). Soil liquefaction modeling by Genetic Expression Programming and Neuro-Fuzzy. *Expert Systems with Applications, 38*(4), 4080–4087. doi:10.1016/j.eswa.2010.09.071

Kecman, V. (2001). *Learning and Soft Computing: Support Vector Machines, Neural Networks, And Fuzzy Logic Models*. Cambridge, Massachusetts, London, England: MIT press.

Ku, C. S., Lee, D. H., & Wu, J. H. (2004). Evaluation of soil liquefaction in the Chi-Chi Taiwan earthquake using CPT. *Soil Dynamics and Earthquake Engineering, 24*(9-10), 659–673. doi:10.1016/j.soildyn.2004.06.009

Kumar, M.A., & Gopal, M. (2009). Least squares twin support vector machines for pattern classification. *Expert Systems with Applications, 36*(4), 7535–7543. doi:10.1016/j.eswa.2008.09.066

Mianji, F. A., & Zhang, Y. (2011). Robust Hyperspectral Classification Using Relevance Vector Machine. *Geoscience and Remote Sensing IEEE Transactions, 49*(6), 2100–2112.

Mukherjee, S., Osuna, E., & Girosi, F. (1997). Nonlinear prediction of chaotic time series using support vector machine. *Proceedings of IEEE Workshop on Neural Networks for Signal Processing 7, Institute of Electrical and Electronics Engineering*, New York (pp. 511–520) doi:10.1109/NNSP.1997.622433

Olsen, R. S. (1997). Cyclic liquefaction based on the cone penetrometer test. In T. L. Youd, & I. M. Idriss, (Eds.), *Proceedings NCEER Workshop on Evaluation of Liquefaction Resistance of Soils* (pp. 225–276). Buffalo: National Center for Earthquake Engineering Research.

Park, D. J., & Rilett, L. (1999). Forecasting freeway link travel times with a multilayer feed-forward neural network. *Computer-Aided Civil and Infrastructure Engineering, 14*(5), 357–367. doi:10.1111/0885-9507.00154

de Kruif, B. J., & de Vries, T. J. A. (2003). Pruning Error Minimization in Least Squares Support Vector Machines. *IEEE Transactions on Neural Networks, 14*(3), 696–702. doi:10.1109/TNN.2003.810597 PMID:18238050

Bowd, C., Medeiros, F. A., Zhang, Z., Zangwill, L. M., Hao, J., Lee, T.-W., . . . Goldbaum, M. H. (2005). Relevance Vector Machine and Support Vector Machine Classifier Analysis of Scanning Laser Polarimetry Retinal Nerve Fiber Layer Measurements. *Investigative Ophthalmology & Visual Science, 46*(4), 1322–1329. doi:10.1167/iovs.04-1122 PMID:15790898

Phillips, C. L., Bruno, M.-A., Maquet, P., Boly, M., Noirhomme, Q., Schnakers, C., . . . Laureys, S. (2011). Relevance vector machine consciousness classifier applied to cerebral metabolism of vegetative and locked-in patients. *NeuroImage, 56*(2), 797–808. doi:10.1016/j.neuroimage.2010.05.083 PMID:20570741

Majumder, S. K., Ghosh, N., & Gupta, P. K. (2005). Relevance vector machine for optical diagnosis of cancer. *Lasers in Surgery and Medicine, 36*(4), 323–333. doi:10.1002/lsm.20160 PMID:15825208

Robertson, P. K. & Campanella, R. G. (1985). Liquefaction Potential of Sands Using the Cone Penetration Test. *Journal of Geotech. Div., ASCE, 111*(3), 384-407.

Robertson, P. K., & Wride, C. E. (1998). Evaluating cyclic liquefaction potential using the cone penetration test. *Canadian Geotechnical Journal, 35*(3), 442–459. doi:10.1139/t98-017

Seed, H. B., & De Alba, P. (1986). *Use of SPT and CPT tests for evaluating the liquefaction resistance of sands. Use of in situ tests in geotechnical engineering* (p. 6). Geotechnical Special Publication ASCE.

Shahin, M. A., Jaksa, M. B., & Maier, H. R. (2000). *Predicting the Settlement of Shallow Foundations on Cohesionless Soils Using Back-Propagation Neural Networks. Research Report No. R 167.* University of Adelaide.

Silva, C., & Ribeiro, B. (2006). Scaling Text Classification with Relevance Vector Machines. In *Systems, Man and Cybernetics* (*Vol. 5*). Taipei: IEEE. doi:10.1109/ICSMC.2006.384791

Lee, Y.-J., & Mangasarian, O. L. (2001). SSVM: A Smooth Support Vector Machine for Classification. *Computational Optimization and Applications, 20*(1), 5–22. doi:10.1023/A:1011215321374

Stark, T. D., & Olson, S. M. (1995). Liquefaction resistance using CPT and field case histories. *Journal of Geotechnical Engineering*, *121*(12), 856–869. doi:10.1061/(ASCE)0733-9410(1995)121:12(856)

Sun, A., & Lim, E.P., (2002). Web classification using support vector machine. *Proceedings of the 4th international workshop on Web information and data management* (pp. 96 – 99). New York, USA.

Tong, S., & Koller, D. (2001). Support Vector Machine Active Learning with Applications to Text Classification. *Journal of Machine Learning Research*, 2001, 45–66.

Oskoei, M. A., & Huosheng Hu (2008). Support Vector Machine-Based Classification Scheme for Myoelectric Control Applied to Upper Limb. *IEEE Transactions on Bio-Medical Engineering*, *55*(8), 1956–1965. doi:10.1109/TBME.2008.919734 PMID:18632358

Furey, T. S., Cristianini, N., Duffy, N., Bednarski, D. W., Schummer, M., & Haussler, D.(2000). Support vector machine classification and validation of cancer tissue samples using microarray expression data. *Bioinformatics (Oxford, England)*, *16*(10), 906–914. doi:10.1093/bioinformatics/16.10.906 PMID:11120680

Chapelle, O., Haffner, P., & Vapnik, V. N. (1999). Support Vector Machines for Histogram-Based Image Classification. *IEEE Transactions on Neural Networks*, *10*(5), 1055–1064. doi:10.1109/72.788646 PMID:18252608

Suykens, J. A. K., Van Gestel, T., De Brabanter, J., De Moor, B., & Vandewalle, J. (2002). *Least Squares Support Vector Machines*. Singapore: World Scientific.

Suykens, J. A. K., & Vandewalle, J. (1999). Least Squares Support Vector Machine Classifiers. *Neural Processing Letters*, *9*(3), 293–300. doi:10.1023/A:1018628609742

Suykens, J. A. K., Vandewalle, J., & De Moor, B. (2001). Optimal control by least squares support vector machines. *Neural Networks*, *14*(1), 23–35. doi:10.1016/S0893-6080(00)00077-0 PMID:11213211

Tang, X. W., Zhang, X. W., & Uzuoka, R. (2015). Novel adaptive time stepping method and its application to soil seismic liquefaction analysis. *Soil Dynamics and Earthquake Engineering*, *71*, 100–113. doi:10.1016/j.soildyn.2015.01.016

Mitra, V., Wang, C.-J., & Banerjee, S. (2007). Text classification: A least square support vector machine approach. *Applied Soft Computing*, *7*(3), 908–914. doi:10.1016/j.asoc.2006.04.002

Tipping, M. E. (2000). The relevance vector machine. *Advances in Neural Information Processing Systems*, *12*, 625–658.

Valyon, J., & Horvath, G. (2004). A sparse least squares support vector machine classifier. In *Neural Networks* (vol. 1). IEEE. doi:10.1109/IJCNN.2004.1379967

Vapnik, V. N. (1995). *The nature of statistical learning theory*. New York: Springer. doi:10.1007/978-1-4757-2440-0

Vapnik, V. N. (1998). *Statistical learning theory*. New York: Wiley.

Weiss Ron, J., & Ellis Daniel, P. W. (2006). Estimating Single-Channel Source Separation Masks: Relevance Vector Machine Classifiers vs. Pitch-Based Masking. In *ISCA Tutorial and Research Workshop on Statistical and Perceptual Audition: SAPA2006*. Pittsburgh, PA: International Speech Communication Association.

Youd, T. L., & Idriss, I.M. (1997a). Magnitude scaling factors. *Proceedings of NCEER Workshop on Evaluation of Liquefaction Resistance of Soils* (pp. 149–165) Buffalo: National Center for Earthquake Engineering Research.

Yuangui, L., Chen, L., & Weidong, Z. (2006). Improved sparse least-squares support vector machine classifiers. *Neurocomputing, 69*(13–15), 1655–1658.

Zhang, H.F.X., Heller, K.A., Hefter, I., Leslie, C.S., & Chasin, L.A. (2003). Sequence Information for the Splicing of Human Pre-mRNA Identified by Support Vector Machine Classification. *Genome Research, 13*(12), 2637–2650. doi:10.1101/gr.1679003 PMID:14656968

ADDITIONAL READING

Unutmaz, B. (2014). 3D liquefaction assessment of soils surrounding circular tunnels. *Tunnelling and Underground Space Technology, 40*, 85–94. doi:10.1016/j.tust.2013.09.006

Dash, S. R., Govindaraju, L., & Bhattacharya, S. (2009). A case study of damages of the Kandla Port and Customs Office tower supported on a mat–pile foundation in liquefied soils under the 2001 Bhuj earthquake. *Soil Dynamics and Earthquake Engineering, 29*(2), 333–346. doi:10.1016/j.soildyn.2008.03.004

Yu, B., & Xu, Z. (2008). A comparative study for content-based dynamic spam classification using four machine learning algorithms. *Knowledge-Based Systems, 21*(4), 355–362. doi:10.1016/j.knosys.2008.01.001

Lashkari, A., & Latifi, M. (2009). A constitutive model for sand liquefaction under continuous rotation of principal stress axes. *Mechanics Research Communications, 36*(2), 215–223. doi:10.1016/j.mechrescom.2008.08.003

Wu, Q., Law, R., Wu, E., & Lin, J. (2013). A hybrid-forecasting model reducing Gaussian noise based on the Gaussian support vector regression machine and chaotic particle swarm optimization. *Information Sciences, 238*, 96–110. doi:10.1016/j.ins.2013.02.017

Wan, C. H., Lee, L. H., Rajkumar, R., & Isa, D. (2012). A hybrid text classification approach with low dependency on parameter by integrating K-nearest neighbor and support vector machine. *Expert Systems with Applications, 39*(15), 11880–11888. doi:10.1016/j.eswa.2012.02.068

Alham, N. K., Li, M., Liu, Y., & Qi, M. (2013). A MapReduce-based distributed SVM ensemble for scalable image classification and annotation. *Computers & Mathematics with Applications (Oxford, England), 66*(10), 1920–1934. doi:10.1016/j.camwa.2013.07.015

Ehret, B., Safenreiter, K., Lorenz, F., & Biermann, J. (2011). A new feature extraction method for odour classification. *Sensors and Actuators. B, Chemical, 158*(1), 75–88. doi:10.1016/j.snb.2011.05.042

Hwang, J. P., Park, S., & Kim, E. (2011). A new weighted approach to imbalanced data classification problem via support vector machine with quadratic cost function. *Expert Systems with Applications*, *38*(7), 8580–8585. doi:10.1016/j.eswa.2011.01.061

Yang, X., Tan, L., & He, L. (2014). A robust least squares support vector machine for regression and classification with noise. *Neurocomputing*, *140*, 41–52. doi:10.1016/j.neucom.2014.03.037

Abuomar, O., Nouranian, S., King, R., Ricks, T. M., & Lacy, T. E. (2015). Comprehensive mechanical property classification of vapor-grown carbon nanofiber/vinyl ester nanocomposites using support vector machines. *Computational Materials Science*, *99*, 316–325. doi:10.1016/j.commatsci.2014.12.029

Alavi, A. H., & Gandomi, A. H. (2012). Energy-based numerical models for assessment of soil liquefaction. *Geoscience Frontiers*, *3*(4), 541–555. doi:10.1016/j.gsf.2011.12.008

Li, T.-S. (2009). Applying wavelets transform and support vector machine for copper clad laminate defects classification. *Computers & Industrial Engineering*, *56*(3), 1154–1168. doi:10.1016/j.cie.2008.09.018

Li, T.-S. (2009). Applying wavelets transform, rough set theory and support vector machine for copper clad laminate defects classification. *Expert Systems with Applications*, *36*(3), 5822–5829. doi:10.1016/j.eswa.2008.07.040

Cetin, K. O., Unutmaz, B., & Jeremic, B. (2012). Assessment of seismic soil liquefaction triggering beneath building foundation systems. *Soil Dynamics and Earthquake Engineering*, *43*, 160–173. doi:10.1016/j.soildyn.2012.07.021

Xue, H., Wang, H., Chen, P., Li, K., & Song, L. (2013). Automatic diagnosis method for structural fault of rotating machinery based on distinctive frequency components and support vector machines under varied operating conditions. *Neurocomputing*, *116*, 326–335. doi:10.1016/j.neucom.2012.02.048

Azadeh, A., Saberi, M., Kazem, A., Ebrahimipour, V., Nourmohammadzadeh, A., & Saberi, Z. (2013). A flexible algorithm for fault diagnosis in a centrifugal pump with corrupted data and noise based on ANN and support vector machine with hyper-parameters optimization. *Applied Soft Computing*, *13*(3), 1478–1485. doi:10.1016/j.asoc.2012.06.020

Ku C. S., , L D. H., , & Wu J. H., (2004). Evaluation of soil liquefaction in the Chi-Chi, Taiwan earthquake using CPT. *Soil Dynamics and Earthquake Engineering*, *24*(9–10), 659–673.

Chen, S.-J., Chang, C.-Y., Chang, K.-Y., Tzeng, J.-E., Chen, Y.-T., Lin, C.-W., Hsu, W.-C., & Wei, C.-K. (2010). Classification of the Thyroid Nodules Based on Characteristic Sonographic Textural Feature and Correlated Histopathology Using Hierarchical Support Vector Machines. *Ultrasound in Medicine & Biology*, 36(12), 2018-2026.

de la Paz-Marín, M., Gutiérrez, P. A., & Hervás-Martínez, C. (2015). Classification of countries' progress toward a knowledge economy based on machine learning classification techniques. *Expert Systems with Applications*, *42*(1), 562–572. doi:10.1016/j.eswa.2014.08.008

Wu, B., Xiong, Z.-., Chen, Y.-., & Zhao, Y. (2009). Classification of quickbird image with maximal mutual information feature selection and support vector machine. *Procedia Earth and Planetary Science*, *1*(1), 1165–1172. doi:10.1016/j.proeps.2009.09.179

Matsumoto, M., & Hori, J. (2014). Classification of silent speech using support vector machine and relevance vector machine. *Applied Soft Computing*, *20*, 95–102. doi:10.1016/j.asoc.2013.10.023

Ren, Y., Liu, H., Xue, C., Yao, X., Liu, M., & Fan, B. (2006). Classification study of skin sensitizers based on support vector machine and linear discriminant analysis. *Analytica Chimica Acta*, *572*(2), 272–282. doi:10.1016/j.aca.2006.05.027 PMID:17723489

Chang, M., Kuo, C.-., Shau, S.-., & Hsu, R. (2011). Comparison of SPT-N-based analysis methods in evaluation of liquefaction potential during the 1999 Chi-chi earthquake in Taiwan. *Computers and Geotechnics*, *38*(3), 393–406. doi:10.1016/j.compgeo.2011.01.003

Yao, J., Dwyer, A., Summers, R. M., & Mollura, D. J. (2011). Computer-aided Diagnosis of Pulmonary Infections Using Texture Analysis and Support Vector Machine Classification. *Academic Radiology*, *18*(3), 306–314. doi:10.1016/j.acra.2010.11.013 PMID:21295734

Choudhury, A., Nair, P. B., & Keane, A. J. (2006). Constructing a speculative kernel machine for pattern classification. *Neural Networks*, *19*(1), 84–89. doi:10.1016/j.neunet.2005.06.051 PMID:16300928

Gong, G., Lin, P., Qin, Y., & Wei, J. (2012). Dem simulation of liquefaction for granular media under undrained axisymmetric compression and plane strain conditions. *Acta Mechanica Solida Sinica*, *25*(6), 562–570. doi:10.1016/S0894-9166(12)60051-2

Park, J.-G., & Kim, K.-J. (2013). Design of a visual perception model with edge-adaptive Gabor filter and support vector machine for traffic sign detection. *Expert Systems with Applications*, *40*(9), 3679–3687. doi:10.1016/j.eswa.2012.12.072

Ruan, J., Wang, X., & Shi, Y. (2013). Developing fast predictors for large-scale time series using fuzzy granular support vector machines. *Applied Soft Computing*, *13*(9), 3981–4000. doi:10.1016/j.asoc.2012.09.005

Korkmaz, S., Zararsiz, G., & Goksuluk, D. (2014). Drug/nondrug classification using Support Vector Machines with various feature selection strategies. *Computer Methods and Programs in Biomedicine*, *117*(2), 51–60. doi:10.1016/j.cmpb.2014.08.009 PMID:25224081

Rahmani, A., & Pak, A.(2012). Dynamic behavior of pile foundations under cyclic loading in liquefiable soils. *Computers and Geotechnics*, *40*, 114–126. doi:10.1016/j.compgeo.2011.09.002

Unjoh, S., Kaneko, M., Kataoka, S., Nagaya, K., & Matsuoka, K. (2012). Effect of earthquake ground motions on soil liquefaction. *Soil and Foundation*, *52*(5), 830–841. doi:10.1016/j.sandf.2012.11.006

Tian, Y., Ju, X., Qi, Z., & Shi, Y. (2013). Efficient sparse least squares support vector machines for pattern classification. *Computers & Mathematics with Applications (Oxford, England)*, *66*(10), 1935–1947. doi:10.1016/j.camwa.2013.06.028

Shahir, H., Pak, A., Taiebat, M., & Jeremić, B. (2012). Evaluation of variation of permeability in liquefiable soil under earthquake loading. *Computers and Geotechnics*, *40*, 74–88. doi:10.1016/j.compgeo.2011.10.003

Shengxian, C., Yanhui, Z., Jing, Z., & Dayu, Y. (2012). Experimental Study on Dynamic Simulation for Biofouling Resistance Prediction by Least Squares Support Vector Machine. *Energy Procedia, 17*, 74–78. doi:10.1016/j.egypro.2012.02.065

Hamedi, M., Salleh, S.-H., & Noor, A. M. (2015). Facial neuromuscular signal classification by means of least square support vector machine for MuCI. *Applied Soft Computing, 30*, 83–93. doi:10.1016/j.asoc.2015.01.034

Guo, J., Yi, P., Wang, R., Ye, Q., & Zhao, C. (2014). Feature selection for least squares projection twin support vector machine. *Neurocomputing, 144*, 174–183. doi:10.1016/j.neucom.2014.05.040

Kaytez, F., Taplamacioglu, M. C., Cam, E., & Hardalac, F. (2015). Forecasting electricity consumption: A comparison of regression analysis, neural networks and least squares support vector machines. *International Journal of Electrical Power & Energy Systems, 67*, 431–438. doi:10.1016/j.ijepes.2014.12.036

Fokoué, E., Sun, D., & Goel, P. (2011). Fully Bayesian analysis of the relevance vector machine with an extended hierarchical prior structure. *Statistical Methodology, 8*(1), 83–96. doi:10.1016/j.stamet.2010.05.005

Fung, G., , & Mangasarian, O.L. (2003). Finite Newton method for Lagrangian support vector machine classification. *Neurocomputing, 55*(1–2), 39–55.

Li, D.-F., Hu, W.-C., Xiong, W., & Yang, J.-B. (2008). Fuzzy relevance vector machine for learning from unbalanced data and noise. *Pattern Recognition Letters, 29*(9), 1175–1181. doi:10.1016/j.patrec.2008.01.009

Abe, S. (2015). Fuzzy support vector machines for multilabel classification. *Pattern Recognition, 48*(6), 2110–2117. doi:10.1016/j.patcog.2015.01.009

García, S. R., Romo, M. P., & Botero, E. (2008). A neurofuzzy system to analyze liquefaction-induced lateral spread. *Soil Dynamics and Earthquake Engineering, 28*(3), 169–180. doi:10.1016/j.soildyn.2007.06.014

Goh, A. T. C., & Goh, S. H. (2007). Support vector machines: Their use in geotechnical engineering as illustrated using seismic liquefaction data. *Computers and Geotechnics, 34*(5), 410–421. doi:10.1016/j.compgeo.2007.06.001

Cao, Z., Leslie Youd, T., & Yuan, X. (2011). Gravelly soils that liquefied during 2008 Wenchuan, China earthquake, Ms=8.0. *Soil Dynamics and Earthquake Engineering, 31*(8), 1132–1143. doi:10.1016/j.soildyn.2011.04.001

Hanna, A. M., Ural, D., & Saygili, G. (2007, June). Neural network model for liquefaction potential in soil deposits using Turkey and Taiwan earthquake data. *Soil Dynamics and Earthquake Engineering, 27*(6), 521–540. doi:10.1016/j.soildyn.2006.11.001

Hanna, A. M., Ural, D., & Saygili, G. (2007, January 09). Evaluation of liquefaction potential of soil deposits using artificial neural networks. *Engineering Computations, 24*(1), 5–16. doi:10.1108/02644400710718547

Hanna, A. M., Ural, D., & Saygili, G. (2007a). Neural network model for liquefaction potential in soil deposits using Turkey and Taiwan earthquake data. *Soil Dynamics and Earthquake Engineering, 27*(6), 521–540. doi:10.1016/j.soildyn.2006.11.001

Hanna, A. M., Ural, D., & Saygili, G. (2007b). Evaluation of liquefaction potential of soil deposits using artificial neural networks. *International Journal for Computer Aided Engineering and Software, 24*(1), 5–16. doi:10.1108/02644400710718547

Hong, Y. Y., Xiang, Y. W., & Zhong, K. F. (2012). A new image denoising scheme using support vector machine classification in shiftable complex directional pyramid domain

Alonso, J., Villa, A., & Bahamonde, A. (2015). Improved estimation of bovine weight trajectories using Support Vector Machine Classification. *Computers and Electronics in Agriculture, 110*, 36–41. doi:10.1016/j.compag.2014.10.001

García, S.R., Romo, M.P., & Botero, E. (2008). A neurofuzzy system to analyze liquefaction-induced lateral spread. *Soil Dynamics and Earthquake Engineering, 28(3)*, 169–180.

Juang, C.H., Lu, C.-C., & Hwang, J.-H., (2009). Assessing probability of surface manifestation of liquefaction at a given site in a given exposure time using CPTU. *Engineering Geology, 104*(3–4), 223–231.

Kamagata, S., & Takewaki, I. (2015). Non-linear transient behavior during soil liquefaction based on re-evaluation of seismic records. *Soil Dynamics and Earthquake Engineering, 71*, 163–184. doi:10.1016/j.soildyn.2015.01.017

Khozaghi, S.S.H., & Choobbasti, A. J. A. (2007). Predicting of liquefaction potential in soils using artificial neural networks. *Electronic Journal of Geotechnical Engineering, 12*C.

Kunlei, Z., Wenmiao, L., & Marziliano, P. (2013). Automatic knee cartilage segmentation from multi-contrast MR images using support vector machine classification with spatial dependencies

Laroche, D., Tolambiya, A., Morisset, C., Maillefert, J. F., French, R. M., Ornetti, P., & Thomas, E. (2014). A classification study of kinematic gait trajectories in hip osteoarthritis. *Computers in Biology and Medicine, 55*, 42–48. doi:10.1016/j.compbiomed.2014.09.012 PMID:25450217

Mokhtar, A.-S. A., Abdel-Motaal, M. A., & Wahidy, M. M.(2014). Lateral displacement and pile instability due to soil liquefaction using numerical model. *Ain Shams Engineering Journal, 5*(4), 1019–1032. doi:10.1016/j.asej.2014.05.002

Choi, Y.-S. (2009). Least squares one-class support vector machine. *Pattern Recognition Letters, 30*(13), 1236–1240. doi:10.1016/j.patrec.2009.05.007

Cai, G., Liu, S., & Puppala, A. J. (2012). Liquefaction assessments using seismic piezocone penetration (SCPTU) test investigations in Tangshan region in China. *Soil Dynamics and Earthquake Engineering, 41*, 141–150. doi:10.1016/j.soildyn.2012.05.008

Liu, H., Jeng, D.-S. (2007). A semi-analytical solution for random wave-induced soil response and seabed liquefaction in marine sediments. *Ocean Engineering, 34*(8–9), 1211–1224.

Löw, F., Michel, U., Dech, S., & Conrad, C. (2013). Impact of feature selection on the accuracy and spatial uncertainty of per-field crop classification using Support Vector Machines. *ISPRS Journal of Photogrammetry and Remote Sensing, 85*, 102–119. doi:10.1016/j.isprsjprs.2013.08.007

Luts, J., & Ormerod, J. T. (2014). Mean field variational Bayesian inference for support vector machine classification. *Computational Statistics & Data Analysis*, *73*, 163–176. doi:10.1016/j.csda.2013.10.030

Rahman, M. M., Desai, B. C., & Bhattacharya, P. (2008). Medical image retrieval with probabilistic multi-class support vector machine classifiers and adaptive similarity fusion. *Computerized Medical Imaging and Graphics*, *32*(2), 95–108. doi:10.1016/j.compmedimag.2007.10.001 PMID:18037271

Wang, F., Gou, B., & Qin, Y. (2013). Modeling tunneling-induced ground surface settlement development using a wavelet smooth relevance vector machine. *Computers and Geotechnics*, *54*, 125–132. doi:10.1016/j.compgeo.2013.07.004

Clark, A. R. J., & Everson, R. M. (2012). Multi-objective learning of Relevance Vector Machine classifiers with multi-resolution kernels. *Pattern Recognition*, *45*(9), 3535–3543. doi:10.1016/j.patcog.2012.02.025

Xue, T., Bai, L., Chen, S., Zhong, C., Feng, Y., Wang, H., Liu, Z., You, Y., Cui, F., Ren, Y., Tian, J., & Liu, Y. (2011). Neural specificity of acupuncture stimulation from support vector machine classification analysis. *Magnetic Resonance Imaging*, *29*(7), 943–950. PMID:21531109

Daoud, E. A., & Turabieh, H.(2013). New empirical nonparametric kernels for support vector machine classification. *Applied Soft Computing*, *13*(4), 1759–1765. doi:10.1016/j.asoc.2013.01.010

Zhang, Q., Tian, Y., & Liu, D. (2013). Nonparallel Support Vector Machines for Multiple-Instance Learning. *Procedia Computer Science*, *17*, 1063–1072. doi:10.1016/j.procs.2013.05.135

Ye, B., Ye, G., & Zhang, F. (2012). Numerical modeling of changes in anisotropy during liquefaction using a generalized constitutive model. *Computers and Geotechnics*, *42*, 62–72. doi:10.1016/j.compgeo.2011.12.009

Pitilakis, D., Dietz, M., Wood, D. M., Clouteau, D., & Modaressi, A. (2008). Numerical simulation of dynamic soil–structure interaction in shaking table testing. *Soil Dynamics and Earthquake Engineering*, *28*(6), 453–467. doi:10.1016/j.soildyn.2007.07.011

Wang, Z., Lu, Y., & Bai, C. (2011). Numerical simulation of explosion-induced soil liquefaction and its effect on surface structures. *Finite Elements in Analysis and Design*, *47*(9), 1079–1090. doi:10.1016/j.finel.2011.04.001

Lee, L.H., Rajkumar, R., Lo, L.H., Wan, C.H., & Isa, D. (2013). Oil and gas pipeline failure prediction system using long range ultrasonic transducers and Euclidean-Support Vector Machines classification approach. *Expert Systems with Applications*, *40*(6), 1925–1934. doi:10.1016/j.eswa.2012.10.006

Cheng, D., Nguyen, M. N., Gao, J., & Shi, D. (2013). On the construction of the relevance vector machine based on Bayesian Ying-Yang harmony learning. *Neural Networks*, *48*, 173–179. doi:10.1016/j.neunet.2013.08.005 PMID:24055959

Valsamis, A. I., Bouckovalas, G. D., & Papadimitriou, A. G. (2010). Parametric investigation of lateral spreading of gently sloping liquefied ground. *Soil Dynamics and Earthquake Engineering*, *30*(6), 490–508. doi:10.1016/j.soildyn.2010.01.005

Petropoulos, G. P., Kalaitzidis, C., & Prasad Vadrevu, K. (2012). Support vector machines and object-based classification for obtaining land-use/cover cartography from Hyperion hyperspectral imagery. *Computers & Geosciences*, *41*, 99–107. doi:10.1016/j.cageo.2011.08.019

Phillips, C., Bruno, M.-A., Maquet, P., Boly, M., Schnakers, C., Vanhaudenhuyse, A., & Laureys, S. et al. (2011). Relevance Vector Machine" Consciousness Classifier Applied to Vegetative and Locked-in Patients. *NeuroImage*, *56*(2), 797. doi:10.1016/S1053-8119(09)70548-8 PMID:20570741

Wang, Y.-R., Yu, C.-Y., & Chan, H.-H. (2012). Predicting construction cost and schedule success using artificial neural networks ensemble and support vector machines classification models. *International Journal of Project Management*, *30*(4), 470–478. doi:10.1016/j.ijproman.2011.09.002

Jafarian, Y., Sadeghi Abdollahi, A., Vakili, R., & Baziar, M. H. (2010). Probabilistic correlation between laboratory and field liquefaction potentials using relative state parameter index (ξR). *Soil Dynamics and Earthquake Engineering*, *30*(10), 1061–1072. doi:10.1016/j.soildyn.2010.04.017

Rajasekaran, S., Gayathri, S., & Lee, T. L. (2008). Support vector regression methodology for storm surge predictions. *Ocean Engineering*, *35*(16), 1578–1587. doi:10.1016/j.oceaneng.2008.08.004

Ji-yong, S., Xiao-bo, Z., Xiao-wei, H., Jie-wen, Z., Yanxiao, L., Limin, H., & Jianchun, Z. (2013). Rapid detecting total acid content and classifying different types of vinegar based on near infrared spectroscopy and least-squares support vector machine. *Food Chemistry*, *138*(1), 192–199. doi:10.1016/j.foodchem.2012.10.060 PMID:23265476

Phillips, C. L., Bruno, M.-A., Maquet, P., Boly, M., Noirhomme, Q., Schnakers, C., . . . Laureys, S. (2011). Relevance vector machine consciousness classifier applied to cerebral metabolism of vegetative and locked-in patients. *NeuroImage*, *56*(2), 797–808. doi:10.1016/j.neuroimage.2010.05.083 PMID:20570741

Liyang Wei., Yongyi Yang., Nishikawa, R. M., Wernick, M. N., & Edwards, A. (2005). Relevance vector machine for automatic detection of clustered microcalcifications. *IEEE Transactions on Medical Imaging*, *24*(10), 1278–1285. doi:10.1109/TMI.2005.855435 PMID:16229415

Jha, S. K., & Suzuki, K. (2009). Reliability analysis of soil liquefaction based on standard penetration test. *Computers and Geotechnics*, *36*(4), 589–596. doi:10.1016/j.compgeo.2008.10.004

Rezania, M., Javadi, A., & Giustolisi, O., (2010). Evaluation of liquefaction potential based on CPT results using evolutionary polynomial regression. *Computers and Geotechnics*, *37*(1–2), 82–92.

Bao, Y., Ye, G., Ye, B., & Zhang, F. (2012). Seismic evaluation of soil–foundation–superstructure system considering geometry and material nonlinearities of both soils and structures. *Soil and Foundation*, *52*(2), 257–278. doi:10.1016/j.sandf.2012.02.005

Rumpf, T., Römer, C., Weis, M., Sökefeld, M., Gerhards, R., & Plümer, L. (2012). Sequential support vector machine classification for small-grain weed species discrimination with special regard to Cirsium arvense and Galium aparine. *Computers and Electronics in Agriculture*, *80*, 89–96. doi:10.1016/j.compag.2011.10.018

Liang, S., & Sun, Z. (2008). Sketch retrieval and relevance feedback with biased SVM classification. *Pattern Recognition Letters*, *29*(12), 1733–1741. doi:10.1016/j.patrec.2008.05.004

Youn, E., Koenig, L., Jeong, M. K., & Baek, S. H. (2010). Support vector-based feature selection using Fisher's linear discriminant and Support Vector Machine. *Expert Systems with Applications, 37*(9), 6148–6156. doi:10.1016/j.eswa.2010.02.113

Adib, H., Sharifi, F., Mehranbod, N., Kazerooni, N. M., & Koolivand, M. (2013). Support Vector Machine based modeling of an industrial natural gas sweetening plant. *Journal of Natural Gas Science and Engineering, 14*, 121–131. doi:10.1016/j.jngse.2013.06.004

Meier, T. B., Desphande, A. S., Vergun, S., Nair, V. A., Song, J., Biswal, B. B., . . . Prabhakaran, V. (2012). Support vector machine classification and characterization of age-related reorganization of functional brain networks. *NeuroImage, 60*(1), 601–613. doi:10.1016/j.neuroimage.2011.12.052 PMID:22227886

Cervantes, J., Li, X., Yu, W., & Li, K. (2008). Support vector machine classification for large data sets via minimum enclosing ball clustering. *Neurocomputing, 71*(4–6), 611–619. doi:10.1016/j.neucom.2007.07.028

Chau, A. L., Li, X., & Yu, W. (2014). Support vector machine classification for large datasets using decision tree and Fisher linear discriminant. *Future Generation Computer Systems, 36*, 57–65. doi:10.1016/j.future.2013.06.021

Zheng, W., Tian, D., Wang, X., Tian, W., Zhang, H., Jiang, S., He, G., Zheng, Y., & Qu, W.. (2013). Support vector machine: Classifying and predicting mutagenicity of complex mixtures based on pollution profiles. *Toxicology, 313*(2–3), 151–159. PMID:23395826

Güraksın, G. E., Haklı, H., & Uğuz, H. (2014). Support vector machines classification based on particle swarm optimization for bone age determination. *Applied Soft Computing, 24*, 597–602. doi:10.1016/j.asoc.2014.08.007

Suresh, R. D., Bhattacharya, S., & Blakeborough, A. (2010). Bending–buckling interaction as a failure mechanism of piles in liquefiable soils. *Soil Dynamics and Earthquake Engineering, 30*(1–2), 32–39.

Rosado, P., Lequerica-Fernández, P., Villallaín, L., Peña, I., Sanchez-Lasheras, F., & de Vicente, J. C. (2013). Survival model in oral squamous cell carcinoma based on clinicopathological parameters, molecular markers and support vector machines. *Expert Systems with Applications, 40*(12), 4770–4776. doi:10.1016/j.eswa.2013.02.032

Chen, S.-M., & Kao, P.-Y. (2013). TAIEX forecasting based on fuzzy time series, particle swarm optimization techniques and support vector machines. *Information Sciences, 247*, 62–71. doi:10.1016/j.ins.2013.06.005

Shao, Y.-H., Chen, W.-J., Huang, W.-B., Yang, Z.-M., & Deng, N.-Y. (2013). The Best Separating Decision Tree Twin Support Vector Machine for Multi-Class Classification. *Procedia Computer Science, 17*, 1032–1038. doi:10.1016/j.procs.2013.05.131

Gao, X., Chu, C., Li, Y., Lu, P., Wang, W., Liu, W., & Yu, L. (2015). The method and efficacy of support vector machine classifiers based on texture features and multi-resolution histogram from 18F-FDG PET-CT images for the evaluation of mediastinal lymph nodes in patients with lung cancer. *European Journal of Radiology, 84*(2), 312–317. doi:10.1016/j.ejrad.2014.11.006 PMID:25487819

Khader, A. I., & McKee, M.(2014). Use of a relevance vector machine for groundwater quality monitoring network design under uncertainty. *Environmental Modelling & Software*, *57*, 115–126. doi:10.1016/j.envsoft.2014.02.015

Uzuoka, R., Sento, N., Kazama, M., Zhang, F., Yashima, A., & Oka, A. (2007). Three-dimensional numerical simulation of earthquake damage to group-piles in a liquefied ground. *Soil Dynamics and Earthquake Engineering*, *27*(5), 395–413. doi:10.1016/j.soildyn.2006.10.003

Tang, L.-J., Jiang, J.-H., Wu, H.-L., Shen, G.-L., & Yu, R.-Q. (2009). Variable selection using probability density function similarity for support vector machine classification of high-dimensional microarray data. *Talanta*, *79*(2), 260–267. doi:10.1016/j.talanta.2009.03.044 PMID:19559875

Vessia, G., & Venisti, N. (2011). Liquefaction damage potential for seismic hazard evaluation in urbanized areas. *Soil Dynamics and Earthquake Engineering*, *31*(8), 1094–1105. doi:10.1016/j.soildyn.2011.02.005

Moshou, D., Pantazi, X.-E., Kateris, D., & Gravalos, I. (2014). Water stress detection based on optical multisensor fusion with a least squares support vector machine classifier. *Biosystems Engineering*, *117*, 15–22. doi:10.1016/j.biosystemseng.2013.07.008

Xiaoyuan, Z., & Jianzhong, Z. (2013). Multi-fault diagnosis for rolling element bearings based on ensemble empirical mode decomposition and optimized support vector machines. *Mechanical Systems and Signal Processing*, *41*(1–2), 127–140.

Yao, X. J., Panaye, A., Doucet, J. P., Chen, H. F., Zhang, R. S., Fan, B. T., & Hu, Z. D. et al. (2005). Comparative classification study of toxicity mechanisms using support vector machines and radial basis function neural networks. *Analytica Chimica Acta*, *535*(1–2), 259–273. doi:10.1016/j.aca.2004.11.066

Yilmaz, Y., Mollamahmutoglu, Y., Ozaydin, V., & Kayabali, K. (2008). Experimental investigation of the effect of grading characteristics on the liquefaction resistance of various graded sands. *Engineering Geology*, *100*(3–4), 91–100. doi:10.1016/j.enggeo.2007.12.002

Yuan, Y. (2013). Forecasting the movement direction of exchange rate with polynomial smooth support vector machine. *Mathematical and Computer Modelling*, *57*(3–4), 932–944.

KEY TERMS AND DEFINITIONS

Cone Penetration Test: Cone Penetration Test (CPT) is in situ method for determining the geotechnical engineering properties.

Cone Resistance: For any depth the resistance of the cone is called cone penetration resistance (qc). These values can be then correlated to shear strength parameters using proposed empirical curves.

Earthquake: Earthquake is defined as the movements in earth crust which results in sudden shaking of the ground that causes major destruction to life and property.

Least Square Support Vector Machine: Least Square Support Vector Machine (LSSVM) least squares version of SVM. In this, the solutions can be obtained by solving the set of linear equations.

Liquefaction: Liquefaction is the observational fact in which the strength and the stiffness of the soil get reduced as a result of earthquake or dynamic loading.

Peak Ground Acceleration: Peak Ground Acceleration (PGA) is a measure of the acceleration of the ground during earthquake. This is the most important parameter for the designing purpose.

Relevance Vector Machine: Relevance Vector Machine (RVM) uses Bayesian inference to get the solutions for classification and regression problems. It has same functional form of SVM, but provides the probabilistic classification.

Support Vector Machine: Support Vector Machine (SVM) is supervised learning algorithm used for analyzing data and recognizes designs, also used for classification and regression analysis.

Chapter 6

Soft-Computational Techniques and Spectro-Temporal Features for Telephonic Speech Recognition:
An Overview and Review of Current State of the Art

Mridusmita Sharma
Gauhati University, India

Kandarpa Kumar Sarma
Gauhati University, India

ABSTRACT

Speech is the natural communication means, however, it is not the typical input means afforded by computers. The interaction between humans and machines would have become easier, if speech were an alternative effective input means to the keyboard and mouse. With advancement in techniques for signal processing and model building and the empowerment of computing devices, significant progress has been made in speech recognition research, and various speech based applications have been developed. With rapid advancement of the speech recognition technology, telephone speech technology are getting more involved in many new applications of spoken language processing. From the literature it has been found that the spectro-temporal features gives a significant performance improvement for telephone speech recognition system in comparison to the robust feature techniques used for the recognition purpose. In this chapter, the authors have reported the use of various spectral and temporal features and the soft computing techniques that have been used for the telephonic speech recognition.

DOI: 10.4018/978-1-4666-9474-3.ch006

INTRODUCTION

Speech is the vocalized form of communication between one speaker and one or more listeners and is the most effective, reliable and common medium of sending messages in real time systems. Speech is the result of time varying vocal tract system excited by the time varying excitation source signal. According to Information Theory, speech can be represented in terms of its message content, or information. An alternative way of characterizing speech is in terms of signal carrying the message information that is the acoustic waveform. Speech is a natural phenomenon which is easy, fast to communicate and do not require any technical knowledge. The bandwidth of human speech communication is approximately the frequency range up to 7 kHz (O'Shaughnessy, 2000). From the very childhood a human being starts to learn the basic linguistic information without any strict instructions and hence develop a large vocabulary in the brain throughout their lives. The physiology of human speech production is however not an easy process. It requires the co-functioning of biological organs such as the lungs, larynx, pharynx, etc. The human vocal tracts and the articulators are biological organs with non-linear properties whose parameters are largely affected by the factors ranging from gender to upbringing to emotional state. As a result, vocalization is largely influenced by the accent, pronunciation and various other vocal tract parameters (Sarma & Sarma, 2014). With the advent of the speech processing technology the human-machine interaction has become much easier. It is much comfortable on the part of the human being to communicate directly with the machine than to use primitive interfaces such as keyboard, mouse or other pointing devices because of the fact that the primitive interfaces like keyboard and pointing devices require certain amount of skill for their effective usage. In order to use the computer efficiently, apart from a certain level of literacy, the user is also expected to have a sound proficiency in English and a proper typing skill. However, a physically challenged person finds it difficult to use the computer as well the interfacing devices. Further, non-English literate persons also find it difficult to use these interface devices. For a language with dialectal and ethnographic variations, the complexities grow further. These difficulties can be overcome with the speech based interfaces. The interfacing of the human being with the machine with a user friendly interface has always been an important technological issue. This is one of the most widely followed issues in human computer interaction (HCI). Recognition of speech with native content enables the common man to make use of the benefits of information technology and hence facilitates better HCI in a much easier way (Kurian, 2014). Now-a-days, telephone speech technology is getting more acceptance in many new applications of spoken language processing such as Voice Service Centre in hotels and restaurants, voice navigations in traffic and transportation systems, call center support in medical, banking, agriculture etc. sectors and many more. However, there are significant challenges that need solutions while designing system for real time telephone speech recognition with better accuracy. Greater reliability in real time telephonic speech recognition is another constraint often seen while dealing with the speech that comes through a telephone channel. Recording over the telephone lines introduces severe distortions due to the variations in the transmission channels (Zuo, Liu & Ruan, 2003). Speech recognition over the lines has also become an integral part of the various applications of Large Vocabulary Continuous Speech Recognition (LVCSR).

From the literature it has also been found that over the past decades, there has been considerable amount of works done in the field of English Conversational Telephone Speech Recognition (CTSR). Also, India being a country with vast linguistic variations, it provides a sound area of research toward language-specific speech recognition technology. However, not much work has been done in Assamese as well as other north-eastern languages of the country in telephonic speech recognition. This chapter provides certain description related to the basic foundations of spectro-temporal features and applications in telephonic conversation recognition. Speech signals are rich in acoustic variations that contain the textures of emotion, content, individuality and commonality in human vocalization. Mel Frequency Cepstral Coefficient (MFCC) and Perpetual Linear Predictive Coefficient (PLP) features are used to capture the spectral characteristics in the speech signal and the temporal fluctuations may be captured by dynamic delta and delta-delta features as well as by filtering approaches of Temporal Patterns (TRAPs) and Relative Spectra Filtering of Log Domain Coefficients (RASTA). Studies revealed that the auditory cortexes of the mammalian neurons are highly sensitive to specific modulations. These spectro-temporal modulations can be extracted using the 2D Gabor filters. It has also been stated that there is ample need of exploring these spectro-temporal features and their applications in speech recognition. Also, the chapter focuses on the use of soft computing techniques for such purposes. Speech recognition related applications are expanding areas of testing the capabilities of soft computing tools. This is more so for a linguistically rich language like Assamese which is spoken by around 30 million people mostly in north-east India. Some of the basic techniques and reported works have also been included in the chapter.

The rest of the chapter is organized in the following sections. The second section provides an overview of the basic considerations, theoretical background and other related topics that are required to understand Speech Recognition problems. A detailed literature survey of the previous work done related to telephone speech recognition with the implementation of soft computational techniques as well as spectral and temporal features is presented in the third section. The fourth section concludes the chapter.

BASIC CONSIDERATIONS

In order to get a proper understanding of the speech recognition problems, it is necessary to study the basic theoretical considerations of speech recognition and other such related topics. This section provides a brief overview of the basic theoretical considerations related to speech recognition, various feature extraction methods and soft computing techniques.

1. **Speech Recognition Basics:** Speech is the natural way to interact and communicate adopted by human beings with specific characteristics uniquely representing an individual. Speech processing is the study of speech signals and the processing methods of such waveforms. The signals are usually processed in a digital hardware therefore, require an equivalent representation. Speech processing involves the representation of the signal in the given model and then application of some higher level transformation in order to obtain the signal in a more convenient form. The foremost requirement of a speech based application is the design of a robust recognition system so that it enhances HCI and the communication between human and machines (Kurain, 2014).

    Speech recognition can be defined as the ability of a machine or program to identify words or phrases in spoken language and translate it to a machine readable format. It is the process of converting a speech signal into word sequences by implementing computer algorithms or programming. The design of a speech recognition system depends upon the following components: various categories of speech classes, representation and pre-processing, different feature extraction techniques, various classifiers used, database and performance of the system. Speech recognition has been one of the most exciting areas of signal processing. Speech recognition technology has facilitated better HCI and has brought technology closer

Figure 1. Structure of a standard speech recognition system

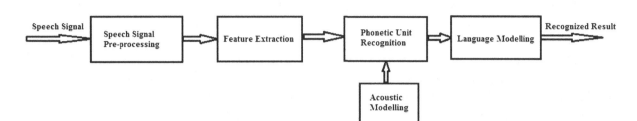

to the common man. It has also made possible for the computer to follow human voice commands and understand various languages. The main objective of speech recognition system is to develop efficient techniques and methods for inputting speech data to machine permitting it to generate interpretation and use such samples for performing certain tasks. It basically means talking to the machine and the machine being able to understand or recognize what is being said. The major advances in the field of speech processing and the development of various statistical tools have lead to the widespread application of speech recognition in various fields such as automatic call processing in telephone networks, and query based information systems that provide updated travel information, stock price quotations, weather reports, data entry, voice dictation, access to information: travel, banking, commands, avionics, automobile portal, speech transcription, support to people with special needs, railway reservations etc (Anusuya & Katti, 2009). Figure 1 shows the basic block diagram for a speech recognition system:

2. **Types of Speech Recognition:** Speech recognition has become a complex and a challenging task because of the variability of the signals. Speech recognition requires certain definitions for its proper understanding. Speech recognition systems can be separated in several different classes by describing the types of utterances that they can recognize. Utterance is the speaking of a word or words that defines a single meaning to the computer. Utterances can be a single word, multiple words, a sentence, or even multiple sentences. The types of speech utterance are as follows:

   a. **Isolated Words:** Isolated word recognizers usually require each utterance to have silence part or absence of audio on both sides of the sample window. This type of recognition system accepts single word or single utterance at a time. These systems have "Listen/Not-Listen" states, where the speakers are required to wait or pause between the utterances.

   b. **Connected Words:** Connect words or connected utterances are same as the isolated words but in connected words a minimal pause is maintained between the utterances of the words.

   c. **Continuous Speech:** In continuous speech recognizers the users are allowed to speak almost in a natural manner. Here the computer determines the content and is basically known as computer dictation.

   d. **Spontaneous Speech:** At a basic level, spontaneous speech can be thought of as speech that is natural sounding and not rehearsed. An ASR system with spontaneous speech should be able to handle a variety of natural speech features such as words being run together, "ums" and "ahs", and even slight stutters (Anusuya & Katti, 2009).

Automatic speech recognition has been playing a vital role in almost every task that involves interfacing with the computer. Some of the common ASR applications can be listed to be dictation, translation, military purposes, domestic appliances, education sector, command and control, telephony, aid to medical/disabilities situation, embedded applications, etc.

3. **Feature Extraction Techniques in Speech Recognition:** Feature extraction can be defined as the method of gaining the useful information of a signal that can represent the signal thereby removing the unwanted information. In short, it can be said to be the process which does analysis of the given input signal. In speech recognition, the main goal of feature extraction is to find a set of properties or feature vectors that have acoustic correlation with the speech sample which can provide a compact representation of the given signal. The objective behind feature extraction is to transform the input signal space to an output signal in a feature space with the help of prior knowledge in order to achieve some desired criteria. Feature extraction in speech processing is necessary to reduce the complexity of the problem before the next stage starts to work with the data. The feature extraction process is usually carried out in three different phases. The first phase is the acoustic analysis of the speech sample where some kind of spectro-temporal analysis is carried out to generate some raw features which describes the envelope of the power spectrum of short speech intervals.

The second phase is comprised of an extended feature vectors which is composed of static and dynamic features. At the last stage these extended feature vectors are transformed into more compact and robust vectors that are then supplied to the speech recognizer (Anusuya & Katti, 2009).

There are various techniques for feature extraction like Mel Frequency Cepstral Coefficients (MFCC), Perceptual Linear Predictive Coefficients (PLP), Relative Spectra Filtering of Log Domain Coefficients (RASTA), Linear Predictive Cepstral coefficients (LPCC), but mostly used technique is MFCC.

a. **Linear Predictive Coding (LPC):** It is a dominant method of determining the basic parameter of speech and can be treated as the linear combination of previous speech samples. LPC is an important tool used in the Audio Signal Processing and also Speech Processing which represents the spectral envelope of a digital speech signal in compressed form with the information of a linear predictive model. The speech signal is analyzed by estimating their formants, their effects are removed and their intensity and frequency are stored or transmitted elsewhere. The speech signal is synthesized by LPC by reversing the process using the buzz parameters and the residue in order to produce a source signal. This process is done in short frames of the speech signal which varies with time. LPC is one of the most powerful speeches analyzing technique which is useful for encoding good quality speech at a low bit rate. It provides an extremely accurate estimate of speech parameters. Figure 2 shows the schematic diagram of LPCC analysis.

    i. **Sampling:** To achieve a better recognition rate, higher sampling frequency or more sampling precision is needed. Commercial speech recognizers typically use comparable parameter values and achieve impressive results.

    ii. **Pre-Emphasis:** The speech waveform which is digitized has a high dynamic range and it suffers from additive noise. So pre-emphasis is applied to spectrally flatten the signal.

Figure 2. Schematic diagram for LPCC analysis

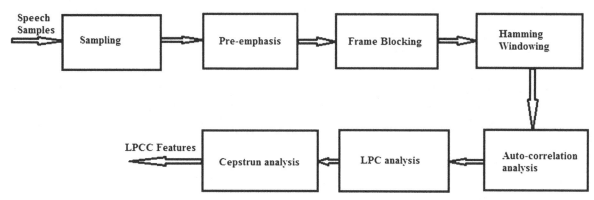

iii. **Frame Blocking:** The speech signal is dynamic or time variant in nature. According to Rabiner, the speech signal is assumed to be stationary when it is examined over a short period of time. In order to analyze the speech signal, it has to be blocked in frames of N samples, with adjacent frames being separated by M samples. If M≡N, then LPC spectral estimates from frame to frame will be quite smooth. On the other hand, if M>N, there will be no overlap between adjacent frames.

iv. **Windowing:** Each frame is windowed in order to minimize the signal discontinuities or the signal is tapered to zero at the starting and ending of each frame. Let the window be defined as $w(n)$ such that

$$y(n) = x(n)w(n), 0 \equiv n \equiv N - 1$$

where $y(n)$ is the windowed output of the signal $x(n)$.

A typical window used is the Hamming window, which has a form given as,

$$w(n) = 0.54 - 0.46 \cos 2n(N - 1), 0 \equiv n \equiv N - 1$$

The value of the analysis frame length N must be long enough so that tapering effects of the window do not seriously affect the result.

v. **Auto-Correlation Analysis:** Auto-correlation analysis can be used to find the fundamental frequency or pitch of the signal. It can also be used to find the correlation between the signal and the delayed version of itself. It can also be used for finding the repeating pattern in a signal or identifying the missing fundamental frequency.

vi. **LPC Analysis:** The LPC parameters can be the LPC coefficients. The method of converting auto-correlation coefficients to LPC coefficients is known as Durbin's method. Levinson Durbin recursive algorithm is used for LPC analysis.

$$E_0 = R_0 \tag{1}$$

$$K_i = R_i - \coprod_j -1_i - 1a_{ij} - 1R_j - \frac{j}{E_i} - 1,1 \equiv i \equiv P \tag{2}$$

$$a_{ii} = K_i \tag{3}$$

$$a_{ii} = a_{ii} - l - K_i a_i - ji - l, l \equiv j \equiv i - 1 \tag{4}$$

$$E_i = \left(1 - K_{12}\right) E_i - 1 \tag{5}$$

The above set of equations is solved recursively for $i = 1,2,...P$ where P PP is the order of the LPC analysis. The K_i are the reflection coefficients. The a_j are the LPC coefficients. The final solution for the LPC coefficients is given as

$$a_j = a_j(P), 1 \equiv j \equiv P \tag{6}$$

vii. **Cepstrum Analysis:** The parametric representations are divided into two groups- those that are based on the Fourier spectrum and the others that are based on the linear prediction spectrum. The first group consists of Mel Frequency Cepstral Coefficients (MFCC) and Linear frequency Cepstral Coefficients (LFCC) while the second group consists of Linear Predictive Coding (LPC), Reflection coefficient (RC) and Cepstral Coefficients derived from LPC. The LPCC are the extension of LPC.

Cepstral features based on short time spectral analysis are the dominant features used in the speaker recognition process. Once the vocal tract filters coefficients $\alpha_i = 1,2,..P$ are estimated by the linear predictive analysis for each frame of speech, the filter coefficients are converted to cepstral coefficients using the following equations

$$C_m = \alpha_m + \sum_{i=1}^{n-1} \frac{i}{m} C_m \alpha_{m-i}, 1 < m \leq P \tag{7}$$

where C_m are the m th coefficient and P are is the order of the LP analysis or the number of LP coefficients (Venkateshwarlu, Raviteja & Rajeev, 2012).

b. **Mel-Frequency Cepstral Coefficient (MFCC):** There are various methods of parametric representation for the acoustic signals. Among them MFCC is the most widely used technique. They are captured from cepstral representation of the audio clip. MFCCs are based on the known variation of the human ear's critical bandwidths with frequency (Yadav & Mukhedkar,

Figure 3. Steps involved in MFCC extraction

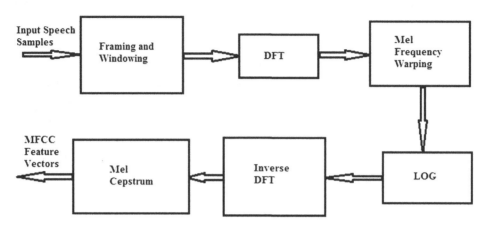

2013). The reason behind the extensive use of MFCC features is that it approximates the human system response more closely than any other system because the frequency bands are positioned logarithmically in MFCC. Figure 3 below shows the steps involved in MFCC feature extraction.

The computation of MFCC vector is based on short term analysis and thus from each frame MFCC vector is computed. To minimize the discontinuities of the input speech sample, Hamming window is applied to the sample to extract the coefficients. It also decreases spectral distortions created by overlapping. Then Discrete Fourier Transform (DFT) is used to generate the Mel filter bank. According to Mel frequency warping, the width of the triangular filters varies and so the log total energy in a critical band around the center frequency is included. After warping the numbers of coefficients are obtained. Finally the Inverse DFT is used for the cepstral coefficients calculation. For phonetically important characteristics, speech signal is expressed in Mel Frequency Scale (C & Radha, 2012). The general formula for calculating MFCC is-

$$Mel(f) = 2595 * \log 10 \left(1 + \frac{f}{700}\right) \tag{8}$$

c.   **Perceptual Linear Prediction (PLP):** PLP is first introduced by H. Hermansky in 1990 and can be said to be the combination of the Discrete Fourier Transform (DFT) and Linear Prediction (LP) techniques. This technique uses concepts from psychophysics of hearing to evaluate more auditory. It has been found in literature that as compared to the conventional LPC, the PLP coefficients are more consistent. The computation of PLP features consists of two main steps. The first step is to get the auditory spectrum and then approximating the spectrum by an all pole model. Auditory spectrum is derived from the speech waveform by critical-band filtering. PLP is more consistent with human hearing is computationally more efficient and functions as low-dimensional representation of speech. This is basically used in speaker independent automatic speech recognition system (Yadav & Mukhedkar, 2013).

4. **Various Speech Recognition Techniques:** There exist three main approaches to Speech Recognition. They are:

    a. **Acoustic Phonetic Approach:** The basis of the acoustic phonetic approaches was postulated by Hedmal and Huges in 1967, which states that there exists finite number of distinctive phonemes in spoken languages. These phonetic units are characterized by a set of acoustic properties. The acoustic properties which represent the phonetic units are highly varying with time because of the co-articulation effect (both with speaker and with neighboring sounds). Despite of the variations in the acoustic properties, it is assumed that the rules governing the acoustic phonetic approach are straight forward and can be easily adapted or learned by a machine. There are various steps involved in the acoustic phonetic approach. The first step deals with the spectral analysis of the speech signal combined with a feature detection technique which converts the spectral measurements to a set of features which describes the acoustic properties of the different phonemes. The next step is the segmentation and labeling of the speech signal into stable acoustic regions followed by attaching one or more phonetic labels to each segmented labels resulting in the formation of a phoneme lattice characterization of the speech sample. In the last step attempts are made to determine a valid word from the phonetic label sequences produced by the segmentation to labeling. The acoustic phonetic approach is not been used commercially to a large extent (Arora & Singh, 2012).

    b. **Pattern Recognition Approach:** The pattern matching approach is used to extract patterns and separate on class from the other. The pattern matching approach involves four essential steps namely feature extraction, pattern training, and pattern matching and decision logic. Well formulated mathematical framework, consistent speech pattern representation, reliable pattern comparison from a set of labeled training samples implementing a training algorithm are the essential features of the pattern recognition approach. In order to test an input pattern a sequence of measurements is made on the input signal thereby creating a reference pattern by taking into consideration one or more test patterns. A speech pattern representation can be in the form of a speech template or a statistical model (e.g. HMM) and can be applied to a sound, word or a phrase. In the pattern comparison stage of the approach, a direct comparison is made between the speech to be recognized and each possible pattern learned in the training stage. The decision logic stage determines the identity of the unknown sample according to the percentage of match between the patterns. The pattern recognition approach has become the prime method for speech recognition in the last six decades. Some of the methods related to this approaches are as follows-

        i. **Template Based Approach:** In this approach a collection of prototypical speech patterns are stored as reference patterns for representing the dictionary of candidates' words. For an unknown utterance, recognition is then carried out by matching the utterance with each of the reference templates and selecting the category of a best matching pattern. The template based approach to speech recognition has provided lots of techniques that have advanced the field considerably during the last six decades. One of the key features of the Template based approach is to derive sequences of speech frames for a pattern implementing some averaging procedure and to use the local spectral distance measures to compare patterns.

ii. **Stochastic Approach:** In Stochastic modeling, the use of probabilistic models is ensured to deal with incomplete and uncertain information. Confusable sounds, speaker variability, contextual effects and homophone words are the sources for the production of uncertain and incomplete information in speech recognition. That is why the stochastic models prove to be suitable for speech recognition. Hidden Markov Model (HMM) is considered to be the most popular stochastic model for speech recognition among the researchers. HMM is characterized by a finite set Markov Model and a set of output distributions. The transition parameters in the Markov models are temporal variability's, while the spectral variability's are the parameters in the output distribution model. In comparison to the template based modeling, the HMM modeling is found to be more general and has a sound mathematical background (Arora & Singh, 2012).

iii. **Dynamic Time Warping (DTW):** The DTW algorithm is used to measure the similarity between two sequences which may vary in time or speed. Linear representation of any data such as video, audio and graphics can be analyzed with DTW. DTW finds its application in Automatic Speech Recognition (ASR) to cope with the different speaking speeds of the speakers. It allows a machine to find an optimal match between two sequences with certain restrictions. Continuity is less important in DWT than in other pattern matching algoritms. For long segments, the DTW algorithm is appropriate for matching the sequences with missing information. The DTW is named so because the optimization process is performed using dynamic programming (Anusuya & Katti, 2009).

iv. **Vector Quantization (VQ):** VQ is very often used in ASR because of its efficient data reduction and its usefulness as Speech Coders. The most successful text independent recognition method uses VQ. The utility of VQ lies in the efficient use of compact codebooks for reference models and codebook searchers instead of more compact costly evaluation methods. In this method, a codebook is produced by grouping the training features of each speaker separately. In the recognition stage an input speech is vector quantized by the reference codebook of the speakers and the VQ distortion of the entire input sample is used for decision making. VQ however does not contain the time information. T. Matsui and S. Furui in their research have found that VQ method is stronger than a continuous HMM method (Anusuya & Katti, 2009).

c. **Artificial Intelligence (AI) Approach:** The AI approach is a hybrid of the acoustic phonetic approach and the pattern recognition approach. It incorporates the concepts of Acoustic Phonetics and pattern recognition methods.

i. **Knowledge Based Approach:** Knowledge based approaches uses the information related to linguistic, phonetic and spectrogram. From the literature, it has been found that for the classification of the speech sounds, recognition systems that use acoustic phonetic knowledge have been developed. Template based approaches proved effective in various speech recognition system but its inability to provide much insight to the human speech processing made error analysis and knowledge based system enhancement difficult. On the other hand, many literatures can be found which provides proper understanding to human speech processing. Design of the knowledge engineering involves the incorporation of the expert knowledge of speech which can be derived from the study of spectrogram and implemented using rules and proper procedure. The disadvantages related to this approach are the difficulty in incorporating expert knowledge and in the integration of human knowledge like phonetics, phonotactic, lexical access, syntax, semantics and pragmatics. This form of knowledge based system however plays an important role in the selection of a suitable input representation, the definition of unit of speech and the design of recognition algorithm (Anusuya & Katti, 2009).

ii. **Connectionist Approach (Artificial Neural Network):** Artificial Neural Network (ANN) also known as Neural Network (Yadav & Mukhedkar, 2013), is similar to the mechanism of the biological neurons where intelligence is applied in visualizing, analyzing and characterizing speech based on certain feature set. This AI approach uses lexical, syntactic knowledge for segmentation and labeling and uses tools like ANN for learning and classification of the phonetic units. Connectionist models also known as ANN or NN rely critically on the availability of good training and learning algorithms. Multi layer Neural Networks can be trained to generate rather complex non-linear classifiers. The basic reason behind the implementation of connectionist model in hardware is its simplicity and uniformity of the processing elements which enables the operation of a net to be simulated efficiently (Anusuya & Katti, 2009).

Neural networks include a large family of methods which are built from simple interconnected units which cooperates in order to implement the global transfer function of the networks. The architecture and dynamics of the neural networks defines the functional form of the network. Complex systems with non-linear transfer functions and sophisticated dynamics can be built with these networks.

Neural Networks which have found its application in many different tasks in several domains have proved its efficiency by effectively learning complex input output mappings. The performance of the neural network however relies upon the theoretical properties as well as the training procedures applied. Neural Networks can be considered as the non-parametric statistical model for function approximation. Several researchers have found that the neural nets can give a desired level of accuracy for most of the usual classes of measurable functions. These systems are trained with effective optimization algorithms in accordance with the performance criterion. Implementation of discriminations, non-linear feature extraction, etc. taking into consideration account context information, can be done with the help of these nets. For very large applications in the field of speech processing, Feed Forward Neural Network (FFNN) and networks with local recurrent connections have been used. Recurrent Neural Networks (RNN) can be used through sophisticated dynamics which can be used for data analysis techniques, pattern recognition, signal and speech processing. RNNs are the natural candidates for capturing the dynamic structure of sequences. Training algorithms are used to estimate the parameters of these systems. Neural Networks are found to have shown very good performance in tasks related to a large variety of classifications. They can be shown to approximate a posteriori probabilities of classes. The discriminative property of these systems enhances its performance in the classification task. Neural networks can also be implemented for the purpose of identification of unknown process or for modeling of signal sources which can be done by training the network to predict the sequences originated from the source. The neural networks also finds its application for clustering or for classification based on the distance to learn reference patterns as in Learning Vector Quantization (LVQ) (Bennani and Gallinari, 1995).

iii. **Support Vector Machine (SVM):** SVM can be considered to be one of the powerful tools for pattern recognition that uses a discriminative approach. SVM uses linear and non-linear hyper-planes for classification of the data. The demerit of SVM approach is

Figure 4. Classification of speech recognition approaches

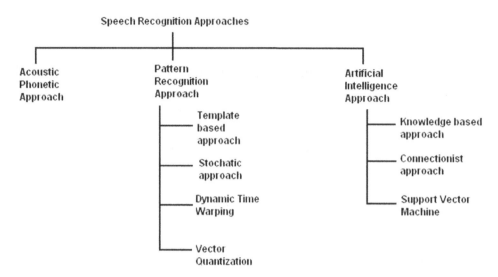

its ability to classify only fixed length data for which it cannot be used for the classification of data having variable length. However the variable length data can be converted to fixed length data before being fed to the SVM for classification. It is a generalized linear classifier with maximum margin fitting function which provides regularization thus allowing the classifier to generalize in a better manner. Unlike the conventional statistical models and Neural Network methods, the SVM controls the model complexity by controlling the VC dimensions of its model (Anusuya & Katti, 2009).

Figure 4 shows the classification of the speech recognition approaches.

5. **Soft Computing Techniques for Speech Recognition:** Soft computing is the collection of computational techniques which finds its application in various fields of engineering disciplines. The major advantage of using soft computational tool is that they can address and analyze many complex problems where conventional methods fail to provide solutions at a low cost. ANN, Fuzzy Logic and Evolutionary Computation (EC) like Genetic Algorithm (GA) are the major components of soft computing. ANN is an information processing model. The basic idea behind the design of the ANN is its biological equivalent which is effective, functional and is extensively used in the human body. The architecture of the ANN consists of highly interconnected neurons working together to model and analyze specific problems. The ANN simulation using software tools has resulted the design of the soft-computational tools that has found its application in wide range of areas. ANN finds real time applications because it can be defined to be a parallel, distributed processor that has a natural capacity of retaining knowledge and thus using that knowledge in the subsequent stages of the experiment. For the last few decades, ANN has been an area of interest for the researchers and is successfully used for solving various problems. Non-linearity, learning capacity, input-output mapping, ability to adapt, neurobiological analogy, etc. is some of the key factors behind the success of the ANN as a soft computational tool. Fuzzy Logic is another soft computational technique which is used to solve the problems related to control system. It was envisaged by Lotfi

Zadef. It deals with imprecise data which are considered as the fuzzy sets. Fuzzy logic finds its application in many control system related problems. GA is yet another adaptive computational algorithm which is designed keeping in view the natural genetic systems. ANN trained with GA provides a more precise and optimal solutions (Nemade & Shah, 2013).

LITERATURE SURVEY OF VARIOUS WORKS DONE RELATED TO OUR TOPIC OF DISCUSSION

A number of works across the globe have been carried out all over the world in the last few decades that deals with the recognition of telephonic speech as well as the use of the spectral and the temporal features implemented on soft computational tools for the recognition purpose.

Review of Previous Work Done for Telephone Speech Recognition using Soft Computing Techniques

The following section provides a detailed survey on the study of the literature related to the work that deals with Telephone Speech Recognition.

1. Yuk and Flanagan (1999), in the paper have mentioned that even the performance of well trained speech recognizers using high quality full bandwidth data also degrades when it is used in the real world environment. In such a situation, telephone speech recognition is of extreme difficulty because of the extreme difficulty due to the limited bandwidth of transmission channels. The authors here have used an ANN based adaptation methods to telephone speech recognition. They have also proposed new supervised model adaptation method which does not require transcriptions and can be used with the ANN. They have found the ANN approach to be advantageous in that the retraining of the speech recognizers for telephone speech is avoided. The authors have also mentioned that the Multi layer Neural Network (MLNN) is able to compute non-linear functions and can accommodate for the non-linear mapping between full bandwidth speech and telephone speech. This method however does not require transcriptions and can be used with Neural Networks. For their work the authors have considered telephone speech and the feature vector is composed of 12 dimensional MFCC, normalized energy and first and second order time derivatives resulting in a 39 dimensional vector for 25 ms Hamming windowed signals in every 10 ms repetition. From the experiments the authors have found that for robust telephone speech recognition the performance improves further when the neural network is combined with additional multi layer training or unsupervised adaptation.

2. With growing research in the field of ASR, such systems have become available for more and more languages. As a result the availability of standardized, multi-lingual speech corpora will increase. These large corpora has facilitated the training and testing of the ASR systems that models language dependencies more accurately then is possible with just language dependent phoneme recognizers. Large corpora facilitate the training of separate male and female models. The use of language dependent word spotters and/or continuous speech recognizers in case of Language Identification (LID) system may help in achieving a better performance rate. Zissman and Singer (1994) in their paper have compared the performance of four different approaches to Automatic

Language Identification (LID) of Telephone speech messages. The four approaches are Gaussian Mixture Model classification (GMM), Language Independent Phoneme recognition followed by Language-dependent Language Modeling (PRLM), parallel PRLM (PRLM-P) and Language Dependent Parallel Phoneme Recognition. From the experiment the authors have found that the system performance is directly related to system complexity and the performance of PRLM-P and PPR systems were found to be best.

3. Zhu, Chen, Morgan and Stolcke (2005), in their paper have discussed the characteristics of MLP based features and their use for the tandem approach. This paper shows that the MLP transformations yield variables that have regular distributions and can be further modified by using logarithmic functions to make the distribution easier to model by a Gaussian-HMM hybrid model. The authors have mentioned that over the last decade the dominant paradigm for speech recognition have incorporated the use of the hybrid structure of GMM and HMM. To get the maximum benefit from the hybrid structure of MLP-HMM and Gaussian-HMM, the tandem approach was proposed in 2001 using modified MLP outputs for a Gaussian-HMM model. One of the advantages is that two or more such feature vectors can be easily combined without increasing the feature dimension. The authors have also mentioned that even when large amount of training data, discriminant training and other system enhancements are used, MLP based features can improve ASR performance on a large conversational telephone speech recognition task. MLP based features provide a data driven front end approach to feature extraction which further improves discrimination and provides ease of modeling. When properly used, the MLP based features can improve automatic speech recognition performance in the conversational telephone speech recognition by significantly reducing the errors from 5% to 9%.

4. Hagen and Neto (2003) have developed an automatic speech recognizer for Portuguese telephone speech which is a state-of-art HMM/MLP hybrid system. Various kind of robust acoustic features have been employed in the system proposed in the work. The recorded speech signals are highly influenced by the quality of the microphone used for the purpose and also recording over the telephone line introduces large amount of distortions due to the telephony transmission channels. The authors have mentioned that with large number of advanced telephone gadgets available now-a-days, these distortions are hard to predict. The availability of large, telephone recorded database is also an important in research and development of a competitive speech recognizer for teleservice application. Another important factor as mentioned by the authors is the use of reliable feature set in the design of an automatic speech recognition system. In their work, the authors have investigated three feature streams which have served their purpose. The features investigated are 12 PLP cepstra and the log energy, 12 RASTA-PLP cepstra and the log energy and 28 Modulation Spectrogram (MSG) features, which were extracted on windows of 20 ms with a 10 ms frame shift. The extraction of the PLP and the RASTA-PLP features took place from the auditory spectrum after filtering the power spectrum with trapezoidal shaped filters applied at intervals equal to loudness pre-emphasis and cube root compression. 13 cepstral coefficients are calculated for cepstral analysis. After decomposition of the spectrum into critical bands, an additional filtering is applied for the RASTA-PLP features. The low modulation frequencies which are the result of the channel effects rather that the speech characteristics, are suppressed by the RASTA filter. For the extraction of the MSG features the frequency domain is divided into ¼ octave bands resulting into 14 bands, each of which is filtered with two modulation frequency pass bands. The concatenation of these two sets of 14 coefficients gives the MSG feature vector of 28 coefficients.

5. Gajsek, Zibert and Mihelic (2008) in their work have evaluated different techniques of acoustic modeling for speech recognition in the case of limited audio resource. As mentioned, the objective of their work was to develop different set of acoustic models that was first trained on a small set of telephone speech samples and then adapted to a different audio environment. Different adaptation methods such as Maximum Likelihood Linear Regression (MLLR), Maximum a Posteriori Adaptation (MAP) were examined in combination with various feature sets like MFCC, PLP and Revised Perceptual Linear Prediction coefficients (RPLP). The authors have shown that using different adaptation methods that are used mainly for the speaker adaptation purpose can increase the robustness of speech recognition in case of mismatched training and working acoustic environment conditions. They have mentioned that the performance of a speech recognizer in applications where speech input is acquired through telephone line is more crucial because of the fact that the error rates are higher compared to the systems that are designed to work in a studio like environment. The lack of sufficient amount of telephone speech can be a problem for training acoustic models, also acquiring a large amount of telephone recordings would be time consuming. From the experiment the authors have gone through the recognition of phonemes and have found that the PLP features gives a better performance than the MFCC features while dealing with samples in the noisy environment. They have also mentioned that the combination of RPLP and MAP adaptation were a suitable approach.

6. Mporas, Ganchev and Fakotakis (2008) have reported a recent progress in development of dialect recognition system for the standard Modern Greek and Cypriot dialect of Greek language. The authors here have relied upon a compound recognition scheme where the outputs of multiple phone recognizers trained on different European language are combined. They have found that the scheme have provided a higher recognition accuracy than the main stream phone recognizer. The evaluation results reported by the authors here indicate high recognition accuracy up to 95% which makes the proposed solution a feasible one with addition to the existing spoken dialogue systems such as voice banking applications, call routes, voice portals, etc. As mentioned, one of the challenging research area related to Language Identification (LID) is Dialect Identification (DID), where the system is supposed to identify correctly one among the different dialects of a given language from a spoken utterance. The authors have also added that the most successful approach for the Language Identification (LID) and Dialect Identification (DID) is the phonotactic approach where the speech signal is decomposed to its corresponding phone sequence and further fed as input to the dialect specific language models. The language models then recognizes the dialects with the maximum probability score. The decomposition of the speech signal into phonetic sequence can be achieved by using a single phone recognizer followed by the target language models (PRLM) or using parallel phone recognizers (PPRLM). In present day speech recognition, large corpora of speech database is used which helps in the creation of the statistical models of speech. However, collection of such large database is a major constraint. As a consequence the speakers are not in a position that would allow them to comfortably take advantage of the modern day technology. The authors have also mentioned that the use of combined phone recognition scheme improves dialect identification rates when compared to the use of the mainstream phone recognizer alone.

7. Automatic recognition of spoken alphabets proves to be one of the difficult areas of computer speech recognition. Various researchers have targeted the field of automatic speech recognition with spoken alphabets for different languages as there are of research. Alotaibi, Alghamdi and Alotaiby (2010) in their work have investigated spoken Arabic alphabets from the speech recognition point of view.

They have designed a system to recognize spelling of an isolated word where HMM toolkit (HTK) is used to implement the isolated word recognizer with phoneme based HMM models and MFCCs were used as the feature set. The HMM Toolkit is a portable toolkit for building and manipulating HMM models which is mainly used for the designing, testing and implementation of ASR. In the training and the testing phase of their system they have used isolated alphabets data sets from the telephony Arabic Speech Corpus. The authors have designed an HMM based speech recognition system and tested the same with Automatic Arabic alphabets recognition. ASR researchers in general targets the spoken alphabets for different languages. HMM is considered to be a widely used statistical tool for characterizing the spectral features of speech frame which started gaining popularity in the mid 1980's. The HMM method provides a natural and highly reliable way of recognizing speech for a wide range of applications.

8. Rodriguez et al. (1997) in their have presented a speaker recognition voice based system. The recognition rates obtained by the system was found to be around 93% for microphone recorded speech and that for the speech that came from a telephone line was found to be 90%. In their work the authors have developed a speaker verification voice system based on HMM/GMM hybrid model. The authors here have mentioned the use of security systems when accessing services through the network communications and the need of improving it. The use of own user characteristics such as fingerprints, voice, etc. can prove to be a reliable means for such security systems. In their experiment the authors have extracted the spectral features from the sample speech and modeled them in a statistical way. The speech sample is isolated from the noisy background and the spectral representations are modeled by a function density of probability (Fdp). The spectral envelope is then fitted to a number of Gaussian. A model for each user is created and stored in the database and is ready for future use whenever accessed by the users. They have mentioned that the task of speaker identification through telephone line is a difficult one as the recognition accuracy decreases because of the fact that telephone channel introduces noise and distortion in the communication channel.

9. Kundu and Bayya (1998) have discussed the use of an integrated HMM/NN classifier for speech recognition which combines the time normalization property of the HMM classifier with the superior discriminative ability of the ANN classifier. The authors have mentioned that the ANN has been successful in many classification problems but the success rate as compared to HMM is secondary in the field of speech recognition because of the lack of time normalization characteristics of most neural net structures. In their proposed hybrid HMM/ANN classifier, the authors have used a left to right HMM module to segment the observation sequence into a fixed number of states. All the frames belonging to the same state are then replaced by one average frame. In this way every sample is converted into a static pattern. The ANN is then used as a classifier. The proposed system was tested using some telephone speech database.

10. Gauvain et al. (2003) have described the development of a speech recognition system for the processing of telephone conversations. They have identified the major changes and improvements in acoustic and languages modeling that are basic requirement for achieving the state-of-art performance in conversational telephonic speech. As mentioned some of the major changes on the acoustic side are the use of speaker normalization, channel variability, efficient speaker adaptation and better pronunciation modeling. On the other hand the limited amount of language model training data is the major challenge in the linguistic side. The authors have used a data selection technique and a smoothing technique based on a neural network language model in order to cope with the acoustic as well as the linguistic sides of speech recognition system.

11. Hwang et al. (2004) in their work have presented their effort to extend language independent technologies into Mandarin Conversational Telephone Speech (CTS) as well as addressing language dependent issues such as tone. In their paper they have shown the impact of the following factors such as simplified Mandarin phone set, pitch features, auto retrieved web text for augmenting n-gram training, speaker adaptive training, maximum mutual information estimation, decision tree based parameter sharing, cross word co-articulation modeling. They have also used a combination of MFCC and PLP features in their work which have helped in reducing the Chinese character error rate (CER). Further, the authors have stated that improvement of CER can be obtained by taking into consideration all the improvements.

12. Glass and Hazen (1998) have developed a telephone based speech recognizer as a part of a conversational system in the weather information domain called JUPITER which can be used to query a relational database of current weather conditions using natural, conversational speech. Here the authors have collected the data by recording conversations from local telephone handsets in different environments which have been used as a source of both recognition and understanding errors. The recognizer developed by the authors has however proved to be effective and can be improved further by increasing the database.

13. Zuo, Liu and Ruan (2003) in their paper have mentioned that speech recognition over the lines plays an important role in various applications of Large Vocabulary Continuous speech Recognition (LVCSR). The authors describe an implementation system completely in software form to produce simulated telephone data form clean databases. The experimental results show the effectiveness and feasibility of the software simulation. The authors in their experiment have focused on the simulation of frequency characteristics of analogue facilities and different noise behaviors in telephone transmission channel. The authors by controlling the parameters have approximated clean speech to different actual telephone situations which provides an operable and economical solution to the problem on insufficiency of real telephone data.

14. Mary and Yegnanarayana (2008) in their work have examined the effectiveness of prosodic features for language identification. Prosodic differences among the various languages of the world include variation in the intonation, rhythm and stress. The variations in the prosodic differences can be represented by using features derived from fundamental frequency (F0) contour, duration and energy contour. In their experiment, the authors have extracted the prosodic features by segmenting the speech samples into syllable-like units by locating vowel-onset points (VOP) automatically. Various parameters are derived to represent F0 contour, duration and energy contour characteristics for each syllable-like unit. The features obtained by concatenating the parameters derived from the three consecutive syllable-like units were used to represent the prosodic characteristic of a language. The prosodic features thus derived from different languages were used to train a Multi Layer Feed Forward Neural Network (MLFFNN) classifier for language identification which was found to be effective by the authors when verified using the multi language telephone speech corpus.

15. Reynolds and Rose (1995) in this paper have introduced the use of Gaussian Mixture Model (GMM) for robust text independent speaker identification. The authors have mentioned that the individual Gaussian component of a GMM represents some general speaker dependent spectral shapes that are effective for modeling speaker identity. In their work the authors have concentrated on the application part that requires a very high recognition rate using short utterance from unconstrained conversational speech and robustness to degradations produced by transmission over a telephone channel. They have performed their experiment taking into consideration 49 speakers and conver-

sational telephone speech database. Algorithmic issues like initializations, variance limiting, model order selection and spectral variability robustness techniques, large population performance and comparisons to other speaker modeling techniques like uni-modal Gaussian, Vector Quantization (VQ) codebook, tied Gaussian mixture and radial basis functions were examined in their experiment. The results obtained were as follows- the Gaussian mixture speaker model attains an identification accuracy of 96.8% using 5 seconds clean speech utterance and 80.8% identification accuracy using 15 seconds telephone speech utterance with a 49 speakers population. The authors have found that their technique have outperformed the other speaker modeling techniques on an identical 16 speaker telephone speech task.

16. In this paper, Wegmann, McAllaster, Orloff and Peskin (1996) have reported a simplified system for determining vocal tract normalization. The authors have mentioned that such normalization have led to significant gains in recognition accuracy by reducing variability among speakers and allowing the pooling of training data and the construction of the shaper models. As mentioned, it has been an extremely cumbersome task to determine the warp scale by the standard method which requires multiple recognition passes. The authors have therefore presented a new system for warp scale selection which uses a simple generic voiced speech model to rapidly select appropriate frequency scales. The selection is sufficiently streamlined that it can be moved completely into the front end processing. The authors have used this system on a standard test of the switchboard corpus and have achieved a relative reduction of the word error rates (WER) of 12% over un-normalized gender independent models and 6% over the un-normalized gender-dependent models.

17. In the paper Zissman (1996) the author has compared the performance of four approaches for automatic language identification of speech utterances. The approaches were Gaussian mixture model (GMM) classification, single language phone recognition followed by language dependent, interpolated n-gram language modeling (PRLM), parallel PRLM which uses multiple single language phone recognizers each trained in different language and language dependent parallel phone recognition (PPR). These approaches which span a wide range of training requirements and levels of recognition complexity were evaluated with the Oregon Graduate Institute Multi-language Telephone speech corpus. The authors from their experiment have found that the systems containing phone recognizers performed better that the simpler Gaussian mixture model classifier and also the parallel PRLM system was found to be the top performing system.

Table 1 summarizes some of the relevant works depicting the use of composite classifiers and spectral as well as temporal features like MFCC, PLP, and PCA etc. It also highlights the use of prosodic features and certain composite features for performing tasks like classification and identification. The recognition rate for the performed tasks ranges between 60% to 95% approximately. It has also been reported that there has been a significant improvement in the WER using the above mentioned approaches.

Literature Review of Previous Work Done for Telephone Speech Recognition using Spectral and Temporal Features

Studies in the Neuroscience have revealed that neurons in the mammalian auditory cortex are highly tuned to specific spectro-temporal modulations. Humans are highly sensitive to temporal modulation frequencies up to 16 Hz and spectral modulation frequencies up to 2 cycles per octave. There is a need to explore the saliency of spectro-temporal features in different environment as well as methods that allow the dynamic selection of these features (Zhao and Morgan, 2008).

Table 1. Summary of works depicting the use of composite classifiers and spectral, temporal, and composite features

SL No.	Authors	Database	Feature Parameters	Algorithm Model	Task Performed	Reference
1	Yuk, Flanagan	3,696 utterances, TIMIT	12 Dimensional Mel Frequency Cepstral oefficients (MFCC)	HMM, MLNN	Recognition	(Yuk and Flanagan, 1999)
2	Zissman, Singer	The Oregon Graduate Institute Telephone Speech Corpus (OGI-TS)	Centisecond mel scale cepstra and delta cepstra, RASTA	GMM, PRLM-P, PRLM, PPR	Identification	(Zissman and Singer, 1994)
3	Zhu, Chen, Morgan, Stolcke	Switchboard Corpus	MLP features, PLP	MLP, HMM	Recognition	(Zhu, Chen Morgan and Stolcke, 2005)
4	Hagen, Neto	Portuguese SPEECHDAT Database	12 PLP Cepstra and the log energy, 12 RASTA-PLP Cepstra and the log energy, 28 Modulation Spectrogram features (MSG)	HMM/MLP Hybrid System	Recognition	(Hagen and Neto, 2003)
5	Rodriguez, Ruiz, Crespo, Gracia	Recorded Speech Database (Carlos III and Polycode II)	10 Mel Cepstrums, 10 differential Mel Cepstrums, the energy and the differential energy	HMM/ GMM Hybrid model	Verification	(Rodriguez, Ruiz, Crespo and Gracia, 1997)
6	Kundu, Bayya	Discretely spoken telephone digit corpus compiled by Bellcore	10 MFCC coefficients and 10 Delta MFCC coefficients	Integrated HMM/NN Classifier	Recognition	(Kundu and Bayya, 1998)
7	Glass, Hazen	Telephone Based Weather information system (JUPITER)	MFCC, Principal Component Analysis (PCA)	Bigram and trigram language model	Recognition	(Glass and Hazen, 1998)
8	Zissman	Oregon Graduate Institute (OGI) multi language telephone speech corpus, NTIMIT	Mel-cepstral coefficients	GMM, PRLM, PRLM-P, PPR	Identification	(Zissman, 1996)
9	Ganapathy, Thomas, Hermansky	HTIMIT database	Autoregressive models of Hilbert Envelopes	Hybrid HMM-ANN model	Recognition	(Ganapathy, Thomas and Hermansky, 2010)
10	Rao, Koolagudi	Hindi Dialect Speech corpus and IIT Kharagpur-Simulated Emotions Hindi Speech Corpus (IITKGP-SEHSC)	MFCC, Duration of Syllables, Pitch and Energy Contour	Auto Associative Neural Network (AANN) Support Vector Machine (SVM)	Identification	(Rao and Koolagudi, 2011)
11	Bouvrie, Ezzat, Poggio	TIMIT database	2D- Discrete Cosine Transform (2D-DCT)	Regularized Least Square (RLS) classifiers and SVM	Classification	(Bouvrie, Ezzat and Poggio, 2008)

Various researchers across the globe have also reported the use of spectral and temporal features with the implementation of soft computational tools for speech recognition purpose. Some of the previous works in relation to this has been discussed below-

1. Ruske (1982) in his paper has presented an Automatic Speech Recognition system which starts from a demi-syllable segmentation of a speech signal. A set of Spectral and temporal acoustic features, which are automatically extracted from LPC spectra and ensemble as one feature vector for each demi-syllable, are used for recognition of the segments. The feature vector used in the experiment is composed of 24 components which consists formants, formant loci, formant transitions, formant like links for characterization of the nasals, liquids or glides, the spectral distribution of fricative noise or bursts (turbulences) and duration of pauses. In this paper the author have not used any context dependent rules by the feature extraction procedures. The author has mentioned that as long as no context dependent rules are applied, the feature representation can be considered as the reduction of the dimension of the speech segment into low dimensional subspace where the feature vector components represents the co-ordinates in the subspace. It is expected by the author that the dependencies between the feature components can be accounted for by statistical evaluation of a training set of demi-syllables. The transformation of the features is highly non linear because of the threshold decision which could be reduced by calculating the degree of similarity. As mentioned by the author, the advantage of this method lies in the feature vector size. The feature vector for a complete demi-syllable has only 24 components where as a spectral-temporal demi-syllable segment need a component of size 200 which have to be further compared by appropriate distance measurement.

2. Ganapathy, Thomas and Hermansky (2010) in their work have presented a robust spectro-temporal feature extraction technique using Autoregressive (AR) models of sub band Hilbert envelopes. Frequency Domain Linear Prediction (FDLP) is used to derive the AR models of Hilbert envelopes. The spectral features are derived by integrating the sub-band Hilbert envelopes in short term frames and the temporal features are formed by converting the envelopes into modulation frequency components. The spectral and the temporal features are then combined in the later stage and the composite feature set is used as the input feature vector for the recognition purpose. For the proposed features, robustness is achieved by using novel techniques of noise compensation and gain normalization. For their work the authors have used telephone speech in the HTIMIT database and found that the proposed feature set when compared to other robust feature techniques provides considerable improvements for phoneme recognition tasks in noisy environment.

3. It has mostly been found that the state-of-art speech recognition systems use the MFCCs as the acoustic features for the recognition purpose. Sharifzadeh, Serrano and Carrabina (2012) in their work have proposed a new discriminative analysis of acoustic features based on spectrogram analysis. The authors in their experiment have considered both the spectral and temporal variations of speech signal. They have found that considering both the variations has helped the recognition performance to improve especially in case of noisy situation and phonemes with time domain modulations.

4. Bouvrie, Ezzat and Poggio (2008) in their paper have presented a novel speech feature analysis technique which is based on localized spectro-temporal cepstral analysis of speech. They have extracted the localized 2D patches from the spectrogram and projected onto a 2-D Discrete Cosine (2D DCT) basis. A set of feature vector is then formed by concatenating the low order 2D DCT coefficients from the set of corresponding patches for each time frame. The authors have stated that

their framework has significant advantages over the standard one dimensional MFCC features. They have found that their features are more robust to noise and better capture temporal modulations that are important for recognition of plosive sounds. Extraction of localized spectro-temporal patches and low dimensional spectro-temporal tuning using the 2D-DCT are the two main steps presented by the authors for feature analysis. They have also mentioned that even features incorporating more temporal information per frame is not sufficient, both time and frequency localization is necessary.

5.   Hermansky and Sharma (1999) have proposed a new approach to process temporal information for ASR. The authors have studied the use of long time Temporal Patterns (TRAPS) of spectral energies instead of the conventional spectral patterns for ASR and have mentioned that the neural TRAPs that have been used in their experiment have been found to yield significant amount of complementary information to that of the conventional spectral features. In the experiment the authors have used two datasets one of which is the telephone quality conversational speech. They have provided a complete ASR system based on the concept of independent processing of temporal trajectories and showed that the system is competitive with the current conventional ASR system. They have also mentioned that the complementary information provided by the TRAP system can be further used to improve robustness of ASR by using the TRAP system in combination with the conventional system.

6.   Xu and Zheng (2007) stated that due to the fact that the cochlear implant users receive limited spectral and temporal information, their speech recognition deteriorates to a great extent in noise. The authors in their work have determined the relative contributions of spectral and temporal cues to speech recognition. From their experiment they have found that increased spectral information can improve vowel recognition in noise whereas increased temporal information does not improve phoneme recognition in noise. They have also mentioned that increasing the effective number of channels may help in improving speech recognition in noisy environment for cochlear implant users.

7.   It has been found that the transcription of conversational speech from telephone data as well as in-person interactions has remained a challenging task. Chen, Zhu and Morgan (2005) in their paper have developed a technique to incorporate long term temporal features using Multi Layer Perceptrons (MLP). In their experiments the authors have used widened acoustic context by using more number of frames of full band speech energies as input to the MLP They have also compared the approach with a more constrained two stage approach that first focuses on long term temporal patterns in each critical band separately and later combines them together. They have mentioned that the two stage approach utilizes hidden activation values of MLPs trained on the log critical band energies (LCBEs) of 51 consecutive frames. From their experiment they have found that combining the two stage approach with the conventional short term features significantly reduces the word error rates. The authors have also mentioned that explicitly computing new and complementary functions of the time frequency plane has the potential of changing the performance of the recognizers for these difficult tasks.

8.   Rosen (1992) in his work have mentioned that the temporal properties of speech appear to play a major role in linguistic contrasts. The author has developed a framework of acoustic structure of speech which is based on purely temporal aspects. Envelope, Periodicity and Fine structure are said to be the three main temporal features comprised by speech. In his work the author have also discussed the usability of these three temporal features related to hearing impaired and normal listeners.

9. Speech can be said to be one of the most interesting and complex sounds which is dealt by the auditory system. Young (2008) in his paper said that the need of neural representation is to capture those features of signals on which the brain depends on language communication. Here the author has represented the speech in the auditory nerve and central nervous system from the perspective of neural coding of important aspects of signal. The representation is tonotopic, meaning that the speech is decomposed by frequency and different frequency components are represented in different populations of neurons. The author has also mentioned that the frequencies into which the speech signal is decomposed are used to represent different populations of neurons.

10. Rao and Koolagudi (2011) have studied speech features for dialects, which is the distinguishable variety of a language spoken by a group of people, and emotion recognition in Hindi language. The emotions considered are anger, disgust, fear, happy, neutral and sad. The authors have used prosodic features such as duration of syllables, pitch and energy contour and spectral features i.e. mel frequency cepstral coefficients (MFCC) for their purpose. Auto-associative neural network (AANN) models and Support Vector Machine (SVM) are used for recognition of the dialects and emotions respectively. The AANN models captures the non-linear information related to emotions and dialects whereas the SVM classifies the dialects and the emotions based on the discriminative features present among them. The recognition rates obtained are 81% and 78% respectively for dialects and emotion recognition. From the experimentally derived results the authors have concluded that the prosodic features contain more dialect specific information than spectral features.

11. Hanson and Applebaum (1990) discusses speaker independent recognition of Lombard and noisy speech by a recognizer trained with normal speech where static, dynamic and accelerating features were used for representing the speech. The authors have found strong interactions between the temporal features, the frequency differentiation due to cepstral weighting, and the degree of smoothing in the spectral analysis. From the experiment the author concluded that the dynamic and accelerating features gave better performance than the static features.

12. Reddy, Maity and Rao (2013) have explored the spectral and prosodic features extracted from different levels for analyzing the language specific information present in speech. Frame wise calculation of the pitch cycle and the glottal closure regions were done to extract the spectral features. Prosodic features extracted from syllable, tri-syllable and multi-word levels were proposed in addition to the spectral features for capturing the language specific information. The authors have represented the language specific prosody by intonation, rhythm and stress features at syllable and tri-syllable levels. They have also represented the prosodic features at the multi-syllable level by temporal variations in frequency (F0) and temporal variations in intensities. Language specific information may be present in the speech signal at various levels. Speech features such as the spectral or acoustic, phonetic, phonotactic and prosody are used to discriminate the language at the lower level, whereas at the higher level, the discrimination of the language is based on the morphology, syntax and semantics of the speech. The authors have used the Gaussian mixture models (GMM) for capturing the language specific information in their work. The experimental conclusion says that with the combination of features the performance of language identification can be improved manifold.

13. Koolagudi and Krothapalli (2012) have used the spectral features from the sub-syllabic regions and pitch synchronous analysis for speech emotion recognition. The authors have used LPCC, MFCC and feature extracted from high amplitude regions of the spectrum to represent emotion specific spectral information. They have extracted these features from consonants, vowels and transition

regions of each syllable to study the contribution of these regions towards emotions recognition of speech. Consonants, vowels and the transition regions are determined by using the vowel onset point. The spectral features extracted from each pitch cycles are also used for the recognition of the emotions present in the speech samples. Anger, fear, sad, happy and neutral are the types of emotions dealt with by the authors in their study. The authors have compared the results of emotion recognition using sub-syllabic speech segments with the conventional block processing approach where the speech samples are processed frame by frame. They have developed the emotion recognition system by using the Gaussian Mixture Models (GMM) and auto associative neural networks. From the experimental results the authors have concluded saying that formant features combined with spectral features have always improved the emotion performance.

14. Studies from the Physiological and Psychoacoustic fields reveal that spectrally and temporally localized time-frequency envelope patterns provides a base for auditory perception. This in-turn motivates new approaches in the feature extraction process for automatic speech recognition which utilizez two dimensional spectro-temporal modulation filters. Kleinschmidt (2003) has provided a brief overview on the work related to Localized spectro-temporal features (LSTF). The author further focuses on the Gabor feature approach where a feature selection scheme is applied to automatically obtain a suitable set of Gabor features for future implementation. The statistical properties of these feature sets are further analyzed and are examined in ASR experiments with respect to their robustness.

15. Thomas, Ganapathy and Hermansky (2008) have presented a spectro-temporal feature extraction technique using sub-band Hilbert envelope of relatively long segments of speech signals. Hilbert envelopes of the sub bands are estimated using Frequency Domain Linear Prediction (FDLP). Spectral features are derived by integrating the sub band Hilbert envelopes in short term frames and the temporal features are found by converting the FDLP envelopes into modulation frequency components. These components are then combined and used as the input features in the later stage. The authors have mentioned that the phoneme recognition system on telephone speech shows significant performance improvements for the proposed features when compared to the robust feature techniques used for speech recognition problems.

16. The acoustic representation of speech signal is based on the short time analysis of the spectral features over windows of 10-30 ms. Any information below this time scale is considered to be lost and also the temporal structures above these time is weakly represented. To overcome this limitation, Ellis and Athineos (2003) in their work have proposed a novel representation of the temporal envelope in different frequency bands by exploring the dual of conventional Linear Prediction Coefficients (LPC) when applied in the transform domain. In the techniques of Frequency Domain Linear prediction (FDLP), the poles of the model describe the temporal peaks rather that the spectral peaks. The procedure automatically distributes the poles to model the temporal features within the windows used. The authors here have performed the experiment by taking into consideration one amongst the various speech features offered by the approach. They have considered an index describing the sharpness of individual poles within a window frame and have achieved a relatively large word error rate (WER) improvement from 4.97% to 3.81% in a recognizer trained on general conversational telephone speech and tested on a spontaneous numbers task.

17. In this study, Zhao and Morgan (2008) have investigated the multi-stream approach of utilizing the large number of spectro-temporal features that are used for speech recognition. The authors have mentioned that instead of reducing the feature space dimension, this method divides the features

into streams so that each stream represents a patch of information in the spectro-temporal response field. From their work the authors have found that the combination of these features with the mel frequency cepstral coefficients (MFCCs) for the recognition of speech under both noisy and clean environments provides roughly a 30% relative improvement in Word Error Rate (WER) over using MFCCs alone. They have stated that the use of multiple streams of spectro-temporal features along with MFCCs in Tandem system have resulted in improved performance in the number recognition task in clean and noisy environments. From the results the authors have concluded that the multi-stream approach may be an effective way to handle and utilize spectro-temporal features for various speech applications.

Table 2 summarizes the various reported works that have dealt with single classifier for performing tasks like identification and recognition of various speech samples using prosodic, spectral and temporal features. Some of the recognition rates obtained by the authors for their work lie in the range of 64% to 97% approximately.

CONCLUSION

Speech is considered to be the most natural means for conveying messages and information between human beings. The main idea behind speech recognition is to convert speech signal into a sequence of word by computer program which a machine can understand. As the main mode of communication, the goal of speech recognition is to facilitate the communication between human and machine more naturally and effectively. This chapter gives a basic overview of the various speech recognition works related to telephone speech recognition as well as the features used for the purpose. It has been found that telephonic speech technologies are getting more involved into various new applications related to spoken language processing such as voice service, voice navigation, etc., but the recognition of telephonic speech becomes cumbersome due to the limited bandwidth of the transmission channels. Another drawback of telephone recorded speech is that during recording of the samples over the line, severe distortions are introduced due to the transmission channel. Also the availability of large amount of telephone recorded database is another constraint.

From the literature it has been found that the use of various spectral and temporal features provides significant performance improvements when compared to other common features. It has also been mentioned in some of the works that the combination of these features provides even better performance.

In a number of reported works related to telephone speech recognition, various soft computational tools have been implemented for the recognition purpose. Statistical tools such as HMM and GMM along with ANN have been implemented in various works. The uses of ANN for speech recognition tasks have received greater attention for some years now. The trend is to use such tools more frequently in combinations with traditional methods. Early experiments have been dedicated to small vocabulary isolated word recognition and extensive comparisons of the results with classical systems were performed. Researchers have developed hybrid systems combining ANNs and dynamic speech alignment techniques for both isolated word recognition as well as continuous speech recognition. According to the researchers, the ANN proves to be advantageous and more so in combination with other systems because of its capacity to retain the learning and use it subsequently for which a generalized system can be formulated instead of designing task specific speech recognizer. The true mimicking of the biological speech recognition process is only possible by using learning based approaches which is achieved by application of ANN in such cases.

Table 2. Summary of works depicting the use of single classifiers and spectral and temporal features

SL No.	Authors	Database	Feature Parameters	Algorithm Model	Task Performed	Reference
1	Gajsek, Zibert, Mihelic	Voicetran Database (Gopolis, K211d, VNTV in total duration of 12.6 hours)	PLP features	HMM Tool Kit (HTK)	Recognition	(Gajsek, Zibert, Mihelic, 2008)
2	Mporas, Ganchev, Fakotakis	Standard Modern Greek and Cypriot Dialect (SpeechDat (II) FDB5000 Greek Database and the Oriental Cypriot Greek Database)	12 first MFCCs together with the 0th coefficients.	HMM Tool Kit (HTK)	Recognition	(Mporas, Ganchev and Fakotakis , 2008)
3	Alotaibi, Alghamdi, Alotaiby	Telephony Arabic Speech corpus, SAAVB	MFCC	HMM Tool Kit (HTK)	Recognition	(Alotaibi, Alghamdi and Alotaiby 2010).
4	Gauvain, Lamel, Schwenk, Adda, Chen, Lefevre	SwitchBoard resources, CallHome Data	PLP like cepstral features derived from a Mel Frequency Spectrum	Neural Network Language model	Recognition	(Gauvain et al. 2003)
5	Hwang, Lei, Ng, Bulyko, et al.	BBN-2003 Data set	MFCC and PLP	HMM	Recognition	(Hwang et al., 2004)
6	Mary, Yegnanarayana	Oregon Graduate Institute (OGI) multi language speech corpus and National Institute of Science and Technology (NIST) 2003 language Identification database.	Prosodic Features (Fundamental frequency (F0), energy contour, duration)	Multilayer Feed Forward Neural Network (MLFFNN)	Identification	(Mary and Yegnanarayana, 2008)
7	Reynolds, Rose	KING speech database	Mel-cepstral features	GMM	Identification	(Reynolds and Rose, 1995)
8	Ruske	Recorded samples of 360 German words	Formants, formants loci, formant transitions, formant- like links for characterization of nasals, glides or liquids, spectral distribution of fricative noise or burst and duration of pauses.	Nearest neighbor rule	Recognition	(Ruske, 1982)
9	Chen, Zhu, Morgan	2001 NIST Hub-5 conversational telephone speech (CTS) and OGI database	TRAP and log critical band energies (LCBEs)	MLP	Recognition	(Chen, Zhu and Morgan, 2005)

REFERENCES

Alotaibi, Y. A., Alghamdi, M., & Alotaiby, F. (2010). Speech Recognition System of Arabic Alphabet Based on a Telephony Arabic Corpus. In A. Elmoataz et al. (Eds.), Image and Signal Processing (pp. 122-129). Springer Berlin Heidelberg. doi:10.1007/978-3-642-13681-8_15

Anusuya, M. A., & Katti, S. K. (2009). Speech Recognition by Machine: A Review. *International Journal of Computer Science and Information Security*, 6(3), 181–205.

Arora, S. J., & Singh, R. P. (2012). Automatic Speech Recognition: A Review. *International Journal of Computers and Applications*, 60(9), 34–44.

Bennani, Y., & Gallinari, P. (1995). Neural networks for discrimination and modelization of speakers. *Speech Communication*, 17(1-2), 159–175. doi:10.1016/0167-6393(95)00014-F

Bouvrie, J., Ezzat, T., & Poggio, T. (2008). Localized Spectro-Temporal Cepstral Analysis of Speech. *Proceedings of the 2008 IEEE International Conference on Acoustics, Speech and Signal Processing (ICASSP)*, Las Vegas, NV, USA (pp. 4733-4736). doi:10.1109/ICASSP.2008.4518714

C, V. & Radha, V. (2012). A Review on Speech Recognition Challenges and Approaches. *World of Computer Science and Information Technology Journal*, 2(1), 1-7.

Chen, B., Zhu, Q., & Morgan, N. (2005). Long-Term Temporal Features for Conversational Speech Recognition. In S. Bengio & H. Bourland (Eds.), *Machine Learning for Multimodal Interaction* (pp. 232–242). Springer Berlin Heidelberg. Doi: doi:10.1007/978-3-540-30568-2_19

Ellis, D. P. W., & Athineos, M. (2003). Frequency-domain Linear Prediction for Temporal Features. In *Proceedings of 2003 IEEE workshop on Automatic Speech Recognition and Understanding (ASRU)* (pp. 261-266).

Gajsek, R., Zibert, J., & Mihelic, F. (2008). Acoustic Modeling for Speech Recognition in Telephone Based Dialog System Using Limited Audio Resources. In P. Sojka et al. (Eds.), *Text, Speech and Dialogue* (pp. 311–316). Springer Berlin Heidelberg. doi:10.1007/978-3-540-87391-4_40

Ganapathy, S., Thomas, S., & Hermansky, H. (2010). Robust Spectro-Temporal Features based on Autoregressive Models of Hilbert Envelopes. *Proceedings of the 2010 IEEE International Conference on Acoustics, Speech and Signal Processing (ICASSP)*, Dallas, TX (pp. 4286-4289). DOI: doi:10.1109/ICASSP.2010.5495668

Gauvain, J. L., Lamel, L., Schwenk, H., Adda, G., Chen, L., & Lefevre, F. (2003). Conversational Telephone Speech Recognition. *Proceedings of the 2003 IEEE International Conference on Acoustics, Speech and Signal Processing* (Vol. 1, pp. 212-215).

Glass, J. R., & Hazen, T. J. (1998). Telephone-based Conversational Speech Recognition in the Jupiter Domain. *Proceedings of the 1998 fifth International Conference on spoken Language processing* (Vol. 98, pp. 1327-1330). Sydney, Australia.

Hagen, A., & Neto, J. P. (2003). HMM/MLP Hybrid Speech Recognizer for the Portuguese Telephone SpeechDat Corpus. In N. J. Mamede et al. (Eds.), *Computational Processing of the Portuguese Language* (pp. 126–134). Springer Berlin Heidelberg. doi:10.1007/3-540-45011-4_19

Hanson, B., & Applebaum, T. H. (1990). Robust Speaker-independent Word Recognition using Static, Dynamic and Acceleration Features: Experiments with Lombard and noisy Speech. *Proceedings of the 1990 IEEE International Conference on Acoustics, Speech and Signal Processing (ICASSP)* Albuquerque, NM, USA (Vol. 2, pp. 857-860). doi:10.1109/ICASSP.1990.115973

Hermansky, H., & Sharma, S. (1999). Temporal Patterns (TRAPs) in ASR of Noisy Speech. *Proceedings of the 1999 IEEE International Conference on Acoustics, Speech and Signal Processing (ICASSP)* Phoenix, AZ, USA (Vol. 1, pp. 289-292). doi:10.1109/ICASSP.1999.758119

Hwang, M. Y. et al.. (2004). Progress on Mandarin Conversational Telephone Speech Recognition. *Proceedings of the 2004 International Symposium on Chinese Spoken Language Processing* (pp. 1-4). DOI: doi:10.1109/CHINSL.2004.1409571

Kleinschmidt, M. (2003). *Localized Spectro-Temporal Features for Automatic Speech Recognition* (pp. 2573–2576). Geneva, Switzerland: EUROSPEECH.

Koolagudi, S. G., & Krothapalli, S. R. (2012). Emotion Recognition from Speech using Sub-syllabic and Pitch Synchronous Spectral Features. *International Journal of Speech Technology*, *15*(4), 495–511. doi:10.1007/s10772-012-9150-8

Kundu, A., & Bayya, A. (1998). Speech Recognition Using Hidden Markov Model and NN Classifier. *International Journal of Speech Technology*, *2*(3), 227–240. doi:10.1007/BF02111210

Kurian, C. (2014). A Survey on Speech Recognition in Indian Languages. *International Journal of Computer Science and Information Technologies*, *5*(5), 6169–6175.

Mary, L., & Yegnanarayana, B. (2008). Prosodic Features for Language Identification. *Proceedings of the International Conference on Signal Processing, Communications and Networking, (ICSCN),* Chennai (pp. 57-62).

Mporas, I., Ganchev, T., & Fakotakis, N. (2008). Phonotactic Recognition of Greek and Cypriot Dialects from Telephone Speech. In J. Darzentas et al. (Eds.), *Artificial Intelligence: Theories, Models and Applications* (pp. 173–181). Springer Berlin Heidelberg. doi:10.1007/978-3-540-87881-0_16

Nemade, M. U., & Shah, S. K. (2013). Survey of Soft Computing based Speech Recognition Techniques for Speech Enhancement in Multimedia Applications. *International Journal of Advanced Research in Computer and Communication Engineering*, *2*(5), 2039–2043.

O'Shaughnessy, D. (2000). *Speech Communications- Human and Machine*. New York: IEEE Press.

Rao, K. S., & Koolagudi, S. G. (2011). Identification of Hindi Dialects and Emotions using Spectral and Prosodic Features of Speech. *International journal of Systemic. Cybernetics and Informatics*, *9*(4), 24–33.

Reddy, V. R., Maity, S., & Rao, K. S. (2013). Identification of Indian Languages using Multi-level Spectral and Prosodic Features. *International Journal of Speech Technology*, *16*(4), 489–511. doi:10.1007/s10772-013-9198-0

Reynolds, D. A., & Rose, R. C. (1995). Robust Text-independent Speaker Identification using Gaussian Mixture Speaker Models. *IEEE Transactions on Speech and Audio Processing*, *3*(1), 72–83. doi:10.1109/89.365379

Rodriguez, E., Ruiz, B., Crespo, A. G., & Gracia, F. (1997). Speech/ Speaker Recognition using a HMM/ GMM Hybrid Model. In J. Bigun et al. (Eds.), *Audio and Video Based Biometric Person Authentication* (pp. 227–234). Springer Berlin Heidelberg. doi:10.1007/BFb0016000

Rosen, S. (1992). Temporal Information in Speech: Acoustic, Auditory and Linguistic Aspects. *Philosophical Transactions of the Royal Society of London. Series B, Biological Sciences*, *336*(1278), 367–373. doi:10.1098/rstb.1992.0070 PMID:1354376

Ruske, G. (1982). Automatic Recognition of Syllabic Speech Segments using Spectral and Temporal Features. *Proceedings of the 1982 IEEE International Conference on Acoustic Speech and Signal Processing* (Vol. 7, pp. 550-553). DOI: doi:10.1109/ICASSP.1982.1171663

Sarma, M., & Sarma, K. K. (2014). *Phoneme-Based Speech Segmentation Using Hybrid Soft Computing Framework*. India: Springer. doi:10.1007/978-81-322-1862-3

Sharifzadeh, S., Serrano, J. & Carrabina, J. (2012). Spectro-Temporal Analysis of Speech for Spanish Phoneme Recognition. *Proceedings of the 2012 19th International Conference on Systems, Signals and Image Processing (IWSSIP),* Vienna (pp. 548-551).

Thomas, S., Ganapathy, S., & Hermansky, H. (2008). *Hilbert Envelope Based Spectro-Temporal Features for Phoneme Recognition in Telephone Speech* (pp. 1521–1524). INTERSPEECH.

Venkateshwarlu, R. L. K., Raviteja, R., & Rajeev, R. (2012). The Performance Evaluation of Speech Recognition by Comparative Approach. In A. Karahoca (Ed.), *Advances in Data Mining Knowledge Discovery and Applications*. doi:10.5772/50640

Wegmann, S., McAllaster, D., Orloff, J., & Peskin, B. (1996). Speaker Normalization on Conversational Telephone Speech. *Proceedings of 1996 IEEE International Conference on Acoustics, Speech and Signal Processing, (ICASSP),* Atlanta, GA (Vol. 1, pp 339-341). doi:10.1109/ICASSP.1996.541101

Xu, L., & Zheng, Y. (2007). Spectral and Temporal Cues for Phoneme Recognition in Noise. *The Journal of the Acoustical Society of America*, *122*(3), 1758–1764. doi:10.1121/1.2767000 PMID:17927435

Yadav, K. S., & Mukhedkar, M. M. (2013). Review on Speech Recognition. *International Journal of Science and Engineering*, *1*(2), 61–70.

Young, E. D. (2008). Neural Representation of Spectral and temporal Information in Speech. *Philosophical Transactions of the Royal Society of London. Series B, Biological Sciences*, *363*(1493), 923–945. doi:10.1098/rstb.2007.2151 PMID:17827107

Yuk, D., & Flanagan, J. (1999). Telephone Speech Recognition Using Neural Networks and Hidden Markov Models. *Proceedings of the 1999 IEEE International Conference on Acoustics, Speech and Signal Processing,* Phoenix, AZ (*Vol. 1*, pp. 157-160). IEEE Press.

Zhao, S. Y., & Morgan, N. (2008). *Multi-stream Spectro-Temporal features for Robust Speech Recognition* (pp. 898–901). INTERSPEECH.

Zhu, Q., Chen, B., Morgan, N., & Stolcke, A. (2005). Tandem Connectionist Feature Extraction for Conversational Speech Recognition. In S. Bengio & H. Bourland (Eds.), *Machine Learning for Multimodal Interaction* (pp. 223–231). Springer Berlin Heidelberg. doi:10.1007/978-3-540-30568-2_19

Zissman, M. A. (1996). Comparison of Four Approaches to Automatic Language Identification of Telephone Speech. *IEEE Transactions on Speech and Audio Processing*, *4*(1), 31–44. doi:10.1109/TSA.1996.481450

Zissman, M. A., & Singer, E. (1994). Automatic Language Identification of Telephone Speech Message Using Phoneme Recognition and N-Gram Modeling. *Proceedings of the 1994 IEEE International Conference on Acoustics, Speech and Signal Processing,* Adelaide, SA (Vol. 1, pp. 305-308). doi:10.1109/ICASSP.1994.389377

Zuo, G., Liu, W., & Ruan, X. (2003). Telephone Speech Recognition Using Simulated Data from Clean Database. *Proceedings of the 2003 IEEE International Conference on Robotics, Intelligent Systems and Signal Processing* (Vol. 1, pp. 49-53). Changsha, China. doi:10.1109/RISSP.2003.1285547

KEY TERMS AND DEFINITIONS

Acoustic Phonetics: The study of the acoustic characteristics of speech in terms of its physical properties such as fundamental frequency, formants, intensity and duration.

Artificial Neural Network: ANNs are non-parametric computational tools which resembles the operation of biological nervous systems and work by learning from the surrounding.

Feature Extraction: Feature extraction is the process of transforming the input data into a set of features which can very well represent the input data. It is a special form of dimensionality reduction.

Multi Layer Perceptron (MLP): MLP is a feed forward neural network with one or more layers between input and output layer and are used to solve non-linearly separable problems. MLPs are trained using the back propagation algorithm. MLPs are widely used in pattern classification, recognition, prediction, etc.

Pattern Recognition: A branch of machine learning that recognizes and separates the patterns of one class from the other.

Soft Computation: A technique of solving problems which deals with imprecision, uncertainty, partial truth and approximation to achieve practicability, robustness and a low cost solution.

Speech Processing: Speech Processing is the study of the characteristics and the processing methods of the speech signals.

Speech Recognition: Speech Recognition can be defined as the ability of a machine or program to identify words or phrases in spoken language to a machine readable format. It is the process of converting a speech signal into word sequences by implementing computer algorithms or programming.

Chapter 7
Evolutionary Algorithms:
Concepts, Designs, and Applications in Bioinformatics

Ka-Chun Wong
City University of Hong Kong, Hong Kong SAR

ABSTRACT

Inspired from nature, evolutionary algorithms have been proven effective and unique in different real world applications. Comparing to traditional algorithms, its parallel search capability and stochastic nature enable it to excel in search performance in a unique way. In this chapter, evolutionary algorithms are reviewed and discussed from concepts and designs to applications in bioinformatics. The history of evolutionary algorithms is first discussed at the beginning. An overview on the state-of-the-art evolutionary algorithm concepts is then provided. Following that, the related design and implementation details are discussed on different aspects: representation, parent selection, reproductive operators, survival selection, and fitness function. At the end of this chapter, real world evolutionary algorithm applications in bioinformatics are reviewed and discussed.

INTRODUCTION

Since genetic algorithm was proposed by John Holland (Holland, 1975) in the early 1970s, the study of evolutionary algorithm has emerged as a popular research field (Civicioglu & Besdok, 2013). Researchers from various scientific and engineering disciplines have been digging into this field, exploring the unique power of evolutionary algorithms (Hadka & Reed, 2013). Many applications have been successfully proposed in the past twenty years. For example, mechanical design (Lampinen & Zelinka, 1999), electromagnetic optimization (Rahmat-Samii & Michielssen, 1999), environmental protection (Bertini, De, Moretti, & Pizzuti, 2010), finance (Larkin & Ryan, 2010), musical orchestration (Esling, Carpentier, & Agon, 2010), pipe routing (Furuholmen, Glette, Hovin, & Torresen, 2010), and nuclear reactor core design (Sacco, Henderson, Rios-Coelho, Ali, & Pereira, 2009). In particular, its function optimization capability was highlighted (Goldberg & Richardson, 1987) because of its high adaptability to different function landscapes, to which we cannot apply traditional optimization techniques (Wong, Leung, & Wong, 2009).

DOI: 10.4018/978-1-4666-9474-3.ch007

BACKGROUND

Evolutionary algorithms draw inspiration from nature. An evolutionary algorithm starts with a randomly initialized population. The population then evolves across several generations. In each generation, fit individuals are selected to become parent individuals. They cross-over with each other to generate new individuals, which are subsequently called offspring individuals. Randomly selected offspring individuals then undergo certain mutations. After that, the algorithm selects the optimal individuals for survival to the next generation according to the survival selection scheme designed in advance. For instance, if the algorithm is overlapping (De Jong, 2006), then both parent and offspring populations will participate in the survival selection. Otherwise, only the offspring population will participate in the survival selection. The selected individuals then survive to the next generation. Such a procedure is repeated again and again until a certain termination condition is met (Wong, Leung, & Wong, 2010). Figure 1 outlines a typical evolutionary algorithm.

In this book chapter, we follow the unified approach proposed by De Jong (De Jong, 2006). The design of evolutionary algorithm can be divided into several components: representation, parent selection, crossover operators, mutation operators, survival selection, and termination condition. Details can be found in the following sections.

- **Representation:** It involves genotype representation and genotype-phenotype mapping. (De Jong, 2006). For instance, we may represent an integer (phenotype) as a binary array (genotype): '19' as '10011' and '106' as '1101010'. If we mutate the first bit, then we will get '3' (00011) and '42' (0101010). For those examples, even we have mutated one bit in the genotype, the phenotype may vary very much. Thus we can see that there are a lot of considerations in the mapping.

Figure 1. Major components of a typical evolutionary algorithm

---

Algorithm 1 A Typical Evolutionary Algorithm

Choose suitable representation methods;

$P(t)$: Parent Population at time t
$O(t)$: Offspring Population at time t

$t \leftarrow 0$;
Initialize $P(t)$;
while not termination condition **do**
    $temp$ = Parent Selection from $P(t)$;
    $O(t+1)$ = Crossover in $temp$;
    $O(t+1)$ = Mutate $O(t+1)$;
    if overlapping **then**
        $P(t+1)$ = Survival Selection from $O(t+1) \cup P(t)$;
    else
        $P(t+1)$ = Survival Selection from $O(t+1)$;
    end if
    $t \leftarrow t+1$;
end while

Good individuals can then be found in $P(t)$;

- **Parent Selection:** It aims at selecting good parent individuals for crossovers, where the goodness of a parent individual is quantified by its fitness. Thus most parent selection schemes focus on giving more opportunities to the fitter parent individuals than the other individuals and vice versa such that "good" offspring individuals are likely to be generated.
- **Crossover Operators:** It resembles the reproduction mechanism in nature. Thus they, with mutation operators, are collectively called reproductive operators. In general, a crossover operator combines two individuals to form a new individual. It tries to split an individual into parts and then assemble those parts into a new individual.
- **Mutation Operators:** It simulates the mutation mechanism in which some parts of a genome undergoes random changes in nature. Thus, as a typical modeling practice, a mutation operator changes parts of the genome of an individual. On the other hand, mutations can be thought as an exploration mechanism to balance the exploitation power of crossover operators.
- **Survival Selection:** It aims at selecting a subset of good individuals from a set of individuals, where the goodness of individual is proportional to its fitness in most cases. Thus survival selection mechanism is somehow similar to parent selection mechanism. In a typical framework like 'EC4' (De Jong, 2006), most parent selection mechanisms can be re-applied in survival selection.
- **Termination Condition:** It refers to the condition at which an evolutionary algorithm should end.

EVOLUTIONARY ALGORITHMS: CONCEPTS AND DESIGNS

Representation

Representation involves genotype representation and genotype-phenotype mapping. In general, designers try to keep genotype representation as compact as possible while keeping it as close to the corresponding phenotype representations as possible such that measurement metrics, say distance, in the genotype space can be mapped to those in phenotype space without the loss of semantic information.

In general, there are many types of representations that an evolutionary algorithm can adopt. For example, fixed-length linear structures, variable-length linear structures, and tree structures...... Figure 2 depicts three examples. Figure 2a is a vector of integers. We can observe that its genotype is a binary array with length equal to 10. To map it into the phenotype space, the first 5 binary digits (10011) are mapped to the first element (19) of the vector whereas the remaining 5 binary digits (11110) are mapped to the second element (30) of the vector. Figure 2b is the relative encoding representation of a protein on the HP lattice model (Krasnogor, Hart, Smith, & Pelta, 1999). Its genotype is an array of moves and its length is set to the amino acid sequence length of the protein. The array of moves encodes the relative positions of amino acids from their predecessor amino acids. Thus we need to follow the move sequence to compute the 3D structure of the protein (phenotype) for further evaluations. Figure 2c is the tree representation of a mathematical expression. Obviously, such tree structure is a variable length structure, which has the flexibility in design. If the expression is short, it can be shrunk during the evolution. If the expression is long, it can also be expanded during the evolution. Thus we can observe that the structure has an advantage over the previous representations. Nevertheless, there is no free lunch. It imposes several implementation difficulties to translate it into phenotypes.

Figure 2. Some representations of evolutionary algorithms: (a) integer representation (b) protein structure representation on a lattice model (c) tree representation for a mathematical expression

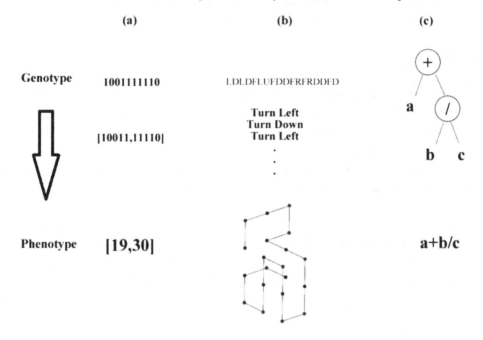

Parent Selection

Parent selection aims at selecting "good" parent individuals for crossover, where the goodness of a parent individual is positively proportional to its fitness for most cases. Thus most parent selection schemes focus on giving more opportunities to the fitter parent individuals than the other individuals and vice versa. The typical methods are listed as follows:

- **Fitness Proportional Selection:** The scheme is sometimes called roulette wheel selection. In the scheme, the fitness values of all individuals are summed. Once summed, the fitness of each individual is divided by the sum. The ratio then becomes the probability for each individual to be selected.

- **Rank Proportional Selection:** Individuals with high ranks are given more chances to be selected. Unlike fitness proportional scheme, the rank proportional scheme does not depend on the actual fitness values of the individuals. It is a double-edged sword. On the positive side, it can help us prevent the domination of very high fitness values. On the negative side, it imposes additional computational costs for ranking.

- **Uniform Deterministic Selection:** The scheme is the simplest among the other schemes. All individuals are selected, resulting in uniform selection.

- **Uniform Stochastic Selection:** The scheme is the probabilistic version of uniform deterministic selection. All individuals are given equal chances (equal probabilities) to be selected.

- **Binary Tournament:** Actually, there are other tournament selection schemes proposed in the past literature. In this book chapter, the most basic one, binary tournament, is selected and described. In each binary tournament, two individuals are randomly selected and competed with each other by fitness. The winner is then selected. Such a procedure is repeated until all vacancies are filled.

- **Truncation:** The top individuals are selected deterministically when there is a vacancy for selection. In other words, the bottom individuals are never selected. For example, if there are 100 individuals and 50 slots are available, then the top 50 fittest individuals will be selected.

Crossover Operators

Crossover operators resemble the reproduction mechanism in nature. Thus they, with mutation operators, are collectively called reproductive operators. In general, a crossover operator combines two individuals to form a new individual. It tries to partition an individual into parts and then assemble the parts of two individuals into a new individual. The partitioning is not a trivial task. It depends on the representation adopted. Thus it is not hard to imagine that crossover operators are representation-dependent. Nevertheless, without loss of generality, a list of classic crossover operators is listed as follows:

- **One Point Crossover:** One point crossover is a commonly used crossover operator because of its simplicity. Given two individuals, it randomly chooses a cut point in their genomes. Then it swaps the parts after (or before) the cut point between the two genomes.
- **Two Points Crossover:** Two points crossover is another commonly used crossover operator because people argue that one point crossover has a positional bias toward the terminal positions. For instance, when making a one point crossover, the rightmost (or leftmost) part is always swapped. Thus people propose two point crossovers to avoid the positional bias.
- **Uniform Crossover:** Uniform crossover is a general one. Each gene is given an equal probability to be swapped.
- **Blend Crossover:** Blend crossover is commonly used in real number optimization. Instead of swapping genes, it tries to blend two genes together by arithmetic averaging to obtain the intermediate values. For instance, if we are going to make a crossover between two vectors [1 2 3] and [4 5 6], then the blended vector will be [2.5 3.5 4.5]. Weights can be applied here.

Mutation Operators

Mutation operators resemble the mutation mechanism in which some parts of genome undergo random changes in nature. Thus, as a typical modeling, a mutation operator changes parts of the genome of an individual probabilistically. Similar to crossover operators, mutation operators are representation-dependent. Nevertheless, without loss of generality, a list of commonly used mutation operators is shown below:

- **Bitflip Mutation:** It is commonly used in binary genomes. Specified by a pre-defined probability, each bit in a binary genome is probabilistically inverted.
- **Random Mutation:** Random mutation is generalized from bitflip mutation. It can be applied in many genomes. Specified by a pre-defined probability, each part in a genome is probabilistically changed to a random value within domain bounds.
- **Delta Mutation:** Delta mutation is commonly used in real number genomes. Specified by a pre-defined probability, each real number in a real number genome is probabilistically incremented/ decremented by a certain step size (called delta), where the step size is pre-specified. Nonetheless, it is straightforward to make the step size adaptive, similar to the trial vector generations in differential evolution (Storn & Price, 1997).

- **Gaussian Mutation:** Gaussian mutation is also commonly used in real number genomes. Similar to delta mutation, each real number in a real number genome is probabilistically increased / decreased by a step size. The difference is that the step size is a Gaussian random number. (De Jong, 2006).

Survival Selection

Survival selection aims at selecting a subset of good individuals from a population, where the goodness of individual is proportional to its fitness for most cases. Thus survival selection mechanism is somehow similar to parent selection mechanism. In a typical framework like EC4 (De Jong, 2006), most parent selection mechanisms can be re-applied in survival selection. For example, the fitness proportional selection can be applied as survival selection.

Termination Condition

Termination condition refers to the condition at which an evolutionary algorithm should end. For historical reasons, the number of generations is often adopted as the termination measurement: an evolutionary algorithm terminates when a certain number of generations has been reached (e.g. 1000 generations). Nonetheless, it has been pointed out that fitness function evaluations are computationally expensive in certain domains. Thus the number of fitness function evaluations is also adopted in some problems. If computing resources are limited, CPU time is also adopted. Nonetheless, convergence is not guaranteed. Thus people have calculated the fitness improvement of each generation as another condition for termination.

Examples

- **Genetic Algorithm:** Genetic algorithm is the most classic evolutionary algorithm. It draws inspiration from the Darwin's Evolution Theory. The difference between genetic algorithm and evolutionary algorithm becomes blurred nowadays. The words 'genetic algorithm' and 'evolutionary algorithm' are sometimes interchanged in use. To clearly explain the working mechanism of a genetic algorithm, we chose the canonical genetic algorithm (Whitley, 1994) as a representative example.

In the canonical genetic algorithm, each individual has a fixed-length binary array as its genotype. Then the fitness of each individual is divided by the average fitness to calculate the normalized probability to be selected. The algorithm then adopts them to select parents for one point crossover to produce offspring individuals, which subsequently undergo mutations. The offspring individuals become the population in the next generation and so forth.

- **Genetic Programming:** Genetic programming is indeed a special type of genetic algorithm. The difference lies in their representations. Genetic programming adopts trees as genotypes to represent programs or expressions. (Figure 2 depicts an example). The typical selection schemes of evolutionary algorithms can still be used as parent selection and survival selection in genetic programming. The distinct features of genetic programming are their crossover and mutation operators. For instance, swapping sub-trees between two trees and random generation of sub-trees. A list of common crossover and mutation operators for genetic programming is tabulated in Table 1.

Table 1. A list of crossover and mutation operators for genetic programming

	Description
Crossover	• **Subtree Exchange Crossover:** Exchange subtrees between individuals. • **Self Crossover:** Exchange subtrees within an individual. • **Module Crossover:** Exchange modules between individuals. • **SCPC:** Exchange subtrees if coordinates match exactly. • **WCPC:** Exchange subtrees if coordinates match approximately.
Mutation	• **Point Mutation:** Change the value of a node. • **Permutation:** Change the argument order of a node. • **Hoist:** Use a subtree to become a new individual. • **Expansion Mutation:** Exchange a subtree against a terminal node. • **Collapse Subtree Mutation:** Exchange a terminal node against a subtree. • **Subtree Mutation:** Replace a subtree by another subtree. • **Gene Duplication:** Replace a subtree by a terminal.

(Banzhaf, Nordin, Keller, & Francone, 1998).

- **Differential Evolution:** Differential Evolution was first proposed by Price and Storn in the 1990s (Storn & Price, 1997). It demonstrated great potential for real function optimization in the subsequent contests (Price, 1997). Without loss of generality, a typical strategy of differential evolution (DE/rand/1) (Feoktistov, 2006) is shown in Figure 3.

For each individual in a generation, the algorithm randomly selects three individuals to form a trial vector. One individual forms a base vector, whereas the value difference between the other two individuals forms a difference vector. The sum of those two vectors forms a trial vector, which recombines

Figure 3. Outline of differential evolution (DE/rand/1)

Algorithm 2 Differential Evolution

P_t: Population at time t
TP: Transient population

$t \leftarrow 0$;
Initialize P_t;
Evaluate P_t;
while not termination condition **do**
  $TP \leftarrow \emptyset$;
  for $\forall indiv_i \in P_t$ **do**
    Offspring $\leftarrow$ TRIALVECTORGENERATION($indiv_i$);
    Evaluate *Offspring*;
    if *Offspring* is fitter than $indiv_i$ **then**
      Put *Offspring* into TP;
    else
      Put *Parent* into TP;
    end if
  end for
  $t = t + 1$;
  $P_t \leftarrow TP$;
end while

---

with the individual to form an offspring. Replacing the typical crossover and mutation operation by this trial vector generation, manual parameter tuning of crossover and mutation is no longer needed. It can provide differential evolution a self-organizing ability and high adaptability for choosing suitable step sizes which demonstrated its potential for continuous optimization in the past contests. A self-organizing ability is granted for moving toward the optima. A high adaptability is achieved for optimizing different landscapes (Feoktistov, 2006). With such self-adaptability, differential evolution is considered as one of the most powerful evolutionary algorithms for real function optimization. For example, mechanical engineering design (Lampinen & Zelinka, 1999) and nuclear reactor core design (Sacco, Henderson, Rios-Coelho, Ali, & Pereira, 2009).

- **Evolution Strategy:** Evolution Strategy was proposed in 1968 (Beyer & Schwefel, 2002). It is even older than genetic algorithm. Schwefel and Klockgether originally used evolution strategy as a heuristic to perform several experimental optimizations in air flow. They found that evolution strategy was better than other discrete gradient-oriented strategy, which raised people's interests in evolution strategy. Comparing to the previous evolutionary algorithms, evolution strategy draws less inspiration from nature. Instead, it was artificially created as a numerical tool for optimization. Thus the structure of evolution strategy is quite different from the other evolutionary algorithms. For example, evolution strategy scholars call the mutation step size and probability as endogenous parameters encoded in the genome of an individual. Thus, besides the gene values, a genome is also composed of the parameter settings which control the convergence progress of the whole algorithm. The notation of evolution strategy is quite interesting. $(\mu / \rho^+, \lambda)$ - ES denotes an evolution strategy where μ denotes parent population size; ρ denotes breeding size; $(\mu / \rho + \lambda)$ - ES denotes the algorithm is overlapping; $(\mu / \rho, \lambda)$ denotes the algorithm is not overlapping; λ denotes the offspring population size.
- **Swarm Intelligence:** Ant Colony Optimization (Dorigo & Gambardella, 1997), Particle Swarm Optimization (Poli, Kennedy, & Blackwell, 2007), and Bee Colony Optimization (Karaboga, Akay, & Ozturk, 2007)......etc are collectively known as Swarm Intelligence. Swarm intelligence is a special class of evolutionary algorithm. It does not involve any selection (i.e. birth and death). Instead, it maintains a fixed-size population of individuals for search across generations. After each generation, the individuals report their findings which are recorded and used to adjust the search strategy in the next generation. Some of the algorithms were originally designed for shortest path finding. Nevertheless, people have further generalized them for other applications. For instance, Bi-Criterion Opitmization (Iredi, Merkle, & Middendorf, 2000), Load Balancing in Telecommunication Network (Schoonderwoerd, Bruten, Holland, & Rothkrantz, 1996), Protein Folding Problem (Shmygelska & Hoos, 2005), and Power System (Del Venayagamoorthy, Mohagheghi, Hernandez, & Harley, 2008).
- **Multimodel Optimization:** Real world problems always have different multiple solutions. For instance, optical engineers need to tune the recording parameters to get as many optimal solutions as possible for multiple trials in the varied-line-spacing holographic grating design problem because the design constraints are too difficult to be expressed and solved in mathematical forms. Unfortunately, most traditional optimization techniques focus on solving for a single optimal solution. They need to be applied several times; yet all solutions are not guaranteed to be found. Thus the multimodal optimization problem was proposed. In that problem, we are interested in not only a single optimal point, but also the others. Given an objective function, an algorithm is expected

to find all optimal points in a single run. With strong parallel search capability, evolutionary algorithms are shown to be particularly effective in solving this type of problem. Although the objective is clear, it is not easy to be satisfied in practice because some problems may have too many optima to be located. Nonetheless, it is still of great interest to researchers how these problems are going to be solved because the algorithms for multimodal optimization usually not only locate multiple optima in a single run, but also preserve their population diversity throughout a run, resulting in their global optimization ability on multimodal functions.

The work by De Jong (De Jong, 2006) is one of the first known attempts to solve the multimodal optimization problem by an evolutionary algorithm. He introduced the crowding technique to increase the chance of locating multiple optima. In the crowding technique, an offspring replaces the parent which is most similar to the offspring itself. Such a strategy can preserve the diversity and maintain different niches in a run. Twelve years later, Goldberg and Richardson (Goldberg & Richardson, 1987) proposed a fitness-sharing niching technique as a diversity preserving strategy to solve the multimodal optimization problem. They proposed a shared fitness function, instead of an absolute fitness function, to evaluate the fitness of a individual in order to favor the growth of the individuals which are distinct from the others. With this technique, a population can be prevented from the domination of a particular type of individuals. Species conserving genetic algorithm (SCGA) (Wong, Leung, & Wong, An evolutionary algorithm with species-specific explosion for multimodal optimization, 2009) is another technique for evolving parallel subpopulations. Before crossovers in each generation, the algorithm selects a set of species seeds which can bypass the subsequent procedures to the next generation. Since then, many researchers have been exploring different ways to deal with the problem. Notably, SCGA was claimed that the technique was considered as an effective and efficient method for inducing niching behavior into GAs. However, in our experiments, we find that the performance of the technique still has space for improvement. It always suffers from genetic drifts though each species is conserved with one individual. The results of the comparison test conducted by Singh et al. (Singh & Deb, 2006) also reveals that the species conserving technique performs the worst among the algorithms tested. As a result, Wong et al. have proposed a novel algorithm to remedy the species conserving technique. The novel algorithm is called Evolutionary Algorithm with Species-specific Explosion (EASE) for multimodal optimization (Wong, Leung, & Wong, An evolutionary algorithm with species-specific explosion for multimodal optimization, 2009). EASE is built on the Species Conserving Genetic Algorithm (SCGA), and the design is improved in several ways. In particular, it not only identifies species seeds, but also exploits the species seeds to create multiple mutated copies in order to further converge to the respective optimum for each species. Evolutionary Algorithm with Species-specific Explosion (EASE) is an evolutionary algorithm which identifies and exploits species seeds to locate global and local optima. There are two stages in the algorithm: Exploration Stage and Species-specific Stage. The exploration stage targets for roughly locating all global and local optima. It not only undergoes normal genetic operations: selection and crossover, but also involves the addition of randomly generated individuals for preserving the diversity. On the other hand, the species-specific stage targets for gently locating the optimum for each species. Species-specific genetic operations are applied. Only the individuals within the same species are allowed to perform selection and crossover to each other. No inter-species selection and crossover are allowed. Such a strategy is to provide more chances for each species to converge to its respective optimum, with the trade-off that diversity is no longer preserved. To have a better global picture for locating optima, EASE starts with the exploration stage. It will switch to the species-specific stage only after the stage switching condition is satisfied. No matter in which stage, a local operation called Species-specific Explosion is always executed so as to help species to climb and converge to its corresponding optimum. Briefly, in SCGA, Li et al. proposed conserving one individual for each species. However, just one individual for each species is not enough for the algorithm to well-conserve and nurture the species. In a run of SCGA, it is often the case that the algorithm does conserve species with low fitness values, but they are present in a small proportion. Once they form new offspring, their offspring are often removed quickly in subsequent generations due to their low fitness values. Thus most individuals are always of the species with high fitness values. In atypical run of SCGA, we can observe that the individuals gradually converge to the three optima fitness-proportionally. Though different species are preserved with an individual as the species seed, it cannot converge to some of the low-fitness local optima. Merely SCGA itself actually cannot provide enough indiscriminate condition for species to nurture, evolve, and converge to its respective optimum in each run. Hence EASE incorporates a local operation called Species-specific Explosion to nurture species and remedy their convergences. Species-specific explosion is the local operation in which we create multiple copies for each species seed and mutate them. In summary, EASE is divided into two stages: Exploration Stage and Species-specific Stage. EASE starts with the exploration stage. Once the stage switching condition is satisfied, it will be changed to species-specific stage. Throughout the two stages, a local operation: Species-specific Explosion is applied so as to help each species to converge to its respective optimum.

Though different methods were proposed in the past, they were all based on the same fundamental idea: it is to strike an optimal balance between convergence and population diversity in order to locate optima.

- **Others:** Other evolutionary computation methods have been proposed; for instance, Cuckoo-search (Civicioglu & Besdok, 2013), Lévy flight (Vuswabatgab, et al., 1996), Bacterial Colony Optimization (Niu & Wang, 2012), and Intelligent Water Drops algorithm (Shah-Hosseini, 2009).

APPLICATIONS TO BIOINFORMATICS

An Overview of Bioinformatics

Since the 1990s, the whole genomes of a large number of species have been sequenced by their corresponding genome sequencing projects. In 1995, the first free-living organism *Haemophilus influenzae* was sequenced by the Institute for Genomic Research (Fleischmann, et al., 1995). In 1996, the first eukaryotic genome (*Saccharomyces cerevisiase*) was completely sequenced (Goffeau, et al., 1996). In 2000, the first plant genome *Arabidopsis thaliana*, was also sequenced by Arabidopsis Genome Initiative (Initiative, 2000). In 2004, the Human Genome Project (HGP) announced its completion (Consortium I. H., 2004). Following the HGP, the Encyclopedia of DNA Elements (ENCODE) project was started, revealing massive functional putative elements on the human genome in 2011 (Consortium E., 2012). The drastically decreasing cost of sequencing also enables the 1000 Genomes Project to be carried out, resulting in an integrated map of genetic variation from 1,092 human genomes published in 2012 (Abecasis, Auton, Brooks, DePristo, & Durbin, 2012). Nonetheless, the massive genomic data generated by those projects impose an unforeseen challenge for large-scale data analysis at the scale of gigabytes or even terabytes (Wong, Peng, Li, & Chan, 2014).

In particular, computational methods are essential in analyzing the massive genomic data (Wong, Li, Peng, & Zhang, 2015). They are collectively known as bioinformatics or computational biology. For instance, motif discovery (GuhaThakurta, 2006) helps us distinguish real signal subsequence patterns from background sequences. Multiple sequence alignment (Altschul, Gish, Miller, Myers, & Lipman, 1990) can be used to analyze the similarities between multiple sequences. Protein structure prediction (McGuffin, Bryson, & Jones, 2000) can be applied to predict the 3D tertiary structure from an amino acid sequence. Gene network inference (D'Haeseleer, Liang, & Somogyi, 2000) are the statistical methods to infer gene networks from correlated data (e.g. microarray data). Promoter prediction (Abeel, Van de Peer, & Saeys, 2009) help us annotate the promoter regions on a genome. Phylogenetic tree inference (Ronquist & Huelsenbeck, 2003) can be applied to study the hierarchical evolution relationship between different species. Drug scheduling (Liang, Leung, & Mok, 2008) can help solve the clinical scheduling problems in an effective manner. Although the precisions of those computational methods are usually lower than the existing biotechnology, they can still serve as useful preprocessing tools to significantly narrow search spaces (Wong & Zhang, 2014). Thus prioritized candidates can be selected for further validation by wet-lab experiments, saving manual time and funding (Wong, Chan, Peng, Li, & Zhang, 2013).

Evolutionary Algorithms for Protein Structure Prediction

A polypeptide is a chain of amino acid residues. Once folded into its native state, it is called protein. Proteins play vital roles in living organisms. They perform different tasks to maintain a body's life. For instance, material transportations across cells and catalyzing metabolic reactions and body defenses against viruses. Nevertheless, functions of proteins substantially depend on their structural features. In other words, researchers need to know a protein's native structure before its function can be completely deduced. It gives rises to the protein structure prediction problem.

The protein structure prediction problem is often referred as the "holy grail" of biology. In particular, Anfinsen's dogma (Anfinsen, 1973) and Levinthal's paradox (Levinthal, 1968) are the central rules in this problem. Anfinsen's dogma postulates that a protein's native structure (tertiary structure) only depends on its amino acid residue sequence (primary structure). On the other hand, Levinthal's paradox postulates that it is too time-consuming for a protein to randomly sample all the feasible confirmation regions for its native structure. On the other hand, the proteins in nature can still spontaneously fold into its native structures in about several milliseconds.

Based on the above ideas, researchers have explored the problem throughout several years. In particular, the protein structural design and sequence degeneracy have been studied by Li et. al. (Li, Helling, Tang, & Wingreen, 1996). The computational complexity has also been examined (Aluru, 2005).

Numerous prediction approaches have been proposed. In general, they can be classified into two categories, depending on whether any prior knowledge other than sequence data has been incorporated (Baker & Sali, 2001). This book chapter focuses on *de novo* (or *ab initio*) protein structure prediction on 3D Hydrophobic-Polar (HP) lattice model using evolutionary algorithms (Krasnogor, Hart, Smith, & Pelta, 1999). In other words, only sequence data is considered.

Different protein structure models have been proposed in the past (Silverio, 2008). Their differences mainly lie in their resolution levels and search space freedom. At the highest resolution level, all the atoms and bond angles can be simulated using molecular dynamics. Nevertheless, there is no free lunch. The simulation is hard to be completed by the current computational power. On the other hand, a study indicated that protein folding mechanisms might be simpler than previously thought (Baker, 2000). Thus this book chapter focuses on HP lattice model to capture the physical principles of protein folding process (Duan & Kollman, 2001).

In this problem, it assumes that the main driving forces are the interactions among the hydrophobic amino acid residues. The twenty amino acids are experimentally classified as either hydrophobic (H) or polar (P). An amino acid sequence is thus represented as a string {H,P}$^+$. Each residue is represented as a non-overlapping bead in a cubic lattice L. Each peptide bond in the main chain is represented as a connecting line. A protein is thus represented as a non-overlapping chain in L.

Based on the above model, the objective of the protein structure prediction problem is to find the conformation with the minimal energy for each protein. Mathematically, it is to minimize the following function (Li, Helling, Tang, & Wingreen, 1996):

$$H = \sum_{i+1<j} E\left(r_i, r_j\right) \Delta\left(r_i, r_j\right)$$

where r_i and r_j are amino acid residues at sequence position i and j. The constraint $i+1<j$ is to ensure that r_i and r_j are not next to each other on their sequence and they are examined together once only. $\Delta\left(r_i, r_j\right) = 1$ when r_i and r_j are adjacent in L; Otherwise $\Delta\left(r_i, r_j\right) = 0$. As stated in the previous section, each residue is represented as either H or P. Thus $E(\sigma_i, \sigma_j)$ could be $E\left(H,H\right)$, $E\left(H,P\right)$, $E\left(P,H\right)$., or $E\left(P,P\right)$. For their values, three schemes have been proposed. The most widely used scheme is $E\left(H,H\right) = -1$, $E\left(H,P\right) = 0, E\left(P,H\right) = 0$, and $E\left(P,P\right) = 0$. The second scheme $E\left(H,H\right) = -2.3,$ ⫲⫲, $E\left(P,H\right) = -1$, and $E\left(P,P\right) = 0$ was proposed. The last scheme $E\left(H,H\right) = -2$, $E\left(H,P\right) = 1$, $E\left(P,H\right) = 1$, and $E\left(P,P\right) = 1$ is called functional model protein (or "shifted" HP model) (Cutello, Nicosia, Pavone, & Timmis, 2007). As mentioned in (Silverio, 2008), the results are insensitive to the value of *E(H,H)* as long as the physical constraints (Li, Helling, Tang, & Wingreen, 1996) are satisfied. Thus we have chosen the first scheme in this book chapter.

For the representation of an amino acid residue sequence, there are two conditions to be satisfied: (Krasnogor, Hart, Smith, & Pelta, 1999) (1) Sequence connectivity (2) Self-avoidance. Among the proposed representations (Cutello, Nicosia, Pavone, & Timmis, 2007), *Internal Coordinate* should be a favorable choice since it can handle the first condition implicitly. Internal coordinate is a representation system which residue positions depend on their sequence-predecessor residues. There are two types of internal coordinate representation: *Absolute Encoding* and *Relative Encoding*. Absolute encoding represents each residue position as the aolute direction from the previous residue. A sequence is represented as {U,D,L,R,F,B}$^{n-1}$ (Up, Down, Left,ight, Forward, Backward) (Unger & Moult, 1993). On the other hand, relative encoding represents those as relatively directional changes based on the directions of the two predecessor residues. Backward direction is omitted for one-step self-avoiding. Thus a sequence is represented as {F,R,L,U,D}$^{n-2}$ (Patton, Punch III, & Goodman, 1995). Except the forward move, a cyclic conformation is formed if a move is repeated four times. Krasnogor et al. (Krasnogor, Hart, Smith, & Pelta, 1999) have examined both representations on square lattices. Their results showed that relative encoding had better performance than absolute encoding on square lattices.

Although the 3D HP model seems relatively simple among other models, it has been proved that the protein structure prediction problem on the model is NP-Complete (Berger & Leighton, 1998). Thus researchers propose heuristics as compromising solutions. In particular, the seminal work by Unger et al. (Unger & Moult, 1993) experimentally showed that genetic algorithm approaches were better than Monte Carlos simulations. Thus researchers tried genetic algorithm as one of the heuristics to solve the problem. Nevertheless, the genetic algorithm approach by Unger et al. (Unger & Moult, 1993) was actually hybridized with Monte Carlo moves. Hence Patton et al. (Patton, Punch III, & Goodman, 1995) further generalized it into a standard genetic algorithm approach, which search space included infeasible regions penalized by a penalty function. Furthermore, they proposed "relative encoding" so that one-step self-avoiding constraints could be implicitly incorporated in the genome representation. Few years later, Krasnogor et al. (Krasnogor, Hart, Smith, & Pelta, 1999) published a work discussing the basic algorithmic factors affecting the problem. Since then, researchers explored different ways to tackle the problem. For instance, Krasnogor et al. further applied a multimeme algorithm, which adaptively chose multiple local searchers to reach optimal structures (Krasnogor, Blackburnem, Hirst, & Burke, 2002). Cox et al. (Cox, Mortimer-Jones, Taylor, & Johnston, 2004) and Hoque et al. (Hoque, Chetty, & Dooley, 2006) utilized heavy machinery of specific genetic operators and techniques. Ant colony algorithm (Shmygelska & Hoos, 2005), differential evolution (Bitello & Lopes, 2006), immune algorithm (Cutello, Nicosia, Pavone, & Timmis, 2007) and estimation of distribution algorithm (Santana, Larranaga, & Lozano, 2008) were also customized and reported in literatures. In particular, diversity preserving techniques were often incorporated in them. For instance, Duplicate Predator (Cox, Mortimer-Jones, Taylor, & Johnston, 2004), Aging Operator (Cutello, Nicosia, Pavone, & Timmis, 2007), and additional renormalization of the pheromone (Shmygelska & Hoos, 2005). They can be deemed as the signs of the multimodality in the problem. However, the necessity of multimodal optimization techniques has not been emphasized.

For the protein structure prediction problem, it is generally believed that the native state of protein should be at the conformation with the lowest energy. Thus previous works mainly focus on the minimal energy they could achieve: the minimal energy ever found and the average and standard deviation of the minimal energy across several runs. Nevertheless, Jahn et al. (Jahn & Radford, 2008) has shown that the native state is not necessarily a single global optimum. It may also be a local optimum in Fig.1 of (Jahn & Radford, 2008). For the HP lattice model, Unger et al. (Unger & Moult, 1993) have observed that there can be multiple conformations for each energy value. A recent fitness landscape study also indicated that HP landscapes were highly multimodal (Flores & Smith, 2003). Thus Wong et al. have proposed multimodal optimization techniques for the protein structure prediction problem (Wong, Leung, & Wong, 2010).

The most widely used distance measure should be the root mean square deviation (RMSD) (Holm & Sander, 1993). RMSD calculates the average absolute distances between two superimposed conformations' points. Nevertheless, if two conformations differ by only one point direction in relative encoding, their RMSD cannot reflect such small change. For instance, some conformations of the benchmark UM20 (Cotta, 2003) are visualized in Figure 4.

To be mutated to the optimal conformation, Example A is only needed to change its move between a1 and a2 to R whereas example b is needed to change nearly all of its moves between b1 and b8. However, the RMSD of Example A with the optimal conformation (5 diagonal point changes a2 to a6) is larger than that of example B (4 diagonal point changes b2,b3,b5,b6). RMSD cannot capture the move information in relative encoding. Furthermore, if RMSD is applied, it will be quite computationally intensive. To calculate the RMSD between two conformations, the corresponding relative encoding genomes are

Figure 4. The left most confirmation depicts an optimal conformation (LDLDFLUFDDFRFRDDFD) on the benchmark UM20. The other two confirmations (LDLDFLUFDDFRFEDDFD and LDLDDLL-RLLDRFRDDFD) depict two candidate conformations after mutations; red beads denote hydrophobic residues (H) while blue beads denote polar residues (P).

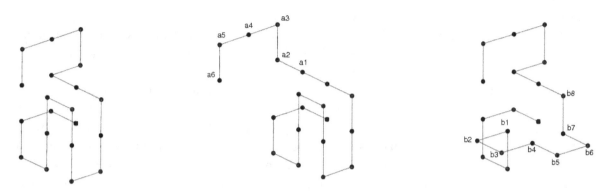

converted to absolute 3D coordinates. Once converted, one of them is then translated and rotated to be optimally superimposed on the other. RMSD is then calculated which involves multiplications and square root calculations. In contrast, Hamming distance calculates the move differences between two relative encoding genomes. It is relatively computational tractable. Thus Hamming distance is usually adopted in this problem.

Basically there are two approaches for handling infeasible conformations:

1.   Delete infeasible conformations;
2.   Tolerate infeasible conformations by adjusting their energy values by a penalty score (either constant or adaptive).

Both approaches were thought beneficial in different view angles (Flores & Smith, 2003). For the first approach, it is conjectured that search space can be narrowed if infeasible conformations are deleted. For the second approach, it is conjectured that the paths to optimal conformations are shorter if infeasible conformations exist. Nevertheless, the study in (Flores & Smith, 2003) had a detailed analysis supporting the first approach.

Evolutionary Algorithms for Protein-DNA Pattern Discovery

Protein-DNA interactions are essential in genetic activities such as transcription, packaging, rearrangement, and replication (Luscombe & Thornton, 2002). Understanding them forms the basis for further deciphering biological systems. In particular, the protein-DNA interactions between Transcription Factors (TFs) and Transcription Factor Binding Sites (TFBSs) play a central role in gene transcription. TFs bind in a sequence-specific manner to TFBSs to regulate gene transcription (Luscombe, Austin, Berman, & Thornton, 2000).

Nevertheless, it is expensive and laborious to experimentally identify the TF-TFBS binding sequence pairs, for example, using DNA footprinting (Galas & Schmitz, 1987) or gel electrophoresis (Garner & Revzin, 1981). The technology of Chromatin immunoprecipitation (ChIP) (Smith, Sumazin, Das, &

Zhang, 2005) measures the binding of a particular TF to DNA of co-regulated genes on a genome-wide scale *in vivo*, but at low resolution. Further processing is needed to extract precise TFBSs (Liu, Brutlag, & Liu, 2002). To share the precious sequence data, researchers have built databases. In particular, TRANSFAC (Matys, et al., 2006) is one of the largest and most representative databases for regulatory elements including TFs, TFBSs, nucleotide distribution matrices of the TFBSs, and regulated genes. The data are expertly annotated and manually corrected from peer-reviewed publications and experimentally verified studies. Other annotation databases of TF families and binding domains are also available (e.g. PROSITE (Hulo, et al., 2008), Pfam (Bateman, et al., 2004)).

On the other hand, high-quality TF-TFBS binding structures can provide valuable insights into putative principles of binding. However, it is difficult and time consuming to extract those high-resolution 3D TF-TFBS complex structures with X-ray crystallography (Smyth & Martin, 2000) or Nuclear Magnetic Resonance (NMR) spectroscopic analysis (Mohan & Hosur, 2009). To share the precious structural data, researchers have also built databases. In particular, the Protein Data Bank (PDB) (Berman, et al., 2000) serves as a representative repository of such experimentally extracted protein-DNA (in particular TF-TFBS) complexes with high resolution at atomic levels. However, the available 3D structures are far from complete. As a result, there is strong motivation to have automatic methods, particularly, computational approaches based on existing abundant data, to provide testable candidates of TF-TFBS binding sequence pairs with high confidence to guide and accelerate the wet-lab experiments.

Most of the previous computational attempts related to TF-TFBS interactions are devoted to discover either the motifs of TF domains or those of TFBSs separately. The TF domains and TFBSs sequences are somewhat conserved due to their functional similarity and importance. By exploiting the conservation, computational methods called motif discovery have been proposed to save the expensive and laborious laboratory experiments (MacIsaac & Fraenkel, 2006). The methods usually make use of comprehensive statistical and scoring models to extract the domain information from the background sequences (Jensen, Liu, Zhou, & Liu, 2004). In addition, data mining methods have been proposed to find the sequence pairs. For instance, support vector machines (SVM) (Ofran, Mysore, & Rost, 2007) and regressions (Zhou & Liu, 2008). Distinct from motif discovery, they utilize the biochemical information in sequence data (e.g. base compositions, structures, thermodynamic properties (Ahmad, Keskin, Sarai, & Nussinov, 2008)) to perform prediction. Nevertheless, most of their results are not concrete sequences (the most explicit and interpretable format).

Thus Leung et al. have proposed a framework based on association rule mining with Apriori algorithm (Agrawal, Imielinski, & Swami, 1993) to discover associated TF-TFBS binding sequence patterns in the most explicit and interpretable form from TRANSFAC (Leung, et al., 2010). With downward closure property, the algorithm guarantees the exact and optimal performance to generate all frequent TFBS k-mer TF k-mer pairs from TRANSFAC where a k-mer is a string with length equal to k. The approach relies merely on sequence information without any prior knowledge in TF binding domains or protein-DNA 3D structure data. From comprehensive evaluations, statistics of the discovered patterns are shown to reflect meaningful binding characteristics. According to independent literature, PDB data and homology modeling, a good number of TF-TFBS binding patterns discovered have been verified by experiments and annotations. They exhibit atomic-level interactions between the respective TF binding domains and specific nucleotides of the TFBS from experimentally determined protein-DNA 3D structures.

Although the above, the sequence pairs discovered are in one-to-one mappings (Leung, et al., 2010). One TF amino acid sequence is coupled with one TFBS DNA sequence. In the biological world, a TF may bind to a promoter using several contact surface subsequences. Some surfaces of the TF may also be interacting surfaces to recruit another TF as a performing complex (White R. J., 2001). For instance, McGuire et al found that there were two conserved parts for the ArcA-P recognition motif in E.coli (McGuire, De Wulf, Church, & Lin, 1999). Kato et al. proposed a novel method to identify combinatorial regulation of transcription factors and binding motifs using chromatin immunoprecipitation (ChIP) data with microarray expression data (Kato, Hata, Banerjee, Futcher, & Zhang, 2004). A case study in the evolution of combinatorial gene regulation in Fungi has also been carried out (Tuch, Galgoczy, Hernday, Li, & Johnson, 2008). Biochemists have used biochemical experiment methods to observe many evidences. For instance, SOX proteins perform their function in a complex interplay with other transcription factors in a manner highly dependent on cell type and promoter context. In particular, multiple TFBSs are found within the enhancer of the FGF4 gene during early embryonic expression. One is a recognition element for POU proteins; the other is a binding site for SOX proteins. The POU and SOX protein partnership is crucial to determine cell fate. Scientists have also used 3D structural determination methods to observe such combinatorial behavior. Some examples can be found in (Kato, Hata, Banerjee, Futcher, & Zhang, 2004). Many experimental evidences can also be found in TransCompel (Matys, et al., 2006) which is a comprehensive database on the composite interactions between TFs binding to their TFBSs. Multiple TF amino acid sequences may be coupled with multiple TFBS DNA sequence, instead of just one-to-one mapping. Considering the huge search space, Wong et al. have further proposed an evolutionary algorithm to learn generalized representations from the original pairs (Wong, Peng, Wong, & Leung, 2011). In particular, the original pairs are evolved to pairs of boolean expressions (trees) of k-mers An example is shown in Figure 5.

Evolving trees (e.g. boolean expressions of k-mers) by evolutionary algorithms are well studied in the genetic programming field. Many design issues have been reviewed in section 2 of (Banzhaf, Nordin, Keller, & Francone, 1998). In particular, researchers are especially concerned about the roles of crossovers and mutations. Some of them argue that crossovers are not beneficial to the evolution, whereas the others hold the opposite view (Spears & Anand, 1991). Some of them also argue that mutations are not needed, whereas the others hold the opposite view (Poli, Langdon, & Mcphee, A Field Guide to Genetic Programming, 2008). Even extensive experiments on comparing crossovers and mutations on a series of well-known problems have been conducted (Luke & Spector, 1998). The results can only reflect that it is problem-dependent (White & Poulding, 2009). The debate is still continuing. Thus, as a compromising solution, both crossover and mutation operators are adopted in (Wong, Peng, Wong, &

Figure 5. Exemplary pair of boolean expressions (trees) of k-mers; the left tree is on the TF side with amino acid k-mers while the right tree is on the TFBS side with DNA k-mers.

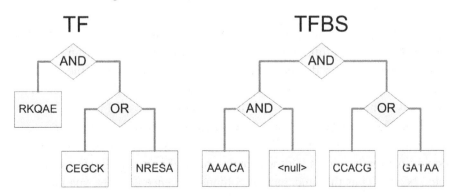

Leung, 2011). Another important topic in genetic programming is to control the "bloat" property. During a typical run of genetic programming, it is often found that some unnecessary components (called "introns") are formed. It is intuitive for us to think that they are not necessary, and thus not good. Soule et al. (Terence, Foster, & Dickinson, 1996) suggested a fitness function which penalizes trees with many introns. Rosca also suggested parsimony pressure on selecting trees was beneficial to grow toward the optimal structures (Rosca, 1997). Some researchers also suggest that the presence of the introns can confuse crossover operators, protecting good modules/components as discussed in Chapter 7 of (Banzhaf, Nordin, Keller, & Francone, 1998). For instance, some of them made use of the bloat property to evolve buffer overflow attack codes which can successfully hide themselves from intrusion detectors (Kayacik, Heywood, & Zincir-Heywood, 2006). Indeed, the bloat property is a double-edged sword.

CONCLUSION

Evolutionary algorithms build a bridge between computer science and nature (Kari & Rozenberg, 2008). Instead of artificial creation, evolutionary algorithm emphasizes on learning from nature. Nature rules are applied or modeled to build novel computational techniques, which can be well adapted and integrated into different contexts. For instance, inspired from the Darwin's evolutionary theory, John Holland has proposed genetic algorithm which simulates the evolutionary process for natural selection. It has been proved successful in different applications widely. Indeed, the design of evolutionary algorithms draws inspiration from nature. They resemble the natural mechanism and are affiliated to nature. It is not surprising for us to expect that they should be among the best methods in bioinformatics to decipher nature in the future.

Besides, we suspect that most of the evolutionary algorithms applied to bioinformatics are always stuck in local optima. People are either not aware of the issue, or too lazy to study and handle it as long as the local optima found are good enough in practice. Thus we can foresee, if we further apply some evolutionary algorithms for multimodal optimization to the bioinformatics problems, promising results will be probably obtained.

Notably, Wong et al. have proposed robust and competitive methods for multimodel optimization (Wong, Wu, Mok, Peng, & Zhang, 2012). In those methods, to explore the locality principle in evolutionary computation, crowding differential evolution (CrowdingDE) is incorporated with locality for multimodal optimization. Instead of generating trial vectors randomly, the first method proposed takes advantage of spatial locality to generate trial vectors. Temporal locality is also adopted to help generate offspring in the second method proposed. Temporal and spatial localities are then applied together in the third method proposed.

If diversity maintenance techniques are not applied, most evolutionary algorithms will prematurely converge and get stuck in a local optimum. To cope with the problem, the algorithms are usually equipped with their own local operations for diversity maintenance. In CorwdingDE, the local operation is the crowding technique, in which each offspring can only replace the individual which is most similar to itself. Looking at this technique more deeply, a restriction is proposed in the individual replacement method so that a individual gets replaced only when another individual is generated and evaluated fitter than the former within the same niche. The algorithm is forced to passively wait for the trial vector generations for feasible replacements. Unfortunately, the trial vector generations of CrowdingDE are random, as stated before. Thus the fundamental computer science concept, spatial locality, is applied to the trial vector generations in order to increase the chance of successful replacements in this work.

Close individuals tend to have similar characteristics. In a run of evolutionary algorithm, the population is usually divided into different niches. Within each niche, the individuals exhibit similar positions and step-sizes for improvement. After several generations, the differences between niches may be large. It will be a disaster if a single evolutionary strategy is applied to all of them regardless of their niches. Interestingly, it is a double-edged sword. Such a property also gives us spatial locality: the crossovers between close individuals can have higher chance to generate better offspring in their niche, comparing with the crossovers between distinct individuals. Thus the individuals which are closer to the parent than the others in the same generation should be given more chance of trial vector generations within a population. We should be aware that such an evolutionary policy may not be applicable for the problem domains other than multimodal optimization because the selected individuals may be similar to each other. Such a similarity may generally reduce the step size. To bring such a neighborhood idea into trial vector generations, spatial locality is proposed as a measure for selecting individuals to form trial vectors. The distances between the parent and all candidate individuals are computed and transformed into proportions which form a roulette-wheel. Within the roulette-wheel, a larger portion is given to the candidate individual which is closer to the parent than the others in the same generation. It follows that closer individuals are given higher chance of trial vector generations and vice versa.

By doing so, each trial vector generation becomes a local operation tailor-made for the parent individual. Crowding Differential Evolution (CrowdingDE) is reformulated as a hybrid algorithm which takes advantage of spatial locality. Thus we call the proposed algorithm as Crowding Differential Evolution using Spatial Locality (CrowdingDE-SL).

Besides spatial locality, temporal locality is also an intrinsic feature we can make use of. For instance, the most typical application is the use of cache in a computer system. If some data is accessed at a given time, then it is very likely that these data will be referenced again. Thus it is useful to store these data into high speed caches. Based on the same idea, such a temporal locality concept can also be incorporated into CrowdingDE. If an individual is replaced by another fitter individual under the crowding selection, then the vector difference between them is a improvement step within their niche. If the step is reused in a correct situation, it can contribute to improvements within their niche again. Thus it is advantageous for an algorithm to save and reuse these vectors for improvement. Nevertheless, as several generations pass by, a vast amount of these vectors are accumulated. It is impossible to store them all. As an intuitive solution, these vectors should be summarized on the fly. To do that, there are lots of existing techniques available. Considering the heavily iterative property of evolutionary algorithms, computational efficiency needs be taken into account seriously. Thus a simple summation technique with a discount factor is proposed.

In that technique, each individual is allocated with an array called delta which is of the same size as the genome. The main use of the array is to store the temporal locality history. Whenever an offspring generated is fitter than its nearest neighbor, the method records and stores their vector difference, plus the array delta of the nearest neighbor (with a discount factor), into the array delta of the offspring. After that, one more offspring is generated by summing the genome of the offspring and the array delta of the offspring together. If the new offspring is fitter than the original offspring, then the new offspring replaces the nearest neighbor. Otherwise, the original offspring replaces the nearest neighbor. Combined with this local operation, Crowding Differential Evolution (CrowdingDE) is reformulated as a hybrid algorithm which takes advantage of temporal locality. Thus we call it Crowding Differential Evolution using Temporal Locality (CrowdingDE-TL).

Having incorporated spatial and temporal locality into CrowdingDE separately, it is intuitive for us to apply them together since they belong to different modules: spatial locality takes effect in trial vector generations, whereas temporal locality takes effect in the selection stage after trial vector generations. Thus CrowdingDE can be combined with both spatial and temporal locality together, which is subsequently called Crowding Differential Evolution using Spatial and Temporal Locality (CrowdingDE-STL).

Numerical experiments are conducted to compare the proposed methods with the state-of-the-art methods on benchmark functions extensively. Experimental analysis is undertaken to observe the effect of locality and the synergy between temporal locality and spatial locality. Further experiments are also conducted on two application problems. One is the varied-line-spacing holographic grating design problem, while the other is the protein structure prediction problem. The numerical results demonstrate the effectiveness of those methods (Wong, Wu, Mok, Peng, & Zhang, 2012).

REFERENCES

Abecasis, G. R., Auton, A., Brooks, L. D., DePristo, M. A., & Durbin, R. M. (2012, November). An integrated map of genetic variation from 1,092 human genomes. *Nature*, *491*(7422), 56–65. PMID:23128226

Abeel, T., Van de Peer, Y., & Saeys, Y. (2009). Toward a gold standard for promoter prediction evaluation. *Bioinformatics (Oxford, England)*, *25*(12), i313–i320. doi:10.1093/bioinformatics/btp191 PMID:19478005

Agrawal, R., Imielinski, T., & Swami, A. (1993). Mining association rules between sets of items in large databases. *Proceedings of the 1993 ACM SIGMOD international conference on Management of data SIGMOD '93* (pp. 207-216). doi:10.1145/170035.170072

Ahmad, S., Keskin, O., Sarai, A., & Nussinov, R. (2008, October). Protein-DNA interactions: Structural, thermodynamic and clustering patterns of conserved residues in DNA-binding proteins. *Nucleic Acids Research*, *36*(18), 5922–5932. doi:10.1093/nar/gkn573 PMID:18801847

Altschul, S. F., Gish, W., Miller, W., Myers, E. W., & Lipman, D. J. (1990, October). Basic local alignment search tool. *Journal of molecular biology, 215*(3), 403-410. doi:10.1006/jmbi.1990.9999

Aluru, S. (2005). Handbook of Computational Molecular Biology. Chapman & Hall/CRC.

Anfinsen, C. B. (1973). Principles that Govern the Folding of Protein Chains. *Science, 181*(4096), 223–230. Retrieved from http://www.sciencemag.org doi:10.1126/science.181.4096.223 PMID:4124164

Baker, D. (2000, May). A surprising simplicity to protein folding. *Nature, 405*(6782), 39-42. Retrieved from10.1038/35011000

Baker, D., & Sali, A. (2001). Protein Structure Prediction and Structural Genomics. *Science, 294*(5540), 93–96. Retrieved from http://www.sciencemag.org/cgi/content/abstract/sci;294/5540/93 doi:10.1126/science.1065659 PubMed doi:10.1126/science.1065659 PMID:11588250

Banzhaf, W., Nordin, P., Keller, R. E., & Francone, F. D. (1998, January). *Genetic Programming -- An Introduction; On the Automatic Evolution of Computer Programs and its Applications.* San Francisco, CA, USA: Morgan Kaufmann. Retrieved from http://www.elsevier.com/wps/find/bookdescription. cws_home/677869/description#description

Bateman, A., Coin, L., Durbin, R., Finn, R. D., & Hollich, V. (2004). The Pfam protein families database. *Nucleic Acids Research, 32*(90001), D138–D141. doi:10.1093/nar/gkh121 PMID:14681378

Berger, B., & Leighton, T. (1998). Protein folding in the hydrophobic-hydrophilic (HP) is NP-complete. *Proceedings of the second annual international conference on Computational molecular biology RE-COMB '98* (pp. 30-39). New York, NY, USA: ACM. doi:10.1145/279069.279080

Berman, H. M., Westbrook, J., Feng, Z., Gilliland, G., Bhat, T. N., Weissig, H., . . . Bourne, P. E. (2000, January). The Protein Data Bank. *Nucl. Acids Res., 28*(1), 235-242. doi:10.1093/nar/28.1.235

Bertini, I., De, M., Moretti, F., & Pizzuti, S. (2010). Start-Up Optimisation of a Combined Cycle Power Plant with Multiobjective Evolutionary Algorithms. *EvoApplications* (Vol. 2, pp. 151-160).

Beyer, H., & Schwefel, H. (2002, March). Evolution strategies - A comprehensive introduction. *Natural Computing, 1*(1), 3-52. doi:10.1023/A:1015059928466

Bitello, R., & Lopes, H. S. (2006, September). A Differential Evolution Approach for Protein Folding. Proceedings of the *IEEE Symposium on Computational Intelligence and Bioinformatics and Computational Biology CIBCB '06*, Toronto, Ontario, Canada (pp. 1-5).

Civicioglu, P., & Besdok, E. (2013). A conceptual comparison of the Cuckoo-search, particle swarm optimization, differential evolution and artificial bee colony algorithms. *Artificial Intelligence Review, 39*(4), 315–346. doi:10.1007/s10462-011-9276-0

Liu, J. S., Zhou, Q., Liu, X. S., & Jensen, S. T. (2004). Computational discovery of gene regulatory binding motifs: A Bayesian perspective. *Statistical Science, 19*(1), 188–204. doi:10.1214/088342304000000107

Human Genome Sequencing Consortium, . (2004, October). Finishing the euchromatic sequence of the human genome. *Nature, 431*(7011), 931–945. doi:10.1038/nature03001 PMID:15496913

Consortium, E. (2012, September). An integrated encyclopedia of DNA elements in the human genome. *Nature, 489*(7414), 57–74. PMID:22955616

Cotta, C. (2003). Protein Structure Prediction Using Evolutionary Algorithms Hybridized with Backtracking. *Proceedings of the 7th International Work-Conference on Artificial and Natural Neural Networks IWANN '03* (pp. 321-328). Berlin, Heidelberg: Springer-Verlag. doi:10.1007/3-540-44869-1_41

Cox, G. A., Mortimer-Jones, T. V., Taylor, R. P., & Johnston, R. L. (2004). Development and optimisation of a novel genetic algorithm for studying model protein folding. *Theoretical Chemistry Accounts: Theory, Computation, and Modeling, 112*(3), 163–178. doi:10.1007/s00214-004-0601-4

Cutello, V., Nicosia, G., Pavone, M., & Timmis, J. (2007, February). An Immune Algorithm for Protein Structure Prediction on Lattice Models. *IEEE Transactions on Evolutionary Computation, 11*(1), 101-117.

D'Haeseleer, P., Liang, S., & Somogyi, R. (2000, August). Genetic network inference: from co-expression clustering to reverse engineering. *Bioinformatics (Oxford, England), 16*(8), 707-726. doi:10.1093/bioinformatics/16.8.707

De Jong, K. A. (2006). *Evolutionary Computation. A Unified Approach.* Cambridge, MA, USA: MIT Press.

Del Venayagamoorthy, G. K., Mohagheghi, S., Hernandez, J. C., & Harley, R. G. (2008). Particle Swarm Optimization: Basic Concepts, Variants and Applications in Power Systems. *Evolutionary Computation, IEEE Transactions, 12*(2), 171-195. doi:10.1109/TEVC.2007.896686

Dorigo, M., & Gambardella, L. M. (1997). Ant colony system: a cooperative learning approach to the traveling salesman problem. *Evolutionary Computation, IEEE Transactions on, 1*(1), 53-66. doi:10.1109/4235.585892

Duan, Y., & Kollman, P. A. (2001). Computational protein folding: From lattice to all-atom. *IBM Systems Journal, 40*(2), 297–309. doi:10.1147/sj.402.0297

Esling, P., Carpentier, G., & Agon, C. (2010). Dynamic Musical Orchestration Using Genetic Algorithms and a Spectro-Temporal Description of Musical Instruments. *EvoApplications* (Vol. 2, pp. 371-380).

Feoktistov, V. (2006). Differential Evolution. In *Search of Solutions*. Secaucus, NJ, USA: Springer-Verlag New York, Inc.

Fleischmann, R. D., Adams, M. D., White, O., Clayton, R. A., Kirkness, E. F., Kerlavage, A. R., & Merrick, J. M. et al. (1995, July). Whole-genome random sequencing and assembly of Haemophilus influenza Rd. *Science, 269*(5223), 496–512. doi:10.1126/science.7542800 PMID:7542800

Flores, S. D., & Smith, J. (2003, #dec#). Study of fitness landscapes for the HP model of protein structure prediction. Proceedings of the *2003 Congress on Evolutionary Computation CEC '03* (pp. 2338-2345).

Furuholmen, M., Glette, K., Hovin, M., & Torresen, J. (2010). Evolutionary Approaches to the Three-dimensional Multi-pipe Routing Problem: A Comparative Study Using Direct Encodings. EvoCOP, 71-82.

Galas, D. J., & Schmitz, A. (1987, September). DNAse footprinting: A simple method for the detection of protein-{DNA} binding specificity. *Nucleic Acids Research, 5*(9), 3157–3170. doi:10.1093/nar/5.9.3157 PMID:212715

Garner, M. M., & Revzin, A. (1981, July). A gel electrophoresis method for quantifying the binding of proteins to specific DNA regions: Application to components of the Escherichia coli lactose operon regulatory system. *Nucleic Acids Research, 9*(13), 3047–3060. doi:10.1093/nar/9.13.3047 PMID:6269071

Goffeau, A., Barrell, B., Bussey, H., Davis, R., Dujon, B., Feldmann, H., & Oliver, S. et al. (1996, October). Life with 6000 genes. *Science, 274*(5287), 563–567. doi:10.1126/science.274.5287.546 PMID:8849441

Goldberg, D. E., & Richardson, J. (1987). Genetic algorithms with sharing for multimodal function optimization. *Proceedings of the Second International Conference on Genetic algorithms and their application* (pp. 41-49). Hillsdale, NJ, USA: L. Erlbaum Associates Inc.

GuhaThakurta, D. (2006). Computational identification of transcriptional regulatory elements in DNA sequence. *Nucleic Acids Research, 34*(12), 3585–3598. doi:10.1093/nar/gkl372 PMID:16855295

Hadka, D., & Reed, P. (2013). Borg: An Auto-Adaptive Many-Objective Evolutionary Computing Framework. *Evolutionary Computation, 21*(2), 231–259. doi:10.1162/EVCO_a_00075 PMID:22385134

Holland, J. H. (1975). *Adaptation in natural and artificial systems*. Ann Arbor: University of Michigan Press.

Holm, L., & Sander, C. (1993, September). Protein structure comparison by alignment of distance matrices. *Journal of Molecular Biology*, *233*(1), 123–138. doi:10.1006/jmbi.1993.1489 PMID:8377180

Hoque, T., Chetty, M., & Dooley, L. S. (2006). A Guided Genetic Algorithm for Protein Folding Prediction Using 3D Hydrophobic-Hydrophilic Model. Proceedings of the *IEEE Congress on Evolutionary Computation CEC '06,* Vancouver, BC, Canada (pp. 2339-2346).

Hulo, N., Bairoch, A., Bulliard, V., Cerutti, L., Cuche, B. A., de Castro, E., . . . Sigrist, C. J. (2008, January). The 20 years of PROSITE. *Nucl. Acids Res., 36*(suppl_1), D245--249.

Initiative, A. G.The Arabidopsis Genome Initiative. (2000, December). Analysis of the genome sequence of the flowering plant Arabidopsis thaliana. *Nature*, *408*(6814), 796–815. doi:10.1038/35048692 PMID:11130711

Iredi, S., Merkle, D., & Middendorf, M. (2000). Bi-Criterion Optimization with Multi Colony Ant Algorithms. *Proceedings of the First International Conference on Evolutionary Multi-Criterion Optimization (EMO 2001)* (pp. 359-372). Springer.

Jahn, T. R., & Radford, S. E. (2008, January). Folding versus aggregation: Polypeptide conformations on competing pathways. *Archives of Biochemistry and Biophysics*, *469*(1), 100–117. doi:10.1016/j.abb.2007.05.015 PMID:17588526

Karaboga, D., Akay, B., & Ozturk, C. (2007). Artificial Bee Colony (ABC) Optimization Algorithm for Training Feed-Forward Neural Networks. In V. Torra, Y. Narukawa, & Y. Yoshida (Eds.), MDAI 4617 (pp. 318–329). Springer; Retrieved from http://dblp.uni-trier.de/db/conf/mdai/mdai2007.html#KarabogaAO07 doi:10.1007/978-3-540-73729-2_30

Kari, L., & Rozenberg, G. (2008). The many facets of natural computing. *Communications of the ACM*, *51*(10), 72–83. doi:10.1145/1400181.1400200

Kato, M., Hata, N., Banerjee, N., Futcher, B., & Zhang, M. Q. (2004). Identifying combinatorial regulation of transcription factors and binding motifs. *Genome Biology*, *5*(8), R56. doi:10.1186/gb-2004-5-8-r56 PMID:15287978

Kayacik, H., Heywood, M., & Zincir-Heywood, N. (2006). On evolving buffer overflow attacks using genetic programming. *Proceedings of the 8th annual conference on Genetic and evolutionary computation* (pp. 1667-1674). New York: ACM. doi:10.1145/1143997.1144271

Krasnogor, N., Blackburnem, B., Hirst, J., & Burke, E. (2002, September). Multimeme Algorithms for Protein Structure Prediction. Proceedings of the *7th International Conference Parallel Problem Solving from Nature,* Granada, Spain (Vol. 2439, pp. 769-778). Springer Berlin / Heidelberg. Retrieved from http://www.cs.nott.ac.uk/~nxk/PAPERS/ppsn2002.pdf

Krasnogor, N., Hart, W., Smith, J., & Pelta, D. (1999). Protein Structure Prediction With Evolutionary Algorithms. International Genetic and Evolutionary Computation Conference (GECCO99) (pp. 1569–1601). Morgan Kaufmann. Retrieved from http://www.cs.nott.ac.uk/~nxk/PAPERS/gecco99.pdf

Lampinen, J., & Zelinka, I. (1999). Mechanical engineering design optimization by differential evolution. *New Ideas in optimization*, 127-146.

Larkin, F., & Ryan, C. (2010). Modesty Is the Best Policy: Automatic Discovery of Viable Forecasting Goals in Financial Data. *EvoApplications* (Vol. 2, pp. 202-211).

Leung, K. S., Wong, K. C., Chan, T. M., Wong, M. H., Lee, K. H., Lau, C. K., & Tsui, S. K. (2010, October). Discovering protein-DNA binding sequence patterns using association rule mining. *Nucleic Acids Research*, *38*(19), 6324–6337. doi:10.1093/nar/gkq500 PMID:20529874

Levinthal, C. (1968). Are there pathways for protein folding? *The Journal of Chemical Physics*, *65*, 44–45.

Li, H., Helling, R., Tang, C., & Wingreen, N. (1996). Emergence of Preferred Structures in a Simple Model of Protein Folding. *Science*, *273*(5275), 666–669. Retrieved from http://www.sciencemag.org/cgi/content/abstract/273/5275/666 doi:10.1126/science.273.5275.666 PMID:8662562

Liang, Y., Leung, K. S., & Mok, T. S. (2008). Evolutionary drug scheduling models with different toxicity metabolism in cancer chemotherapy. *Applied Soft Computing*, *8*(1), 140–149. doi:10.1016/j.asoc.2006.12.002

Liu, X. S., Brutlag, D. L., & Liu, J. S. (2002). An algorithm for finding protein DNA binding sites with applications to chromatinimmunoprecipitation microarray experiments. *Nature Biotechnology*, *20*(8), 835–839. doi:10.1038/nbt717 PMID:12101404

Luke, S., & Spector, L. (1998). A Revised Comparison of Crossover and Mutation in Genetic Programming. *Proceedings of the Third Annual Genetic Programming Conference (GP98)* (pp. 208-213). Morgan Kaufmann.

Luscombe, N. M., Austin, S. E., Berman, H. M., & Thornton, J. M. (2000, June). An overview of the structures of protein-DNA complexes. *Genome Biol.*, *1*(1).

Luscombe, N. M., & Thornton, J. M. (2002, July). Protein-DNA interactions: Amino acid conservation and the effects of mutations on binding specificity. *Journal of Molecular Biology*, *320*(5), 991–1009. Retrieved from http://view.ncbi.nlm.nih.gov/pubmed/12126620 doi:10.1016/S0022-2836(02)00571-5 PMID:12126620

MacIsaac, K. D., & Fraenkel, E. (2006). Practical strategies for discovering regulatory DNA sequence motifs. *PLoS Computational Biology*, *2*(4), e36. doi:10.1371/journal.pcbi.0020036 PMID:16683017

Matys, V., Kel-Margoulis, O. V., Fricke, E., Liebich, I., Land, S., Barre-Dirrie, A., & Wingender, E. et al. (2006). TRANSFAC and its module TRANSCompel: Transcriptional gene regulation in eukaryotes. *Nucleic Acids Research*, *34*(90001), 108–110. doi:10.1093/nar/gkj143 PMID:16381825

McGuffin, L. J., Bryson, K., & Jones, D. T. (2000, April). The PSIPRED protein structure prediction server. *Bioinformatics (Oxford, England)*, *16*(4), 404-405. Retrieved from 10.1093/bioinformatics/16.4.404

McGuire, A. M., De Wulf, P., Church, G. M., & Lin, E. C. (1999, April). A weight matrix for binding recognition by the redox-response regulator ArcA-P of Escherichia coli. *Molecular Microbiology*, *32*(1), 219–221. doi:10.1046/j.1365-2958.1999.01347.x PMID:10216875

Mohan, P. M., & Hosur, R. V. (2009, September). Structure-function-folding relationships and native energy landscape of dynein light chain protein: Nuclear magnetic resonance insights. *Journal of Biosciences*, *34*(3), 465–479. doi:10.1007/s12038-009-0052-0 PMID:19805907

Niu, B., & Wang, H. (2012). Bacterial Colony Optimization. *Discrete Dynamics in Nature and Society*, 698057.

Ofran, Y., Mysore, V., & Rost, B. (2007, July). Prediction of DNA-binding residues from sequence. *Bioinformatics, 23*(13), i347--353. doi:10.1093/bioinformatics/btm174

Patton, A. L., Punch, W. F. III, & Goodman, E. D. (1995). A Standard GA Approach to Native Protein Conformation Prediction. *Proceedings of the 6th International Conference on Genetic Algorithms* (pp. 574-581). San Francisco, CA, USA: Morgan Kaufmann Publishers Inc.

Poli, R., Kennedy, J., & Blackwell, T. (2007, June). Particle swarm optimization. *Swarm Intelligence, 1*(1), 33-57. doi:10.1007/s11721-007-0002-0

Poli, R., Langdon, W. B., & Mcphee, N. F. (2008, March). *A Field Guide to Genetic Programming.* Lulu Enterprises, UK Ltd. Retrieved from http://www.amazon.com/exec/obidos/redirect?tag=citeulike07-20&path=ASIN/1409200736

Price, K. V. (1997, April). Differential evolution vs. the functions of the 2nd ICEO. *Evolutionary Computation, 1997., IEEE International Conference on,* (pp. 153-157). Indianapolis, IN, USA.

Rahmat-Samii, Y., & Michielssen, E. (Eds.). (1999). Electromagnetic Optimization by Genetic Algorithms. New York, NY, USA: John Wiley \& Sons, Inc.

Ronquist, F., & Huelsenbeck, J. P. (2003, August). MrBayes 3: Bayesian phylogenetic inference under mixed models. *Bioinformatics, 19*(12), 1572-1574. Retrieved from10.1093/bioinformatics/btg180

Rosca, J. P. (1997). Analysis of Complexity Drift in Genetic Programming. *Genetic Programming 1997: Proceedings of the Second Annual Conference* (pp. 286-294). Morgan Kaufmann.

Sacco, W. F., Henderson, N., Rios-Coelho, A. C., Ali, M. M., & Pereira, C. M. (2009, June). Differential evolution algorithms applied to nuclear reactor core design. *Annals of Nuclear Energy.* doi:10.1016/j.anucene.2009.05.007

Santana, R., Larranaga, P., & Lozano, J. A. (2008, August). Protein Folding in Simplified Models with Estimation of Distribution Algorithms. *IEEE Transactions on Evolutionary Computation, 12*(4), 418-438.

Schoonderwoerd, R., Bruten, J. L., Holland, O. E., & Rothkrantz, L. J. (1996). Ant-based load balancing in telecommunications networks. *Adaptive Behavior, 5*(2), 169–207. doi:10.1177/105971239700500203

Shah-Hosseini, H. (2009). The intelligent water drops algorithm: A nature-inspired swarm-based optimization algorithm. *International Journal of Bio-inspired Computation, 1*(1/2), 71–79. doi:10.1504/IJBIC.2009.022775

Shmygelska, A., & Hoos, H. (2005). An ant colony optimisation algorithm for the 2D and 3D hydrophobic polar protein folding problem. *BMC Bioinformatics, 6*(1), 30. http://www.biomedcentral.com/1471-2105/6/30 doi:10.1186/1471-2105-6-30 PMID:15710037

Silverio, H. (2008). Evolutionary Algorithms for the Protein Folding Problem: A Review and Current Trends. *Computational Intelligence in Biomedicine and Bioinformatics*, 297-315. Retrieved from http://www.springerlink.com/content/e810504k11t13107

Singh, G., & Deb, K. (2006). Comparison of multi-modal optimization algorithms based on evolutionary algorithms. *Proceedings of the 8th annual conference on Genetic and evolutionary computation GECCO '06* (pp. 1305-1312). doi:10.1145/1143997.1144200

Smith, A. D., Sumazin, P., Das, D., & Zhang, M. Q. (2005). Mining ChIP-chip data for transcription factor and cofactor binding sites. *Bioinformatics. Suppl, 1*(20), i403–i412.

Smyth, M. S., & Martin, J. H. (2000, February). X ray crystallography. *Molecular pathology: MP, 53*(1), 8-14. Retrieved from http://view.ncbi.nlm.nih.gov/pubmed/10884915

Spears, W. M., & Anand, V. (1991). A Study of Crossover Operators in Genetic Programming. *Proceedings of the 6th International Symposium on Methodologies for Intelligent Systems ISMIS '91* (pp. 409-418). London, UK: Springer-Verlag. doi:10.1007/3-540-54563-8_104

Storn, R., & Price, K. (1997, December). Differential Evolution - A Simple and Efficient Heuristic for global Optimization over Continuous Spaces. *Journal of Global Optimization, 11*(4), 341–359. http://www.springerlink.com/content/x555692233083677/ doi:10.1023/A:1008202821328

Terence, S., Foster, J. A., & Dickinson, J. (1996). Code growth in genetic programming. *Proceedings of the 1st annual conference on genetic programming* (pp. 215-223). Cambridge, MA: MIT Press.

Tuch, B. B., Galgoczy, D. J., Hernday, A. D., Li, H., & Johnson, A. D. (2008, February). The evolution of combinatorial gene regulation in fungi. *PLoS Biology, 6*(2), e38. doi:10.1371/journal.pbio.0060038 PMID:18303948

Unger, R., & Moult, J. (1993). Genetic Algorithm for 3D Protein Folding Simulations. *Proceedings of the 5th International Conference on Genetic Algorithms* (pp. 581-588). San Francisco, CA, USA: Morgan Kaufmann Publishers Inc.

Vuswabatgab, G. M., Afanasyer, V., Buldyrev, S. V., Murphy, E. J., Prince, P. A., & Stanley, H. E. (1996). Levy flight search patterns of wandering albatrosses. *Nature, 381*(6581), 413–415. doi:10.1038/381413a0

White, D. R., & Poulding, S. (2009). A Rigorous Evaluation of Crossover and Mutation in Genetic Programming. *Proceedings of the 12th European Conference on Genetic Programming* EuroGP '09 (pp. 220-231). Berlin, Heidelberg: Springer-Verlag.

White, R. J. (2001). *Gene Transcription: Mechanisms and Control.* Wiley-Blackwell.

Whitley, D. (1994, June). A genetic algorithm tutorial. *Statistics and Computing, 4*(2), 65-85. doi:10.1007/BF00175354

Wong, K. C., Chan, T. M., Peng, C., Li, Y., & Zhang, Z. (2013, September). DNA motif elucidation using belief propagation. *Nucleic Acids Research, 41*(16), e153. doi:10.1093/nar/gkt574 PMID:23814189

Wong, K. C., Leung, K. S., & Wong, M. H. (2009). An evolutionary algorithm with species-specific explosion for multimodal optimization. *Proceedings of the 11th Annual conference on Genetic and evolutionary computation GECCO '09* (pp. 923-930). New York, NY, USA: ACM. doi:10.1145/1569901.1570027

Wong, K. C., Leung, K. S., & Wong, M. H. (2010). Effect of Spatial Locality on an Evolutionary Algorithm for Multimodal Optimization. *EvoApplications, Part I, LNCS 6024.* Springer-Verlag.

Wong, K. C., Leung, K. S., & Wong, M. H. (2010). Protein Structure Prediction on a Lattice Model via Multimodal Optimization Techniques. *Proceedings of the 12th annual conference on Genetic and evolutionary computation* (pp. 155-162). Portland: ACM. doi:10.1145/1830483.1830513

Wong, K. C., Li, Y., Peng, C., & Zhang, Z. (2015). SignalSpider: Probabilistic pattern discovery on multiple normalized ChIP-Seq signal profiles. *Bioinformatics (Oxford, England), 31*(1), 17–24. doi:10.1093/bioinformatics/btu604 PMID:25192742

Wong, K. C., Peng, C., Li, Y., & Chan, T. M. (2014, December). Herd Clustering: A synergistic data clustering approach using collective intelligence. *Applied Soft Computing, 23*, 61–75. doi:10.1016/j.asoc.2014.05.034

Wong, K. C., Peng, C., Wong, M. H., & Leung, K. S. (2011, August). Generalizing and learning protein-DNA binding sequence representations by an evolutionary algorithm. *Soft Comput., 15*(8), 1631-1642. Doi:10.1007/s00500-011-0692-5

Wong, K. C., Wu, C. H., Mok, R., Peng, C., & Zhang, Z. (2012). Evolutionary multimodal optimization using the principle of locality. *Information Sciences, 194*, 138–170. doi:10.1016/j.ins.2011.12.016

Wong, K. C., & Zhang, Z. (2014). SNPdryad: Predicting deleterious non-synonymous human SNPs using only orthologous protein sequences. *Bioinformatics (Oxford, England), 30*(8), 1112–1119. doi:10.1093/bioinformatics/btt769 PMID:24389653

Zhou, Q., & Liu, J. S. (2008, July). Extracting sequence features to predict protein-DNA interactions: a comparative study. *Nucl. Acids Res., 36*(12), 4137-4148. doi:10.1093/nar/gkn361

Chapter 8
Discovering Behavioural Patterns within Customer Population by using Temporal Data Subsets

Goran Klepac
Raiffeisenbank Austria d.d., Croatia

ABSTRACT

Chapter represents discovering behavioural patterns within non-temporal and temporal data subsets related to customer churn. Traditional approach, based on using conventional data mining techniques, is not a guarantee for discovering valuable patterns, which could be useful for decision support. Business case, as a part of the text, illustrates such type of situation, where an additional data set has been chosen for finding useful patterns. Chosen data set with temporal characteristics was the key factor after applying REFII model on it, for finding behavioural customer patterns and for understanding causes of the increasing churn trends within observed portfolio. Text gives a methodological framework for churn problem solution, from customer value calculation, to developing predictive churn model, as well as using additional data sources in a situation where conventional approaches in churn analytics do not provide enough information for qualitative decision support. Revealed knowledge was a base for better understanding of customer needs and expectations.

1. INTRODUCTION

Understanding of customer behaviour is a key factor of market success, especially in competitive market conditions (Bang, 2009; Berry, 1997; Berry, 2000; Giudici, 2003).

Extracting important behavioural information from transactional customer data, and enabling better decision-making throughout an organization is one of the aims when a company wants to understand their customers (Hemalatha, 2012).

DOI: 10.4018/978-1-4666-9474-3.ch008

New era of big data and social networks contributes in complexity of data sources for analytical purposes, and offers new challenges and also additional useful information for understanding customer behaviour (Scot, 2012; Raine, 2012). That leads us to taking in account social network analysis as an important factor for understanding hidden relations within a portfolio.

One of the frequent topics related to customer behaviour, which is important for business, is a problem of churn detection and churn mitigation (Hadden, 2006; Rashid, 2010).

Churn detection and nature of churn is closely related to customer behaviour patterns. Understanding of customer behaviour, leads us to finding solutions for successful churn detection and mitigation.

Telecom industry is very interested in churn issues. Because of that fact, the presented case study, which connects consumer behaviour, churn detection and mitigation will be from the telecom industry.

Churn detection and mitigation is also a frequent topic in data mining literature (Berry, 1997; Berry, 2000; Giudici, 2003). Telecommunication companies are also interested in churn problem solving, especially in dynamic market environment (Klepac, 2006). Customer acquisition is important, but only as a starting point of each customer lifetime cycle. Companies attempt to extend customer lifetime period as long as possible in order to return initial costs and to make profit.

Production control, planning, and scheduling are forms of decision making, which play a crucial role in manufacturing industries. In the current competitive environment, effective decision-making has become a necessity for survival in the marketplace. (Elamvazuthi, 2012)

Telecom companies are no exception, and they also use advanced analytical models for better decision making in everyday business.

With the evolution of wireless technologies, mobile networks can provide much more interesting services and resources to users than before. Consequently storing, sharing and delivering resources efficiently have become popular topics in the field of mobile networks. (Feng, 2009)

This is not the case only for wireless technologies, but for the telecom industry in general, and the other industries as well, which act in competitive environment.

Churn modelling trend is present in technologies like IP TV, fixed phone line, and other services provided by telecom companies.

There are many areas in telecom companies in which collected data could be useful for decision-making, and churn is one of them (Hemalatha, 2012).

Churn prediction modelling is one of the major tasks in successful churn mitigation (Abbasimehr, 2011).

Predictive data mining techniques play a major role in predictive churn model development (Kotsiantis, 2009).

The reasons for customer churn are diverse. They range from the unexpected moves of competitors trying to gain a bigger piece of the market share by using swift campaigns (possibly directly endangering your company's market position) to the unsatisfied clients suddenly starting to churn (Berry, 2000).

There are no available cookbook methodologies regarding churn detection and churn prediction. In general, we can talk about some common approaches in churn detection (Giudici, 2009), but it depends on situation and business area for which we try to build an adequate model.

For the purposes of churn mitigation and detection, it is not unusual to chain several data mining methods and use analytical strategies, which fit into a specific business problem.

Traditional approach is mainly focused on using predictive models like logistic regression or neural networks, which calculate probability of churning. This could be sufficient in projects highly focused on client detection with highest evaluated probability of churn. Following case studies are much more complex, because *Veza* company wants to understand existing client structure, their segments, their needs, product adequacy, customer values and motivators for service usage as a base for long term customer relationship management.

2. BACKGROUND

The telecommunications industry was one of the first to adopt data mining technology. This is most likely because telecommunication companies routinely generate and store enormous amounts of high-quality data, have a very large customer base, and operate in a rapidly changing and highly competitive environment. (Weiss, 2009)

Case studies based on churn detection are topic in several books (Berry, 2000; Berry, 2003; Giudici 2003). Common data mining approach for churn detection is using logistic regression (Larose, 2005; Larose, 2006), survival models (Berry, 2003), neural networks (Alexander, 1995), self-organizing maps (Kohonen, 2001). A mutual characteristic of denominated method is the usage of historical data for future trends prediction. This isa dominant approach in churn detection, but the fact is that we should be aware that knowledge about events in history sometimes does not reflect future trends. Because of that, it is recommendation to use SNA as a tool which does not make judgement about churn based on history (Kazienko, 2011). SNA takes in consideration the present states in portfolio connectivity and calculates the strength of influence between the observed subjects (subscribers). This gives us insight into potential damage from perspective of churn, what will happened if some network member would leave portfolio, and how many churners would be generated because of that fact.

Traditional data mining methods based on historical data like logistic regression result ininformation about the probability that some subscriber will make churn in future period of time. SNA does not care about probabilities in classical way; it is concentrated on object influence in network on other objects in network. This means that with the help of SNA we could evaluate potential danger if a subscriber breaks a contract, because he or she could have significant influence on other subscribers.

Social network analysis became an important area for churn and behaviour understanding within some segments of population. (Varnali, 2013).

There is a lot of hidden potential in telecom databases, which remain unused for predictive modelling (Landow, 2008), and some of the papers (Qi, 2009) represent innovative approaches in integrated methodological system of telecommunication customer detainment management, including telecommunication customer churn prediction and strategy formulation of customer detainment management.

"In the telecom industry, high installation and marketing costs make it six to ten times more expensive to acquire a new customer than it is to retain an existing one. Prediction and prevention of customer churn is therefore a key priority for industrial research. While all the motives of customer decision to churn are highly uncertain, there is a lot of related temporal data generated as a result of customer interaction with the service provider." (Ruta, 2009).

Customer prospective value calculation is an important element of churn project.

In communications services, the continued competitiveness and growth of a company depends vitally on customer value. As the market nears the point of saturation, carriers are focusing on winning over competitors' subscribers, at the same time on retaining their existing customers. Customer satisfaction is the widely acknowledged primary determinant of customer behaviour. (Kim, 2009)

This element is very often neglected in churn modelling projects, but it gives us the answer to: which customers are worth spending the limited budget on. If you had a limited budget, you would like to spend it on the most valuable customers and find out who your most valuable customers are, for whom you should calculate prospective customer value.

Fuzzy expert system was used for prospective customer value calculation.

Fuzzy logic could be effective not only in prospective value calculation, but also in other areas like forecasting and planning in construction industry (Vasant, 2008; Vasant, 2012).

All mentioned elements were used for enterprise churn detection/mitigation solution, which relays on customer behaviour patterns.

The business case presented in this chapter gives an innovative, holistic solution, which combines traditional data mining models for churn probability calculation, SNA analysis and fuzzy expert system. It uses data subsets with temporal characteristics and this was a key factor of project's success.

3. CHAPTER ORGANIZATION

Chapter will show hybridization in action, in way of integration different data mining methods for solving practical problem in domain of churn in telecommunication company.

Central part of the chapter is REFII model, as a base for innovative solution, and which acts central role in hybridization process.

In the first part of the chapter, we will introduce problem with which telecom company has faced.

We will also introduce concept of using expert system as an important element of churn prediction.

Next part of the chapter is dedicated to REFII model and it application on temporal data.

Finally, key findings will be presented, as well as recommendation for churn mitigation.

4. VEZA COMPANY: GOALS OF THE PROJECT

Veza company is telecommunication company in the Croatian market which started to operate in 1998.

In the beginning of its lifetime, *Veza* company operated at relatively peaceful market with few competitors, with which it shared market without much unpredictable market situations.

During time, more and more competitors entered the market, and conditions changed. *Veza* company has been faced with increasing problems of subscriber churn, and company also realized the need for developing telecommunication products more related to customer needs.

One of the major problems was a limited budget, and company needed to recognize the most valuable subscribers, to spend that budget on them. Important part of the project was data sources (databases), and there were several major difficulties during the development of the final solution.

Veza's top management wanted to find a long-term churn solution. They did not want only to detect the clients with high churn probability. They wanted a complete solution which would show a complete picture of client's portfolio, and which would have a long-term value.

Regarding that, following four functionalities in a future solution were recognised as important:

- Prospective customer value calculation engine for recognizing the most valuable subscribers with periodical evaluation.
- Churn probability calculation on subscriber level with possibility of model monitoring and redevelopment in line with changes in subscriber portfolio structure.
- Testing the adequacy of existing telecommunication services packages while taking into consideration the subscriber portfolio segment.
- Recognizing potentially dangerous subscribers from a perspective of social network leadership influence. This subscriber does not need to have highly calculated churn probability, but in case of churn, they could cause serious damage to *Veza's* company because they have great influence on other subscribers. They might not be conscious of their position, but it is important to recognize them and to try to keep them into subscriber's portfolio.

Some of the mentioned aims are common goals in churn prediction data mining projects (Dresner, 2008), (Berry, 2000), (Berry, 1997), (Faulkner, 2003).

5. PROPOSED SOLUTION FROM THE PERSPECTIVE OF DATA MINING METHODS

It is evident that the requested solution given by top management was very complex, and it is not possible to finish the whole project by using a single data mining method. On the other hand, using only data mining methods does not guarantee a successful solution. It is much more important to find an optimal analytical strategy considering the existing data sources and to connect it with appropriate data mining methods/methodology.

Regarding the first request, which was focused on prospective customer value calculation for detecting the most valuable subscribers and to evaluate their value periodically, it was decided to use the fuzzy expert system.

Fuzzy expert systems are based on expert knowledge, and they are intuitive and easily understandable for management. Prospective value calculations are focused on loyalty evaluation, profitability calculation, perceptivity evaluation and evaluation of similar categories. As a final result, a developed solution should provide a single category for each subscriber, and that category should point on subscriber's value from the perspective of *Veza* company. Given results could be easily explainable by triggered rules within the expert system.

When we talk about periodical evaluation of each subscriber from the perspective of customer value, expert systems provide a solution, because they can be run periodically, and they can measure customer value trends.

In order to fulfil the second request related to churn probability calculation on subscriber level with the possibility of model monitoring and redevelopment in line with changes in subscriber portfolio structure, traditional modelling based on predictive models was used. As it will be shown, after attribute relevance analysis and model predictive power evaluation, neural networks and logistic regression were used. This methodology is commonly used, and it is expected that the developed model should be monitored and redeveloped periodically to be in line with market/subscriber structure changes.

Third request was generally most doubtful from the perspective of data mining model usage. Main reason for that lies in fact that there was an unclear adequacy of existing data sources. *Veza* company offers various service packages which include fixed phone lines, mobile phone lines, internet connection and IP TV in many different options. General idea was to recognize adequacy of created service packages for existing subscribers. For customer profile recognition, we need a lot of specific data, which on first sight was not visible from the existing data sources. First idea was the usage of data mining models like self organizing maps, segmentation methods or decision trees. Problem was in data adequacy for this kind of purpose. Data, which was recognized as potentially valuable, was socio demographic data from contracts, and behavioural data collected during service usage, and derived behavioural attributes as well.

Fourth request, aimed at the recognition of thr subscribers who has a strong influence on other subscribers (influencer), was planned to be solved by using the Social Network Analysis.

Proposed solution takes into consideration the specifics, which are related to specific company, and does not take into consideration only the traditional approach with stress on predictive model development. Proposed solution also takes into consideration the fact of limited budget, which means that we should recognise the most valuable customers. It takes into consideration the fact that we should recognise subscribers who are risky in sense of breaking the contract. On the other hand, the knowledge about who are the most valuable and risky subscribers will not stop them in intention to break their contracts. To stop them, we have to understand their behaviour, motivators and lifestyle.

For this kind of purpose we should use adequate methods, which will help us in creating services and meet their needs and mitigate churn rate.

Final step in this holistic solution was the SNA analysis, which gives us the answer to who is the greatest influencer within a portfolio, and who can damage the portfolio as a leader in of churn.

The entire analytical process is described with following steps:

1. Fuzzy expert system creation for prospective customer value.
2. Apply Fuzzy expert system on subscribers portfolio and categorise all subscribers within following categories (*Very high customer value, High customer value, Average customer value, Low customer value, Very low customer value*).
3. Exclude subscribers with *Low customer value* and *Very low customer value* for further analytical process.
4. Find subscriber behaviour and segments on reduced data set (*Low customer value* and *Very low customer value* categories are excluded from the sample).
5. Create predictive (probabilistic) churn model on reduced data set. Also use recognised patterns from step 4. as potential predictors for churn model (*Low customer value* and *Very low customer value* categories are excluded from the sample).
6. Apply SNA analysis on the entire portfolio (*Very high customer value, High customer value, Average customer value, Low customer value, Very low customer value*).
7. Make decisions based on given results.

Fuzzy expert system in its first step recognised the most valuable subscribers, and company can put focus on that population for future marketing activities regarding churn reduction.

For most valuable subscribers, understanding their needs, behaviour, and wishes is an important element in intention to decrease the churn rate.

Next activity was concentrated in predictive model development, and in this process reduced samples were used (most valuable subscribers) and recognised patterns from previous step were also used as predictors into model.

SNA analysis was applied on total population, because subscribers with low values potentially could have great influence on other subscribers and they are potentially dangerous in a way that they could motivate other valuable subscribers to churn. It is important to recognise all subscribers, who have great influence on other subscribers in sense of stopping potential churn, which could be caused by social network relations.

At the end, company creates a strategy with the focus on the most valuable subscribers, who have high probability of churn, and subscribers, who were recognised as influencers. Strategy should be in line with recognised customer behaviour, needs and motivators. If somebody (or specific segment) has the intention to break their contract the company should offer some conditions or benefits, which would be attractive to them.

6. DATA FOUNDATION

Key factor for project success is the appropriate data, which enters into data mining models. *Veza* company had mostly unconnected data sources, which were based in core systems. They started to develop a data warehouse, but at the moment when churn-solving project started, it was far away from an adequate solution.

They had several main data sources like a contracting transaction system which also had information about services in use, billing system, call centre system which was semi connected with other existing systems, and IP TV system which was not transactional oriented, but was recognized as valuable data source.

Socio demographic data, which mainly existed in contracting transaction system, was not good choice for model development as single source of data. It is a well-known fact that best predictors in churn models are behavioural attributes.

First step in data cleansing and preparation was finding ways to connect all disposable data sources at the subscriber level. That includes establishing connection between all existing data sources (contracts, used services, call centre, IP TV system, mobile phone data centre, fixed phone data centre). Basic idea was to use hidden data potential from existing data sources with stress on derived data attributes, which have behavioural character and consolidate all existing business segments.

This approach in data integration was the base for holistic view on subscribers. It provides an opportunity to find out specifics derived from usage of specific services, such as IP TV in combination with mobile phone services and insight on subscribers' potential activities in the call centre.

7. MODELING SOLUTION FOR PROSPECTIVE CUSTOMER VALUE CALCULATION

7.1 Importance of Prospective Customer Value Calculation

As it was already mentioned, the main reason why *Veza* company started churn detection/mitigation project was to observe the increasing churn rate. Due to limited budget, which could be spent with the intention to retain subscribers; the most important thing was to recognize the most valuable customers for the company. Contrary to conviction that profitability is the only criteria for customer value evaluation, the aim was to build a system which could be able to calculate other factors like loyalty, perspective, long-term perspective, and riskiness as elements for customer value evaluation.

This model had the task to recognize the most valuable subscribers, who are worthy of spending budget on, because they are the most valuable customers for *Veza* company.

The Problem of customer value calculation is often neglected in two ways. Firstly, it neglects the fact that within a portfolio, there are clients with different degree of worthiness. Secondly, one trivializes the way how to calculate customer value. Frequently, ambitious projects' first step for customer value calculation becomes trivial in later phases, after the system designer realizes that there are too many rules, which should be incorporated into SQL statements. After that, conclusion, customer value calculation often becomes the profitability value calculation, and other aspect of customer worthiness like loyalty, perspective, and potentials as elements for customer value calculation are neglected.

Practice often shows Pareto effect within subscriber portfolio, and we can say that we have a small number of customers, who generate most of the profit. Often, to generate profit does not only mean to be profitable, because profitability in one point of time does not mean that customer/subscriber will be profitable also in the near future period. The reason for that can be soft churn trends, less buying potential in future, seasonal oscillations or other reasons. Because of all mentioned facts, for the precise customer value evaluation we should take in consideration different subscriber characteristics. To achieve this aim we should operate with a large amounts of data and numerous business rules. That means that we need a powerful tool, which can operate with huge databases and large number of rules.

A fuzzy expert system shows good performance for solving these types of problems (Klepac, 2010).

7.2 Model Development Process

First task in model development process was aimed on knowledge elicitation from the experts. There are numerous knowledge elicitation techniques (Pedricz, 1998; Siler, 2005), but for this project, *typical case method* was used.

Model development process contained following steps:

1. Knowledge elicitation (interviews with experts).
2. Recognising main meta categories in model based on interviews (like profitability, loyalty…).
3. Linguistic variable definition and its connection to meta categories.
4. Model structure development.
5. Data pre-processing from database.
6. Rule definition.
7. Model testing.
8. Model application.

For successful knowledge elicitation clearly defined target variable on expert system level is prescribed. Beside a clearly defined target, useful auxiliary tool is hypothesis consideration. Hypothesis deliberation leads us to understanding and discovering causalities of an observed problem. We recommend that analytical process should not only be pure pattern extraction from disposable data sources. It should be supervised and supported by business experts, which can express their opinions about causalities that can be proved or disproved in an analytical way.

In that case, any incorrect assumption, which has an influence on business decisions by decision makers, could be challenged and rejected.

It is possible to skip this stage, but it is not recommended, because that way the company has an opportunity for better understanding the causalities of the observed problem.

A hypothesis is, widely, potential explanation or conclusion, which is tested by collecting and presenting evidences (Heuer, 2010.). It is a statement, which was not confirmed to be true, or, in other words, temporary explanation based on an observation, which has to be confirmed or rejected.

A typical case method, gives a task to experts to describe the characteristics of the most valuable customer (customer value is target variable). This task has several iterations in correlation with the level of abstraction. The first iteration was concentrated at the highest level of abstraction, and experts defined which terms best describe the most valuable customer. After brainstorming, it was clear that we could operate with four major abstract terms:

- Profitability.
- Loyalty.
- Perspective.
- Riskiness.

First level of abstraction was used as a base for the further development of the fuzzy expert system structure. Next iteration was concentrated on the deeper definition of the recognized terms. For example, perspective was defined through campaign responding ratio in a one year period, trend of product usage in one year period, number of calls in the call center for inquiring about new products and services, paying bills on time, and some other behavioural characteristic.

Next iteration comes closer to data definition in database, what was the final aim.

The idea was, to find path from terms in highest level of abstraction to database attributes, and to connect them through rule blocks within the fuzzy expert system.

After the process of knowledge elicitation, basic relations from the high level abstract terms to database attributes were presented with the mind map.

It was a solid basic point for fuzzy expert system shell construction.

Next task in expert system development was to concentrate on linguistic variable definition, and rules definition.

Figure 1 shows the structure of developed fuzzy expert system for customer value calculation.

As it is visible on Figure 1, fuzzy expert system at the end gives unique value, which represents customer value. This value is represented through five linguistic categories:

Figure 1. Structure of developed fuzzy expert system

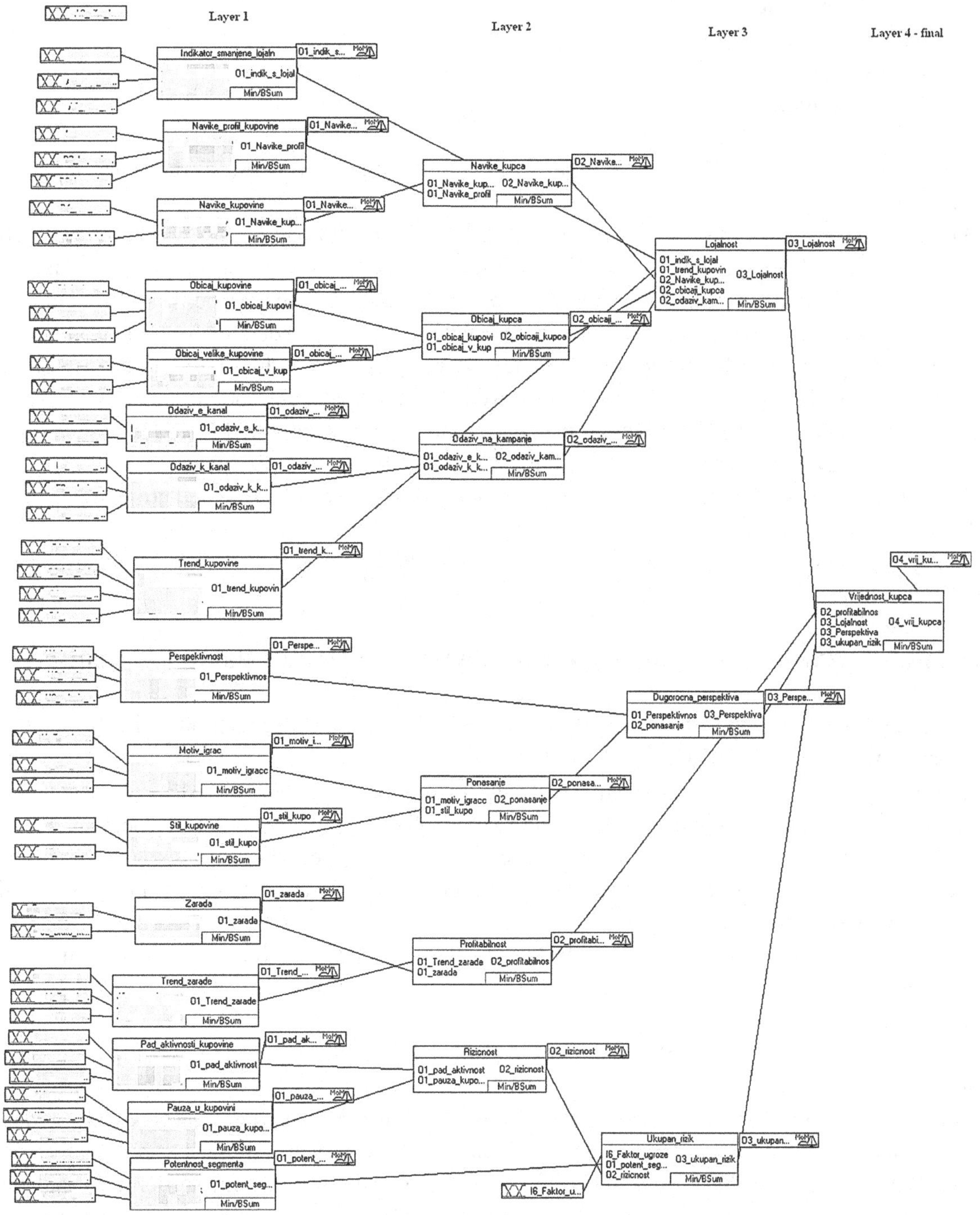

- Very high customer value;
- High customer value;
- Average customer value;
- Low customer value;
- Very low customer value.

The entire system had 597 rules, 46 input variables, 26 output variables, 26 rule blocks, and 200 linguistic terms.

For the purpose of data entry into the model, Extract,Transform & Load process was developed on the existing databases. After applying the model on extracted data, all subscribers were categorized into one of the final linguistic categories, which represent subscriber value from the perspective of *Veza* company.

Predictive models as a central solution for churn detection and churn reduction has a lot of advantages in practice. The problem with that approach became evident in a situation, which is described in this paper.

Contrary to predictive model development which demands attribute relevance analysis on the existing database attributes and derived attributes due to target variable for an observed period in past, variables for fuzzy expert systems could be recognized in a process of knowledge elicitation.

For this purpose, traditional knowledge elicitation methods could be used, and structured analytic techniques as well (Heurer, 2010).

Fuzzy expert systems give an opportunity for an individual approach for each client regarding customer value from company perspective.

7.3 Using Fuzzy Expert System for Prospective Customer Value Calculation

An additional benefit from the model was the ability to find the reason why each subscriber was categorized into one of the defined category.

For example, a customer can have an average customer value, because he or she is averagely profitable for the company but not perspective, and medium risky. He or she is not perspective, because campaign responding ratio is low, trend of product usage in a one year period is low, number of calls in the call center for inquiry about new products and services are low, and he or she does not have the habit of paying bills on time.

On the other hand, a fuzzy expert system gives us the opportunity to look at customer structure on a very high level, and to make judgment of what is our weakest or strongest characteristic of portfolio structure.

Figure 2 shows the main portfolio structure calculated through concentrations within four major abstract terms.

It is visible that the major factors, which cause downgrade into lower category, were loyalty and perspective. Subscriber value downgrading is in correlation with loyalty and subscriber perspective. This fact leads us to conclusion that loyalty and perspective are the weakest factors into subscriber population.

Main hypothesis was that subscribers during their lifecycle migrate from the best to the worst level of loyalty and perspective. To prove that hypothesis, Cox regression model was developed.

Model shows that in average 25% of all subscribers migrate from the zone of very high customer value to the zone of high customer value in the period of one year. Model also shows that in average 18% of all subscribers migrate in zone of high customer value to average customer value in period of one year.

Figure 2. Portfolio structure calculated through concentrations within four major abstract terms

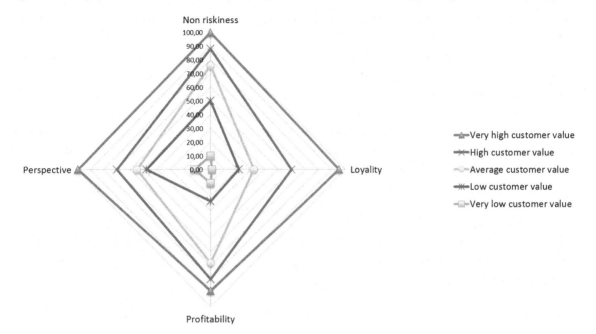

Same model shows that key driven factors for those migrations are loyalty and perceptiveness, which became weaker and weaker as the period of existence in portfolio becomes close to one year.

Main factors which were recognized, as influencers on loyalty and perceptiveness are the intensity of usage contracted services, responding on campaigns, and stopping the usage of some contracted services.

Recognized trend were mainly responsible for downgrades in the zone of most valuable subscribers.

Most valuable customers were in scope of the analysis with the intention to find out the reasons for migrations to the less valuable categories.

Data, which was used for the, analysis had limits regarding the information about subscriber profiles. With the exception of basic socio-demographic data from the contract, product usage data, and billing information, there was no additional data which can be useful for profiling and deeper investigation of the reason why subscribers have a decreased trend in usage of contracted services, why they do not respond to campaigns, and why they stop using some of the contracted services.

7.4 Using REFII Model for Deeper Investigation

Due to the limited information insufficient for profiling, additional data sources were investigated. Regarding the fact that about 82% of all subscribers use IP TV as a service, IP TV was recognized as potentially valuable data source for profiling purposes. Mitigating circumstance was the fact that around 92% customers who were recognized as most valuable use IP TV. The idea was to analyze their behavior in IP TV usage through watched channels and period of time when they watch those channels with the intention to find out more information about their profiles.

This step was crucial for customer behavior recognition, and recognizing important patterns vital for making customer segments.

Basis for such conclusion was time series from IP TV data sources on which the REFII model was applied. Analysis was done only on the most valuable customer segments recognized by Fuzzy expert system.

If we take into consider that most of the subscribers live with their families, it would be a mistake to neglect the time component of the analysis. Some of the family members could watch some of the channels during the week at same period of time, and other family members could watch some other channels during the week at other period of time. Watching specific channels, or group of specific channel, in correlation with days and specific day of the week, gives us an opportunity for profile recognition.

Challenge was to make segmentation based on watching habits, while taking into account temporal factors. For this purpose REFII model was used (Klepac, 2013).

Basic functionality of REFII model is time series transformation into form adequate for temporal data mining with conventional (clustering, decision trees, self organizing maps...) and unconventional data mining techniques.

Transformation process of time series into REFII model is given by following algorithm (Klepac, 2013):

Time series can be expressed as a sequences of values S(s1,..,sn), where S represents the time series and (s1,..,sn) represent the elements in the S series.

Step 1: Time interpolation.

Creation of auxiliary time series Vi(vi1,..,vin) on interval <1..n> (days, weeks, months, quarters, years) with the value 0. Based on the created sequence, interpolation of the missing values in S(s1,..,sn) with the value 0 based on the created sequence Vi is carried out. The result of processing is the series S(s1,..,sn) with interpolated missing values from the series Vi(vi1,..,vin).

Step 2: Time granulation.

In this step the degree of compression of time series S(s1,..,sn) in the elementary time unit (day, week, month...) is defined. In the second step, the elements of the existing time series are compressed by using statistical functions such as sum, average and mode on the level of the granulated segment. In that way, the time series can be converted to a higher degree of granulation (days into weeks, weeks into months...), resulting in the time series S(s1,..,sn) with a higher degree of granulation.

Depending on the objectives, we can return to this step during the process of analysis, which means that the processes described in the following steps must also be repeated.

Step 3: Standardization.

The standardization procedure consists of transformation of the time series S(s1,..,sn) into the time series T(t1,..,tn), in which each element in the series is subjected to min-max standardization on interval <0,1>, where

    a.   Time series T consists of the elements (t1,.., tn), where ti is calculated as $t_i = ((s_i - \min(S))/(\max(S) - \min(S))$, in which $\min(S)$ and $\max(S)$ represent the minimum and maximum value of time series S.

b. The time variation between elementary patterns (time complexity measure) of the segment on the X axis is defined as d(ti,ti+1)=a

Step 4: Transformation to REF notation.

According to the formula Tr=ti+1- ti Tr > 0 =>R; Tr< 0 =>F; Tr=0 =>E, where Yi are elements of series Ns.

Step 5: Calculation of angle coefficient.

Angle coefficient=>

Tr > 0 (R) Coefficient = t i+1-t i

Tr < 0 (F) Coefficient = t i -t i+1

Tr = 0 (E) Coefficient = 0

Step 6: Calculation of area beneath the curve.

Method of numeric integration based on the rectangle

p= ((t i*a)+(t i+1*a))/2

Step 7: Creation of time indices.

Building of a hierarchical index tree depending on the characteristics of the analysis, in which an element of the structured index can also be an attribute, such as the client code.

Step 8: Creating categories.

Creation of derived attribute values based on the area beneath the curve and the angle coefficient. It is possible to create categories by application of standard *crisp* logic or by application of *fuzzy* logic.

Step 9: Connecting the REFII model transformation tables with relational tables containing attributes which do not have a temporal dimension.

As a final result of transformation into REFII model each subscriber (account) was represent as it is shown in Table 1.

Basis for time series creation was minutes within one day when IP TV was switched on. Granularity level was day as elemental time span, and each subscriber was represented by time series, which were two years long. This REFII representation gives us an opportunity for temporal data mining, and profiling because additional attributes on daily level were ratio of watching specific group of channels.

Table 1. Subscriber habits in REFII notation

Subscriber Number	Time Segment Index	REF Mark	Angle Coefficient	Area of Time Segment	Channel A	Channel B	...	Channel N
1	I1	REF1	Angle coefficient 1	P1	%	%	%	%
1	I3	REF2	Angle coefficient 2	P2	%	%	%	%
1	I3	REF3	Angle coefficient 3	P3	%	%	%	%
...	...	...	...	...	...	...	...	...
n	In	REFn	Angle coefficient n	Pn	%	%	%	%

Channel grouping was done by channel thematic like sport, documentary, movies, local TV channels, national channels, cartoon channels, the comedy channel...

Each record within table represents data for the one subscriber and his behavior within one specific day determined with time segment index. Time segment index was constructed so it represents specific day within two years. Index contains information about day, month, and specific day of the year with stress on the day in week. This index structure is suitable for deeper analysis about subscriber habits on daily level and trends regarding the usage of IP TV.

REF mark, angle coefficient and area beneath time segments derived from minutes of watching IP TV are core elements of REFII model. Additional attributes represented as "Channel A", "Channel B", "Chanel n", represents ratio in watching a specific channel within one day and period within one day when IP TV was switched on.

Area beneath the curve was used as a tool for calculation the intensity of watching channels.

During analysis process, one unusual segment was discovered. This segment represents undecided watchers, or a watcher, which continuously changes program channels. This segment was assigned to channel grouping as an additional attribute.

REFII transformation and assignation of channel groups gave good foundation for a deeper data investigation.

First analysis was aimed on finding out expected combination of watching channels in global (during the entire observation period), and on daily basis for each subscriber.

Next step was concentrated on creating clusters based on previous findings.

A final result shows a few interesting patterns:

- 18% subscribers mostly watch movies only.
- 9% subscribers mostly watch movies in combination with cartoons, and during the remaining period they act as undecided watchers.
- 7% subscribers mostly watch sport channels, and during the remaining period they act as undecided watchers.
- 3% subscribers mostly watch the comedy channel, documentary channels, and cartoon channels.
- 14% subscribers mostly watch cartoon channels only, and during the remaining period they act as undecided watchers.

- 5% subscribers mostly watch documentary channels only, and during the remaining period they act as undecided watchers.

Next question was: is there any temporal relation between the observed patterns? For this purpose REFII notation was also used in combination with OLAP reports. This combination reveled some new facts:

- Subscribers, who mostly watch only movies, watch TV very rarely during week, and they watch TV mostly during weekend. Intensity of watching IP TV grows during the period of weekend, and it falls during rest of the week.
- Subscribers, who mostly watch movies in combination with cartoons, and during the remaining period they acts as undecided watchers, watch movies mostly during week, and they watch cartoons mostly during weekend. Intensity of watching IP TV during week is much higher than during weekend.
- Subscribers, who mostly watch sport channels, and during the remaining period act as undecided watchers watch TV mainly in the second part of the day. Their intensity of watching IP TV is mostly the same during the whole week.
- Subscribers, who mostly watch only cartoon channels, during the remaining period act as undecided watchers. They act as undecided watchers during the whole week, and they watch cartoon channels during weekend. For those subscribers it is evident that they more intensively use IP TV during the weekend.

Revealed knowledge gives us some idea about profiles and needs among subscribers. Term "mostly" in analysis means watching a specific channel group more than 20% into the observed time span.

Regarding watching the cartoon channels, we can assume the existence of children and families, and regarding watching a specific channel group we can roughly set up hypothesis about subscriber profiles.

Recognized segments were used in the next analytical stage for churn probability measurement.

Undecided watchers were extracted as additional segment, and all subscribes which showed those characteristic within a certain recognized segment were assigned to additional stand-alone group.

OLAP analysis on REFII transformation gave additional relations and patterns, including details about watching preferences of subscribers, which prefer some specific group of channels, within those groups.

This analysis finds out, for example, that subscribers who are mostly watching movies in combination with cartoons, and during the remaining period act as undecided watchers, watch movies mostly during week, and they watch cartoons mostly during weekend, prefer to watch channels with old movies.

Also, subscribers, which mostly watch only documentary channels, and during the remaining period they act as undecided watchers, prefer to watch documentary channels dedicated to history and UFO related themes.

After analytical activities related to IP TV, similar models were developed for fix telephone line users, and mobile telephone users. Recognized segments were compared with discovered segments within IP TV users who already use mobile phone or fix line.

Most interesting findings were:

- Subscribers, who mostly watch sport channels, and during the remaining period act as undecided watchers, watch TV mainly in the second part of the day. Their intensity of watching IP TV is mostly the same during the whole week. They intensively use mobile phones in the first part of the day, and during weekend they increase their mobile phone usage during the whole day.
- Subscribers, who mostly watch only cartoon channels, and during the remaining period act as undecided watchers, act as undecided watchers during the whole week, and they watch cartoon channels during the weekend. For those subscribers it is evident that they more intensively use IP TV during the weekend. These subscribers prefer fix line, mostly at the evening during the whole week, and their activities regarding the usage of fix line drops during the period of weekend.

Reveled information gives a general overview about existence of subscriber segments, and it could be useful for setting important hypothesis for finding main churn triggers. Presented analysis does not provide answers on question why, and who will break contract, but it was valuable for understanding the existing subscribers behavior.

7. CHURN PREDICTION MODELLING

When we are talking about classical churn predictive models, major task is to build a model which should be able to calculate probability of churn for each subscriber, who already signed a contract.

For this purpose logistic regression and neural network were used.

Churn prediction modeling was divided in following steps:

1. Data sample creation (most valuable customers included only).
2. Splitting basic sample in two samples (development and test sample).
3. Attribute relevance analyses.
4. Creating dummy variables.
5. Correlation calculation on created dummy variables.
6. Model development using logistic regression and neural network.
7. Predictive power measuring using ROC curve and KS test.
8. Selecting most appropriate model regarding ROC and KS.
9. Calculation churn probability for the most valuable customers and expressing probabilities as score.

Before the modeling, it is important to construct appropriate development sample, and to recognize attributes which are most relevant for model development.

During the process of model development it is the most important thing to understand reasons of churn (Gorman, 2013). On the one hand, in modeling process existing variables from data sources could be used, but variables, which show most predictive characteristic, are behavioral variables. They describe subscriber behavior in service usage. This kind of variables are mostly derived from the existing ones. In their construction analyst should consult the business owner, because they can suggest additional variable construction based on experience.

It is not unusual, that in the first phase after cooperation with the experts, numerous derived variables are generated. In this phase, a huge number of potential predictors (variables) exist in the initial sample.

During the process of attribute relevance analysis, for each variable a predictive power is measured, and in that way we also test hypothesis about importance of variables derived by experts, or variables which have been selected from the databases.

After attribute relevance assessment, it is possible to make rough expertise about churner profile, based on the most predictive variables.

8.1. Data Preparation and Data Sampling

An important thing in building predictive models is appropriate sample construction. Predictive models should reflects business reality and expectance, which means that constructed sample should represent holistic picture of the subscriber portfolio, with an adequate segment of churner population which is sufficient for model building.

Predictive churn models are almost synonym for churn modeling. Building predictive churn models is the most widely used approach in churn solution development.

Aimed outputs from those models are churn probability in a defined future period of time.

There are a few recommended characteristics, which every predictive model should have, and predictive churn models are no exception:

- Reliability;
- Usability;
- Stability;
- Robustness.

Reliability in light of churn predictive modeling means that a model should have significant power to predict which customers/consumers/clients will make churn in a defined future period (e.g. 6 months). Predictive power could be measured using statistical measures like Kolmogorov Smirnoff test, or ROC curve on test sample. This methodology will be explained in detail in the following chapter.

Usability means that developed model has integrated business logic, and that it is in line with business perception of the existing customer portfolio.

Stability is an important characteristic for the models, which should be used periodically, and it implies that model should not contain unstable variables, which could cause instability of the whole model and imprecise probability calculation.

A robustness criterion implies that a model is resistant to business environment changes and resistant to market changes. It is unrealistic to expect that it is possible to develop a completely resistant model on significant market condition changes, or portfolio structure changes. Robustness means that model will not overreact and will not become unusable in a short period of time after market conditions start to change, or portfolio structure starts to change.

Each predictive modeling project demands almost 80% of time spending on data preparation. Contrary to rooted belief that data preparation process consists on Extract Transform Load processes, data quality improvement, or data extraction from different data sources only, it is a much more broader process.

Data preparation starts with data sample construction planning.

As it is shown in Figure 3, sample for model developing should be constructed while taking in consideration three main parts:

Figure 3. Data sample structure

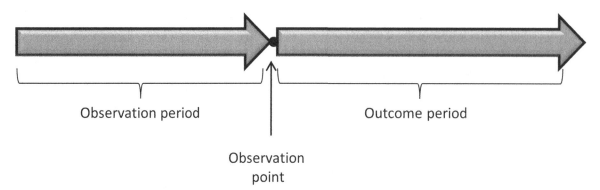

- Outcome period;
- Observation point;
- Observation period;

Outcome period is used for churn recognition. If subscriber brakes contract in this period, he is marked as a churner. In model development sample attribute *churn* in that case has value *churn="Yes"*, otherwise *churn="No"*.

Observation point has orientation role during sample construction, it defines border, which splits observation period from outcome period. If we take into account subscriber's socio demographic, and other static characteristic like for example "number of services used", this is point in time from which we take those characteristics.

Observation period was used for calculating characteristics of derived variables such as: average minutes in the evening when IP TV was turned on during observation period, or average number of late night calls from mobile phone during observation period, average number of calls in call center during observation period.

Presented technique is known as fixed window sample creation technique, and it is convenient for situations when we do not have significant number on newcomers during observed period.

Veza company in their portfolio had contractors which mostly signed contracts few years ago, and those contractors show bad performance regarding churn in period of last observed year.

Sample of part time contractors, which entered into portfolio 4 months before observation point, as a result of one specific campaign, was removed from the sample.

It was evident that most of the contracts were stopped 7 months from observation point. Churn rate was 6,9%.

In case of *Veza* company outcome period was 9 months long (9 months from observation point), and observation period was 12 months long. This sample had relatively statistically sufficient number of churners for the purpose of predictive model development. In case when it became problem, one of the possible solution is to extend outcome period. With this technique, we can extend outcome period too much in way that we can capture historically irrelevant period. It has implication also on observation period, because we are doing calculation of behavioral characteristic on old data.

Those activities could result with unrealistic and unstable models. *Veza* company had good performance from statistical point of view, regarding ratio between number of churners, and data freshness.

8.2. Attribute Relevance Analysis

Main task of attribute relevance analysis is reducing number of predictors, which entered into the model by predictive power criteria.

A robust and stable predictive model has few attributes incorporated into model. It could be 6-10 of most predictive attributes. As it is evident initial data sample could contain more than hundreds of potential predictors. Some of them are original variables from databases as socio demographic values assigned to each customer, and other has behavioral characteristics defined by experts and extracted from existing transactional data.

Attribute relevance analysis has two important functions:

Recognition of most important variables which has greatest impact on target variable

Understanding relations and logic between most important predictor and target variable, and understanding relations and logic between most important predictors from target variable perspective.

Contrary to assurance that powerful hardware and sophisticated software can substitute need for attribute relevance analysis, attribute relevance analysis is important part of each analysis, which operates with target variable. Recognition of most important variables, which has greatest impact on target variable, reduces redundancy and uncertainty at model development process stage. It provides robustness of the model and model reliability. Attribute relevance analysis besides importance measuring, evaluates attribute characteristics. Attribute characteristics evaluation includes measuring attribute values impact on target variables. It helps on understanding relations and logic between most important predictors and target variable, and understanding relations and logic between most important predictors from target variable perspective. After attribute relevance analysis stage, analyst has initial picture about churner profile and behavior. This stage often opens many additional questions related to reveled relations and sometimes induces construction of new behavioral (derived) variables, which also should pass attribute relevance analysis process.

In situation when target variable has two states (it is common situation in churn modeling), as attribute relevance analysis method information value calculation could be used.

First step in information value calculation is calculating weight of evidence. Weight of evidence gives a detailed insight to variable distribution and their partial impact on aim variable. This stage is crucial for understanding relations within predictors and aim variable. With this information it is possible to find out patterns, which has strongest impact aim variable (churn flag).

For prediction model development in specific area like in finance, logical weight of evidence trend could be also another selection beside predictive power criteria for model building (Thomas, 2002).

In churn modeling, logical weight of evidence trend is welcome, but variable with strong predictive power could be removed from the building sample only if weight of evidence trend are extremely illogical.

Information value calculation uses weight of evidence calculation for predictive power calculation.

Final calculation should provide list of most predictive variables due to aim variable. Strong predictive models in average contain 6-10 predictors, which is selected through attribute relevance analysis process.

Formulas for weight of evidence calculation and information value calculation are shown below:

$$WoE = \ln\left(\frac{Dnc}{Dc}\right)$$

$$\sum_{i=1}^{n} \left(Dnc_i - Dc_i\right) \ln\left(\frac{Dnc_i}{Dc_i}\right)$$

Weight of evidence is calculated as a natural logarithm of ratio between distribution of non-churners (Dnc) and churners (Dc) in distribution spans.

Information value is calculated as sum of differences between distribution of non-churners and churners in distribution spans and product of corresponding weight of evidence.

Regarding task for the churn predictive model development for *Veza* company, weight of evidence and information value were calculated. As a base for calculation 183 variables (potential predictors) were used. Those 183 variables were socio-demographic variables, behavior variables, variables derived by expert (mostly ratio oriented), segments reveled after applying fuzzy expert system described in first part of the chapter.

After calculation some variables with highest predictive power in sample were:

- Undecided watchers (yes/no).
- Segment of subscribers which mostly looking cartoon channels only, and in remain period acts as undecided watchers acts as undecided watchers during whole week, and they watch cartoon channels during weekend (member of the segment: yes/no).
- Number of used services.
- Number of long distance calls.
- County.
- Age.
- Average number of rejected calls (mobile phone) by operator within month.
- Number of calls to *Veza's* call center in last observed quarter.
- Usage trend of contracted services.

There were also more variables with average significant predictive power, but enumerated variables had highest predictive power in the sample. Those variables after dummy variable creation based on weight of evidence calculation and correlation calculation were used for model development.

8.3. Model Development using Logistic Regression, Survival Analyze, And SNA

After recognition of most predictive variables, and correlation calculation between them, logistic regression and neural network were used for building predictive churn models on development sample.

Initial sample has been split on development sample and test sample in ratio 80%: 20%.

It is important to keep in mind that data preparation process takes almost 80% of time in modeling. Churn is no exception in that. Data preparation on the other hand contains business logic. Sampling process and data preparation process follows business needs. It could manifest as requests for unprofitable customers rejection, exclusions of some categories from the sample or inclusion of other categories into data sample is in direct connection with business way of thinking. Data sample construction is one way of integrating business logic within models. Other disposable way for integrating business requirements within churn solution is tweaking data mining techniques by chaining methods, or input data modification. Applying some of the data mining method is about 20% of all work on designing final churn solution. There are numerous ways how to apply it, and two different modelers could reach satisfying results on totally different ways. It implies that puzzles could be connected on different ways for reaching same aims.

Idea of building traditional predictive churn models is to develop tool for calculation churn probability.

Model based on logistic regression showed better performance on test sample with area under ROC curve 78.4%, versus model based on neural network with area under ROC curve 71.8%.

Model was applied on recent sample, with result presented in Figure 4.

Subscribers with lower score given from the model has higher probability of churn, and there are mostly concentrated on scale from 0-200, other subscribers with higher probability of churn are spread on scale from 200-600, but their concentration in given bins are not so high like in zone from 0-200.

It is important to mention that we are talking about most valuable subscribers, recognized through fuzzy expert system. Decision was to set up the cut off for churn observation on 300 points, because this scale contains about 80% of all potentially recognized churners. Model recognized 21% potential churners in future period. Subscriber, which has more than 300 points, is not so risky in relation with subscriber, which has less than 300 points.

After predictive model development, survival analysis (Cox's regression) was used on each variable recognized as relevant for churn prediction. Survival analysis was done for period of 12 months. Survival analysis discovered some new fact from the data:

- Segment of subscribers which mostly look cartoon channels only, and in remain period acts as undecided watchers acts as undecided watchers during whole week, and they watch cartoon channels during weekend have worst survival rate than other segments. This segment from initial 100% dropped to 70% after 12 months
- Subscribers with more services has better survival rate than subscribers with less services.
- Subscribers with more long distance calls have worst survival rate than subscribers without or few long distance calls.

Figure 4. Churner concentration by model score

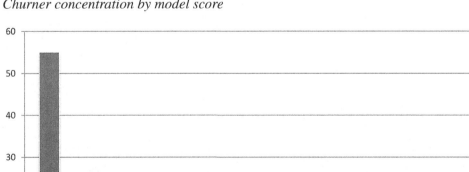

- Younger and middle aged subscribers has worst survival rate than older subscribers
- Subscribers with more rejected calls (mobile phone) by operator within month has worst survival rate than subscribers without rejected calls or few rejected calls
- Subscribers with more number of calls to *Veza's* call center in last observed quarter has worst survival rate than subscribers without calls to call center or few calls

Most surprising discovered fact was evident difference about survival rate between Undecided watchers segment, and other segments, which does not belong to this category.

Results are presented in Figure 5.

As it is visible from Figure 5, if subscribes belongs to undecided watcher segment after 12 months only 20% of population will survive. This segment was defined through results of REFII model and represent subscribes in any other segment, which additionally has characteristic of undecided watchers.

Finally, Social Network Analysis was applied on whole subscriber population, not only on most valuable ones. Reason for that laid in fact that subscribers which could have strong influence on other subscribers, does not have to be valuable for the *Veza* company or with high probability of churn. Problem is, if they will sometime in the future commit churn, it could cause serious damage from churn perspective on significant part of portfolio. Social Network Analysis has task to recognize those influencers.

For this purpose following Social Network Analysis metrics was used:

- Closeness;
- Eigenvector;
- Degree;
- Betweenness.

Figure 5. Survival rate undecided watchers vs. watchers within this category

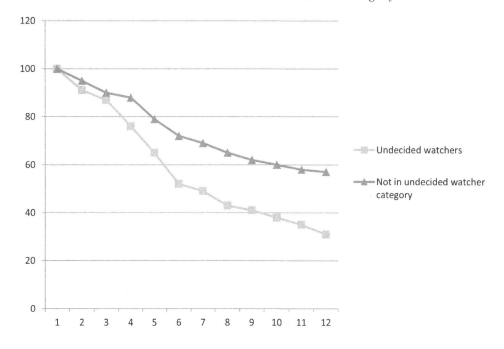

Using mentioned metrics 3% of influencers within subscriber population have been recognized. Most interesting thing was that:

- 34% of them was not recognized as valuable subscribers.
- 28% of them belongs to *undecided watchers* segment.
- 14% of them has churn score less than 300 which imply on high churn probability.

Regarding to the given results, it has been potentially high danger within recognized influencers. Recognized subscribers had great influence on other subscribers, and if they churn it could cause uncontrolled churn of other subscribers.

If we take in consider influencer's structure, 34% of them are not valuable subscribers, which means that regarding on focus at most valuable subscriber we could neglect it in case that we did not apply Social Network Analysis on whole population .

On the other hand, *undecided watchers* segment (28%) has bad survival rate, which means that 80% of them will probably churn of and it could have a consequence on great part of the other subscribers. Similar situation is with 14% of influencers with calculated high churn probability.

9. REVEALED KNOWLEDGE AS A BASE FOR THE CHURN MITIGATION STRATEGIES AND THE NEW PRODUCTS DEVELOPMENT

Every analysis from business perspective does not have sense, if it cannot be used for making business decision. Regarding that, all given results have been consolidated, and observed as one big picture.

First step has been focused on most valuable customer recognition. This step helped in budget saving, and precise sample creation for further model development as well. As a result *Veza* company realized that it has problem with subscriber's loyalty, and perspective of existing subscribers.

After REFII model has been applied on reduced sample of existing subscribers (most valuable), several subscriber segments and their characteristics have been discovered.

Developed logistic regression model was used for churn probability calculation. After calculating churn probability, as most important segments with highest probability of churn, following segment were recognized:

1. Subscribers, which mostly watch sport channels, and in remaining period act as undecided watchers, intensively use mobile phones in the first part of the day, and during weekend they raise in mobile phone usage during whole day.
2. Subscribers which mostly watch cartoons, and in remaining period, act as undecided watchers and act as undecided watchers during whole week, watch cartoons during whole weekend, use fixed line at the evening during whole week, except weekend.
3. Subscribers which mostly watch documentary channels, and in remain period, act as undecided watchers, prefer to watch channels dedicated to history and UFO related themes.

Common characteristic for the all recognized segments is that all of them has subscribers, which act as undecided watchers. Undecided watchers characteristic has been recognized as a strong predictor at attribute relevance analysis stage. Same characteristic showed strong negative influence on survival rate.

Hypothesis about more than one users of IP TV behind one subscriber should not be neglected, and resulting hypothesis is that offered channel packages should adapt to recognized segments.

The other visible fact has been that characteristic of "to use IP TV" has highest influence in segmentation and churn analysis then characteristic of "use fix line " or "to use mobile phone".

For the first segment, additional analysis was done, and there were no additional useful information after analysis about reasons why do they behave as undecided watchers. Decision was to offer them option with lower prices on fix line with few new cartoon channels in existing IP TV service package.

Members of the second segment were obviously families with small kids. Decision was to offer them option with lower prices on mobile services with few new cartoon channels in existing IP TV service package.

Members of the third segment got new sport channels dedicated to history and UFO related themes within existing IP TV service package.

During model development process two interesting facts have been noticed:

- Subscribers with more rejected calls (mobile phone) by operator within month has worst survival rate than subscribers without rejected calls or few rejected calls
- Subscribers with more number of calls to *Veza's* call center in last observed quarter has worst survival rate than subscribers without calls to call center or few calls

Calls can be rejected in existing service packages if subscriber does not have enough additional money on account for establishment of call. Existing package offers some amount of data transfer in MB, number of minutes for calls and SMS for fixed price, which should be paid at the beginning of the month, but each establishment of call should be paid additionally. That means if subscriber can have unused minutes for calls, but it could not be used if does not have money on account (or he/she already spend it) for establishment of call.

Surprisingly this finding was in connection with other one- number of calls to *Veza's* call center in last observed quarter. There were significant percentage of customers who has many short calls by mobile phones and they have problems with additional payments. They made complaints to *Veza's* call center regarding that situation. As it became evident, that situation has serious impact on churn.

Management of *Veza's* company decided to decrease for 50% establishment of call fees, regarding discovered pattern.

Finally, it was decided that all influencer recognized by Social Network Analysis should get additional benefits and discounts, regarding to segment to which they have been recognized. For the non-valuable customers recognized as influencers *Veza* company will give additional discounts on used services.

Regarding changes in prices and services adoption, as well as other measures, *Veza* company mitigated in following next 12 month period. Created models are still in use and quarterly reviewed as a tool for churn detection.

Developed churn solution is a result of current portfolio state. It is unrealistic to expect that developed solution will be usable, predictive or reliable without periodical redesign. Changes in market conditions, implies changes on developed churn solution. To achieve this aim it is prescribed to make periodic validation of existing solution, and in case that it shows poor performance it should be recalibrated or redesigned.

Due to different potential changes in the market, competitor's movement, macro economical changes or other factors, developed churn solution could become inappropriate for function for which it was made. To be aware is developed churn solution is still valid or it needs recalibration or redevelopment, it should be periodically validated. There is no rule how often validation should be done, but there is simple rule that turbulent markets needs more frequent checks on developed models than steady markets. This trend became obvious in situation when new competitor enters into market, and churn solution is one of the instruments for having control what is going on into existing portfolio due to amended market condition, where changes could be very often and invisible without deeper data analysis.

Each type of the developed data mining models, which makes final churn solution, could be stricken by market changes. Predictive models could lose their predictive power due to fact that some other type of customers and their behavior became more risky than at the previous period. It simply could be explained with the fact that competitors could target different market segments from company portfolio as a result of changing its market strategy. Changes in competitor's strategy will not cause loss of predictive power in predictive models immediately; it will be relatively long process. It is important to realize those trends in early stage, which could give an opportunity to company which is threatened with those strategy to make right decisions on time and to calibrate and redesign existing churn models. If model validation is performed very often (e.g. monthly), these trends will not be so explicit, than if model validation is performed less often. Frequent validation performing assures early warning systems recognition. Changing in competitors strategy could also affect on developed segmentation models, prospective customer values and all other developed models, which are integral part of, churn solution. Regarding all that facts it is important to perform periodic validation process, which assures solution, which is applicable for current market situation.

Frequent validation process is welcomed, but problem is that within short time spans there could be too few sample elements for analysis, which will capture new trends into portfolio. One of the technique is using part of period on which model was developed (most recent one) to achieve reliable data sample. This technique has a weakness, because it does not captures real recent sample only, it combines it with part of the sample on which mode was developed. Mitigating circumstance is that it takes most recent on periods and it shows real picture in current portfolio state. As mentioned before, some of the tools which analyst has in performing validation process (mostly for predictive models) are:

- ROC curve;
- Kolmogorov-Smirnov test;
- Stability index.

With applying ROC curve and Kolmogorov-Smirnov test on recent sample for existing predictive models it is possible to realize does model lost in predictive power or not. Also, it is possible to monitoring trends of the model in predictive power, does it loose it power as time goes by or it is evident some different type of trend. Continuous losing in predictive power of the model implies evident changes in churner's portfolio structure. It could be early warning signal for significant changes in market which could be caused by competitors activities or because some other reasons. It does not mean that predictive model should lose it predictive power in way that it is unusable. Predictive model could still have great predictive power, but fact that it continuously loses its power implies that obviously some other characteristics of churners became much more significant. For finding out what is the reason for that, it is recommended to repeat attribute relevance analysis (Weight of evidence, Information Value). Regarding satisfying predictive power, for sure it would not be dramatically changes in results, but indications of rising trends which causes predictive power drop will be visible. Regarding those trends, company can make or redesign churn strategy for further period. It also can put focus on revealed (now relatively weak) indicators, especially on periodic validations to reject or accept some hypothesis about market changes, competitor's new strategy, or macroeconomic influence on existing portfolio. Usage of Weight of evidence and Information Value measures, could also be useful during validation process, even churn solution does not contain predictive model. On that way company could recognize mentioned trends, churners profile, their motivators, behavior, and changes in them.

Stability index is another great tool for recognizing changes in portfolio structure (churners structure). It could be used in combination with predictive models, where some classification regarding churn probability exists, and portfolio is categorized within churn probability by binned probability scales. In that case it is common way how stability index could be applied. In case where predictive model is not part of the churn solution, stability index could be applied on some other categories/groups like clusters from self-organizing maps, or prospective customer values expressed as categories from e.g. fuzzy expert system. Stability index shows potential layering within recent sample (most fresh one) and existing portfolio.

10. DISCUSSION

Real data-mining projects requests usage of several data mining methods for achieving defined goals. Churn projects in telecom industry is no exception. Presented case study is a description of one real data-mining project for an east European telecommunication company which had problems with increasing churn trends. Traditional solutions for churn prediction are mostly based on developing predictive models, which calculates probabilities that customer will break contract.

Advantage of presented solution was holistic approach, which takes into consideration the fact that every subscriber does not have the same value for the company, and company should concentrate on spending budget on most valuable clients, instead of spending budget for churn mitigation to whole client portfolio.

After realizing who is worth for further marketing activities, next movement is concentrated on finding behavioral patterns and churn probabilities for the most valuable clients. That approach leads us to the fact that we could spend more of the budget on valuable customers.

Client evaluation, presented through soft aspects as loyalty or riskiness, instead of client evaluation based on profitability is much more objective, but also much more complicated. Thanks to Fuzzy expert systems chapter shows how it was done for this case study.

This step was crucial for following activities, revealing customer habits and creation traditional probabilistic churn model on most valuable customer data sample.

Project would be insufficient without SNA analytics on whole portfolio, because less valuable customers can cause problems in case that they commit churn as a network leaders.

Presented approach showed good results for the specific company taking in consider their market position, data sources and market conditions.

Chapter does not have intention for introducing some new churn method. It shows how real world problem in domain of churn could be solved by chaining different data mining methods, and how the given results could be used for better decision making in domain of churn mitigation takin in consider customer behavioral patterns.

Presented solution shoved good performance in presented case, but success of presented methodological approach on some other telecom company depend on portfolio structure, data sources and many other factors.

In general, idea that predictive models and behavioral characteristics models should be developed on most valuable customer sample is universal, as a fact that SNA analytics should be done on whole population.

11. FUTURE RESEARCH

As it was already mentioned chapter does not have the intention for introducing some new churn method. It shows how real world problem in domain of churn could be solved by chaining different data mining methods, and how the given results could be used for better decision making in domain of churn mitigation.

Taking into consideration that fact, it is possible to introduce some new elements and analysis into churn detection/mitigation solution as using clustering methods for customer segments recognition.

Revealed segments could be used as input variables for survival analysis, and also could be investigated with methods like decision trees for segment profiling.

It could be much alternative ways for reaching similar information usable in decision support for presented case study.

There is no cookbook for churn detection. Same company at same time with same data sources, with same problem, but in different market conditions probably needs some different solution for successful decision-making.

Introducing new data mining methods into presented solution as potentially useful elements, could discover some new dimensions and ideas for better decision-making process and understanding of consumer behavior.

Unstructured data (different kind of text data) with natural language processing could also be used as the elements for business predictive models.

Textual data from call center (customer comments written by operators in call center) could be valuable data source for churn prediction. Collected textual data contains variety of information, questions, and comments from customers entered into textual fields by operators. It contains questions about new services/products, notifications about equipment failure, questions about bills etc.

Natural language processing could show some patterns within textual data, which can show impact on churn commitment. Recognized textual patterns could lead company to conclusion about churn nature and causes. This approach could give an opportunity for company to learn churn patterns on internal data sources structured and unstructured, and to connect knowledge from both sources for extracting holistic picture and better churn understanding.

12. CONCLUSION

Real world data mining solutions are always complex in way of chaining and usage of more than one data mining method. Presented churn project in telecommunication industry is no exception in complexity.

Usage of numerous data mining methods is not guarantee of project success. More than that it is cooperation between analyst, business insider within company, which initiate project, and creativity of all project members.

Traditional assurance, that churn modeling is developing predictive model, which calculates probabilities, is not correct. It is more than that. We should understand why churn has begun, who are the churners, do we concentrate on most valuable customers because of limited budget and how to stop them in the future.

Simple predictive models calculate probabilities, and in process of developing we can get a rough picture about churn reasons without deeper expertise. For deeper expertise usage of various data mining methods is a must.

Unfortunately there is no cookbook for the churn modeling, each business case is a unique story, and each step forward in analysis can change initial analysis direction.

Most important of all things is to derive useful information for decision support, because main aim of business modeling with data mining methods is knowledge recognition, understanding of customer behavior which can be applied in decision-making.

Presented case study shows business cooperation synergy of all team members and data mining method usage regarding recognized business problem.

REFERENCES

Abbasimehr, H., Tarokh, M. J., & Setak, M. (2011). Determination of Algorithms Making Balance Between Accuracy and Comprehensibility in Churn Prediction Setting. *International Journal of Information Retrieval Research, 1*(2), 39–54. doi:10.4018/IJIRR.2011040103

Agosta, L. (2000). *The Essential Guide to Data Warehousing.* Upper Saddle River, N.J.: Prentice Hall.

Aleksander, I., & Morton, H. (1995). *An introduction to neural computing.* NY: International Thompson Computer Press.

Aracil, J., & Gordillo, F. (Eds.). (2000). *Stability Issues in Fuzzy Control.* Heidelberg: Physica-Verlag.

Bang, J., Dholakia, N., Hamel, L., & Shin, S. (2009). Customer Relationship Management and Knowledge Discovery in Database. In J. Erickson (Ed.), *Database Technologies: Concepts, Methodologies, Tools, and Applications* (pp. 1778–1786). Hershey, PA: Information Science Reference. doi:10.4018/978-1-60566-058-5.ch107

Linoff G.S., & Berry, M.J.A. (1997). Data mining techniques for marketing sales and customer support. NY: John Wiley &Sons Inc.

Dresner, H. (2008). *Performance management revolution.* NY: John Wiley &Sons Inc.

Elamvazuthi, I., Vasant, P., & Ganesan, T. (2012). Integration of Fuzzy Logic Techniques into DSS for Profitability Quantification in a Manufacturing Environment. In M. Khan & A. Ansari (Eds.), *Handbook of Research on Industrial Informatics and Manufacturing Intelligence: Innovations and Solutions* (pp. 171–192). Hershey, PA: Information Science Reference. doi:10.4018/978-1-4666-0294-6.ch007

Faulkner, M. (2003). *Customer management excellence*. NY: John Wiley &Sons Inc.

Feng, J., Xu, L., & Ramamurthy, B. (2009). Overlay Construction in Mobile Peer-to-Peer Networks. In B. Seet (Ed.), *Mobile Peer-to-Peer Computing for Next Generation Distributed Environments: Advancing Conceptual and Algorithmic Applications* (pp. 51–67). Hershey, PA: Information Science Reference. doi:10.4018/978-1-60566-715-7.ch003

Giudici, P. (2003). *Applied Data Mining: Statistical Methods for Business and Industry*. NY: John Wiley &Sons Inc.

Giudici, P., & Figini, S. (2009). *Applied Data Mining for Business and Industry (Statistics in Practice)*. NY: Wiley. doi:10.1002/9780470745830

Gorman, M. F., Wynn, D. E., & Salisbury, W. D. (2013). Searching for Herbert Simon: Extending the Reach and Impact of Business Intelligence Research through Analytics. *International Journal of Business Intelligence Research*, *4*(1), 1–12. doi:10.4018/jbir.2013010101

Hadden, J., Ashtoush, T., Rajkumar, R., & Ruta, D. (2006). Churn Prediction: Does Technology Matter? *Iranian Journal of Electrical and Computer Engineering*, *1*, 6.

Hampel, R., Wagenknecht, M., & Chaker, N. (Eds.). (2000). *Fuzzy Control: Theory and Practice*. Heidelberg, Germany: Physica-Verlag. doi:10.1007/978-3-7908-1841-3

Han, J., & Kamber, M. (2000). *Data Mining: Concepts and Techniques*. NY: Morgan Kaufmann.

Hemalatha, M. (2012). A Predictive Modeling of Retail Satisfaction: A Data Mining Approach to Retail Service Industry. In P. Ordóñez de Pablos & M. Lytras (Eds.), *Knowledge Management and Drivers of Innovation in Services Industries* (pp. 175–189). Hershey, PA: Information Science Reference. doi:10.4018/978-1-4666-0948-8.ch014

Heurer, R., & Pherson, R. (2010). *Structured analytic techniques for intelligence analysis*. Washington, DC: CQ Press College.

Kazienko, P., & Ruta, D. (2011). The Impact of Customer Churn on Social Value Dynamics. In I. Management Association (Ed.), Virtual Communities: Concepts, Methodologies, Tools and Applications (pp. 2086-2096). Hershey, PA: IGI Global. doi:10.4018/978-1-60960-100-3.ch613

Kim, M., Park, M., & Park, J. (2009). When Customer Satisfaction Isn't Good Enough: The Role of Switching Incentives and Barriers Affecting Customer Behavior in Korean Mobile Communications Services. In I. Lee (Ed.), *Handbook of Research on Telecommunications Planning and Management for Business* (pp. 351–363). Hershey, PA: Information Science Reference. doi:10.4018/978-1-60566-194-0.ch022

Klepac, G. (2010). Preparing for New Competition in the Retail Industry. In A. Syvajarvi & J. Stenvall (Eds.), *Data Mining in Public and Private Sectors: Organizational and Government Applications* (pp. 245–266). Hershey, PA: Information Science Reference; doi:10.4018/978-1-60566-906-9.ch013

Klepac, G. (2013). Risk Evaluation in the Insurance Company Using REFII Model. In S. Dehuri, M. Patra, B. Misra, & A. Jagadev (Eds.), *Intelligent Techniques in Recommendation Systems: Contextual Advancements and New Methods* (pp. 84–104). Hershey, PA: Information Science Reference; doi:10.4018/978-1-4666-2542-6.ch005

Klepac, G. (2014). Data Mining Models as a Tool for Churn Reduction and Custom Product Development in Telecommunication Industries. In P. Vasant (Ed.), *Handbook of Research on Novel Soft Computing Intelligent Algorithms: Theory and Practical Applications* (pp. 511–537). Hershey, PA: Information Science Reference. doi:10.4018/978-1-4666-4450-2.ch017

Klepac, G., & Mršić, L. (2006). *Poslovna inteligencija kroz poslovne slučajeve*. Zagreb: Liderpress.

Klepac, G., & Panian, Ž. (2003). *Poslovna inteligencija*. Zagreb: Masmedia.

Kohonen, T. (2001). *Self-organizing maps*. NY: Springer. doi:10.1007/978-3-642-56927-2

Kotsiantis, S., & Pintelas, P. (2009). Predictive Data Mining: A Survey of Regression Methods. In M. Khosrow-Pour (Ed.), *Encyclopedia of Information Science and Technology* (2nd ed., pp. 3105–3110). Hershey, PA: Information Science Reference; doi:10.4018/978-1-60566-026-4.ch495

Landow, K. C., Fandre, M., Nambiath, R., Shringarpure, N., Gates, H., Lugmayr, A., & Barker, S. (2008). Internet Protocol Television. In Y. Dwivedi, A. Papazafeiropoulou, & J. Choudrie (Eds.), *Handbook of Research on Global Diffusion of Broadband Data Transmission* (pp. 538–562). Hershey, PA: Information Science Reference. doi:10.4018/978-1-59904-851-2.ch034

Larose, D. T. (2005). *Discovering Knowledge in Data: An Introduction to Data Mining*. NY: John Wiley &Sons Inc.

Larose, D. T. (2006). *Data mining methods and models*. NY: John Wiley &Sons Inc.

Mannila, H., & Hand, D. (2001). *Principles of Data Mining*. Cambridge: The MIT press.

Michaell, B. J. A., & Gordon, L. (2000). *Mastering data mining*. NY: John Wiley &Sons Inc.

Michaell, B. J. A., & Gordon, L. (2003). *Mining the web*. NY: John Wiley &Sons Inc.

Namid, R. N., & Christopher, D. B. (Eds.). (2004). *Organizational Data Mining: Leveraging Enterprise Data Resources for Optimal Performance*. PA: Idea Group.

Pedrycz, W., & Gomide, F. (1998). *An Introduction to Fuzzy Sets: Analysis and Design of Complex Adaptive Systems*. Cambridge, Massachusetts: MIT Press.

Pyle, D. (1999). *Data preparation for Data Mining*. NY: Morgan Kaufmann.

Qi, J., Li, Y., Li, C., & Zhang, Y. (2009). Telecommunication Customer Detainment Management. In I. Lee (Ed.), *Handbook of Research on Telecommunications Planning and Management for Business* (pp. 379–399). Hershey, PA: Information Science Reference. doi:10.4018/978-1-60566-194-0.ch024

Raine, L., & Wellman, B. (2012). *Networked. The new social operating system*. Cambridge: MIT Press.

Rashid T. (2010) Classification of Churn and non-Churn Customers for Telecommunication Companies. *International Journal of Biometrics and Bioinformatics*, 3(5).

Ruta, D., Adl, C., & Nauck, D. (2009). New Churn Prediction Strategies in the Telecom Industry. In H. Wang (Ed.), *Intelligent Data Analysis: Developing New Methodologies Through Pattern Discovery and Recovery* (pp. 218–235). Hershey, PA: Information Science Reference; doi:10.4018/978-1-59904-982-3.ch013

Scott, J. (2012). *Social Network Analysis*. London: SAGE Publications.

Siler, W., & Buckley, J. J. (2005). *Fuzzy expert sytems and fuzzy reasoning*. NY: John Wiley &Sons Inc.

Thomas, L., Edelman, D., & Crook, J. (2002). *Credit Scoring and Its Application*. NY: SIAM. doi:10.1137/1.9780898718317

Varnali, K. (2013). Mobile Social Networks: Communication and Marketing Perspectives. In I. Lee (Ed.), *Strategy, Adoption, and Competitive Advantage of Mobile Services in the Global Economy* (pp. 248–258). Hershey, PA: Information Science Reference. doi:10.4018/978-1-4666-1939-5.ch014

Vasant, P., Barsoum, N., Kahraman, C., & Dimirovski, G. (2008). Application of Fuzzy Optimization in Forecasting and Planning of Construction Industry. In I. Vlahavas & D. Vrakas (Eds.), *Artificial Intelligence for Advanced Problem Solving Techniques* (pp. 254–265). Hershey, PA: Information Science Reference. doi:10.4018/978-1-59904-705-8.ch010

Vasant, P., Ganesan, T., & Elamvazuthi, I. (2012). Hybrid Tabu Search Hopfield Recurrent ANN Fuzzy Technique to the Production Planning Problems: A Case Study of Crude Oil in Refinery Industry. [IJMMME]. *International Journal of Manufacturing, Materials, and Mechanical Engineering*, 2(1), 47–65. doi:10.4018/ijmmme.2012010104

Vose, D. (2000). *Quantitative Risk Analysis*. New York: John Wiley & Sons.

Weiss, G. (2009). Data Mining in the Telecommunications Industry. In J. Wang (Ed.), *Encyclopedia of Data Warehousing and Mining* (2nd ed., pp. 486–491). Hershey, PA: Information Science Reference. doi:10.4018/978-1-60566-010-3.ch076

Williams, J., Weiqiang, L., & Mehmet, O. (2002). An Overview of Temporal Data Mining. In S.J. Simoff, G.J. Williams, M. Hegland (Eds.), *Proceedings of the 1st Australian Data Mining Workshop* (ADM02) Canberra, Australia (pp. 83-90). University of Technology, Sydney.

Willis, R., Serenko, A., & Turel, O. (2009). Contractual Obligations between Mobile Service Providers and Users. In D. Taniar (Ed.), *Mobile Computing: Concepts, Methodologies, Tools, and Applications* (pp. 1929–1936). Hershey, PA: Information Science Reference; doi:10.4018/978-1-60566-054-7.ch155

ADDITIONAL READING

Almeida, F., & Santos, M. (2014). A Conceptual Framework for Big Data Analysis. In I. Portela & F. Almeida (Eds.), *Organizational, Legal, and Technological Dimensions of Information System Administration* (pp. 199–223). Hershey, PA: Information Science Reference. doi:10.4018/978-1-4666-4526-4.ch011

Bakshi, K. (2014). Technologies for Big Data. In W. Hu & N. Kaabouch (Eds.), *Big Data Management, Technologies, and Applications* (pp. 1–22). Hershey, PA: Information Science Reference; doi:10.4018/978-1-4666-4699-5.ch001

Bhattacharyya, S., & Dutta, P. (2012). Fuzzy Logic: Concepts, System Design, and Applications to Industrial Informatics. In M. Khan & A. Ansari (Eds.), *Handbook of Research on Industrial Informatics and Manufacturing Intelligence: Innovations and Solutions* (pp. 33–71). Hershey, PA: Information Science Reference. doi:10.4018/978-1-4666-0294-6.ch003

Bird, S., Klein, E., & Loper, E. (2009). *Natural Language Processing with Python*. Sebastopol: O'Reilly.

Casabayó, M., & Agell, N. (2012). A Fuzzy Segmentation Approach to Guide Marketing Decisions. In A. Meier & L. Donzé (Eds.), *Fuzzy Methods for Customer Relationship Management and Marketing: Applications and Classifications* (pp. 291–311). Hershey, PA: Business Science Reference. doi:10.4018/978-1-4666-0095-9.ch013

Chen, G., & Hoon Joo, Y. (2009). Fuzzy Control Systems: An Introduction. In J. Rabuñal Dopico, J. Dorado, & A. Pazos (Eds.), *Encyclopedia of Artificial Intelligence* (pp. 688–695). Hershey, PA: Information Science Reference. doi:10.4018/978-1-59904-849-9.ch103

Dagiasis, A. P. (2013). Logistics Modeling and Forecasting with Regression. In D. Folinas (Ed.), *Outsourcing Management for Supply Chain Operations and Logistics Service* (pp. 223–237). Hershey, PA: Business Science Reference. doi:10.4018/978-1-4666-2008-7.ch013

Donzé, L., & Meier, A. (2013). Applying Fuzzy Logic and Fuzzy Methods to Marketing. In IRMA International (Ed.), Supply Chain Management: Concepts, Methodologies, Tools, and Applications (pp. 1056-1068). Hershey, PA: Business Science Reference. doi: 10.4018/978-1-4666-2625-6.ch062

Feng, J., Xu, L., & Ramamurthy, B. (2009). Overlay Construction in Mobile Peer-to-Peer Networks. In B. Seet (Ed.), *Mobile Peer-to-Peer Computing for Next Generation Distributed Environments: Advancing Conceptual and Algorithmic Applications* (pp. 51–67). Hershey, PA: Information Science Reference. doi:10.4018/978-1-60566-715-7.ch003

Han, J., & Kamber, M. (2000). *Data Mining: Concepts and Techniques*. San Francisco: Morgan Kaufmann.

Hemalatha, M. (2012). A Predictive Modeling of Retail Satisfaction: A Data Mining Approach to Retail Service Industry. In P. Ordóñez de Pablos & M. Lytras (Eds.), *Knowledge Management and Drivers of Innovation in Services Industries* (pp. 175–189). Hershey, PA: Information Science Reference. doi:10.4018/978-1-4666-0948-8.ch014

Hu, W., & Kaabouch, N. (2014). *Big Data Management, Technologies, and Applications* (pp. 1–342). Hershey, PA: IGI Global; doi:10.4018/978-1-4666-4699-5

Kantardžić, M. (2003). *Data Mining: Concepts, Models, Methods and Algorithms*. New York, USA: John Wiley & Sons.

Kazienko, P., & Ruta, D. (2011). The Impact of Customer Churn on Social Value Dynamics. In I. Management Association (Ed.), Virtual Communities: Concepts, Methodologies, Tools and Applications (pp. 2086-2096). Hershey, PA: Information Science Reference. - doi:10.4018/978-1-60960-100-3.ch613

Kim, M., Park, M., & Park, J. (2009). When Customer Satisfaction Isn't Good Enough: The Role of Switching Incentives and Barriers Affecting Customer Behavior in Korean Mobile Communications Services. In I. Lee (Ed.), *Handbook of Research on Telecommunications Planning and Management for Business* (pp. 351–363). Hershey, PA: Information Science Reference. doi:10.4018/978-1-60566-194-0.ch022

Kolomvatsos, K., & Hadjiefthymiades, S. (2012). On the Use of Fuzzy Logic in Electronic Marketplaces. In V. Mago & N. Bhatia (Eds.), *Cross-Disciplinary Applications of Artificial Intelligence and Pattern Recognition: Advancing Technologies* (pp. 609–632). Hershey, PA: Information Science Reference. Doi: 10.4018/978-1-61350-429-1.ch030

Landow, K. C., Fandre, M., Nambiath, R., Shringarpure, N., Gates, H., Lugmayr, A., & Barker, S. (2008). Internet Protocol Television. In Y. Dwivedi, A. Papazafeiropoulou, & J. Choudrie (Eds.), *Handbook of Research on Global Diffusion of Broadband Data Transmission* (pp. 538–562). Hershey, PA: Information Science Reference. doi:10.4018/978-1-59904-851-2.ch034

Marvuglia, A., Cellura, M., & Pucci, M. (2012). A Generalization of the Orthogonal Regression Technique for Life Cycle Inventory. *International Journal of Agricultural and Environmental Information Systems*, *3*(1), 51–71. doi:10.4018/jaeis.2012010105

Mehran, K., Zahawi, B., & Giaouris, D. (2011). Fuzzy Logic for Non-smooth Dynamical Systems. In Y. Dai, B. Chakraborty, & M. Shi (Eds.), *Kansei Engineering and Soft Computing: Theory and Practice* (pp. 147–168). Hershey, PA: Engineering Science Reference. doi:10.4018/978-1-61692-797-4.ch008

Merlin, B., & Raynal, M. (2012). Soft Keyboard Evaluations: Integrating User's Background in Predictive Models. In E. Alkhalifa & K. Gaid (Eds.), *Cognitively Informed Intelligent Interfaces: Systems Design and Development* (pp. 21–40). Hershey, PA: Information Science Reference. doi:10.4018/978-1-4666-1628-8.ch002

Pomazalová, N. (2013). Public Sector Transformation Processes and Internet Public Procurement: Decision Support Systems. IGI Global. doi:10.4018/978-1-4666-2665-2

Prilop, M., Tonisson, L., & Maicher, L. (2013). Designing Analytical Approaches for Interactive Competitive Intelligence. *International Journal of Service Science, Management, Engineering, and Technology*, *4*(2), 34–45. doi:10.4018/jssmet.2013040103

Qi, J., Li, Y., Li, C., & Zhang, Y. (2009). Telecommunication Customer Detainment Management. In I. Lee (Ed.), *Handbook of Research on Telecommunications Planning and Management for Business* (pp. 379–399). Hershey, PA: Information Science Reference. doi:10.4018/978-1-60566-194-0.ch024

Raine, L., & Wellman, B. (2012). *Networked. The new social operating system*. Cambridge: MIT Press.

Rokach, L. (2009). Incorporating Fuzzy Logic in Data Mining Tasks. In J. Rabuñal Dopico, J. Dorado, & A. Pazos (Eds.), *Encyclopedia of Artificial Intelligence* (pp. 884–891). Hershey, PA: Information Science Reference. doi:10.4018/978-1-59904-849-9.ch131

Ruta, D., Adl, C., & Nauck, D. (2009). New Churn Prediction Strategies in the Telecom Industry. In H. Wang (Ed.), *Intelligent Data Analysis: Developing New Methodologies Through Pattern Discovery and Recovery* (pp. 218–235). Hershey, PA: Information Science Reference. doi:10.4018/978-1-59904-982-3.ch013

Scott, J. (2012). *Social Network Analysis*. London: SAGE Publications.

Sirkeci, I., & Mannix, R. (2010). Segmentation Challenges Posed by 'Transnationals' in Mobile Marketing. In K. Pousttchi & D. Wiedemann (Eds.), *Handbook of Research on Mobile Marketing Management* (pp. 94–114). Hershey, PA: Business Science Reference. Doi: 10.4018/978-1-60566-074-5.ch006

Varnali, K. (2013). Mobile Social Networks: Communication and Marketing Perspectives. In I. Lee (Ed.), *Strategy, Adoption, and Competitive Advantage of Mobile Services in the Global Economy* (pp. 248–258). Hershey, PA: Information Science Reference. doi:10.4018/978-1-4666-1939-5.ch014

Vasant, P., Barsoum, N., Kahraman, C., & Dimirovski, G. (2008). Application of Fuzzy Optimization in Forecasting and Planning of Construction Industry. In I. Vlahavas & D. Vrakas (Eds.), *Artificial Intelligence for Advanced Problem Solving Techniques* (pp. 254–265). Hershey, PA: Information Science Reference. doi:10.4018/978-1-59904-705-8.ch010

Vasant, P., Ganesan, T., & Elamvazuthi, I. (2012). Hybrid Tabu Search Hopfield Recurrent ANN Fuzzy Technique to the Production Planning Problems: A Case Study of Crude Oil in Refinery Industry. *International Journal of Manufacturing, Materials, and Mechanical Engineering*, 2(1), 47–65. doi:10.4018/ijmmme.2012010104

Venkateswaran, P., Kundu, M., Shaw, S., Orea, K., & Nandi, R. (2013). Fuzzy Logic-based Mobility Metric Clustering Algorithm for MANETs. In V. Sridhar & D. Saha (Eds.), *Web-Based Multimedia Advancements in Data Communications and Networking Technologies* (pp. 207–219). Hershey, PA: Information Science Reference. doi:10.4018/978-1-4666-2026-1.ch011

Vose, D. (2000). *Quantitative Risk Analysis*. New York, USA: John Wiley & Sons.

Weiss, G. (2009). Data Mining in the Telecommunications Industry. In J. Wang (Ed.), *Encyclopedia of Data Warehousing and Mining* (2nd ed., pp. 486–491). Hershey, PA: Information Science Reference. doi:10.4018/978-1-60566-010-3.ch076

Werro, N., & Stormer, H. (2012). A Fuzzy Logic Approach for the Assessment of Online Customers. In A. Meier & L. Donzé (Eds.), *Fuzzy Methods for Customer Relationship Management and Marketing: Applications and Classifications* (pp. 252–270). Hershey, PA: Business Science Reference. doi:10.4018/978-1-4666-0095-9.ch011

Willis, R., Serenko, A., & Turel, O. (2007). Contractual Obligations between Mobile Service Providers and Users. In D. Taniar (Ed.), *Encyclopedia of Mobile Computing and Commerce* (pp. 143–148). Hershey, PA: Information Science Reference; doi:10.4018/978-1-59904-002-8.ch025

Willis, R., Serenko, A., & Turel, O. (2009). Contractual Obligations Between Mobile Service Providers and Users. In D. Taniar (Ed.), *Mobile Computing: Concepts, Methodologies, Tools, and Applications* (pp. 1929–1936). Hershey, PA: Information Science Reference. doi:10.4018/978-1-60566-054-7.ch155

Yang, Y. (2009). Behavioral Pattern-Based Customer Segmentation. In J. Wang (Ed.), *Encyclopedia of Data Warehousing and Mining* (2nd ed., pp. 140–145). Hershey, PA: Information Science Reference. doi:10.4018/978-1-60566-010-3.ch023

KEY TERMS AND DEFINITIONS

Churn: Interruption of the contract or using product or services.

Cox Regression: One of the method for survival analysis.

Data Mining: Discovering hidden useful knowledge in large amount of data (databases).

Fuzzy Expert System: Expert system based on fuzzy logic.

Fuzzy Logic: Logic which presumes possible membership to more than one category with degree of membership, and which is opposite to (exact) crisp logic.

Keywords: Data Mining, Fuzzy logic, Fuzzy expert system, Scoring, Churn, Survival analysis, Cox regression, SNA, Segmentation, Customer relationship management.

Scoring: Process of assignation of some usually numeric value as grade which show as performance of observed case/object.

Survival Analysis: Analysis that shows survival rate (example: from population of customers) in defined period of time.

APPENDIX: PREDICTIVE CHURN MODEL DEVELOPMENT USING LOGISTIC REGRESSION

Let zi $(i = 1, 2, \ldots, n)$ be empirical values of a churn, which can take only the values 0 for non churners and for churners 1.

A logistic regression model calculates probabilities that churn occurs in different subpopulation .

$$\prod_i = p\left(Z_i = 1\right) for \ i = 1, 2, 3, .., n \tag{1}$$

Logistic regression model for churn probability calculation specifies that an appropriate function of the fitted probability of the event within linear function of the variables recognized in process of attribute relevance analysis in form:

$$\log\left[\frac{\prod_i}{1 - \prod_i}\right] = b + a_1 x_{i1} + a_2 x_{i2} + \ldots + a_m x_{im} \tag{2}$$

As a result we have probability that some subscriber will become churner or non-churner in certain period of time.

By inverting the definition of the logit function, we obtain:

$$\prod_i = \frac{e^{b + a_1 x_{i1} + a_2 x_{i2} + .. + a_m x_{im}}}{1 - e^{b + a_1 x_{i1} + a_2 x_{i2} + .. + a_m x_{im}}} \tag{3}$$

After applying model on empirical data, score bands were created based on probability calculation for

$$P\left(Z_i = 1_{churner} \ i\right) = 1, 2, 3, .. n \ .$$

Chapter 9
Hybrid Intelligence for Smarter Networking Operations

Bassem Mahmoud Mokhtar
Alexandria University, Egypt

Mohamed Eltoweissy
Virginia Military Institute, USA

ABSTRACT

The ever-growing and ever-evolved Internet targets supporting billions of networked entities to provide a wide variety of services and resources. Such complexity results in network-data from different sources with special characteristics, such as widely diverse users, multiple media, high-dimensionality and various dynamic concerns. With huge amounts of network-data with such characteristics, there are significant challenges to a) recognize emergent and anomalous behavior in network-traffic and b) make intelligent decisions for efficient network operations. Endowing the semantically-oblivious Internet with Intelligence would advance the Internet capability to learn traffic behavior and to predict future events. In this chapter, the authors discuss and evaluate the hybridization of monolithic intelligence techniques in order to achieve smarter and enhanced networking operations. Additionally, the authors provide systematic application-agnostic semantics management methodology with efficient processes for extracting and classifying high-level features and reasoning about rich semantics.

1. INTRODUCTION

Due to semantically-oblivious networking operations, the current Internet cannot effectively or efficiently cope with the explosion in services with different requirements, number of users, resource heterogeneity, and widely varied user, application and system dynamics (Feldmann, 2007). This leads to increasing complexity in Internet management and operations, thus multiplying challenges to achieve better security, performance and Quality of Service (QoS) satisfaction. The current Internet largely lacks capabilities to extract network-semantics to efficiently build behavioral models of Internet elements at different levels of granularity and to pervasively observe and inspect network dynamics. For example, a network host might know the role of TCP; however, it might not know the behavior of TCP in a mobile *ad hoc* network.

DOI: 10.4018/978-1-4666-9474-3.ch009

We refer to the limited utilization of Internet traffic semantics in networking operations as the Internet semantic gap. Additionally, many evolutionary cross-layer networking enhancements and clean-slate architectures, see for example (Bouabene et al., 2010; Day, Matta, & Mattar, 2008; Hassan, Eltoweissy, & Youssef, 2009; Zafeiropoulos, Liakopoulos, Davy, & Chaparadza, 2010), did not consider capabilities for representing, managing, and utilizing the inherent multi-dimensional networking data patterns. Also, these architectures lack facilities to learn network-semantics and utilize them to dynamically allocate and predict "right-sized" services/resources on demand for example.

The current and future internetworks (for example, Internet of things (IoT) (Khan, Khan, Zaheer, & Khan, 2012; Zhiming, Qi, & Hong, 2011)) support a massive number of Internet elements with extensive amounts of data. Fortunately, these data generally exhibit multi-dimensional patterns (for example, patterns with dimensions such as time, space, and users) that can be learned in order to extract network-semantics (Srivastava, Cooley, Deshpande, & Tan, 2000). These semantics can help in learning normal and anomalous behavior of the different networking elements (for example, services, protocols, etc.) in the Internet, and in building behavior models for those elements accordingly. Recognizing and maintaining semantics as accessible concepts and behavior models related to various Internet elements will aid in possessing intelligence thus helping elements in predicting future events (for example, QoS degradation and attacks) that might occur and affect performance of networking operations. Furthermore, learning behavior of those elements will better support self-* properties such as awareness with unfamiliar services and also advance reasoning about their behavior. For instance, a router can classify a new running service in a network as a specific type of TCP-based file transfer service when it finds similarity between behavior of the new service and that of an already known service.

The lack of efficient methodology and capabilities for analyzing and learning patterns of high- and multi-dimensional big network-data and reasoning about network-semantics presents challenges including but not limited to the following:

- Recognizing emergent and abnormal behavior of various Internet elements;
- Making effective decisions for efficient network operations;
- Ensuring availability of resources on-demand; and
- Efficient utilization of networked entities' capabilities to store, access and process data and extract valuable network-semantics.

Many research works targeted intelligence-based solutions to enhance operation performance in different fields (e.g., networks, speech and image recognition). Those works present solutions either using monolithic or hybrid intelligence techniques for achieving intelligence in different areas, such as speech recognition, language modeling and networking. In this chapter, we discuss the hybridization of monolithic intelligence techniques in order to achieve smarter and enhanced operations, especially in the networking field. Endowing the semantically-oblivious Internet with Intelligence would advance the Internet capability to learn traffic behavior and to predict future events. Additionally, we present our proposed network-semantics reasoner which is designed via hybridizing hidden Markov models (HMM) and latent Dirichlet allocation (LDA) for enabling latent features extraction with semantics dependencies.

In literature, some works have targeted intelligence-based solutions to enhance operation performance in different fields (e.g., speech and image recognition). In (Willett & Rigoll, 1998), authors integrated HMM and Neural Networks (NN) to form a hybrid speech recognition system. They employed NN to extract discriminative speech features by processing multiple instances of the same feature vector.

Extracted features are then directed to HMM to model the acoustic behavior of speech. HMM helps overcome NN's limitations in extracting valuable information from highly-dynamic traffic data. Another system uses support vector machine (SVM) for data analysis, classification and pattern recognition plus Fuzzy rules (Nii, Nakai, Takahashi, Higuchi, & Maenaka, 2011) for discovering human behavior. The system performs abstraction of data using SVM-based classification into sequence of actions, and constructs Fuzzy rules for each behavior, defined by a sequence of actions. In (Griffiths, Steyvers, Blei, & Tenenbaum, 2004), the authors provided a system for language learning based on using LDA and HMM. They adopted the ability of LDA and HMM to simultaneously learn and find syntactic classes and semantic topics despite having no knowledge of syntax or semantics beyond statistical dependency.

Internet (or network) intelligence (referred to here as InetIntel) is defined in the literature as the capability of Internet elements to understand network-semantics to be able to make effective decisions and use resources efficiently (Li, Xiao, Han, Chen, & Liu, 2007). InetIntel has to support Internet elements with the capability for learning normal and dynamic/emergent behavior of various elements and in turn building dynamic behavior models of those elements. Consequently, this will enable elements to be conscious of surrounding contexts enabling them to enhance their performance, utilization of resources and QoS satisfaction.

InetIntel provides facilities to understand network traffic by identifying correlation among users, services, and protocols; and it might be able to represent acquired knowledge in a unified model. InetIntel is considered as a middleware where it forms an information layer with metadata from IP traffic. These data are fed to applications to enrich their information about network-based activity. Furthermore, InetIntel relates data from different traffics to enhance situational awareness and better cyber security and IP services. Here are some of the services that can be offered by InetIntel:

- Optimization for QoS of running services and applications and enhancing protocols operation based on end-to-end (e2e) and non e2e principles.
- Unified representation "metadata" for different types of traffic to be used by applications.
- Real-time traffic analysis and situational awareness.
- Behavior analysis based on statistics, for various Internet elements, such as users, services, applications and protocols.
- Accumulated and evolvable knowledge services within time for better decision making processes in different situations as anomaly discovery.

InetIntel can be achieved via employing intelligence techniques to design intelligence systems. InetIntel systems can employ monolithic and/or hybrid (or combinations of more than one monolithic technique) intelligence techniques. Each implemented monolithic technique for InetIntel has its mechanisms for learning data patterns, extracting features and reasoning about data semantics. The environment of Internet has tremendous and ever-growing scale. It is noisy and dynamic with dissimilar communicating networks and heterogeneous entities, running services and resources. Accordingly, generated and transmitted Internet data have special characteristics, such as massive volume with high- and multi-dimensionality. Those characteristics might affect negatively performance of monolithic intelligence techniques. Hybrid intelligence techniques (HIT) can mitigate that challenge (Abraham & Nath, 2000; Peddabachigari, Abraham, Grosan, & Thomas, 2007). HIT will integrate more than one monolithic intelligence technique. HIT can mitigate limitations of monolithic techniques that it can combine their significant capabilities to extract valuable information with good level of accuracy and timeliness. For example, in (Kumar, Kumar, & Sachdeva, 2010), comparisons among various InetIntel techniques-based intrusion detection systems showed the outperformance of HIT in achieving higher detection accuracy.

In the networking literature, monolithic- and hybrid intelligence-based solutions have been investigated to provide intelligence for networks and Internet to realize self-* properties, address intrusion detection and achieve improved network performance and operation. Kumar *et al.* in (Kumar et al., 2010) discussed artificial intelligence-based techniques that can help in enhancing intrusion detection in Internet. A classification for those techniques was provided. Machine leaning and genetic algorithm based techniques are examples of artificial intelligence-based techniques. In (Idris & Shanmugam, 2005), Idris *et al.* provided a software-based middleware solution via a HIT for intrusion detection system (IDS). The implemented HIT comprises Fuzzy logic and a data mining mechanism with the usage of neural networks (NN). The IDS system depended on extracting features or attributes from large sets of real network-data and applying those features over simple *if-then* Fuzzy rules. The proposed system combines: a) misuse detection (e.g., detect attacks based on learning patterns and matching with already known attack patterns); and b) anomaly detection (e.g., learning unfamiliar attacks or threats by applying statistical analysis methods over data and compare results with historical knowledge).

In this chapter, we discuss the importance of embedding Internet with Intelligence via employing monolithic and hybrid semantics reasoning techniques. We propose hybrid intelligence technique (HIT) integrating HMM and LDA for reasoning about network semantics and targeting intelligence-based networking operations. Additionally, we highlight the importance and impact of attaching Intelligence to operating and communicating Internet elements; such as hosts and routers, and show how this capability can aid in better and smarter networking operations like optimizing at runtime QoS of running applications and learning abnormal traffic and strengthening security. The chapter is organized as follows. Section 2 provides background of concepts underlying our work and explores some related work. Hybrid intelligence-based methodology for reasoning about network semantics is presented in Section 3. Also, Section 3 highlights the differences between utilizing monolithic and hybrid intelligence techniques for learning network semantics and having smarter networking operations. Section 4 evaluates via conducting simulation the performance analysis of the studied intelligence techniques. Future directions are presented in Section 5. Finally, Section 6 concludes the chapter.

2. BACKGROUND AND RELATED WORK

In this section, we first highlight some definitions related to network-semantics management methodology. Then, we survey some research work related to network-semantics management in literature.

2.1 Background

In this subsection, we present definitions related to the methodology, as shown in Figure 1, which we adopt to reasoning about and manage network-semantics. These definitions are as follows.

- **Big Network-Data:** Data generated from different sources (e.g., Internet traffic, offline databases, management information bases (MIB)) with special characteristics, such as massive volume, information diversity (e.g., text, audio, video, etc.), high- and multi-dimensionality (e.g., large sets of attributes related to different Internet elements) and various dynamics concerns (e.g., time-sensitive data). With big network-data, there are challenges regarding content, structure and behavior.

Figure 1. Semantics management methodology

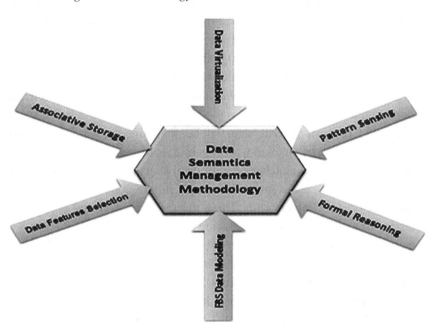

- **Big Network:** A network that generates big network-data and can benefit from big data management in their operations. Examples of big networks include the current Internet, the emerging Internet of Things (Khan et al., 2012) and social networks.

- **Data Virtualization:** Voluminous data are generated with different formats and representation modes from various sources in big networks. To have efficient data collection, data virtualization (DV) techniques ("[Online] "; IBM; informatica; queplix) should be used. This would enable data abstraction and federation from different sources employing unified data representation. We are inspired here by the sensory system in humans (Hawkins & Blakeslee, 2005), which collects huge amount of data from five senses and sends it to the brain via nerve signals in a unified representation.

- **Data Feature Selection:** Big network-data are high- and multi-dimensional. This requires huge storage and computation capabilities to analyze patterns of these data. To have efficient big network-data processing, dimensionality reduction algorithms with the capability of directive data feature selection process will be used. Inspired by functionalities of the human memory, capturing raw data from various sources can lead to retrieving some distinguished features which are already maintained in the memory. For example, seeing an unfamiliar restaurant across a road aids us in easily remembering and retrieving some known special restaurant features like the existence of dining tables, chairs, restrooms, etc. (not the locations of restrooms or number and color of chairs and tables).

- **Function-Behavior-Structure (FBS) Data Modeling:** Representing data uniformly, clarifying their functional, behavioral and structural aspects (Dorst & Vermaas, 2005; Gero, 1990) will facilitate data pattern learning. In the human memory, there are connectivity patterns established via synapses amongst neurons in different brain cortex areas. Those connectivity patterns refer to three different connectivity modes, namely, structural connectivity, functional connectively and effective connectivity between neurons. Structural connectivity gives information about the established links or synapses between neurons. Functional connectivity provides information about statistical dependencies and correlations between neurons. Effective connectivity refers to the information flow carried by electrochemical signals between neurons. The analysis of connectivity patterns using the previously discussed modes helps in learning the behavior and characteristics of neurons (e.g., specialized neurons) and related synapses and transferred electrochemical signals in different cortex areas.

- **Associative Storage:** To learn patterns, data will be maintained in warehouses, which will be extendible. That storage would be enabled with capabilities of identifying storage locations by their content or part of contents. This matches operations of short-term and long-term memories in human. Low or high levels of neurons fire in different cortex regions when they capture data, which indicate to different types of information. These groups of neurons are connected as sequences. They are referring to lots of detailed or abstracted data.

- **Pattern Sensing:** States the ability to discover big data patterns based on data attributes (or features) extraction and classification processes. In the human memory, sequences of neurons in certain cortex areas (e.g. visual and vocal areas) with certain connection pattern lead to identifying characteristics of that pattern. For instance, hearing and seeing a cat lead to a certain neurons pattern in our brain based on learned concepts (e.g., expectation of listening to cat *meow* voice).

- **Formal Reasoning:** A well-founded artificial intelligence functionality based on integrated statistical reasoning models to perform semantic reasoning and matching. Those models will be used to extract semantics from learned data patterns and already known semantics. Constructed chains of neurons in different cortex locations (e.g., vocal and visual cortex areas) of the human brain result in formation of high level neurons that will be fired along the human life. Capturing data via different senses (e.g., sight and hearing) result in having sequences of correlated fired neurons in various cortex areas.

2.2 Related Work

In this subsection, we compare various techniques that can be used in network-semantics reasoning and management. Table 1 shows a comparison between different schemes for implementing models for semantics reasoning, such as HMM (Rabiner & Juang, 1986), LDA (Blei, Ng, & Jordan, 2003), neural networks (Cross, Harrison, & Kennedy, 1995), Latent Semantics Analysis (LSA) (Landauer, Foltz, & Laham, 1998), Simulated Annealing (SA) (Van Laarhoven & Aarts, 1987) and Support Vector Machine (SVM) (Cristianini & Shawe-Taylor, 2000). The comparison highlights the advantages and the limitations of each technique.

3. HYBRID INTELLIGENCE TECHNIQUE-BASED REASONER FOR SMARTER NETWORKING

In this section, we discuss network-semantics management processes using monolithic and hybrid intelligence techniques. We will highlight three different monolithic intelligence techniques in literature for semantics reasoning where we show the operation and performance of each technique. Then, we present our hybrid intelligence techniques. Finally, we provide a qualitative comparison between the presented intelligence techniques for showing their capabilities and performance.

Table 1. Comparison between different schemes for network-semantics reasoning

Scheme	Description	Operation Technique	Application	Advantage	Limitation
HMM (Rabiner & Juang, 1986)	• HMM is a statistical Markov model for categorical sequence labeling (i.e., pattern recognition by statistical inference) based on using supervised/unsupervised learning algorithms (e.g., Baum-Welch algorithm (Baum, 1972)). • Sequence labeling can be treated as a set of independent classification tasks. • HMM is a structured architecture that is able to predict sequences of semantic topics based on hidden sequences of input data attributes or features.	Based on continuous input sequence with different Gaussian distributions then making distribution mixture for obtaining most likelihood output sequence.	• Labeling documents/ motions with certain tags or topics for information retrieval • Gesture imitation in robots	• HMM depends on a mathematical model with parameters) that can be adjusted for supporting different semantic topics in many contexts • HMM's statistical foundations are computationally efficient and well-suited to handle new data • HMM can support multi-dimensional data • HMM can be adjusted as prototype to extract spedific semanti topics	• The floating-point underflow problem. • discovering high-level features with long-range semantics dependencies • lot of HMM parameters to be calculated at large input states • require large sets of data to be trained • Low performance at operation with reduced-dimensional data
LDA (Blei et al., 2003)	• LDA is a generative probabilistic dynamic model that can be used for extracting hidden topics in group of observed unlabeled input data profiles and known words or attributes. • LDA has the capability to discover high-level features in data profiles where it has a well-defined inference methodology to associate a data profile with group of attributes with several semantic topics. • LDA is capable of extracting data semantics based on prior probabilities for data profile-semantic topic and attribute-semantic topic associations.	Based on supervised learning process and training data with prior probabilities that associate topics with words and documents and using sampling tech. (e.g., Gibbs)	• Modeling a mixture of topics with documents • Topic models for image and text recognition	• LDA models are extendible to support more associations amongst semantic topics and data attributes • Can be integrated with functionalities of other semantic reasoning models (e.g., HMMs) • discovering high-level latent features	• Randomization process for assigning parameters' values of attribute-topic • Probability for the overfitting problem at large number of training data sets • Big bag of attributes lead to topic misclassification process based on random topic sampling process
LDA-HMM (Hybrid) (Griffiths et al., 2004)	Probabilistic and Categorical sequence labeling supervised/ unsupervised algorithms for allocating latent topic and estimating semantics based on hidden sequence of input latent words	Based on sampling process for hidden topic bases on multinomial probability distribution and using Gaussian distributions with maximum likelihood estimation for outputting semantics	Topic modeling for many applications such as pattern and image recognition, and information retrieval	• Combine advantages of both LDA and HMM schemes • Number of input features or states to train the HMM is lower than operation with HMM alone • Mitigate the effect of topic misclassification and overfitting by LDA where final semantics output depends on group of syntactic states formed by extracted features by LDA	• The time complexity worsens to some extent compared to comprised monolithic schemes • The floating-point underflow problem. • Require large sets of data to be trained
Simple statistical-analysis-based models	Models for learning statistics of input words and based on some defined rules, they can extract semantics	Collecting statistics about words, documents and using defined rules (e.g., Fuzzy rules) and thresholds that outputs depend on meeting those rules	Rule-based Reasoning (extraction of information related to specific semantic topics)	• Can be designed to be directed to specific types of semantic-topics or information ; achieving good performance • Low computation complexity	• Specific to certain semantic topics • Inefficient design lead to incorrect extracted information • No capability to extract high-level latent features

continued on following page

Table 1. Continued

Scheme	Description	Operation Technique	Application	Advantage	Limitation
Neural network (Cross et al., 1995)	• Classification algorithms (supervised algorithms predicting categorical labels) • Learning is by training and used to model complex relationships between inputs and outputs, to find patterns in data, or to capture the statistical structure in an unknown joint probability distribution between observed variables	• Based on a hidden layer that relates group of input with other group of output via defined weights. • Connection weight based on relation between inputs and outputs and affect results (i.e. outputs) • Depending on composition of functions where components of each neural network layer are independent of each other	• System identification and control • Decision making • Pattern recognition • Data mining	• Flexibility: it can be applied to many applications • Robustness: it can work properly and mitigate the failure of some Internet elements • It can handle noisy data and analyze complex data patterns	• Design complexity: o Complicated group of neural units connected based on weighted inputs to outputs and passing thresholds o Long processing time in case of large neural network • More trainings is needed to operate efficiently • Its operation might face overfitting
Latent Semantic Analysis (LSA) (Landauer et al., 1998)	Probabilistic models which relates documents to topics based on weighted relationship specified by probabilities (mapping documents' words into concepts)	Building models for mixtures of topics and documents through training examples	Modeling a mixture of topics and concepts with documents and their words	Reduces dimensionality of documents for better representation, finding synonyms and minimizing computational complexity.	• Assuming Gaussian distribution for words in documents. • No directed capabilities for selecting efficient dimensions of reduced documents (based on heuristics)
Simulated Annealing (SA) (Van Laarhoven & Aarts, 1987)	Its name is inspired from annealing in metallurgy. It is a Probabilistic metaheuristic algorithm for searching for global optimum solutions of objective functions and with large search space.	Its operation methodology depends on a slow decreasing in probability for accepting worse solutions and moving from state to another state depending on a defined acceptance probability function, generated new solutions by mutation and a generated random number for making decision through number of iterations or until getting no more better solutions.	Optimizing operations of online information searching through massive number of Internet web pages and related information	• Capability to operate with arbitrary problems (e.g., combinatorial problems) and systems. • Easy to be coded and implemented for complex problems.	• Slow according to its sequential nature. • One candidate solution per iteration and capability for building quick overall view of search space. • Overstated for problems with few local minima.
Support Vector Machine (SVM) (Cristianini & Shawe-Taylor, 2000)	Machine learning models depending on supervised learning algorithms. SVM is used for analyzing data and learning patterns	Non-probabilistic binary linear and non-linear classifier using numerical quadratic programming It depends on a set of training examples via support vectors (to build an assignment model) and data input where it will classifies each input to one category	• Data classification • Anomaly detection • Regression analysis • Feature and online searching • Text and hypertext categorization	• Easy for training • No local minima • Versatile through using different kernel functions for modeling complex problems and decision making	• Poor performances at long feature dimensions compared with number of samples or support vectors • High complexity (long training time) with extensive memory requirements at large scale tasks • Selection of appropriate kernel functions to suit problems.

3.1 Introduction

Monolithic and hybrid intelligence techniques can be used to design reasoning models to manage network-semantics. The capability (e.g., latent features extraction ability, high prediction accuracy, etc.) of adopted reasoning model for learning rich semantics depends on the operation performance of the used intelligence techniques. In the following subsections, we discuss different semantics reasoning models, which can be implemented to reason about semantics related to various network concerns. Various monolithic intelligence techniques using Latent Dirichlet Allocation (LDA) (Blei et al., 2003) and Hidden Markov Models (HMM) (Rabiner & Juang, 1986) are presented for designing semantics reasoning models. Additionally, we propose hybrid intelligence technique (HIT)-based reasoning model integrating LDA and HMM to efficiently extract semantics and know high-level data features. We will show characteristics and capabilities of adopted reasoning models clarifying their advantages and limitations.

3.2 Monolithic Intelligence Technique-Based Reasoners

In this subsection, we discuss reasoning models implemented for extracting network-semantics using monolithic intelligence techniques.

3.2.1 Simple Statistical-Analysis-Based Reasoner

Characteristics of big data, such as massive volume and complexity, impede regular data monitoring and analysis tools to anticipate data contents and structure and to interpret patterns meaningfully. Construction of statistical models (Breiman, 2001; Vasconcelos & Lippman, 2000) can help in understanding patterns of big data. This would lead to a capability of extracting features and semantics. One of the problems with those models is that they are specific to certain semantic topics (i.e., those models have limitations in extracting latent features). Inefficient design (e.g., inadequate algorithmic model) for those models can lead to incorrect extracted information. There is a need for a data training phase to test accuracy of models. Some rules (e.g., Fuzzy rules) can be constructed to fit certain semantic topics. Adoption of classification techniques with rules can help statistical models to extract high level data features.

We provide a simple statistical-analysis-based model (via statistics and rules) for a network-semantics manager (SM) to extract semantics related to various Internet elements (e.g., behavior of TCP protocol or TCP hosts' storage memory). Figure 2 illustrates the algorithm of the proposed simple statistical-analysis-based model. Adopting this model, SM would learn patterns of N different data profiles represented in a related storage memory to derive semantics with higher levels of abstraction. There are K targeted attributes that can be extracted and classified from stored profiles. Using data pattern learning algorithms (e.g., ARL (Paul, 2010)) and a classification technique (e.g., FMF (Winter, 2007)), SM will learn group of attributes (A_p) per each data profile in the storage memory that match required K attributes. An assumption is made that attributes per profiles are independent with equal probabilities of existence at each analyzed profile (i.e., attributes have same weights per profile). SM searches every reasoning time period (t_R) for similar data profiles (N_{Pn}) of each (n) profile of total (N) profiles.

Figure 2. Simple statistical-analysis-based reasoning model

Input: *K*: targeted attributes, *A$_p$*: number of attributes per data profile, *P$_n$* : data profile which contains attributes, *N$_{Pn}$*: similar data profiles, *min_support*:: define the minimum number of data profiles that have common attributes (based on number of captured data profiles)
Operations:
For (*n*=2; *n* ≤ A$_p$; *n*++) {
        Initialize *count*; counter for calculating number of data profiles' instances
        Generate candidate group C$_A$ of *n* attributes;
        For N data profiles in the storage memory do {
            For all attributes in each P$_n$ do {
                if (comprised attributes found in C$_A$) *count* **++;**
            }

        }
        if (*count* ≥ min_support)   K = C$_A$; learn group of attributes that found in most data profiles
}
For N data profiles in the storage memory do {
    For all attributes in each P$_n$ do {
        calculate attributes membership using FMFs
    }
    calculate profile weight W$_{Pn}$
    }
Learn group of N$_{Pn}$
For each N$_{Pn}$ profiles do {
    calculate accuracy according to K, W$_{Pn}$, N, N$_{Pn}$ and A$_p$
    apply defined Fuzzy rules for N$_{Pn}$ with high accuracy
    generate semantics
}
Output: *Semantics that are maintained as concept classes*

Equations (1) and (2) describe the initial attribute weight and data profile weight, respectively. $I - A_{i,Pn}$ is the initial attribute i weight per data profile P$_n$ where:

$$I - A_{i,Pn} = \frac{1}{K}$$

(1)

and $1 \le n \le N$, N number of profiles kept in the storage memory

$$Data\ profile\ P\ weight\left(W_{Pn}\right) = \sum_i \left(I - A_{i,Pn} \times M - A_{i,Pn}\right)$$

(2)

for each attribute i per data profile, where $1 \le i \le K$, where M_A$_{i,Pn}$ is the membership value of the attribute i in a data profile P$_n$ calculated by defined FMFs. The previous simple equations calculate group of low level features that can be used to extract semantics. SM has definitions for sets of fuzzy rules to aid in extracting semantics. Those rules can be used, for example, in determining normal behavior of the storage memory in TCP hosts. With Fuzzy rules, SM adopts a vector (T) of thresholds, which are determined by experts or via SM experience and history. Based on results from profiles analysis process and thresholds' values, SM can abstract semantics. Figure 3 depicts a trapezoidal FMF used for calculating membership values of the bandwidth attribute. The figure shows three different classes for the bandwidth attribute which are low; medium; and high based on the attribute's value. The accuracy for the semantics management processes executed in SM is calculated using (3).

Figure 3. Trapezoidal fuzzy membership function for the bandwidth attribute

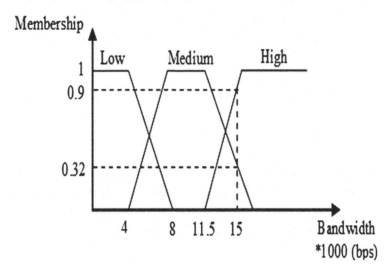

$$SM\ Accuracy = W_{Pn} \times \left(\frac{A_p}{K} \right) \times \left(\frac{N_{Pn}}{N} \right) \tag{3}$$

where $A_p \leq K$

Table 2 shows some statistics calculated using the above equations to learn patterns of 10 data profiles kept in the storage memory concerning a file transfer service operated by TCP protocol (Bassem Mokhtar, Eltoweissy, & El-Sayed, 2013). We assumed that three attributes, i.e., K=3, are considered in learning patterns by the ARL algorithm. Hence, SM will inspect data profiles in the storage memory and search for those attributes. Here, the problem is attribute extraction and classification (discrete target

Table 2. Statistics of different TCP data profiles calculated by SM for learning TCP protocol patterns

Attributes (A_p) per the Service Data Profile			Number of Similar Profiles (N_{Pn})	Total Number of Profiles (N)	Data Profile Weight (W_{Pn})	Profile Rank (P_r)	SM Accuracy
Bandwidth (bps) Membership	Buffer Size (Packets) Membership	Service Duration (Seconds) Membership					
15000 0.9 (high)	7000 1 (high)	1000 1 (high)	5	10	1	1	48.33%
10000 1 (medium)	3000 1 (low)	200 1 (low)	1	10	1	2	10%
14000 0.82 (high)	6000 0.4(medium)	500 0.5(medium)	1	10	0.57276	4	5.7276%
---	6500 0.55 (high)	1000 1 (high)	1	10	0.51615	6	3.441%
15000 0.9 (high)	5000 1 (medium)	---	1	10	0.666	5	4.22%
12000 0.9(medium)	6000 0.4(medium)	1000 1 (high)	1	10	0.7659	3	7.659%

attributes) using discriminative functions, i.e., FMF. SM has definitions for Fuzzy rules which are used in, for example, determining normal behavior of the TCP communication protocol using an assigned vector (T) of thresholds, which are determined by experts or by SM via its experience and maintained history. Here is an example of a rule:

$$IF\left(\left(W_{Pn} > T_a\right) \& \& \left(N_{Pn} > T_b\right) \& \& \left(\left(N_{Pn} / N\right) \times t_R < T_c\right) \& \& \left(A_p == K\right)\right)$$

THEN normal behavior **ELSE** abnormal behavior

T_a, T_b and T_c are thresholds defined in T vector for profile weight, number, and arrival ratio, respectively. According to the above rule, SM will extract semantics for the TCP protocol as follows:

```
IF behavior = normal THEN develop semantics (S_normal);
S_normal = largeNumberOfProfiles,CompleteDataProfile, NormalProfileWeight.
IF behavior =abnormal THEN develop semantics (S_abnormal);
S_abnormal = SmallNumberOfProfiles,InCompleteDataProfile, AbnormalProfileWeight.
```

largeNumberOfProfiles means that N_{Pn} exceeds the threshold T_b, CompleteDataProfile means that the data profile maintains all interesting attributes, NormalProfileWeight means that W_{Pn} is above threshold T_a. The semantics for the abnormal behavior will reveal that profiles do not satisfy the above conditions.

3.2.2 Hidden Markov Models-Based Reasoner

Hidden Markov models (HMM) (Rabiner & Juang, 1986; Ramage, 2007) are a structured architecture that is able of predicting sequences of semantic-topics based on input sequences of extracted network attributes or features. Depending on input sequences or pattern of high discriminative network-data features, HMM with forward and backward algorithms can learn semantics efficiently. HMM is widely used in learning processes and extracting information (Jiten, Merialdo, & Huet, 2006; Seymore, McCallum, & Rosenfeld, 1999) in different fields, such as in image and speech recognition, detection of network attacks (Ourston, Matzner, Stump, & Hopkins, 2003), and robotics for gesture imitation (J. Yang & Xu, 1994). HMM is a statistical Markov model for categorical sequence labeling (i.e., pattern recognition by statistical inference) based on using supervised/unsupervised learning algorithms (e.g., Baum-Welch algorithm). Sequence labeling can be treated as a set of independent classification tasks. HMM depends on a mathematical model with parameters (i.e., initial (π), state transition (A), and observation (B) probabilities) that can be adjusted for supporting different semantic topics in many contexts. With sets of training data, Baum-Welch's forward-backward algorithm can be applied to HMM to discover unknown HMM parameters (i.e., unsupervised learning). HMM can support multi-dimensional data (e.g., big network-data with time-based, domain-based, and service-based features). Each input state in an HMM can be specific to an output semantics domain. Considering input states as Markovian processes might affect degree of accuracy for output data. This can be mitigated, to some extent, by adjusting parameters of HMM. For example, the forward and backward transition probabilities among specific states can have the same value. This will give equal weights for get certain semantic topics if transition occurs among those states.

HMM can extract low-level data features from variable length data attributes' sequence using unsupervised learning. HMM's statistical foundations are computationally efficient and well-suited to handle new data (Seymore et al., 1999). A single HMM can be built by combining a verity of knowledge sources (J. Yang & Xu, 1994) with the consideration of their properties. This enables an efficient design of an HMM to reason about semantics related to various Internet elements. One of HMM problems is the floating-point underflow problem. This can affect extracted correct semantics. It can be overcome by taking logarithm for values of probabilities and performing summation process instead of multiplication to calculate forward probabilities. HMM have limitations in discovering high-level features with long-range syntactic dependencies. Another limitation for HMM can be found if it is required to design an HMM with large input states. This means a lot of HMM parameters to be calculated. This might affect performance (e.g., timeliness) of a semantics reasoning model implemented with HMM. HMM can be combined to form a hybrid or multi-stage model constituting matrix of HMM models. This can aid in enhancing the performance if there is a need to separate of feeding large scale of parameters and/or focusing on specific set of parameters related to certain operation domains. HMM might require large sets of data to be trained. This can be found in case of big network-data if the system can sample some sets for training. Since HMM can be considered as static models or prototypes for semantic reasoning, HMM models face challenges at operation reduced-dimension data. This will affect accuracy of operations for obtaining right semantics. This can be mitigated via using an algorithm for latent features discovery from low and reduced dimension data. Then, those features can be supplied to HMM.

For instance, a semantic manager (SM) might employ HMM for semantics reasoning and extraction as shown in Figure 4 (B. Mokhtar & Eltoweissy, 2012). As shown in the figure, the HMM-based model depends on defining set of HMM parameters as will be discussed later. Then, a training phase is executed using sets of maintained data profiles to adjust the HMM parameters. After that, the operations of HMM-based model begin by calculating the probability of partial observation sequence according to his process will continue until reaching the whole input sequence length (i.e., the termination phase). Based on sequence and length of input attributes with stateless operation; calculated HMM parameters; and maximum likelihood estimation, HMM can extract features. These features will constitute associated semantics related to specific fields (e.g., behavior of Internet elements) or network concerns (application, communication, and resource).

Figure 4. HMM-based reasoning model

Input: Using HMM model $\lambda=(A,B,\pi)$ and the forward algorithm:
α: the probability of partial observation sequence at certain detection time t giving that there is a certain input state (i.e., feature or attribute) at that time

Operations:

a) Initialization:

$\alpha_1(i) = \pi_i B_i(concept(1))$, $1 \leq i \leq K$, where K: number of defined features, $B_i(concept(1))$ is the probability to have first concept from feature i

b) Induction:

$\alpha_{t+1}(j) = [\sum_i \alpha_t(i) A_{ij}] B_j(concept(t+1))$, $1 \leq i \leq K, 1 \leq j \leq K, 1 \leq t \leq T-1$

c) Termination:

$P(concept\ sequence/\lambda) = \sum_i \alpha_T(i)$, $1 \leq i \leq K$, considering accumulated value of α of T (length of sequence) states

1. The input to HMM-based models which is sequence of profiles' attributes;
2. The transition probability A among input attributes;
3. The observation probability B between each input attribute and each possible output feature.

HMM Performance Measure

A HMM is defined as $\lambda = (A, B, \pi)$ with the following notation:

π is the initial probability distribution for HMM states. For K discrete (feature) states and input sequence of T states, $\pi_i = p\left(state_{(t=1)} = i\right)$ where $1 \leq i \leq K$.

A is the state transition probability matrix, which is square matrix and it shows probabilities for transition from a state (i.e., feature) to another state. $A_{ij} = p\left(\dfrac{\left(state_{(t+1)} = j\right)}{\left(state_{(t)} = i\right)}\right)$ where $1 \leq i \leq K$ and

$1 \leq t \leq T$.

B is the observable concept or semantic topic probability distribution. If there is a probability distribution over output concepts (i.e., observations) for each input feature (i.e., input state) that this distribution will show the probability to have a concept from a specific feature where there M discrete observations $\{1, 2, ..., M\}$. $B_j\left(concept(t)\right) = p\left(\dfrac{\left(concept_{(t)} = m\right)}{\left(state_{(t)} = j\right)}\right)$ where $1 \leq m \leq M$, $1 \leq j \leq K$ and

$1 \leq t \leq T$.

As mentioned in (Chatterjee & Russell, 2012), the time and space complexity of a HMM are $O(K^2T)$ and $O(K^2+KT)$, respectively.

3.2.3 Latent Dirichlet Allocation-Based Reasoner

Latent Dirichlet Allocation (LDA) is a generative probabilistic dynamic model that can be used for data semantics reasoning based on learned data attributes (Blei et al., 2003). LDA has the capability to discover high-level features of data profiles where it has a well-defined inference methodology to associate a data profile with group of attributes with several semantic topics. LDA is capable of extracting data semantics based on prior probabilities for data profile-semantic topic and attribute-semantic topic associations. For example, the operation of LDA to discover feature or semantic topics in *M* analyzed profiles is executed every defined reasoning window or through other criteria as initiating triggering signals. LDA samples a hidden semantic topic *z* for each *m* data profile through calculating sampled posterior probability vector *θ* of topic-data profile association which depends on prior association weight *α*, number of the *m*th profile's attributes related to a certain topic *z*, and *N* total number of attributes in the m profile. Also, LDA calculates sampled posterior probability *φ* of attribute-topic association based on prior attribute-topic association weight *β*, number of attribute instances assigned to topic *z*, and total number of attributes in all *M* profiles assigned to topic *z*.

Figure 5 shows LDA algorithm for semantics reasoning processes. Through certain number of iterations, the posterior probability to have a specific semantic topic assigned to data profiles and attributes is enforced. This is because that semantic topics with high association probabilities will have great chances to be assigned to data profiles and related attributes after finishing all iterations. For instance,

Figure 5. LDA-based reasoning model

<u>*Initialization:*</u>
- Define Z semantic topics, input M profiles each has N attributes of total V attributes, α a real value Z-dimension vector (prior weight of topic z in a profile), β a real value V-dimension vector (prior weight of attribute v in a topic)
- Assign randomly a topic for each attribute in a data profile and build matrix z[M][N]

<u>*Definitions:*</u>
nw[i][j]: # of instance of attribute i assigned to topic j, nd[i][j] number of attributes in document i assigned to topic j, nwsum[j] total number of attributes assigned to topic j, ndsum[i] total number of attributes in document i

<u>*Generative Process:*</u>
For iter = 1:Iterations
    For m = 1: M (number of profiles)
        For n=1:N (number of attributes per each profile m)
            remove current state topic z from the count variables for each attribute n in
profile m

            for z= 1 : Z (number of semantic topics)
                $p(topic\ z) = (nw[profiles[m][n]][z] + \beta)/(nwsum[z] +$
                    $V * \beta) * (nd[m][z] + \alpha)/(ndsum[m] + Z * \alpha)$
            end
            sample topic z from p
            Add newly estimated topic z to count variables
        end
    end
end

assume a data profile which has prior association probabilities with four semantic topics (p(1)=0.1, p(2)=0.2,p(3)=0.3,p(4)=0.4). After using Gibbs sampling and choosing a random number (e.g., u) from the total summation of all probabilities (i.e., p_tot=1), u will be less than 1. So, the assigned topic to that data profile should be for a topic that its prior association probability greater than u.

LDA-based reasoning models provide semantic-topics models that enable discovery of hidden topic-based patterns through supervised learning process. LDA gives a systematic and well-defined way for inferring latent semantic topics in large scale of multi-dimensional data sets. LDA assign random values for prior probabilities semantic topics and related attributes based on data sampling (e.g., Gibbs sampling (Casella & George, 1992; Darling, 2011)), multivariate distribution (e.g., dirichlet distribution) and training data sets. LDA models have the capability of extracting latent features and semantics based on prior probabilities for data attribute- data profile and data attribute-semantic topic associations. LDA assumes that attributes of data are related to random chosen semantic topics. The selection of semantic topics is based on random values of multivariate probability distribution parameter. LDA executes semantic topic sampling for each data attribute in every data profile for all profiles, and the updating processes for profile-semantic topic and attribute-topic associations, which are iterated many times. LDA models have the ability to estimate semantics based on small scope of extracted features with long-range semantic dependencies. LDA supports semantic extraction from big data with high dimension. Semantic-topics selection parameters and prior probabilities can be directed to relate to specific attributes to group of topics (i.e., having specific distribution of semantic-topics over group of attributes). This enables LDA models to work with low-dimensional data, such as reduced-dimension data obtained through an LSH algorithm.

One of the main advantages for LDA models that these models are extendible (Bíró & Szabó, 2009) to support more associations amongst semantic topics and data attributes. LDA models can be used to enhance functionalities of other semantic reasoning models (e.g., HMM) to strengthen their capability of extracting latent features and semantics. Some limitations of LDA models can be found due to their randomization process for assigning parameters' values of attribute-topic associations. This can result in inaccurate predictions and semantic topics. LDA models, at large number of training data sets, can face the overfitting problem. LDA has some limitations (Newman, Asuncion, Smyth, & Welling, 2007), such as the bag of words or attributes assumption where there is a possibility of semantic topic sampling process to allow attributes, related to same semantic topics, to be assigned to other semantic topics. Furthermore, the LDA's probabilistic inference process for topics is computational complexity where that process takes polynomial time in case of inferring document's topics using a small number of semantic topics (Sontag & Roy, 2011).

LDA Performance Measure

Equations (4) and (5) is used to calculate the perplexity where that equation was derived based on the one mentioned at (Blei et al., 2003). Calculating perplexity helps in evaluating performance of the LDA models in detecting and categorizing attributes in data profiles based on learned parameters (e.g., prior profile-topic association weight or probabilities). A data profile is represented by a network-data storage model where it comprises data attributes related to traffic among Internet elements. So, based on M data profiles and their N related attributes and number of defined semantic topics K, we can get the value of perplexity.

$$Perplexity = \exp^{-\left(\frac{\left(\sum_{m=1}^{M} \log\left(p\left(attribute_m\right)\right)\right)}{\left(\sum_{m=1}^{M} N_m\right)}\right)}$$

(4)

where

$$p\left(attribute_m\right) = \prod_{n=1}^{N_m}\left(\sum_{j=1}^{K} p\left(\frac{attribute_n}{topic_j}\right) p\left(\frac{topic_j}{profile_m}\right)\right)$$

(5)

and N_m is the number of attributes per each data profile m.

In (Sontag & Roy, 2011), the authors investigated the inference problem, or the maximum a posteriori (MAP) problem, at LDA. That problem relates to the most likely assignment process of semantic topics to profile's attributes. Due to that problem, it was proved in (Sontag & Roy, 2011) that the time complexity of LDA is: a) *"polynomial"* $O((N_mK)^k(N_m+k)^3)$ in case of having small k topics appear in document (or data profile) where k << K; and b) non-deterministic polynomial (NP)-hard in case of LDA general settings with arbitrary topics per data profiles where each profile might have K topics in its MAP assignment. Henderson *et al.* in (Henderson & Eliassi-Rad), investigated the LDA inference using standard Gibbs sampling approach. Based on that approach, the runtime and space complexity of LDA with Gibbs sampling were $O(MKN_m)$ and $O(M(K+N_m))$, respectively.

3.3 Hybrid Intelligence Technique (HIT)-Based Reasoner

In this subsection, we discuss the proposed HIT-based reasoning methodology for reasoning about network-semantics.

3.3.1 HIT Overview

We propose and implement a HIT to build efficient reasoning model to reason about network-semantics based on learning patterns of full or reduced-dimensional data. The HIT integrates LDA (Blei et al., 2003) and HMM (Rabiner & Juang, 1986). Our HIT is designed to overcome limitations of the semantics reasoning operation with only adopting HMM. The hybridization of HMM and LDA enables latent features extraction with semantics dependencies not just based on learning features with syntax dependencies. On the one hand, LDA has the capability to discover high-level features of data profiles with full or reduced dimensionality. LDA possesses extendible operation (Bíró & Szabó, 2009) where it can support more associations amongst semantic topics and extracted high-level data features. LDA has a well-defined inference methodology to associate a data profile with groups of attributes with several semantic topics. However, adopting LDA alone in semantics reasoning might produce some shortcomings due to LDA's limitations, such as the bag of words assumption (Newman et al., 2007) that might result in semantic topics misclassification where there is a possibility of semantic topic sampling process to allow attributes, related to same semantic topics, to be assigned to other semantic topics. Furthermore, the LDA's probabilistic inference process for topics is computationally complex where that process has NP-hard complexity in case of inferring document's topics using a large number of semantic topics (Sontag & Roy, 2011). On the other hand, HMM can efficiently extract data semantics from variable-length input sequence of data features, extracted by LDA, using unsupervised learning algorithms (Jiang, 2009). HMM's statistical foundations are computationally efficient and well-suited to handle new data (Seymore et al., 1999). A single HMM can be built by combining a verity of knowledge sources (J. Yang & Xu, 1994) with the consideration of their properties. This enables an efficient design of an HMM to reason about semantics related to various Internet elements. However, utilizing HMM singularly for semantic reasoning might result in some deficiencies due to HMM incapability: a) to discover high-level features with long-term semantics dependencies due to the assumption about data using the Markovian process and the usage of maximum likelihood estimator (Merhav & Ephraim, 1991); and b) to work efficiently with reduced-dimension data since HMM needs large amounts of data for training and adjusting HMM's unstructured parameters.

We propose the HIT to overcome limitations of the operation with only HMM or LDA (Bassem Mokhtar & Eltoweissy, 2014). Integrating LDA with HMM enables latent features extraction with semantics dependencies not just based on learning features with syntax dependencies. Our proposed HIT can enhance the operation of LDA by assuming Markovianity of attribute sequences (Blei et al., 2003) which can mitigate the LDA limitation caused by the bag of words assumption (Newman et al., 2007) . Also, the designed HIT will consider advantages of comprised intelligence techniques; HMM and LDA. We are motivated in our HIT design by the capability of LDA to discover latent high-level features from multi-dimensional network-data patterns with long-range semantics dependencies. Those features will be grouped as sequences that enable semantics reasoning operation via HMM with higher accuracy. LDA models are extendible (Bíró & Szabó, 2009) in that they can support more associations amongst semantic topics and extracted data features. Hence, HMM will be able to efficiently reason

Figure 6. Pseudo code of the HIT-based semantic reasoning model

```
Input: operation time t and reasoning period tR, LDA-parameters: Z hidden topics, K feature topics and
hyperparameters α & β, Gibbs sampling iterations J, HMM λ-model parameters (A,B,π) for N states & T
semantic topics
Operations:
1.1 Repeat every tR
1.2    Attribute corpus a = {a¹, a², ......, a^L} ← getAttributes()
1.3    Data/Concept Class Profiles corpus P = {P¹, P², ......, P^M} ← captureDataConceptClassProfiles()
1.4    for j = 1:J do
1.5       for m = 1:M do
1.6          sample topic z of Z topics for the mᵗʰ data profile based on Gibbs sampling & prior probabilities
             α & β
1.7       end for
1.8    end for
          1.9    calculate  θᵐ = Dir(α) for Z feature topics in each data profile & calculate φᶻ = Dir(β)
          for attributes in each m profile
1.10   for m = 1:M do
1.11      draw zᵐ ~ multinomial(θᵐ)
1.12      for n = 1:N (where N of attributes per profiles & N ≤ L) do
1.13         sample feature topic fₙᵐ from K topics for each n attribute in the mᵗʰ data profile, draw fₙᵐ ~
             multinomial(φᶻᵐ)
1.14      end for
1.15   end for
1.16   initialize HMM models and run Baum-Welch algorithm for learning models' parameters
1.17   for m = 1:M
1.18      for i = 1:T
1.19         calculate observation probability Bfₙᵐ(semantic-topicᵢ) for each n input state (i.e., classified
             feature fₙ )
1.20      end for
1.21      get maximum likelihood semantic-topics sequence of length T with high probability for each
             implemented HMM
1.22   end for
1.23 until operation time
Output: set of semantic topics that are related to various concerns and represented as associated concept
classes
```

about data semantics related to input sequences of high-level data features. HMM (Rabiner & Juang, 1986) are structured architectures that are able to predicting sequences of semantic-topics based on input sequences of extracted network attributes or features. Depending on input sequences or pattern of high discriminative network-data features, HMM with forward and backward algorithms can learn semantics efficiently. The output from feature extraction process executed by LDA (i.e., input to HMM) is random based on analyzed data. This agrees with the characteristics of HMM to predict output based on hidden data sequences.

3.3.2 Semantics Reasoning Process using the HIT

For instance, a semantic manager (SM) has tasks that depend on learning patterns of multi-dimensional dynamic network-data in a storage memory. Based on learned patterns, SM will reason about semantics and maintain them as associated and classified concepts. Figure 6 shows the pseudo code of the HIT-based semantics reasoning process which is executed by SM. SM learns group of attributes in data profiles kept in the storage memory through utilizing associative rule learning (Paul, 2010) and simple statistical-analysis-based models using FMF (Winter, 2007). Construction of statistical models (Breiman, 2001) can help in understanding patterns and analyzing low-level features of big data. SM adopts LDA for extracting and classifying high-level data features with long-range semantics dependencies. SM integrates the capabilities of LDA with HMM for semantics reasoning. Integration of LDA and HMM forms a hybrid model for semantics reasoning. LDA are extendible (Bíró & Szabó, 2009) that they can support more associations amongst semantic topics and extracted data features. Classified features by LDA are input to HMM as sequences.

Figure 7. The LDA-HMM-based reasoning model

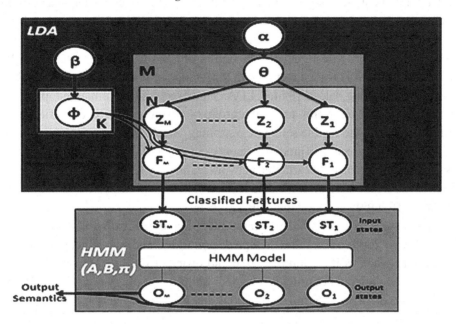

Figure 7 describes the semantics extraction process implemented by the LDA-HMM-based reasoning model. Network-data characteristics include massive volume, high- and multi-dimensionality, dynamicity, complexity (variety in representation models and languages). In (Griffiths et al., 2004), authors proposed a generative model based on Latent Dirichlet Allocation (LDA) (Blei et al., 2003) and HMM for learning words with short-range syntax and long-range semantics dependencies. Consequently, this aids in forming richer ontology with more associated semantic topics and classes. There is similarity between characteristics (e.g., huge volume, high dimensionality, and complexity) of datasets in networks and language modeling. So, we provide the hybrid LDA-HMM-based reasoning model integrating LDA and HMM for combining the advantages of both algorithms in efficiently:

1. Learning patterns of big data with reduced-/high- and multi-dimensionality; and
2. Building dynamic network-concept ontology (DNCO) showing different and correlated concept classes (Rajpathak & Chougule, 2011).

We provide a semantic reasoning model for intelligent network entities using the proposed HIT in order to have highly abstracted and associated semantics at different levels of granularity and relate to various network concerns. At using HIT-based reasoning model, LDA is able to extract latent features with long-range semantics dependencies based on adopting inference models. Those models define correlations of semantic topics among data attributes and related data profiles. Relied on determined inference models, LDA can extract hidden semantic topics related to each data profile's attribute and also assign an overall topic to every data profile. HMM, as individual reasoning techniques, can be used to extract low-level features with short-range semantics dependencies (Jiang, 2009). Based on extracted semantic topics or features by LDA, HMM output depends on the sequence of input data features related to diverse network concerns. HMM can be designed and trained to get output based on sequences of data features, independent of features' order. In other words, the outcome from a HMM-based reasoning process can focus only on the existence of certain data features regardless of features' order.

We are motivated in our HIT design by the capability of LDA to discover latent high-level features from multi-dimensional network-data patterns with long-range semantics dependencies. Using correlations of semantic topics among data attributes, LDA can extract hidden semantic topics related to each data attribute and also assign an overall topic of a group of attributes. Those classified semantic topics of features will be sequenced to enable semantic reasoning via HMM with higher accuracy. HMM are structured architectures that are able to predict sequences of semantic topics (related to different network concerns) based on input sequences of extracted network features by LDA. Depending on input sequences or pattern of highly-discriminative network-data features, HMM with forward and backward algorithms can learn semantics efficiently showing their FBS aspects.

Some related work (e.g., (Idris & Shanmugam, 2005; Schuler, Bastos-Filho, & Oliveira, 2009; C. C. Yang, Yen, & Chen, 2000; Yao, 1999)) adopted monolithic and hybrid techniques for enhancing networking operations, such as intrusion detection and efficient routing. However, those works were application-specific and they did not provide a way for building ontology of associated concept classes related to various Internet elements (e.g., applications and services).

3.3.3 Operation of HIT-Based Reasoner

In our HIT-based reasoning model, LDA (Blei et al., 2003) is able to extract latent features with long-range semantics dependencies based on adopting inference models. Those models define correlations of semantic topics among data attributes and related data profiles. Relying upon determined inference models, LDA can extract hidden semantic topics related to each data profile's attribute and also assign an overall topic to every data profile. Based on extracted semantic topics or features by LDA, HMM (Rabiner & Juang, 1986) output depends on the sequence of input data features related to diverse network concerns. HMM can be designed and trained to get output based on sequences of data features, independent of features' order. Table 3 shows the parameters used within the HIT.

LDA Operation in HIT

LDA gives a systematic and well-defined way for inferring latent semantic topics in large scale of multi-dimensional data sets. LDA assigns random values for prior probabilities of semantic topics and related attributes based on data sampling (e.g., Gibbs sampling), multivariate distribution (e.g., dirichlet distribution) and training data sets. LDA has the capability of extracting latent features and semantics based on prior probabilities, using dirichlet distribution, for data-attribute data profile and data-attribute semantic topic associations. LDA assumes that attributes of data are related to randomly chosen semantic topics. The selection of semantic topics is based on random values of multivariate probability distribution parameters. LDA executes semantic topic sampling for each data attribute in every data profile for all profiles, and the updating processes for profile-semantic topic and attribute-topic associations, which are iterated many times. LDA looks at each data attribute and generates its related latent feature within each data profile (i.e., LDA makes semantic topic modeling for each data profile based on its comprised attributes). LDA randomly assigns a semantic topic for each attribute based on initially defined weights

Table 3. The LDA-HMM-based model's parameters

Symbol	Description
K	Number of feature topics
Z	Identity of hidden semantic topics
V	Number of attributes in all data profiles (or profiles)
N	Number of attributes per each data profiles, N ≤ V
M	Number of data profiles
F	Identity of feature topics of all attributes
α	Prior feature topics/profile weight for feature topic-profile association
β	Prior attribute/topic weight for attribute-feature topic association
θ	Sampled posterior feature topics/profile weight vector of length Z for feature topic-profile association
φ	Sampled posterior attribute/profile weight vector of length V for profile attribute-feature topic association
π	Initial state probability vector of length N
A	State transition probability matrix of size N×N
B	Observation (or output semantics) probability matrix of size N×N
ST_i	Input HMM state i (or feature topic), i ≤ N
O_i	Output semantics based on input state i

of topic-attribute associations. Accordingly, the weight of the assigned topic with respect to related attributes is increased. For certain number of iterations, the process repeats and LDA will provide posterior weights of topic-attributes association and accordingly profile-topic association.

Through a certain number of iterations and using Gibbs sampling (Casella & George, 1992), LDA extracts and classifies high-level features associated with each analyzed m data profile of total M profiles in the storage memory. LDA samples a hidden semantic topic z for each m data profile through calculating sampled posterior probability vector θ of topic-data profile association which depends on prior association weight α, number of the mth profile's attributes related to a certain topic z, and total number of attributes in the m profile. Also, LDA calculates sampled posterior probability φ of attribute-topic association based on prior attribute-topic association weight β, number of attribute instances assigned to topic z, and total number of attributes in all M profiles assigned to topic z. For example, three feature or semantic topics (i.e., K=3) are defined in LDA: ("normal TCP packet", "normal comm-flow", "TCP comm-protocol"). Ten data profiles (M=10) in the storage memory have the same three attributes (i.e., N=V=3). Each attribute and profile has a prior topic association weight vector. Based on the overall prior weight vectors $(\alpha$ and $\beta)$ and number of semantic topics, a sampled topic association probability vector p_{assoc} of length equals the number of available semantic topics is calculated like p_{assoc}=p(semantic_topic_1)=0.75, p(s_2)=0.2, p(s_3)=0.05. In each LDA iteration, the current assigned topics for a data profile and comprised attributes are removed. Then, a random number u is sampled based on p_{assoc} and the summation of its contents. The higher p topic association value will be chosen and the related topic is assigned. For example, if u equals 0.6, number of attributes and related profiles assigned to the first semantic topic (i.e., the new topic) increases since p(s_1) which equals 0.75 is greater than 0.6. Thereafter, updates will be happened to posterior association weights θ and φ according to changes in number of attributes and profiles that relate to first semantic topic. Hence, the posterior association weight of the first topic with data profiles and comprised topic-related attributes increases.

HMM Operation in HIT

HMM comprises categorical sequence labeling supervised/unsupervised algorithms for estimating observations based on sequence of hidden input words (i.e, data attributes or features). Extracted and classified features, output from LDA, form a sequence and convey to parameters of HMM to generate semantics. The estimation process for HMM observations relies on continuous input sequence with different Gaussian distributions. Then, HMM performs distribution mixture for obtaining the most likelihood output sequence. HMM looks at the group and the sequence of data attributes or features. The order of states in an input sequence might change the output observations. In other words, the existence of the same data features, however, with different order might result in different outputs adopting the same HMM. However, the HMM can be designed to have outputs based on having specific group of input states (or features) without considering their sequence order.

The HMM parameters (A, B, π), discussed shortly, are trained and assigned using the unsupervised Baum-welch learning algorithm (Baum, 1972). That algorithm depends on an initial developed HMM for finding the maximum likelihood HMM parameters through iteratively training the parameters of the initial model relied on the observed output sequence. The ability of input to HMM sequence of data features related to diverse network concerns enables getting output sequence with associated semantic topics or concept classes at different levels of abstraction. For example, an input sequence to HMM might be ("normal TCP packet size", "normal comm-flow", "TCP comm-protocol") with equal initial state probability π (i.e., $\pi = 1/3$) and state transition probabilities A (i.e., $A_{ij} = 1/2$ for i$\neq$j and $A_{ij} = 0$ for i=j where A_{ij} is the transition probability form state i to state j). The first feature can be classified as an application concern and the other two features as communication concerns. Accordingly, the expected HMM output observation based on the previous sequence with any feature order might be "normal TCP-based service". To get the previous output, the observation probability B matrix, which relates each input state with an output, regarding that concept class (i.e., output) will be high. For instance, B matrix might consist of three rows r and three columns c; and it might equal ((0.3,0.5,0.2),(0.2,0.8,0.0), (0.4,0.45,0.05)) where the number of r equals the number of input features and the number of c equals the number of output concept classes. According to the previous example, all input features have high observation probability with the "normal TCP-based service" concept.

3.4 HIT-Based vs. Monolithic Reasoners

We highlight in this subsection, via working example, the differences between semantics reasoning process using monolithic intelligence techniques, adopting HMM or LDA algorithms, and HIT (i.e., the hybrid LDA-HMM algorithm). The discussed example concerns reasoning about semantics of a TCP-based file transfer service based on capturing raw network-data related to TCP-based services and learning data patterns. Through a defined reasoning window, a semantic manager (SM), which adopts reasoning models, learns patterns of reduced-dimensional data profiles for recognizing and classifying attributes, respectively. SM recognizes the frequency of each data profile and its comprised attributes. For example, a captured profile might have multiple instances with the following attributes: P:={date, time, src_IP, dest_IP, packet_size, packet_type, service, protocol, port_number, sequence_number, MAC_address}. SM adopts locality sensitive hashing (LSH) algorithm to reduce the dimensionality of each profile (Mimaroglu & Simovici, 2008). The profile P after applying LSH for selecting specific attributes and with a hash function length equals five will be P_LSH:={packet_size, packet_type, service, protocol, port_number}. SM analyzes the data profile P_LSH and it gets the following information: 10000 profile's instances with the attributes vector Attr: {a^1= large_TCP-SYN_packet_size, a^2= TCP-SYN_packets, a^3= file_transfer_service, a^4=abnormal_ port_number}.

We show in the next paragraphs the operation technique for three implemented algorithms (HMM, LDA and HIT) for semantics reasoning based on processes of data representation and dimensionality reduction which are discussed in the last paragraph. Due to adopting different algorithms for semantics reasoning, various output semantics will be formed and kept.

Firstly, HMM-based reasoning model is used to extract semantics regarding the behavior of TCP-based file transfer services. The input states to HMM are described as sequences. Each input state represents one learned and classified data-attribute. For example, "large TCP-SYN packet size" is a learned and classified attribute based on captured values in the TCP *packet size* and *packet type fields* in a data profile. For HMM operation, we assume that we have four possible input states ST_1, ST_2, ST_3 and ST_4 to HMM for estimating the behavior of those services. Those input states represent the extracted and classified data attributes per each data profile. Those states are data attributes defined in the *Attr* vector. The estimated observation (or concept class) based on any sequence of the previously mentioned attributes is "O: *Abnormal TCP-based service*". HMM extracts that concept class based on its defined operation parameters. For instance, the observation probabilities B, using the maximum likelihood estimator, for the concept class O and the other concepts are high (e.g., 0.9) based on having any input attribute (i.e., state ST_i and i ≤ 4) of the defined *Attr* attributes vector (a^1, a^2, a^3, a^4) . Also, the transition probability A between any two input features (ST_i and ST_j, and i≠j) has the same value. This increases the probability of having the targeted O based on using the trained HMM with the forward algorithm over sequences of interesting attributes.

Secondly, LDA-based reasoning model is used to reason about semantics for TCP-based file transfer services, LDA after 1000 iterations assigns attributes in P_LSH to the following feature topics: "Abnormal TCP-SYN packet size", "TCP-based File transfer service", "Abnormal TCP control packet", "Abnormal TCP-based file transfer service". LDA samples the feature topics as the following example. The classified attribute $\mathbf{a^1}$, large_TCP-SYN_ packet_size, has high prior association weight β (e.g. β > 0.75) with the semantic topic, *Abnormal TCP-SYN packet size*. So, the updated attribute-topic posterior association weight φ for $\mathbf{a^1}$ after 1000 iterations will be high with respect to the assigned feature topic. In addition, the prior association weight (α) of P_LSH with the feature topic "Abnormal TCP-based file transfer service" is high (e.g., α > 0.8). Then, LDA samples P_LSH that specific topic based on the updated topic-profile posterior association weight θ taking into consideration the number of profile's attributes assigned to that topic (e.g., two attributes) and the total number of profiles' attributes (e.g., P_LSH has four attributes).

Finally, the hybrid LDA-HMM algorithm is designed to produce more meaningful information from analyzed data profiles and to form richer associations amongst extracted semantics. The hybrid algorithm extracts latent features of each data attribute in analyzed data profiles relying on learned and classified attributes in analyzed data profiles in the storage memory. Then, the hybrid algorithm outputs data semantics for each data profile based on a sequence of extracted latent features of the whole data profile. The LDA-HMM algorithm looks at both a) data attributes and related latent features within data profiles and b) the sequence of extracted latent features within each data profile. The implemented LDA algorithm performs semantic of feature topics modeling for analyzed data profiles and their comprised attributes. The output of that modeling process is a set of syntax states per each profile that is fed to HMM to reason about semantics concerning each profile. Utilizing simple feature classification techniques, e.g., using

FMF, enables assignment of membership degrees for some extracted feature topics which have related designed FMF. These degrees enable SM to build and update DNCO. In the example of reasoning about TCP-based file transfer service semantics and using the same operation parameters of LDA in the previous semantics reasoning case, the latent feature topics T extracted by the LDA algorithm from P_LSH and its comprised attributes might be T:={ t^1= Abnormal TCP-SYN packet size, t^2= TCP-based File transfer service, t^3= Abnormal TCP control packet,t^4= Abnormal TCP-based file transfer service }. An input sequence comprised the previous latent feature topics (i.e., any sequence order of (t^1,t^2,t^3,t^4)) to a designed HMM might yield the following semantics or observations: O:={O_1=File_Transfer_Service_Behavior,O_2=TCP_based_Service_Behavior,O_3=Abormal_TCP_based_Service_Operation, O_4=TCP_SYN_Flood_Attack}Accordingly, a simple DNCO can be built via the obtained observations or concept classes. For instance, the top parent class will be O_1 and it will have three child classes O_2, O_3 and O_4. The concept class O_3 will be a child class for the parent class O_2 and so on. In addition, the four classified attributes in the *Attr* vector will be registered as FBS aspects for the lower child concept class O_4.

4. PERFORMANCE ANALYSIS

In this section, we discuss the effectiveness of semantics reasoning processes using monolithic and hybrid intelligence techniques-based reasoning models. We evaluate reasoning models via conducting a set of simulation scenarios. Semantics reasoning processes are implemented as an application written in Java including Java classes for the operations learning data patterns and extracting high-level latent features. We run simulation scenarios via integrating reasoning models' Java classes with java-based network simulator (J-Sim) (Sobeih, Viswanathan, Marinov, & Hou, 2007). A simulation scenario for a network of 50 nodes is conducted, with the aid of real offline KDD datasets (S. Hettich & S. D. Bay, 1999), to investigate the impact of learning concepts related to file transfer services and communication protocols over improving QoS of running services on top of TCP and UDP protocols. Our simulation studies include implementation of different semantics reasoning models (using simple statistical-analysis-based, LDA-based, HMM-based, and the hybrid LDA-HMM-based models).

4.1 Network Simulation Scenario using Real Offline Datasets

In this scenario, we study the effectiveness of semantics reasoning operations using various reasoning models and adopting real offline datasets for learning patterns and extracting semantics of normal/abnormal flows of TCP- and UDP-based services and related attacks (e.g., TCP-SYN flood attacks). Extracted semantics are represented as accessible correlated concept classes and maintained in a shared database. Networking entities can access and learn those concept classes at runtime and on-demand to enhance QoS of their operations.

The simulation scenario is run at adopting various semantics reasoning models. The utilized semantics reasoning models are: LDA-based model, HMM-based model and the hybrid model (or the LDA-HMM model). We study the impact of employing those reasoning models by an intelligent network host on networking operations performance. Such host learns data traffic, analyzes data patterns and reasons about semantics accordingly. Also, the host accesses real offline datasets to learn other information and to update what it learnt before. Other network hosts in the scenario can learn extracted semantics, registered at shared database. Table 4 shows the addressed metrics for analyzing performance of the semantics reasoning process made by various models.

Table 4. Performance analysis metrics of semantics reasoning techniques

Metric	Function	Equation	Unit
Average Throughput (Thp)	Describes data throughput at a current simulation time by the summation of current captured data packets' sizes (S_p) in a defined window divided by the window size (5 seconds)	$Thp = \sum (S_p)/(5$ seconds window size$)$.	bytes/sec
Network Latency (L)	Measures the consumed time from the beginning of simulation until learning all behavior classes of running file transfer services	$L = T_R + T_S$ where T_R is the time-overhead caused by the reasoning technique and T_S is the time period measured from simulation start	mseconds
Prediction Accuracy (A_c)	Calculates ratio of true positive (Tp) classes and true negative (Tn) classes that are learned with respect to all behavior classes (N_c) that should be learned	$A_c = (Tp+Tn) / N_c$	--
False Negative (Fn) Ratio	Calculates ratio of abnormal behavior classes that misclassified to normal classes according to N_c	Fn / N_c	--

Our simulator is based on J-Sim. We adapted already existing java codes of HMM and LDA. We implemented a code for the LDA-HMM model and integrated it with J-Sim. Random fully-connected static network topologies were generated for 50 nodes using minimum degree proximity algorithm (Onat & Stojmenovic, 2007). TCP- and UDP-based file transfer services were run among nodes. Some nodes were chosen to send malicious and/or abnormal data (e.g., attacks like TCP SYN-flood attack and UDP flood attack). Exchanged data among hosts are represented and maintained in the intelligent host as profiles of attribute-value pairs with/without using LSH for dimensionality reduction. Those attributes give information about, for example, service type, packet type and packet size. KDD'99 dataset (S. Hettich & S. D. Bay, 1999)with 41 data attributes was used as offline dataset by the intelligent host to learn semantics of normal TCP flows and some denial-of-service (DoS) attacks, such as TCP SYN-flood attack. The intelligent host learns patterns of registered data, recognizes their group of attributes and classifies those attributes utilizing a simple statistical-analysis-based model. SM extracts and classifies high-level latent features using the implemented semantics reasoning model. We tested three different semantics reasoning models which are

1. LDA-based model;
2. HMM-based model; and
3. The LDA-HMM or hybrid model.

We studied the capability of these models to learn data semantics and to know various concept classes related to normal/abnormal flows and attacks.

The intelligent host executes behavior classification for analyzed network flows of TCP- and UDP-based services. Extracted semantics concerning those flows will form ontology of concept classes which show for example classes for the normal_TCP-based_service, normal_UDP-based_service, attack_TCP-based_service and attack_UDP-based_service. An effective semantics reasoning model is the model which has the ability to discover all or most classes of concepts related to running services in the network. The intelligent host generates alerts when it detects matching between what it learns at real-time and maintained concept classes. A performance analysis was done for the operation of semantics reasoning process. Each implemented semantics reasoning model was evaluated based on the detected true positives (Tp) and negatives (Tn) besides false positives (Fp) and negatives (Fn). Table 5 shows simulation parameters and their default values.

Table 5. Simulation parameters of the network simulation scenario

Parameter	Default Value	Unit
Number of nodes	50	node
Number of attributes/KDD data set	41	attribute
Link data rate	1	Mbps
Router buffer size	7000	packet
TCP MSS (normal/abnormal)	512/1024,2048	byte
TCP MCWS	128	byte
TCP Time to Live	255	seconds
UDP packet size (normal/ abnormal)	512/512,2048	byte
UDP Client/Reply Timeout	30	seconds
Propagation model	Free space model	--
Propagation delay	100	mseconds
MAC protocol	IEEE 802.11	--
Routing protocol	AODV	--
Rate of database access by hosts	1	time/11 seconds
Rate of patterns learning	1	time/10 seconds
HMM approach/number of training sequences	Unsupervised with Baum-Welch algorithm/1000	--
LSH (L hash tables, K hash function length)	(L=6,K=3)	--
LDA (# of iterations)	20000	--
Simulation Time	100	seconds

For statistical validation for results, we repeated the experiment nine times for each implemented semantics reasoning model (LDA, HMM or LDA-HMM) and also when operation at different cases which are: a) without using LSH; b) using undirected LSH and c) using directed LSH. Directed LSH mechanism means that the implemented LSH algorithm adopts a specific attributes' group smaller than the one used by the undirected LSH and related to interesting file transfer services. Semantics reasoning models were designed to reason about data semantics clarifying the normal and abnormal behavior of TCP- and UDP-based service flows. Recognized semantics of abnormal service flows' behavior might refer to known attacks (e.g., TCP-SYN-flood attack and UDP-flood attack). We have 13 behavior concept classes which have to be learned. Five classes represent normal behavior and nine classes define abnormal behavior. The effectiveness of the adopted reasoning model by the intelligent host and its impact over networking operations was studied via measuring some network performance metrics such as average network throughput and latency. Figure 8 illustrates average network throughput measured at network destination with/without using LSH. The LDA-HMM model learned most data semantics (i.e., behavior concept classes) of normal/abnormal flows earlier, besides clarifying attacks in the network. This enabled intelligent host to generate early alerts that allowed nodes to recognize semantics and to subsequently suppress abnormal flows and attacks. Figure 9 illustrates the effectiveness of the implemented reasoning model to learn, in a timely manner, semantics of normal/abnormal flows and to detect running malicious flows and attacks accordingly. Due to the time-overhead caused by semantics reasoning models to learn patterns and extract semantics, there was time delay experienced in the network to accomplish reasoning tasks.

Figure 8. Average network throughput

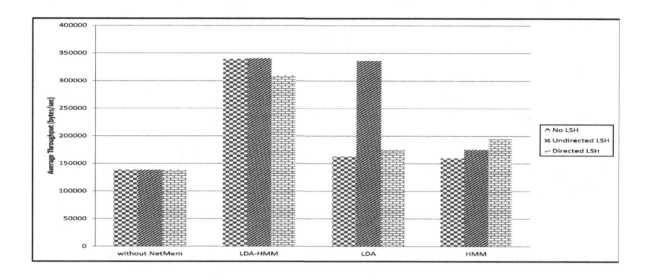

In Figure 10, The LDA-HMM or the HIT model was able to learn semantics with higher level of accuracy through the simulation time compared with LDA and HMM. This showed the ability of the HIT to mitigate challenges faced by the HMM to work with reduced- dimensional data. Also, it can be concluded from obtained results that reasoning operations with the hybrid reasoning model achieved low false negative ratios compared with operations at adopting monolithic intelligence-based models. Figure 11 shows Fn ratio at using different semantics reasoning models. The hybrid model for semantics

Figure 9. Network latency due to the usage of various reasoning models

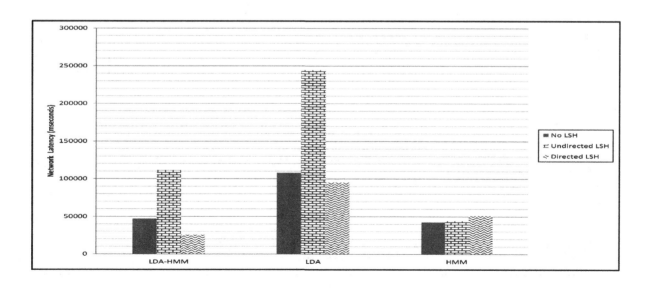

reasoning achieved better values compared with other models. This means that the HIT model was able to decrease the percentage of misclassified data profiles according to its internal capabilities of detecting successfully abnormal traffic with knowing small set of attributes.

From the above results, we conclude the following:

1. The LDA-HMM-based model for semantics reasoning has overcome limitations of other models with individual intelligence techniques (LDA or HMM). Consequently, better performance (higher accuracy with low Fn ratio) of semantics reasoning process was achieved in case of using the LDA-HMM model; and
2. The LDA-HMM model was able to learn features in case of having full- or reduced-dimensional data profiles and reason about network-semantics. This led to recognize, in case of using or not using LSH, almost all behavior classes which are related to different Internet elements (normal file transfer services and attacks). Consequently, this aided in enhancing QoS of running services.

Figure 10. Accuracy for learning semantics

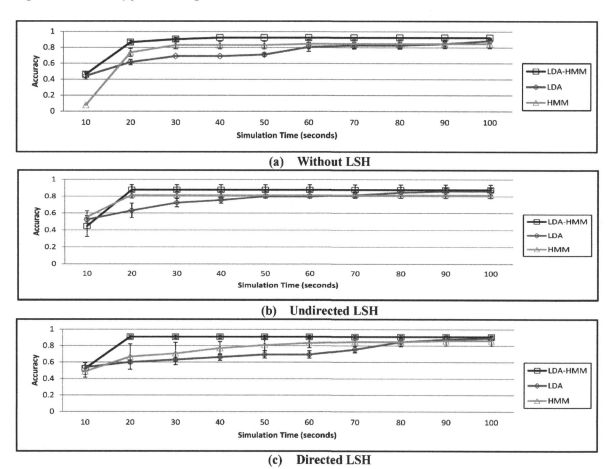

(a)   Without LSH

(b)   Undirected LSH

(c)   Directed LSH

Figure 11. False negative (Fn) ratio for learning semantics

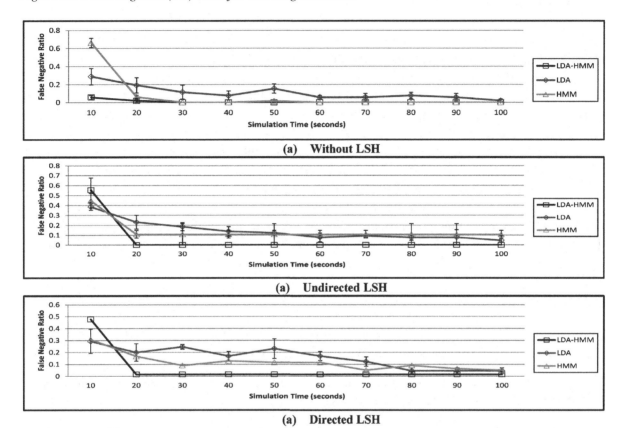

(a) **Without LSH**

(a) **Undirected LSH**

(a) **Directed LSH**

5. FUTURE RESEARCH DIRECTIONS

Today's and prospective coming technology-based applications are heterogeneous and related to various interesting fields such as healthcare, networking, food processing, renewable energy systems, etc. Those applications involve parameters of importance that can be captured and measured. Learning and analyzing set of correlated applications' parameters and extracting semantics (or high level information) accordingly will aid in enhancing applications' security, output and QoS and optimizing resource utilization. Easy measurements for application-specific parameters can be made with developing reliable small portable smart collaborative devices that minimize required implementation space and consumed energy resources. Capturing multi-dimensional application data with multi-sensors is needed for enabling combining data attributes related to various dimension. Also, there is a need to have a system with a means of coordinating and feeding the readouts of the sensors into sets of reasoning models' matrices to generate output from which efficient human decisions could be made. In other words, there will be intelligent processing unit that perform efficiently such roles.

For example, investigating real-life systems, such as smart grids, and implementing autonomous reconfigurable semantic reasoning capabilities for them would help in improving the performance of the system operations and jobs. Semantic reasoning processes can strengthen the security of state estimation processes in smart grids by providing dynamic models for state estimation which clarify the normal/abnormal behavior of multiple smart grid elements, like remote terminal units, power generation units, and network entities (e.g., routers) in communication networks of smart grids.

6. CONCLUSION

In this chapter, we have discussed network-semantics management methodology using monolithic and hybrid intelligence techniques for extracting semantics and building dynamic ontology of network concepts. The hybridization of more than one monolithic intelligence technique can help in integrating the capabilities of each technique when it is used separately. Additionally, we discussed the operations of semantics reasoning via designing multiple reasoning models using monolithic and hybrid intelligence techniques. We discussed the effectiveness of the implemented reasoning models via simulation over real Internet traffic data. Simulation results showed the capability of reasoning models to learn patterns of large-scale data with full or reduced dimensionality and reason about semantics that are used in a) enhancing QoS of running services; b) detection of anomalies and attacks; and c) learning normal/abnormal behavior classes of some Internet elements (e.g., services and attacks). The presented hybrid LDA-HMM-based reasoning model achieved higher effectiveness whether using full- or reduced data dimensionality compared with the other monolithic intelligence-based reasoning models.

REFERENCES

Abraham, A., & Nath, B. (2000). Hybrid intelligent systems design: A review of a decade of research. *IEEE Transactions on Systems, Man and Cybernetics (Part-C),* August.

Baum, L. E. (1972). An Inequality and Associated Maximization Technique in Statistical Estimation for Probabilistic Functions of a Markov Process. *Inequalities, 3.*

Bíró, I., & Szabó, J. (2009). *Latent dirichlet allocation for automatic document categorization.* Paper presented at the ECML PKDD '09 Proceedings of the European Conference on Machine Learning and Knowledge Discovery in Databases. doi:10.1007/978-3-642-04174-7_28

Blei, D. M., Ng, A. Y., & Jordan, M. I. (2003). Latent dirichlet allocation. *Journal of Machine Learning Research, 3,* 993-1022.

Bouabene, G., Jelger, C., Tschudin, C., Schmid, S., Keller, A., & May, M. (2010). The autonomic network architecture (ANA). *IEEE Journal on Selected Areas in Communications, 28*(1), 4–14.

Breiman, L. (2001). Statistical modeling: The two cultures (with comments and a rejoinder by the author). *Statistical Science, 16*(3), 199–231. doi:10.1214/ss/1009213726

Casella, G., & George, E. I. (1992). Explaining the Gibbs sampler. *The American Statistician, 46*(3), 167–174.

Chatterjee, S., & Russell, S. (2012). A temporally abstracted Viterbi algorithm. *arXiv preprint arXiv:1202.3707.*

Cristianini, N., & Shawe-Taylor, J. (2000). *An introduction to support vector machines and other kernel-based learning methods.* Cambridge university press. doi:10.1017/CBO9780511801389

Cross, S. S., Harrison, R. F., & Kennedy, R. L. (1995). Introduction to neural networks. *Lancet, 346*(8982), 1075–1079. doi:10.1016/S0140-6736(95)91746-2 PMID:7564791

Darling, W. M. (2011). *A Theoretical and Practical Implementation Tutorial on Topic Modeling and Gibbs Sampling.* Paper presented at the 49th Annual Meeting of the Association for Computational Linguistics: Human Language Technologies.

Data virtualization by denodo technologies. (2012, December). from http://www.denodo.com/en/solutions/technology/data_virtualization.php

Day, J., Matta, I., & Mattar, K. (2008). *Networking is IPC: A guiding principle to a better Internet.* Paper presented at the 2008 ACM CoNEXT Conference. doi:10.1145/1544012.1544079

Dorst, K., & Vermaas, P. E. (2005). John Gero's Function-Behaviour-Structure model of designing: A critical analysis. *Research in Engineering Design, 16*(1), 17–26. doi:10.1007/s00163-005-0058-z

Dvb queplix, (2012, September). Retrieved from http://www.queplix.com

Feldmann, A. (2007). Internet clean-slate design: What and why? *Computer Communication Review, 37*(3), 59–64. doi:10.1145/1273445.1273453

Gero, J. S. (1990). Design prototypes: A knowledge representation schema for design. *AI Magazine, 11*(4), 26.

Griffiths, T. L., Steyvers, M., Blei, D. M., & Tenenbaum, J. B. (2004). *Integrating topics and syntax.* Paper presented at the Advances in Neural Information Processing Systems.

Hassan, H., Eltoweissy, M., & Youssef, M. (2009). *CellNet: a bottom-up approach to network design.* Paper presented at the 3rd International Conference on New Technologies, Mobility and Security (NTMS). doi:10.1109/NTMS.2009.5384680

Hawkins, J., & Blakeslee, S. (2005). On Intelligence: St. Martin's Press.

Henderson, K., & Eliassi-Rad, T. *Applying latent dirichlet allocation to group discovery in large graphs.* Paper presented at the 2009 ACM symposium on Applied Computing. doi:10.1145/1529282.1529607

Hettich, S., & Bay, S. D. (1999). *The UCI KDD Archive.* Irvine, CA: University of California, Department of Information and Computer Science.

IBM. (n. d.). Retrieved from http://www.ibm.com

Idris, N. B., & Shanmugam, B. (2005). *Artificial intelligence techniques applied to intrusion detection.* Paper presented at the IEEE INDICON '05.

informatica, D. v. b. (2013, January). Retrieved from http://www.informatica.com

Jiang, J. (2009). *Modeling syntactic structures of topics with a nested hmm-lda.* Paper presented at the 9th IEEE International Conference on Data Mining. doi:10.1109/ICDM.2009.144

Jiten, J., Merialdo, B., & Huet, B. (2006). *Semantic feature extraction with multidimensional hidden Markov model.* Paper presented at the Proceedings of SPIE. doi:10.1117/12.650590

Khan, R., Khan, S. U., Zaheer, R., & Khan, S. (2012). *Future Internet: The Internet of Things Architecture, Possible Applications and Key Challenges.* Paper presented at the 10th International Conference on Frontiers of Information Technology (FIT). doi:10.1109/FIT.2012.53

Kumar, G., Kumar, K., & Sachdeva, M. (2010). The use of artificial intelligence based techniques for intrusion detection: A review. *Artificial Intelligence Review, 34*(4), 369–387. doi:10.1007/s10462-010-9179-5

Landauer, T. K., Foltz, P. W., & Laham, D. (1998). An introduction to latent semantic analysis. *Discourse Processes, 25*(2-3), 259–284. doi:10.1080/01638539809545028

Li, D., Xiao, L., Han, Y., Chen, G., & Liu, K. (2007). Network Thinking and Network Intelligence. In N. Zhong, J. Liu, Y. Yao, J. Wu, S. Lu, & K. Li (Eds.), *Web Intelligence Meets Brain Informatics* (Vol. 4845, pp. 36–58). Springer Berlin Heidelberg. doi:10.1007/978-3-540-77028-2_3

Merhav, N., & Ephraim, Y. (1991). Maximum likelihood hidden Markov modeling using a dominant sequence of states. *IEEE Transactions on Signal Processing, 39*(9), 2111–2115. doi:10.1109/78.134449

Mimaroglu, S., & Simovici, D. A. (2008). *Approximate computation of object distances by locality-sensitive hashing.* Paper presented at the Proceedings of the 2008 International Conference on Data Mining, Washington, DC.

Mokhtar, B., & Eltoweissy, M. (2012). *Biologically-inspired network "memory" for smarter networking.* Paper presented at the 8th International Conference on Collaborative Computing: Networking, Applications and Worksharing (CollaborateCom).

Mokhtar, B., & Eltoweissy, M. (2014). *Hybrid Intelligence for Semantics-Enhanced Networking Operations.* Paper presented at the The Twenty-Seventh International Flairs Conference.

Mokhtar, B., Eltoweissy, M., & El-Sayed, H. (2013). *Network "memory" system for enhanced network services.* Paper presented at the 9th International Conference on Innovations in Information Technology (IIT).

Newman, D., Asuncion, A., Smyth, P., & Welling, M. (2007). Distributed inference for latent dirichlet allocation. Advances in Neural Information Processing Systems, 20(1081-1088), 17-24.

Nii, M., Nakai, K., Takahashi, Y., Higuchi, K., & Maenaka, K. (2011). *Behavior extraction from multiple sensors information for human activity monitoring.* Paper presented at the IEEE International Conference on Systems, Man, and Cybernetics (SMC). doi:10.1109/ICSMC.2011.6083831

Onat, F. A., & Stojmenovic, I. (2007). *Generating random graphs for wireless actuator networks.* Paper presented at the IEEE International Symposium on World of Wireless, Mobile and Multimedia Networks WoWMoM '07. doi:10.1109/WOWMOM.2007.4351712

Ourston, D., Matzner, S., Stump, W., & Hopkins, B. (2003). *Applications of hidden markov models to detecting multi-stage network attacks.* Paper presented at the 36th Annual International Conference on System Sciences, Hawaii. doi:10.1109/HICSS.2003.1174909

Paul, S. (2010). An Optimized distributed association rule mining algorithm in parallel and distributed data mining with xml data for improved response time. *International Journal of Computer Science and Information Technology, 2*(2), 90–103. doi:10.5121/ijcsit.2010.2208

Peddabachigari, S., Abraham, A., Grosan, C., & Thomas, J. (2007). Modeling intrusion detection system using hybrid intelligent systems. *Journal of Network and Computer Applications, 30*(1), 114–132. doi:10.1016/j.jnca.2005.06.003

Rabiner, L., & Juang, B. (1986). An introduction to hidden Markov models. *ASSP Magazine, IEEE, 3*(1), 4–16. doi:10.1109/MASSP.1986.1165342

Rajpathak, D., & Chougule, R. (2011). A generic ontology development framework for data integration and decision support in a distributed environment. *International Journal of Computer Integrated Manufacturing, 24*(2), 154–170. doi:10.1080/0951192X.2010.531291

Ramage, D. (2007). Hidden Markov Models Fundamentals. *CS229 Section Notes.*

Schuler, W., Bastos-Filho, C., & Oliveira, A. (2009). A novel hybrid training method for hopfield neural networks applied to routing in communications networks. *International Journal of Hybrid Intelligent Systems, 6*(1), 27–39.

Seymore, K., McCallum, A., & Rosenfeld, R. (1999). *Learning hidden Markov model structure for information extraction.* Paper presented at the AAAI-99 Workshop on Machine Learning for Information Extraction.

Sobeih, A., Viswanathan, M., Marinov, D., & Hou, J. C. (2007). *J-Sim: An integrated environment for simulation and model checking of network protocols.* Paper presented at the Parallel and Distributed Processing Symposium, 2007. IPDPS 2007. IEEE International. doi:10.1109/IPDPS.2007.370519

Sontag, D., & Roy, D. M. (2011). *Complexity of inference in latent dirichlet allocation.* Advances in Neural Information Processing Systems NIPS.

Srivastava, J., Cooley, R., Deshpande, M., & Tan, P.-N. (2000). Web usage mining: Discovery and applications of usage patterns from web data. *ACM SIGKDD Explorations Newsletter, 1*(2), 12–23. doi:10.1145/846183.846188

Van Laarhoven, P. J., & Aarts, E. H. (1987). *Simulated annealing.* Springer. doi:10.1007/978-94-015-7744-1

Vasconcelos, N., & Lippman, A. (2000). Statistical models of video structure for content analysis and characterization. *Image Processing. IEEE Transactions on, 9*(1), 3–19.

Willett, D., & Rigoll, G. (1998). Hybrid NN/HMM-based speech recognition with a discriminant neural feature extraction. *Advances in Neural Information Processing Systems,* 763–772.

Winter, M. (2007). *Goguen categories: a categorical approach to L-fuzzy relations.* Springer Publishing Company, Incorporated.

Yang, C. C., Yen, J., & Chen, H. (2000). Intelligent internet searching agent based on hybrid simulated annealing. *Decision Support Systems, 28*(3), 269–277. doi:10.1016/S0167-9236(99)00091-3

Yang, J., & Xu, Y. (1994). Hidden markov model for gesture recognition: *Tech. Report CMU-RI-TR-94-10.*

Yao, X. (1999). Evolving artificial neural networks. *Proceedings of the IEEE, 87*(9), 1423–1447. doi:10.1109/5.784219

Zafeiropoulos, A., Liakopoulos, A., Davy, A., & Chaparadza, R. (2010). *Monitoring within an autonomic network: a GANA based network monitoring framework.* Paper presented at the Service-Oriented Computing. ICSOC/ServiceWave 2009 Workshops. doi:10.1007/978-3-642-16132-2_29

Zhiming, D., Qi, Y., & Hong, W. (2011). *Massive Heterogeneous Sensor Data Management in the Internet of Things.* Paper presented at the 2011 International Conference on Internet of Things and 4th International Conference on Cyber, Physical and Social Computing (iThings/CPSCom).

Chapter 10
Epidemic Estimation over Social Networks using Large Scale Biosensors

João Sousa Andrade
Instituto Superior Tecnico, Portugal

Artur M. Arsénio
Universidade da Beira Interior, Portugal

ABSTRACT

Infectious diseases, such as the recent Ebola outbreak, can be especially dangerous for large communities on today's highly connected world. Countermeasures can be put in place if one is able to predict determine which people are more vulnerable to infections or have been in contact with the disease, and where. Contact location, time and relationship with the subject are relevant metrics that affect the probability of disease propagation. Sensors on personal devices that gather information from people, and social networks analysis, allow the integration of community data, while data analysis and modelling may potentially indicate community-level susceptibility to an epidemic. Indeed, there has been interest on social networks for epidemic prediction. But the integration between large-scale sensor networks and these initiatives, required to achieve epidemic prediction, is yet to be achieved. In this context, an opportunistic system is proposed and evaluated for predicting an epidemic outbreak in a community, while guaranteeing user privacy.

INTRODUCTION

Distributed systems have been employed as platforms for allowing the interaction between groups of individuals and set of devices. As technology advances, sensing, computation, storage and communications become widespread, ubiquitous sensing devices will become a part of global distributed sensing systems (Lane et al., 2010) (Campbell et al., 2008).

DOI: 10.4018/978-1-4666-9474-3.ch010

Recently, the predominance of mobile phones equipped with sensors, the explosion in social networks and the deployment of sensor networks have created an enormous digital footprint that can be harnessed (Zhang et al., 2010). Furthermore, developments in sensor technology, communications and semantic processing, allow the coordination of a large network of devices and large dataset processing with intelligent data analysis (Lane et al., 2010).

The sensing of people constitutes a new application domain that broadens the traditional sensor network scope of environmental and infrastructure monitoring. People become the carriers of sensing devices and both producers and consumers of events (Miluzzo et al., 2010). As a consequence, the recent interest by the industry in open programming platforms and software distribution channels is accelerating the development of people-centric sensing applications and systems (Miluzzo et al., 2010)(Lane et al., 2010).

To take advantage of these emerging networks of mobile people-centric sensing devices, researchers arrived at the concept of Mobiscopes, i.e. taskable mobile sensing systems that are capable of high coverage. They represent a new type of infrastructure, where mobile sensors have the potential to logical belong to more than one network, while being physically attached to their carriers (Abdelzaher et al., 2007). By taking advantage of these systems, it will be possible to mine and run computations on enormous amounts of data from a very large number of users (Lane et al., 2010).

A people-centric sensing system imbues the individuals it serves in a symbiotic relationship with itself (Kansal et al., 2007) (Campbell et al., 2008). People-centric sensing enables a different approach to sensing, learning, visualizing and data sharing, not only self-centered, but focused on the surrounding world. The traditional view on mesh sensor networks is combined with one where people, carrying sensors turn opportunistic coverage into a reality (Campbell et al., 2008). These sensors can reach into regions static sensors cannot, proving to be especially useful for applications that occasionally require sensing (Abdelzaher et al., 2007). By employing these systems, one can aim to revolutionize the field of context-aware computing (Zhang et al., 2010).

An alternative based on worldwide coverage of static sensors to develop people-centric systems is unfeasible in terms of monetary costs, management and permissions (Kansal et al., 2007)(Campbell et al., 2008). In addition, it is extremely challenging in static sensing models, due to band limits and issues that arise from covering a vast area, to satisfy the required density requirements (Abdelzaher et al., 2007). Thanks to their mobility, mobile sensors overcome spatial coverage limitations (Abdelzaher et al., 2007)(Kansal et al., 2007).

Adoption issues might come up as potential users are usually unaware of the benefits that arise from technological developments. However, with the advent of smartphones, a direct impact in daily life is easier to achieve, making advantages clearer. By using opportunistic sensing, functionality can be offered in a transparent fashion (Lane et al., 2010), leaving the user agnostic of system activity and circumventing adoption obstacles that might be present in participatory sensing.

Behavioral modeling requires large amounts of accurate data (Peebles et al., 2010). These systems constitute an opportunity for intelligent analysis systems, as relevant information can be obtained from large-scale sensory data and employed in statistical models (Peebles et al., 2010)(Lane et al., 2010). Great benefits can be taken from this unconstrained human data, in opposition to the traditional carefully setup experiments (Peebles et al., 2010). With these developments it is now possible to distribute and run experiments in a worldwide population rather than in a small laboratory controlled study (Lane et al., 2010).

By leveraging the behavioral patterns related to individuals, groups and society, a new multi- disciplinary field is created: Social Community Intelligence (SCI) (Zhang et al., 2010). Real-time user contributed data is invaluable to address community-level problems and provide an universal access to information, contributing to the emergence of innovative services (Zhang et al., 2010)(Campbell et al., 2008)(Lane et al., 2010). For instance, services for the prediction and tracking of epidemic outbreaks across populations (Zhang et al., 2010). Thus, technological benefits are shifted from a restricted group of scientists to the whole society (Campbell et al., 2008).

Healthcare is a possible application, where these systems can facilitate monitoring and sharing of automatically gathered health data (Campbell et al., 2008). Epidemics are a major public health concern and it has been shown impact can be reduced by early detection of the disease activity. For instance, it has been shown that the level of influenza-like illness in regions of the US can be estimated with a reporting lag of one day, when compared to clinical methods whose results take a week to be published (Zhang et al., 2010).

The advent of ubiquitous networks of mobile sensing devices constitute a paradigm shift, offering researchers challenges in network architecture, protocol design and data abstractions (Abdelzaher et al., 2007).

Results from mobile sensing networks, pervasive computing and methods of statistical analysis can be exploited. However, new unaddressed challenges arise. These challenges range from growing volumes of multi-modal sensor data, dynamic operating conditions and the increasing mobility of the sensing devices (Lane et al., 2010).

Enabling user participation, while minimizing mobile sensing devices resource consumption and protecting user privacy, are addressed in the proposed solution. This chapter's solution considers performing robust data analysis in a dynamic environment and system scaling from a personal to a community-level, while providing useful feedback to its users.

The chosen application area of epidemic prediction has an inherent lack of adequate data that does not result from potentially biased simulations (Rothenberg & Costenbader, 2011). To counter this, similarities between computer and biological infectious agents are exploited (Pastor-Satorras & Vespignani, 2001).

Epidemic Estimation

In an infectious disease it is necessary to detect, monitor and foresee the advent of an epidemic in a real-time environment. To operate in such a scenario the system should know who can get infected and which people have been in contact and where. Contact location, time and relationship with the subject are relevant metrics that affect the probability of disease propagation. Sensors and social networks analysis allow the integration of these concerns into personal devices, while developments in data analysis and modeling allow more accurate results regarding this data, potentially indicating community-level susceptibility to an epidemic.

This work comprises data gathering and management, intelligent analysis and privacy respecting pervasive computing applied to epidemiological disease prediction in a population. A community is the target population of the analysis. It consists of the set of sensing devices belonging to people that are users plus their associated social contact network.

Sampling is only possible when privacy requirements are met. Participation in the system is managed in an opportunistic fashion. The developed system is capable of exploiting large sets of multimodal sensorial data (contact and network data). Information extraction from raw data is based on the application of data analysis strategies in a dynamic environment.

These operations occur with some degree of distribution in the mobile sensing device and data processing backend. The criteria for this is based upon privacy, communication and resource management concerns.

There are other solutions targeting these problems, but none of them has been applied to epidemic prediction, as it is the case with this chapter's proposed solution. Information is fed to an epidemic model-based algorithm, predicting the possibility of an epidemic and notifying users about the risk.

Hence, this chapter is organized as follows. It first reviews previous work on sensing architectures, computational epidemiology and social network analysis. Based on the identified limitations, it is proposed a network solution based on social network data. Its experimental evaluation is discussed afterwards, together with recommendations for improving the outcomes of this work. The chapter ends giving directions for future research and presenting the main conclusions.

BACKGROUND ON SENSING ARCHITECTURES

This section addresses the first of the three main areas that constitute the multi-disciplinary field where the contribution of this work is inserted, namely Sensing Architectures, Computational Epidemiology and Social Network Analysis.

Sensing devices enjoy a high degree of heterogeneity. Typically, sensed data has varying time-space resolutions and may become biased depending on the sensing context. Nonetheless, the heterogeneity in sensing data can be harnessed to increase system robustness by exploiting distinct views that may complement each other (Abdelzaher et al., 2007). Sensing devices usually have resource limitations that require careful consideration as to where data processing takes place (Campbell et al., 2008). One approach is to persist data by employing local buffering capabilities (Abdelzaher et al., 2007). However, for analysis requiring large amounts of data, local storage limitations may promote the need to have data persistence on remote servers (Campbell et al., 2008)(Kansal et al., 2007). Privacy issues also need to be considered, as it may be inappropriate to store sensitive data in a remote untrusted system.

Connectivity issues in the system affect sensing performance. In this sensing networks, at a given time, a greater amount of data is gathered when compared to data that can be delivered. To circumvent this issues and avoid resource waste, data prioritization schemes (Abdelzaher et al., 2007), to be used when multiple nodes cover the same area, have been suggested. Opportunistic data diffusion schemes between sensing devices, with possible data aggregation, aim to improve connectivity and data quality despite data incongruence (Abdelzaher et al., 2007).

Information needed by an application may only be available by integrating data from multiple sensing modalities. As such, transmitted data must be compatible across heterogeneous networks (Abdelzaher et al., 2007).

Data analysis techniques require a systemic view, considering the sensing devices' resource constraints, communication costs to remote servers and the sampling rate required to detect and characterize interesting phenomena (Campbell et al., 2008).

There is a high correlation between data accesses and user location. Because of the dynamic nature of sensor densities in both time and space, system performance depends on the mobility patterns of the sensing devices. Uniform coverage for a given is area is hard to achieve as sensors tend to visit zones in a given area in a non-uniform fashion. As such and adding the fact that interesting events might be rare, sparse data models need to be considered. For such cases data-mining techniques can be applied.

Another approach is to have actuated sensing devices, i.e. sensors that are tasked to visit uncovered areas (Abdelzaher et al., 2007).

Some authors have provided a systematical architecture that can be used as a viewpoint to face these issues, consisting of five layers: pervasive sensing, data anonymization, hybrid learning, semantic inference, and application (Zhang et al., 2010).

- The pervasive sensing layer involves the gathering of data from the different data sources (mobile devices, static sensors, social web).
- The data anonymization layer anonymizes sensed data, offering different anonymization algorithms that can be applied according to the nature of the requirements.
- The hybrid-learning layer applies data analysis algorithms to convert low-level single-modality sensing data into high-level features or micro-context. Its focus is to mine data patterns and derive behaviour and single space context, before multi-modal intelligence is extracted.
- The semantic inference layer is needed when different micro-contexts need to be aggregated. Its objective is to match the inputted micro-contexts with an expected high-level result.
- The application layer provides a set of accessible services that are sustained on the other layers. Applications may be installed directly on a mobile sensing device or on remote servers, communicating with the sensors.

Other work (Campbell et al., 2008)(Lane et al., 2010) proposes a three stage Sense, Learn and Share architecture.

- In the sense layer, sensing interaction-based mobility-enabled data is acquired from the heterogeneous sensors that are part of the system (Campbell et al., 2008) (Lane et al., 2010). The delivery of application sampling requests and the delivery of sampled data are part of this layer. A sampling request specifies at least one required sensor type and the required sampling context, i.e. the set of conditions required. Related applications may be present on the mobile sensing devices or remote server, communicating wirelessly (Campbell et al., 2008).
- In the learn layer, information extracted from raw data is analysed using statistical measures, data mining or machine-learning techniques to infer higher-level meaning (Campbell et al., 2008). Data analysis techniques and features to analyse are chosen to best fit the availability and characteristics of the sensed data and the target application (Campbell et al., 2008) (Lane et al., 2010).
- In the share layer, learned information is visualized and shared according to its application (Campbell et al., 2008). A personal application will inform its user and a community application will share aggregated information with its target group, while obfuscating their identity. Resulting information can also be used to persuade users to make positive behavioural changes (Lane et al., 2010).

These architectural views, presented in Table 1, complement each other.

Miluzzo et al. (2010) investigate the usage of phone sensors to automatically classify events in the lives of community people. These classifications can be selectively shared using online social networks, replacing manual actions that are currently performed daily (Miluzzo et al., 2010)(Lane et al., 2010). Lu et al. (2009) provide a lightweight and scalable hierarchical audio classification system, designed

Table 1. Architecture comparison

Architecture	
Share	Application
Learn	Semantic inference Hybrid learning
Sense	Data anonymization Pervasive sensing

with resource limited mobile phones in mind, while remaining capable of recognizing a broad set of events. In opposition with offline audio context recognition systems, classification is performed online at a lower computational cost, while yielding comparable results.

Conventional ways of evaluating environmental impact rely on aggregate statistical data that applies to a community (Lane et al., 2010). Mun et al., (2009) propose a personalized environmental impact approach, allowing the tracking of human actions and their impact towards urban problem exposure and contribution. Continuous physical activity data is captured and related to personal health goals in the form of user feedback (Lane et al., 2010). These applications have been proven to be effective in impacting the way health is assessed, helping the improvement of behavioural patterns.

BACKGROUND ON COMPUTATIONAL EPIDEMIOLOGY

Computational epidemiology consists on the development and use of computer models to understand the diffusion of disease through populations with regard to space and time (Barret et al., 2008). In epidemiology, contact tracing is the process of controlling the spread of an infectious disease by identifying individuals who were previously exposed to it (Chen, Tseng & King, 2007).

In order to accurately predict and understand the propagation of diseases, the data used in these models should be representative (Lopes et al., 2009). Nonetheless, decisions have to be made with limited information. An effective prediction is difficult, especially if initial data is not expressive enough (Gorder, 2010). Hybrid Intelligence techniques have been employed to address epidemics estimation, for instance propagation of the HIV virus (Teweldemedhin et al., 2004), or detection of public health events (Fisichella et al., 2010).

Traditional systems obtain model data either through periodic online questionnaires (Noort et al., 2007), trusted web news sources (Brownstein & Freifeld, 2007) or by exploiting web search queries to monitor health-seeking behaviour (Ginsberg et al., 2009). Social contact networks constitute a potential new data source as large-scale relevant user-related data can be acquired instantaneously and in real-time (Lopes et al., 2009). As a consequence of their capability to estimate disease propagation, these models are powerful tools to evaluate the course of a disease in response to public health interventions (Barret et al., 2008) (Kretzschmar et al., 2010) (El-Sayed et al., 2012) (Christley et al., 2005) (Christakis & Fowler, 2009).

The more is understood about infectious disease spreading, the more efficiently it is possible to deploy outbreaks' counter measures, such as vaccines (Li & Shao, 2009) (Ginsberg et al., 2009) (Noort et al., 2007). The following terminology is relevant in epidemiology:

- N population size;
- β effective contact rate, i.e. rate of disease contraction;
- δ recovery rate, i.e. rate of disease recovery;
- R_0 basic reproductive number, i.e. number of susceptible individuals with no immunity that an infected individual will infect (Longini et al., 2005);
- $1/\varepsilon$ average latent period, i.e. period in which infected individuals cannot transmit the disease;
- $1/\gamma$ average infectious period, i.e. period in which infected individuals can transmit the disease;

One approach for the approximation of δ, which is analogous for other rates, is determining the mean time associated to the said rate and inverting that value. For instance, one person is sick with influenza for a period that can range from three to seven days. Hence, the mean time spent as infectious is five days and the recovery rate, measured in units of days^{-1} is 0.2. R_0 is usually estimated from the average number of secondary cases resulting from one primary case in a population of susceptible individuals (Meyers et al., 2005) (Chao et al., 2010). It stands for the total number of expected cases for every generation of infection in a disease. A generation is the mean time between an individual getting infected and transmitting the infection to others (Meyers et al., 2005). R_0 is highly dependant on the contact patterns that determine the disease transmission. Thus, measuring it in a location where the rate of contact is unusually high will lead to estimates that have poor generalisation. Contact rates in the population may be considerably lower, thus affecting the estimation of the value of R_0 (Meyers et al., 2005). Moreover, this parameter assumes that the population is constituted of susceptible individuals only (i.e. no a priori immunity). This is not the case for certain epidemics, such as the seasonal influenza (Chao et al., 2010).

Samples of values estimated for R_0 are present in (Longini et al., 2005). It should be noted that A(X) stands for influenza A virus subtype X.

- **Pandemic Influenza:** $1 < R_0 \leq 2.4$.
- **A(H3N2) in Hong Kong (1968-69):** $R_0 \approx 1.7$.
- **A(H1N1) in the USA (1918, Second Wave):** $R_0 \approx 2.0$.

Associated to this number, there is the transmissibility parameter or effective contact rate (usually known as β or T). Contrarily to R_0, this parameter can be extrapolated from one location to another, even in cases where the contact patterns diverge in a significant way (Meyers et al., 2005). An example is provided by Meyers et al. (2005): in a given place with $R_0 = 2.7$, an individual may come in contact with one hundred other individuals. As such, the probability an individual will get infected from an infected contact is 2.7% or $T = 0.027$ (in an uniform contact network). If this individual moves to another location where there are 10 potential contacts and R_0 is extrapolated, it implies that on average 2.7 out of every 10 contacts or 27% of the contacts will become infected. On the other hand, if T is extrapolated, one can still verify that 2.7% of all contacts get infected (Meyers et al., 2005).

$$\beta = pc \tag{1}$$

Equation (1) defines the effective contact rate of a given infection. p is the probability that a contact will result in an infection, while c is the rate at which individuals come into contact with each other, *i.e.* the contact rate (Meyers et al., 2005). Some models rely on a set of fixed values for c, which vary according to population characteristics, such as age and place of contact (Chao et al., 2010).

It is relevant to distinguish between epidemics and outbreaks. An epidemic results from the spread of an infection from its initial set of cases to a community level, resulting in an incidence that has population-wide impact. An outbreak is associated with cases, whose transmissibility is inherently low. In this way, the infection dies out before reaching the general population (Meyers et al., 2005).

Another important concept is the epidemic threshold. It is calculated by the quotient between the epidemic agent's death and birth rate. It refers to the threshold above which agents can spread explosively and cause epidemics.

Endemic equilibrium is reached, when the number of infective individuals remains strictly positive for a significant amount of time. As a result, a disease remains in a population, becoming endemic. It is important to note that the end of an epidemic is caused by the decline in the number of infected individuals rather than an absolute lack of susceptible subjects. Thus, at the end of an epidemic, not all individuals have recovered.

Model

An epidemic model is a mathematical abstraction that describes the evolution of a transmittable disease in a population. Various parameters impact model construction. By taking them into account, while relating them appropriately, models can be defined and refined to better reflect reality and potentially go towards real-time epidemic detection rather than prediction (Noort et al., 2007).

- **Mixing:** Under homogeneous mixing, individuals belonging to the population are neighbours with every other individual, making contact at random and not mixing into smaller subgroups (Kephart, 1994). Here, the probability of any infected individual contacting any other susceptible individual is well approximated by the average. This is often a problematic model assumption, but it can be relaxed in complex models. In this situation, the set of infected individuals has little meaning to the overall population dynamics and the relevant metric is the number of infected individuals (Kephart, 1994). Examples of this approach are (Chao et al., 2010), where individuals are members of social mixing groups inside which a disease is transmitted by random mixing. In non-homogeneous mixing, the structure of the considered social network greatly influences disease proliferation as it conditions contact between individuals (Barret et al., 2008). Examples of this approach are present by Schumm et al. (2007), Danon et al. (2011) and Ames et al. (2011).
- **Spatial Distribution:** Simple models assume uniform spatial distribution. More complex lattice-based models can cope with non-uniform distributions (Kephart, 1994). For an epidemic model to be realistic in a large population, long-distance travelling is necessary. Nonetheless, depending on the scope of the model (i.e. if the model has a reduced scope), this kind of travelling may be dismissed (Chao et al., 2010). Epidemic models pertaining a sufficiently large area may be adequate for determining national level impact of given epidemic. However, their epidemic peak will appear later. This is due to the time it takes for the epidemic to affect surrounding areas (Chao et al., 2010).
- **Genotypes:** The genotype of the afflicted population constitutes its inherited genetic information and can determine its vulnerability against a given infectious agent and resistance towards another (Kretzschmar et al., 2010). Recent observations suggest that the relation between ethnicity and health may be heterogeneous, and that generalising this information without considering social context may be a flawed approach (El-Sayed et al., 2012). The genotype of the infectious agent

influences its behaviour, infectivity, and resistance to public health measures, and may contribute to the appearance of new sub-strains with different characteristics. The interaction between these two variables conditions epidemic dynamics (Kretzschmar et al., 2010).

- **Transmission:** There are two directions in disease progression: within-host progression and between-host transmission. The start of within-host progression is triggered by between-host transmission.

There is a latent period between the time an individual becomes infected and the time when the capability to infect others is acquired (Barret et al., 2008). Between-host transmission can occur in different directions: horizontal and vertical. Horizontal disease transmission may be triggered through various forms of contact: direct contact; indirect contact (e.g. contact with a contaminated surface); droplet contact (e.g. sneezing), airborne contact (if the pathogen is resilient enough to survive in the air); fecal-oral contact (e.g. contact with contaminated food or resources) (Kretzschmar et al., 2010). Vertical disease transmission occurs from mother to child (e.g. in the case of AIDS and Hepatitis B).

- **Infectivity:** An individual's capability to transmit disease varies over time and is viral load related. In the case of influenza, symptomatic individuals can be twice as infectious as asymptomatic ones (Chao et al., 2010).
- **Age Structure:** A rectangular age structure assumes people live to reach the average life expectancy of the population. This model is suitable for developed countries. For other countries a triangular age structure is considered more appropriate (Abbas et al., 2004). Infectivity can also be age-dependent. For instance, children tend to infect and get infected more often than adults. Consequently, in the early stages of an epidemic, the number of cases involving children is likely to be higher (Chao et al., 2010).
- **Epidemic Reaction:** The behaviour of people is changed in response to the menacing nature of an epidemic. One future direction in computational epidemiology is to take this into account (Noort et al., 2007).
- **Granularity:** A model unit can be defined to represent a single individual or larger social units (groups, families, a small location, organisations or a country) (Schumm et al., 2007) (Handcock & Gile, 2010). Aggregate models assume a population is partitioned into sub-populations with a predictable interaction structure within and between them. While, these models are useful for obtaining parameters, such as the total number of infections, they lack the capability to capture the complexity of human interactions that serve as a major infectious disease transmission mechanism. Also, they are incapable of providing causal explanations. The capability to provide specific details about the flow of disease spread may be required to provide insights to researchers investigating interventions against the epidemic. As the granularity of sub-populations is considered to be high, parameters such as the base reproductive number (R0) and the contact rate are hard to observe (Barret et al., 2008). Models under this category may group the population into a hierarchical set of mixing groups with decreasing social proximity (e.g. from a family household to a community), providing an explicit community structure. For these models, the attack rate of the epidemic, i.e. the ratio of the number of people infected with the disease over the number of exposed people, is lower than the one for models with random mixing (Chao et al., 2010). Disaggregate models (or individual-based models) use a representation of individual agents with explicit interactions between them to model the disease spread across a social network, offering a

much finer granularity (Barret et al., 2008). If one aims to obtain an history of the disease evolution or tackle detailed intervention strategies these models represent the most suitable solution (Chao et al., 2010).

Epidemiological models can be classified depending on their mathematical formulation (Kretzschmar et al., 2010), as described hereafter.

Deterministic Models

Deterministic models can be used to study an epidemic analytically and constitute the most popular approach for disease modelling (Chao et al., 2010). Under this formulation, individuals are assumed to be uniformly distributed in space and to mix at a certain rate, i.e. the effective contact rate β. They are usually based on the Susceptible-Infected-Recovered (SIR) compartmental models (Kretzschmar et al., 2010) (Chao et al., 2010), while predicting that an outbreak with an $R_0 > 1$ will originate an epidemic (Meyers et al., 2005).

They are defined by differential equations, and create the partition of individuals across model-dependent compartments. System behaviour depends on parameter choices (Kretzschmar et al., 2010). These reductionist models impose limitations. Population dynamics, in terms of health and disease, emerge from interactions between the heterogeneous individuals that are part of these models (El-Sayed et al., 2012). This results in complex relations between individuals and originates complex social networks (Noort et al., 2007), impacting on the social fabric of health and disease (El-Sayed et al., 2012). Hence these models may be inappropriate since they lack to account for social factors interactions. One example (Barros et al., 2001) is people's high degree of mobility people, easily travelling abroad while carrying an infectious disease with them (Noort et al., 2007).

Stochastic Models

In the Stochastic formulation, the probability distribution of potential outcomes in disease propagation is estimated by allowing input data to vary randomly over time. Systems may be modelled as a Discrete Event System (DES), in which system state only changes upon the occurrence of an event (Barret et al., 2008). A Finite State Machine (FSM) variant, called a Probabilistic Timed Transition System (PTTS) may be used to represent within-host disease progression. In this approach, state transitions are probabilistic and timed and the considered states depend upon the chosen implementation (Barret et al., 2008).

Stochastic models (Barret et al., 2008)(Eubank, 2002) usually run in discrete time and may even consider different steps in the simulation to account for periods where the mixing between individuals differs (such as night and day). The running time of these models is dependant on the number of infected individuals (Chao et al., 2010).

An Agent-based Model (ABM) (El-Sayed et al., 2012) provides information on all simulated individuals and all the significant interest factors that relate to them (i.e. infection, incapacitation, and treatment with the associated time and location), resulting in large simulations (Schumm et al., 2007). By simulating individuals, over a simulated space and time, one aims to clarify in which way macro-level insights on health and disease distribution patterns may emerge from pre-defined micro-level rules (e.g. health behaviours, individual-related interactions, and mobility in frequented environments). Following a bottom-up approach enables the identification of macro-level patterns (El-Sayed et al., 2012).

They are most appropriate when:

- Individual behaviour is complex (comprised of learning, adaptation, feedback, etc.)
- Heterogeneous environments can impact behaviour and interaction, and individuals are dynamic over either space or time.
- Interaction between individuals is complex, non-linear, and can influence others' behaviours.

Individual behaviour is thus a function of individual's attributes and characteristics, environments, and social interactions over time. In every simulated unit of time, researchers update simulation parameters, resulting in stochastically applied changes in behaviour and characteristics. Hereon, they can go into experimental simulations that fork from an initially well-defined control one. This can promote causal thinking in the analysis, thus improving the understanding on the social production of health and disease. This contrasts with deterministic and regression methods, which feed on aggregated data and whose results are a priori bound to it. In the model implementation process, it is important to define the trade-off between system precision and performance, since new stochastic models' variables may increase the already high computational costs and the degree of uncertainty in simulation outcomes (El-Sayed et al., 2012).

As such, for obtaining absolute population-level metrics, such as disease prevalence or incidence, these models might not be appropriate. Another problem may be a resulting bias, due to the parameterization of these models by data that results from reductionist approaches. Finally, complete validation in systems models is often difficult. To attempt model validation, a researcher might:

- Use real data to parameterize the model.
- Construct a model from conceptual relations. Its findings can be compared to real world observations.

Either the relationships between factors in the model or the outcomes of the model can be validated, but rarely both. In the first approach, the validity of the simulations depends on the valid extraction and implementation of factors in the model, which is nearly impossible to verify, even when those factors are extracted from real data. In the second approach there is a threat resulting from the fact that while a particular model configuration might produce outcomes that predict the observed data, it is possible that there is any other number configurations that would also result in the observed data. As a consequence there is no way to ensure that the configuration that leads to the results observed in reality has been isolated (El-Sayed et al., 2012).

Network-Based Epidemic Models

Developments in epidemic spreading have emphasized the importance of network topology in epidemic modelling. Social and biological systems can be described by complex networks, whose nodes represent the system actors, and its links the relationships between the nodes (Pastor-Satorras & Vespignani, 2001). They may be modelled as a computational network, which is itself modelled as a graph. A graph consists of a set of points called nodes or vertices. Interconnections between these nodes are named links or edges and, in this application, they represent a form of contact or relation. The degree of a node k corresponds to the number of neighbours it has (Schumm et al., 2007).

Network-based epidemic models predict that there is a probability S (often $S<<1$) that an outbreak with an $R_0 > 1$ will result in an epidemic. Two networks with identical R_0 may have different outbreak probabilities. For the cases where $S<<1$ and $R_0>1$, networks that share similar contact patterns are likely to show disparity on their results (minor outbreaks versus large epidemics) (Meyers et al., 2005).

An important result in network models is the prediction of a non-zero epidemic threshold (λ_c). The higher it is node's connectivity, the smaller the epidemic threshold, and consequently, the higher the probability of infection (Pastor-Satorras & Vespignani, 2001).

$$\beta_a \delta^{-1} \leq \left(\lambda_{1,A} \right)^{-1} \tag{2}$$

Equation (2) represents the bounding of the epidemic threshold and defines a condition, that when not met implies the existence of an epidemic. $\lambda_{1,A}$ corresponds to the modulus of the largest eigenvalue of the adjacency matrix of the associated contact network topology, also known as the dominant eigenvalue or spectral radius of the network graph. β_a stands for the average rate of infection along a network edge and δ is the recovery rate of an infected node (Schumm et al., 2007).

The strength of an epidemic can be evaluated with resort to the generalized isoperimetric constant $(\lambda_{1,A})^{-1}$ of the associated social contact network, also known as Cheeger's constant (Schumm et al., 2007).

The smaller the spectral radius of the network graph, the higher is the isoperimetric constant and the resistance of the network against the spread of infectious agents (Jamakovic et al., 2006).

Contextually, this constant is equivalent to the epidemic threshold. When the ratio between infections and cures is lower than the epidemic threshold, an infection dies out quickly (exponentially fast). Conversely, if it is higher an infection will die out slowly, resulting in an epidemic (Schumm et al., 2007) (Pastor-Satorras & Vespignani, 2001).

In these models, one way to accommodate asymmetric and variable contact is by weighting the links of the contact networks. The weighted links distribute the contact rate parameter β_a over the network. The weight value and its distribution can have a significant effect on the epidemic resistance of the topology, offering the possibility to alter a network without changing its topology. One can hence define weight clusters that can boost infectious agent spread through the network (Schumm et al., 2007).

$$\beta_a = \beta_f \hat{w} \tag{3}$$

Equation (3) introduces a weighting parameter $\hat{w}$ that accounts for the average contact rate on the network topology. β_f stands for the full contact measure of the effective contact rate β (Schumm et al., 2007).

$$\begin{cases} \beta_f w_{ij} \leq 1 \\ w_{ij} \leq 1 \\ \beta_a \leq \hat{w} \leq 1 \end{cases} \tag{4}$$

The upper bound for the link weight parameter for an edge from node i to j and its impact on the average link weight $\hat{w}$ is presented on equation (4). The weights for a given link ω_{ij} take values on the $[0...1]$ interval. As for matrices A and B with a_{ij} and b_{ij}, $\lambda_{1,A} \leq \lambda_{1,B}$, the upper bound ensures the link weights do not directly alter the epidemic threshold of the network (Schumm et al., 2007).

In these models, specific network topologies are favoured. Scale-free networks are the family of networks whose degree distribution obeys a power-law, made explicit in equation (5). γ is a coefficient that in this context of analysis is subjected to the condition $2 < \gamma \leq 3$ (Schumm et al., 2007) (Pastor-Satorras & Vespignani, 2001), and k constitutes the number of connections per node, *i.e.* the average node degree.

$$P\left(k\right) = k^{-\gamma} \tag{5}$$

Scale-free networks are constituted of nodes with few edges, having a minority of nodes with a high degree (Meyers et al., 2005). Each node has a statistically significant probability of having a very large number of edges, when compared to the average connectivity of the network k. This notion is distinct from conventional random networks, where each node has approximately k links (Pastor-Satorras & Vespignani, 2001). Thus, a scale-free network has considerably more nodes of high degree than a random network (Christakis & Fowler, 2009). This inherent large fluctuation among the number of connections in each vertex makes them appropriate to model real social networks (Schumm et al., 2007) and computer virus epidemics (Pastor-Satorras & Vespignani, 2001). These variations lead to the existence of local clustering, i.e. the existence of nodes with a very large number of connections. However, for these topologies, even the best power law model may fail to predict a valid epidemic threshold for certain diseases (Rothenberg & Costenbader, 2011).

In these networks, the final size and persistence time of a given epidemic are highly sensitive to the multi-scale hierarchical structure of the considered population (Li & Shao, 2009). For instance, nodes that are in contact with a large number of other nodes are easily infected and constitute a bridge for the spreading of infections (Li & Shao, 2009)(Kretzschmar et al., 2010) (Christakis & Fowler, 2009). These well-connected nodes will enable the potential for an outbreak if there is a non-negligible probability that an infection will reach them, resulting, in the case of large scale-free networks, on the vanishment of the epidemic threshold, i.e. $\lambda_c = 0$ (Pastor-Satorras & Vespignani, 2001)(Li & Shao, 2009). This suggests that even weak infections can spread (Li & Shao, 2009)(Meyers et al., 2005)(Pastor-Satorras & Vespignani, 2001). Moreover, this indicates that infections can spread regardless of their spread rate or effective contact rate ($\beta \ll 1$) (Pastor-Satorras & Vespignani, 2001).

In networks with bounded connectivity, epidemic prevalence is always below the epidemic threshold, resulting in the eventual death of all infections. In scale-free networks, the unbounded nature of the fluctuations in node degree leads to a state of infinite connectivity in the limit of network size. As a consequence, if network size increases, an infection will last longer (Pastor-Satorras & Vespignani, 2001).

Network-based models may be analysed using integrated statistical and intelligent analysis methods to produce stochastic model input data, effectively representing a labelled social contact network. Modelling challenges come from the large size, irregularity and dynamism of the underlying social contact network (Barret et al., 2008).

BACKGROUND ON SOCIAL NETWORK ANALYSIS

Recently, there has been a surge of interest on systems approaches applied to epidemiological research, especially well-suited for social epidemiology (El-Sayed et al., 2012). Such approaches rely on an implicit assumption that the dynamics of a system is different, qualitatively, from those of the sum of its parts.

As such, the relation between system components is more relevant than the attributes of its components by themselves. In the case of network approaches, this means a bigger emphasis on the structural characteristics rather than on nodes characteristics. Therefore, the social ties that influence network actors have important consequences in the analysis (El-Sayed et al., 2012).

Social network analysis involves the characterization of social networks to infer how network structures may influence the exposure risk among its nodes. It pertains the characterization of the components and subcomponents of social networks in order to understand their impact on health and disease. It constitutes the framework in which to analyse factors that have an impact on populations. Moreover, it is a major improvement when compared with techniques base upon the assumption of independence of observations (deterministic and regression-based techniques) (El-Sayed et al., 2012) . This assumption is not verified in network data, as it is inherently relational (Christakis & Fowler, 2009) (El-Sayed et al., 2012).

Disease, information and social support are among health-relevant factors of interest that may impact networks nodes (El-Sayed et al., 2012). Upon the appearance of the Acquired Immunodeficiency Syndrome (AIDS), social network analysis was demonstrated to be suited for infectious contact tracing (Chen, Tseng & King, 2007).

Social networks for the investigation of infectious diseases are typically built with resort to personal contacts only, as these contacts are the most traceable means for disease transmission. Nonetheless, in the case of diseases that transmit through other mechanisms besides personal contacts, the inclusion of geographical contacts into social network analysis methods has been proven to reveal hidden contacts (Chen, Tseng & King, 2007).

Social network analysis is comprised of three main branches:

- **Network Visualization:** Which focuses on diagramming network connections in order to visualize network structure and relationships.
- **Network Characterization:** Directed towards understanding the roles played by individual actors, subgroups of actors, or global network structure while analysing the flow of factors of interest within the network. One example of such an analysis is the comparison of connections an actor possesses in relation to others.
- **Stochastic and Longitudinal Network Analysis:** Intend to perform inferential analysis on networks. While longitudinal analysis allows researchers to study the dynamics of temporal changes, stochastic analysis permits the construction of models targeted at network simulations (El-Sayed et al., 2012).

Representation

Networks constitute a useful construct to represent data that possesses properties with a greater scope than its nodes attributes. Therefore, one can map relationships with resort to network edges. In this context, networks can be used to model different concepts, such as the behaviour of epidemics. For networks whose vertexes stand for individualised social actors and whose edges represent actor relationships, random graph model representations have been the target of recent social network studies (Handcock & Gile, 2010).

Social network data can be represented by a set of N actors and a variable that constitutes their relational tie Y_{ij}, for all ordered actor pairs *(i,j)*, such that $i,j \leq n$ and $i \neq j$. Y_{ij} is usually dichotomous and it indicates the absence or presence of a relationship between two nodes. It can represent disease transmission, academic collaboration, contacts, friendship, or any other form of relationship. This data can be thought of as a $n \times n$ matrix denoted Y, whose diagonal elements represent relations between a node and itself (whose value is typically zero). When considering binary relations between actors, this data can also be represented as a graph, whose nodes map the social actors and edges correspond to their relations. The relations between actors are said to be undirected if $Y_{ij} = Y_{ji}$ for $i, j \leq N$ (Handcock & Gile, 2010), i.e., matrix Y is symmetrical.

Sampling

Sampling is an important factor on the definition of a credible mathematical basis for statistical inference over a social network. This can be shown in the bias that arises from missing data in modelling approaches (Rothenberg & Costenbader, 2011).

Populations of actors can be hard to find, and it is often difficult to obtain data representing all actors and relations. Furthermore, most inference social network models assume that the information obtained is reliable and that the necessary measurements result in no errors. In practice, this is not verified as individuals and links between individuals are typically missed (i.e. they are not part of the recorded data) (Christakis & Fowler, 2009) (Handcock & Gile, 2010).

In sampling, the unit is the node, while the unit of analysis is most commonly the dyad or relation. Under many sampling designs the set of sampled nodes determines the set of sampled relations (Handcock & Gile, 2010).

A sampling design is:

- Conventional if it does not take advantage of the information collected to direct subsequent sampling of individuals.
- Adaptive if it employs the information collected to direct subsequent sampling, and the sampling design depends only on the observed data.

Various sampling strategies may be employed. They are supported on different approaches for network sampling and are grouped under conventional and adaptive designs.

Egocentric sampling is a conventional network sampling design whose steps are:

1. The selection of individuals at random with a given probability.
2. The observation of all dyads involving the selected individuals (i.e. the complete observation of the relations originating from them).

Alternative conventional designs consider the probability sampling of pairs and auxiliary variables (Handcock & Gile, 2010). Examples of adaptive designs are: One-wave link-tracing, Multi-wave link-tracing and Saturated link-tracing.

The process for One-wave link-tracing is comprised by:

1. The selection of individuals at random with a given probability.
2. The observation of all dyads involving the selected individuals (i.e. complete observation of the relations originating from them).

3. The identification of all individuals that have at least one relation with the initial sample, and their selection with probability 1.
4. The observation of all dyads involving these individuals.

For Multi-wave link-tracing or snowball sampling, the process described for one-wave link-tracing is executed k times. If k is a fixed value, then it is called k-wave link-tracing.

Saturated link-tracing is a variant of k-wave link-tracing design, in which sampling continues until wave m is reached, $k < m$ and for which samples$_m = \varnothing$. K is the bound on the number of sampled waves. Since this design does not explicitly limit the number of waves, k = ∞ (Handcock & Gile, 2010).

Nonetheless, these methods possess limitations. Snowball sampling finds people in proportion to their contact centrality, but equilibrium might require a number of waves that is unreasonable. In random walk sampling, sampling is proportional to degree, and convergence can be reached quickly for small groups, but the issues associated with undiscoverable nodes still persist (Rothenberg & Costenbader, 2011).

Lastly, random sampling techniques designed to improve result generalizability may not be suited to network approaches, as the resulting relational data may lack sufficient completeness and accuracy. More concretely, in a population sample, these techniques may collect data about disease exposure, its health outcomes, and the number of social contacts each actor has. However, they will not gather exposures and outcome data that is actor-relational (El-Sayed et al., 2012).

Limitations

Theoretical and empirical data seem to be part of two separate discussions in the process of analysing social networks under the scope of epidemic inquiries. This is reflected in the notion of abduction, a concept that exists between induction (generating theory from data) and deduction (testing theory with data).

The different skill sets that are required and the substantial obstacles to the collection of human network data promote data deficiencies. These along with the ease at which data can be generated by simulations contribute to this issue (Rothenberg & Costenbader, 2011).

Analysis requires network data, which may impose restrictions on result generalizability. Causal inference from currently used network analysis methods is limited, as there are considerable limitations resulting from observational models. Population dynamics are non-linear processes, i.e. a change in disease risk is not always proportional to the change in disease exposure. Furthermore, these relations can be affected by feedback, resulting in confounding, i.e. situations where disease can modulate exposure and vice versa.

The conceptual framework that supports epidemiological inquiry is not enough when taking into account both low-level social causes and macro-social causes for disease (El-Sayed et al., 2012).

Some other factors that contribute to the chasm between the theoretical and empirical approaches are:

- The cost of acquiring the appropriate social network structure is prohibitive, especially for hard-to-reach populations.
- The way in which the relations between individuals and nodes are sampled is not standardised, leading to missing data and hindering information interpretation.
- There is no standard network model to measure against empirical results.

This mismatch results in an increase in theory-based network simulation, where the researcher controls the sampling procedure, creates a standard and measures the effect of the imposed parameters. In these approaches, the assumption of theoretical validity can be emphasized in such a way that empirical verification is missed completely. Researchers are then unable to assess if the reached answers are the valid ones, the reviving the problem of inductive reasoning, which directs epidemiological analysis.

Empirical network descriptions, both qualitative and quantitative, have the potential to find abstract characteristics of a pattern, a task for which theory and simulation are not well suited by themselves. Theoretical analysis is suited to exploring patterns, and they often do it best while decoupled from reality. Nonetheless, they should be directed towards demonstrating mechanisms and testing observations, i.e. the deductive processes (Rothenberg & Costenbader, 2011).

SOLUTIONS

The following architectural modules compose the proposed solution, as depicted in Figure 1.

Both the data sampling and data filtering modules constitute the Sensing layer of the system. The aim of this layer is to obtain processed input data. Sampling complies with user privacy requirements, meaning that both a user's network and contact data are not disclosed to the system without explicit permission.

The data analysis and epidemic prediction modules constitute the learning layer. In this layer, obtained data is transformed and integrated into a model, contributing to the extraction of intelligence in the context of the application problem. Information dissemination comprises the Sharing layer, where system output is returned to its users.

An analysis round constitutes a end-to-end system run, i.e. the flow of data from through these modules. From when it leaves the data source to the instant in which results are returned to the users. An actor is an entity that is part of a social contact network. All sourced actors have a corresponding system mapping, but not all of them carry sensing devices, i.e. they do not take part in the system directly. This means that not all actors are users.

Figure 1. Solution architecture

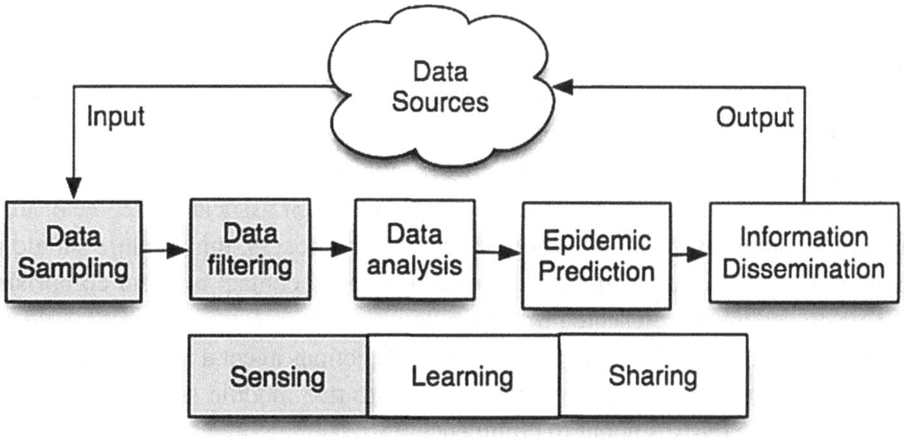

Another important distinction is the one between users and clients. Users are the individuals that participate in the system. Clients are the entities responsible for opportunistic data sampling.

Hereafter, a description of each module is presented.

Data Sampling

In this module, raw data is gathered periodically from the data sources. The delivery of application sampling requests and sampled data are part of this layer. For each individual taking part in the system, the data gathered may belong to one of the following categories, depending on its modality.

- **Network Data:** i.e. Relational data constituting an individual's social network.
- **Contact Data:** i.e. Inferred meetings between individuals.

While network data does not vary significantly, contact data is prone to change more frequently.

Data Filtering

This module performs data anonymization and filtering. To ensure that user identification does not reach the next modules in the chain, it is mapped to another value in an irreversible transformation. This transform has to preserve context, so that the properties required for data merging and processing are respected. Data deemed relevant for the application is kept, while data that may lead to erroneous system behaviour is discarded.

Data Analysis

As the acquired data by the system constitutes different data modalities for different users, it has to be aggregated in a meaningful way.

The purpose of this module is to correlate data that may bear distinct viewpoints and resolutions, processing and merging data and enabling the extraction of higher-meaning information. Previously acquired contact and network data is merged, concluding for all users with whom they met and which social connections exist for them.

The merging process attributes different importance to the relations associated to user ties observed in the network data by measuring them against perceived user meetings. Given that infectious disease spread is primarily achieved by direct contact, contact-related data has a higher impact in this estimation. This process consists in the weighting of network links with the information provided by contact data, as shown in equation (3). Following equation (4), these weights are then scaled based on their average.

The merged data originates a social contact network, containing all the considered individuals. This network accounts for the relationships between all actors with their associated degree of importance in epidemic spread. As data analysis is a computationally costly process, this module should perform on the set of all aggregated data. For each analysis round the social contact network comprising all users is evaluated. This procedure is represented in Figure 2a.

The resulting social contact network is joined with an infectious agent data, constituting an epidemic model. The infectious agent data is predefined and fed into this module as a parameter. The module requests user data when analysis is about to commence.

Figure 2a. Solution epidemic model

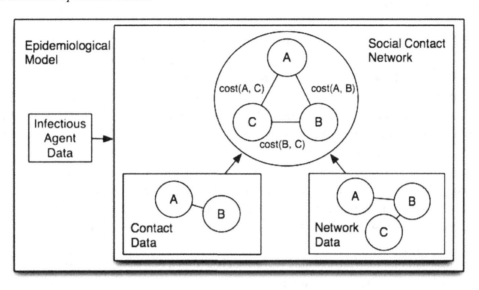

Figure 2b. Social contact network model

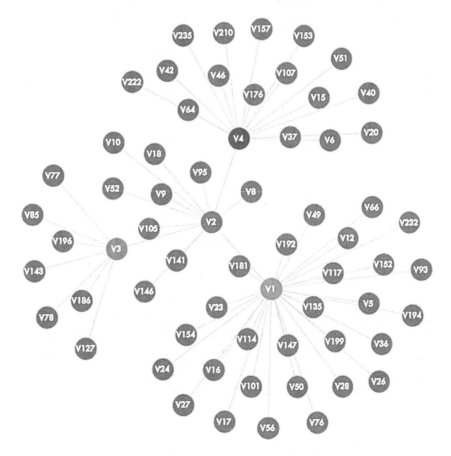

Epidemic Prediction

This module receives the epidemic model resulting from data analysis. By employing the appropriate mathematical formulation and metrics, the evaluation of social contact network for a given epidemic agent's properties is made possible. As a result, the assessment of the dawning of an epidemic is enabled.

Social contact networks may exhibit a wide variety of properties. A network's node degree distribution and isoperimetric constant (or epidemic threshold) are among the most relevant in this area of application. A network configuration is shown in Figure 2b. Since its node degrees are arranged in an exponentially distributed way, it is a scale-free network. Colours are mapped according to node degree.

The idea behind this module is the correlation of network properties and analytical methods applied to epidemiology. More precisely, it is the relation between the isoperimetric constant and the epidemic threshold, as verified in equation (2). By determining and comparing these metrics, it is assessed the network susceptibility to disease outbreaks. Consequently, it is possible to assess a Boolean measure of epidemic risk.

This module is paramount to the learning layer, as it is within it that intelligence is applied to epidemic prediction. Implementation-wise, in conformance with methodology criteria and for scalability reasons, it was desired that this module would use memory parsimoniously and run quickly, while for extensibility reasons, its code should be relatively easy to read and modify. Additionally, it was necessary to find a process through which obtain viable data analysis.

Simulation-oriented strategies demand an extremely complex validation process. Furthermore they are potentially impossible to validate completely (Rothenberg & Costenbader, 2011). These approaches attempt to validate the model by measuring the output of computationally expensive simulations against the public health statistics of an ongoing epidemic (Gorder, 2010). Alternatively, one may employ data from past epidemics, which compromises the results generalization. There is however a significant lack of data in the joint area of social network analysis and epidemiology (Rothenberg & Costenbader, 2011).

In response to the validation demands of epidemic simulation, an analytic network topology approach was selected. The main idea behind the predictive power of this module is the notion that the topological properties of a social contact network can be used to assess epidemic persistence (Schumm et al., 2007) and, thus, its advent. While this approach provides a limited context, it provides accurate results for the data family in analysis.

The prediction algorithm consists in identifying the spectral radius (the maximum of the absolute of the eigenvalues of the adjacency matrix) of the social contact network.

For this purpose, Numeric.js possesses an eigenvalue calculation method, which may be invoked for a square matrix (i.e. a Javascript vector containing n vectors with size n). This feature returns all eigenvalues and eigenvectors for a symmetric matrix and it resorts to the QR algorithm (Parlett, 2000).

However, for a single iteration step, its complexity is of the order of $O(n^3)$, which is prohibitively expensive for large matrices. Additionally, the QR algorithm computes all eigenvalues (and eventually all eigenvectors), which is rarely desirable for sparse matrices (Parlett, 2000). Given these issues behind this computational endeavor for the determination of the dominant eigenvalue, this is even less reasonable. A computationally less expensive trace iteration algorithm can however be employed, given by equation (6),

$$\lambda_{dom} = \lim_{n \to \infty} \left(Tr \left(A^n \right) \right)^{\frac{1}{n}} \qquad (6)$$

where *n* stands for the iteration number and *Tr* is the trace of the matrix A. Nonetheless, this is still a computationally expensive method is expensive. Restricting the number of allowed iterations can lessen its cost, provided that there is an approximation error that is suitable enough for the area of application (Jelonek, 2012). As such, this algorithm was implemented and used in conjunction with Numeric.js.

More sophisticated and effective iterative approaches, like the Arnoldi iteration can be tried to obtain a reduced error. Nonetheless, such would be achieved at the expense of code re-usability and flexibility, which are deemed heavier criteria.

The obtained spectral radius and the infectious agent parameters are inserted into equation (2), which relates the epidemic threshold of the graph associated to the network and the rate of infection transmission and recovery.

This process verifies if there is a subset of actors that possess enough connections, of a relatively high weight, to constitute a weight cluster, and thus form a network bridge. If this subset is representative enough, the existence of network weight bottlenecks will be high enough for the successful spread of disease and the creation of an epidemic. The equations yield a Boolean value, which can be translated into network epidemic vulnerability, if false, or the lack of risk if true. This value is forwarded to the next layer, the Sharing layer.

Information Dissemination

In the Sharing layer, for information dissemination, prediction metrics are transformed into notifications that are forwarded to users. This is done without breaching any of the aforementioned privacy requirements. These notifications result from the translation of epidemic prediction dichotomous results into information that is interpretable by users.

After the system broadcasts this information, an analysis round is deemed concluded. Figure 3 depicts the relation between the previous module and information dissemination.

Figure 3. Solution epidemic prediction and information dissemination

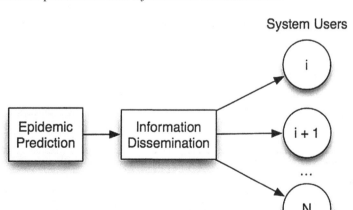

EXPERIMENTAL EVALUATION

The purpose of this section is to assess the general model behaviour with scenarios that can exclude model and implementation shortcomings. Validation is done through the comparison of test outputs with the results of other authors.

Learning Layer Validation and Testing

The main metric to measure is the epidemic threshold λ_c for a given network. Its correct evolution according to other model parameters, such as network size and number of contacts between its actors, is also analysed. With this goal in mind, the data analysis and epidemic prediction modules are used in the aggregation of user contact and network data into a social contact network and subsequent epidemic threshold computations. Data was generated randomly, as previously described.

Social contact networks may result from contact data with zero contacts between its actors. In these cases, the network will still possess an epidemic threshold, as it results from the relations present in network data (i.e. relations analogous to a Facebook friendship).

For the experiments in this section, 50 network samples of different sizes were generated. Their sizes S are included in $\{4, 8, 16, 32, 64, 128, 256\}$. Given the choice of a representative number of contacts, for each of these network sizes S_i, the contact range C_i^R was calculated. It has the form $[0, S_i]$. For each of these intervals, its quartiles were extracted. These were used to generate the set of contact sample sizes C_i, following the expression *{0, 0.25 S_i, 0.5 S_i, 0.75 S_i, S_i}*.

Finally it was determined C_S, the union of all C_i sets, yielding the final set of contact samples sizes. For every number of contacts in this set, 50 samples were generated. Table 2 illustrates the instantiation of C_i for every S_i and the union set C_S.

As for the infectious agent data, it was assumed that the effective contact rate was $\beta_a = 0.025$ and the recovery rate $\delta = 0.2$. The recovery rate value is taken from seasonal influenza. The ratio between both values is in the same order of magnitude as in (Schumm et al., 2007).

In order to acquire statistics, the average for all epidemic threshold approximations is found and placed in a 95% confidence interval. In the experimental charts, the reported average values are marked in black, and the error bars, when present, represent the calculated confidence interval. The following experiments were executed based on the generated data and the system's Learning layer.

Table 2. Contacts per network size and their set union

S_i	C_i
4	$\{0,1,2,3,4\}$
8	$\{0,2,4,6,8\}$
16	$\{0, 4, 8, 12, 16\}$
32	$\{0, 8, 16, 24, 32\}$
64	$\{0, 16, 32, 48, 64\}$
128	$\{0, 32, 64, 96, 128\}$
256	$\{0, 64, 128, 192, 256\}$
S	$\{0,1,2,3,4,6,8,12,16,24,32,48,64,96,128,192,256\}$

Epidemic Threshold Approximation

The purpose of this experiment is the verification of the iterative eigenvalue method used in the epidemic prediction module, whose results are used to calculate the epidemic threshold. This method yields an approximated value and it is necessary to verify that it is both numerically and theoretically correct.

The network data generated as described previously, with resort to *R*, is used. As the aggregation of contact data is independent from these metrics, it is not considered in this experiment.

To have a basis to compare numerical results with, a comparison with R was used. The epidemic prediction approximation of the epidemic threshold is compared with the threshold results produced by R. These results are computed with the maximum of the absolute value of the eigenvalues produced by R's eigenvalue approximation methods. Theoretical correction is ensured if the plotted values follow the epidemic threshold trend foreseen by other authors.

The chart, as shown in Figure 4a, plots the average epidemic threshold for different network sizes and number of iterations. As in (Schumm et al., 2007) and (Pastor-Satorras & Vespignani, 2001), it is verified that as a scale-free network's size increases the epidemic threshold decreases exponentially, eventually leading to its vanishment ($\lambda_c = 0$).

Figure 4a. Epidemic threshold calculated by the system versus R

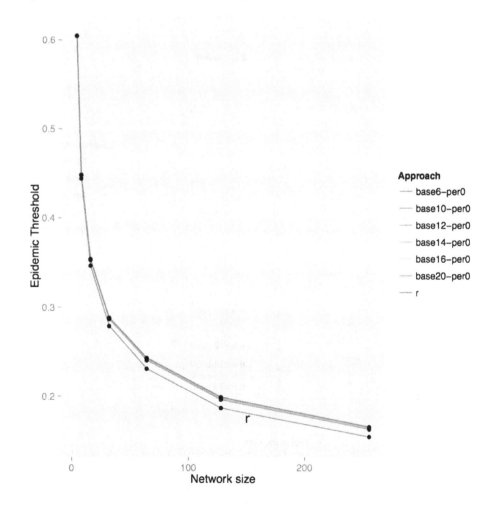

The error between approximations and R should be low enough for the number of iterations used. It can be minimised by increasing the number of iterations used by the algorithm. There is, however, a compromise between algorithm accuracy and computational complexity.

Only even iterations provide usable values, as on odd iterations, the trace of the matrices produced from the social contact network adjacency matrix becomes zero. In Figure 4b, the error between R and the algorithm with different iterations is plotted. It is shown that the error can be greatly reduced with the number of iterations. As such, the implemented algorithm, when properly parameterised, yields results comparable to R.

This algorithm is adequate for being employed in the system. However, as system performance is a concern, one needs to determine a suitable number of iterations to be used. It is visible that from the plotted iteration curves, the one representing 20 iterations provides the best fit. Nonetheless, it was chosen 16 iterations as it yields comparable results for a lower computational cost.

Figure 4b. Epidemic threshold approximation error versus R

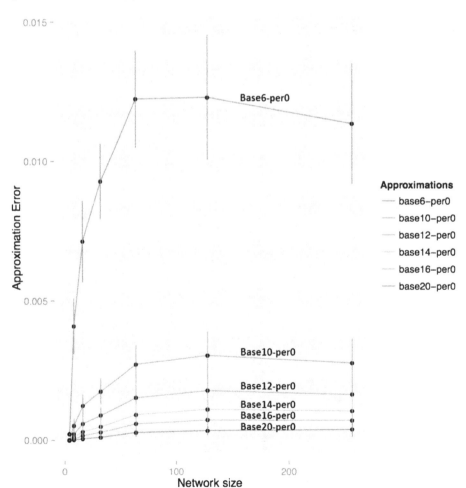

Epidemic Threshold with Weighting and Scaling

This experiment is aimed at assessing if the epidemic threshold is directly increased by the weighting of a network and that scaling is required, as verified in the works of (Schumm et al., 2007) and (Yan et al., 2005).

For the same infectious agent parameters, a given weighted network is more resilient than its weightless counterpart. There is a need to lessen weighting impact, so that network and contact data can be combined without significantly affecting the epidemic threshold. This creates the need for scaling.

To verify this principle, the epidemic threshold for networks of different sizes, produced for these experiments, was plotted in their un-weighted, weighted, and both weighted and scaled versions. The results are presented in Figure 5.

As expected, it is visible that the weighting process clearly boosts the epidemic threshold. Scaling compensates this increase, bringing the epidemic threshold down to values on the same order of magnitude as the original network data.

Figure 5. Epidemic threshold for un-weighted (perG), weighted (perG-w), and both weighted and scaled (perG-ws) networks

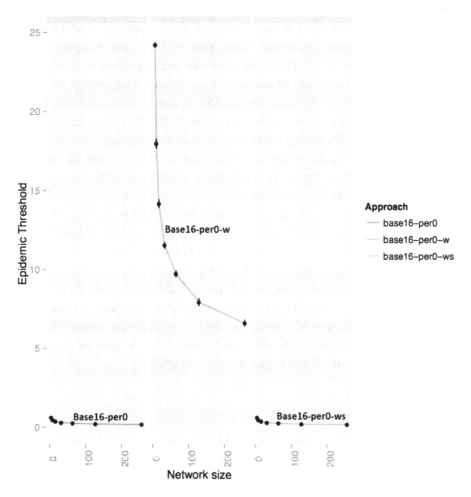

Epidemic Threshold Evolution and Contact Modalities

This experiment is aimed at assessing that the weighting algorithm, performed to merge network and contact data, correctly supports the model assumptions. With this goal in mind, it will be now assessed how different contact modalities impact the epidemic threshold, both in the number and distribution of contacts. It is assumed that more contact diversity in the network should lead to a higher chance of an epidemic.

A contact distribution, in this experiment, can be either egocentric or uniform. In a uniform distribution, contacts are spread evenly between the actors and over the network. Egocentric distributions assign all contacts to a given actor. Contact distribution contributes to the creation and stress of network bottlenecks. In a network configuration with bottlenecks, there are relatively few links between highly clustered sub-networks. Some individuals constitute the sole link between their cluster and the rest of network. Their presence constitutes a bridge to epidemic spread. A small positive epidemic threshold or isoperimetric constant indicates the presence of network bottlenecks. In this way, the creation of network bottlenecks may directly impact the decrease of the isoperimetric constant of a graph. Furthermore, the assignment of a significant number of contacts to a single node should impact the epidemic threshold decrease more significantly than the uniform distribution of the same contacts over more nodes. The number of significant contacts is a function of network size.

These premises can be analytically verified by looking for evidence of a decreasing epidemic threshold. To make this verification possible, for every analysed network size, contact-free control network samples are included for comparison with samples with contacts. If the model implementation is correct, contact-free networks should always yield a higher epidemic threshold than networks with contacts.

Contact data is pre-generated and its attribution within a network is sequential, implying that for different analysis it does not change for a given network. In this data, it is not possible for a node to have a contact with itself, meaning that network loops are not part of the data. Also, contacts are established between members of the network. If external actors were included, the epidemic threshold would decrease due to the introduction of new network nodes and consequent increase in network size.

In Figure 6, the independent axis stands for a relative measure of contacts for network size, denoted as C_n. C_n is the amount of contacts spread on the network and S_n the network size. It should be noted that when $C_n = 0$, there is no contact attribution to the network. The name code for the curves is S_n, standing n for their size.

Figure 6a depicts the epidemic threshold for networks of different network sizes with an increasing contact percentage. This percentage results from the uniform distribution of contacts, which affects the epidemic threshold. It can be concluded that, in this model, a relatively small number of contacts per individual has impact in the creation of network bottlenecks and thus direct impact in epidemic persistence. In a more intuitive explanation, if each individual in a group encounters the same number of individuals, there is an increase in contacts between susceptible individuals in the group that is sufficient for an infectious disease to boost itself and for an epidemic to emerge.

Figure 6a. Epidemic threshold for uniform contacts as a percentage of network size

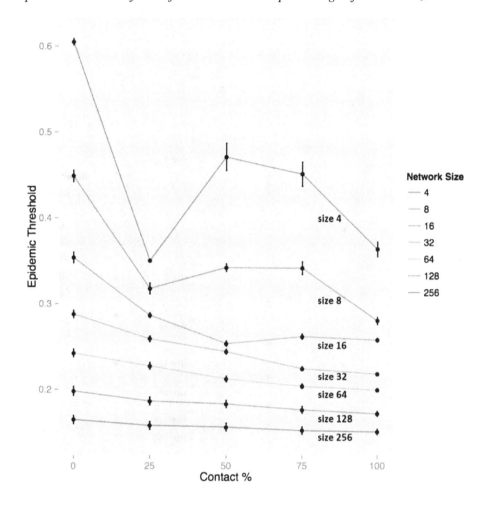

In Figure 6b, the impact of the variation of network size is compared with an increase in contact percentage. The contact distribution is now egocentric. It is noticeable that concentrated contacts lead to a faster decrease in the epidemic threshold, which results from the larger relative bottleneck presence on the resulting network.

In other words, if individuals in a group contact a significant amount of people, a "would be" infectious agent would have more paths to spread and, eventually, break through in the form of an epidemic.

In both scenarios, in networks of relatively smaller size, the contact introduction process greatly impacts the topology (Schumm et al., 2007), effectively reshaping it into providing a threshold that would be expected with larger network sizes. This is associated with their lower size and, thus higher susceptibility to weight clusters.

It is visible that the increase in contacts results in a decrease in epidemic threshold from the initial point of zero contacts in the network. Hence, the impact of contact data in the network is a dominant factor in its susceptibility to an infection (Schumm et al., 2007), in the limit, eclipsing the shape of network data. Thus, with a weighting scheme, it is possible to impact the model without being constrained by the topology of the sampled network. Finally, it is verified that the introduction of random contacts has an impact over network data, resulting in a lower epidemic threshold (Schumm et al., 2007) that decreases with network size.

Figure 6b. Epidemic threshold for egocentric contacts as a percentage of network size

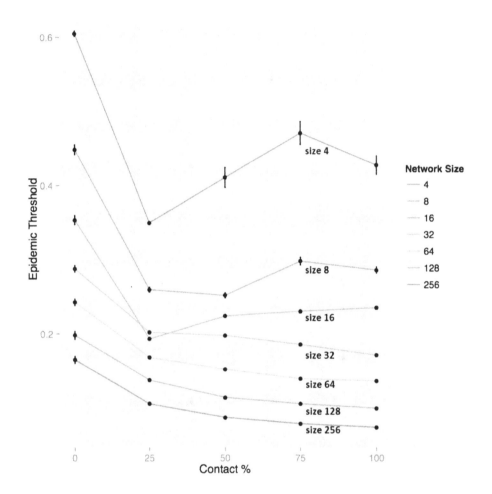

RECOMMENDATIONS

Aiming for improving the outcomes of this work, there are some issues that should be mentioned.

The system explores the assumption that social networks can be modeled as scale-free networks, due to the existing lack of data. Although the model has been assessed to be fit to this assumption, more detailed and realistic social network data on the natural evolution of infectious diseases and their transmission is needed. If access to such data remains unfeasible, more forms of validation including more network topologies and other suitable network-oriented models should be attempted.

Better sampling of relational data can help uncover more interaction patterns. Different approaches to this problematic should be tried, while taking into account heuristic metrics for appropriate sampling size and the shortest path distance between actors. If Facebook is used as a data source, studies presented by Backstrom et al. (2012) can serve as a suitable parameter source.

The case of disconnected users is not covered in the present work, i.e. if two system users do not possess any social contact network neighbor of any degree between them. A more distributed analysis component could help tackle the separate outputs that are required to face this issue.

The bottleneck to system inference is in the size of the sampled network. Furthermore, significant performance improvements and system scalability can be unleashed by taping the potential of divide-and-conquer matrix analysis techniques and by extrapolating the validated analysis to the cloud.

The principle underlying the executed systems approach is that the whole may be different from the sum of its parts. Consequently, it is legitimate that systems models outcomes may contradict the results that are originated from other reductionist approaches (El-Sayed et al., 2012).

The usefulness of system results can be improved and more complex metrics can be produced. When attempting more forms of analysis, often result generalization will become a barrier. In computational epidemiology, future research should aim for a clearer synergy between theory and empiricism, providing the field with a more systemic approach to experimentation and inference (Rothenberg & Costenbader, 2011).

FUTURE RESEARCH DIRECTIONS

The proposed solution deals with privacy concerns within some limitations. Nonetheless, complete data anonymization and data analysis are two areas with somehow contradictory goals. The resulting system solves the issue of distributed resource management distribution by placing most of the concerns on a centralized entity, liberating the mobile sensing devices of unnecessary computation. Other approaches might be superior, but their impact has to be properly assessed and studied.

Cloud technologies constitute a major step in enabling large-scale data merging, analysis and result dissemination. They are the most immediate sound basis for permitting scaling to a population-level analysis and their potential should be harnessed in future work.

Another interesting area of future research concerns the integration with real data from large-scale health sensors. Since only a sample of the users will be carrying sensors, the accuracy of the estimation of epidemics propagation based solely on such a sample needs to be assessed on a real deployment.

CONCLUSION

In the future, mobile sensing systems will provide scaled views of communities and individuals, contributing to solve problems affecting society (Lane et al., 2010). When mobility issues affecting the resolution and accuracy of these systems are finally circumvented, a new area of information extraction will bloom and its numerous applications will bring benefits to the various domains of science. Furthermore, once technical issues are solved, this field has all the potential to constitute an innovative ground-breaking technology applicable to various domains in society, namely social networking, transports, health and energy (Lane et al., 2010).

This chapter presents an innovative system aimed at addressing these technical challenges. A new system architecture to concretize opportunistic mobile sensing systems with the applicational context of epidemic prediction was proposed, implemented and validated. Problems related to the integration of all the requirements imposed on the solution were addressed and possible solutions to such problems proposed by previous scientific work were discussed. The system considers the real-time processing of multi-modal data, such as social network and location data from mobile devices. User data is anonymized and it is only shared after an initial consent, while subsequent sampling occurs opportunistically. Such data is integrated with user social network data (originated from Facebook) and fed into a data merge and analysis algorithm for epidemic prediction.

The system is hence fully automated on an end-to-end perspective. Epidemic prediction is based on the analysis of the epidemic threshold of the sensed network and the infectious agent parameters, resulting in an aggregate metric for epidemic prediction. This analysis is centered on the sampled data and, as such, it is not generalizable to the whole population. Nonetheless, it sets the ground for algorithmic extensions for large-scale data merge and processing.

REFERENCES

Abbas, K., Mikler, A., Ramezani, A., & Menezes, S. (2004). Computational epidemiology: Bayesian disease surveillance. *Proc. of the International Conference on Bioinformatics and its Applications*, USA, pp. 1–12.

Abdelzaher, T., Anokwa, Y., Boda, P., Burke, J., Estrin, D., & Guibas, L. et al. (2007). Mobiscopes for human spaces. *Pervasive Computing, IEEE*, *6*(2), 20–29. doi:10.1109/MPRV.2007.38

Ames, G., George, D., Hampson, C., Kanarek, A., McBee, C., Lockwood, D., Achter, J., & Webb, C. (2011). Using network properties to predict disease dynamics on human contact networks. Proceedings Biological sciences, The Royal Society, 278(1724) 3544–3550.

Backstrom, L., Boldi, P., Rosa, M., Ugander, J., & Vigna, S. (2012). Four degrees of separation. *Proceedings of the 4th Annual ACM Web Science Conference (WebSci '12)*, New York, NY, USA (pp. 33-42). ACM doi:10.1145/2380718.2380723

Barrett, C., Bisset, K., Eubank, S., Feng, X., & Marathe, M. (2008). EpiSimdemics: An efficient algorithm for simulating the spread of infectious disease over large realistic social networks. *International Conference for High Performance Computing Networking Storage and Analysis* (pp. 1–12). doi:10.1109/SC.2008.5214892

Barros, L., Bassanezi, R., Oliveira, R., & Leite, M. (2001). A disease evolution model with uncertain parameters. Proceedings of the IEEE Joint 9th IFSA World Congress and 20th NAFIPS International Conference, vol. 3, no. C., pp. 1626–1630. doi:10.1109/NAFIPS.2001.943794

Brownstein, J., & Freifeld, C. (2007). HealthMap: The development of automated real-time internet surveillance for epidemic intelligence. *Eurosurveillance*, *12*(11). Retrieved from http://www.eurosurveillance.org/ViewArticle.aspx?ArticleId=3322 PMID:18053570

Campbell, A., Eisenman, S., Lane, N., Miluzzo, E., Peterson, R., & Lu, H. et al. (2008). The rise of people-centric sensing. *IEEE Internet Computing*, *12*(4), 12–21. doi:10.1109/MIC.2008.90

Chao, D., Halloran, M., Obenchain, M., & Longini, J. Jr. (2010). FluTE, a Publicly Available Stochastic Influenza Epidemic Simulation Model. *PLoS Computational Biology*, *6*(1), e1000656. doi:10.1371/journal.pcbi.1000656 PMID:20126529

Chen, Y., Tseng, C., & King, C. (2007). Incorporating geographical contacts into social network analysis for contact tracing in epidemiology: A study on Taiwan SARS data. In *Advances in Disease Surveillance: Abstracts from the 2007 Conference of the International Society for Disease Surveillance*. doi:10.1007/978-3-540-72608-1_3

Christakis, N., & Fowler, J. (2009). Social Network Visualization in Epidemiology. Norwegian Journal of Epidemiology [Norsk epidemiologi], 19(1), 5–16.

Christley, R., Pinchbeck, G., Bowers, R., Clancy, D., French, N., Bennett, R., & Turner, J. (2005). Infection in social networks: Using network analysis to identify high-risk individuals. *American Journal of Epidemiology*, *162*(10), 1024–1031. doi:10.1093/aje/kwi308 PMID:16177140

Danon, L., Ford, A., House, T., Jewell, C., Keeling, M., & Roberts, G. et al. (2011). Networks and the epidemiology of infectious disease. *Interdisciplinary Perspectives on Infectious Diseases*, *2011*, 1–28. doi:10.1155/2011/284909 PMID:21437001

El-Sayed, A., Scarborough, P., Seemann, L., & Galea, S. (2012). Social network analysis and agent-based modeling in social epidemiology. Epidemiologic perspectives & innovations: EP+I, 9(1).

Eubank, S. (2002). Scalable, efficient epidemiological simulation. *Proceedings of the 2002 ACM symposium on Applied computing* (pp. 139–145). doi:10.1145/508791.508819

Fisichella, M., Stewart, A., Denecke, K., & Nejdl, W. (2010). Unsupervised public health event detection for epidemic intelligence. *Proceedings of the 19th ACM international conference on Information and knowledge management*, New York, USA. ACM. doi:10.1145/1871437.1871753

Ginsberg, J., Mohebbi, M., Patel, R., Brammer, L., Smolinski, M., & Brilliant, L. (2009). Detecting influenza epidemics using search engine query data. *Nature*, *457*(7232), 1012–1014. doi:10.1038/nature07634 PMID:19020500

Gorder, P. (2010). Computational Epidemiology. *Computing in Science & Engineering*, *12*(1), 4–6. doi:10.1109/MCSE.2010.7

Handcock, M., & Gile, K. (2010). Modeling social networks from sampled data. *The Annals of Applied Statistics*, *4*(1), 5–25. doi:10.1214/08-AOAS221

Jamakovic, A., Kooij, R., Van Mieghem, P., & van Dam, E. (2006). Robustness of networks against viruses: the role of the spectral radius. Proceedings of the Symposium on Communications and Vehicular Technology (Vol. 3, pp. 35–38). doi:10.1109/SCVT.2006.334367

Jelonek, Z. (2012). Solving polynomial equations. *Mathematica Aeterna*, *2*(8), 651–667.

Kansal, A., Goraczko, M., & Zhao, F. (2007). Building a sensor network of mobile phones. In Information Processing in sensor Networks (pp. 547–548).

Kephart, J. (1994). How topology affects population dynamics. In C. Langton (Ed.), *Artificial Life III Studies in the Sciences of Complexity* (pp. 447–463). Addison-Wesley Publishing Co.

Kretzschmar, M., Gomes, M., Coutinho, R., & Koopman, J. (2010). Unlocking pathogen genotyping information for public health by mathematical modeling. *Trends in Microbiology, 18*(9), 406–412. doi:10.1016/j.tim.2010.06.008 PMID:20638846

Lane, N., Miluzzo, E., Lu, H., Peebles, D., Choudhury, T., Campbell, A., & College, D. (2010). A Survey of Mobile Phone Sensing. *IEEE Communications Magazine, 48*(9), 140–150. doi:10.1109/MCOM.2010.5560598

Li, Z., & Shao, G. (2009). Halting Infectious Disease Spread in Social Network. Proceedings of the IEEE IWCFTA'09 International Workshop on Chaos-Fractals Theories and Applications (pp. 305–308). doi:10.1109/IWCFTA.2009.70

Longini, I., Nizam, A., Xu, S., Ungchusak, K., Hanshaoworakul, W., Cummings, D., & Halloran, M. (2005). Containing pandemic influenza at the source. *Science, 309*(5737), 1083–1087. doi:10.1126/science.1115717 PMID:16079251

Lopes, L., Zamite, J., Tavares, B., Couto, F., Silva, F., & Silva, M. (2009). Automated social network epidemic data collector. Proceedings of INForum informatics symposium, Lisboa, (pp. 1–10).

Lu, H., Pan, W., Lane, N., Choudhury, T., & Campbell, A. (2009). SoundSense: scalable sound sensing for people-centric applications on mobile phones. *Proceedings of the 7th international conference on Mobile systems, applications, and services* (pp. 165–178). doi:10.1145/1555816.1555834

Meyers, L., Pourbohloul, B., Newman, M., Skowronski, D., & Brunham, R. (2005). Network theory and SARS: Predicting outbreak diversity. *Journal of Theoretical Biology, 232*(1), 71–81. doi:10.1016/j.jtbi.2004.07.026 PMID:15498594

Miluzzo, E., Lane, N., Fodor, K., Peterson, R., Lu, H., & Musolesi, M. et al. (2008). Sensing meets mobile social networks: the design, implementation and evaluation of the cenceme application. *Proceedings of the 6th ACM conference on Embedded network sensor systems* (pp. 337–350). doi:10.1145/1460412.1460445

Mun, M., Reddy, S., Shilton, K., Yau, N., Burke, J., & Estrin, D. et al. (2009). PEIR, the personal environmental impact report, as a platform for participatory sensing systems research. *Proceedings of the 7th international conference on Mobile systems applications and services Mobisys 09* (pp. 55–68). doi:10.1145/1555816.1555823

Noort, S., Muehlen, M., & Rebelo, A. (2007). Gripenet: An internet-based system to monitor influenza-like illness uniformly across Europe. *Eurosurveillance, 12*(7), 1–14. http://www.ncbi.nlm.nih.gov/pubmed/17991409 PMID:17991409

Parlett, B. (2000). *"The QR algorithm" in Computing in Science & Engineering* (pp. 51–76). College Park, MD: American Institute of Physics. IEEE Computer Society.

Pastor-Satorras, R., & Vespignani, A. (2001). Epidemic Spreading in Scale-Free Networks. *Physical Review Letters, 86*(14), 3200–3203. doi:10.1103/PhysRevLett.86.3200 PMID:11290142

Peebles, D., Lu, H., Lane, N., Choudhury, T., & Campbell, A. (2010). Community-guided learning: Exploiting mobile sensor users to model human behavior. *Proc. of 24th AAAI Conference on Artificial Intelligence.*

Rothenberg, R., & Costenbader, E. (2011). Empiricism and theorizing in epidemiology and social network analysis. *Interdisciplinary Perspectives on Infectious Diseases, 2011,* 1–5. doi:10.1155/2011/157194 PMID:21127746

Schumm, P., Scoglio, C., Gruenbacher, D., & Easton, T. (2007). Epidemic spreading on weighted contact networks. Proceedings of the 2007 IEEE 2nd BioInspired Models of Network Information and Computing Systems (Vol. 1, pp. 201–208).

Teweldemedhin, E., Marwala, T., & Mueller, C. (2004). Agent-based modelling: a case study in HIV epidemic. Proceedings of the 4th International Conference on Hybrid Intelligent Systems.

Yan, G., Zhou, T., Wang, J., Fu, Z., & Wang, B. (2005). Epidemic Spread in Weighted Scale-Free Networks. *Chinese Physics Letters, 22*(2), 510–513. doi:10.1088/0256-307X/22/2/068

Zhang, D., Guo, B., Li, B., & Yu, Z. (2010). Extracting social and community intelligence from digital footprints: an emerging research area. In *Ubiquitous Intelligence and Computing* (pp. 4–18). Springer. doi:10.1007/978-3-642-16355-5_4

KEY TERMS AND DEFINITIONS

Computational Epidemiology: Consists on the development and use of computer models to understand the diffusion of disease through populations with regard to space and time.

Data Sampling: Taking a subset of data for analysis.

Disease Outbreak: The surge of a contagious disease that spreads at a higher rate than usual, among a specific social environment or geographic region during a specific time interval.

Epidemic Prediction: Capability of providing accurate estimates on the epidemic evolution.

Epidemiology Models: Computational mathematical formalism that represents the mechanics behind the propagation of an epidemic.

Scale-Free Networks: Family of networks whose degree distribution obeys a power-law.

Social Network Analysis: Characterization of social networks to infer how network structures may influence the exposure risk among its nodes.

Section 2
Hybrid Intelligent Techniques:
Applications

Chapter 11
Multilevel and Color Image Segmentation by NSGA II Based OptiMUSIG Activation Function

Sourav De
The University of Burdwan, India

Siddhartha Bhattacharyya
RCC Institute of Information Technology, India

Susanta Chakraborty
Indian Institute of Engineering Science and Technology, India

ABSTRACT

A self-supervised image segmentation method by a non-dominated sorting genetic algorithm-II (NSGA-II) based optimized MUSIG (OptiMUSIG) activation function with a multilayer self-organizing neural network (MLSONN) architecture is proposed to segment multilevel gray scale images. In the same way, another NSGA-II based parallel version of the OptiMUSIG (ParaOptiMUSIG) activation function with a parallel self-organizing neural network (PSONN) architecture is purported to segment the color images in this article. These methods are intended to overcome the drawback of their single objective based counterparts. Three standard objective functions are employed as the multiple objective criteria of the NSGA-II algorithm to measure the quality of the segmented images.

INTRODUCTION

Basically, segmentation is the segregation of similar patterns out of dissimilar patterns. A basic and important technique of segregating an image space into multiple non-overlapping meaningful homogeneous regions is on the basis of some characteristics of the pixels, such as, color, intensity or texture, etc. The successful classification of the pixels in an image is done on the basis of the inherent features of that image and for that reason, some *a priori* knowledge or/and presumptions about the image are usually required (Das, Abraham, & Konar, 2008). Due to the variety of the gray scale and color intensity gamut,

DOI: 10.4018/978-1-4666-9474-3.ch011

the problem of segmentation turns more severe for multilevel gray scale and color images. Different fuzzy techniques have been applied successfully for image segmentation as it is quite capable to deal with the varied amount of uncertainty, vagueness and imprecision in the real life images. Zhao *et al.* (Zhao, Fu, & Yan, 2001) proposed an entropy function in the search for fuzzy thresholding parameters by exploiting the relationship between the fuzzy *c*-partition and the probability partition. A spatially weighted fuzzy *c*-means (SWFCM) clustering algorithm is invented by Yang *et al.* (Yang, Zheng, & Lin, 2004). In this method, the global spatial neighboring information is used into the standard FCM clustering algorithm. A good literature survey of the color image segmentation using fuzzy logic is presented in the literature (Bhattacharyya, 2011). A color image segmentation algorithm named, eigen space FCM (SEFCM) algorithm, is efficient to segment the images that have the same color as the pre-selected pixels (Yang, Hao, & Chung, 2002).

Genetic algorithms (GAs) (Goldberg, 1989; Davis, 1991) are randomized search and optimization techniques guided by the principles of evolution and natural genetics. GAs are employed to solve the image segmentation problem without knowing the segmentation techniques applied and only require a segmentation quality measurement criterion due to generality of the GAs. Population generation, natural selection, crossover and mutation are applied over a number of generations for generating potentially better solutions. Alander (Alander, 2000) presented a complete survey of GA based image segmentation. A combined approach of genetic algorithm with the *K*-means clustering algorithm has been employed for image segmentation in (Li & Chiao, 2003). GA is applied in the unsupervised color image segmentation method as it executes multi-pass thresholding (Zingaretti, Tascini, & Regini, 2002) and the different thresholds are employed in different iterations of the genetic algorithm to segment a wide variety of non-textured images successfully. A three-level thresholding method for image segmentation on the basis of probability partition, fuzzy partition and entropy theory is presented by Tao *et al.* (Tao, Tian & Liu, 2003).

Neural networks are very much efficient for the processing of the images as neural networks have different important properties like high degree of parallelism, nonlinear mapping, ability of approximation, error tolerance etc. The segmentation of gray scale images as well as color images are quite efficiently handled by the neural network. Kohonen's self-organizing feature map (SOFM) (Kohonen, 1989) is a renowned and efficient competitive neural network due to its properties such as the input space approximation, topological ordering, and density matching (Chi, 2011). The utility of SOFM in the field of image segmentation, such as segmentation of printed fabric images, or in sonar images is fully accounted in (Xu & Lin, 2002; Yao *et. al.*, 2000). Kohonen's SOFM in accordance with the hybrid genetic algorithm (HGA) is employed efficiently to segment the satellite images (Awad, Chehdi & Nasri, 2007). A fast convergent network named Local Adaptive Receptive Field Self-organizing Map (LARFSOM) is applied to segment color images efficiently (Arajo & Costa, 2009).

A single multilayer self-organizing neural networks (MLSONN) (Ghosh, Pal & Pal, 1993) is capable to extract the binary objects from a noisy binary image scene. In this network, the network weights are adjusted with a view to derive a stable solution using the standard backpropagation algorithm (Ghosh, Pal & Pal, 1993). The multilevel objects cannot be extracted with this network architecture since it is characterized by the generalized bilevel/bipolar sigmoidal activation function. A functional modification has been incorporated in the MLSONN architecture by Bhattacharyya *et al.* (Bhattacharyya, 2008, 2011). They introduced the multilevel sigmoidal (MUSIG) (Bhattacharyya, 2008, 2011) activation function that is employed for mapping multilevel input information into multiple scales of gray. The different transition levels of the MUSIG activation function is determined by the number of gray scale objects and the representative gray scale intensity levels. Since this activation function employ fixed and uniform thresholding parameters, they assume homogeneous image information content, which on the contrary, generally exhibit a varied amount of heterogeneity. The parallel version of the MLSONN (PSONN) architecture (Bhattacharyya, 2003, 2007, 2012) which consists of three independent and parallel MLSONNs, is employed to extract the pure color images from a noisy color image background and the individual MLSONNs of the PSONN are responsible to process the individual color components. Like the MLSONN architecture, the MUSIG activation function has been also introduced in the PSONN architecture for true color image segmentation. To overcome this drawback, De *et al.* (De, Bhattacharyya, & Dutta, 2010) proposed the optimized MUSIG (OptiMUSIG) activation function which is capable to segment multilevel gray scale images by incorporating the heterogeneous information content in the MUSIG activation function. The color images are segmented by the parallel version of the OptiMUSIG (ParaOptiMUSIG) activation function (De, Bhattacharyya, & Chakraborty, 2012, 2010) in connection with the PSONN architecture. These methods may or may not generate a good quality segmented image as the segmentation criteria of these methods are based on a single objective or single segmentation evaluation criterion. Usually, there will be a set of alternative solutions instead of a single optimal solution when we consider different criterions of a problem at a go. Simultaneous optimization of multiple segmentation evaluation measures serves to handle with different characteristics of segmentation and generates good segmented images when all constraints are considered. Instead of getting a single optimal solution, a set of optimal solutions are generated and these set of optimal solutions are defined as the Pareto-optimal solutions. Motivated by this, a popular evolutionary multiobjective optimization technique, named Non-dominated Sorting Genetic Algorithm-II (NSGA-II) (Deb, 2001) has been applied in this proposed image segmentation technique that optimizes some evaluation/ goodness measures simultaneously. A good survey of image segmentation by several multiobjective optimization (MOO) techniques is depicted in the literature (Chin-Wei & Rajeswari, 2010). Multiobjective genetic clustering based method is applied to segregate the pixels of remote sensing images in (Bandyopadhyay, Maulik, & Mukhopadhyay, 2007). A good use of MOO in image segmentation with thresholding techniques has been prevailed by Nakib *et al.* (Nakib, Oulhadj, & Siarry, 2010). Bandyopadhyay *et al.* (Bandyopadhyay, Srivastava, & Pal, 2002) proposed a multi objective genetic algorithm based classifier, named CEMOGA-classifier, for segmenting the remote sensing images. This classifier can able to recognize the pixels belonging to a class, given its intensity values in multiple bands.

The drawback of the single objective based OptiMUSIG activation function for segmentation of multilevel gray scale images and the single objective based parallel OptiMUSIG (ParaOptiMUSIG) activation function for color images are attempted to overcome in this proposed article. In this article, the multilevel gray scale images are segmented into different number of classes with the NSGA II based optimized class levels which are employed to generate an optimized MUSIG (OptiMUSIG) activation function. This activation function is applied in a single MLSONN architecture for segmenting multilevel gray scale images. Like the gray scale image segmentation, the optimized class levels for distinct color components which are generated in parallel by means of NSGA II based optimization techniques are applied to generate the ParaOptiMUSIG activation function. The individual SONNs in a PSONN architecture are fed with the distinct color components after segregating the input true color images into different color components. The NSGA II based ParaOptiMUSIG activation function is employed in PSONN architecture to segment the color images. The application of the proposed NSGA II based OptiMUSIG activation function approach is presented using two real life multilevel gray scale images, viz. the Baboon and Peppers images. The color version of these images have been applied to demonstrate the applications of the proposed NSGA II based ParaOptiMUSIG activation function approach. The standard measure of correlation coefficient (ρ) (Bhattacharyya, 2008), F due to Liu and Yang (Liu, & Yang, 1994) and F' due to Borsotti *et al.* (Borsotti, Campadelli, & Schettini, 1998) are used as the fitness functions and to be optimized in this NSGA II based proposed method. Ultimately, it has been proved on the basis of the results that the segmentation using the proposed NSGA II based OptiMUSIG and ParaOptiMUSIG activation functions perform better than the conventional MUSIG activation function employing heuristic class responses.

The outline of this chapter is as follows. The next section demonstrates about the multiobjective optimization problem. A brief overview of the multilayer self-organizing neural network (MLSONN) architecture and the parallel version of the self-organizing neural network (PSONN) are presented in the subsequent section with reference to the basic neuronal model, its mathematical formalism, constituent components, structure and topology. The operational mechanism and the characteristics of the NSGA II based optimized multilevel sigmoidal (OptiMUSIG) activation function and the NSGA II based parallel optimized multilevel sigmoidal (ParaOptiMUSIG) activation function are illustrated in the following two sections. Different image segmentation metrics those are used in this article are demonstrated in the next section. The next section is followed by the detailed representation of the proposed methodology to segment the multilevel gray scale as well as true color images. The image segmentation results, both in qualitative and quantitative nature, are detailed in the next section. The chapter ends with a brief concluding section.

MULTIOBJECTIVE OPTIMIZATION

Optimization of many real world problems are basically based on several conflicting objectives instead of a single objective. Multiobjective optimization is discerned as findings of one or more optimal solutions as the optimization problem optimizes more than one objective functions. Formally, the definition of the multiobjective optimization is represented as (Deb, 2001): determine the vector function

$$\bar{f}(\bar{x}) = \left[\bar{f}_1(\bar{x}), \bar{f}_2(\bar{x}), ..., \bar{f}_k(\bar{x}) \right]^T \tag{1}$$

subject to the *m* inequality constraints, $g_i(\bar{x}) \geq 0, i = 1, 2, ..., m$ and the *p* equality constraints (Deb, 2001), $h_i(\bar{x}) = 0, i = 1, 2, ..., p$, where *k* is the number of objective functions ... The vector of *n* decision variables $\bar{x} = \left(x_1, x_2, ..., x_n \right)^T$ is resultant solution, $\bar{x}$, where $x_i^L \leq \bar{x} \leq x_i^U, i = 1, 2, .., n$. Each decision variable x_i is limited in between the lower bound $\left(x_i^L \right)$ and upper bound $\left(x_i^U \right)$. The feasible region F which contains all the admissible solutions is defined by the equality and inequality constraints. Any solutions outside of this region will not be considered as it violates one or more constraints. A multiobjective optimization problem can be expressed mathematically only in terms of non-dominated solutions or Pareto optimal solutions. From the standpoint of minimization problem, the formal definition of Pareto optimality may be defined as (Deb, 2001; Mukhopadhyay, & Maulik, 2011): a decision vector $\bar{x}^*$ is defined as Pareto optimal if and only if there is no $\bar{x}$ that dominates $\bar{x}^*$, i. e., there is no $\bar{x}$ such that $\forall i \in \left\{ 1, 2, .., n \right\} : f_i\left(x_1^* \right) \geq f_i\left(x_2^* \right)$ and $\exists j \in \left\{ 1, 2, .., n \right\} : f_j\left(x_1^* \right) > f_j\left(x_2^* \right)$. The Pareto optimal solutions are usually referred as the nondominated solutions. Among several modern multiobjective optimization techniques, the GA based elitist multiobjective techniques are NSGA II (Deb, 2001), SPEA (Zitzler, & Thiele, 1998) and SPEA 2 (Zitzler, Laumanns, & Thiele, 2001) are very much popular. Amongst these algorithms, NSGA-II has been applied in this article for the generation of NSGA-II based OptiMUSIG and ParaOptiMUSIG activation function for multilevel gray scale and color image segmentation, respectively.

MULTILAYER SELF-ORGANIZING NEURAL NETWORK (MLSONN) ARCHITECTURE

The multilayer self-organizing neural network (MLSONN) (Ghosh, Pal & Pal, 1993) architecture is a feed forward neural network architecture that comprises an input layer, any number of hidden layers and an output layer. It works in a self-supervised manner to extract binary objects from noisy backgrounds. The input image intensity information which are received from the outside world in the range [0, 1] is fed into the input layer of the network. The neuron of each layer is however, connected to the corresponding neuron in the previous layer and to its neighbors in that layer following a neighborhood based topology. The hidden layer accepts the processed information from the input layer neurons of the network. The different layer neurons process this incoming information using the standard bilevel sigmoidal activation function. The network system errors at the output layer neurons are calculated from the corresponding linear indices of fuzziness (Ghosh, Pal & Pal, 1993) as the network operates in a self-supervised manner and there are no target outputs to compare with. The standard backpropagation algorithm (Haykin, 1999; Rojas, 1996) is employed to determine the system errors which are applied to adjust the neighborhood topology-based interconnection weights between the different network layers. After weight adjustment, the outputs derived at the output layer of the network are fed back to the input layer via output-input layer connections. The next stage of processing of the initial input information is repeated till the interconnection weights stabilize or the system errors are reduced below some tolerable limits. In this way, the different noise-free binary objects and background regions are segregated from the input information. Interested readers are suggested to go through (Ghosh, Pal & Pal, 1993) for details regarding the architecture and operational characteristics of the MLSONN network architecture.

The parallel version of the self-organizing neural network (PSONN) (Bhattacharyya, 2003, 2007, 2012) is capable to extract pure color/binary color objects from a pure color image. This network consists of three independent single three-layer self-organizing neural network (SONN) (Bhattacharyya, 2003, 2007, 2012) for component level processing in accordance with a source layer for inputs to the network and a sink layer for generating the final network output. The source layer disseminates the primary color component information of true color images into the three parallel SONN architectures. After processing of each color components at these three parallel SONN architectures, the sink layer fuses and generates the final pure color output images. However, the three parallel self-organizing neural network architectures operate in a self-supervised mode on multiple shades of color component information (Bhattacharyya, 2003). The functionality of the individual SONN of the PSONN is same as the functionality of the previously discussed MLSONN. The architecture and operational characteristics of the PSONN architecture is discussed in (Bhattacharyya, 2003, 2007, 2012) in detail.

The MLSONN network architecture (Ghosh, Pal & Pal, 1993) and PSONN (Bhattacharyya, 2003, 2007, 2012) network architecture are not capable to segment multilevel input images i. e. inputs which consist of different heterogeneous shades of image pixel intensity levels. The use of the standard bilevel sigmoidal activation function in these network architectures is the main cause for this drawback. For this reason, a multilevel version of the generalized bilevel sigmoidal activation function is introduced by Bhattacharyya *et al.* (Bhattacharyya, 2008, 2011). The novelty of the multilevel sigmoidal (MUSIG) activation (Bhattacharyya, 2008, 2011) function lies in its ability to map inputs into multiple output levels and can efficiently able to segment the multilevel gray scale as well as color images.

NSGA II BASED OPTIMIZED MULTILEVEL SIGMOIDAL (OPTIMUSIG) ACTIVATION FUNCTION

One of the targets of this article is to segment multilevel gray scale images using MLSONN architecture (Ghosh, Pal & Pal, 1993) by NSGA-II based optimized activation function. Neural network is quite efficient enough to manage the segmentation of the multidimensional datapoints of the dataset due to its parallelism characteristics. The researchers are keen to apply neural networks for processing of gray scale images as well. The neural networks reach their goals by updating the network weights dynamically. The operational characteristics of the neural networks mainly depend on the activation function. It will be quite helpful if the activation function is capable to handle multilevel characteristics of the dataset instead of including multiple layers for multilevel datasets.

The multiscaling ability is incorporated into a MLSONN architecture by the modified version of the standard bilevel sigmoidal activation function of the MLSONN architecture which has been proposed by Bhattacharyya *et al.* (Bhattacharyya, 2008, 2011). The multilevel sigmoidal (MUSIG) activation function is presented in (Bhattacharyya, 2008, 2011). The detailed characteristics and functionality of MUSIG activation function is narrated in those articles. This function is not dependent on the nature as this function is generated with the randomly chosen class boundaries from the feature histograms of the input datapoints. The heterogeneity of the underlying features of the datapoints has been overlooked. The class levels of the datapoints can be integrated in the characteristics neuronal activations by the optimized class boundaries deduced from the dataset. The optimized version of the MUSIG activation (OptiMUSIG) (De, 2010) function, using optimized class boundaries, can be represented as (De, 2010)

$$f_{OptiMUSIG}\left(x; \eta_{\alpha_{opt}}, cl_{\alpha_{opt}}\right) = \sum_{\alpha_{opt}=1}^{K-1} \frac{1}{\eta_{\alpha_{opt}} + e^{-\lambda\left[x-\left(\alpha_{opt}-1\right)cl_{\alpha_{opt}} - \theta_{var}\right]}} \tag{2}$$

where, α_{opt} represents the optimized feature class index ($1 \leq \alpha_{opt} < K$) and the total number of feature classes is represented as K. The slope of the activation function is denoted as λ. $cl_{\alpha_{opt}}$ and $cl_{\alpha_{opt}-1}$ are the optimized feature contributions corresponding to optimized class boundaries of the α_{opt}^{th} and $\left(\alpha_{opt}-1\right)^{th}$ classes, respectively. $\eta_{\alpha_{opt}}$ represents the multilevel optimized class responses and it is denoted as

$\eta_{\alpha_{opt}} = \dfrac{C_N}{cl_{\alpha_{opt}} - cl_{\alpha_{opt}-1}}$. The variable threshold, θ_{var}, depends on the optimized class boundaries and is represented as (De, 2010) $\theta_{var} = cl_{\alpha_{opt}} + \dfrac{cl_{\alpha_{opt}} - cl_{\alpha_{opt}-1}}{2}$. Basically, the single objective based OptiMU-SIG activation function is efficient to segment the multilevel gray scale images. It does not assured that the derived multilevel gray scale segmented output image is the good one in respect of all other fitness criterions.

In this article, the optimized class levels are generated on the basis of more than one criterion to overcome the problem. The popular and efficient multiobjective based algorithm, NSGA-II, is applied to generate the optimized class levels. The NSGA II based OptiMUSIG activation function $\left(\overline{f}_{Opti_{NSGA}} \left(\overline{x} \right) \right)$ is proposed in this article and it is denoted as

$$\overline{f}_{Opti_{NSGA}} \left(\overline{x} \right) = \left[\overline{f}_{Opti_{F_1}} \left(\overline{x} \right), \overline{f}_{Opti_{F_2}} \left(\overline{x} \right), ..., \overline{f}_{Opti_{Fn}} \left(\overline{x} \right) \right]^T \qquad (3)$$

subject to $g_{Opti_{F_i}} \left(\overline{x} \right) \geq 0, i = 1, 2, ..., m$ and $h_{Opti_{F_i}} \left(\overline{x} \right) = 0, i = 1, 2, ..., p$ where, $f_{Opti_{F_i}} \left(\overline{x} \right) \geq 0, i = 1, 2, ..., n$ are different objective functions in the NSGA II based OptiMUSIG activation function. $g_{Opti_{F_i}} \left(\overline{x} \right) \geq 0, i = 1, 2, ..., m$ and $h_{Opti_{F_i}} \left(\overline{x} \right) = 0, i = 1, 2, ..., p$ are the inequality and equality constraints of this function, respectively.

NSGA II BASED PARALLEL OPTIMIZED MULTILEVEL SIGMOIDAL (PARAOPTIMUSIG) ACTIVATION FUNCTION

Another objective of this article is the color image segmentation, using the PSONN architecture (Bhattacharyya, 2003, 2007, 2012) by embedding optimized functional characteristics in the constituent SONN primitives obtained from the color image context. This problem can be treated as an extension of the multidimensional dataset in which the segmentation of every feature can be accomplished in parallel. After obtaining the segmented value of all the features in the parallel, segmentation process is combined to get the resultant segmented value of that datapoint. Same as the single dimensional dataset, the different class levels for the segmentation of such a dataset can be usually selected heuristically from the histograms of the kth features of the dataset. The heterogeneity of the underlying information has been ignored as the datapoints in a real life dataset generally manifest a fair amount of heterogeneity and the class levels generally differ from one dataset to another. Applying the parallelism characteristics of the neural network, the segmentation of the multidimensional datapoints of the dataset can be easily managed. The individual neural networks are applied to process the individual feature of the multidimensional datapoints in parallel and independently. The way of component level processing of incident feature of the multidimensional datapoints is quite effectively dealt with the PSONN architecture (Bhattacharyya, 2003, 2007, 2012).

Each constituent SONN primitive of PSONN (Bhattacharyya, 2003, 2007, 2012) architecture is characterized with individual and separate OptiMUSIG activation function with appropriate optimized parameter settings. The parallel representation of the OptiMUSIG (ParaOptiMUSIG) activation function for the *R*, *G* and *B* color component of a color image is referred as (De, Bhattacharyya, & Chakraborty, 2012, 2010)

$$f_{ParaOptiMUSIG} = \sum_{t \in \{t_R, t_G, t_B\}} f_{t_{OptiMUSIG}} \qquad (4)$$

where t_R, t_G, t_B denotes the different layers of the neural network for R, G and B color components, respectively. The $f_{t_{OptiMUSIG}}$ denotes the OptiMUSIG activation function for one layer of the network (De, 2012). The collection of the OptiMUSIG functions of different layers is denoted by the Σ sign. The optimized class boundaries for different OptiMUSIG activation functions of different layers are generated by the genetic algorithm in parallel.

Like the OptiMUSIG activation function, the optimized class levels for the different color components of the ParaOptiMUSIG activation function are generated with the help of the single objective based algorithm and it does not ensure that the resultant segmented color images are good for the other criterions. The NSGA-II based ParaOptiMUSIG activation function $\left(\overline{f}_{Para_{NSGA}} \left(\overline{x} \right) \right)$ is presented in this article to segment the color images on the basis of more than one criterions. This function $\left(\overline{f}_{Para_{NSGA}} \left(\overline{x} \right) \right)$ is represented as

$$\overline{f}_{Para_{NSGA}} \left(\overline{x} \right) = \left[\overline{f}_{Para_{F_1}} \left(\overline{x} \right), \overline{f}_{Para_{F_2}} \left(\overline{x} \right), ..., \overline{f}_{Para_{Fn}} \left(\overline{x} \right) \right]^T \qquad (5)$$

subject to

$$g_{Para_{F_i}} \left(\overline{x} \right) \geq 0, i = 1, 2, ..., m \text{ and } h_{Para_{F_i}} \left(\overline{x} \right) = 0, i = 1, 2, ..., p$$

where, $f_{Para_{F_i}} \left(\overline{x} \right) \geq 0, i = 1, 2, ..., n$ are different objective functions in the NSGA II based ParaOptiMUSIG activation function.

$$g_{Para_{F_i}} \left(\overline{x} \right) \geq 0, i = 1, 2, ..., m \text{ and } h_{Para_{F_i}} \left(\overline{x} \right) = 0, i = 1, 2, ..., p$$

are the inequality and equality constraints of this function, respectively.

WELL KNOWN IMAGE SEGMENTATION QUALITY EVALUATION METRICS

The goodness of the segmented image of the existing segmentation algorithms have been determined by several unsupervised approaches (Zhang, 1996). Some of these measures are discussed in the following subsections.

Correlation Coefficient

The correlation coefficient (ρ) (Bhattacharyya, 2008), applied to evaluate the quality of the segmented images, is denoted as (Bhattacharyya, 2008)

$$\rho = \frac{\dfrac{1}{n^2}\sum_{i=1}^{n}\sum_{j=1}^{n}\left(H_{ij}-\bar{H}\right)\left(G_{ij}-\bar{G}\right)}{\sqrt{\dfrac{1}{n^2}\sum_{i=1}^{n}\sum_{j=1}^{n}\left(H_{ij}-\bar{H}\right)^2}\sqrt{\dfrac{1}{n^2}\sum_{i=1}^{n}\sum_{j=1}^{n}\left(G_{ij}-\bar{G}\right)^2}} \tag{6}$$

where, $H_{ij}, 1 \leq i, j \leq n$ and $G_{ij}, 1 \leq i, j \leq n$ are the original and the segmented images respectively, each of dimensions $n \times n$. H and G are the respective mean intensity values of H_{ij} and G_{ij}, respectively. The better quality of segmentation is denoted by the higher value of ρ.

Empirical Measures (F (M), F' (M), and Q (M))

Liu and Yang (Liu, & Yang, 1994) proposed a quantitative evaluation function (EF), F (M), denoted as (Liu, & Yang, 1994)

$$F\left(M\right) = \sqrt{N}\sum_{r=1}^{N}\frac{e_r^2}{\sqrt{S_r}} \tag{7}$$

where, the entire image is denoted as M and N signifies the number of arbitrarily shaped regions of the image. RE_r represents the number of pixels in region r. The area of the r region is represented as $S_r = |RE_r|$. e_r^2 the squared color error of region r, is given as (Liu, & Yang, 1994)

$$e_r^2 = \sum_{v\in(R,G,B)}\sum_{px\in RE_r}\left(C_v\left(px\right)-\overline{C_v}\left(RE_r\right)\right)^2.$$

Here, $\overline{C_v}\left(RE_r\right)$ is the average value of feature v (Red, Green or Blue) of a pixel px in region r and

denoted as (Liu, & Yang, 1994) $\overline{C_v}\left(RE_r\right) = \dfrac{\sum_{px\in RE_r}C_v(px)}{S_r}$,where, $C_v(px)$ denotes the value of component v for pixel px. The lower value of F signifies the better quality of segmentation.

Borsotti *et al.* (Borsotti, Campadelli, & Schettini, 1998) suggested another EF, F' (M), that improved the performance of Liu and Yang's method (Liu, & Yang, 1994) and it is denoted as

$$F'(M) = \frac{1}{1000\cdot S_M}\sqrt{\sum_{u=1}^{Maxarea}\left[N\left(u\right)\right]^{1+\frac{1}{u}}}\sum_{r=1}^{N}\frac{e_r^2}{\sqrt{S_r}} \tag{8}$$

where, S_M is the area of an image (M) to be segmented. *Maxarea* is represented as the area of the largest region in the segmented image. N (u) denotes the number of regions in the segmented image having an area of exactly u. The quality of segmentation increases as the $F'(M)$ value of the segmented image decreases.

Borsotti *et al*. (Borsotti, Campadelli, & Schettini, 1998) proposed another *EF*, Q (M), represented as

$$Q\left(M\right) = \frac{1}{1000 \cdot S_M} \sqrt{N} \sum_{r=1}^{N} \left[\frac{e_r^2}{1 + \log S_r} + \left(\frac{N\left(S_r\right)}{S_r} \right)^2 \right] \tag{9}$$

where, $N(S_r)$ stands for the number of regions having an area S_r. As the Q (M) value of the segmented image decreases, the quality of the segmentation enhances.

These measures have been employed as different objective functions for the proposed NSGA II based optimization procedure to design the optimized multilevel sigmoidal activation function.

PROPOSED METHODOLOGY

The proposed methodology has been rendered into two parts in this article. In the first subsection, the gray scale image segmentation by NSGA II based OptiMUSIG activation function with a MLSONN architecture is discussed and after that, color image segmentation by NSGA II based ParaOptiMUSIG activation function with a PSONN architecture is depicted. The flow diagrams of both the methods are depicted in Figure 1.

Gray Scale Image Segmentation

In this section, the gray scale image segmentation process has been discussed using the NSGA II based OptiMUSIG activation function with a MLSONN architecture and it has been operated in three phases. The different phases of this method are depicted in Figure 1 (a) and elaborated in the following subsections.

1. **Generation of Optimized Class Boundaries for Gray Scale Images by NSGA II Algorithm:** This is the most important phase of the proposed approach. The NSGA II based optimization procedure is employed to generate the optimized class boundaries $\left(cl_{\alpha_{opt}} \right)$ of the proposed NSGA II based OptiMUSIG activation function. The detailed description of this stage is described as follows:

    a. **Initialization Phase:** The pixel intensity levels of the gray scale image and the number of classes (K) to be segmented are supplied as inputs to this NSGA II based optimization procedure in this phase.

    b. **Chromosome Representation and Population Generation:** The real numbered chromosomes are applied in the NSGA II algorithm and the real numbers are generated randomly between maximum and minimum gray scale value of the test images. A population size of 200 has been utilized in this treatment.

Figure 1. (a) Flow diagram of gray scale image segmentation using NSGA II based OptiMUSIG activation function; (b) flow diagram of color image segmentation using NSGA II based ParaOptiMUSIG activation function

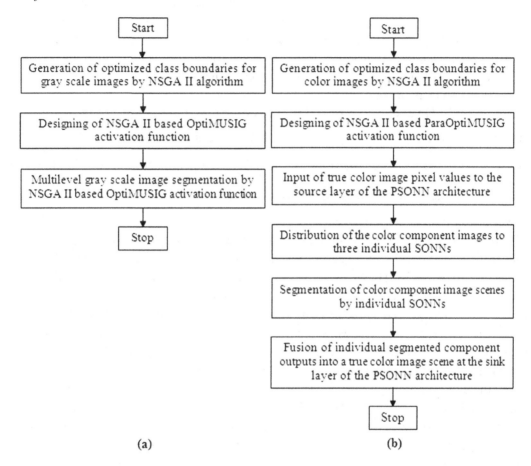

(a)   (b)

c. **Fitness Computation:** In this phase, three segmentation evaluation metrices (ρ, F, F') given in equations 6, 7 and 8 respectively, are applied as the fitness functions.

d. **Genetic Operators:** Selection, crossover and mutation, three common genetic operators, are applied in this method. The selection operator, the crowded binary tournament selection, is applied in NSGA-II. After selection, the selected chromosomes are put in the mating pool for the crossover and mutation operation. The crossover probability is taken as 0.8 and the mutation probability is chosen as 0.01 in this approach. In the next generation of NSGA II, the non-dominated solutions among the parent and child populations are propagated. In this approach, this process continued for 10^4 iterations. After the last generation, the near-pareto-optimal strings render the desired solutions.

e. **Selecting a Solution from the Non-Dominated Set:** A particular solution has to be selected from the set of non-dominated solutions those have rank one in the NSGA-II algorithm to design the OptiMUSIG activation function. For that reason, a suitable cluster validity index is needed to determine the particular solution. Some well-known clustering algorithms, like Davies-Bouldin (DB) index (Davies, & Bouldin, 1979), CDbw (Composed Density between and within clusters) (Halkidi, & Vazirgiannis, 2002) cannot be employed in every sector of clustering application. DB index works efficiently only for spherical clusters (Pal, & Biswas, 1997) as it is very much noise sensitive. The image segmentation evaluation index like entropy-based index (Zhang, Fritts, & Goldman, 2004) or quantitative-based index (Borsotti, Campadelli, & Schettini, 1998) are efficient enough to assess the image clustering results. A lower quantitative value or entropy value signifies to better segmentations. The empirical measure, Q index has been employed to select the better chromosomes from the selected chromosome pool in this approach.

2. **Designing of NSGA II Based OptiMUSIG Activation Function:** The NSGA II based OptiMUSIG activation function has been designed with the help of the optimized class boundaries $\left(cl_{\alpha_{opt}} \right)$ those are selected in the Pareto optimal set. The $\eta_{\alpha_{opt}}$ parameters are determined using the optimized $\left(cl_{\alpha_{opt}} \right)$. These parameters are further employed to obtain the different transition levels of the NSGA II based OptiMUSIG activation function.

3. **Multilevel Gray Scale Image Segmentation by NSGA II based OptiMUSIG Activation Function:** The real-life multilevel gray scale images are segmented by the single MLSONN architecture characterized by NSGA II based OptiMUSIG activation function in this last phase. The succeeding network layers propagate the processed input information. Different gray level responses of the input image have been assessed by the neurons of the different layers of the MLSONN architecture. As it is a self-supervised neural network, the MLSONN architecture has no *a priori* knowledge about the outputs. The subnormal linear index of fuzziness (Bhattacharyya, 2008) is employed to determine the system errors at the output layer of the MLSONN architecture. These errors are used to adjust the interconnection weights between the different layers using the standard backpropagation algorithm (Haykin, 1999; Rojas, 1996). The outputs of the output layer of the network is transferred to the input layer of the network to minimize the system errors for further processing. The original input image gets segmented into different multilevel regions depending upon the optimized transition levels of the OptiMUSIG activation function after the self-supervision of the network attains stabilization.

Color Image Segmentation

The color image segmentation process by the NSGA II based ParaOptiMUSIG activation function with a PSONN architecture has been described in this section and the flow diagram of this process is shown in Figure 1 (b). The following subsections detailed the different phases of the proposed approach.

1. **Generation of Optimized Class Boundaries for Color Images by NSGA II Algorithm:** In this part of the article, the NSGA II based optimization procedure is employed to generate the optimized class boundaries $\left(cl_{\alpha_{opt}} \right)$ for the proposed NSGA II based ParaOptiMUSIG activation function. The procedure applied in this phase is detailed as follows.

   a. **Input Phase:** The pixel intensity levels of the color image and the number of classes (K) to be segmented are furnished as inputs to this NSGA II based optimization procedure.

b. **Chromosome Representation and Population Generation:** The real coded chromosomes are applied in NSGA II based optimization procedure and the real numbers are generated randomly from the input color image information content. The three color components, viz. red, green and blue color components are differentiated from each pixel intensity of the true color image information. Three different chromosome pools are developed for the three individual color components and individual chromosome pool is employed to generate the optimized class levels for the individual color component. In this treatment, a population size of 200 has been applied.

c. **Fitness Computation:** Three segmentation efficiency measures (ρ, F, F'), given in equations 6, 7 and 8 respectively, are utilized as the evaluation functions in the NSGA II algorithm. These fitness functions are applied on three chromosome pools in cumulative fashion.

d. **Genetic Operators:** Same genetic operators, like gray scale image segmentation, are also used is this phase. Like the gray scale segmentation, the crowded binary tournament selection operator, the crossover probability and the mutation probability are selected as same. The near-pareto-optimal strings furnish the desired solutions in the last generation.

e. **Selecting a Solution from the Non-Dominated Set:** Q index (Borsotti, Campadelli, & Schettini, 1998) is applied to select the particular solution from the Pareto-optimal non-dominated set of solutions after the final generation.

2. **Designing of NSGA II Based ParaOptiMUSIG Activation Function:** The optimized class boundaries $\left(cl_{\alpha_{opt}} \right)$ those are selected in the Pareto optimal set are employed to design the NSGA II based ParaOptiMUSIG activation function. The optimized class boundaries for individual color component in the selected chromosomes are applied to generate the individual OptiMUSIG activation function for that color component, viz. the class boundaries for the red component is employed to generate OptiMUSIG activation function for red and so on. The NSGA II based ParaOptiMUSIG activation function is rendered using equation 5.

3. **Input of True Color Image Pixel Values to the Source Layer of the PSONN Architecture:** The source layer of the PSONN architecture is inputted with the pixel intensity levels of the true color image. The input pixel intensities of the true color image are assigned to each of the neurons of the source layer.

4. **Distribution of the Color Component Images to Three Individual SONNs:** The pixel intensity levels of the input color image are segregated into three individual primary color components and the three individual three-layer component SONNs are fed with these independent primary color components, viz. the red component is utilized to one SONN, the green component to another SONN and the remaining SONN accepts the blue component information at their respective input layers. The fixed interconnections of the respective SONNs with the source layer are responsible for this scenario.

5. **Segmentation of Color Component Images by Individual SONNs:** The corresponding SONN architecture guided by the designed NSGA II based ParaOptiMUSIG activation function at the constituent primitives/neurons are applied to segment the individual color component of the true color images. Depending on the number of transition lobes of the ParaOptiMUSIG activation function, the neurons of the different layers of individual three layer SONN architecture render different output color component level responses. The subnormal linear index of fuzziness (Bhattacharyya, 2008) is employed to decide the system errors at the corresponding output layers as the network

has no *a priori* knowledge about the outputs. Like the gray scale image segmentation, these errors are employed to adjust the interconnection weights between the different layers using the standard backpropagation algorithm (Haykin, 1999; Rojas, 1996). After attaining stabilization in the corresponding networks, the respective output layers of the independent SONNs generate the final color component images.

6. **Fusion of Individual Segmented Component Outputs into a True Color Image at the Sink Layer of the PSONN Architecture:** In this final stage, the segmented outputs deduced at the three output layers of the three independent three-layer SONN architectures are fused at the sink layer of the PSONN architecture to derive the segmented true color image. The number of segments are a combination of the number of transition lobes of the designed NSGA II based ParaOptiMUSIG activation functions used during component level segmentation.

RESULT ANALYSIS

Two real life images viz. Baboon and Peppers each of dimensions 128×128 have been used to demonstrate the proposed multilevel gray scale image segmentation approach using the MLSONN architecture guided by NSGA II based OptiMUSIG activation function. The proposed multilevel true color image segmentation approach using the PSONN architecture guided by the NSGA II based ParaOptiMUSIG activation function is demonstrated using the color version of the same real life images. Experiments have been carried with $K = \{6, 8\}$ classes. Both the activation functions have been designed with a fixed slope, $\lambda = \{2, 4\}$. But the results are reported for 8 classes and a fixed slope of $\lambda = 4$. To generate the class levels, the population size for NSGA II algorithm is 100. The crossover probability (μ_c) and the mutation probability (μ_p) for the proposed method are 0.8 and 0.01, respectively. The segmentation efficiency of the proposed approach is demonstrated in the following subsection and it is compared with the segmentation derived by means of the conventional MUSIG activation function with same number of class responses and heuristic class levels. In the next subsection, the quantitative comparison of the above mentioned methods are manifested and after that, the comparative study as regards to its efficacy in the segmentation of test images of the segmented outputs by the proposed methods and the conventional MUSIG activation function based methods are detailed.

Quantitative Performance Analysis of Segmentation

In this section, the efficiency of the proposed NSGA II based OptiMUSIG and ParaOptiMUSIG activation function and the conventional MUSIG activation functions for $K = 8$ have been exemplified quantitatively. Three segmentation efficiency functions viz. correlation coefficient (ρ), and two empirical evaluation function (F and F') have been employed in the NSGA II based approach to generate the nondominated set of chromosomes. Another empirical evaluation function, Q, has been employed for the selection of the chromosome that is applied in the corresponding network in the proposed method. The results obtained with the NSGA II based OptiMUSIG and ParaOptiMUSIG activation function have been discussed in the next subsection and the corresponding results obtained with the conventional fixed class response based MUSIG activation function are furnished after that.

1. **Segmentation Evaluation using NSGA II Based OptiMUSIG Activation Function for Gray Scale Images and NSGA II Based ParaOptiMUSIG Activation Function for Color Images:**
In Tables 1-2, the optimized set of class boundaries $\left(cl_{\alpha_{opt}} \right)$ for the gray scale images obtained using NSGA II based optimization with the three evaluation functions (ρ, F and F') are tabulated. In the same manner, the optimized set of class boundaries for the color images obtained using NSGA II based algorithm with the three evaluation functions (ρ, F and F') are depicted in Tables 5-6. Three fitness values (ρ, F and F') of individual chromosome set are also reported in these tables. Two set of Pareto optimal set of chromosomes of each images are tabulated in the above mentioned tables. The Q values of individual set of class boundaries for gray scale Baboon and Peppers images which have been used for the gradation system for that particular set of class boundaries are presented in Tables 3 and 4, respectively and in the same way, the Q values of individual set of class boundaries for color Baboon and Peppers images are tabulated in Tables 7 and 8, respectively. The last columns of the Tables 1-2 and 5-6 show the quality measures κ [graded on a scale of 1 (best) onwards] obtained by the segmentation of the test images based on the corresponding set of optimized class boundaries. The first four good Q valued chromosomes are indicated in those tables for easy reckoning. In this article, all evaluation function values are tabulated in normalized form.

Table 1. NSGA II based set of optimized class boundaries and corresponding evaluated segmentation quality measures for 8 classes of gray scale Baboon image

Set No.		Class Level	ρ	F	F'	κ
1	(i)	4, 70, 95, 116, 137, 159, 184, 217	0.9764	0.4904	0.1734	
	(ii)	4, 78, 89, 114, 127, 147, 154, 217	0.9442	0.4447	0.1572	1
	(iii)	4, 68, 95, 116, 137, 159, 182, 217	0.9760	0.4880	0.1725	
	(iv)	4, 74, 93, 118, 132, 159, 163, 217	0.9543	0.4462	0.1578	2
	(v)	4, 76, 93, 118, 135, 159, 174, 217	0.9576	0.4531	0.1602	
	(vi)	4, 74, 95, 116, 136, 159, 167, 217	0.9570	0.4514	0.1596	
	(vii)	4, 74, 93, 118, 135, 159, 172, 217	0.9666	0.4692	0.1659	
	(viii)	4, 72, 95, 116, 137, 159, 182, 217	0.9753	0.4850	0.1715	
	(ix)	4, 72, 95, 118, 137, 161, 180, 217	0.9677	0.4705	0.1663	
	(x)	4, 70, 95, 114, 136, 157, 167, 217	0.9740	0.4820	0.1704	4
	(xi)	4, 71, 95, 116, 136, 155, 167, 217	0.9638	0.4646	0.1643	3
2	(i)	4, 78, 84, 115, 121, 148, 152, 217	0.9358	0.4327	0.1530	2
	(ii)	4, 68, 95, 117, 138, 160, 185, 217	0.9767	0.4949	0.1750	
	(iii)	4, 68, 93, 115, 136, 153, 165, 217	0.9626	0.4672	0.1652	
	(iv)	4, 78, 95, 117, 135, 160, 177, 217	0.9682	0.4731	0.1672	
	(v)	4, 71, 95, 115, 134, 155, 165, 217	0.9619	0.4643	0.1641	
	(vi)	4, 71, 95, 115, 134, 153, 165, 217	0.9756	0.4865	0.1720	
	(vii)	4, 68, 96, 117, 137, 160, 181, 217	0.9614	0.4611	0.1630	
	(viii)	4, 69, 95, 115, 134, 155, 163, 217	0.9719	0.4766	0.1685	4
	(ix)	4, 78, 86, 115, 121, 148, 154, 217	0.9595	0.4571	0.1616	3
	(x)	4, 78, 88, 115, 121, 148, 152, 217	0.9578	0.4534	0.1603	1

Table 2. NSGA II based set of optimized class boundaries and corresponding evaluated segmentation quality measures for 8 classes of gray scale Peppers image

Set No.		Class Level	ρ	F	F'	κ
1	(i)	0,40,78,107,139,168,195,248	0.9831	0.7697	0.2721	
	(ii)	0,52,71,111,140,166,189,248	0.9780	0.7317	0.2587	
	(iii)	0,42,78,107,139,168,195,248	0.9831	0.7653	0.2706	
	(iv)	0,42,75,107,139,168,195,248	0.9830	0.7600	0.2687	
	(v)	0,44,78,109,140,168,195,248	0.9830	0.7633	0.2699	2
	(vi)	0,52,71,111,140,166,191,248	0.9788	0.7327	0.2591	
	(vii)	0,54,73,111,139,166,191,248	0.9789	0.7345	0.2597	4
	(viii)	0,44,78,109,140,166,195,248	0.9808	0.7400	0.2616	1
	(ix)	0,47,76,109,141,166,193,248	0.9805	0.7385	0.2611	
	(x)	0,47,73,109,140,166,191,248	0.9816	0.7445	0.2632	
	(xi)	0,49,73,109,139,166,191,248	0.9829	0.7568	0.2676	
	(xii)	0,44,76,109,139,166,195,248	0.9823	0.7495	0.2650	
	(xiii)	0,46,76,109,140,166,191,248	0.9820	0.7466	0.2640	3
2	(i)	0,42,76,110,138,168,196,248	0.9700	0.7653	0.2706	
	(ii)	0,61,67,114,137,170,187,248	0.9829	0.7188	0.2541	
	(iii)	0,42,76,108,142,166,196,248	0.9828	0.7610	0.2691	
	(iv)	0,42,76,108,140,168,194,248	0.9822	0.7587	0.2683	
	(v)	0,50,76,108,140,166,194,248	0.9819	0.7510	0.2655	4
	(vi)	0,44,76,110,140,166,193,248	0.9811	0.7484	0.2646	
	(vii)	0,50,76,108,140,166,191,248	0.9825	0.7441	0.2631	1
	(viii)	0,52,71,110,140,166,191,248	0.9813	0.7546	0.2668	
	(ix)	0,50,73,110,140,166,193,248	0.9828	0.7457	0.2637	
	(x)	0,50,76,110,140,166,193,248	0.9825	0.7567	0.2675	2
	(xi)	0,44,78,108,142,166,194,248	0.9799	0.7537	0.2665	
	(xii)	0,50,76,108,140,166,193,248	0.9784	0.7377	0.2608	3

Table 3. The evaluated segmentation quality measure Q of the each optimized class boundaries of Table 1

Set	No.	(i)	(ii)	(iii)	(iv)	(v)	(vi)	(vii)
1	Q	0.3058	0.2494	0.3022	0.2745	0.2872	0.2840	0.2856
	No.	(viii)	(ix)	(x)	(xi)			
	Q	0.3004	0.2975	0.2823	0.2758			
2	No.	(i)	(ii)	(iii)	(iv)	(v)	(vi)	(vii)
	Q	0.2557	0.3044	0.2704	0.2940	0.2709	0.2708	0.2995
	No.	(viii)	(ix)	(x)				
	Q	0.2701	0.2579	0.2525				

Table 4. The evaluated segmentation quality measure Q of the each optimized class boundaries of Table 2

Set	No.	(i)	(ii)	(iii)	(iv)	(v)	(vi)	(vii)
1	Q	0.8813	0.8911	0.8800	0.8881	0.8696	0.8943	0.8794
	No.	(viii)	(ix)	(x)	(xi)	(xii)	(xii)	
	Q	0.8688	0.8837	0.8828	0.8843	0.8879	0.8762	
2	No.	(i)	(ii)	(iii)	(iv)	(v)	(vi)	(vii)
	Q	0.8841	0.8876	0.8945	0.8850	0.8793	0.8811	0.8718
	No.	(viii)	(ix)	(x)	(xi)	(xii)		
	Q	0.8931	0.8852	0.8760	0.8814	0.8769		

Table 5. NSGA II based set of optimized class boundaries and corresponding evaluated segmentation quality measures for 8 classes of color Baboon image

Set No.		Class Level	ρ	F	F'	κ
1	(i)	$R=\{27, 95, 104, 137, 173, 197, 239, 252\}$; $G=\{24, 76, 93, 119, 133, 158, 182, 209\}$; $B=\{0, 45, 72, 97, 127, 161, 221, 249\}$	0.9820	0.2016	0.0713	
	(ii)	$R=\{27, 95, 100, 139, 148, 186, 219, 252\}$; $G=\{24, 78, 91, 119, 135, 165, 182, 209\}$; $B=\{0, 45, 72, 97, 127, 161, 221, 249\}$	0.9821	0.2018	0.0714	2
	(iii)	$R=\{27, 95, 97, 135, 148, 184, 217, 252\}$; $G=\{24, 76, 93, 119, 135, 163, 182, 209\}$; $B=\{0, 45, 78, 109, 136, 161, 221, 249\}$	0.9856	0.2158	0.0763	
	(iv)	$R=\{27, 95, 96, 137, 148, 186, 219, 252\}$; $24, 76, 93, 119, 135, 165, 182, 209\}$; $B=\{0, 45, 72, 97, 127, 161, 221, 249$	0.9856	0.2040	0.0721	1
	(v)	$R=\{27, 99, 104, 137, 173, 186, 219, 252\}$; $G=\{24, 76, 91, 119, 135, 165, 182, 209\}$; $B=\{0, 45, 72, 97, 127, 161, 221, 249$	0.9815	0.2016	0.0713	
	(vi)	$R=\{27, 95, 98, 137, 148, 198, 210, 252\}$; $G=\{24, 76, 93, 115, 131, 145, 176, 209\}$; $B=\{0, 45, 80, 107, 138, 175, 208, 249\}$	0.9855	0.2033	0.0719	4
	(vii)	$R=\{27, 95, 98, 139, 148, 186, 217, 252\}$; $G=\{24, 76, 91, 119, 137, 163, 182, 209\}$; $B=\{0, 45, 72, 97, 125, 163, 221, 249\}$	0.9820	0.2018	0.0713	3
2	(i)	$R=\{27, 64, 94, 124, 140, 180, 192, 252\}$; $G=\{24, 74, 99, 123, 145, 172, 190, 209\}$; $B=\{0, 49, 75, 102, 132, 165, 218, 249\}$	0.9856	0.2050	0.0725	
	(ii)	$R=\{27, 64, 94, 126, 140, 182, 192, 252\}$; $G=\{24, 74, 97, 123, 141, 170, 190, 209\}$; $B=\{0, 49, 75, 102, 132, 163, 222, 249\}$	0.9856	0.2055	0.0726	
	(iii)	$R=\{27, 66, 97, 124, 140, 180, 192, 252\}$; $G=\{24, 74, 91, 123, 141, 170, 190, 209\}$; $B=\{0, 47, 75, 102, 132, 165, 216, 249\}$	0.9855	0.2043	0.0722	3
	(iv)	$R=\{27, 64, 94, 126, 140, 180, 190, 252\}$; $G=\{24, 74, 97, 123, 141, 172, 190, 209\}$; $B=\{0, 49, 75, 102, 132, 163, 218, 249\}$	0.9856	0.2047	0.0724	
	(v)	$R=\{27, 66, 97, 124, 140, 180, 192, 252\}$; $G=\{24, 76, 91, 123, 141, 170, 190, 209\}$; $B=\{0, 47, 77, 102, 132, 165, 216, 249\}$	0.9855	0.2045	0.0723	1
	(vi)	$R=\{27, 66, 97, 124, 140, 180, 190, 252\}$; $G=\{24, 74, 99, 121, 141, 172, 190, 209\}$; $B=\{0, 47, 75, 102, 132, 163, 218, 249\}$	0.9855	0.2046	0.0723	
	(vii)	$R=\{27, 66, 97, 124, 140, 180, 192, 252\}$; $G=\{24, 74, 97, 123, 141, 170, 190, 209\}$; $B=\{0, 47, 75, 102, 132, 165, 216, 249\}$	0.9856	0.2052	0.0725	2
	(viii)	$R=\{27, 66, 97, 124, 140, 182, 192, 252\}$; $G=\{24, 74, 97, 121, 141, 170, 190, 209\}$; $B=\{0, 47, 75, 102, 132, 163, 222, 249\}$	0.9856	0.2052	0.0726	
	(ix)	$R=\{27, 66, 97, 124, 142, 180, 190, 252\}$; $G-\{24, 74, 97, 123, 139, 172, 190, 209\}$; $B=\{0, 47, 75, 102, 130, 163, 220, 249\}$	0.9855	0.2043	0.0723	4

Table 6. NSGA II based set of optimized class boundaries and corresponding evaluated segmentation quality measures for 8 classes of color Peppers image

Set No.		Class Level	ρ	F	F'	κ
1	(i)	$R=\{13, 66, 83, 112, 119, 151, 161, 224\}$; $G=\{0, 35, 49, 99, 121, 165, 167, 234\}$; $B=\{0, 37, 60, 84, 113, 159, 194, 224\}$	0.9799	0.6321	0.2235	1
	(ii)	$R=\{13, 66, 83, 112, 143, 156, 186, 224\}$; $G=\{0, 35, 51, 106, 129, 174, 191, 234\}$; $B=\{0, 37, 60, 82, 101, 132, 167, 224\}$	0.9815	0.6531	0.2309	
	(iii)	$R=\{13, 66, 81, 112, 119, 151, 161, 224\}$; $G=\{0, 37, 51, 108, 121, 163, 167, 234\}$; $B=\{0, 37, 60, 84, 113, 157, 194, 224\}$	0.9801	0.6336	0.2240	
	(iv)	$R=\{13, 66, 81, 114, 143, 156, 188, 224\}$; $G=\{0, 35, 49, 106, 129, 176, 193, 234\}$; $B=\{0, 37, 60, 82, 101, 134, 169, 224\}$	0.9815	0.6527	0.2308	
	(v)	$R=\{13, 68, 81, 112, 143, 156, 188, 224\}$; $G=\{0, 35, 51, 106, 129, 176, 193, 234\}$; $B=\{0, 35, 58, 80, 101, 132, 167, 224\}$	0.9816	0.6539	0.2312	
	(vi)	$R=\{13, 66, 83, 114, 149, 162, 192, 224\}$; $G=\{0, 35, 51, 108, 133, 180, 193, 234\}$; $B=\{0, 37, 60, 82, 103, 136, 167, 224\}$	0.9816	0.6570	0.2323	
	(vii)	$R=\{13, 66, 83, 112, 143, 156, 188, 224\}$; $G=\{0, 35, 51, 106, 129, 176, 193, 234\}$; $B=\{0, 35, 58, 80, 101, 134, 169, 224\}$	0.9814	0.6500	0.2298	
	(viii)	$R=\{13, 66, 83, 112, 119, 147, 159, 224\}$; $G=\{0, 35, 51, 106, 121, 165, 167, 234\}$; $B=\{0, 37, 60, 84, 113, 153, 194, 224\}$	0.9816	0.6580	0.2326	
	(ix)	$R=\{13, 66, 83, 112, 145, 160, 188, 224\}$; $G=\{0, 37, 51, 106, 129, 176, 193, 234\}$; $B=\{0, 37, 60, 82, 103, 136, 165, 224\}$;	0.9802	0.6381	0.2256	
	(x)	$R=\{13, 66, 83, 112, 145, 154, 190, 224\}$; $G=\{0, 35, 53, 104, 129, 176, 193, 234\}$; $B=\{0, 35, 58, 80, 101, 132, 169, 224\}$	0.9816	0.6660	0.2355	
	(xi)	$R=\{13, 66, 83, 112, 119, 151, 161, 224\}$; $G=\{0, 37, 51, 108, 121, 163, 167, 234\}$; $B=\{0, 37, 60, 84, 113, 157, 194, 224\}$	0.9812	0.6480	0.2291	2
	(xii)	$R=\{13, 68, 81, 110, 145, 156, 188, 224\}$; $G=\{0, 35, 51, 106, 127, 176, 193, 234\}$; $B=\{0, 35, 58, 80, 101, 132, 167, 224\}$	0.9816	0.6618	0.2340	
	(xiii)	$R=\{13, 66, 79, 114, 149, 162, 192, 224\}$; $G=\{0, 35, 49, 106, 133, 180, 193, 234\}$; $B=\{0, 37, 60, 82, 103, 134, 167, 224\}$	0.9801	0.6346	0.2243	
	(xiv)	$R=\{13, 66, 85, 112, 119, 151, 161, 224\}$; $G=\{0, 41, 49, 99, 121, 163, 167, 234\}$; $B=\{0, 37, 62, 84, 113, 157, 194, 224\}$	0.9816	0.6570	0.2323	
	(xv)	$R=\{13, 66, 81, 114, 143, 160, 190, 224\}$; $G=\{0, 35, 51, 106, 133, 180, 193, 234\}$; $B=\{0, 37, 60, 82, 103, 136, 167, 224\}$	0.9816	0.6577	0.2325	
	(xvi)	$R=\{13, 66, 81, 112, 119, 151, 161, 224\}$; $G=\{0, 41, 51, 99, 121, 165, 169, 234\}$; $B=\{0, 37, 60, 87, 119, 157, 194, 224\}$	0.9814	0.6520	0.2305	4
	(xvii)	$R=\{13, 66, 83, 112, 119, 151, 161, 224\}$; $G=\{0, 35, 51, 108, 121, 163, 167, 234\}$; $B=\{0, 37, 60, 84, 113, 157, 194, 224\}$	0.9815	0.6528	0.2308	3

continued on following page

2. **Segmentation Evaluation using MUSIG Activation Function for Gray Scale Images and Color Images:** The heuristically selected class boundaries are applied in the conventional MUSIG activation function for gray scale images and for color images in the same manner and they are depicted in Tables 9 and 10, respectively. The evaluation procedure is exercised for the individual set of class boundaries along with the same evaluation functions and the results are reported in those tables. After the segmentation process using the MUSIG activation function, the quality of the segmented images are evaluated using the Q evaluation function and the results are tabulated in Tables 11 and 12 for gray scale and color images, respectively.

Table 6. Continued

Set No.		Class Level	ρ	F	F'	κ
2	(i)	R={13, 73, 82, 123, 135, 173, 187, 224}; G={0, 21, 54, 91, 113, 157, 166, 234}; B={0, 37, 60, 83, 110, 145, 179, 224}	0.9815	0.6255	0.2211	
	(ii)	R={13, 73, 78, 123, 135, 173, 185, 224}; G={0, 21, 54, 91, 111, 155, 166, 234}; B={0, 37, 60, 83, 108, 143, 179, 224}	0.9816	0.6578	0.2326	
	(iii)	R={13, 73, 78, 123, 135, 173, 187, 224}; G={0, 21, 54, 91, 113, 157, 166, 234}; B={0, 37, 60, 83, 110, 145, 179, 224}	0.9812	0.6200	0.2192	2
	(iv)	R={13, 73, 80, 125, 137, 176, 185, 224}; G={0, 19, 58, 91, 142, 162, 209, 234}; B={0, 37, 60, 83, 104, 139, 174, 224}	0.9815	0.6202	0.2193	1
	(v)	R={13, 73, 80, 123, 135, 176, 187, 224}; G={0, 19, 58, 93, 144, 162, 209, 234}; B={0, 37, 60, 81, 104, 139, 174, 224}	0.9811	0.6191	0.2189	
	(vi)	R={13, 73, 78, 123, 133, 173, 187, 224}; G={0, 21, 54, 91, 111, 155, 166, 234}; B={0, 37, 60, 83, 106, 145, 179, 224}	0.9812	0.6192	0.2189	
	(vii)	R={13, 65, 69, 125, 133, 173, 187, 224}; G={0, 35, 50, 91, 113, 157, 166, 234}; B={0, 38, 60, 83, 106, 145, 179, 224}	0.9817	0.6585	0.2328	
	(viii)	R={13, 65, 80, 123, 137, 173, 187, 224}; G={0, 35, 50, 93, 113, 157, 166, 234}; B={0, 38, 60, 83, 104, 145, 179, 224}	0.9817	0.6603	0.2335	
	(ix)	R={13, 73, 78, 123, 135, 173, 187, 224}; G={0, 21, 54, 91, 111, 157, 168, 234}; B={0, 37, 60, 83, 108, 147, 179, 224}	0.9815	0.6212	0.2196	
	(x)	R={13, 65, 67, 125, 133, 173, 187, 224}; G={0, 33, 50, 91, 113, 155, 166, 234}; B={0, 38, 60, 83, 106, 143, 179, 224}	0.9817	0.6591	0.2330	
	(xi)	R={13, 73, 80, 123, 135, 173, 187, 224}; G={0, 21, 56, 91, 113, 157, 166, 234}; B={0, 37, 60, 83, 110, 145, 179, 224}	0.9811	0.6148	0.2174	
	(xii)	R={13, 71, 82, 125, 137, 176, 185, 224}; G={0, 23, 58, 89, 142, 162, 209, 234}; B={0, 37, 60, 83, 102, 139, 174, 224}	0.9810	0.6134	0.2169	
	(xiii)	R={13, 65, 69, 123, 137, 173, 187, 224}; G={0, 35, 50, 93, 113, 157, 166, 234}; B={0, 38, 60, 83, 106, 145, 179, 224}	0.9813	0.6202	0.2193	3
	(xiv)	R={13, 73, 82, 123, 137, 171, 187, 224}; G={0, 19, 56, 91, 142, 157, 166, 234}; B={0, 37, 60, 83, 104, 143, 179, 224}	0.9814	0.6238	0.2205	4

Table 7. The evaluated segmentation quality measure Q of the each optimized class boundaries of Table 5

Set	No.	(i)	(ii)	(iii)	(iv)	(v)	(vi)	(vii)
1	Q	0.3996	0.2863	0.4020	0.2844	0.4182	0.2929	0.2875
2	No.	(i)	(ii)	(iii)	(iv)	(v)	(vi)	(vii)
	Q	0.3225	0.3262	0.3171	0.3291	0.3144	0.3206	0.3162
	No.	(viii)	(ix)					
	Q	0.3237	0.3195					

Table 8. The evaluated segmentation quality measure Q of the each optimized class boundaries of Table 6

Set	No.	(i)	(ii)	(iii)	(iv)	(v)	(vi)	(vii)
1	Q	0.6371	0.6868	0.6470	0.7013	0.6721	0.6857	0.6739
	No.	(viii)	(ix)	(x)	(xi)	(xii)	(xiii)	(xiv)
	Q	0.6661	0.6680	0.6672	0.6429	0.6709	0.6873	0.6501
	No.	(xv)	(xvi)	(xvii)				
	Q	0.6624	0.6457	0.6446				
2	No.	(i)	(ii)	(iii)	(iv)	(v)	(vi)	(vii)
	Q	0.6456	0.6815	0.6882	0.6807	0.7001	0.6799	0.6994
	No.	(viii)	(ix)	(x)	(xi)	(xii)	(xiii)	
	Q	0.6391	0.7059	0.6986	0.6589	0.6465	0.6788	

Table 9. Fixed class boundaries and corresponding evaluated segmentation quality measures for 8 classes of gray scale Baboon and Peppers image

Image	Set No.	Class Level	ρ	F	F'
Baboon	1	4,50,80,105,130,165,205,217	0.9691	0.8849	0.8849
	2	4,49,74,100,135,160,200,217	0.9724	0.8180	0.8180
	3	4,36,76,105,142,172,212,217	0.9664	0.9711	0.9711
	4	4,30,80,105,145,180,205,217	0.9656	1.0000	1.0000
Peppers	1	0,35,80,110,152,175,200,248	0.9852	0.9187	0.9187
	2	0,30,75,115,150,185,205,248	0.9825	0.9996	0.9996
	3	0,40,78,112,155,188,208,248	0.9835	1.0000	1.0000
	4	0,30,73,106,145,178,200,248	0.9849	0.9445	0.9445

Table 10. Fixed class boundaries and corresponding evaluated segmentation quality measures for 8 classes of color Baboon and Peppers image

Image	Set No.	Class Level	ρ	F	F'
Baboon	1	$R=\{27, 60, 110, 130, 160, 190, 210, 252\}$; $G=\{24, 50, 70, 90, 115, 145, 175, 209\}$; $B=\{0, 45, 90, 116, 145, 175, 200, 249\}$	0.9422	0.7881	0.7881
	2	$R=\{27, 40, 60, 110, 180, 215, 225, 252\}$; $G=\{24, 50, 70, 100, 145, 175, 190, 209\}$; $B=\{0, 35, 90, 160, 185, 205, 230, 249\}$	0.9297	1.0000	1.0000
	3	$R=\{27, 45, 75, 130, 150, 200, 235, 252\}$; $G=\{24, 55, 70, 85, 130, 170, 185, 209\}$; $B=\{0, 55, 80, 115, 125, 185, 225, 249\}$	0.9406	0.7408	0.7408
	4	$R=\{27, 50, 70, 120, 185, 215, 230, 252\}$; $G=\{24, 45, 65, 95, 140, 175, 195, 209\}$; $B=\{0, 35, 100, 150, 185, 215, 230, 249\}$	0.9314	0.9800	0.9800
Peppers	1	$R=\{0, 20, 60, 120, 150, 190, 210, 253\}$; $G=\{0, 40, 75, 90, 190, 215, 230, 255\}$; $B=\{0, 35, 60, 100, 125, 160, 175, 245\}$	0.9745	1.0000	1.0000
	2	$R=\{0, 25, 70, 130, 145, 175, 205, 253\}$; $G=\{0, 45, 80, 100, 170, 200, 225, 255\}$; $B=\{0, 30, 60, 90, 115, 150, 180, 245\}$	0.9803	0.8734	0.8734
	3	$R=\{0, 30, 75, 135, 150, 180, 215, 253\}$; $G=\{0, 55, 90, 105, 175, 195, 215, 255\}$; $B=\{0, 40, 65, 105, 135, 170, 195, 245\}$	0.9761	0.8612	0.8612
	4	$R=\{0, 50, 75, 125, 155, 192, 220, 253\}$; $G=\{0, 60, 85, 130, 180, 206, 235, 255\}$; $B=\{0, 37, 60, 85, 109, 150, 195, 245\}$	0.9847	0.8430	0.8430

Table 11. The evaluated segmentation quality measure Q of the each fixed class boundaries of Table 9

Image	Set No.	Q	Image	Set No.	Q
Baboon	1	0.3590	Peppers	1	0.9142
	2	0.3787		2	0.9674
	3	1.0000		3	1.0000
	4	0.8502		4	0.9399

Table 12. The evaluated segmentation quality measure Q of the each fixed class boundaries of Table 10

Image	Set No.	Q	Image	Set No.	Q
Baboon	1	0.3917	Peppers	1	0.8744
	2	0.8139		2	0.8978
	3	1.0000		3	0.8995
	4	0.4959		4	1.0000

It is quite evident from Tables 3-4 and 11 that the fitness values derived by the NSGA II based OptiMUSIG activation function for gray scale images are better than those obtained by the conventional MUSIG activation function. In most of the cases, the Q value in Tables 3-4 is lower than the same value in Table 11 for both images. The lower value of Q denotes the better segmentation as it is known from the above discussion. In the same manner, the Q values depicted in the Tables 7-8 are compared with the Q values tabulated in Table 12 for both the images. It is discernible from those tables that the image segmentation done by the proposed method generates the lower Q value than the image segmentation done by the heuristically selected class levels. This can also be proved from the Tables 1-2, 5-6 and 9-10 if we observe these tables minutely. In those tables, the ρ, F and F' values derived by the NSGA II based OptiMUSIG activation function for gray scale images and the NSGA II based ParaOptiMUSIG activation function for color images are better than those derived by the conventional MUSIG activation function for the respective images.

Image Segmentation Outputs

The segmented gray scale and color output images obtained for the $K=8$ classes, with the proposed optimized approach vis-a-vis those obtained with the heuristically chosen class boundaries, are demonstrated in this section.

1. **Segmented Outputs using Proposed Optimized Approach:** The networks are applied to segment the test images using the first four better results on the basis of the evaluation metric, Q, value. The segmented multilevel gray scale test images obtained with the MLSONN architecture using the NSGA II based OptiMUSIG activation function for $K = 8$ are presented in Figures 2-3 and the segmented color test images derived with the PSONN architecture using the NSGA II based ParaOptiMUSIG activation function for $K = 8$ are shown in Figures 4-5.

Figure 2. 8-class segmented 128 × 128 gray scale Baboon image with the optimized class levels referring to (a-d) set 1 (e-h) set 2 of Table 1 for first four better quality measure Q with NSGA II based OptiMUSIG activation function

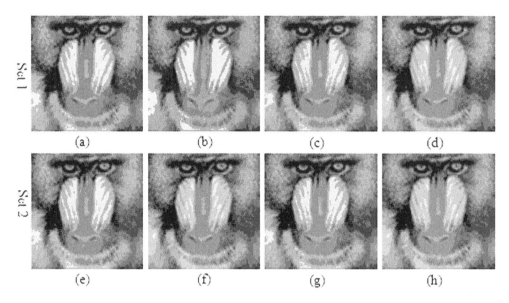

2. **Segmented Outputs using MUSIG Activation Function:** The fixed class responses are employed to generate the segmented multilevel gray scale test images in connection with the MLSONN architecture and the segmented multilevel color test images obtained with the PSONN architecture characterized by the conventional MUSIG activation. The segmented output gray scale and color images for *K*=8 are shown in Figures 6 and 7, respectively.

Figure 3. 8-class segmented 128 × 128 gray scale Peppers image with the optimized class levels referring to (a-d) set 1 (e-h) set 2 of Table 2 for first four better quality measure Q with NSGA II based OptiMUSIG activation function

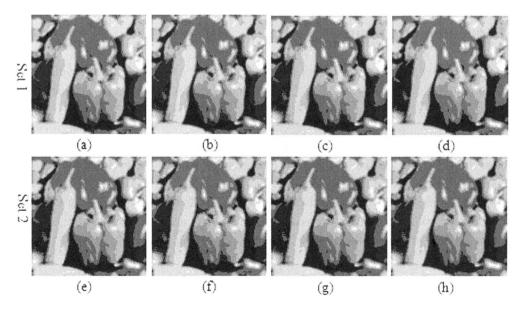

Figure 4. 8-class segmented 128 × 128 color Baboon image with the optimized class levels referring to (a-d) set 1 (e-h) set 2 of Table 5 for first four better quality measure Q with NSGA II based ParaOpti-MUSIG activation function

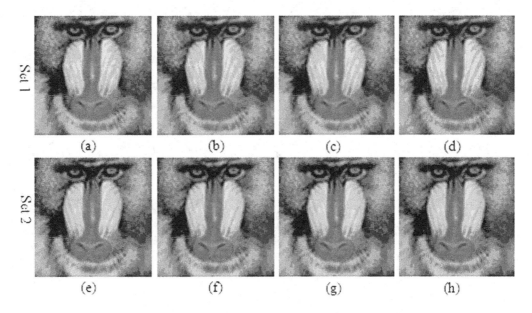

Figure 5. 8-class segmented 128 × 128 color Peppers image with the optimized class levels referring to (a-d) set 1 (e-h) set 2 of Table 6 for first four better quality measure Q with NSGA II based ParaOp-tiMUSIG activation function

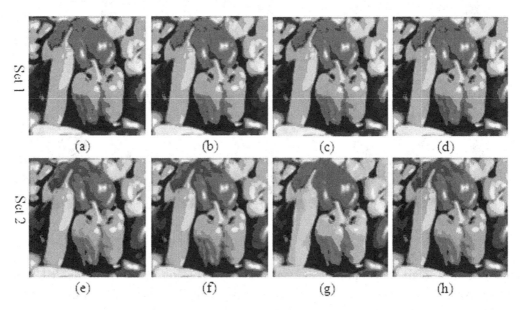

Figure 6. 8-class segmented 128 × 128 (a-d) gray scale Baboon image and (e-h) gray scale Peppers image with the fixed class levels of Table 9 with MUSIG activation function

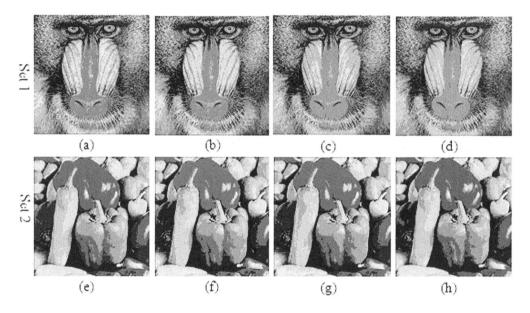

Figure 7. 8-class segmented 128 × 128 (a-d) color Baboon image and (e-h) color Peppers image with the fixed class levels of Table 10 with MUSIG activation function

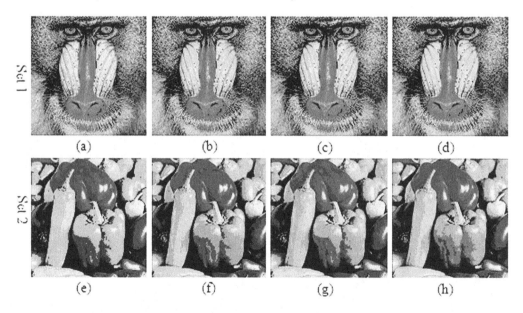

From the results obtained, the image segmentation method using the conventional MUSIG activation function is outperformed by the image segmentation method by the NSGA II based OptiMUSIG activation function for gray scale images and the NSGA II based ParaOptiMUSIG activation function for color images as regards to the segmentation quality of the images for the different number of classes. It is also be evident that the proposed approach incorporates the image heterogeneity as it can handle a wide variety of image intensity distribution prevalent in real life.

CONCLUSION

The multiscaling capabilities in the MLSONN network is induced by the optimized multilevel MUSIG activation function and the parallel optimized multilevel MUSIG activation function incorporates the parallelism property in the PSONN architecture. The NSGA II based OptiMUSIG activation function for gray scale images and the NSGA II based ParaOptiMUSIG activation function for true color images are accounted for in this article. In this method, the optimized class boundaries are derived on the basis of different image segmentation evaluation criterions. The selection of a particular set of class boundaries is performed based on another quantitative quality measure that is applied in the network. The performance of the proposed NSGA II based OptiMUSIG activation function for the segmentation of real life gray scale images and NSGA II based ParaOptiMUSIG activation function for the segmentation of real life color images show superior performance in most of the cases as compared to the conventional MUSIG activation function with heuristic class responses.

REFERENCES

Alander, J. T. (2000) *Indexed bibliography of genetic algorithms in optics and image processing*, (Technical Report 94-1-OPTICS). University of Vaasa, Vaasa, Finland.

Arajo, A. R. F., & Costa, D. C. (2009). Local adaptive receptive field self-organizing map for image color segmentation. *Image and Vision Computing*, 27(9), 1229–1239. doi:10.1016/j.imavis.2008.11.014

Awad, M., Chehdi, K., & Nasri, A. (2007). Multicomponent Image Segmentation Using a Genetic Algorithm and Artificial Neural Network. *IEEE Geoscience and Remote Sensing Letters*, 4(4), 571–575. doi:10.1109/LGRS.2007.903064

Bandyopadhyay, S., Maulik, U., & Mukhopadhyay, A. (2007). Multiobjective Genetic Clustering for Pixel Classification in Remote Sensing Imagery. *IEEE Transactions on Geoscience and Remote Sensing*, 45(5), 1506–1511. doi:10.1109/TGRS.2007.892604

Bandyopadhyay, S., Srivastava, A. K., & Pal, S. K. (Eds.). (2002) Multiobjective Variable String Genetic Classifier: Application of Remote Sensing Image. World Scientific, 2002.

Bhattacharyya, S. (2011). A Brief Survey of Color Image Preprocessing and Segmentation Techniques. *Journal of Pattern Recognition Research*, 1(1), 120–129. doi:10.13176/11.191

Bhattacharyya, S., & Dasgupta, K. Color Object Extraction From A Noisy Background Using Parallel Multilayer Self-Organizing Neural Networks. *Proceedings of CSI-YITPA(E) 2003* (pp. 32-36).

Bhattacharyya, S., Dutta, P., & Maulik, U. (2008). Self organizing neural network (SONN) based gray scale object extractor with a multilevel sigmoidal (MUSIG) activation function. *Foundations of Computing and Decision Sciences*, 33(2), 131–165.

Bhattacharyya, S., Dutta, P., Maulik, U., & Nandi, P. K. (2007). Multilevel activation functions for true color image segmentation using a self supervised parallel self organizing neural network (PSONN) architecture: A comparative study. *International Journal on Computer Sciences*, 2(1), 9-21.

Bhattacharyya, S., Maulik, U., & Dutta, P. (2011). Multilevel image segmentation with adaptive image context based thresholding. *Applied Soft Computing*, *11*(1), 946–962. doi:10.1016/j.asoc.2010.01.015

Bhattacharyya, S., Maulik, U., & Dutta, P. (2012, June). A Parallel Bi-Directional Self Organizing Neural Network (PBDSONN) Architecture for Color Image Extraction and Segmentation. *Neurocomputing*, *86*, 1–23. doi:10.1016/j.neucom.2011.11.025

Borsotti, M., Campadelli, P., & Schettini, R. (1998). Quantitative evaluation of color image segmentation results. *Pattern Recognition Letters*, *19*(8), 741–747. doi:10.1016/S0167-8655(98)00052-X

Chi, D. (2011). Self-Organizing Map-Based Color Image Segmentation with k-Means Clustering and Saliency Map. *ISRN Signal Processing*, 2011. doi:.10.5402/2011/393891

Chin-Wei, B., & Rajeswari, M. (2010). Multiobjective Optimization Approaches in Image Segmentation - The Directions and Challenges. *International Journal of Advanced Soft Computing Application*, *2*(1), 40–64.

Das, S., Abraham, A., & Konar, A. (2008). Automatic Clustering Using an Improved Differential Evolution Algorithm. *IEEE Transactions on Systems, Man, and Cybernetics. Part A, Systems and Humans*, *38*(1), 218–237. doi:10.1109/TSMCA.2007.909595

Davies, D. L., & Bouldin, D. W. (1979). A cluster separation measure. *IEEE Transactions on Pattern Recognition and Machine Intelligence*, *1*(2), 224–227. doi:10.1109/TPAMI.1979.4766909 PMID:21868852

Davis, L. (Ed.). (1991). *Handbook of Genetic Algorithms*. New York: Van Nostrand Reinhold.

De, S., Bhattacharyya, S., & Chakraborty, S. (2010). True Color Image Segmentation by an Optimized Multilevel Activation Function. *Proceedings of 2010 IEEE International Conference on Computational Intelligence and Computing Research* (pp. 545-548). doi:10.1109/ICCIC.2010.5705833

De, S., Bhattacharyya, S., & Chakraborty, S. (2012). Color image segmentation using parallel OptiMUSIG activation function. *Applied Soft Computing*, *12*(10), 3228–3236. doi:10.1016/j.asoc.2012.05.011

De, S., Bhattacharyya, S., & Dutta, P. (2010). Efficient grey-level image segmentation using an optimised MUSIG (OptiMUSIG) activation function. *International Journal of Parallel. Emergent and Distributed Systems*, *26*(1), 1–39. doi:10.1080/17445760903546618

Deb, K. (2001). *Multi-Objective Optimization using Evolutionary Algorithms*. England: John Wiley & Sons, Ltd.

Ghosh, A., Pal, N. R., & Pal, S. K. (1993). Self-organization for object extraction using a multilayer neural network and fuzziness measures. *IEEE Transactions on Fuzzy Systems*, *1*(1), 54–68. doi:10.1109/TFUZZ.1993.390285

Goldberg, D. E. (1989). *Genetic Algorithm in Search Optimization and Machine Learning*. New York: Addison-Wesley.

Halkidi, M., & Vazirgiannis, M. (2002). Clustering validity assessment using multi representatives. *Proceedings of the Hellenic Conference on Artificial Intelligence* (SETN '02), Thessaloniki, Greece.

Haykin, S. (1999). *Neural Networks: A Comprehensive Foundation*. Upper Saddle River, NJ: Prentice Hall.

Kohonen, T. (1989). *Self-Organization and Associative Memory*. Berlin, Germany: Springer-Verlag. doi:10.1007/978-3-642-88163-3

Li, C.-T., & Chiao, R. (2003). Multiresolution genetic clustering algorithm for texture segmentation. *Image and Vision Computing, 21*(11), 955–966. doi:10.1016/S0262-8856(03)00120-3

Liu, J., & Yang, Y. H. (1994). Multi-resolution color image segmentation. *IEEE Transactions on Pattern Analysis and Machine Intelligence, 16*(7), 689–700. doi:10.1109/34.297949

Mukhopadhyay, A., & Maulik, U. (2011). A multiobjective approach to MR brain image segmentation. *Applied Soft Computing, 11*(1), 872–880. doi:10.1016/j.asoc.2010.01.007

Nakib, A., Oulhadj, H., & Siarry, P. (2010). Image thresholding based on Pareto multiobjective optimization. *Engineering Applications of Artificial Intelligence, 23*(3), 313–320. doi:10.1016/j.engappai.2009.09.002

Pal, N. R., & Biswas, J. (1997). Cluster validation using graph theoretic concepts. *Pattern Recognition, 30*(6), 847–857. doi:10.1016/S0031-3203(96)00127-6

Rojas, R. (1996). *Neural Networks: A Systematic Introduction*. Berlin: Springer-Verlag. doi:10.1007/978-3-642-61068-4

Tao, W. B., Tian, J. W., & Liu, J. (2003). Image segmentation by three-level thresholding based on maximum fuzzy entropy and genetic algorithm. *Pattern Recognition Letters, 24*(16), 3069–3078. doi:10.1016/S0167-8655(03)00166-1

Xu, B., & Lin, S. (2002). Automatic color identification in printed fabric images by a fuzzy-neural network. *AATICC Rev, 2*(9), 42–45.

Yang, J. F., Hao, S. S., & Chung, P. C. (2002). Color image segmentation using fuzzy C-means and eigenspace projections. *Signal Processing, 82*(3), 461–472. doi:10.1016/S0165-1684(01)00196-7

Yang, Y., Zheng, C., & Lin, P. (2004). Image thresholding based on spatially weighted fuzzy C-means clustering. *Proceedings of the 4th International Conference on Computer and Information Technology (CIT04)* (pp. 184-189). doi:10.1109/CIT.2004.1357194

Yao, K., Mignotte, M., Collet, C., Galerne, P., & Burel, G. (2000). Unsupervised segmentation using a self-organizing map and a noise model estimation in sonar imagery. *Pattern Recognition, 33*(9), 1575–1584. doi:10.1016/S0031-3203(99)00135-1

Zhang, H., Fritts, J. E., & Goldman, S. A. (2004). An entropy-based objective evaluation method for image segmentation. *Proceedings of SPIE Storage and Retrieval Methods and Applications for Multimedia*, 38-49.

Zhang, Y. (1996). A survey on evaluation methods for image segmentation. *Pattern Recognition, 29*(8), 1335–1346. doi:10.1016/0031-3203(95)00169-7

Zhao, M. S., Fu, A. M. N., & Yan, H. (2001). A technique of three level thresholding based on probability partition and fuzzy 3-partition. *IEEE Transactions on Fuzzy Systems, 9*(3), 469–479. doi:10.1109/91.928743

Zingaretti, P., Tascini, G., & Regini, L. (2002). Optimising the colour image segmentation. *Proceedings of VIII Convegno dell Associazione Italiana per Intelligenza Artificiale*.

Zitzler, E., Laumanns, M., & Thiele, L. (2001). *SPEA2: Improving the Strength Pareto Evolutionary Algorithm* (Tech. Rep. 103). Zurich, Switzerland.

Zitzler, E., & Thiele, L. (1998). An evolutionary algorithm for multiobjective optimization: The strength pareto approach. *Tech. Rep. 43, Gloriastrasse 35, CH-8092 Zurich, Switzerland.*

KEY TERMS AND DEFINITIONS

Fuzzy Set: The ambiguity, vagueness and uncertainty in real world knowledge bases can be determined by this soft computing technique.

Genetic Algorithm: A probabilistic search technique for attaining an optimum solution to combinatorial problems that works in the principles of genetics.

Image Segmentation: A collection of image pixels, similar to one another within the same segment, dissimilar to the pixels in other segments with respect to some features.

Multiobjective Optimization: A method to determine one or more optimum solutions from an optimization problem that have multiple objective functions.

Optimization: A method for finding single or more feasible solutions which corresponds to minimum or maximum values of single or more objectives.

Self-Organizing Feature Map: A topology maintaining artificial neural network architecture capable of learning through self-supervision of incident input features.

Chapter 12

Optimum Gray Level Image Thresholding using a Quantum Inspired Genetic Algorithm

Sandip Dey
Camellia Institute of Technology, India

Siddhartha Bhattacharyya
RCC Institute of Information Technology, India

Ujjwal Maulik
Jadavpur University, India

ABSTRACT

In this article, a genetic algorithm inspired by quantum computing is presented. The novel algorithm referred to as quantum inspired genetic algorithm (QIGA) is applied to determine optimal threshold of two gray level images. Different random chaotic map models exhibit the inherent interference operation in collaboration with qubit and superposition of states. The random interference is followed by three different quantum operators viz., quantum crossover, quantum mutation and quantum shifting produce population diversity. Finally, the intermediate states pass through the quantum measurement for optimization of image thresholding. In the proposed algorithm three evaluation metrics such as Brinks's, Kapur's and Pun's algorithms have been applied to two gray level images viz., Lena and Barbara. These algorithms have been applied in conventional GA and Han et al.'s QEA. A comparative study has been made between the proposed QIGA, Han et al.'s algorithm and conventional GA that indicates encouraging avenues of the proposed QIGA.

INTRODUCTION

The concept of quantum computing (QC) has been originated from the discipline of quantum physics. In the upcoming twenty-second century, QC may be visualized as one of the most challenging research areas for the scholars of computer science and engineering (Mcmohan, 2008; Gonzalez, 2002). The inher-

DOI: 10.4018/978-1-4666-9474-3.ch012

ent dynamism of QC has been derived from the Schrödinger equation (SE) (Talbi, 2006). QC has some physical phenomena in its own like superposition, interference, coherence & decoherence, entanglement etc., which facilitate the parallelism capability. The features of QC can be embedded into the classical algorithms via a proper coupling to construct quantum inspired algorithms. The new quantum version of classical algorithms may possess exponentially speed up as compared with the pure classical algorithms (Dey, 2011). So the reflection of the research activities have been turned into designing quantum versions of the conventional algorithms such that these would fit on the quantum computer when invented (Dey, 2011). According to Richard Feynman, the efficacy of classical computers is very low when the quantum mechanical activities are concerned. His observation postulates that the effect of quantum mechanics would compensate the said problem fully (Talbi, 2004). The parallelism potential makes QC to be superior to its counterpart in the context of time complexity (Talbi, 2006; Reiffel, 2000). The application of QC conceited its existence when applied into some complex optimization problems that need larger solution space (Han, 2002). Grover's database search algorithm (Grover, 1998) and Shor's quantum factoring algorithm (Shor, 1997) are two popular quantum inspired algorithm that have been already discovered.

There are some renowned soft computing approaches used in this direction so far. Heuristic search and various optimization techniques or image analysis using intensity distribution are appropriate examples in this regards (Ren, 2009; Filho, 2008; Nakiba, 2010; Bazi, 2007). Thresholding plays a very important role in image segmentation, which acquiesce a binary image. The basic purpose of image thresholding is to separate object with its background (Pal, 1993). Threshold converts a given gray scale or color image into its corresponding binary image based on a predefined threshold intensity value. The pixel intensity values greater than the threshold value are grouped into one category, called foreground (F). The remaining pixels are fallen into other category, called background (B) or vice-versa (Sahoo, 1997; Jawahar, 1997). The pixels belonging to set (F) are set to 1 (white), while the remaining pixels in the other set are set to 0 (black) (Pal, 1988; Dey, 2011).

Let $I = \left[I_{pq} \right]_{a \times b}$ be the gray scale image of the dimension $a \times b$ where, $\left(p, q \right)$ signifies a pixel coordinate of the test image and T is said to be the predefined threshold value satisfying the following properties [6]

$$F = \left\{ I_{pq} \middle| I_{pq} > T \right\} \tag{1}$$

$$B = \left\{ I_{pq} \middle| I_{pq} \leq T \right\} \tag{2}$$

Here, $I_{pq} \in \left[0, L \right]$ where, L represents the maximum threshold value of the image. It has been observed that some severe complications may arise for determining the optimum threshold due to some unwanted phenomena. A few typical examples of such complications may include poor contrast, abrupt illumination changes, immobile and correlated noise, no apposite objective measures etc. (Sezgin, 2004 ; Dey, 2011). Image thresholding are widely used in image processing (Sezan, 1990), video change detection (Su, 2006), Magnetic Resonance Image (MRI) (Atkins, 1998), Optical Character Recognition (OCR) (Sezgin, 2004), infrared gait recognition (Xue, 2010) to name a few.

In 1948, Shannon described and recognized entropy as a statistical measure that can recapitulate the random property of the used variables. By his observation, the increase of randomness in turn increases the entropy for the said variable (Talbi, 2006).

Let Y be a probability distribution of some given random variables and the probability of each variable y_j is defined by p_j. Then the entropy Y is defined by (Talbi, 2006)

$$H(Y) = -\sum p_j \log_2(p_j)$$ (3)

Let there are two probability distributions Y and Z defined for two random variables. When Y and Z are not independent to each other, the joint entropy can be illustrated as (Talbi, 2006)

$$H(Y, Z) = -\sum\sum p(y, z) \log_2(y, z)$$ (4)

The aforesaid joint distribution will be converted to marginal distribution when Y and Z are totally independent to each other as depicted by (Talbi, 2006).

$$P(Y, Z) = P(Y) \cdot P(Z)$$ (5)

Equation (5) leads to the following equation when entropy is concerned (Talbi, 2006).

$$H(Y, Z) = H(Y) + H(Z)$$ (6)

Mutual information is another measure that depicts the reduction on the entropy of Z when Y is given. This can be depicted as (Talbi, 2006).

$$MI(Y, Z) = H(Y) + H(Z) - H(Y, Z)$$ (7)

If Y and Z are totally dependent, $MI(Y;Z)$ is maximized (Talbi, 2006).

The entropy of the two segmented regions resort the result for entropy-based methods and the cross-entropy between the real images with its binary version is fabricated (Sezgin, 2004). Exploration and exploitation of gray level image distribution resort to the entropy of foreground and background image in this category. Some authors struggle for maximizing the entropy for the input image (Pun, 1980; Kapur, 1985), some others go for minimization for the same (Brink, 1996). Somewhere minimization of the cross-entropy is considered between the gray-level image and the resulting binary image (Li, 1998).

Since the intelligent systems have already been initiated, the researchers have been trying to improve its performance by applying the principles of QC. Now the challenge for the researchers has turned into combining the traditional soft computing approaches like fuzzy systems, artificial neural networks, swarm intelligence, evolutionary computing, and various hybrids soft computing methods with the basic inherent features of QC like interference, coherence, decoherence, superposition principle of participating states.

Before describing quantum-inspired evolutionary algorithm (QEA) proposed by Han *et al.* (Han, 2002), QC needs to be addressed first because it is the backbone of the above algorithm. The basic properties of QC are used to construct such powerful and complex algorithms that need large solutions spaces (Han, 2002; Narayanan, 1996). Though we are on the eve of new era of computer world, the researchers have been trying to design the quantum version of conventional algorithms that can be fitted efficiently on QC while invented. As QEA is inspired by QC, it can be described as qubit individuals that form population dynamics. Each qubit individual is probabilistic is nature. A qubit is referred to as the smallest unit of information in QC while a group of qubits can form a qubit individual (Han, 2002). The qubit individual causes better population diversity in the solution space for its inherent characteristics. In the process, it can use different Q-gate operators to get a better solution that finally converge to a single state. Though QEA is inspired by QC, QEA cannot be recognized as a quantum algorithm, but instead an evolutionary algorithm for the conventional computer (Kim, 2006).

The following sections depict the structure of this article presented here. Section II portrays the basic of quantum computing. Section III describes the basic ideas on quantum evolutionary algorithm (QEA) (Han, 2002). Section IV illustrates about the image thresholding optimization. Different methods used as the evaluation functions are described briefly in Section V. Section VI presents the proposed quantum inspired genetic algorithm in details. In Section VII, experimental results of QIGA are summarized and comparisons are made between the proposed QIGA and conventional GA (Holland, 1975; Reeves, 1993) and later with the algorithm proposed by Han *et al.* (Han, 2002). Finally, we present a discussion and conclusion section where some conclusions are drawn in Section VIII.

BASICS OF QUANTUM COMPUTING

A wave function which belongs to a Hilbert space is deemed to describe quantum machines. This Hilbert space encompasses the basic set of states (Mcmohan, 2008; Dey, 2011). The basic components needed for designing a QC are illustrated briefly in the following subsections.

Qubit

Qubit can be considered as a repository for storing the smallest unit of information in a two-state quantum system (Hey, 1999). In QC, $|0\rangle$ and $|1\rangle$ are the two-state vector of a quantum bit that are employed for bit representation as given by (Dey, 2011).

$$|0\rangle = \begin{bmatrix} 1 \\ 0 \end{bmatrix} \text{ and } |1\rangle = \begin{bmatrix} 0 \\ 1 \end{bmatrix} \tag{8}$$

where, two bracket notations $|.\rangle$ and $\langle.|$ were introduced by Paul Dirac for representing qubits (Araujo, 2008). These two notations are called *ket* and *bra* respectively. The first one is equivalent to a column vector and the second notation is referred to as the complex conjugate transpose of the first notation.

Quantum Gate

From the quantum computing perspective, quantum gates and quantum logic operations are very essential parts that are implemented for processing quantum algorithms (Dey, 2011). A quantum gate resort to the necessary changes for the basic qubit states. The quantum gates are reversible in nature that are represented as a unitary operator, U satisfying the relation $U^+ = U^{-1}$ where, U operates on the qubit basis states. The Hermitian unitary operator, U holds the relationships given by (Han, 2002)

$$UU^+ = U^+U = I \text{ and } U = e^{iHt} \tag{9}$$

Some typical examples of the quantum gates may include rotation gate, Hadamard gate, NOT gate, controlled NOT gate, etc. (Hey, 1999; Araujo, 2008). Finally, among the participating qubits, all states collapses to a single state (Han, 2002). Schrödinger's equation is a basic part for performing QC's operation (Han, 2002). The Q-gates which perform the transformation operation, preserves the orthogonality of the qubits.

Quantum Superposition

Quantum superposition is an interesting feature for QC. Linear superposition may be thought as an analogous to the linear combination representing vectors. The qubit may be in "0" state, "1" state or any linear combination called superposition of these two state vectors as depicted in the following equation (Han, 2002).

$$|\psi\rangle = \alpha|0\rangle + \beta|1\rangle \tag{10}$$

where, α, β are two complex numbers. Each qubits must satisfy the following equation in respect of the normalization of the participating qubit states (Han, 2002).

$$|\alpha|^2 + |\beta|^2 = 1 \tag{11}$$

When the superposition between the participating qubits states are considered, the probability of measurement of the states $|0\rangle$ and $|1\rangle$ will be $|\alpha|^2$ and $|\beta|^2$, respectively (Han, 2002). For a p qubits quantum computer, the root of the state space can be illustrated as $\underbrace{|0000\rangle}_{4\ qubits}, \underbrace{|0001\rangle}_{4\ qubits}, \underbrace{|0010\rangle}_{4\ qubits}, \cdots, \underbrace{|1111\rangle}_{4\ qubits}$
(Araujo, 2008).

The dot product of the complex numbers α and β is calculated as (Araujo, 2008).

$$d = \alpha \cdot \beta \tag{12}$$

The angle between the qubit phase, ξ is expressed by (Araujo, 2008)

$$\xi = \arctan\left(\beta \Big/ \alpha\right) \tag{13}$$

Quantum Coherence and Decoherence

Coherence and decoherence are considered with the concept of linear superposition of the basic qubit states in QC. Coherence between two parts of the wave functions $\left|\psi\right\rangle$ must exist for the qubit states as illustrated in (10). Here, a constant phase relationship must be preserved between these wave functions. When this phase relationship is destroyed or the linear superposition between the basis states are collapsed, decoherence occurs. The probabilities required for collapsing to the basic states are calculated as $\left|\alpha\right|^2$ and $\left|\beta\right|^2$, respectively (Han, 2002; Patel, 2009; Han, 2003).

QUANTUM EVOLUTIONARY ALGORITHM

The basis of QC is qubit and superposition of states. The principle of Quantum Evolutionary Algorithm (QEA) (Han, 2002) is comparable to the concept of QC. In QEA, the population dynamics are preserved and updated with different generations according to the evaluation function provided. As the business progresses, this algorithm discovers the best individual that ensembles the evaluation function and preserves for the next generation. The probabilistic representation of qubit of QEA is illustrated in the following subsection.

Quantum Inspired Representation

Qubit is acknowledged as the smallest unit of information for a two state QC which has state "0" and state "1". QEA exploits a probabilistic representation of these two states and their superposition for its application. The qubit individual may be represented in many ways. One of such representation is given below (Han, 2002; Araujo, 2008; Han, 2003).

Representation 1: A Q-bit individual formed by Q-bit strings collectively, is defined

$$t = \begin{bmatrix} \alpha_1 & \alpha_2 & \alpha_3 & \cdots & \alpha_p \\ \beta_1 & \beta_2 & \beta_3 & \cdots & \beta_p \end{bmatrix} \tag{14}$$

Here each α_j and β_j satisfy equations (9), (10), (11), (12), and (13) $\forall j = 1, 2, \ldots, p$.

Elegance of superposition principle between the states boots the aptitude of storing information for QC. An example of one q-individual figuring with four qubits $\left(p = 4\right)$ is expressed as follows.

$$u = \begin{bmatrix} \dfrac{1}{\sqrt{2}} & -\dfrac{\sqrt{3}}{2} & \dfrac{1}{\sqrt{2}} & \dfrac{1}{2} \\ \dfrac{1}{\sqrt{2}} & -\dfrac{1}{2} & -\dfrac{1}{\sqrt{2}} & \dfrac{\sqrt{3}}{2} \end{bmatrix} \tag{15}$$

The states for equation (15) can be represented as

$$u = -\left(\frac{\sqrt{3}}{8}\right)|0000\rangle - \left(\frac{3}{8}\right)|0001\rangle + \left(\frac{\sqrt{3}}{8}\right)|0010\rangle - \left(\frac{3}{8}\right)|0011\rangle - \left(\frac{1}{8}\right)|0100\rangle - \left(\frac{\sqrt{3}}{8}\right)|0101\rangle$$

$$+ \left(\frac{1}{8}\right)|0110\rangle + \left(\frac{\sqrt{3}}{8}\right)|0111\rangle - \left(\frac{\sqrt{3}}{8}\right)|1000\rangle - \left(\frac{3}{8}\right)|1001\rangle + \left(\frac{\sqrt{3}}{8}\right)|1010\rangle + \left(\frac{3}{8}\right)|1011\rangle$$

$$- \left(\frac{1}{8}\right)|1100\rangle - \left(\frac{\sqrt{3}}{8}\right)|1101\rangle + \left(\frac{1}{8}\right)|1110\rangle + \left(\frac{\sqrt{3}}{8}\right)|1111\rangle \qquad (16)$$

According to equation (16), 16 states are required for the q-individual presented in equation (15). These are

$$\underbrace{|0000\rangle}_{4\ qubits}, \underbrace{|0001\rangle}_{4\ qubits}, \underbrace{|0010\rangle}_{4\ qubits}, \cdots, \underbrace{|1111\rangle}_{4\ qubits}$$

having probabilities

$$\frac{3}{64}, \frac{9}{64}, \frac{3}{64}, \frac{9}{64}, \frac{1}{64},$$

$$\frac{3}{64}, \frac{1}{64}, \frac{3}{64}, \frac{3}{64}, \frac{9}{64}, \frac{3}{64}, \frac{9}{64}, \frac{1}{64}, \frac{3}{64}, \frac{1}{64}, \frac{3}{64},$$

respectively. In QC, one q-individual is adequate to represent these sixteen states as affirmed in equation (15) but for classical representation sixteen different strings viz. $(0000),(0001),\ldots,(1111)$ are obligatory (Han, 2002; Araujo, 2008). The interested readers may refer to (Han, 2002) for other forms of representation.

Details of QEA

The probabilistic quantum inspired evolutionary algorithm (QEA) is presented in this subsection. In this algorithm, $S(z) = \{r_1^z, r_2^z, r_3^z, \ldots, r_m^z\}$ denote a population of m qubit individuals which is generated at generation z. Here, we define each q-individual by r_k^z as depicted by

$$r_k^z = \begin{bmatrix} \alpha_{k1}^z & \alpha_{k2}^z & \alpha_{k3}^z & \cdots & \alpha_{kn}^z \\ \beta_{k1}^z & \beta_{k2}^z & \beta_{k3}^z & \cdots & \beta_{kn}^z \end{bmatrix} \qquad (17)$$

where, the string length of all the q-individuals for $k = 1, 2, \ldots, m$ is determined by n number of qubits. Initially, each α_p, β_p are initialized as $\alpha_p^0 = \beta_p^0 = \dfrac{1}{\sqrt{2}}$ for $p = 1, 2, \ldots, n \ \forall \ r_q^0 = r_q^z \big| z = 0$ for $q = 1, 2, \ldots, m$ to generate the population of m individuals that point to have superposition between all possible states with a same probability. The states of q-individuals in $S(z)$ possess a binary solution T_z where this solution may be represented as $T_z = \left\{ y_1^z, y_2^z, y_3^z, \ldots, y_m^z \right\}$ if it is attained at z-th generation. In T_z, each y_j^z is binary string of length n for $j = 1, 2, \ldots, m$ i.e., $y_j^z = c_1 c_2 c_3 \ldots c_n$ and each c_k for $k = 1, 2, \ldots, n$ where c_k may be either 0 or 1. A random number $r_d \in [0,1]$ is generated for each $\left(\alpha_i, \beta_i \right)^T$ where $i = 1, 2, \ldots, n \times m$ for all the participating qubit in the population S(z) during the observation phase. The qubit is set as 0 if $r_d \geq |\beta|^2$; otherwise it is set as 1.

In this algorithm, various Q-gates can be implemented in the QC for updating each q-individual in $S(z)$. The algorithm is executed for a number of times and if it is observed that the solution is not being improved for a number of iterations then all the solutions are replaced by b. QEA is portrayed at Figure 1 (Han, 2002; Araujo, 2008).

Figure 1. Quantum evolutionary algorithm

Require: A population of qubit individuals of size n
Ensure: Best solution for a particular application
1: Initialize $S(0)$ with n participating individuals
2: Create the state $T(0)$ by examining the state $S(0)$
3: **for** each element $y \in T(0)$ do
4:    Use evaluation function to exercise $Fitness(y)$
5:    Make a copy of $T(0)$ in $A(0)$
6: **end for**
7: **while** end condition not reached do
8:    Examine state $S(t-1)$ to create state $T(t)$
9:    **for** $y \in T(t)$ do
10:    Calculate $Fitness(y)$ considering probability constraints if applicable
11:    **end for**
12:    Use Q-gate to update the elements of $S(t)$
13:    Store the better solution among $B(t-1)$ and $T(t)$ in $B(t)$
14:    Store the optimum solution in $B(t)$
15:    **if** solution is not improved for many generations **then**
16:    All the solutions of $B(t)$ is replaced by b
17:    **end if**
18: **end while**

In (Han, 2002), the authors have developed QEA and applied on knapsack problem which is combinatorial optimization problem in nature. The characteristic of QEA is that it initiates with a random search for optimization. Starting with the local search, it automatically looks for global search while the probability of getting the solution increases. After several successful runs the observed probability of getting a solution converges to 1. Some rotation gates need to be implemented to perform some required operations in accordance with some predefined lookup tables that in turn provide the population diversity. The shortcoming of QEA is also observed. It is not expedient to espouse the coding and decoding process in QEA in an effortless way. It has a very low searching efficacy when applied for numerical methods oriented optimization processes as QEA is not capable to espouse to handle the dimensions and related precisions for these numerical problems for optimization. Above all, since it depends on look up tables for optimization, then it cannot be a good process for taking in (Han, 2002; Araujo, 2008; Hossain, 2010).

IMAGE THRESHOLDING OPTIMIZATION

In the present computer world, thresholding holds the impression to be a very effective and simplest method. This process translates a given gray level image into its corresponding binary image. For this purpose, a predefined intensity value that belongs to the intensity span in the image spectrum is compared with the entire image content on a pixel to pixel basis (Dey, 2011). The pixels in the image are grouped into two categories viz., background and foreground. All the pixels in the image which are greater than the predefined intensity value (referred to as threshold) are classified as foreground. The remaining pixels in the image are classified as background (or vice versa). There are two well-known thresholding methods called as local methods and global methods. For the former one, there may be more than one threshold value, which varies across the image neighborhoods while the later guarantees to have a fixed threshold for the entire image (Bazi, 2007).

Optimization results in pixel intensity value yield for a given evaluation function. Histogram can be applied as a tool that helps to find out a unique peak in an image intensity gamut for thresholding that can easily differentiate the foreground and background pixels in the image. Unimodal histogram is easy to handle because a single lobe is present compared to a multimodal one which consists of multiple lobes. Thus, the problem arises to an optimized search heuristic. In short, thresholding can be envisaged as a classical optimization problem, which can be attended by different optimization heuristics in nature.

IMAGE THRESHOLDING EVALUATION METRICS

In (Bhattacharyya, 2011), the author has presented a brief survey on different image thresholding and image segmentation techniques. Apart from that, Sezin and Sankur presented a detailed investigation on different thresholding techniques with their performance evaluation in (Sezgin, 2004). They have categorized their research works into six groups. Among the various entropy based thresholding algorithms described in (Sezgin, 2004), three methods have been selected in this article. These are Entropy-Brink (Brink, 1996), Entropy-Pun (Pun, 1980) and Entropy-Kapur (Kapur, 1985). The entropy-based methods judge the entropy of the entire foreground and background areas. The methods also calculate the corresponding cross entropy between the original images with their binary version of images (Sezgin, 2004). In practice, the attention of this kind reflects on image histograms. These algorithms regulate each pixel element by its total number in the image. Therefore, the probability of each pixel in the image is given by

$$p_j = \frac{n_j}{N}, j \in [0, 255] \tag{18}$$

and

$$P(T) = \sum_{j=0}^{T} p_j \tag{19}$$

where, n_j represents the number of pixels in the gray scale image, N represents the total number of pixels in the image. p_j is the probability of j_{th} pixel in the image and $P(T)$ is calculated by summing up the probability distributions up to the threshold T. The selected algorithms are presented in the following subsections.

Pun's Algorithm

Pun has proposed an entropy-based algorithm (Entropy-Pun) in (Pun, 1980; Sezgin, 2004). Pun has mulled over g-symbol source where, $g = 256$ for gray-level histogram, statistically independent in nature. The ratio of the following entropy (Pun, 1980).

$$H'(T) = -P(T)\log[P(T)] - [1 - P(T)]\log[1 - P(T)] \tag{20}$$

to the source entropy given by (Pun, 1980)

$$H(T) = H_b(T) + H_f(T) \tag{21}$$

produces,

$$\frac{H'(T)}{H(T)} \geq Pu(\beta) = \beta \frac{\log P(T)}{\log\left(\max\left(p_0, p_1, \ldots, p_T\right)\right)} + (1 - \beta)\frac{\log\left(1 - P(T)\right)}{\log\left(\max\left(p_{T+1}, p_{T+2}, \ldots, p_g\right)\right)} \tag{22}$$

where,

$$H_b(T) = \beta H(T) \tag{23}$$

Here, $H_b(T)$ and $H_f(T)$ can be depicted by (Pun, 1980)

$$H_b(T) = -\sum_{j=0}^{T} p_j \log(p_j) \tag{24}$$

and

$$H_f\left(T\right) = -\sum_{j=T+1}^{g} p_j \log\left(p_j\right) \tag{25}$$

The optimum threshold is acquired by the particular T which persuades equation (23) with the argument β that maximizes $Pu\left(\beta\right)$ in (22) (Pun, 1980).

Kapur's Algorithm

This entropy-based algorithm was proposed by Kapur, Sahoo and Wong (Entropy-Kapur) (Kapur, 1985; Sezgin, 2004). They have taken into consideration two dissimilar signal sources known as foreground and background images for determining the optimum threshold value of the given images (Kapur, 1985). The class distribution of the object O with its background B are illustrated below (Kapur, 1985)

$$O : p\left(j\right) = \frac{p_j}{P\left(T\right)}, j \in \left[0, T\right] \tag{26}$$

and

$$B : p\left(j\right) = \frac{p_j}{P\left(T\right)}, j \in \left[T+1, g\right] \tag{27}$$

where, p_j and $P\left(T\right)$ are determined by the equations (18) and (19), respectively. $H_b\left(T\right)$ and $H_f\left(T\right)$ are known as the background and foreground class entropies which are calculated using the equations (24) and (25), respectively with $p\left(j\right) = p_j$ (Kapur, 1985). Two class entropies, one for foreground and another for background image are judged separately and whenever the sum of the said entropies enriches its maximum value, the threshold T is taken as the optimum threshold value. The optimum threshold value is determined by maximizing $H\left(T\right)$ as given in equation (21) (Kapur, 1985) and the values of $H_b\left(T\right)$ and $H_f\left(T\right)$ are determined using the equations (24) and (25), respectively (Kapur, 1985).

Brink's Algorithm

A. D. Brink and N. E. Pendock are the inventors of this cross entropy-based (Entropy-Brink) (Brink, 1996; Sezgin, 2004) thresholding algorithm. In this method, the original grayscale images are used as the preceding distribution with the existing gray level intensity values for threshold selection among the test images. The averages comprising the above and below threshold values $\left(T\right)$ of the image are considered. These two means are referred to as $\mu_f(T)$ and $\mu_b(T)$, respectively and can be utilized as the two gray levels for determining the threshold value of binary thresholded image as given by (Brink, 1996).

$$\mu_b(T) = \sum_{i=0}^{T} ip_i \text{ and } \mu_f(T) = \sum_{i=T+1}^{255} ip_i \tag{28}$$

where, each p_i for $i \in [0, 255]$ are determined by the equation (18) (Brink, 1996). Let us consider two probability distribution functions; one is called *priori* probability distribution, $p(y)$ and other is referred to *posteriori* probability distribution, $q(y)$. The cross-entropy distance is described as follows (Brink, 1996):

$$Z_{CE}(q,p) = \int q(y) \log \frac{q(y)}{p(y)} dy \tag{29}$$

The integration given in equation (29) is substituted to summation for discrete probability distributions. For the discrete cross-entropy distance for q_y and p_y, the following equation is satisfied (Brink, 1996).

$$Z_{CE}(q,p) = \sum_{y=1}^{N} q_y \log \frac{q_y}{p_y} \tag{30}$$

subject to,

$$\sum_{y=1}^{N} p_y = \sum_{y=1}^{N} q_y (= 1)$$

where, N represents the number of discrete points in the discrete probability distribution. Equation (29) is non-symmetric in nature. It is important to get the symmetry to have a metric distance measure. This is achieved by the following equation (Brink, 1996).

$$Z_{MD}(p,q) = Z_{CE}(q,p) + Z_{CE}(p,q)$$

$$= \sum_{y=1}^{N} q_y \log \frac{q_y}{p_y} + \sum_{y=1}^{N} p_y \log \frac{p_y}{q_y} \tag{31}$$

The condition for equation (31) can be satisfied using the means as determined by equation (28). This in turn gives (Brink, 1996)

$$\sum_{j=0}^{M} g_j = \left[\sum_{j=0}^{M} \mu_b\left(T\right) \right]_{g_j \le T} + \left[\sum_{j=0}^{M} \mu_f\left(T\right) \right]_{g_j > T} \tag{32}$$

where, M represents the number of pixels in the test image and $g_j \in \left[0, 255\right]$ are the pixel intensity values in the image. In a similar fashion, we can rewrite equation (31).

Since a large image has larger number of pixel intensity values, it will be time consuming to calculate the threshold value using equation (32) and by its equivalent version as given in equation (31). To improve the computational efficacy, gray level frequency histogram is considered. From this histogram, it is easy to calculate the frequency $\left(f\right)$ of each gray level g. This condition may lead to equation (32) in the following form (Brink, 1996):

$$Z_{CE}\left(T\right) = \sum_{j=0}^{T} f\mu_b\left(T\right) \log \frac{\mu_b\left(T\right)}{j} + \sum_{j=T+1}^{255} f\mu_f\left(T\right) \log \frac{\mu_f\left(T\right)}{j} \tag{33}$$

Similarly, equation (31) can be rewritten as (Brink, 1996)

$$Z_{MD}\left(T\right) = \sum_{j=0}^{T} f\left[\mu_b\left(T\right) \log \frac{\mu_b\left(T\right)}{j} + j \log \frac{j}{\mu_b\left(T\right)} \right] + \sum_{j=T+1}^{255} f\left[\mu_f\left(T\right) \log \frac{\mu_f\left(T\right)}{j} + j \log \frac{j}{\mu_f\left(T\right)} \right] \tag{34}$$

The most simplest and efficient scheme for determining the optimum threshold is to minimize $Z_{CE}\left(T\right)$ or $Z_{MD}\left(T\right)$ as determined by the equations (33) and (34), respectively (Brink, 1996; Sezgin, 2004).

RANDOM INTERFERENCE BASED QUANTUM INSPIRED GENETIC ALGORITHM

Now a day, many researchers of the field of computer science and engineering are trying to design various quantum-inspired evolutionary algorithms (QIEA). They basically try to incorporate the principles of quantum mechanics into suitable algorithmic structure (Han, 2002; Kim, 2006). QIEA is mainly employed to solve diverse combinatorial optimization problems (Dey, 2011). In (Bhattacharyya, 2010), the authors have used the fitness function of correlation coefficient as a standard measure of the participating chromosomes in the form of encoded qubits. Later, a convex combination of two dissimilar fuzzy thresholding was considered as an evaluation function for the same purpose (Dey, 2011). The QEA proposed by Han *et al.* was about the notion of qubit that comply with certain probability constraints and superposition of various states. This algorithm used different Q-gate to confer a better solution space (Han, 2002). Another quantum GA approach was taken by Talbi *et al.* for solving TSP problem (Talbi, 2004).

In this paper, a quantum version of genetic algorithm namely, quantum-inspired genetic algorithm (QIGA) has been presented. QIGA comprises the following phases as depicted in the flow diagram in Figure 2. The outline of the proposed QIGA is described in the subsections given below.

Figure 2. The proposed algorithm

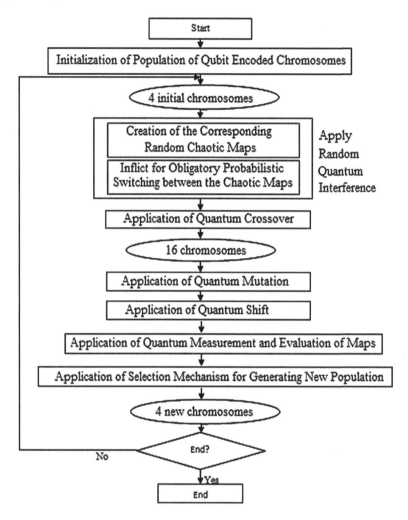

Initialization of Population of Qubit Encoded Chromosomes

In this earliest phase of the proposed algorithm, the initial population in the form of qubit encoded chromosomes was generated. For the gray scale image having G possible intensity values, an initial matrix of dimension $G \times G$ is formed. Each element of the above matrix was formed using qubits of two superposed quantum states as given by (Talbi, 2004; Dey, 2011).

$$|\psi\rangle = \begin{bmatrix} \alpha_{11}\langle\psi_1| + \beta_{11}\langle\psi_2| \cdots\cdots \alpha_{1G}\langle\psi_1| + \beta_{1G}\langle\psi_2| \\ \alpha_{21}\langle\psi_1| + \beta_{21}\langle\psi_2| \cdots\cdots \alpha_{2G}\langle\psi_1| + \beta_{2G}\langle\psi_2| \\ \cdots\cdots\cdots\cdots\cdots\cdots\cdots\cdots\cdots\cdots\cdots\cdots\cdots \\ \cdots\cdots\cdots\cdots\cdots\cdots\cdots\cdots\cdots\cdots\cdots\cdots\cdots \\ \alpha_{L1}\langle\psi_1| + \beta_{L1}\langle\psi_2| \cdots\cdots \alpha_{GG}\langle\psi_1| + \beta_{GG}\langle\psi_2| \end{bmatrix} \tag{35}$$

$\left|\alpha_{ij}\right|^2$ and $\left|\beta_{ij}\right|^2$ are probabilities for measuring the values of $\left|0\right\rangle$ and $\left|1\right\rangle$, respectively for qubit (i,j) where, $i = 1, 2, \ldots, G$ and $j = 1, 2, \ldots, G$.

Apply Random Quantum Interference

The constituents of the matrix specified in (35) is a structure of two quantum states in superposed fashion for the participating qubits. Each element of this matrix must assure the relationship as given in equation (11). The effect of quantum interference for a participating qubit e.g., $\left\{\left(0.0119\right),\left(0.9937\right)\right\}$ would actually mean the superposition of the states yielding $\left(0.0119\right)^2 + \left(0.9937\right)^2 = 1$. Similarly, for another participating qubit $\left\{\left(0.2395\right),\left(0.9708\right)\right\}$, $\left(0.2395\right)^2 + \left(0.9708\right)^2 = 1$ must holds. The quantum interference is the conjunction of following two random phases as described in the following two subsections.

1. **Creation of the Corresponding Random Chaotic Map:** The first step of this phase causes for the instigation of random quantum interference of the participating qubits. To endure quantum interference for the qubits, the states should be symbolized in terms of real chaotic maps (Dey, 2011). The very basic property of QIGA is that it maintains dynamic time discreteness and pursue the properties of Sri Jayachamarajendra College of Engineering, Mysore

    a. **Automorphism:** When K is considered as an automorphism, the following equation must be satisfied (Boyarsky, 2010; Dey, 2011)

$$\lim_{n\to\infty} \frac{1}{n} \sum_{j=0}^{n-1} g\left(K^j z\right) = \lim_{n\to\infty} \frac{1}{n} \sum_{j=0}^{n-1} g\left(K^{-j} z\right) \tag{36}$$

that in turn can be written as

$$\frac{1}{2n+1} \sum_{j=-n}^{n} g\left(K^j z\right) \overset{def}{=} \overline{g}\left(z\right) \tag{37}$$

    b. **Endomorphism:** When K is considered as an endomorphism, the following equation must be satisfied (Boyarsky, 2010; Dey, 2011):

$$\lim_{n\to\infty} \frac{1}{n} \sum_{j=0}^{n-1} g\left(K^j z\right) \overset{def}{=} \overline{g}\left(z\right) \tag{38}$$

    c. **Flow:** When $\left\{K^t\right\}_{t\in R}$ (assuming R to be in the measurement space) is considered as a flow, the equation given below must be satisfied (Boyarsky, 2010; Dey, 2011)

$$\lim_{t \to \infty} \frac{1}{t} \int_0^t g\left(K^\tau z\right) d\tau = \lim_{t \to \infty} \frac{1}{t} \int_0^t g\left(K^{-\tau} z\right) d\tau \tag{39}$$

that in turn can be specified as

$$\lim_{t \to \infty} \frac{1}{2t} \int_{-t}^t g\left(K^\tau z\right) d\tau \stackrel{def}{=} \overline{g}\left(z\right) \tag{40}$$

    d.   **Semiflow:** When $\left\{M^t\right\}_{t \in R}$ (assuming R to be in the measurement space) is considered as a semiflow, the equation given below must be satisfied (Boyarsky, 2010; Dey, 2011)

$$\lim_{t \to \infty} \frac{1}{2t} \int g\left(M^\tau z\right) d\tau \stackrel{def}{=} \overline{g}\left(z\right) \tag{41}$$

By summarizing the above four properties, we can write the following equation (Boyarsky, 2010; Dey, 2011)

$$\overline{g}\left(Kz\right) = \overline{g}\left(z\right) \text{ or } \overline{g}\left(K^t z\right) = \overline{g}\left(z\right) \text{ or } \overline{g}\left(M^t z\right) = \overline{g}\left(z\right) \tag{42}$$

To be invariant with respect to the above four properties, the transformation must satisfies the equations (36), (38), (39), and (41). A system is Ergodic when the value of the measure $\mu\left(B\right)$ of any invariant set B is either 0 or 1 under these transformations (Boyarsky, 2010). It can be stated that the participating qubits

$$\left(\left|\psi\right\rangle = \alpha_k \left|\psi_k\right\rangle + \beta_k \left|\psi_k\right\rangle, k = 1, 2\right)$$

pursue a dynamical ergodic system. Boyarsky and Góra applied the Birkhoff's Ergodic theorem as an effective tool to ascertain the equivalence between the chaotic map and quantum state (Boyarsky, 2010).

An invariant point transformation V should be pertained to the qubits to bag the corresponding assortment of chaotic maps as $V = \left\{t_1, t_2, I, p_1, p_2, 1 - p_1, 1 - p_2\right\}$ (Boyarsky, 2010). Here, $\tau_p \left(p = 1, 2\right) = g \circ V \circ g^{-1}$ with nonlinear point transformations and is differentially conjugate to V and I is the identity map. The weighting probabilities p_1 and p_2 of τ_1 and τ_2 are established by the equation given by

$$p_j = \frac{b_j g_j}{\displaystyle\sum_{j=1}^2 b_j g_j} \tag{43}$$

where, b_j for $j = 1, 2$ are the positive constants and $g_j = |\psi_j\rangle\langle\psi_j| = \psi_j^*\psi_j$ are probability density function corresponding to each τ_j (Dey, 2011).

2. **Inflict for Obligatory Probabilistic Switching between the Chaotic Maps:** This is the second step of this phase where a probabilistic switching relevant to interference is invoked between the maps. The upshot of this switching may alter states of the chaotic maps that are shaped with the participating qubits. As a result of fact, an expected interference may come into existence between them. This random interference is simply the effect of superposition applied between two wave functions if some order is maintained. Thus, the beauty of the proposed method is its randomness which is achieved due to the probabilistic transformation V discussed in the previous subsection. Due to random nature, no predefined order needs to be followed for interference.

- **Application of Quantum Crossover:** This phase initiates the quantum inspired genetic crossover in QIGA to persuade assortment in the population of chaotic maps. Two offspring are being fashioned from the participating chaotic maps by swapping their parts with each other. To settle on the position within the participating chromosome for crossover, a random number (say p_{cr}) referred to as crossover probability is generated for each chromosome.

- **Application of Quantum Mutation:** In addition to quantum crossover, this phase can also be a cause of diversity in the augmented population of chaotic maps. Unlike quantum crossover, any position in a chaotic map may undergo for mutation depending on a predefined mutation probability (say p_m).

- **Application of Quantum Shift:** With quantum mutation, this phase enhances the assortment in the population of chaotic maps. Like quantum mutation, four random numbers are subsequently generated in this phase. The first number is used to decide whether a particular chaotic map will be selected for shifting or not by comparing with a predefined selection probability (say $shthrs$). The three other random numbers (say r_1, r_2, and r_3) are used for intermediate calculations within the selected chaotic maps.

- **Application of Quantum Measurement and Evaluation of Maps:** In QIGA, the previous states need to be indemnified from loss for evaluating the iterations. The proposed algorithm preserves the states fo `r future evaluation. Quantum measurement leads to destruct the superposition between the states to substantiate the required measurement by figuring out the fitness values of each participating chaotic maps (Dey, 2011). To attain the best possible solutions, the proposed algorithm generates a random number (N_r) and compare with p_2. The positions of τ_2 within all participating chaotic maps where $|p_2|^2 > N_r$ may lead to possible solutions.

Let us take an example to describe how the procedure actually works in the proposed QIGA. Let $G = \{0, 1, 2, \ldots, G-1\}$ be the set of G possible gray level intensity values of a gray scale image. In these procedure comparisons takes place between a randomly generated numbers N_r and all p_2 as given by the equation (43). Let us assume the condition $|p_2|^2 > N_r$ holds at the position $(16, 8)$ as shown in Figure 3. Then the possible solution is at row 16 and column 8 of the qubit (now transformed into chaotic maps) encoded chromosome in population as shown in equation (35). The optimum threshold is given by $128 (= 16 \times 8)$.

Figure 3. The solution matrix

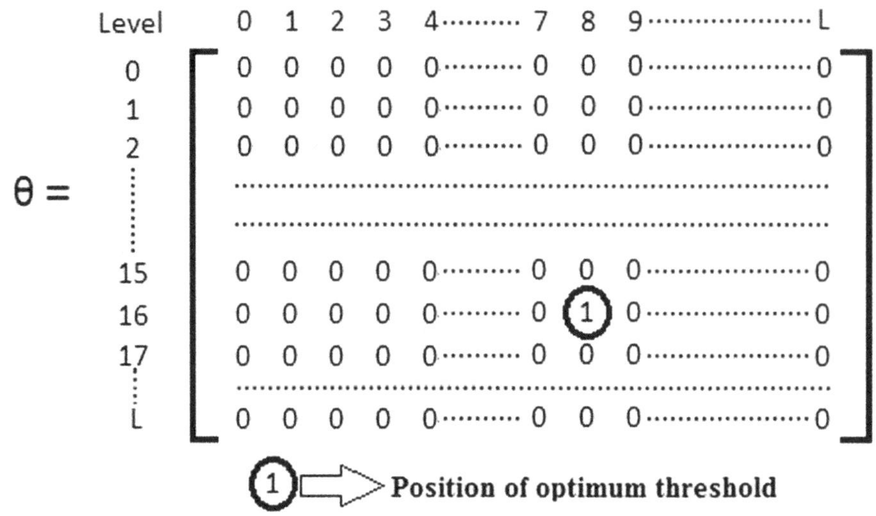

$$
\theta =
\begin{array}{c}
\text{Level} \\
0 \\
1 \\
2 \\
\vdots \\
15 \\
16 \\
17 \\
\vdots \\
L
\end{array}
\quad
\begin{bmatrix}
0 & 1 & 2 & 3 & 4 \cdots 7 & 8 & 9 \cdots L \\
0 & 0 & 0 & 0 & 0 \cdots 0 & 0 & 0 \cdots 0 \\
0 & 0 & 0 & 0 & 0 \cdots 0 & 0 & 0 \cdots 0 \\
0 & 0 & 0 & 0 & 0 \cdots 0 & 0 & 0 \cdots 0 \\
& & & & & & \\
0 & 0 & 0 & 0 & 0 \cdots 0 & 0 & 0 \cdots 0 \\
0 & 0 & 0 & 0 & 0 \cdots 0 & \textcircled{1} & 0 \cdots 0 \\
0 & 0 & 0 & 0 & 0 \cdots 0 & 0 & 0 \cdots 0 \\
& & & & & & \\
0 & 0 & 0 & 0 & 0 \cdots 0 & 0 & 0 \cdots 0
\end{bmatrix}
$$

$\textcircled{1} \Longrightarrow$ **Position of optimum threshold**

- **Application of Selection Mechanism for Generating New Population:** This section expresses the selection strategy adopted by QIGA. At every generation the best fitness value for the chaotic map that costume the selection strategy are preserved for the next iteration. The entire practice is repeated over until and unless the best solution attained at any generation surpasses the overall best solution.

EXPERIMENTAL RESULTS

Results Obtained with Proposed QIGA and Conventional GA

The proposed QIGA algorithm has been run on two gray scale images of dimensions 256×256 to get their optimum thresholds. The selected test images are Lena (intensity dynamic range varies from 23 and 255) and Barbara (intensity dynamic range varies from 2 and 248) (Websource, 2000). For this purpose three entropy-based methods viz., Brink's algorithm (Brink, 1996), Kapur's algorithm (Kapur, 1985) and Pun's algorithm (Pun, 1980) have been used as the evaluation functions. The proposed QIGA algorithm has been executed for 10 different runs with 500 iterations each for all the three measures individually. The conventional GA has been also tested on the two test images with the three evolution metrics as fitness functions.

The list of results for the selected evaluation methods are shown in Tables 1-3. Fitness value (μ), optimum threshold (θ) and the execution time (t) (in seconds) for each method have been documented both for QIGA and the conventional genetic algorithm (GA) for the two test images. Finally, the optimum threshold (θ_{op}) value for each of the test images are listed among 10 individual runs using each of the particular measure.

Table 1. Experimental results of QIGA and GA for two gray scale images using Brink's method

TN	Lena						Barbara					
	QIGA			GA			QIGA			GA		
	θ	υ	t	θ	υ	t	θ	υ	t	θ	υ	t
1	131	-41.910	344	131	-41.910	344	115	-37.606	343	115	-37.606	440
2	131	-41.910	344	131	-41.910	344	115	-37.606	344	115	-37.606	428
3	131	-41.910	343	131	-41.910	343	115	-37.606	343	115	-37.606	445
4	131	-41.910	343	131	-41.910	343	115	-37.606	344	115	-37.606	443
5	131	-41.910	344	131	-41.910	344	115	-37.606	344	115	-37.606	433
6	131	-41.910	344	131	-41.910	344	115	-37.606	343	115	-37.606	451
7	131	-41.910	343	131	-41.910	343	115	-37.606	344	115	-37.606	439
8	131	-41.910	343	131	-41.910	343	115	-37.606	343	115	-37.606	437
9	131	-41.910	343	131	-41.910	343	115	-37.606	344	115	-37.606	440
10	131	-41.910	344	131	-41.910	344	115	-37.606	344	115	-37.606	442
θ_{op}	131			131			115			115		
υ_{op}	-41.910			-41.910			-37.606			-37.606		

(Holland, 1975; Reeves, 1993); (Brink, 1996).

Considering two qubit states in QIGA, for a test image of dimensions $a \times b$ having pixel intensity of size d each, total size is supposed to be $P = 2 \times a \times b \times d \times 8 = 16abd$ bits. Now for the same test image having each pixel intensity size of c for GA, the total size can be calculated as $Q = a \times b \times c \times 8 = 8abc$ bits. So, $\dfrac{Q}{P} = \dfrac{8abc}{16abd} = \dfrac{c}{2d}$. In our proposed algorithm, we have chosen 16 chromosomes each of double data type for QIGA and 8192 chromosomes each of integer data type $\left(2^8 = 256\right)$ for GA for performing the respective operations. The size of the selected test images are 256×256. In this respect, the size required in QIGA is given by

$$16 \times 2 \times 256 \times 256 \times 8 \times 8 = 134217728$$

bits and that of conventional GA is $8192 \times 8 \times 4 \times 8 = 2097152$ bits. So, it can be easily shown that the size in GA is $\dfrac{134217728}{2097152} = 64$ times bigger that of QIGA. The effective time is listed for each measure in the aforementioned tables using both for QIGA and GA. The comparison in time efficacy proves that QIGA is superior to its GA counterpart. The convergence graph for each method for the proposed QIGA is given in Figure 4. Finally, the thresholded images for each of the three measures are depicted in Figures 5-7.

Table 2. Experimental results of QIGA and GA for two gray scale images using Pun's method

TN	Lena						Barbara					
	QIGA			GA			QIGA			GA		
	θ	υ	t	θ	υ	t	θ	υ	t	θ	υ	t
1	130	0.154	343	130	0.154	389	113	0.151	343	113	0.151	463
2	130	0.154	343	130	0.154	406	113	0.151	342	113	0.151	478
3	130	0.154	344	130	0.154	416	113	0.151	343	113	0.151	494
4	130	0.154	344	130	0.154	421	113	0.151	344	113	0.151	474
5	130	0.154	343	130	0.154	410	113	0.151	343	113	0.151	468
6	130	0.154	343	130	0.154	385	113	0.151	342	113	0.151	466
7	130	0.154	344	130	0.154	43	113	0.151	344	113	0.151	472
8	130	0.154	343	130	0.154	413	113	0.151	342	113	0.151	482
9	130	0.154	344	130	0.154	396	113	0.151	343	113	0.151	488
10	130	0.154	344	130	0.154	422	113	0.151	342	113	0.151	490
θ_{op}	130			130			113			113		
υ_{op}	0.154			0.154			0.151			0.151		

Figure 4. Convergence curves for Brink's method, for Pun's method, and for Kapur's method for QIGA (Brink, 1996); (Pun, 1980); (Kapur, 1985).

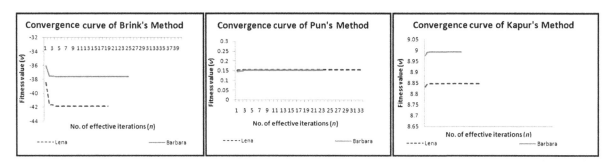

(Holland, 1975; Reeves, 1993); (Pun, 1980).

Results Obtained with QEA

In (Han, 2002) proposed by Han *et al.*, the same evaluation functions have been applied on the selected test images as used in the proposed QIGA. Results have been taken for 10 individual runs of 500 iterations each. As the random interference in the algorithm proposed by Han *et al.* is solely dependent on

Table 3. Experimental results of QIGA and GA for two gray scale images using Kapur's method

TN	Lena						Barbara					
	QIGA			GA			QIGA			GA		
	θ	υ	t	θ	υ	t	θ	υ	t	θ	υ	t
1	125	8.846	343	125	8.846	444	117	8.992	343	117	8.992	420
2	125	8.846	343	125	8.846	456	117	8.992	344	117	8.992	426
3	125	8.846	344	125	8.846	436	117	8.992	344	117	8.992	436
4	125	8.846	342	125	8.846	436	117	8.992	342	117	8.992	428
5	125	8.846	342	125	8.846	451	117	8.992	343	117	8.992	430
6	125	8.846	344	125	8.846	429	117	8.992	344	117	8.992	431
7	125	8.846	344	125	8.846	439	117	8.992	342	117	8.992	419
8	125	8.846	343	125	8.846	431	117	8.992	344	117	8.992	425
9	125	8.846	343	125	8.846	450	117	8.992	343	117	8.992	447
10	125	8.846	344	125	8.846	449	117	8.992	343	117	8.992	442
θ_{op}	**125**			**125**			**117**			**117**		
υ_{op}	**8.846**			**8.846**			**8.992**			**8.992**		

(Holland, 1975 ; Reeves, 1993); (Kapur, 1985) .

Figure 5. Thresholded images of Lena and Barbara using Brink's method in Figures 5(a) and Figures 5(b) with θ_{op} for QIGA
(Brink, 1996).

(a) Thresholded Lena image with of 131   (b) Thresholded Barbara image with of 115

Figure 6. Thresholded images of Lena and Barbara using Pun's method in Figures 6(a) and Figures 6(b) with θ_{op} for QIGA
(Pun, 1980).

(a) Thresholded Lena image with of 130 (b) Thresholded Barbara image with of 11з

Figure 7. Thresholded images of Lena and Barbara using Kapur's method in Figures 7(a) and Figures 7(b) with θ_{op} for QIGA
(Kapur, 1985).

(a) Thresholded Lena image with of 125 (b) Thresholded Barbara image with of 117

the predefined lookup table (Han, 2002), 6 different lookup tables for two test images (two for each method) were built for this purpose. For each test image, two different threshold values have been chosen preferably from near the average value of the dynamic intensity range of the selected image. It has been observed that the intensity dynamic range varies from 23 to 255 for Lena and 2 to 248 for Barbara. The chosen thresholded vales for Lena are $108\left(=12\times9\right)$ and $116\left(=4\times29\right)$, and for Barbara $124\left(=31\times4\right)$ and $120\left(=24\times5\right)$ respectively. The corresponding lookup tables have been generated accordingly. The average and best results among the 10 runs for each individual method are listed in Tables 4-6. Finally, the convergence curve attained for the three methods for the QEA proposed by Han *et al.* (Han, 2002) is depicted in Figure 8 and the thresholded images obtained from this method are shown in Figures 9-11.

Table 4. Experimental results of QEA for two gray scale images using Brink's method

TN	Lena						Barbara					
	108			116			120			124		
	θ	υ	t	θ	υ	t	θ	υ	t	θ	υ	t
Average	131	-41.910	344	131	-41.910	344	115	-37.606	343	115	-37.606	343
Best	131	-41.910	343	131	-41.910	343	115	-37.606	343	115	-37.606	342
θ_{op}	131			131			115			125		
υ_{op}	-41.910			-41.910			-37.606			-37.606		

(Han, 2002); (Brink, 1996)

Table 5. Experimental results of QEA for two gray scale images using Pun's method

TN	Lena						Barbara					
	108			116			120			124		
	θ	υ	t	θ	υ	t	θ	υ	t	θ	υ	t
Average	130	0.154	344	130	0.154	345	113	0.151	344	113	0.151	344
Best	130	0.154	342	130	0.154	342	113	0.151	343	113	0.151	343
θ_{op}	130			130			113			113		
υ_{op}	0.154			0.154			0.151			0.151		

(Han, 2002); (Pun, 1980).

Figure 8. Convergence curves for Brink's method for Pun's method and for Kapur's method for QIGA for QEA
(Brink, 1996); (Pun, 1980); (Kapur, 1985).

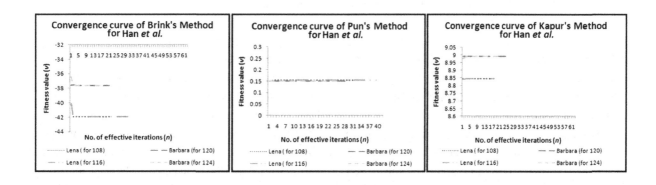

Figure 9. Thresholded images of Lena and Barbara using Brink's method in Figures 9(a) and Figures 9(b) with θ_{op} for QEA
(Brink, 1996).

(a) Thresholded Lena image with of 131   (b) Thresholded Barbara image with of 115

Figure 10. Thresholded images of Lena and Barbara using Pun's method in Figures 10(a) and Figures 10(b) with θ_{op} for QEA
(Pun, 1980).

(a) Thresholded Lena image with of 130   (b) Thresholded Barbara image with of 113

Comparative Study of Proposed QIGA, Conventional GA and Algorithm Proposed by Han et al.

The performances of proposed QIGA, the conventional GA (Reeves, 1993) and the algorithm proposed by Han et al. (Han, 2002; Araujo, 2008) have been evaluated in this article. For this purpose, these three algorithms have been executed for the same number of runs with same number of iterations. As said before, the performance of QIGA is greatly influenced by its inherent properties. The parallelism capability with random interference for search heuristics turns QIGA superior in terms of time efficacy. The concerned time complexities both for the proposed QIGA and the conventional GA have been discussed in the above subsection. The algorithm proposed by Han *et al.* (Han, 2002) uses a predefined look up table for its random interference. The lookup tables have been made up heuristically. In QEA (Han, 2002),

Table 6. Experimental results of QEA for two gray scale images using Kapur's method

TN	Lena						Barbara					
	108			116			120			124		
	θ	υ	t	θ	υ	t	θ	υ	t	θ	υ	t
Average	125	8.846	343	125	8.846	343	117	8.992	343	117	8.992	344
Best	125	8.846	343	125	8.846	342	117	8.992	342	117	8.992	343
θ_{op}	125			125			117			117		
υ_{op}	8.846			8.846			8.992			8.992		

(Han, 2002); (Kapur, 1985).

Figure 11. Thresholded images of Lena and Barbara using Kapur's method in Figures 11(a) and Figures11(b) with θ_{op} for QEA
(Kapur, 1985).

(a) Thresholded Lena image with of 125   (b) Thresholded Barbara image with of 117

rotation is used to enhance the probability of getting population diversity. In the proposed algorithm only the probabilistic approach was made for random interference. Moreover, the approach followed in Han *et al.*'s QEA (Han, 2002; Araujo, 2008) is to continue a random search until and unless the probability converges to 1 for the best fit qubit individual. It can be shown that the QEA proposed by Han *et al.* (Han, 2002) enjoys the features of exploration and exploitation (Han, 2002) because random searching initiates global search followed by local search (Han, 2002). The convergence curve as depicted in Figure 4 and Figure 8 are the evidences of elapsing least time for the global search mechanism as compared with the QEA proposed by Han *et al.* (Han, 2002; Araujo, 2008). Here Figure 8 illustrates the behavioral pattern of Han *et al.*'s QEA (Han, 2002; Araujo, 2008) for the three selected evaluation metrics. Therefore, it can be concluded that QIGA succeeds over QEA in context of searching mechanism (Han, 2002; Araujo, 2008). So QIGA outperforms QEA (Han, 2002; Araujo, 2008) for determining optimum threshold due to its inherent features.

DISCUSSIONS AND CONCLUSION

In this article, a quantum inspired genetic algorithm (QIGA) has been proposed and applied to determine the optimum threshold of gray level images. In QIGA, Birkhoffs Ergodic theorem advocates the random interference of the participating chaotic maps and resort to time discreteness. As discussed in the previous section, the best solution needs not to be stored in advance to execute the proposed QIGA. The inherent features of QIGA helps to reduce the time complexity of the proposed algorithm compared to its classical counterpart that opens up encouraging avenues.

The authors are in the direction of investigating the proposed QIGA to find the optimum thresholding for pure and true color images.

REFERENCES

Araujo, T., Nedjah, N., & Mourelle, L. (2008). Quantum-Inspired Evolutionary State Assignment for Synchronous Finite State Machines. *Journal of Universal Computer Science*, *14*(15), 2532–2548.

Atkins, M., & Mackiewich, B. (1998). Fully Automatic Segmentation of the Brain in MRI, *Proceedings of 1998. IEEE Transactions on Medical Imaging*, *17*(1), 98–107. doi:10.1109/42.668699 PMID:9617911

Bazi, Y., Bruzzone, L., & Melgani, F. (2007). Image thresholding based on the EM algorithm and the generalized Gaussian distribution. *Pattern Recognition*, *40*(2), 619–634. doi:10.1016/j.patcog.2006.05.006

Bhattacharyya, S. (2011). A Brief Survey of Color Image Preprocessing and Segmentation Techniques. *Journal of Pattern Recognition Research*, *1*(1), 120–129. doi:10.13176/11.191

Bhattacharyya, S., & Dey, S. (2011). An Efficient Quantum Inspired Genetic Algorithm with Chaotic Map Model based Interference and Fuzzy Objective Function for Gray Level Image Thresholding. *Proceedings of 2011 International Conference on Computational Intelligence and Communication Systems*, *Gwalior, India* (pp. 121-125). doi:10.1109/CICN.2011.24

Bhattacharyya, S., Dutta, P., Chakraborty, S., Chakraborty, R., & Dey, S. (2010). Determination of Optimal Threshold of a Gray-level Image Using a Quantum Inspired Genetic Algorithm with Interference Based on a Random Map Model. *Proceedings of 2010 IEEE International Conference on Computational Intelligence and Computing Research (ICCIC 2010)*. doi:10.1109/ICCIC.2010.5705806

Boyarsky, A., & G'ora, P. (2010). A random map model for quantum interference. *Communications in Nonlinear Science and Numerical Simulation*, *15*(8), 1974–1979. doi:10.1016/j.cnsns.2009.08.018

Brink, A. D., & Pendock, N. E. (1996). Minimum cross entropy threshold selection. *Pattern Recognition*, *29*(1), 179–188. doi:10.1016/0031-3203(95)00066-6

Filho, C. B., Mello, C. A., Andrade, J., Lima, M., Santos, W. d., Oliveira, A., & Falcao, D. (2008). Image Thresholding of Historical Documents Based on Genetic Algorithms. In P. Fritzsche (Ed.), Tools in Artificial Intelligence (pp. 93-100).

Gonzalez, R. C., & Woods, R. E. (2002). *Digital Image Processing*. Englewood Cliffs, NJ: Prentice-Hall.

Grover, L. K. (1998). Quantum computers can search rapidly by using almost any transformation. *Physical Review Letters*, *80*(19), 4329–4332. doi:10.1103/PhysRevLett.80.4329

Han, K., & Kim, J. (2002). Quantum-Inspired Evolutionary Algorithm for a Class Combinational Optimization. *IEEE Transactions on Evolutionary Computation*, *6*(6), 580–593. doi:10.1109/TEVC.2002.804320

Han, K., & Kim, J. (2003). On setting the parameters of quantum-inspired evolutionary algorithm for practical application. *Proceedings of IEEE Congr. Evol. Comput. (Vol. 1*, 178–194

Hey, T. (1999). Quantum computing: An introduction. Computing & Control Engineering Journal, 10(3), 105–112

Holland, J. (1975). *Adaptation in Natural and Artificial Systems*. Ann Arbor: University of Michigan Press.

Hossain, M., Hossain, M. & Hashem, M. (2010). A Generalizes Hybrid Real-Coded Quantum Evolutionary Algorithm Based On Particle Swarm Theory With Arithmetic Crossover. *International Journal of Computer Science & Information Technology (IJCSIT), 2(4)*

Jawahar, C., Biswas, P., & Ray, A. (1997). Investigations on Fuzzy Thresholding Based On Fuzzy Clustering. *Pattern Recognition*, *30*(10), 1605–1613. doi:10.1016/S0031-3203(97)00004-6

Kapur, J. N., Sahoo, P. K., & Wong, A. K. C. (1985). A new method for gray-level picture thresholding using the entropy of the histogram. *Graphical Models and Image Processing*, *29*(3), 273–285. doi:10.1016/0734-189X(85)90125-2

Kim, Y., Kim, J., & Han, K. (2006). Quantum-inspired Multiobjective Evolutionary Algorithm for Multiobjective 0/1 Knapsack Problems. *Proceedings of 2006 IEEE Congress on Evolutionary Computation, Sheraton Vancouver Wall Centre Hotel, Vancouver, BC, Canada* (pp. 16–21).

Li, C. H., & Tam, P. K. S. (1998). An iterative algorithm for minimum cross-entropy thresholding. *Pattern Recognition Letters*, *19*(8), 771–776. doi:10.1016/S0167-8655(98)00057-9

Mcmohan, D. (2008). *Quantum computing explained*. Hoboken, New Jersey: John Wiley & Sons, Inc.

Nakiba, A., Oulhadja, H., & Siarry, P. (2010). Image thresholding based on Pareto multiobjective optimization. *Engineering Applications of Artificial Intelligence*, *23*(3), 313–320. doi:10.1016/j.engappai.2009.09.002

Narayanan, A., & Moore, M. (1996). Quantum inspired genetic algorithms. *Proceedings of Int. Conf. Evol. Comput.* (pp. 61–66). doi:10.1109/ICEC.1996.542334

Pal, N., & Bhandari, D. (1993). Image thresholding: Some new techniques. *Signal Processing*, *33*(2), 139–158. doi:10.1016/0165-1684(93)90107-L

Pal, S., & Rosenfeld, A. (1988). Image enhancement and thresholding by optimization of fuzzy compactness. *Pattern Recognition Letters*, *7*(2), 77–86. doi:10.1016/0167-8655(88)90122-5

Platel, M. D., Schliebs, S., & Kasabov, N. (2009). Quantum-Inspired Evolutionary Algorithm: A Multimodel EDA. *IEEE Transactions on Evolutionary Computation*, *13*(6), 1218–1231. doi:10.1109/TEVC.2008.2003010

Pun, T. (1980). A new method for gray-level picture threshold using the entropy of the histogram. *Signal Processing*, *2*(3), 223–237. doi:10.1016/0165-1684(80)90020-1

Reeves, C. (1993). *Using Genetic Algorithms with Small Populations, Proceedings of Fifth International Conference on Genetic Algorithms* (pp. 92–99). San Mateo, CA: Morgan Kaufman.

Reiffel, E., & Polak, W. (2000). An Introduction to Quantum Computing for Non-Physicists. Retrieved from arxive.org.quant-ph/9809016v2

Ren, X. (2009). An Optimal Image Thresholding Using Genetic Algorithm. *Proceedings of International Forum on Computer Science-Technology and Applications (IFCSTA '09)* (pp. 169-172). doi:10.1109/IFCSTA.2009.48

Sahoo, P., Wilkins, C., & Yeager, J. (1997). Threshold Selection Using Renyi's Entropy. *Pattern Recognition*, *30*(1), 71–84. doi:10.1016/S0031-3203(96)00065-9

Sezan, M. I. (1990). A peak detection algorithm and its application to histogram-based image data reduction. *Computer Vision Graphics and Image Processing*, *49*(1), 36–51. doi:10.1016/0734-189X(90)90161-N

Sezgin, M., & Sankur, B. (2004). Survey over image thresholding techniques and quantitative performance evaluation. *Journal of Electronic Imaging*, *13*(1), 146–165. doi:10.1117/1.1631315

Shor, P. W. (1997). Polynomial-time algorithms for prime factorization and discrete logarithms on a quantum computer. *SIAM Journal on Computing*, *26*(5), 1484–1509. doi:10.1137/S0097539795293172

Su, C., & Amer, A. (2006). A Real-time Adaptive Thresholding for Video Change Detection, *Proceedings of 2006 IEEE International Conference, Image Processing*, Atlanta, Georgia, USA (pp. 157–160). doi:10.1109/ICIP.2006.312373

Talbi, H., Draa, A., & Batouche, M. (2004). A New Quantum-Inspired Genetic Algorithm for Solving the Travelling Salesman Problem. *Proceedings of IEEE International Conference on Industrial Technology (ICIT'04)* (Vol. 3, pp. 1192–11970. doi:10.1109/ICIT.2004.1490730

Talbi, H., Draa, A., & Batouche, M. (2006). A Novel Quantum-Inspired Evolutionary Algorithm for Multi-Sensor Image Registration. *The International Arab Journal of Information Technology*, *3*(1), 9–15.

WebSource. (2000). Retrieved from http://www.math.tau.ac.il/~turkel/images.html

Xue, Z., Ming, D., Song, W., Wan, B., & Jin, S. (2010). Infrared gait recognition based on wavelet transform and support vector machine. *Pattern Recognition*, *43*(8), 2904–2910. doi:10.1016/j.patcog.2010.03.011

KEY TERMS AND DEFINITIONS

Genetic Algorithm: The concept of basic genetics is applied to form a meta-heuristic optimization search technique.

Gray Scale Image: The pixel intensities of an image consist of 256 different pixel values ranging from 0 to 255.

Image Thresholding: It bifurcate an objects and its corresponding background in a gray level image.

Optimization: A term used to find maximum or minimum value of any defined objective function.

Population: It consists of set of participating vectors.

Quantum Computing: Quantum computing is originated from the basic principles of quantum physics. It has more efficacies while comparing to its classical counterpart when time is concerned.

Quantum Evolutionary Algorithms: The algorithms that are built on quantum principles.

Chapter 13

The Application of Rough Set Theory and Near Set Theory to Face Recognition Problem

K R Singh
Yeshwantrao Chavan College of Engineering,
India

M A Zaveri
Sardar Vallabhbhai National Institute of
Technology, India

M M Raghuwanshi
Yeshwantrao Chavan College of Engineering,
India

James Peters
University of Manitoba, Canada

ABSTRACT

Computer vision is a process of electronically perceiving and understanding of an image like human vision system (HVS) do. Face recognition techniques (FRT) determines the identity of the individual by matching the facial images with the one stored in the facial database. The performance of FRT is greatly affected by variations in face due to different factors. It is interesting to study how well these issues are being handled by RST and near set theory to improve the performance. The variation in illumination and plastic surgery changes the appearance of face that introduces imprecision and vagueness. One part of chapter introduces the adaptive illumination normalization technique using RST that classifies the image illumination into three classes based on which illumination normalization is performed using an appropriate filter. Later part of this chapter introduces use of near set theory for FRT on facial images that have previously undergone some feature modifications through plastic surgery.

INTRODUCTION

In real world, human interaction with one another depends on their capability of recognition. This inherent capability to effortlessly identify and recognize human being is generally referred as human vision system (HVS). When such HVS is emulated through computer or machine it is referred as computer vision. Computer vision is a field that includes methods for acquiring, processing, analyzing, and understanding the images like HVS do. It is a process of electronically perceiving and understanding of

DOI: 10.4018/978-1-4666-9474-3.ch013

an image. The image can take many forms, such as video sequences, views from multiple cameras, or multi-dimensional data from a medical scanner. Understanding of HVS helps to build a powerful computer vision system where some useful information is extracted from image by a machine that is necessary for solving a particular problem. Face recognition is one such problem from computer vision domain.

FRT determines the identity of the individual by matching the facial images with the one stored in the facial database. It brings together the promises of other biometric systems and familiar functionality of visual security systems. FRT has emerged as a rapidly growing application in various fields. For example, the law enforcement and surveillance applications include closed circuit television video (CCTV) analysis, post event analysis, drug offenders (M. Bryant, 2011) *etc*. The usage of FRT have also been extended to few prohibited and safety related public areas such as airport (Big Brother, 2010)8, railways (Vicente, Fernandez & Coves, 2009) *etc*. In order to maintain the authenticity of a person, FRTs have also been employed in login system, driver license, voter registration, smart cards immigration, access control to buildings, email authentication on multimedia, automatic teller machine (ATM) *etc*. Recently, the government of India has also launched the concept of Aadhar Card as national identity that also uses FRT along with other biometrics. Not limited to this face recognition is also used for different commercial purposes (Apple Invents Facial Recognition, 2012) (Face Recognition Toshiba, 2013) and available with a product as a software application such as Apple Facial Recognition Locking&Unlocking System (Apple Invents Facial Recognition, 2012), Toshiba Face Recognition (Face Recognition Toshiba, 2013) *etc*.

In most of the aforesaid applications, identifying or recognizing the person based on the facial image is an important task, called as face identification or face recognition (Zhao, Chellappa, Phillips, & Rosenfeld, 2003). FRT basically constitutes of four main stages (Zhao, Chellappa, Phillips, & Rosenfeld, 2003)*viz*;

1. Face localization,
2. Pre-processing,
3. Feature extraction, and
4. Face recognition as shown in Figure 1.

Face localization is the initial and most important stage, where face portion is cropped either manually or automatically from the input image in order to remove the irrelevant information present in the background. Face pre-processing enhances the quality of cropped face image either by reducing the

Figure 1. Face recognition system

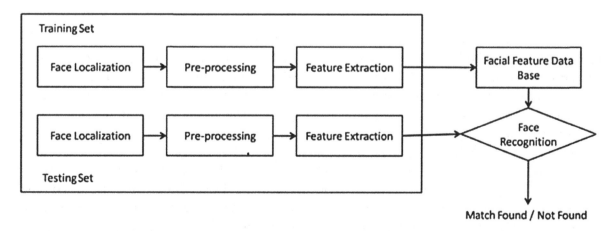

effect of noise, illumination variation, alignment of faces, resizing the faces to equal sizes *etc.*, which is required for better feature extraction. Feature extraction phase extracts the facial characteristics needed for recognition of an individual. The extracted facial features are further used to perform face recognition.

However, in real world applications like any other biometric entity face is subjected to variation due to various factors such as illumination, pose, plastic surgery, age, expression and partial occlusion. The variations in aforesaid factors can occur either deliberately such as plastic surgery, partial occlusion or as sometimes it is not possible to have control over some factors such as illumination, pose *etc.*, while capturing the image or video. Since acquiring images under controlled condition is not always in user's control that results in large variations in appearances of the faces. The variations in appearances of the face greatly affect the performance of FRT. It is interesting to study how well these issues are being handled by FRT to improve the performance. These challenges make the face recognition under varying conditions an active area of research.

This chapter specifically focus on two challenging issues namely, illumination variation and plastic surgery for discussion. The variation in illumination is due to uneven distribution of light from different sources on face. The variation in illumination changes the appearance of face that introduces imprecision and vagueness. The imprecision and vagueness can be termed as ambiguity present in a face that make face recognition a challenging issue. However, a human being may not perceive these variations brilliantly because such decisions are subjective and therefore different people may judge the degree of variations in different way. This difference in decision is due to the vagueness and ambiguity present in the perceived information for a decision. Rough set theory (RST) is a formal approximation of a crisp set that can deal with imprecision and vagueness effectively. This chapter introduces an adaptive illumination normalization technique using RST. A rough membership function (*rmf*)-based classifier (K. R. Singh, M. A. Zaveri & M. M. Raghuwanshi, 2013) caters the need of adaptive illumination normalization. The adaptive illumination normalization approach first classifies the image illumination into three classes such as, *dark*, *normal* and *shadow* based on which illumination normalization is performed using an appropriate filter. The advantage is that it avoids applying the same normalization technique to all images irrespective of type of variation in illumination or applying chain of illumination normalization techniques to compensate the variation in illumination.

In facial plastic surgery certain features of the face are altered. These alterations in the facial features are up to such an extent that human being often struggle to identify a person after facial plastic surgery. This introduces new and different challenge to face recognition. The facial plastic surgery can change the appearance of facial features and texture to such an extent that it is very difficult to predict which features are invariant (a region without surgery effects) with unavailable surgery information. This difficulty can be handled if each feature is represented as an object with description. This significant characteristic is present in near set theory. Later part of this chapter introduces use of near set theory for FRT on facial images that have previously undergone some feature modifications through plastic surgery. The work concerns only geometrically obtained feature values and their approximation using near sets.

This chapter makes two main contributions. First, it tries to establish a context for soft computing techniques that can be used as the part of development of hybrid intelligent system. Second, it discusses rough set and near set approach to tackle the issues of illumination variation and plastic surgery in face recognition respectively.

This chapter is organized as follows. The background of rough set theory and near set theory is presented in background section. Face recognition section of the chapter discuses the illumination and plastic surgery problem with respect to rough set theory and near set theory respectively. Finally, the chapter is concluded in conclusion section and the scope of future work is discussed.

BACKGROUND

Uncertainty and imprecision are the two terms that are very well dealt with soft computational intelligence techniques that have origin from the theory of sets. The basic concept of set theory originates with crisp set which contains members with a characteristic membership of 1 and ignore remaining elements of the universe set. Further, one such technique that emerged was fuzzy set theory (A. Skowron & J.F. Peters, 2007) (L. Zadeh, 1965) defined by employing the fuzzy membership function involving advance mathematical structures, numbers and functions that generalizes the traditional characteristic function. Fuzzy sets deal with impression and uncertainties observed in real world problems with the help of linguistic information and perform approximate reasoning. It uses fuzzy sets, logical connectives to model real-world reasoning. Unlike the crisp set, a fuzzy set includes all elements of the universal set of the domain but with a varying membership values in the interval (A. I. Dimitras, S. H. Zanakis & C. Zopounidis, 1996). Few decades later Z.Pawlak proposed rough set theory as a new approach to uncertainties and imprecision.

Rough Sets: An Overview

Rough set theory (Y. Sun, J. Liu & L. Wang, 2011) (Z. Pawlak, 1981) was put forth by mathematician Z.Pawlak in the beginning of the eighties as a new mathematical approach to model imperfect knowledge and problems in the areas of artificial intelligence and computer vision. Apart from fuzzy set theory pointed out in the preceding section, rough set theory is another approach to tackle the real world uncertainties. For instance, in contrast to set of real numbers or set of natural numbers, the concept of love for a person does not have a well defined boundary. The fuzzy set theory deals with the ill-definition of the boundary of a class through a continuous generalization of set characteristic functions. RST takes into consideration the indiscernibility between objects; typically characterized by an equivalence relation as discussed later in this chapter. The indiscernibility between objects is not used in fuzzy set theory. The main advantage of rough set is that at one side, it does not need any preliminary information or additional information about dataunlike probability in statistics, or basic probability assignment in Dampster-Shafer theory, or grade membership or the value of possibility in fuzzy set theory. At another side, the uncertainty and imprecision is expressed by the boundary region of a set in rough set theory, as opposed to the partial membership as in fuzzy set theory. The different properties of rough set make it an efficient technique for feature/attribute reduction, knowledge recovery, finding hidden values, classification *etc*. These properties attracted many researchers and rough set have been used in many diverse areas. In (Pawlak, 1982) authors have presented the application of rough set theory for recognition of bridges over water in aerial photography IR image. Authors have detected the bridge based on indiscernibility relation of RST and recognized based on the geometric characters of bridges. In another application, authors in (Ming Hu and Qiang Zhang Zhiping Wang, 2008) proposed the use of rough set theory for face detection as a pre-processing method for face color image. Not limited to computer domain problems, rough set theory have also been successfully used in civil applications (Weijie Wang, Gang Ren & Wei Wang, 2010). In (Ramani, Maya Ingle & Parag Kulkarni, 2012) authors have presented few facial expressions as a vague concept represented with rough sets and some facial expressions that are universal represented with fuzzy set as they definitely belong to that membership set. In one of the recent application proposed in (Geetha Mary & Akhilesh Saklecha, 2013) authors have proposed an algorithm for facial recognition using CCTV images based on rough set theory and Scale Invariant Feature Transform. One application as feature selection for best emotional feature criteria based on rough set theory has been proposed in (Ayesha Butalia, Maya Ingle & Parag Kulkarni, 2012). Yet in another paper (Hesham Arafat, Elawady, Barakat & Elrashidy, 2013) authors proposed fast and effective approximate algorithms to generate a set of discriminatory features based on rough ret theory with Ant Colony Optimization (ACO) in data mining. Rough set theory has also been effectively used in (Fang Chunsheng, Chen Fending, Wei Qiang, Wang Shouchao & Wang, 2010) as sources analysis of atmospheric particulates. Few of the listed applications very well states the effective use of RST in various domains.

Rough Sets: Basics

RST consists of various concepts mainly feature reduction/selection, rough membership function, decision system, cuts, and significance of attributes *etc.*, that make the rough set theory a preferable option to deal with real life problems (Dimitras, Zanakis & Zopounidis, 1996) (Kostek, Szczuko & Zwan, 2004) (H. Arafat, S. Barakat & Goweda, 2012) (Peters, Z. Suraj, S. Shan, S. Ramanna, W. Pedrycz & Pizzi, 2003) (K. Mannar & D. Ceglarek, 2004) (S.Nguyen, T. Nguyen & H. Nguyen, 2005) (S. Rubin, Michalowski & R. Slowinski, 1996). In this section, few of these concepts like decision system, indiscernibility relation, approximations and rough membership function are explained in brief for better understanding of the work presented here. In RST, information about the real world is expressed in the form of an information table. An information table can be represented as a pair $\mathcal{A} = \left(U, A\right)$, where, U is a non-empty finite set of objects called the universe and A is a non-empty finite set of attributes such that information function $f_a : u \rightarrow V_a$, for every $a \in A$. The set V_a is called the value set of a. Furthermore, a decision system is any information table of the form $\mathcal{A} = \left(U, A \bigcup \{d\}\right)$, where $d \notin A$ is a decision attribute. For every set of attributes $B \subseteq A$, an indiscernibility relation $IND\left(B\right)$ is defined in the following way: two objects, x_i and x_j, are indiscernible by the set of attributes $B \subseteq A$, if $b\left(x_i\right) = b\left(x_j\right)$ for every $b \subseteq B$. The equivalence class of $IND\left(B\right)$ is called elementary set in b because it represents the smallest discernible groups of objects. For any element x_i of u, the equivalence class of x_i in relation $IND\left(B\right)$ is represented as $\left[x_i\right]_{IND(B)}$. The notation $\left[x\right]_B$ denotes equivalence classes. Thus the family of all equivalence classes, partition the universe for all b will be denoted by $U\big/B$. This partitions induced by an equivalence relation can be used to build new subsets of the universe. The construction of equivalence classes is the first step in classification with rough sets.

Rough sets can also be defined by rough membership functions instead of approximation. A rough membership function (*rmf*) makes it possible to measure the degree that any specified object with a given attribute values belongs to a given decision set x. let $B \subseteq A$ and let x be a set of observations of interest. The degree of overlap between x and $\left[x\right]_B$ containing x can be quantified with an *rmf* given by equation 2.

$$\mu_X^B :\rightarrow \left[0,1\right] \tag{1}$$

$$\mu_X^B\left(x\right) = \frac{\left|\left[x\right]_B \cap X\right|}{\left|\left[x\right]_B\right|} \tag{2}$$

where, $\left|\bullet\right|$ denotes the cardinality of a set. The rough membership value μ_X^B may be interpreted as the conditional probability that an arbitrary element x belongs to X given B. The decision set x is called a generating set of the rough membership μ_X^B. Thus rough membership function quantifies the degree of relative overlap between the decision set x and the equivalence class to which x belongs. It has been suggested that rough set when used as a classifier, objects can be classified by means of their attributes (Z. Pawlak, 1996). The concept of rough sets was further extended by J. Peters and a new set theory called near set theory (J. Peters, 2007) was introduced in the year of 2006. A brief overview of the near set theory is presented ahead.

Near Sets: An Overview

Before going into the details of the near sets, out of many questions that can be answered on the basis of near set approach are how near the facial image of a person will be after plastic surgery or how near the Himalayan peaks are after the effect of global warming? The basic idea of this approach is object recognition by comparing the object descriptions. Near set is the theory of finding the approximation of sets of perceptual objects that are qualitatively near each other (*i.e.,* objects with at least partial matching descriptions). Perceptual objects can be represented by their descriptions. A *description* is a tuple of values of functions representing features of an object. Readers can refer the description of symbols from (J. Peters, 2007). Thus, the near set theory provides a formal basis for observation, relationship and classification of perceptual elements. Near set results from the introduction of a description-based approach to perceptual elements/objects and a generalization of the traditional rough set approach to granulation that is independent of the notion of the boundary of a set approximation. Near set theory has strength gained from rough set theory, starting with extensions of the traditional indiscernibility relation. Near set is an approach that solves the problem of what it means for objects with common features to be near each other qualitatively but not necessarily spatially. From a rough sets point-of-view, the main focus is on the approximation of sets with non-empty boundaries. In contrast, in the near sets approach to set approximation, the focus is on the discovery of near sets in the case where there is either a non-empty or an empty approximation boundary.

The various different domains where the near set has been successfully applied are: feature selection (J. Peters & S. Ramanna, 2007), object recognition in images (Henry & Peters, 2007) (Peters & Wasilecoski, 2009), image processing (M. Borkowski & J. Peters, 2006), granular computing (A. Skowron & J.F. Peters, 2007) (J. Peters, 2007) and in various forms of machine learning (Henry, Lockery, J. Peters & Borkowski, 2006) (Lockery & J. Peters, 2007) (J. Peters, 2007) (J. Peters & Henry, 2006) (J. Peters, Borkowski, Henry, Lockery & Gunderson, 2006) (J. Peters, S. Shahfar, Ramanna & Szturm, 2007) (Z. Pawlak, 1996). Literature shows that near set has been already used for frontal face recognition in (S. Gupta & K. Patnaik, 2008) where authors have presented an automated facial feature extraction procedure and make use of near set approach to choose the best feature among the considered one which significantly improves face recognition efficiency of SVM.

Near Sets: Basics

In near set theory, each object is described by the list of feature values. The word feature corresponds to an observable property of physical objects in the environment. For instance, for the feature such as nose on a human face, nose length or nose width will be the feature values. Comparing the list of feature values, similarity between the objects can be determined and can be grouped together in a set, called as near set. Thus the near set theory provides a formal basis for the observation, comparison and recognition or classification of objects. The nearness of objects can be approximated using near sets. Approximation can be considered in the context of information granules (neighbourhoods). Any approximation space is a tuple given in equation 3.

$$AS = \left(U, \mathcal{F}, v\right) \tag{3}$$

where $\mathcal{F}$ is a covering of finite universe of object U, *i.e.*, $\cup \mathcal{F} = U = U$ and

$$v : P\left(U\right) \times P\left(U\right) \to \left[0,1\right] \tag{4}$$

maps a pair of set to a number in $\left[0,1\right]$ representing the degree of overlap between the sets and $P\left(U\right)$ is a power set of U [4].

For a given approximation space $AS = \left(U, \mathcal{F}, v\right)$, we define a binary link relations $link_{\mathcal{F}} \subseteq U$

For any $X \subseteq U$, $\mathcal{F}$-lower approximation of X, and $\mathcal{F}$-upper approximation of X is defined respectively by equations 5 and 6.

$$\mathcal{F}_* X = \cup \left\{ Y \in \mathcal{F} | v\left(X,Y\right) = 1 \right\}. \tag{5}$$

$$\mathcal{F}^* X = \cup \left\{ Y \in \mathcal{F} | v\left(X,Y\right) > 0 \right\} \tag{6}$$

The *lower approximation* of a set X is the set of all objects, which can be for *certain* classified as X. The *upper approximation* of a set X is the set of all objects which can be *possibly* classified as X. The lower and upper approximations of a set lead naturally to the notion of a boundary region of an approximation. Let $BND_{\mathcal{F}} X$ denote the boundary region of an approximation defined as in [4]. Thus, the lower-and upper- approximations result in an increase in the number of neighbourhoods used to assess the nearness of a classification.

FACE RECOGNITION PROBLEMS

Despite a good number of approaches reported in the literature, face recognition is still an open research problem due to various challenging issues such as pose, illumination, plastic surgery and expression variations. The variations in these factors bring large inconsistencies and vagueness in the facial information extracted for recognition. This makes the face recognition a challenging problem. This section presents how two recent set theories as soft computing tools *viz.*; rough set theory and near set theory can be used to solve the different problems of face recognition. This section of chapter presents how the variation in illumination can be formulated using rough set theory and how plastic surgery in face recognition can be effectively tackled using near set theory.

Rough Set Theory: Illumination Problem in Face Recognition

For real world application like surveillance at airport or public gathering places, it is not possible to have control over illumination while capturing the image or video and there will be variations in illumination. Generally, pre-processing is performed to eliminate the effect of illumination variation called as illumination normalization. Different types of methods exist to normalize the effect of illumination variations. Examples of such illumination normalization techniques include histogram equalization, Homomorphic, self-quotient image (SQI) and gamma correction (Shashua & Riklin-Raviv, 2001) (Lakshmiprabha, J. Bhattacharya & Majumder, 2011) (Gonzalez,Woods & Eddins, 2009).

Although several techniques have been proposed for normalizing the effect of varying illumination, the selection of any particular normalization technique on illuminated face image is subjective in nature. Generally, the same illumination normalization technique is applied to all the face images irrespective of the degree of illumination variation. It is not possible to predict how much illumination variation is present at the time of capturing the set of images of the same subject. It is very much the case of uncontrolled environment, for example, the set of images captured by surveillance camera where the movement of the camera may be controlled but the illumination cannot be controlled when the images are captured in different direction. The appearance of a face changes from one image to another during acquisition. Therefore, if any of the illumination normalization techniques applied to all the face images, irrespective of the knowledge of illumination variation in a given image, might result in uneven effect. This will affect the feature extraction and recognition also. So it is important to have an adaptive mechanism where the amount of illumination will be classified and an appropriate illumination normalization technique may be applied which not only helps in enhancing the features in the given image but it will also reduce the computational cost as the same illumination technique is not applied now to all the images. The amount of illumination variation is very much imprecise and hence, vagueness exists in defining the same. This imprecise and vagueness can be termed as illumination ambiguity present in an image.

Next, it is required to represent this imprecision and vagueness present in illumination in the form of different degree of variation so that the illumination may be classified into different classes. For this task, there may be several ways. One simple way is to have crisp representation for classification using intensity value itself. Classical set theory allows setting a crisp value as a threshold for illumination classification. Further, for classifying a given image based on illumination, it is required to represent the whole image by some parameters. For example, the average intensity value of a given image that is mean value will be good enough to use further for illumination classification. This is illustrated using an example as shown in Figure 2 where mean value of a given image is used for illumination classification. In Figure 2, the gray level bar shows at the bottom represent the average intensity value of an image. For example, let the threshold (gray level value) be 50, as observed from the gray level bar shown in Figure 2. Then all the gray levels between 0 and 50 define a *dark* set for illumination. Suppose an image having a mean gray value 51 is to be classified then as per the threshold defined, it does not belong to the *dark* set even though it is a *dark* image. It is obvious that, in this case the boundary between two gray levels *viz*; 50 and 51 is indistinct or vague in nature.

Figure 2. Gray level representation of different illumination types of image with crisp set

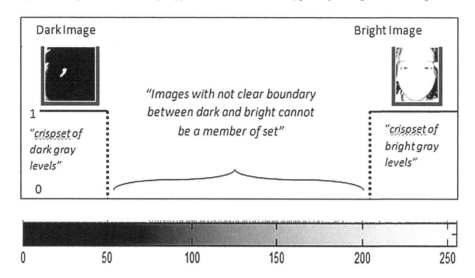

Another important point is that imprecision and vagueness in illumination variation cannot be modelled using one parameter like, mean value, but it requires more than one statistical feature such as, average mean level, standard deviation *etc*. At the same time using these parameters, how to define the degree of imprecision and vagueness present in illumination variation is a challenging issue. The imprecise and vagueness can be very well handled by fuzzy logic (A. Skowron & J. Peters, 2007) and rough set theory (Z. Pawlak, 1981). As discussed earlier, the rough set theory is preferred to handle such imprecision and vagueness that exists in the information. So in this work, the degree of imprecision and vagueness in an image illumination which is also termed as illumination ambiguity, is resolved using rough set theory. The rough set theory allows one to map this ambiguity into different illumination classes using rough membership function. It is also called as rough membership function (*rmf*)-based classifier (K. Singh, M. Zaveri & M. Raghuwanshi, 2013).

Based on the above discussion, an illumination can be expressed using some statistical features for estimating the variations in illumination that is the first task towards the illumination classification for a given image. Next, three different classes are defined, namely, *normal, dark* and *shadow* for illumination classification to incorporate the degree of illumination variation (K. Singh, M. Zaveri & M. Raghuwanshi, 2013). As discussed it is very important to determine the amount of illumination variation and then choose the appropriate illumination normalization technique. In this view, this chapter discusses *rmf*-based classifier which classifies the image based on the amount of illumination variation. The advantage of the *rmf*-based classifier is that it allows one to determine pre-processing required or not and hence, reduces the computational complexity.

Adaptive Approach to Illumination Normalization

This section presents a completely adaptive approach to illumination normalization which consists of mainly two steps. In the first step the set of statistical parameters are derived and then these parameters are used to define *rmf*-based classifier for illumination classification of an image in to three classes, namely, *dark, normal* and *shadow*. This is called as illumination classification step. The second step is

Figure 3. Architecture of adaptive approach to illumination normalization
(K. Singh, M. Zaveri & M. Raghuwanshi, 2013).

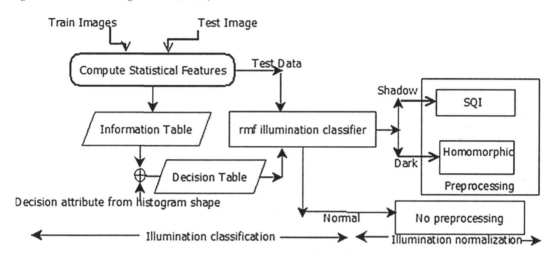

application of an illumination technique to different images of the same subject based on class of an image. Illumination normalization is adaptively applied only if an image is classified into *dark* and *shadow* type. For *normal* image any illumination normalization operation is not performed and thus reduces the computational complexity. The overview of this adaptive system is presented in Figure 3.

Statistical Parameters for Illumination Classification

As mentioned earlier, to map the degree of imprecision and vagueness present due to illumination variation *i.e.*, illumination ambiguity, one need statistical parameters. From literature review, the following four statistical features such as average mean level, standard deviation, entropy, and uniformity (Gonzalez, Woods & Eddins, 2009) have been used extensively for image or texture descriptor. The reason behind the choice of these statistical parameters is that the illumination variation from image to image is indirectly depicted by image intensity values. So, the same parameters have been used for illumination classification. Let, B presents the set of statistical parameters or attributes that have been derived from a given image. It is defined as:

$$B = \left\{ b_i \middle| = 1 \ldots N \right\}$$

where b is a statistical parameter and N is the total number of statistical parameters. Here, N is set equal to 4 and each of these parameters is defined as below:

$$B = \left\{ b_i \middle| i = 1 \; to \; 4 \right\} = \left\{ mean \; level \; value, standard \; deviatio, uniformity, entropy \right\}$$

These statistical parameters are used further for defining *rmf*-based classifier. These parameters are termed as feature values. These feature values are used to create an information table for rough membership function which is described ahead in the following section in detail.

Illumination Classification using *rmf*-Based Classifier

In this section, chapter presents the rough set-based classifier, namely, rough membership function (*rmf*)-based classifier. The basic concepts of rough set theory described in background section, can be illustrated by following examples of facial images with respect to illumination classification as the main objective of this chapter is to exploit the rough set theory for illumination classification. For this, first define information table $\mathcal{A} = (U, A)$, where $U = \{I_i | i = 1 \text{ to } N\}$ and I_i are the input facial images, where $i = 1$ to N, N being the total of samples of all subjects. Next, define attribute set using extracted large number of attributes *i.e.*, feature depending on given application. For example $A = \{b_i | i = 1 \text{ to } m\}$ and b_i is the ith feature such as mean value, standard deviation, kurtosis, variance, entropy, *etc.*

Using this, information about an illuminated image can be represented as shown in Table 1. In Table 1, total 10 objects, *i.e.*, images I_i, ($i=1$ to 10) from universal U are depicted. For each object, B is represented by different attributes values *i.e.*, feature values of mean level (b_1), standard deviation (b_2), uniformity (b_3) and entropy (b_4). The resultant information table is depicted in Table 1 for understanding of the problem. Next, partition the given U into equivalence classes for *rmf* calculation. From Table 1 it is observed that for any real world problem, such as face recognition, attribute values are continuous values. These set of continuous values are proven to be rather unsuitable for depiction of crisp decision class, so the attribute values have to be disjointedly discretized. Let us consider S is a set of continuous attribute value and let the domain of S be the interval $[p, q]$. A partition on φ_S $[p, q]$ is defined as the following set of m subintervals shown in equation 11.

$$\varphi_S = \left\{ \left[p_0, p_1 \right), \left[p_1, p_2 \right), \dots \left[p_{m-1}, p_m \right] \right\}$$ (11)

where, $p_0 = p, p_{i-1} > p_i$ for i= 1, 2 . . . *m,* and $p_m = q$. Thus, discretization is the process that produces a partition φ_S on $\left[p, q \right]$. The range values are determined dynamically based on the applications and how the different values are distributed.

Table 1. Information table using statistical features

Images	b_1	b_2	b_3	b_4
I_1	114.63	33.94	0.0094	6.9713
I_2	15.6989	28.2042	0.0488	4.9039
I_3	68.2056	52.8680	0.0100	7.1198
I_4	50.2189	51.5113	0.0283	6.4132
I_5	1.1633	1.4617	0.2969	2.1322
I_6	49.5600	52.6033	0.0287	7.0573
I_7	72.2911	63.8979	0.0088	7.3086
I_8	45.2411	59.6705	0.0279	6.3013
I_9	1.3078	2.0016	0.3293	2.1271
I_{10}	21.3889	36.1836	0.0548	5.1068

Table 2. Defined interval for each attribute (extended YaleB face database)

b_1	b_2	b_3	b_4
1, $b \leq 50$ 2, $50 < x < 100$ 3, $x \geq 100$	1, $x \leq 30$ 2, $30 < x < 50$ 3, $x \geq 50$	1, $x \leq 0.0100$ 2, $0.0100 < x < 0.0300$ 3, $x \geq 0.0300$	1, $x < 5$ 2, $x \geq 5$

For simplicity, the range of continuous value for each attribute is represented using symbolic representation which is depicted in Table 2. Using these range values shown in Table 2, one shall create a discretized information table using the algorithm given in (K. Singh, M. Zaveri & M. Raghuwanshi, 2013). Discretized information is shown in Table 3 of the original information table shown in Table 1. For illustration, the value of attribute b_1 for object I_1 from Table 1 is 114.63 which are greater than the range value 100 as shown in Table 2. This value of b_1 is represented as 3 in Table 3 for I_1. Similarly, one can ensure for b_2, b_3 and b_4 for I_1 object and also for other objects in the universe U.

Similar to information table for illumination classification, decision system is also required for enabling the decision process. Continuous attribute value set $B = \{b_1, b_2, b_3, b_4\}$ after discretization are redefined as function values $F = \{f_1, f_2, f_3, f_4\}$. Using these redefined function values discretized information table is shown in Table 3.

This discretized information table is used to construct a decision table $\mathcal{A} = \left(U, A \cup d\right)$, where $\{d\}$ is the decision attribute. The set of decision attributes can be defined as:

$$\left\{ d_i \middle| d_i = 1 \; to \; q \right\}$$

where d_i is decision attribute for i[th] given class and q is the total number of decision classes. In our case, we define three illumination classes such as:

$$\left\{ d \right\} = \left\{ dark, \; normal, \; shadow \right\}, q = 3$$

Table 3. Discretized information table

Objects	f_1	f_2	f_3	f_4
I_1	3	2	1	2
I_2	1	1	3	1
I_3	2	3	1	2
I_4	2	3	3	2
I_5	1	1	3	1
I_6	2	3	3	2
I_7	2	3	1	2
I_8	1	3	3	2
I_9	1	1	3	1
I_{10}	1	2	3	2

These three illumination classes can be represented as *dark*=0, *normal*=1 and *shadow*=2. In this context, *d* will be a decision set for three illumination classes as depicted:

$$\{d\} = \{0,1,2\}$$

Next, it is also important to derive the value of decision attributes for each given image as object in information table to construct the decision table or system. Here, the shape of histogram distribution of each illuminated image is used to assign the value to d_i for each given image in information table. The histogram distributions for few sample images are shown in Figure 4 for understanding. Experimentally, it has been observed that, for *dark* face images gray level histogram shown in Figure 4(a) is negatively-skewed, for *normal* face images the shape of histogram shown in Figure 4(b) is bell shaped and for *shadow* face images histogram distribution shown in Figure 4(c) is not well defined. These shapes can be considered as facts for known illumination; and the value of decision attribute is assigned to each illumination type. For instance, sample decision table is shown in Table 4, where I_1 represent a *normal* image with *d*=1, since the histogram shape of I_1 is bell shape. It is to be noted that the decision table we created will be used as training table for determining the illumination type unknown illuminated image.

It is very much clear from the Table 4 that face images I_4 and I_6 have same attribute values but belongs to different decision classes. In this context, images I_4 and I_6 are indiscernible with respect to given attribute values. This illustrates that there is anuncertainty or ambiguity in decision for the same range of attribute values. This can be very well resolved with rough membership function as discussed in background section. To calculate rough membership function first the objects of the decision table has to be partitioned into different equivalence classes for the given function values in set *F* derived from attribute values in *B*. The elements of each equivalence class formed are represented in Table 5. From the Table 5, it has been observed that there are seven equivalence classes *viz.*; $[1]_B$, $[2]_B$, … $[7]_B$. The set of all decision classes *d* related to an equivalence class is called the generalized decision set of this

Table 4. Sample decision table

Objects	Discretized Attributes Values				Decision Attribute
	b1	*b2*	*b3*	*b4*	*d*
I_1	3	2	1	2	1
I_2	1	1	3	1	0
I_3	2	3	1	2	2
I_4	2	3	3	2	2
I_5	1	1	3	1	0
I_6	2	3	3	2	1
I_7	2	3	1	2	2
I_8	1	3	3	2	2
I_9	1	1	3	1	0
I_{10}	1	2	3	2	0

Figure 4. Histogram distribution of facial images from extended YaleB database

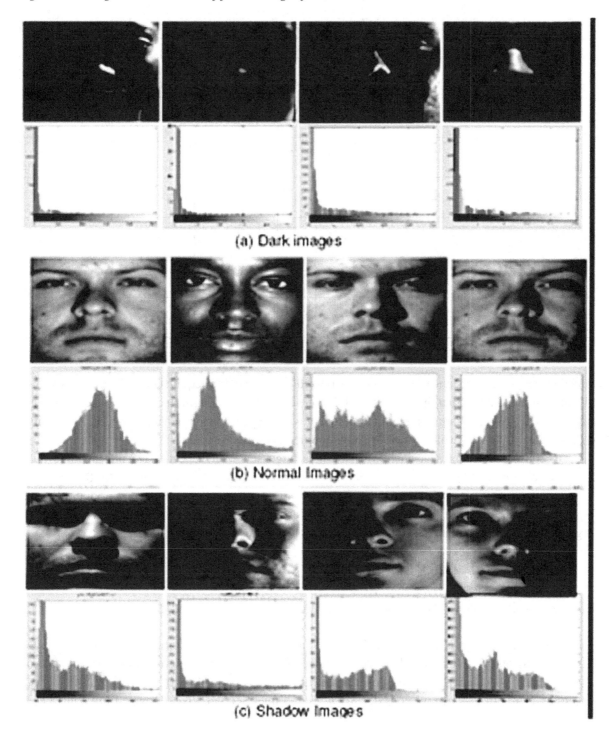

(a) Dark images

(b) Normal images

(c) Shadow images

Table 5. Set of equivalence classes for decision Table 3

Equivalence Classes	Function Values				Decision Attribute
	f_1	f_2	f_3	f_4	D
$[1]_B = \{I_1\}$	3	2	1	2	{1}
$[2]_B = \{I_2, I_5, I_9\}$	1	1	3	1	{0}
$[3]_B = \{I_{10}\}$	1	2	3	2	{0}
$[4]_B = \{I_3, I_7\}$	2	3	1	2	{2}
$[5]_B = \{I_4, I_6\}$	2	3	3	2	{2,1}
$[6]_B = \{I_8\}$	1	3	3	2	{2}
$[7]_B = \{I_6\}$	2	2	1	2	{1}

equivalence class. For instance, set {1} is generalized decision set for equivalence class $[1]_B$. It is also evident from the Table 5 that the generalize decision set {2, 1} for *shadow* and *normal* face images are rough sets because they cannot be defined uniquely with respect togiven attribute values. Such rough sets can however be very well defined by rough membership function.

Let us consider, decision sets which we also call as target sets with respect to decision attributevalue. For instance, *normal* Target Set={x: d(x) =1}. For the defined three decision classes for the proposed algorithm, three different target sets can be formed from the information tabulated in Table 4. For example, images I_5, I_2, I_9, and I_{10} have same value for decision attribute, so these images belong to *dark* Target Set. Similarly, one can also define other target sets as represented:

- *Dark Target Set* 0= $\{I_5, I_2, I_9, I_{10}\}$
- *Normal Target Set* 1= $\{I_1, I_6\}$
- *Shadow Target Set* 2 = $\{I_3, I_4, I_7, I_8\}$

Now, the approximation that an image belongs to a particular defined illumination class is computed with rough membership function. The degree of overlap is calculated using *rmf* as shown in equation 2. For instance, consider the degree of overlap of equivalence class $[1]_B$ with the decision sets *normal* Target Set. Here, for instance we consider X= *normal* Target Set and x is the image from equivalence class $[1]_B$ i.e., I_1

$$\mu^B_{normalTargetSet}(I1) = \frac{\left| [1]_B \cap normalTargetSet \right|}{\left| [1]_B \right|} = \frac{1}{2} = 0.5$$

This demonstrates that the degree to which the face image I_1 in class $[1]_B$ belongs to *normal* Target Set is 50%. For the understanding of the reader, this chapter presents the concept of rough membership function with respect to *shadow* class as depicted in Figure 5. From the Figure 5 it is clear that X represent the set of *shadow* images; x is a query image with varying illumination. If the query image is x1, the rough membership function value is 0, as it does not belong to defined *shadow* class. On the other hand, for another query image x2 decision is not clearly defined, so rough membership function value lies between the ranges 0 to 1. For example, if query image x3 completely belongs to defined *shadow* class, the rough membership function value is 1. Once the illuminations of facial images have been classified in one of the desired illumination type next step is to pre-process them using appropriate illumination normalization technique.

Figure 5. Concepts of rough membership function through illuminated images
(Source image from extended YaleB face database).

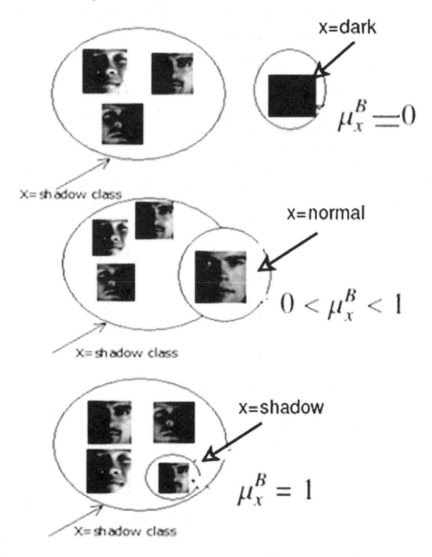

EXPERIMENTAL RESULTS

The adaptive method for illumination classification followed by normalization is evaluated on extended YaleB [55] face database. Extended YaleB face database consists of whole range of illumination consisting of 2496 facial images of 39 different subjects. Performance of the adaptive illumination normalization is evaluated on 1500 images of 30 subjects (50 different illumination conditions of each subject) selected randomly which were not used in training. Since this chapter emphasizes on illumination variation problem, only frontal faces under different illumination conditions have been chosen from the face database. Separate training sets and testing sets are created for the database. In order to select the number of images used for training, experimentation has been performed with 3, 4, 5 and 6 train face samples/subject. It has been observed that 5 train samples per subject give better result and no significant improvement in performance have been noticed for 6 samples per subject. Due to this 5 training sample face images per subject have been to train the *rmf*-based classifier. Testing has been performed on those images that were not used for training. Firstly, simulation has been performed for illumination classification using the four statistical parameters as feature values as described earlier. Secondly, classified *dark* and *shadow* images are adaptively normalized with Homomorphic and SQI illumination normalization techniques respectively to surmount the effect of illumination.

To evaluate the performance of adaptive approach, the statistical features were extracted for each test image and an information table has been created. Information table for few of the test samples is shown in Table 6. Using the *rmf*-based classifier the class of illumination for each test image is determined and the results are tabulated in Table 7. In Table 7, number 0 represents the *dark* class, 1 represent the *normal* class and similarly 2 represents the *shadow* class.

The performance has been evaluated using two parameters, namely, accuracy and sensitivity. The overall performance is summarized in Table 9. Table 9 depicts 99% accuracy for the *normal* images, 98% accuracy for *shadow* and 100% accuracy for *dark* images. It is clear from Table 10, that 300 *dark* images are correctly predicted as *dark* images by *rmf*-based classifier. Since, we are interested in *shadow* images, what is most likely to note from Table 8 is that the accuracy in case of *shadow* illumination type is not 100%. This is due to the fact that overall statistics of the *shadow* images changes much since there is uneven distribution of lighting from all direction. Due to this uneven distribution of lighting, degree of uncertainty in *shadow* images is more. For instance, out of 600 actual *shadow* images 588 images are predicted as *shadow* images. Thus, the *rmf*-based classifier has shown 98.8% overall performance for illumination classification on a wider range of variations for extended YaleB face database. Sample face images from correctly classified face images have been shown in Figure 6.

Results of normalized face images with appropriate illumination normalization technique after it has been classified as *dark*, *normal* or *shadow* is shown in Figure 7. From experiment, it has been observed that Homomorphic and SQI have shown excellent and smooth results for *dark* and *shadow* face images respectively. The resultant face images in Figure 7 shows that instead of applying any particular normalization technique on all range of variations in illumination, if images are first classified based on the illumination type and then the normalization technique is applied, yields better result.

The classification results of rough set based *rmf*-based classifier are compared against state-of-art classifiers such as *k*-nearest neighbor classifier (K. Singh & M. Raghuwanshi, 2009) (K. Singh, M. Zaveri & M. Raghuwanshi, 2010), SVM (S. Nishida & M. Shinya, 1998), and neural network (Lawrence, Giles, Tsoi & Back, 1995) (Y. Kung & Taur, 2002). The performance of each approach has been evaluated using the parameters such as accuracy and sensitivity used previously. Figure 8 depict the performance of the *rmf*-based classifier for illumination for extended YaleB (YaleB Face Database, 2010).

Table 6. Information table for test images from extended YaleB face database

Name of Images	b_1	b_2	b_3	b_4
yaleB01ffP00A+000E+45.pgm	106.8144	59.4886	0.0059	7.5639
yaleB01ffP00A+050E-40.pgm	55.8167	41.7339	0.0114	6.8590
yaleB01ffP00A+110E+65.pgm	16.6433	19.0644	0.0420	5.0881
yaleB01ffP00A+120E+00.pgm	20.8200	31.8857	0.0525	5.0555
yaleB01ffP00A-035E+65.pgm	58.2189	60.3417	0.0153	6.8680
yaleB02ffP00A-005E+10.pgm	105.5667	34.4156	0.0098	6.9489
yaleB02ffP00A-060E+20.pgm	1.0078	1.1609	0.3089	1.9511
yaleB02ffP00A-060E-20.pgm	71.7856	65.0749	0.0167	6.9371
yaleB02ffP00A-110E+40.pgm	18.7067	33.8856	0.0671	4.8989
yaleB02ffP00A-130E+20.pgm	7.3044	2.7237	0.1068	3.4512
yaleB09ffP00A+050E-40.pgm	1.2889	1.9835	0.3343	2.1072
yaleB09ffP00A+110E+40.pgm	32.2311	50.3209	0.0293	5.8038
yaleB09ffP00A-060E-20.pgm	65.2089	64.0055	0.0188	6.8058
yaleB09ffP00A-070E+00.pgm	74.0522	82.1786	0.0260	6.6247
yaleB09ffP00A-110E+15.pgm	37.1756	60.7276	0.0419	5.6358
yaleB12ffP00A+000E-35.pgm	67.6889	26.6021	0.0120	6.5923
yaleB12ffP00A+110E+65.pgm	20.6000	33.4694	0.0484	5.1013
yaleB12ffP00A-010E-20.pgm	79.0489	31.8043	0.0097	6.8921
yaleB12ffP00A-110E+15.pgm	1.7822	5.7769	0.2398	2.3655
yaleB12ffP00A-120E+00.pgm	37.4833	62.4265	0.0583	5.3677
yaleB15ffP00A+000E+45.pgm	109.7867	61.2981	0.0055	7.6686
yaleB15ffP00A+000E+90.pgm	38.2733	52.7381	0.0404	5.9524
yaleB15ffP00A+050E-40.pgm	43.3978	46.5906	0.0301	6.2067
yaleB15ffP00A+070E-35.pgm	42.9056	51.1402	0.0386	6.0955
yaleB15ffP00A+130E+20.pgm	19.8711	42.8228	0.0595	4.6644
yaleB20ffP00A-050E+00.pgm	77.1944	58.2857	0.0112	7.0905
yaleB20ffP00A-050E-40.pgm	47.0733	37.3828	0.0161	6.5292
yaleB20ffP00A-070E+45.pgm	43.4533	53.0917	0.0779	5.6808
yaleB20ffP00A-110E+15.pgm	28.1300	44.1848	0.0961	5.0011
yaleB20ffP00A-110E+65.pgm	7.5922	18.8344	0.1804	3.3891
yaleB21ffP00A-020E+10.pgm	123.7589	58.4000	0.0057	7.6348
yaleB21ffP00A-035E+40.pgm	94.3156	71.8023	0.0080	7.5166
yaleB21ffP00A-035E+65.pgm	43.2056	51.1245	0.0221	6.4562
yaleB21ffP00A-085E+20.pgm	67.3633	76.5736	0.0295	6.5508
yaleB21ffP00A-110E+15.pgm	36.7667	56.9809	0.0528	5.6193
yaleB22ffP00A+000E+45.pgm	52.1722	42.7283	0.0116	6.8281
yaleB22ffP00A+000E+90.pgm	12.5611	22.8374	0.0779	4.3908
yaleB22ffP00A+025E+00.pgm	60.1256	41.7926	0.0092	6.9897
yaleB22ffP00A+070E+45.pgm	41.5856	57.6199	0.0352	6.0446

continued on following page

Table 6. Continued

Name of Images	b_1	b_2	b_3	b_4
yaleB22ffP00A-110E-20.pgm	43.5644	70.8834	0.0678	5.4119
yaleB28ffP00A+000E+20.pgm	110.0256	58.9625	0.0060	7.5465
yaleB28ffP00A+000E+90.pgm	14.7544	29.3593	0.0600	4.6954
yaleB28ffP00A+120E+00.pgm	9.9400	18.9832	0.0720	4.1447
yaleB28ffP00A-050E-40.pgm	63.0211	56.2551	0.0117	7.0400
yaleB28ffP00A-070E-35.pgm	46.4578	54.1518	0.0368	6.1635
yaleB29ffP00A-005E-10.pgm	144.9911	47.0159	0.0070	7.3621
yaleB29ffP00A-035E+15.pgm	112.8733	88.7960	0.0107	7.3542
yaleB29ffP00A-035E-20.pgm	97.8600	76.7625	0.0101	7.3887
yaleB29ffP00A-070E+00.pgm	73.3700	84.5433	0.0488	6.2074
yaleB29ffP00A-110E-20.pgm	22.0678	43.4294	0.0808	4.8274
yaleB30ffP00A+095E+00.pgm	45.3567	56.7469	0.0479	5.8266
yaleB30ffP00A+110E+15.pgm	34.5411	54.6382	0.0581	5.3618
yaleB30ffP00A+120E+00.pgm	18.4000	34.4349	0.0747	4.5907
yaleB30ffP00A-005E+10.pgm	78.3444	26.9677	0.0115	6.6660
yaleB30ffP00A-035E+65.pgm	41.3678	45.2530	0.0245	6.3788
yaleB34ffP00A-005E-10.pgm	125.7822	39.6469	0.0086	7.1017
yaleB34ffP00A-035E+65.pgm	30.6967	39.4925	0.0261	6.0494
yaleB34ffP00A-050E-40.pgm	72.7778	55.8167	0.0090	7.1813
yaleB34ffP00A-070E+00.pgm	62.2600	64.3743	0.0236	6.5966
yaleB34ffP00A-110E+40.pgm	16.1189	30.0740	0.0692	4.8130
yaleB35ffP00A-035E+65.pgm	22.2533	30.8973	0.0598	5.3862
yaleB35ffP00A-050E+00.pgm	61.0000	48.2749	0.0111	6.9318

From this figure it is clear that *rmf*-based classifier out performs in comparison of all other algorithms. It is also important to note that illumination type *dark* is classified with high sensitivity using almost all approaches but as illumination varies from *dark* to *normal*, the efficacy of the illumination classifier is very much evident. The most challenging task is to deal with the images having variations in illumination due to *shadow* effect. From figure 8 it is very much evident that the *shadow* images that have been classified are comparable with high sensitivity values using the *rmf*-based classifier in comparison to other algorithms such as SVM, neural network *etc*.

Thus the main contributions of the adaptive illumination normalization using *rmf*-based classifier are; firstly, instead of applying two or three normalization technique in cascaded way as in (Bozorgtabar, Azami & Noorian, 2012) (Tan & Triggs, 2010), this approach automatically choose appropriate illumination normalization technique based on the decision given by the *rmf*-based classifier. This makes adaptive illumination normalization computationally more efficient. Secondly, instead of taking decision using a *single* parameter (average intensity value) as in (Y. Sun, Liu & Wang (2011); adaptive approach uses four parameters like average mean level, standard deviation; uniformity and entropy to make the decision about the illumination type of the image. This leads to a more robust and reliable adaptive system.

Table 7. Resultant table showing the decision of rmf-based classifier

Name of Image	0	1	2	d
yaleB01ffP00A+000E+45.pgm	0	0.6923	0.2308	1
yaleB01ffP00A+050E-40.pgm	0	0.1111	0.7778	2
yaleB01ffP00A+110E+65.pgm	0	0.5000	0	1
yaleB01ffP00A+120E+00.pgm	0.2857	0	0.6429	2
yaleB01ffP00A-035E+65.pgm	0	0.1111	0.7778	2
yaleB02ffP00A-005E+10.pgm	0	0.6923	0.2308	1
yaleB02ffP00A-060E+20.pgm	0.9091	0	0	0
yaleB02ffP00A-060E-20.pgm	0	0.1111	0.7778	2
yaleB02ffP00A-110E+40.pgm	0.7143	0	0.1429	0
yaleB02ffP00A-130E+20.pgm	0.9091	0	0	0
yaleB09ffP00A+050E-40.pgm	0.9091	0	0	0
yaleB09ffP00A+110E+40.pgm	0.2857	0	0.6429	2
yaleB09ffP00A-060E-20.pgm	0	0.1111	0.7778	2
yaleB09ffP00A-070E+00.pgm	0	0.1111	0.7778	2
yaleB09ffP00A-110E+15.pgm	0.2857	0	0.6429	2
yaleB12ffP00A+000E-35.pgm	0	0.5000	0	1
yaleB12ffP00A+110E+65.pgm	0.2857	0	0.6429	2
yaleB12ffP00A-010E-20.pgm	0	0.6923	0.2308	1
yaleB12ffP00A-110E+15.pgm	0.9091	0	0	0
yaleB12ffP00A-120E+00.pgm	0.2857	0	0.6429	2
yaleB15ffP00A+000E+45.pgm	0	0.6923	0.2308	1
yaleB15ffP00A+000E+90.pgm	0.2857	0	0.6429	2
yaleB15ffP00A+050E-40.pgm	0.2857	0	0.6429	2
yaleB15ffP00A+070E-35.pgm	0.2857	0	0.6429	2
yaleB15ffP00A+130E+20.pgm	0.7143	0	0.1429	0
yaleB20ffP00A-050E+00.pgm	0	0.1111	0.7778	2
yaleB20ffP00A-050E-40.pgm	0.2857	0	0.6429	2
yaleB20ffP00A-070E+45.pgm	0.2857	0	0.6429	2
yaleB20ffP00A-110E+15.pgm	0.2857	0	0.6429	2
yaleB20ffP00A-110E+65.pgm	0.9091	0	0	0
yaleB21ffP00A-020E+10.pgm	0	0.6923	0.2308	1
yaleB21ffP00A-035E+40.pgm	0	0.6923	0.2308	1
yaleB21ffP00A-035E+65.pgm	0.2857	0	0.6429	2
yaleB21ffP00A-085E+20.pgm	0	0.1111	0.7778	2
yaleB21ffP00A-110E+15.pgm	0.2857	0	0.6429	2
yaleB22ffP00A+000E+45.pgm	0	0.1111	0.7778	2
yaleB22ffP00A+000E+90.pgm	0.9091	0	0	0
yaleB22ffP00A+025E+00.pgm	0	0.6923	0.2308	1
yaleB22ffP00A+070E+45.pgm	0.2857	0	0.6429	2

continued on following page

Table 7. Continued

Name of Image	0	1	2	d
yaleB22ffP00A-110E-20.pgm	0.2857	0	0.6429	2
yaleB28ffP00A+000E+20.pgm	0	0.6923	0.2308	1
yaleB28ffP00A+000E+90.pgm	0.9091	0	0	0
yaleB28ffP00A+120E+00.pgm	0.9091	0	0	0
yaleB28ffP00A-050E-40.pgm	0	0.1111	0.7778	2
yaleB28ffP00A-070E-35.pgm	0.2857	0	0.6429	2
yaleB29ffP00A-005E-10.pgm	0	0.6923	0.2308	1
yaleB29ffP00A-035E+15.pgm	0	0.1111	0.7778	2
yaleB29ffP00A-035E-20.pgm	0	0.1111	0.7778	2
yaleB29ffP00A-070E+00.pgm	0	0.1111	0.7778	2
yaleB29ffP00A-110E-20.pgm	0.7143	0	0.1429	0
yaleB30ffP00A+095E+00.pgm	0.2857	0	0.6429	2
yaleB30ffP00A+110E+15.pgm	0.2857	0	0.6429	2
yaleB30ffP00A+120E+00.pgm	0.7143	0	0.1429	0
yaleB30ffP00A-005E+10.pgm	0	0.5000	0	1
yaleB30ffP00A-035E+65.pgm	0.2857	0	0.6429	2
yaleB34ffP00A-005E-10.pgm	0	0.6923	0.2308	1
yaleB34ffP00A-035E+65.pgm	0.2857	0	0.6429	2
yaleB34ffP00A-050E-40.pgm	0	0.6923	0.2308	1
yaleB34ffP00A-070E+00.pgm	0	0.1111	0.7778	2
yaleB34ffP00A-110E+40.pgm	0.7143	0	0.1429	0
yaleB35ffP00A-035E+65.pgm	0.2857	0	0.6429	2
yaleB35ffP00A-050E+00.pgm	0	0.1111	0.7778	2

Table 8. Overall performance of rmf classifier on extended YaleB face database

	0	1	2	Sensitivity
0	300	0	0	100%
1	0	594	6	99%
2	2	10	588	98%
Accuracy	99.3%	98.34%	98.98	98.8%

Table 9. Comparative classification rate in % for different classifiers for extended YaleB

k-nn	Neural Network	SVM	*rmf*-Based Classifier
80.70	84.1	92.01	98.8

Table 10. Feature names

Types of Surgery	Features Name	Symbolic Representation
Rhinoplasty (Nose surgery)	Noselength	NL
	NoseWidth	NW
	Eyeballdist	EBD
Blepharoplasty (Eyelid surgery)	Eyelipdist	ELD
	Eyenosedist	END
	Noselipdist	NLD
Lip Augmentation	AngleEL	AEL
	AngleEN	AEN
	AngleNL	ANL

Figure 6. Top left: examples of correctly classified normal face images; top right: examples of correctly classified shadow face images; bottom: examples of correctly classified dark face images

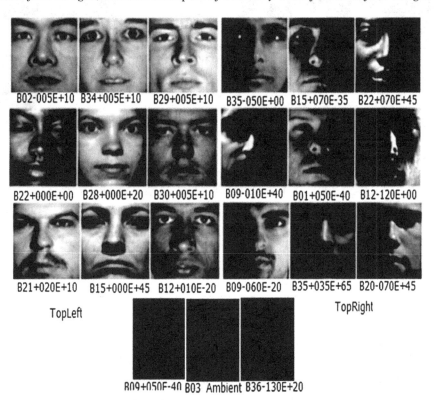

Figure 7. (a) Effect of different illumination normalization techniques on shadow face images, (b) effect of different illumination normalization techniques on dark face images

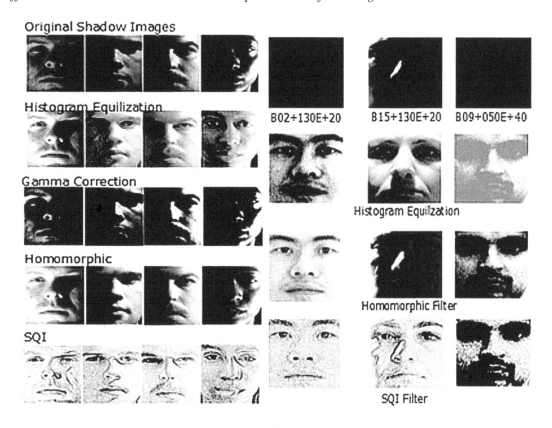

Figure 8. Plots for different classifiers using extended YaleB face database

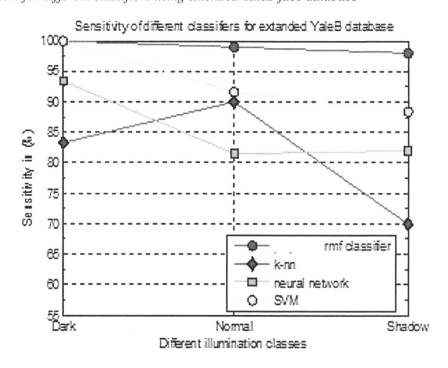

Near Set Theory: Plastic Surgery Problem in Face Recognition

In face recognition plastic surgery is a new challenge that makes the face recognition a complex and unsolved problem. Facial plastic surgery a sophisticated operational technique is still an unexplored area from medical background. Being one of the challenges in face recognition, plastic surgery is related with ethical, social and engineering domain also. Generally, facial plastic surgery is performed under two main circumstances. First is medical reasons and second one is individual's choice (*i.e.,* cosmetic surgery). Under any circumstances whenever plastic surgery has been performed it changes the appearances of facial images of any individual. This alteration in facial appearances can be significantly brought either globally or locally, thereby making plastic surgery a computer vision challenge to face recognition. Due to this the growing popularity of plastic surgery introduces new challenges in designing future face recognition systems. To the best of our knowledge, much literature is not available that exhibit any simulation for recognizing faces that have undergone local or global plastic surgery. Very few researchers till now have contributed in this field. In paper (R.Singh & M.Vatsa, 2009) authors have shown the comparative study of different face recognition algorithms for plastic surgery. Based on the experimentation carried out by the authors, it has been concluded that face recognition algorithms such as PCA, FDA, GF, LLA, LBP and GNN have shown recognition rate not more than 40% for local plastic surgery. Moreover, for global surgery it was merely up to 10%. Among all the algorithms, geometrical feature-based approach has proven to a great extent comparatively for local plastic surgery. The forthcoming section presents a brief overview of facial plastic surgery for the understanding of reader.

Facial Plastic Surgery

Plastic surgery being a new challenge to face recognition is a specialized area of surgery. With respect to face recognition, facial plastic surgery can be broadly classified in two categories.

- **Global Plastic Surgery:** In this category, surgery changes the complete facial structure. The appearance, texture and facial features of an individual are reconstructed in such a way that the surgical faces are not same as the original one. This surgery can be boon to burned or severely injured patients. But there are people who have used it for changing their looks completely. From the examples shown in Figure 9(a) and Figure 9(b) it can be seen that how the total facial appearances has been changed after plastic surgery.

From the examples depicted in figure it is clear that, after global surgery appearance of many people changes to such an extent that it becomes very difficult to recognize even with bare eye. The facial feature and texture gets drastically altered after surgery and hence makes face recognition under global plastic surgery an ineffective task. Very few researchers till now have contributed in this field. Furthermore, since global plastic surgery entirely change the face appearance, it can also be misused by criminals or individuals who want to remain elusive from law enforcement and pose a great threat to society despite all the security mechanism in-place. For instance, Rhytidectomy is a type of face surgery which is used to treat the patients to correct the burns, faces with injuries.

Figure 9. Examples of global plastic surgery
(Plastic surgery faces, 2009).

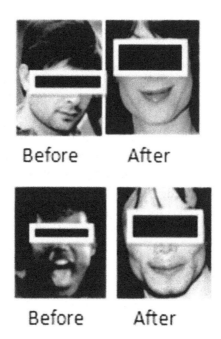

- **Local Plastic Surgery:** Local plastic surgery is used to correct individual part of faces such as certain defects, anomalies or to improve skin texture. It can be used to correct several features on face such as teeth structure, jaw, nose structure, chin, cheek, forehead and eyelids. Local plastic surgery will lead to some amount of changes in the geometric distance between these facial features. Such changes may lead to the verification accuracy. Few people who have undergone local plastic surgery on different parts of faces are listed in Figure 2. These images are collected from (Plastic surgery faces, 2009) and are simply used for experimentation. Different types of local plastic surgery are: rhinoplasty, blepharoplasty, forehead surgery, cheek implant, otoplasty, lip augmentation, and craniofacial. Rhinoplasty is used to correct the defects such as birth defects in nose or damaged nose in cases of accidents. Another form *i.e.,* cosmetic rhinoplasty is used for those who desire to change the shape of their nose to improve their facial appearance. Blepharoplasty is used to reshape both upper as well as lower eyelid in cases where unnecessary growth of skin tissues on the eyelid causes visualization problem. Forehead surgery is generally performed on those old aged people who suffer from flagging eyebrows which obstruct the vision and also for removing the wrinkles. Shape of ears also plays a dramatic role in the looks of an individual. Otoplasty is a kind of surgery that involves bringing the ears closer to the face, reducing the size of ears and orienting/pruning some structural ear elements. Another facial part *i.e.,* nose whose shape and look is also a concerned for many females. Thus lip augmentation is a technique that correct, enhance the shape of lips and play an important role in an individual's beauty.

Most of the existing face recognition algorithms have predominantly focused on mitigating the effects of pose, illumination and expression, and no attempt has been made to study the effect of local and global plastic surgery on face recognition. As facial plastic surgery procedures become more and more

Figure 10. Examples of local plastic surgery on different parts of faces
(Plastic surgery faces, 2009).

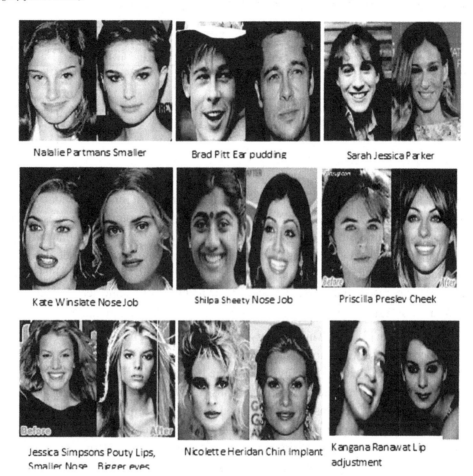

Natalie Partmans Smaller

Brad Pitt Ear pudding

Sarah Jessica Parker

Kate Winslate Nose Job

Shilpa Sheety Nose Job

Priscilla Presley Cheek

Jessica Simpsons Pouty Lips, Smaller Nose Bigger eyes

Nicolette Heridan Chin Implant

Kangana Ranawat Lip adjustment

prevalent, face recognition systems will be challenged to recognize individuals after plastic surgery has been performed. In this section, chapter investigate different aspects related to plastic surgery and face recognition.

The problem considered here is how to approximate surgical faces that are qualitatively alike in one or more respects. The term qualitatively alike/near is used here to mean closeness of description of distinctive characteristic of faces. The term near applied to surgical faces or sets of surgical faces means closely related. Means the description of surgical faces partially or completely matches the description of earlier non-surgical faces. The extent that description match is determine by considering the correspondence between measurement associate with the feature of objects that are in some sense near to each other. This near set will surely reduce the search space and in forth enhance the performance in terms of accuracy and speed. This chapter discusses an approach to plastic surgery based face recognition using near set theory.

The overall approach as shown in Figure 11 is basically classified into two modules: First module defines the image processing technique such as feature extraction where as second module defines the procedure for finding near sets of objects under consideration, which helps in classification. The train set contains

Figure 11. The overall architecture of near set theory based face recognition

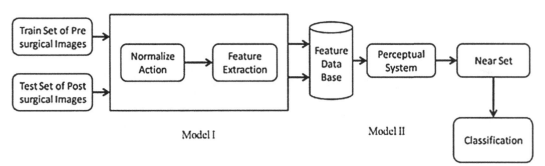

Model I   Model II

the pre-surgical images and test set contains the post-surgical images. In this chapter, local plastic surgery has been considered for discusion as local surgery leads to varying amount of changes in the geometric distance between facial features but the overall texture and appearance may look similar to the original face.

Based on the above facts and conclusion, it can be said that recognizing someone based on facial geometry makes human recognition a more automated process. Suppose an image which is a pre-plastic surgery face it can be represented as $\mathcal{F} \in O$, where O is a non empty finite set of objects/faces and $\mathcal{F}$ an be defined as a set of features $\{f_1, f_2, f_3, \dots f_n\}$, where $1 \leq n \leq |A|$. These feature values are extracted using the algorithm given in [31, 34]. This chapter explores three different types of surgery with nine facial features like nose length, nose width and distance between some fiducial points *etc.*, as listed in Table 10. From the listed nine features chapter initially concentrated on three facial features such as Nose Length (NL), Nose Width (NW) and Distance between Eye Balls (EBD) for calculating the nearness measure.

Using the above listed features plastic surgery facial decision system is shown in Table 11 with eight facial samples. At this point chapter present the formation of nearness relation for surgical faces using near set theory. Let x_1 to x_4 are the pre-surgical faces and x_5 to x_8 are post-surgical faces as shown in Table 11. Let, x_1 is a pre surgical face of one subject and x_8 is the post-surgical face of the same subject.

As a first step neighborhood of feature NL denoted as $N_{NL}(B)$ will be calculated. Based on the notation used in [85, 86],

$$\text{Let } D = \left\{ x \in Object \big| d(x) = 1 \right\} = \left\{ x_2, x_3, x_4, x_6, x_7 \right\},$$

Table 11. Sample decision table

Object	NL	NW	DEB	D
x_1	14	11	06	0
x_2	11	09	03	1
x_3	13	11	02	1
x_4	12	10	04	1
x_5	12	10	06	0
x_6	14	12	03	1
x_7	11	09	04	1
x_8	14	11	02	0

$B= \{NL, NW, DEB\}$, where B is the set of features.

The following neighborhoods are in $N_{NL}(B)$:

$$B_{NL}(x_1) = link_{NL}[x_1] = \{x_1, x_6, x_8\}$$

$$B_{NL}(x_2) = link_{NL}[x_2] = \{x_2, x_7\}$$

$$B_{NL}(x_3) = link_{NL}[x_3] = \{x_3\}$$

$$B_{NL}(x_4) = link_{NL}[x_4] = \{x_4, x_5\}$$

$$B_{NW}(x_1) = link_{NW}[x_1] = \{x_1, x_3, x_8\}$$

$$B_{NW}(x_2) = link_{NW}[x_2] = \{x_2, x_7\}$$

$$B_{NW}(x_4) = link_{NW}[x_4] = \{x_4, x_5\}$$

$$B_{NW}(x_6) = link_{NW}[x_6] = \{x_6\}$$

$$B_{EBD}(x_1) = link_{EBD}[x_1] = \{x_1, x_5\}$$

$$B_{EBD}(x_2) = link_{EBD}[x_2] = \{x_2, x_6\}$$

$$B_{EBD}(x_3) = link_{EBD}[x_3] = \{x_3, x_8\}$$

$$B_{EBD}(x_4) = link_{EBD}[x_4] = \{x_4, x_7\}$$

The Upper approximation based on the features, denoted by

$$(N_{NL}(B))^*(D) =$$
$$B_{NL(x1)} \cup B_{NL(x2)} \cup B_{NL(x3)} \cup B_{NL(x4)} \cup B_{NW(x1)} \cup B_{NW(x2)} \cup B_{NW(x4)} \cup B_{NW(x6)} \cup B_{DEB(x2)} \cup B_{DEB(x3)} \cup B_{DEB(x4)} =$$
$$\{x_1, x_2, x_3, x_4, x_5, x_6, x_7, x_8\}$$

Next, the lower approximation based on the features, denoted by

$$
\left(N_{NL}\left(B\right)\right)_{*}\left(D\right) =
$$
$$
B_{NL}\left(x_{2}\right) \cup B_{NL}\left(x_{3}\right) \cup B_{NW}\left(x_{2}\right) \cup B_{NW}\left(x_{6}\right) \cup B_{EBD}\left(x_{2}\right) \cup B_{EBD}\left(x_{4}\right) =
$$
$$
\left\{x_{2}, x_{3}, x_{4}, x_{6}, x_{7}\right\}
$$

Finally, the boundary region can be obtained as,

$$
BNDN_{NL}\left(B\right)\left(D\right) = \left(N_{NL}\left(B\right)\right)^{*}\left(D\right) / \left(N_{NL}\left(B\right)\right)_{*}\left(D\right) = \left\{x_{1}, x_{5}, x_{8}\right\}
$$

This set will be termed as a "near set" relative to neighborhood of nose length $N_{NL}(B)$. This means that objects x_{1}, x_{5}, x_{8} can certainly be classified. The extent that descriptions of these objects match is determined by considering the correspondence between measurements associated with features of objects [26].

Using the above concept of near set theory the chapter presents Algorithm 1 to measure the nearness between pre-surgical and post-surgical faces as explained in algorithm. The first step is to measure the nearness is to initially retrieve every image i, from set of images I, where $i \in I$. Let the value of preset threshold ε as 0.1. If $\phi_{B}(x)$ and $\phi_{B}(y)$ are the probe functions of an object x and y belonging to the set and if the difference comes to be less than or equals to preset threshold ε, then features are near to each other and classify the post-surgical faces to the correct class. The figure 11 shows the overall process of matching the pre- surgical and post-surgical faces.

Experimentation Result

In order to evaluate the performance of the near set approach for local plastic surgery face recognition, specifically, a plastic surgery face database is prepared that consists of facial images of some celebrities who have under gone plastic surgery (Plastic surgery faces, 2009). The database is partition into two parts: train set and test set. The train set consist of 3 images of pre-surgical faces of one individual. The feature vector is created by extracting the feature from train and test images respectively. On those feature values, the perfect matching is performed by near set approach. Initially the near set approach has been evaluated with 9 different pre-plastic surgical faces with post-plastic surgical faces out of which 5 were surely matched as shown in Table 12. From the table it is evident that face recognition under nose surgery is more effective compared to other type of local plastic surgery under consideration. The near set approach to plastic surgery faces have also been evaluated against standard algorithm of PCA, LBP and GNN. As shown in table 15, one can observe that out of this four different face recognition algorithm near sets has yield better performance accuracy of 55.55%. Match scores obtained from near sets yield the best verification accuracy demonstrating the effectiveness of near set theory for face recognition under plastic surgery.

Thus this chapter presented an approach to find the nearness between the pre-plastic surgical face to the post-plastic surgical face using the concept of near sets. Three features such as nose, eyes and lips have been used for nearness measure. Using those features, chapter has shown the process of calculation of near set which will assist in classification.

Algorithm 1. Measuring the nearness between pre-surgical and post-surgical faces

Input: Face images, i ∈ I. Feature vector of surgical faces, set of feature $\{f_1, f_2, f_3, \ldots \ldots f_n\} \subseteq$ A, **Facial feature:** Nose Length (NL), Nose Width (NW) and eyes balls distance (EBD).

Output: Match Face with error ξ.

While *True* do

For (i=0, i <= I; i++) do

Repeat (for number of faces);

Retrieve image I;

Let ε = 0,1

Calculate (nearness between pre-surgical faces with post-surgical faces);

If $\| \phi_B(x) - \phi_B(y) \|_2 \leq \varepsilon$ Feature near to each other and matching is form with observable error ξ;

Otherwise

Face does not classified in the correct class,

Until all features are extracted from facial images.

End

End

Table 12. Different 9 facial images which have undergone certain type of surgery with their matching score

Subject	Type of Surgery	Matched and Unmatched
Sarah Parker	Nose Surgery	Matched
Natalie Portman	Nose Surgery	Matched
Brad Pitt	Ear pinning surgery	Unmatched
Kate Winslet	Nose Surgery	Matched
Koena Mitra	Nose Surgery	Unmatched
Prioscilla Resley	Chick Implant	Matched
Jessica Simpson	Lips, Nose and eyes surgery	Matched
Nicolette Heridan	Chin Implant	Unmatched
Kangna Ranawat	Lip adjustment	Unmatched

Table 13. Performance of face recognition algorithms on local plastic surgery with verification accuracy

Procedure	PCA	LBP	GNN	Near Sets
Local Plastic Surgery	22.2%	34.5%	38.8%	55.55%

FUTURE RESEARCH DIRECTIONS

It should be observed that rough set or near set by themselves or in combination with other hybrid computational intelligence technologies work remarkably well in tackling different issues in face recognition. Reader can also see that how the uncertainties and vagueness present either due to variation in illumination or plastic surgery can be mapped with rough set theory and near set theory respectively. In this context this chapter specifically tried to focus on how different issues still present in face recognition can be tackled with these set theories. Presently, for adaptive approach to illumination normalization the range of interval for each feature is subjected to face databases. In future, possibilities can be explored to generalize these ranges for any type of facial image. It will be interesting also to evaluate adaptive based illumination normalization with video-based face recognition system because when a video is captured in real time environment, effect of lighting is not in human control. For a subject moving around in a video, there will be no constant lighting from all the direction. In such videos there will be variations in illumination from one frame to another frame for the same subject, use of any particular illumination normalization technique will not be sufficient for illumination compensation. It has been observed that near set methods can be useful in object recognition, especially in solving face recognition problems and has shown greatest promise for plastic surgery. However, experimentation has been done on a very small number of samples. So in the future work can be extended for large plastic surgical face databases. Furthermore, from the perspective of rough sets and near sets, further explorations into possible hybridizations of rough sets and near sets with other technologies are necessary to build a more complete picture of rough set or near set based applications in face recognition.

CONCLUSION

By way of introducing the face recognition as computer vision problem and its challenges this chapter also presented the brief overview of rough set theory and near set theory. The basic concept of rough sets such as indesirnibility relation, equivalence class and rough membership function has been discussed. This theory has been used to formulate the illumination problem of face recognition and thus an adaptive approach to illumination normalization to compensate the effect of variations in illumination has been discussed. The adaptive approach to illumination normalization allows one to choose appropriate illumination normalization techniques automatically depending upon the type of illumination. From simulation result it has been also seen that it is reliable and computationally efficient as one can choose illumination normalization technique adaptively. In addition, this chapter also presented various nearness relations that define partitions of sets of perceptual objects that are near each other. Furthermore, this chapter presented the formal foundation of near sets to tackle the issue of plastic surgery in face recognition. Chapter also discussed different categories of facial plastic surgery with brief description.

From the simulation results it is evident that near set theory has shown promising result for plastic surgery and possibilities for future exploration. From the problem formulated for illumination variation and plastic surgery it is seen that while rough sets provide a powerful tool to objects classification by means of their attributes, near sets presents a nearness approach based on the fact of comparing similarities between facial images.

REFERENCES

Dimitras, A. I., Zanakis, S. H., & Zopounidis, C. (1996). A survey of business failure with an emphasis on prediction methods and industrial applications. *Elsevier European Journal of Operational Research*, *90*(3), 487–513. doi:10.1016/0377-2217(95)00070-4

Patently Apple. (2012, September 20). Apple Invents Facial Recognition Locking & Unlocking System. Retrieved from http://www.patentlyapple.com/patently-apple/2012/09/apple-invents-facial-recognition-locking-unlocking-system.html

Skowron, A., & Peters, J. F. (2007). Rough granular computing. In W. Pedrycz, A. Skowron, & V. Kreinovich (Eds.), Handbook on Granular Computing. New York: Wiley.

Skowron, A., & Stepaniuk, J. (1996). Tolerance approximation spaces. Fundamental Informaticas, 27(2-3), 245-253.

Shashua, A., & Riklin-Raviv, T. (2001).The Quotient Image: Class-based re-rendering and recognition with varying illuminations. *Proceedings of IEEE Transactions on Pattern Analysis and Machine Intelligence*, 23(2), 129–139. doi:10.1109/34.908964

Butalia, A., Ingle, M., & Kulkarni, P. (2012). Best emotional feature selection criteria based on rough set theory. *International Journal of Computer Application and Engineering Technology*, *1*(2), 49–71.

Bozorgtabar, B., Azami, H., & Noorian, F. (2012). Illumination Invariant Face Recognition Using Fuzzy LDA and FFNN. *Scientific Research Journal of Signal and Information Processing*, *3*(1), 45–50. doi:10.4236/jsip.2012.31007

Big brother. (2010, July). Retrieved from http://www.theforbiddenknowledge.com/hardtruth/face_recognition _airports.htm

Chanda, B., & Majumder, D. D. (2004). *Digital image processing and analysis*. PHI Learning Pvt. Ltd.

Kostek, B., Szczuko, P., & Zwan, P. (2004). Processing of Musical Data Employing Rough Sets and Artificial Neural Networks. Proceedings of International Conference on Rough Sets and Current Trends in Computing (Vol. 3066, pp. 539–548). doi:10.1007/978-3-540-25929-9_65

Henry, C., & Peters, J. F. (2007). Image Pattern Recognition Using Approximation Spaces and Near Sets. Proceedings of Eleventh International Conference on Rough Sets, Fuzzy Sets, Data Mining and Granular (Vol. 4482, pp. 475-482). doi:10.1007/978-3-540-72530-5_57

Henry, C., Lockery, D., Peters, J. F., & Borkowski, M. (2006). Monocular vision system that learns with approximation spaces. In A. Ella, P. Lingras, D. Slezak, & Z. Suraj (Eds.), Rough Set Computing: Toward Perception Based Computing (pp. 186-203). Hershey, PA: Information Science Reference. doi:10.4018/978-1-59904-552-8.ch009

Lockery, D., & Peters, J. F. (2007). Robotic target tracking with approximation space-based feedback during reinforcement learning. Proceedings of Eleventh International Conference on Rough Sets, Fuzzy Sets, Data Mining and Granular Computing, Joint Rough Set Symposium, Lecture Notes in Artificial Intelligence (Vol. 4482, pp. 483-490). doi:10.1007/978-3-540-72530-5_58

Ramani, A.K., Ingle, M., & Kulkarni, P. (2012). Classification of Sentiments through Rough Fuzzy Approach Butalia. *International Journal of Computer Science And Information Technology & Security*, 2(2), 209-309.

Toshiba. (n. d.). Face Recognition. Retrieved from http://explore.toshiba.com/innovation-lab/face-recognition

Chunsheng, F., Fending, C., Qiang, W., Shouchao, W., & Ju, W. (2010). Application of Rough Sets Theory to Sources Analysis of Atmospheric Particulates. Bioinformatics and Biomedical Engineering, 1-5.

Geetha, M. A., & Saklecha, A. (2013). Facial Recognition using CCTV images based on Rough Set Theory and Scale Invariant Feature Transform. *International Journal of Emerging Trends in Engineering and Development*, 2(3), 203–209.

Arafat, H., Barakat, S., & Goweda, A. F. (2012). Using Intelligent Techniques for Breast Cancer Classification. *International Journal of Emerging Trends & Technology in Computer Science*, 1(3), 26–36.

Arafat, H., Elawady, R. M., Barakat, S., & Elrashidy, N. M. (2013). Using Rough Set and Ant Colony optimization In Feature Selection. *International Journal of Emerging Trends and Technology in Computer Science*, 2(1), 148–155.

Plastic surgery faces. (2009). Retrieved from http://glamour-news-blog.com/2009/10/stars-before-after-plastic-surgery.html

Zimmermann, H. J. (2001). *Fuzzy Set Theory and Its Applications*. Springer.

Peters, J. F. (2007). Near Sets. Proceedings of Applied Mathematical Sciences, 11(53), 2609-2629.

Peters, J. F. (2007). Perceptual granulation in ethology-based reinforcement learning. In W. Pedrycz, A. Skowron, & V. Kreinovich (Eds.), Handbook on Granular Computing. Wiley, NY.

Peters, J. F., & Henry, C. (2006). Reinforcement learning with approximation spaces. Fundamental Informaticas, 71(23), 323-349.

Peters, J. F., Borkowski, M., & Henry, C., D. Lockery' D.S. Gunderson (2006). Line-Crawling Bots that Inspect Electric Power Transmission Line Equipment. Proceedings of the Third International Conference on Autonomous Robots and Agents (pp. 39-44).

Peters, J. F., & Wasilecoski, P. (2009). Foundations of near sets. *International Journal of Information Sciences*, 179(18), 3091–3109. doi:10.1016/j.ins.2009.04.018

Peters, J. F., & Ramanna, S. (2007). Feature Selection: Near Set Approach. *Lecture Notes in Computer Science, 4944*, 57–71. doi:10.1007/978-3-540-68416-9_5

Peters, J. F., Shahfar, S., Ramanna, S., & Szturm, T. (2007). Biologically-inspired adaptive learning: A near set approach. Proceedings of Frontiers in the Convergence of Bioscience and Information Technologies (Vol. 11, pp. 403 – 408).

Peters, J. F., Suraj, Z., Shan, S., Ramanna, S., Pedrycz, W., & Pizzi, N. (2003). Classification of meteorological volumetric radar data using rough set methods. Pattern Recognition Letters, 24(6), 911–920. doi:10.1016/S0167-8655(02)00203-9

Mannar, K., & Ceglarek, D. (2004). Continuous Failure Diagnosis for Assembly Systems using Rough Set Approach. Manufacturing Technology, 53(1), 39–42. doi:10.1016/S0007-8506(07)60640-4

Singh, K. R., & Raghuwanshi, M. M. (2009). Face Recognition with Rough-Neural Network: A Rule Based Approach. *Proceedings of International workshop on Machine Intelligence Research* (Vol. 38, pp. 123-129).

Singh, K. R., Zaveri, M. A., & Raghuwanshi, M. M. (2010). Extraction of Pose Invariant Feature. Information and Communications Technologies, 101(3), 535-539.

Singh, K. R., Zaveri, M. A., & Raghuwanshi, M. M. (2013). Rough Membership Function based Illumination Classifier for Illumination Invariant Face Recognition. *Applied Soft Computing, 13*(10), 4105–4117. doi:10.1016/j.asoc.2013.04.012

Zadeh, L. (1965). Fuzzy Sets. Information and Control, 8(3), 338–353. doi:10.1016/S0019-9958(65)90241-X

M. A. Vicente, C. Fernandez, and A. M. Coves. (2009). Supervised Face Recognition for Railway Stations Surveillance. *Advanced Concepts for Intelligent Vision Systems* (pp. 710–719).

Borkowski, M., & Peters, J. F. (2006). Matching 2D image segments with genetic algorithms and approximation spaces. Transactions on Rough Sets (Vol. 4100, pp. 63-101).

Bryant, M. (2011). 10 Great Uses of Image and Face Recognition. Retrieved from http://thenextweb.com/apps/2011/08/19/10-great-uses-of-image-and-face-recognition

Hu, M., & Qiang, Z. Z. W. (2008). Application of Rough Sets to Image Pre-processing for Face Detection. *Proceedings of the 2008 IEEE International Conference on Information and Automation* (pp. 545-548).

Lakshmiprabha, N. S., Bhattacharya, J., & Majumder, S. (2011). Face recognition using multimodal biometric features. *Proceedings of IEEE International Conference on Image Information Processing* (pp. 1–6).

Gonzalez, R. C., Woods, R. E., & Eddins, S. L. (2009). *Digital image processing using MATLAB.* Gatesmark Publishing Knoxville.

Singh, R., & Vatsa, M. (2009). *Effect of Plastic Surgery on Face Recognition: A Preliminary Study.* Morgantown, USA: West Virginia University.

Fleming, R. W., Dror, R. O., & Adelson, E. H. (2003). Real-world illumination and the perception of surface reflectance properties. *Association for Research in Vision and Ophthalmology Journal of Vision*, *3*(5), 347–368. PMID:12875632

Gupta, S., & Patnaik, K.S. (2008). Enhancing performance of face recognition system by using near set approach for selecting facial features. Journal of Theoretical and Applied Information Technology, 4(5), 433.

Nguyen, S. H., Nguyen, T. T., & Nguyen, H. S. (2005). Rough Set Approach to Sunspot Classification Problem. *Proceedings of International Conference on Rough Sets, Fuzzy Sets, Data Mining and Granular Computing, Lecture Notes in Artificial Intelligence* (Vol. 3642, pp. 263–2720. doi:10.1007/11548706_28

Choi, S. I., & Choi, C. H. (2007). An effective Face Recognition under Illumination and Pose Variation. *Proceedings of IEEE International Joint Conference on Neural Networks* (pp. 914–919). doi:10.1109/IJCNN.2007.4371080

Nishida, S., & Shinya, M. (1998). Use of image-based information in judgments of surface reflectance properties. *Journal of the Optical Society of America*, *15*(12), 2951–2965. doi:10.1364/JOSAA.15.002951 PMID:9857525

Lawrence, S., Giles, C. L., Tsoi, A. C., & Back, A. D. (1995). Face Recognition: A convolutional neural-network approach. *IEEE Transactions on Neural Networks*, *8*(1), 98–113. doi:10.1109/72.554195 PMID:18255614

Rubin, S., Michalowski, W., & Slowinski, R. (1996). Developing an emergency room diagnostic check list using rough sets-a case study of appendicitis. In J. Anderson, M. Katzper (Eds.), Simulation in the Medical Sciences (pp. 19–24).

Kung, S. Y., & Taur, J. S. (2002). Decision-based neural networks with signal/image classification applications. *IEEE Transactions on Neural Networks*, *6*(1), 170–181. doi:10.1109/72.363439 PMID:18263296

Wang, W., Ren, G., & Wang, W. (2010). The Applications of Rough Set Theory in Civil Engineering. *Proceedings of International Conference on Artificial Intelligence and Computational Intelligence*. doi:10.1007/978-3-642-16527-6

Zhao, W., Chellappa, R., Phillips, P. J., & Rosenfeld, A. (2003). Face Recognition: A Literature Survey. *Association for Computing Machinery Computing Surveys*, *35*(4), 390–458.

Tan, X., & Triggs, B. (2010). Enhanced local texture feature sets for face recognition under difficult lighting conditions. *IEEE Transactions on Image Processing*, *19*(6), 1635–1650. doi:10.1109/TIP.2010.2042645 PMID:20172829

Zou, X., Kittler, J., & Messer, K. (2007). Illumination invariant face recognition: A Survey. *Proceedings of First IEEE International Conference on Biometrics: Theory, Applications, and Systems* (pp. 1–8).

He, X.-J., Zhang, Y., Lok, T.-M. & Lyu, M.R. (2005). A new feature of uniformity of image texture directions coinciding with the human eyes perception. Fuzzy Systems and Knowledge Discovery (Vol. 3614, pp. 727–730).

YaleB Face Database. (2010, June). Retrieved from http://cvc.yale.edu/projects/yalefacesB/yalefacesB.html

Sun, Y., Liu, J., & Wang, L. (2011). A Multi-Scale TVQI-based Illumination Normalization Model. *Proceedings of International Multi Conference of Engineers and Computer Scientists* (Vol. 1, pp. 1-6).

Pawlak, Z. (1996). Rough sets, rough relations and rough functions. Fundamental Informaticas, 27(2), 103–108.

Pawlak, Z. (1981). Classification of objects by means of attributes. Proceedings of Polish Academy of Sciences.

Pawlak, Z. (1982). Rough Sets. *International Journal of Computer and Information Sciences*, *11*(5), 341–356. doi:10.1007/BF01001956

Junjie, Z. H. E. N. G., Xiaoke, Y. A. N., Caicheng, S. H. I., & Peikun, H. E. (2006). Recognition of bridges over water based on fracatal and rough sets theory in aerial photography in image. *Proceedings of IEEE ICSP* (pp. 1-4).

Chapter 14
Automation in Sputum Microscopy:
A Hybrid Intelligent Technique in Diagnostic Device Automation

Pramit Ghosh
RCC Institute of Information Technology, India

Debotosh Bhattacharjee
Jadavpur University, India

Mita Nasipuri
Jadavpur University, India

ABSTRACT

This chapter describes an automatic intelligent diagnostic system for Tuberculosis. Sputum microscopy is the most common diagnostic technique to diagnose Tuberculosis. In Sputum microscopy, Sputum are examined using a microscope for Mycobacterium tuberculosis. This manual process is being automated by image processing, where classification is performed by using a hybrid approach (color based and shape based). This hybrid approach reduces the false positive and false negative rate. Final classification decision is taken by a fuzzy system. Image processing, soft-computing, mechanics, and control system plays a significant role in this system. Slides are given as input to the system. System finds for Mycobacterium tuberculosis bacteria and generates reports. From designing point of view ARM11 based, 32 bit RISC processor is used to control the mechanical units. The main mathematical calculation (including image processing and soft computing) is distributed between ARM11 based group and Personal Computer (Intel i3). This system has better sensitivity than manual sputum microscopy.

INTRODUCTION

Tuberculosis (TB) is an infectious disease that is caused by a bacterium called Mycobacterium tuberculosis (Centers for Disease Control and Prevention [CDC], 2014). TB primarily affects the lungs called Pulmonary TB, but it can also affect organs in the central nervous system, lymphatic system, and cir-

DOI: 10.4018/978-1-4666-9474-3.ch014

culatory system among others. TB is spread from person to person through the air. The TB bacteria are put into the air when a person with TB disease of the lungs or throat coughs, sneezes, speaks, or sings. People nearby may breathe in these bacteria and become infected. If TB is not treated properly, it can be fatal. However, TB is not spread by shaking someone's hand, sharing food or drink, sharing toilet seats, etc. People, who have TB disease, do feel sick, have symptoms, and may spread TB bacteria to others. The active TB disease symptoms are:

- Overall sensation of feeling unwell;
- Cough, possibly with bloody saliva;
- Fatigue;
- Shortness of breath;
- Slight fever;
- Weight loss;
- Pain in the chest;
- Night sweats.

The occurrence of additional symptoms depends on where the disease has spread beyond the chest and lungs. For example, if TB spreads to the lymph nodes, it can cause swollen glands on the sides of the neck or under the arms. When TB spreads to the bones and joints, it can cause pain and swelling in the knee or hip. About one-third of the world's population has latent TB, which means people have been infected by TB bacteria, but they are not yet sick with disease, do not have symptoms and cannot transmit the disease. Persons infected with TB bacteria have a lifetime risk of falling ill due to TB with a certainty of 10%. However individuals with compromised immune systems, such as persons living with HIV, malnutrition or diabetes, or people who use tobacco, have a much higher risk of falling ill. When a person develops active TB disease, the symptoms of cough, fever, night sweats, weight loss, etc. may be mild for many months. This can lead to delay in seeking care and results in transmission of the bacteria to others. People sick with TB can infect up to 10-15 other persons through close contact over the course of a year. Without proper treatment, up to two-third of people, who are ill with TB, will die (World Health Organization [WHO], 2015). The following factors may play a role in promoting active disease in someone who has an inactive TB infection:

- Diabetes;
- Cancer;
- Illnesses that suppress the immune system, such as HIV or AIDS;
- Kidney disease;
- Long-term steroid use;
- Malnutrition;
- Medications that suppress the immune system, such as anticancer medications (e.g., cyclosporine);
- Pregnancy;
- Radiotherapy.

The Relation between Diabetes and TB

Most of the people from a weak immune system are suffering from chronic disease like diabetes. They are at a higher risk of moving ahead from latent to active tuberculosis. Diabetes affected people have 2-3 times higher risk of TB compared to the persons without diabetes. The risk of death and TB relapse rate after treatment completion are much higher for the people with diabetes. WHO-recommended treatments should be thoroughly implemented for people with TB or diabetes (WHO, 2008).

The Relation between Cancer and TB

American Thoracic Society and Centers for Disease Control and Prevention have recognized that cancer increases the risk of tuberculosis since 1970. Specific cancers listed in the initial guideline included leukemia and Hodgkin disease. Cancer care has changed in such a way that it increases the risk of tuberculosis (Kamboj, 2006). Nowadays new and more intensive treatments are available like purine analogues, hematopoietic stem cell transplantation etc. The other fact is that improved cancer survivals in the United States have increased the number of people at high TB risk.

The Relation between TB and HIV (The AIDS Virus)

People infected with HIV (the virus that causes AIDS) are more likely than uninfected people to get sick with other infections and diseases. Tuberculosis (TB) is one of these illnesses (Granich, Akolo, Gunneberg, Getahun, Williams, & Williams, 2010).

The Relation between TB and Chronic Kidney Disease (CKD)

Patients with advanced chronic kidney disease (CKD) are susceptible to tuberculosis infection and illness. CKD is more prevalent in foreign born individuals—a population with high rates of latent tuberculosis infection (LTBI). More importantly, however, immunity is impaired in CKD patients through reduced function of T and B cells and neutrophils. Once infected with Mycobacterium tuberculosis, dialysis patients have a 20-fold increased risk of developing active disease. Renal transplant patients are at even higher risk due to added immunosuppressive therapy. The occurrence of an active infectious case of TB in a dialysis unit is highly disruptive, putting both staff and other patients at risk (Moore, Lightstone, & Friedland, 2002) .

According to world health organization report of 2014 (WHO, Global tuberculosis report, 2014), an estimated 8.6 million people developed TB and 1.3 million died from the disease (including 320 000 deaths among HIV-positive people). The number of TB deaths is unacceptably large given that most are preventable. This report reveals that over 95% of TB deaths occur in low- and middle-income countries, and it is among the top three causes of death for women aged 15 to 44. Furthermore in 2012, an estimated 530 000 children became ill with TB and 74 000 HIV-negative children died of TB. From the above discussion, it is clear that the most important thing is to prediction of TB.

THE DIAGNOSIS OF TB

There are four available tests to diagnosis TB. These are skin test, sputum test, blood test and imaging test.

The TB Skin Test

The TB skin test (Huebner 1993) (Lordi, Reichman, 1994) is a widely used diagnostic TB test, and sometimes it is used to verify for latent TB infection. The TB skin test involves injecting a small amount of fluid called tuberculin into the skin in the lower part of the arm. Then the person must return after 3 to 4 days to have a trained health care worker look at their arm. The health care worker will look for a raised hard area or swelling, and if there is one then they will measure its size. They will not include any general area of redness. The TB skin test result depends on the size of the raised hard area or swelling, and the larger the size of the affected area the greater the likelihood that the person has been infected with TB bacteria at some time in the past. But interpreting the TB skin test result, that is whether it is a positive result, may also involve considering the lifestyle factors of the person being tested for TB. The TB skin test also cannot tell if the person has latent TB or active TB disease. False positive results happen with the TB skin test because the person has been infected with a different type of bacteria, rather than the one that causes TB. It can also happen because the person has been vaccinated with the BCG vaccine, and this vaccine is widely used in countries with high rates of TB infection. False negative results mainly happen with children, older people, and people with HIV. Figure 1 shows TB skin test. The swelling area is measured by a special type of scale.

Figure 1. Skin test for TB detection

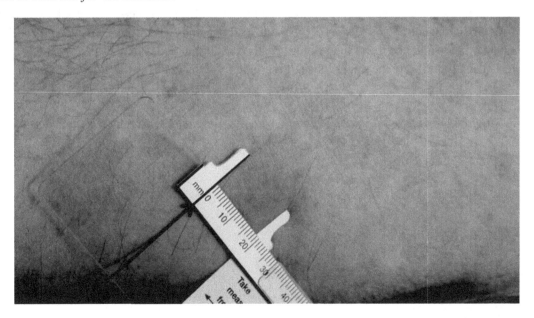

Sputum Test

Sputum microscopy (Levy & Feldman, 1989) (Feng-zeng, Levy & Wen, 1997) is one of the widely used non-invasive techniques to confirm a diagnosis of TB. Sputum tests are used to diagnose tuberculosis (TB) when other tests show that a person probably has TB. One of the best ways to diagnose TB is through a sputum culture. A culture uses a sample of mucus from the lungs (sputum) that is placed under special conditions that allow TB bacteria to grow. If TB bacteria grow, then the person has tuberculosis. The test also can show if a lung infection is caused by some other kind of bacteria. But a sputum culture can take 1 to 8 weeks to provide results because every sample slides are checked manually using microscope. That case Rapid sputum test helps to diagnose. Rapid sputum tests can tell if a person has TB within 24 hours. Figure 2 shows the microscopic image of Tuberculosis bacteria which are stained with pink color (Epstein, & Schluger, 1998).

Blood Test

The TB blood test is a specialized test that was developed in recent years. It is basically a particular type of antigen test. This test is also called Gamma Release Assay or IGRA. The IGRA test measures the release of a substance called gamma interferon by white blood cells in a sample of blood. These blood cells are exposed to specific TB antigens. This test requires viable white blood cells. It helps to identify people infected with latent TB. However this test is not used for people who are sick with active TB disease. A positive TB blood test tells us that at which stage people became infected with Mycobacterium tuberculosis. The TB blood test gives more accurate result than skin test.

X-Ray Imaging Test

The most common diagnostic test to predict the suspicion of infection is chest X-ray. Chest X-rays are valuable for predicting pulmonary lesions of tuberculosis. In primary infection of TB, an X-ray will show an abnormality in the mid and lower lung fields. In this case lymph nodes may be enlarged. Reactivated TB bacteria usually infiltrate the upper lobes of the lungs. X-Ray changes the characteristics of active

Figure 2. Magnified image of the sputum sample, with the presence of mycobacterium Tuberculosis

TB. The main disadvantage of using X-Ray frequently is the radiation used in X-Ray sometimes damage the body cells, DNA structure which leads to cancer. Figure 3 shows the X-Ray images of the chest, where lung is affected by TB. In Figure 3, two arrows are used.

- **Cavities (Left Arrow):** Hollow spaces within the lung which contains bacteria.
- **Infiltrates (Right Arrow):** White areas that shows accumulation of fluid in the lung tissue.

In the TB scenario, a chest x-ray was performed on a patient, who had a normal left lung and infiltrated in the right lung. If abnormalities are present, the patient has possible pulmonary TB. A negative chest x-ray indicates that the patient has either latent TB, negative TB or EPTB. In both cases, a sputum analysis needs to be performed to confirm the provisional diagnosis.

DRUGS AND TREATMENT PROCEDURE

The treatments of tuberculosis may take much longer time than other bacterial infectious disease. Medications are the keystone of tuberculosis treatment. Tuberculosis affected patient must take antibiotics for at least six to nine months. The exact drugs and length of treatment depend on the patient's age, overall health condition, possible drug resistance, the type of TB i.e. latent or active and the infection's location in the body.

Recent research suggests that a shorter term of treatment. TB patients used to take medication for nine months but according to recent research patient will take medicine four months instead of nine. The combined medication may be effective in keeping latent TB from becoming active TB. With the shorter course of treatment, people are more likely to take all their medication and the risk of side effects is lessened. Studies are ongoing in this field.

Figure 3. Chest x-ray showing pulmonary Tuberculosis

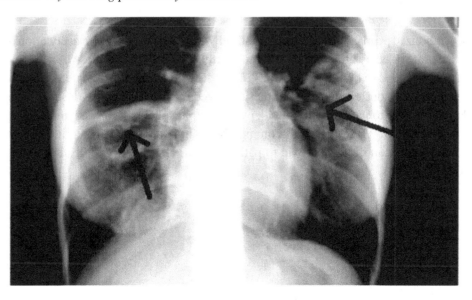

Most Widely Used TB Drugs

It is very important that when one patient has latent TB, then he/she must take at least one type of TB drug prescribed by doctor. Active tuberculosis will require several drugs at once in case of its drug resistance staining. The most popular medication used to treat tuberculosis is Isoniazid which is an antibacterial available as 100 mg and 300 mg tablets for oral administration. Each tablet mainly contains as inactive ingredients such as colloidal silicon dioxide, lactose monohydrate, pregelatinized starch, povidone and stearic acid. Chemical name of Isoniazid is isonicotinyl hydrazine or isonicotinic acid hydrazide. It has an empirical formula of $C_6H_7N_3O$ and a molecular weight of 137.14. Within 1 to 2 hours after oral administration, isoniazid produces peak blood levels which decline to 50 percent or less within 6 hours. It diffuses readily into all body fluids (cerebrospinal, pleural and ascitic fluids), tissues, organs, and excreta (saliva, sputum, and feces). The drug also passes through the placental barrier in concentrations comparable to those in the plasma. Near about 50 to 70 percent of a dose of isoniazid is excreted in the urine in 24 hours. Isoniazid inhibits the synthesis of mycoloic acids, an essential component of the bacterial cell wall. At therapeutic levels isoniazid is bacteriocidal against actively growing intracellular and extracellular Mycobacterium tuberculosis organisms. Isoniazid resistant Mycobacterium tuberculosis bacilli develop rapidly when isoniazid monotherapy is administered. In this case, a combination of antibiotics called fluoro-quinolones and injectable medications, such as amikacin, kanamycin or capreomycin, are generally used for 20 to 30 months. Some types of TB are developing resistance to these medications as well. A number of new drugs are being looked at as add-on therapy to the current drug-resistant combination treatment including:

- Bedaquiline;
- Delamanid;
- PA-824;
- Linezolid;
- Sutezolid.

Medication Side Effects

Isoniazid is metabolized primarily by acetylation and dehydrazination. The rate of acetylation is genetically determined. The rate of acetylation does not significantly alter the effectiveness of isoniazid. However, slow acetylation may lead to higher blood levels of the drug and, thus, to an increase in toxic reactions. Pyridoxine (vitamin B6) deficiency is sometimes observed in adults with high doses of isoniazid and is considered probably due to its competition with pyridoxal phosphate for the enzyme apotryptophanase.

Serious side effects of TB drugs aren't common but can be dangerous when it is activated. All tuberculosis medications can be highly toxic to patient's liver. During TB medication patient may have the following side effects.

- Nausea or vomiting;
- Loss of appetite;
- A yellow color to your skin (jaundice);
- Dark urine.

However if patients have some of the above mentioned symptom then they should contact a doctor.

Completing Treatment Is Essential

Patients may start to feel better after a few weeks of medication. It is crucial that patients should finish the full course of therapy and take the medications exactly as prescribed by the doctor. Stopping treatment too soon or skipping doses can allow the bacteria that are still alive to become resistant to those drugs, leading to TB that is much more dangerous and difficult to treat.

To help people stick with their treatment, a program called directly observed therapy (DOT) is recommended. In this approach, a health care worker administers your medication so that you don't have to remember to take it on your own.

Prevention

Doctor may advise patient to take medications to reduce the risk of developing active tuberculosis if someone has latent TB infection. The only type of tuberculosis that is contagious is the active variety, when it affects the lungs. So if one can prevent their latent tuberculosis from becoming active, then they won't transmit tuberculosis to anyone else.

Protect Your Family and Friends

If anyone has active TB, then they should keep their germs to themselves. It generally takes a few weeks of treatment with TB medications before patient are not contagious anymore. Follow these tips to help keep our friends and family from getting sick:

- *Stay home.* Don't go to work or school or sleep in a room with other people during the first few weeks of treatment for active tuberculosis.
- *Ventilate the room.* Tuberculosis germs spread more easily in small closed spaces where air doesn't move. If it's not too cold outdoors, open the windows and use a fan to blow indoor air outside.
- *Cover your mouth.* Use a tissue to cover your mouth anytime you laugh, sneeze or cough. Put the dirty tissue in a bag, seal it and throw it away.
- *Wear a mask.* Wearing a surgical mask when you're around other people during the first three weeks of treatment may help lessen the risk of transmission.

It will be very helpful for doctors if an automatic system compatible with the telemedicine system can be deployed at the remote places of the country to identify and classify the stain of tuberculosis from the cough samples. Moreover, it would be advantageous if only school education is sufficient to operate such diagnosis system in a remote place.

The objective of this work is to design a low cost device which is capable of detecting and classifying the tuberculosis bacteria from the microscopic images of cough samples to speed up the diagnosis process.

REVIEW ON EXISTING DIAGNOSTIC SYSTEMS

TB lesion near clavicles will invisible in X-rays images. Hence, medicine dose estimation for patients would probably go wrong, which results in drug resistance problem. To overcome this problem, an automated segmentation technique is needed which will work with CT images or any other imaging techniques. Gradient inverse coefficient of variation and circularity measures is used to classify detected features and confirm right TB lesions. Classification of the infectious stages based on their intensity property is crucial to recover from the TB (Myronenko, & Song 2009). Chest radiograph is the primary detection tool (Ginneken, & Romeny, 2000). TB diagnosis usually occurs after a combination of skin, blood, and imaging tests. In routine diagnosis, skin and blood tests are taken in case of the latent stage of disease in which patients does not have symptoms. The combination of radiographic discoveries and demographic data helps physicians to decide the possibility of infectious TB (Ginneken, Katsuragawa, Romeny, & Viergever 2002). Manually the detection of TB lesions is done by just looking at the X-rays/CT images by the doctors. Because of this wrong prediction of the lesion, the physicians may not prescribe the correct dosage of medicine. They may prescribe high or low dosage of medicine which is actually very harmful to the patient. Hence, proper lesion detection technique is required. Tuberculin Skin Testing (TST) test is the standard method of determining whether a person is infected with M. Tuberculosis. Some persons may react to the TST even though they are not infected with TB. But, in some cases, persons may not react to the TST even though they are infected with TB. This makes the detection process complex. By means of the proposed technique, the complexity can be reduced by finding their intensities, and the disease can be identified directly and accurately. Numerous techniques for segmenting lung fields have been proposed (Ruberto, & Dempster 2000) (Comaniciu, Ramesh, &. Meer, 2000).

Traditionally, X-rays were used for the detection of disease. An X-ray will only produce a two dimensional shadows of an object. It does not provide any details about the disease. So, CT scan is used in order to generate a three-dimensional image of two-dimensional X-ray picture, a narrow slice of a time. A CT scan thus takes this axial image, compiles them together, and recreates how the tissues and organs are located inside the body, assisting doctors to arrive at an accurate diagnosis. By following this technique, power of infection would be accurately determined. By analyzing the images, we can easily infer that the cavities shown by the arrow in X-ray image are not definite and cannot be viewed correctly.

But, in case of CT image the arrow clearly indicates the lesions. Image segmentation methods can be broadly classified into mainly three categories. They are boundary-based techniques, region-based techniques and pixel-based direct classification methods. In practice, region-based methods are mostly used to detect the TB affected lesion. It is very fast and easy to manipulate (MacMahon, Engelmann, Roberts, & Armato, 2008). To improve performance of region-based methods and their results, preprocessing techniques are must require. The segmentation of the lesions could be done semi automatically using active contour (AC) models (or snakes) (Yoshida, & Doi 2000) (Zhao, 2001) (Song, &. Yang 2010). This is commonly used as segmentation techniques for medical images. Performance of AC models in segmenting multiple lesion is very good when more than one TB lesion exists in infected lungs. A common weakness of most AC models is the necessity to define an initial contour close to the Region of Interest (ROI). In (Osman, Mashor, &. Jaafar 2009, a technique has been proposed to detect TB. This method is based on binarization, process to set edge lines of ribs, Gradient vector flow model for segmentation and K-means algorithm for classification. Also, in (Xu, Cheng, Long, &. Mandal, 2013), a method has been discussed to detect TB by using Ziehl-Neelsen Stained Tissue Slide Images. Active shape model was used for texture analysis. Multilevel Image Enhancement for Pulmonary TB Analysis is the task of auto detecting the tiny nodules that will help to get more information on pulmonary tuberculosis. In (Ginneken, 2009), the authors have proposed an efficient coarse-to-fine dual scale technique for lesion detection in chest radiographs. Gaussian-based matching, local binary pattern, and gradient orientation features are applied at the coarse level. In a recent survey, van Ginneken told that forty-five years after the initial work on computer-aided diagnosis in chest radiology, there are still lack of the application which can accurately read chest radiographs (Lodwick, 1996) (Lodwick, Keats, & Dorst, 1963) (Shen, Cheng, & Basu, 2010). Hogeweg et al.(2010) combined a textural abnormality detection system with a clavicle detection system to suppress false positive responses (Pavlopoulos, Kyriacou, Berler, & Dembeyiotis, 1998). Presence of a lesion in the upper lung zones strongly indicates that TB has developed into an extremely infectious state. Shen et al. developed a hybrid knowledge-based approach using Bayesian classifier to detect lesion in these regions automatically (Ginneken, Stegmann, & Loog 2006). For lung segmentation, several different methods have been proposed. For example, van Ginneken et al. compared various techniques for lung segmentation, including active shapes, rule-based methods, pixel classification, and different combinations, etc (Ginneken, Van, & Romeny 2000) (Dawoud, 2010). Another approach given by Dawoud used an iterative segmentation method that combines intensity information with shape priors. Systems based on ANNs and SVMs, Fuzzy rule related offer a convenient format for representing the knowledge underlying a system in the form of transparent and linguistic conditional statements.

OVERVIEW AND DESIGN PRINCIPAL

Automation on sputum microscopy is focused in this work. Microscopic images of the sputum (stained with Ziehl-Neelsen) are used here for diagnoses. Appendix 1 describes the detail staining process and the working principal. This approach performs hybrid (color base and shape based) matching in order to achieve efficiency and robustness. This hybrid approach reduces the false positive and false negative rate. Final classification decision is taken by a fuzzy system.

This section describes two independent processes to diagnosis the TB. The approach uses color feature and the second one on the shape basis. The image acquisition and filtering steps are common to both processes. The system is explained with the help of a block diagram, shown in Figure 4. The implementation is divided in to two parts preprocessing and object detection is. Pre processing part includes image acquisition, image enhancement, extract color information and segment the image based in color information. Object detection part describes the techniques to remove false contours and classify the disease severity. All the steps of the system are described next.

Image Acquisition

Image Acquisition is the first step of the system. Microscopic images of the sputum samples of the slides are acquired with a CCD camera which is mounted upon the eyepiece of a compound microscope. A fully automatic slide movement system is introduced to control the slide movement under the objective lens for different site images of the same sample slide. Two stepper motors are used for the sample slide movement in the X and Y direction shown in Figure 5. Figure 6 shows the driving circuit of the stepper

Figure 4. Block diagram of the system

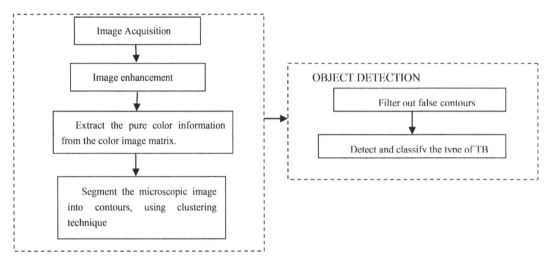

Figure 5. Slide control using a stepper motor

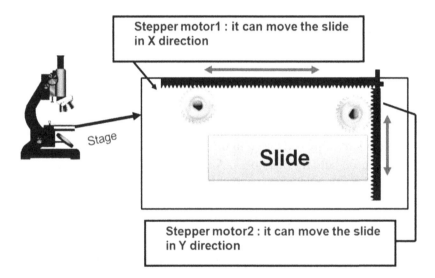

motor through ARM 11 based control system. ARM chips are RISC processors. It is very prevalent in low power embedded applications. TB6600HG (H-bridge) IC is used for current amplification to control the stepper, apply voltage to each of the coils in a particular sequence. The sequence is shown in Table 1.

The TB6600HG is a PWM chopper-type single-chip bipolar sinusoidal micro-step stepping motor driver. In 2-phase, 1-2-phase, W1-2-phase, 2W1-2-phase, and 4W1-2-phase excitation modes, forward and reverse rotation has been controlled. 2-phase bipolar-type stepping motor can be also driven.

TB6600 is a 25 pin IC. Table 2 describes the pins of TB6600. TB6600 requires I/O pins to control the direction of the stepper motor along with speed. PCF8574A is used to hand shake between ARM 11 and TB6600. PCF8574A is an I2C I/O expansion I.C. I2C (Inter integrated Circuit) is Philips proprietary low speed peripheral device data transfer protocol. It supports up to 100kbits/sec data transfer speed. It is a two wire data communication, one for data line (SDA), and another for the clock line (SCL). More than one slave device can be connected in parallel with a master device. Operating clock frequency is

Figure 6. Block diagram of the driver ckt

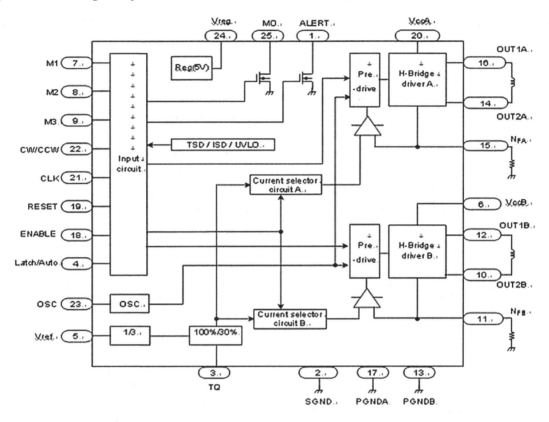

Table 1. The pulse sequences to drive a stepper motor

Step	Wire 1	Wire 2	Wire 3	Wire 4
1	high	low	high	low
2	low	high	high	low
3	low	high	low	high
4	high	low	low	high

controlled by the master device. It identifies each slave devices by their unique 7 bit address. 111 slave devices can be attached to the master devices (128-17 reserved = 111). I2C data transfers are byte oriented where MSB is transmitted first. In this protocol master device control the clock. Communication starts up by placing low logic into SDA and high logic to SCL. This is initiated by master device. After that master sends 7 bit slave address on next 7 clock pulse. Slave address is required to select the slave device. After sending slave address, master sends one additional bit which is read/write request bit. If this bit is low then master wants to write (send) data to slave the device and if it is high then master wishes to read (receive) data from the slave device. If the addressed slave device is ready to work then it acknowledge the request by pulling SDA line low on next clock pulse. The next phase is data transfer. When communication is open as "write to the slave" then 8 bit data is sent to particular slave device within next 8 clock pulses. After receiving data from the master device, the slave device acknowledges the by pulling SDA low in next clock pulses. Master device can send the next 8 bit data after releasing the SDA by slave device. Stop signal is sent by making a low to high transition on SDA with SCL is going to high. The TB6600 is a compact single axis bipolar, up to 5A/phase stepper motor driver. It supports micro stepping with step and direction inputs, M1, M2, M3 are input pins; they are used to configure micro levels.

Micro stepping is the winding current approximates a sinusoidal AC waveform. Micro stepping is often called "sine cosine micro stepping". Sine cosine micro stepping is the most common form, but other waveforms can also be used. As the micro steps become smaller, motor operation becomes more smooth, thereby significantly reducing resonance in any parts the motor may be connected to, as well as the motor itself. Resolution will be limited by the use of mechanical stiction, backlash, and other sources of error between the motor and the end device. Gear reducers may be used to increase resolution of positioning. Step size repeatability is a significant step motor feature and a fundamental reason

Table 2. Pin configuration of TB6600

Pin No.	I/O	Symbol	Function
1	Output	ALERT	TSD / ISO monitor pin
2	—	SGND	Signal ground
3	Input	TQ	Torque (output current) setting input
4	Input	Latch/Auto	Select a return type for TSD
5	Input	Vref	Voltage in. for 100% current level
6	Input	VccB	B channel Power supply
7	Input	M1	Excitation mode setting input pin
8	Input	M2	Excitation mode setting input pin
9	Input	M3	Excitation mode setting input pin
10	Output	OUT2B	B channel output 2
11	—	NFB	B channel output current detection pin
12	Output	OUT1B	B channel output 1
13	—	PGNDB	Power ground
14	Output	OUT2A	A channel output 2
15	—	NFA	A channel output current detection PIN
16	Output	OUT1A	A channel output 1
17	—	PGNDA	Power ground
18	Input	ENABLE	Enable signal input pin
19	Input	RESET	Reset signal input pin
20	Input	VCCA	A channel Power supply
21	Input	CLK	CLK pulse input pin
22	Input	CW/CCW	Forward/reverse control pin
23	—	OSC	Register connection pin for internal oscillation setting
24	Output	Vreg	Control side connection pin for power capacitor
25	Output	MO	Electrical angle monitor pin

for their use in positioning. Example: many modern hybrid step motors are rated such that the travel of every full step (example 1.8 degrees per full step or 200 full steps per revolution) will be within 3% or 5% of the travel of every other full step, as long as the motor is operated within its specified operating ranges. Several manufacturers show that their motors can easily maintain the 3% or 5% equality of step travel size. If step size is reduced from full stepping down to 1/10 stepping. Then, as the micro stepping divisor number grows, step size repeatability degrades. At large step size reductions it is possible to issue many micro step commands before any motion occurs at all. Then the motion can be a "jump" to a new position. Pin 18 is used to enable the IC. Pin 19 to 22 are input pins. 19 are used to reset the system. 21 are used to give the pulse. Pin 22 is used to set the direction of the rotation, clock wise or anti clock wise. Pin 3 is used to set the output current. Pin 14 and 16 are used to connect coil 1 and pin 10 12 for coil 2. The TB6600 converts step and direction signals to Pulse Width Modulated high voltage drive signals. It can also send the appropriate current to the four coils of a bipolar stepper motor. The TB6600 is capable of driving stepper motors continuously at 4.5A and up to 45VDC.

Image Enhancement

The images obtained from the CCD camera are not up to the mark. Wiener filtering (Goldstein, Irving, & Louis, 1998). is an efficient linear image restoration approach, and it is used here. In signal processing, the Wiener filter is a filter used to produce an estimate of a desired or target random process by linear time-invariant filtering of an observed noisy process, assuming known stationary signal and noise spectra, and additive noise. The Wiener filter minimizes the mean square error between the estimated random process and the desired process. The task is to find the estimate of the "best" image $\hat{f}$ is usually done in the frequency domain:

$$\hat{F}(u,v) = \frac{|H(u,v)|^2}{H(u,v)|H(u,v)|^2 + |N(u,v)|^2 / |F(u,v)|^2} G(u,v) \tag{1}$$

where, H(u,v) is the degradation function, G(u,v) is the Fourier transform of the degraded image, $N(u,v)^2$ is the power spectrum of noise, $F(u,v)^2$ is the power spectrum of the un-degraded image. The goal of the Wiener filter is to compute a statistical estimate of an unknown signal using a related signal as an input and filtering that known signal to produce the estimate as an output.

The Wiener filter performs de-convolution in the sense of minimizing the least squares error i.e.:

$$e^2 = E\left\{ \left(f - \hat{f} \right)^2 \right\} \tag{2}$$

where E is the mean value, f is the un-degraded image which is usually not known. In the case of omitting the noise the Wiener filter changes to a simple inverse filter. The Wiener filter is applied separately to Red, Green and Blue components of the color images obtained from the CCD camera. Figure 7 shows the image after applying Wiener filter.

Figure 7. Comparatively clear image after applying Wiener filter upon Figure 2

Identify Mycobacterium Tuberculosis from Color Feature

Information Extraction

A huge no of pink threadlike elements are present in Figure 2 and Figure 7; actually they are Mycobacterium tuberculosis bacteria. Due to variation in staining technique and the strength of stain the stained color is not always the same; it varies from radish to pink. It is very difficult task to extract pure color information from red, green and blue components from the RGB microscopic images.

The RGB color model is an additive color model. In this model red, green, and blue light are added together in different ways to replicate a broad array of colors. The name of the model comes from the initials of the three additive primary colors such as red, green, and blue. The main purpose of the RGB color model is for the sensing images from CCD transducer, and display of images in display device, such as televisions and computers. Before the electronic age, the RGB color model already has a solid theory behind it, based in human perception of colors. Zero intensity for each component gives the darkest color (no light, considered the black), and full intensity of each gives a white. The quality of this white depends on the nature of the primary light sources, but if they are properly balanced, the result is a neutral white matching the system's white point. When the intensities for all the components are the same, the result is a shade of gray, darker or lighter depending on the intensity. When one of the components has the strongest intensity, then the color is a tone near this primary color (reddish, greenish, or bluish), and when two components have the same strongest intensity, then the color is a tone of a secondary color (a shade of cyan, magenta or yellow). A secondary color is formed by the sum of two primary colors of equal intensity: cyan is combination of green and blue, magenta is combination of red and blue, and yellow is combination of red and green. Every secondary color is the complement of one primary color. At the time of a primary and its complementary secondary color are added together, the result is white like cyan complements red, magenta complements green and yellow complements blue.

The HSI color space is very important color model for image processing applications because it represents colors similarly how the human eye senses colors. The HSI color model represents every color with three components: hue (H), saturation (S), intensity (I). The H and S axes are polar coordinates on the plane orthogonal to I. H is the angle, specified such that red is at zero, green at 120 degrees, and blue at 240 degrees. Hue thus represents what humans implicitly understand as color. S is the magnitude of the color vector projected in the plane orthogonal to I. In simpler form it can be said that the Hue component describes the pure color itself in the form of an angle between [0,360] degrees and it is invariant to color intensity. That means Hue value is same for light pink or dark pink. The Saturation component indicates how much the color is diluted with white light. The range of the S component is [0,1]. The Intensity range is between [0,1] and 0 means black, 1 means white.

HSI (Ghosh, Bhattacharjee, Nasipuri & Basu, 2010) (Gonzalez, Richard, &Woods 2002) color format is used to extract pink colored regions because it eliminates light intensity variation. The RGB to HSI color space conversion process is performed by using the equations (eq3-eq5).

$$H = \begin{cases} \theta & if \ B \leq G \\ 360° - \theta & otherwise \end{cases} \tag{3}$$

where,

$$\theta = \cos^{-1}\left\{ \frac{\frac{1}{2}\left[(R - G) + (R - B)\right]}{\sqrt{\left[(R - G)(R - G) + (R - B)(G - B)\right]}} \right\}$$

$$S = 1 - \frac{3}{(R + G + B)}\left[\min(R, G, B)\right] \tag{4}$$

$$I = \frac{1}{3}\left(R + G + B\right) \tag{5}$$

where, H stands for Hue i.e. Pure color, S for saturation, i.e. the degree by which the pure color is diluted using white light and me for intensity i.e. Gray level.

Segmentation

By analyzing Hue components obtained from equation 3, it is inferred that the area of the image occupied by the Tuberculosis bacteria has a HUE value very close to the HUE value of pink and high intensity variation with respect to another area of the image (Ghosh et al., 2013). So, partial supervised clustering techniques (Pedrycz, & Waletzky, 1997), are applied, where initial cluster centers are the Hue value of pink, blue, white and violate. Algorithm 1 is used to detect the contour of Mycobacterium tuberculosis.

Algorithm 1: To find out image clusters that contain Mycobacterium tuberculosis.

Let X = {x1, x2, x3 ..., xn} be the set of data points, Hue values of the image and V = {v1, v2, v3, v4} be the set of centers.

Step 1: Select 'c' cluster centers with the Hue values of pink, blue, white, and violate. Say c= 4
Step 2: Calculate the fuzzy membership 'µij' using

$$\mu_{ij} = \frac{1}{\sum_{k=1}^{c=4} \left(d_{ij} / d_{ik} \right)^{(2/m-1)}} \tag{6}$$

where µij: is the element of U-matrix and dij is the element of the distance matrix, where dij is the Euclidian distance between ith object and jth cluster center, m is constant.

Step 3: Compute the new fuzzy centers 'vj' using:

$$v_j = \frac{\left(\sum_{i=1}^{n} \left(\mu_{ij} \right)^m x_i \right)}{\left(\sum_{i=1}^{n} \left(\mu_{ij} \right)^m \right), \forall j = 1, 2, \dots c} \tag{7}$$

Step 4: Repeat Step 2 and 3 until the minimum 'J' value is achieved or $\|U(k+1) - U(k)\| < \beta$. where,
'k' is the iteration step.
'β' is the termination criterion between [0, 1].
'U = (µij)n*c' is the fuzzy membership matrix.
'J' is the objective function.
Step 5: Find out all points which belong to the "pink" cluster. Pink cluster contains the pixels of the image that contains the images of Mycobacterium tuberculosis bacteria. Figure 8 shows the output.
Step 6: Stop.

Figure 8. Images of Mycobacterium tuberculosis bacteria after applying algorithm1 upon Figure 7

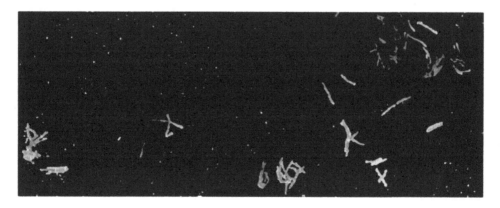

Remove the Noise Contours

The output image from algorithm1 contains some dotted they are basically noise. This small sub-contours are removed by closing ((Ghosh et al., 2011), (Forero, Sroubek, & Cristóbal, 2004), which is dilation followed by erosion. Erosion is able to remove unnecessary contours, which are small in size. The dilation of A by B, denoted $A \oplus B$, is defined as the set operation

$$A \oplus B = \left\{ z \middle| \left(\hat{B} \right)_z \cap A \neq \varphi \right\} \tag{8}$$

where Ø is the empty set, and B is the structuring element. In words, the dilation of A by B is the set consisting of all the structuring element origin locations where the reflected and translated B overlaps at least one element of A. The erosion of A by B, denoted $A \ominus B$, is defined as

$$A \ominus B = \left\{ z \middle| \left(B \right)_z \cap A^c = \varphi \right\} \tag{9}$$

Here, erosion of A by B is the set of all structuring element origin locations where no part of B overlaps the background of A. Figure 9 shows the cleared mask and Figure 10 shows the image where TB bacteria are visible.

Figure 9. The mask after opening

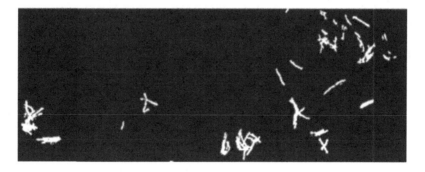

Figure 10. The clean images of mycobacterium Tuberculosis bacteria

Detection of Mycobacterium Tuberculosis

The next step is detection. If the number of bacteria present in the image is greater than 15 then severity is very high, and if it is less than 3 then severity is less, but affected by TB. The severity is determined by taking the ratio of the number of pixels used to show the Mycobacterium tuberculosis bacteria to the number of pixels present in the image.

Identification of Mycobacterium Tuberculosis from Shape Feature

Every image is a set of pixels (picture elements). Each pixel contains information about the image. In the color image, pixel can be considered as a vector of 3 elements. The vector contains the color information of that pixel in the form of primary color i.e. Red, Green, and Blue. As discussed earlier the color of stained Tuberculosis Bacterium is pink, and the rest of the area is whitish where red, green and blue components have almost equal value. Pink is a combination of red and blue color. Hence, the green component value is very less to the lesion (area) that contains stained Tuberculosis Bacterium. These two dimensional array (matrix) of green components will be used for contour detection. This green component area converted into a binary image using a threshold value which is calculated using the given equations.

f(i, j) is the gray-scale value at pixel (i, j), and Ti is the segmentation threshold value at step "i". To obtain a new threshold value, one have to threshold the original image using Ti to separate the image into two areas, where μ_0^i and μ_1^i are the mean values for the two areas.

$$\mu_0^i = \frac{\sum (i,j) \in f(i,j)}{Number\ of\ Pixels} \tag{10}$$

$$\mu_1^i = \frac{\sum (i,j) \in\ Background\ of\ f(i,j)}{Number\ of\ Pixels} \tag{11}$$

The threshold value for step i+1 can be obtained as

$$T_{i+1} = \frac{\mu_1^i + \mu_0^i}{2} \tag{12}$$

It is clear from Figure 2 that Tuberculosis bacterium looks like pink ribbon (Makkapati, Ravindra & Raviraja, 2009), (Grady, 2006), so ribbon like structures should be detected accurately. In the binary image, some unnecessary contours exist; which are actually noise. After the individual contours in the binary image are segmented by label matrix technique, they are checked whether they represent valid contours or noise. This is done by the following algorithm.

Algorithm 2: To find out valid contours.

This algorithm is used to find out the valid contours of the binary image.

Step 1: Apply label matrix technique in the binary image and store the output matrix in LB variable. LB will have the same dimension as the binary image. The value '1' in each contour in the binary image will be replaced by an integer number in the LB.

Step 2: Count = maximum integer value stored in LB; So "count" will contain the number of contours in the input image.

Step 3: Index = 1

Step 4: Val = maximum gray level value of the pixels in the high pass filtered image.

Step 5: Find the coordinates of the pixels of the LB where value of the pixel == index;

Step 6: Local_Value = maximum intensity level value of the pixels in the inverse green components (matrix)

Step 7: If local_Value > 0.85* val // 0.85 is choosen based on experimental data the contour is valid and segment the contour for processing.

Else
Not a valid contour.

Step 8: Index = index + 1;

Step 9: Repeat step 5 to step 8 until index > count

Step 10: Stop.

Valid contours are segmented (separated) after applying algorithm 2.

In some situation, two contours may overlap with each other. It is paramount to ensure that one contour must contain a single TB bacterium, otherwise shape based classification will not work correctly The algorithm 3 is used to do a segment overlapped contours.

Algorithm 3: To separate the overlapped contours.

This algorithm checks whether two contours are overlapped or not.

Step 1: Output image of algorithm 2 is dilated and then from this dilated image that output image is subtracted pixel wise to obtain the shape of contours. This subtracted binary image is actually the mask to get the pixel values just outside the TB bacterium.

Step 2: Find out nucleus pixel values from the high pass filtered image by applying the mask obtained in the step 1.

Step 3: Value = average of the pixel values obtained in step 2.

Step 4: Build an image with the same dimension of the original image; where all the pixels are filled with "value" except the coordinates of the mask; these points are filled with the value of the inverse green components.

Step 5: Convert the newly created image into a binary image using a threshold value. This threshold is calculated by the equation 12.

Step 6: Segment the contour using label matrix technique.

Step 7: Now each contour contains only TB bacterium.

Step 8: Send all contours for shape based object recognition module.

Step 9: Stop.

After applying algorithm 3, each contour is ready for shape based classification.

Shape Based Feature Extraction

TB bacteria are ribbon like, so line detection algorithm is suitable to detect them. Line detection based on tangent, work upon single pixel thick line. So the ribbons like contours are converted into a single pixel thin line using

Algorithm 4: it is used to convert a single pixel thin line.

Assume black pixels are one and white pixels zero, and that the input image is a rectangular N by M array of ones and zeroes.

The algorithm operates on all black pixels P1 that can have eight neighbors. The neighbors are, in order, arranged as: P1= pixel value at ith row and jth column, P2= pixel value at (i-1)th row and jth column, P3= pixel value at (i-1)th row and (j+1)th column, P4= pixel value at ith row and (j+1)th column, P5= pixel value at (i+1)th row and (j+1)th column, P6= pixel value at (i+1)th row and jth column, P7= pixel value at (i+1)th row and (j-1)th column, P8= pixel value at ith row and (j-1)th column, P9= pixel value at (i-1)th row and(j-1)th column,

Obviously the boundary pixels of the image cannot have the full eight neighbors.

Define A(P1) = the number of transitions from white to black, (0 -> 1) in the sequence P2,P3,P4,P5,P6,P7,P8,P9,P2. (Note the extra P2 at the end - it is circular).

Define B(P1) = The number of black pixel neighbours of P1. (= sum(P2 .. P9))

Step 1: All pixels are tested, and pixels satisfying all the following conditions (simultaneously) are just noted at this stage.

1. The pixel is black and has eight neighbours.
2. $2 <= B(P1) <= 6$.
3. A(P1) = 1.
4. At least one of P2 and P4 and P6 is white.
5. At least one of P4 and P6 and P8 is white.

After iterating over the image and collecting all the pixels satisfying all step 1 conditions, all these condition satisfying pixels are set to white.

Step 2: All pixels are again tested, and pixels satisfying all the following conditions are just noted at this stage.

1. The pixel is black and has eight neighbours.
2. $2 <= B(P1) <= 6$.
3. A(P1) = 1.
4. At least one of P2 and P4 and P8 is white.
5. At least one of P2 and P6 and P8 is white.

434

After iterating over the image and collecting all the pixels satisfying all step 2 conditions, all these condition satisfying pixels are again set to white.

Step 3: Stop

A Cartesian coordinate system is a coordinate system that specifies each point uniquely in a plane by a pair of numerical coordinates, which are the signed distances from the point to two fixed perpendicular directed lines, measured in the same unit of length.

Lines in a Cartesian plane can be described algebraically by linear equations. In two dimensions, the equation for non-vertical lines is often given in the slope-intercept form: y = mx + b where m is the slope or gradient of the line. b is the y-intercept of the line. x is the independent variable of the function y = f(x). The slope of the line through points $A(x_a, y_a)$ and $B(x_b, y_b)$, when $x_a \neq x_b$, is given by $m = (y_b - y_a)/(x_b - x_a)$ and the equation of this line can be written $y = m(x - x_a) + y_a$. This m is constant for all points of a straight line segment. So it can be said a set of points belongs to a single straight line if and only if the m is constant in any two points.

After thinning, slopes are calculated between two consecutive points. If slopes are almost in similar value, then the contour is almost considered as a ribbon like and the result is "Mycobacterium tuberculosis bacteria are found".

Mathematically it is define as

$$p = \frac{1}{(n-1)} \sum_{i=1}^{n-1} \left| z_i - z_{i+1} \right| \tag{13}$$

where

$$z_i = \frac{1}{(n-1)} \sum_{j=1, j \neq i}^{n} \frac{y_i - y_j}{x_i - x_j} \tag{14}$$

p is an index value and this value will determine the presence of Mycobacterium tuberculosis. n is the number of points in the contour and xi and yi is the Cartesian coordinates of the points. Zi denotes the average slopes between ith point and all other points of the thinned contour. p is the average difference between two consecutive z points.

Final Classification

Crisp sets are the sets that are mostly used in real life. In a crisp set, an element is either a member of the set or not. In other word a crisp relation represents the presence or absence of association, interaction, or interconnectedness between the elements of two or more sets. This concept can be generalized to allow for various degrees or strengths of relation or interaction between elements. Crisp set works based on the differential equation. Hence it is very difficult to define crisp set to identify the presence of Mycobacterium tuberculosis bacteria from the feature value. Another one fact is that crisp set is purely linear in nature. For incomplete amount of data, crisp set does not give accurate result. Whereas fuzzy set can handle incomplete data set to some degree and it is completely rule based i.e. logistic.

Hence, fuzzy set is used. Fuzzy sets are the sets whose elements are degrees of membership. Fuzzy logic just evolved from the need to model the type of indefinite or ill-defined systems that are difficult to handle using conventional binary valued logic, but the methodology itself is based on mathematical theory. A fuzzy set X can be described by a membership function $\left\{\mu_X\left(x\right)\right\}$. A membership function defines to what extent a certain element (e.g. x) belongs to a (fuzzy) set (e.g. X). Membership functions only get values between 0 and 1. A membership function associated with a given fuzzy set maps an input value to its appropriate membership value. In other word the membership function of a fuzzy set is a generalization of the indicator function in classical sets. In fuzzy logic, it represents the degree of truth as an extension of valuation. Degrees of truth are often perplexed with probabilities, although they are theoretically distinct, because fuzzy truth represents membership in loosely defined sets, not likelihood of some event or condition.

In this system, the fuzzy membership function is built from a reference/ training data set. The advantage of this membership function is flexibility, i.e. by changing the reference data set or training set the response of the membership function can quickly be modify.

In terms of mathematics, interpolation is a method of constructing new data points within the range of a discrete set of known data sets (points). In engineering and science, one often has a number of data points, obtained by sampling or experimentation, which represent the values of a function for a limited number of values (incomplete data set) of the independent variable. It is often required to interpolate (i.e. estimate) the value of that function for an intermediate value of the independent variable. That's why interpolation is used to build membership function. There are different types of interpolation techniques available. Piecewise constant interpolation, Linear interpolation, Polynomial interpolation, Spline interpolation, Multivariate interpolation and Quadratic interpolation are most common. Piecewise constant interpolation is the simplest interpolation method. It locates the nearest data value, and assign the same value for unknown point. In simple problems, this method is used.

Linear interpolation is a method of curve fitting using linear polynomials. If the two known points are given by the coordinates (X0,Y0) and (X1,Y1), the linear interpolation is the straight line between these points.

Polynomial interpolation is a generalization of linear interpolation. Linear interpolant is a linear function where interpolant is replaced with a polynomial of higher degree. In other word polynomial interpolation is the interpolation of a given data set by a polynomial: given some points, find a polynomial which goes exactly through these points.

Spline interpolation is a form of interpolation where the interpolant is a special type of piecewise polynomial called a spline. Spline interpolation is often preferred over polynomial interpolation because the interpolation error can be made small even when using low degree polynomials for the spline. Spline interpolation avoids the problem of Runge's phenomenon, in which oscillation can occur between points when interpolating using high degree polynomials.

Multivariate interpolation or spatial interpolation is interpolation on functions of more than one variable. The function to be interpolated is known at given points (xi, yi, zi, ...)and the interpolation problem consist of yielding values at arbitrary points (x, y, z, ...).

Quadratic interpolation (Dodgson, 1997), (Gregory, &. Delbourgo, 1982) method is used to build fuzzy membership functions for "TB detected" and "TB not detected". Six training data set are used to construct each member ship function. $(X_1,Y_1, F(X_1,Y_1))$, $(X_2,Y_2, F(X_2,Y_2))...(X_6,Y_6, F(X_6,Y_6))$ are 6 the data set, where X denotes the index value obtain from "Identify Mycobacterium tuberculosis from color feature" and Y denotes the value obtain from previous section. F(Xi, Yi) denotes the percentage of infection found in that image.

Vandermonde Shammas matrix is always a square matrix with the number of rows (or columns) equal to the number of coefficients used in the interpolation model. The first column is typically populated with 1 to reflect the presence of a constant term in the interpolation model. In the case of quadratic interpolation with two independent variables, we have used the following model:

F(X,Y) = C1 + C2X + C3X$_2$ + C4Y + C5Y$_2$ +C6XY . C1, C2, C3, C4, C5, C6 are the constants. The Vandermonde-Shammas (Macon, & Spitzbart 1958) matrix for the bi-quadratic interpolation is:

$$A = \begin{bmatrix} 1 & X_1 & X_1^2 & Y_1 & Y_1^2 & X_1 \ Y_1 \\ 1 & X_2 & X_2^2 & Y_2 & Y_2^2 & X_2 \ Y_2 \\ 1 & X_3 & X_3^2 & Y_3 & Y_3^2 & X_3 \ Y_3 \\ 1 & X_4 & X_4^2 & Y_4 & Y_4^2 & X_4 \ Y_4 \\ 1 & X_5 & X_5^2 & Y_5 & Y_5^2 & X_5 \ Y_5 \\ 1 & X_6 & X_6^2 & Y_6 & Y_6^2 & X_6 \ Y_6 \end{bmatrix} \tag{15}$$

The above matrix A has six rows and six columns, because the target model has six coefficients. The constant vector b has the function values at (X_1, Y_1) through (X_6, Y_6) and is:

$$b = \begin{bmatrix} F(X_1,Y_1) \\ F(X_2,Y_2) \\ F(X_3,Y_3) \\ F(X_4,Y_4) \\ F(X_5,Y_5) \\ F(X_6,Y_6) \end{bmatrix} \tag{16}$$

As before, the following matrix equation calculates the coefficients for the above linear model:
C = A-1b C is a vector and its elements are C1, C2 .... C6.
F(X,Y) is the unknown value, then F(X,Y) is defined as

F(X,Y) = C1 + C2 X + C3 X$_2$ + C4 Y + C5 Y$_2$ + C6 X Y

Finding value F(X,Y) for each membership function is the final step.

Majority voting is a decision rule that selects alternatives which have a majority, that is, the highest votes. It is the binary decision rule used most often in influential decision-making system. Using majority voting technique, upon the outcomes of membership functions for the value F(X,Y), the final decision is to be taken.

RESULTS AND DISCUSSION

The sample slides are collected from K. C. Roy Tuberculosis hospital, Jadavpur, Kolkata, India. The authors and their institutes are not directly involves with sputum sample collection, staining, slide preparation etc. As per WHO recommendation a slide may be declare negative if and only if no Tuberculosis bacterium has found at least 100 fields. So huge number of field images for each slides has to be examined. For example, if numbers of slides are 50 then a total 5000 images has to be examined. So it is not possible for a single processor system to handle huge work load.

The entire computation is distributed upon ARM 11 quad core processor and Intel i3 series system. ARM 11 is a 32 bit RISC processor with pipeline support. System level C programming is used to instruct the ARM system and Matlab is used for i3 system. The CCD camera, which is mounted upon the eye-piece of the microscope, is connected with the ARM system. Input image filtering and RGB to HIS conversion portion is performed upon 4 cores of ARM system. Wiener filter involves a lot of computation upon Red, Green and Blue component of an image. These computations upon three color components are distributed in three threads which run independently on three separate cores. List 1 in APPENDIX 2 shows corresponding C code segment.

Table 3. A comparative study of performance for 640X480 pixel images

Assign Task	MatLab Platform	In ARM 11 Single Thread	In ARM 11 Multithread with Separate Cores
Filtering	2450 ms	1340 ms	750 ms
RGB to HSI	250 ms	150 ms	98 ms
Rest of the work	45000 ms to 97000 ms	Coding is pending	Coding is pending

Figure 11. The decision from the system for the input image shown in Figure 2

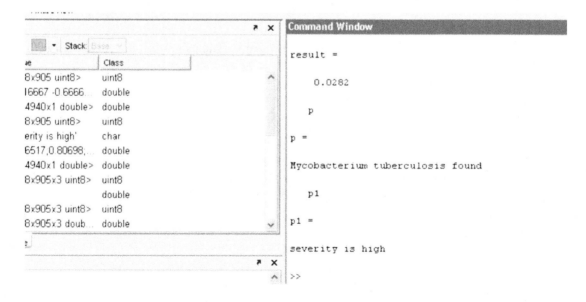

After filtration the output matrixes are recombine to get the filtered images. The filtered image is again supplied as an input image to another multi threaded function for HIS conversion. After that these data are supplied to Matlab (MATLAB User's Guide 2015)for further processing through socket programming List 2 and List 3 in APPENDIX 2 shows the code segments for socket programming between C programs and Matlab. This Matlab code is valid only for Matlab 7.1. Table 3 shows a comparative study of performance. "ARM 11 Multithread with separate cores" shows improvement of performance because of four cores utilization; but it has additional overhead to handle thread and CPU affinity.

The image shown in Figure 2 is fed as input. After analysis, system finds the presence of Mycobacterium tuberculosis bacteria in the sample slide and the severity is high. The snapshot of the output is shown in Figure 11. Figure 2 contains cluster that contains 4 to 8 bacterium in a single contour. Color based segmentation detects that contours but shape based detection fails to detect all the contours. This affects the final decision; actually the severity is very high but it results that the severity is high. For another test image, the result is satisfactory. The input image is shown in Figure 12, and the corresponding output is shown in Figure 14. Figure 13 is an intermediate stage. Figure 15 is an input image with no TB bacteria, and Figure 16 is the corresponding output.

Figure 12. The new input image which is fed to the system

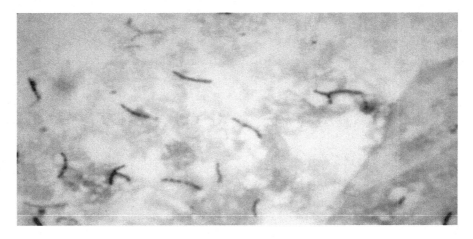

Figure 13. The clean Images of mycobacterium Tuberculosis bacteria

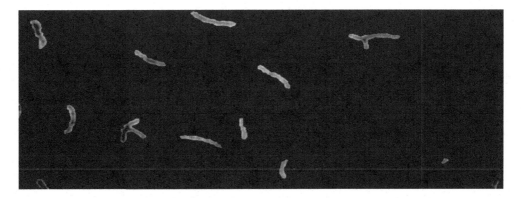

Figure 14. The decision from the system for the input image shown in Figure 10

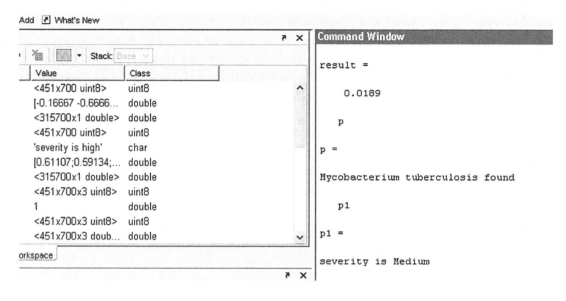

Figure 15. The input image with no TB bacteria

Table 4. Comparative study between the proposed system and manual system

Metric	Proposed System	Manual System
False positive	8	15
Real negative	43	36
True positive	90	80
False negative	9	19

Figure 16. The decision from the system for the input image shown in Figure 15

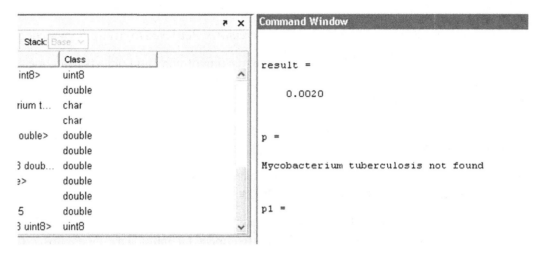

150 slides are used here to test the system out of which 99 slides contains TB bacterium. Table 4 shows a comparative study between the proposed system and manual system.

FUTURE SCOPE

Shape based identification sometimes fails to segment overlapped contours; that is discussed in the previous section. Overlapped contour segmentation algorithm need to be improved. A few portions of the algorithms are migrated into ARM 11 system. As a next phase of work, authors are planning to implement all the algorithms in multi core, multi-threaded mobile processing units like ARM 11 to improve portability and speed.

CONCLUSION

In this research work, we have discussed a portable system for diagnosis of Tuberculosis disease at any place. The system can send the reports and suspicious microscopic images to other node when it is connected with a network i.e. intranet or internet. So it is compatible with telemedicine infrastructure. This system is cheaper than other test kits exist as a present state of the art. This system does not require any special technical skill. So, this can be used by the people of remote places with very basic level of education. It may reduce the probability of wrong treatment which happens due to non-availability of diagnosis systems in remote and economically backward areas. The shape based and color based diagnosis systems works independently, but in this work they are combined (hybridized) to strengthen the decision. In classification section fuzzy based classification technique is used rather than probability based classification because probability theory only allows the modeling of stochastic uncertainty. Probability theory cannot be used to model this decision making logic because it does not follow or compatible with the human decision axioms. But the fuzzy set theory follows those axioms.

REFERENCES

Centers for Disease Control and Prevention. (2014). *Tuberculosis*. Retrieved from http://www.cdc.gov/tb/

Comaniciu, D., Ramesh, & Meer, P. (2000). Real-time tracking of non-rigid objects using mean shift. Proceedings of the IEEE Conference on Computer Vision and Pattern Recognition (pp. 142–149). IEEE. doi:10.1109/CVPR.2000.854761

Dawoud, A (2010). Fusing shape information in lung segmentation in chest radiographs. *Image Analysis and Recognition* (Vol. 6112, pp. 70–78).

Dodgson, N. A. (1997). Quadratic interpolation for image re-sampling. *IEEE Transactions on Image Processing*, *6*(9), 1322–1326. doi:10.1109/83.623195

Epstein, M. D., & Schluger, N. W. (1998). Time to detection of Mycobacterium tuberculosis in sputum culture correlates with outcome in patients receiving treatment for pulmonary tuberculosis. *CHEST Journal*, *113*(2), 379–386. doi:10.1378/chest.113.2.379

Feng-zeng, Z., Levy, M. H., & Wen, S. (1997). Sputum microscopy results at two and three months predict outcome of tuberculosis treatment Notes from the Field. *The International Journal of Tuberculosis and Lung Disease*, *1*(6), 570–572.

Forero, M.G., Sroubek, F., & Cristóbal, G. (2004). Identification of tuberculosis bacteria based on shape and color. *Real-time imaging*, 10(4), 251-262.

Ghosh, P., Bhattacharjee, D., Nasipuri, M., & Basu, D. K. (2010), Round-the-clock urine sugar monitoring system for diabetic patients. Proceedings of Systems International Conference on Medicine and Biology (ICSMB) (pp 326 – 330). IEEE. doi:10.1109/ICSMB.2010.5735397

Ghosh, P., Bhattacharjee, D., Nasipuri, M., Basu, D.K. (2011). Medical Aid for Automatic Detection of Malaria. *Computer Information Systems–Analysis and Technologies* (Vol. 245, pp. 170-178). Springer Berlin Heidelberg.

Ghosh, P., Bhattacharjee, D., Nasipuri, M., & Basu, D. K. (2013). Child Obesity Control through Computer Game. *Biomedical Engineering Research*, *2*(2), 88–95. doi:10.5963/BER0202005

Ginneken, B., & Romeny, H. (2000). Automatic segmentation of lung fields in chest radiographs. *Medical Physics*, *27*(10), 2445–2455. doi:10.1118/1.1312192

Ginneken, B., van, , Katsuragawa, S., & Romeny, K. (2002). Automatic detection of abnormalities in chest radiographs using local texture analysis. *IEEE Transactions on Medical Imaging*, *21*(2), 139–149. doi:10.1109/42.993132

Ginneken, B. V., & ter Haar Romeny, B. (2000). Automatic segmentation of lung fields in chest radiographs. *Medical Physics*, *27*(10), 2445–2455. doi:10.1118/1.1312192

Goldstein, J. S., Irving, S. R., & Louis, L. S. (1998). A multistage representation of the Wiener filter based on orthogonal projections. *IEEE Transactions on Information Theory*, *44*(7), 2943–2959. doi:10.1109/18.737524

Gonzalez, R. C., & Richard, R. E. Woods (Eds.), (2002). Digital image processing. Prentice Hall Press.

Grady, L. (2006). Random walks for image segmentation. *IEEE Transactions on Pattern Analysis and Machine Intelligence, 28*(11), 1768–1783. doi:10.1109/TPAMI.2006.233

Granich, R., Akolo, C., Gunneberg, C., Getahun, H., Williams, P., & Williams, B. (2010). Prevention of tuberculosis in people living with HIV. *Clinical Infectious Diseases, 50*(3), 215–222. doi:10.1086/651494

Gregory, J. A., & Delbourgo, R. (1982). Piecewise rational quadratic interpolation to monotonic data. *IMA Journal of Numerical Analysis, 2*(2), 123–130. doi:10.1093/imanum/2.2.123

Hogeweg, C., Mol, C., de Jong, P.A., Dawson, R., Ayles, H., & van Ginneken, B. (2010). Fusion of local and global detection systems to detect tuberculosis in chest radiographs. Proceedings of Medical Image Computing and Computer-Assisted Intervention MICCAI 2010 (pp. 650–657).

Huebner, R. E., Maybelle, F. S., & Bass, J. B. (1993). The tuberculin skin test. *Clinical Infectious Diseases, 17*(6), 968–975. doi:10.1093/clinids/17.6.968

Kamboj, M., & Sepkowitz, K. A. (2006). The risk of tuberculosis in patients with cancer. *Clinical Infectious Diseases, 42*(11), 1592–1595. doi:10.1086/503917

Levy, H., Feldman, C., & Sacho, H. (1989). A reevaluation of sputum microscopy and culture in the diagnosis of pulmonary tuberculosis. *CHEST Journal, 95*(6), 1193–1197. doi:10.1378/chest.95.6.1193

Lodwick, G. (1996). Computer-aided diagnosis in radiology: A research plan. *Investigative Radiology, 1*(1), 72–80. doi:10.1097/00004424-196601000-00032

Lodwick, G., Keats, T., & Dorst, J. (1963). The coding of roentgen images for computer analysis as applied to lung cancer. *Radiology, 81*(2), 185–200. doi:10.1148/81.2.185

Lordi, G. M., & Reichman, L. B. (1994), Tuberculin skin testing - Tuberculosis (pp. 63-68). New York: Springer.

MacMahon, H., & Feng, F. R. (2008). Dual energy subtraction and temporal subtraction chest radiography. *Journal of Thoracic Imaging, 23*(2), 77–85. doi:10.1097/RTI.0b013e318173dd38

Macon, N., & Spitzbart, A. (1958). Inverses of Vandermonde matrices. *The American Mathematical Monthly, 65*(2), 95–100. doi:10.2307/2308881

Makkapati, V., Agrawal, R., & Acharya, R. (2009). *Segmentation and classification of tuberculosis bacilli from ZN-stained sputum smear images. Automation Science and Engineering.* IEEE.

MATLAB User's Guide. (2015). The Mathworks. Retrieved from http://www.mathworks.com

Moore, D. A., Lightstone, L., Javid, B., & Friedland, J. S. (2002). High rates of tuberculosis in end-stage renal failure: The impact of international migration. *Emerging Infectious Diseases, 8*(1), 77–78. doi:10.3201/eid0801.010017

Myronenko, A., & Song, X. (2009). Global active contour-based image segmentation via probability alignment. *Proceedings of the IEEE Computer Society Conference on Computer Vision and Pattern Recognition Workshops* (pp. 2798–2804). IEEE. doi:10.1109/CVPR.2009.5206552

Osman, M. K., Mashor, M. Y., Saad, Z., & Jaafar, H. (2009). Contrast enhancement for Ziehl-Neelsen tissue slide images using linear stretching and histogram equalization technique. *Proceedings of the IEEE Symposium on Industrial Electronics and Applications (ISIEA '09)* (pp. 431–435). doi:10.1109/ISIEA.2009.5356411

Pavlopoulos, S., Kyriacou, E., Berler, A., Dembeyiotis, S., & Koutsouris, D. (1998). A novel emergency telemedicine system based on wireless communication technology-AMBULANCE. *IEEE Transactions on Information Technology in Biomedicine*, *2*(4), 261–267. doi:10.1109/4233.737581

Pedrycz, W. (1985). Algorithms of fuzzy clustering with partial supervision Pattern Recognition. *Letters*, *2*(1), 13-20.

Pedrycz, W., & Waletzky, J. (1997). Fuzzy clustering with partial supervision. *IEEE Transactions on Systems, Man, and Cybernetics. Part B, Cybernetics*, *27*(5), 787–795. doi:10.1109/3477.623232

DiRuperto, C., & Dempster, A. (2000). Circularity measures based on mathematical morphology. *Electronics Letters*, *36*(20), 1691–1693.

Shen, R., Cheng, I., & Basu, A. (2010). A hybrid knowledge-guided detection technique for screening of infectious pulmonary tuberculosis from chest radiographs. *Biomedical Engineering,* *57*(11), 2646–2656.

Song, Y.-L., & Yang, Y. (2010). Localization algorithm and implementation for focal of pulmonary tuberculosis chest image. *Proceedings of the International Conference on Machine Vision and Human-Machine Interface (MVHI '10)* (pp. 361–364). doi:10.1109/MVHI.2010.180

van Ginneken, B., Hogeweg, L., & Prokop, M. (2009). Computer-aided diagnosis in chest radiography: Beyond nodules. *European Journal of Radiology*, *72*(2), 226–230. doi:10.1016/j.ejrad.2009.05.061

Van Ginneken, B., Stegmann, M., & Loog, M. (2006). Segmentation of anatomical structures in chest radiographs using supervised methods: A comparative study on a public database. *Medical Image Analysis*, *10*(1), 19–40. doi:10.1016/j.media.2005.02.002

World Health Organization. (2008). *Implementing the WHO stop TB strategy: A handbook for national TB control programs*. World Health Organization Press.

World Health Organization. (2015). *Global tuberculosis report 2014*. Retrieved from http://www.who.int/tb/publications/global_report/en/

World Health Organization. (2015). *Fact Sheet Tuberculosis*. Retrieved from http://www.who.int/mediacentre/factsheets/fs104/en/

Xu, T., Cheng, I., Long, R., & Mandal, M. (2013). Novel coarse-to-fine dual scale technique for tuberculosis lesion detection in chest radiographs. *EURASIP Journal on Image and Video Processing*, *2013*(3), 1–18.

Yoshida, H., & Doi, K. (2000). Computerized detection of pulmonary nodules in chest radiographs: reduction of false positives based on symmetry between left and right lungs. *Proceedings of SPIE Medical Imaging* (Vol. 3979). doi:10.1117/12.387732

Zhao, H., Lo, S.-C. B., Freedman, M. T., & Seong Ki Mun, S. K. M. (2001). On automatic temporal subtraction of chest radiographs and its enhancement for lung cancers. *Proceedings of SPIE Medical Imaging* (Vol. 4322, pp. 1867–1872). doi:10.1117/12.431078

KEY TERMS AND DEFINITIONS

ARM11 Processor Family: The ARM11 is a 32-bit RISC processor cores. The ARM11 micro architecture (announced 29 April 2002) introduced the ARMv6 architectural. This micro architecture includes SIMD media instructions, multiprocessor support and a new cache architecture.

Binary Image: Binary images are images whose pixels have only two possible intensity values. They are normally displayed as black and white. Numerically, the two values are often 0 for black, and either 1 or 255 for white.

CCD: A charge-coupled device (CCD) is a device for the movement of electrical charge, usually from within the device to an area where the charge can be manipulated CCDs move charge between capacitive bins in the device, with the shift allowing for the transfer of charge between bins. In a CCD sensor, points are represented by p-doped MOS capacitors.

CCD Camera: A CCD camera is a camera whose imaging system uses three separate charge-coupled devices (CCDs), each one taking a separate measurement of the primary colors, red, green, or blue light. Light coming through the lens is split by a trichroic prism assembly, which directs the appropriate wavelength ranges of light to their respective CCDs. The system is employed by still cameras, telecine systems, professional video cameras etc.

Closing: It is a morphological operators, the exact operation is determined by a structuring element. The effect of the operator is to preserve foreground regions that have a similar shape to this structuring element, or that can completely contain the structuring element, while eliminating all other regions of foreground pixels.

Dilation: The basic effect of the operator on a binary image is to gradually enlarge the boundaries of regions of foreground pixels (i.e. white pixels, typically). Thus areas of foreground pixels grow in size while holes within those regions become smaller.

Erosion: It is typically applied to binary images, but there are versions that work on grayscale images. The basic effect of the operator on a binary image is to erode away the boundaries of regions of foreground pixels (i.e. white pixels, typically). Thus areas of foreground pixels shrink in size, and holes within those areas become larger.

H Bridge: An H bridge is an electronic circuit that enables a voltage to be applied across a load in either direction. These circuits are often used in robotics and other applications to allow DC motors to run forwards and backwards.

HSI Color Space: The HSI color model represents every color with three components: hue (H), saturation (S), intensity (I). The Hue component describes the color in the form of an angle between [0,360] degrees. The Saturation component describes how much the color is diluted with white light. The range of the S varies between [0,1]. The Intensity range is between [0,1] and 0 means black, 1 means white.

Image Segmentation: In computer vision, image segmentation is the process of partitioning a digital image into multiple segments.

Opening: Opening is normally applied to binary images. The basic effect of an opening is somewhat like erosion in that it tends to remove some of the foreground (bright) pixels from the edges of regions of foreground pixels.

Pulse Width Modulation: Pulse Width Modulation, or PWM, is a technique for getting analog results with digital means. Digital control is used to create a square wave, a signal switched between on and off. This on-off pattern can simulate voltages in between full on (5 Volts) and off (0 Volts) by changing the portion of the time the signal spends on versus the time that the signal spends off. The duration of "on time" is called the pulse width.

Stepper Motor: A stepper motor (or step motor) is a brushless DC electric motor that divides a full rotation into a number of equal steps. The motor's position can be commanded to move and hold on one of steps without any feedback sensor (an open-loop controller).

Thinning: Thinning is a morphological operation that is used to remove selected foreground pixels from binary images, somewhat like erosion or opening. It can be used for several applications, but is particularly useful for skeletonization. The thinning operation is related to the hit-and-miss transform.

APPENDIX 1

Ziehl-Neelsen (ZN) Staining Procedure and Principal

Working Principle

The property of acid-fastness is based on the presence of mycolic acids in the cell wall of mycobacteria. The lipoid capsule of the acid-fast organism takes up carbol-fuchsin and resists decolorization with a dilute acid rinse. The lipoid capsule of the mycobacterium is of such high molecular weight that it is waxy at room temperature and successful penetration by the aqueous based staining solutions (such as Gram's) is prevented. The mycobacterium retains the red colour of fuchsine. Counter staining (with methylene blue) provides a contrasting background. While mycobacterium is AFB, very few other bacteria possess the property of acid-fastness. AFB found in respiratory specimens of patients from countries with high TB prevalence is almost always TB bacilli. Non-TB mycobacteriums are more commonly found in countries where TB prevalence is low. In high-burden countries, however, some patients suspected of having MDR-TB may actually have disease caused by non-TB mycobacterium. AFB found in extra pulmonary specimens, particularly gastric washings, stool or urine, should never be automatically assumed to represent TB bacilli.

Specimens

Any incoming specimen must be properly labelled, as a minimum with a unique identification number. Sputa from suspects should be rejected only if they are liquid and clear as water, with no particles or streaks of mucous material. However, they should be accepted if the patient cannot produce a better specimen on a repeated attempt. Sputa from follow-up patients should be accepted and examined even if they look like saliva, since these patients often cannot produce mucous specimens.

- **Induced Sputa:** These specimens resemble saliva but have to be processed as adequate specimens.
- Decontaminated sputa, concentrated by centrifugation.
- Laryngeal swabs, gastric lavages, bronchial washings, brushings and transtracheal aspirates.
- Urine.
- Body fluids (spinal, pleural, pericardial, synovial, fluids from ascites, blood, pus, bone marrow).
- Tissue biopsies.

Equipment and Materials

- Alcohol sand jar (only if a loop is used, not needed with disposable sticks).
- Bunsen burner or spirit lamp.
- Gas or burning spirit torch.
- Diamond pencil or lead pencil (if frosted-end slides are available).
- Filter paper, small, and appropriate for funnel size.
- Funnels, small, for filtering solutions in use.
- Forceps.

- Lens paper or soft tissue paper.
- Plastic bag for waste disposal.
- Bamboo or wooden sticks or wire loops.
- Microscope, preferably binocular, with par focal lenses, electric light source or mirror, mechanical stage, 100x objective, 10x eyepiece (see Appendix 2).
- Immersion oil, synthetic, refractive index 1.5180 ± 0.0004 (according to DIN/ISO recommendations). Do not use cedar wood oil.
- Slide drying rack.
- Slide staining rack.
- Slide boxes.
- New, clean slides (rinse in alcohol and dry if necessary).
- Timer.
- Staining reagents.
- Staining bottles, 250 ml, with spout.
- Beaker for rinsing water.
- Sink and water supply.
- Oil-absorbing paper.
- Disinfectant solution (see relevant SOP).

Reagents and Solutions

The formulations of reagents given here below are consistent with current recommendations and differ from those in previous WHO guidelines. The fuchsine concentration is higher but with a lower methylene blue concentration, which results in stronger red staining of bacilli on a weak blue background, with generally better contrast and visibility. However, the preparation of staining solutions or if the staining solutions are supplied centrally and the method used or recommended by the NTP should be inserted or described, if different.

- Carbol fuchsin staining solution, 1%.
- Acid decolourizing solution, 25% H_2SO_4.
- Methylene blue counterstaining solution, 0.1%.

Colour-blind workers are advised to use picric acid solution (7 g/l in water) which yields a yellow background.

Detailed Instructions

Label the slides properly using the laboratory register serial number marked on the sputum container. Place each slide on its corresponding container. Proceed to smearing, taking the labelled slides and opening containers one by one; do the smearing behind the flame of a Bunsen burner or spirit lamp. for a direct sputum smear, select a small portion of purulent or mucopurulent material with the stick/loop and transfer it to the slide; If a smear is prepared after specimen decontamination, the concentrated material must be transferred to the slide with a sterilized loop to avoid splashing. Note: If a loop is used, it must be sterilized before use by heating until red-hot within the glass chimney of the Bunsen burner. After use, plunge the loop into the alcohol sand jar, moving it up and down to remove any remaining material, then heat it again until red-hot.

Spread the material carefully over an area equal to about 2–3 cm x 1–2 cm using repeated circular movements, without touching the edge of the slide. Make the smear as even as possible by continuing this process until no thick parts remain. The thickness of the smear should be such that a newspaper held under the slide can barely be read through the dried smear.

Disinfect the Working Area after Smear Preparation

Let the smears air-dry at room temperature; do not use heat to speed the drying. Where humidity is high, gentle warming will be needed on a slide warmer (or locally made box with glass top under which there is a 20-W light bulb). When dry, hold the slides in forceps and fix them by passing three times slowly through the flame of a spirit lamp or quickly through that of a Bunsen burner, smear upwards; do not overheat or AFB staining will be poor. Always keep smears out of direct sunlight.

Staining Method

Place the slides, smear upwards, on the staining rack over a sink, about 1 cm apart. Place a new filter paper in a small funnel, keep it over the first slide and fill it up with carbol fuchsine staining solution. Let the solution filter through the paper, covering each slide completely. Prepare the torch by dipping its cotton wool end in burning spirit; light it. Heat all the slides, keeping the torch a little below them and moving it continuously back and forth along the line until steam rises. This is repeated twice at intervals of 3–5 minutes. Do not allow the staining solution to dry on the slides – add fresh solution as required. Contact time of the staining solution with the smear should total at least 10 minutes. Using forceps tilt each slide to drain off the stain solution. Rinse the slides well with distilled water or clean tap water from a beaker (not directly from the tap). Pour the acid solution over the smears, covering them completely, and allow acting for 3 minutes. Using forceps tilt each slide to drain off the acid solution. Gently rinse each slide again with distilled water or clean tap water from a beaker (not directly from the tap). If necessary, repeat the acid treatment and rinsing until all macroscopically visible stain has been washed away.

Flood Smears with Methylene Blue Solution for 1 Minute

Using forceps tilt each slide to drain off the methylene blue solution. Rinse the slides well with distilled water or clean tap water from a beaker (not directly from the tap). Using forceps, take each slide from the rack and let the water drain off. Stand the slide on edge on the drying rack and allow air-drying. Note: The stained smear should show a light blue colour. A dark blue colour usually indicates that the smear is too thick or that the methylene blue staining time was too long; this will hide the red AFB in the background. Acid-fast bacilli appear bright red against the background material counterstained in blue. Report as positive for AFB when the background is bluish and at least one red AFB is seen in a well de-stained smear (even if the AFB may be mycobacterium other than tubercle bacilli). Tubercle bacilli are quite variable in shape, from very short fragments to elongated types. The typical appearance is usually of rather long and slender, slightly curved rods. They may be uniformly stained or with one or many gaps, or even granular. They occur singly or in small groups, and rarely in large clumps.

Table 5.

Finding	Recording
No AFB found in at least 100 fields	negative
1–9 AFB per 100 fields	exact figure/100
10–99 AFB per 100 fields	+
1–10 AFB per field (count at least 50 fields)	++
More than 10 AFB per field (count at least 20 fields)	+++

Recording

Shown in Table 5.

Quality Control and Evaluation of Smear Quality

Internal QC of Freshly Made Staining Solutions

Prepare batches of control slides from suitable sputum specimens. These are negatives that have been thoroughly examined, and low positive sputum (1+, 10–99 AFB/100 fields) homogenized after liquefaction by standing overnight at room temperature. Prepare at least 20 smears of each, as nearly identical in size and thickness as possible, giving each series the same QC identification number. Check 2–3 of each after good staining, and note the average number of AFB for the 1+ in the QC logbook. Check every newly prepared staining solution with unstained control smears, using at least one positive, with known approximate number of AFB, and one negative slide. Stain the positive smear(s) as in section 1.5.2 repeat the cycle for the negative(s) at least once to ensure that contaminants present in decolourizer or counterstaining solution will be visible.

Waste Management

At the end of each day, seal contaminated material (used sputum containers, sticks, etc.) in a bag and incinerate as soon as possible. Keep the bag in a safe, closed bin or large bucket until it can be incinerated. In intermediate or central laboratories where there is an autoclave, infectious waste should be collected in an auto clavable bag and should be autoclaved before incineration.

APPENDIX 2

Code Segments in C and Matlab for Job Scheduling and Data Transfer

All devices in linux is considered as a file fopen function is used to open camera device file which is located in "/dev/video0". pthread_create function is used to create a separate thread for a function called "filter_task". "filter_task" performs filtration upon the input matrix. in "filter_task" function "pthread_setaffinity_np" function is used to assign CPU (core) for that thread. "pthread_setaffinity_np" takes current thread ID as an input. This current thread ID is obtained from the function "pthread_self".

The code revolves "Addr" which is a struct of type sockaddr_in. This struct stores information about the machine, user want to connect. The socket() function tells OS that the user want a file descriptor for a socket which can use for a network stream connection. This tells OS to use the socket sock to create a connection to the machine specified in "Addr".

Listing 1. Multithreaded program with dedicated core assignment (CPU affinity)

```
-------------------------------------
-------------------------------------
-------------------------------------
FILE *camera1;
    Camera1 = fopen("/dev/video0", "rb");
// open camera device file /dev/video0
// do other initialization works
-------------------------------------
fread(data, sizeof(data[0]), SIZE, camera1);
// read raw data from web cam
// rearrange raw data and fit it into 3 matrixes namely R, G and B
-------------------------------------
-------------------------------------
pthread_t thread[3]; // create thread variable
rc1 = pthread_create(&thread[0], NULL, filter_task, (void *)R);
rc2 = pthread_create(&thread[1], NULL, filter_task, (void *)G);
rc3 = pthread_create(&thread[2], NULL, filter_task, (void *)B);
// create 3 filter thread for 3 matrix.

if (rc1 < 1 || rc2 < 1 || rc1 < 1) {
     printf("ERROR: return code from pthread_create() is %d %d  %d \n", rc,
rc, rc);
     exit(-1);

// create threads for filtering
-------------------------------------
-------------------------------------
// do other works
// there are 4 cores. The main thread will run on core 1 and 3 cores are as-
sign for other 3 threads.
core_id =1;
cpu_set_t cpuset;
CPU_ZERO (&cpuset);
CPU_SET (core_id, &cpuset);
```

continued on following page

Listing 1. Continued

```
// core_id represent the id of each core
   pthread_t current_thread = pthread_self();  // get self thread id
   pthread_setaffinity_np (current_thread, sizeof (cpu_set_t), &cpuset);


------------------------------------
------------------------------------
// do other works

pthread_join (thread[0], NULL);
pthread_join (thread[1], NULL);
pthread_join (thread[2], NULL);

// weight until each thread completes execution.
// divide the RGB to HIS convertion in multi thread and assign cores to each
of them.


------------------------------------
------------------------------------
------------------------------------
 // In filter function the coding structure is like that.

void * filter_task (void  matrix[][])
{
------------------------------------
------------------------------------
  //the CPU we whant to use
  int cpu = 2;

  CPU_ZERO(&cpuset);        //clears the cpuset
  CPU_SET(cpu, &cpuset); //set CPU 2 on cpuset



  // cpu affinity for the calling thread
  pthread_t current_thread = pthread_self();  // get self thread id
  pthread_setaffinity_np (current_thread, sizeof (cpu_set_t), &cpuset);
------------------------------------
------------------------------------
// code for filtering
------------------------------------
------------------------------------
}
```

Listing 2. C code for socket communication in Linux

```
int sock;                           /* Socket */
struct sockaddr_in Addr;            /* Broadcast address */
char *IP;                           /* IP broadcast address */
unsigned short Port;                /* Server port */
char *sendData;                     /* String to broadcast */
int Permission;          /* Socket opt to set permission to broadcast */
unsigned int sendStringLen;        /* Length of string to broadcast */
IP = "192.168.0.2";      /* First arg:  broadcast IP address */
Port = 1500;             /* Second arg:  broadcast port */

sock = socket(PF_INET, SOCK_DGRAM, IPPROTO_UDP))
/* Set socket to allow communication */
Permission = 1;
setsockopt(sock, SOL_SOCKET, SO_BROADCAST, (void *) &Permission,
      sizeof(Permission))
/* Construct local address structure */
memset(&Addr, 0, sizeof(Addr));    /* Zero out structure */
Addr.sin_family = AF_INET;         /* Internet address family */
Addr.sin_addr.s_addr = inet_addr(IP); /*Broadcast IP address */
Addr.sin_port = htons(Port);       /* Broadcast port */
------------------------------------
------------------------------------
// ptepare data that need to send and send that data
------------------------------------
------------------------------------
sendto(sock, data, sendDataLen, 0, (struct sockaddr *)&Addr, sizeof(Addr)
------------------------------------
------------------------------------
```

Listing 3. Code segment for socket communication in Matlab 7.1

```
input_socket = tcpip(IP, 1500);
        fopen(input_socket);
        Data = fread(input_socket, buffer)
------------------------------------
------------------------------------
------------------------------------
% re-arrange data to build RGB image
fclose(input_socket)
delete(input_socket)
```

453

Chapter 15
Application of Meta-Models (MPMR and ELM) for Determining OMC, MDD and Soaked CBR Value of Soil

Vishal Shreyans Shah
VIT University, India

Henyl Rakesh Shah
VIT University, India

Pijush Samui
VIT University, India

ABSTRACT

This chapter examines the capability of Minimax Probability Machine Regression (MPMR) and Extreme Learning Machine (ELM) for prediction of Optimum Moisture Content (OMC), Maximum Dry Density (MDD) and Soaked California Bearing Ratio (CBR) of soil. These algorithms can analyse data and recognize patterns and are proved to be very useful for problems pertaining to classification and regression analysis. These regression models are used for prediction of OMC and MDD using Liquid limit (LL) and Plastic limit (PL) as input parameters. Whereas Soaked CBR is predicted using Liquid limit, Plastic limit, OMC and MDD as input parameters. The predicted values obtained from the MPMR and ELM models have been compared with that obtained from Artificial Neural Networks (ANN). The accuracy of MPMR and ELM models, their performance and their reliability with respect to ANN models has also been evaluated.

INTRODUCTION

Developing countries, especially India, are experiencing a current boom in infrastructure update. Many of the old structures are getting redeveloped and also encroachment on open land for new structures has become a routine. With the rapid growth in world population and limited land availability, the need for

DOI: 10.4018/978-1-4666-9474-3.ch015

quickly developing and delivering infrastructure projects is at its peak. From highways to runways, from houses to multi-storey buildings, each project has a limited schedule and failure to deliver within the time frame causes immense losses. Project managers and planners seek to reduce the amount of time required in each and every step and activity in order to bring down the total time required to complete the project. Many new projects are surfacing in Mumbai in a bid to emulate the excellent Shanghai road network. The Eastern Freeway is the perfect example of this. Even the golden quadrilateral connecting Mumbai, Kolkata, Delhi and Chennai is undergoing widening and redevelopment. All these past year projects and even the newer upcoming projects are just short on one realm - time. This "time" is a major shortcoming of most undergoing projects. For example the Eastern Freeway project in Mumbai was supposed to be completed by the 2011 but finally got completed in 2013 (a two year delay). The cost spike was more than seventy percent- from an original estimate of Rs 847 crore to a final cost of Rs 1463 crore. Thus we learn that time and economy in a project can be a real issue in its efficient delivery. The new Indian government, under the guidance of Prime Minister Narendra Modi, planning to build or update a 100 smart cities with a plan to build 15000kms of road networks. This is simply a dream to complete in the coming years if correct measures and newer, more efficient technologies are not soon introduced into daily practice. This chapter is focused on giving an alternate method, which is reliable and can save significant amount of time, in one of the most important and preliminary stages of a project – Soil Testing.

Pavement is a road surface made of durable material that will be able to resist foot and/or vehicular load. It is a relatively stronger and stable surface designed in layers of subgrade, sub-base course, base course and the surface course. Pavements are designed keeping in mind the various load that will act in the complete duration of a structures life and how much resistance the subgrade layer is able to offer. Thus the design and performance of a flexible pavement is highly dependent on the resistance the compacted subgrade layer will offer. Due to this it is important to assess the strength of the sub-base layer. For this assessment the California Department of Transportation developed a technique of penetration for mechanical strength evaluation of the subgrade layer. This technique called the California Bearing Ratio test was developed before World War 2 and soon it came to use widely in the construction world. The test procedures can be obtained from *ASTM standards D1883-05 (lab prepared samples), D4429 (for soils in place in field) and IS2720 Part 16 (1979)* for soaked California Bearing Ratio test. It is important to note the difference and significance of using soaked CBR over normal CBR test. This will be describe later in the chapter.

The tests used to determine the engineering properties of soil are time consuming, expensive and are extremely prone to human error. If not double checked, these tests may give wrong values. Also the equipment required to carry out these tests are not readily available on site and soil samples need to be sent to laboratory for testing. On the other hand, the index properties of soil are lot easier to determine and although the tests are equally prone to human error, they are not at all time consuming and double even triple checking the properties is very much possible during the preliminary analysis of the site. Also, during preliminary analysis and testing of soil samples taking samples along the entire stretch of a major long road construction and then testing it for its index properties and finally soaked CBR value can be really difficult. Even if attempted such amount of work would take days of laboratory testing for just a single sample. This can cause major delay in the work resulting in late delivery of the final completed project by the concerned contractor. Delay in work will eventually lead to cost spikes. This is where a model with the ability to predict CBR value, by using index properties like Liquid and Plastic Limit, and engineering properties like OMC and MDD as inputs, may contribute immensely to save time and thus save the project from cost spikes.

This chapter aims at developing a correlation between some index properties of soil such as Liquid Limit, Plastic Limit and engineering properties like OMC, MDD and Soaked CBR of soil such that this relationship can be used to predict the engineering properties of a range of soils by simply calculating their required index properties. Thus, the important results that may take days to arrive will be approximately predicted within matter of minutes and work on designing the geotechnical components of the project can be commenced at the earliest.

BACKGROUND

Soil Properties and Their Correlation

The determination of soil properties are of great importance as all construction works are dependent on soil strength and stability. The engineering properties of soil such as compressibility, permeability and shear strength may not have the desired capacity of handling heavy loads on each and every site. Thus, these soil properties are artificially improved by the process of compaction. Optimum level of compaction is when the soil has the highest degree of mentioned engineering properties especially shear strength. This is achieved when the soil has the highest dry density. Standard Proctor test is the laboratory test carried out to give the compaction characteristics. The tests results are plotted to obtain a curve that shows relationship between dry density and water content of the soil. It is observed that dry density increases with water content till the Maximum Dry Density (MDD) is reached and thereafter decreases with the increase in water content. The water content at which MDD is attained is of the utmost importance since the compaction is to be done at exactly this water content. This water content is called the Optimum Moisture Content (OMC).

The tests used for determining engineering properties of soils are very time consuming and recommended to be done in a laboratory environment. Hence we determine the index properties for rough evaluation of soil during preliminary site analysis. Atterberg's Limits are amongst the major index properties of soil. These tests give the water contents at which soil change from one state to another.

With increasing water content, the water content at which soil changes from semi solid to plastic is known as plastic limit. It is determined by the thread rolling test. Further increasing water content, liquid limit is the water content at which the soil starts to behave as liquid. The liquid limit is determined using Casagrande's apparatus. Both liquid and plastic limits depend on the *clay* content in soil.

Another important engineering property, the bearing ratio of soil is determined for pavement design. California Baring Ratio, an empirical penetration test developed by California Highway Dept. in 1920s, is an indicator of soil strength and is one of the most widely used methods to determine the stiffness and suitability of subgrade.

CBR test is conducted on soil by collecting a representative sample from which specimen is remoulded. The laboratory specimen is compacted at predetermined OMC using standard proctor compaction. The compacted specimen is soaked under water for 4 days and penetration is conducted.

Definitions

- **Liquid Limit:** A soil containing high water content is in a liquid state. It offers no shearing resistance and can flow like liquids. As the water content is reduced, the soil becomes stiffer and starts developing shear resistance. At some particular water content, the soil becomes plastic. The water content at which the soil changes from liquid state to plastic state is known as *Liquid Limit.*

- **Plastic Limit:** The soil in plastic state can be moulded into various shapes. As the water content is reduced, the plasticity of the soil decreases. Ultimately soil passes from the plastic from plastic state to the semi solid state when it stops behaving like plastic. The water content at which the soil becomes semi-solid is known as *Plastic Limit.*

- **Compaction:** Compaction means pressing of soil particles close to each other by mechanical methods. Compaction generally increases the shear strength of soil and hence the stability and bearing capacity. Thus the mass density is increased and engineering properties are improved.

- **MDD and OMC:** A compaction curve is plotted between the water content as abscissa and corresponding dry density (after compaction) as the ordinate. It is observed that the dry density initially increases with the increase in water content till *Maximum Dry Density (MDD)* is attained. With further increase in water content, the dry density decreases. The water content corresponding to the maximum dry density is called *Optimum Moisture Content (OMC).*

- **California Bearing Ratio:** The California Bearing Ratio is a penetration test to evaluate the mechanical strength of subgrades and base courses in a road. This technique was developed by the California Department of Transportation before World War 2. The soil sample is penetrated by a plunger of standard area. The measured pressure is then divided by the standard pressure that achieves penetration in standard crushed rock material. This technique was thus developed to measure the load bearing capacity of soils forming pavement or road foundation. There are two types of CBR tests performed in a laboratory:
  - ○ Unsoaked CBR test is performed on soil samples from regions which are not very much prone to rainfall. The soil is compacted at OMC and is directly placed on the CBR equipment for penetration.
  - ○ Soaked CBR test is most commonly performed on soil samples from regions which receive rainfall. In this test the soil sample is first compacted at OMC and then is covered by filter on both sides and weights on the open side (opposite the mould base). This set up is then immersed in water for 96 hours before the penetration test is performed thus providing a simulated condition for the rainfall that would affect the soil in that region from where the sample is collect for design of pavement.

Literature Review

Some of the existing models to estimate CBR:

Several attempts have been made by researchers to develop a correlation between CBR value at OMC and simple field tests like Liquid Limit, Plastic Limit and other important soil engineering and index parameters. Some of these correlations have been listed and described below.

- **NCHRP (2001):** The National Cooperative Research Program of the United States of America developed some correlations to establish relationships between CBR value and index properties of soil. An equation was developed for soils containing 12% fines and exhibit some plasticity. Their suggested equation is as shown below:

$$CBR = 75/\left[1 + 0.728(w \times PL)\right]$$

where 'w' is the percentage passing No. 200 US sieve and PI is Plasticity Index.

- **Satyanarayana Reddy and Pavani (2006):** They considered parameters Liquid Limit and MDD to obtain an equation from their model.
- **Gregory and Gross (2007):** They obtained and equation for estimation of CBR value for both cohesive and cohesionless soils using undrained cohesion and ultimate bearing capacity values for the soils respectively.
- **Vinod and Cletus (2008):** Proposed a relationship based on the liquid limit and gradation characteristics of soil based on their experimental study on lateritic soils as described in the equation below:

$$CBR = -0.889(WLM) + 45.616$$

where WLM is modified Liquid Limit and is given by

$$WLM = LL(1 - C/10)$$

where LL is Liquid Limit on soil passing 425 micron sieve (in percent) and C is fraction of soil coarser than 425 micron (percent).

- **Roy et al (2009):** Proposed a method to predict CBR value of soil in correlation with OMC and MDD data of that soil. They used the following relationship

$$\log(CBR) = \log\left(\gamma_d \max/\gamma_w\right) - \log\left(OMC\right)$$

where, γ_d max and γ_w are in same unit.

- **Patel and Desai (2010):** They proposed a model to develop a relationship between OMC, MDD and Plasticity Index. They had proposed a few correlations for alluvial soils to obtain CBR value from Liquid and Plastic Limits.

$$CBR(Soaked) = 43.907 - 0.093(PI) - 18.78(MDD) - 0.3081(OMC)$$

where, MDD is in gm/cc.

Table 1 made by Ramasubbarao and Siva Sankar (2013) sums up the works done previously.

- **Yildirim and Gunaydin (2011); Venkatasubramanian and Dhinakaran (2011); Saklecha et al (2012):** Used soft computing systems like ANN to develop a correlation between CBR value and LL, PL,OMC, MDD and unconfined compressive strength values.

Table 1. Models proposed by earlier investigators

No.	Investigator	Parameters Considered and Their Range	Model	Statistical Parameter
1	NCHRP, 2001	Non-plastic coarse-grained soils	CBR= 5%, if $D_{60} \leq 0.01mm$ CBR= $28.09(D_{60})^2$, if $0.01mm \leq D_{60} \leq 30mm$ CBR= 95%, if $D_{60} \geq 30mm$	$R^2 = 0.84$
		Plastic, fine-grained soils	$$CBR = \frac{75}{1 + 0.7288(w \times PL)}$$	$R^2 = 0.67$
2	Satyanarayana Reddy & Pavani, 2006	FF=9.0-34.8%, LL=22-48%, MDD=1.90-2.32g/cc CBR$_s$ = 12.8-56.8%	$CBR_s = -0.388F - 0.064LL + 20.38MDD$	R=0.96
3	(Gregory & Gross, 2007)	For cohesive soils	CBR = 0.09 C_u	-
		For cohesionless soils	$$CBR = \frac{q_{ult} \times 100}{6895}$$	-
4	(Vinod & Cletus, 2008)	C = 33-65%, LL = 38.10-63.00%, CBR$_s$ = 8.9-30.4%	$CBR = -0.889(WLM) + 45.616$ where, $WLM = LL(1 - C/10)$	R=0.979
5	(Patel & Desai, 2010)	LL=52.98-70.78%, PL=17.09-26.8%, SL=8.03-19.5%, MDD=1.58-1.73g/cc OMC=17.23-24.70% PI=24.19-47.78%, CBR$_u$=2.80-8.94%, CBR$_s$=1.54-4.42%	$CBR_u = 17.009 - 0.0696(PI) - 0.296(MDD)$ $+0.0648(OMC)$	%error=-2.5%
			$CBR_s = 43.907 - 0.093(PI) - 18.78(MDD)$ $-0.3081(OMC)$	%error=-5%
6	(Yildirim & Gunaydin, 2011)	G=0-78%, S=1-49%, F=10-99%, LL=2089%, PL=11-43% MDD=1.21-2.18 g/cc, OMC=7.20-40.20%	$CBR = 0.2353G + 3.0798$	$R^2 = 0.86$
			$CBR = -0.1805F + 18.508$	$R^2 = 0.80$
			$CBR = 0.22G + 0.045S + 4.739MDD + 0.122OMC$	$R^2 = 0.88$
			$CBR = 0.62OMC + 58.9MDD + 0.11LL + 0.53PL$ -126.18	$R^2 = 0.63$

Where, CBRs = Soaked California Bearing Ratio, CBRu = Unsoaked California Bearing Ratio, D60 = Diameter at 60% passing from grain size distribution (in mm), w = Percentage passing No.200 U.S. sieve (in decimal), LL= Liquid Limit of soil (in percent) and C is fraction of soil coarser than 425micron (percent), PL=Plastic Limit, SL=Shrinkage Limit, Ip =PI=Plasticity Index, MDD=Maximum Dry Density, OMC = Optimum Moisture Content (%), cu= undrained cohesion (kPa), qult=Ultimate bearing capacity (in kPa).

Pandian et al (1997) in their works suggest a method of predicting the OMC and MDD in terms of Liquid Limit. Study by Sridharan and Nagraj (2005) point out that compaction characteristics correlate with plastic limit and do not correlate with plasticity index and liquid limit.

Various attempts have been made by researchers (Venkatraman et al., 1995; Kumar et al., 2000; Karunaprema and Edirisinghe, 2002) to develop correlation between CBR value of soil compacted at OMC and results of field tests or soil characteristics.

Varghese et al (2013) suggests accurate predictions on soaked CBR of fine grained soil is obtained by ANN prediction using OMC, MDD, PL and LL as input parameters. Also the compaction characteristics can be predicted using two input parameters namely PL and LL.

Factors Affecting CBR Value of Soil

As explained above various researchers have known that there exist a relationship between CBR and other soil parameters and thus have constantly tried to develop relations between them. It is important to know and then correlate the factor that affects CBR value the most. The reliability of prediction of any CBR value by a proposed model will be dependent on how reliable or rather how important an incorporated factor is and its influence on the predicted value. This amount of reliability can be obtained by doing sensitivity analysis of the model as done in this chapter later.

Application of Prediction Models to Predict Soil Properties

Determination of soaked CBR, OMC and MDD of soils in the laboratory require considerable time and effort. Thus the exigency to use a software model which will aid in the prediction of these parameters without the need for tedious experimentation. The preliminary tests for suitability of soil at the project site include determination of properties of soil properties such as Liquid Limit, Plastic Limit and the indices. Soil suitability is predicted from these basic properties.

Minimax Probability Machine Regression (MPMR) is an only recently developed model proposed in the year 2003 by Thomas Strohmann and Gregory Grudic from Computer Science Department at University of Colorado, Boulder. The regression problem is formulated in such a way so as to maximise the minimum probability to predict outcomes within a certain bound of the true regression function. In this processes minimum assumptions are taken to maximise the accuracy for practical use. MPMR is a regression form of Minimax Probability Machine Classification and has been used extensively since for the prediction of chaotic time series (Liu Zunxiong et al 2006) and prediction of gaseous emissions from industrial stacks (C.I. Anghel et al 2006) Maximizing sensitivity in medical diagnosis (Huang, K., Yang, H., King, I., & Lyu, M. R., 2006) and Supervised tensor learning (Tao, D., Li, X., Hu, W., Maybank, S., & Wu, X., 2005) but has rarely been optimised for use in prediction of soil parameter or any other geotechnical area- thus the motivation to use MPMR for this study.

A major bottleneck in the past decades' applications of feedforward neural networks has been it's slower than required speed reasons being:

1. The use of slow gradient based algorithms to train neural networks.
2. All parameters of the network are tuned iteratively by such learning algorithms.

These were identified by Guan-Bin Huang (2006) from the Electrical and Electronics department of Nanyang Technological University who then proposed a new neural networks based learning algorithm called Extreme Learning Machine or single layer feedforward networks (SLFN). This randomly chooses hidden nodes and analytical determines the output weights of SLFNs. This algorithm is known for providing a good generalisation performance, not usually as accurate as other prediction models, but at extremely fast learning speeds than the previously used artificial neural network based algorithms. This machine has been used widely for prediction of protein secondary structures (Guoren Wang et al., 2008) and dynamic model hypothesis for fish trajectory tracking in fish ethology (Rui Nian, et al., 2014, among others).

Literature Review

MPMR

Strohmann & Grudic (2002) developed the Minimax probability machine regression based on the Minimax probability Machine Classification algorithm (Lanckriet et al.) and used Mercer Kernels to obtain nonlinear regression models. The goal of the problem was to maximize the minimum probability (Ω) of future predicted outputs of a regression model to be within some minimum $\pm\varepsilon$ bound of the true regression function. The authors have asserted that MPMR is tested in both artificial and natural environment and have verified the accuracy of the function and efficacy of the regression models.

Anghel & Ozunu (2006) used the MPMR to predict the gaseous emissions from industrial stacks. This new technique is able to predict the concentration of required pollutants by combining regression and classification problem into a unified technique, minimax decision regression model. The MPMR, which forms the core of this procedure, uses the trends from experimental databases of pollutant emissions and level of pollution. The work is numerically validated to provide close estimates against tested results from one industrial thermal power station thus confirming the accuracy of this method.

Cheng & Liu (2006) used the MPMR in Chaotic load series forecasting. After exploring the theory of MPMR, The authors verified the chaotic property of the load series from a certain power system by predicting one-day ahead points for 24 hours using MPMR. The results demonstrated that MPMR had excellent prediction efficiency.

Ng, Zhong & Yang (2007) used MPMR approach for face recognition. Minimax Probability Machine (MPM) and its extension, Minimum Error Minimax Probability Machine, have been incorporated into their face recognition system for further study. The performance of this new system is tested and compared with SVM, PCA-based and a LDA-based algorithms on the FERET database for both verification and identification. The experimental results demonstrated that MPM-based approaches are promising for automatic face recognition.

Huang et al (2006) have used a biased minimax probability machine to maximize sensitivity in medical diagnosis. The goal of the diagnosis is to favour the ill class over the healthy class making the objective of the BMPM to focus on improving the sensitivity of "ill" diagnosis and maintaining the specificity of "healthy" diagnosis rather than increasing the overall accuracy of the process. Earlier methods have adopted roundabout ways to impose bias towards "ill" class using intermediate factors to influence the classification. It has been uncertain as to whether these methods did improve the classification performance significantly. The BMPM directly approaches the objective by controlling the worst case accuracy to incorporate bias towards "ill" class. The decision rule thus derived is distribution-free and it maximizes the worst case sensitivities while maintaining an acceptable specificity. In such a way, the BMPM distinguishes itself from a large family of generative classifiers. The performance of BMPM has been compared to three traditional classifiers – nearest neighbour, naïve Bayesian and C4.5 and the results show that BMPM completely performs the rest proving itself to be a primary choice of classifier.

ELM

Huang, Zhu & Siew (2006) developed the Extreme learning machine based on neural networks mainly to increase the speed of training the model. According to them, the slow learning speeds of neural networks, which has been a major issue over the past decade, can be attributed to two reasons:

1. The slow gradient-based learning algorithms are extensively used to train neural networks, and
2. All the parameters of the networks are tuned iteratively by using such learning algorithms.

The proposed ELM algorithm uses single-hidden layer feed forward neural network (SLNF) which randomly chooses hidden nodes and analytically determines the output weights. The experimental results of this new algorithm provided a very good generalisation performance in most cases and it learned thousands of times faster than the conventional feed forward neural network algorithm.

Nian et al (2014) used the Extreme learning machine for dynamic model hypothesis in fish ethology research. One dynamic hypothesis is used to perform fish trajectory tracking and relevant mathematical criterion is developed based on ELM. Multiple historical cues and current predictions like stat vector motion, colour distribution and appearance recognition are used to conduct non-linear and non-Gaussian tracking. These predictions can be extracted from the SLFN at diverse levels of ELM. The hierarchical hybrid ELM combined the individual SLFN of tracking cues to improve the performance. Simulation results have shown excellent performance in both accuracy and robustness of the ELM approach

Wang et al. (2008) developed an ELM based protein secondary structure prediction framework which successfully provided good performance at extremely fast speeds. According to the authors, better performance is achieved by

1. Independently predicting the three secondary structures using a binary ELM classifier;
2. Using a probability based combination (PBC) method to combine the binary prediction results into the expected three-classification results; and
3. Using a helix post processing (HPP) method to further improve the overall performance of the framework based on biological features.

The experimental results concluded that this algorithm can match the performance of other popular methods and obviously at much faster learning speeds.

ANN

Bechtler et al. (2001) have used ANN for dynamic modelling of vapour-compression liquid chillers. The authors use ANN to train the model which requires the inputs as only those parameters that are easily measurable. The resulting outputs are relevant performance parameters such as co-efficient of performance or compressor work input. They have successfully applied the model to two dynamic processes of two different chillers.

Varghese et al. (2013) have used Artificial Neural Networks to predict the Engineering Properties of Fine-Grained Soils. They have used properties like LL, PL compaction characteristics in ANN to predict Soaked CBR values of Soil samples. They have also predicted compaction characteristics of a different set of samples using PL and LL as the input to the ANN. The authors have concluded that ANN, although is very capable of giving close results, the results can deviate drastically from the actual values if in case fewer input parameters are used.

Shahin et al. (2008) analyse the uses and shortcomings of artificial neural networks in geotechnical engineering. According to them, ANNs do show great promise in this field but suffer from number of shortcomings such as knowledge extraction, extrapolation and uncertainty. The work elaborates on the applications of ANN in geotechnical engineering and provides insights into the modelling issues of ANN.

MAIN FOCUS OF THE CHAPTER

1. Objectives of Present Work

As seen in introduction, the tests to determine the engineering properties of the soil are time consuming, cumbersome and only suitable for testing in laboratory environments. The index properties are rather easier to determine and can be obtained quickly on the site in the preliminary tests although, their experimental methods - Casagrande Liquid limit test, Thread rolling test for plastic limit - are subjected to manual error. This work aims to eliminate any discrepancies in the evaluation and provide a quick and efficient yet reliable method to determine the engineering properties like OMC, MDD and Soaked CBR values using the meta-models MPMR and ELM. The main objective is to determine the efficiency of MPMR and ELM models for prediction of these engineering properties.

The OMC and MDD values are predicted using the Liquid and Plastic limits of soils as input parameters to the MPMR and ELM models. Also Soaked CBR is predicted using LL, PL, MDD and OMC input to MPMR and ELM models. The predicted values obtained from MPMR and ELM will be compared with that obtained from Artificial Neural Networks. The aim is to evaluate the accuracy of MPMR and ELM models and their performance and reliability with respect to ANN.

2. Laboratory Tests

This section gives an insight into the level of difficulty faced by each and every test that was described in the introduction. The briefly mentioned test procedures are referenced from *the Indian Standards (IS 2720, 1983-1992)*. The complexity of the tests required to obtain the compaction parameters and soaked CBR value and the relative ease in obtaining Liquid Limit and Plastic Limit shows why there is a need of reliable A.I. models to predict the complex properties of soil by processing the basic properties.

2.1 Liquid Limit Test

The liquid limit of soil is the water content beyond which the soil starts to behave like a liquid. Soil has small shear strength at and after liquid limit.

2.1.1 Apparatus

- Casagrande's Liquid limit device,
- Grooving tool,
- Oven,
- Spatula,
- 425μ IS sieve,
- Weighing Machine.

2.1.2 Procedure

120g of air dried passing through 425μ IS sieve is taken. It is mixed with distilled water in a dish for 30 minutes till a uniform paste is obtained. The liquid limit device is adjusted such that the drop of the cup is 1 cm. A portion of the paste is placed on the cup using a spatula. A groove is cut in the sample using standard grooving tool. The handle of the device is turned at the rate of 2 revolutions per second.

The number of blows is noted down until the groove closes by flow of the soil. A representative soil sample is collected at right angle to the groove to determine the water content. The remaining soil sample is mixed with the paste and water content of the paste is varied. The test is repeated 3 to 4 times. Each time the water content (w) and number of blows (N) are noted. A flow curve is plotted between log N and w. The water content corresponding to N=25 on the flow curve gives the liquid limit of the sample.

2.2 Plastic Limit Test

Plastic limit is when soil begins to crumble when rolled into threads of 3 mm diameter.

2.2.1 Apparatus

- Glass plate,
- Oven,
- 425µ sieve.

2.2.2 Procedure

About 30 g of air dried soil passing through 425µ sieve is taken. The soil is mixed with water and shaped into a small ball. A small portion of the plastic soil is taken and rolled on a glass plate into threads of 3 mm diameter. If the thread doesn't crumble below a diameter of 3 mm then knead the soil again. Repeat the process until the thread crumbles. The pieces are collected to determine the water content by oven drying method. Repeat the test 2 to 3 times. The water content determined is the plastic limit of the soil.

2.3 Proctor Compaction Test (Indian Standard Light Compaction Test)

Compaction is the method of reducing air voids in the soil and thereby increasing density. The dry density is maximum at optimum moisture content. We have

$$Dry\ Density = Bulk\ Density \big/ (1 + w)$$

where

Bulk density = mass of soil/Volume of soil

w= water content.

2.3.1 Apparatus

- Compaction mould, 1000 ml,
- Rammer, 2.6 kg,
- Collar,

- Detachable base plate,
- 4.75 mm IS sieve,
- Oven,
- Weighing balance,
- Mixing pan.

2.3.2 Procedure

2 kg of air dried soil passing through 4.75 mm sieve is taken. The mould is greased md weighed with the base plate. Water is added to soil. Collar is attached to the mould. Soil is placed in the mould in 3 equal layers. Each layer is given 25 blows using the rammer. The blows should be uniformly distributed over the surface of each layer. The collar is removed and excess soil is trimmed off. The mould containing the compacted soil is weighed with the base plate. Soil is extruded from the mould and sample is taken for water content determination. The dry density is calculated using the above mentioned formula. The test is repeated for different water contents. A curve is plotted between water content and dry density. The water content corresponding to maximum dry density in the plot gives the value of optimum moisture content.

2.4 Soaked California Bearing Ratio Test

The test gives the CBR value from the penetration curve. CBR value is the penetration load expressed as percentage of standard load at the respective penetration level of 2.5 mm or 5.0 mm. The greater of these values are used for pavement design.

CBR value = Penetration load / Standard load x   100

2.4.1 Apparatus

- CBR mould,
- Detachable collar,
- Detachable base plate,
- Spacer disc,
- Rammer, 2.6 kg,
- Slotted mass,
- Penetration piston,
- Loading device,
- Dial gauges, 2 nos,
- IS sieve, 4.75 mm and 20 mm.

2.4.2 Procedure

5 kg of sample passing through 20 mm sieve and retained on 4.75 mm sieve is taken. The soil is mixed with required quantity of water (likely OMC). The mould is fixed to the base plate and extension collar is attached. The spacer disc is placed over base plate and filter paper disc is placed on top of it. Soil sample is taken in the mould. It is compacted using the rammer in 3 equal layers. Each layer is given 56

blows. The extension collar is removed and excess soil is trimmed off. The base plate is removed and the mould is weighed with the compacted soil. A filter paper disc is placed on the base plate. The mould with the sample is inverted. The mould is clamped to base plate. A perforated disc with an extension stem is placed on the top of the specimen after placing a filter disc. A surcharge of 2.5 kg annular mass is placed on the specimen. The mould is immersed in a tank full of water for a period of 96 hours. The mould with the soaked sample is weighed. The mould containing the specimen is placed on the loading machine. Required surcharge mass is placed. The penetration plunger is seated on the specimen. A seating load of 40 N is applied. Load dial gauge and displacement dial gauge are set to zero. The load is applied on the plunger. The rate of penetration must be 1.25 mm/minute. The load is recorded corresponding to penetrations of 0.0, 0.5, 1.0, 1.5, 2.0, 2.5, 3.0, 4.0, 5.0, 7.5, 10.0 and

12.5 mm. At the end the plunger is raised and the mould is removed from the loading machine. The load-penetration graph is plotted. The corrected load is found after zero correction corresponding to 2.5 mm and 5.0 mm penetration. The CBR value is calculated using the following equation.

$$CBR = (Corrected\ load\ at\ 2.5mm/13.44) \times 100$$

$$CBR = (Corrected\ load\ at\ 5mm/20.16) \times 100$$

3. Details of Prediction Models

3.1 Minimax Probability Machine Regression (MPMR)

Recently, Minimax Probability Machine (MPM), a discriminant classifier, has been proposed. It has shown comparative performance with models such as Support Vector Machine (Wang, 2005) in machine learning literature as cited by Johnny K.C. Ng et al .(2007). The model is derived in a probability based structure it differs from generative models that require distributional assumption (Jaakkola and Haussler, 1998).

Minimax Probability Machine Regression is a new model based on Minimax Probability Machine Classification (MPMC) and has only recently been proposed. MPMC is the first to put forward the linear classification that maximises the minimum probability of correct classification on future data (Liu ZunXiong, 2006) and can be further extended to nonlinear classifier by utilizing Mercer Kernels. While constructing a regression model one needs to maximise the minimum probability of future prediction within bounds of the true regression function. This regression can be referred to as Minimax Probability Machine Regression (MPMR).

For use of MPMR in practise, minimum assumptions should be taken about the distributions underlying the true regression function.

In our regression problem we maximise the minimum probability, symbol Ω. The future predicted results of the regression model will be within some bound $\pm\ \varepsilon$ of the true regression function. Here we test MPMR on real world data using liquid limit and plastic limit inputs to predict compaction parameters like OMC and MDD and further predict CBR of soil. By this we then identify and validate the accuracy of this Ω bound and thus the practicality and usefulness of such a regression model.

It is developed by constructing dichotomy classifier (Strohmann and Grudic, 2002). The relation between input(x) and output(y) is given below.

$$y = \sum_{i=1}^{N} \beta_i K(x_i, x) + b \qquad (1)$$

where N is the number of datasets, $K(x_i, x)$ is kernel function, β_i and b is the output of MPMR. In this, PL and LL has been used as inputs of the MPMR. The output of MPMR is OMC and MDD.

The total datasets will be divided into the following two classes.

$$u_i = \left(y_i + \varepsilon, x_{i1}, x_{i2}, \ldots x_{in} \right) \qquad (2)$$

$$v_i = (y_i - \varepsilon, x_{i1}, x_{i2}, \ldots x_{in}) \qquad (3)$$

The classification boundary between u_i and v_i is regression surface.

For developing MPMR, the dataset have been divided into the following two groups:

1. **Training Dataset:** This is adopted to develop the MPMR model. This article uses 120 dataset as training dataset (Table 2).
2. **Testing Dataset:** This is used to verify the developed MPMR. The remaining 25 dataset has been used as testing dataset (Table 2).

Similar method is adopted for the case of Soaked CBR value with the inputs being PL, LL, OMC and MDD (Table 3). Likewise, the dataset is divided into 95 training and 17 testing.

The dataset is normalized between 0 and 1. Radial basis function has been adopted as kernel function. The program of MPMR has been constructed by using MATLAB.

3.2 Extreme Learning Machine (ELM)

Artificial Neural Network (ANN) has been playing major role in the development of machine learning models due to advantages in flexibility, nonlinearity, fault tolerance, etc. Recently Extreme Learning Machine (ELM) has made great progress in single-layer hidden feedforward neural network (SLFN) instead of classical gradient based algorithms like the Gaussian distribution.

ELM has not only developed for conventional SLFN but also has extended towards generalized SLFN that need not be neural like and this has further led to state-of-the-art results in many applications both for regression problems and pattern recognition problems (R. Nian et al., 2014). Here hidden node parameters are randomly chosen and the output weights can be analytically determined at extremely fast learning speeds and requiring least human interference.

Many ELM variation have been proposed that have numerous regression based applications. For instance random hidden layer feature mapping based ELM improves stability during calculation of output weights in ridge regression theory. Kernel based ELM uses corresponding kernel instead of hidden layer feature and the dimensionality of the hidden layer feature space need not be specified. The fully complex ELM has universal approximation capability. The incremental ELM shows efficiently and practically to build a incremental feed-forward network with wide activation capabilities, where hidden nodes are added individually. The OS-ELM (online sequential ELM) can be trained by feeding data not only in-

Table 2. Database for OMC and MDD prediction of fine-grained soils

Sl. No.	LL (%)	PL (%)	OMC (%)	MDD (g/cc)	Sl. No.	LL (%)	PL (%)	OMC (%)	MDD (g/cc)
Training									
1	47.5	22	19	16.66663	61	39	20	21.1	16.0784
2	28	18	16.8	18.03918	62	85	38	28	13.19605
3	73.4	51.9	44.4	11.09801	63	46	20.2	16.8	16.27447
4	61	28	19	16.0784	64	46.5	20	18	16.66663
5	48.8	20.8	18.7	16.60781	65	43	23	15.9	16.01957
6	42	21	20	16.0784	66	59	24	16	16.96075
7	65	24	16.8	16.86271	67	42.5	20	19.5	16.47055
8	45	26	18	15.90193	68	39	24	19	16.49996
9	23.5	15	14	17.3333	69	43	22	19	16.47055
10	37.5	21	16.5	16.56859	70	35	18	17.6	17.8431
11	40	20	17	16.76467	71	27	16	16.4	17.54898
12	23.4	15.1	12.8	19.098	72	44	24	20	16.19996
13	26.5	12.5	14	18.33329	73	36.5	20	14.9	16.78428
14	48.3	22.5	15.5	16.88232	74	62	24	20.5	15.78428
15	58	26	17.5	16.76467	75	48.9	20.5	18.2	17.17643
16	31.5	17.5	14.5	17.5882	76	57	27	23.2	16.19604
17	36.5	22	16	16.66663	77	61	42	29	13.49997
18	58.7	45.2	39.7	12.19605	78	59	27	21.1	14.70585
19	64	27	22	15.49016	79	59.5	27	19.8	14.80389
20	29	19	14	17.74506	80	41.6	21	19.4	16.82349
21	38.5	20.6	21	16.0784	81	43	18	19	16.5882
22	38	19	18.68	16.66663	82	42	24	19.2	16.49996
23	44	24	20	16.19604	83	57	25	18.5	16.56859
24	41	23	20.9	16.15683	84	60	29	21	15.88232
25	63	27	18.7	16.0784	85	66	29	20.5	16.27447
26	27.5	16.5	14	17.598	86	43	19.2	17.7	15.88232
27	25	14	15	18.23525	87	29	15	14.57	16.76467
28	28.2	17.6	13.7	18.3	88	47	24	20.5	16.96075
29	56	28	17	16.66663	89	36	21.5	17	17.15683
30	44.5	23	21.9	16.56859	90	39	20	15	17.32349
31	29.5	17.5	15	17.49996	91	71	29.7	22	14.51958
32	38	19	20	17.45094	92	44.4	22	18.6	17.25486
33	39	29.5	24	15.19605	93	25	18	12	18.07839
34	30	16	17.6	17.54898	94	56	24	18.8	16.47055
35	47	21	19	16.68624	95	69	31	24	15.69604
36	36	19	16	16.66663	96	53	26	25.5	15.29408
37	60	25	19	16.40192	97	28.5	16.5	14.5	17.91173
38	25.5	14.5	17.9	17.15683	98	37	20.5	16.5	16.76467

continued on following page

Table 2. Continued

Sl. No.	LL (%)	PL (%)	OMC (%)	MDD (g/cc)	Sl. No.	LL (%)	PL (%)	OMC (%)	MDD (g/cc)
39	58	25	15.9	17.15683	99	48	21.3	21.2	15.99996
40	42	17	17.4	16.56859	100	23	15	11.5	18.52937
41	33	20	14.3	17.51957	101	25.5	13.5	13	17.74506
42	31	12	16.5	18.52937	102	36	24.9	21	16.3
43	59.8	27.5	20.8	16.76467	103	55.5	21	20	16.00977
44	40.5	18	18.8	17.45094	104	60	25	19	16.37251
45	60	30	17.3	14.70585	105	60	28	22	16.01957
46	24.5	12.5	14	18.16663	106	26.5	17	13	17.90192
47	37	18	16.2	17.90192	107	65	24	19.5	15.98036
48	39	18	19.5	17.94114	108	68	49.7	29.4	12.94115
49	45	20	18.6	17.45094	109	26.5	17	12.8	17.91173
50	28	19	13.9	17.96074	110	36	21.5	17	17.15683
51	43	22	18	15.39212	111	37	20	17.88	14.99997
52	55	30	21	15.95095	112	58.5	32.1	28	14.19605
53	29	18	13.4	17.26467	113	24	14	16.5	17.44114
54	40.4	21.9	18.5	16.18624	114	58	28	20	16.17644
55	38.7	21	19.2	16.37251	115	78	26	24	15.75487
56	53	24	13	17.05879	116	38	21	20	16.0784
57	28	21	14.3	17.2	117	26	15	14.5	17.45094
58	35.5	21.5	16.5	16.76467	118	112	43	25	14.51958
59	37	17.9	16.5	16.72545	119	58.5	25	22	15.99996
60	40.5	19.5	17	16.17644	120	31	17	15.6	17.74506
Testing 1					**Testing 2**				
1	56	24	14.8	17.549	1	55	25	15	17.598
2	59	25	14.9	17.4509	2	54	26	14.1	18.0392
3	60	25	19	16.3725	3	26.5	15	18	16.7647
4	89	47	32	14.3	4	37.2	24.1	17.8	16.5838
5	52	27	17	17.66	5	100	27	34	13.598
6	50	18	16.04	15.96	6	44	22	17.49	16.26
7	32.5	32.5	15.5	18.0392	7	52	26	14.6	17.7451
8	57	27	15.3	17.2549	8	63.3	51.5	30.53	13.7255
9	39	18.5	20.85	15.9804	9	32.8	19.2	20.19	16.5686
10	37	20	21	15.9804	10	28.1	15.7	13.8	18.1385
11	42	21	19.89	14.9019					
12	42.5	17	19.7	16.2745					
13	35.8	22.5	18.6	16.6623					
14	53	23	14.4	17.8431					
15	22.3	16.2	13.8	18.0914					

dividually but in bundles or chunks. It discards the observations as soon as the learning procedure has been completed. The optimally pruned ELM starts with many hidden nodes but gradually eliminates the non-essential nodes that have low relevance to the learning process.

In SLFN, the relation between input(x) and output(y) is given below:

$$\sum_{i=1}^{L} \beta_i g_i x_j \left(\ \right) = \sum_{i=1}^{L} \beta_i G\left(a_i, b_i, x_j\right) = y_j \tag{4}$$

where L is the number of hidden layers, g denotes the non-linear activation function and β is weight.

The above equation (4) can be written in the following way.

$$H\beta = T \tag{5}$$

where

$$H = \begin{bmatrix} G\left(a_1, b_1, x_1\right) & \cdots & G\left(a_L, b_L, x_1\right) \\ \vdots & \ddots & \vdots \\ G\left(a_1, b_1, x_N\right) & \cdots & G\left(a_L, b_L, x_N\right) \end{bmatrix}_{N \times L} , \ \beta = \begin{bmatrix} \beta_1^T \\ \vdots \\ \beta_L^T \end{bmatrix} \text{ and } T = \begin{bmatrix} y_1^T \\ \vdots \\ y_N^T \end{bmatrix}_{N \times m} .$$

The value of β is determined from the following equation

$$\beta = H^{-1}T \tag{6}$$

where H^{-1} is the Moore–Penrose generalized inverse of hidden layer output matrix.

ELM employs the same training dataset, testing dataset and normalization technique as used by the MPMR model. Radial basis function has been used as activation function for developing the ELM model. The program of ELM has been constructed by using MATLAB.

3.3 Limitations of Artificial Neural Networks

Varghese et al. (2013) used Artificial Neural Network (ANN) for prediction of OMC and MDD based on Liquid Limit (LL) and Plastic Limit (PL). He suggests that for ANN model it is more efficient to use all influential input parameters which can be determined by laboratory tests. A major drawback was that ANN gives less insight into the underlying physical relationship between each input variable and predicted variable.

Along with this, ANN has the following limitations which indicate the need of improved algorithms like MPMR and ELM:

- ANN has some inherent drawbacks such as slow convergence speed, less generalizing performance, arriving at local minimum and over-fitting problems.

Table 3. Database for Soaked CBR prediction of fine grained soils

Sl. No.	LL (%)	PL (%)	OMC (%)	MDD (g/cc)	Soaked CBR (%)	Sl. No.	LL (%)	PL (%)	OMC (%)	MDD (g/cc)	Soaked CBR (%)
Training											
1	57	27	23.2	1.652	1.4	49	36	19	16	1.7	5.5
2	66	29	20.5	1.66	3.8	50	37	20.5	16.5	1.71	4.12
3	56	24	18.8	1.68	4.1	51	37	20	17.88	1.53	3
4	57	25	18.5	1.69	4.3	52	35.5	21.5	16.5	1.71	2.65
5	61	28	19	1.64	3	53	36	21.5	17	1.75	4
6	26.5	12.5	14	1.87	7.8	54	43	23	15.9	1.634	4.98
7	26.5	17	13	1.826	10.86	55	36.5	20	14.9	1.712	4.64
8	38	21	20	1.64	2.5	56	40.5	19.5	17	1.65	2.38
9	38.5	20.6	21	1.64	2.4	57	46.5	20	18	1.7	5.64
10	23.5	15	14	1.768	10.88	58	44.5	23	21.9	1.69	4.12
11	25.5	13.5	13	1.81	13	59	42	21	20	1.64	3.5
12	58	26	17.5	1.71	4.5	60	38	19	18.68	1.7	3
13	60	30	17.3	1.5	2.5	61	29.5	17.5	15	1.785	6.31
14	65	24	16.8	1.72	3.9	62	43	22	19	1.68	4
15	64	27	22	1.58	1.8	63	47	24	20.5	1.73	3.2
16	60	25	19	1.67	4	64	40.5	18	18.8	1.78	4.45
17	26.5	17	12.8	1.827	11.5	65	40	20	17	1.71	2.5
18	56	28	17	1.7	4.6	66	45	20	18.6	1.78	4.45
19	78	26	24	1.607	2.4	67	47	21	19	1.702	2.65
20	28.5	16.5	14.5	1.827	7.3	68	36.5	22	16	1.7	4.85
21	37	17.9	16.5	1.706	3.2	69	41	23	20.9	1.648	3.91
22	29	18	13.4	1.761	11	70	48.8	20.8	18.7	1.694	3.5
23	41.6	21	19.4	1.716	3.9	71	40.4	21.9	18.5	1.651	4.41
24	24	14	16.5	1.779	7.75	72	48.3	22.5	15.5	1.722	3.9
25	59	27	21.1	1.5	1.8	73	36	21.5	17	1.75	4
26	27.5	16.5	14	1.795	7.27	74	46	20.2	16.8	1.66	3.5
27	30	16	17.6	1.79	6.5	75	25	14	15	1.86	8.5
28	47.5	22	19	1.7	2.3	76	43	18	19	1.692	3.36
29	37.5	21	16.5	1.69	2.5	77	42	17	17.4	1.69	4.58
30	31	17	15.6	1.81	8.5	78	39	20	15	1.767	4.5
31	43	19.2	17.7	1.62	3	79	43	22	18	1.57	2.24
32	25	18	12	1.844	18.3	80	42.5	20	19.5	1.68	4.8
33	39	20	21.1	1.64	2.2	81	48.9	20.5	18.2	1.752	3.25
34	26	15	14.5	1.78	10	82	44.4	22	18.6	1.76	3.75
35	33	20	14.3	1.787	7.3	83	53	24	13	1.74	4.5
36	58	28	20	1.65	2.5	84	53	26	25.5	1.56	1.69
37	24.5	12.5	14	1.853	7.9	85	58.5	25	22	1.632	2.51
38	38.7	21	19.2	1.67	2.8	86	28	19	13.9	1.832	10.25

continued on following page

Table 3. Continued

Sl. No.	LL (%)	PL (%)	OMC (%)	MDD (g/cc)	Soaked CBR (%)	Sl. No.	LL (%)	PL (%)	OMC (%)	MDD (g/cc)	Soaked CBR (%)
39	60	28	22	1.634	2	87	59.5	27	19.8	1.51	2
40	23	15	11.5	1.89	15.1	88	28	18	16.8	1.84	7.5
41	59	24	16	1.73	4.7	89	58	25	15.9	1.75	4.9
42	31	12	16.5	1.89	7	90	63	27	18.7	1.64	3.2
43	39	18	19.5	1.83	5.8	91	31.5	17.5	14.5	1.794	5.6
44	38	19	20	1.78	4	92	29	19	14	1.81	9.18
45	35	18	17.6	1.82	6.5	93	65	24	19.5	1.63	3.5
46	62	24	20.5	1.61	2.3	94	25.5	14.5	17.9	1.75	6.8
47	27	16	16.4	1.79	5.9	95	55.5	21	20	1.633	1.7
48	60	29	21	1.62	2.5						
Testing 1						**Testing 2**					
1	37	20	21	1.63	3.21	1	55	25	15	1.795	4.88
2	42	21	19.89	1.52	3.28	2	63.5	25.5	15.9	1.8	3.52
3	42.5	17	19.7	1.66	3	3	62	30	15.7	1.77	3.9
4	52	26	14.6	1.81	5.6	4	53	23	14.4	1.82	5.4
5	56	24	14.8	1.79	5.2	5	54	26	14.1	1.84	5.8
6	59	25	14.9	1.78	5.1	6	57	27	15.3	1.76	5.1
7	60	25	19	1.67	4	7	39	18.5	20.85	1.63	2.4
8	26.5	15	18	1.71	5	8	47	25.3	22.6	1.5	2.26
9	37	21.5	21.4	1.55	3.14						

- Park and Rilett (1999) stated that unlike other statistical models, ANN does not provide information about the relative importance of the various parameters
- According to Kecman (2001), the knowledge acquired during the training of the model is stored in an implicit manner and hence it is very difficult to come up with reasonable interpretation of the overall structure of the network.
- The neural network parameters, are optimized, based on a training dataset. Silverman et al. (2000) suggest if the distribution of the training datasets changes dramatically, the method usually does not project, i.e., ANN is usually considered to have good skills when the input data belong to a distribution similar or close to the distribution of the training dataset.

4. Dataset Used for Training Both the Models

This study uses the dataset used by Varghese et al. (2013) for formulation of Multiple Regression Model and Artificial Neural Network Model for OMC, MDD and Soaked CBR.

4.1 OMC and MDD

The following table (Table 2) lists the dataset used to train both MPMR and ELM models for the prediction of OMC and MDD using input as Liquid Limit (LL) and Plastic Limit (PL). The table has 3 Datasets namely Training, Testing 1 and Testing 2. The Testing 2 data was used by Varghese et al (April 2013) to validate their ANN model. This study uses combined Testing 1 and Testing 2 data to validate the MPMR and ELM models developed here.

4.2 Soaked CBR

The following table (Table 3) lists the dataset used to train both MPMR and ELM models for the prediction of soaked CBR using input as LL, PL, OMC and MDD. The table has 3 Datasets namely Training, Testing 1 and Testing 2. The Testing 2 data was used by Varghese et al. (April 2013) to validate their ANN model. This study uses combined Testing 1 and Testing 2 data to validate the MPMR and ELM models developed here.

5. Results and Discussion

5.1 Performance of MPMR

For developing MPMR, the design values of ε and σ have been determined by trial and error approach. The developed MPMR gives best performance at $\varepsilon = 0.007$ and $\sigma = 0.2$ for prediction of OMC. Figure 1 depicts the performance of MPMR for prediction of OMC using 2 input parameters – Liquid Limit and Plastic Limit (Table 2). This article uses Coefficient of Correlation (R) to assess the performance of the developed MPMR. For a good model, the value of R should be close to one. It is observed from figure 1 that the value of R is close to 1 for training as well as testing datasets. For prediction of MDD the design values of ε and σ are 0.001 and 0.3 respectively. Figure 2 illustrates the performance of

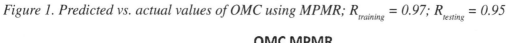

Figure 1. Predicted vs. actual values of OMC using MPMR; $R_{training} = 0.97$; $R_{testing} = 0.95$

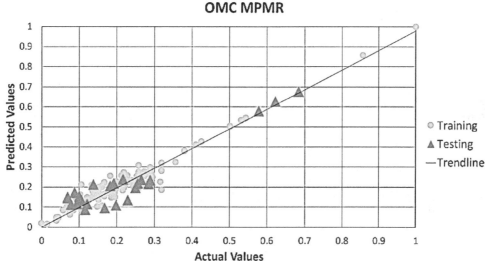

Figure 2. Predicted vs. actual values of MDD using MPMR; $R_{training}$ = 0.97; $R_{testing}$ = 0.97

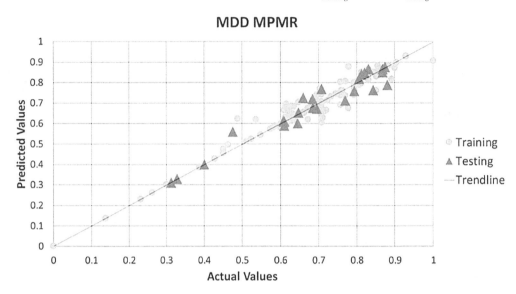

MPMR for prediction of MDD again using the inputs Plastic Limit and Liquid Limit. The dataset used is the same as that used in previous case (Table 2). As shown in figure 2, the value of R is close to one for training as well as testing datasets. The data used for Soaked CBR (Table 3) was different from that used for OMC and MDD and the input parameters this time were 4 – LL, PL, OMC and MDD. This time, the best performance was achieved at ε = 0.002 and σ = 0.4. Figure 3 shows the performance of the MPMR model developed for Prediction of Soaked CBR. With higher number of inputs, the results are even better in case of soaked CBR. So, the developed models prove their ability for prediction of OMC, MDD and Soaked CBR.

Figure 3. Predicted vs. actual values of Soaked CBR using MPMR; $R_{training}$ = 0.99; $R_{testing}$ = 0.99

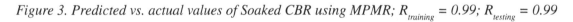
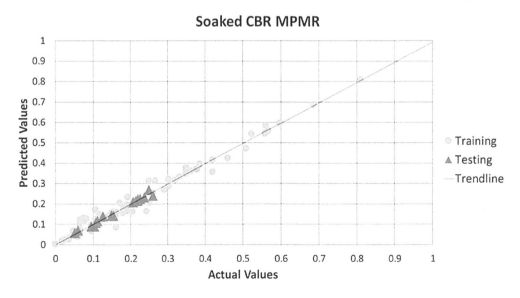

5.2 Performance of ELM

The performance of ELM depends on the number of hidden nodes. The design number of hidden nodes is determined by trial and error approach. For prediction of OMC, the developed ELM gives best performance for 5 hidden nodes. It uses the same input parameters as used for the case of OMC using MPMR (Table 2). Figure 4 depicts the performance of ELM for prediction of OMC. For the case of MDD, the developed ELM gives best performance at 7 hidden nodes. Again, the same input dataset used for the MPMR model of MDD is used. Figure 5 illustrates the performance of ELM for prediction of MDD. Finally, the ELM prediction model soaked CBR is developed using the Table 3 dataset (same as the MPMR model of Soaked CBR) with the best performance observed at 4 hidden nodes. Figure 6 shows the performance of the ELM model developed for Soaked CBR. As shown in figures 4, 5 and 6, the value of R is close to one.

5.3 Comparison with ANN Model of Varghese et al. (2013)

The performance of ANN model developed by Varghese et al (2013) gives close results for the prediction of OMC which are slightly better than MPMR and ELM but the difference in performance was not enormous and both MPMR and ELM are as reliable as ANN for the case of OMC. However, the accuracy of the ANN predictions for MDD casts serious doubts on its performance. In this case, The MPMR performs exceptionally with the ELM not far behind. The Soaked CBR predictions were very accurate for all the three cases with MPMR once again taking the credit of giving the best results. As seen in the Table 4, the MPMR model has the best accuracy of prediction in two cases. The ELM model, although not as accurate as MPMR, certainly is a better substitute for ANN.

Figure 4. Predicted vs. actual values of OMC using ELM; $R_{training} = 0.96$; $R_{testing} = 0.94$

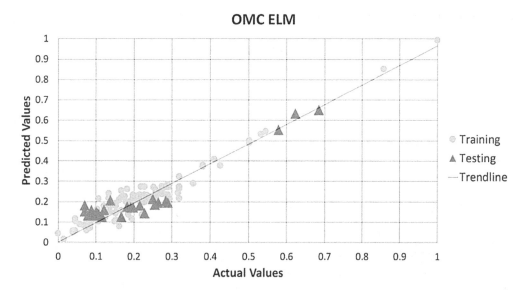

Figure 5. Predicted vs. actual values of MDD using ELM; $R_{training}$ = 0.94; $R_{testing}$ = 0.9

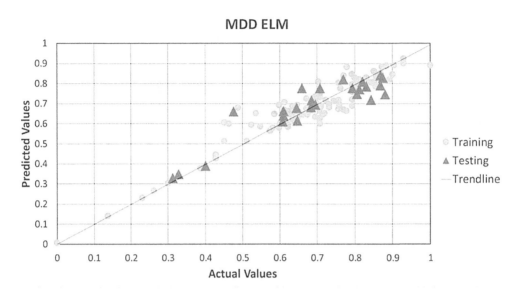

5.4 Sensitivity Analysis

To further investigate the weightage and influence of the considered parameters namely Plastic Limit, Liquid Limit, Optimum Moisture Content and Maximum Dry Density a sensitivity analysis is performed. The sensitivity analysis investigates the contribution of the input parameters to the output prediction. For the sensitivity analysis, a simple procedure is proposed. The sensitivity percentage of the output to each input parameter is determined using the following formulae:

Figure 6. Predicted vs. actual values of Soaked CBR using ELM; $R_{training}$ = 0.97; $R_{testing}$ = 0.966

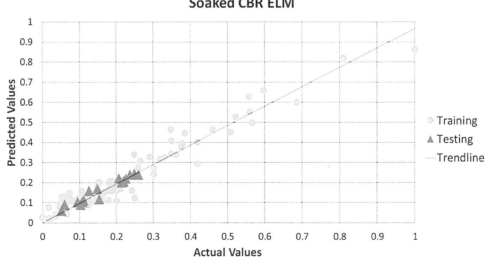

Table 4. Comparison of Co-relation Coefficient (R) values obtained from testing data for MPMR & ELM models developed in this study and ANN model developed by Varghese et al (2013)

Predicted Engineering Properties of Fine Grained Soils	Input Parameters Used	Co-Relation Coefficient (R) for MPMR Model	Co-Relation Coefficient (R) for ELM Model	Co-Relation Coefficient (R) for ANN Model*
OMC	PL and LL (Table 2)	0.95	0.94	0.97
MDD	PL and LL (Table 2)	0.97	0.94	0.77
Soaked CBR	PL, LL, OMC and MDD (Table 3)	0.99	0.966	0.93

* The Co-relation Coefficient obtained in the ANN model is only from the Testing 2 data (Table 2 and 3).

$$N_i = f_{max}\left(x_i\right) - f_{min}\left(x_i\right)$$

$$S_i = \frac{N_i}{\sum_{j=1}^{n} N_j} \times 100$$

where $f_{max}(xi)$ and $f_{min}(xi)$ are, respectively, the maximum and minimum of the predicted output over the ith input domain, where other variables are equal to their mean values.

The resulting analysis points towards how much a certain parameter would influence the models' (MPMR and ELM) decision to predict the initial OMC and MDD values from the basic PL and LL values and finally how much of an influence all of PL, LL, OMC and MDD values will have on the final prediction of soaked CBR value by our MPMR and ELM models. It can be asserted, from Table 5 and Table 6, that when both MPMR and ELM models try to predict the OMC and MDD values its decision is considerably influenced by the Plastic Limit of the soil. Finally, while predicting the soaked CBR

Table 5. Sensitivity Analysis of Output parameters when MPMR was used

% Sensitivity	PL	LL	OMC	MDD
OMC	65.13	34.86		
MDD	60.45	39.55		
Soaked CBR	6.758878	26.9276	29.90975	36.40377

Table 6. Sensitivity Analysis of Output parameters when ELM was used

% Sensitivity	PL	LL	OMC	MDD
OMC	67.78	32.22		
MDD	66.21	33.79		
Soaked CBR	4.2387	28.6547	32.30456	34.8

value using LL, PL, OMC and MDD as new inputs, the MPMR model's decision is most influenced by the MDD value followed by the OMC and LL values while the PL value has very little significance here. Similarly while predicting the soaked CBR value using LL, PL, OMC and MDD as new inputs, the ELM model's decision is most influenced by the MDD value followed by the OMC value and then LL value. Even while using ELM it is shown that PL value has very little significance.

5.5 Error and Performance Analysis

Error and Correlation Functions

$$MAE = \frac{\sum_{i=1}^{n} |h_i - t_i|}{n}$$

$$RMSE = \sqrt{\frac{\sum_{i=1}^{n} (h_i - t_i)^2}{n}}$$

$$\rho = \frac{RMSE}{mean(h_i)} \frac{1}{R+1}$$

where h_i and t_i are respectively the measured and predicted OMC, MDD or Soaked CBR values for the ith output, mean(h_i) is the average of the measured outputs, and n is the total number of samples.

The performance and errors for both MPMR and ELM models is shown in Table 7 and Table 8 The performance of MPMR and ELM is encouraging.

Table 7. Error and performance analysis for MPMR

MPMR	Training Data of OMC	Testing Data of OMC	Training Data of MDD	Testing Data of MDD	Training Data of Soaked CBR	Testing Data of Soaked CBR
MAE	0.02316	0.04362	0.02304	0.02987	0.01578	0.00761
RMSE	0.03393	0.05199	0.03680	0.04114	0.02471	0.01007
R	0.97000	0.94900	0.97100	0.96700	0.99000	0.98800
ρ	0.07931	0.12135	0.02747	0.03033	0.05872	0.03096

Table 8. Error and performance analysis for ELM

ELM	Training Data of OMC	Testing Data of OMC	Training Data of MDD	Testing Data of MDD	Training Data of Soaked CBR	Testing Data of Soaked CBR
MAE	0.03028	0.04862	0.03693	0.04929	0.03341	0.01422
RMSE	0.04064	0.05604	0.05161	0.06735	0.04548	0.01756
R	0.95700	0.94200	0.94300	0.94300	0.96800	0.96600
ρ	0.09564	0.13129	0.03908	0.05027	0.10927	0.05462

CONCLUSION

Along with describing the methodology of MPMR and ELM, this study describes as to how these two alternative models can be used for prediction OMC, MDD and Soaked CBR. Two types of dataset have been utilized to construct the MPMR and ELM models. The study also compares the resulting MPMR and ELM models and the accuracy of their predictions of soaked CBR and compaction characteristics with the accuracy of predictions given by ANN model. The result is that values predicted using MPMR and ELM are more accurate than those predicted using neural network models.

As stated by Varghese et al (2013), the performance of neural networks improves as the number of input parameters increase. Thus for neural network analysis, the use of relatively less influential input parameters along with stronger parameters is definitely beneficial. Although, as it is seen from the results, the neural network model for MDD gave rather unreliable values and the level of accuracy was too low to implement in practice. The reason being lack of input parameters. This is where both MPMR and ELM prove themselves a lot more accurate and reliable over the neural networks. Both the models have maintained high standards of accuracy even in the scarcity of input data. Obviously, the MPMR and ELM were bound to perform well when the number of input parameters were increased i.e. in case of Soaked CBR. It was also not at all surprising that both of them bettered the already close accuracy shown by ANN.

Researchers can use the developed models as quick tools for prediction of Compaction Characteristics and Soaked CBR value. The developed models can be employed to solve different problems in geotechnical engineering.

REFERENCES

Anghel, C. I., & Ozunu, A. (2006). Prediction of gaseous emissions from industrial stacks using an artificial intelligence method. *Chemical Papers*, *60*(6), 410–415. doi:10.2478/s11696-006-0075-z

Bechtler, H., Browne, M. W., Bansal, P. K., & Kecman, V. (2001). New approach to dynamic modelling of vapour-compression liquid chillers: Artificial neural networks. *Applied Thermal Engineering*, *21*(9), 941–953. doi:10.1016/S1359-4311(00)00093-4

Chandrasekhar, B. P., Vinayak Rao, V. R., & Prasada Raju, G. V. R. (2003). A comprehensive study of soil CBR assessment through Clegg's Impact test, Field and Laboratory CBR test. *Indian Highways*, *31*(7), 39–45.

Cheng, Q. H., & Liu, Z. X. (2006, August). Chaotic load series forecasting based on MPMR. In *Machine Learning and Cybernetics 2006 International Conference* (pp. 2868-2871). IEEE. doi:10.1109/ICMLC.2006.259071

Gandomi, A. H., Yun, G. J., & Alavi, A. H. (2013). An evolutionary approach for modeling of shear strength of RC deep beams. *Materials and Structures*, *46*(12), 2109–2119. doi:10.1617/s11527-013-0039-z

Gandomi, M., Soltanpour, M., Zolfaghari, M. R., & Gandomi, A. H. (2014). Prediction of peak ground acceleration of Iran's tectonic regions using a hybrid soft computing technique. *Geoscience Frontiers*. doi:10.1016/j.gsf.2014.10.004

Gregory, G. H., & Cross, S. A. (2007, June 24-27). Correlation of CBR with Shear Strength Parameters. *Proceedings of 9th International Conference on Low Volume Roads*, Austin, Texas.

Huang, G. B., Zhu, Q. Y., & Siew, C. K. (2006). Extreme learning machine: Theory and applications. *Neurocomputing, 70*(1), 489–501. doi:10.1016/j.neucom.2005.12.126

Huang, K., Yang, H., King, I., & Lyu, M. R. (2006). Maximizing sensitivity in medical diagnosis using biased minimax probability machine. *Biomedical Engineering. IEEE Transactions on, 53*(5), 821–831.

Indian Standards. (1982). *Specification for compaction mould assembly for light and heavy compaction test for soils* (IS 10078-1982).

Indian Standards. (1983). *Methods of Test for Soils: Part 8 - Determination of Water Content – Dry Density Relation using Heavy Compaction* (IS 2720.8-1983).

Indian Standards. (1985). *Methods of Test for Soils: Part 5 - Determination of Liquid and Plastic Limit* (IS 2720.5-1985).

Indian Standards. (1987). *Methods of Test for Soils: Part 16 - Laboratory Determination of CBR* (IS 2720.16-1987).

Indian Standards. (1993). *Methods of Test for Soils: Part 9 - Determination of Dry Density-Moisture Content Relation by Constant Mass of Soil Method* (IS 2720.8-1983).

IRC. (n. d.). 37-1970,Guidelines for Flexible Pavement Design, *Indian Road Congress*, New Delhi 1970

IRC. (n. d.). 37-2001, Guidelines for Flexible Pavement Design. *Indian Road Congress*, New Delhi 2001

Jaakkola, T., & Haussler, D. (1999). Probabilistic kernel regression models. *Proceedings of the 1999 Conference on AI and Statistics* (Vol. 126, pp. 00-04).

Karunaprema, K.A.K., & Edirisinghe, A.G.H.J. (2002). A Laboratory study to establish some useful relationship for the case of Dynamic Cone Penetration. Electronic journal of Geotechnical Engineering, 7.

Kaur, S., Boveja, V. B., & Agarwal, A. (2011). Artificial Neural Network Modeling for Prediction of CBR. *Indian Highways, 39*(1), 31–38.

Kecman, V. (2001). *Learning and soft computing: support vector machines, neural networks, and fuzzy logic models*. MIT press.

Kumar, P., et el (2000). An Indigenous Impact Tester for measuring Insitu CBR of Pavement Materials (No 63, 13-22). Highway Research Bulletin, IRC.

NCHRP. (2003). *Guide for mechanistic-empirical design of new and rehabilitated pavement structures* (p. 61820). Illinois: National Co–operative Highway Research Program Transportation Research Board National Research Council.

Ng, J. K., Zhong, Y., & Yang, S. (2007). A comparative study of Minimax Probability Machine-based approaches for face recognition. *Pattern Recognition Letters, 28*(15), 1995–2002. doi:10.1016/j.patrec.2007.05.021

Nian, R., He, B., Zheng, B., Van Heeswijk, M., Yu, Q., Miche, Y., & Lendasse, A. (2014). Extreme learning machine towards dynamic model hypothesis in fish ethology research. *Neurocomputing, 128,* 273–284. doi:10.1016/j.neucom.2013.03.054

Pandian, N. S., Nagaraj, T. S., & Manoj, M. (1997). Re-examination of compaction characteristics of fine-grained soils. *Geotechnique, 47*(2), 363–366. doi:10.1680/geot.1997.47.2.363

Park, D., & Rilett, L. R. (1999). Forecasting freeway link travel times with a multilayer feedforward neural network. *Computer-Aided Civil and Infrastructure Engineering, 14*(5), 357–367. doi:10.1111/0885-9507.00154

Patel, R. S., & Desai, M. D. (2010). CBR Predicted by Index Properties of Soil for Alluvial Soils of South Gujarat. *Proceedings of the Indian Geotechnical Conference (Vol. I,* 79-82).

Ramasubbarao, G. V., & Siva Sankar, G. (2013). Predicting Soaked CBR value of fine grained soils using index and compaction characteristics. *Jordan Journal of Civil Engineering, 7*(3).

Roy, T. K., Chattopadhyay, B. C., & Roy, S. K. (2009). Prediction of CBR from Compaction Characteristics of Cohesive Soil. *Highway Research Journal*, July-Dec., 77-88.

Saklecha, P. P., Katpatal, Y. B., Rathore, S. S., & Agarwal, D. K. (2012). ANN Modeling for Strength Characterization of Subgrade Soil in a Basaltic Terrain. *Proceedings of ICAMB-2012* (pp. 1215–1220).

Satyanarayana Reddy, C. N. V., & Pavani, K. (2006). Mechanically Stabilised Soils-Regression Equation for CBR Evaluation, Dec. 14-16, 731-734, *Proceedings of Indian Geotechnical Conference*-2006, Chennai, India.

Shahin, M. A., Jaksa, M. B., & Maier, H. R. (2008). State of the art of artificial neural networks in geotechnical engineering. *Electronic Journal of Geotechnical Engineering, 8,* 1–26.

Silverman, D., & Dracup, J. A. (2000). Artificial neural networks and long-range precipitation prediction in California. *Journal of Applied Meteorology, 39*(1), 57–66. doi:10.1175/1520-0450(2000)039<0057:AN NALR>2.0.CO;2

Sridharan, A., & Nagaraj, H. B. (2005). Plastic limit and compaction characteristics of fine grained soils. *Proceedings of the ICE-Ground Improvement, 9*(1), 17–22. doi:10.1680/grim.2005.9.1.17

Strohmann, T., & Grudic, G. Z. (2002). *A formulation for minimax probability machine regression* (pp. 769–776). Advances in Neural Information Processing Systems.

Tao, D., Li, X., Wu, X., Hu, W., & Maybank, S. J. (2005, November). Supervised tensor learning. In *Data Mining Fifth IEEE International Conference* (p. 8). IEEE. doi:10.1007/s10115-006-0050-6

Varghese, V. K., Babu, S. S., Bijukumar, R., Cyrus, S., & Abraham, B. M. (2013). Artificial Neural Networks: A Solution to the Ambiguity in Prediction of Engineering Properties of Fine-Grained Soils. *Geotechnical and Geological Engineering, 31*(4), 1187–1205. doi:10.1007/s10706-013-9643-5

Venkatasubramanian, C., & Dhinakaran, G. (2011). ANN model for predicting CBR from index properties of soils. *International Journal of Civil & Structural Engineering, 2*(2), 614–620.

Venkatraman, T. S., & Samson, M., & Ambili, T.S. (1995). Correlation between CBR and Clegg Impact Value. Proc. Nat. Sem. On emerging trends in Highway Engineering, Centre for Transportation Engineering, Bangalore (Vol. 1, pp. 25.1-25.5).

Vinod, P., & Reena, C. (2008). Prediction of CBR Value of Lateritic Soils Using Liquid Limit and Gradation Characteristics Data. *Highway Research Journal, IRC, 1*(1), 89–98.

Wang, G., Zhao, Y., & Wang, D. (2008). A protein secondary structure prediction framework based on the extreme learning machine. *Neurocomputing, 72*(1), 262–268. doi:10.1016/j.neucom.2008.01.016

Wang, L. (Ed.). (2005). *Support Vector Machines: theory and applications* (Vol. 177). Springer.

Yildrim, B., & Gunaydin, O. (2011). Estimation of CBR by Soft Computing Systems. *Expert Systems with Applications* (Vol. *38*, 6381–6391). Elsevier. doi:10.1016/j.eswa.2010.12.054

Chapter 16
An Intelligent Approach for Virtual Chemistry Laboratory

Shikha Mehta
Jaypee Institute of Information Technology, India

Monika Bajaj
University of Delhi, India

Hema Banati
Dyal Singh College, India

ABSTRACT

Formal learning has shifted from the confines of institutional walls to our home computers and even to our mobiles. It is often felt that the concept of e-learning can be successfully applied to theoretical subjects but when it comes to teaching of science subjects like chemistry where hands on practical training is must, it is inadequate. This chapter presents a hybrid approach (amalgamation of concepts of machine learning technique with soft computing paradigm) to develop an intelligent virtual chemistry laboratory (IVCL) tool for simulating chemical experiments online. Tool presents an easy to use web based interface, which takes as input the reactants and presents results in the form of - type of reaction occurred and the list of possible products. Technically, the IVCL tool utilizes naïve bayes algorithm to classify the type of reactions and then applies genetic algorithm inspired approach to generate the products. Subsequently it employs system of equations method to balance the reactions. Experimental evaluations reveal that proposed IVCL tool runs with 95% accuracy.

1. INTRODUCTION

The emergence of Internet and information technologies has given an unprecedented boost to e-learning. Learning over internet has added a new dimension to traditional education system. It has enabled the learners to not only access the educational resources across the globe but also interact with others and engage in effective and attractive learning experiences (Welsh et al., 2003). Recent findings of Project Tomorrow (2014) revealed that 50% of middle school students who took online classes apart from their

DOI: 10.4018/978-1-4666-9474-3.ch016

regular school level felt that online learning makes it easier for them to succeed. Around 50 percent of virtual high school students preferred their way of learning in school and 32 percent of traditional high school students also preferred the e-learning mode. It was also observed that 53% of students wanted their schools to allow them use their own mobile devices to support their schoolwork. These e-learning systems seek to bridge the digital divide i.e. to fill the gap in the skills of teachers and learners and focus on providing the facilities of online teachers / mentors and virtual laboratories to implement the taught theory in the virtual world. For example massive open online course (MOOC) is an online course aimed at unlimited participation and open access via the web. In addition to traditional course materials such as videos, readings, and problem sets, MOOCs facilitates the interactions of the users with students, professors, and teaching assistants, thereby forming the virtual communities (Pappano, 2014; Lewin, 2013). EdX (https://www.edx.org) provides a platform for students and institutions seeking to transform themselves through cutting-edge technologies, innovative pedagogy, and rigorous courses. Coursera (https://www.coursera.org/) is an education platform that partners with top universities and organizations worldwide, to offer free online courses. MIT OpenCourseWare (OCW) (ocw.mit.edu) is an open web-based publication of virtually all MIT course content and is available to the world. OCW enables the educators to improve courses and curricula, making their schools more effective. Students find additional resources to help them succeed and enrich their lives by tackling difficult challenges. Open Yale Courses (oyc.yale.edu) provide free and open access to a selection of introductory courses taught by distinguished teachers and scholars at Yale University. Thus, this digital era has completely transformed the conventional teaching and learning styles. Although a big advantage, these platforms provide only the course materials to be studied and understood by the students without any practical experience. However learning theory without practice is like body without soul. Laboratory experience is a key factor in technical and scientific education. The concept of "learning by doing" (Bruner, 1990) emphasizes that laboratories are important components of education to make students to gain experience. The importance of laboratory experience in engineering education (and other fields) has long been recognized such that experimental skills are considered crucial in the sciences as well as computer science (Tichy, 1998). Thus in this era of technology assisted education, virtual laboratories are indeed essential for the students. Virtual Laboratories concept was defined as "laboratory experiment without real laboratory with its walls and doors. It enables the learner to link between the theoretical aspect and the practical one, without papers and pens. It is electronically programmed in computer to simulate the real experiments inside the real laboratories." (Harry & Edward, 2005). Woodfield (2005) defined virtual laboratories as the learning environments in which students convert their theoretical knowledge into practical knowledge by conducting experiments. In addition, it was defined as "A virtual studying and learning environment aims at developing the lab skills of students. This environment is located on one of the internet pages. Usually, this page has main page & many links, which are related to laboratory activities and its achievements (Zaitoon, 2005). These laboratories provide an opportunity to the students to repeat any incorrect experiment and deepen the intended experiences (Ardac & Akaygun, 2004 Jeschke, Richter, & Zorn, 2010). Thus, virtual laboratories offer the learning experience of a physical laboratory without the limitations of time, location, material and equipments (Harding, 2003). It was also emphasized that virtual laboratories are not only beneficial from the organization and economic point but also enhance learning of the students (Wolf, 2010). Virtual Laboratory concept has been expanded to advanced opportunities for integrated teaching, research and promoting cross-disciplinary research (Rauwerda et al., 2006). Studies have been performed to identify what students can learn from virtual labs. Results indicate that students found virtual lab experiments likeable, easy and quick to do (Wendy &

Kurt, 2013). Although, they could have learned more by doing real world labs, it took less time and was less stressful and gave them better grades. It was also established that lectures alone can only partially contribute to student learning, lab components are almost equally important. Bose (2013) observed that virtual labs were commonly used outside regular lab hours, often late in the night and over the weekend. Thus virtual laboratories provide an opportunity to the students to learn and practice at their own pace. To create online interactive media which would help students learn difficult concepts in various domains, "Virtual Labs (2014)" Project initiative has been taken by the Ministry of Human Resource Development (MHRD), Govt. of India, under the National Mission on Education through ICT. As a part of this initiative, a virtual laboratory for Basic Electronics has been developed with the objective to perform experiments in the Basic Electronics labs virtually, and yet have close to real life experience. The success of virtual laboratories has already been realized in various domains such as development of multimedia-based laboratory experiments or virtual lab was found to be effective for civil engineers (Yarbrough and Gilbert, 1999), molecular biology (2001), virtual geotechnical laboratory (Wyatt et al., 2000) and networking laboratory (Kinnari et al., 2007). Wang et al. (2013) reviewed the various studies that incorporate technologies in school science laboratories. Investigations revealed that majority of these studies addressed the areas of physics, chemistry and biology. Among these, Chemistry plays an important role in every person's daily activities from the moment they are born, for example chemical reactions occur in all our activities of breathing, eating, sitting or reading etc. It is one of the subjects whose understanding remains totally curtailed without performing laboratory experiments.

Chemistry is the branch of science that deals with molecules and their transformations. Chemical principles (NCERT, 2013) prevail in all spheres of life such as weather patterns, functioning of brain and operations of a computer etc. Chemical industries manufacturing fertilizers, pesticides, dyes, drugs, polymers, soaps, shampoos, detergents, metals, alloys and other inorganic and organic chemicals etc play a significant role in improving the national economy. Human needs such as food, health care products and other materials aimed at improving the quality of life are all met through chemicals. This is exemplified by the production of a variety of life saving drugs such as cisplatin and taxol, are effective in cancer therapy and AZT (Azidothymidine) used for helping AIDS victims, have been isolated from plant and animal sources or prepared by synthetic methods. Due to its immense usage and huge significance in real life, teaching and learning chemistry has been observed as the crucial requisite of entire education system. Thus chemistry is taught as mandatory course in K-12 curriculum and subsequently the whole carrier can be pursued in this field. Practice makes a man perfect is the best demonstrated by a subject like chemistry. Laboratory experiments are the bridge that connects theoretical knowledge to the practical application. Thus all organizations need to maintain laboratories for learning and performing chemical reactions. Laboratory experiments are an imperative part for development and testing of all chemical products. However, in developing / under developed countries, there are large numbers of constraints to perform experiments in the chemistry laboratories due to the non-availability of necessary reactants, experiment apparatus etc. Besides, a number of safety measures also need to be taken and all experiments have to be performed in a constrained environment. Some experiments may be hazardous and all laboratories may not be suitably furnished for such experiments. Lack of resources such as laboratory or equipment or insufficient lab conditions therefore make laboratory accessibility a critical issue. Therefore, there is no option for the students or teachers who want to prepare or practice at home. Besides, the common problem among students community is that they find it is exasperating to physically go into a chemistry lab and perform different experiments. Thus, several studies have emphasized the development of virtual laboratories in chemistry education. Mintz (1993) accentuated that one of the most promising computer applications in science instruction is the use of simulations for teaching material that cannot be taught by conventional laboratory experimentation. However the question is, whether these simulations should be used as supplementary or complementary. Climent-Bellido et al. (2003) performed a study to evaluate the software's influence on engineering student understanding of basic organic chemistry laboratory techniques. It was observed that virtual chemistry laboratories help students gain better understanding of the subject and contributed more towards improving the performance of students with greatest learning difficulties. Kerr et al. (2004) compared achievement among students instructed using hands-on chemistry labs versus those instructed using virtual chemistry labs (elabs). Their study demonstrated that students who completed the virtual labs performed equally well as the students who completed the traditional, hands-on labs. Josephsen and Kristensen (2006) performed a study to elucidate the undergraduate chemistry students' response to the SimuLab computer-based learning environment. Laboratory assignments were simulated to enhance the students' experience and knowledge of chemical reactions and the physical and chemical properties of common inorganic compounds. The results revealed that the students enjoyed working with the simulated programs and found it motivating and easy to learn. Winberg et al (2007) developed a computer-simulated pre-lab with the aim to prepare students cognitively to real lab activity about acid-base titration. It was observed that simulation influenced students toward posing more theoretical questions during their laboratory work and exhibited a more complex, correct use of chemistry knowledge in their interviews. Tuysuz (2010) studied the effect of virtual laboratory on 9th grade students' achievement and attitude in chemistry. Results established that virtual laboratory applications made positive effects when compared to conventional methods.

All these studies emphasize that technology assisted laboratory experiments may serve as boon for the chemistry education. In this respect various tools are available for simulating chemical experiments for the organic chemistry e.g. Virtual Chemistry Lab v2.0 (www.chemistry.dortikum.net) tool provides a multimedia interface that allows the user to select apparatus for an experiment, and a limited number of reactants to drag into the experiment area and gives the name of the product formed. Although due efforts have been made to provide real chemistry laboratory experience, it is limited in database and does not imbibe any intelligence to inform the user about the kind of reaction taking place. A VRML (Virtual Chemistry Laboratory Incorporating Reusable Prototypes for Object Manipulation) (Dalgarno, B. (2005)) deals completely with the interface part, and has no functionality. It employs VRML (Virtual Reality Modeling Language) to design 3D models of the virtual chemistry laboratory for navigation and motion control and for manipulating objects within the environment. It provides a good 3D experience of a chemistry laboratory but there is no provision to perform any experiments. Virtual Computational Chemistry Laboratory (www.vcclab.org) provides a series of web based software tools based on three-tier architecture that allow the users to perform molecular properties calculations and data analysis on Internet. However, the software tools are very rigid as they cannot be transferred between different computer platforms and laboratories and does not provide results and explanations of reactions which is the basic necessity of a chemistry student or enthusiast. Virtlab: A Virtual Laboratory tool developed by Simpson & Company (www.virtlab.com/index.aspx) provides a web based platform for students and teachers to perform experiments and then review them. However, this tool does not provide an extensive set of reactions and experiments and it requires paid registration to perform the simulations. The ChemCollective (chemcollective.org/vlabs) is a collection of virtual labs with scenario-based learning activities which can be used by students and teachers as pre-lab activities rather than actual laboratory experiments. The set

Model ChemLab (http://modelscience.com/products.html) and Online Chem Labs (www.onlinechemlabs.com/) are both commercial software platforms to perform interactive chemistry laboratory experiments virtually. However, these tools are too costly to be afforded by the student community.

These studies indicate that the prevailing virtual chemistry laboratories either provide limited functionality for the learners to perform experiments or a big amount needs to be paid to fulfill their needs. Moreover, these software tools have been developed using database and graphics programs that have replaced the manual approaches. Although, these tools are time saving, employ algorithms for simply creating a solution path that requires a complete set of data and a predicate set of steps defined by the programmer(Padhy, 2010). Since chemistry is the branch of science that is not limited to the amount of knowledge that a person has. It imbibes multiple laws that define the principles of chemistry which a user may not be aware of yet. This derives a need to develop a virtual chemistry laboratory tool using artificial intelligence techniques that would have the capability to overcome this weakness by studying the behavior of many substances under varied conditions. This tool would ultimately learn to account for the intricate details when computing the results of a given reaction. This chapter presents a framework to develop an intelligent virtual chemistry laboratory (IVCL) tool to automate the task of simulating inorganic chemical equations for learning practical aspects of chemistry. The framework primarily employs naïve bayes algorithm to classify the type of reactions that will occur based on the inputs provided by the user. Thereafter, genetic algorithm based approach is used to generate the products. Finally, the IVCL tool utilizes system of equations method to balance the reactions. The organization of the chapter is as follows: section 2 presents the related work followed by the framework for intelligent virtual chemistry laboratory tool in section 3. Experiments and results are given in section 4, followed by conclusion and future work in section 5.

2. RELATED WORK

Intelligent Systems have witnessed a significant growth in the recent years. Researchers have identified and acknowledged the potential of intelligence systems to deal large complex and dynamic real world problems. These systems transformed the human cognitive process into machine intelligence and the center of this revolution is soft computing techniques that include fuzzy systems, probabilistic reasoning, neural networks and evolutionary computation. Zadeh (Zadeh, 1981) asserted that soft computing techniques provide a solid foundation for the conception, design, and application of intelligent systems employing its methodologies symbiotically rather than in isolation. Fuzzy systems (Zadeh 1965, 1973) are associated with approximate reasoning which attempts to model the human reasoning process at a cognitive level (Kosko, 1997). It acquires knowledge from domain experts which is encoded within the algorithm in terms of the set of if-then rules. The system employs this rule-based approach and interpolative reasoning to respond to new inputs (Cherkassky, 1998). Neural networks focuses on simulation of neurological mechanisms of human brain. It stores knowledge in a distributive manner within its weights which have been determined by learning from known samples. The generalization ability of new inputs is then based on the inherent algebraic structure of the neural network. Probabilistic reasoning such as Bayesian belief networks (Bayes, 1763) and the DempsterShafer theory of belief (Dempster, 19967; Shafer 1976), provides a mechanism for evaluating the outcome of systems affected by randomness or other types of probabilistic uncertainty. An important advantage of probabilistic reasoning is its ability to update previous outcome estimates by conditioning them with newly available evidence (Judea, 1997). Evolutionary Computation refers to computing techniques that mimic the organizational principal of natural creatures into mathematical models to solve complex problems. These computing techniques are mainly categorized into evolutionary algorithms and swarm intelligence based algorithms. Swarm intelligence represents the algorithms and distributed problems-solvers that are inspired by the cooperative group intelligence of swarm or collective behaviour of insect colonies and other animal societies (Bonabeau et. al., 1999). These algorithms are composed of many individuals that are self-organized and coordinate using decentralized control. In order to accomplish complex and difficult tasks these system focuses on the collective behavior that results from local interactions of the individuals with each other and with their environment. Evolutionary algorithm is a term used to describe algorithms that are inspired by 'survival of the fittest' or 'natural selection' principles (Holland, 1975). The generic evolutionary algorithm starts with problem specific fixed sized population called chromosomes. Each chromosome in the population represents a randomly generated solution to the problem and has fitness value that is determined by the value of the function to be optimized. These chromosomes evolve over generations and reproduce better solutions. During each generation genetic new population is produced by applying crossover and mutation operators on current population. Crossover is the key operator, which makes these algorithms converge to a good solution. The idea behind crossover is that two or more individuals with high fitness values will create one or more new offspring (children) that inherits the features of their parents. Mutation is another reproduction operator used for finding new points in the search space. It is performed by randomly selecting one chromosome from the population and then arbitrarily changing some of its information. It is generally used with a crossover operator to diversify the population. It helps in avoiding premature convergence to a sub-optimal solution by introducing new genetic material to the evolutionary process. This iterative process goes on till the fitness value has reached some predefined threshold or maximum number of generations has passed. The main paradigms of evolutionary computation include ant colony optimization (ACO), particle swarm optimization (PSO), artificial bee colony (ABC), firefly algorithm (FA), differential algorithm (DE) and genetic algorithm (GA).

Due to their vast success in diverse fields, genetic algorithms have gained more popularity over other algorithms. Genetic algorithms (Mitchell, 1998) are adaptive heuristic search techniques inspired by the Darwin's theory of survival of the fittest and Goldberg's (Goldberg, 1989) idea of natural evolution. They are randomized search and optimization techniques guided by the principle of natural genetic systems. Genetic algorithms (GA) were developed by John Holland and colleagues at the University of Michigan in 1965. In GA, solution to a given problem is represented in the form of a string called as chromosome. Each string consists of a set of elements called 'genes'. In GA, new chromosomes are produced through crossover and mutation operators. Crossover involves the selection of two chromosomes and thereafter exchange of genetic material to the right of the meeting point of these two chromosomes. Fitness of each chromosome is computed using its objective function. Mutation is a rare process that resembles a sudden change in the genes of an individual. Due to its immense capability to model complex and dynamic real world problems GA has been used in varied applications of science and engineering (Eiben and Smith 2003; Mitchell, 1997) ranging from jet engines to autonomous adaptive agents (Forrest 1993; Lipson and Pollack 2000). The potential of GA has also been established in varied web based applications and one of its prominent applications is E-learning. E-learning refers to, education via Internet, network, or stand-alone computer etc. Its applications and processes include web-based learning, computer-based learning, virtual classrooms and digital collaboration. It is essentially the network-enabled transfer of skills and knowledge. It enables the learners to connect and explore educational resources around the globe. Selection and delivery of appropriate learning contents to learners are the main challenging tasks of e-learning, because the learning content must be provided to an acceptable level of the learner's understanding. Thus many researchers have explored the utility of genetic algorithms for developing personalized e-learning systems (Tan et al, 2012), determining an optimal learning path for each learner (Huang et al., 2007), evaluating learning achievements (Cheng et al., 2011), to optimize the performance of e-learning system for recommending appropriate study material to the users (Salehi et al., 2013), to create the appropriate sequence of the teaching resources from the set of all possible (Hovakimyan, 2004) and to seek an optimal path starting from the learner profile to the pedagogic objective passing by intermediate courses (Azough, 2010) etc. Nevertheless all these studies employed genetic algorithm to provide appropriate study material of theoretical courses only and that too in general. Practical aspect of the courses is also left untouched by these web based education systems. Although, for some courses, practical experiments may not be vital but understanding science subject like chemistry cannot be imagined without laboratory experiments. Therefore chemistry scientists have employed genetic algorithm to solve the problems prevailing in this domain such as Macromolecular Structure Prediction (Lucasius et al., 1991), QSAR (Rogers & Hopfinger, 1994), Molecular Design (Jones, 1994), Chemical Structure Handling (Fontain, 1992), Crystallography (Chang & Lewis, 1997), predicting atomic clusters (Mestres & Scuseria, 1995), Combinatorial Libraries and Library Synthesis (Sheridan & Kearsley, 1995), and Drug Design (Douguet et al., 2000) etc. The versatility of evolutionary algorithms in various real world problems related to chemistry has also been highlighted in various books such as evolutionary algorithms in molecular design (Clark 2000) and Soft Computing approaches in Chemistry (Hugh and Les, 2003). The wide range of research problems solved using these computational methods include conformational analysis, de novo molecular design, chemical structure handling, combinatorial library design, and the study of protein folding etc.

Thus, it can be inferred from the above studies that research scientist have either aimed at developing intelligent systems to optimize the performance of e-learning systems or to generate optimal solutions in chemical industries. The development of web based intelligent system for the students to learn and practice chemistry is left to be studied. In this respect, the chapter presents an intelligent approach to develop virtual chemistry laboratory for the chemistry enthusiast. Next section presents the detailed framework for intelligent virtual chemistry laboratory.

3. FRAMEWORK FOR INTELLIGENT VIRTUAL CHEMISTRY LABORATORY (IVCL)

Chemistry is a vast subject with major classification into organic and inorganic chemistry. Organic chemistry is the study of carbon and its compounds. Industries like polymer industries, petrochemical industries and pharmaceutical industries etc depend on organic chemists. On the other hand inorganic chemistry involves the study of inorganic compounds such as salts. It is the study of everything except carbon. Other classifications include physical chemistry, industrial chemistry, analytical chemistry, biochemistry and nuclear chemistry etc. A wide range of tools have been developed for organic chemistry, and large databases are already available as it is more methodical and systematic. Inorganic chemistry on the other hand can be quantified but has a large number of exceptions and anomalies. Nevertheless, this branch of chemistry also runs on a set of rules and methods. Presented IVCL tool provides solutions for the inorganic chemistry reactions. The various categories of reactions in inorganic chemistry are as shown in Table 1.

Table 1. Classification of reactions

S. No.	Type of Reaction	General Form	Example
1	Decomposition Reactions	$XY \rightarrow X + Y$	$2\,H_2O \rightarrow 2H_2 + O_2$ $2\,HgO \rightarrow 2Hg + O_2$
2	Synthesis/Combustion Reaction	$X + Y \rightarrow XY$	$2CO(g) + O_2\,(g) \rightarrow 2\,CO_2\,(g)$
3	Single Displacement Reaction	$X + YZ \rightarrow XZ + Y$(if X is a metal) $X + YZ \rightarrow YX + Z$(if X is a nonmetal)	$Zn\,(s) + CuSO_4\,(aq) \rightarrow Cu\,(s) + ZnSO_4\,(aq)$
4	Double Displacement Reaction	$WX + YZ \rightarrow WY + XZ$	$CaCl_2\,(aq) + 2AgNO_3\,(aq)$ $\rightarrow Ca(NO_3)_2(aq) + AgCl(s)$

1. **Decomposition Reaction:** In a decomposition reaction one chemical compound is broken down into smaller compounds or separate elements under the suitable conditions. It is the reverse of a synthesis reaction. These reactions are found in abundance in nature but do not take place under normal laboratory circumstances. They usually require heat, light, electric current or some other external catalyst to propagate such phenomenon.

2. **Synthesis/Combustion Reaction:** Synthesis reaction or a direct combination reaction is a type of chemical reaction in which two or more simple substances combine to form a complex compound. The reactants may be elements or compound. The product is always a compound. A combustion reaction is a type of redox reaction in which a combustible material combines with an oxidizer to form oxidized products and generate heat.

3. **Single Displacement Reaction:** A single displacement reactions occur when one element replaces another in a compound. These reactions are characterized by an atom or ion of a single compound replacing an atom of another element that is a metal can replace a metal (+) or a nonmetal can replace a nonmetal (-).

4. **Double Displacement**: In double displacement reactions, elements from two compounds displace each other to form new compounds i.e. reactions occur when a metal replaces a metal in a compound and a nonmetal replaces a nonmetal in a compound. These reactions may also occur when one product is removed from the solution as a gas or precipitate to form a weak electrolyte in solution.

Therefore, the presented tool primarily identifies the class of chemical reaction and thereafter generates the products and balances the equations. The Figure 1 depicts the framework of Intelligent Virtual Chemistry Laboratory (IVCL) tool for inorganic chemical reactions. It begins with input data given by the user in the form of reactants of the chemical equation to be solved. The reactants are primarily classified based on their characteristics to identify the type of reaction to take place. Classification of chemical reaction is performed using artificial intelligence technique- Naïve Bayes classifier. Subsequently, based on the category of reaction and the type of reactants, products are formed using an evolutionary algorithm inspired approach that is Genetic algorithm. After forming the products, an important task in chemistry is to balance the equations. It is performed using System of Equations method. As a result, balanced chemical equations with potential products are presented to the user. Overall functionality of the tool is divided into three phases:

Figure 1. Framework for Virtual Chemistry Laboratory (VCL)

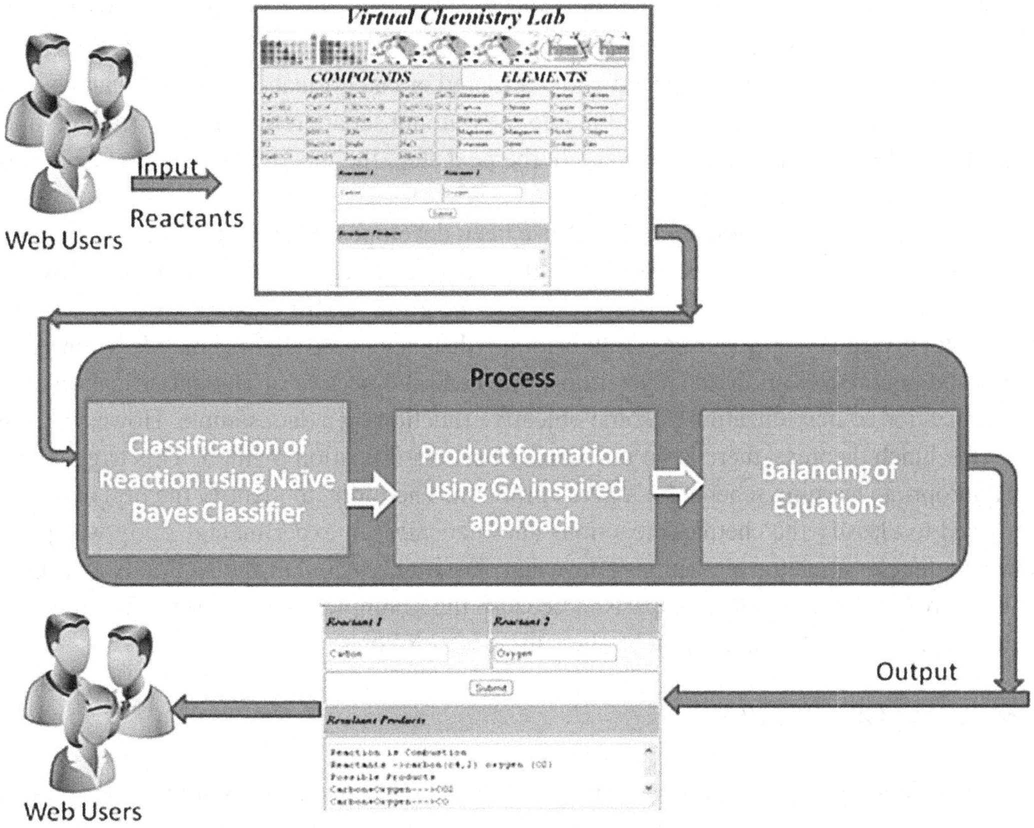

Phase I: Classification using Naïve Bayes classifier.
Phase II: Product formation using Genetic Algorithm inspired approach.
Phase III: Balancing of Equations.

3.1 Classification using Naïve Bayes Classifier

Classification is one of the most popular data mining technique that refers to the task of assigning objects to one of several predefined categories (Steinbach et al., 2007) It is a well-known problem that encompasses many diverse applications such as image and pattern recognition, detecting spam email messages, categorizing cells as malignant or benign, loan approval, detecting faults in industry applications and classifying galaxies based on their shapes etc.

Definition (Classification). Classification is the task of learning a *target function f* that maps each attribute set *x* to one of the predefined label *y*. The target function is also known informally as a *classification model* (Dunham, 2003).

To solve real world problems, classification is implemented as a two-step process. In the first step, a classifier is built describing a predetermined set of data classes or concepts. This is known as the learning step or training phase. In this step, a classification algorithm is used to build the classifier by analyzing or "learning from" a training set made up of database tuples and their associated class labels. A tuple, P, is represented by an n-dimensional attribute vector, $P = (p_1, p_2, \ldots, p_n)$, depicting n measurements made on the tuple from n database attributes, respectively, $A_1, A_2, \ldots, A_n$. Each tuple P is assumed to belong to a predefined class as determined by another database attribute called the class label attribute. The class label attribute may be discrete-valued and unordered or categorical in that each value serves as a category or class. The individual tuples making up the training set are referred to as training tuples and are selected from the database under analysis. In the next step, the model is used for classification i.e. to classify tuples from the target database.

A wide variety of classification algorithms have been developed during the last few decades. These algorithms employ different theories to generate the model such as decision tree, probabilistic model, network of interconnected neurons etc. Based on these theories, various classification algorithms (Figure 2) are categorized as statistical based algorithms, distance based algorithms, decision tree based algorithms and neural network based algorithms. The central objective of any classification algorithm is the minimization or maximization of some objective function on a data sample. However, according to the no-free lunch theorem, there is no universally best classification method. This triggers the need to select appropriate learning scheme for a given problem. Therefore, to identify the best algorithm that could be used to classify the chemical reactions automatically, an experimental study was performed over four popular classification algorithms (Bayesian classifier, C4.5, ID3 and Neural Networks). Other algorithms have not been used for comparison because their complexity increases with the increase in size of datasets. The detailed discussion of algorithms is as follows:

3.1.1 Bayesian Classification

Bayesian classifiers are one of the most popular and widely used statistical classifiers. They predict class membership based on probabilities such as the probability that a given tuple belongs to a particular class. Bayesian classification is based on Bayes theorem and assumes that the effect of an attribute value on a given class is independent of the values of other attributes. The Naïve Bayesian classifier works as follows (Han & Kamber, 2000):

Figure 2. Classification algorithms

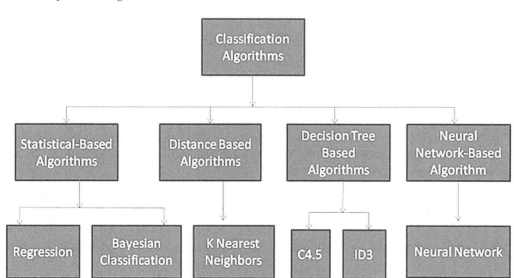

Step 1: Let D be the training set of tuples and their associated class labels. Each tuple is represented by an n-dimensional attribute vector, $X = (x_1, x_2, …, x_n)$, depicting n measurements made on the tuple from n attributes, respectively, $A_1, A_2, …., A_n$.

Step 2: Suppose that there are m classes, $C_1, C_2, …., C_m$. Given a tuple, X, the classifier predicts that X belongs to the class having the highest posterior probability, conditioned on X. That is, the naïve Bayesian classifier predicts that tuple X belongs to the class C_i if and only if

$$P\left(C_i \mid X\right) > P\left(C_j \mid X\right) \text{ for } 1 \leq j \leq m, j \neq i \tag{1}$$

Thus, $P\left(C_i \mid X\right)$ is maximized. The class C_i for which $P\left(C_i \mid X\right)$ s maximized is called the maximum posteriori hypothesis. By Bayes' theorem (Equation 2),

$$P(C_i \mid X) = P(X \mid C_i)P(C_i) / P(X) \tag{2}$$

Step 3: As P(X) is constant for all classes, only $P(X|C_i)$ $P(C_i)$ need to be maximized. If the class prior probabilities are not known, then it is commonly assumed that the classes are equally likely, that is, $P(C_1) = P(C_2) = …….. = P(C_m)$, and $P(X|C_i)$ is maximized else $P(X|C_i)$ $P(C_i)$ is maximized. The class prior probabilities may be estimated by $P\left(C_i\right) = \dfrac{\left|C_{i,D}\right|}{|D|}$. where $\left|C_{i,D}\right|$ is the number of training tuples of class C_i in D.

Step 4: In the data sets with large number of attributes, it is extremely computationally expensive to compute $P(X|C_i)$. Therefore, to reduce computation in evaluating $P(C_i)$, it is assumed that the values of the attributes are conditionally independent of one another, given the class label of the tuple (i.e., that there are no dependence relationships among the attributes). Thus,

$$P\left(X \mid C_i\right) = \prod_{k=1}^{n} P\left(x_k \mid C_i\right) = P\left(x_1 \mid C_i\right) \times P\left(x_2 \mid C_i\right) \times ….. \times P\left(x_2 \mid C_i\right) \tag{3}$$

The probabilities $P\left(x_1 \mid C_i\right) \times P\left(x_2 \mid C_i\right) \times …… \times P\left(x_n \mid C_i\right)$ n be easily estimated from the training tuples. Here x_k refers to the value of attribute A_k for tuple X. Computation of $P(X|C_i)$ is performed based on whether the attribute is categorical or continuous-valued as follows:

If A_k is categorical, then $P\left(x_k \mid C_i\right)$ is the number of tuples of class C_i in D having the value x_k for A_k, divided by $|C_{i,D}|$, the number of tuples of class C_i in D.

If A_k is continuous-valued, it assumes to have a Gaussian distribution with a mean μ and standard deviation, defined by

$$g(x, \mu, \sigma) = \frac{1}{\sqrt{2\pi}\sigma} e^{\frac{(x-\mu)^2}{2\sigma^2}} \tag{4}$$

so that

$$P\left(x_k \mid C_i\right) = g\left(x_k, \mu_{c_i}, \sigma_{c_i}\right)$$

where μ_{c_i} and σ_{c_i}, are the mean and standard deviation values respectively of the values of attribute A_k for training tuples of class C_i.

Step 5: To predict the class label of X, $P(X|C_i)P(C_i)$ is evaluated for each class C_i. The classifier predicts that the class label of tuple X is the class C_i if and only if

$$P\left(X \mid C_i\right)P\left(C_i\right) > P\left(X \mid C_j\right)P\left(C_j\right) \; for 1 \leq j \leq m, j \neq i \tag{5}$$

So, the predicted class label is the class C_i for which $P(X|C_i)P(C_i)$ is the maximum.

3.1.2 Classification using Decision Tree

The Decision tree approach is one of most useful and popular technique in classification problems. This technique involves construction of a tree to model the classification process. Once the tree is built, it is applied to each tuple in the database and results in a classification of that tuple.

Definition: Given a database $D = \{t_1, \ldots, t_n\}$ where $t_i = (t_{i1}, \ldots, t_{ih})$ and the database schema contains the following attributes $\{A_1, A_2, \ldots, A_h\}$. Also given is a set of classes $C = \{C_1, C_2, \ldots, C_h\}$. A decision tree (DT) or classification tree is a tree associated with D that has the following properties (Dunham, 2003):

- Each internal node is labeled with an attribute A_i.
- ch arc is labeled with a predicate that can be applied to the attribute associated with the parent.
- Each leaf node is labeled with a class C_j.

Thus solving a classification problem is a two-step process:

- Decision tree induction: Construct a DT using training data (Figure 3).
- For each $t_i \in D$, apply the DT to determine its class.

In the algorithm, parameter D refers to a data partition. Initially, it is the complete set of training tuples and their associated class labels. The parameter attribute_list is a list of attributes describing the tuples. Attribute_selection_method specifies a heuristic procedure for selecting the attribute that "best" discriminates the given tuples according to class. Decision tree algorithms vary mainly according to an attribute selection measure adopted, such as information gain (ID3 algorithm) or the gain ratio (C4.5 algorithm) as discussed in the subsequent sections.

Figure 3. Decision tree algorithm
(Han & Kamber, 2000).

Algorithm: Generate_decision_tree. Generate a decision tree from the training tuples of data partition D.

Input:

- Data partition,D,which is a set of training tuples and their associated class labels;
- attribute_list,the set of candidate attributes;
- Attributte _selection_method,a procedure to determine the splitting criterion that "best" partitions data tuples into individual classes. This criterion consists of a splitting_attribute nd,possibly, either a split point or splitting subset.

Output: A decision tree.

Method:
```
(1) create a node N;
(2) if tuples in D are all of the same class,C then
(3)     return N as a leaf node labeled with the class C;
(4) if attribute_list is empty then
(5)     return N as a leaf node labeled with the majority class in D;
// majority voting
(6) apply Attribut_ selection_method(D,attribute_list) to find the
"best" splitting_criterion;
(7) label node N with splitting_criterion;
(8) if splitting_attribute is discrete-valued and multiway splits
allowed then // not restricted to binary trees
     attribute_list ← attribute_ list-splitting_attribute; //
remove splitting attribute
(10) for each outcome j of splitting_criterion
     // partition the tuples and grow subtrees for each partition
(11) let Dj be the set of data tuples in D satisfying outcome j; // a
partition
(12) if Dj is empty then
        attach a leaf labeled with the majority class in D to node N;
(14) else attach the node returned by
Generate_decision_tree(Dj,attribute list) to node N;
     endfor
(15) return N;
```

3.1.2.1 ID3 Algorithm

ID3 algorithm employs information gain as its attribute selection measure. This measure is based on the concept of information theory by Claude Shannon which studied the value or "information content" of messages (Shannon, 1948). Let node N represents the tuples of partition D. The attribute with the highest information gain is chosen as the splitting attribute for node N. The expected information needed to classify a tuplc in D is given by (Han & Kamber, 2000)

$$Info(D) = -\sum_{i=1}^{m} \log_2(p_i) \tag{6}$$

where p_i is the probability that an arbitrary tuple in D belongs to class C_i, which is estimated by $|C_{i,D}|/|D|$. A log function to the base 2 is used as the information is encoded in bits. Info (D) refers to the average amount of information needed to identify the class label of a tuple in D. Info (D) is also known as the entropy of D.

Suppose, the tuple D is partitioned on some attribute A having v distinct values, $\{a_1, a_2, \ldots.a_v\}$, as observed from the training data. Attribute A can be used to split D into v partitions or subsets, $\{D_1, D_2, \ldots.., D_v\}$, where Dj contains those tuples in D that have outcome a_j of A. This amount is measured by

$$Info_A(D) = \sum_{j=1}^{v} \frac{|D_j|}{|D|} \times Info(D_j) \tag{7}$$

where $\dfrac{|D_j|}{|D|}$ acts as the weight of the jth partition. $Info_A(D)$ is the expected information required to classify a tuple from D based on the partitioning by A. It is assumed that smaller the expected information required, greater is the purity of the partition. Thus, information gain is computed as the difference between the original information requirement (i.e., based on just the proportion of classes) and the new requirement (i.e., obtained after partitioning on a particular attribute A).

$$Info\_gain = Info(D) - \sum_{j=1}^{m} p(D_j) Info(D_j) \tag{8}$$

In other words, Info_gain tells us how much would be gained by branching on A. It is the expected reduction in the information requirement caused by knowing the value of A. The attribute A with the highest information gain, Info_gain, is chosen as the splitting attribute at node N. This approach minimizes the expected number of tests needed to classify a given tuple and guarantees that a simple tree is found.

3.1.2.2 C4.5 Algorithm

The information gain measure as discussed in the previous section is biased toward tests with many outcomes. It prefers to select the attributes having large number of values as the information gained by partitioning on this attribute is maximam. C4.5, a successor of ID3, uses an extension to information gain known as gain ratio, which attempts to overcome this bias. It applies a kind of normalization to information gain using a "split information" value defined analogously with Info (D) as

$$SplitInfo_A(D) = -\sum_{j=1}^{v} \frac{|D_j|}{|D|} \times \log_2\left(\frac{|D_j|}{|D|}\right) \tag{9}$$

This value represents the potential information generated by splitting the training data set, D, into v partitions, corresponding to the v outcomes of a test on attribute A. The gain ratio is defined as

$$GainRatio(A) = \frac{Info\_gain}{SplitInfo(A)} \tag{10}$$

Thus, the attribute with the maximum gain ratio is selected as the splitting attribute to generate the tree.

3.1.3 Neural Networks

Neural Network (NN) is an information processing paradigm that is inspired by the information processing mechanism of biological nervous systems, such as the brain. The information processing system is composed of a large number of highly interconnected processing elements (neurons) working in unison to solve specific problems. A neural network is a learning algorithm associated with a set of connected input/output units in which each connection has a weight associated with it. During the learning phase, the network learns by adjusting the weights in order to predict the correct class label of the input tuples. Neural networks involve long training times and are therefore more suitable for applications where this is feasible. The basic neural network algorithm used for data classification is Backpropagation algorithm which is as follows (Figure 4):

- **Initialize the Weights:** The weights in the network are initialized to small random numbers (e.g., ranging from-1.0 to 1.0 or -0.5 to 0.5). Each unit has a *bias* associated with it that is initialized to small random numbers. Each training tuple, X, is processed by the following steps.
- **Propagate the Inputs Forward:** First, the training tuple is fed to the input layer of the network. The inputs pass through the input units without any change e.g. for an input unit, j, its output, O_j, is equal to its input value, I_j. Thereafter, the net input and output of each unit in the hidden and output layers are computed. The net input to a unit in the hidden or output layers is computed as a linear combination of its inputs. Given a unit j in a hidden or output layer, the net input, I_j, to unit j is

$$I_j = \sum_i w_{ij} o_i + \theta_j \tag{11}$$

where w_{ij} is the weight of the connection from unit i in the previous layer to unit j; O_i is the output of unit i from the previous layer; and θ_j is the bias of the unit. The bias acts as a threshold as it tends to vary the activity of the unit. Each unit in the hidden and output layers takes its net input and then applies an activation function to it. The function symbolizes the activation of the neuron represented by the unit. Commonly used activation functions are logistic, or sigmoid, functions. Given the net input I_j to unit j, then O_j, the output of unit j, is computed as

$$O_j = \frac{1}{1 + e^{-I_j}} \tag{12}$$

Figure 4. Backpropagation algorithm
(Han & Kamber, 2000).

Algorithm: *Backpropagation. Neural network learning for classification, using the backpropagation algorithm.*

Input:
- *D, a data set consisting of the training tuples and their associated target values;*
- *l, the learning rate;*
- *network, a multilayer feed-forward network.*

Output: *A trained neural network.*

Method:

(1) *Initialize all weights and biases in network;*
(2) **while** *terminating condition is not satisfied {*
(3)   **for** *each training tuple X in D {*
(4)   *// Propagate the inputs forward:*
(5)   *for each input layer unit j {*
(6)   *$O_j = I_j$; //output of an input unit is its actual input value*
(7)   *for each hidden or output layer unit j {*
(8) $I_j = \sum_i w_{ij}o_i + \theta_j$ *//compute the net input of unit j with respect*

                To the previous layer, i

(9) $O_j = \dfrac{1}{1+e^{-I_j}}$*;}* *// compute the output of each unit j*

(10)   *// Backpropagate the errors:*
(11)   **for each** *unit j in the output layer*
(12)   *$Err_j = O_j(1-O_j)(T_j - O_j)$; // compute the error*
(13)   **for** *each unit j in the hidden layers, from the last to*
        the first hidden layer
(14)   *$Err_j = O_j(1-O_j)\sum_k Err_k w_{jk}$; // compute the error with respect to the*
                next higher layer, k
(15)   *for each weight w_{ij} in network {*
(16)   *$\Delta w_{ij} = (l)Err_j O_i$; // weight increment*
(17)   *$w_{ij} = w_{ij} + \Delta w_{ij}$;} // weight update*
(18)   *for each bias θ_j in network {*
(19)   *$\Delta\theta_j = (l)Err_j$; // bias increment*
(20)   *$\theta_j = \theta_j + \Delta\theta_j$;} // bias update*
(21)   *} }*

This function is also referred to as a *squashing function*, because it maps a large input domain onto the smaller range of 0 to 1. The logistic function is nonlinear and differentiable, allowing the backpropagation algorithm to model classification problems that are linearly inseparable. The output values, O_j, computed for each hidden layer including the output layer provide the network's prediction.

- **Backpropagate the Error:** The error is propagated backward by updating the weights and biases to reflect the error of the network's prediction. For a unit j in the output layer, the error Err_j is computed by

$$Err_j = O_j(1 - O_j)(T_j - O_j) \tag{13}$$

where O_j is the actual output of unit j, and T_j is the known target value of the given training tuple. To compute the error of a hidden layer unit j, the weighted sum of the errors of the units connected to unit j in the next layer is considered. The error of a hidden layer unit j is

$$Err_j = O_j(1 - O_j)\sum_k Err_k w_{jk} \tag{14}$$

where w_{jk} is the weight of the connection from unit j to a unit k in the next higher layer, and Err_k is the error of unit k. The weights and biases are updated to reflect the propagated errors. Weights are updated by the following equations, where Δw_{ij} is the change in weight w_{ij}:

$$\Delta w_{ij} = (l)Err_j O_i \tag{15}$$

$$w_{ij} = w_{ij} + \Delta w_{ij} \tag{16}$$

The variable l is the learning rate, a constant typically having a value between 0.0 and 1.0. The learning rate helps avoid getting stuck to a local minimum in decision space and helps in finding the global optimal value. Biases are updated according to the equations given below, where $\Delta\theta j$ is the change in bias θj:

$$\Delta\theta_j = (l)Err_j \tag{17}$$

$$\theta_j = \theta_j + \Delta\theta_j \tag{18}$$

- **Terminating Condition:** Training may be stopped when
  - All w_{ij} in the previous epoch are below some specified threshold, or
  - The percentage of tuples misclassified in the previous epoch is below some threshold, or
  - A pre specified number of epochs have expired. In practice, several hundreds of thousands of epochs may be required before the convergence of weights.

3.1.4 Comparative Study of Classification Algorithms over Benchmark Problems

Discover the best classification algorithm (discussed in Section 3.1) that could be employed to classify the chemical equations, a comparative study was performed over benchmark datasets. These dataset were primarily divided into training and test dataset. To evaluate the classification algorithm, training dataset was used to develop the classifier model and the test data was utilized to compute the accuracy of model. The efficacy of particular classifier to recognize tuples of different classes is analyzed on the basis of the confusion matrix (Table 2). As depicted in the confusion matrix for two classes, true positives refer to the positive tuples that were correctly labeled by the classifier, while true negatives are the negative tuples that were correctly labeled by the classifier. False positives are the negative tuples that were incorrectly labeled. Similarly false negatives are the positive tuples that were incorrectly labeled.

The various evaluation parameters computed using confusion matrix and used for comparison are as follows:

1. **Accuracy:** It is measured as the percentage of test set tuples that are correctly classified by the classifier

$$Accuracy = \frac{\left(TP + TN\right)}{\left(TP + TN + FP + FN\right)}$$

2. **Sensitivity and Specificity:** These parameters are mainly used for the medical data where even a small percentage of false positives or false negatives may have a severe effect. Sensitivity is referred to as the true positive rate while specificity is the true negative rate. These measures are defined as

$$Sensitivity = \frac{TP}{\left(TP + FP\right)}$$

$$Specificity = \frac{TN}{\left(TN + FN\right)}$$

3. **Receiver Operating Curve (ROC):** It is a graph based technique to visualize and select the classifiers based on their performance. These are two-dimensional graphs that depict the relative tradeoffs between costs (false positives) and benefits (true positives). Earliest usage of ROC was traced in signal detection theory to depict the tradeoff between hit rates and false alarm rates of classifiers (Eagan, 1975; Swets et al., 2000). It has been realized that measuring simple classification accuracy is often a weak metric to assess the performance (Provost and Fawcett, 1997, Provost et al., 2001). ROC graphs are computed using the confusion matrix in which fp rate is plotted on the X axis and tp rate is plotted on the Y axis where

Table 2. Confusion matrix

Actual Class		Predicted Class	
		C1	C2
	C1	True Positives(TP)	False Negatives(FN)
	C2	False Positives(FP)	True Negatives(TN)

$$TP\ rate = \frac{Positives\ Correctly\ Classified}{Total\ Positives}$$

$$FP\ rate = \frac{Negatives\ Incorrectly\ Classified}{Total\ Negatives}$$

3.1.5 Results

Study was carried out to assess the various classifiers such as Bayesian algorithm, ID3 algorithm, C4.5 algorithm and Neural Network Backpropagation algorithm over 16 real world benchmark problems (Blake and Merz, 1998). These problems were taken from varied application domains with varying number of attributes and tuples (Table 3).

Experimental study was performed using WEKA toolkit (Hall et al., 2009). Figure 5, Figure 6 and Figure 7 depict the results obtained by executing the classification algorithms over the bench mark problems. These results have been averaged over the results of all the datasets. Accuracy results (Figure 5) of the various algorithms indicate that C4.5 algorithm perform better than ID3, Naïve Bayes and the backpropagation algorithm. On the contrary, results of sensitivity (Figure 6) and specificity (Figure 7) parameters signify that Naïve Bayes algorithm shows better performance. To establish these results, cost-benefit analysis was performed using the ROC curve. Table 4 depicts the false positive (FP) rate and the True positive (TP) rate values to plot the graph.

Table 3. Benchmark datasets used to compare classification algorithms

Sr. No.	Dataset /Algorithms	No. of Attributes	No. of Instances
1	ANNEAL	33	898
2	AUDIOLOGY	70	226
3	AUTOS	11	205
4	BREAST-CANCER	10	286
5	HORSE-COLIC	16	368
6	CREDIT RANKING	10	690
7	HEART DISEASES	8	303
8	HEART DISEASES	8	294
9	HEPATITIS	14	155
10	HYPOTHROID	23	3772
11	KR-VS-KP	37	3196
12	LABOUR	9	57
13	LYMPHOGRAPHY	16	148
14	PRIMARY TUMOR	18	339
15	SICK	23	3772
16	SOYBEAN	36	683

In the graph (Figure 8), lower left point (0, 0) represents the policy of never giving a positive classification and the upper right point (1, 1) indicates the conditionally issuing positive classifications and point (0, 1) means perfect classification. Line joining the points (0,0) and point (1, 1) is known as line of no discrimination as all the point lying above this line are better classifiers while the points below this line show worse results (Fawcett, 2006). As seen in the graph, TP rate and FP rate points of Backpropagation algorithm, and Naïve bayes algorithm lie above the line of no discrimination, are thus better classifiers whereas Decision Tree algorithms such as ID3 and C4.5, both lie below the discrimination line, are thus worse classifier for the given data. Although, TP rate and FP rate points of neural networks

Figure 5. Accuracy of ID3, C4.5, Naive Bayes simple and backpropagation algorithms

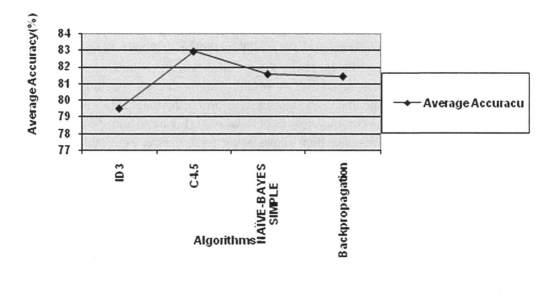

Figure 6. Sensitivity of ID3, C4.5, Naive Bayes simple and backpropagation algorithms

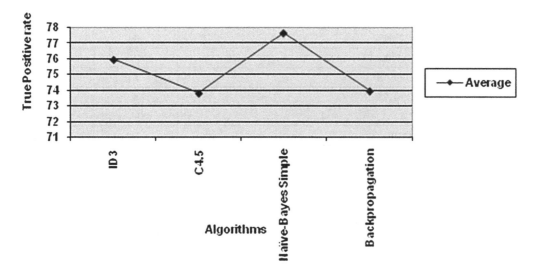

Figure 7. Specificity of ID3, C4.5, Naive Bayes simple and backpropagation algorithm

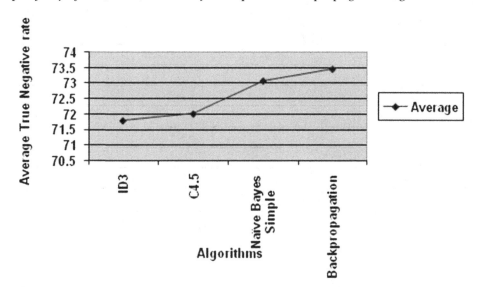

Table 4. True positive and false positive rate

Parameters/Algorithms	ID3	C4.5	Naïve Bayes Algorithm	Backpropagation Algorithm
Average False Positive Rate	38.7	39.2	36.7	36.2
Average True Positive Rate	73.56	74.56	77.22	71.22

(Backpropagation algorithm) qualify as better classifiers, they lie very close to the discrimination line. Besides neural network algorithms involve long training times and are therefore more suitable for applications where this is feasible and they are also criticized for their poor interpretability. Thus Naïve Bayes algorithm is employed to classify the chemical reactions.

3.1.6 Classification of Chemical Reactions Using Naïve Bayes Classifier

In this phase, IVCL tool takes chemical reactants as an input from the user and classifies the reaction into one of the many broad reaction classes as specified in Figure 9. IVCL tool employs Naïve-Bayes algorithm to identify the reaction class of the chemical reactants given by the user. The algorithm works on the salient features of the data on the basis of which it classifies the given data into various classes.

An empirical analysis of around 130 chemical reactions was done to identify the set of features to be used for classification. All these features were identified by taking into account the chemical properties and unique features for each reaction class. The various features or attributes which are utilized by the IVCL tool for classification are:

- Single Reactant.
- State of 1st reactant is not solid.
- State of 2nd reactant is not solid.

Figure 8. ROC plot of ID3, C4.5, Naive Bayes simple and backpropagation algorithms

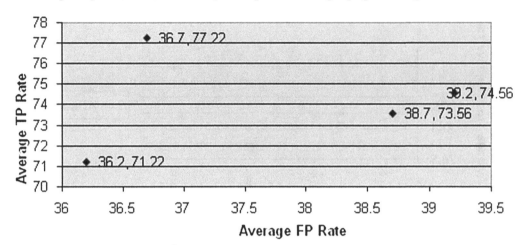

Figure 9. Classification of reactions

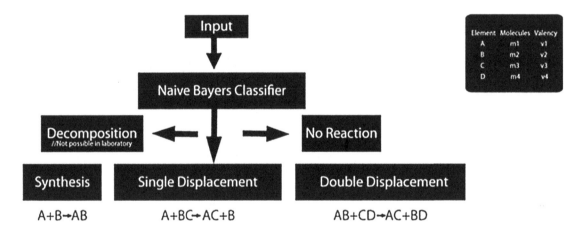

- Presence of Oxygen.
- Presence of Single Element in 1st reactant.
- Presence of Single Element in 2nd reactant.
- Presence of cation/anion in 1st reactant.
- Presence of cation/anion in 2nd reactant.
- Relative Position on reactivity series.

All these features were stored in the database and were assigned binary values (Figure 10). When the user provides set of the reactants as input, tool analyzes and identifies the salient features of the reactants to be used for classification. Subsequently Naïve-Bayes classifier utilizes the trained model based on identified features of chemical reactions to classify it into one of the reaction classes. Naïve-Bayes classifier computes the percentage probability of the reactant pair to be in each reaction class. Subsequently the reaction is classified with class bearing highest percentage.

3.2 Product Formation using Genetic Algorithm Inspired Approach

Once the category of user specified reactants is classified using Naïve-Bayes algorithm, products are generated in the next phase based on the class of reaction. IVCL tool employs Genetic algorithm inspired approach to generate the products. A genetic algorithm (GA) is categorized as global search heuristic technique used in computing to find true or approximate solutions to optimization and search problems. It is a class of evolutionary algorithm that employs techniques inspired by evolutionary biology such as inheritance, mutation, selection, and crossover. In GA, solution to a given problem is represented in the form of a string called as chromosome. Each chromosome consists of a set of elements called 'genes' which are typically binary (0/1) numbers. Here, new chromosomes are produced in each and every generation by the repetition of two-stage cycle. This involves first encoding and evolving the chromosome and then decoding each individual chromosome for assessing its ability to solve the problem. Fitness of each chromosome is computed using its objective function. In the second stage, fittest chromosome is preferentially chosen for recombination. It involves the selection of two chromosomes and thereafter exchange of genetic material to the right of the meeting point of these two chromosomes. This is called crossover. Several approaches have been developed in literature to perform crossover operation e.g. single point crossover, multipoint crossover, uniform crossover etc. Another genetic operator is mutation. Mutation is a rare process that resembles a sudden change in the genes of an individual. It is performed by randomly selecting one chromosome from the population and then arbitrarily changing some of its information. It is used to maintain genetic diversity within a small population of chromosomes. A small mutation rate of less than 0.1 is usually preferred.

For the given problem, a reactant refers to the chromosome in genetic algorithm. Structure and number of genes in the chromosome vary accordingly if the reactant is a single element or compound element. For a single element, chromosome consists of the symbol of the element, its valency in ionic form, and its existence state i.e. number of molecules that exist together in nature. When the reactant is a compound, the chromosome structure is defined as the cationic or positively charged part, the positive charge or valency of cation in ionic form, number of molecules of that cation present in the compound,

Figure 10. Training data with features used for classification of reactions

Sno	Chemical Reactions	Single reactant	State of 1st reactant is not solid	State pf 2nd reactant is not solid	Presence of Oxygen	Presence of single element in 1st reactant	Presence of single element in 2nd reactant	Presence of Cation/anion n in 1st reactant	Presence of cation/anion in 2nd reactant	RelativePosition on reactivity series of single element with respective cationic/anionic part of compound	Category
1	Cu + 2AgNO3 → 2Ag + Cu(NO3)2	0	0	1	0	1	0	0	1	1	2
2	Fe + Cu(NO3)2 → Fe(NO3)2 + Cu	0	0	1	0	1	0	0	1	1	2
3	Ca + 2H2O → Ca(OH)2 + H2	0	0	1	0	1	0	0	1	1	2
4	Zn + 2HCl → ZnCl$_2$ + H$_2$	0	0	1	0	1	0	0	1	1	2
5	Ag + Cu(NO$_3$)$_2$ → No reaction	0	0	1	0	1	0	0	1	0	9
6	Au + HCl → No reaction	0	0	1	0	1	0	0	1	0	9
7	Cl$_2$ + 2NaBr → 2NaCl + Br$_2$	0	1	1	0	1	0	0	1	1	2
8	Br$_2$ + 2KI → 2KBr + I$_2$	0	1	1	0	1	0	0	1	1	2
9	I$_2$ + 2KBr → no reaction	0	1	1	0	1	0	1	1	0	9
10	Cu + Zn → No reaction	0	0	0	0	1	1	0	0	0	9
11	Cu + Fe → No reaction	0	0	0	0	1	1	0	0	0	9
12	HCl + NaOH → NaCl + H$_2$O	0	1	1	0	0	0	1	1	1	3
13	AgNO3 + NaCl → AgCl + NaNO3	0	1	1	0	0	0	1	1	1	3
14	Na$_2$SO$_4$ + BaCl$_2$ → BaSO$_4$ + 2NaCl	0	1	1	0	0	0	1	1	1	3
15	CH$_3$COOH + NaHCO$_3$ → CH$_3$COONa + CO$_2$ + H$_2$O	0	1	1	0	0	0	1	1	1	3
16	ZnBr$_2$ + 2AgNO$_3$ → Zn(NO$_3$)$_2$ + 2AgBr	0	1	1	0	0	0	1	1	1	3
17	H$_2$SO$_4$ + 2NaOH → Na$_2$SO$_4$ + 2H$_2$O	0	1	1	0	0	0	1	1	1	3
18	C H OH + O → CO H O	0	1		0				0		

the anionic or negatively charged part, the negative charge or valency of anion in ionic form, number of molecules of that anion present in the compound. An initial population of the chromosomes is initialized with such basic information about the reactants. For example the structure of chromosome for a compound PxQy, where P and Q are elements in their ionic form and x and y are the number of molecules in the compound. For an element exhibiting variable valency, the structure of the chromosome changes dynamically to accommodate more than one valency (Box 1 and Box 2).

3.2.1 Crossover Operator

VCL tool adapts the crossover mechanism (Mehta, 2013) of genetic algorithms to generate the offspring for the next generation. This approach varies with the class of chemical reaction as follows (Box 3).

- **Synthesis/Combustion Reaction:** Both these types of reactions consist of two elements joining together to form a compound. Thus the methodology for product formation is same for both of them. These reactions do not occur between two metals, thus two positively charged ions do not react together to form a compound. These reactions are of the form Px + Qy → PyQx. When the reaction is classified as a Synthesis or a Combustion reaction, it is taken into consideration that two or more reactants will form one product. The same procedure as above follows, where the individual elements or compounds on the reactant side are taken along with their valances and electro-negativities. Depending on which reactant is more electronegative, the donor and acceptor are determined. Reactants combine with each other to attain stability, hence losing or gaining electrons is a method of achieving a full orbit or a stable state. Once the donor/acceptor is determined, the valences are interchanged between the elements. These values now become the number of molecules for each element in the resultant compound, and the more electronegative one is written on the right and the less electronegative one is written on the left.

- **Single Displacement:** These reactions are typically of the form Px + QyRz with one element and one compound. A similar crossover process as stated for combustion or synthesis reaction is followed except that in this case, products include a compound and a single element. However, for a single displacement to be successful, the single element needs to be more reactive than the ion in the compound which is in the same ionic state as the single element. Product formation in single displacement reactions depends on the ability of the single element in displacing the cation part of the other reactant. The capability of the single element is determined by the reactivity of the cation part. In these reactions the cation part of the compound is left alone in the form of an ion or element.

- **Double Displacement:** These reactions are of the form PxQy + RvSw→ PwSx + RyQv where P, Q, R, S are elements in their ionic forms and x, y, v, w are corresponding molecules of those elements in that compound. For a chemical reaction with reactants PxQy + RvSw, the structure of chromosomes is given in Box 4.

Box 1. Chromosome A

Ion P	Molecules of P	Valency of P	Variable Valency	Ionic State

Box 2. Chromosome B

Ion Q	Molecules of Q	Valency of Q	Variable Valency	Ionic State

Box 3.

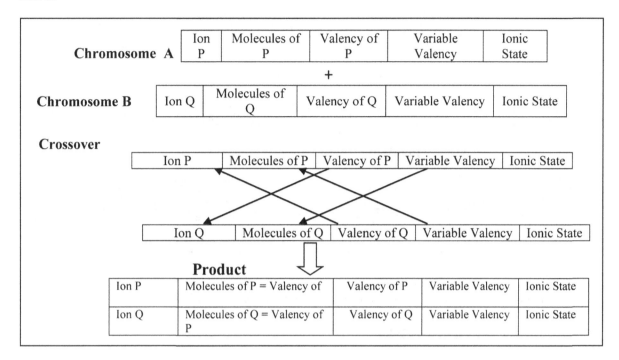

Then the methodology to perform crossover operation for double displacement reaction is as follows: Assuming that ion P and R are positively charged, and Q and S are negatively charged, the crossover is performed such that the valences of the ions are interchanged but they take the molecules position as shown in Box 5.

Similar crossover takes place for the other pair of oppositely charged ions. For elements with more than one valency, multiple products are formed. Final products are PwSx + RyQv (Box 6).

3.3 Balancing of Equations

After product formation, next step is to balance the equations. The system of equations method is employed in the VCL tool to balance the reactions. A system of equations is a collection of two or more equations with a same set of unknown variables. While solving a system of equations, values for each of the unknowns are identified such that they will satisfy every equation in the system as follows:

Box 4.

Ion P	Molecules of P	Valency of P	Variable Valency	Ionic State
Ion Q	Molecules of Q	Valency of Q	Variable Valency	Ionic State
		+		
Ion R	Molecules of R	Valency of R	Variable Valency	Ionic State
Ion S	Molecules of S	Valency of S	Variable Valency	Ionic State

Box 5.

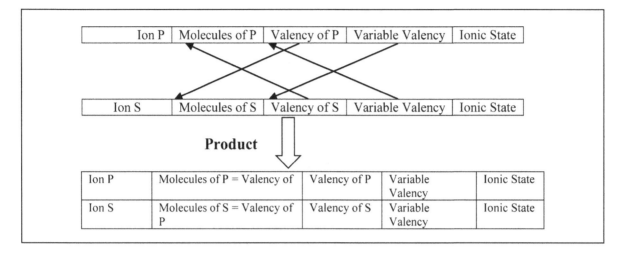

- Let A,B,C and D be the coefficients of reactants and products as follows

$APxQy + BRvSw \rightarrow CPwSx + DQyRv$

- Then the equations formed by equating the molecules of a particular element on both sides are:

$Ax - Cw = 0$

$Ay - Dv = 0$

$Bv - Dy = 0$

$Bw - Cx = 0$

- Subsequently a 4*4 matrix (D) is created and number of molecules of the reactants and products are initialized in each row as

Box 6.

Ion P	Molecules of P = Valency of S	Valency of P	Variable Valency	Ionic State
Ion S	Molecules of S = Valency of P	Valency of S	Variable Valency	Ionic State
+				
Ion Q	Molecules of Q = Valency of R	Valency of Q	Variable Valency	Ionic State
Ion R	Molecules of R = Valency of Q	Valency of R	Variable Valency	Ionic State

Table 5. Results of manual testing of tool

S. No.	Reactants (Input)	Expected Product	Product Formed
1	AgNO3 + HCl	AgCl + HNO3	AgCl + HNO3
2	AgCl + HNO3	AgNO3 + HCl	AgNO3 + HCl
3	BaCl2 + H2SO4	BaSO4 + HCl	BaSO4 + HCl
4	Ca(OH)2 + H3PO4	Ca3(PO4)2 + H2O	Ca3(PO4)2 + H2O
5	Cu(NO3)2 + NH4Cl	CuCl2 + NH4NO3	CuCl2 + NH4NO3
6	CaSO4 + AgCl	CaCl2 + Ag2SO4	CaCl2 + Ag2SO4
7	NaBr + HCl	NaCl + HBr	NaCl + HBr
8	Fe(NO3)2 + H2SO4	FeSO4 + HNO3	FeSO4 + HNO3
9	H2O + AgCl	AgOH + HCl	AgOH + HCl
10	BaSO4 + KI	BaI2 + K2SO4	BaI2 + K2SO4
11	KClO3 + NaHCO3	KHCO3 + NaClO3	KHCO3 + NaClO3
12	KBr + NaNO3	KNO3 + NaBr	KNO3 + NaBr
13	H2O + H3PO4	H2O + H3PO4	H2O + H3PO4
14	ZnCl2 + Ca(OH)2	Zn(OH)2 + CaCl2	Zn(OH)2 + CaCl2
15	CH3COOH + AgCl	AgCH3COO + HCl	AgCH3COO + HCl
16	Al + AgCl	AlCl3 + Ag	AlCl3 + Ag
17	Ba2 + BaSO4	Ba2 + BaSO4	Ba2 + BaSO4
18	Al + NaCl	No reaction	No reaction
19	Ca + NaOH	No reaction	No reaction
20	Na + Ca(OH)2	NaOH + Ca2	NaOH + Ca2
21	Ag + NaCl	No reaction	No reaction
22	Na + AgCl	NaCl + Ag	NaCl + Ag
23	Cu + BaCl2	CuCl2 + Ba2 + CuCl	CuCl2 + Ba2 + CuCl
24	Fe + HCl	FeCl2 + FeCl3 + H2	FeCl2 + FeCl3 + H2
25	Mg + BaSO4	MgSO4 + Ba2	MgSO4 + Ba2
26	Li + KBr	No reaction	No reaction
27	K + NH4Cl	KCl + NH4	KCl + NH4
28	Zn + CH3COOH	Zn(CH3COO)2 + H2	Zn(CH3COO)2 + H2
29	Mn + Na2SO4	No reaction	No reaction
30	Ca + BaCl2	CaCl2 + Ba2	CaCl2 + Ba2
31	Ca + Cl2	CaCl2	CaCl2
32	H2 + O2	H2O	H2O
33	Na + Br2	NaBr	NaBr
34	S2 + O2	SO2	SO2
35	Mg + H2O	Mg(OH)2	Mg(OH)2

$$D = \begin{pmatrix} Ax & 0 & -Cw & 0 \\ Ay & 0 & 0 & -Dv \\ 0 & Bv & 0 & -Dy \\ 0 & Bw & -Cx & 0 \end{pmatrix}$$

- Similarly four 4*4 matrices (D1....D4) are created replacing one column with constant column like matrix created for D1 as given below. In the same way matrices for D2, D3 and D4 are developed.

$$D1 = \begin{pmatrix} Ax & 0 & -Cw & 0 \\ Ay & 0 & 0 & 0 \\ 0 & Bv & 0 & 0 \\ 0 & Bw & -Cx & 0 \end{pmatrix}$$

- Next, for each matrix, determinant is computed. Subsequently the determinant of each of these matrices is divided by the original matrix D to generate values of A, B, C and D.
- Finally, the LCM of these values is computed and multiplied to each to convert decimal numbers into whole numbers.

4. EXPERIMENTS AND RESULTS

With the tremendous growth and development of information and communication technology, internet is easily accessible and available everywhere. Thus, a web based prototype system for IVCL tool was developed for experimental purpose as shown in Figure 13. System was developed using Java, JSP and MySql database and executed on Core2 Duo 1.67 GHz processor and 2-GB RAM computer. For inorganic reactions, there were no readily available benchmark datasets for experimental analysis. Thus the datasets were generated manually by referring to various standard chemistry books, journals, lab manuals and also by consulting various chemistry teachers from schools and universities. A data set of 130 reactions was populated as training dataset to be used by Naïve bayes classifier (Figure 11). All these chemical reactions were analyzed to identify their salient features which are subsequently mapped with the different categories of reactions. Properties which identify the reactions were also identified and then each reaction was given boolean values against each property.

Meticulous experiments were performed to evaluate the classification and product formation accuracy of presented approach. Figure 13 depicts the working of naïve Bayes classifier and its classification accuracy along with the products formed using GA inspired approach. As demonstrated in the Figure 12, for input reactants NaCl and H_2SO_4, Naïve Bayes classifier predicts that there is high probability for the reaction to be double displacement and subsequently the products formed using proposed approach are Na_2SO_4 and HCl.

The efficacy of IVCL tool was tested on a set of reactants chosen randomly as shown in Table 5. The testing was performed manually by giving input reactants to the web interface of the IVCL tool and recording the results. These results indicate that presented approach runs with 95% accuracy. The approach is accurately able to distinguish between the different reaction types, has the capability to determine whether the input reaction will take place or not, and form resultant products. The web based interface (Figure13) for the Virtual Chemistry Laboratory allows the user enters the values of the first and second reactant. As the user clicks on the submit button, tool displays the necessary information like type of reaction that occurs between the reactants and the set of possible products. For example for the reactants carbon and oxygen, tool displays that reaction is combustion reaction and possible products are CO2 and CO. With this web based virtual chemistry laboratory (VCL) tool, chemical experiments are just internet connection away.

Thus, chapter presents an effective web based virtual chemistry laboratory for the whole web community to practice and perform experiments from their workstations without going to a chemistry laboratory physically. Like others, VCL tool also has certain limitations for ambiguous cases like

- In Single Displacement, where a non metal has to displace a non metal in a few cases where displacement capability is not quantifiable Eg.
  - $2KBr + I2 \rightarrow 2KI + Br2$
  - $CaF2 + Br2 \rightarrow CaBr2 + F2$
- Few synthesis reactions which depend on lone pairs and covalent bond sharing (when elements exist in abnormal states) Eg.
  - $8Fe + S8 \rightarrow 8FeS$
- Synthesis cases where two non metals react to form a compound, and one of the non metals which is less electronegative takes the form of a positive ion Eg.
  - $I2 + F2 \rightarrow IF2$

Figure 11. Snapshot of chemical reactions used for training Naïve Bayes classifier

#					
1	$Cu + 2AgNO_3 \rightarrow 2Ag + Cu(NO_3)_2$	$P_4O_{10}(s) + 6 H_2O(l) = 4 H_3PO_4(aq)$	$H_2(g) + Cl_2(g) ==> 2HCl(g)$	$CaCO_3 ===> CaO + CO_2$	$Cl_2(aq) + 2I^-(aq) \; 2Cl^-(a$
2	$Fe + Cu(NO_3)_2 \rightarrow Fe(NO_3)_2 + Cu$	$2 Mg(s) + O_2(g) = 2 MgO(s)$	$2Na(s) + Cl_2(g) ==> 2NaCl(s)$	$Mg + 2HCl ===> MgCl_2 + H_2$	$4Na(s) + O_2(g) \; 2Na_2O(s)$
3	$Ca + H_2O \rightarrow Ca(OH)_2 + H_2$	$2 H_2O(l) = 2 H_2 + O_2$	$2Al(s) + 3Cl_2(g) ==> 2AlCl_3(s)$	$Zn + CuSO_4 ===> ZnSO_4 + Cu$	$2Mg (s) + O_2 (g) \; 2MgO ($
4	$Zn + 2HCl \rightarrow ZnCl_2 + H_2$	$2 HgO(s) = 2 Hg(l) + O_2(g)$	$2Fe(s) + 3Cl_2(g) ==> 2FeCl_3(s)$	$HCl + AgNO_3 ===> HNO_3 + AgCl$	$4Al(s) + 3O_2(g) \; 2Al_2O_3$ (s
5	$Ag + Cu(NO_3)_2 \rightarrow No\ reaction$	$2 KClO_3(s) = 2 KCl(s) + 3 O_2(g)$	$2NaCl(aq) + 2H_2O(l) + elec.\ energy ==> 2N\ NaCl$	$AgNO_3 ===> NaNO_3 + AgCl$	$Si(s) + O_2(g) \; SiO_2 (s)$
6	$Au + HCl \rightarrow No\ reaction$	$4Li (s) + O_2 (g) \; 2Li_2O (s)$	$NaOH + KNO_3 --> NaNO_3 + KOH$	$2HNO_3 + H_2S ===> 2H_2O + 2NO_2 + S$	$4P(s) + 5O_2(g) \; P_4O_{10} (s)$
7	$Cl_2 + 2NaBr \rightarrow 2NaCl + Br_2$	$2Na(s) + O_2(g) \; Na_2O_2(s)$	$CH_4 + 2 O_2 --> CO_2 + 2 H_2O$	$2KMnO_4 + 2H_2O + 5O_2 ===> K_2SO_4 + 2MnSO_4 + 2H_2SO_4$	$S(s) + O_2(g) \; SO_2(g)$
8	$Br_2 + 2KI \rightarrow 2KBr + I_2$	$K(s) + O_2(g) \; KO_2(s)$	$2 Fe + 6 NaBr --> 2 FeBr_3 + 6 Na$	$Ag^+(aq) + Cl^-(aq) \; AgCl(s)$	$2Na(s) + Cl_2(g) \; 2NaCl(s)$
9	$I_2 + 2KBr \rightarrow no\ reaction$	$2Li(s) + 2H_2O(l) \; 2LiOH(aq) + H_2(g)$	$CaSO_4 + Mg(OH)_2 --> Ca(OH)_2 + MgSO_4$	$Ag^+(aq) + Br^-(aq) \; AgBr(s)$	$Mg(s) + Cl_2(g) \; MgCl_2(s)$
10	$Cu + Zn \rightarrow No\ reaction$	$2Mg (s) + O_2(g) \; 2MgO(s)$	$NH_4OH + HBr --> H_2O + NH_4Br$	$Ag^+(aq) + I^-(aq) \; AgI(s)$	$2Al(s) + 3Cl_2(g) \; 2AlCl_3(s$
11	$Cu + Fe \rightarrow No\ reaction$	$Mg(s) + Cl_2(g) \; MgCl_2(s)$	$Pb + O_2 --> PbO_2$	$AgCl(s) + 2NH_3(aq) \; [Ag(NH_3)_2]^+(aq) + Cl^-(aq)$	$Si(s) + 2Cl_2(g) \; SiCl_4(l)$
12	$HCl + NaOH \rightarrow NaCl + H_2O$	$Mg(s) + H_2O(g) \; MgO(s) + H_2(g)$	$Na_2CO_3 --> Na_2O + CO_2$	$AgBr(s) + 2NH_3(aq) \; [Ag(NH_3)_2]^+(aq) + Br^-(aq)$	$2P(s) + 3Cl_2(g) \; 2PCl_3(l)$
13	$AgNO_3 + NaCl \rightarrow AgCl + NaNO_3$	$Ca(s) + 2H_2O(l) \; Ca(OH)_2(aq) + H_2($	$HBr + NaOH ---> NaBr + H_2O$	$NaCl(s) + H_2SO_4(l) \; NaHSO_4(s) + HCl(g)$	$PCl_3(l) + Cl_2(g) \; PCl_5(s)$
14	$Na_2SO_4 + BaCl_2 \rightarrow BaSO_4 + 2NaCl$	$Li_2O(s) + H_2O(l) \; 2LiOH(aq)$	$Pb(NO_3)_2 + 2 KI ---> PbI_2 + 2 KNO_3$	$NaBr(s) + H_2SO_4(l) \; NaHSO_4(s) + HBr(g)$	$2S(l) + Cl_2(g) \; S_2Cl_2(l)$
15	$CH_3COOH + NaHCO_3 \rightarrow CH_3COONa + CO_2$	$Na_2O_2(s) + 2H_2O(l) \; 2NaOH(aq) +$	$Mg + 2 H_2O ---> Mg(OH)_2 + H_2$	$2HBr(g) + H_2SO_4(l) \; Br_2(g) + SO_2(g) + 2H_2O(l)$	$2Na(s) + 2H_2O(l) \; 2NaOH$
16	$ZnBr_2 + 2AgNO_3 \rightarrow Zn(NO_3)_2 + 2AgBr$	$2KO_2(s) + H_2O(l) \; 2KOH(aq) + H_2O_2$	$2 H_2 + O_2$	$NaI(s) + H_2SO_4(l) \; NaHSO_4(s) + HI(g)$	$Mg(s) + H_2O(g) \; MgO(s)$
17	$H_2SO_4 + 2NaOH \rightarrow Na_2SO_4 + 2H_2O$	$MgO(s) + H_2O(l) \; Mg(OH)_2(aq)$	$8 Fe + S_8 ---> 8 FeS$	$2HI(g) + H_2SO_4(l) \; I_2(s) + SO_2(g) + 2H_2O(l)$	$2Al(s) + 3H_2O(g) \; Al_2O_3(s$
18	$C_2H_5OH + O_2 \rightarrow CO_2\ H_2O$	$Li_2O(s) + 2H^+(aq) \; 2Li^+(aq) + H_2O(l)C_{12}H_6 + 12 O_2 ---> 10 CO_2 + 4 H_2O$		$6HI(g) + H_2SO_4(l) \; 3I_2(s) + S(s) + 4H_2O(l)$	$Na_2O (s) + H_2O (l) \; 2NaO$
19	$S(s) + O_2(g) = SO_2(g)$	$Na_2O_2(s) + 2H^+(aq) \; 2Na^+(aq) + H_2O_2 2Mg + O_2 ===> 2MgO$		$8HI(g) + H_2SO_4(l) \; 4I_2(s) + H_2S(s) + 4H_2O(l)$	$Na^+ (aq) + OH^- (aq) + H^+ (a$
20	$H_2(g) + Cl_2(g) = 2HCl(g)$	$2KO_2(s) + 2H^+(aq) \; 2K^+(aq) + H_2O_2(l) Fe + S ===> FeS$		$Cl_2(aq) + H_2O(l) \; HOCl(aq) + HCl (aq)$	$MgO (s) + 2H^+ (aq) \; Mg^2$
21	$Fe(s) + S(s) = FeS(s)$	$MgO(s) + 2H^+(aq) \; Mg^{2+}(aq) + H_2O(l) 2KClO_3 ===> 2KCl + 3O_2$		$Cl_2(aq) + 2NaOH(aq) \; NaCl (aq) + NaOCl (aq) + H_2$	$Mg(OH)_2 (s) + 2H^+ (aq) \;$
22	$NH_2(g) + HCl(g) = NH_4Cl$	$Cl_2(aq) + 2KBr(aq) ==> 2KCl(aq) + Br_2(aq)$	$SiO_2 (s) + 2 OH^- (aq) \; SiO_2^{2-} (aq) +$	$3Cl_2(aq) + 6NaOH(aq) \; 5NaCl(aq) + NaClO_3(aq) + 3$	$Al_2O_3 (s) + 6H^+ (aq) \; 2Al$
23	$2 Na(s) + Cl_2(g) = 2 NaCl(s)$	$Cl_2(aq) + 2KI(aq) ==> 2KCl(aq) + I_2(aq)$	$P_4O_{10} (s) + 2H_2O (l) \; 4HPO_2(s)$	$3 OCl^- (aq) \; ClO_3^- (aq) + 2Cl^- (aq)$	$Al(OH)_3 (s) + 3H^+ (aq) \; A$

Figure 12. Results of classification algorithm and formation of products

```
compile-single:
run-single:

COMPOUNDS

1.AgCl2.AgNO33.BaCl24.BaSO45.Ca(OH)26.CaSO47.CH3COOH8.Cu(NO3)29
17.KI18.Na2SO419.NaBr20.NaCl21.NaHCO322.NaNO323.NaOH24.NH4C125.
ELEMENTS

27.Aluminium28.Barium29.Bromine30.Calcium31.Carbon32.Chlorine33
nesium40.Manganese41.Nickel42.Oxygen43.Potassium44.Silver45.Sod

Enter the 1st component:
NACL
Enter the 2nd component:
H2SO4

 Single Displacement %age:0.058175083
 Double Displacement %age:47.221657
 combustion %age:0.0016915179
 Synthesis %age:3.5762787E-4
 Noreaction %age:0.09144948
Reaction is double displacement
One of the product will be Na2SO41

Other product will beH1Cl1
```

Figure 13. Web Based user interface

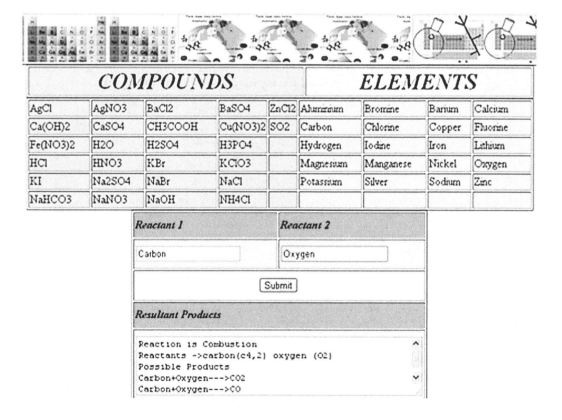

COMPOUNDS					ELEMENTS			
AgCl	AgNO3	BaCl2	BaSO4	ZnCl2	Aluminium	Bromine	Barium	Calcium
Ca(OH)2	CaSO4	CH3COOH	Cu(NO3)2	SO2	Carbon	Chlorine	Copper	Fluorine
Fe(NO3)2	H2O	H2SO4	H3PO4		Hydrogen	Iodine	Iron	Lithium
HCl	HNO3	KBr	KClO3		Magnesium	Manganese	Nickel	Oxygen
KI	Na2SO4	NaBr	NaCl		Potassium	Silver	Sodium	Zinc
NaHCO3	NaNO3	NaOH	NH4Cl					

Reactant 1	Reactant 2
Carbon	Oxygen

Submit

Resultant Products

```
Reaction is Combustion
Reactants ->carbon(c4,2) oxygen (O2)
Possible Products
Carbon+Oxygen--->CO2
Carbon+Oxygen--->CO
```

5. CONCLUSION

The ease of internet access in this digital era has enabled the educationist to reach beyond boundaries. Teaching and learning is no more restricted to the physical walls of schools and libraries. WWW has become the largest source of information to enhance teaching and learning. Massive work has been done to teach theory courses online. However, virtual laboratories have the potential to bring paradigm shift in the way practical courses are taught today. This chapter presented an intelligent approach to simulate inorganic chemical reactions online. The prototype intelligent system that is intelligent virtual chemistry laboratory tool (IVCL) was developed using artificial intelligence techniques. The IVCL tool employed naïve bayes classification to classify the reaction. Thereafter, it used genetic algorithm inspired approach to generate the products. Finally system of equations methods was utilized to balance the equations. IVCL is an interactive user friendly tool that allows the learners to input the set of reactants and generate the output in the form of type of reaction occurred and the potential products generated. Thus IVL empowers students, scientists, and other chemistry enthusiasts by providing a virtual chemistry laboratory where anyone with even very basic computer knowledge can learn and perform most chemistry experiments. Future work involves adding multimedia 3-d experience to the interface and overcoming the limitations of the existing system. Development of mobile application to provide a complete virtual laboratory experience to the chemistry enthusiasts anywhere anytime would be an added advantage for the digital community.

REFERENCES

Ardac, D., & Akaygun, S. (2004). Effectiveness of multimedia-based instruction that emphasizes molecular representations on students' understanding of chemical change. *Journal of Research in Science Teaching*, *41*(4), 317–337. doi:10.1002/tea.20005

Azough, S., Bellafkih, M., & Bouyakhf, E. H. (2010). Adaptive E-learning using Genetic Algorithms. *IJCSNS International Journal of Computer Science and Network Security*, *10*(7), 237–244.

Bayes, T., & Price, M. (1763). Essay towards Solving a Problem in the Doctrine of Chances. By the Late Rev. Mr. Bayes, F. R. S. Communicated by Mr. Price, in a Letter to John Canton, A. M. F. R. S. *Philosophical Transactions of the Royal Society of London*, *53*(0), 370–418. doi:10.1098/rstl.1763.0053

Blake, C., & Merz, C. J. (1998). *UCI repository of machine learning databases*. University of California, Irvine, Dept. of Information and Computer Sciences. Retrieved from http://www.ics.uci.edu/mlearn/MLRepository.html

Bonabeau, E., Dorigo, M., & Theraulaz, G. (1999). *Swarm Intelligence: From Natural to Artificial Systems*. New York: Oxford University Press.

Bose, R. (2013). Virtual Labs Project: A Paradigm Shift in Internet-Based Remote Experimentation. *Practical Innovations: Open Solutions*, *1*, 718–725.

Bruner, J. S. (1990). *Acts of meaning*. Cambridge, MA: Harvard University Press.

Buyya, R. (2001). The Virtual Laboratory Project. *IEEE Distributed Systems Online*, *2*(5), 2001.

Chang, G., & Lewis, M. (1997). Molecular replacement using genetic algorithms. *Acta Crystallographica. Section D, Biological Crystallography, 53*(3), 279–289. doi:10.1107/S0907444996014990 PMID:15299931

Cheng, H., Wei, L., & Chen, Y. (2011). A New E-learning Achievement Evaluation Model Based on RoughSet and Similar Filter. *Computational Intelligence, 27*(2), 260–279. doi:10.1111/j.1467-8640.2011.00380.x

Cherkassky, V. (1998). In O. Kayak et al. (Eds.), *Fuzzy Inference Systems: A Critical Review, Computational Intelligence: Soft Computing and Fuzzy-Neuro Integration with Applications* (pp. 177–197). Springer. doi:10.1007/978-3-642-58930-0_10

Clark, D. E. (2000). *Evolutionary Algorithms in Molecular Design (Methods and Principles in Medicinal Chemistry)*. Wiley-VCH. doi:10.1002/9783527613168

Climent-Bellido, M. S., Martínez-Jiménez, P., Pontes-Pedrajas, A., & Polo, J. (2003). Learning in Chemistry with Virtual Laboratories. *Journal of Chemical Education, 80*(3), 346–352. doi:10.1021/ed080p346

Dalgarno, B. (2005). A VRML virtual chemistry laboratory incorporating reusable prototypes for object manipulation. In P. Beckett (Ed.), *SimTect 2005, the annual conference of the Simulation Industry Association of Australia*, Sydney, Australia, 1-6.

Dempster, A. P. (1967). Upper and Lower Probabilities induced by a Multivalued Mapping. *Annals of Mathematical Statistics, 38*(2), 325–339. doi:10.1214/aoms/1177698950

Douguet, D., Thoreau, E., & Grassy, G. (2000). A genetic algorithm for the automated generation of small organic molecules: Drug design using an evolutionary algorithm. *Journal of Computer-Aided Molecular Design, 14*(5), 449–466. doi:10.1023/A:1008108423895 PMID:10896317

Dunham, M. H. (2003). *Data Mining: Introductory and Advanced Topics*. Prentice Hall.

Egan, J. P. (1975). *Signal detection theory and ROC analysis, Series in Cognition and Perception*. New York: Academic Press.

Eiben, A. E., & Smith, J. E. (2003). *Introduction to evolutionary computing*. Berlin: Springer. doi:10.1007/978-3-662-05094-1

Fawcett, T. (2006). An introduction to ROC analysis. *Pattern Recognition Letters, 27*(8), 861–874. doi:10.1016/j.patrec.2005.10.010

Forrest, S. (1993). Genetic algorithms: Principles of natural selection applied to computation. *Science, 261*(5123), 872–878. doi:10.1126/science.8346439 PMID:8346439

Goldberg, D. E. (1989). *Genetic algorithms in search, optimization and machine learning*. Reading, MA: Addison-Wesley Publishing Co.

Hall, M., Frank, E., Holmes, G., Pfahringer, B., Reutemann, P., & Witten, I. H. (2009). The WEKA Data Mining Software: An Update. *SIGKDD Explorations, 11*(1), 10. doi:10.1145/1656274.1656278

Han, J., & Kamber, M. (2000). *Data Mining: Concepts and Techniques Data mining: concepts and techniques*. San Francisco, CA, USA: Morgan Kaufmann Publishers Inc.

Harding, D. P. (2003). The Virtual Laboratory: Technology Assisted Education. *Proceedings of The National Conference On Undergraduate Research (NCUR)*, University of Utah, Salt Lake City, Utah.

Harry, E. & Edward, B. (2005). Making Real Virtual Lab. The Science Education Review, 4(1).

Holland, J. (1975). *Adaptation in Natural and Artificial Systems*. Ann Arbour: The University of Michigan Press.

Hovakimyan, A., Sargsyan, S., & Barkhoudaryan, S. (2004). Genetic Algorithm and the Problem of Getting Knowledge in e-Learning Systems. *Proceedings of the IEEE International Conference on Advanced Learning Technologies* (pp. 336-339). doi:10.1109/ICALT.2004.1357431

Huang, M., Huang, H., & Chen, M. (2007). Constructing a personalized e-learning system based on genetic algorithm and case-based reasoning approach. *Expert Systems with Applications*, *33*(3), 551–564. doi:10.1016/j.eswa.2006.05.019

Hugh, M. C., & Les, M. S. (2003). *Soft Computing Approaches in Chemistry*. Springer Science & Business Media.

Jeschke, S., Richter, T., & Zorn, E. (2010). Virtual labs in mathematics and natural sciences. International Conference on Technology Supported Learning & Training: Online Educa Berlin. Retrieved from http://www.ibi.tuberlin.de/diskurs/veranst/online_educa/ oeb_04/Zorn%20TU.pdf

Jones, D. T. (1994). De novo protein design using pairwise potentials and a genetic algorithm. *Protein Science*, *3*(4), 567–574. doi:10.1002/pro.5560030405 PMID:8003975

Josephsen, J. & Kristensen, A. K. (2006). Simulation of laboratory assignments to support students' learning of introductory inorganic chemistry. *Chemistry Education Research and practice*, 7(4), 266-279.

Judea, P. (1997). *Probabilistic Reasoning in Intelligent Systems: Networks of Plausible Inference*. USA: Morgan Kaufmann Publishers.

Kerr, M. S., Rynearson, K., & Kerr, M. C. (2004). Innovative educational practice: Using virtual labs in the secondary classroom. *The Journal of Educators Online*, *1*(1), 1–9.

Kinnari, S., Suhonen, A., Harju, J., & Räihä, K.-J. (2007). Evaluating a remote access networking laboratory as a learning environment. *Proc. WBED*, Chamonix, France (pp. 73–79).

Kosko, B. (1997). *Fuzzy Engineering*. Upper Saddle River, NJ: Prentice Hall.

Lewin, T. (2013). Universities Abroad Join Partnerships on the Web. *New York Times*.

Lipson, H., & Pollack, J. (2000). Automatic design and manufacture of robotic life forms. *Nature*, *406*(6799), 974–978. doi:10.1038/35023115 PMID:10984047

Lucasius, C. B., Blommers, M. J. J., Buydens, L. M. C., & Kateman, G. (1991). In L. Davis (Ed.), *Iin Handbook of the genetic algorithm* (pp. 251–281). New York: Van Nostrand Reinhold.

Mehta, S. (2013). Bio-inspired approach to solve chemical equations. *International Conference on Contemporary Computing* (pp. 461-466).

Mestres, J., & Scuseria, G. E. (1995). Genetic Algorithms, A robust scheme for geometery optimizations and global minimum structure problems. *Journal of Computational Chemistry*, *16*(6), 729–742. doi:10.1002/jcc.540160609

Mintz, R. (1993). Computerized simulation as an inquiry tool. *School Science and Mathematics*, *93*(2), 76–80. doi:10.1111/j.1949-8594.1993.tb12198.x

Mitchell, M. (1998). *An Introduction to Genetic Algorithms*. Cambridge, MA: MIT Press.

NCERT. (2013). Chemistry Part 1.

Padhy N.P. (2010). Artificial Intelligence and Intelligence Systems. OXFORD University Press, Impression010.

Pappano, L. (2014). The Year of the MOOC. *The New York Times*.

Project Tomorrow. (2014, June). Trends in Digital Learning: Students' Views on Innovative Classroom Models. Project Tomorrow and Blackboard K-12 Speak Up 2013 National Data.

Provost, F., & Fawcett, T. (1997). Analysis and visualization of classifier performance: Comparison under imprecise class and cost distributions. *Proc. Third International Conference on Knowledge Discovery and DataMining (KDD-97)*, Menlo Park, CA (pp. 43–48). AAAI Press.

Provost, F., & Fawcett, T. (2001). Robust classification systems for imprecise environments. *Machine Learning*, *42*(3), 203–231. doi:10.1023/A:1007601015854

Rauwerda, H., Roos, M., Hertzberger, B., & Breit, T. (2006). The promise of a virtual lab in drug discovery. *Drug Discovery Today*, *11*(5-6), 228–236. doi:10.1016/S1359-6446(05)03680-9 PMID:16580600

Rogers, D., & Hopfinger, A. J. (1994). Genetic function approximation to generate a family of QSAR equations using genetic algorithms. *Journal of Chemical Information and Modeling*, *34*, 854–866. doi:10.1021/ci00020a020

Salehi, M., Pourzaferani, M., & Razavi, S. A. (2013). Hybrid attribute-based recommender system for learning material using genetic algorithm and a multidimensional information model. *Egyptian Informatics Journal*, *14*(1), 67–78. doi:10.1016/j.eij.2012.12.001

Shafer, G. (1976). *A Mathematical Theory of Evidence*. Princeton, NJ: Princeton University Press.

Shannon, C.E. (1948). A Mathematical Theory of Communication. *Bell System Technical Journal*, *27*(July & October), 379–423 & 623–656.

Sheridan, R. P., & Kearsley, S. K. (1995). Using Genetic Algorithm to suggest combinatorial libraries. *Journal of Chemical Information and Computer Sciences*, *35*(2), 310–320. doi:10.1021/ci00024a021

Steinbach, M., Tan, P., & Kumar, V. (2007). *Introduction to Data Mining (English)* (1st ed.). Pearson Education.

Swets, J. A., Dawes, R. M., & Monahan, J. (2000). Better decisions through science. *Scientific American*, *283*(4), 82–87. doi:10.1038/scientificamerican1000-82 PMID:11011389

Tan, X., Shen, R., Wang, Y. (2012). Personalized course generation and evolution based on genetic algorithms. *Journal of Zhejiang Univ-Sci C (Comput & Electron)*, 13(12), 909-917.

Tichy, W. F. (1998). Should computer scientists experiment more? *Computer*, *31*(5), 32–40. doi:10.1109/2.675631

TÜYSÜZ C. (2010). The Effect of the Virtual Laboratory on Students' Achievement and Attitude in Chemistry. *International Online Journal of Educational Sciences*, 2(1), 37–53.

Virtual Computational Chemistry Laboratory. (2001) Retrieved from www.vcclab.org

Virtual Labs. (n. d.), Mission Document of National Mission on Education Through ICT. Government of India.

Wang, C.-Y., Wu, H.-K., Lee, S. W.-Y., Hwang, F.-K., Chang, H.-Y., Wu, Y.-T., & Tsai, C.-C. et al. (2014). A review of research on technology-assisted school science laboratories. *Journal of Educational Technology & Society*, *17*(2), 307–320.

Welsh, E. T., Wanberg, C. R., Brown, K. G., & Simmering, M. J. (2003). E-learning: Emerging uses, empirical results and future directions. *International Journal of Training and Development*, 7(4), 245–258. doi:10.1046/j.1360-3736.2003.00184.x

Wendy, K., & Kurt, W. (2013). *What Can Students Learn from Virtual Labs?* ACS CHED CCCE Newsletter.

Winberg, T. M., & Berg, C. A. R. (2007). Students' cognitive focus during a chemistry laboratory exercise: Effects of a computer-simulated prelab. *Journal of Research in Science Teaching*, *44*(8), 1108–1133. doi:10.1002/tea.20217

Wolf, T. (2010). Assessing Student Learning in a Virtual Laboratory Environment. *IEEE Transactions on Education*, *53*(2), 216–222. doi:10.1109/TE.2008.2012114

Wyatt, T. R., Arduino, P., & Macari, E. J. (2000). Assessment of a virtual laboratory for geotechnical engineering education. *Comput. Educ. J.*, *10*(2), 27–35.

Yarbrough, S. E., & Gilbert, R. B. (1999). Development, implementation, and preliminary assessment of virtual laboratory. *Journal of Professional Issues in Engineering Education and Practice*, *125*(4), 147–151. doi:10.1061/(ASCE)1052-3928(1999)125:4(147)

Zadeh, L. A. (1965). Fuzzy Sets. *Information and Control*, *8*(3), 338–353. doi:10.1016/S0019-9958(65)90241-X

Zadeh, L. A. (1973). Outline of a New Approach to the Analysis of Complex Systems and Decision Process. *IEEE Transactions on Systems, Man, and Cybernetics*, *3*(1), 28–44. doi:10.1109/TSMC.1973.5408575

Zadeh, L. A. (1981). Possibility Theory and Soft Data Analysis. In Cobb and R. Thrall (Eds), Mathematical Frontiers of Social and Policy Sciences (pp. 69-129). Boulder, CO, USA: Westview Press.

Zaitoun, H. (2005). *New Vision in Electronic Learning*. Riyadh: Aldar Al-Soltiah.

Chapter 17

A Novel Fuzzy Anomaly Detection Algorithm Based on Hybrid PSO–Kmeans in Content–Centric Networking

Amin Karami
Universitat Politecnica de Catalunya, Spain

ABSTRACT

In Content-Centric Networks (CCNs) as a promising network architecture, new kinds of anomalies will arise. Usually, clustering algorithms would fit the requirements for building a good anomaly detection system. K-means is a popular anomaly detection method; however, it suffers from the local convergence and sensitivity to selection of the cluster centroids. This chapter presents a novel fuzzy anomaly detection method that works in two phases. In the first phase, authors propose an hybridization of Particle Swarm Optimization (PSO) and K-means algorithm with two simultaneous cost functions as well-separated clusters and local optimization to determine the optimal number of clusters. When the optimal placement of clusters centroids and objects are defined, it starts the second phase. In this phase, the authors employ a fuzzy approach by the combination of two distance-based methods as classification and outlier to detect anomalies in new monitoring data. Experimental results demonstrate that the proposed method can yield high accuracy as compared to preexisting algorithms.

INTRODUCTION

Content-Centric Networking (CCN, also referred to as Data-Centric Networking or Named Data Networking) has emerged to overcome the inherent limitations of the current Internet regarding content security and privacy, and to provide a better trust model (Ahlgren et al., 2011; Jacobson et al., 2009). Unlike the current Internet (host-centric approach) in which security mechanisms are based on the communication channels between hosts, in the content-centric network, security mechanisms must be applied to the Information Objects (IOs) themselves independent of its storage location and physical

DOI: 10.4018/978-1-4666-9474-3.ch017

representation. Consequently, new information-centric security concepts based on the information itself are required (Ahlgren et al., 2011). With this new paradigm, new kinds of attacks and anomalies –from Denial of Service (DoS) to privacy attacks– will arise (Karami & Guerrero-Zapata, 2015). Attacks and anomalies are deliberate actions against data, contents, software or hardware that can destroy, degrade, disrupt or deny access to a computer network (Louvieris et al., 2013). Hence, the contents should be resilient against both DoS and new forms of (unknown) attacks or at least limit their effectiveness (Gasti et al., 2013). In order to disarm new kinds of attacks, anomalous traffics, and any deviation, not only the detection of the malevolent behavior must be achieved, but also the network traffic belonging to the attackers should be also blocked (Liao et al., 2013; Kolias et al., 2011; Peddabachigari et al., 2007). In an attempt to tackle with the new kinds of anomalies and the threat of future unknown attacks, many researchers have been developing Intrusion Detection Systems (IDS) to help filter out known malware, exploits and vulnerabilities (Louvieris et al., 2013, Patcha & Park, 2007). Anomaly detection systems are becoming increasingly vital and valuable tools of any network security infrastructure in order to mitigate disruptions in normal delivery of network services due to malicious activities, Denial of Service (DOS) attacks and network intrusions (Palmieri & Fiore, 2010; Perdisci et al., 2009). An IDS dynamically monitors logs and network traffics, applying detection algorithms to identify potential intrusions and anomalies within a network (Faysel & Haque, 2010; Krawczyk & Woźniak, 2014). In recent years, data mining techniques specially unsupervised anomaly detection have been employed with much success in the area of intrusion detection (Krawczyk & Woźniak, 2014; Fiore et al., 2013; Chandola et al., 2009). Generally, unsupervised learning or cluster analysis algorithms have been utilized to discover natural groupings of objects and find features inherent and their deviations with similar characteristics to solve the detection problems of the abnormal traffics and unknown forms of new attacks (Corral et al., 2009; Wang & Megalooikonomou, 2010). Data clustering algorithms can be either hierarchical or partitioning (Jain et al., 1999; Karami, 2013). In this paper, we focus on the partitioning clustering and in particular, a popular method called K- means clustering algorithm. The K-means algorithm is one of the most efficient clustering algorithms (Kao et al., 2008; Laszlo & Mukherjee, 2007; Zalik, 2008). This algorithm is simple, easy to implement, straightforward, suitable for large data sets, and very efficient with linear time complexity (Chen & Ye, 2004). However, it suffers from two main drawbacks: (1) the random selection of centroid points and determining the number of clusters may lead to different clustering results, (2) the cost function is not convex and the K-means algorithm may contain many local optimum (Selim & Ismail, 1984). In the previous work (Karami, 2013), we employed K-means clustering in our anomaly detection system over CCN. But, the results were not appropriate due to the large number of clusters, trapping in the local optimum solution, and changing results by running the algorithm with the constant parameters in several times. However, if good initial clustering centroids can be assigned by any of other global optimal searching techniques, the K-means would work well in refining the cluster centroids to find the optimal centroids (Naldi & Campello, 2014; Anderberg, 1973).

To overcome these drawbacks, we present a fuzzy anomaly detection system in two phases: training and detection. In the training phase, we apply a meta-heuristic algorithm called PSO (Particle Swarm Optimization) which can find the optimal or the near optimal solution by the least iterations (Quan et al., 2014; Carlisle & Dozier, 2001; Kennedy & Eberhart, 2001). We employ the combination of the ability of global search of the PSO with a novel boundary handling approach and the fast convergence of the K-means to avoid being trapped in a local optimal solution. On the other hand, the most clustering methods usually try to minimize the Mean Square Error (MSE) between data points and their cluster centroids (Everitt, 1993; Kaufman & Rousseeuw, 1990). The MSE is not suitable for determining the optimal number of clusters. Since the MSE decreases, the number of the clusters increases. We develop our method for globally optimal placement of data points as well-separated clusters by low intra-cluster cohesion and high inter-cluster separation. But the optimal placement can increase MSE (Kärkkäinen & Fränti, 2000). Thus, we apply MSE for local optimization, i.e., in the case of each cluster separately to decrease the error caused by corresponding data points and their cluster centroids. This simultaneous approach –application of two cost functions (well-separated clusters and local optimization) – in PSO can lead to the optimal number of clusters and well-separated clusters. When the optimal placement of clusters centroids and objects are defined, they are sent to the second phase. In the detection phase, we apply a novel fuzzy decision approach to give a fuzzy detection of normal or abnormal results in the new monitoring data that do not appear in the training data set. Because fuzzy approach can reduce the false positive rate with higher reliability in determining intrusive activities, due to any data (normal or attack) may be similar (closest distance) to some clusters.

RELATED WORK

So far, there has been no attempt to further evaluate and compare hybrid intelligent algorithms for anomaly detection in CCN. In this chapter, we are concerned with a first attempt to investigate and compare the performance of some hybrid intelligent algorithms for anomaly detection over CCN's traffics, then introduce a novel method to outperform preexisting algorithms. Using hybrid algorithms for improving the clustering performance is not a novel idea. The novelty of our proposed method is using a swarm intelligence algorithm, specifically PSO algorithm, with K-means in order to optimize clustering results based on two simultaneous metrics: (1) well-separated clusters by low intra-cluster and high inter-cluster distances and (2) local optimization by MSE (Mean Square Error). We apply a new boundary handling approach for PSO algorithm to not only select linearly the best set of parameters but fulfill also exploration and exploitation issues. Then, we propose a fuzzy detection method by the combination of two distance-based methods as classification and outlier. We design this hybrid system over CCNs to find the optimal number of clusters with high separation from neighbor clusters and low compactness of local data points, increase detection rate, and decrease false positive rate at the same time. Table 1 summarizes the comparison of applied PSO with K-means in different domains and with various parameters.

CONTENT-CENTRIC NETWORKS

The main idea in the CCN is that, an Interest request for a content object is routed towards the location of the content's origin where it has been published. Any router or intermediate node on the way checks its cache for matching copies of the requested content. If a cached copy of any piece of Interest request is found, it is returned to the requester along the path the request came from. On the way back, all the intermediate nodes store a copy of content in their caches to answer to probable same Interest requests from subsequent requesters (Conti et al., 2013; Xie et al., 2012). CCN routers must include the following components:

Table 1. Comparison of hybrid PSO + K-means approaches in clustering problems

Author	Raw Data	Parameter Value	Cost Function	Contribution
Junyan Chen (2012)	A commercial website log le with 726 clients and 52 pages which clustered separately to 15, 25 and 35 classes	iteration: 50	$\sum_{j=1}^{m} \sum_{\forall x_n} d(x_n, z_{i,j})$, x_n is the data point and $z_{i,j}$ refers to the j_{th} cluster centroid of the i_{th} particle	A hybrid PSO for initial seeds in K-means by incorporating the multidimensional asynchronism and stochastic disturbance model to the velocity, called MSPSO-K.
Zhenkui et al. (2008)	City coordinates of Hop eld-10 TSP (10 records) and Iris (150 records)	$c1 = c2 = 1:3$, w linearly reduces from 1.0 to 0.3, iteration: 10, population size: 10 (first data), 130 (second data)	$(1) \max \left(\sum_{\forall x_i \in y_j} \dfrac{d(x_i, y_j)}{|y_j|} \right)$ $(2) \min(d(y_i, y_j)), \forall_{i,j,i \neq j}$ (1): The maximum value of the mean of distances within same classes, and (2): The minimum value of distances between classes.	A combination of the core idea of K-means with PSO, which it leads to the clustering algorithm with low error rate as compared to K-means.
Cui & Potok (2005)	Artificial data sets: ds1 (414, 6429, 9), ds2 (313, 5804, 8), ds3 (204, 5832, 6), ds4 (878, 7454, 10) (1st: number of documents, 2nd: number of terms, 3rd: number of classes)	$c1 = c2 = 1:49$, $w = 0:72$ (in the PSO, w reduces 1% at each iteration but for hybrid it is constant), iteration: 50, population size: 50	$ADVDC =$ $\dfrac{\sum_{i=1}^{N_c} \left[\dfrac{\sum_{j=1}^{P_i} d(O_i, m_{i,j})}{P_i} \right]}{N_c}$ $m_{i,j}$ denotes the j_{th} document vector belongs to the cluster i, O_i is the centroid vector of i_{th} cluster, P_i stands for the document number belongs to the cluster C_i, and N_c stands for the cluster number.	A hybrid PSO-Kmeans document clustering algorithm presents to perform fast document clustering. The cluster quality measured with ADVDC (average distance between documents and the cluster centroid) which the smaller ADVDC value results the more compact clusters.
Merwe & Engelbrecht (2003)	Two 2-dimensional artificial data set (n=400 with c=2 and n=600 with c=4), Iris (n=150, c=3, d=4), Wine (n=178, c=3, d=13), Breast-cancer (d=9, c=2), Automotive (n=500, d=11), n: number of data, c: number of class, d: number of attribute	$c1 = c2 = 1:49$, $w = 0:72$, iteration: 1000, population size: 10	$\dfrac{\sum_{j=1}^{N_c} \left[\sum_{\forall Z_p \in C_{i,j}} \dfrac{d(Z_p, m_j)}{|C_{ij}|} \right]}{N_c}$, $|C_{ij}|$ is the number of data vectors belonging to cluster C_{ij}, *Practical methods of optimization* refers to the j_{th} cluster centroid, Z_p denotes the centroid vector of cluster j, and N_c is the number of the cluster centroid vectors.	The result of the K-means algorithm utilized as one particle, while the rest of the swarm is initialized randomly. The quality is measured by the low intra-cluster (distance between data within a cluster), and high inter-cluster distance (distance between the centroids of the clusters).

continued on following page.

Table 1. Continued

Author	Raw Data	Parameter Value	Cost Function	Contribution
Xiao et al. (2006)	1st data set for training and developing normal clusters (97,278 normal samples) and the 2nd data set for evaluation (60,593 normal and 250,436 attack samples) from KDDCup 1999	w decreases linearly by $$\left(\omega_1 - \omega_2\right)^* \frac{Max_{iter} - iter}{Max_{iter}} + \omega_2$$	$$f = \frac{1}{1 + J_c}, J_c = \sum_{j=1}^{k} \sum_{X_i \in C_j} d\left(X_i, Z_j\right),$$ $d(X_i, Z_j)$ is Euclidean distance between a data point X_i and the cluster center Z_j	It is an anomaly intrusion detection system based on combination of PSO (for initializing K cluster centroids) and K-means (for local search ability to stable the centroids). The results show a false positive rate of 2.8% and the detection rate of 86%.
Our method	1st data set for training (5,240 normal and 530 attack instances), 2nd and 3rd data sets for evaluation (2,110 normal and 866 attack, and 1,545 normal and 486 attack instances) from three CCN scenarios	$c1=c2=2$, w linearly decreases by w * *Wdamp* (Inertia Weight Damping Ratio), position and velocity limit by Eqs. (3) and (4), iteration: 1000, number of particles: 25	Well-separated clusters through DBI (Eq. (11)) and local optimization through MSE (Eq. (7)).	Fuzzy anomaly detection method in two phases, training and detection. This method leads to well-separated clusters, high detection rate, and low false positive rate at the same time as compared to some other well-known methods.

1. **Content Store (CS):** A storage space for content caching and retrieval.
2. **Forwarding Interest Base (FIB):** A table with name prefixes and corresponding outgoing interfaces for routing incoming Interests packets.
3. **Pending Interest Table (PIT):** A table with the currently unsatisfied interests and their corresponding incoming interfaces.

The following is a list of some of the main security issues in CCN:

1. **Architectural Risks:** Since contents can be cached on each CCN router, the caches can jeopardize user privacy, content privacy and perform cache pollution attacks. Because users leave communication and exchanged data traces in the caches and content can be extracted by attackers (Conti et al., 2013; Xie et al., 2012; Widjaja, 2012). And since any attacker can get that information from the caches by either using Interest packets with special query features or by probing the caches, user's privacy is very vulnerable.
2. **DoS Attacks:** There are new ways to perform DoS attacks by either making content unreachable for requests or forcing fake responses (Gasti et al., 2013; Lauinger, 2010; Compagno et al., 2013). To make content unreachable for requests, a source can be disrupted by sending large numbers of new and distinct Interests (Interest Flooding Attacks) or an attacker can decline the cache performance by overloading the cache when a cache receives a legal traffic. When attackers get high access control in a router, they can make disruption in routing by do not forwarding requests or enforce misbehaving in Pending Interest Table (PIT) routers in order to prevent content retrieval. To serve fake responses, an attacker can make routers believe a valid content is invalid and reply a

"not valid" response, deliberately. A content can also be spoofed by injecting fake responses that are not signed or are signed with a wrong key, hoping that the user accepts the response in source. An old content (which may be unsecured) signed with the right key can also be replaced with the original one, or an attacker may get high access to the source's signing key to sign content with the correct key. Another possible threat is the misbehavior of the distributed directory system (a digital certificate storage of authority identities) where a client should query for a digital certificate of a content provider, e.g., not replying to a query (Wong & Nikander, 2010; Karami, 2013).

PARTICLE SWARM OPTIMIZATION (PSO)

The PSO was firstly introduced by Kennedy and Eberhart in 1995 (Kennedy & Eberhart, 1995). It was inspired by the social behavior of a bird flock or fish school. It is a population based meta-heuristic method that optimizes a problem by initializing a flock of birds randomly over the search space where each bird is referred as a "particle" and the population of Particles is called "swarm". The Particles move iteratively around in the search space according to a simple mathematical formula over the Particle's position and velocity to find the global best position. In the n -dimensional search space, the position and the velocity of ith Particle at tth iteration of algorithm is denoted by vector $X_i(t) = (X_{i1}(t), X_{i2}(t), ..., X_{in}(t))$ and vector $V_i(t) = \left(V_{i1}(t), V_{i2}(t), ..., V_{in}(t)\right)$, respectively. This solution is evaluated by a cost function for each Particle at each stage of algorithm to provide a quantitative value of the solution's utility. Afterwards, a record of the best position of each Particle based on the cost value is saved. The best previously visited position of the Particle i at current stage is denoted by vector $P_i = (P_{i1}, P_{i2}, ..., P_{in})$ as the personal bests. During this process, the position of all the Particles that gives the best cost until the current stage is also recorded as the global best position denoted by $G = (g_1, g_2, ..., g_n)$. The structure of the velocity and the position updates is depicted in Figure 1. Each iteration is composed of three movements: in the first movement, Particle moves slightly toward the front in the previous direction with the same speed. In the second movement, it moves slightly toward the previous itself best position. Finally, in the third movement, moves slightly toward the global position.

Figure 1. Description of velocity and position updates in PSO for a 2-dimensional parameter space

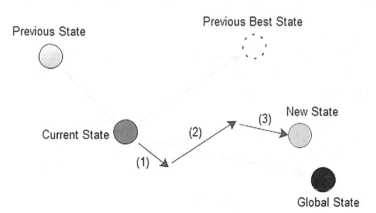

At each iteration, the velocity and the position of each Particle are defined according to Eqs. 1 and 2, respectively:

$$V_i(t) = \omega * V_i(t-1) + c_1\varphi_1(P_i - X_i(t-1)) + c_2\varphi_2(G - X_i(t-1)) \tag{1}$$

$$X_i(t) = X_i(t-1) + V_i(t) \tag{2}$$

where, ω denotes the nonzero inertia weight factor that introduces a preference for the Particle to continue moving in the same direction. Decreasing the inertia over time introduces a shift from the exploratory (global search) to the exploitative (local search) mode (Li et al., 2014; Settles, 2005). Generally, the inertia weight ω is reduced linearly. There are several selection strategies of inertia weight ω which have been described in (Shi & Eberhart, 1998; Eberhart & Shi, 2000). c_1 and c_2 are positive constant (social) parameters called acceleration coefficients which control the maximum step size between successive iterations. φ_1 and φ_2 are two independently positive random number drawn form a uniform distribution between 0.0 and 1.0. According to (Settles, 2005), a good starting point is to set ω start to 0.9, ω end to 0.4, and $c_1 = c_2 = 2$. The velocity and position of a Particle might end up positioning the Particle beyond the boundary $[Var_{\min}, Var_{\max}]$ of the search space. Therefore, the need of having a scheme which can bring such Particles back into the search space. We apply *Set On Boundary* strategy. According to this strategy the Particle is reset on the bound of the variable which it exceeds (Padhye et al., 2012). Let X_c denote a current velocity or position of a solution, then X_c is set to X_c^{new} as follows:

$$X_c \rightarrow X_c^{new} = \begin{cases} -0.1 * (Var_{\max} - Var_{\min}) \text{ if } X_c < lowerbound \\ 0.1 * (Var_{\max} - Var_{\min}) \text{ if } X_c > upperbound \end{cases} \tag{3}$$

An additional strategy called velocity reflection is also applied. Velocity reflection allows those Particles that move toward the outside the boundary to move back into the search space according to Eq. (4).

$$V_i(t+1) \rightarrow -V_i(t+1) \tag{4}$$

K-MEANS CLUSTERING ALGORITHM

The K-means algorithm groups the set of data points into a predefined number of the clusters in terms of a distance function. The most widely used method is the Euclidean distance in which a small distance implies a strong similarity whereas a large distance implies a low similarity. Eq. (5) shows the Euclidean distance calculation between two data points (x and y) with N objects in a n-dimensional space:

$$Dis\tan ce(x,y) = \sqrt{\sum_{i=1}^{n}(X_i - y_i)^2} \tag{5}$$

The standard K-means algorithm is summarized as follows:

1. Randomly initialize the K cluster centroids.
2. Assign each object to the group with the closest centroid. Euclidean distance measures the minimum distance between data objects and each cluster centroid.
3. Recalculate the cluster centroid vector, using

$$m_j = \frac{1}{n_j} \sum_{\forall data_p \in C_j} data_p \tag{6}$$

where, m_j denotes the centroid vector of the cluster j, n_j is the number of the data vectors in cluster j, c_j is the subset of the data vectors from cluster j, and $data_p$ denotes the pth data vector.

4. Repeat step 2 until the centroids do not change any more in the predefined number of iteration or a maximum number of iterations has been reached.

CLUSTERING PROBLEM

Mean Square Error (MSE) is the average pairwise distance between the data points and the corresponding cluster centroids. Usually distance is the Euclidean distance, but other metrics are also used. Given the set of cluster centroids (c), the set of corresponding data points (x), c_x denotes the cluster centroid corresponding to the x, and N is the number of data points, MSE can be calculated as:

$$MSE = \frac{1}{N} \sum_{i=1}^{N} d(x_i, c_x)^2 \tag{7}$$

In order to determine the correct and the optimal number of clusters, we must choose the validation criteria. There are several methods (such as K-means) which try to minimize the MSE between data vectors and their cluster centroid to verify the clustering goodness (Everitt, 1993; Gersho & Gray, 1992). But, MSE is not enough and suitable metric for determining the number of the clusters, since it decreases as the number of cluster increases. In fact, the optimal MSE would be the number of cluster that equals data set points, and the MSE=0. Therefore, we apply Davies Bouldin Index (DBI) (Davies & Bouldin, 1979) as the criterion since, in our experiments, we have found it to be quite reliable among the variety of alternative internal clustering validation metrics with regard to pointing out the correct number of clusters. DBI takes into account both compactness (intra-cluster diversity) and separation (inter-cluster diversity) criteria that makes similar data points within the same clusters and places other data points in distinct clusters. The intra-cluster diversity of a cluster j is calculated as

$$MSE_j = \frac{1}{N} \sum_{i=1}^{N} d\left(x_i, c_x\right)^2 \tag{8}$$

The inter-cluster distance of the cluster i and j is measured as the distance between their centroids c_i and c_j. According to Eq. (9), the closeness of the two clusters can be calculated by the sum of their MSE divided by the distance of their centroids:

$$Closeness_{i,j} = \frac{MSE_i + MSE_j}{d(c_i, c_j)} \tag{9}$$

Small value of $Closeness_{i,j}$ denotes that the clusters are separated and a large value denotes that the clusters are close to each other. To calculate DBI value, the highest value from Eq. (9) is assigned to cluster as its cluster similarity:

$$Closeness_i = \max(Closeness_{i,j}), i \neq j \tag{10}$$

Finally, the overall DBI validity is defined according to Eq. (11), which the lower DBI value means better clustering result:

$$DBI = \frac{1}{M} \sum_{i=1}^{M} Closeness_i \tag{11}$$

FUZZY SETS (FS)

In classical set theory, an element either belongs or not to a set of elements. Therefore, the membership evaluation is Boolean. A more flexible approach would be fuzzy set theory, where elements belong to sets with certain degree of membership that takes its value in the interval [0 1]. This makes fuzzy set theory suitable for complex models where some things are not either entirely true nor entirely false and where the problems are somehow ambiguous or it is needed to manage subjective judgments or opinions (Karami & Guerrero-Zapata, 2014). FS is appropriate for anomaly detection for two major reasons (Izakian & Pedrycz, 2014; Wu & Banzhaf, 2010):

1. The anomaly detection problem involves many numeric attributes in collected audit data and various derived statistical measurements. Building models directly on numeric data causes high detection errors, and
2. The security itself involves fuzziness, because the boundary between the normal and abnormal is not well defined.

Fuzzy logic also can work with other popular data mining technique as outlier detection. Since malicious behavior is naturally different from normal behavior, abnormal behavior should be considered as outliers (Chimphlee et al., 2005; He et al., 2005). Fuzzy logic can help to construct more abstract and flexible patterns for intrusion detection and thus greatly increase the robustness and adaption ability of detection systems (Wu & Banzhaf, 2010). Hence, fuzzy approach can reduce the false positive rate with higher reliability in determining intrusive activities, due to any data (normal or attack) may be similar (closest distance) to some clusters.

PROPOSED FUZZY ANOMALY DETECTION SYSTEM

This section presents the details of our proposed method. Proposed fuzzy anomaly detection system consists of two phases: training and detection. Figure 2 shows the proposed fuzzy anomaly detection system steps. Each phase is also described as follows.

Figure 2. Two steps of the proposed fuzzy anomaly detection system

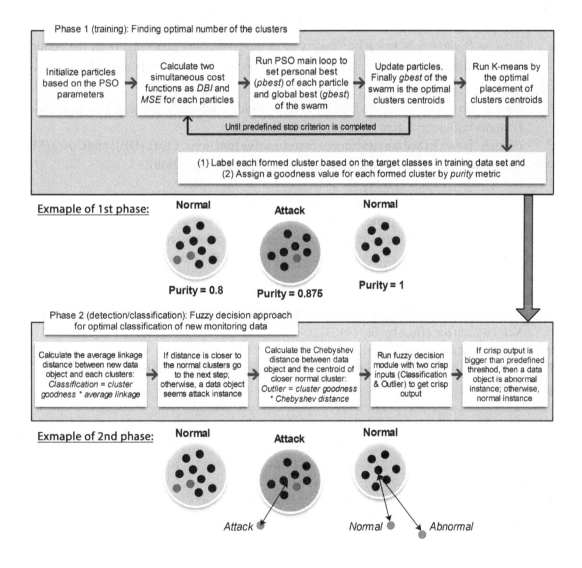

Training Phase

The training phase is based on the hybridization of PSO and K-means clustering algorithm with two simultaneous cost functions: well-separated clusters (low intra-cluster distance and high inter-cluster distance) by DBI and local optimization by MSE to find the optimal number of clusters. Before training process, data samples should be normalized into [0 1], when dealing with parameters of different units and scales (Karami, 2011; Karami & Johansson, 2014). The steps of the training phase is presented as follow.

Step 1: Define Problem and PSO Parameters

1. *nVar*: number of the cluster centroids, *nPop*: size of the population;
2. Define constriction coefficients parameters, $c_1 = c_2 = 2$ and initially $\omega = 1$;
3. Define inertia weight damping ratio (*Wdamp* = 0.99) to linearly decrease ω;
4. Define position and velocity limits as $Var_{max} = 1$ and $Var_{min} = 0$;
5. An initial population is generated based on the *nPop* with following parameters:
   a. *Particle.Position* = a $m \times nVar$ matrix of random numbers generated from the continuous uniform distributions with lower $\left(Var_{min}\right)$ and upper $\left(Var_{max}\right)$ endpoints. M denotes size of the data set features;
   b. *Particle.Cost* = calculate the DBI for each Particle based on the generated *Particle.Position*;
   c. *Particle.Velocity* = a zero matrix in $m \times nVar$ size;
   d. *Particle.Sol* = [], (Sol is a structure of two objective functions: Cost1 (DBI) and Cost2 (MSE));
   e. *Particle.Best.Position* = [] (keep the personal best of the position);
   f. *Particle.Best.Cost* = [] (keep the personal best of the cost);
   g. *Particle.Best.Sol* = [] (keep the personal best of the Sol);
      6. *Globalbest* = [] (keep the global best of swarm);
7. Repeat the following loop until the target or maximum iteration is completed:
8. Select *Particle(i); i = 1, 2, ..., nPop* and run the following PSO algorithm for *Particle(i)*:
   a. Update velocity by Eq. (1);
   b. Apply velocity limits by Eq. (3);
   c. Update position by Eq. (2);
   d. Velocity mirror effect by Eq. (4);
   e. Apply position limits by Eq. (3);
   f. Evaluation of two objective functions, DBI by Eq. (11) and MSE by Eq. (7);
   g. Update personal best:

```
If (Particle(i).Cost = Particle(i).Best.Cost) AND (Particle(i).Sol.MSE <
Particle(i).Best.Sol.MSE)
        Particle(i).Best.Position = Particle(i).Position;
        Particle(i).Best.Sol = Particle(i).Sol;
    else if (Particle(i).Cost < Particle(i).Best.Cost)
        Particle(i).Best.Position = Particle(i).Position;
        Particle(i).Best.Cost = Particle(i).Cost;
        Particle(i).Best.Sol = Particle(i).Sol;
```

```
      end
  end;
```

h.   Update global best:

```
  if ((Particle(i).Best.Cost == GlobalBest.Cost) AND (Particle(i).BestSol.
MSE < GlobalBest.Sol.MSE)) OR (Particle(i).Best.Cost < GlobalBest.Cost)
      GlobalBest = Particle(i).Best;
  end;
```

9.   if $i > nPop$ go to the step 10; otherwise, set $i = i + 1$ and go to the step 8;
10.   Update ω by $\omega = \omega * Wdamp$;
11.   If the maximum iteration or predefined target is not reached, set $i = 1$ and go to the step 7; Otherwise, run K-means clustering algorithm by the obtained positions of cluster centroids from PSO algorithm.

After the main procedure of training phase, each formed cluster is labeled based on the target (original) classes in training data set. It is highly probable that the clusters containing normal data (correct classification) will have a number of abnormal data (incorrect classification) and vice versa. Therefore, we assigned a goodness value in range of [0...1] for each formed cluster by purity metric. The purity metric determines the frequency of the most common category/class into each cluster:

$$Purity = \frac{1}{n} \sum_{q=1}^{k} \max_{1 \le j \le l} n_q^j \qquad (12)$$

where, n is the total number of samples; l is the number of categories, n_q^j is the number of samples in cluster q that belongs to the original class j ($1 \le j \le l$). A large purity (close to 1) is desired for a good clustering. If the all samples (data) in a cluster have the same class, the purity value set to 1 as a pure cluster. This purity metric (goodness value) is used in the detection phase.

Detection Phase

The defined optimal placement of cluster centroids and data objects from training phase are sent to the second phase for outlier and anomaly detection when new monitoring data enter. In the detection phase, a fuzzy decision approach applied to detect attacks and anomalies. We deploy a combination of two distance-based methods, i.e., classification and outlier:

1.   **Classification:** The distances between a data object and each clusters are calculated using the *goodness value of the cluster* × average linkage. Average linkage approach considers small variances, because it considers all members in the cluster rather than just a single point. However, it tends to be less influenced by extreme values than other distance methods (Verma, 2013). A data object is classified as normal if it is closer to the one of the normal clusters than to the anomalous ones, and vice versa. This distance-based classification allows detecting known kind of abnormal or normal traffics with similar characteristics as in the training data set.

2. **Outlier:** An outlier (noise) is a data object that differs considerably from most other objects, which can be considered as an anomaly. For outlier detection, only the distance to the normal clusters (obtained from classification phase) is calculated by *goodness value of the closer normal cluster* ×Chebyshev distance. In the Chebyshev distance (Eq. (13)), distance between two vectors is the greatest of their differences along any coordinate dimension. It allows to detect better new anomalies that do not appear in the training data set. Because it takes into account the maximum value distance approach between any coordinate dimensions that would lead to become stricter against data objects measurement.

$$D_{chebyshev}(p,c) = \max(|p_i - c_i|) \tag{13}$$

where, p is the data object and c is the centroids of the normal cluster with standard coordinates p_i and c_i. The proposed fuzzy detection method consists of two inputs (classification and outlier), one output, and four main parts: fuzzification, rules, inference engine, and defuzzification. In fuzzification step, a crisp set of input data are converted to a fuzzy set using fuzzy linguistic terms and membership functions. In step 2, we construct rule base. Afterwards, an inference is made and combined based on a set of rules. In the defuzzification step, the results of fuzzy output are mapped to a crisp (non-fuzzy) output using the membership functions. Finally, if the crisp output is bigger than a predefined threshold, an object is considered as an abnormal instance; otherwise, an object is a normal instance. This fuzzy approach can improve our performance criteria (high detection rate and low false positive rate at the same time) as compared to a non-fuzzy approach.

EXPERIMENTAL RESULTS AND DISCUSSION

Performance Measurement

We compared and evaluated the training phase of our proposed method with standalone PSO and K-means algorithms as well as preexisting methods from the literature as (Chen, 2012; Zhenkui et al., 2008; Cui & Potok, 2005; Merwe & Engelbrecht, 2003; Xiao et al., 2006) which used different parameters and cost functions. We also employed both MSE and DBI criteria on all evaluations. In order to evaluate the performance of each method, we use the Detection Rate (DR), False Positive Rate (FPR) and F-measure criteria. The detection rate is the number of intrusions detected by the system from Eq. (14), the false positive rate is the number of normal traffics that was incorrectly classified as intrusion from Eq. (15) and F-measure is the weighted harmonic mean of precision (positive predictive value) and recall (detection rate) from Eq. (17):

$$DR(Recall) = \frac{TruePositive}{TruePositive + FalseNegative} \tag{14}$$

$$FPR = \frac{FalsePositive}{FalsePositive + TrueNegative} \tag{15}$$

$$Precision = \frac{TruePositive}{TruePositive + FalsePositive} \tag{16}$$

$$F - measure = 2 \times \frac{Precision \times Recall}{Precision + Recall} \tag{17}$$

True negative and true positive correspond to a correct operation of the system when traffics are successfully predicted as normal and attacks, respectively. False positive refers to normal traffics when are predicted as attack, and false negative is attack traffic when incorrectly predicted as normal traffic.

Benchmarking the Proposed Method

To assess the robustness and accuracy of our proposed method, we applied the five classic benchmark problems from the UCI machine learning repository (Asuncion & Newman, 2007). Table 2 shows the main characteristics of these data sets. All experiments were run 20 times, and the average classification error (Ave.) and its standard deviation (S.D.) were computed. In the experiments, 70% of data set is used as training data set in the training phase and the rest is considered as testing data set in the detection phase in order to validate the functionality of the proposed method. We assume that the normal clusters denote the correct classification and abnormal (attack) clusters denote the incorrect classification. For instance, given a data object d in a test data set belongings to class A. If it gets assigned to class B by the proposed classification method in the second phase, class B is an incorrect class/category for data object d. Hereby, the formed cluster belongings to class B is assumed to be an abnormal cluster for the data object d. In contrast, if data object d is closer to a cluster labeled class A (we called it normal cluster), the outlier distance should be calculated. Then, according to the detection/classification phase of the proposed method, both classification and outlier values are sent to the fuzzy module. If the crisp output is smaller than the predefined threshold, data object d seems normal instance (correct classification); otherwise, it seems anomalous instance (incorrect classification). The results have been summarized in Table 3. It can be seen in the table that our proposed fuzzy method tends to obtain a more accurate classification rate (Ave.) and lower standard deviation (S.D.) as compared to other methods.

Table 2. The five applied benchmark data sets

Data Set	No. of Features	No. of Classes	No. of Patterns
Iris	4	3	150
Glass	9	6	214
Wine	13	3	178
Ionosphere	34	2	351
Zoo	17	7	101

Table 3. Classification error (%) for our proposed method and applied methods

Method	Type	Criteria	Data Sets				
			Iris	Glass	Wine	Ionosphere	Zoo
K-means	Training	Ave.	6.86	19.54	18.2	11.64	10.83
		S.D.	2.34	3.61	3.66	3.28	2.73
	Test	Ave.	5.53	17.59	18.26	11.12	9.42
		S.D.	2.32	3.12	3.76	3.1	2.6
PSO (MSE)	Training	Ave.	5.42	17.41	17.08	10.66	10.35
		S.D.	2.14	3.08	3.01	2.86	2.73
	Test	Ave.	4.84	16.41	16.81	9.59	9.64
		S.D.	2.24	3.3	2.98	2.78	2.2
PSO (DBI, MSE)	Training	Ave.	4.9	16.85	17.46	10.75	9.98
		S.D.	1.73	3.01	2.56	3.14	2.48
	Test	Ave.	4.59	16.08	16.41	9.17	8.64
		S.D.	1.62	2.85	2.41	2.72	2.6
PSO-Kmeans (MSE)	Training	Ave.	5.1	16.89	17.54	11.94	11.4
		S.D.	1.23	3.08	3.56	2.91	2.55
	Test	Ave.	4.77	16.81	17.48	9.96	9.35
		S.D.	1.26	3.1	3.26	2.78	2.6
Chen, 2012	Training	Ave.	4.87	16.32	15.24	11.16	8.58
		S.D.	1.28	3.32	3.4	2.48	2.4
	Test	Ave.	5.4	16.07	15.08	9.92	8.06
		S.D.	1.4	3.63	2.92	2.39	2.02
Zhenkui, 2008	Training	Ave.	5.92	16.54	16.34	10.42	10.03
		S.D.	1.35	3.47	3.4	3.36	3.3
	Test	Ave.	5.76	16.43	15.6	9.88	10.05
		S.D.	1.5	3.51	3.04	2.68	2.75
Cui, 2005	Training	Ave.	5.84	18.72	16.98	12.24	11.52
		S.D.	1.34	3.78	3.3	3.79	3.17
	Test	Ave.	5.48	17.18	15.82	11.86	9.56
		S.D.	1.32	3.61	2.98	3.61	3.25
Merwe, 2003	Training	Ave.	6.01	18.59	17.65	10.45	9.31
		S.D.	1.97	4.54	4.76	4.87	5.01
	Test	Ave.	5.98	17.64	16.16	11.06	9.11
		S.D.	1.75	4.85	5.02	4.85	3.97
Xiao, 2006	Training	Ave.	4.91	16.29	15.62	11.18	9.49
		S.D.	1.23	3.33	3.9	2.98	2.35
	Test	Ave.	4.52	16.18	15.14	10.22	8.09
		S.D.	1.38	3.11	3.01	2.84	2.23
Our method PSO-Kmeans (DBI, MSE)	Training	Ave.	4.01	14.44	14.88	10.04	7.98
		S.D.	1.03	2.29	2.16	2.31	2.11
	Test	Ave.	3.58	13.14	13.04	9.03	7.47
		S.D.	0.98	2.12	2.01	2.26	1.88

Feature Construction

We employed simple features that can be extracted by inspecting the headers of the network packets. These intrinsic features are the duration of the connection, source host, destination host, source interface, and destination interface (Lee & Stolfo, 2000). We also used the following features in each 2 seconds time interval:

1. Total number of packets sent from and to the given interface in the considered time interval,
2. Total number of bytes sent from and to the given interface in the considered time interval,
3. Number of different source-destination pairs matching the given content name that being observed in the considered time interval.

The motivation of the first two features is that the number of packets and bytes allow to detect anomalies in traffic volume, and the third feature allows to detect network and interface scans as well as distributed attacks, which both result in increased number of source-destination pairs (Münz et al., 2007).

Training Phase

Since there is no reference data for content-centric networks as well as real Internet traffic, we used the CCNx software of PARC (www.ccnx.org) to run a scenario for generating of CCN traffics in a local testbed. This local testbed includes 13 Linux machines (9 clients, 2 servers and 2 routers). We performed the following experiments with the main tools in CCNx: ccnsendchunks (to upload objects/files into the CCN repository), ccncatchunks2 (to receive desired contents and to write them to stdout), ccnputfile (to publish a local file in the CCNx repository), ccngetfile (to retrieve published content and writes it to the local file), ccndsmoketest (to send the large number of Interests -Interest flooding attacks- toward a host/ network), and ccnchat (to run a chat channel). We conducted three attack instances for both training and detection phases including Interest flooding attacks, flooding a victim router by sending too many small contents from owner of origin content (we called it Abnormal Source Behavior) and making content unreachable for requesters (we called it Abnormal Unreachable Content Behavior). We also carried out an anomaly instance in the detection phase as serving fake response (we called it Abnormal Forwarder Capacity Behavior) which does not appear in the training data set. The structure of the generated traffics are shown in Table 4 for training and Tables 5 and 6 for testing data sets. The proposed hybrid method was implemented by the MATLAB software on an Intel Pentium 2.13 GHz CPU, 4 GB RAM running Windows 7 Ultimate.

Detection Phase

We use MATLAB fuzzy logic toolbox for fuzzy rule based intrusion detection. The detection phase is structured with the following components:

1. Two fuzzy set of input variables: Classification and Outlier.
   a. *Classification membership*: Very Close, Close, Average, Far, Very Far;
   b. *Outlier membership:* Close, Average, Far.

Table 4. CCNx traffic generation

Type of Traffic	Applied Tools
Normal (5240 records)	(1) *ccnsendchunks* with *ccncatchunks2* (2) *ccnputfi le* with *ccngetfile* (3) *ccnchat*
Attack (530 records)	(1) *ccndsmoketest* for (distributed) Interest flooding attack (2) make abnormal traffics to saturate channels by sending very small contents (decreasing buffer size) from owner of origin, called *Abnormal Source Behavior* (3) do not forward contents deliberately to requester(s), called *Abnormal Unreachable Content Behavior*

Table 5. First scenario of CCNx traffic

Type of Traffic	Applied Tools
Normal (2110 records)	(1) *HttpProxy* application to run a HTTP proxy that converts HTTP Gets to CCN data. (2) *ccnput file* with *ccnget file* (3) *ccnchat*
Attack (866 records)	(1) *ccndsmoketest* for Interest flooding attack (2) *Abnormal Source Behavior* (3) make capacity limitation in count of content objects by forwarder/router to discard cached content objects deliberately as *Abnormal Forwarder Capacity Behavior*

Table 6. Second scenario of CCNx traffic

Type of Traffic	Applied Tools
Normal (1545 records)	(1) *ccnsendchunks* with *ccncatchunks2* (2) *ccnputfi le* with *ccngetfi le* (3) *HttpProxy* application
Attack (492 records)	(1) *Abnormal Source Behavior* (2) *Abnormal Unreachable Content Behavior* (3) *Abnormal Forwarder Capacity Behavior*

2. A fuzzy set of output variable: Alarm.

    a. *Alarm membership:* Normal, Less Prone, High Prone, Abnormal.

3. Fuzzy membership functions: See Figure 9.

4. Fuzzy rules: 15 rules (Tables 7 and 8).

5. Inference: Mamdani fuzzy inference by fuzzy set operations as max and min for OR and AND, respectively.

6. Defuzzifier: Center of Gravity algorithm:

$$Center\ of\ Gravity = \frac{\int_{min}^{max} u\mu(u)d(u)}{\int_{min}^{max} \mu(u)d(u)} \qquad (18)$$

where, u denotes the output variable, μ is the membership function after accumulation, and min and max are lower and upper limit for defuzzification, respectively.

A sample solution area (fuzzy inference) of proposed fuzzy detection phase is given in Figure 3.

Figure 9. Seven applied membership functions in detection phase (two inputs and one output)

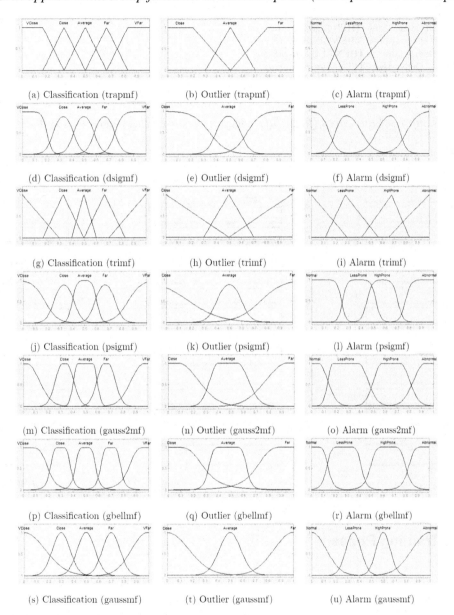

(a) Classification (trapmf)   (b) Outlier (trapmf)   (c) Alarm (trapmf)

(d) Classification (dsigmf)   (e) Outlier (dsigmf)   (f) Alarm (dsigmf)

(g) Classification (trimf)   (h) Outlier (trimf)   (i) Alarm (trimf)

(j) Classification (psigmf)   (k) Outlier (psigmf)   (l) Alarm (psigmf)

(m) Classification (gauss2mf)   (n) Outlier (gauss2mf)   (o) Alarm (gauss2mf)

(p) Classification (gbellmf)   (q) Outlier (gbellmf)   (r) Alarm (gbellmf)

(s) Classification (gaussmf)   (t) Outlier (gaussmf)   (u) Alarm (gaussmf)

Table 7. Rules matrix

Outlier	Classification (Cls.)				
	Very Close	**Close**	**Average**	**Far**	**Very Far**
Close	Normal	Normal	Normal	Low prone	Low prone
Average	Low prone	Low prone	High prone	High prone	High prone
Far	High prone	High prone	Abnormal	Abnormal	Abnormal

Table 8. Some fuzzy rules in proposed fuzzy system

IF Cls.=*Average* and Outlier=*Close* **THEN** Alarm=*Normal*
IF Cls.=*Close* and Outlier=*Average* **THEN** Alarm=*LowProne*
IF Cls.=*High* and Outlier=*Average* **THEN** Alarm=*HighProne*
IF Cls.=*Very far* and Outlier=*Far* **THEN** Alarm=*Abnormal*

Figure 3. The sample solution area (fuzzy inference) of proposed fuzzy detection system

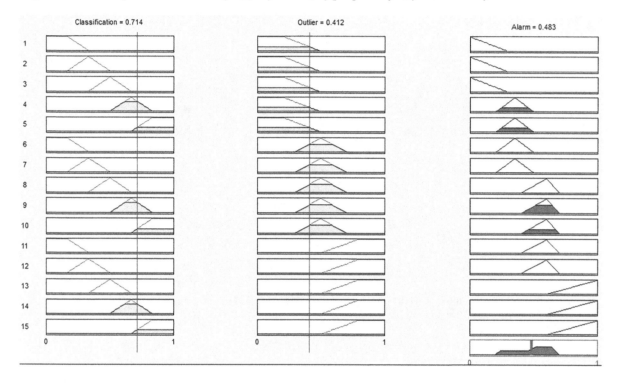

Results of Training Phase

In this section, the performance of proposed method and preexisting methods from the literature are compared. Since null clusters might appear in the results, these clusters are removed and we count the correct number of *K*. The experiments on each method were repeated 10 times independently with several *K* values. The trends of minimum and maximum ratio of the DR and the FPR at the same time for applied methods are shown in Figure 4. Detailed results are also given in Table 9. The proposed method outperforms other preexisting methods in terms of the DR, the FPR and the F-measure at the same time. The PSO (DBI and MSE) could satisfy DR by 99% when initial K is between 300 and 500. However, it could not satisfy a suitable FPR. By the hybridization of K-means algorithm and PSO (DBI and MSE), we could gain suitable results by very low FPR and very high DR at the same time. In contrast, none of other methods meet very high DR and very low FPR at the same time. According to the Table 9, by increasing of initial parameter K, results are more efficient with the optimal number of clusters, high detection rate, low false positive rate and greater F-measure at the same time.

Figure 4. The trends of minimum and maximum combination of DR and FPR at the same time

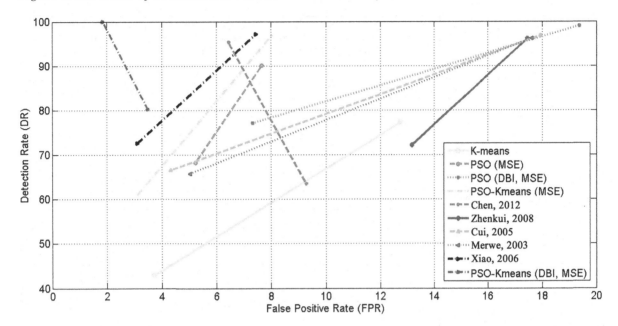

The results clearly show that our proposed method offers the best optimized solution in comparison with the other methods when K=400 by DR=100%, FPR=1.847%, F-measure=98.99% and the correct number of K=27. We show the fluctuation of variations of two cost functions during the training phase in Figures 5 and 6. The results clearly show that by changing of clustering values based on DBI, MSE changes in an irregular manner through the different iterations. For instance, in the last iteration, the minimum MSE is 8.391, but the lowest MSE is in iteration 915 by 8.3458.

When DBI is decreasing to find optimal clustering results in the iterations between 100 and 800, there are many fluctuations for MSE value. We also show the trend of changes of DBI and MSE values during the training phase when the DR was 100% and K is between 300 and 500 (Figures 7 and 8). According to Figure 7, the best and the worst procedure of reducing the DBI value are for K=300 and 400, respectively. In contrast, the best and the worst procedure of reducing the MSE value are for K=500 and 300 as shown in Figure 8. The best DBI value for K=300 led to the worst value in MSE. Moreover, the highest changes for minimizing the two applied cost functions during the training phase are for K=400 and 500. These results verify that the MSE parameter cannot be singly used as a good performance criterion for finding the optimal placement of clusters centroids and data objects. We send the optimal outcomes from our proposed method (DR = 100%, FPR = 1.847%, F-measure = 89.99% and K = 27) and the best combination of the DR, the FPR and the F-measure from other methods to the second phase for fuzzy anomaly detection.

Results of Detection Phase

In order to obtain results on how the proposed fuzzy anomaly detection system can perform in real scenarios, we applied it to packet traces recorded at two scenarios with 17 Linux machines (10 clients, 4 servers, and 3 routers). These traces are from CCNx data repository of the Universitat Politecnica de

Table 9. Comparison of our proposed method with some other methods

K	Criteria	Kmeans	PSO (MSE)	PSO (MSE, DBI)	PSO-Kmeans (MSE)	Chen, 2012	Zhenkui, 2008	Cui, 2005	Merwe, 2003	Xia, 2006	Our Method
100	Correct K	15	15	14	15	16	17	20	19	16	14
	DR (%)	47.24	68.18	77.11	67.14	64.5	72.14	76.55	75.83	76.12	80.22
	FPR (%)	8.55	6.43	7.83	7.81	7.18	12.31	8.12	9.12	12.8	3.48
	F-measure (%)	60.61	78.06	83.35	76.72	75.11	78.17	82.85	80.68	80.52	87.32
125	Correct K	17	10	15	18	18	15	21	21	17	11
	DR (%)	56.18	68.18	77.11	65.12	66.5	72.14	66.55	67.89	77.12	80.22
	FPR (%)	4.73	4.1	3.505	3.93	8.13	9.63	2.98	3.78	10.02	3.48
	F-measure (%)	69.81	79.31	85.37	77.02	76.12	79.33	78.5	78.95	82.38	87.32
150	Correct K	11	14	16	13	14	14	15	16	17	16
	DR (%)	42.93	68.18	77.11	71.14	71.11	72.14	76.55	77.93	77.14	80.22
	FPR (%)	3.73	1.34	1.34	2.1	5.98	12.5	8.88	7.64	12.2	1.31
	F-measure (%)	58.53	80.43	86.41	82.12	80.28	78.09	82.51	85.89	81.43	88.38
175	Correct K	22	22	20	21	25	31	30	32	17	20
	DR (%)	71.9	68.18	77.11	70.54	72.11	83.34	78.95	76.89	77.06	80.22
	FPR (%)	4.48	3.13	3	2.44	3.98	15.98	14.14	13.54	3.09	2.73
	F-measure (%)	81.51	79.58	85.61	81.55	81.88	83.55	81.71	82.48	85.53	87.68
200	Correct K	16	18	18	19	22	21	20	19	20	18
	DR (%)	64.24	71.11	77.11	74.34	72.11	73.34	72.95	74.35	81.66	80.22
	FPR (%)	2.73	3	1.37	2.73	9.98	12.43	12.15	13.14	14.09	1.31
	F-measure (%)	76.81	81.67	88.71	83.95	79.16	78.9	78.76	80.32	83.37	88.38
250	Correct K	16	17	15	19	19	16	21	18	18	15
	DR (%)	64.24	70.34	77.11	71.01	82.11	72.24	75.95	79.45	72.66	80.22
	FPR (%)	2.73	2.01	3.91	4.11	15.95	5.86	1.16	3.12	3.01	2.73
	F-measure (%)	76.81	81.61	85.18	81.08	82.85	81.1	85.74	86.83	82.66	87.7
300	Correct K	21	20	14	20	21	18	18	19	17	14
	DR (%)	74.82	88.27	99	88.13	81.44	89.91	90.1	88.34	94.1	100
	FPR (%)	10.31	9.12	17.35	9.19	11.2	17.33	24.51	26.93	16.91	9.11
	F-measure (%)	80.74	89.36	91.44	89.28	84.5	86.59	83.36	81.14	88.71	95.64
350	Correct K	21	25	26	22	23	23	26	25	20	26
	DR (%)	77.22	90.12	99	88.66	88.44	95.22	92.2	93.67	97.1	100
	FPR (%)	12.38	16.98	9.67	10.25	9.2	9.16	12.12	11.39	7.45	6.8
	F-measure (%)	81.4	86.96	94.84	89.1	89.45	93.13	90.19	90.83	94.91	96.71
400	Correct K	16	21	25	19	21	28	28	26	27	27
	DR (%)	77.22	90.12	99	92.55	95.29	94	96.2	94.23	97.07	100
	FPR (%)	12.38	16.98	17.99	10.45	6.45	15.45	13.12	14.67	14.96	1.84
	F-measure (%)	81.37	86.95	90.89	91.21	94.64	89.82	91.92	88.45	91.76	98.99
500	Correct K	23	24	21	22	25	31	33	33	27	21
	DR (%)	77.22	90.12	99	96.68	94.29	96	96.78	96.15	96.8	100
	FPR (%)	12.73	7.67	19.36	8.01	16.45	17.45	17.94	17.63	12.21	12.37
	F-measure (%)	81.25	91.09	90.59	94.43	89.42	89.88	90.01	90.03	92.54	94.17

Figure 5. 1st cost function (DBI) in 1000 iterations

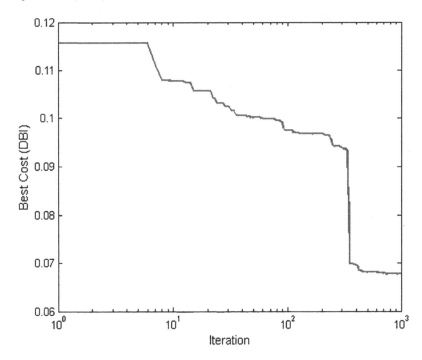

Figure 6. 2nd cost function (MSE) in 1000 iterations

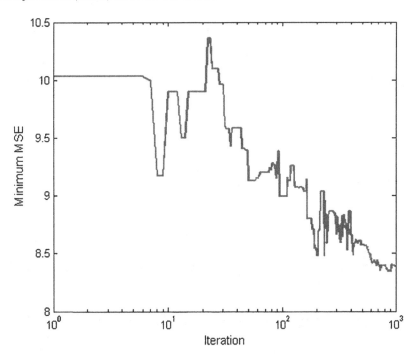

Figure 7. The best cost (DBI) of four clustering results

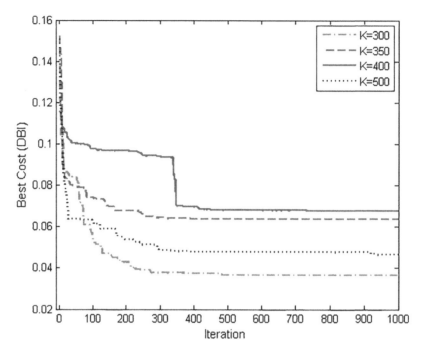

Figure 8. The MSE value of four clustering results

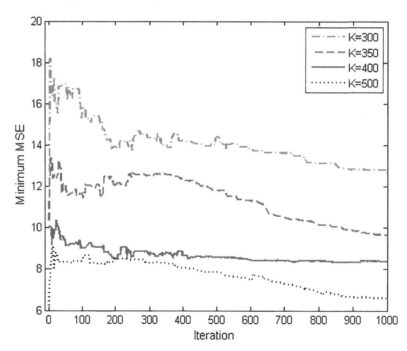

Catalunya (UPC) which are shown in Tables 5 and 6. Each trace file contains about 20 minutes of monitored traffic. According to Tables 5 and 6, there is a new type of normal traffic (HttpProxy) and a new type of anomaly traffic (Abnormal Forwarder Capacity Behavior) which have not appeared in the training data set. We also define a threshold as $d_{threshold} = 0.5$. Each new monitored CCN packet is sent as input to the fuzzy detection phase in order to detect attacks and anomalies. According to the proposed fuzzy anomaly detection system, we calculate the classification distance to find the nearest cluster. If the distance is closer to one of the normal clusters, we calculate the outlier. If the outlier outcome is bigger than a predefined threshold, the packet is treated as an anomaly. In contrast, if the classification distance is closer to one of the attack clusters, it gets treated as an attack packet.

Based on the different fuzzy membership functions, the fuzzy detection method produces different results. To find the most ideal system, we apply seven membership functions for each applied methods including trapmf (Trapezoidal-shaped), dsigmf (Difference between two sigmoidal functions), trimf (Triangular-shaped), psigmf (Product of two sigmoidal), gauss2mf (Gaussian combination), gbellmf (Generalized bell-shaped), and gaussmf (Gaussian curve). Figure 9 illustrates the applied membership functions. We integrated each method by optimal results gained from the training phase (Table 4) with our proposed fuzzy detection method in the second phase. Afterwards, we compare the performance of each method based on the RMSE, minimum and maximum error between target output and predicted output. The comparison results between methods in two applied data sets (Tables 5 and 6) are summarized in Table 10. We found out that the RMSE between target and predicted output is absolutely different. We marked the three best results for each membership function. The most appropriate results based on the RMSE, minimum and maximum error include our proposed method (PSO-Kmeans (DBI, MSE)), PSO (DBI, MSE), methods [36] and [40], respectively. By the integration of DBI (well-separated cost) and MSE (local optimization cost), PSO could considerably improve the results in detection phase. As shown, our proposed method is very well suited for most of the membership functions based on the less RMSE, minimum and maximum error values. Performance of trapmf and gauss2mf MF in our proposed method are better than other MF and applied methods.

For anomaly detection performance measurement, we continue our experiment by applying well-performing and preexisting methods from Table 10 on the aforementioned data sets. The performance of fuzzy detection approach is also compared with the non-fuzzy approach. In order to validate the CCNx traffic classification performance of our fuzzy detector, we use the Receiver Operating Characteristic (ROC) curve analysis, Area Under the Curve (AUC), accuracy, specificity and sensitivity (recall). The ROC curve provides a way to visually represent how the trade-off between false positive and detection rate varies for different values of the detection threshold (Bradley, 1997). The AUC summarizes the classification performance of the classifier in the range [0 1] in which the higher the AUC, the easier to distinguish attacks from normal traffic (Cortes & Mohri, 2005). The other applied performance measures can be summarized as a 2×2 table (confusion matrix in Table 11):

1. **Accuracy:** (a + d) = (a + b + c + d)
2. **Specificity (true Negative Rate):** a = (a + b)
3. **Sensitivity (Recall):** d = (c + d)

Table 12 shows the results of fuzzy and non-fuzzy (crisp) anomaly detection for two applied testing data sets. As shown in this table, our proposed method classifies data objects better than the other

Table 10. Comparison of membership functions for fuzzy anomaly detection purposes

Methods	Data Set	Criteria	trapmf	dsigmf	trimf	psigmf	gauss2mf	gbellmf	gaussmf
Kmeans	Table 5.	RMSE	0.103	0.237	0.271	0.226	0.303	0.194	0.194
		Min error	-0.253	-0.299	-0.221	-0.975	-1.589	-1.058	-0.424
		Max error	0.893	0.863	0.995	0.933	1.002	0.968	0.987
	Table 6.	RMSE	0.066	0.159	0.121	0.123	0.22	0.27	0.2
		Min error	-0.881	-0.208	-0.432	-0.36	-1.177	-0.45	-0.666
		Max error	0.999	0.935	0.625	0.356	0.996	0.988	1.008
PSO (MSE)	Table 5.	RMSE	0.075	**0.092**	0.103	0.116	0.095	0.104	**0.086**
		Min error	-0.262	**-0.776**	-0.301	-0.727	-0.603	-0.63	**-0.65**
		Max error	0.486	**0.792**	0.436	0.991	0.398	0.865	**0.833**
	Table 6.	RMSE	0.129	0.159	0.212	0.26	0.166	0.178	0.172
		Min error	-0.944	-0.238	-0.2	-1.02	-0.354	-1.21	-0.444
		Max error	0.894	0.826	1.03	0.95	0.868	0.413	0.961
PSO (DBI, MSE)	Table 5.	RMSE	0.652	0.187	0.154	0.143	0.202	**0.0723**	0.158
		Min error	-0.745	-0.276	-0.654	-0.462	-0.264	**-0.584**	-0.923
		Max error	0.937	0.885	0.43	0.939	0.948	**0.557**	0.83
	Table 6.	RMSE	**0.052**	0.089	0.125	0.122	**0.066**	0.25	0.925
		Min error	**-0.583**	-0.538	-0.724	-0.286	**-0.632**	-0.925	-0.405
		Max error	**0.659**	0.829	0.948	0.761	**0.567**	0.961	0.846
PSO-Kmeans (MSE)	Table 5.	RMSE	0.109	0.138	0.258	0.26	0.325	0.173	0.193
		Min error	-0.541	-0.283	-0.305	-1.173	-1.015	-0.151	0.846
		Max error	0.854	0.99	1.116	0.915	0.999	0.942	0.842
	Table 6.	RMSE	0.2	0.159	**0.097**	0.146	0.233	0.264	0.168
		Min error	-1.125	-1.115	**-0.571**	-1.307	-1.005	-0.198	-0.457
		Max error	0.952	0.608	**0.592**	0.108	0.998	1.043	0.945
Chen, 2012	Table 5.	RMSE	0.0927	0.109	**0.072**	**0.113**	0.093	**0.076**	**0.058**
		Min error	-0.317	-0.565	**-0.346**	**-0.512**	-0.092	**-0.662**	**-0.606**
		Max error	0.468	0.878	**0.88**	**0.876**	1.003	**0.586**	**0.613**
	Table 6.	RMSE	0.115	0.343	0.182	0.231	0.281	0.23	0.239
		Min error	-0.527	-0.653	-0.807	-0.982	-0.964	-0.171	-0.565
		Max error	0.882	0.921	0.727	0.825	1.011	0.988	1.032
Zhenkui, 2008	Table 5.	RMSE	0.15	0.258	0.186	0.291	0.252	0.111	0.296
		Min error	-0.422	-0.649	-0.872	-0.339	-1.074	-0.462	-1.038
		Max error	0.943	0.794	0.78	0.836	1.008	0.389	0.965
	Table 6.	RMSE	0.191	0.244	0.097	0.174	0.137	0.128	0.11
		Min error	-0.227	-0.649	-0.308	-0.554	-0.625	-0.796	-0.31
		Max error	1.024	0.869	0.812	0.897	0.969	0.914	0.862

continued on following page

Table 10. Continued

Methods	Data Set	Criteria	trapmf	dsigmf	trimf	psigmf	gauss2mf	gbellmf	gaussmf
Cui, 2005	Table 5.	RMSE	0.091	0.197	0.28	0.205	0.289	0.173	0.156
		Min error	-0.588	-0.494	-0.925	-0.773	-0.893	-0.918	-0.614
		Max error	0.786	0.985	0.991	1.408	1.479	1.007	0.604
	Table 6.	RMSE	0.174	0.13	0.252	0.128	0.248	0.209	0.178
		Min error	-0.543	-0.596	-0.602	-0.362	-0.946	-1.139	-0.902
		Max error	0.971	0.431	0.716	1.051	1.085	1.005	0.391
Merwe, 2003	Table 5.	RMSE	0.092	0.201	0.261	0.211	0.276	0.187	0.169
		Min error	-0.593	-0.514	-0.898	-0.875	-0.901	-0.921	-0.624
		Max error	0.795	0.993	0.998	1.414	1.502	1.019	0.65
	Table 6.	RMSE	0.179	0.125	0.248	0.143	0.251	0.215	0.188
		Min error	-0.555	-0.604	-0.608	-0.37	-0.933	-1.114	-0.924
		Max error	0.978	0.439	0.722	1.046	1.094	1.055	0.403
Xiao, 2006	Table 5.	RMSE	0.144	**0.0948**	0.12	**0.0811**	0.096	**0.084**	0.11
		Min error	-0.352	**-0.568**	-0.651	**-0.582**	-0.209	**-0.518**	-0.341
		Max error	1.015	**0.872**	0.556	**0.71**	0.835	**0.822**	0.865
	Table 6.	RMSE	0.288	0.187	0.224	0.204	0.184	0.196	0.379
		Min error	-1.391	-1.005	-0.812	-1.152	-0.803	-0.202	-1.363
		Max error	1.038	0.805	1.056	0.48	0.967	0.929	0.822
Our Method: PSO-Kmeans (DBI, MSE)	Table 5.	RMSE	**0.061**	0.252	0.119	**0.0653**	**0.066**	0.117	**0.321**
		Min error	**-0.415**	-1.014	-1.081	**-0.543**	**-0.581**	-0.365	**-1.018**
		Max error	**0.6002**	0.999	0.667	**0.512**	**0.456**	0.879	**1.003**
	Table 6.	RMSE	**0.0531**	**0.073**	**0.069**	0.216	**0.065**	0.149	**0.051**
		Min error	**-0.521**	**-0.528**	**-0.671**	-0.526	**-0.575**	-0.734	**-0.533**
		Max error	**0.52**	**0.536**	**0.488**	0.895	**0.646**	0.806	**0.598**

Table 11. The contingency table (confusion matrix)

True Label	Predicted Label	
	Negative	Positive
Negative	a	b
Positive	c	d

Table 12. Fuzzy (non-fuzzy) anomaly detection for two applied testing data sets

Method	AUC	Accuracy		Sensitivity (Recall)		Specificity	
		Mean	S.D.	Mean	S.D.	Mean	S.D.
Data Set 1: Table 5							
Our Method	97.44	94.48	0.97	96.88	1.54	95.52	0.79
	(93.26)	(89.07)	(2.35)	(90.15)	(1.41)	(93.51)	(1.02)
PSO (DBI, MSE)	95.36	91.38	1.34	91.02	2.45	94.18	1.51
	(91.41)	(87.3)	(2.48)	(89.15)	(2.03)	(91.12)	(1.29)
Xiao, 2006	92.39	89.61	2.73	89.2	2.83	91.4	1.28
	(89.87)	(81.74)	(3.9)	(82.76)	(2.97)	(88.4)	(1.37)
Chen, 2012	91.92	88.18	2.84	88.21	2.89	90.98	1.94
	(87.37)	(81.64)	(3.71)	(83.33)	(3.7)	(87.73)	(1.17)
Zhenkui, 2008	91.37	89.29	2.98	87.07	3.04	90.11	2.08
	(87.14)	(81.18)	(3.88)	(82.13)	(3.57)	(87.61)	(2.21)
Cui, 2005	90.87	88.63	3.02	87.1	3.12	90.01	2.18
	(86.78)	(80.51)	(3.76)	(82.21)	(3.85)	(87.15)	(2.4)
Merwe, 2003	89.4	87.74	3.01	86.63	3.31	89.41	2.15
	(86.12)	(80.2)	(3.58)	(81.68)	(3.72)	(87.05)	(2.31)
Data Set 2: Table 6							
Our Method	97.41	94.45	0.99	97.65	0.67	96.7	0.99
	(92.29)	(88.14)	(2.84)	(89.15)	(2.03)	(91.57)	(1.36)
PSO (DBI, MSE)	95.91	92.01	1.01	93.81	1.43	94.93	1.8
	(90.98)	(86.8)	(2.68)	(88.18)	(3.96)	(90.3)	(1.39)
Xiao, 2006	92.92	89.84	2.83	88.49	2.19	91.58	1.74
	(88.64)	(81.06)	(3.49)	(82.3)	(3.19)	(86.32)	(1.83)
Chen, 2012	92.18	89.14	2.78	87.3	0.75	90.43	1.14
	(86.67)	(80.19)	(3.9)	(81.82)	(3.09)	(85.55)	(1.98)
Zhenkui, 2008	91.71	87.11	2.74	87.21	0.8	90.1	1.22
	(86.11)	(80.1)	(3.99)	(81.9)	(3.18)	(85.33)	(2.05)
Cui, 2005	91.47	86.98	2.86	87.17	0.91	90.02	1.34
	(85.61)	(80.06)	(3.92)	(81.76)	(3.41)	(85.3)	(2.03)
Merwe, 2003	90.08	85.49	3.03	86.66	1.03	89.43	1.53
	(85.86)	(80.01)	(3.99)	(80.54)	(3.68)	(85.11)	(2.61)

approaches based on AUC, accuracy, sensitivity and specificity. In addition, the non-fuzzy anomaly detection approach is often not sufficient in detecting many types of attacks as compared to a fuzzy detection method.

Computational Order

The computational order of standard PSO algorithm is $O(I \times S \times Cost)$, where I is the required generation number, S is the population size, and $Cost$ is the cost function. The computational complexity of evaluating the cost function depends on the particular cost function under consideration. The applied cost functions in preexisting methods are $O(N \times K)$, where N is the number of data samples and K is the number of clusters. The computational order of K-means algorithm is $O(T \times N \times K)$, where T is the number of iterations. The computational order of proposed training method and preexisting methods from the literature are shown in Table 13.

Time Complexity

We compare the computational time of algorithms on the training data set. Table 14 shows the computational time and the times of increment on computational time of the six methods. Table 14 demonstrates that the proposed method (PSO+Kmeans (DBI, MSE)) seems to be less time consuming than the other methods except methods by (Cui & Potok, 2005; Merwe & Engelbrecht, 2003) due to the application of a single cost function. But the proposed method can find the better solution with less times of increment on computational time than the other five methods due to its fast convergence speed. The results show that the proposed method with the new strategy of cost function -application of two simultaneous cost functions- can yield high accuracy as compared to other methods without very much computational cost.

Table 13. The computational order of the six methods

Methods	Cost Function	Algorithm
Our Method	$O(MSE) + O(DBI) = O(N \cdot K) + O(K^2)$	$O(PSO) + O(K - means)$
Xiao, 2006	$O(MSE) = O(N \cdot K)$	$O(PSO) \times O(K - means)$
Chen, 2012	$O(MSE) = O(N \cdot K)$	$O(PSO) \times O(K - means)$
Zhenkui, 2008	$O(MSE) = O(N \cdot K)$	$O(PSO) \times O(K - means)$
Cui, 2005	$O(MSE) = O(N \cdot K)$	$O(PSO) + O(K - means)$
Merwe, 2003	$O(MSE) = O(N \cdot K)$	$O(PSO) + O(K - means)$

Table 14. The computational time of the six methods

Methods	Computational Time (Sec)	Increment Time (Sec)
Our Method	791.412	92.381
Xiao, 2006	1348.297	478.146
Chen, 2012	1203.459	401.678
Zhenkui, 2008	1301.763	424.829
Cui, 2005	711.359	207.412
Merwe, 2003	723.286	289.764

CONCLUSION

We proposed a novel fuzzy anomaly detection system based on the hybridization of PSO and K-means clustering algorithms over Content-Centric Networks (CCNs). This system consists of two phases: the training phase with two simultaneous cost functions as well-separated clusters by DBI and local optimization by MSE, and the detection phase with two combination-based distance approaches as classification and outlier. Experimental results and analysis show the proposed method in the training phase is very effective in determining the optimal number of clusters, and has a very high detection rate and a very low false positive rate at the same time. In the detection phase, the proposed method clearly outperforms other applied method in terms of AUC (area under the ROC curve), accuracy, sensitivity and specificity. In addition, the times of increment on computational time of proposed method is relative smaller than the other considered methods.

We are currently working on several improvements of the presented approach with the application of computational intelligence methodologies (such as multi-objective optimization techniques) to propose a robust method to improve the accuracy of detection rate and reduce false positive rate over different CCNs traffics.

REFERENCES

Ahlgren, B., Dannewitz, C., Imbrenda, C., Kutscher, D., & Ohlman, B. (2011). A survey of information-centric networking (draft). Proceedings of Information-Centric Networking. Schloss Dagstuhl - Leibniz-Zentrum fuerInformatik, Germany.

Anderberg, M. R. (1973). *Cluster Analysis for Applications*. New York, NY: Academic Press, Inc.

Asuncion, A., & Newman, D. (2007). UCI machine learning repository. Retrieved from http://www.ics.uci.edu

Bradley, A. (1997). The use of the area under the ROC curve in the evaluation of machine learning algorithms. *Pattern Recognition*, *30*(7), 1145–1159. doi:10.1016/S0031-3203(96)00142-2

Carlisle, A., & Dozier, G. (2001). An off-the-shelf PSO. *Proceedings of the Particle Swarm Optimization Workshop* (Vol. 1, pp. 1-6). Indianapolis.

Chandola, V., Banerjee, A., & Kumar, V. (2009). Anomaly detection: a survey. *ACM Computing Surveys*, 41(3), 15, 1-15:58.

Chen, C. Y., & Ye, F. (2004). Particle swarm optimization algorithm and its application to clustering analysis. *Proceedings of the IEEE International Conference on Networking, Sensing and Control* (Vol. 2, pp. 789-794). doi:10.1109/ICNSC.2004.1297047

Chen, J. (2012). Hybrid clustering algorithm based on pso with the multidimensional asynchronism and stochastic disturbance method. *Journal of Theoretical and Applied Information Technology*, 46(1), 434–440.

Chimphlee, W., Abdullah, A. H., Chimphlee, S., & Srinoy, S. (2005). Unsupervised clustering methods for identifying rare events in anomaly detection. In: *Proceedings of the Sixth International Enformatika Conference* (pp. 26-28).

Compagno, A., Conti, M., Gasti, P., & Tsudik, G. (2013). Poseidon: mitigating interest flooding DDoS attacks in named data networking. In: *Proceedings of IEEE 38th Conference on Local Computer Networks* (pp. 630-638). Sydney, NSW. doi:10.1109/LCN.2013.6761300

Conti, M., Gasti, P., & Teoli, M. (2013). A lightweight mechanism for detection of cache pollution attacks in named data networking. *Computer Networks*, 57(16), 3178–3191. doi:10.1016/j.comnet.2013.07.034

Corral, G., Armengol, E., Fornells, A., & Golobardes, E. (2009). Explanations of unsupervised learning clustering applied to data security analysis. *Neurocomputing*, 72(13-15), 2754–2762. doi:10.1016/j.neucom.2008.09.021

Cortes, C., & Mohri, M. (2005). Confidence intervals for the area under the roc curve. *Advances in Neural Information Processing Systems*, 17, 305.

Cui, X., & Potok, T. E. (2005). Document clustering analysis based on hybrid pso+k-means algorithm. *Journal of Computer Science (special issue)*, 27-33.

Davies, D. L., & Bouldin, D. W. (1979). A cluster separation measure. *IEEE Transactions on Pattern Analysis and Machine Intelligence*, PAMI-1(2), 224–227. doi:10.1109/TPAMI.1979.4766909 PMID:21868852

Eberhart, R. C., & Shi, Y. (2000). Comparing inertia weights and constriction factors in particle swarm optimization. *Proceedings of the Evolutionary Computation*, 1, 84–88.

Everitt, B. S. (1993). *Cluster Analysis* (3rd ed.). London: Edward Arnold / Halsted Press.

Faysel, M. A., & Haque, S. S. (2010). Towards cyber defense: Research in intrusion detection and intrusion prevention systems. *International Journal of Computer Science and Network Security*, 10(7), 316–325.

Fiore, U., Palmieri, F., Castiglione, A., & De Santis, A. (2013). Network anomaly detection with the restricted boltzmann machine. *Neurocomputing*, 122(25), 13–23. doi:10.1016/j.neucom.2012.11.050

Gasti, P., Tsudik, G., Uzun, E., & Zhang, L. (2013). DoS and DDoS in Named-Data Networking. In *Proceedings of the 22nd International Conference on Computer Communications and Networks,* Nassau, USA (pp. 1-7).

Gersho, A., & Gray, R. M. (1992). *Vector Quantization and Signal Compression*. Dordrecht: Kluwer Academic Publishers. doi:10.1007/978-1-4615-3626-0

He, H.-T., Luo, X.-N., & Liu, B.-l. (2005). Detecting anomalous network traffic with combined fuzzy-based approaches. *Proceedings of International Conference on Intelligent Computing (ICIC)* Hefei, China, (Part II, pp. 433–442).

Izakian, H., & Pedrycz, W. (2014). Agreement-based fuzzy c-means for clustering data with blocks of features. *Neurocomputing, 127*, 266–280. doi:10.1016/j.neucom.2013.08.006

Jacobson, V., Smetters, D. K., Thornton, J. D., Plass, M. F., Briggs, N. H., & Braynard, R. L. (2009) Networking named content. *Proceedings of the Fifth International Conference on Emerging Networking Experiments and Technologies* (pp. 1-12). ACM, New York, NY, USA. doi:10.1145/1658939.1658941

Jain, A. K., Murty, M. N., & Flynn, P. J. (1999). Data clustering: A review. *ACM Computing Surveys, 31*(3), 264–323. doi:10.1145/331499.331504

Kao, Y. T., Zahara, E., & Kao, I. W. (2008). A hybridized approach to data clustering. *Expert Systems with Applications, 34*(3), 1754–1762. doi:10.1016/j.eswa.2007.01.028

Karami, A. (2011). *Utilization and comparison of multi attribute decision making techniques to rank Bayesian network options* [Master's Thesis]. University of Skövde, Skövde, Sweden.

Karami, A. (2013). Data clustering for anomaly detection in content-centric networks. *International Journal of Computers and Applications, 81*(7), 1–8. doi:10.5120/14021-2180

Karami, A., & Guerrero-Zapata, M. (2014). Mining and Visualizing Uncertain Data Objects and Named Data Networking Traffics by Fuzzy Self-Organizing Map. *Proceedings of the Second International Workshop on Artificial Intelligence and Cognition,* Turin, Italy (Vol. 1315, pp. 156-163).

Karami, A., & Guerrero-Zapata, M. (2015). A hybrid multiobjective RBF-PSO method for mitigating DoS attacks in Named Data Networking. *Neurocomputing, 151*(Part 3), 1262–1282.

Karami, A., & Johansson, R. (2014). Choosing DBSCAN parameters automatically using differential evolution. *International Journal of Computers and Applications, 91*(7), 1–11. doi:10.5120/15890-5059

Kärkkäinen, I., & Fränti, P. (2000). Minimization of the value of Davies–Bouldin index. *Proceedings of the LASTED International Conference Signal Processing and Communications* (pp. 426-432). Marbella, Spain.

Kaufman, L., & Rousseeuw, P. J. (Eds.), (1990). *Finding Groups in Data: An Introduction to Cluster Analysis*. New York: John Wiley Sons. doi:10.1002/9780470316801

Kennedy, J., & Eberhart, R. (1995). Particle swarm optimization. *Neural Networks, 4*, 1942–1948.

Kennedy, J., & Eberhart, R. (2001). *Swarm Intelligence*. San Francisco, CA: Morgan Kaufmann.

Kolias, C., Kambourakis, G., & Maragoudakis, M. (2011). Swarm intelligence in intrusion detection: A survey. *Computers & Security, 30*(8), 625–642. doi:10.1016/j.cose.2011.08.009

Krawczyk, B., & Woźniak, M. (2014). Diversity measures for one-class classifier ensembles. *Neurocomputing, 126*, 36–44. doi:10.1016/j.neucom.2013.01.053

Lauinger, T. (2010). *Security & Scalability of Content-centric Networking*. Doctoral dissertation, TU Darmstadt.

Lee, W., & Stolfo, S. J. (2000). A framework for constructing features and models for intrusion detection systems. *ACM Transactions on Information and System Security, 3*(4), 227–261. doi:10.1145/382912.382914

Li, N.-J., Wang, W.-J., James Hsu, C.-C., Chang, W., Chou, H.-G., & Chang, J.-W. (2014). Enhanced particle swarm optimizer incorporating a weighted particle. *Neurocomputing, 124*, 218–227. doi:10.1016/j.neucom.2013.07.005

Liao, H.-J., Richard Lin, C.-H., Lin, Y.-C., & Tung, K.-Y. (2013). Intrusion detection system: A comprehensive review. *Journal of Network and Computer Applications, 36*(1), 16–24. doi:10.1016/j.jnca.2012.09.004

Louvieris, P., Clewley, N., & Liu, X. (2013). Effects-based feature identification for network intrusion detection. *Neurocomputing, 121*, 265–273. doi:10.1016/j.neucom.2013.04.038

Merwe, D. W. V. D., & Engelbrecht, A. P. (2003). Data clustering using particle swarm optimization. *Proceedings of the IEEE Congress on Evolutionary Computation*, Canberra, Australia. (vVol. 1, pp. 215-220)

Münz, G., Li, S., & Carle, G. (2007). Traffic anomaly detection using k-means clustering. *Proceedings of Performance, Reliability and Dependability Evaluation of Communication Networks and Distributed Systems, 4GI/ITG Workshop MMBnet*, Hamburg, Germany.

Naldi, M., & Campello, R. (2014). Evolutionary k-means for distributed data sets. *Neurocomputing, 127*, 30–42. doi:10.1016/j.neucom.2013.05.046

Padhye, N., Deb, K., & Mittal, P. (2013). Boundary handling approaches in particle swarm optimization. *Advances in Intelligent Systems and Computing, 201*, 287–298. doi:10.1007/978-81-322-1038-2_25

Palmieri, F., & Fiore, U. (2010). Network anomaly detection through nonlinear analysis. *Computers & Security, 29*(7), 737–755. doi:10.1016/j.cose.2010.05.002

Patcha, A., & Park, J. M. (2007). An overview of anomaly detection techniques: Existing solutions and latest technological trends. *Computer Networks, 51*(12), 3448–3470. doi:10.1016/j.comnet.2007.02.001

Peddabachigari, S., Abraham, A., Grosan, C., & Thomas, J. (2007). Modeling intrusion detection system using hybrid intelligent systems. *Journal of Network and Computer Applications, 30*(1), 114–132. doi:10.1016/j.jnca.2005.06.003

Perdisci, R., Ariu, D., Fogla, P., Giacinto, G., & Lee, W. (2009). Mcpad: A multiple classifier system for accurate payload-based anomaly detection. *Computer Networks, 53*(6), 864–881. doi:10.1016/j.comnet.2008.11.011

Quan, H., Srinivasan, D., & Khosravi, A. (2014). Particle swarm optimization for construction of neural network-based prediction intervals. *Neurocomputing, 127*, 172–180. doi:10.1016/j.neucom.2013.08.020

Selim, S. Z., & Ismail, M. A. (1984). K-means-type algorithms: A generalized convergence theorem and characterization of local optimality. *IEEE Transactions on Pattern Analysis and Machine Intelligence, 6*(1), 81–87. doi:10.1109/TPAMI.1984.4767478 PMID:21869168

Settles, M. (2005). *An Introduction to Particle Swarm Optimization*. Moscow: Department of Computer Science, University of Idaho.

Shi, Y., & Eberhart, R. (1998). A modified particle swarm optimizer. *Proceedings of IEEE World Congress on Computational Intelligence,* Anchorage, AK (pp. 69-73).

Verma, J. P. (2013). *Data Analysis in Management with SPSS Software*. Berlin: Springer. doi:10.1007/978-81-322-0786-3

Wang, Q., & Megalooikonomou, V. (2010). A performance evaluation framework for association mining in spatial data. *Journal of Intelligent Information Systems, 35*(3), 465–494. doi:10.1007/s10844-009-0115-6 PMID:21170170

Widjaja, I. (2012). Towards a flexible resource management system for content centric networking. *Proceedings of IEEE International Conference on Communications* (pp. 2634-2638). IEEE.

Wong, W., & Nikander, P. (2010). Secure naming in information-centric networks. *Proceedings of the Re-architecting the Internet Workshop,* Philadelphia, Pennsylvania (pp. 12:1-12:6).

Wu, S. X., & Banzhaf, W. (2010). The use of computational intelligence in intrusion detection systems: A review. *Journal of Applied Soft Computing, 10*(1), 1–35. doi:10.1016/j.asoc.2009.06.019

Xiao, L., Shao, Z., & Liu, G. (2006). K-means algorithm based on particle swarm optimization algorithm for anomaly intrusion detection. *Proceedings of the Sixth World Congress on Intelligent Control and Automation,* Dalian, China (pp. 5854-5858). doi:10.1109/WCICA.2006.1714200

Xie, M., Widjaja, I., & Wang, H. (2012). Enhancing cache robustness for content-centric networking. *Proceedings of INFOCOM*, Orlando, FL (pp. 2426-2434).

Zalik, K. R. (2008). An efficient k-means clustering algorithm. *Pattern Recognition Letters, 29*(9), 1385–1391. doi:10.1016/j.patrec.2008.02.014

Zhenkui, P., Xia, H., & Jinfeng, H. (2008). The clustering algorithm based on particle swarm optimization algorithm. *Proceedings of the International Conference on Intelligent Computation Technology and Automation* (pp. 148-151). IEEE Computer Society, Washington, DC, USA.

Chapter 18
Cluster Based Medical Image Registration Using Optimized Neural Network

Joydev Hazra
Heritage Institute of Technology, India

Aditi Roy Chowdhury
B.P.C. Institute of Technology, India

Paramartha Dutta
Visva-Bharati University, India

ABSTRACT

Registration of medical images like CT-MR, MR-MR etc. are challenging area for researchers. This chapter introduces a new cluster based registration technique with help of the supervised optimized neural network. Features are extracted from different cluster of an image obtained from clustering algorithms. To overcome the drawback regarding convergence rate of neural network, an optimized neural network is proposed in this chapter. The weights are optimized to increase the convergence rate as well as to avoid stuck in local minima. Different clustering algorithms are explored to minimize the clustering error of an image and extract features from suitable one. The supervised learning method applied to train the neural network. During this training process an optimization algorithm named Genetic Algorithm (GA) is used to update the weights of a neural network. To demonstrate the effectiveness of the proposed method, investigation is carried out on MR T1, T2 data sets. The proposed method shows convincing results in comparison with other existing techniques.

INTRODUCTION

Image registration or alignment and matching of two or more images, establishes a one-to-one spatial correspondence of a single 2-D/3-D scene or several similar scenes captured at different time instants or from various viewpoints or by different sensors. In image processing this is one of the important steps

DOI: 10.4018/978-1-4666-9474-3.ch018

used in a variety of applications including remote sensing and cartography, autonomous navigation, robot vision, and medical imaging to mention a few. It is a powerful tool for integrating or fusing image data collected from different sensors (mono-modal or multi-modality), tracking the temporal evolution (changes in images taken at different times), making inter-patient comparisons, reconstructing 3-D (volumetric) images from multiple 2-D (planar) images, etc. When one image is registered to another image, the latter is typically referred to as a reference image, and the former is called a target or sensed image. Medical images are very important for diagnosis, treatment, and supervising disease progression. The term 'medical image' spreads over a vast area of different types of images. Now-a-days medical researchers used medical images to investigate disease processes and to understand different developments like a tumor. Multiple images are acquired of common subjects at different times, or from different imaging modalities. Comparing two or more unregistered images can lead to incorrect diagnostic conclusions. Medical image registration generally deals with the technique to align two or more images of different modalities like inter-modality or intra-modality. Different topographic medical images like computed tomography (CT), magnetic resonance imaging (MRI), single photon emission computed tomography (SPECT), and positron emission tomography (PET) are generally used for research in image registration. Computer-aided diagnosis (CAD) systems use image registration to investigate how human anatomy is altered by disease, age, gender, handedness, and other clinical or genetic factors. Over the last decade, researches on automatic rigid registration methods of medical images have been widely developed. Rigid registration generally deals with some popular global geometric transformations include similarity, affine transformation, perspective projection, and polynomial models etc. Affine geometric transformation was used by Scale-invariant feature transform (SIFT) introduced by Lowe (Lowe, 2004). Multiple point-wise correspondences between local areas in two images determine the transformation parameters. Different retinal images collected with the 1-day time difference is analyzed using this method to estimation transformation parameters. Affine transformation deals with translation, rotation, scaling, and skewness of a target with respect to a reference. For negligible deformation in the image the affine transformations are sufficient. To address the deformable nature of a medical image like different organs, tissues etc. nonrigid registration methods have been developed. However, the global mapping is unable to capture intrinsically local large deformations of anatomical structures. Thus, frequently more flexible elastic transformations that locally warp a target to align with a reference image are needed. Most popular such transformations include large deformation models (diffeomorphisms), radial basis functions (RBF), physical continuum models (viscous fluids). Soft Computing techniques like GA (Genetic Algorithm), ANN (Artificial Neural network) etc. are also used in medical image registration. A powerful advantage of soft computing is the complementary nature rather than competitive. For this reason more than one soft computing technique is used collectively named hybrid technique. Hybrid soft computing models have been applied to a large number of classification and prediction. In this chapter a hybrid technique is described to register images of same modality. Here weight optimization of neural network is done by GA.

BACKGROUND

Image Registration is a technique to align two images, with one being referenced (fixed) image whiles the other being sensed (transformed) image of the same scene taken over different times or from different viewpoints. Over the years, research on image registration has offered a lot of methods. Typical examples include methods like image correlation functions, principal axis method, Fourier transform based methods, image feature based methods and so on. It has enormous importance in areas encompassing medical diagnosis and treatment. Medical image registration can be categories as manual, landmark-based, surface-based, intensity based depends on type of matching. Manual registration is to align images from mono-modality or multi-modality based on the user's judgment. In different articles (Habboush, Mitchell, Mulkern, Barnes, & Treves, 1996) both internal and surface features are used to achieve accurate alignment. In Landmark registration (Maurer et al., 1997), (Fox, Perlmutter, & Raichle, 1985), (Evans, Marrett, Collins, & Peters, 1989), (Strother et al., 1994), (Morris et al., 1993), (Pietrzyk, 1994), (Soltys, Beard, Carrasco, Mukherji, & Rosenman, 1995) researchers manually identify the locations of corresponding points within different images. The sum of distances between homogeneous point pairs of the two image sets (Evans et al., 1989) are used as a cost function. Minimize or maximize the values of certain cost functions are used to achieve the global optimized matching of the images. Two types of landmark techniques are there: internal landmark and external landmark. The internal landmark mainly deals with anatomical structure of an image. So it is also known as anatomical markers. In external landmark (Evans, Marrett, Torrescorzo, Ku, & Collins, 1991), (Maguire et al., 1991) artificial objects are attached to the patient body before image acquisition. Different errors occur in rigid landmark-based registration can be described as (Fitzpatric, West, & Maurer, 1998)

1. Fiducial localization error (FLE),
2. Target registration error (TRE),
3. Fiducial registration error (FRE).

Another is surface based registration (Grimpson et al., 1996), (Herring et al., 1998), (Kanatani, 1994), (Declerc, Feldmar, Betting, & Goris, 1997), (Collignon, Geraud, Vandarmeulen, Suetens, & Marchal, 1993), (Hill, Hawkes, Harrison, & Ruff, 1993), (Grimson et al., 1994), (Scott et al., 1995) technique. Here surface of an image reconstructed from a stack of contours generated by the segmentation. Minimizing the distance between the corresponding surface models transformation parameters can be detected. Iterative Closest Point (ICP) (Besl & McKay, 1992) is a popular technique, introduced by Besl and Mckay, to register the closest point in one surface to all the points relative to another surface.

In image registration algorithms, three types of interaction can be recognized. First and widely used technique is automatic (Evans et al., 1991), where the user only supplies the algorithm with the image data and possibly information on the image acquisition. Second is interactive, where the user does the registration himself. Softwares are there to assist the user by supplying a visual or numerical impression of the current transformation, and also an initial transformation guess. Third is semi-automatic, (Pietrzyk, 1994) where the nature of interaction can be of two different types: the user needs to initialize the algorithm or steer the algorithm. Fully interactive methods are reported on very little literature (Morris et al., 1993), (Pietrzyk, 1994).

Image registration can also be categorized as intensity based and feature based (Goshtaby, 2005) based on nature of matching. Matching algorithms based on local invariant features have smaller calculations, better robustness. Rigid body, affine (Collins, Neelin, Peters, & Evans, 1994), linear elastic (Gee, Reivich, & Bajacsy, 1993), (Bagcsy, & Koyacic, 1989), viscous fluid (Christensen, Rabitt, & Miller, 1996), (Christensen, 1996),, radial basis function (Bookstein, 1989), (Rueckert et al., 1999) etc. are popular image registration technique. Image intensities are directly used in intensity based method to estimate the transformation paramcters likc rotation, scaling and translation both in x and y dircction ctc. (Kim & Fessler, 2004), (Hazra, Roy Chowdhury, & Dutta, 2013) of gray as well as color images (Hazra, Roy

Chowdhury, & Dutta, 2014)). Image features are used to determine corresponding feature pairs from the pair of images and then the transformation parameters are determined. Lowe (Lowe, 2004) proposed SURF (speeded up robust features) algorithm based on feature information. The feature-based registration is highly effective in remote sensing, robotic vision etc. It has a wide area of application due to its robust nature and low time complexity. Recently, mutual information (MI) (Pluim, Maintz, & Viergever, 2003), cross-correlation (Langevin & Didon, 1995) etc. are commonly used registration techniques. Mutual information (Rangarajan, Chui, & Duncan, 1999) can be effectively utilized to solve the correspondence problem. Other than mutual information, information theory offers many more other measures that may be suitable for image registration. The distance between a joint probability distribution and the product of the marginal distributions are *information* measures. Information measures constitute a subclass of the *divergence* measures. A measure of the distance between two arbitrary distributions is called divergence measure. A specific class of information (divergence) measure is formed by the *f*-information (*f*-divergence) measures. Authors (Pluim, Maintz, & Viergever, 2004,) used mutual information with f-information measures to register two images. Feature descriptors and similarity functions of both reference and target images are used to establish the point-wise correspondence (Zitova & Flusser, 2003). The study shows that feature-based registration depends on many factors, including, areas of overlaps between the images, severity of geometric distortions, noise, blurring, and other signal (photometric) distortions, and similarities between dominant uniform (smooth) or textured image areas (Yasein & Agathoklis, 2008). Well-known examples of similarity functions are the sum of squared differences (SSD) and ratio–image uniformity (RIU) (Hipwell, Tanner, Crum, & Hawkes, 2006), cross-correlation (CC) (Subsol, Thirion, & Ayache, 1998), phase correlation (PC) (Kuglin & Hines, 1975) (based on the Fourier shift theorem (Bracewell, 1965)), mutual information (MI) (Viola & Wells, 1997), and normalized mutual information (NMI) (Studholme, Hill, & Hawkes, 1999). The SSD and CC are common for registering images of the same modality, while the MI and NMI are suitable for multiple modalities, too. The area based registration is one of the alternatives of feature based image registration techniques (Zitova & Flusser, 2003), (Pope & Theiler, 2003). This registration technique is not so popular due to higher computational complexity and its nature to trap frequently in local minima than the other feature based methods (Xia & Liu, 2004).

Mono-modal image registration is used to identify neuropsychiatric disorders Huntington's disease etc. (Puri, 2004). Brain imaging plays an important role in image registration. A mono-modal image registration technique based on Non-Subsampled Coutourlet Transform (NSCT), Mutual Information (MI) and Particle Swarm Optimization (PSO) is described in (Al-Azzawi & Abdullah, 2012).. Mutual information (MI) (Viola, Wells, 1997), (Collignon, 1995) and normalized mutual information (NMI) (Studholme, Hill, & Hawkes, 1999), (Studholme, 1997) are the most successful and commonly used techniques for image registration. Now a day, MI is used for aligning mono-modal and multimodal images (Wang, Reinstein, Hanley, & Meek, 1996), (Wells, Viola, Atsumi, Nakajima, & Kikinis, 1996) as well as for rigid and nonrigid registration (Maes, Vandermeulen, & Suetuns, 2003). MI and NMI use statistical point of view to register two images. Statistically, the reference and target image pairs are independent samples, and the MI and NMI calculate the amount of information in a reference image about a target image to find the dependencies among corresponding points of the samples.

Medical image registration can be considered as (Roche, Malandain, Ayache, (2000) a maximum likelihood estimation problem and it used different methods of similarity measures, e.g. correlation ratio, MI etc. Mutual Information (MI) which was proposed independently by Viola and Wells (Viola, & Wells, 1997) and by Maes (Maes, Collignon, Vandermeulen, Marchal, & Suetens, 1997),. For mon-modality as well as multi-modality images it gives good accuracy in comparison to other techniques (Hipwell, Tanner, Crum, Schnabel, & Hawkes, 2007), (Wells et al., 1996). So many researchers use this method in both rigid and affine transformations due to impressive registration results (Maes et al., 2003), (Rueckert et al., 1999). Computationally expensive methods like elasticity (Davatzikos, 1997), (Gee et al., 1993) or fluid mechanics (Bro-Nielsen & Gramkow, 1993), (Christensen et al., 1996), report good result, but due to timing factor, it is not so popular. In (Likar & Pernus, 2001) authors proposed an elastic registration of three differently stained serial transverse sections. A Markov random-field (MRF)-based objective function is used in elastic image registration (Mahapatra, & Sun, 2012). MRFs are suitable for discrete labeling problems. The labels are defined as the joint occurrence of displacement fields (for registration) and segmentation class probability. The smoothness is a function of the interaction between the defined labels. A nonrigid 3D image registration technique (Khader, & HamzaI, 2011) used cubic B-splines to model non-rigid deformation. Quasi-Newton method was used as an optimization technique between the fixed and moving 3-D image pairs. Using elastic interpolation of multiple local image registration the nonrigid matching problem was decomposed. For PET-CT image registration (Mattes, Haynor, Vesselle, Lewellen, & Eubank, 2003), inherent differences in the two imaging protocols produce significant nonrigid motion between the two acquisitions. A rigid transformation is combined with localized cubic B-splines are used to capture this motion. A method to register x-ray mammograms by projecting the resulting known 3-D displacements into 2-D was proposed (Hipwell, Tanner, Crum, Schnabel, & Hawkes, 2007). Thus generating pseudo-mammograms from these same compressed magnetic resonance (MR) volumes, different images with known 2-D displacements was generated which is used to validate registration. Most of registration techniques rely upon the assumption that there exists a relationship between the intensities of images to be registered and that this relationship remains the same all over the image domains (Studholme et al., 1999), (Woods, Mazziotta, & Cherry, 1993), (Roche, Malandain, Pennec, & Ayache, 1998), (Malandain, 2006),. This assumption is true when applying registration techniques based on intensity, such as the sum of squared differences (SSD), the correlation ratio, the correlation coefficient, or the mutual information (Pohl, Fisher, Grimson, Kikinis, & Wells, 2006),. But such an assumption is not always applicable especially for medical images (Tanner et al., 2000), (Rohlfing & Maurer, 2001). Several works have been done with image registration in the presence of multiple pixel classes. Robust estimation is a statistical approach which has been widely applied to image processing (Sebe & Lew, 2003). More general robust estimation approaches are based on mixture models. Some specific probability distributions are used as outliers (Schroeter, Vesin, Langenberger, & Meuli, 1998), (Jepson & Black, 1993). In Bayesian frameworks, image segmentation has also been combined with atlas-based registration (Pohl, Fisher, Grimson, Kikinis, & Wells, 2006), (Hachama, D esolneux, & Richard, 2012), where mixture models were used to represent pixel intensities of different anatomical structures. The authors (Hachama et al., 2012) deal with the issue of registering images whose intensity relationships are spatially dependent. The registration is simultaneously combined to a pixel classification. This classification provides some spatial information about intensity relationships.

Traditionally soft computing has four technical disciplines like probabilistic, fuzzy logic, Neuro computing, and evolutionary computing. They fall into two categories, namely knowledge-driven and data driven. Neuro Computing (NC) and Evolutionary Computing (EC), are optimization technique categorize as data driven search. These types of techniques such as neural network, genetic algorithm, fuzzy logic, Neuro-fuzzy etc. are recently being explored. An artificial neural network (ANN) is a mathematical or computational model based on the principles of biological neural networks. They can be used to model simple as well as the complex relationships between inputs and outputs. Registration methods using neural networks have been reported (Elhanany et al., 2000), (Mostafa, Farag, & Essock, 2000). A neural network technique was proposed (Mostafa et al., 2000) for multi modality image registration. The technique employs a feedforward neural network to perform the transformation, scaling, and resampling processes required for the fusion. Radial basis functions (Davis, Khotanzad, & Flaming, 1996), self-organizing maps (Sabisch, Ferguson, & Bolouri, 1998) can be used for different computational aspects. Principal component analysis (PCA) (Shang, Lv, & Yi, 2006) has been used in the neural network for CT-MR and MR-MR registration. A genetic algorithm (GA) (Goldberg, 1989) is an optimization search technique used to find exact or approximate solutions with any problems. Some authors (Chalermwat, El-Ghazawi, & LeMoigneb, 2001), proposed 2-phase GA-based image registration algorithms. Since it is two phase, the first phase near optimal transformations of the registration are found using low-resolution version of the images. But the second phase deals with full resolution images. To refine the results from the first phase and obtain the best solution second phase is very useful. The transformation, consisting of rotation, translations is encoded into a bit string of chromosome and is decoded for an evaluation of the fitness values.

Clustering plays an important role in image registration. Clustering deals with splitting the image into different segments. In the spatial transformation histogram of intensities are used for this purpose. In image clustering total number of cluster are set a priori and each intensities are mapped to some segments. Different clustering techniques like k-means, c-means, fuzzy c-means etc. are very popular methods. But the image intensities of MR brain images are not necessarily constant for each tissue and so it is very difficult to automatically segment the image. To register two images, (Tsao & Lauterbur, 1998), Clusters are formed when the images are registered. The degree of clustering is assessed by assigning a clustering measure (local density of the IMP) to every point in the IMP, and summing the local density of all points. Important factors in this regard are the choice of monotonically increasing functions for evaluating the local density, the effects of normalization, and the effects of background elimination. An image registration framework based on a hierarchical image clustering and atlas synthesis strategy was proposed (Wang, Chen, Yap, Wu, & Shen, 2010). Based on affinity propagation images are hierarchically clustered into several classes. Intraclass group-wise registration will be performed on these clusters. All images in the group will be registered onto the referenced image based on their respective transformation routes. Fuzzy clustering techniques are also used in image registration. Fuzzy clustering (Mahmoud, Masulli, & Rovetta, 2007) is used to automatically detect robust candidate regions for a registration method based on the Scale Invariant Feature Transform (SIFT) (Lowe, 1999) which is also a popular feature-based image registration method matching points based on similarity measure. A mathematical transformation describes the geometrical relationship between two images (Seedahmed & Martucci 2002). The basic steps are feature extraction, geometric invariant features construction, and then parameter space clustering. Parameter space clustering was used to identify parameter distribution function of the scale factor from the derived norms from the first and the second data sets.

MAIN FOCUS OF THE CHAPTER

In this section at first a brief description on affine transformation, feature extraction mechanism, neural network and genetic algorithm is provided.

Affine Transformation

All the mapping models fall into two basic categories: rigid (global) and nonrigid (elastic) transformations. The rigid models (Viola & Wells, 1997), (West et al., 1997) transform uniformly the whole 2-D or 3-D images, e.g., translate, rotate, scale, and/or shear every depicted object just in the same manner. While these models are sufficient in many applications, medical objects to be co-aligned always have spatially variant geometric differences. Such complex deformations of images suggest more flexible elastic models that register a target to a reference image by spatially variant local warping (see, e.g., (Hurvitz, Joskowicz, 2008), (D'Agostino, Maes, Vandermeulen, & Suetens, 2003), (Arsigny, Pennec, & Ayache, 2005), (Bookstein, 1989)). One of the commonly used global models includes affine transformations. A rigid transformation is one where the pre-image and the image after transforming both have the exact same shape. Transformations such as rotation, translation, reflection, scaling is rigid in nature. In affine transform the relationship between the two sets of image coordinates (x', y') and (x, y) is often modeled as

$$
\begin{pmatrix} x' \\ y' \\ 1 \end{pmatrix} = \begin{pmatrix} m_1 & m_2 & m_3 \\ m_4 & m_5 & m_6 \\ 0 & 0 & 1 \end{pmatrix} \cdot \begin{pmatrix} x \\ y \\ 1 \end{pmatrix}
\tag{1}
$$

Mathematically, affine model is the product of translations, scaling and rotations. These transformations like rotation, scaling, translation can be represented as,

$$
T' = RST
\tag{2}
$$

where, order may be different.

Rotation R about the image center at an angle θ represented by,

$$
R = \begin{pmatrix} \cos\theta & \sin\theta \\ -\sin\theta & \cos\theta \end{pmatrix}
\tag{3}
$$

S is the scaling factor with Sx and Sy representing scaling factors along X and Y axes respectively, i.e,

$$
s = \begin{pmatrix} s_x & 0 \\ 0 & s_y \end{pmatrix}
\tag{4}
$$

and Tr is the translation effect with Tx and Ty representing translation factors along X and Y axes respectively, i.e,

$$
\begin{aligned}
x' &= x + Tx \\
y' &= y + Ty
\end{aligned}
\tag{5}
$$

Clustering Technique

Clustering is the classification of objects into different groups. The main objective of clustering is to find out the similar type of objects based on features and form a group and dissimilar objects in another group (Aldenderfer & Blashfield, 1985), (Everitt, Handau, & Leese, 2001), (Duda, Hart, & Stork, 2001). The criterion of good clustering is that maximizes the similarity within a group and maximizes the dissimilarity between the groups. Clustering is represented as a set of subsets $C = C_1, C_2, ..., C_k$ of U, such that:

$$U = \bigcup_{i=1}^{k} C_i \text{ and } C_i \cap C_j = \varphi \text{ for } i \neq j.$$

It is true for any element in U that belongs to exactly one and only one subset. An important step in any clustering technique is to select a suitable distance measure. This is useful because that will determine the similarity or dissimilarity of two elements. The shape of the cluster more or less depends on this factor since as some elements may be close to one another according to one distance measure technique and farther away according to other. Different types of distance functions are used like the Euclidean distance (2-norm distance), the Manhattan distance (1-norm), the maximum norm (infinity norm), the Mahalanobis distance (corrects data for different scales). For high dimensional data slightly different technique is used like the angle between two vectors can be used as a distance measure. The Hamming distance measures the minimum number of substitutions required to change one member into another.

The measurement of similarity or dissimilarity for grouping the objects in terms of distance that means how closer or farther from the cluster head of the cluster. The objects belong in a same cluster are closer to each other's i.e. intra-cluster distance should be minimized, but well separated between the other clusters i.e. inter-cluster distance should be maximized. In clustering the measurement of distance is called metric. Minkowski metric is a popular metric for higher dimensional data. Let two d-dimensional instances Xi = (Xi1, Xi2, ..., Xid) and Xj = (Xj1, Xj2, ..., Xjd). The Minkowski metric is

$$D_P\left(X_i, X_j\right) = \left(\left|X_{i1} - X_{j1}\right|^P + \left|X_{i2} - X_{j2}\right|^P + \text{.......} + \left|X_{id} - X_{jd}\right|^P\right)^{1/P}$$

$$D_P\left(X_i, X_j\right) = \left(\sum_{k=1}^{d} \left|X_{ik} - X_{jk}\right|^P\right)^{1/P}$$

Varying the value of P it represents the different distance metric. For example, P = 2 means it is Euclidean distance and P = 1 means Manhattan metric.

The clustering is commonly divided into following category:

1. **Hierarchical:** If the clusters are divided into sub-clusters, then form a hierarchical clustering. It is represented as a tree and each node is union of its child nodes except the leaf nodes. The root node of the tree contains all the instances.
2. **Partitional:** Here a set of data divides into non-overlapping subsets in such a way that each element belongs in exactly one subset.

3. **Exclusive:** Each object is assigned to a single cluster. No object may place more than one cluster.
4. **Fuzzy:** In fuzzy clustering, each object belongs to every cluster with some membership value. The membership value is in between 0 and 1, 0 means no membership and 1 means full membership of a cluster.
5. **Complete:** In complete clustering, every object must be assign to a cluster.
6. **Partial:** Here some objects may not be assigned to any clusters. If the object is not well-defined for belonging to a cluster then the object is not assigned in a cluster.

FEATURE EXTRACTION USING GLCM

A statistical method for describing features of an image is a gray level co-occurrence matrix (GLCM) (Haralick, Shanmugam, & Dinstein, 1973), (Renzetti & Zortea, 2011). The co-occurrence matrix will help to provide valuable information about the relative position of the neighboring pixels in an image. These methods analyze the spatial distribution of gray values and compute local features at each point in the image. The statistical features could be based on the number of pixels like first-order (one pixel), second-order (two pixel), or higher-order (three or more pixels) statistics of gray level of an image. GLCM calculates how often a pixel with gray-level value i occurs either horizontally, vertically, or diagonally to adjacent pixels with the gray-level value j. For any image GLCM can be calculated using displacement vector v. The displacement vector can be defined based on radius and orientation.

Various research activities have been done to find out the radius of the displacement vector. Very large value cannot detect detail information of an image. Generally its value is ranging from 1 to 10. For best result value of radius is limited to 1 or 2. Every pixel has eight neighboring pixels at angles 0°, 45°, 90°, 135°, 180°, 225°, 270° or 315°. The calculation of angle in 0° and 180° is equal and so for others. So, in GLCM calculation one has to consider only 0^0, 45°, 90° and 135°.

GLCM Features

q(i, j) is (i, j)th entry in a normalized gray color spatial dependence matrix, G is the number of distinct gray levels in the quantized image, and $q_i(i)$ and $q_j(j)$ are the ith and j^{th} entry in the marginal probability matrix respectively.

Following notations are used to explain the various textural features:

$$q_i(i) = \sum_{j=1}^{G} q(i, j) \tag{6}$$

$$q_j(j) = \sum_{i=1}^{G} q(i, j) \tag{7}$$

i and j are the mean of q_i and q_j

$$\mu_i = \sum_{i=1}^{G} q_i(i),$$ (8)

$$\mu_j = \sum_{j=1}^{G} q_j(j)$$ (9)

i and j are the standard deviation of p_i and p_j

$$\sigma_i^2 = \sum_{i=1}^{G} \left(i - \mu_i\right)^2 q_i(i),$$ (10)

$$\sigma_j^2 = \sum_{j=1}^{G} \left(j - \mu_j\right)^2 q_j(j)$$ (11)

$$q_{x+y} = -\sum_{i=1}^{G}\sum_{j=1}^{G} q(i,j), i+j = k \text{ and k=2,3, ...,2G}$$ (12)

$$q_{x-y} = -\sum_{i=1}^{G}\sum_{j=1}^{G} q(i,j), |i+j| = k \text{ and k=0,1,...,G-1}$$ (13)

Important features (Haralick) of GLCM can be represented as follows ((Haralick et al., 1973):

1. **Energy or Angular Second Moment:** Homogeneous property of any image can be detected by this feature. It has a normalize range where maximum value is one. For any homogeneous image that has a uniform or periodic gray level distribution reaches a maximum value. So,

$$\text{Energy} = \sum_{i,j} q(i,j)^2$$ (14)

2. **Variance or Sum of Squares:** It is correlated with first order statistics namely standard deviation. If gray value of any pixel differs from their mean then variance becomes large.

$$\text{Variance} = \sum_{i,j} \left(q(i,j)\frac{1}{N}\right)^2$$ (15)

3. **Entropy:** Complexity property of any image can be measure by entropy property. Basically entropy is complement of energy. So, for any non-uniform or aperiodic gray level distribution entropy value is large.

$$\text{Entropy} = -\sum_{i,j} q(i,j) \log(q(i,j)) \tag{16}$$

4. **Inverse Difference Moment or Homogeneity:** For any pair of pixels small gray value differences can be detected easily by this property. It attains maximum value for same gray value of all pixels. GLCM contrast and homogeneity are strongly, but inversely, correlated. It means homogeneity decreases if contrast increases while energy is kept constant.

$$\text{Homogeneity} = \sum_{i=0}^{G-1} \sum_{j=0}^{G-1} \frac{1}{1 + (i-j)^2} q(i,j) \tag{17}$$

5. **Correlation:** Measures the linear dependency among gray values of an image.

$$\text{Correlation} = \sum_{i=0}^{G-1} \sum_{j=0}^{G-1} q(i,j) \frac{\left(i - \mu_x\right)\left(j - \mu_y\right)}{\sigma_x \sigma_y} \tag{18}$$

6. **Contrast:** Spatial frequency of any image can be measure by this feature. Through this feature we can measure the amount of variations present among pixels in an image.

$$\text{Contrast} = \sum_{n=0}^{G-1} n^2 \{ \sum_{i=1}^{G} \sum_{j=1}^{G} q(i,j) \}, |\, i - j \,| = n \tag{19}$$

The rest of the features are derived from above mentioned features.

$$\text{Sum Average} = \sum_{i=2}^{2G} i q_{x+y}(i) \tag{20}$$

$$\text{Sum Entropy} = -\sum_{i=2}^{2G} q_{x+y}(i) \log \left\{ q_{x+y}(i) \right\} \tag{21}$$

$$\text{Sum Variance} = \sum_{i=2}^{2G} (i - vii)^2 q_{x+y}(i) \tag{22}$$

Difference Variance $=$ Variance of q_{x+y} (23)

Difference Entropy $= -\sum\limits_{i=0}^{G-1} q_{x-y}(i) \log\{q_{x-y}(i)\}$ (24)

Information measure of correlation $= \dfrac{HXY - HXY1}{\max\{Hx, Hy\}}$ (25)

Information measure of correlation $= \left(1 - e^{[-2(HXY2-HXY)]}\right)^{\frac{1}{2}}$ (26)

where,

$HXY = -\sum\limits_{i}\sum\limits_{j} q(i,j) \log q(i,j))$, (26 a)

$HXY1 = -\sum\limits_{i}\sum\limits_{j} q(i,j) \log\{q_x(i) q_y(j)\}$ (26 b)

$HXY2 = -\sum\limits_{i}\sum\limits_{j} q_x(i) q_y(j) \log\left\{q_x(i) q_y(j)\right\}$ (26 c)

Maximal correlation coefficient$=$ (Second largest eigen value of A)$^{1/2}$ where,

$A = \sum\limits_{k} \dfrac{q(i,k) q(j,k)}{q_x(i) q_y(k)}$ (27)

Neural Network

An artificial Neural Network is basically a mathematical model of biological neural networks (Haykin, 1999), (Meva, Kumbharana, & Kothari, 2012). This network mainly consists of some artificial inter-connected neurons. Every computational unit can be represented as neuron. After processing the input neurons produce some outputs. The connections between the neurons determine the information flow. Neurons basically consist of inputs, which are multiplied by weights (strength of the respective signals). Then it is computed by a mathematical function (activation/transfer function) such as hard limit, linear, sigmoidal etc. This function determines the activation characteristics of the neuron. In Figure 1, x_i, i $=$ 1, 2,...., n are the input values. Each input is multiplied by the corresponding weight W_i and a bias b is associated with each neuron. Their sum goes through a transfer function f. Output neuron Y gives the desired output as represented in the Figure 1.

Figure 1. A sample neuron

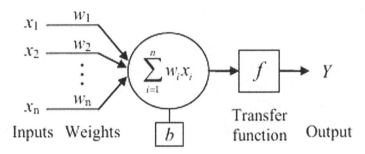

The neural network is useful since it acts as an adaptive system that changes its structure during its learning phase. In ANN three major learning paradigms comprise supervised learning, unsupervised learning and reinforcement learning. In supervised learning, a network is trained using a set of inputs and outputs (targets). A learning network estimates an unknown function from representative observations of the relevant variables. One of the well-known and frequently used learning techniques is back-propagation learning (BPL).

Multilayer perceptron uses back-propagation learning (BPL) for training purposes. It is basically a simple iterative gradient descent algorithm designed to minimize the mean squared error (MSE) between the desired response output and the actual output. The weights in batch BPL can be updated only after the presentation of the complete set of training data. So, a training iteration incorporates one complete pass through all the training patterns. On the other hand, the sequential BPL adjusts the network parameters as and when one training pattern is provided.

Genetic Algorithm

Genetic Algorithm (GA) is an optimization technique based on the combination of biological natural selection and genetics (Goldberg, 1989), (Malhotra, Singh & Singh, 2011). It works with a group of candidate solution called population. Each individuals or chromosome of the population is represented by a sequence of genes. The process of representation of individual genes is called encoding scheme. Depending on the problem encoding scheme can be of different types like: binary, octal, hexadecimal, permutation and value encoding.

1. **Binary Encoding:** It is the most common representation of chromosomes in genetic algorithm. Here the chromosomes are represented by binary strings.
2. **Octal Encoding:** The chromosomes are represented by the octal numbers (0-7).
3. **Hexadecimal Encoding:** Here the strings of chromosomes are represented by hexadecimal numbers (0-9, A-E).
4. **Permutation Encoding:** Every chromosome is a string of numbers that represent a position in a sequence. This scheme is used in ordering problems such as travelling salesman problem.
5. **Value Encoding or Real Encoding:** Every chromosome is a string of some values. Values can be anything connected to the problem. This scheme is generally used in neural network.

Three basic biological operations namely selection, crossover and mutation are main building blocks of genetic algorithm.

- **Selection:** Select individuals from the group of samples based on the fitness value of each individual. Fitness function varies from problem to problem. Any individual with higher fitness value has more chance to participate in the reproduction.
- **Crossover:** In crossover operation parents exchange some part based on randomly selected crossover point. There are different types of crossover namely one point, two point, uniform, arithmetic schemes.
- **One Point Crossover:** Let, we have two parents A (110011) and B (001100). For one point crossover if the randomly chosen point is 3 then after crossover two individuals will be generated: 110100 and 001011 (Box 1).
- **Two Point Crossover:** In this crossover scheme two points are selected from the string randomly. From the beginning of chromosome to the first crossover point is copied from one parent, the part from the first to the second crossover point is copied from the second parent and the rest is copied from the first parent. If the crossover points are 3 and 5 then after crossover two individuals will be generated (Box 2).

Box 1.

A	110011	After crossover	A1	**110**100
B	001100		B1	001**011**

↓

Crossover point

Box 2.

A	110011	After crossover	A1	**110**101
B	001100		B1	001**011**

↓ ↓

Crossover point

Box 3.

A	110011	After crossover	A1	**111110**
B	001100		B1	000**0**01

Box 4.

A	110011
B	111000
A AND B	110000

- **Uniform Crossover:** In this crossover scheme the bits are randomly copied from the first or from the second parent (Box 3).
- **Arithmetic Crossover:** In this crossover scheme some arithmetic operations is performed to make a new offspring. For example AND, OR etc. are some arithmetic operations (Box 4).
- **Tree Encoding Crossover:** One point of crossover is selected in both parent tree chromosomes, which are divided at point. The parts of tree below crossover point are exactly exchanged to produce new child.

Figure 2. Parent 1 and Parent 2 before crossover

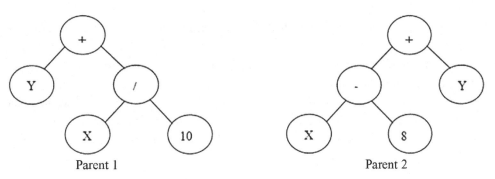

Figure 3. Child 1 and Child 2 after crossover

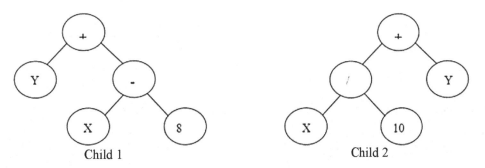

● **Mutation:** Premature convergence is a critical problem in GA based optimized techniques, due to highly fit parent chromosomes breed many similar off springs. These chromosomes are again of high fitness value. Crossover operation can generate different off springs but not always the solution of the previous mentioned problem. For better alternative mutation operation is used to explore new search area. To generate new individuals some bits of the parent are flip. These bits are selected randomly. Mutation generally takes place with small probability to avoid local optima. Like crossover, mutation can be performed for all types of encoding techniques mentioned above.

1.   **Binary Encoding Mutation:** The bits selected for creating new offspring are inverted.

   If parent A(001110) is selected to do mutation and the mutated bit is second bit the newly generated offspring is 011110.

2.   **Permutation Encoding Mutation:** The order of the two numbers given in a sequence is exchanged (Box 5 and Box 6).
3.   **Value Encoding Mutation:** A small numerical value is either added or subtracted from the selected values of chromosomes to create new offspring (Box 7 and Box 8).

   The working principle of GA as shown in figure is described as follows:

1.   Randomly generate an initial population. These populations may be created for multidimensional search space.
2.   Evaluate the fitness of each individual of the initial population. Fitness function varies from problem to problem.
3.   Repeat the following natural selection operation until the termination condition is reached
   a.   Select the individuals with highest fitness value in the current population as parents.
   b.   Using crossover operation among the selected parents new populations are created.

Box 5. Parent chromosome

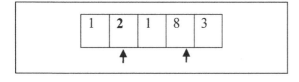

Box 6. Child chromosome

Box 7. Parent chromosome

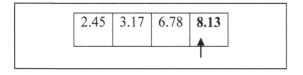

Box 8. Child chromosome

c.   Mutate the new parents to generate the new individuals.

d.   Again calculate the fitness value of the current individuals and update the fixed size population based on the fitness value.

e.   After reaching the termination condition (max. no. of iteration or no change in the fitness value) the best individuals are selected. These individuals are the solutions of the present problem. If not then go back to (a) and repeat the whole process.

Figure 4. Flowchart of the genetic algorithm

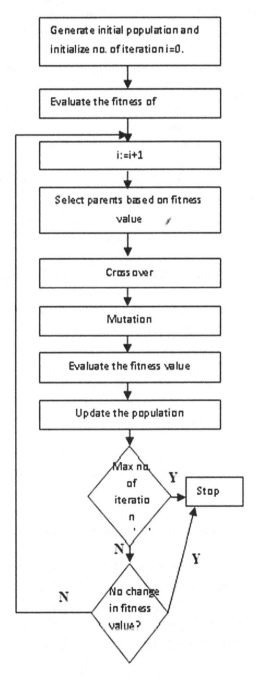

PROPOSED METHOD

Feature extraction, feature matching, and geometric transformation are three popular steps that have evolved into a general paradigm for automatic image registration. In our proposed technique at first we used K-means algorithm to cluster the image into different segments. K-means clustering algorithm used in the proposed method is described in next section (algorithm 1). GLCM is used to extract features of different clusters. These cluster based features are used as input of the Neural Network. Here multilayer perceptron is used as ANN. The problem with MLP is that the rate of convergence is higher than other optimization techniques like GA. So, to reduce this problem we used GA to optimize weights of ANN. In the proposed technique the weights of the input to hidden layer and hidden to output layer are optimized by GA in such a way that the output of the neural network meets the target output as close as possible i.e. to minimize the error.

K-means algorithm (Algorithm 1): Algorithm to partition an image into several clustered image.

Step 1: Input the image.
Step 2: Create histogram of the given image.
Step 3: /* Select the initial cluster head */

Sort the intensities $\{v_1, v_2, v_3, \ldots v_{max}\}$ of the image based on the number of occurrence of specific intensities in descending order.

Step 4: Based on the number of cluster (u) first u intensities $\{v_1, v_2, \ldots, v_u\}$ are selected as the initial cluster head.
Step 5: Each cluster has a specified area of radius r, using trail-n-error we select the suitable radius of the clusters.
Step 6: At first calculate whether or not any cluster head belongs to the radius of another cluster head. If so then change the cluster head with next suitable pixel intensity among the pool of sorted pixel intensities.
Step 7: For any arbitrary pixel intensity x, calculate the distance from each cluster head v_i, i=1, 2, ..., u.
Step 8: If the absolute distance $\mid v_i - x \mid \bullet$ r then x belongs to cluster with cluster head v_i.
Step 9: So, each cluster head v_i has cluster members like $\{C_{i1} + C_{i2} + \ldots + C_{ik}\}$ etc.
Step 10: Now, calculate new cluster head V_i.

$$V_i = \bullet \left(\frac{1}{k} \sum_{j=1}^{k} C_{ij} \right) \bullet \text{ where k is the number of cluster members in cluster i.}$$

Step 11: If no change in cluster head then stops the process otherwise repeat step (g) to step (j).

Figure 5(a) is decomposed into five clusters by k-means algorithm represented from (b) to (f).

After identifying clusters in each medical image feature extraction mechanism named GLCM is used to identify features of each cluster separately. These extracted features are used as input value of the multilayer perceptron network (MLP). Our proposed neural network is constructed of single hidden layer. The input layer of the ANN is denoted by L_{in}. Hidden layer is denoted by L_h and the output layer is denoted by L_{out} i.e.

Figure 5. Different clusters of an image segmented by k-means algorithm mentioned above

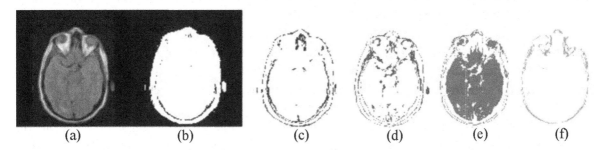

(a)   (b)   (c)   (d)   (e)   (f)

$L_{in}(i)$ i^{th} node of L_{in} where $i = 1$ to $2m$

$L_h(j)$ j^{th} node of L_h where $j=1$ to m

$W_{Lin(i)Lh(j)}$ is the weight along i^{th} node of input layer and j^{th} node of hidden layer and () is the activation function

Activation function from input to hidden layer and hidden to output layer is sigmoidal. Output of the neural network is 5 representing five transformational parameter as rotation, translation on both X and Y axes and scaling on both X and Y axes. The weights of input to hidden layer as well as hidden to output layer of neural network are optimized by Genetic Algorithm. Initial population in GA is 50 consists of weights from input to hidden layer followed by hidden to output layer. Each chromosome is encoded by real value. The best chromosome is selected using fitness function given in equation (28). Initial selection of chromosome for single point crossover operation is done by proportion of fitness value. In this proposed technique we used the mutation probability 0.1 for better solutions.

Fitness function is $\displaystyle Min_{s \in \zeta} \sum_{k=1}^{5} \left| \theta_k^d - \theta_k^a \right|$ (28)

where,

$$\theta_k^d = f\left(\sum_{j=1}^{m} f\left(\sum_{i=1}^{2m} f\left(I_{n(i)}\right).W_{Lin(i)Lh(j)} \right) \cdot W_{Lh(j)Lout(k)} \right)$$

and θ_k^a is the actual output value.

SOLUTIONS AND RECOMMENDATIONS

To evaluate the performance of the proposed method, several experiments were performed on different MRI images of brain. Registration of MR T1 and T2 weighted images is probably the best test case for a gradient based method. We perform different experiments on twenty mono-modal intra-subject MRI brain image datasets. In this article, we only present four such datasets as indicated in figures 6, 7, 8, 9. Before conducting the experiment, normalization of data has been done. The training of the network is performed by presenting the network a set of 50 artificial affine transformation applied on the original image. For the whole experiments as well as comparison, some initial constraints are applied on the given datasets. Rotational angle is maintained within -30^0 to 30^0. Scaling parameters along both X and Y co-ordinate axes are maintained within 0.5 to 5 while translational parameters along X and Y axes are kept within 1 to 10.

Result of proposed technique in Figure 6 is represented in Table 1. Comparing actual value and the resultant value after applying the proposed technique shows that the proposed technique gives convincing result.

Similarly we apply this technique on Figures 7, 8, 9 and report the result in Table 2.

Figure 6. A T1 weighted MR image slice of brain with different transformations

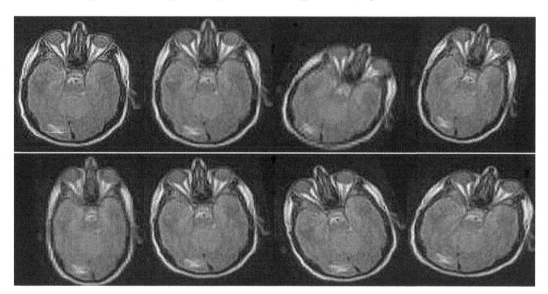

Table 1. Result of proposed technique on datasets given in Figure 6

Actual Value					Proposed Technique				
R	**Sx**	**Sy**	**Tx**	**Ty**	**R**	**Sx**	**Sy**	**Tx**	**Ty**
3	1.0	2.0	5	2	3.092	1.021	2.133	4.991	1.850
-18	0.5	2.0	7	9	-18.011	0.581	2.005	6.912	8.896
-12	1.5	1.0	10	1	-12.112	1.537	1.010	9.612	0.938
4	2.5	0.5	2	8	3.979	2.522	0.508	2.136	7.948
8	1.0	2.0	3	6	7.928	1.066	2.041	2.984	6.832
20	1.5	2.5	10	1	19.972	1.494	2.5	9.741	1.034
-10	1.0	3.0	5	10	-10.028	1.005	3.107	5.146	10.041

Figure 7. A T2 weighted MR image slice of brain

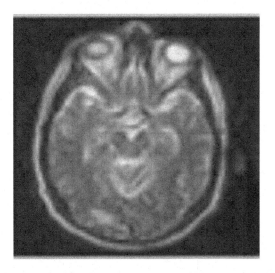

Figure 8. A T1 weighted MR image corpus of brain

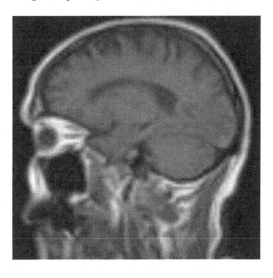

Figure 9. A T1 weighted MR image corpus of brain

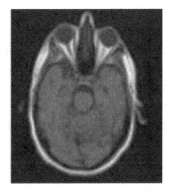

Table 2. Result of proposed technique on datasets given in Figures 7, 8 and 9

Actual Value					Proposed Technique				
R	Sx	Sy	Tx	Ty	R	Sx	Sy	Tx	Ty
Figure 7									
6	2.0	2.5	6	4	5.983	1.898	2.530	5.991	4.021
-8	1.5	3.0	8	8	-8.014	1.5	3.074	7.917	8.170
11	1.0	1.5	10	5	10.968	1.113	1.519	10.001	5.017
5	3.5	1.5	6	2	4.918	3.531	1.552	5.981	2.102
9	5.0	4.0	4	9	9.028	4.961	4.003	4.349	9.053
-20	3.5	2.0	3	1	-19.971	3.490	2.021	3.047	0.982
-13	3.0	3.5	5	2	-12.963	3.112	3.493	4.989	2.116
Figure 8									
-15	2.5	3.0	6	10	-15.096	2.497	3.003	6.082	10.013
-20	4.5	2.5	1	5	-20.012	4.611	2.548	0.983	4.939
12	1.5	1.5	4	8	12.156	1.537	1.418	4.014	7.779
9	2.0	1.5	9	1	9.021	2.052	1.5	9.138	0.947
20	3.0	2.0	2	6	20.061	3.160	2.019	1.884	6.024
13	1.5	4.5	3	10	12.963	1.602	4.501	2.993	9.887
10	3.0	3.5	7	2	10.030	2.981	3.514	6.974	2.120
Figure 9									
20	1.0	2.0	5	1	19.959	1.079	2.033	4.982	1.007
-18	4.5	3.5	4	3	-18.012	4.521	3.485	3.991	3.137
-2	1.0	1.0	8	7	-2.156	1.537	1.019	8.088	6.996
9	4.5	1.5	10	1	9.072	4.552	1.558	10.138	0.945
-14	1.0	3.0	9	9	-13.937	1.066	3.049	8.784	9.056
17	1.0	4.5	2	10	16.916	0.890	4.502	2.191	10.030
3	1.5	3.0	6	10	3.068	1.381	2.999	5.744	10.212

We carry out MR-MR registration using PCA method (Shang et al., 2006) and combination of NSCT (nonsubsampled coutourlet transform) and PSO based method (Al-Azzawi & Abdullah, 2012) and our proposed method and show the comparative study in Table 3. In the paper (Al-Azzawi & Abdullah, 2012), authors used a combination of both Nonsubsampled Contourlet Transform (NSCT) and PSO based method to register medical images. According to (Cunha, 2006), (Zhou, Cunha & Do, 2005) image features can be captured by NSCT method. After decomposing images using the NSCT, the edge and CP were extracted from bandpass directional sub band of NSCT coefficients. Then mutual information (MI) was adopted for the registration of feature points and then Particle Swarm Optimization (PSO) was use to calculate transformation parameters. There are three main steps edge detection using NSCT transform, optimization the MI based on particle swarm optimization and transformation parameter estimation. In this method (Shang et al., 2006) principal component analysis (PCA) neural network is used to calculate the first principal directions from feature images. The proposed registration method is accomplished by simply aligning feature images' first principal directions and centroids.

We perform comparison on more than 20 data sets and here we mentioned only result of our experiments performed on three data sets given in Figures 7, 8 and 9. The best results are marked in bold. From this comparison it is clear that the proposed hybrid methodology outperforms all the other two methods used in our experiment (reported in Table 3).

Table 3. Overall result comparison between PCA, NSTC based and the proposed methods for different data sets given in Figures 7, 8, and 9

PCA			NSTC and PSO					Propose Method				
R	T_x	T_y	R	S_x	S_y	T_x	T_y	R	S_x	S_y	T_x	T_y
Figure 7												
5.63	5.91	3.89	5.59	**2.013**	2.35	5.876	3.881	**5.983**	1.898	**2.530**	**5.991**	**4.021**
-8.029	**7.982**	**8.017**	-7.68	1.438	2.818	7.903	7.724	**-8.014**	**1.5**	**3.074**	7.917	8.170
10.906	9.395	4.697	**11.017**	**1.011**	**1.503**	9.913	5.131	10.968	1.113	1.519	**10.001**	**5.017**
4.09	3.44	5.89	4.77	2.90	1.53	6.02	1.83	**4.918**	3.531	1.552	5.981	2.102
8.881	3.911	8.818	8.994	4.595	3.618	4.004	8.774	**9.028**	4.961	4.003	4.349	9.053
-20.017	2.837	0.992	-19.759	3.387	1.763	2.917	0.912	-19.971	**3.490**	**2.021**	3.047	0.982
-12.638	4.875	1.886	-13.049	2.783	3.591	4.918	1.947	**-12.963**	3.112	3.493	4.989	2.116
Figure 8												
-14.738	5.871	10.061	-14.616	2.384	2.697	5.961	9.893	**-15.096**	2.497	3.003	6.082	10.013
-19.984	0.973	4.976	-20.049	4.381	2.712	1.130	4.971	**-20.012**	4.611	2.548	0.983	4.939
11.684	3.884	7.797	12.311	1.597	1.386	4.112	8.341	**12.156**	1.537	1.418	4.014	7.779
8.887	8.235	.696	9.271	1.899	1.321	8.366	.932	**9.021**	2.052	**1.5**	9.138	0.947
19.973	1.977	5.669	20.284	**2.965**	1.596	1.781	5.787	**20.061**	3.160	2.019	1.884	6.024
12.594	2.912	**10.011**	12.868	**1.491**	4.368	2.749	9.548	**12.963**	1.602	4.501	2.993	9.887
10.001	6.667	1.743	9.457	2.674	3.381	6.792	2.841	10.030	2.981	3.514	6.974	2.120
Figure 9												
19.529	4.769	0.858	19.947	0.739	1.846	4.561	1.011	**19.959**	1.079	2.033	4.982	1.007
-18.017	3.866	2.874	-17.911	4.367	3.569	3.962	3.436	**-18.012**	4.521	3.485	3.991	3.137
-2.261	7.877	6.697	-1.481	**0.865**	0.643	7.851	6.973	**-2.156**	1.537	1.019	8.088	6.996
8.914	9.737	0.913	8.954	4.381	1.583	9.588	0.882	**9.072**	4.552	1.558	10.138	0.945
-14.106	8.414	8.761	-13.916	0.918	2.898	8.522	8.847	**-13.937**	1.066	3.049	8.784	9.056
16.717	1.991	9.896	16.694	**0.898**	4.367	1.883	9.668	**16.916**	0.890	4.502	2.191	10.030
2.892	5.597	10.007	3.108	**1.492**	2.913	5.649	9.117	**3.068**	1.381	2.999	5.744	10.212

The best results are marked in bold

CONCLUSION

In this article, a cluster based image registration technique is proposed using artificial neural network. GLCM method is used as a feature extractor from each cluster. The weight of the neural network is optimized by Genetic Algorithm. The performance of the proposed method is very satisfactory comparing with the actual value of transformation parameters as well as with some other well-known registration methods.

REFERENCES

Al-Azzawi, N., & Ahmed K. Wan Abdullah, W. (2012). MRI monomodal feature based registration based on the efficiency of multiresolution representation and mutual information. *American Journal of Biomedical Engineering*, *2*(3), 98–104. doi:10.5923/j.ajbe.20120203.02

Aldenderfer, M. S., & Blashfield, R. K. (1985). *Cluster Analysis*. Los Angeles: Sage Publication.

Arsigny, V., Pennec, X., & Ayache, N. (2005). Polyrigid and polyaf□ne transformations: A novel geometrical tool to deal with non-rigid deformations application to the registration of histological slices. *Medical Image Analysis*, *9*(6), 507–523. doi:10.1016/j.media.2005.04.001 PMID:15948656

Bajcsy, R., & Kovacic, S. (1989). Multiresolution elastic matching. *Computer Vision Graphics and Image Processing*, *46*(1), 1–21. doi:10.1016/S0734-189X(89)80014-3

Besl, P. J., & McKay, N. D. (1992). A Method for Registration of 3-D Shapes. *IEEE Transaction on Pattern Recognition and Machine Intelligence*, *14*(2), 239–256. doi:10.1109/34.121791

Bookstein, F. L. (1989). Principal Warps: Thin-Plate Splines and the Decomposition of Deformations. *IEEE Transactions on Pattern Analysis and Machine Intelligence*, *11*(6), 567–585. doi:10.1109/34.24792

Bracewell, R. N. (1965). *The Fourier transform and its applications*. New York: McGraw-Hill.

Bro-Nielsen, M., & Gramkow, C. (1993). *Fast)uid registration of medical images*. Paper presented at Int. Conf. Vis. Biomed. Comput. (pp. 267–276).

Chalermwat, P., El-Ghazawi, T., & LeMoigneb, J. (2001). 2-phase GA-based image registration on parallel clusters. *Future Generation Computer Systems*, *17*(4), 467–476. doi:10.1016/S0167-739X(99)00131-4

Christensen, G. E., Miller, M. I., Vannier, M. W., & Grenander, U. (1996). Individualizing neuroanatomical atlases using a massively parallel computer. *Computer*, *29*(1), 32–38. doi:10.1109/2.481434

Christensen, G. E., Rabitt, R. D., & Miller, M. I. (1996). Deformable Templates Using Large Deformation Kinematics. *IEEE Transactions on Medical Imaging*, *5*(10), 1435–1447. PMID:18290061

Collignon, A., Geraud, T., Vandermeulen, D., Suetens, P., & Marchal, G. (1993). New high-performance 3D registration algorithms for 3D medical images. Medical imaging: image processing, 1898, 779–788.

Collignon, A., Maes, F., Delaere, D., Vandermeulen, D., Suetens, P., & Marchal, G. (1995), *Automated multimodality medical image registration using information theory*. Paper presented at 14th international conference on information processing in medical imaging (IPMI'95) (pp. 263–274).

Collins, D. L., Neelin, P., Peters, T. M., & Evans, A. C. (1994). Automatic 3D intersubject registration of MR volumetric data in standardized Talairach space. *Journal of Computer Assisted Tomography*, *18*(2), 192–205. doi:10.1097/00004728-199403000-00005 PMID:8126267

Cunha, A. L. (2006). The nonsubsampled contourlet transform: Theory, design, and applications. *IEEE Transactions on Image Processing*, *15*(10), 3089–3101. doi:10.1109/TIP.2006.877507 PMID:17022272

D'Agostino, E., Maes, F., Vandermeulen, D., & Suetens, P. (2003). A viscous)uid model for multi-modal non-rigid image registration using mutual information. *Medical Image Analysis*, *7*(4), 565–575. doi:10.1016/S1361-8415(03)00039-2 PMID:14561559

Davatzikos, C. (1997). Spatial transformation and registration of brain images using elastically deformable models. *Computer Vision and Image Understanding*, *66*(2), 207–222. doi:10.1006/cviu.1997.0605 PMID:11543561

Davis, M. H., Khotanzad, A., & Flaming, D. P. (1996) 3d image matching using radial basis function neural network. Paper presented at *WCNN'96: World Congress on Neural Networks* (pp. 1174–1179).

Declerc, J., Feldmar, J., Betting, F., & Goris, M. L. (1997). Automatic registration and alignment on a template of cardiac stress and rest SPECT images. *IEEE Transactions on Medical Imaging*, *16*(6), 727–737. doi:10.1109/42.650870 PMID:9533574

Duda, R. O., Hart, P. E., & Stork, D. G. (2001). *Pattern Classification*. New York: John Wiley and Sons.

Elhanany, I., Sheinfeld, M., Beck, A., Kadmon, Y., Tal, N., & Tirosh, D. (2000). *Robust image registration based on feedforward neural networks*. Paper Presented at 2000 IEEE International Conference on Systems, Man and Cybernetics, TN, USA (pp. 1507–1511). doi:10.1109/ICSMC.2000.886068

Evans, A. C., Marrett, S., Collins, L., & Peters, T. M. (1989), Anatomical-functional correlative analysis of the human brain using three dimensional imaging systems. *Medical imaging processing*, *1092*, 264-274.

Evans, A. C., Marrett, S., Torrescorzo, J., Ku, S., & Collins, L. (1991). MRI-PET correlation in three dimensions using a volume of interest (VOI) atlas. *Journal of Cerebral Blood Flow and Metabolism*, *11*, A69–A78. doi:10.1038/jcbfm.1991.40 PMID:1997491

Everitt, B. S., Handau, S., & Leese, M. (2001). *Cluster Analysis* (4th ed.). London: Arnold Publication.

Fitzpatrick, J. M., West, J. B., & Maurer, C. R. (1998). Predicting error in rigid-body pointbased registration. *IEEE Transactions on Medical Imaging*, *17*(5), 694–702. doi:10.1109/42.736021 PMID:9874293

Fox, P. T., Perlmutter, J. S., & Raichle, M. E. (1985). A Stereotactic Method of Anatomical Localization of Positron Emission Tomography. *Journal of Computer Assisted Tomography*, *9*(1), 141–153. doi:10.1097/00004728-198501000-00025 PMID:3881487

Gee, J., Reivich, M., & Bajacsy, R. (1993). Elastically deforming 3D atlas to match anatomical brain images. *Journal of Computer Assisted Tomography, 17*(2), 225–236. doi:10.1097/00004728-199303000-00011 PMID:8454749

Goldberg, D. E. (1989). *Genetic Algorithm in Search*. Optimization and Machine Learning, Addison-Wesley Professional.

Goshtaby, A. (2005). *2-d and 3-d image registration for medical, remote sensing, and industrial applications*. J. Wiley and Sons.

Grimson, W. E. L., Ettinger, G. J., White, S. J., Lozano-Perez, T., Wells, W. M., & Kikinis, R. (1996). An automatic registration method for frameless stereotaxy, image guided surgery, and enhanced reality visualization. *IEEE Transactions on Medical Imaging, 15*(2), 129–140. doi:10.1109/42.491415 PMID:18215896

Grimson, W. E. L., Lozano-P'erez, T., Wells, W. M. III, Ettinger, G. J., White, S. J., & Kikinis, R. (1994). *An automatic registration method for frameless stereotaxy, image guided surgery, and enhanced reality visualization, Computer vision and pattern recognition* (pp. 430–436). Los Alamitos, CA: IEEE Computer Society press.

Habboush, I. H., Mitchell, K. D., Mulkern, R. V., Barnes, P. D., & Treves, S. T. (1996). Registration *and Alignment of Three-Dimensional Images: An Interactive Visual Approach. Radiology, 199*(2), 573–578. doi:10.1148/radiology.199.2.8668816 PMID:8668816

Hachama, M., Desolneux, A., & Richard, F. J. P. (2012). Bayesian Technique for Image Classifying Registration. *IEEE Transactions on Image Processing, 21*(9), 4080–4091. doi:10.1109/TIP.2012.2200495 PMID:22645269

Haralick, R. M., Shanmugam, K., & Dinstein, I. (1973). Textural features for image classification. *IEEE Transactions on Systems, Man, and Cybernetics, 3*(6), 610–621. doi:10.1109/TSMC.1973.4309314

Haykin, S. (1999). *Neural networks: A comprehensive foundation* (2nd ed.). Prentice-Hall.

Hazra, J., Roy Chowdhury, A., & Dutta, P. (2013). An approach for determining angle of rotation of a gray image using weighted statistical regression. *International Journal of Scientific and Engineering Research, 4*(8), 1006–1013.

Hazra, J., Roy Chowdhury, A., & Dutta, P. (2014). Statistical Regression based Rotation Estimation Technique of Color Image. *International Journal of Computers and Applications, 102*(15), 1–4. doi:10.5120/17888-8903

Herring, J. L., Dawant, B. M., Maurer, C. R. Jr, Muratore, D. M., Galloway, R. L., & Fitzpatrick, J. M. (1998). Surface-based registration of CT images to physical space for image-guided surgery of the spine: A sensitivity study. *IEEE Transactions on Medical Imaging, 17*(5), 743–752. doi:10.1109/42.736029 PMID:9874298

Hill, D. L. G., Hawkes, D. J., Harrison, N. A., & Ruff, C. F. (1993), A strategy for automated multimodality image registration incorporating anatomical knowledge and imager characteristics. Paper presented as Information processing in medical imaging, 687, 182–196, Berlin, Springer-Verlag doi:10.1007/BFb0013788

Hipwell, J., Tanner, C., Crum, W., & Hawkes, D. (2006), *X-ray mammogram registration: a novel validation method.* Paper presented at 8th international workshop on digital mammography (IWDM'06), Manchester, UK (Vol. 4046, pp. 197–204). doi:10.1007/11783237_28

Hipwell, J., Tanner, C., Crum, W., Schnabel, J. A., & Hawkes, D. (2007). A New Validation Method for X-ray Mammogram Registration Algorithms Using a Projection Model of Breast X-ray Compression. *IEEE Transactions on Medical Imaging*, *26*(9), 1190–1200. doi:10.1109/TMI.2007.903569 PMID:17896592

Hurvitz, A., & Joskowicz, L. (2008). *Registration of a CT-like atlas to fluoroscopic X-ray images using intensity correspondences. International Journal of Computer Assisted Radiology and Surgery*, *3*(6), 493–504

Jepson, A., & Black, M. (1993). Mixture models for optical $\phi\lambda$ow computation. *Computer Vision and Pattern Recognition* (pp. 760–761).

Kanatani, K. (1994). Analysis of 3-D rotation fitting. *IEEE Transactions on Pattern Analysis and Machine Intelligence*, *16*(5), 543–549. doi:10.1109/34.291441

Khader, M., & Hamza, I. A. (2011). Nonrigid Image Registration Using an Entropic Similarity. *IEEE Transactions on Information Technology in Biomedicine*, *15*(5), 681–690. doi:10.1109/TITB.2011.2159806 PMID:21690017

Kim, J., & Fessler, J. A. (2004). Intensity-based image registration using robust correlation coefficients. *IEEE Transactions on Medical Imaging*, *23*(11), 98–104. doi:10.1109/TMI.2004.835313 PMID:15554130

Kuglin, C. D., & Hines, D. C. (1975) *The phase correlation image alignment method.* Paper presented at IEEE International Conference Cybern Society (pp. 163–165).

Langevin, F., & Didon, J. P. (1995). Registration of MR images: from 2d to 3d, using a projection based cross correlation method. In: Engineering in Medicine and Biology Society, *IEEE 17th Annual Conference,* Canada (Vol. 1).

Likar, B., & Pernus, F. (2001). A hierarchical approach to elastic registration based on mutual information. *Image and Vision Computing*, *19*(1–2), 33–44. doi:10.1016/S0262-8856(00)00053-6

Liu, J. X., Chen, Y. S., & Chen, L. F. (2008). Nonlinear Registration Based on the Approximation of Radial Basis Function Coefficient. *Journal of Medical and Biological Engineering*, *28*(3), 119–126.

Lowe, D. G. (1999), *Object recognition from local scale-invariant features.* Paper presented at International Conference on Computer Vision, 1150–1157.

Lowe, D. G. (2004). Distinctive image features from scale invarient keypoints. *International Journal of Computer Vision*, *60*(2), 91–110. doi:10.1023/B:VISI.0000029664.99615.94

Maes, F., Collignon, A., Vandermeulen, D., Marchal, G., & Suetens, P. (1997). Multimodality image registration by maximization of mutual information, *IEEE Transaction on. Medical. Image, 16*(2), 187–198.

Maes, F., Vandermeulen, D., & Suetuns, P. (2003) *Medical image registration using mutual information. IEEE Proc 91(10),* 1699–1722 doi:10.1109/JPROC.2003.817864

Maguire, G. Q., Noz, M., Rusinek, H., Jaeger, J., Kramer, E. L., Sanger, J. J., & Smith, G. (1991). Graphics applied to medical image registration. *IEEE Computer Graphics and Applications, 11*(2), 20–28. doi:10.1109/38.75587

Mahapatra, D., & Sun, Y. (2012). Integrating Segmentation Information for Improved MRF-Based Elastic Image Registration. *IEEE Transactions on Image Processing, 21*(1), 170–183. doi:10.1109/TIP.2011.2162738 PMID:21791411

Mahmoud, H., Masulli, F., & Rovetta, S. (2007) Feature-Based Medical Image Registration using a zzy Clustering Segmentation Approach. *IEEE Transaction,* 172-184

Malandain, G. (2006). *Les mesures de similarité pour le recalage des images médicales, Habilitation à Diriger Recherches, Univ.* Nice Sophia-Antipolis, Nice, France: Tech. Rep.

Malhotra, R., Singh, N., & Singh, Y. (2011). *Genetic Algorithms: Concepts* (Vol. 4, p. 2). Design for Optimization of Process Controllers.

Mattes, D., Haynor, D. R., Vesselle, H., Lewellen, T. K., & Eubank, W. (2003). PET-CT Image Registration in the Chest Using Free-form Deformations. *IEEE Transactions on Medical Imaging, 22*(1), 120–128. doi:10.1109/TMI.2003.809072 PMID:12703765

Maurer, C. R., Fitzpatrick, J. M., Wang, M. Y., Galloway, R. L., Maciunas, R. J., & Allen, G. G. (1997). Registration of head volume images using implantable fiducial markers. *IEEE Transactions on Medical Imaging, 16*(4), 447–462. doi:10.1109/42.611354 PMID:9263002

Meva, D. T., Kumbharana, C. K., & Kothari, A. D. (2012). The study of adoption of neural network approach in fingerprint recognition. *International Journal of Computers and Applications, 40*(11), 8–11. doi:10.5120/5007-7326

Morris, E. D., Muswick, G. J., Ellert, E. S., Steagall, R. N., Goyer, P. F., & Semple, W. E. (1993). Computer-aided techniques for aligning interleaved sets of non-identical medical images. Medical imaging: image processing (Vol. 1898, pp. 146–157). Bellingham, WA: SPIE Press.

Mostafa, M. G., Farag, A. A., & Essock, E. (2000). Multimodality image registration and fusion using neural network. *FUSION, 2,* 10–13.

Pietrzyk, U., Herholz, K., Fink, G., Jacobs, A., Mielke, R., Slansky, I., & Heis, W. et al. (1994). An interactive technique for three-dimensional image registration: Validation for PET, SPECT, MRI and CT brain studies. *Journal of Nuclear Medicine, 35,* 2011–2018. PMID:7989986

Pluim, J. P. W., Maintz, J. B. A., & Viergever, M. A. (2003). Mutual-information based registration of medical images: A survey. *IEEE Transactions on Medical Imaging, 22*(6), 986–1004. doi:10.1109/TMI.2003.815867 PMID:12906253

Pluim, J. P. W., Maintz, J. B. A., & Viergever, M. A. (2004). f-Information Measures in Medical Image Registration. *IEEE Transactions on Medical Imaging, 23*(12), 1508–1516. doi:10.1109/TMI.2004.836872 PMID:15575408

Pohl, K., Fisher, J., Grimson, W., Kikinis, R., & Wells, W. (2006). A Bayesian model for joint segmentation and registration. *NeuroImage, 31*(1), 228–239. doi:10.1016/j.neuroimage.2005.11.044 PMID:16466677

Pope, P., & Theiler, J. (2003) *Automated image registration (AIR) of MTI imagery*. Paper presented at SPIE 27, Orlando, Florida (pp. 294–305).

Puri, B. K. (2004). Monomodal rigid-body registration and applications to the investigation of the effects of eicosapentaenoic acid intervention in neuropsychiatric disorders. *Prostaglandins, Leukotrienes, and Essential Fatty Acids, 71*(3), 137–200. doi:10.1016/j.plefa.2004.03.010 PMID:15253887

Rangarajan, A., Chui, H., & Duncan, J. S. (1999). Rigid point feature registration using mutual information. *Medical Image Analysis, 3*(4), 425–440. doi:10.1016/S1361-8415(99)80034-6 PMID:10709705

Renzetti, F. R., & Zortea, L. (2011). Use of a gray level coccurrence matrix to characterize duplex stainless steel phases microstructure. *Frattura ed Integrita Strutturale*, 16, 43-51

Roche, A., Malandain, G., & Ayache, N. (2000). Unifying maximum likelihood approaches in medical image registration. *International Journal of Imaging Systems and Technology, 11*(1), 71–80. doi:10.1002/(SICI)1098-1098(2000)11:1<71::AID-IMA8>3.0.CO;2-5

Roche, A., Malandain, G., Pennec, X., & Ayache, N. (1998), The *correlation ratio as a new similarity measure for multimodal image registration*. Paper presented as 1st Int. Conf. Med. Image Comput. Comput.-Assisted Intervent., (Vol. 1496, pp. 1115–1124).

Rohling, T., & Maurer, C. R., Jr. (2001), *Intensity-based non-rigid registration using adaptive multilevel free-form deformation with an incompressibility constraint*. Paper presented as: 4th Int. Conf. Medical Image Comput. Comput.-Assisted Intervent., (Vol. 2208, pp. 111–119). doi:10.1007/3-540-45468-3_14

Rueckert, D., Sonoda, L. I., Hayes, C., Hill, D. L. G., Leach, M. O., & Hawkes, D. J. (1999). Non-rigid registration using free-form deformation: Application to breast MR images. *IEEE Transactions on Medical Imaging, 18*(8), 712–721. doi:10.1109/42.796284 PMID:10534053

Sabisch, T., & Ferguson, A. & Bolouri (1998). Automatic Registration Of Complex Images Using A Self Organizing Neural System. *Proceedings of 1998 Int. Joint Conf. on Neural Networks* (pp. 165–170).

Schroeter, P., Vesin, J. M., Langenberger, T., & Meuli, R. (1998). Robust parameter estimation of intensity distributions for brain magnetic resonance images. *IEEE Transactions on Medical Imaging, 17*(2), 172–186. doi:10.1109/42.700730 PMID:9688150

Scott, A. M., Macapinlac, H., Zhang, J., Daghighian, F., Montemayor, N., Kalaigian H., Sgouros, G., Graham, M. C., Kolbert, K., Yeh, S. D. J., Lai, E., Goldsmith, S. J., & Larson, S. M. (1996), Image registration of SPECT and CT images using an external fiduciary band and three-dimensional surface fitting in metastatic thyroid cancer. *Journal of image registration using GA.*, 36, 100–103.

Sebe, N., & Lew, M. (2003). *Robust Computer Vision: Theory and Applications (Computational Imaging and Vision)* (p. 26). New York: Springer-Verlag. doi:10.1007/978-94-017-0295-9

Seedahmed, G., & Martucci, L. (2002), Automated Image Registration Using Geometrically Invariant Parameter Space Clustering (Gipsc). Paper presented at Potogrammetic Computer Vision, Graz, Austria.

Shang, L., Cheng L. v. J., & Yi, Z. (2006). Rigid medical image registration using pca neural network. *Neurocomputing, 69(13-15),* 1717-1722

Soltys, M., Beard, D. V., Carrasco, V., Mukherji, S., & Rosenman, J. (1995). FUSION: a tool for registration and visualization of multiple modality 3D medical data. Medical imaging: image processing, 2434, 74–80.

Strother, S. C., Anderson, J. R., Xu, X., Liow, J., Bonar, D. C., & Rottenberg, D. A. (1994). Quantitative comparisons of image registration techniques based on high-resolution MRI of the brain. *Journal of Computer Assisted Tomography, 18*(6), 954–962. doi:10.1097/00004728-199411000-00021 PMID:7962808

Studholme, C. (1997). Measures of 3-D medical image alignment [Ph.D. thesis]. University of London, London, UK.

Studholme, C., Hill, D. L. G., & Hawkes, D. J. (1999). An overlap invariant entropy measure of 3-D medical image alignment. *Pattern Recognition, 32*(1), 71–86. doi:10.1016/S0031-3203(98)00091-0

Subsol, G., Thirion, J. P., & Ayache, N. (1998). A general scheme for automatically building 3-D morphometric anatomical atlases: Application to a skull atlas. *Medical Image Analysis, 2*(1), 37–60. doi:10.1016/S1361-8415(01)80027-X PMID:10638852

Tanner, C., Schnabel, J. A., Chung, D., Clarkson, M. J., Rueckert, D., Hill, D., & Hawkes, D. J. (2000). Volume and shape preservation of enhancing lesions when applying non-rigid registration to a time series of contrast enhancing MR breast images. Paper presented at the *3rd Int. Conf. Med. Image Comput. Comput.-Assisted Intervent., London,* U.K. (pp 327–337).

Tsao, J., & Lauterbur, P. (1998). Generalized clustering-based image registration for multi-modality images. Paper presented at 20th Annual International Conference of the IEEE (Vol. 2, pp. 667-670).

Viola, P., & Wells, W. M. III. (1997). Alignment by maximization of mutual information. *International Journal of Computer Vision, 24*(2), 137–154. doi:10.1023/A:1007958904918

Wang, J., Reinstein, L. E., Hanley, J., & Meek, A. G. (1996). Investigation of a phase-only correlation technique for anatomical alignment of portal images in radiation therapy. *Physics in Medicine and Biology, 41*(6), 1045–1058. doi:10.1088/0031-9155/41/6/008 PMID:8794484

Wang, Q., Chen, L., Yap, P., Wu, G., & Shen, D. (2010). Groupwise Registration Based on Hierarchical Image Clustering and Atlas Synthesis. *Human Brain Mapping, 31*(8), 1128–1140. PMID:20063349

Wells, W. M. III, Viola, P., Atsumi, H., Nakajima, S., & Kikinis, R. (1996). Multi-modal volume registration by maximization of mutual information. *Medical Image Analysis, 1*(1), 35–51. doi:10.1016/S1361-8415(01)80004-9 PMID:9873920

West, J., Fitzpatrick, J. M., Wang, M. Y., Dawant, B. M., Maurer, C. R. Jr, Kessler, R. M., & Woods, R. P. et al. (1997). Comparison and evaluation of retrospective intermodality brain image registration techniques. *Journal of Computer Assisted Tomography, 21*(4), 554–566. doi:10.1097/00004728-199707000-00007 PMID:9216759

Woods, R., Mazziotta, J., & Cherry, S. R. (1993). MRI-PET registration with automate algorithm. *Journal of Computer Assisted Tomography, 17*(4), 536–546. doi:10.1097/00004728-199307000-00004 PMID:8331222

Xia, M., & Liu, B. (2004). Image registration by super-curves. *IEEE Transactions on Image Processing, 13*(4), 720–732. doi:10.1109/TIP.2003.822611 PMID:15376603

Yasein, M. S., & Agathoklis, P. (2008) A feature-based image registration technique for images of different scale. Paper presented at IEEE international symposium on circuits and systems (ISCAS'08), Seattle, WA (pp. 3558–3561). doi:10.1109/ISCAS.2008.4542228

Zhou, J., Cunha, A. L., & Do, M. N. (2005), Nonsubsampled contourlet transform: construction and application in enhancement. Proceedings of the *IEEE International Conference on Image Processing (ICIP '05)*, Genova, Italy (Vol. 1, pp. 469–472).

Zitova, B., & Flusser, J. (2003). Image registration methods: A survey. *Image and Vision Computing, 21*(11), 977–1000. doi:10.1016/S0262-8856(03)00137-9

Compilation of References

Dvb queplix, (2012, September). Retrieved from http://www.queplix.com

He, X.-J., Zhang, Y., Lok, T.-M. & Lyu, M.R. (2005). A new feature of uniformity of image texture directions coinciding with the human eyes perception. Fuzzy Systems and Knowledge Discovery (Vol. 3614, pp. 727–730).

Abbasimehr, H., Tarokh, M. J., & Setak, M. (2011). Determination of Algorithms Making Balance Between Accuracy and Comprehensibility in Churn Prediction Setting. *International Journal of Information Retrieval Research, 1*(2), 39–54. doi:10.4018/IJIRR.2011040103

Abbas, K., Mikler, A., Ramezani, A., & Menezes, S. (2004). Computational epidemiology: Bayesian disease surveillance. *Proc. of the International Conference on Bioinformatics and its Applications*, USA, pp. 1–12.

Abdelzaher, T., Anokwa, Y., Boda, P., Burke, J., Estrin, D., & Guibas, L. et al. (2007). Mobiscopes for human spaces. *Pervasive Computing, IEEE, 6*(2), 20–29. doi:10.1109/MPRV.2007.38

Abecasis, G. R., Auton, A., Brooks, L. D., DePristo, M. A., & Durbin, R. M. (2012, November). An integrated map of genetic variation from 1,092 human genomes. *Nature, 491*(7422), 56–65. PMID:23128226

Abeel, T., Van de Peer, Y., & Saeys, Y. (2009). Toward a gold standard for promoter prediction evaluation. *Bioinformatics (Oxford, England), 25*(12), i313–i320. doi:10.1093/bioinformatics/btp191 PMID:19478005

Abraham, A., & Nath, B. (2000). Hybrid intelligent systems design: A review of a decade of research. *IEEE Transactions on Systems, Man and Cybernetics (Part-C)*, August.

Acur, N. (2005). Classification of ECG beats by using a fast least square support vector machines with a dynamic programming feature selection algorithm. *Neural Computing & Applications, 14*(4), 299–309. doi:10.1007/s00521-005-0466-z

Adamatzky, A. (1994). *Identification of Cellular Automata*. London: Taylor & Francis Ltd.

Agarwal, S., & Xaxa, D. K. (2014). Survey on Image Segmentation Techniques and Color Models.[IJCSIT]. *International Journal of Computer Science and Information Technologies, 5*(3), 3025–3030.

Agosta, L. (2000). *The Essential Guide to Data Warehousing*. Upper Saddle River, N.J.: Prentice Hall.

Agrawal, R., Imielinski, T., & Swami, A. (1993). Mining association rules between sets of items in large databases. *Proceedings of the 1993 ACM SIGMOD international conference on Management of data SIGMOD '93* (pp. 207-216). doi:10.1145/170035.170072

Ahlgren, B., Dannewitz, C., Imbrenda, C., Kutscher, D., & Ohlman, B. (2011). A survey of information-centric networking (draft). Proceedings of Information-Centric Networking. Schloss Dagstuhl - Leibniz-Zentrum fuerInformatik, Germany.

Ahmad, S., Keskin, O., Sarai, A., & Nussinov, R. (2008, October). Protein-DNA interactions: Structural, thermodynamic and clustering patterns of conserved residues in DNA-binding proteins. *Nucleic Acids Research, 36*(18), 5922–5932. doi:10.1093/nar/gkn573 PMID:18801847

Alami, M. E. (2014). A new matching strategy for content based image retrieval system. *Applied Soft Computing, 14*, 407–418. doi:10.1016/j.asoc.2013.10.003

Alander, J. T. (2000) *Indexed bibliography of genetic algorithms in optics and image processing*, (Technical Report 94-1-OPTICS). University of Vaasa, Vaasa, Finland.

Al-Azzawi, N., & Ahmed K. Wan Abdullah, W. (2012). MRI monomodal feature based registration based on the efficiency of multiresolution representation and mutual information. *American Journal of Biomedical Engineering, 2*(3), 98–104. doi:10.5923/j.ajbe.20120203.02

Aleksander, I., & Morton, H. (1995). *An introduction to neural computing*. NY: International Thompson Computer Press.

Alotaibi, Y. A., Alghamdi, M., & Alotaiby, F. (2010). Speech Recognition System of Arabic Alphabet Based on a Telephony Arabic Corpus. In A. Elmoataz et al. (Eds.), Image and Signal Processing (pp. 122-129). Springer Berlin Heidelberg. doi:10.1007/978-3-642-13681-8_15

Altavista. (n. d.). Retrieved from http://www.altavista.com/sites/search/simage

Altschul, S. F., Gish, W., Miller, W., Myers, E. W., & Lipman, D. J. (1990, October). Basic local alignment search tool. *Journal of molecular biology, 215*(3), 403-410. doi:10.1006/jmbi.1990.9999

Aluru, S. (2005). Handbook of Computational Molecular Biology. Chapman & Hall/CRC.

Ames, G., George, D., Hampson, C., Kanarek, A., McBee, C., Lockwood, D., Achter, J., & Webb, C. (2011). Using network properties to predict disease dynamics on human contact networks. Proceedings Biological sciences, The Royal Society, 278(1724) 3544–3550.

Anderberg, M. R. (1973). *Cluster Analysis for Applications*. New York, NY: Academic Press, Inc.

Anderson, D. C., Li, W., Payan, D. G., & Noble, W. S. (2003). A New Algorithm for the Evaluation of Shotgun Peptide Sequencing in Proteomics: Support Vector Machine Classification of Peptide MS/MS Spectra and SEQUEST Scores. *Journal of Proteome Research, 2*(2), 137–146. doi:10.1021/pr0255654 PMID:12716127

Anfinsen, C. B. (1973). Principles that Govern the Folding of Protein Chains. *Science, 181*(4096), 223–230. Retrieved from http://www.sciencemag.org doi:10.1126/science.181.4096.223 PMID:4124164

Anghel, C. I., & Ozunu, A. (2006). Prediction of gaseous emissions from industrial stacks using an artificial intelligence method. *Chemical Papers, 60*(6), 410–415. doi:10.2478/s11696-006-0075-z

Anghelescu, P., Ionita, S., & Iana, V. (2013). High-speed PCA Encryption Algorithm using Reconfigurable Computing. *Journal of Cybernetics and Systems, 44*(4), 285–304.

Anghelescu, P., Ionita, S., & Sofron, E. (2010). Encryption Technique with Programmable Cellular Automata. *Journal of Cellular Automata, 5*(1-2), 79–106.

Anusuya, M. A., & Katti, S. K. (2009). Speech Recognition by Machine: A Review. *International Journal of Computer Science and Information Security, 6*(3), 181–205.

Aracil, J., & Gordillo, F. (Eds.). (2000). *Stability Issues in Fuzzy Control*. Heidelberg: Physica-Verlag.

Arafat, H., Barakat, S., & Goweda, A. F. (2012). Using Intelligent Techniques for Breast Cancer Classification. *International Journal of Emerging Trends & Technology in Computer Science*, *1*(3), 26–36.

Arafat, H., Elawady, R. M., Barakat, S., & Elrashidy, N. M. (2013). Using Rough Set and Ant Colony optimization In Feature Selection. *International Journal of Emerging Trends and Technology in Computer Science*, *2*(1), 148–155.

Arajo, A. R. F., & Costa, D. C. (2009). Local adaptive receptive field self-organizing map for image color segmentation. *Image and Vision Computing*, *27*(9), 1229–1239. doi:10.1016/j.imavis.2008.11.014

Araujo, T., Nedjah, N., & Mourelle, L. (2008). Quantum-Inspired Evolutionary State Assignment for Synchronous Finite State Machines. *Journal of Universal Computer Science*, *14*(15), 2532–2548.

Ardac, D., & Akaygun, S. (2004). Effectiveness of multimedia-based instruction that emphasizes molecular representations on students' understanding of chemical change. *Journal of Research in Science Teaching*, *41*(4), 317–337. doi:10.1002/tea.20005

Arora, S. J., & Singh, R. P. (2012). Automatic Speech Recognition: A Review. *International Journal of Computers and Applications*, *60*(9), 34–44.

Arsigny, V., Pennec, X., & Ayache, N. (2005). Polyrigid and polyaf□ne transformations: A novel geometrical tool to deal with non-rigid deformations application to the registration of histological slices. *Medical Image Analysis*, *9*(6), 507–523. doi:10.1016/j.media.2005.04.001 PMID:15948656

Asif, S., & Kong, Y. (2014). Low-area Wallace multiplier. *VLSI Design*, *2014*, 1–6. doi:10.1155/2014/343960

Asuncion, A., & Newman, D. (2007). UCI machine learning repository. Retrieved from http://www.ics.uci.edu

Atkins, M., & Mackiewich, B. (1998). Fully Automatic Segmentation of the Brain in MRI, *Proceedings of 1998. IEEE Transactions on Medical Imaging*, *17*(1), 98–107. doi:10.1109/42.668699 PMID:9617911

Awad, M., Chehdi, K., & Nasri, A. (2007). Multicomponent Image Segmentation Using a Genetic Algorithm and Artificial Neural Network. *IEEE Geoscience and Remote Sensing Letters*, *4*(4), 571–575. doi:10.1109/LGRS.2007.903064

Azough, S., Bellafkih, M., & Bouyakhf, E. H. (2010). Adaptive E-learning using Genetic Algorithms. *IJCSNS International Journal of Computer Science and Network Security*, *10*(7), 237–244.

Backstrom, L., Boldi, P., Rosa, M., Ugander, J., & Vigna, S. (2012). Four degrees of separation. *Proceedings of the 4th Annual ACM Web Science Conference (WebSci '12)*, New York, NY, USA (pp. 33-42). ACM doi:10.1145/2380718.2380723

Bailer, W., Schallauer, P., Haraldsson, H. B., & Rehatschek, H. (2005). Optimized Mean Shift Algorithm for Color Segmentation in Image Sequences. In IS&T/SPIE Electronic Imaging (Vol. 5685, pp. 593–600).

Bajcsy, R., & Kovacic, S. (1989). Multiresolution elastic matching. *Computer Vision Graphics and Image Processing*, *46*(1), 1–21. doi:10.1016/S0734-189X(89)80014-3

Baker, D. (2000, May). A surprising simplicity to protein folding. *Nature*, *405*(6782), 39-42. Retrieved from 10.1038/35011000

Baker, D., & Sali, A. (2001). Protein Structure Prediction and Structural Genomics. *Science*, *294*(5540), 93–96. Retrieved from http://www.sciencemag.org/cgi/content/abstract/sci;294/5540/93 doi:10.1126/science.1065659 PubMed doi:10.1126/science.1065659 PMID:11588250

Baldevbhai, P. J., & Anand, R. S. (2012). Review of Graph, Medical and Color Image base Segmentation Techniques. *IOSR Journal of Electrical and Electronics Engineering (IOSRJEEE)*, *1*(1), 1-19.

Baltazar, A., Aranda, J. I., & Gonzalez-Aguilar, G. (2008). Bayesian classification of ripening stages of tomato fruit using acoustic impact and colorimeter sensor data. *Computers and Electronics in Agriculture*, *60*(2), 113–121. doi:10.1016/j. compag.2007.07.005

Bandyopadhyay, S., Srivastava, A. K., & Pal, S. K. (Eds.). (2002) Multiobjective Variable String Genetic Classifier: Application of Remote Sensing Image. World Scientific, 2002.

Bandyopadhyay, S., Maulik, U., & Mukhopadhyay, A. (2007). Multiobjective Genetic Clustering for Pixel Classification in Remote Sensing Imagery. *IEEE Transactions on Geoscience and Remote Sensing*, *45*(5), 1506–1511. doi:10.1109/ TGRS.2007.892604

Bang, J., Dholakia, N., Hamel, L., & Shin, S. (2009). Customer Relationship Management and Knowledge Discovery in Database. In J. Erickson (Ed.), *Database Technologies: Concepts, Methodologies, Tools, and Applications* (pp. 1778–1786). Hershey, PA: Information Science Reference. doi:10.4018/978-1-60566-058-5.ch107

Banzhaf, W., Nordin, P., Keller, R. E., & Francone, F. D. (1998, January). *Genetic Programming -- An Introduction; On the Automatic Evolution of Computer Programs and its Applications.* San Francisco, CA, USA: Morgan Kaufmann. Retrieved from http://www.elsevier.com/wps/find/bookdescription.cws_home/677869/description#description

Barrett, C., Bisset, K., Eubank, S., Feng, X., & Marathe, M. (2008). EpiSimdemics: An efficient algorithm for simulating the spread of infectious disease over large realistic social networks.*International Conference for High Performance Computing Networking Storage and Analysis* (pp. 1–12). doi:10.1109/SC.2008.5214892

Barros, L., Bassanezi, R., Oliveira, R., & Leite, M. (2001). A disease evolution model with uncertain parameters. Proceedings of the IEEE Joint 9th IFSA World Congress and 20th NAFIPS International Conference, vol. 3, no. C., pp. 1626–1630. doi:10.1109/NAFIPS.2001.943794

Bartlett, M.S., Movellan, J.R., & Sejnowski, T.J. (2002). Face recognition by independent component analysis. *Neural Networks, IEEE Transactions,* 13(6), 1450-1464.

Bateman, A., Coin, L., Durbin, R., Finn, R. D., & Hollich, V. (2004). The Pfam protein families database. *Nucleic Acids Research*, *32*(90001), D138–D141. doi:10.1093/nar/gkh121 PMID:14681378

Baugh, C. R., & Wooley, B. A. (1973). A Two's complement parallel array multiplication algorithm. *IEEE Transactions on Computers*, *C-22*(12), 1045–1047. doi:10.1109/T-C.1973.223648

Baum, L. E. (1972). An Inequality and Associated Maximization Technique in Statistical Estimation for Probabilistic Functions of a Markov Process. *Inequalities, 3.*

Bayes, T., & Price, M. (1763). Essay towards Solving a Problem in the Doctrine of Chances. By the Late Rev. Mr. Bayes, F. R. S. Communicated by Mr. Price, in a Letter to John Canton, A. M. F. R. S. *Philosophical Transactions of the Royal Society of London*, *53*(0), 370–418. doi:10.1098/rstl.1763.0053

Baykasoğlu, A., Çevik, A., Özbakır, L., & Kulluk, S. (2009). Generating prediction rules for liquefaction through data mining. *Expert Systems with Applications*, *36*(10), 12491–12499. doi:10.1016/j.eswa.2009.04.033

Baziar, M. H., & Jafarian, Y. (2007). Assessment of liquefaction triggering using strain energy concept and ANN model: Capacity energy. *Soil Dynamics and Earthquake Engineering*, *27*(12), 1056–1072. doi:10.1016/j.soildyn.2007.03.007

Bazi, Y., Bruzzone, L., & Melgani, F. (2007). Image thresholding based on the EM algorithm and the generalized Gaussian distribution. *Pattern Recognition*, *40*(2), 619–634. doi:10.1016/j.patcog.2006.05.006

Bechtler, H., Browne, M. W., Bansal, P. K., & Kecman, V. (2001). New approach to dynamic modelling of vapour-compression liquid chillers: Artificial neural networks. *Applied Thermal Engineering*, *21*(9), 941–953. doi:10.1016/S1359-4311(00)00093-4

Belaid, L. J., & Mourou, W. (2009). Image Segmentation: A Watershed Transformation Algorithm. *Journal of Image Analysis and Stereology by International Society for Stereology*, *28*(2), 93–102. doi:10.5566/ias.v28.p93-102

Belhumeur, P. N., Hespanha, J. P., & Kriegman, D. J. (1997). Eigenfaces vs fisherfaces: Recognition using class specific linear projection. *IEEE Transactions on Pattern Analysis and Machine Intelligence*, *19*(7), 711–720. doi:10.1109/34.598228

Belongie, S., Hellerstein, J.M., Carson, C., Thomas, M., & Malik, J. (1999). Blobworld: A system for region-based image indexing and retrieval. *Proceedings of the Third International Conference VISUAL* (pp. 509– 517).

Bennani, Y., & Gallinari, P. (1995). Neural networks for discrimination and modelization of speakers. *Speech Communication*, *17*(1-2), 159–175. doi:10.1016/0167-6393(95)00014-F

Benson, E. R., Reid, J. F., & Zhang, Q. (2003). Machine vision–based guidance system for an Agricultural small–grain harvester. *Transactions of the American Society of Agricultural Engineers*, *46*(4), 1255–1264. doi:10.13031/2013.13945

Berger, B., & Leighton, T. (1998). Protein folding in the hydrophobic-hydrophilic (HP) is NP-complete.*Proceedings of the second annual international conference on Computational molecular biologyRECOMB '98* (pp. 30-39). New York, NY, USA: ACM. doi:10.1145/279069.279080

Berman, H. M., Westbrook, J., Feng, Z., Gilliland, G., Bhat, T. N., Weissig, H., . . . Bourne, P. E. (2000, January). The Protein Data Bank. *Nucl. Acids Res., 28*(1), 235-242. doi:10.1093/nar/28.1.235

Bertini, I., De, M., Moretti, F., & Pizzuti, S. (2010). Start-Up Optimisation of a Combined Cycle Power Plant with Multiobjective Evolutionary Algorithms. *EvoApplications* (Vol. 2, pp. 151-160).

Besl, P. J., & McKay, N. D. (1992). A Method for Registration of 3-D Shapes. *IEEE Transaction on Pattern Recognition and Machine Intelligence*, *14*(2), 239–256. doi:10.1109/34.121791

Beyer, H., & Schwefel, H. (2002, March). Evolution strategies - A comprehensive introduction. *Natural Computing*, *1*(1), 3-52. doi:10.1023/A:1015059928466

Bhattacharyya, S., & Dasgupta, K. Color Object Extraction From A Noisy Background Using Parallel Multilayer Self-Organizing Neural Networks. *Proceedings of CSI-YITPA(E)2003* (pp. 32-36).

Bhattacharyya, S., Dutta, P., Maulik, U., & Nandi, P. K. (2007). Multilevel activation functions for true color image segmentation using a self supervised parallel self organizing neural network (PSONN) architecture: A comparative study. *International Journal on Computer Sciences*, *2*(1), 9-21.

Bhattacharyya, S. (2011). A Brief Survey of Color Image Preprocessing and Segmentation Techniques. *Journal of Pattern Recognition Research*, *1*(1), 120–129. doi:10.13176/11.191

Bhattacharyya, S., & Dey, S. (2011). An Efficient Quantum Inspired Genetic Algorithm with Chaotic Map Model based Interference and Fuzzy Objective Function for Gray Level Image Thresholding. *Proceedings of 2011 International Conference on Computational Intelligence and Communication Systems, Gwalior, India* (pp. 121-125). doi:10.1109/CICN.2011.24

Bhattacharyya, S., Dutta, P., Chakraborty, S., Chakraborty, R., & Dey, S. (2010). Determination of Optimal Threshold of a Gray-level Image Using a Quantum Inspired Genetic Algorithm with Interference Based on a Random Map Model. *Proceedings of 2010 IEEE International Conference on Computational Intelligence and Computing Research (ICCIC 2010)*. doi:10.1109/ICCIC.2010.5705806

Bhattacharyya, S., Dutta, P., & Maulik, U. (2008). Self organizing neural network (SONN) based gray scale object extractor with a multilevel sigmoidal (MUSIG) activation function. *Foundations of Computing and Decision Sciences*, *33*(2), 131–165.

Bhattacharyya, S., Maulik, U., & Dutta, P. (2011). Multilevel image segmentation with adaptive image context based thresholding. *Applied Soft Computing*, *11*(1), 946–962. doi:10.1016/j.asoc.2010.01.015

Bhattacharyya, S., Maulik, U., & Dutta, P. (2012, June). A Parallel Bi-Directional Self Organizing Neural Network (PBDSONN) Architecture for Color Image Extraction and Segmentation. *Neurocomputing*, *86*, 1–23. doi:10.1016/j.neucom.2011.11.025

Bhoyar, K., & Kakde, O. (2010). Colour Image Segmentation using Fast Fuzzy C-Means Algorithm. *Electronic Letters on Computer Vision and Image Analysis*, *9*(1), 18–31.

Big brother. (2010, July). Retrieved from http://www.theforbiddenknowledge.com/hardtruth/face_recognition_airports.htm

Bíró, I., & Szabó, J. (2009). *Latent dirichlet allocation for automatic document categorization.* Paper presented at the ECML PKDD '09 Proceedings of the European Conference on Machine Learning and Knowledge Discovery in Databases. doi:10.1007/978-3-642-04174-7_28

Bishop, C. (2006). *Pattern Recognition and Machine Learning*. Springer.

Bitello, R., & Lopes, H. S. (2006, September). A Differential Evolution Approach for Protein Folding. Proceedings of the *IEEE Symposium on Computational Intelligence and Bioinformatics and Computational Biology CIBCB '06*, Toronto, Ontario, Canada (pp. 1-5).

Blake, C., & Merz, C. J. (1998). *UCI repository of machine learning databases.* University of California, Irvine, Dept. of Information and Computer Sciences. Retrieved from http://www.ics.uci.edu/mlearn/MLRepository.html

Blaser, A. (Ed.), (1979). Database Techniques for Pictorial Applications, Lecture Notes in Computer Science (Vol. 81). Springer Verlag.

Blei, D. M., Ng, A. Y., & Jordan, M. I. (2003). Latent dirichlet allocation. *Journal of Machine Learning Research, 3,* 993-1022.

Bobda, C. (2007). *Introduction to Reconfigurable Computing – Architectures, algorithms and applications*. Springer.

Bonabeau, E., Dorigo, M., & Theraulaz, G. (1999). *Swarm Intelligence: From Natural to Artificial Systems*. New York: Oxford University Press.

Bookstein, F. L. (1989). Principal Warps: Thin-Plate Splines and the Decomposition of Deformations. *IEEE Transactions on Pattern Analysis and Machine Intelligence*, *11*(6), 567–585. doi:10.1109/34.24792

Booth, A. D. (1951). A signed binary multiplication technique. *The Quarterly Journal of Mechanics and Applied Mathematics*, *4*(2), 237–240. doi:10.1093/qjmam/4.2.236

Borkowski, M., & Peters, J. F. (2006). Matching 2D image segments with genetic algorithms and approximation spaces. Transactions on Rough Sets (Vol. 4100, pp. 63-101).

Borsotti, M., Campadelli, P., & Schettini, R. (1998). Quantitative evaluation of color image segmentation results. *Pattern Recognition Letters*, *19*(8), 741–747. doi:10.1016/S0167-8655(98)00052-X

Bose, R. (2013). Virtual Labs Project: A Paradigm Shift in Internet-Based Remote Experimentation. *Practical Innovations: Open Solutions, 1,* 718–725.

Boser, B. E., Guyon, I. M., & Vapnik, V. N. (1992). A training algorithm for optimal margin classifier. *Proceedings of the fifth annual workshop on Computational learning theory,* Pittusburgh, PA, USA (pp. 27-29). doi:10.1145/130385.130401

Bouabene, G., Jelger, C., Tschudin, C., Schmid, S., Keller, A., & May, M. (2010). The autonomic network architecture (ANA). *IEEE Journal on Selected Areas in Communications, 28*(1), 4–14.

Bouvrie, J., Ezzat, T., & Poggio, T. (2008). Localized Spectro-Temporal Cepstral Analysis of Speech. *Proceedings of the 2008 IEEE International Conference on Acoustics, Speech and Signal Processing (ICASSP),* Las Vegas, NV, USA (pp. 4733-4736). doi:10.1109/ICASSP.2008.4518714

Bowd, C., Medeiros, F. A., Zhang, Z., Zangwill, L. M., Hao, J., Lee, T.-W., . . . Goldbaum, M. H. (2005). Relevance Vector Machine and Support Vector Machine Classifier Analysis of Scanning Laser Polarimetry Retinal Nerve Fiber Layer Measurements. *Investigative Ophthalmology & Visual Science, 46*(4), 1322–1329. doi:10.1167/iovs.04-1122 PMID:15790898

Boyarsky, A., & G'ora, P. (2010). A random map model for quantum interference. *Communications in Nonlinear Science and Numerical Simulation, 15*(8), 1974–1979. doi:10.1016/j.cnsns.2009.08.018

Boykov, Y. V., & Jolly, M. P. (2001). Interactive graph cuts for optimal boundary & region segmentation of objects in n-d images. *Proceedings of IEEE International Conference on Computer Vision* (Vol. 1, pp. 105–112). doi:10.1109/ICCV.2001.937505

Bozorgtabar, B., Azami, H., & Noorian, F. (2012). Illumination Invariant Face Recognition Using Fuzzy LDA and FFNN. *Scientific Research Journal of Signal and Information Processing, 3*(1), 45–50. doi:10.4236/jsip.2012.31007

Bracewell, R. N. (1965). *The Fourier transform and its applications*. New York: McGraw-Hill.

Bradley, A. (1997). The use of the area under the ROC curve in the evaluation of machine learning algorithms. *Pattern Recognition, 30*(7), 1145–1159. doi:10.1016/S0031-3203(96)00142-2

Breiman, L. (2001). Statistical modeling: The two cultures (with comments and a rejoinder by the author). *Statistical Science, 16*(3), 199–231. doi:10.1214/ss/1009213726

Brink, A. D., & Pendock, N. E. (1996). Minimum cross entropy threshold selection. *Pattern Recognition, 29*(1), 179–188. doi:10.1016/0031-3203(95)00066-6

Bro-Nielsen, M., & Gramkow, C. (1993). *Fast)uid registration of medical images*. Paper presented at Int. Conf. Vis. Biomed. Comput. (pp. 267–276).

Brownstein, J., & Freifeld, C. (2007). HealthMap: The development of automated real-time internet surveillance for epidemic intelligence. *Eurosurveillance, 12*(11). Retrieved from http://www.eurosurveillance.org/ViewArticle.aspx?ArticleId=3322 PMID:18053570

Bruner, J. S. (1990). *Acts of meaning*. Cambridge, MA: Harvard University Press.

Bryant, M. (2011). 10 Great Uses of Image and Face Recognition. Retrieved from http://thenextweb.com/apps/2011/08/19/10-great-uses-of-image-and-face-recognition

Burges, C. (1988). A tutorial on support vector machines for pattern recognition. *Knowledge Discovery and Data Mining, 2*, 1–47.

Butalia, A., Ingle, M., & Kulkarni, P. (2012). Best emotional feature selection criteria based on rough set theory. *International Journal of Computer Application and Engineering Technology, 1*(2), 49–71.

Buyya, R. (2001). The Virtual Laboratory Project. *IEEE Distributed Systems Online, 2*(5), 2001.

C, V. & Radha, V. (2012). A Review on Speech Recognition Challenges and Approaches. *World of Computer Science and Information Technology Journal, 2*(1), 1-7.

Campbell, A., Eisenman, S., Lane, N., Miluzzo, E., Peterson, R., & Lu, H. et al. (2008). The rise of people-centric sensing. *IEEE Internet Computing, 12*(4), 12–21. doi:10.1109/MIC.2008.90

Capitaine, H. L., & Frelicot, C. (2011). A fast fuzzy c-means algorithm for color image segmentation.*Proceedings of International Conference of the European Society for Fuzzy Logic and Technology (EUSFLAT'2011)*, France (pp. 1074-1081). doi:10.2991/eusflat.2011.9

Cappello, P. R., & Steiglitz, K. (1983). A VLSI layout for a pipe-lined Dadda multiplier. *ACM Transactions on Computer Systems, 1*(2), 157–17. doi:10.1145/357360.357366

Carlisle, A., & Dozier, G. (2001). An off-the-shelf PSO.*Proceedings of the Particle Swarm Optimization Workshop* (Vol. 1, pp. 1-6). Indianapolis.

Carson, C., & Ogle, V. E. (1996). Storage and retrieval of feature data for a very large online mage collection. *IEEE Computer Society Bulletin of the Technical Committee on Data Engineering, 19*(4), 19–27.

Casella, G., & George, E. I. (1992). Explaining the Gibbs sampler. *The American Statistician, 46*(3), 167–174.

Catanzaro, B., Sundaram, N., & Keutzer, K., (2008). Fast support vector machine training and classification on graphics processors.*Proceedings of the 25th international conference on Machine learning*, New York, USA (pp. 104-111).

Celenk, M. (1990). A color clustering technique for image segmentation. *Computer Vision Graphics and Image Processing, 52*(2), 145–170. doi:10.1016/0734-189X(90)90052-W

Centers for Disease Control and Prevention. (2014). *Tuberculosis*. Retrieved from http://www.cdc.gov/tb/

Chaabane, B. S., Sayadi, M., Fnaiech, F., & Brassart, E. (2008). *Color Image Segmentation using Automatic Thresholding and the Fuzzy C-Means Techniques. Electro technical conference, 14th IEEE Mediterranean* (pp. 857–861). Ajaccio: ISBN.

Chalermwat, P., El-Ghazawi, T., & LeMoigneb, J. (2001). 2-phase GA-based image registration on parallel clusters. *Future Generation Computer Systems, 17*(4), 467–476. doi:10.1016/S0167-739X(99)00131-4

Chanda, B., & Majumder, D. D. (2004). *Digital image processing and analysis*. PHI Learning Pvt. Ltd.

Chandola, V., Banerjee, A., & Kumar, V. (2009). Anomaly detection: a survey.*ACM Computing Surveys*, 41(3), 15, 1-15:58.

Chandrakasan, A. P., & Brodersen, R. W. (1995). Minimizing power consumption in digital CMOS circuits. *Proceedings of the IEEE, 83*(4), 498–523. doi:10.1109/5.371964

Chandrakasan, A. P., Sheng, S., & Brodersen, R. W. (1992). Low- power CMOS digital design. *IEEE Journal of Solid-State Circuits, 27*(4), 473–484. doi:10.1109/4.126534

Chandrasekhar, B. P., Vinayak Rao, V. R., & Prasada Raju, G. V. R. (2003). A comprehensive study of soil CBR assessment through Clegg's Impact test, Field and Laboratory CBR test. *Indian Highways, 31*(7), 39–45.

Chang, G., & Lewis, M. (1997). Molecular replacement using genetic algorithms. *Acta Crystallographica. Section D, Biological Crystallography, 53*(3), 279–289. doi:10.1107/S0907444996014990 PMID:15299931

Chang, S. K., & Hsu, A. (1992). Image information systems: Where do we go from here. *IEEE Transactions on Knowledge and Data Engineering, 5*(5), 431–442. doi:10.1109/69.166986

Chao, D., Halloran, M., Obenchain, M., & Longini, J. Jr. (2010). FluTE, a Publicly Available Stochastic Influenza Epidemic Simulation Model. *PLoS Computational Biology, 6*(1), e1000656. doi:10.1371/journal.pcbi.1000656 PMID:20126529

Chapelle, O., Haffner, P., & Vapnik, V. N. (1999). Support Vector Machines for Histogram-Based Image Classification. *IEEE Transactions on Neural Networks*, *10*(5), 1055–1064. doi:10.1109/72.788646 PMID:18252608

Chatterjee, S., & Russell, S. (2012). A temporally abstracted Viterbi algorithm. *arXiv preprint arXiv:1202.3707*.

Chen, Y., Tseng, C., & King, C. (2007). Incorporating geographical contacts into social network analysis for contact tracing in epidemiology: A study on Taiwan SARS data. In *Advances in Disease Surveillance:Abstracts from the 2007 Conference of the International Society for Disease Surveillance*. doi:10.1007/978-3-540-72608-1_3

Chen, B., Zhu, Q., & Morgan, N. (2005). Long-Term Temporal Features for Conversational Speech Recognition. In S. Bengio & H. Bourland (Eds.), *Machine Learning for Multimodal Interaction* (pp. 232–242). Springer Berlin Heidelberg. Doi: doi:10.1007/978-3-540-30568-2_19

Chen, C. Y., & Ye, F. (2004). Particle swarm optimization algorithm and its application to clustering analysis.*Proceedings of the IEEE International Conference on Networking, Sensing and Control* (Vol. 2, pp. 789-794). doi:10.1109/ICNSC.2004.1297047

Cheng, Q. H., & Liu, Z. X. (2006, August). Chaotic load series forecasting based on MPMR. In *Machine Learning and Cybernetics 2006 International Conference* (pp. 2868-2871). IEEE. doi:10.1109/ICMLC.2006.259071

Cheng, G., Han, J., Zhou, P., & Guo, L. (2014). Multi-class geospatial object detection and geographic image classification based on collection of part detectors. *ISPRS Journal of Photogrammetry and Remote Sensing*, *98*, 119–132. doi:10.1016/j.isprsjprs.2014.10.002

Cheng, H., Wei, L., & Chen, Y. (2011). A New E-learning Achievement Evaluation Model Based on RoughSet and Similar Filter. *Computational Intelligence*, *27*(2), 260–279. doi:10.1111/j.1467-8640.2011.00380.x

Cheng, Y. Z. (1995). Mean shift, Mode seeking and clustering. *IEEE Transactions on Pattern Analysis and Machine Intelligence*, *17*(8), 790–799. doi:10.1109/34.400568

Chen, J. (2012). Hybrid clustering algorithm based on pso with the multidimensional asynchronism and stochastic disturbance method. *Journal of Theoretical and Applied Information Technology*, *46*(1), 434–440.

Chen, J. L., & Kundu, A. (1994). Rotational and gray-scale transform invariant texture identification using wavelet decomposition and hidden Markov model. *IEEE Transaction in Machine Intelligence*, *16*(2), 208–214. doi:10.1109/34.273730

Chen, S., Gunn, S. R., & Harris, C. J. (2001). The relevance vector machine technique for channel equalization application. *IEEE Transactions on Neural Networks*, *12*(6), 1529–1532. doi:10.1109/72.963792 PMID:18249985

Chen, T. Q., & Lu, Y. (2002). Color image segmentation - an innovative approach. *Pattern Recognition*, *35*(2), 395–405. doi:10.1016/S0031-3203(01)00050-4

Cherkassky, V. (1998). In O. Kayak et al. (Eds.), *Fuzzy Inference Systems: A Critical Review, Computational Intelligence: Soft Computing and Fuzzy-Neuro Integration with Applications* (pp. 177–197). Springer. doi:10.1007/978-3-642-58930-0_10

Chhabra, M., Gour, R., & Reel, P. S. (2012). Detection of Fully and Partially Riped Mango by Machine vision. *Proceeding of the International Conference on Recent Trends in Information Technology and Computer Science ICRTITCS* (pp. 26-31). doi:10.1007/978-81-322-0491-6_15

Chi, D. (2011). Self-Organizing Map-Based Color Image Segmentation with k-Means Clustering and Saliency Map. *ISRN Signal Processing*, 2011. doi:.10.5402/2011/393891

Chih-Wei Hsu., & Chih-Jen Lin (2002). A Comparison of Methods for Multiclass Support Vector Machines. *IEEE Transactions on Neural Networks*, *13*(2), 415–425. doi:10.1109/72.991427 PMID:18244442

Chimphlee, W., Abdullah, A. H., Chimphlee, S., & Srinoy, S. (2005). Unsupervised clustering methods for identifying rare events in anomaly detection. In: *Proceedings of the Sixth International Enformatika Conference* (pp. 26-28).

Chin-Wei, B., & Rajeswari, M. (2010). Multiobjective Optimization Approaches in Image Segmentation - The Directions and Challenges. *International Journal of Advanced Soft Computing Application*, *2*(1), 40–64.

Cho, S.-J., Choi, U.-S., Hwang, Y.-H., Kim, H.-D., Pyo, Y.-S., Kim, K.-S., & Heo, S.-H. (2004). Computing Phase Shifts of Maximum-Length 90/150 Cellular Automata Sequences. Proceeding of the *6*th *International Conference on Cellular Automata for Research and Industry, ACRI 2004*, Amsterdam (pp. 31-39). doi:10.1007/978-3-540-30479-1_4

Choi, S. I., & Choi, C. H. (2007). An effective Face Recognition under Illumination and Pose Variation. *Proceedings of IEEE International Joint Conference on Neural Networks* (pp. 914–919). doi:10.1109/IJCNN.2007.4371080

Christakis, N., & Fowler, J. (2009). Social Network Visualization in Epidemiology. Norwegian Journal of Epidemiology [Norsk epidemiologi], *19*(1), 5–16.

Christensen, G. E., Miller, M. I., Vannier, M. W., & Grenander, U. (1996). Individualizing neuroanatomical atlases using a massively parallel computer. *Computer*, *29*(1), 32–38. doi:10.1109/2.481434

Christensen, G. E., Rabitt, R. D., & Miller, M. I. (1996). Deformable Templates Using Large Deformation Kinematics. *IEEE Transactions on Medical Imaging*, *5*(10), 1435–1447. PMID:18290061

Christley, R., Pinchbeck, G., Bowers, R., Clancy, D., French, N., Bennett, R., & Turner, J. (2005). Infection in social networks: Using network analysis to identify high-risk individuals. *American Journal of Epidemiology*, *162*(10), 1024–1031. doi:10.1093/aje/kwi308 PMID:16177140

Christopher Bishop, M., & Michael Tipping, E. (2000). Variational relevance vector machines.*Proceedings of the Sixteenth conference on Uncertainty in artificial intelligence*, San Francisco, CA, USA (pp. 46-53). Morgan Kaufmann Publishers Inc.

Chuang, K. S., Tzeng, H. L., Chen, S., Wu, J., & Chen, T. J. (2006). Fuzzy c-means clustering with spatial information for image segmentation. *Journal of Computerized Medical Imaging and Graphics*, *30*(1), 9–15. doi:10.1016/j.compmedimag.2005.10.001 PMID:16361080

Chunsheng, F., Fending, C., Qiang, W., Shouchao, W., & Ju, W. (2010). Application of Rough Sets Theory to Sources Analysis of Atmospheric Particulates. Bioinformatics and Biomedical Engineering, 1-5.

Cinque, L., Ciocca, G., Levialdi, S., Pellicanò, A., & Schettini, R. (2001). Color-based image retrieval using spatial-chromatic histogram. *Image and Vision Computing*, *19*(13), 979–986. doi:10.1016/S0262-8856(01)00060-9

Civicioglu, P., & Besdok, E. (2013). A conceptual comparison of the Cuckoo-search, particle swarm optimization, differential evolution and artificial bee colony algorithms. *Artificial Intelligence Review*, *39*(4), 315–346. doi:10.1007/s10462-011-9276-0

Clark, D. E. (2000). *Evolutionary Algorithms in Molecular Design (Methods and Principles in Medicinal Chemistry).* Wiley-VCH. doi:10.1002/9783527613168

Climent-Bellido, M. S., Martínez-Jiménez, P., Pontes-Pedrajas, A., & Polo, J. (2003). Learning in Chemistry with Virtual Laboratories. *Journal of Chemical Education*, *80*(3), 346–352. doi:10.1021/ed080p346

Collignon, A., Geraud, T., Vandermeulen, D., Suetens, P., & Marchal, G. (1993). New high-performance 3D registration algorithms for 3D medical images. Medical imaging: image processing, 1898, 779–788.

Collignon, A., Maes, F., Delaere, D., Vandermeulen, D., Suetens, P., & Marchal, G. (1995), *Automated multimodality medical image registration using information theory*. Paper presented at 14th international conference on information processing in medical imaging (IPMI'95) (pp. 263–274).

Collins, D. L., Neelin, P., Peters, T. M., & Evans, A. C. (1994). Automatic 3D intersubject registration of MR volumetric data in standardized Talairach space. *Journal of Computer Assisted Tomography*, *18*(2), 192–205. doi:10.1097/00004728-199403000-00005 PMID:8126267

Comaniciu, D., Ramesh, & Meer, P. (2000). Real-time tracking of non-rigid objects using mean shift. Proceedings of the IEEE Conference on Computer Vision and Pattern Recognition (pp. 142–149). IEEE. doi:10.1109/CVPR.2000.854761

Compagno, A., Conti, M., Gasti, P., & Tsudik, G. (2013). Poseidon: mitigating interest flooding DDoS attacks in named data networking. In: *Proceedings of IEEE 38th Conference on Local Computer Networks* (pp. 630-638). Sydney, NSW. doi:10.1109/LCN.2013.6761300

Consortium, E. (2012, September). An integrated encyclopedia of DNA elements in the human genome. *Nature*, *489*(7414), 57–74. PMID:22955616

Conti, M., Gasti, P., & Teoli, M. (2013). A lightweight mechanism for detection of cache pollution attacks in named data networking. *Computer Networks*, *57*(16), 3178–3191. doi:10.1016/j.comnet.2013.07.034

Corral, G., Armengol, E., Fornells, A., & Golobardes, E. (2009). Explanations of unsupervised learning clustering applied to data security analysis. *Neurocomputing*, *72*(13-15), 2754–2762. doi:10.1016/j.neucom.2008.09.021

Cortes, C., & Mohri, M. (2005). Confidence intervals for the area under the roc curve. *Advances in Neural Information Processing Systems*, *17*, 305.

Cortes, C., & Vapnik, V. N. (1995). Support-vector networks. *Machine Learning*, *20*(3), 273–297. doi:10.1007/BF00994018

Cotta, C. (2003). Protein Structure Prediction Using Evolutionary Algorithms Hybridized with Backtracking. *Proceedings of the 7th International Work-Conference on Artificial and Natural Neural Networks IWANN '03* (pp. 321-328). Berlin, Heidelberg: Springer-Verlag. doi:10.1007/3-540-44869-1_41

Cox, G. A., Mortimer-Jones, T. V., Taylor, R. P., & Johnston, R. L. (2004). Development and optimisation of a novel genetic algorithm for studying model protein folding. *Theoretical Chemistry Accounts: Theory, Computation, and Modeling*, *112*(3), 163–178. doi:10.1007/s00214-004-0601-4

Cox, S. (2002). Information technology: The global key to precision agriculture and sustainability. *Computers and Electronics in Agriculture Journal*, *36*(2-3), 93–111. doi:10.1016/S0168-1699(02)00095-9

Cristianini, N., & Shawe Taylor, J. (2000). *An introduction to Support vector machine*. London: Cambridge University press.

Cristianini, N., & Shawe-Taylor, J. (2000). *An introduction to support vector machines and other kernel-based learning methods*. Cambridge university press. doi:10.1017/CBO9780511801389

Cross, S. S., Harrison, R. F., & Kennedy, R. L. (1995). Introduction to neural networks. *Lancet*, *346*(8982), 1075–1079. doi:10.1016/S0140-6736(95)91746-2 PMID:7564791

Csurka, G., Dance, C., Fan, L., Willamowski, J., & Bray, C. (2004). Visual categorization with bags of keypoints. Proceedings of *Workshop on Statistical Learning in Computer Vision, ECCV* (pp 1-22).

Cui, X., & Potok, T. E. (2005). Document clustering analysis based on hybrid pso+k-means algorithm. *Journal of Computer Science (special issue)*, 27-33.

Cunha, A. L. (2006). The nonsubsampled contourlet transform: Theory, design, and applications. *IEEE Transactions on Image Processing, 15*(10), 3089–3101. doi:10.1109/TIP.2006.877507 PMID:17022272

Cusick, T., & Stanica, P. (2009). *Cryptographic Boolean functions and applications.* Elsevier.

Cutello, V., Nicosia, G., Pavone, M., & Timmis, J. (2007, February). An Immune Algorithm for Protein Structure Prediction on Lattice Models. *IEEE Transactions on Evolutionary Computation, 11*(1), 101-117.

Czarnecki, W. M., & Tabor, J. (2014). Two ellipsoid Support Vector Machines. *Expert Systems with Applications, 41*(18), 8211–8224.

D'Agostino, E., Maes, F., Vandermeulen, D., & Suetens, P. (2003). A viscous)uid model for multimodal non-rigid image registration using mutual information. *Medical Image Analysis, 7*(4), 565–575. doi:10.1016/S1361-8415(03)00039-2 PMID:14561559

D'Haeseleer, P., Liang, S., & Somogyi, R. (2000, August). Genetic network inference: from co-expression clustering to reverse engineering. *Bioinformatics (Oxford, England), 16*(8), 707-726. doi:10.1093/bioinformatics/16.8.707

Daasch, W., Lim, C., & Cai, G. (2002). Design of VLSI CMOS Circuits under Thermal Constraint. *IEEE Transactions on Circuits and Systems II: Analog and Digital Signal Processing, 49*(8), 589–593. doi:10.1109/TCSII.2002.806247

Dachselt, F., & Schwarz, W. (2001). Chaos and Cryptography. *IEEE Transactions on Circuits and Systems, 48*(12), 1498–1509. doi:10.1109/TCSI.2001.972857

Dadda, L. (1965). Some schemes for parallel multipliers. *Alta Frequenza, 34,* 349–356.

Dakua, P., & Sinha, A., & Gourab. (2012). Hardware implementation of MAC unit. *International Journal of Electronics Communication and Computer Engineering, 3,* 79–82.

Dalgarno, B. (2005). A VRML virtual chemistry laboratory incorporating reusable prototypes for object manipulation. In P. Beckett (Ed.), *SimTect 2005, the annual conference of the Simulation Industry Association of Australia,* Sydney, Australia, 1-6.

Danon, L., Ford, A., House, T., Jewell, C., Keeling, M., & Roberts, G. et al. (2011). Networks and the epidemiology of infectious disease. *Interdisciplinary Perspectives on Infectious Diseases, 2011,* 1–28. doi:10.1155/2011/284909 PMID:21437001

Danti, A., & Suresha, M. (2012a). Arecanut Grading Based on Three Sigma Controls and SVM, Proceedings of the IEEE-International Conference On Advances In Engineering, Science And Management (ICAESM), Nagapattinam, Tamilnadu, India (pp. 372-376).

Danti, A., & Suresha, M. (2012b). Segmentation and classification of raw arecanuts based on three sigma control limits. Journal Procedia Technology. *Sciverse Science Direct, 4,* 215–219.

Danti, A., & Suresha, M. (2012c).Texture Based Decision Tree Classification for Arecanut, *Proceedings of the CUBE International Information Technology Conference* (pp. 113-117). ACM Publications.

Darling, W. M. (2011). *A Theoretical and Practical Implementation Tutorial on Topic Modeling and Gibbs Sampling.* Paper presented at the 49th Annual Meeting of the Association for Computational Linguistics: Human Language Technologies.

Das, S., Abraham, A., & Konar, A. (2008). Automatic Clustering Using an Improved Differential Evolution Algorithm. *IEEE Transactions on Systems, Man, and Cybernetics. Part A, Systems and Humans, 38*(1), 218–237. doi:10.1109/TSMCA.2007.909595

Data virtualization by denodo technologies. (2012, December). from http://www.denodo.com/en/solutions/technology/data_virtualization.php

Datta, R., Joshi, D., Li, J., & Wang, J. Z. (2008). Image retrieval: Ideas, influences, and trends of the new age. *ACM Computing Surveys, 40*(2), 1–60. doi:10.1145/1348246.1348248

Davatzikos, C. (1997). Spatial transformation and registration of brain images using elastically deformable models. *Computer Vision and Image Understanding, 66*(2), 207–222. doi:10.1006/cviu.1997.0605 PMID:11543561

Davies, D. L., & Bouldin, D. W. (1979). A cluster separation measure. *IEEE Transactions on Pattern Recognition and Machine Intelligence, 1*(2), 224–227. doi:10.1109/TPAMI.1979.4766909 PMID:21868852

Davis, M. H., Khotanzad, A., & Flaming, D. P. (1996) 3d image matching using radial basis function neural network. Paper presented at *WCNN'96: World Congress on Neural Networks* (pp. 1174–1179).

Davis, L. (Ed.). (1991). *Handbook of Genetic Algorithms*. New York: Van Nostrand Reinhold.

Dawoud, A (2010). Fusing shape information in lung segmentation in chest radiographs. *Image Analysis and Recognition* (Vol. 6112, pp. 70–78).

Day, J., Matta, I., & Mattar, K. (2008). *Networking is IPC: A guiding principle to a better Internet*. Paper presented at the 2008 ACM CoNEXT Conference. doi:10.1145/1544012.1544079

De Jong, K. A. (2006). *Evolutionary Computation. A Unified Approach*. Cambridge, MA, USA: MIT Press.

de Kruif, B. J., & de Vries, T. J. A. (2003). Pruning Error Minimization in Least Squares Support Vector Machines. *IEEE Transactions on Neural Networks, 14*(3), 696–702. doi:10.1109/TNN.2003.810597 PMID:18238050

De Mori, R. (1965). Suggestions for an IC fast parallel multiplier. *Electronics Letters, 5*(3), 50–51. doi:10.1049/el:19690034

De, V. & Borkar S. (1999, August). *Technology and Design Challenges for Low Power and High Performance*. Paper presented at Proceedings of International Symposium on Low Power Electronics. San Diego, CA, USA. doi:10.1145/313817.313908

Deb, K. (2001). *Multi-Objective Optimization using Evolutionary Algorithms*. England: John Wiley & Sons, Ltd.

Declerc, J., Feldmar, J., Betting, F., & Goris, M. L. (1997). Automatic registration and alignment on a template of cardiac stress and rest SPECT images. *IEEE Transactions on Medical Imaging, 16*(6), 727–737. doi:10.1109/42.650870 PMID:9533574

del Rey, Á.M. (2004). A Novel Cryptosystem for Binary Images. *Grant SA052/03, Studies in Informatics and Control, 13*(1).

Del Venayagamoorthy, G. K., Mohagheghi, S., Hernandez, J. C., & Harley, R. G. (2008). Particle Swarm Optimization: Basic Concepts, Variants and Applications in Power Systems. *Evolutionary Computation, IEEE Transactions, 12*(2), 171-195. doi:10.1109/TEVC.2007.896686

Demir, B., & Erturk, S. (2007). Hyperspectral Image Classification Using Relevance Vector Machines. *Geoscience and Remote Sensing Letters, 4*(4), 586–590. doi:10.1109/LGRS.2007.903069

Dempster, A. P. (1967). Upper and Lower Probabilities induced by a Multivalued Mapping. *Annals of Mathematical Statistics, 38*(2), 325–339. doi:10.1214/aoms/1177698950

De, S., Bhattacharyya, S., & Chakraborty, S. (2010). True Color Image Segmentation by an Optimized Multilevel Activation Function.*Proceedings of 2010 IEEE International Conference on Computational Intelligence and Computing Research* (pp. 545-548). doi:10.1109/ICCIC.2010.5705833

De, S., Bhattacharyya, S., & Chakraborty, S. (2012). Color image segmentation using parallel OptiMUSIG activation function. *Applied Soft Computing*, *12*(10), 3228–3236. doi:10.1016/j.asoc.2012.05.011

De, S., Bhattacharyya, S., & Dutta, P. (2010). Efficient grey-level image segmentation using an optimised MUSIG (OptiMUSIG) activation function. *International Journal of Parallel. Emergent and Distributed Systems*, *26*(1), 1–39. doi:10.1080/17445760903546618

Dimitras, A. I., Zanakis, S. H., & Zopounidis, C. (1996). A survey of business failure with an emphasis on prediction methods and industrial applications. *Elsevier European Journal of Operational Research*, *90*(3), 487–513. doi:10.1016/0377-2217(95)00070-4

DiRuperto, C., &Dempster, A. (2000). Circularity measures based on mathematical morphology. *Electronics Letters*, *36*(20), 1691–1693.

Dodgson, N. A. (1997). Quadratic interpolation for image re-sampling. *IEEE Transactions on Image Processing*, *6*(9), 1322–1326. doi:10.1109/83.623195

Donald, F. (1990). Probabilistic Neural Networks. *Neural Networks*, *3*(1), 109–118. doi:10.1016/0893-6080(90)90049-Q

Dorigo, M., & Gambardella, L. M. (1997). Ant colony system: a cooperative learning approach to the traveling salesman problem. *Evolutionary Computation, IEEE Transactions on, 1*(1), 53-66. doi:10.1109/4235.585892

Dorst, K., & Vermaas, P. E. (2005). John Gero's Function-Behaviour-Structure model of designing: A critical analysis. *Research in Engineering Design*, *16*(1), 17–26. doi:10.1007/s00163-005-0058-z

Douguet, D., Thoreau, E., & Grassy, G. (2000). A genetic algorithm for the automated generation of small organic molecules: Drug design using an evolutionary algorithm. *Journal of Computer-Aided Molecular Design*, *14*(5), 449–466. doi:10.1023/A:1008108423895 PMID:10896317

Dresner, H. (2008). *Performance management revolution*. NY: John Wiley &Sons Inc.

Duan, Y., & Kollman, P. A. (2001). Computational protein folding: From lattice to all-atom. *IBM Systems Journal*, *40*(2), 297–309. doi:10.1147/sj.402.0297

Dubey, S. K., & Ghosh, S. (2013). Comparative analysis of k-means and fuzzy cmeans algorithms. *International Journal of Advanced Computer Science and Applications*, *4*, 35–39.

Duda, R. O., Hart, P. E., & Stork, D. G. (2001). *Pattern Classification*. New York: John Wiley and Sons.

Dunham, M. H. (2003). *Data Mining: Introductory and Advanced Topics*. Prentice Hall.

Eberhart, R. C., & Shi, Y. (2000). Comparing inertia weights and constriction factors in particle swarm optimization. *Proceedings of the Evolutionary Computation*, *1*, 84–88.

Egan, J. P. (1975). *Signal detection theory and ROC analysis, Series in Cognition and Perception*. New York: Academic Press.

Eiben, A. E., & Smith, J. E. (2003). *Introduction to evolutionary computing*. Berlin: Springer. doi:10.1007/978-3-662-05094-1

Elamvazuthi, I., Vasant, P., & Ganesan, T. (2012). Integration of Fuzzy Logic Techniques into DSS for Profitability Quantification in a Manufacturing Environment. In M. Khan & A. Ansari (Eds.), *Handbook of Research on Industrial Informatics and Manufacturing Intelligence: Innovations and Solutions* (pp. 171–192). Hershey, PA: Information Science Reference. doi:10.4018/978-1-4666-0294-6.ch007

Elbalaoui, A., Fakir, M., Idrissi, N., & Marboha, A. (2013). Review of Color Image Segmentation. *International Journal of Advanced Computer Science and Applications* (Special Issue on Selected Papers from Third international symposium on Automatic Amazigh processing), 15-21. doi:10.14569/SpecialIssue.2013.030204

Elhanany, I., Sheinfeld, M., Beck, A., Kadmon, Y., Tal, N., & Tirosh, D. (2000). *Robust image registration based on feedforward neural networks*. Paper Presented at 2000 IEEE International Conference on Systems, Man and Cybernetics, TN, USA (pp. 1507–1511). doi:10.1109/ICSMC.2000.886068

Ellis, D. P. W., & Athineos, M. (2003). Frequency-domain Linear Prediction for Temporal Features. In *Proceedings of 2003 IEEE workshop on Automatic Speech Recognition and Understanding (ASRU)* (pp. 261-266).

El-Sayed, A., Scarborough, P., Seemann, L., & Galea, S. (2012). Social network analysis and agent-based modeling in social epidemiology. Epidemiologic perspectives & innovations: EP+I, 9(1).

Epstein, M. D., & Schluger, N. W. (1998). Time to detection of Mycobacterium tuberculosis in sputum culture correlates with outcome in patients receiving treatment for pulmonary tuberculosis. *CHEST Journal, 113*(2), 379–386. doi:10.1378/chest.113.2.379

Eshtawie, M., Hussin, S., & Othman, M. (2010, June). *Analysis of results obtained with a new proposed low area low power high speed fixed point adder*. Paper presented at IEEE International Conference on Semiconductor Electronics (ICSE), Melaka, Malaysia. doi:10.1109/SMELEC.2010.5549387

Esling, P., Carpentier, G., & Agon, C. (2010). Dynamic Musical Orchestration Using Genetic Algorithms and a Spectro-Temporal Description of Musical Instruments. *EvoApplications* (Vol. 2, pp. 371-380).

Eubank, S. (2002). Scalable, efficient epidemiological simulation.*Proceedings of the 2002 ACM symposium on Applied computing* (pp. 139–145). doi:10.1145/508791.508819

Evans, A. C., Marrett, S., Collins, L., & Peters, T. M. (1989), Anatomical-functional correlative analysis of the human brain using three dimensional imaging systems. *Medical imaging processing, 1092*, 264-274.

Evans, A. C., Marrett, S., Torrescorzo, J., Ku, S., & Collins, L. (1991). MRI-PET correlation in three dimensions using a volume of interest (VOI) atlas. *Journal of Cerebral Blood Flow and Metabolism, 11*, A69–A78. doi:10.1038/jcbfm.1991.40 PMID:1997491

Everitt, B. S. (1993). *Cluster Analysis* (3rd ed.). London: Edward Arnold / Halsted Press.

Farnoosh, R., & Zarpak, B. (2008). Image Segmentation using Gaussian mixture model. *International Journal of Engineering Science, 19*(1-2), 29–32.

Faulkner, M. (2003). *Customer management excellence*. NY: John Wiley &Sons Inc.

Fawcett, T. (2006). An introduction to ROC analysis. *Pattern Recognition Letters, 27*(8), 861–874. doi:10.1016/j.patrec.2005.10.010

Faysel, M. A., & Haque, S. S. (2010). Towards cyber defense: Research in intrusion detection and intrusion prevention systems. *International Journal of Computer Science and Network Security, 10*(7), 316–325.

Fei-Fei, L., Fergus, R., & Perona, P. (2004). Learning generative visual models from few training examples. Proceedings of *Workshop on Computer Vision and Pattern Recognition.*

Feldmann, A. (2007). Internet clean-slate design: What and why? *Computer Communication Review, 37*(3), 59–64. doi:10.1145/1273445.1273453

Feng, J., Xu, L., & Ramamurthy, B. (2009). Overlay Construction in Mobile Peer-to-Peer Networks. In B. Seet (Ed.), *Mobile Peer-to-Peer Computing for Next Generation Distributed Environments: Advancing Conceptual and Algorithmic Applications* (pp. 51–67). Hershey, PA: Information Science Reference. doi:10.4018/978-1-60566-715-7.ch003

Feng-zeng, Z., Levy, M. H., & Wen, S. (1997). Sputum microscopy results at two and three months predict outcome of tuberculosis treatment Notes from the Field. *The International Journal of Tuberculosis and Lung Disease, 1*(6), 570–572.

Feoktistov, V. (2006). Differential Evolution. In *Search of Solutions*. Secaucus, NJ, USA: Springer-Verlag New York, Inc.

Fergus, R., Perona, P., & Zisserman, A. (2003). Object class recognition by unsupervised scale invariant learning. *Proceedings of theIEEE Computer Society Conference on Computer Vision and Pattern Recognition* (Vol.2, p. 264). doi:10.1109/CVPR.2003.1211479

Filho, C. B., Mello, C. A., Andrade, J., Lima, M., Santos, W. d., Oliveira, A., & Falcao, D. (2008). Image Thresholding of Historical Documents Based on Genetic Algorithms. In P. Fritzsche (Ed.), Tools in Artificial Intelligence (pp. 93-100).

Fiore, U., Palmieri, F., Castiglione, A., & De Santis, A. (2013). Network anomaly detection with the restricted boltzmann machine. *Neurocomputing, 122*(25), 13–23. doi:10.1016/j.neucom.2012.11.050

Fisher, S. Teman, A. Vaysman, D. , Gertsman, A. , Yadid-Pecht O., & Fish A. (2008, December). *Digital sub-threshold logic design - motivation and challenges.* Paper presented at 25th IEEE Convention of Electrical and Electronics Engineers in Israel, Eilat.

Fisichella, M., Stewart, A., Denecke, K., & Nejdl, W. (2010). Unsupervised public health event detection for epidemic intelligence.*Proceedings of the 19th ACM international conference on Information and knowledge management*, New York, USA. ACM. doi:10.1145/1871437.1871753

Fitzpatrick, J. M., West, J. B., & Maurer, C. R. (1998). Predicting error in rigid-body pointbased registration. *IEEE Transactions on Medical Imaging, 17*(5), 694–702. doi:10.1109/42.736021 PMID:9874293

Fleischmann, R. D., Adams, M. D., White, O., Clayton, R. A., Kirkness, E. F., Kerlavage, A. R., & Merrick, J. M. et al. (1995, July). Whole-genome random sequencing and assembly of Haemophilus influenza Rd. *Science, 269*(5223), 496–512. doi:10.1126/science.7542800 PMID:7542800

Fleming, R. W., Dror, R. O., & Adelson, E. H. (2003). Real-world illumination and the perception of surface reflectance properties. *Association for Research in Vision and Ophthalmology Journal of Vision, 3*(5), 347–368. PMID:12875632

Fletcher, R. (1987). *Practical methods of optimization.* Chichester, New York: Wiley.

Flores, S. D., & Smith, J. (2003, #dec#). Study of fitness landscapes for the HP model of protein structure prediction. Proceedings of the *2003 Congress on Evolutionary Computation CEC '03* (pp. 2338-2345).

Foody, G. M., & Mathur, A. (2004). A Relative Evaluation of Multiclass Image Classification by Support Vector Machines. *IEEE Transactions on Geoscience and Remote Sensing, 42*(6), 1335–1343. doi:10.1109/TGRS.2004.827257

Forero, M.G., Sroubek, F., & Cristóbal, G. (2004). Identification of tuberculosis bacteria based on shape and color. *Real-time imaging, 10*(4), 251-262.

Forrest, S. (1993). Genetic algorithms: Principles of natural selection applied to computation. *Science, 261*(5123), 872–878. doi:10.1126/science.8346439 PMID:8346439

Forsyth, D. A., & Fleck, M. M. (1997). Body plans.*Proceedings of the IEEE Conference on Computer Vision and Pattern Recognition* (pp. 678–683). doi:10.1109/CVPR.1997.609399

Fowlkes, C., Malik, J., Arbelaez, P., & Maire, M. (2009). *From contours to regions: An empirical evaluation* (pp. 2294–2301). IEEE CVPR.

Fowlkes, C., Malik, J., Arbelaez, P., & Maire, M. (2011). Contour detection and hierarchical image segmentation. *IEEE PAMI, 33*(5), 898–916. doi:10.1109/TPAMI.2010.161 PMID:20733228

Fowlkes, C., Martin, D., & Malik, J. (2004). Learning to detect natural image boundaries using local brightness, color and texture cues. *IEEE-PAMI, 26*(5), 530–549. doi:10.1109/TPAMI.2004.1273918 PMID:15460277

Fox, P. T., Perlmutter, J. S., & Raichle, M. E. (1985). A Stereotactic Method of Anatomical Localization of Positron Emission Tomography. *Journal of Computer Assisted Tomography, 9*(1), 141–153. doi:10.1097/00004728-198501000-00025 PMID:3881487

Fraser, G. D., Chan, A. D. C., Green, J. R., & Macisaac, D. T. (2014). Automated biosignal quality analysis for electromyography using a one-class support vector machine. *IEEE Transactions on Instrumentation and Measurement, 63*(12), 2919–2930. doi:10.1109/TIM.2014.2317296

Fu, K. S., & Mui, J. K. (1981). A Survey on image segmentation. *Pattern Recognition Journal, 13*(1), 3–16. doi:10.1016/0031-3203(81)90028-5

Fukunaga, K. (1990). *Introduction to statistical Pattern recognition* (2nd ed.). Academic press.

Furey, T. S., Cristianini, N., Duffy, N., Bednarski, D. W., Schummer, M., & Haussler, D.(2000). Support vector machine classification and validation of cancer tissue samples using microarray expression data. *Bioinformatics (Oxford, England), 16*(10), 906–914. doi:10.1093/bioinformatics/16.10.906 PMID:11120680

Furfaro, R., Ganapol, B. D., Johnson, L. F., & Herwitz, S. R. (2007). Neural Network Algorithm for Coffee Ripeness Evaluation Using Airborne Images. *Applied Engineering in Agriculture, 23*(3), 379–387. doi:10.13031/2013.22676

Furuholmen, M., Glette, K., Hovin, M., & Torresen, J. (2010). Evolutionary Approaches to the Three-dimensional Multi-pipe Routing Problem: A Comparative Study Using Direct Encodings. EvoCOP, 71-82.

Fuster-Sabater, A., & Cabalerro-Gil, P. (2010). Chaotic Cellular Automata with Cryptographic Application. Proceedings of the 9th *International Conference on Cellular Automata for Research and Industry* (pp. 251–260). Springer-Verlag Berlin Heidelberg

Gajsek, R., Zibert, J., & Mihelic, F. (2008). Acoustic Modeling for Speech Recognition in Telephone Based Dialog System Using Limited Audio Resources. In P. Sojka et al. (Eds.), *Text, Speech and Dialogue* (pp. 311–316). Springer Berlin Heidelberg. doi:10.1007/978-3-540-87391-4_40

Galas, D. J., & Schmitz, A. (1987, September). DNAse footprinting: A simple method for the detection of protein-{DNA} binding specificity. *Nucleic Acids Research, 5*(9), 3157–3170. doi:10.1093/nar/5.9.3157 PMID:212715

Ganapathy, S., Thomas, S., & Hermansky, H. (2010). Robust Spectro-Temporal Features based on Autoregressive Models of Hilbert Envelopes.*Proceedings of the 2010 IEEE International Conference on Acoustics, Speech and Signal Processing (ICASSP),*Dallas, TX (pp. 4286-4289). DOI: doi:10.1109/ICASSP.2010.5495668

Gandomi, A. H., Yun, G. J., & Alavi, A. H. (2013). An evolutionary approach for modeling of shear strength of RC deep beams. *Materials and Structures, 46*(12), 2109–2119. doi:10.1617/s11527-013-0039-z

Gandomi, M., Soltanpour, M., Zolfaghari, M. R., & Gandomi, A. H. (2014). Prediction of peak ground acceleration of Iran's tectonic regions using a hybrid soft computing technique. *Geoscience Frontiers*. doi:10.1016/j.gsf.2014.10.004

Gao, S. Wai Hung Tsang, I., Tien Chia, L., & Zhao, P. (2010). Local features are not lonely. Laplacian sparse coding for image classification. In IEEE CVPR (pp 3555-3561).

Gao, H., Siu, W. C., & Hou, C. H. (2001). Improved Techniques for Automatic Image Segmentation. *IEEE Transactions on Circuits and Systems for Video Technology, 11*(12), 1273–1280. doi:10.1109/76.974681

Garner, M. M., & Revzin, A. (1981, July). A gel electrophoresis method for quantifying the binding of proteins to specific DNA regions: Application to components of the Escherichia coli lactose operon regulatory system. *Nucleic Acids Research, 9*(13), 3047–3060. doi:10.1093/nar/9.13.3047 PMID:6269071

Gasti, P., Tsudik, G., Uzun, E., & Zhang, L. (2013). DoS and DDoS in Named-Data Networking. In *Proceedings of the 22nd International Conference on Computer Communications and Networks,*Nassau, USA (pp. 1-7).

Gauvain, J. L., Lamel, L., Schwenk, H., Adda, G., Chen, L., & Lefevre, F. (2003). Conversational Telephone Speech Recognition.*Proceedings of the 2003 IEEE International Conference on Acoustics, Speech and Signal Processing* (Vol. 1, pp. 212-215).

Gee, J., Reivich, M., & Bajacsy, R. (1993). Elastically deforming 3D atlas to match anatomical brain images. *Journal of Computer Assisted Tomography, 17*(2), 225–236. doi:10.1097/00004728-199303000-00011 PMID:8454749

Geetha, M. A., & Saklecha, A. (2013). Facial Recognition using CCTV images based on Rough Set Theory and Scale Invariant Feature Transform. *International Journal of Emerging Trends in Engineering and Development, 2*(3), 203–209.

Gero, J. S. (1990). Design prototypes: A knowledge representation schema for design. *AI Magazine, 11*(4), 26.

Gersho, A., & Gray, R. M. (1992). *Vector Quantization and Signal Compression*. Dordrecht: Kluwer Academic Publishers. doi:10.1007/978-1-4615-3626-0

Ghosh, P., Bhattacharjee, D., Nasipuri, M., & Basu, D. K. (2010), Round-the-clock urine sugar monitoring system for diabetic patients. Proceedings of Systems International Conference on Medicine and Biology (ICSMB) (pp 326 – 330). IEEE. doi:10.1109/ICSMB.2010.5735397

Ghosh, P., Bhattacharjee, D., Nasipuri, M., Basu, D.K. (2011). Medical Aid for Automatic Detection of Malaria. *Computer Information Systems–Analysis and Technologies* (Vol. 245, pp. 170-178). Springer Berlin Heidelberg.

Ghosh, A., Pal, N. R., & Pal, S. K. (1993). Self-organization for object extraction using a multilayer neural network and fuzziness measures. *IEEE Transactions on Fuzzy Systems, 1*(1), 54–68. doi:10.1109/TFUZZ.1993.390285

Ghosh, P., Bhattacharjee, D., Nasipuri, M., & Basu, D. K. (2013). Child Obesity Control through Computer Game. *Biomedical Engineering Research, 2*(2), 88–95. doi:10.5963/BER0202005

Ginneken, B., & Romeny, H. (2000). Automatic segmentation of lung fields in chest radiographs. *Medical Physics, 27*(10), 2445–2455. doi:10.1118/1.1312192

Ginneken, B., van, , Katsuragawa, S., & Romeny, K. (2002). Automatic detection of abnormalities in chest radiographs using local texture analysis. *IEEE Transactions on Medical Imaging, 21*(2), 139–149. doi:10.1109/42.993132

Ginsberg, J., Mohebbi, M., Patel, R., Brammer, L., Smolinski, M., & Brilliant, L. (2009). Detecting influenza epidemics using search engine query data. *Nature, 457*(7232), 1012–1014. doi:10.1038/nature07634 PMID:19020500

Giudici, P. (2003). *Applied Data Mining: Statistical Methods for Business and Industry*. NY: John Wiley &Sons Inc.

Giudici, P., & Figini, S. (2009). *Applied Data Mining for Business and Industry (Statistics in Practice)*. NY: Wiley. doi:10.1002/9780470745830

Glass, J. R., & Hazen, T. J. (1998). Telephone-based Conversational Speech Recognition in the Jupiter Domain. *Proceedings of the 1998 fifth International Conference on spoken Language processing* (Vol. 98, pp. 1327-1330). Sydney, Australia.

Godwin, R. J., & Miller, P. C. H. (2003). A Review of the Technologies for Mapping Within-field Variability. *Biosystems Engineering Journal*, *84*(4), 393–407. doi:10.1016/S1537-5110(02)00283-0

Goense, D., Hofstee, J. W., & Bergeijk, J. V. (1996). An information model to describe systems for spatially variable field operations. *Computers and Electronics in Agriculture Journal*, *14*(2-3), 197–214. doi:10.1016/0168-1699(95)00048-8

Goffeau, A., Barrell, B., Bussey, H., Davis, R., Dujon, B., Feldmann, H., & Oliver, S. et al. (1996, October). Life with 6000 genes. *Science*, *274*(5287), 563–567. doi:10.1126/science.274.5287.546 PMID:8849441

Goh, A. T. C. (1994). Seismic liquefaction potential assessed by neural networks. *Journal of Geotechnical Engineering*, *120*(9), 1467–1480. doi:10.1061/(ASCE)0733-9410(1994)120:9(1467)

Gold, C., & Sollich, P., (2003). Model selection for support vector machine classification. *Neurocomputing*, *55*(1–2), 221–249.

Goldberg, D. E. (1989). *Genetic Algorithm in Search Optimization and Machine Learning*. New York: Addison-Wesley.

Goldberg, D. E. (1989). *Genetic Algorithm in Search*. Optimization and Machine Learning, Addison-Wesley Professional.

Goldberg, D. E. (1989). *Genetic algorithms in search, optimization and machine learning*. Reading, MA: Addison-Wesley Publishing Co.

Goldberg, D. E., & Richardson, J. (1987). Genetic algorithms with sharing for multimodal function optimization. *Proceedings of the Second International Conference on Genetic algorithms and their application* (pp. 41-49). Hillsdale, NJ, USA: L. Erlbaum Associates Inc.

Goldstein, J. S., Irving, S. R., & Louis, L. S. (1998). A multistage representation of the Wiener filter based on orthogonal projections. *IEEE Transactions on Information Theory*, *44*(7), 2943–2959. doi:10.1109/18.737524

Gonzalez, R. C., & Richard, R. E. Woods (Eds.), (2002). Digital image processing. Prentice Hall Press.

Gonzalez, R. C., & Woods, R. E. (2009). *Digital Image Processing* (3rd ed.). Pearson Prentice Hall.

Gonzalez, R. C., Woods, R. E., & Eddins, S. L. (2009). *Digital image processing using MATLAB*. Gatesmark Publishing Knoxville.

Goovaerts, P. (2000). Estimation or simulation of soil properties- An optimization problem with conflicting criteria. *Geoderma*, *3*(3-4), 165–186. doi:10.1016/S0016-7061(00)00037-9

Gorder, P. (2010). Computational Epidemiology. *Computing in Science & Engineering*, *12*(1), 4–6. doi:10.1109/MCSE.2010.7

Gorman, M. F., Wynn, D. E., & Salisbury, W. D. (2013). Searching for Herbert Simon: Extending the Reach and Impact of Business Intelligence Research through Analytics. *International Journal of Business Intelligence Research*, *4*(1), 1–12. doi:10.4018/jbir.2013010101

Goshtaby, A. (2005). *2-d and 3-d image registration for medical, remote sensing, and industrial applications*. J. Wiley and Sons.

Gracy, C. P., Nagashree, N., Nayak, A., & Girisha, K. (2010). Recent Posts on Indian Scenario of arecanut. Retrieved from http://krishisewa.com/cms/articles/production-technology/61-arecanut.html

Grady, L. (2006). Random walks for image segmentation. *IEEE Transactions on Pattern Analysis and Machine Intelligence*, *28*(11), 1768–1783. doi:10.1109/TPAMI.2006.233

Granich, R., Akolo, C., Gunneberg, C., Getahun, H., Williams, P., & Williams, B. (2010). Prevention of tuberculosis in people living with HIV. *Clinical Infectious Diseases*, *50*(3), 215–222. doi:10.1086/651494

Gregory, G. H., & Cross, S. A. (2007, June 24-27). Correlation of CBR with Shear Strength Parameters. *Proceedings of 9th International Conference on Low Volume Roads*, Austin, Texas.

Gregory, J. A., & Delbourgo, R. (1982). Piecewise rational quadratic interpolation to monotonic data. *IMA Journal of Numerical Analysis*, *2*(2), 123–130. doi:10.1093/imanum/2.2.123

Griffin, G., Holub, A., & Perona, P. (2007). *Caltech 256 object category dataset* [Technical Report UCB/CSD-04-1366]. California Institute of Technology.

Griffiths, T. L., Steyvers, M., Blei, D. M., & Tenenbaum, J. B. (2004). *Integrating topics and syntax.* Paper presented at the Advances in Neural Information Processing Systems.

Grimson, W. E. L., Ettinger, G. J., White, S. J., Lozano-Perez, T., Wells, W. M., & Kikinis, R.(1996). An automatic registration method for frameless stereotaxy, image guided surgery, and enhanced reality visualization. *IEEE Transactions on Medical Imaging*, *15*(2), 129–140. doi:10.1109/42.491415 PMID:18215896

Grimson, W. E. L., Lozano-P'erez, T., Wells, W. M. III, Ettinger, G. J., White, S. J., & Kikinis, R. (1994). *An automatic registration method for frameless stereotaxy, image guided surgery, and enhanced reality visualization, Computer vision and pattern recognition* (pp. 430–436). Los Alamitos, CA: IEEE Computer Society press.

Grover, L. K. (1998). Quantum computers can search rapidly by using almost any transformation. *Physical Review Letters*, *80*(19), 4329–4332. doi:10.1103/PhysRevLett.80.4329

Gualtieri, J. A., Chettri, S. R., Cromp, R. F., & Johnson, L. F. (1999). Support vector machine classifiers as applied to AVIRIS data.*Proceedings of the 8th JPL Airborne Earth Science Workshop.*

GuhaThakurta, D. (2006). Computational identification of transcriptional regulatory elements in DNA sequence. *Nucleic Acids Research*, *34*(12), 3585–3598. doi:10.1093/nar/gkl372 PMID:16855295

Gupta, S., & Patnaik, K.S. (2008). Enhancing performance of face recognition system by using near set approach for selecting facial features. Journal of Theoretical and Applied Information Technology, 4(5), 433.

Gupta, A., Santini, S., & Jain, R. (1997). In search of information in visual media. *Communications of the ACM*, *40*(12), 34–42. doi:10.1145/265563.265570

Guru, D. S., Mallikarjuna, P. B., Manjunath, S., & Shenoi, M. M. (2012). Machine vision based classification of tobacco leaves for automatic harvesting. *Intelligent Automation and Soft Computing Journal*, *18*(5), 581–590. doi:10.1080/10798587.2012.10643267

Gutowitz, H. (1994). *Methods and Apparatus for Encryption, Decryption and Authentication using Dynamical Systems.*

Habboush, I. H., Mitchell, K. D., Mulkern, R. V., Barnes, P. D., & Treves, S. T. (1996). Registration *and Alignment of Three-Dimensional Images: An Interactive Visual Approach. Radiology*, *199*(2), 573–578. doi:10.1148/radiology.199.2.8668816 PMID:8668816

Hachama, M., Desolneux, A., & Richard, F. J. P. (2012). Bayesian Technique for Image Classifying Registration. *IEEE Transactions on Image Processing*, *21*(9), 4080–4091. doi:10.1109/TIP.2012.2200495 PMID:22645269

Hadden, J., Ashtoush, T., Rajkumar, R., & Ruta, D. (2006). Churn Prediction: Does Technology Matter? *Iranian Journal of Electrical and Computer Engineering*, *1*, 6.

Hadka, D., & Reed, P. (2013). Borg: An Auto-Adaptive Many-Objective Evolutionary Computing Framework. *Evolutionary Computation*, *21*(2), 231–259. doi:10.1162/EVCO_a_00075 PMID:22385134

Hagen, A., & Neto, J. P. (2003). HMM/MLP Hybrid Speech Recognizer for the Portuguese Telephone SpeechDat Corpus. In N. J. Mamede et al. (Eds.), *Computational Processing of the Portuguese Language* (pp. 126–134). Springer Berlin Heidelberg. doi:10.1007/3-540-45011-4_19

Halkidi, M., & Vazirgiannis, M. (2002). Clustering validity assessment using multi representatives. *Proceedings of the Hellenic Conference on Artificial Intelligence* (SETN '02), Thessaloniki, Greece.

Hall, M., Frank, E., Holmes, G., Pfahringer, B., Reutemann, P., & Witten, I. H. (2009). The WEKA Data Mining Software: An Update. *SIGKDD Explorations*, *11*(1), 10. doi:10.1145/1656274.1656278

Hampel, R., Wagenknecht, M., & Chaker, N. (Eds.). (2000). *Fuzzy Control: Theory and Practice*. Heidelberg, Germany: Physica-Verlag. doi:10.1007/978-3-7908-1841-3

Handcock, M., & Gile, K. (2010). Modeling social networks from sampled data. *The Annals of Applied Statistics*, *4*(1), 5–25. doi:10.1214/08-AOAS221

Han, J., & Kamber, M. (2000). *Data Mining: Concepts and Techniques Data mining: concepts and techniques*. San Francisco, CA, USA: Morgan Kaufmann Publishers Inc.

Han, J., & Kamber, M. (2000). *Data Mining: Concepts and Techniques*. NY: Morgan Kaufmann.

Han, K., & Kim, J. (2002). Quantum-Inspired Evolutionary Algorithm for a Class Combinational Optimization. *IEEE Transactions on Evolutionary Computation*, *6*(6), 580–593. doi:10.1109/TEVC.2002.804320

Han, K., & Kim, J. (2003). On setting the parameters of quantum-inspired evolutionary algorithm for practical application.*Proceedings of IEEE Congr. Evol. Comput. (Vol. 1*, 178–194

Hanson, B., & Applebaum, T. H. (1990). Robust Speaker-independent Word Recognition using Static, Dynamic and Acceleration Features: Experiments with Lombard and noisy Speech.*Proceedings of the 1990 IEEE International Conference on Acoustics, Speech and Signal Processing (ICASSP)*Albuquerque, NM, USA (Vol. 2, pp. 857-860). doi:10.1109/ICASSP.1990.115973

Haralick, R. M., Shanmugam, K., & Dinstein, I. (1973). Textural features for image classification. *IEEE Transactions on Systems, Man, and Cybernetics*, *3*(6), 610–621. doi:10.1109/TSMC.1973.4309314

Haralick, R. M., & Shapiro, L. G. (1985). Image segmentation techniques. *Computer Vision Graphics and Image Processing*, *29*(1), 100–132. doi:10.1016/S0734-189X(85)90153-7

Harding, D. P. (2003). The Virtual Laboratory: Technology Assisted Education.*Proceedings of The National Conference On Undergraduate Research (NCUR)*, University of Utah, Salt Lake City, Utah.

Harry, E. & Edward, B. (2005). Making Real Virtual Lab. The Science Education Review, 4(1).

Hassan, H., Eltoweissy, M., & Youssef, M. (2009). *CellNet: a bottom-up approach to network design*. Paper presented at the 3rd International Conference on New Technologies, Mobility and Security (NTMS). doi:10.1109/NTMS.2009.5384680

Hassankhani, R., & Navid, H. (2012). Potato Sorting Based on Size and Color in Machine Vision System. *The Journal of Agricultural Science*, *4*(5), 235–244.

Hawkins, J., & Blakeslee, S. (2005). On Intelligence: St. Martin's Press.

Haykin, S. (1999). *Neural networks: A comprehensive foundation* (2nd ed.). Prentice-Hall.

Haykin, S. (1999). *Neural Networks: A Comprehensive Foundation*. Upper Saddle River, NJ: Prentice Hall.

Hazra, J., Roy Chowdhury, A., & Dutta, P. (2013). An approach for determining angle of rotation of a gray image using weighted statistical regression. *International Journal of Scientific and Engineering Research*, *4*(8), 1006–1013.

Hazra, J., Roy Chowdhury, A., & Dutta, P. (2014). Statistical Regression based Rotation Estimation Technique of Color Image. *International Journal of Computers and Applications*, *102*(15), 1–4. doi:10.5120/17888-8903

He, H.-T., Luo, X.-N., & Liu, B.-l. (2005). Detecting anomalous network traffic with combined fuzzy-based approaches. *Proceedings of International Conference on Intelligent Computing (ICIC)* Hefei, China, (Part II, pp. 433–442).

Hemalatha, M. (2012). A Predictive Modeling of Retail Satisfaction: A Data Mining Approach to Retail Service Industry. In P. Ordóñez de Pablos & M. Lytras (Eds.), *Knowledge Management and Drivers of Innovation in Services Industries* (pp. 175–189). Hershey, PA: Information Science Reference. doi:10.4018/978-1-4666-0948-8.ch014

Henderson, K., & Eliassi-Rad, T. *Applying latent dirichlet allocation to group discovery in large graphs*. Paper presented at the 2009 ACM symposium on Applied Computing. doi:10.1145/1529282.1529607

Henry, C., & Peters, J. F. (2007). Image Pattern Recognition Using Approximation Spaces and Near Sets. Proceedings of Eleventh International Conference on Rough Sets, Fuzzy Sets, Data Mining and Granular (Vol. 4482, pp. 475-482). doi:10.1007/978-3-540-72530-5_57

Henry, C., Lockery, D., Peters, J. F., & Borkowski, M. (2006). Monocular vision system that learns with approximation spaces. In A. Ella, P. Lingras, D. Slezak, & Z. Suraj (Eds.), Rough Set Computing: Toward Perception Based Computing (pp. 186-203). Hershey, PA: Information Science Reference. doi:10.4018/978-1-59904-552-8.ch009

Hermansky, H., & Sharma, S. (1999). Temporal Patterns (TRAPs) in ASR of Noisy Speech.*Proceedings of the 1999 IEEE International Conference on Acoustics, Speech and Signal Processing (ICASSP)*Phoenix, AZ, USA (Vol. 1, pp. 289-292). doi:10.1109/ICASSP.1999.758119

Herring, J. L., Dawant, B. M., Maurer, C. R. Jr, Muratore, D. M., Galloway, R. L., & Fitzpatrick, J. M. (1998). Surface-based registration of CT images to physical space for image-guided surgery of the spine: A sensitivity study. *IEEE Transactions on Medical Imaging*, *17*(5), 743–752. doi:10.1109/42.736029 PMID:9874298

Hettich, S., & Bay, S. D. (1999). *The UCI KDD Archive*. Irvine, CA: University of California, Department of Information and Computer Science.

Heurer, R., & Pherson, R. (2010). *Structured analytic techniques for intelligence analysis*. Washington, DC: CQ Press College.

Hey, T. (1999). Quantum computing: An introduction. Computing & Control Engineering Journal, 10(3), 105–112

Hill, D. L. G., Hawkes, D. J., Harrison, N. A., & Ruff, C. F. (1993), A strategy for automated multimodality image registration incorporating anatomical knowledge and imager characteristics. Paper presented as Information processing in medical imaging, 687, 182–196, Berlin, Springer-Verlag doi:10.1007/BFb0013788

Hipwell, J., Tanner, C., Crum, W., & Hawkes, D. (2006), *X-ray mammogram registration: a novel validation method*. Paper presented at 8th international workshop on digital mammography (IWDM'06), Manchester, UK (Vol. 4046, pp. 197–204). doi:10.1007/11783237_28

Hipwell, J., Tanner, C., Crum, W., Schnabel, J. A., & Hawkes, D. (2007). A New Validation Method for X-ray Mammogram Registration Algorithms Using a Projection Model of Breast X-ray Compression. *IEEE Transactions on Medical Imaging*, *26*(9), 1190–1200. doi:10.1109/TMI.2007.903569 PMID:17896592

Hogeweg, C., Mol, C., de Jong, P.A., Dawson, R., Ayles, H., & van Ginneken, B. (2010). Fusion of local and global detection systems to detect tuberculosis in chest radiographs. Proceedings of Medical Image Computing and Computer-Assisted Intervention MICCAI 2010 (pp. 650–657).

Holland, J. (1975). *Adaptation in Natural and Artificial Systems*. Ann Arbor: University of Michigan Press.

Holland, J. H. (1975). *Adaptation in natural and artificial systems*. Ann Arbor: University of Michigan Press.

Holm, L., & Sander, C. (1993, September). Protein structure comparison by alignment of distance matrices. *Journal of Molecular Biology*, *233*(1), 123–138. doi:10.1006/jmbi.1993.1489 PMID:8377180

Holub, A., Welling, M., & Perona, P. (2005). Exploiting unlabelled data for hybrid object classification. Proceedings of the *NIPS Workshop* (Vol.7).

Hoque, T., Chetty, M., & Dooley, L. S. (2006). A Guided Genetic Algorithm for Protein Folding Prediction Using 3D Hydrophobic-Hydrophilic Model. Proceedings of the *IEEE Congress on Evolutionary Computation CEC '06,* Vancouver, BC, Canada (pp. 2339-2346).

Hortensius, P. D., McLeod, R. D., & Card, H. (1989). Parallel Random Number Generation for VLSI Systems using Cellular Automata. *IEEE Transactions on Computers*, *38*(10), 1466–1473. doi:10.1109/12.35843

Hortensius, P. D., & Podaima, R. D. (1990). Cellular Automata Circuits for Built-in Self-test. *IBM Journal of Research and Development*, *34*(2/3), 389–405. doi:10.1147/rd.342.0389

Hossain, M., Hossain,M. & Hashem,M. (2010). A Generalizes Hybrid Real-Coded Quantum Evolutionary Algorithm Based On Particle Swarm Theory With Arithmetic Crossover. *International Journal of Computer Science & Information Technology (IJCSIT), 2(4)*

Hovakimyan, A., Sargsyan, S., & Barkhoudaryan, S. (2004). Genetic Algorithm and the Problem of Getting Knowledge in e-Learning Systems.*Proceedings of the IEEE International Conference on Advanced Learning Technologies* (pp. 336-339). doi:10.1109/ICALT.2004.1357431

Huang, G. B., Zhu, Q. Y., & Siew, C. K. (2006). Extreme learning machine: Theory and applications. *Neurocomputing*, *70*(1), 489–501. doi:10.1016/j.neucom.2005.12.126

Huang, K. Y. (2012). Detection and classification of areca nuts with machine vision. *Journal Computers and Mathematics with Applications*, *64*(5), 739–746. doi:10.1016/j.camwa.2011.11.041

Huang, K., Yang, H., King, I., & Lyu, M. R. (2006). Maximizing sensitivity in medical diagnosis using biased minimax probability machine. *Biomedical Engineering. IEEE Transactions on*, *53*(5), 821–831.

Huang, M., Huang, H., & Chen, M. (2007). Constructing a personalized e-learning system based on genetic algorithm and case-based reasoning approach. *Expert Systems with Applications*, *33*(3), 551–564. doi:10.1016/j.eswa.2006.05.019

Huebner, R. E., Maybelle, F. S., & Bass, J. B. (1993). The tuberculin skin test. *Clinical Infectious Diseases*, *17*(6), 968–975. doi:10.1093/clinids/17.6.968

Hugh, M. C., & Les, M. S. (2003). *Soft Computing Approaches in Chemistry*. Springer Science & Business Media.

Hulo, N., Bairoch, A., Bulliard, V., Cerutti, L., Cuche, B. A., de Castro, E., . . . Sigrist, C. J. (2008, January). The 20 years of PROSITE. *Nucl. Acids Res., 36*(suppl_1), D245--249.

Hu, M., & Qiang, Z. Z. W. (2008). Application of Rough Sets to Image Pre-processing for Face Detection.*Proceedings of the 2008 IEEE International Conference on Information and Automation* (pp. 545-548).

Human Genome Sequencing Consortium, . (2004, October). Finishing the euchromatic sequence of the human genome. *Nature, 431*(7011), 931–945. doi:10.1038/nature03001 PMID:15496913

Hurvitz, A., & Joskowicz, L. (2008). *Registration of a CT-like atlas to fluoroscopic X-ray images using intensity correspondences.International Journal of Computer Assisted Radiology and Surgery*, 3(6), 493–504

Hwang, M. Y. et al.. (2004). Progress on Mandarin Conversational Telephone Speech Recognition.*Proceedings of the 2004 International Symposium on Chinese Spoken Language Processing* (pp. 1-4). DOI: doi:10.1109/CHINSL.2004.1409571

IBM. (n. d.). Retrieved from http://www.ibm.com

Idris, N. B., & Shanmugam, B. (2005). *Artificial intelligence techniques applied to intrusion detection.* Paper presented at the IEEE INDICON '05.

Ilachinski, A. (2001). Cellular Automata – A Discrete Universe. Singapore: World Scientific Publishing Co. Pte. Ltd.

Indian Standards. (1982). *Specification for compaction mould assembly for light and heavy compaction test for soils* (IS 10078-1982).

Indian Standards. (1983). *Methods of Test for Soils: Part 8 - Determination of Water Content – Dry Density Relation using Heavy Compaction* (IS 2720.8-1983).

Indian Standards. (1985). *Methods of Test for Soils: Part 5 - Determination of Liquid and Plastic Limit* (IS 2720.5-1985).

Indian Standards. (1987). *Methods of Test for Soils: Part 16 - Laboratory Determination of CBR* (IS 2720.16-1987).

Indian Standards. (1993). *Methods of Test for Soils: Part 9 - Determination of Dry Density-Moisture Content Relation by Constant Mass of Soil Method* (IS 2720.8-1983).

informatica, D. v. b. (2013, January). Retrieved from http://www.informatica.com

Initiative, A. G.The Arabidopsis Genome Initiative. (2000, December). Analysis of the genome sequence of the flowering plant Arabidopsis thaliana. *Nature, 408*(6814), 796–815. doi:10.1038/35048692 PMID:11130711

IRC. (n. d.). 37-1970,Guidelines for Flexible Pavement Design, *Indian Road Congress*, New Delhi1970

IRC. (n. d.). 37-2001, Guidelines for Flexible Pavement Design.*Indian Road Congress*, New Delhi2001

Iredi, S., Merkle, D., & Middendorf, M. (2000). Bi-Criterion Optimization with Multi Colony Ant Algorithms. *Proceedings of the First International Conference on Evolutionary Multi-Criterion Optimization (EMO 2001)* (pp. 359-372). Springer.

Izakian, H., & Pedrycz, W. (2014). Agreement-based fuzzy c-means for clustering data with blocks of features. *Neurocomputing, 127*, 266–280. doi:10.1016/j.neucom.2013.08.006

Jaakkola, T., & Haussler, D. (1999). Probabilistic kernel regression models.*Proceedings of the 1999 Conference on AI and Statistics* (Vol. 126, pp. 00-04).

Jacobson, V., Smetters, D. K., Thornton, J. D., Plass, M. F., Briggs, N. H., & Braynard, R. L. (2009) Networking named content.*Proceedings of the Fifth International Conference on Emerging Networking Experiments and Technologies* (pp. 1-12). ACM, New York, NY, USA. doi:10.1145/1658939.1658941

Jahn, T. R., & Radford, S. E. (2008, January). Folding versus aggregation: Polypeptide conformations on competing pathways. *Archives of Biochemistry and Biophysics, 469*(1), 100–117. doi:10.1016/j.abb.2007.05.015 PMID:17588526

Jain, A. K., Murty, M. N., & Flynn, P. J. (1999). Data clustering: A review. *ACM Computing Surveys, 31*(3), 264–323. doi:10.1145/331499.331504

Jamakovic, A., Kooij, R., Van Mieghem, P., & van Dam, E. (2006). Robustness of networks against viruses: the role of the spectral radius. Proceedings of the Symposium on Communications and Vehicular Technology (Vol. 3, pp. 35–38). doi:10.1109/SCVT.2006.334367

Jamil, N., Mahmood, R., & Muhammad, R. (2012). A New Cryptographic Hash Function Based on Cellular Automata Rules 30, 134 and Omega-Flip Network. Proceedings of the *2012 International Conference on Information and Computer networks (ICICN 2012)*, Singapore (Vol. 27, pp. 163-169). IACSIT Press.

Jawahar, C., Biswas, P., & Ray, A. (1997). Investigations on Fuzzy Thresholding Based On Fuzzy Clustering. *Pattern Recognition, 30*(10), 1605–1613. doi:10.1016/S0031-3203(97)00004-6

Jelonek, Z. (2012). Solving polynomial equations. *Mathematica Aeterna, 2*(8), 651–667.

Jepson, A., & Black, M. (1993). Mixture models for optical φλow computation. *Computer Vision and Pattern Recognition* (pp. 760–761).

Jeschke, S., Richter, T., & Zorn, E. (2010). Virtual labs in mathematics and natural sciences. International Conference on Technology Supported Learning & Training: Online Educa Berlin. Retrieved from http://www.ibi.tuberlin.de/diskurs/veranst/online_educa/ oeb_04/Zorn%20TU.pdf

Jianchao, K. Y., Gongz, Y., & Huang, T. (2009). Linear Spatial Pyramid Matching Using Sparse Coding for Image Classification. In IEEE CVPR (pp 1794-1801).

Jiang, J. (2009). *Modeling syntactic structures of topics with a nested hmm-lda.* Paper presented at the 9th IEEE International Conference on Data Mining. doi:10.1109/ICDM.2009.144

Jiten, J., Merialdo, B., & Huet, B. (2006). *Semantic feature extraction with multidimensional hidden Markov model.* Paper presented at the Proceedings of SPIE. doi:10.1117/12.650590

Johnson, L. F., Herwitz, S. R., Lobitz, B. M., & Dunagan, S. E.L. F. Johnson; S. R. Herwitz; B. M. Lobitz; S. E. Dunagan. (2004). Feasibility of Monitoring Coffee Field Ripeness with Airborne Multispectral imagery. *Applied Engineering in Agriculture, 20*(6), 845–849. doi:10.13031/2013.17718

Jones, D. T. (1994). De novo protein design using pairwise potentials and a genetic algorithm. *Protein Science, 3*(4), 567–574. doi:10.1002/pro.5560030405 PMID:8003975

Josephsen, J. & Kristensen, A. K. (2006). Simulation of laboratory assignments to support students' learning of introductory inorganic chemistry. *Chemistry Education Research and practice, 7*(4), 266-279.

Judea, P. (1997). *Probabilistic Reasoning in Intelligent Systems: Networks of Plausible Inference.* USA: Morgan Kaufmann Publishers.

Junjie, Z. H. E. N. G., Xiaoke, Y. A. N., Caicheng, S. H. I., & Peikun, H. E. (2006). Recognition of bridges over water based on fracatal and rough sets theory in aerial photography in image.*Proceedings of IEEE ICSP* (pp. 1-4).

Kamboj, M., & Sepkowitz, K. A. (2006). The risk of tuberculosis in patients with cancer. *Clinical Infectious Diseases, 42*(11), 1592–1595. doi:10.1086/503917

Kanatani, K. (1994). Analysis of 3-D rotation fitting. *IEEE Transactions on Pattern Analysis and Machine Intelligence, 16*(5), 543–549. doi:10.1109/34.291441

Kansal, A., Goraczko, M., & Zhao, F. (2007). Building a sensor network of mobile phones. In Information Processing in sensor Networks (pp. 547–548).

Kao, Y. T., Zahara, E., & Kao, I. W. (2008). A hybridized approach to data clustering. *Expert Systems with Applications*, *34*(3), 1754–1762. doi:10.1016/j.eswa.2007.01.028

Kapur, J. N., Sahoo, P. K., & Wong, A. K. C. (1985). A new method for gray-level picture thresholding using the entropy of the histogram. *Graphical Models and Image Processing*, *29*(3), 273–285. doi:10.1016/0734-189X(85)90125-2

Karaboga, D., Akay, B., & Ozturk, C. (2007). Artificial Bee Colony (ABC) Optimization Algorithm for Training Feed-Forward Neural Networks. In V. Torra, Y. Narukawa, & Y. Yoshida (Eds.), MDAI 4617 (pp. 318–329). Springer; Retrieved from http://dblp.uni-trier.de/db/conf/mdai/mdai2007.html#KarabogaAO07 doi:10.1007/978-3-540-73729-2_30

Karami, A. (2011). *Utilization and comparison of multi attribute decision making techniques to rank Bayesian network options* [Master's Thesis]. University of Skövde, Skövde, Sweden.

Karami, A. (2013). Data clustering for anomaly detection in content-centric networks. *International Journal of Computers and Applications*, *81*(7), 1–8. doi:10.5120/14021-2180

Karami, A., & Guerrero-Zapata, M. (2014). Mining and Visualizing Uncertain Data Objects and Named Data Networking Traffics by Fuzzy Self-Organizing Map.*Proceedings of the Second International Workshop on Artificial Intelligence and Cognition,*Turin, Italy (Vol. 1315, pp. 156-163).

Karami, A., & Guerrero-Zapata, M. (2015). A hybrid multiobjective RBF-PSO method for mitigating DoS attacks in Named Data Networking. *Neurocomputing*, *151*(Part 3), 1262–1282.

Karami, A., & Johansson, R. (2014). Choosing DBSCAN parameters automatically using differential evolution. *International Journal of Computers and Applications*, *91*(7), 1–11. doi:10.5120/15890-5059

Kari, L., & Rozenberg, G. (2008). The many facets of natural computing. *Communications of the ACM*, *51*(10), 72–83. doi:10.1145/1400181.1400200

Kärkkäinen, I., & Fränti, P. (2000). Minimization of the value of Davies–Bouldin index.*Proceedings of the LASTED International Conference Signal Processing and Communications* (pp. 426-432). Marbella, Spain.

Karunaprema, K.A.K., & Edirisinghe, A.G.H.J. (2002). A Laboratory study to establish some useful relationship for the case of Dynamic Cone Penetration. Electronic journal of Geotechnical Engineering, 7.

Kato, M., Hata, N., Banerjee, N., Futcher, B., & Zhang, M. Q. (2004). Identifying combinatorial regulation of transcription factors and binding motifs. *Genome Biology*, *5*(8), R56. doi:10.1186/gb-2004-5-8-r56 PMID:15287978

Kaufman, L., & Rousseeuw, P. J. (Eds.), (1990). *Finding Groups in Data: An Introduction to Cluster Analysis*. New York: John Wiley Sons. doi:10.1002/9780470316801

Kaur, S., Boveja, V. B., & Agarwal, A. (2011). Artificial Neural Network Modeling for Prediction of CBR. *Indian Highways*, *39*(1), 31–38.

Kayacik, H., Heywood, M., & Zincir-Heywood, N. (2006). On evolving buffer overflow attacks using genetic programming.*Proceedings of the 8th annual conference on Genetic and evolutionary computation* (pp. 1667-1674). New York: ACM. doi:10.1145/1143997.1144271

Kayadelen, C. (2011). Soil liquefaction modeling by Genetic Expression Programming and Neuro-Fuzzy. *Expert Systems with Applications*, *38*(4), 4080–4087. doi:10.1016/j.eswa.2010.09.071

Kazienko, P., & Ruta, D. (2011). The Impact of Customer Churn on Social Value Dynamics. In I. Management Association (Ed.), Virtual Communities: Concepts, Methodologies, Tools and Applications (pp. 2086-2096). Hershey, PA: IGI Global. doi:10.4018/978-1-60960-100-3.ch613

Kecman, V. (2001). *Learning and Soft Computing: Support Vector Machines, Neural Networks, And Fuzzy Logic Models.* Cambridge, Massachusetts, London, England: MIT press.

Kecman, V. (2001). *Learning and soft computing: support vector machines, neural networks, and fuzzy logic models.* MIT press.

Kennedy, J., & Eberhart, R. (1995). Particle swarm optimization. *Neural Networks, 4,* 1942–1948.

Kennedy, J., & Eberhart, R. (2001). *Swarm Intelligence.* San Francisco, CA: Morgan Kaufmann.

Kephart, J. (1994). How topology affects population dynamics. In C. Langton (Ed.), *Artificial Life III Studies in the Sciences of Complexity* (pp. 447–463). Addison-Wesley Publishing Co.

Kerr, M. S., Rynearson, K., & Kerr, M. C. (2004). Innovative educational practice: Using virtual labs in the secondary classroom. *The Journal of Educators Online, 1*(1), 1–9.

Khader, M., & Hamza, I. A. (2011). Nonrigid Image Registration Using an Entropic Similarity. *IEEE Transactions on Information Technology in Biomedicine, 15*(5), 681–690. doi:10.1109/TITB.2011.2159806 PMID:21690017

Khan, A. M., & Ravi, S. (2013). Image Segmentation Methods: A Comparative Study. *International Journal of Soft Computing and Engineering, 3*(4), 84-92.

Khan, R., Khan, S. U., Zaheer, R., & Khan, S. (2012). *Future Internet: The Internet of Things Architecture, Possible Applications and Key Challenges.* Paper presented at the 10th International Conference on Frontiers of Information Technology (FIT). doi:10.1109/FIT.2012.53

Khan, Z., Arslan, T., Thompson, J., & Erdogan, A. (2006). Analysis and implementation of multiple–input, multiple–output VBLAST receiver from area and power efficiency perspective. *IEEE Transactions on Very Large Scale Integration (VLSI). Systems, 14,* 1281–1286.

Kim, J. B., & Kim, H. J. (2003). Multiresolution-based watersheds for efficient image segmentation. *Pattern Recognition Letters, 24*(1–3), 473–488. doi:10.1016/S0167-8655(02)00270-2

Kim, J., & Fessler, J. A. (2004). Intensity-based image registration using robust correlation coefficients. *IEEE Transactions on Medical Imaging, 23*(11), 98–104. doi:10.1109/TMI.2004.835313 PMID:15554130

Kim, M., Park, M., & Park, J. (2009). When Customer Satisfaction Isn't Good Enough: The Role of Switching Incentives and Barriers Affecting Customer Behavior in Korean Mobile Communications Services. In I. Lee (Ed.), *Handbook of Research on Telecommunications Planning and Management for Business* (pp. 351–363). Hershey, PA: Information Science Reference. doi:10.4018/978-1-60566-194-0.ch022

Kim, Y., Kim, J., & Han, K. (2006). Quantum-inspired Multiobjective Evolutionary Algorithm for Multiobjective 0/1 Knapsack Problems. *Proceedings of 2006 IEEE Congress on Evolutionary Computation, Sheraton Vancouver Wall Centre Hotel, Vancouver, BC, Canada* (pp. 16–21).

Kinnari, S., Suhonen, A., Harju, J., & Räihä, K.-J. (2007). Evaluating a remote access networking laboratory as a learning environment. *Proc. WBED,* Chamonix, France (pp. 73–79).

Kleinschmidt, M. (2003). *Localized Spectro-Temporal Features for Automatic Speech Recognition* (pp. 2573–2576). Geneva, Switzerland: EUROSPEECH.

Klepac, G. (2010). Preparing for New Competition in the Retail Industry. In A. Syvajarvi & J. Stenvall (Eds.), *Data Mining in Public and Private Sectors: Organizational and Government Applications* (pp. 245–266). Hershey, PA: Information Science Reference; doi:10.4018/978-1-60566-906-9.ch013

Klepac, G. (2013). Risk Evaluation in the Insurance Company Using REFII Model. In S. Dehuri, M. Patra, B. Misra, & A. Jagadev (Eds.), *Intelligent Techniques in Recommendation Systems: Contextual Advancements and New Methods* (pp. 84–104). Hershey, PA: Information Science Reference; doi:10.4018/978-1-4666-2542-6.ch005

Klepac, G. (2014). Data Mining Models as a Tool for Churn Reduction and Custom Product Development in Telecommunication Industries. In P. Vasant (Ed.), *Handbook of Research on Novel Soft Computing Intelligent Algorithms: Theory and Practical Applications* (pp. 511–537). Hershey, PA: Information Science Reference. doi:10.4018/978-1-4666-4450-2.ch017

Klepac, G., & Mršić, L. (2006). *Poslovna inteligencija kroz poslovne slučajeve*. Zagreb: Liderpress.

Klepac, G., & Panian, Ž. (2003). *Poslovna inteligencija*. Zagreb: Masmedia.

Koc, C.K. (Ed.), (2009). Cryptographic engineering. Springer Science + Business Media, LLC. doi:10.1007/978-0-387-71817-0

Kocarev, L., & Lian, S. (2011). *Chaos-Based Cryptography – Theory, Algorithms and Applications*. Springer-Verlag Berlin Heidelberg. doi:10.1007/978-3-642-20542-2

Koch, B., and Khosla, R.(2003). The Role of Precision Agriculture in Cropping Systems. *Journal of Crop Production*, 9(1/2), 361-381.

Kohonen, T. (1989). *Self-Organization and Associative Memory*. Berlin, Germany: Springer-Verlag. doi:10.1007/978-3-642-88163-3

Kohonen, T. (2001). *Self-organizing maps*. NY: Springer. doi:10.1007/978-3-642-56927-2

Kolias, C., Kambourakis, G., & Maragoudakis, M. (2011). Swarm intelligence in intrusion detection: A survey. *Computers & Security*, 30(8), 625–642. doi:10.1016/j.cose.2011.08.009

Koolagudi, S. G., & Krothapalli, S. R. (2012). Emotion Recognition from Speech using Sub-syllabic and Pitch Synchronous Spectral Features. *International Journal of Speech Technology*, 15(4), 495–511. doi:10.1007/s10772-012-9150-8

Kosko, B. (1997). *Fuzzy Engineering*. Upper Saddle River, NJ: Prentice Hall.

Kostek, B., Szczuko, P., & Zwan, P. (2004). Processing of Musical Data Employing Rough Sets and Artificial Neural Networks. Proceedings of International Conference on Rough Sets and Current Trends in Computing (Vol. 3066, pp. 539–548). doi:10.1007/978-3-540-25929-9_65

Kotsiantis, S., & Pintelas, P. (2009). Predictive Data Mining: A Survey of Regression Methods. In M. Khosrow-Pour (Ed.), *Encyclopedia of Information Science and Technology* (2nd ed., pp. 3105–3110). Hershey, PA: Information Science Reference; doi:10.4018/978-1-60566-026-4.ch495

Ko, U., Balsara, P. T., & Lee, W. (1995). Low-power design techniques for high-performance CMOS adders. *IEEE Transactions on Very Large Scale Integration (VLSI). Systems*, 3, 327–333.

Krasnogor, N., Blackburnem, B., Hirst, J., & Burke, E. (2002, September). Multimeme Algorithms for Protein Structure Prediction. Proceedings of the *7th International Conference Parallel Problem Solving from Nature,* Granada, Spain (Vol. 2439, pp. 769-778). Springer Berlin / Heidelberg. Retrieved from http://www.cs.nott.ac.uk/~nxk/PAPERS/ppsn2002.pdf

Krasnogor, N., Hart, W., Smith, J., & Pelta, D. (1999). Protein Structure Prediction With Evolutionary Algorithms. International Genetic and Evolutionary Computation Conference (GECCO99) (pp. 1569–1601). Morgan Kaufmann. Retrieved from http://www.cs.nott.ac.uk/~nxk/PAPERS/gecco99.pdf

Krawczyk, B., & Woźniak, M. (2014). Diversity measures for one-class classifier ensembles. *Neurocomputing, 126,* 36–44. doi:10.1016/j.neucom.2013.01.053

Kretzschmar, M., Gomes, M., Coutinho, R., & Koopman, J. (2010). Unlocking pathogen genotyping information for public health by mathematical modeling. *Trends in Microbiology, 18*(9), 406–412. doi:10.1016/j.tim.2010.06.008 PMID:20638846

Ku, C. S., Lee, D. H., & Wu, J. H. (2004). Evaluation of soil liquefaction in the Chi-Chi Taiwan earthquake using CPT. *Soil Dynamics and Earthquake Engineering, 24*(9-10), 659–673. doi:10.1016/j.soildyn.2004.06.009

Kuglin, C. D., & Hines, D. C. (1975) *The phase correlation image alignment method.* Paper presented at IEEE International Conference Cybern Society (pp. 163–165).

Kumar, P., et el (2000). An Indigenous Impact Tester for measuring Insitu CBR of Pavement Materials (No 63, 13-22). Highway Research Bulletin, IRC.

Kumar, G., Kumar, K., & Sachdeva, M. (2010). The use of artificial intelligence based techniques for intrusion detection: A review. *Artificial Intelligence Review, 34*(4), 369–387. doi:10.1007/s10462-010-9179-5

Kumar, M.A., & Gopal, M. (2009). Least squares twin support vector machines for pattern classification. *Expert Systems with Applications, 36*(4), 7535–7543. doi:10.1016/j.eswa.2008.09.066

Kundu, A., & Bayya, A. (1998). Speech Recognition Using Hidden Markov Model and NN Classifier. *International Journal of Speech Technology, 2*(3), 227–240. doi:10.1007/BF02111210

Kung, S. Y., & Taur, J. S. (2002). Decision-based neural networks with signal/image classification applications. *IEEE Transactions on Neural Networks, 6*(1), 170–181. doi:10.1109/72.363439 PMID:18263296

Kurian, C. (2014). A Survey on Speech Recognition in Indian Languages. *International Journal of Computer Science and Information Technologies, 5*(5), 6169–6175.

Lakshmiprabha, N. S., Bhattacharya, J., & Majumder, S. (2011). Face recognition using multimodal biometric features. *Proceedings of IEEE International Conference on Image Information Processing* (pp. 1–6).

Lampinen, J., & Zelinka, I. (1999). Mechanical engineering design optimization by differential evolution. *New ideas in optimization,* 127-146.

Landauer, T. K., Foltz, P. W., & Laham, D. (1998). An introduction to latent semantic analysis. *Discourse Processes, 25*(2-3), 259–284. doi:10.1080/01638539809545028

Landow, K. C., Fandre, M., Nambiath, R., Shringarpure, N., Gates, H., Lugmayr, A., & Barker, S. (2008). Internet Protocol Television. In Y. Dwivedi, A. Papazafeiropoulou, & J. Choudrie (Eds.), *Handbook of Research on Global Diffusion of Broadband Data Transmission* (pp. 538–562). Hershey, PA: Information Science Reference. doi:10.4018/978-1-59904-851-2.ch034

Lane, N., Miluzzo, E., Lu, H., Peebles, D., Choudhury, T., Campbell, A., & College, D. (2010). A Survey of Mobile Phone Sensing. *IEEE Communications Magazine, 48*(9), 140–150. doi:10.1109/MCOM.2010.5560598

Langevin, F., & Didon, J. P. (1995). Registration of MR images: from 2d to 3d, using a projection based cross correlation method. In: Engineering in Medicine and Biology Society, *IEEE 17th Annual Conference,* Canada (Vol. 1).

Langlois, D., Chartier, S., & Gosselin, D. (2010). An introduction to independent component analysis: Infomax and fastica algorithms. *Tutorials in Quantitative Methods for Psychology*, *6*(1), 31–38.

Larkin, F., & Ryan, C. (2010). Modesty Is the Best Policy: Automatic Discovery of Viable Forecasting Goals in Financial Data. *EvoApplications* (Vol. 2, pp. 202-211).

Larose, D. T. (2005). *Discovering Knowledge in Data: An Introduction to Data Mining*. NY: John Wiley &Sons Inc.

Larose, D. T. (2006). *Data mining methods and models*. NY: John Wiley &Sons Inc.

Lauinger, T. (2010). *Security & Scalability of Content-centric Networking*. Doctoral dissertation, TU Darmstadt.

Lawrence, S., Giles, C. L., Tsoi, A. C., & Back, A. D. (1995). Face Recognition: A convolutional neural-network approach. *IEEE Transactions on Neural Networks*, *8*(1), 98–113. doi:10.1109/72.554195 PMID:18255614

Lazebnik, S., Schmid, C., & Ponce, J. (2006). *Beyond bags of features: Spatial pyramid matching for recognizing natural scene categories*. CVPR.

Lee, D. J., Chang, Y., Archibald, J. K., & Greco, C. G. (2008a). Color quantization and image analysis for automated fruit quality evaluation. Proceedings of the IEEE International Conference on Automation Science and Engineering (pp. 194-199). doi:10.1109/COASE.2008.4626418

Lee, Y., & Lee, C.-K. (2003). Classification of multiple cancer types by multicategory support vector machines using gene expression data. *Bioinformatics (Oxford, England)*, *19*(9), 1132–1139. doi:10.1093/bioinformatics/btg102 PMID:12801874

Lee, Y.-J., & Mangasarian, O. L. (2001). SSVM: A Smooth Support Vector Machine for Classification. *Computational Optimization and Applications*, *20*(1), 5–22. doi:10.1023/A:1011215321374

Lee, D., Archibald, J. K., Chang, Y., & Greco, C. R. (2008b). Robust color space conversion and color distribution analysis techniques for date maturity evaluation. *Journal of Food Engineering*, *88*(3), 364–372. doi:10.1016/j.jfoodeng.2008.02.023

Lee, D., Archibald, J. K., & Xiong, G. (2011). Rapid Color Grading for Fruit Quality Evaluation Using Direct Color Mapping. *IEEE Transactions on Automation Science and Engineering*, *8*(2), 292–302. doi:10.1109/TASE.2010.2087325

Lee, P. H., Pei, S. C., & Chen, Y. Y. (2003). Generating chaotic stream ciphers using chaotic systems. *The Chinese Journal of Physiology*, *41*, 559–581.

Lee, W., & Stolfo, S. J. (2000). A framework for constructing features and models for intrusion detection systems. *ACM Transactions on Information and System Security*, *3*(4), 227–261. doi:10.1145/382912.382914

Leung, K. S., Wong, K. C., Chan, T. M., Wong, M. H., Lee, K. H., Lau, C. K., & Tsui, S. K. (2010, October). Discovering protein-DNA binding sequence patterns using association rule mining. *Nucleic Acids Research*, *38*(19), 6324–6337. doi:10.1093/nar/gkq500 PMID:20529874

Levinthal, C. (1968). Are there pathways for protein folding? *The Journal of Chemical Physics*, *65*, 44–45.

Levy, H., Feldman, C., & Sacho, H. (1989). A reevaluation of sputum microscopy and culture in the diagnosis of pulmonary tuberculosis. *CHEST Journal*, *95*(6), 1193–1197. doi:10.1378/chest.95.6.1193

Lewin, T. (2013). Universities Abroad Join Partnerships on the Web. *New York Times*.

Li, Z., & Shao, G. (2009). Halting Infectious Disease Spread in Social Network. Proceedings of the IEEE IWCFTA'09 International Workshop on Chaos-Fractals Theories and Applications (pp. 305–308). doi:10.1109/IWCFTA.2009.70

Liang, Y., Leung, K. S., & Mok, T. S. (2008). Evolutionary drug scheduling models with different toxicity metabolism in cancer chemotherapy. *Applied Soft Computing*, *8*(1), 140–149. doi:10.1016/j.asoc.2006.12.002

Liao, H.-J., Richard Lin, C.-H., Lin, Y.-C., & Tung, K.-Y. (2013). Intrusion detection system: A comprehensive review. *Journal of Network and Computer Applications, 36*(1), 16–24. doi:10.1016/j.jnca.2012.09.004

Li, C. H., & Tam, P. K. S. (1998). An iterative algorithm for minimum cross-entropy thresholding. *Pattern Recognition Letters, 19*(8), 771–776. doi:10.1016/S0167-8655(98)00057-9

Li, C.-T., & Chiao, R. (2003). Multiresolution genetic clustering algorithm for texture segmentation. *Image and Vision Computing, 21*(11), 955–966. doi:10.1016/S0262-8856(03)00120-3

Li, D., Xiao, L., Han, Y., Chen, G., & Liu, K. (2007). Network Thinking and Network Intelligence. In N. Zhong, J. Liu, Y. Yao, J. Wu, S. Lu, & K. Li (Eds.), *Web Intelligence Meets Brain Informatics* (Vol. 4845, pp. 36–58). Springer Berlin Heidelberg. doi:10.1007/978-3-540-77028-2_3

Li, H., Helling, R., Tang, C., & Wingreen, N. (1996). Emergence of Preferred Structures in a Simple Model of Protein Folding. *Science, 273*(5275), 666–669. Retrieved from http://www.sciencemag.org/cgi/content/abstract/273/5275/666 doi:10.1126/science.273.5275.666 PMID:8662562

Li, J. (2001). SIMPLIcity: Semantics-sensitive Integrated Matching for Picture Libraries. *IEEE Transactions on Pattern Analysis and Machine Intelligence, 23*(9), 947–963. doi:10.1109/34.955109

Likar, B., & Pernus, F. (2001). A hierarchical approach to elastic registration based on mutual information. *Image and Vision Computing, 19*(1–2), 33–44. doi:10.1016/S0262-8856(00)00053-6

Li, N.-J., Wang, W.-J., James Hsu, C.-C., Chang, W., Chou, H.-G., & Chang, J.-W. (2014). Enhanced particle swarm optimizer incorporating a weighted particle. *Neurocomputing, 124*, 218–227. doi:10.1016/j.neucom.2013.07.005

Linoff G.S., & Berry, M.J.A. (1997). Data mining techniques for marketing sales and customer support. NY: John Wiley &Sons Inc.

Lipson, H., & Pollack, J. (2000). Automatic design and manufacture of robotic life forms. *Nature, 406*(6799), 974–978. doi:10.1038/35023115 PMID:10984047

Liu, J. S., Zhou, Q., Liu, X. S., & Jensen, S. T. (2004). Computational discovery of gene regulatory binding motifs: A Bayesian perspective. *Statistical Science, 19*(1), 188–204. doi:10.1214/088342304000000107

Liu, B.-D., Wang, Y.-X., Zhang, Y.-J., & Shen, B. (2013). Learning dictionary on manifolds for image classification. *Pattern Recognition, 46*(7), 1879–1890. doi:10.1016/j.patcog.2012.11.018

Liu, B., Wang, Y., Zhang, Y., & Zheng, Y. (2012). Discriminant sparse coding for image classification: *Proceedings of the 37th International Conference on Acoustics, Speech and Signal Processing* (pp. 2193–2196).

Liu, J. X., Chen, Y. S., & Chen, L. F. (2008). Nonlinear Registration Based on the Approximation of Radial Basis Function Coefficient. *Journal of Medical and Biological Engineering, 28*(3), 119–126.

Liu, J., & Yang, Y. H. (1994). Multi-resolution color image segmentation. *IEEE Transactions on Pattern Analysis and Machine Intelligence, 16*(7), 689–700. doi:10.1109/34.297949

Liu, T., Xie, J., He, Y., Xu, M., & Qin, C. (2009). An Automatic Classification Method for Betel Nut Based on Computer Vision, *Proceedings of the IEEE International Conference on Robotics and Biomimetics*, Guilin, China (pp. 19-23). doi:10.1109/ROBIO.2009.5420823

Liu, X. S., Brutlag, D. L., & Liu, J. S. (2002). An algorithm for finding protein DNA binding sites with applications to chromatinimmunoprecipitation microarray experiments. *Nature Biotechnology, 20*(8), 835–839. doi:10.1038/nbt717 PMID:12101404

Lockery, D., & Peters, J. F. (2007). Robotic target tracking with approximation space-based feedback during reinforcement learning. Proceedings of Eleventh International Conference on Rough Sets, Fuzzy Sets, Data Mining and Granular Computing, Joint Rough Set Symposium, Lecture Notes in Artificial Intelligence (Vol. 4482, pp. 483-490). doi:10.1007/978-3-540-72530-5_58

Lodwick, G. (1996). Computer-aided diagnosis in radiology: A research plan. *Investigative Radiology*, *1*(1), 72–80. doi:10.1097/00004424-196601000-00032

Lodwick, G., Keats, T., & Dorst, J. (1963). The coding of roentgen images for computer analysis as applied to lung cancer. *Radiology*, *81*(2), 185–200. doi:10.1148/81.2.185

Longini, I., Nizam, A., Xu, S., Ungchusak, K., Hanshaoworakul, W., Cummings, D., & Halloran, M. (2005). Containing pandemic influenza at the source. *Science*, *309*(5737), 1083–1087. doi:10.1126/science.1115717 PMID:16079251

Lopes, L., Zamite, J., Tavares, B., Couto, F., Silva, F., & Silva, M. (2009). Automated social network epidemic data collector.Proceedings of INForum informatics symposium, Lisboa, (pp. 1–10).

Lordi, G. M., & Reichman, L. B. (1994), Tuberculin skin testing - Tuberculosis (pp. 63-68). New York: Springer.

Louvieris, P., Clewley, N., & Liu, X. (2013). Effects-based feature identification for network intrusion detection. *Neurocomputing*, *121*, 265–273. doi:10.1016/j.neucom.2013.04.038

Lowe, D. G. (1999), *Object recognition from local scale-invariant features*. Paper presented at International Conference on Computer Vision, 1150–1157.

Lowe, D. G. (2004). Distinctive image features from scale invarient keypoints. *International Journal of Computer Vision*, *60*(2), 91–110. doi:10.1023/B:VISI.0000029664.99615.94

Lu, Z., & Ip, H. H. (2009). Image categorization by learning with context and consistency. In IEEE CVPR, (pp 2719-2726).

Lucasius, C. B., Blommers, M. J. J., Buydens, L. M. C., & Kateman, G. (1991). In L. Davis (Ed.), *Iin Handbook of the genetic algorithm* (pp. 251–281). New York: Van Nostrand Reinhold.

Lucchese, L., & Mitra, S. K. (2001). Color image segmentation: a state-of-the-art survey. In Proceedings of the Indian National Science Academy (INSA-A), New Delhi, India (Vol. 67, pp. 207–221).

Lu, G., Liu, Y., Zhang, D., & Ma, W.-Y. (2007). A survey of content based image retrieval with high-level semantics. *Pattern Recognition*, *40*(1), 262–282. doi:10.1016/j.patcog.2006.04.045

Lu, H., Pan, W., Lane, N., Choudhury, T., & Campbell, A. (2009). SoundSense: scalable sound sensing for people-centric applications on mobile phones.Proceedings of the 7th international conference on Mobile systems, applications, and services (pp. 165–178). doi:10.1145/1555816.1555834

Lu, H., Wang, S., Li, X., Tang, G., Kuang, J., Ye, W., & Hu, G. (2004). A new spatiotemporally chaotic cryptosystem and its security and performance analyses. *Chaos (Woodbury, N.Y.)*, *14*(3), 617–629. doi:10.1063/1.1772731 PMID:15446972

Luke, S., & Spector, L. (1998). A Revised Comparison of Crossover and Mutation in Genetic Programming.*Proceedings of the Third Annual Genetic Programming Conference (GP98)* (pp. 208-213). Morgan Kaufmann.

Luscombe, N. M., Austin, S. E., Berman, H. M., & Thornton, J. M. (2000, June). An overview of the structures of protein-DNA complexes. *Genome Biol.*, *1*(1).

Luscombe, N. M., & Thornton, J. M. (2002, July). Protein-DNA interactions: Amino acid conservation and the effects of mutations on binding specificity. *Journal of Molecular Biology*, *320*(5), 991–1009. Retrieved from http://view.ncbi.nlm.nih.gov/pubmed/12126620 doi:10.1016/S0022-2836(02)00571-5 PMID:12126620

M. A. Vicente, C. Fernandez, and A. M. Coves. (2009). Supervised Face Recognition for Railway Stations Surveillance. *Advanced Concepts for Intelligent Vision Systems* (pp. 710–719).

MacIsaac, K. D., & Fraenkel, E. (2006). Practical strategies for discovering regulatory DNA sequence motifs. *PLoS Computational Biology, 2*(4), e36. doi:10.1371/journal.pcbi.0020036 PMID:16683017

MacMahon, H., & Feng, F. R. (2008). Dual energy subtraction and temporal subtraction chest radiography. *Journal of Thoracic Imaging, 23*(2), 77–85. doi:10.1097/RTI.0b013e318173dd38

Macon, N., & Spitzbart, A. (1958). Inverses of Vandermonde matrices. *The American Mathematical Monthly, 65*(2), 95–100. doi:10.2307/2308881

Maes, F., Vandermeulen, D., & Suetuns, P. (2003) *Medical image registration using mutual information.IEEE Proc 91(10),* 1699–1722 doi:10.1109/JPROC.2003.817864

Maes, F., Collignon, A., Vandermeulen, D., Marchal, G., & Suetens, P. (1997). Multimodality image registration by maximization of mutual information, *IEEE Transaction on. Medical. Image, 16*(2), 187–198.

Maguire, G. Q., Noz, M., Rusinek, H., Jaeger, J., Kramer, E. L., Sanger, J. J., & Smith, G. (1991). Graphics applied to medical image registration. *IEEE Computer Graphics and Applications, 11*(2), 20–28. doi:10.1109/38.75587

Mahantesh, K., Manjunath Aradhya, V. N., & Niranjan, S. K. (2013). An impact of complex hybrid color space in image segmentation. *Proceedings of 2nd International Symposium on Intelligent Informatics* (Vol.235, pp.73-82).

Mahantesh, K., Manjunath Aradhya, V. N., & Niranjan, S. K. (2015). Coslets: A Novel Approach to Explore Object Taxonomy in Compressed DCT Domain for Large Image Datasets. *Proceedings of 3rd International Symposium on Intelligent Informatics* (Vol. 320, pp. 39-48).

Mahantesh, K., Yashaswini, T. S., & Manjunath Aradhya, V. N. (in press). A Weighted Dominant Visual Descriptor for Object Categorization in Large Image Datasets. Proceedings of the *2nd International Conference on Applied Information and Communications Technology (ICAICT 2014)*, Muscat, Oman.

Mahapatra, D., & Sun, Y. (2012). Integrating Segmentation Information for Improved MRF-Based Elastic Image Registration. *IEEE Transactions on Image Processing, 21*(1), 170–183. doi:10.1109/TIP.2011.2162738 PMID:21791411

Mahmoud, H., Masulli, F., & Rovetta, S. (2007) Feature-Based Medical Image Registration using a zzy Clustering Segmentation Approach. *IEEE Transaction,* 172-184

Majumder, S. K., Ghosh, N., & Gupta, P. K. (2005). Relevance vector machine for optical diagnosis of cancer. *Lasers in Surgery and Medicine, 36*(4), 323–333. doi:10.1002/lsm.20160 PMID:15825208

Makkapati, V., Agrawal, R., & Acharya, R. (2009). *Segmentation and classification of tuberculosis bacilli from ZN-stained sputum smear images. Automation Science and Engineering.* IEEE.

Malandain, G. (2006). *Les mesures de similarité pour le recalage des images médicales, Habilitation à Diriger Recherches, Univ.* Nice Sophia-Antipolis, Nice, France: Tech. Rep.

Malhotra, R., Singh, N., & Singh, Y. (2011). *Genetic Algorithms: Concepts* (Vol. 4, p. 2). Design for Optimization of Process Controllers.

Manjunath, B. S. (1995). Image browsing in the Alexandria digital library project. *D-Lib Magazine.* Retrieved from http://www.dlib.org/dlib/august95/alexandria/08manjunath.html

Mannar, K., & Ceglarek, D. (2004). Continuous Failure Diagnosis for Assembly Systems using Rough Set Approach. Manufacturing Technology, 53(1), 39–42. doi:10.1016/S0007-8506(07)60640-4

Mannila, H., & Hand, D. (2001). *Principles of Data Mining*. Cambridge: The MIT press.

Markovic, D., Nikolic, B., & Oklobdzija, V. G. (2000). A general method in synthesis of pass-transistor circuits. *Microelectronics Journal*, *31*(11-12), 991–998. doi:10.1016/S0026-2692(00)00088-4

Mary, L., & Yegnanarayana, B. (2008). Prosodic Features for Language Identification.*Proceedings of the International Conference on Signal Processing, Communications and Networking, (ICSCN)*,Chennai (pp. 57-62).

Masuda, N., & Aihara, K. (2002). Cryptosystems with discretized chaotic maps. *IEEE Trans. Circuits Syst. I*, *49*(1), 28–40. doi:10.1109/81.974872

MATLAB User's Guide. (2015). The Mathworks. Retrieved from http://www.mathworks.com

Mattes, D., Haynor, D. R., Vesselle, H., Lewellen, T. K., & Eubank, W. (2003). PET-CT Image Registration in the Chest Using Free-form Deformations. *IEEE Transactions on Medical Imaging*, *22*(1), 120–128. doi:10.1109/TMI.2003.809072 PMID:12703765

Matthews, J. (1983). Some challenges for engineers in agriculture. *Journal of the Royal Agricultural Society of England*, *144*, 146–158.

Matys, V., Kel-Margoulis, O. V., Fricke, E., Liebich, I., Land, S., Barre-Dirrie, A., & Wingender, E. et al. (2006). TRANSFAC and its module TRANSCompel: Transcriptional gene regulation in eukaryotes. *Nucleic Acids Research*, *34*(90001), 108–110. doi:10.1093/nar/gkj143 PMID:16381825

Maurer, C. R., Fitzpatrick, J. M., Wang, M. Y., Galloway, R. L., Maciunas, R. J., & Allen, G. G. (1997). Registration of head volume images using implantable fiducial markers. *IEEE Transactions on Medical Imaging*, *16*(4), 447–462. doi:10.1109/42.611354 PMID:9263002

Mc Cann, S., & *Lowe, D. G.* (2012). Local Naive Bayes Nearest Neighbor for Image Classification.

McGuffin, L. J., Bryson, K., & Jones, D. T. (2000, April). The PSIPRED protein structure prediction server. *Bioinformatics (Oxford, England)*, *16*(4), 404-405. Retrieved from10.1093/bioinformatics/16.4.404

McGuire, A. M., De Wulf, P., Church, G. M., & Lin, E. C. (1999, April). A weight matrix for binding recognition by the redox-response regulator ArcA-P of Escherichia coli. *Molecular Microbiology*, *32*(1), 219–221. doi:10.1046/j.1365-2958.1999.01347.x PMID:10216875

Mcmohan, D. (2008). *Quantum computing explained*. Hoboken, New Jersey: John Wiley & Sons, Inc.

Mead C. (1989). Analog VLSI and neural systems. *Addison-Wesley VLSI Systems Series*, 1- 371.

Mehrotra, R., & Gary, J. E. (1995). Similar-shape retrieval in shape data management, *IEEE*. *Computation*, *28*(9), 57–62.

Mehta, S. (2013). Bio-inspired approach to solve chemical equations.*International Conference on Contemporary Computing* (pp. 461-466).

Melgani, F., & Bruzzone, L. (2004). Classification of Hyperspectral Remote Sensing Images with Support Vector Machines. *IEEE Transactions on Geoscience and Remote Sensing*, *42*(8), 1778–1790. doi:10.1109/TGRS.2004.831865

Menezes, A., Oorschot, P., & Vanstone, S. (1996). *Handbook of applied cryptography*. CRC Press. doi:10.1201/9781439821916

Merhav, N., & Ephraim, Y. (1991). Maximum likelihood hidden Markov modeling using a dominant sequence of states. *IEEE Transactions on Signal Processing*, *39*(9), 2111–2115. doi:10.1109/78.134449

Merwe, D. W. V. D., & Engelbrecht, A. P. (2003). Data clustering using particle swarm optimization.*Proceedings of the IEEE Congress on Evolutionary Computation*, Canberra, Australia. (vVol. 1, pp. 215-220)

Mestres, J., & Scuseria, G. E. (1995). Genetic Algorithms, A robust scheme for geomety optimizations and global minimum structure problems. *Journal of Computational Chemistry*, *16*(6), 729–742. doi:10.1002/jcc.540160609

Meva, D. T., Kumbharana, C. K., & Kothari, A. D. (2012). The study of adoption of neural network approach in fingerprint recognition. *International Journal of Computers and Applications*, *40*(11), 8–11. doi:10.5120/5007-7326

Meyers, L., Pourbohloul, B., Newman, M., Skowronski, D., & Brunham, R. (2005). Network theory and SARS: Predicting outbreak diversity. *Journal of Theoretical Biology*, *232*(1), 71–81. doi:10.1016/j.jtbi.2004.07.026 PMID:15498594

Mianji, F. A., & Zhang, Y. (2011). Robust Hyperspectral Classification Using Relevance Vector Machine. *Geoscience and Remote Sensing IEEE Transactions*, *49*(6), 2100–2112.

Michaell, B. J. A., & Gordon, L. (2000). *Mastering data mining*. NY: John Wiley &Sons Inc.

Michaell, B. J. A., & Gordon, L. (2003). *Mining the web*. NY: John Wiley &Sons Inc.

Miluzzo, E., Lane, N., Fodor, K., Peterson, R., Lu, H., & Musolesi, M. et al. (2008). Sensing meets mobile social networks: the design, implementation and evaluation of the cenceme application.*Proceedings of the 6th ACM conference on Embedded network sensor systems* (pp. 337–350). doi:10.1145/1460412.1460445

Mimaroglu, S., & Simovici, D. A. (2008). *Approximate computation of object distances by locality-sensitive hashing.* Paper presented at the Proceedings of the 2008 International Conference on Data Mining, Washington, DC.

Mintz, R. (1993). Computerized simulation as an inquiry tool. *School Science and Mathematics*, *93*(2), 76–80. doi:10.1111/j.1949-8594.1993.tb12198.x

Mitchell, M. (1998). *An Introduction to Genetic Algorithms*. Cambridge, MA: MIT Press.

Mitra, V., Wang, C.-J., & Banerjee, S. (2007). Text classification: A least square support vector machine approach. *Applied Soft Computing*, *7*(3), 908–914. doi:10.1016/j.asoc.2006.04.002

Mohan, P. M., & Hosur, R. V. (2009, September). Structure-function-folding relationships and native energy landscape of dynein light chain protein: Nuclear magnetic resonance insights. *Journal of Biosciences*, *34*(3), 465–479. doi:10.1007/s12038-009-0052-0 PMID:19805907

Mojsilovic, A., & Rogowitz, B. (2001). Capturing image semantics with low-level descriptors.*Proceedings of the ICIP* (pp. 18-21).

Mokhtar, B., & Eltoweissy, M. (2012). *Biologically-inspired network "memory" for smarter networking.* Paper presented at the 8th International Conference on Collaborative Computing: Networking, Applications and Worksharing (CollaborateCom).

Mokhtar, B., & Eltoweissy, M. (2014). *Hybrid Intelligence for Semantics-Enhanced Networking Operations.* Paper presented at the The Twenty-Seventh International Flairs Conference.

Mokhtar, B., Eltoweissy, M., & El-Sayed, H. (2013). *Network "memory" system for enhanced network services.* Paper presented at the 9th International Conference on Innovations in Information Technology (IIT).

Mondal, P., & Tiwari, V. K. (2007). Present status of Precision Farming: A Review. *International Journal of Agricultural Research*, *2*(1), 1–10. doi:10.3923/ijar.2007.1.10

Moore, D. A., Lightstone, L., Javid, B., & Friedland, J. S. (2002). High rates of tuberculosis in end-stage renal failure: The impact of international migration. *Emerging Infectious Diseases*, *8*(1), 77–78. doi:10.3201/eid0801.010017

Morris, E. D., Muswick, G. J., Ellert, E. S., Steagall, R. N., Goyer, P. F., & Semple, W. E. (1993). Computer-aided techniques for aligning interleaved sets of non-identical medical images. Medical imaging: image processing (Vol. 1898, pp. 146–157). Bellingham, WA: SPIE Press.

Moss, R. E., Seed, R. B., Kayen, R. E., Stewart, J. P., Der Kiureghian, A., & Cetin, K. O. (2006). CPT-based Probablistic and Deterministic Assesment of in situ Seismic soil liquefaction potential. *Journal of Geotechnical and Geoenviromental Engineering, 132*(8), 1032–1051. doi:10.1061/(ASCE)1090-0241(2006)132:8(1032)

Mostafa, M. G., Farag, A. A., & Essock, E. (2000). Multimodality image registration and fusion using neural network. *FUSION*, *2*, 10–13.

Mporas, I., Ganchev, T., & Fakotakis, N. (2008). Phonotactic Recognition of Greek and Cypriot Dialects from Telephone Speech. In J. Darzentas et al. (Eds.), *Artificial Intelligence: Theories, Models and Applications* (pp. 173–181). Springer Berlin Heidelberg. doi:10.1007/978-3-540-87881-0_16

Mukherjee, S., Osuna, E., & Girosi, F. (1997). Nonlinear prediction of chaotic time series using support vector machine. *Proceedings of IEEE Workshop on Neural Networks for Signal Processing 7, Institute of Electrical and Electronics Engineering*, New York (pp. 511–520) doi:10.1109/NNSP.1997.622433

Mukhopadhyay, A., & Maulik, U. (2011). A multiobjective approach to MR brain image segmentation. *Applied Soft Computing*, *11*(1), 872–880. doi:10.1016/j.asoc.2010.01.007

Mun, M., Reddy, S., Shilton, K., Yau, N., Burke, J., & Estrin, D. et al. (2009). PEIR, the personal environmental impact report, as a platform for participatory sensing systems research. *Proceedings of the 7th international conference on Mobile systems applications and services Mobisys 09* (pp. 55–68). doi:10.1145/1555816.1555823

Münz, G., Li, S., & Carle, G. (2007). Traffic anomaly detection using k-means clustering. *Proceedings of Performance, Reliability and Dependability Evaluation of Communication Networks and Distributed Systems, 4GI/ITG Workshop MMBnet*, Hamburg, Germany.

Muthukannan, K., & Latha, P. (2012). Clustering Techniques based Crops Image Segmentation. *International Journal of Computer Applications (IJCA)*, *2*, 33-37.

Myronenko, A., & Song, X. (2009). Global active contour-based image segmentation via probability alignment. *Proceedings of the IEEE Computer Society Conference on Computer Vision and Pattern Recognition Workshops* (pp. 2798–2804). IEEE. doi:10.1109/CVPR.2009.5206552

Nakib, A., Oulhadj, H., & Siarry, P. (2010). Image thresholding based on Pareto multiobjective optimization. *Engineering Applications of Artificial Intelligence*, *23*(3), 313–320. doi:10.1016/j.engappai.2009.09.002

Naldi, M., & Campello, R. (2014). Evolutionary k-means for distributed data sets. *Neurocomputing*, *127*, 30–42. doi:10.1016/j.neucom.2013.05.046

Namid, R. N., & Christopher, D. B. (Eds.). (2004). *Organizational Data Mining: Leveraging Enterprise Data Resources for Optimal Performance*. PA: Idea Group.

Nandi, S., Kar, B. K., & Chaudhuri, P. P. (1994). Theory and applications of cellular automata in cryptography. *IEEE Transactions on Computers*, *43*(12), 1346–1356. doi:10.1109/12.338094

Narayanan, A., & Moore, M. (1996). Quantum inspired genetic algorithms. *Proceedings of Int. Conf. Evol. Comput.* (pp. 61–66). doi:10.1109/ICEC.1996.542334

Narendra, S., Shekhar, B., & Vivek, D., Dimitri A., & Anantha C., (2001, August). Scaling *of stack effect and its application for leakage reduction.* Proceedings of the International Symposium on Low Power Electronics and Design, Huntington Beach, CA.

Narendra, S., Tschanz, J., Hofsheier, J., Bloechel, B., Vangal, S., Hoskote, Y., . . . De, V. (2004). *Ultra-Low voltage circuits and processor in 180 nm to 90 nm technologies with swapped- body biasing technique.* Paper presented at IEEE International Conference on Solid-State Circuits, San Francisco, CA.

NCERT. (2013). Chemistry Part 1.

NCHRP. (2003). *Guide for mechanistic-empirical design of new and rehabilitated pavement structures* (p. 61820). Illinois: National Co–operative Highway Research Program Transportation Research Board National Research Council.

Nemade, M. U., & Shah, S. K. (2013). Survey of Soft Computing based Speech Recognition Techniques for Speech Enhancement in Multimedia Applications. *International Journal of Advanced Research in Computer and Communication Engineering*, *2*(5), 2039–2043.

Newman, D., Asuncion, A., Smyth, P., & Welling, M. (2007). Distributed inference for latent dirichlet allocation. Advances in Neural Information Processing Systems, 20(1081-1088), 17-24.

Ng, J. K., Zhong, Y., & Yang, S. (2007). A comparative study of Minimax Probability Machine-based approaches for face recognition. *Pattern Recognition Letters*, *28*(15), 1995–2002. doi:10.1016/j.patrec.2007.05.021

Nguyen, S. H., Nguyen, T. T., & Nguyen, H. S. (2005). Rough Set Approach to Sunspot Classification Problem. *Proceedings of International Conference on Rough Sets, Fuzzy Sets, Data Mining and Granular Computing, Lecture Notes in Artificial Intelligence* (Vol. 3642, pp. 263–2720. doi:10.1007/11548706_28

Nian, R., He, B., Zheng, B., Van Heeswijk, M., Yu, Q., Miche, Y., & Lendasse, A. (2014). Extreme learning machine towards dynamic model hypothesis in fish ethology research. *Neurocomputing*, *128*, 273–284. doi:10.1016/j.neucom.2013.03.054

Nii, M., Nakai, K., Takahashi, Y., Higuchi, K., & Maenaka, K. (2011). *Behavior extraction from multiple sensors information for human activity monitoring.* Paper presented at the IEEE International Conference on Systems, Man, and Cybernetics (SMC). doi:10.1109/ICSMC.2011.6083831

Ning, J., Zhang, L., Zhang, D., & Wu, C. (2009). Interactive image segmentation by maximal similarity based region merging. *Pattern Recognition*, *43*(2), 445–456. doi:10.1016/j.patcog.2009.03.004

Nishida, S., & Shinya, M. (1998). Use of image-based information in judgments of surface reflectance properties. *Journal of the Optical Society of America*, *15*(12), 2951–2965. doi:10.1364/JOSAA.15.002951 PMID:9857525

Niu, B., & Wang, H. (2012). Bacterial Colony Optimization. *Discrete Dynamics in Nature and Society*, 698057.

Noort, S., Muehlen, M., & Rebelo, A. (2007). Gripenet: An internet-based system to monitor influenza-like illness uniformly across Europe. *Eurosurveillance*, *12*(7), 1–14. http://www.ncbi.nlm.nih.gov/pubmed/17991409 PMID:17991409

O'Shaughnessy, D. (2000). *Speech Communications- Human and Machine.* New York: IEEE Press.

Ofran, Y., Mysore, V., & Rost, B. (2007, July). Prediction of DNA-binding residues from sequence. *Bioinformatics*, *23*(13), i347--353. doi:10.1093/bioinformatics/btm174

Ojala, T., Pietikainen, M., & Harwood, D. (1994). Performance evaluation of texture measures with classification based on Kullback discrimination of distributions. *Proceedings of International Conference on Pattern Recognition* (pp 582-585). doi:10.1109/ICPR.1994.576366

Olsen, R. S. (1997). Cyclic liquefaction based on the cone penetrometer test. In T. L. Youd, & I. M. Idriss, (Eds.), *Proceedings NCEER Workshop on Evaluation of Liquefaction Resistance of Soils* (pp. 225–276). Buffalo: National Center for Earthquake Engineering Research.

Onat, F. A., & Stojmenovic, I. (2007). *Generating random graphs for wireless actuator networks.* Paper presented at the IEEE International Symposium on World of Wireless, Mobile and Multimedia Networks WoWMoM '07. doi:10.1109/WOWMOM.2007.4351712

Oskoei, M. A., & Huosheng Hu (2008). Support Vector Machine-Based Classification Scheme for Myoelectric Control Applied to Upper Limb. *IEEE Transactions on Bio-Medical Engineering, 55*(8), 1956–1965. doi:10.1109/TBME.2008.919734 PMID:18632358

Osman, M. K., Mashor, M. Y., Saad, Z., & Jaafar, H. (2009). Contrast enhancement for Ziehl-Neelsen tissue slide images using linear stretching and histogram equalization technique.*Proceedings of the IEEE Symposium on Industrial Electronics and Applications (ISIEA '09)* (pp. 431–435). doi:10.1109/ISIEA.2009.5356411

Ourston, D., Matzner, S., Stump, W., & Hopkins, B. (2003). *Applications of hidden markov models to detecting multi-stage network attacks.* Paper presented at the 36th Annual International Conference on System Sciences, Hawaii. doi:10.1109/HICSS.2003.1174909

Padhy N.P. (2010). Artificial Intelligence and Intelligence Systems. OXFORD University Press, Impression010.

Padhye, N., Deb, K., & Mittal, P. (2013). Boundary handling approaches in particle swarm optimization. *Advances in Intelligent Systems and Computing, 201*, 287–298. doi:10.1007/978-81-322-1038-2_25

Palmieri, F., & Fiore, U. (2010). Network anomaly detection through nonlinear analysis. *Computers & Security, 29*(7), 737–755. doi:10.1016/j.cose.2010.05.002

Pal, N. R., & Biswas, J. (1997). Cluster validation using graph theoretic concepts. *Pattern Recognition, 30*(6), 847–857. doi:10.1016/S0031-3203(96)00127-6

Pal, N., & Bhandari, D. (1993). Image thresholding: Some new techniques. *Signal Processing, 33*(2), 139–158. doi:10.1016/0165-1684(93)90107-L

Pal, S., & Rosenfeld, A. (1988). Image enhancement and thresholding by optimization of fuzzy compactness. *Pattern Recognition Letters, 7*(2), 77–86. doi:10.1016/0167-8655(88)90122-5

Pandian, N. S., Nagaraj, T. S., & Manoj, M. (1997). Re-examination of compaction characteristics of fine-grained soils. *Geotechnique, 47*(2), 363–366. doi:10.1680/geot.1997.47.2.363

Pantofaru, C., & Herbert, M. (2005). A Comparison of image segmentation algorithms [Tech. Report] (CMU-RI-TR-05-40).

Pappano, L. (2014). The Year of the MOOC. *The New York Times.*

Park, D. J., & Rilett, L. (1999). Forecasting freeway link travel times with a multilayer feed-forward neural network. *Computer-Aided Civil and Infrastructure Engineering, 14*(5), 357–367. doi:10.1111/0885-9507.00154

Parlett, B. (2000). *"The QR algorithm" in Computing in Science & Engineering* (pp. 51–76). College Park, MD: American Institute of Physics. IEEE Computer Society.

Pastor-Satorras, R., & Vespignani, A. (2001). Epidemic Spreading in Scale-Free Networks. *Physical Review Letters, 86*(14), 3200–3203. doi:10.1103/PhysRevLett.86.3200 PMID:11290142

Patcha, A., & Park, J. M. (2007). An overview of anomaly detection techniques: Existing solutions and latest technological trends. *Computer Networks, 51*(12), 3448–3470. doi:10.1016/j.comnet.2007.02.001

Patel, R. S., & Desai, M. D. (2010). CBR Predicted by Index Properties of Soil for Alluvial Soils of South Gujarat. *Proceedings of the Indian Geotechnical Conference (Vol. 1*, 79-82).

Patently Apple. (2012, September 20). Apple Invents Facial Recognition Locking & Unlocking System. Retrieved from http://www.patentlyapple.com/patently-apple/2012/09/apple-invents-facial-recognition-locking-unlocking-system.html

Patterson, D. W. (1995). *Artificial neural networks*. Prentice Hall.

Patton, A. L., Punch, W. F. III, & Goodman, E. D. (1995). A Standard GA Approach to Native Protein Conformation Prediction.*Proceedings of the 6th International Conference on Genetic Algorithms* (pp. 574-581). San Francisco, CA, USA: Morgan Kaufmann Publishers Inc.

Paul, S. (2010). An Optimized distributed association rule mining algorithm in parallel and distributed data mining with xml data for improved response time. *International Journal of Computer Science and Information Technology*, *2*(2), 90–103. doi:10.5121/ijcsit.2010.2208

Pavlopoulos, S., Kyriacou, E., Berler, A., Dembeyiotis, S., & Koutsouris, D. (1998). A novel emergency telemedicine system based on wireless communication technology-AMBULANCE. *IEEE Transactions on Information Technology in Biomedicine*, *2*(4), 261–267. doi:10.1109/4233.737581

Pawlak, Z. (1981). Classification of objects by means of attributes. Proceedings of Polish Academy of Sciences.

Pawlak, Z. (1996). Rough sets, rough relations and rough functions. Fundamental Informaticas, 27(2), 103–108.

Pawlak, Z. (1982). Rough Sets. *International Journal of Computer and Information Sciences*, *11*(5), 341–356. doi:10.1007/BF01001956

Peddabachigari, S., Abraham, A., Grosan, C., & Thomas, J. (2007). Modeling intrusion detection system using hybrid intelligent systems. *Journal of Network and Computer Applications*, *30*(1), 114–132. doi:10.1016/j.jnca.2005.06.003

Pedrycz, W. (1985). Algorithms of fuzzy clustering with partial supervision Pattern Recognition. *Letters*, 2(1), 13-20.

Pedrycz, W., & Gomide, F. (1998). *An Introduction to Fuzzy Sets: Analysis and Design of Complex Adaptive Systems*. Cambridge, Massachusetts: MIT Press.

Pedrycz, W., & Waletzky, J. (1997). Fuzzy clustering with partial supervision. *IEEE Transactions on Systems, Man, and Cybernetics. Part B, Cybernetics*, *27*(5), 787–795. doi:10.1109/3477.623232

Peebles, D., Lu, H., Lane, N., Choudhury, T., & Campbell, A. (2010). Community-guided learning: Exploiting mobile sensor users to model human behavior.*Proc. of 24th AAAI Conference on Artificial Intelligence*.

Perdisci, R., Ariu, D., Fogla, P., Giacinto, G., & Lee, W. (2009). Mcpad: A multiple classifier system for accurate payload-based anomaly detection. *Computer Networks*, *53*(6), 864–881. doi:10.1016/j.comnet.2008.11.011

Peters, J. F. (2007). Near Sets. Proceedings of Applied Mathematical Sciences, 11(53), 2609-2629.

Peters, J. F. (2007). Perceptual granulation in ethology-based reinforcement learning. In W. Pedrycz, A. Skowron, & V. Kreinovich (Eds.), Handbook on Granular Computing. Wiley, NY.

Peters, J. F., & Henry, C. (2006). Reinforcement learning with approximation spaces. Fundamental Informaticas, 71(23), 323-349.

Peters, J. F., Borkowski, M., & Henry, C., D. Lockery' D.S. Gunderson (2006). Line-Crawling Bots that Inspect Electric Power Transmission Line Equipment. Proceedings of the Third International Conference on Autonomous Robots and Agents (pp. 39-44).

Peters, J. F., Shahfar, S., Ramanna, S., & Szturm, T. (2007). Biologically-inspired adaptive learning: A near set approach. Proceedings of Frontiers in the Convergence of Bioscience and Information Technologies (Vol. 11, pp. 403 – 408).

Peters, J. F., Suraj, Z., Shan, S., Ramanna, S., Pedrycz, W., & Pizzi, N. (2003). Classification of meteorological volumetric radar data using rough set methods. Pattern Recognition Letters, 24(6), 911–920. doi:10.1016/S0167-8655(02)00203-9

Peters, J. F., & Ramanna, S. (2007). Feature Selection: Near Set Approach. *Lecture Notes in Computer Science, 4944,* 57–71. doi:10.1007/978-3-540-68416-9_5

Peters, J. F., & Wasilecoski, P. (2009). Foundations of near sets. *International Journal of Information Sciences, 179*(18), 3091–3109. doi:10.1016/j.ins.2009.04.018

Phillips, C. L., Bruno, M.-A., Maquet, P., Boly, M., Noirhomme, Q., Schnakers, C., . . . Laureys, S. (2011). Relevance vector machine consciousness classifier applied to cerebral metabolism of vegetative and locked-in patients. *NeuroImage, 56*(2), 797–808. doi:10.1016/j.neuroimage.2010.05.083 PMID:20570741

Pietrzyk, U., Herholz, K., Fink, G., Jacobs, A., Mielke, R., Slansky, I., & Heis, W. et al. (1994). An interactive technique for three-dimensional image registration: Validation for PET, SPECT, MRI and CT brain studies. *Journal of Nuclear Medicine, 35,* 2011–2018. PMID:7989986

Plastic surgery faces. (2009). Retrieved from http://glamour-news-blog.com/2009/10/stars-before-after-plastic-surgery.html

Platel, M. D., Schliebs, S., & Kasabov, N. (2009). Quantum-Inspired Evolutionary Algorithm: A Multimodel EDA. *IEEE Transactions on Evolutionary Computation, 13*(6), 1218–1231. doi:10.1109/TEVC.2008.2003010

Pluim, J. P. W., Maintz, J. B. A., & Viergever, M. A. (2003). Mutual-information based registration of medical images: A survey. *IEEE Transactions on Medical Imaging, 22*(6), 986–1004. doi:10.1109/TMI.2003.815867 PMID:12906253

Pluim, J. P. W., Maintz, J. B. A., & Viergever, M. A. (2004). f-Information Measures in Medical Image Registration. *IEEE Transactions on Medical Imaging, 23*(12), 1508–1516. doi:10.1109/TMI.2004.836872 PMID:15575408

Pohl, K., Fisher, J., Grimson, W., Kikinis, R., & Wells, W. (2006). A Bayesian model for joint segmentation and registration. *NeuroImage, 31*(1), 228–239. doi:10.1016/j.neuroimage.2005.11.044 PMID:16466677

Poli, R., Kennedy, J., & Blackwell, T. (2007, June). Particle swarm optimization. *Swarm Intelligence, 1*(1), 33-57. doi:10.1007/s11721-007-0002-0

Poli, R., Langdon, W. B., & Mcphee, N. F. (2008, March). *A Field Guide to Genetic Programming.* Lulu Enterprises, UK Ltd. Retrieved from http://www.amazon.com/exec/obidos/redirect?tag=citeulike07-20&path=ASIN/1409200736

Pope, P., & Theiler, J. (2003) *Automated image registration (AIR) of MTI imagery.* Paper presented at SPIE 27, Orlando, Florida (pp. 294–305).

Pratt, W. K. (2008). *Image segmentation - Text book of Digital image Processing* (4th ed., pp. 579–622). Wiley.

Price, K. V. (1997, April). Differential evolution vs. the functions of the 2nd ICEO. *Evolutionary Computation, 1997., IEEE International Conference on,* (pp. 153-157). Indianapolis, IN, USA.

Priya, G., Akshay, K., Pratishtha, D., & Anu, G. (2013, August). *Design and Implementation of low power TG full adder design in sub-threshold regime.* Paper presented at IEEE International Conference on Intelligent Interactive Systems and Assistive Technologies, Coimbatore, India.

Priya, G., Anu, G., & Abhijit, A. (2013). A review on ultra low power design technique: Sub-threshold logic. *International Journal of Computer Science and Technology-IJCST., 4*(2), 64–71.

Priya, G., Anu, G., & Abhijit, A. (2014). Design and implementation of n-bit sub-threshold kogge stone adder with improved power delay product. *European Journal of Scientific Research*, *123*(1), 106–116.

Project Tomorrow. (2014, June). Trends in Digital Learning: Students' Views on Innovative Classroom Models. Project Tomorrow and Blackboard K-12 Speak Up 2013 National Data.

Provost, F., & Fawcett, T. (1997). Analysis and visualization of classifier performance: Comparison under imprecise class and cost distributions.*Proc. Third International Conference on Knowledge Discovery and DataMining (KDD-97)*, Menlo Park, CA (pp. 43–48). AAAI Press.

Provost, F., & Fawcett, T. (2001). Robust classification systems for imprecise environments. *Machine Learning*, *42*(3), 203–231. doi:10.1023/A:1007601015854

Pun, T. (1980). A new method for gray-level picture threshold using the entropy of the histogram. *Signal Processing*, *2*(3), 223–237. doi:10.1016/0165-1684(80)90020-1

Puri, B. K. (2004). Monomodal rigid-body registration and applications to the investigation of the effects of eicosapentaenoic acid intervention in neuropsychiatric disorders. *Prostaglandins, Leukotrienes, and Essential Fatty Acids*, *71*(3), 137–200. doi:10.1016/j.plefa.2004.03.010 PMID:15253887

Pyle, D. (1999). *Data preparation for Data Mining*. NY: Morgan Kaufmann.

Qi, J., Li, Y., Li, C., & Zhang, Y. (2009). Telecommunication Customer Detainment Management. In I. Lee (Ed.), *Handbook of Research on Telecommunications Planning and Management for Business* (pp. 379–399). Hershey, PA: Information Science Reference. doi:10.4018/978-1-60566-194-0.ch024

Quan, H., Srinivasan, D., & Khosravi, A. (2014). Particle swarm optimization for construction of neural network-based prediction intervals. *Neurocomputing*, *127*, 172–180. doi:10.1016/j.neucom.2013.08.020

Rabaey, J., Pedram, M., & Landman, P. (2002). *Low power design methodologies. The Springer International Series in Engineering and Computer Science. 336*. Boston, MA: Kluwer Academic Publishers/Springer.

Rabiner, L., & Juang, B. (1986). An introduction to hidden Markov models.*ASSP Magazine, IEEE*, *3*(1), 4–16. doi:10.1109/MASSP.1986.1165342

Rahmani, Z. H., & Cholleti, S. R., & goldman, S. A. (2006). Local image representations using pruned salient points with applications to CBIR. *Proceedings of the ACM International Conference on Multimedia* (pp 287-296).

Rahmat-Samii, Y., & Michielssen, E. (Eds.). (1999). Electromagnetic Optimization by Genetic Algorithms. New York, NY, USA: John Wiley \& Sons, Inc.

Raine, L., & Wellman, B. (2012). *Networked. The new social operating system*. Cambridge: MIT Press.

Rajpathak, D., & Chougule, R. (2011). A generic ontology development framework for data integration and decision support in a distributed environment. *International Journal of Computer Integrated Manufacturing*, *24*(2), 154–170. doi:10.1080/0951192X.2010.531291

Ramage, D. (2007). Hidden Markov Models Fundamentals. *CS229 Section Notes*.

Ramanathan, P., Vanathi, P. T., & Agarwal, S. (2009). High speed multiplier design using decomposition logic. *Serbian Journal of Electrical Engineering*, *6*(1), 33–42. doi:10.2298/SJEE0901033R

Ramani, A.K., Ingle, M., & Kulkarni, P. (2012). Classification of Sentiments through Rough Fuzzy Approach Butalia. *International Journal of Computer Science And Information Technology & Security*, 2(2), 209-309.

Ramasubbarao, G. V., & Siva Sankar, G. (2013). Predicting Soaked CBR value of fine grained soils using index and compaction characteristics. *Jordan Journal of Civil Engineering*, 7(3).

Rangarajan, A., Chui, H., & Duncan, J. S. (1999). Rigid point feature registration using mutual information. *Medical Image Analysis*, 3(4), 425–440. doi:10.1016/S1361-8415(99)80034-6 PMID:10709705

Rao, K. S., & Koolagudi, S. G. (2011). Identification of Hindi Dialects and Emotions using Spectral and Prosodic Features of Speech. *International journal of Systemic. Cybernetics and Informatics*, 9(4), 24–33.

Rashid T. (2010) Classification of Churn and non-Churn Customers for Telecommunication Companies. *International Journal of Biometrics and Bioinformatics*, 3(5).

Rauwerda, H., Roos, M., Hertzberger, B., & Breit, T. (2006). The promise of a virtual lab in drug discovery. *Drug Discovery Today*, 11(5-6), 228–236. doi:10.1016/S1359-6446(05)03680-9 PMID:16580600

Reddy, V. R., Maity, S., & Rao, K. S. (2013). Identification of Indian Languages using Multi-level Spectral and Prosodic Features. *International Journal of Speech Technology*, 16(4), 489–511. doi:10.1007/s10772-013-9198-0

Reeves, C. (1993). *Using Genetic Algorithms with Small Populations, Proceedings of Fifth International Conference on Genetic Algorithms* (pp. 92–99). San Mateo, CA: Morgan Kaufman.

Reiffel, E., & Polak, W. (2000). An Introduction to Quantum Computing for Non-Physicists. Retrieved from arxive.org. quant-ph/9809016v2

Ren, X. (2009). An Optimal Image Thresholding Using Genetic Algorithm. *Proceedings of International Forum on Computer Science-Technology and Applications (IFCSTA '09)* (pp. 169-172). doi:10.1109/IFCSTA.2009.48

Ren, X., & Bo, L. (2012). Discriminatively trained sparse code gradients for contour detection. *Advances in Neural Information Processing Systems*, 25, 593–601.

Renzetti, F. R., & Zortea, L. (2011). Use of a gray level coccurrence matrix to characterize duplex stainless steel phases microstructure. *Frattura ed Integrita Strutturale*, 16, 43-51

Reynolds, D. A., & Rose, R. C. (1995). Robust Text-independent Speaker Identification using Gaussian Mixture Speaker Models. *IEEE Transactions on Speech and Audio Processing*, 3(1), 72–83. doi:10.1109/89.365379

Rigamonti, R., Lepetit, V., González, G., Türetken, E., Benmansour, F., Brown, M., & Fua, P. (2014). On the relevance of sparsity for image classification. *Computer Vision and Image Understanding* (Vol. 125, pp. 115–127). doi:10.1016/j.cviu.2014.03.009

Robertson, P. K. & Campanella, R. G. (1985). Liquefaction Potential of Sands Using the Cone Penetration Test. *Journal of Geotech. Div., ASCE, 111*(3), 384-407.

Robertson, P. K., & Wride, C. E. (1998). Evaluating cyclic liquefaction potential using the cone penetration test. *Canadian Geotechnical Journal*, 35(3), 442–459. doi:10.1139/t98-017

Roche, A., Malandain, G., Pennec, X., &Ayache, N.(1998), The *correlation ratio as a new similarity measure for multimodal image registration.* Paper presented as 1st Int. Conf. Med. Image Comput. Comput.-Assisted Intervent., (Vol. 1496, pp. 1115–1124).

Roche, A., Malandain, G., & Ayache, N. (2000). Unifying maximum likelihood approaches in medical image registration. *International Journal of Imaging Systems and Technology, 11*(1), 71–80. doi:10.1002/(SICI)1098-1098(2000)11:1<71::AID-IMA8>3.0.CO;2-5

Rodriguez, E., Ruiz, B., Crespo, A. G., & Gracia, F. (1997). Speech/ Speaker Recognition using a HMM/ GMM Hybrid Model. In J. Bigun et al. (Eds.), *Audio and Video Based Biometric Person Authentication* (pp. 227–234). Springer Berlin Heidelberg. doi:10.1007/BFb0016000

Rodriguez-Henriquez, F., Saqib, N.A., Días Pérez, A.D., & Koc, C.K. (Eds.), (2006). Cryptographic algorithms on reconfigurable hardware. Springer Science + Business Media, LLC.

Rogers, D., & Hopfinger, A. J. (1994). Genetic function approximation to generate a family of QSAR equations using genetic algorithms. *Journal of Chemical Information and Modeling, 34*, 854–866. doi:10.1021/ci00020a020

Rohl☐ng, T., & Maurer, C. R., Jr. (2001), *Intensity-based non-rigid registration using adaptive multilevel free-form deformation with an incompressibility constraint.* Paper presented as: 4th Int. Conf. Medical Image Comput. Comput.-Assisted Intervent., (Vol. 2208, pp. 111–119). doi:10.1007/3-540-45468-3_14

Rojas, R. (1996). *Neural Networks: A Systematic Introduction.* Berlin: Springer-Verlag. doi:10.1007/978-3-642-61068-4

Ronquist, F., & Huelsenbeck, J. P. (2003, August). MrBayes 3: Bayesian phylogenetic inference under mixed models. *Bioinformatics, 19*(12), 1572-1574. Retrieved from10.1093/bioinformatics/btg180

Rosca, J. P. (1997). Analysis of Complexity Drift in Genetic Programming. *Genetic Programming 1997:Proceedings of the Second Annual Conference* (pp. 286-294). Morgan Kaufmann.

Rosen, S. (1992). Temporal Information in Speech: Acoustic, Auditory and Linguistic Aspects. *Philosophical Transactions of the Royal Society of London. Series B, Biological Sciences, 336*(1278), 367–373. doi:10.1098/rstb.1992.0070 PMID:1354376

Ross, H. D. (1953). The arithmetic element of the IBM type 701 computer.*Proceedings of the IRE*, 1287-1294. doi:10.1109/JRPROC.1953.274302

Rothenberg, R., & Costenbader, E. (2011). Empiricism and theorizing in epidemiology and social network analysis. *Interdisciplinary Perspectives on Infectious Diseases, 2011*, 1–5. doi:10.1155/2011/157194 PMID:21127746

Roy, T.K., Chattopadhyay, B.C., & Roy, S.K. (2009). Prediction of CBR from Compaction Characteristics of Cohesive Soil. *Highway Research Journal*, July-Dec., 77-88.

Rubin, S., Michalowski, W., & Slowinski, R. (1996). Developing an emergency room diagnostic check list using rough sets-a case study of appendicitis. In J. Anderson, M. Katzper (Eds.), Simulation in the Medical Sciences (pp. 19–24).

Rueckert, D., Sonoda, L. I., Hayes, C., Hill, D. L. G., Leach, M. O., & Hawkes, D. J. (1999). Non-rigid registration using free-form deformation: Application to breast MR images. *IEEE Transactions on Medical Imaging, 18*(8), 712–721. doi:10.1109/42.796284 PMID:10534053

Rukhin, A., Soto, J., Nechvatal1, J., Smid, M., Barker, E., Leigh, S., Levenson, M., Vangel, M., Banks, D., Heckert, A., Dray, J., Vo, S. (2010). *A Statistical Test Suite for Random and Pseudorandom Number Generators for Cryptographic Applications* (NIST Special Publication 800-22).

Ruske, G. (1982). Automatic Recognition of Syllabic Speech Segments using Spectral and Temporal Features.*Proceedings of the 1982 IEEE International Conference on Acoustic Speech and Signal Processing* (Vol. 7, pp. 550-553). DOI: doi:10.1109/ICASSP.1982.1171663

Ruta, D., Adl, C., & Nauck, D. (2009). New Churn Prediction Strategies in the Telecom Industry. In H. Wang (Ed.), *Intelligent Data Analysis: Developing New Methodologies Through Pattern Discovery and Recovery* (pp. 218–235). Hershey, PA: Information Science Reference; doi:10.4018/978-1-59904-982-3.ch013

Sabisch, T., & Ferguson, A. & Bolouri (1998). Automatic Registration Of Complex Images Using A Self Organizing Neural System. *Proceedings of 1998 Int.Joint Conf. on Neural Networks* (pp. 165–170).

Sacco, W. F., Henderson, N., Rios-Coelho, A. C., Ali, M. M., & Pereira, C. M. (2009, June). Differential evolution algorithms applied to nuclear reactor core design. *Annals of Nuclear Energy*. doi:10.1016/j.anucene.2009.05.007

Safar, M., Shahabi, C., & Sun, X. (2000). Image Retrieval by Shape: A Comparative Study.*Proceedings of IEEE International Conference on Multimedia and Expo*(pp 141-144). doi:10.1109/ICME.2000.869564

Sahoo, P., Wilkins, C., & Yeager, J. (1997). Threshold Selection Using Renyi's Entropy. *Pattern Recognition, 30*(1), 71–84. doi:10.1016/S0031-3203(96)00065-9

Saklecha, P. P., Katpatal, Y. B., Rathore, S. S., & Agarwal, D. K. (2012). ANN Modeling for Strength Characterization of Subgrade Soil in a Basaltic Terrain. *Proceedings of ICAMB-2012* (pp. 1215–1220).

Salehi, M., Pourzaferani, M., & Razavi, S. A. (2013). Hybrid attribute-based recommender system for learning material using genetic algorithm and a multidimensional information model. *Egyptian Informatics Journal, 14*(1), 67–78. doi:10.1016/j.eij.2012.12.001

Santana, R., Larranaga, P., & Lozano, J. A. (2008, August). Protein Folding in Simplified Models with Estimation of Distribution Algorithms. *IEEE Transactions on Evolutionary Computation, 12*(4), 418-438.

Sarma, M., & Sarma, K. K. (2014). *Phoneme-Based Speech Segmentation Using Hybrid Soft Computing Framework.* India: Springer. doi:10.1007/978-81-322-1862-3

Satyanarayana Reddy, C. N. V., & Pavani, K. (2006). Mechanically Stabilised Soils-Regression Equation for CBR Evaluation, Dec. 14-16, 731-734, *Proceedings of Indian Geotechnical Conference*-2006, Chennai, India.

Scarlet, A. J. (2001). Integrated control of agricultural tractors and implements: A review of potential opportunities relating to cultivation and crop establishment machinery. *Computers and Electronics in Agriculture Journal, 30*(1-3), 167–191. doi:10.1016/S0168-1699(00)00163-0

Schettini, R. (1993). A segmentation algorithm for color images. *Pattern Recognition Letters, 14*(6), 499–506. doi:10.1016/0167-8655(93)90030-H

Schillaci, G., Pennisi, A., Franco, F., & Longo, D. (2012). Detecting tomato crops in greenhouses using a vision based method.*Proc. International Conference on Safety Health and Welfare in Agriculture and in Agro-food Systems*, Ragusa – Italy (pp. 252-258).

Schmitz, R. (2001). Use of Chaotic Dynamical Systems in Cryptography. *Journal of the Franklin Institute, 338*(4), 429-441.

Schoonderwoerd, R., Bruten, J. L., Holland, O. E., & Rothkrantz, L. J. (1996). Ant-based load balancing in telecommunications networks. *Adaptive Behavior, 5*(2), 169–207. doi:10.1177/105971239700500203

Schroeter, P., Vesin, J. M., Langenberger, T., & Meuli, R. (1998). Robust parameter estimation of intensity distributions for brain magnetic resonance images. *IEEE Transactions on Medical Imaging, 17*(2), 172–186. doi:10.1109/42.700730 PMID:9688150

Schuler, W., Bastos-Filho, C., & Oliveira, A. (2009). A novel hybrid training method for hopfield neural networks applied to routing in communications networks. *International Journal of Hybrid Intelligent Systems, 6*(1), 27–39.

Schumm, P., Scoglio, C., Gruenbacher, D., & Easton, T. (2007). Epidemic spreading on weighted contact networks. Proceedings of the 2007 IEEE 2nd BioInspired Models of Network Information and Computing Systems (Vol. 1, pp. 201–208).

Scott, A. M., Macapinlac, H., Zhang, J., Daghighian, F., Montemayor, N., Kalaigian H., Sgouros, G., Graham, M. C., Kolbert, K., Yeh, S. D. J., Lai, E., Goldsmith, S. J., & Larson, S. M. (1996), Image registration of SPECT and CT images using an external fiduciary band and three-dimensional surface fitting in metastatic thyroid cancer. *Journal of image registration using GA., 36*, 100–103.

Scott, J. (2012). *Social Network Analysis*. London: SAGE Publications.

Sebe, N., & Lew, M. (2003). *Robust Computer Vision: Theory and Applications (Computational Imaging and Vision)* (p. 26). New York: Springer-Verlag. doi:10.1007/978-94-017-0295-9

Seedahmed, G., & Martucci, L. (2002), Automated Image Registration Using Geometrically Invariant Parameter Space Clustering (Gipsc). Paper presented at Potogrammetic Computer Vision, Graz, Austria.

Seed, H. B., & De Alba, P. (1986). *Use of SPT and CPT tests for evaluating the liquefaction resistance of sands. Use of in situ tests in geotechnical engineering* (p. 6). Geotechnical Special PublicationASCE.

Selim, S. Z., & Ismail, M. A. (1984). K-means-type algorithms: A generalized convergence theorem and characterization of local optimality. *IEEE Transactions on Pattern Analysis and Machine Intelligence, 6*(1), 81–87. doi:10.1109/TPAMI.1984.4767478 PMID:21869168

Serre, T., Wolf, L., & Poggio, T. (2005). Object recognition with features inspired by visual cortex. Proceedings of *IEEE Computer Society Conference on Computer Vision and Pattern Recognition* (Vol. 2, pp. 994-1000). doi:10.1109/CVPR.2005.254

Sethi, I. K., & Coman, I. L. (2001). Mining association rules between low-level image features and high-level concepts. *Proceedings of the SPIE Data Mining and Knowledge Discovery, 3*, 279–290.

Settles, M. (2005). *An Introduction to Particle Swarm Optimization*. Moscow: Department of Computer Science, University of Idaho.

Seymore, K., McCallum, A., & Rosenfeld, R. (1999). *Learning hidden Markov model structure for information extraction*. Paper presented at the AAAI-99 Workshop on Machine Learning for Information Extraction.

Sezan, M. I. (1990). A peak detection algorithm and its application to histogram-based image data reduction. *Computer Vision Graphics and Image Processing, 49*(1), 36–51. doi:10.1016/0734-189X(90)90161-N

Sezgin, M., & Sankur, B. (2004). Survey over image thresholding techniques and quantitative performance evaluation. *Journal of Electronic Imaging, 13*(1), 146–165. doi:10.1117/1.1631315

Shafer, G. (1976). *A Mathematical Theory of Evidence*. Princeton, NJ: Princeton University Press.

Shah-Hosseini, H. (2009). The intelligent water drops algorithm: A nature-inspired swarm-based optimization algorithm. *International Journal of Bio-inspired Computation, 1*(1/2), 71–79. doi:10.1504/IJBIC.2009.022775

Shahin, M. A., Jaksa, M. B., & Maier, H. R. (2000). *Predicting the Settlement of Shallow Foundations on Cohesionless Soils Using Back-Propagation Neural Networks. Research Report No. R 167*. University of Adelaide.

Shahin, M. A., Jaksa, M. B., & Maier, H. R. (2008). State of the art of artificial neural networks in geotechnical engineering. *Electronic Journal of Geotechnical Engineering, 8*, 1–26.

Shang, L., Cheng L. v. J., & Yi, Z. (2006). Rigid medical image registration using pca neural network. *Neurocomputing, 69(13-15),* 1717-1722

Shannon, C. (1949). Communication Theory of Secrecy Systems. *Bell Sys. Tech. J., 28*, 656–715. Retrieved from netlab.cs.ucla.edu/wiki/files/shannon1949.pdf

Shannon, C.E. (1948). A Mathematical Theory of Communication. *Bell System Technical Journal*, 27(July & October), 379–423 & 623–656.

Sharifzadeh, S., Serrano, J. & Carrabina, J. (2012). Spectro-Temporal Analysis of Speech for Spanish Phoneme Recognition. *Proceedings of the 2012 19th International Conference on Systems, Signals and Image Processing (IWSSIP)*, Vienna (pp. 548-551).

Shashua, A., & Riklin-Raviv, T. (2001).The Quotient Image: Class-based re-rendering and recognition with varying illuminations.*Proceedings of IEEE Transactions on Pattern Analysis and Machine Intelligence*, 23(2), 129–139. doi:10.1109/34.908964

Shaw Robert, F. (1950). Arithmetic operations in a binary computer.*Proceedings of the review of Scientific Instruments*, *21:*687-693.

Shen, R., Cheng, I., & Basu, A. (2010). A hybrid knowledge-guided detection technique for screening of infectious pulmonary tuberculosis from chest radiographs. *Biomedical Engineering,* 57(11), 2646–2656.

Sheridan, R. P., & Kearsley, S. K. (1995). Using Genetic Algorithm to suggest combinatorial libraries. *Journal of Chemical Information and Computer Sciences*, 35(2), 310–320. doi:10.1021/ci00024a021

Shi, J., & Malik, J. (2000). Normalized cuts and image segmentation. *IEEE Transactions on Pattern Analysis and Machine Intelligence*, 22(8), 889–905.

Shi, J., & Malik, J. (2000). Normalized Cuts and Image Segmentation. *IEEE Transactions on Pattern Analysis and Machine Intelligence*, 22(8), 888–905. doi:10.1109/34.868688

Shi, Y., & Eberhart, R. (1998). A modified particle swarm optimizer.*Proceedings of IEEE World Congress on Computational Intelligence,*Anchorage, AK (pp. 69-73).

Shmygelska, A., & Hoos, H. (2005). An ant colony optimisation algorithm for the 2D and 3D hydrophobic polar protein folding problem. *BMC Bioinformatics*, 6(1), 30. http://www.biomedcentral.com/1471-2105/6/30 doi:10.1186/1471-2105-6-30 PMID:15710037

Shor, P. W. (1997). Polynomial-time algorithms for prime factorization and discrete logarithms on a quantum computer. *SIAM Journal on Computing*, 26(5), 1484–1509. doi:10.1137/S0097539795293172

Silburt, A.L., Boothroyd, A.R., & Digiovanni, M. (1988). Automated parameter extraction and modeling of the MOSFET below threshold. *IEEE Transactions on Computer-Aided Design*, 1, 484-488.

Siler, W., & Buckley, J. J. (2005). *Fuzzy expert sytems and fuzzy reasoning*. NY: John Wiley &Sons Inc.

Silva, C., & Ribeiro, B. (2006). Scaling Text Classification with Relevance Vector Machines. In *Systems, Man and Cybernetics* (*Vol. 5*). Taipei: IEEE. doi:10.1109/ICSMC.2006.384791

Silverio, H. (2008). Evolutionary Algorithms for the Protein Folding Problem: A Review and Current Trends. *Computational Intelligence in Biomedicine and Bioinformatics*, 297-315. Retrieved from http://www.springerlink.com/content/e810504k11t13107

Silverman, D., & Dracup, J. A. (2000). Artificial neural networks and long-range precipitation prediction in California. *Journal of Applied Meteorology*, 39(1), 57–66. doi:10.1175/1520-0450(2000)039<0057:ANNALR>2.0.CO;2

Singh, G., & Kamal, N. (2013). Machine Vision System for Tea Quality Determination – Tea Quality Index (TQI). IOSR Journal of Engineering, 3(7), 46-50.

Singh, K. R., Zaveri, M. A., & Raghuwanshi, M. M. (2010). Extraction of Pose Invariant Feature. Information and Communications Technologies, 101(3), 535-539.

Singh, G., & Deb, K. (2006). Comparison of multi-modal optimization algorithms based on evolutionary algorithms. *Proceedings of the 8th annual conference on Genetic and evolutionary computation GECCO '06* (pp. 1305-1312). doi:10.1145/1143997.1144200

Singh, K. K., & Singh, A. (2010). A Study of Image Segmentation Algorithms for Different Types of Images. *International Journal of Computer Science Issues*, 7(5), 414–417.

Singh, K. R., & Raghuwanshi, M. M. (2009). Face Recognition with Rough-Neural Network: A Rule Based Approach. *Proceedings of International workshop on Machine Intelligence Research* (Vol. 38, pp. 123-129).

Singh, K. R., Zaveri, M. A., & Raghuwanshi, M. M. (2013). Rough Membership Function based Illumination Classifier for Illumination Invariant Face Recognition. *Applied Soft Computing*, 13(10), 4105–4117. doi:10.1016/j.asoc.2013.04.012

Singh, R., & Vatsa, M. (2009). *Effect of Plastic Surgery on Face Recognition: A Preliminary Study*. Morgantown, USA: West Virginia University.

Skowron, A., & Peters, J. F. (2007). Rough granular computing. In W. Pedrycz, A. Skowron, & V. Kreinovich (Eds.), Handbook on Granular Computing. New York: Wiley.

Skowron, A., & Stepaniuk, J. (1996). Tolerance approximation spaces. Fundamental Informaticas, 27(2-3), 245-253.

Smith, A. D., Sumazin, P., Das, D., & Zhang, M. Q. (2005). Mining ChIP-chip data for transcription factor and cofactor binding sites. *Bioinformatics. Suppl, 1*(20), i403–i412.

Smyth, M. S., & Martin, J. H. (2000, February). X ray crystallography. *Molecular pathology: MP, 53*(1), 8-14. Retrieved from http://view.ncbi.nlm.nih.gov/pubmed/10884915

Sobeih, A., Viswanathan, M., Marinov, D., & Hou, J. C. (2007). *J-Sim: An integrated environment for simulation and model checking of network protocols*. Paper presented at the Parallel and Distributed Processing Symposium, 2007. IPDPS 2007. IEEE International. doi:10.1109/IPDPS.2007.370519

Sohn, K., Jung, D. Y., Lee, H., & Hero, A. O. (2011). Efficient Learning of Sparse, Distributed, Convolutional Feature Representations for Object Recognition. Proceedings of the *IEEE International Conference on Computer Vision* (pp 2643 – 2650).

Soltys, M., Beard, D. V., Carrasco, V., Mukherji, S., & Rosenman, J. (1995). FUSION: a tool for registration and visualization of multiple modality 3D medical data. Medical imaging: image processing, 2434, 74–80.

Song, Y.-L., & Yang, Y. (2010). Localization algorithm and implementation for focal of pulmonary tuberculosis chest image.*Proceedings of the International Conference on Machine Vision and Human-Machine Interface (MVHI '10)* (pp. 361–364). doi:10.1109/MVHI.2010.180

Sontag, D., & Roy, D. M. (2011). *Complexity of inference in latent dirichlet allocation*. Advances in Neural Information Processing Systems NIPS.

Spears, W. M., & Anand, V. (1991). A Study of Crossover Operators in Genetic Programming.*Proceedings of the 6th International Symposium on Methodologies for Intelligent SystemsISMIS '91* (pp. 409-418). London, UK: Springer-Verlag. doi:10.1007/3-540-54563-8_104

Sridevi, M., & Mala, C. (2012). A Survey on Monochrome Image Segmentation Techniques. *Procedia Technology* (Vol. 6, pp. 548-555).

Sridharan, A., & Nagaraj, H. B. (2005). Plastic limit and compaction characteristics of fine grained soils. *Proceedings of the ICE-Ground Improvement, 9*(1), 17–22. doi:10.1680/grim.2005.9.1.17

Srivastava, J., Cooley, R., Deshpande, M., & Tan, P.-N. (2000). Web usage mining: Discovery and applications of usage patterns from web data. *ACM SIGKDD Explorations Newsletter, 1*(2), 12–23. doi:10.1145/846183.846188

Stafford, J. V. (2000). Implementing Precision Agriculture in the 21st Century [Keynote address]. Proceedings of AgEng (Vol. 76, 267-275).

Stafford, J. V., & Ambler, B. (1994). In-Field location using GPS for spatially variable field operations. *Computers and Electronics in Agriculture Journal, 11*(1), 23–36. doi:10.1016/0168-1699(94)90050-7

Stafford, J. V., Ambler, B., Lark, R. M., & Catt, J. (1996). Mapping and interpreting the yield variation in Cereal Crops. *Computers and Electronics in Agriculture Journal, 14*(2-3), 101–119. doi:10.1016/0168-1699(95)00042-9

Stallings, W. (2003). *Cryptography and Network Security* (3rd ed.). Prentice Hall.

Stark, T. D., & Olson, S. M. (1995). Liquefaction resistance using CPT and field case histories. *Journal of Geotechnical Engineering, 121*(12), 856–869. doi:10.1061/(ASCE)0733-9410(1995)121:12(856)

Steinbach, M., Tan, P., & Kumar, V. (2007). *Introduction to Data Mining (English)* (1st ed.). Pearson Education.

Storn, R., & Price, K. (1997, December). Differential Evolution - A Simple and Efficient Heuristic for global Optimization over Continuous Spaces. *Journal of Global Optimization, 11*(4), 341–359. http://www.springerlink.com/content/x555692233083677/ doi:10.1023/A:1008202821328

Strohmann, T., & Grudic, G. Z. (2002). *A formulation for minimax probability machine regression* (pp. 769–776). Advances in Neural Information Processing Systems.

Strother, S. C., Anderson, J. R., Xu, X., Liow, J., Bonar, D. C., & Rottenberg, D. A. (1994). Quantitative comparisons of image registration techniques based on high-resolution MRI of the brain. *Journal of Computer Assisted Tomography, 18*(6), 954–962. doi:10.1097/00004728-199411000-00021 PMID:7962808

Studholme, C. (1997). Measures of 3-D medical image alignment [Ph.D. thesis]. University of London, London, UK.

Studholme, C., Hill, D. L. G., & Hawkes, D. J. (1999). An overlap invariant entropy measure of 3-D medical image alignment. *Pattern Recognition, 32*(1), 71–86. doi:10.1016/S0031-3203(98)00091-0

Subsol, G., Thirion, J. P., & Ayache, N. (1998). A general scheme for automatically building 3-D morphometric anatomical atlases: Application to a skull atlas. *Medical Image Analysis, 2*(1), 37–60. doi:10.1016/S1361-8415(01)80027-X PMID:10638852

Su, C., & Amer, A. (2006). A Real-time Adaptive Thresholding for Video Change Detection, *Proceedings of 2006 IEEE International Conference, Image Processing*, Atlanta, Georgia, USA (pp. 157–160). doi:10.1109/ICIP.2006.312373

Sun, A., & Lim, E.P., (2002). Web classification using support vector machine.*Proceedings of the 4th international workshop on Web information and data management* (pp. 96 – 99). New York, USA.

Sun, Y., Liu, J., & Wang, L. (2011). A Multi-Scale TVQI-based Illumination Normalization Model.*Proceedings of International Multi Conference of Engineers and Computer Scientists* (Vol. 1, pp. 1-6).

Suykens, J. A. K., Van Gestel, T., De Brabanter, J., De Moor, B., & Vandewalle, J. (2002). *Least Squares Support Vector Machines*. Singapore: World Scientific.

Suykens, J. A. K., & Vandewalle, J. (1999). Least Squares Support Vector Machine Classifiers. *Neural Processing Letters*, *9*(3), 293–300. doi:10.1023/A:1018628609742

Suykens, J. A. K., Vandewalle, J., & De Moor, B. (2001). Optimal control by least squares support vector machines. *Neural Networks*, *14*(1), 23–35. doi:10.1016/S0893-6080(00)00077-0 PMID:11213211

Swets, J. A., Dawes, R. M., & Monahan, J. (2000). Better decisions through science. *Scientific American*, *283*(4), 82–87. doi:10.1038/scientificamerican1000-82 PMID:11011389

Talbi, H., Draa, A., & Batouche, M. (2004). A New Quantum-Inspired Genetic Algorithm for Solving the Travelling Salesman Problem. *Proceedings of IEEE International Conference on Industrial Technology (ICIT'04)* (Vol. 3, pp. 1192–11970. doi:10.1109/ICIT.2004.1490730

Talbi, H., Draa, A., & Batouche, M. (2006). A Novel Quantum-Inspired Evolutionary Algorithm for Multi-Sensor Image Registration. *The International Arab Journal of Information Technology*, *3*(1), 9–15.

Tan, X., Shen, R., Wang, Y. (2012). Personalized course generation and evolution based on genetic algorithms. *Journal of Zhejiang Univ-Sci C (Comput & Electron)*, 13(12), 909-917.

Tang, X. W., Zhang, X. W., & Uzuoka, R. (2015). Novel adaptive time stepping method and its application to soil seismic liquefaction analysis. *Soil Dynamics and Earthquake Engineering*, *71*, 100–113. doi:10.1016/j.soildyn.2015.01.016

Tanner, C., Schnabel, J. A., Chung, D., Clarkson, M. J., Rueckert, D., Hill, D., & Hawkes, D. J. (2000). Volume and shape preservation of enhancing lesions when applying non-rigid registration to a time series of contrast enhancing MR breast images. Paper presented at the *3rd Int. Conf. Med. Image Comput. Comput.-Assisted Intervent., London*, U.K. (pp 327–337).

Tan, X., & Triggs, B. (2010). Enhanced local texture feature sets for face recognition under difficult lighting conditions. *IEEE Transactions on Image Processing*, *19*(6), 1635–1650. doi:10.1109/TIP.2010.2042645 PMID:20172829

Tao, D., Li, X., Wu, X., Hu, W., & Maybank, S. J. (2005, November). Supervised tensor learning. In *Data Mining Fifth IEEE International Conference* (p. 8). IEEE. doi:10.1007/s10115-006-0050-6

Tao, W. B., Tian, J. W., & Liu, J. (2003). Image segmentation by three-level thresholding based on maximum fuzzy entropy and genetic algorithm. *Pattern Recognition Letters*, *24*(16), 3069–3078. doi:10.1016/S0167-8655(03)00166-1

Terence, S., Foster, J. A., & Dickinson, J. (1996). Code growth in genetic programming.*Proceedings of the 1st annual conference on genetic programming* (pp. 215-223). Cambridge, MA: MIT Press.

Teweldemedhin, E., Marwala, T., & Mueller, C. (2004). Agent-based modelling: a case study in HIV epidemic. Proceedings of the 4th International Conference on Hybrid Intelligent Systems.

Thomas, L., Edelman, D., & Crook, J. (2002). *Credit Scoring and Its Application*. NY: SIAM. doi:10.1137/1.9780898718317

Thomas, S., Ganapathy, S., & Hermansky, H. (2008). *Hilbert Envelope Based Spectro- Temporal Features for Phoneme Recognition in Telephone Speech* (pp. 1521–1524). INTERSPEECH.

Tichy, W. F. (1998). Should computer scientists experiment more? *Computer*, *31*(5), 32–40. doi:10.1109/2.675631

Tipping, M. E. (2000). The relevance vector machine. *Advances in Neural Information Processing Systems*, *12*, 625–658.

Tomassini, M., & Perrenoud, M. (2000). Stream Ciphers with One- and Two-Dimensional Cellular Automata. In M. Schoenauer at al. (Eds.), Parallel Problem Solving from Nature - PPSN VI, LNCS (Vol. 1917, pp. 722-731).

Tong, S., & Koller, D. (2001). Support Vector Machine Active Learning with Applications to Text Classification. *Journal of Machine Learning Research*, 2001, 45–66.

Toshiba. (n. d.). Face Recognition. Retrieved from http://explore.toshiba.com/innovation-lab/face-recognition

Townsend, W. J., & Earl, E. Swartzlander & J.A. Abraham. (2003). A comparison of Dadda and Wallace multiplier delays. *Proceedings of the SPIE in Advanced Signal Processing Algorithms, Architectures and Implementations* (*Vol. 5205*, pp. 552-560). Univ. of Texas, Austin, USA.

Tripathy, S., & Nandi, S. (2009). LCASE: Lightweight cellular automata-based symmetric key encryption. *International Journal of Network Security*, 8(2), 243–252.

Tsao, J., & Lauterbur, P. (1998). Generalized clustering-based image registration for multi-modality images. Paper presented at 20th Annual International Conference of the IEEE (Vol. 2, pp. 667-670).

Tsujinishi, D., & Abe, S. (2003). Fuzzy least squares support vector machines for multiclass problems. *Neural Networks*, 16(5–6), 785–792. PMID:12850035

Tuch, B. B., Galgoczy, D. J., Hernday, A. D., Li, H., & Johnson, A. D. (2008, February). The evolution of combinatorial gene regulation in fungi. *PLoS Biology*, 6(2), e38. doi:10.1371/journal.pbio.0060038 PMID:18303948

Turk, M., & Pentland, A. (1991). Eigenfaces for recognition. *Journal of Cognitive Neuroscience*, 3(1), 7186. doi:10.1162/jocn.1991.3.1.71 PMID:23964806

TÜYSÜZ C. (2010). The Effect of the Virtual Laboratory on Students' Achievement and Attitude in Chemistry. *International Online Journal of Educational Sciences*, 2(1), 37–53.

Tu, Z., Dollar, P., & Belongie, S. (2006). Supervised learning of edges and object boundaries. *IEEE-CVPR*, 2, 1964–1971.

Udaiyakumar, R., & Sankaranarayanan, K. (2012). Certain investigations on static power dissipation in various nano-scale CMOS D Flip-Flop structures. *IACSIT International Journal of Engineering and Technology*, 2, 644–651.

Unger, R., & Moult, J. (1993). Genetic Algorithm for 3D Protein Folding Simulations.*Proceedings of the 5th International Conference on Genetic Algorithms* (pp. 581-588). San Francisco, CA, USA: Morgan Kaufmann Publishers Inc.

Upegui, A. (2010). Dynamically Reconfigurable Hardware for Evolving Bio-Inspired Architectures. In R. Chiong (Ed.), *Intelligent Systems for Automated Learning and Adaptation: Emerging Trends and Applications* (pp. 1–22). doi:10.4018/978-1-60566-798-0.ch001

Valyon, J., & Horvath, G. (2004). A sparse least squares support vector machine classifier. In *Neural Networks* (vol. 1). IEEE. doi:10.1109/IJCNN.2004.1379967

Van Gemert, J. C., Geusebroek, J. M., Veenman, C. J., & Smeulders, A. W. M. (2008). Kernel codebooks for scene categorization. *Proceedings of the ACM - European Conference on Computer Vision: Part III* (pp. 696 – 709).

van Gestel, T., Suykens, J. A. K., Baesens, B., Viaene, S., Vanthienen, J., Dedene, G., . . . Vandewalle, J. (2004). Benchmarking Least Squares Support Vector Machine Classifiers. *Machine Learning*, 54(1), 5–32. doi:10.1023/B:MACH.0000008082.80494.e0

van Ginneken, B., Hogeweg, L., & Prokop, M. (2009). Computer-aided diagnosis in chest radiography: Beyond nodules. *European Journal of Radiology*, 72(2), 226–230. doi:10.1016/j.ejrad.2009.05.061

Van Ginneken, B., Stegmann, M., & Loog, M. (2006). Segmentation of anatomical structures in chest radiographs using supervised methods: A comparative study on a public database. *Medical Image Analysis*, 10(1), 19–40. doi:10.1016/j.media.2005.02.002

Van Laarhoven, P. J., & Aarts, E. H. (1987). *Simulated annealing*. Springer. doi:10.1007/978-94-015-7744-1

vanGestel, T., Suykens, J., Lanckriet, G., Lambrechts, A., Moor, B., & Vandewalle, J. (2002). Bayesian Framework for Least-Squares Support Vector Machine Classifiers, Gaussian Processes, and Kernel Fisher Discriminant Analysis. *Neural Computation*, *14*(5), 1115–1147. doi:10.1162/089976602753633411 PMID:11972910

Vapnik, V. (1995). *The nature of statistical learning theory*. New York. doi:10.1007/978-1-4757-2440-0

Vapnik, V. N. (1998). *Statistical learning theory*. New York: Wiley.

Varghese, V. K., Babu, S. S., Bijukumar, R., Cyrus, S., & Abraham, B. M. (2013). Artificial Neural Networks: A Solution to the Ambiguity in Prediction of Engineering Properties of Fine-Grained Soils. *Geotechnical and Geological Engineering*, *31*(4), 1187–1205. doi:10.1007/s10706-013-9643-5

Varnali, K. (2013). Mobile Social Networks: Communication and Marketing Perspectives. In I. Lee (Ed.), *Strategy, Adoption, and Competitive Advantage of Mobile Services in the Global Economy* (pp. 248–258). Hershey, PA: Information Science Reference. doi:10.4018/978-1-4666-1939-5.ch014

Vasant, P., Barsoum, N., Kahraman, C., & Dimirovski, G. (2008). Application of Fuzzy Optimization in Forecasting and Planning of Construction Industry. In I. Vlahavas & D. Vrakas (Eds.), *Artificial Intelligence for Advanced Problem Solving Techniques* (pp. 254–265). Hershey, PA: Information Science Reference. doi:10.4018/978-1-59904-705-8.ch010

Vasant, P., Ganesan, T., & Elamvazuthi, I. (2012). Hybrid Tabu Search Hopfield Recurrent ANN Fuzzy Technique to the Production Planning Problems: A Case Study of Crude Oil in Refinery Industry.[IJMMME]. *International Journal of Manufacturing, Materials, and Mechanical Engineering*, *2*(1), 47–65. doi:10.4018/ijmmme.2012010104

Vasconcelos, N., & Lippman, A. (2000). Statistical models of video structure for content analysis and characterization. *Image Processing. IEEE Transactions on*, *9*(1), 3–19.

Venkatasubramanian, C., & Dhinakaran, G. (2011). ANN model for predicting CBR from index properties of soils. *International Journal of Civil & Structural Engineering*, *2*(2), 614–620.

Venkateshwarlu, R. L. K., Raviteja, R., & Rajeev, R. (2012). The Performance Evaluation of Speech Recognition by Comparative Approach. In A. Karahoca (Ed.), *Advances in Data Mining Knowledge Discovery and Applications*. doi:10.5772/50640

Venkatraman, T. S., & Samson, M., & Ambili, T.S. (1995). Correlation between CBR and Clegg Impact Value. Proc. Nat. Sem. On emerging trends in Highway Engineering, Centre for Transportation Engineering, Bangalore (Vol. 1, pp. 25.1-25.5).

Verma, J. P. (2013). *Data Analysis in Management with SPSS Software*. Berlin: Springer. doi:10.1007/978-81-322-0786-3

Vijay, J., Sohani, M., Shrivas A. (2014). Color Image Segmentation Using K-Means Clustering and Otsu's Adaptive Thresholding. *International Journal of Innovative Technology and Exploring Engineering*, *3*(9), 72-76.

Vinod, P., & Reena, C. (2008). Prediction of CBR Value of Lateritic Soils Using Liquid Limit and Gradation Characteristics Data. *Highway Research Journal, IRC*, *1*(1), 89–98.

Viola, P., & Wells, W. M. III. (1997). Alignment by maximization of mutual information. *International Journal of Computer Vision*, *24*(2), 137–154. doi:10.1023/A:1007958904918

Virtual Computational Chemistry Laboratory. (2001) Retrieved from www.vcclab.org

Virtual Labs. (n. d.), Mission Document of National Mission on Education Through ICT. Government of India.

Vittoz, E., Gerber, B., & Leuenberger, F. (1972). Silicon-Gate CMOS frequency divider for the electronic wrist watch. *IEEE Journal of Solid-State Circuits, SC-7*(2), 100–104. doi:10.1109/JSSC.1972.1050254

von Neumann, J. (1966). *Theory of Self -Reproducing Automata* (Ed., Burks, A.W.). London: Univ. of Illinois Press.

Vose, D. (2000). *Quantitative Risk Analysis*. New York: John Wiley & Sons.

Vuswabatgab, G. M., Afanasyer, V., Buldyrev, S. V., Murphy, E. J., Prince, P. A., & Stanley, H. E. (1996). Levy flight search patterns of wandering albatrosses. *Nature, 381*(6581), 413–415. doi:10.1038/381413a0

Wallace. C. S. (1964). A suggestion for a fast multiplier. *IEEE Transactions on Electronic Computers.* EC-13(1).14-17.

Wang, J., Yang, J., Yu, K., Lv, F., Huang, T., & Gong, Y. (2010). Locality-constrained Linear Coding for Image Classification. In IEEE CVPR (pp 3360 – 3367).

Wang, X., Ye, M., & Duanmu, C. J. (2009). Classification of data from electronic nose using relevance vector machines. *Sensors and Actuators. B, Chemical, 140*(1), 143–148. doi:10.1016/j.snb.2009.04.030

Wang, C.-Y., Wu, H.-K., Lee, S. W.-Y., Hwang, F.-K., Chang, H.-Y., Wu, Y.-T., & Tsai, C.-C. et al. (2014). A review of research on technology-assisted school science laboratories. *Journal of Educational Technology & Society, 17*(2), 307–320.

Wang, G., Zhao, Y., & Wang, D. (2008). A protein secondary structure prediction framework based on the extreme learning machine. *Neurocomputing, 72*(1), 262–268. doi:10.1016/j.neucom.2008.01.016

Wang, J., Reinstein, L. E., Hanley, J., & Meek, A. G. (1996). Investigation of a phase-only correlation technique for anatomical alignment of portal images in radiation therapy. *Physics in Medicine and Biology, 41*(6), 1045–1058. doi:10.1088/0031-9155/41/6/008 PMID:8794484

Wang, L. (Ed.). (2005). *Support Vector Machines: theory and applications* (Vol. 177). Springer.

Wang, Q., Chen, L., Yap, P., Wu, G., & Shen, D. (2010). Groupwise Registration Based on Hierarchical Image Clustering and Atlas Synthesis. *Human Brain Mapping, 31*(8), 1128–1140. PMID:20063349

Wang, Q., & Megalooikonomou, V. (2010). A performance evaluation framework for association mining in spatial data. *Journal of Intelligent Information Systems, 35*(3), 465–494. doi:10.1007/s10844-009-0115-6 PMID:21170170

Wang, W., Ren, G., & Wang, W. (2010). The Applications of Rough Set Theory in Civil Engineering.*Proceedings of International Conference on Artificial Intelligence and Computational Intelligence.* doi:10.1007/978-3-642-16527-6

Wang, X. Y., & Sun, Y. F. (2010). A color- and texture-based image segmentation algorithm. *Machine Graphics and Vision, 19*(1), 3–18.

Wasserman, P. D. (1993). *Advanced methods in Neural Computing* (pp. 155–161).

Waters, R. S., & Swartzlander, E. E. (2010). A reduced complexity Wallace multiplier reduction. *IEEE Transactions on Computers, 59*(8), 1134–1137. doi:10.1109/TC.2010.103

WebSource. (2000). Retrieved from http://www.math.tau.ac.il/~turkel/images.html

Wegmann, S., McAllaster, D., Orloff, J., & Peskin, B. (1996). Speaker Normalization on Conversational Telephone Speech. *Proceedings of 1996 IEEE International Conference on Acoustics, Speech and Signal Processing, (ICASSP),* Atlanta, GA (Vol. 1, pp 339-341). doi:10.1109/ICASSP.1996.541101

Weiser, M. (1999). The computer for the 21st century. *Mobile Computing and Communications Review, 3*(3), 3–11. doi:10.1145/329124.329126

Weiss Ron, J., & Ellis Daniel, P. W. (2006). Estimating Single-Channel Source Separation Masks: Relevance Vector Machine Classifiers vs. Pitch-Based Masking. In *ISCA Tutorial and Research Workshop on Statistical and Perceptual Audition: SAPA2006*. Pittsburgh, PA: International Speech Communication Association.

Weiss, G. (2009). Data Mining in the Telecommunications Industry. In J. Wang (Ed.), *Encyclopedia of Data Warehousing and Mining* (2nd ed., pp. 486–491). Hershey, PA: Information Science Reference. doi:10.4018/978-1-60566-010-3.ch076

Wei-Ying, M., & Manjunath, B. S. (1999). Netra: A toolbox for navigating large image databases. *Multimedia Systems*, *7*(3), 184–198. doi:10.1007/s005300050121

Wells, W. M. III, Viola, P., Atsumi, H., Nakajima, S., & Kikinis, R. (1996). Multi-modal volume registration by maximization of mutual information. *Medical Image Analysis*, *1*(1), 35–51. doi:10.1016/S1361-8415(01)80004-9 PMID:9873920

Welsh, E. T., Wanberg, C. R., Brown, K. G., & Simmering, M. J. (2003). E-learning: Emerging uses, empirical results and future directions. *International Journal of Training and Development*, *7*(4), 245–258. doi:10.1046/j.1360-3736.2003.00184.x

Wendy, K., & Kurt, W. (2013). *What Can Students Learn from Virtual Labs?* ACS CHED CCCE Newsletter.

West, J., Fitzpatrick, J. M., Wang, M. Y., Dawant, B. M., Maurer, C. R. Jr, Kessler, R. M., & Woods, R. P. et al. (1997). Comparison and evaluation of retrospective intermodality brain image registration techniques. *Journal of Computer Assisted Tomography*, *21*(4), 554–566. doi:10.1097/00004728-199707000-00007 PMID:9216759

White, R. J. (2001). *Gene Transcription: Mechanisms and Control*. Wiley-Blackwell.

White, D. R., & Poulding, S. (2009). A Rigorous Evaluation of Crossover and Mutation in Genetic Programming. *Proceedings of the 12th European Conference on Genetic Programming*EuroGP '09 (pp. 220-231). Berlin, Heidelberg: Springer-Verlag.

Whitley, D. (1994, June). A genetic algorithm tutorial. *Statistics and Computing, 4*(2), 65-85. doi:10.1007/BF00175354

Widjaja, I. (2012). Towards a flexible resource management system for content centric networking.*Proceedings of IEEE International Conference on Communications* (pp. 2634-2638). IEEE.

Widodo, A., Kim, E.Y., Son, J.-D., Yang, B.-S., Tan, A.C.C., Gu, D.-S., . . . Mathew, J. (2009). Fault diagnosis of low speed bearing based on relevance vector machine and support vector machine. *Expert Systems with Applications*, *36*(3), 7252–7261. doi:10.1016/j.eswa.2008.09.033

Willett, D., & Rigoll, G. (1998). Hybrid NN/HMM-based speech recognition with a discriminant neural feature extraction. *Advances in Neural Information Processing Systems*, 763–772.

Williams, J., Weiqiang, L., & Mehmet, O. (2002). An Overview of Temporal Data Mining. In S.J. Simoff, G.J. Williams, M. Hegland (Eds.), *Proceedings of the 1st Australian Data Mining Workshop* (ADM02) Canberra, Australia (pp. 83-90). University of Technology, Sydney.

Willis, R., Serenko, A., & Turel, O. (2009). Contractual Obligations between Mobile Service Providers and Users. In D. Taniar (Ed.), *Mobile Computing: Concepts, Methodologies, Tools, and Applications* (pp. 1929–1936). Hershey, PA: Information Science Reference; doi:10.4018/978-1-60566-054-7.ch155

Winberg, T. M., & Berg, C. A. R. (2007). Students' cognitive focus during a chemistry laboratory exercise: Effects of a computer-simulated prelab. *Journal of Research in Science Teaching*, *44*(8), 1108–1133. doi:10.1002/tea.20217

Winter, M. (2007). *Goguen categories: a categorical approach to L-fuzzy relations*. Springer Publishing Company, Incorporated.

Wolfram, S. (1986). Cryptography with Cellular Automata. *Springer, Advances in Cryptology: Crypto '85 Proceedings. LNCS, 218*, 429–432.

Wolfram, S. (2002). *A new kind of science*. Champaign, IL: Wolfram Media Inc.

Wolf, T. (2010). Assessing Student Learning in a Virtual Laboratory Environment. *IEEE Transactions on Education, 53*(2), 216–222. doi:10.1109/TE.2008.2012114

Wong, K. C., Leung, K. S., & Wong, M. H. (2010). Effect of Spatial Locality on an Evolutionary Algorithm for Multi-modal Optimization. *EvoApplications, Part I, LNCS 6024.* Springer-Verlag.

Wong, K. C., Peng, C., Wong, M. H., & Leung, K. S. (2011, August). Generalizing and learning protein-DNA binding sequence representations by an evolutionary algorithm. *Soft Comput., 15*(8), 1631-1642. Doi:10.1007/s00500-011-0692-5

Wong, W., & Nikander, P. (2010). Secure naming in information-centric networks. *Proceedings of the Re-architecting the Internet Workshop,* Philadelphia, Pennsylvania (pp. 12:1-12:6).

Wong, K. C., Chan, T. M., Peng, C., Li, Y., & Zhang, Z. (2013, September). DNA motif elucidation using belief propagation. *Nucleic Acids Research, 41*(16), e153. doi:10.1093/nar/gkt574 PMID:23814189

Wong, K. C., Leung, K. S., & Wong, M. H. (2009). An evolutionary algorithm with species-specific explosion for multimodal optimization.*Proceedings of the 11th Annual conference on Genetic and evolutionary computationGECCO '09* (pp. 923-930). New York, NY, USA: ACM. doi:10.1145/1569901.1570027

Wong, K. C., Leung, K. S., & Wong, M. H. (2010). Protein Structure Prediction on a Lattice Model via Multimodal Optimization Techniques.*Proceedings of the 12th annual conference on Genetic and evolutionary computation* (pp. 155-162). Portland: ACM. doi:10.1145/1830483.1830513

Wong, K. C., Li, Y., Peng, C., & Zhang, Z. (2015). SignalSpider: Probabilistic pattern discovery on multiple normalized ChIP-Seq signal profiles. *Bioinformatics (Oxford, England), 31*(1), 17–24. doi:10.1093/bioinformatics/btu604 PMID:25192742

Wong, K. C., Peng, C., Li, Y., & Chan, T. M. (2014, December). Herd Clustering: A synergistic data clustering approach using collective intelligence. *Applied Soft Computing, 23*, 61–75. doi:10.1016/j.asoc.2014.05.034

Wong, K. C., Wu, C. H., Mok, R., Peng, C., & Zhang, Z. (2012). Evolutionary multimodal optimization using the principle of locality. *Information Sciences, 194*, 138–170. doi:10.1016/j.ins.2011.12.016

Wong, K. C., & Zhang, Z. (2014). SNPdryad: Predicting deleterious non-synonymous human SNPs using only orthologous protein sequences. *Bioinformatics (Oxford, England), 30*(8), 1112–1119. doi:10.1093/bioinformatics/btt769 PMID:24389653

Woods, R., Mazziotta, J., & Cherry, S. R. (1993). MRI-PET registration with automate algorithm. *Journal of Computer Assisted Tomography, 17*(4), 536–546. doi:10.1097/00004728-199307000-00004 PMID:8331222

World Health Organization. (2008). *Implementing the WHO stop TB strategy: A handbook for national TB control programs*. World Health Organization Press.

World Health Organization. (2015). *Fact Sheet Tuberculosis*. Retrieved from http://www.who.int/mediacentre/factsheets/fs104/en/

World Health Organization. (2015). *Global tuberculosis report 2014*. Retrieved from http://www.who.int/tb/publications/global_report/en/

Wu, S. X., & Banzhaf, W. (2010). The use of computational intelligence in intrusion detection systems: A review. *Journal of Applied Soft Computing, 10*(1), 1–35. doi:10.1016/j.asoc.2009.06.019

Wyatt, T. R., Arduino, P., & Macari, E. J. (2000). Assessment of a virtual laboratory for geotechnical engineering education. *Comput. Educ. J., 10*(2), 27–35.

Xia, M., & Liu, B. (2004). Image registration by super-curves. *IEEE Transactions on Image Processing, 13*(4), 720–732. doi:10.1109/TIP.2003.822611 PMID:15376603

Xiao, L., Shao, Z., & Liu, G. (2006). K-means algorithm based on particle swarm optimization algorithm for anomaly intrusion detection.*Proceedings of the Sixth World Congress on Intelligent Control and Automation,*Dalian, China (pp. 5854-5858). doi:10.1109/WCICA.2006.1714200

Xie, L., Ying, Y., & Ying, T. (2009). Classification of tomatoes with different genotypes by visible and short-wave near-infrared spectroscopy with least-squares support vector machines and other chemometrics. *Journal of Food Engineering, 94*(1), 34–39. doi:10.1016/j.jfoodeng.2009.02.023

Xie, M., Widjaja, I., & Wang, H. (2012). Enhancing cache robustness for content-centric networking.*Proceedings of INFOCOM*, Orlando, FL (pp. 2426-2434).

Xilinx. (2011). Spartan 3E Starter kit board data sheet. Retrieved from http://www.xilinx.com/support/documentation/boards_and_kits/ug230.pdf

Xing-yuan, W., Zhi-feng, C., & Jiao-jiao, Y. (2012). An effective method for color image retrieval based on texture. *Computer Standards & Interfaces, 34*(1), 31–35. doi:10.1016/j.csi.2011.05.001

Xi, Y., Feng, D. D., Wang, T., Zhao, R., & Zhang, Y. (2007). Image segmentation by clustering of spatial patterns. *Pattern Recognition Letters, 28*(12), 1548–1555. doi:10.1016/j.patrec.2007.03.012

Xu, B., & Lin, S. (2002). Automatic color identification in printed fabric images by a fuzzy-neural network. *AATICC Rev, 2*(9), 42–45.

Xue, Z., Ming, D., Song, W., Wan, B., & Jin, S. (2010). Infrared gait recognition based on wavelet transform and support vector machine. *Pattern Recognition, 43*(8), 2904–2910. doi:10.1016/j.patcog.2010.03.011

Xu, L. (2009). Strawberry Maturity Neural Network Detecting System Based on Genetic Algorithm. *Computer and Computing Technologies in Agriculture II, 2*, 1201–1208.

Xu, L., & Zheng, Y. (2007). Spectral and Temporal Cues for Phoneme Recognition in Noise. *The Journal of the Acoustical Society of America, 122*(3), 1758–1764. doi:10.1121/1.2767000 PMID:17927435

Xu, T., Cheng, I., Long, R., & Mandal, M. (2013). Novel coarse-to-fine dual scale technique for tuberculosis lesion detection in chest radiographs. *EURASIP Journal on Image and Video Processing, 2013*(3), 1–18.

Yadav, K. S., & Mukhedkar, M. M. (2013). Review on Speech Recognition. *International Journal of Science and Engineering, 1*(2), 61–70.

YaleB Face Database. (2010, June). Retrieved from http://cvc.yale.edu/projects/yalefacesB/yalefacesB.html

Yang, J., & Xu, Y. (1994). Hidden markov model for gesture recognition: *Tech. Report CMU-RI-TR-94-10*.

Yan, G., Zhou, T., Wang, J., Fu, Z., & Wang, B. (2005). Epidemic Spread in Weighted Scale-Free Networks. *Chinese Physics Letters, 22*(2), 510–513. doi:10.1088/0256-307X/22/2/068

Yang, C. C., Yen, J., & Chen, H. (2000). Intelligent internet searching agent based on hybrid simulated annealing. *Decision Support Systems*, *28*(3), 269–277. doi:10.1016/S0167-9236(99)00091-3

Yang, J. F., Hao, S. S., & Chung, P. C. (2002). Color image segmentation using fuzzy C-means and eigenspace projections. *Signal Processing*, *82*(3), 461–472. doi:10.1016/S0165-1684(01)00196-7

Yang, Y., Zheng, C., & Lin, P. (2004). Image thresholding based on spatially weighted fuzzy C-means clustering. *Proceedings of the 4th International Conference on Computer and Information Technology* (CIT04) (pp. 184-189). doi:10.1109/CIT.2004.1357194

Yang, Y., Zheng, Ch., & Lin, P. (2005). Fuzzy C-means clustering algorithm with novel penalty term for image segmentation. *Opto-Electronics Review*, *13*(4), 309–315.

Yao, K., Mignotte, M., Collet, C., Galerne, P., & Burel, G. (2000). Unsupervised segmentation using a self-organizing map and a noise model estimation in sonar imagery. *Pattern Recognition*, *33*(9), 1575–1584. doi:10.1016/S0031-3203(99)00135-1

Yao, X. (1999). Evolving artificial neural networks. *Proceedings of the IEEE*, *87*(9), 1423–1447. doi:10.1109/5.784219

Yarbrough, S. E., & Gilbert, R. B. (1999). Development, implementation, and preliminary assessment of virtual laboratory. *Journal of Professional Issues in Engineering Education and Practice*, *125*(4), 147–151. doi:10.1061/(ASCE)1052-3928(1999)125:4(147)

Yasein, M. S., & Agathoklis, P. (2008) A feature-based image registration technique for images of different scale. Paper presented at IEEE international symposium on circuits and systems (ISCAS'08), Seattle, WA (pp. 3558–3561). doi:10.1109/ISCAS.2008.4542228

Yildrim, B., & Gunaydin, O. (2011). Estimation of CBR by Soft Computing Systems. *Expert Systems with Applications* (Vol. *38*, 6381–6391). Elsevier. doi:10.1016/j.eswa.2010.12.054

Yin H., Chai, Y., Yang, S. X., and Mitta, G. S. (2009). Ripe tomato extraction for a harvesting robotic system. In *Systems, Man and Cybernetics* (pp. 2984-2989). IEEE.

Yoshida, H., & Doi, K. (2000). Computerized detection of pulmonary nodules in chest radiographs: reduction of false positives based on symmetry between left and right lungs.*Proceedings of SPIE Medical Imaging* (Vol. 3979). doi:10.1117/12.387732

Youd, T. L., & Idriss, I.M. (1997a). Magnitude scaling factors. *Proceedings ofNCEER Workshop on Evaluation of Liquefaction Resistance of Soils* (pp. 149–165) Buffalo: National Center for Earthquake Engineering Research.

Young, E. D. (2008). Neural Representation of Spectral and temporal Information in Speech. *Philosophical Transactions of the Royal Society of London. Series B, Biological Sciences*, *363*(1493), 923–945. doi:10.1098/rstb.2007.2151 PMID:17827107

Yuangui, L., Chen, L., & Weidong, Z. (2006). Improved sparse least-squares support vector machine classifiers. *Neurocomputing*, *69*(13–15), 1655–1658.

Yuk, D., & Flanagan, J. (1999). Telephone Speech Recognition Using Neural Networks and Hidden Markov Models. *Proceedings of the 1999 IEEE International Conference on Acoustics, Speech and Signal Processing*, Phoenix, AZ (*Vol. 1*, pp. 157-160). IEEE Press.

Zadeh, L. (1965). Fuzzy Sets. Information and Control, 8(3), 338–353. doi:10.1016/S0019-9958(65)90241-X

Zadeh, L. A. (1981). Possibility Theory and Soft Data Analysis. In Cobb and R. Thrall (Eds), Mathematical Frontiers of Social and Policy Sciences (pp. 69-129). Boulder, CO, USA: Westview Press.

Zadeh, L. A. (1973). Outline of a New Approach to the Analysis of Complex Systems and Decision Process. *IEEE Transactions on Systems, Man, and Cybernetics, 3*(1), 28–44. doi:10.1109/TSMC.1973.5408575

Zafeiropoulos, A., Liakopoulos, A., Davy, A., & Chaparadza, R. (2010). *Monitoring within an autonomic network: a GANA based network monitoring framework.* Paper presented at the Service-Oriented Computing. ICSOC/ServiceWave 2009 Workshops. doi:10.1007/978-3-642-16132-2_29

Zaitoun, H. (2005). *New Vision in Electronic Learning.* Riyadh: Aldar Al-Soltiah.

Zalik, K. R. (2008). An efficient k-means clustering algorithm. *Pattern Recognition Letters, 29*(9), 1385–1391. doi:10.1016/j.patrec.2008.02.014

Zhang, H., Berg, A.C., Maire, M., Malik, J. (2006). Discriminative Nearest Neighbor Classification for Visual Category Recognition. *IEEE-CVPR* (Vol.2, pp. 2126-2136).

Zhang, H.F.X., Heller, K.A., Hefter, I., Leslie, C.S., & Chasin, L.A. (2003). Sequence Information for the Splicing of Human Pre-mRNA Identified by Support Vector Machine Classification. *Genome Research, 13*(12), 2637–2650. doi:10.1101/gr.1679003 PMID:14656968

ZhangD, . (2003). Question classification using support vector machines.*Proceedings of the 26th Annual International ACM SIGIR conference on Research and development in informaion retrieval*, New York, USA (pp. 26-32).

Zhang, D., Guo, B., Li, B., & Yu, Z. (2010). Extracting social and community intelligence from digital footprints: an emerging research area. In *Ubiquitous Intelligence and Computing* (pp. 4–18). Springer. doi:10.1007/978-3-642-16355-5_4

Zhang, H., Fritts, J. E., & Goldman, S. A. (2004). An entropy-based objective evaluation method for image segmentation. *Proceedings of SPIE Storage and Retrieval Methods and Applications for Multimedia*, 38-49.

Zhang, N., Wang, M., & Wang, N. (2002). Precision agriculture worldwide - an overview. *Journal of Computers and Electronics in Agriculture, 36*(2-3), 113–132. doi:10.1016/S0168-1699(02)00096-0

Zhang, Y. (1996). A survey on evaluation methods for image segmentation. *Pattern Recognition, 29*(8), 1335–1346. doi:10.1016/0031-3203(95)00169-7

Zhao, H., Lo, S.-C. B., Freedman, M. T., & Seong Ki Mun, S. K. M. (2001). On automatic temporal subtraction of chest radiographs and its enhancement for lung cancers.*Proceedings of SPIE Medical Imaging* (Vol. 4322, pp. 1867–1872). doi:10.1117/12.431078

Zhao, M. S., Fu, A. M. N., & Yan, H. (2001). A technique of three level thresholding based on probability partition and fuzzy 3-partition. *IEEE Transactions on Fuzzy Systems, 9*(3), 469–479. doi:10.1109/91.928743

Zhao, S. Y., & Morgan, N. (2008). *Multi-stream Spectro-Temporal features for Robust Speech Recognition* (pp. 898–901). INTERSPEECH.

Zhao, W., Chellappa, R., Phillips, P. J., & Rosenfeld, A. (2003). Face Recognition: A Literature Survey. *Association for Computing Machinery Computing Surveys, 35*(4), 390–458.

Zhao, X., Liu, Y., Wang, D., Li, D., & Wang, J. (2014). Multiple kernel-based multi-instance learning algorithm for image classification. *Visual Communication & Image Retrieval, 25*(5), 1112–1117. doi:10.1016/j.jvcir.2014.03.011

Zheng, L., Zhang, J., Wang, Q. (2009). Mean-shift-based color segmentation of images containing green vegetation. *Journal of computers and electronics in agriculture*, 65(1), 93-98.

Zhenkui, P., Xia, H., & Jinfeng, H. (2008). The clustering algorithm based on particle swarm optimization algorithm. *Proceedings of the International Conference on Intelligent Computation Technology and Automation* (pp. 148-151). IEEE Computer Society, Washington, DC, USA.

Zhiming, D., Qi, Y., & Hong, W. (2011). *Massive Heterogeneous Sensor Data Management in the Internet of Things*. Paper presented at the 2011 International Conference on Internet of Things and 4th International Conference on Cyber, Physical and Social Computing (iThings/CPSCom).

Zhou, J., Cunha, A. L., & Do, M. N. (2005), Nonsubsampled contourlet transform: construction and application in enhancement. Proceedings of the *IEEE International Conference on Image Processing (ICIP '05)*, Genova, Italy (Vol. 1, pp. 469–472).

Zhou, Q., & Liu, J. S. (2008, July). Extracting sequence features to predict protein-DNA interactions: a comparative study. *Nucl. Acids Res., 36*(12), 4137-4148. doi:10.1093/nar/gkn361

Zhou, X. S., & Huang, T. S. (2000). CBIR: from low-level features to high level semantics, *Proceedings of the SPIE, Image and Video Communication and Processing* (Vol. 3974, pp. 426-431).

Zhuo, L., Cheng, B., & Zhang, J. (2014). A comparative study of dimensionality reduction methods for large-scale image retrieval. *Neurocomputing, 141*, 202–210. doi:10.1016/j.neucom.2014.03.014

Zimmermann, H. J. (2001). *Fuzzy Set Theory and Its Applications*. Springer.

Zimmermann, R., & Fichtner, W. (1997). Low-power logic styles: CMOS versus pass-transistor logic. *IEEE Journal of Solid-State Circuits, 32*(7), 1079–1090. doi:10.1109/4.597298

Zingaretti, P., Tascini, G., & Regini, L. (2002). Optimising the colour image segmentation.*Proceedings of VIII Convegno dell Associazione Italiana per Intelligenza Artificiale.*

Zissman, M. A. (1996). Comparison of Four Approaches to Automatic Language Identification of Telephone Speech. *IEEE Transactions on Speech and Audio Processing, 4*(1), 31–44. doi:10.1109/TSA.1996.481450

Zissman, M. A., & Singer, E. (1994). Automatic Language Identification of Telephone Speech Message Using Phoneme Recognition and N-Gram Modeling.*Proceedings of the 1994 IEEE International Conference on Acoustics, Speech and Signal Processing,*Adelaide, SA (Vol. 1, pp. 305-308). doi:10.1109/ICASSP.1994.389377

Zitova, B., & Flusser, J. (2003). Image registration methods: A survey. *Image and Vision Computing, 21*(11), 977–1000. doi:10.1016/S0262-8856(03)00137-9

Zitzler, E., & Thiele, L. (1998). An evolutionary algorithm for multiobjective optimization: The strength pareto approach. *Tech. Rep. 43, Gloriastrasse 35, CH-8092 Zurich, Switzerland.*

Zitzler, E., Laumanns, M., & Thiele, L. (2001). *SPEA2: Improving the Strength Pareto Evolutionary Algorithm* (Tech. Rep. 103). Zurich, Switzerland.

Zou, X., Kittler, J., & Messer, K. (2007). Illumination invariant face recognition: A Survey.*Proceedings of First IEEE International Conference on Biometrics: Theory, Applications, and Systems* (pp. 1–8).

Zuo, G., Liu, W., & Ruan, X. (2003). Telephone Speech Recognition Using Simulated Data from Clean Database.*Proceedings of the 2003 IEEE International Conference on Robotics, Intelligent Systems and Signal Processing* (Vol. 1, pp. 49-53). Changsha, China. doi:10.1109/RISSP.2003.1285547

About the Contributors

Siddhartha Bhattacharyya did his Bachelors in Physics, Bachelors in Optics and Optoelectronics and Masters in Optics and Optoelectronics from University of Calcutta, India in 1995, 1998 and 2000 respectively. He completed PhD in Computer Science and Engineering from Jadavpur University, India in 2008. He is the recipient of the University Gold Medalfrom the University of Calcutta for his Masters. He is currently an Associate Professor and Head of Information Technology of RCC Institute of Information Technology, Kolkata, India. In addition, he is serving as the Dean of Research and Development of the institute from November 2013. Prior to this, he was an Assistant Professor in Computer Science and Information Technology of University Institute of Technology, The University of Burdwan, India from 2005-2011. He was a Lecturer in Information Technology of Kalyani Government Engineering College, India during 2001-2005. He is a co-author of a book for undergraduate engineering students of West Bengal University of Technology, Kolkata, India and about 130 research publications in international journals and conference proceedings. He has got a patent titled Low Cost Intelligent Colorimeter Using Color LEDs filed; Patent No. 886/KOL/2015. He was the convener of the AICTE-IEEE National Conference on Computing and Communication Systems (CoCoSys-09) in 2009. He is the co-editor of the Handbook of Research on Computational Intelligence for Engineering, Science and Business; Publisher: IGI Global, Hershey, USA. He is the co-author of the book titled Soft Computing for Image and Multimedia Data Processing; Publisher: Springer-Verlag, Germany. He is the co-editor of the Handbook of Research on Swarm Intelligence in Engineering; Publisher: IGI Global, Hershey, USA. He is the co-author of the book titled Hybrid Soft Computing Approaches: Research and Applications; Publisher: Springer India Ltd. He is the co-author of the book titled Multimedia Programming: A Practical Approach; Publisher: Vikas Publishers Pvt. Ltd. He was the member of the Young Researchers' Committee of the WSC 2008 Online World Conference on Soft Computing in Industrial Applications. He has been the member of the organizing and technical program committees of several national and international conferences. He served as the Editor-In-Chief of International Journal of Ambient Computing and Intelligence (IJACI) published by IGI Global, Hershey, PA, USA from 17th July 2014 to 06th November 2014. He was the General Chair of the IEEE International Conference on Computational Intelligence and Communication Networks (ICCICN 2014) organized by the Department of Information Technology, RCC Institute of Information Technology, Kolkata in association with Machine Intelligence Research Labs, Gwalior and IEEE Young Professionals, Kolkata Section and held at Kolkata, India in 2014. He is the Associate Editor of International Journal of Pattern Recognition Research. He is the member of the editorial board of International Journal of Engineering, Science and Technology and ACCENTS Transactions on Information Security (ATIS). He is also the member of the editorial advisory board of HETC Journal of Computer Engineering and Applications. He is the Associate Editor of the International Journal of Bio-

Info Soft Computing since 2013. He is the Lead Guest Editor of the Special Issue on Hybrid Intelligent Techniques for Image Analysis and Understanding of Applied Soft Computing, Elsevier, B. V. He is the General Chair of the 2015 IEEE International Conference on Research in Computational Intelligence and Communication Networks (ICRCICN 2015) to be organized by the Department of Information Technology, RCC Institute of Information Technology, Kolkata in association with IEEE Young Professionals Affinity Group, Kolkata Section at Kolkata, India in 2015. His research interests include soft computing, pattern recognition, multimedia data processing, hybrid intelligence and quantum computing. Dr. Bhattacharyya is a senior member of Institute of Electrical and Electronics Engineers (IEEE), USA and Association for Computing Machinery (ACM), USA. He is a member of International Rough Set Society and International Association for Engineers (IAENG), Hong Kong. He is a life member of Computer Society of India, Optical Society of India and Indian Society for Technical Education.

Pinaki Banerjee did his diploma in Mechanical Engineering for Govt. Polytechnic, Dhanbad, Bihar, India, in the year 1986. He subsequently completed section A of AMIE in the year 1995. He is presently associated with M/s. Goldstone Infratech Limited, Hyderabad, India, as a Manager in the Rubber Compounding and Rubber Injection Moulding sections since 2005. He was associated with M/s. Polymers (India) Limited, Ahmedabad, Gujarat, India, as an Assistant Manager in the Maintenance Department from 2003 to 2005. Prior to this, he was associated with M/s. Swastik Polyvinyls Limited, New Delhi, India, as an Assistant Manager in the Maintenance Department from 2001 to 2003. He was associated with M/s. Incab Industries Limited, Jamshedpur, India as a Superintendent of the XLPE Plant from 1987 to 2001. His research interests include hybrid intelligence and optimization processes of compounding of rubber compounds.

Dipankar Majumdar did his Bachelors in Electrical Engineering from NIT Silchar, Assam, India and Masters in Computer Technology from Jadavpur University, Kolkata, India in 1999, 2006 respectively. He completed PhD in Computer Science and Engineering from Jadavpur University, India in 2011. He is currently an Associate Professor in Information Technology of RCC Institute of Information Technology, Kolkata, India. Prior to this, he was an Assistant Professor in Information Technology B.P. Poddar Institute of Management and Technology, India from 2003-2010. He is a co-author of about 15 research publications. His research interests include Soft Computing, Quantum Computing and Software Engineering.

Paramartha Dutta did his Bachelors and Masters in Statistics from the Indian Statistical Institute, Calcutta in the years 1988 and 1990 respectively. He afterwards completed his Master of Technology in Computer science from the same Institute in the year 1993 and Doctor of Philosophy in Engineering from the Bengal Engineering and Science University, Shibpur in 2005 respectively. He has served in the capacity of research personnel in various projects funded by Govt. of India, which include Defence Research and Development Organization, Council of Scientific and Industrial Research, Indian Statistical Institute, Calcutta etc. Dr. Dutta is now a Professor in the Department of Computer and System Sciences of the Visva Bharati University, West Bengal, India. Prior to this, he served Kalyani Government Engineering College and College of Engineering and Management, Kolaghat, both in West Bengal as full time faculty members. Apart from this, he has remained associated to The National Institute of Management, Calcutta, Department of Statistics of The University of Calcutta, Department of Computer Science and Technology of The Bengal Engineering and Science University, Shibpur, Department of Computer

Science and Engineering of the University of Kalyani, West Bengal, India, as well as Department of Computer Science and Engineering of The University of Tripura, India either as a Guest Faculty member from time to time. Dr. Dutta has been involved as the principal investigator funded by the All India Council for Technical Education, Govt. of India and Department of Science and Technology, Govt. of India. He has coauthored six books and has also four edited book to his credit. He has published about 160 papers in various journals and conference proceedings, both international and national. Presently, he is supervising four students for their Ph. D programme registered with Visva Bharati University and West Bengal University of Technology, apart from three who have earned their Ph. D already. Dr. Dutta is a Life Fellow of the Optical Society of India (OSI), Life Member of Institution of Electronics and Telecommunication Engineers (OSI), Computer Society of India (CSI), Indian Science Congress Association (ISCA), Indian Society for Technical Education (ISTE), Indian Unit of Pattern Recognition and Artificial Intelligence (IUPRAI) - the Indian affiliate of the International Association for Pattern Recognition (IAPR), Member of Associated Computing Machinery (ACM), IEEE, Computer Society, USA.

***

João Sousa Andrade has a MSc in Communication Network Engineering. Researcher and Entrepreneur.

Petre Anghelescu received a B.E. degree in applied electronics from the University of Pitesti, Romania, in 2002, a M. Tech. in intelligent communication systems and Ph.D. degrees in electrical engineering and telecommunication from the University of Pitesti, Romania, in 2004 and 2008, respectively. In 2002, he joined the Department of Electronics, Communication and Computers at University of Pitesti, as an Assistant, then PhD. Lecturer, and in 2013 became an Associate Professor. His current research interests focus on complex systems and methods of computational and artificial intelligence, mainly on bio-inspired systems – cellular automata & genetic algorithms, self-adaptation and self-organizational systems and reconfigurable computing.

V.N. Manjunath Aradhya received M.S. and Ph.D degrees in Computer Science from the University of Mysore, in 2004 and 2007, respectively. He did his Post Doctoral degree at the University of Genova, Italy in 2010. He is currently working as an Associate Professor in Dept. of MCA, Sri Jayachamarajendra College of Engineering, Mysore. He is a recipient of the "Young Indian Research Scientist" from Italian Ministry of Education, Italy for 2009-2010. He successfully completed two major research projects, one from DST and another from AICTE. His professional recognition includes as a Technical Editor for the Journal of Convergence Information Technology (JCIT), part of the Editor Board of the Journal of Intelligent Systems, reviewer for IEEE Trans. on System, Man and Cybernetics - PART B, the IEEE Trans on Cybernetics, the International Journal of Pattern Recognition (PR), the International Journal of Pattern Recognition Letters (PRL), etc. He also worked as an Evaluation Expert for UGC-NET, New Delhi. He also owns a credit in organizing the prestigious ICACCI 2013 at SJCE, Mysore during Aug 22-25, 2013. He successfully completed one Ph.D and guiding 3 Ph.D's working in different areas of IP and PR. He has published around 80+ research papers in reputed international journals, conference proceedings, and edited books.

Artur Arsenio is YDreams Robotics CEO, an innovative company aiming at turning things into robots. He is also an Invited Professor in Computer Science at the Universidade da Beira Interior. Previously, he headed Innovation at Nokia Siemens Networks, Portugal SA. He also worked as a Senior Solution Architect leading several international R&D teams for Siemens, and as Chief Engineer representing Siemens Networks on IPTV Standardization forums. Artur Arsenio received his doctoral degree in Computer Science from the Massachusetts Institute of Technology (MIT) in 2004. He is the inventor of 6 international patent families, and authored/co-authored more than 100 peer-reviewed scientific publications. He is the recipient of several scientific and innovation awards. He is co-founder and vice-chair of the ACM SIGCOMM Portugal chapter, a Fulbrighter, and President of the MIT alumni association in Portugal.

Abhijit R. Asati completed his B.E. degree (1996) in electrical engineering at Amravati University, Amravati, India; subsequently he completed a M.E. degree (2001) and a Ph. D. degree (2010) in microelectronics at BITS, Pilani, India. He served for more than 16 years as a faculty member at the VNIT, Nagpur, India and BITS Pilani India. His research interest are high performance VLSI data path designs, microprocessor design, micro-coded controller design and NBTI degradation issues in VLSI circuits. He has published more than 40 research papers in the area of microelectronics and VLSI design and is actively involved in research.

Monika Bajaj completed her PhD in 2014 in the Computer Science Department at the University of Delhi. Her research interests include Web engineering, Human Computer Interfaces and E - commerce. She has 10 publications to her credit.

Hema Banati is currently an Associate professor in the Department of Computer Science at Dyal Singh College, University of Delhi, India. She holds a Ph.D in Computer Science and a Masters in Computer Applications both from University of Delhi, India. Currently, she is actively involved in her research work with her doctorate students, many of whom have successfully achieved their doctorate degrees. She has many national and international publications to her credit and is involved in the review process of various national and international journals. Her research interests include Human-Computer Interaction, Multiagent systems, E-learning, E-commerce, and social networks. At present, her work domain focuses on exploring the applicability of nature-inspired solutions to various academic domains.

Debotosh Bhattacharjee received the MCSE and Ph. D. (Eng.) degrees from Jadavpur University, India, in 1997 and 2004, respectively. He was associated with several different institutes in various capacities until March 2007. After that, he joined his Alma Mater, Jadavpur University. His research interests pertain to the applications of computational intelligence techniques like Fuzzy logic, Artificial Neural Network, Genetic Algorithm, Rough Set Theory etc. in Face Recognition, Medical Imaging, and Information Security. He is a life member of the Indian Society for Technical Education (ISTE, New Delhi), Indian Unit for Pattern Recognition and Artificial Intelligence (IUPRAI), and a senior member of IEEE (USA).

Susanta Chakraborty received a Bachelors (B. Tech) and Masters (M.Tech) degrees in Technology from the University of Calcutta in 1983 and 1985, respectively, and a Ph.D(Tech) degree in computer science in 1999 from the University of Calcutta and Research work done at the Advance computing and Microelectronic Unit, Indian Statistical Institute, Kolkata. He is currently a Professor in the department of Computer Science and Technology at the Bengal Engineering Science and University, West Bengal, India. Prior to this, he has served the University of Kalyani as Dean of Engineering, Technology and Management faculty. He has published around 31 research papers, appeared in very reputed International Journals including IEEE Transactions on CAD and refereed international conference proceedings of the IEEE Computer Science Press. Dr. Chakraborty was awarded the INSA-JSPS Fellowship of Indian National Science Academy (INSA) in the session 2003-2004 and collaborated with Professor H. Fujiwara of the Nara Institute of Science and Technology, Japan, in the area of Test Generation of Sequential Circuits and Low Power Design. He has been invited to the Institute of Information Technology, University of Potsdam, Germany with a German Gov. Fellowship, to do research work as a guest scientist with Prof. M. Gossel in the area of VLSI testing and fault diagnosis from September 2000. He has been also invited by the University of Michigan, Advanced Computer Architecture Lab, dept. of Electrical Engineering and Computer Science and works have been done in collaboration with Professor John P. Hays, Shannon Professor of Engineering Science in the area of Quantum circuit and Testable Design of Nano-Circuit in the year 2007. He was also invited to Nara Institute of Science and Technology Nara, Japan to deliver a Lecture on Quantum Circuits in 2013. The 25 years research experience of Dr. Chakraborty has been primarily focused on Logic Synthesis and Testing of VLSI Circuits, DFT, BIST design Test-Pattern Generation, Fault-Tolerant Computing, Image Processing, Fault Diagnosis, Low Power Design and Synthesis and Testing of Quantum Circuit and Micro Fluidic Bio-chips. He has served as: Publicity Co-Chair, at the 18th International Conference on VLSI Design in January 2005 and the Fifteenth Asian test Symposium, India, in December 2005; Publicity Chair & Program Committee member of the 1st and 2nd IEEE International workshops on Reliability Aware system Design and Test (RASDAT), India, January, 2010 and 2011; Advisory Committee member of International Conference on computing and systems, November 19 – 20, 2010, 2011, 2012 and 2013; Publication Chair, IEEE WRTLT-2011 International workshop; Publicity Chair & Program Committee member of 3rd IEEE International workshop on Reliability Aware system Design and Test (RASDAT), India, January 2013.

Sourav De did his Bachelors in Information Technology at the University of Burdwan, Burdwan, India in 2002. He did his Masters in Information Technology from West Bengal University of Technology, Kolkata, India in 2005. He is an Associate Professor in the Department of Computer Science and Information Technology at the University Institute of Technology, University of Burdwan, Burdwan, India since 2006. He served as a Junior Programmer at Apices Consultancy Private Limited, Kolkata, India in 2005. He has several research publications. His research interests include: soft computing, pattern recognition and image processing. Mr. De is a member of IEEE, ACM, IAENG Hong Kong. He is a life member of ISTE, India.

Sandip Dey completed his Bachelors in Mathematics in 1999. He completed B-level from DOEACC society and M.Tech in Software Engineering from West Bengal University of Technology in 2005 and 2008, respectively. Currently, he is pursuing a Ph.D from Jadavpur University. He is currently an Assistant Professor in the department of Information Technology at Cammelia Institute of Technology, Kolkata, India since 2009. Prior to this, he was a Lecturer in the department of Computer Application at the Narula Institute of Technology, Kolkata, India. He has 10 publications in international journals and conference proceedings. His research interests include soft computing, quantum computing and image analysis. He is a member of ACM. He has been the member of the technical program committee of 2014 IEEE International Conference on Computational Intelligence and Communication Networks (ICCICN 2014) to be held in Kolkata.

Mohamed Eltoweissy received his BS and MS degrees in Computer Science and Automatic Control from University of Alexandria, Egypt, in 1986 and 1989 respectively. He received his PhD degree in Computer Science from University of Old Dominion, USA, in 1993. His research interests crosscut the areas of trustworthy engineering, networking architecture and protocols, and distributed systems for large-scale ubiquitous cyber-physical systems. Eltoweissy is a Professor of Electrical and Computer Engineering and Computer and Information Sciences. From March 2010 to March 2012, Eltoweissy served as Chief Scientist for Secure Cyber Systems at Pacific Northwest National Laboratory. Eltoweissy also served on the editorial board of IEEE Transactions on Computers as well as other notable journals.

Pramit Ghosh received the B. Tech. and M. Tech. degrees from the University of Calcutta, India, in 2005 and 2007 respectively. He was associated with TATA Consultancy Service Limited as a system engineers in the R&D section. After that, he joined as an Assistant Professor in RCC Institute of Information Technology, Kolkata. His research interest areas include medical imaging, device automation, and pattern recognition.

Manel Guerrero-Zapata is an Associate Professor in the Computer Architecture Department (DAC) at the Universitat Politècnica de Catalunya (UPC). His research interests include network security, wireless networks, and routing protocols. He is the author of Secure Ad hoc On-Demand Distance Vector (SAODV) routing protocol and of Simple Ad hoc Key Management (SAKM) scheme. Manel Guerrero received his Ph.D., M.Sc. and B.Sc. in Computer Science from the Universitat Politècnica de Catalunya (UPC) in 2006, 1999, and 1997 respectively. From 1998 to 2003, he worked at the Nokia Research Center in Helsinki (first as an Assistant Research Engineer, then as a Research Scientist, and finally as a Senior Research Scientist). From 2003 to 2005, he worked as an Assistant Professor at the Universitat Pompeu Fabra (UPF) in Barcelona.

Prabhakar Gundlapalli, Scientific Officer 'H', working as Additional Chief Engineer (Civil). Involved in design of Structures related to Nuclear Power Plants, including Prestressed and Reinforced Concrete Containment Buildings, Foundation for Turbine-Generator, Diesel Generator, RCC Ventilation Stack, specialized and advanced non-linear analysis, structures to resist blast and explosion loads, aircraft and missile impact on structures, geo-technical investigations, design of steel lined containment structures, etc.

Priya Gupta received B.Tech degree in Electronics & Communication from Bundelkhand University, Jhansi (India) in 2009. She did her M.Tech in VLSI Design from Banasthali University Rajasthan (India) in 2011. She is currently pursuing her Ph.D degree in low power VLSI arithmetic and memory circuits from BITS Pilani.

Joydev Hazra did his Bachelors in Information Technology and Masters in Computer Science from Burdwan University and West Bengal University of Technology in the years 2004 and 2009, respectively. He is now an Assistant Professor in the department of Information Technology, Heritage Institute of Technology, Kolkata, India. He has more than eight years teaching experience in various colleges in West Bengal. His main research interests are in areas of medical image registration, hyperspectral imaging, and pattern recognition.

Jagan J. is currently working as the Junior Research Fellow (JRF) for the Sponsored Research project by BRNS in the Centre for Disaster Mitigation and Management (CDMM), VIT University, Vellore. He is also pursuing the M.S. (By Research) in Geotechnical Engineering in the same department. He had completed his Bachelor of Engineering (B.E.) in Civil Engineering in Adhiyamaan College of Engineering, Hosur.

Mahantesh K. is currently working as Assistant Professor and Research Scholar in Department of Electronics and Communication, SJBIT, Bengaluru. He is currently pursuing his Ph.D degree.

Amin Karami received a M.Sc. degree in Informatics field from the University of Skövde, Sweden, in 2011. He has recently completed Ph.D. degree in the Computer Architecture Department (DAC) at the Universitat Politécnica de Catalunya Barcelona Tech (UPC), Spain. His current research interests include Named Data Networking (NDN), Next-generation Internet on Cloud Computing, Computational Intelligence and learning disciplines and approaches, Information Security, and Uncertainty Visualization.

Goran Klepac, Ph.D., works as a head of Strategic unit in Sector of credit risk in Raiffeisenbank Austria d.d., Croatia. At several universities in Croatia, he has lectured on subjects in the domain of data mining, predictive analytics, decision support system, banking risk, risk evaluation models, expert system, database marketing and business intelligence. As a team leader, he successfully finished many data mining projects in different domains like: retail, finance, insurance, hospitality, telecommunications, and productions. He is an author/coauthor of several books published in Croatian and English in the domain of data mining.

Ujjwal Maulik is a Professor in the Department of Computer Science and Engineering, Jadavpur University, Kolkata, India since 2004. He did his Bachelors in Physics and Computer Science in 1986 and 1989 respectively. Subsequently, he did his Masters and Ph.D. in Computer Science in 1992 and 1997, respectively. He was the Head of the Department of Computer Science and Technology Kalyani Govt. Eng. College, Kalyani, India during 1996-1999. Dr. Maulik has worked in at the Los Alamos National Laboratory, Los Alamos, New Mexico, USA in 1997; the University of New South Wales, Sydney, Australia in 1999; the University of Texas at Arlington, USA in 2001; the Univ. of Maryland Baltimore County, USA in 2004; the Fraunhofer Institute AiS, St. Augustin, Germany in 2005; the Tsinghua University, China in 2007; the University of Rome, Italy in 2008; the University of Heidelberg, Germany in 2009, the German Cancer Research Center (DKFZ) in 2010, 2011 and 2012. He has also visited many Institutes/Universities around the world for invited lectures and collaborative research. He is a senior member of IEEE, USA and CSI, India. Dr. Maulik is a co-author of 7 books and more than 250 research publications. He was the recipient of the Govt. of India BOYSCAST fellowship in 2001; the Alexander Von Humboldt Fellowship for Experienced Researchers in 2010, 2011 and 2012 and the Senior Associate of ICTP, Italy in 2012. He coordinator three Erasmus Mundus Mobility with Asia (EMMA) programs (European-Asian mobility program). Dr. Maulik has been the Program Chair, Tutorial Chair and Member of the program committee of many international conferences and workshops. He is the editorial board member of many journals including the recent one "Protein & Peptide Letters". He is the founding Member of IEEE Computational Intelligence Society (CIS) Chapter, Calcutta Section and has worked as a Secretary and a Treasurer in 2011, as a Vice Chair in 2012 and currently working as the Chair. He is a Fellow of IETE and IE, India. His research interests include Computational Intelligence, Bioinformatics, Combinatorial Optimization, Pattern Recognition, Data Mining.

Shikha Mehta after completing her Ph.D in 2014 from Delhi University, is now guiding Ph.D students from the Department of Computer Science Engineering, JIIT. Currently one student is pursuing PhD under her supervision. She is also a member of the DPMC of students working for their Ph.D with other supervisors. During her teaching career of more than 12 years, she taught subjects like Artificial Intelligence, Distributed Artificial Intelligence, Evolutionary Algorithms, MultiAgent Systems, Fuzzy Logic, Web application Engineering, Information Systems, Recommender systems, Database Applications and Computer Programming. She has participated in many International and National conferences in India and abroad and has actively been involved as a reviewer for many International Journals and Conference Proceedings. She has been actively involved in organizing the International Conference on Contemporary Computing in the years 2008, 2009, 2010, 2011, 2012 and 2013. She has guided approximately 100 graduate and post-graduate project theses.

Bassem M. Mokhtar is an assistant professor in the Department of the Electrical Engineering, in the Faculty of Engineering, University of Alexandria, Egypt. He received his BS and MS degrees in Electrical Engineering from Alexandria University, Egypt, in 2004 and 2008, respectively. He received PhD in Computer Engineering from Virginia Tech, USA in 2014. His research interests include autonomic resilient network, data managements, semantics reasoning, network intelligence, software-defined networking, semantic-driven networking operations, information management, knowledge-based network management and system modeling. He has been involved as a reviewer for various conference papers and journals including IEEE Transactions on Computers and Elsevier Journal of Network and Computer Applications (JNCA). Furthermore, he is researcher and co-founder of the Center of Smart Nanotechnology and Photonics (CSNP), Smart CI Research Center of Excellence, Alexandria University, Egypt.

Mita Nasipuri received her B.E.Tel.E., M.E.Tel.E., and Ph.D. (Eng.) degrees from Jadavpur University, in 1979, 1981 and 1990, respectively. Prof. Nasipuri has been a faculty member of J.U since 1987. Her current research interest includes image processing, pattern recognition, and multimedia systems. She is a senior member of the IEEE, U.S.A., Fellow of I.E (India) and W.B.A.S.T, Kolkata, India.

James F. Peters, B.Sc.(Math), M.Sc.(Math), Ph.D., Constructive Specification of Communicating Systems, Postdoctoral Fellow, Syracuse University, New York (1991), Asst. Prof., University of Arkansas, 1991-1994, and Researcher, Jet Propulsion Laboratory/Caltech, Pasadena, California (1991-1994), Full Professor, ECE Department, University of Manitoba, 1995-present, Visiting Professor, Mathematics Department, Adiyaman University, Adiyaman, Turkey, 2014-present, Visiting Researcher, Universit`a degli Studi di Salerno, Department of Mathematics DIPMAT Fisciano, Italy, 2014-present. He is the author of Topology of Digital Images. Visual Pattern Discovery in Proximity Spaces, Springer, 2014, (with S.A. Naimpally) Topology with Applications. Topological Spaces Near and Far, World Scientific, 2013, as well as over 350 published articles. He introduced near set theory in 2007, followed by the introduction of tolerance near sets in 2009, descriptive proximity spaces in 2013, strongly near Wallman proximity in 2014, proximal Voronoï and Delaunay tessellations in 2015. His main research interests are proximal algebraic structures, topology and proximity spaces in the mathematics of near sets, computational proximity and visual pattern recognition.

Mukesh M. Raghuwanshi received a M.Tech. degree in Computer Sc. and Data Processing from the Indian Institute of Technology (IIT), Kharagpur, in 1991 and a Ph. D. in Computer Sc. & Engineering from Visvesvaraya National Institute of Technology (VNIT), Nagpur, India, in 2007. He is currently a Professor at Computer Technology Department, Yashwantrao Chavan College of Engineering, Nagpur. His current research interests include the area of genetic algorithm, soft computing, language processor, data structures, algorithms and image processing.

Aditi Roy Chowdhury did her MCA and M. Tech from West Bengal University of Technology in the year 2004 and 2009 respectively. Prior to this she did her Bachelors from University of Calcutta in 2000. She is now a lecturer in the department of Computer Science and Technology, B.P.C Institute of Technology, Krishnagar, India. She has more than eight years teaching experience in various colleges in West Bengal. Her main research interests involve hyperspectral imaging, medical image processing.

Niranjan S. K. is currently working as professor in the Department of Master of Computer Applications at Sri Jayachamarajendra College of Engineering, Mysuru, Karnataka, India. He has more than 25 years of experience both in teaching and industry. He received his Bachelor of Business Management (BBM), Master of Computer Applications (MCA), Master of Technology in Software Engineering (M Tech [SE]) and Ph.D in Computer Science from University of Mysore. His area of interest include, Image Processing, Pattern Recognition and Software Engineering. He has published more than 30 technical papers in reputed books, journals and conference proceedings. He is the founder and General Chair of the International Conference on Contemporary Computing and Informatics (IC3I) series.

Siddesha S. is presently working as Assistant Professor in the Department of Master of Computer Applications at Sri Jayachamarajendra College of Engineering, Mysuru, Karnataka, India. Received Bachelor's Degree [1996], Master of Computer Applications [2000] and Master of Science and Technology (by Research) [2013] from University of Mysore. Now Pursuing Ph.D in Visvesvaraya Technological University, Belagavi, Karnataka, India. His research interests include Image processing and Pattern Recognition.

Pjush Samui is a professor at Centre for Disaster Mitigation and Management in VIT University, Vellore, India. He obtained his B.E. at Bengal Engineering and Science University; M.Sc. at Indian Institute of Science; Ph.D. at Indian Institute of Science. He worked as a postdoctoral fellow at University of Pittsburgh (USA) and Tampere University of Technology (Finland). He is the recipient of CIMO fellowship from Finland. Dr. Samui worked as a guest editor in "Disaster Advances" journal. He also serves as an editorial board member in several international journals. Dr. Samui is editor of International Journal of Geomatics and Geosciences. He is the reviewer of several journal papers. Dr. Samui is a Fellow of the International Congress of Disaster Management and Earth Science India. He is the recipient of Shamsher Prakash Research Award for the year of 2011.

Kandarpa Kumar Sarma, currently an Associate Professor in Department of Electronics and Communication Technology, Gauhati University, Guwahati, Assam, India, has over seventeen years of professional experience. He has covered all areas of UG/PG level electronics courses including soft computing, mobile communication, digital signal and image processing. He obtained M.Tech degree in Signal Processing from Indian Institute of Technology Guwahati in 2005 and subsequently completed a PhD programme in the area of Soft-Computational Application in Mobile Communication. He has authored six books, several book chapters, around three hundred peer reviewed research papers in international conference proceedings and journals. His areas of interest are Soft-Computation and its Applications, Mobile Communication, Antenna Design, Speech Processing, Document Image Analysis and Signal Processing Applications in High Energy Physics, Neuro-computing and Computational Models for Social-Science Applications. He is senior member IEEE (USA), Fellow IETE (India), Member International Neural Network Society (INNS, USA), Life Member ISTE (India) and Life Member CSI (India). He is the recipient of INSA SRF in 2009 and IETE N. V. Gadadhar Memorial Award 2014 for contributions towards wireless communication. He serves as an Editor-in-Chief of International Journal of Intelligent System Design and Computing (IJISDC, UK), guest editor of several international journals, reviewer of over thirty international journals and over hundred international conferences.

Henyl Rakesh Shah is currently pursuing Master of Science in Civil Engineering (Concentration in C.E.M.) at the Columbia University in the City of New York, USA. He graduated with a Bachelor of Technology in Civil Engineering from VIT University, Vellore, India in 2015. His primary research interests involve application of computational modeling, Sustainability and Risk Analysis to the field of Civil Engineering.

Vishal Shreyans Shah, is currently pursuing Master of Science in Engineering in Construction Engineering and Management at the University of Michigan, Ann Arbor, USA. He graduated with a Bachelor of Technology in Civil Engineering from VIT University, Vellore, India in 2015. His primary research interests involve application of computational modeling to solve complex quality testing issues in Civil engineering and the use of Constructability techniques and safety planning to enhance job site performance.

Mridusmita Sharma was born in Barpeta Road, Assam, India in 1988. She received the B.E degree in Electronics and Telecommunication Engineering form Girijananda Chowdhury Institute of Management and Technology under Gauhati University in 2011. She got her M.Tech degree in Electronics and Communication Technology from Gauhati University in 2013. Presently she is a pursuing her PhD degree from Gauhati University in the field of Speech Processing.

Kavita R. Singh received her B.E. degree in Computer technology in 2000 from RGCERT, Nagpur, India; M.Tech. degree in Computer Science and Engineering from Birla Institute of Technology, Ranchi, India, in 2007, and Ph.D. degree in Computer Science from Sardar Vallabhbhai National Institute of Technology, Surat, India in 2014. She is currently an Associate Professor in Department of Computer Technology, YCCE, Nagpur. Her current research interests include the area of Data Structures, Database, Rough sets, Near Sets, Image Processing and Pattern Recognisation.

Vijander Singh received his B. Tech in Electrical Engineering from G.B. Pant University of Agriculture and Technology in Uttarakhand in 1995. He received M.E. degree in Electrical Engineering in 2000 and Ph. D in Electrical Engineering in 2007 from IIT Roorkee. He has published many papers in international journals and conferences. He has chaired many international conferences. More than 25 M.Tech theses have been completed under his guidance. At present he has eight Ph.D students under his supervision and 2 Ph.Ds are completed. He is working as an Associate Professor in Instrumentation and Control Engineering Division at Netaji Subhas Institute of Technology, New Delhi, affiliated to the University of Delhi, Delhi. His areas of research are Process control, Biomedical Instrumentation, Artificial Intelligence and Image Processing.

Ka-Chun Wong was born and raised in Hong Kong where he was lucky enough to be immersed in a multi-cultural environment. He received his B.Eng. in Computer Engineering from United College, the Chinese University of Hong Kong in 2008. He has also obtained his M.Phil. degree in the Department of Computer Science and Engineering at the same university in 2010. In 2014, he completed his PhD degree under the supervision of Professor ZHANG ZhaoLei in the Department of Computer Science at the University of Toronto. He joined City University of Hong Kong as assistant professor. His research interests include bioinformatics, computational biology, natural computing, applied machine learning, and big data mining.

Mukesh A. Zaveri received the B.E. degree in Electronics Engineering from Sardar Vallabhbhai Regional College of Engineering and Technology (Now known as, National Institute of Technology (SVNIT)), Surat, India, in 1990, the M.E. degree in Electrical Engineering from Maharaja Sayajirao University, Baroda, India, in 1993, and the Ph.D. degree in Electrical Engineering from the Indian Institute of Technology Bombay, Mumbai, in 2005. He is currently an Associate Professor at Computer Engineering Department, Sardar Vallabhbhai National Institute of Technology. His current research interests include the area of signal and image processing, multimedia, computer networks, machine learning, sensor networks, and wireless communications.

Index

Information Resources Management Association

Become an IRMA Member

Members of the **Information Resources Management Association (IRMA)** understand the importance of community within their field of study. The Information Resources Management Association is an ideal venue through which professionals, students, and academicians can convene and share the latest industry innovations and scholarly research that is changing the field of information science and technology. Become a member today and enjoy the benefits of membership as well as the opportunity to collaborate and network with fellow experts in the field.

IRMA Membership Benefits:

- **One FREE Journal Subscription**

- **30% Off Additional Journal Subscriptions**

- **20% Off Book Purchases**

- Updates on the latest events and research on Information Resources Management through the IRMA-L listserv.

- Updates on new open access and downloadable content added to Research IRM.

- A copy of the Information Technology Management Newsletter twice a year.

- A certificate of membership.

IRMA Membership $195

Scan code to visit irma-international.org and begin by selecting your free journal subscription.

Membership is good for one full year.

Printed in the United States
By Bookmasters